ENCYCLOPEDIA OF PSYCHOLOGY

Alan E. Kazdin

Editor in Chief

VOLUME 3

AMERICAN
PSYCHOLOGICAL
ASSOCIATION

OXFORD
UNIVERSITY PRESS

2000

AMERICAN
PSYCHOLOGICAL
ASSOCIATION

Washington, D.C.

OXFORD
UNIVERSITY PRESS

Oxford   New York
Athens   Auckland   Bangkok   Bogotá   Buenos Aires   Calcutta
Cape Town   Chennai   Dar es Salaam   Delhi   Florence   Hong Kong   Istanbul
Karachi   Kuala Lumpur   Madrid   Melbourne   Mexico City   Mumbai
Nairobi   Paris   São Paulo   Singapore   Taipei   Tokyo   Toronto   Warsaw

and associated companies in
Berlin   Ibadan

Copyright © 2000 by American Psychological Association and Oxford University Press, Inc.

Published by American Psychological Association
750 First Street, NE, Washington, D.C. 20002-4242
www.apa.org
and
Oxford University Press, Inc.
198 Madison Avenue, New York, New York 10016
www.oup.com

Oxford is a registered trademark of Oxford University Press.

Library of Congress Cataloging-in-Publication Data
Encyclopedia of psychology / Alan E. Kazdin, editor in chief
p.   cm.
Includes bibliographical references and index.
1. Psychology—Encyclopedias.   I. Kazdin, Alan E.
BF31 .E52   2000   150'.3—dc21   99-055239
ISBN 1-55798-187-6 (set); ISBN 1-55798-652-5 (vol. 3)

AMERICAN PSYCHOLOGICAL ASSOCIATION STAFF

Gary R. VandenBos, Ph.D., *Publisher*
Julia Frank-McNeil, *Commissioning Editor*
Theodore J. Baroody, *Senior Development Editor*
Adrian Harris Forman, *Project Editor*

OXFORD UNIVERSITY PRESS STAFF

Karen Casey, *Publisher*
Claude Conyers, *Commissioning Editor*
Marion Osmun, *Senior Development Editor*
Matthew Giarratano, *Managing Editor*
Peri Zeenkov and Norina Frabotta, *Project Editors*
Nancy Hoagland, *Production Manager*
Jessica Ryan and Will Moore, *Production Editors*
AEIOU, Inc., *Index Editor*
AEIOU, Inc., Linda Berman, Denise McIntyre,
Space Coast Indexers, Inc., Linda Webster, *Indexers*
Suzanne Holt, *Book Design*
Joan Greenfield, *Cover Design*

3 5 7 9 8 6 4 2

Printed in the United States of America
on acid-free paper

D CONTINUED

DEVELOPMENTAL AGENDA. Biological processes set the parameters of the possible for individual developmental tasks over the life course. Sociocultural context, however, provides the developing individual with both opportunities and limitations at all stages of life. The interaction between biology and context create a developmental agenda characterized by both species-specific universals and culturally determined specifics.

The most well-known formulation of a life-course developmental agenda is that of psychologist Erik Erikson, who proposed that there are eight normative crises of development that occur over the life span (1993). Successful development, he suggested, results from the individual's positive resolution of each of these crises as they come up. Although Erikson's formulation has been influential for thinking about development over the life span, most researchers now recognize that it is culturally biased and does not accurately reflect real developmental changes even for individuals in middle-class Western societies (Gardiner, Mutter, & Kosmitski, 1998).

Despite the limitations of Erikson's formulation, however, it does capture some central themes of development in Western societies, and it establishes the idea that the life span can be conceptualized in terms of a series of stages, each with its own challenges for successful development. Cross-cultural evidence suggests that all societies recognize the age-related stages of infancy, early childhood, middle childhood, adolescence, adulthood, and old age. However, there are cultural differences at the ages when the stages (especially after infancy and childhood) are considered to begin and end, and developmental tasks may be further differentiated according to social class and gender. Current theories of life-course development have proposed specific developmental tasks within each of these major age stages.

Infancy

The first two years of life are universally recognized as a period of special vulnerability. Thus, the first developmental task of the infant is to ensure its own survival past this vulnerable period. Bowlby (1969) proposed that the infant's attachment to its mother was shaped through human evolution by the infant's need for reliable care. Subsequent elaboration of attachment theory has established three different styles of attachment, of which only one, "secure attachment," would be considered successful (the other two are variants of "insecure attachment"). However, cross-cultural studies of attachment have demonstrated that population rates of "insecure attachment" vary considerably, and that these variations seem to mirror the cultural norms of child rearing. This finding is of significance to American policy debates about the possibly harmful effects of day care on infants' attachment to their mothers. Most researchers today agree that although continuity of care is important for infants and young children, it is possible for infants to form successful attachment relationships to their mothers and others under a variety of caretaking arrangements.

An important developmental task for both the infant and its caretakers is the establishment of more mature and regular patterns of eating and sleeping. Cross-cultural research has shown that there are wide variations in how soon babies begin to sleep through the night, with much later establishment of mature sleep schedules in cultures where babies can easily wake up and nurse during the night (Harkness & Super, 1995). The location of the infant during sleep also varies cross-culturally and within U.S. society, with cosleeping (in the same bed or same room) more prevalent among African American, Hispanic, and Appalachian families as well as in other traditional societies around the world.

Early Childhood

As anyone who has interacted with toddlers or preschoolers knows, early childhood is an exciting time of life. Margaret Mead's terms *knee child* and *yard child* highlight the rapidly expanding social world of these children as they move from close proximity to caretakers to a world that includes peers as well as siblings and adults (Whiting & Edwards, 1988). Whereas developmentalists usually define the transition from infancy to early childhood in terms of the acquisition of new skills—notably walking and talking—cultural definitions of this transition may be based on other events outside the child. For example, in traditional African societies, the birth of a younger sibling marks the end of the special attentions given to babies, who now spend less time in the company of their mothers and more with older siblings.

Nevertheless, there are some universally recognized developmental tasks of this life stage. Edwards suggests that these include increased autonomy and independence, the emergence of a sense of self, the beginnings of self-control, and the ability to empathize with others, to learn moral rules, and to identify oneself in relation to gender (1995). As this list makes clear, young children, in contrast to infants, are expected everywhere to take their place as contributing members of their families and social groups. Within this general framework, there are significant cultural differences in which aspects of development are considered most important for the child's future success within its culture. For middle-class Western children, the early acquisition of language is a sign of cognitive competence crucial for successful development, and as the child reaches preschool age, the acquisition of communicative competence comes to include preliteracy skills as well. In contrast even to some European societies, however, middle-class U.S. parents tend to underemphasize the development of social skills. A more extreme contrast can be made with young children in sub-Saharan African communities, who are expected to take on responsibilities for child care and household tasks that would be thought beyond the capabilities of Western children even well into the middle childhood years.

Middle Childhood

Around the ages of 5 to 7 years, children go through qualitative shifts in development, recognized for example by Piaget's formulation of the achievement of concrete operational thinking. These changes are also recognized by cultures around the world as ushering in a new stage of development in which children can begin school, take on more responsible tasks at home, or gain new status within their religion. School in particular becomes a primary context for the development of children in today's world. Whiting and Edwards suggest that school children face four major developmental tasks (1988). First, they must learn to be motivated to work for remote goals promised by doing well in school; second, they must learn to perform individually rather than being identified only with one's family; third, they must learn to manage competition with peers; and finally, they may need to learn to interact with children and adults from different backgrounds. These tasks may not be as new to children who come from highly literate home environments or who may have already encountered cultural differences in preschool or daycare. Nevertheless, children in the middle childhood years are expected to negotiate these new tasks more independently of parents or parent substitutes than are younger children.

For schoolchildren in Western societies, two developmental tasks are particularly important. First, children must establish competence in areas related to their future success in the adult world. Second, children in the middle years must learn how to create and maintain positive relationships with peers, as Collins, Harris, and Susman suggest (1995). Failure at either one of these tasks creates risks for future development, as children enter the later school years lacking necessary competence, self-confidence, and motivation, or find themselves socially isolated in the peer settings that now occupy a large portion of their time. For parents, likewise, the middle childhood years present a new kind of challenge for organizing opportunities for successful development and monitoring their children's progress from a greater distance.

Adolescence

A common view among both psychologists and historians of the family is that adolescence as a recognized stage in the life cycle is relatively new, the product of industrialization, the growth of cities, and the need for schooling past childhood to prepare for adult life. Erikson's conceptualization of the central task of adolescence as establishing a separate identity is consistent with this view, in which development toward adult employment becomes a central concern. Cross-cultural evidence, however, has led anthropologists Schlegel and Barry (1991) to different conclusions. Based on their study of a large worldwide sample of societies, they conclude that social adolescence is a universally recognized developmental stage for both boys and girls, and that its primary purpose is not vocational development but rather preparation for adult reproductive life, generally in the context of marriage. This idea is consistent with the observation that in societies where girls marry too young to experience a prolonged adolescence, such as in India, they tend to marry into the family of their husband and become subject to intimate supervision by their mother-in-law. Even in such societies, however, both boys and girls may be allowed a period of relative freedom from childhood supervision and adult responsibilities.

If the most basic universal developmental task of adolescence is preparation for adult social rather than vocational life, then the development of mature sexuality takes center stage, along with the training for autonomy and responsibility. From this perspective, vocational training can be seen as a necessary component for the support of mature life in the community, rather than as a primary developmental goal in itself. As young people move toward the successful achievement of this agenda, the boundary between late adolescence and early adulthood becomes blurred.

Adulthood

Probably nowhere during the life span is the idea of developmental tasks so present in the consciousness of the developing individual as when making the transition to early adulthood. Increasingly for American young people, this transition occurs after the completion of college or postsecondary vocational training, generally in the early 20s. Within the span of a few short years, the individual is now expected to make vital life-long decisions and commitments—to a career, a life partner, and perhaps to a community or geographic area of residence—all without the direct supervision of adults that has characterized early developmental niches. In contrast, traditional cultures typically pave the way to adulthood through parental involvement in mate choice and through vocational preparation that begins in childhood. In modern Western European societies, the transition to adulthood is also eased by a gentler expectation of independence and separation of young people from their parents, coupled with a strong state-funded social support system.

Developmental textbooks generally divide adulthood into several stages (early, middle and late adulthood), each with its own developmental agenda. In reality, the increasing diversity in life-course trajectories makes any age-based developmental agenda of adulthood problematic. Not only is the "empty nest" left by young adults "refilled" as they seek respite from failed marriages or employment problems, but the processes of family building and career development may take varied paths. Rather than conceptualize the developmental agenda of adulthood in terms of early, middle, and late age stages, it may be more useful to think in terms of early, middle, and late tasks, as these necessarily follow their own developmental sequences.

As conceptualized by Western social scientists, the major tasks of adulthood center around achieving a sense of fulfillment through intimate relationships, work, and parenting (Berger, 1998). In this agenda, successful engagement may include developmental "crises" as well as periods of stability and satisfaction, as the individual adapts to changing circumstances in the workplace and at home. From a cross-cultural perspective, however, this developmental agenda seems overly focused on individual achievement, as well as excessively concerned with individual age-related decline (Shweder, 1998). In traditional cultures, development and change during adulthood are more readily conceptualized in terms of changing family and community roles. Anthropologists have suggested that in all cultures, women's biological changes in mid-life are associated with an increase in status, power, and autonomy (Kerns & Brown, 1992).

Later Adulthood and Old Age

All cultures recognize a period at the end of the life cycle when work and social relationships are modified by the effects of aging. Although Erikson called the life crisis of this stage "integrity versus despair" as the individual comes to terms with the successes and failures of life, it is likely that people in most cultures are not more preoccupied with self-evaluation at this point in their lives than they were earlier. Rather, cultural universals point to a recognition of elders as deserving recipients of increased respect as well as physical care (Keith et al., 1994). From this perspective, the developmental challenge for older adults is to manage a successful transition to greater dependence on others while maintaining their sense of authority and connection with family and community.

Bibliography

Berger, K. S. (1998). *The developing person through the life span.* New York: Worth.

Bowlby, J. (1969). *Attachment and loss: Vol 1. Attachment.* New York: Basic Books.

Collins, W. A., Harris, M. L., & Susman, A. (1995) Parenting during middle childhood. In M. C. Bornstein (Ed.), *Handbook of parenting: Vol. 1. Children and parenting* (pp. 65–90). Mahwah, NJ: Erlbaum.

Edwards, C. P. (1995). Parenting toddlers. In M. C. Bornstein (Ed.), *Handbook of parenting: Vol. 1. Children and parenting* (pp. 41–64). Mahwah, NJ: Erlbaum.

Erikson, E. H. (1963). *Childhood and society* (2nd ed.). New York: Norton.

Gardiner, H. W., Mutter, J. D., & Kosmitski, C. (1998). *Lives across cultures: Cross-cultural human development.* Boston: Allyn & Bacon.

Harkness, S., & Super, C. M. (1995). Culture and parenting. In M. C. Bornstein (Ed.), *Handbook of parenting: Vol. 2. Biology and ecology of parenting* (pp. 211–234). Mahwah, NJ: Erlbaum.

Keith, J., Fry, C. L., Glascock, A. P., Ikels, C., Dickerson-Putman, J., Harpending, H. C., & Draper, P. (1994). *The aging experience: Diversity and commonality across cultures.* Thousand Oaks, CA: Sage.

Kerns, V., & Brown, J. K. (1992). *In her prime: New views of middle-aged women* (2nd ed.). Urbana, IL: University of Illinois Press.

Schlegel, A., & Barry, H., III. (1991). *Adolescence: An anthropological perspective*. New York: Free Press.

Shweder, R. A. (1998). *Welcome to middle age! (and other cultural fictions)*. Chicago: University of Chicago Press.

Whiting, B. B., & Edwards, C. P. (1988). *Children of different worlds: The formation of social behavior*. Cambridge, MA: Harvard University Press.

Sara Harkness

DEVELOPMENTAL DISORDERS.

DEVELOPMENTAL DISORDERS. The field of developmental disorders experienced a very complicated set of scientific and social changes in the 1990s. Many of those advances involved changes in perceptions about disabilities, and have been referred to as a shift in paradigms (Harper, 1991). As a result, modifications in the definition of developmental disorders and substantial changes in societal responses to children and adults with disabilities emerged. In addition, advances in neuropsychological research have refined our understanding of many developmental and learning disorders. The focus of defining developmental disorders, or the more common terminology, *developmental disability*, has evolved in a sociopolitical context (Wiegerink & Pelosi, 1979) combined with the results of scientific advances.

Definition of Developmental Disability

The implications of the developmental disability (DD) classification and resultant diagnostic labels have a major impact on diagnostic systems, scientific study of developmental disorders, and service-based educational and intervention/treatment programs. Whatever particular classification system is used (or its current emphasis) has effects on federal and state distribution of funds for research and educational service at all levels in the United States. The largest impact on children and youth is related to how such DD definitions become incorporated into administrative rules for the delivery of special education services in public schools and related support services in community-based rehabilitation and treatment settings. Classification systems focused on developmental disorders are very important to the lives of children, adults, and families when such disorders are present.

The earliest definition of developmental disability was crafted in Public Law 91-517 by Congress in 1970 (*Summary of existing legislation affecting people with disabilities*, 1992). This law was an outgrowth of the work of several individuals who assisted on the president's panel on mental retardation at the request of President John F. Kennedy in 1961. A very broad panel effort was generated to report on treatment and prevention efforts in mental retardation worldwide. These details set the stage for subsequent legislation related to developmental disabilities. According to Thompson and O'Quinn

(1979) the president's panel made important contributions that expanded the 1970 DD definition. These emphases included: maintaining children in their normal, local environment; supporting those with physical impairments; encouraging a blended continuum of medical, educational, and social care throughout the life span; recognizing a coordinated, interdisciplinary treatment approach; focusing intervention on local and state levels; and encouraging coordination between university professionals and state provider agencies. This thrust was extremely important in that it set the tone for mental retardation services and developmental disabilities for more than the next 35 years. In 1963, President John F. Kennedy, in his message to Congress on mental illness and mental retardation, actualized these recommendations of the panel in proposing a comprehensive approach to combat mental retardation focusing on prevention, community service, research, and training (Thompson & O'Quinn, 1979). Subsequently, legislation in the 1969–1970 era generated the first definition of developmental disabilities, as follows:

> Disabilities attributable to mental retardation, cerebral palsy, epilepsy or another neurological condition of an individual found by the Secretary [Health, Education, and Welfare] to be closely related to mental retardation or to require treatment similar to that required for a mentally retarded individual, which disability originates before such an individual attains age 18, which has continued or can be expected to continue indefinitely, and constitutes a substantial handicap to the individual. (Developmental Disabilities Services and Facilities and Construction Act, 1970)

This initial definition clustered three categorical developmental disorders: mental retardation, cerebral palsy, and epilepsy. These three conditions were contemporarily (circa 1970) viewed as the major causes for substantial handicaps to adults during childhood in the United States. All three of the disorders imply multiple handicap conditions that may require a continuum of highly similar services throughout the life span. The existing services and needs of people were previously classified under disparate and different categorical labels focusing on etiological/medical origins. Furthermore, not all of those who needed services displayed mental retardation, although they did show evidence of multiple handicaps with adaptive delays in life skill functioning. This 1970 DD definition was viewed as "an ecumenical bill since it brought under one umbrella disabled persons with common needs but different diagnostic labels" (Thompson & O'Quinn, 1979, p. 11). A definition of *disability* had now evolved from the early 1960s, reflecting a complicated sociopolitical path, to define and provide services for a wide array of people with diverse and lifelong developmentally based impairments. Concurrently throughout the United States, much additional legislation was being developed relating to early intervention services: Head Start, poverty and developmental care, and university-based training of professionals working in the field of developmental disabilities (*Summary*, 1992).

Over the next 27 years (1970–1997), the definition of DD changed in scope and in complexity. In 1975, Public Law 94-103 broadened the DD definition to include autism and a few specific learning disabilities (e.g., dyslexia, if those learning disabilities related to existing and concurrent developmental disorders). Not all specific learning disabilities were included in this classification. Subsequently, Public Law 94-103, Developmentally Disabled Assistance and Bill of Rights Act, was amended as a result of a national task force on the definition of developmental disabilities, and a report was provided (President's Committee on Mental Retardation, 1977). This definition, adapted as part of Public Law 95-605 (1978), follows:

> For purposes of the Developmental Disabilities Act, a developmental disability is a severe, chronic disability of a person which:
> 1. Is attributable to a mental or physical impairment or combination of mental and physical impairments;
> 2. Is manifest before age 22;
> 3. Is likely to continue indefinitely;
> 4. Results in substantial functional limitation in 3 or more of the following areas of major life activity:
>   a. Self-care,
>   b. Receptive and expressive language,
>   c. Learning,
>   d. Mobility,
>   e. Self-direction,
>   f. Capacity for independent living, or
>   g. Economic self-sufficiency; and
> 5. Reflects the need for a combination and sequence of special, interdisciplinary, or generic care, treatment, or other services which are:
>   a. A lifelong or extended duration and
>   b. Individually planned and coordinated.

Of specific interest is the fact that some of the individuals who generated this definition on the task force were not satisfied with particular terminology, namely, "mental" or "physical" impairments. Consequently, additional clarification was offered to Part 1 of the definition as follows:

> Is attributable to mental retardation, cerebral palsy, epilepsy, or autism; or is attributable to any other condition of a person similar to mental retardation, cerebral palsy, epilepsy, or autism because such condition results in similar impairment of general intellectual functioning and adaptive behavior, and requires treatment and services similar to those required for such persons. (*Summary*, 1992, p. 5)

This new law, signed in 1978 by President Carter, enabled further clarification of the operating definition for developmental disabilities. As is evident, this defi-

nition continued to incorporate broader and more diverse developmental conditions as time went on. The major changes over the prior definitions involved the elimination of specific references to the specific categories of disabling conditions, such as mental retardation and epilepsy, and the more current emphasis on substantial functional limitations. In addition, the term *impairment* was advocated for use because categories or conditions were thought to be confusing and potentially divisive among various groups and organizations involved in the process (Thompson & O'Quinn, 1979).

Contemporary Issues in Defining Developmental Disorders

There has been a move toward using functional perspectives to classify persons with particular developmental disorders or disabilities. This approach focuses on the description of skills, most often adaptive behaviors, that children or young adults need to perform in regard to their daily activities. Again, the relationship between specific diagnostic etiologies and disorders does not capture what most people need with respect to their assistance and functioning on a daily basis. A current trend reflects the importance of support-based paradigms in defining treatments and services for individuals with developmental disorders (Luckasson et al., 1992). A movement away from a deficit (within the person) orientation toward an outcome-based orientation emphasizes the social and community roles for persons with developmental disorders. Fundamental issues underlying this model are that individuals should be maintained and supported in inclusive settings to ensure successful learning, work experiences, and adjustment to the demands of daily community living. An example of this change is in the philosophy evident in the American Association on Mental Retardation (AAMR; Luckasson et al., 1992) definition of mental retardation that emphasizes "level of supports" as a description of the needs of individuals instead of previous levels of disability classification (e.g., mild–moderate–severe–profound mental retardation). Proponents of this support-based orientation of defining disabilities clearly emphasize the opportunity for greater flexibility in diagnosing and classifying such developmental disorders generally. This shift in thinking is not without controversy. For example, others caution that this approach may promote an overemphasis on clinical judgment, rather than empirical sources for decision making, and cite the lack of research and instrumentation to support AAMR's adaptive behavior domains as they are defined in the new system.

The emphasis on these new functionally oriented definitions focuses on chronicity, age-specific onset, multiple areas of functional limitations, and the need for an extended array of long-term services from a multiplicity of providers that are fundamentally unrelated to specific categories of disability. Medical diagnosis, although relevant, is not useful in designing most treatments for developmental disorders. Interestingly, under the newer definitions of developmental disorder, a person with mental retardation who is competent and functioning in his or her environment would not necessarily be considered developmentally disabled. The seemingly simple idea of providing a general diagnostic label based upon functional differences raises many questions about service provision, inclusion, and who has a developmental disorder.

Conceptual Issues in Developmental Disorders

Defining what is a developmental disorder raises numerous problems from a practical intervention, as well as a scientific, standpoint. One of the key issues in defining DD is the concept of severity and substantiality. Recall that one of the major reasons for the definition of DD and its subsequent legislation is to enable treatment and intervention across an array of congenital disorders with different etiologies, but often with similar functional impacts in adaptive behavior. The goal was inclusive diagnostics for functional needs. The definition of DD focuses on defining a degree of functional limitations (e.g., severity and substantiality). This discrimination of adaptive skills has been viewed as a noncategorical issue that might broaden the DD label, at least in terms of its service inclusion. Furthermore, this delineation of functional status is often a clinical decision despite its evaluation based upon adaptive instruments. These key issues (e.g., severity and pervasiveness of impairment) often are the defining factors in obtaining treatment and interventions. However this aspect of the DD definition lacks operational clarity and is very difficult to place into administrative rules for service delivery. A current dilemma of this DD label is evidenced by the occasional finding of early normative milestones in infants with Down syndrome who are not labeled as developmentally delayed or displaying mental retardation at that time in their development, and subsequently are denied early intervention services at a time when they are likely to receive a high benefit and impact from such treatment. When differences are not present, though highly likely, the DD classification can become an administrative impediment to services. In point of fact, this is a misinterpretation of the DD definition, but testifies to problems of operational clarity.

Finally, when considering the DD category, some clarification is necessary with respect to the issues of delay, dissociation, and deviancy (Capute & Accardo, 1996). These concepts are applied in varying degrees to developmental disorders, particularly mental retardation, during the initial stages of identification. *Delay* often refers to a significant lag in one or more areas of development. The degree of delay has biological implications (Capute & Accardo, 1996). Delays that are more severe or more global often imply biological etiologies. As noted by Capute and Accardo, "Although the severity of delay does appear to be directly correlated with the ease of identifying a specific etiology, the absence of a specific etiology in cases of milder delay should not be interpreted as supportive of nonorganic etiologies" (p. 3). However, developmental delay is often used to reflect a less definitive state of disability in a young child (up to 5 years old) when the diagnostic data are equivocal generally. Such confusing and sometimes vague diagnostic statements are often applied to young children with milder learning disorders and less pervasive developmental disorders.

Dissociation suggests a difference between the developmental rates of two areas or skills of development, with one area significantly delayed by comparison (Capute & Accardo, 1996). The dissociation phenomenon is relevant to our understanding of children with more specific learning disorders (e.g., dyslexia). Dissociation in this instance reflects a major discrepancy between the general cognitive skills of a child and his or her reading skills, often a characteristic of a specific language or reading disability.

Deviancy is evidenced by nonsequential unevenness in the attainment of particular milestones or skills within one or more areas of development (Capute & Accardo, 1996). The pattern and presentation of developmental progress is significantly and clinically different in rate and context, irrespective of age. Such examples are found in rote expressive language skills, unusual memory and mnemonics found in certain communication disorders (e.g., autism), and hyperverbal language associated with hydrocephalus.

In summary, developmental disorders are classified as developmental disabilities, sharing similar chronic duration, early onset, multiple physical or mental impairments, and are often pervasive in their lifelong functional effects. Developmental differences in rate, level, and pattern are also reflected in the concepts of delay, dissociation, and deviancy in the common developmental disorders (e.g., mental retardation, learning disabilities, autism).

Key Developmental Disorders

A brief chronological history of mental retardation, autism, and learning disabilities follows.

Mental Retardation. The history of mental retardation is well defined by others and represents a complex social and scientific chronology covering several decades (Irwin & Gross, 1990; Madle & Niesworth, 1990). Much debate currently exists in defining primary key aspects in the category of mental retardation as they relate to particular variables, such as IQ score, age, functional disabilities, and sociocultural circumstances. The current definition of mental retardation is:

Mental retardation refers to substantial limitations in present functioning. It is characterized by significantly subaverage intellectual functioning, existing concurrently with related limitations in two or more of the following applicable adaptive skill areas: Communication, self-care, home living, social skills, community use, self-direction, health and safety, functional academics, leisure and work. Mental retardation manifests before age 18. (Luckasson et al., 1992, p. 15)

This AAMR definition has raised significant discussion among the community of scholars focusing on mental retardation (MacMillan, Gresham, & Siperstein, 1993). Classification of individuals with mental retardation is no longer based primarily on an IQ score, and the categories of mild, moderate, severe, and profound mental retardation are no longer in vogue. This is not true for the *Diagnostic and Statistical Manual of Mental Disorders* (*DSM–IV*; American Psychiatric Association, 1994) or *International Classification of Diseases* (*ICD–10*, World Health Organization, 1989). Instead, AAMR classification is based on particular types and intensities of supports and services needed by the individual, categorized as intermittent, limited, extensive, and pervasive. This supports-based paradigm represents a shift away from the deficit (within the person) orientation toward an outcome-based orientation that emphasizes the social and community roles of persons with mental retardation. Although controversial, fundamental assertions behind this model are that individuals should be maintained and supported in inclusive settings to ensure successful learning, work experiences, and adjustment to the demands of community living. These issues of inclusion are not inconsistent with earlier models of defining mental retardation or the contemporary definitions of *DSM–IV* or *ICD–10*. However, AAMR's 1992 definition of mental retardation makes the diagnosis and definition contingent upon these issues. Key arguments in the application of this definition center around cautions suggesting that AAMR's (Luckasson et al., 1992) approach may promote an overemphasis on clinical judgment, rather than empirical sources for decision making, and those who question it often cite the lack of research and instrumentation to support the development of this definition, specifically adaptive behavior domains (MacMillan et al., 1993). Such paradigm shifts in the definition of such major categorizations of developmental disorders can have profound implications for millions of citizens, primarily in eligibility for services and long-term educational assistance.

Mental retardation may be the end result of one or more of the following categories of risk: biomedical, social, behavioral, educational, and multiple factors (Capute & Accardo, 1996). Evidence is increasing that biomedical factors have a deleterious impact on the child's developing central nervous system (e.g., genetic

disorders, environmental toxins, infections). Etiologies for mental retardation clearly represent a multifactorial continuum of biological and social factors. Finally, the developmental consequences and life outcomes for individuals with particular levels and degrees of mental retardation are related to their associated disabilities, timing of early interventions, and maintenance of ongoing support systems within their daily environments (Capute & Accardo, 1996).

Autism. Autism is a behavioral syndrome of neurologic dysfunction, characterized by impaired reciprocal social interactions, impaired verbal and nonverbal communication, impoverished or diminished imaginative activity, and a markedly restricted repertoire of activities and interests relative to age (Gillberg & Coleman, 1993). Research in the area of autism has exploded in the 1990s. Numerous studies are focusing on neurobehavioral, neuropsychological, genetic, and behavioral functioning.

Although specific etiologies of autism are generally unknown, often an underlying and associated brain disease can be identified (Gillberg & Coleman, 1993). Such examples include congenital infections, developmental brain abnormalities, metabolic diseases, postnatally acquired destructive disorders, neoplasms, and genetic disorders (e.g., tuberous sclerosis and fragile X syndrome; Gillberg & Coleman, 1993). The relationship of etiology to behavioral functioning and adaptive improvement remains equivocal; historical psychogenic explanations are no longer viewed as etiologically valid.

The life outcomes of individuals with autism remain highly variable. Factors that affect outcome relate to initial cognitive levels, language capability, and associated central nervous system disabilities. Treatment of individuals with autism requires a strong behavioral and special education emphasis with a primary focus on the enhancement of communication skills and adaptive behavioral management. In concert with communication, socialization skills must be given high priority as well.

A major determinant of the prognosis of individuals with autism is the presence or absence of an underlying disorder of the brain and accessibility to treatment for associated disorders and impairments that accompany the disorder. Future outcomes of individuals with autism relate to their initial levels of functioning, language skills, and continuous and available support systems to promote functioning in adaptive behavioral skills within community environments (Gillberg & Coleman, 1993).

Learning Disabilities. Learning disabilities (LDs) represent a very broad group of developmental disorders that have a deficit in a particular area of learning as a common characteristic; individuals with LDs display some type of academic or achievement problem.

To get more specific consensus than this among experts is clearly problematic. Contemporary definitions of learning disabilities tend to stress specific disorders, often independent of general deficits (usually cognitive), and are defined within a neurocognitive or a neurobehavioral framework (Obrzut & Hynd, 1991).

Defining learning disabilities is an ongoing issue for practice and science. Generally, the identification and conceptualization of learning disabilities evolved from the work of Strauss and Werner in 1955 (Kavale, 1988). This initial definition of learning disabilities was conceptualized within a medical model associated with or caused by neurological dysfunction, related to particular processing disturbances, and often associated with academic failure defined by discrepancy between various skills. Discrepancy here was frequently noted to be between specific functions, for example, achievement levels and general cognitive status. From these initial definitions, learning disabilities have moved to embrace more fundamental neuropsychological theories of brain functioning and central nervous system information processing (Obrzut & Hynd, 1991).

The National Joint Commission on Learning Disabilities (NJCLD; Baltimore, MD) has consistently passed legislation and promoted definitions similar to those associated with the Developmental Disabilities Act (1970) legislation. The most recent definition of *learning disability* constructed by the NJCLD was stated in a 1988 letter to their membership:

> Learning disability is a general term that refers to a heterogeneous group of disorders manifested by significant difficulties in the acquisition and use of listening, speaking, reading, writing, reasoning, or mathematical abilities. These disorders are intrinsic to the individual, presumed to be due to central nervous system dysfunction, and may occur across the life span. Problems in self-regulatory behaviors, social perception, and social interaction may exist with learning disabilities but do not by themselves constitute a learning disability.
>
> Although learning disabilities may occur concomitantly with other handicapping conditions (for example, sensory impairment, mental retardation, serious emotional disturbance) or with extra influences (such as cultural differences, insufficient or inappropriate instruction) they are not the result of those conditions or influences. (NJCLD, 1988)

For a comprehensive treatment of this history, see Gerber (1993). Findings in this area are moving away from a traditional descriptive medical model and are exploring complex brain-behavior relationships. Research is exploring neurophysiology, brain imaging, event-related cortical potentials, regional cerebral blood flow, and brain electrical activity mapping (Obrzut & Hynd, 1991). Outcomes in relation to learning disability categories and their relationships to particular intervention programs remain an extremely complicated and active area of educational and neuropsychological research (Gerber, 1993). Specific generalizations about outcomes can only be made with respect to very general statements, since many of the disorders that are included in this category have highly specific impacts on cognitive and neuropsychological functioning.

[*See also* Autistic Disorder; Learning Disabilities; *and* Mental Retardation.]

Bibliography

American Psychiatric Association. (1994). *Diagnostic and Statistical manual of mental disorders* (4th ed.). Washington, DC: Author.

Caputo, A. J., & Accardo, P. J. (Eds.). (1996). *Developmental disabilities in infancy and childhood* (2nd ed.): *Vol. 1. Neurodevelopmental diagnosis and treatment; Vol. 2. The spectrum of developmental disabilities.* Baltimore: Paul Brookes. A comprehensive review of the majority of developmental disorders with a biomedical emphasis.

Developmental Disabilities Services and Facilities and Construction Act of 1970, Pub. L. No. 91–517. (HEW/SRS Publication No. 72–25035). Washington, DC: U.S. Government Printing Office.

Gerber, A. (Eds.). (1993). *Language-related learning disabilities: Their nature and treatment.* Baltimore: Paul Brooks. A practical overview of language-based learning disabilities with strong application sections.

Gillberg, C., & Coleman, M. (1993). *The biology of autistic syndromes.* Cambridge, UK: Cambridge University Press. A comprehensive review of the biomedical understanding of autism.

Harper, D. C. (1991). Paradigms for investigating rehabilitation and adaptation to childhood disability and chronic illness. *Journal of Pediatric Psychology, 16*(5), 533–542.

Irwin, A. R., & Gross, A. M. (1990). Mental retardation in childhood. In M. Hersen & C. Last (Eds.), *Handbook of child and adult psychopathology: A longitudinal perspective* (pp. 325–336). New York: Pergamon Press. A contemporary review of the issues of research and practice in mental retardation in children.

Kavale, K. A. (Ed.). (1988). *Learning disabilities: State of the art and practice.* Boston: Little, Brown.

Luckasson, R., Coulter, D. L., Polloway, E. A., Reiss, S., Schalock, R. L., Snell, M. E., Spitalnik, D. M., & Stark, J. A. (1992). *Mental retardation: Definition, classification, and systems of support* (9th ed.). Washington, DC: American Association on Mental Retardation. The 1992 manual on mental retardation, including a brief history and rationale for the revision.

MacMillan, D. L., Gresham, F. M., & Siperstein, G. N. (1993). Conceptual and psychometric concerns about the 1992 AAMR definition of mental retardation. *American Journal on Mental Retardation, 98,* 325–335.

Madle, R. A., & Neisworth, J. T. (1990). Mental retardation in adulthood. In M. Hersen & C. Last (Eds.), *Handbook of child and adult psychopathology: A longitudinal perspective* (pp. 337–352). New York: Pergamon Press. A contemporary review of the issues of research and practice in mental retardation in adults.

Obrzut, J. E., & Hynd, G. W. (Eds.). (1991). *Neuropsychological foundations of learning disabilities: A handbook of issues, methods, and practice*. San Diego, CA: Academic Press. A state-of-the-art text on contemporary research and practice in learning disabilities.

President's Committee on Mental Retardation. (1977). *MR 76. Mental retardation: Past and present* (Stock No. 040-000-00385-1). Washington, DC: U.S. Government Printing Office.

Summary of existing legislation affecting people with disabilities (1992). Washington, DC: Office of Special Education and Rehabilitative Services, U.S. Department of Education. (Contract #433J47100266) This is a comprehensive summary of extant legislation affecting people with disabilities.

Thompson, R. J., & O'Quinn, A. N. (1979). *Developmental disabilities: Etiologies, manifestations, diagnoses, and treatments*. New York: Oxford University Press.

Wiegerink, R., & Pelosi, J. W. (Eds.). (1979). *Developmental disabilities: The DD movement*. Baltimore: Paul Brooks.

World Health Organization. (1989). *International classification of diseases* (10th ed.). Geneva: Author.

Dennis C. Harper

DEVELOPMENTAL PSYCHOLOGY. [*This entry comprises three articles: an overview of the broad history of the field from its inception to the present; a survey of the principal theories that have determined the course of development of the field; and a general descriptive review and evaluation of methods and assessments that have been employed in this field.*]

History of the Field

Human development is the concern of many disciplines, including biology, sociology, anthropology, education, and medicine. In addition, the topic cuts across nations and cultures, adding to the diversity of subject matter and approaches.

Developmental psychology is concerned with constancy and change in psychological functioning over the life span. As a discipline, it arose shortly after the emergence of scientific psychology in the latter part of the nineteenth century. Its antecedents were different from those that led to the founding of experimental psychology.

In its early years, developmental psychology was primarily concerned with child and adolescent development. Later, adult development and aging began to assume more importance. Developmental psychology began as a correlational science, focusing on observation, not on experimentation, and thus differed from traditional research psychology.

Prescientific Antecedents

Views of development have always reflected the culture in which they emerged. In one of the earliest views of the child, *preformationism*, a homunculus or miniature adult was believed to be contained in the semen or egg at conception. The homunculus was only quantitatively different from the adult. Preformationist views were largely abandoned on the biological level with the development of modern science.

Philosophical Bases

From a philosophical perspective, John Locke (1632–1704) and Jean-Jacques Rousseau (1712–1778) are the usual starting points for Western discussions of development. Locke is considered the father of modern learning theory. For him, the child was a *tabula rasa* or blank slate on which experience writes. The role of Locke and later learning theorists was to emphasize the role of the environment in development.

Rousseau is often identified as the father of classical developmental psychology. In his book *Emile* (1762), he championed a view that emphasized the natural unfolding of the child based on an innate blueprint. He was one of the first to argue that development took place in stages.

Baby Biographies

Early attempts to understand development can be found in "baby biographies," descriptive accounts of children, usually written by a parent, and often biased. The German philosopher, Dietrich Tiedemann (1748–1803), is credited with creating the first baby biography (1787), but there was little follow-up to his work. Almost 100 years later, another German, biologist Wilhelm Preyer (1841–1897), kept a detailed account of the mental development of his son during his first four years. He published the results as *Die Seele des Kindes* (The Mind of the Child) (1882), a work frequently cited as beginning the modern child psychology movement. In America, the best known baby biography was a collection of observations of her niece, by Milicent Shinn (1858–1940), which she began in 1890. A popular version was later published as *The Biography of a Baby* (1900).

The Impact of Darwin

The theory of evolution contained in *The Origin of Species* (1859) by Charles Darwin (1809–1882) was the starting point for many Western developmental psychologists, both European and American. In addition, Darwin's emphasis on individual differences and adaptation became important components of developmental psychology.

The German physiologist, Wilhelm Preyer, was inspired by Darwin and, in turn, was the inspiration for other European developmentalists including Karl Bühler (1879–1963), Charlotte Bühler (1893–1974), and William Stern (1871–1938). Darwin's approach also led to the ethological school of development, which includes the work of Konrad Lorenz (1903–1989) and Niko Tinbergen (1907–1988). The research and writing of John Bowlby (1907–1990) and Mary Ainsworth (1913–1999) on loss and attachment are later expressions of this school. More recently, a Darwinian-based approach, "evolutionary psychology," has emerged.

Among the American pioneers deeply affected by Darwin were G. Stanley Hall, one of America's first psychologists, and James Mark Baldwin, also a pioneer psychologist. Hall's main approach to development, recapitulation theory, was derived from Darwin through a German biologist, Ernst Haeckel (1834–1919). Baldwin's approach has been linked to the theories of both Jean Piaget and Lev Vygotsky.

The Child Study Movement and G. Stanley Hall (1844–1924)

Among the many contextual forces which contributed to the rise of developmental psychology in the United States, the child study movement was the most important. This movement, which emerged during the latter part of the nineteenth century, focused on the welfare of children and, among other things, helped to bring about the passage of laws governing child labor and compulsory education. Its leadership was assumed by G. Stanley Hall.

Hall linked the new psychology and the movement. He promised to make an understanding of the child "scientific," an approach that held appeal for many groups, particularly educators. He published a series of questionnaire studies which, though flawed, attempted to establish norms for children in a variety of areas.

In 1891, Hall published the first journal of developmental psychology, *Pedagogical Seminary*, later renamed the *Journal of Genetic Psychology* (the word *genetic* in these early years was a synonym for *development*). He wrote *Adolescence* (1904), a two-volume book, which revived an archaic word and offered a theory of development broader than the title suggested. He also wrote *Senescence* (1922) which was concerned with the second half of life. For all these efforts and more, he is frequently identified as the "father of American developmental psychology."

Four Pioneer Developmentalists

James Mark Baldwin (1861–1934) proposed a stage theory of development which initially focused on cognitive development. Later, he extended it to include social development as well. He was largely a theoretician, not an experimentalist, and there is evidence that his work influenced both Vygotsky and Piaget. John Dewey (1859–1952), an American, is probably best known for

his contributions to philosophy and education, but he also wrote on developmental issues. In contrast to many of his American contemporaries, his theory had a contextual emphasis which has sometimes been compared to that of Vygotsky. He focused on education, in part, because he believed it would establish the agenda for development. He established a "laboratory school" at the University of Chicago in order to observe and experiment with children in a more natural setting. Some of the questions he posed are still being asked today. Which aspects of development are universal? Which are expressions of local culture? Alfred Binet (1857–1911), a Frenchman, and the father of modern intelligence testing, conducted research on cognitive functioning, including memory. In addition to being a prolific writer, he was an advocate for educational reform. The experimental laboratory school he founded was probably the first in Europe. Binet's work in intellectual development introduced many concepts which are still in use today. Maria Montessori (1870–1952), an Italian educator, also wrote extensively on child development. Trained as a physician, she first worked with developmentally disabled children. She investigated the writing of Jean-Marc Itard (1774–1838), whose work is often associated with the beginning of special education and his disciple Edouard Seguin (1812–1880). Many of the techniques she learned from them later became part of her Montessori method.

Psychoanalytic Approaches

Psychoanalytic approaches did not enter mainstream academic psychology until the 1930s, but their influence was eventually profound. Moreover, Sigmund Freud (1856–1939), the founder of the movement, had an impact on popular culture unequalled by any other psychologist. While his method of psychotherapy is well known, it is not always appreciated that his theory is a theory of development. His followers were numerous and produced many different approaches.

Two important followers were his daughter Anna Freud (1895–1982), who became a distinguished psychologist in her own right, and Erik Erikson (1902–1994). Both are "ego psychologists," since they were more concerned with the conscious, rational part of the personality. Erikson is best known for his book *Childhood and Society* (1950), and for his description of the eight stages of man. While accepting S. Freud's notions of psychosexual development, he discussed them within a broader cultural context.

Other psychoanalysts who had an impact on developmental psychology include Karen Horney (1885–1952), particularly for her work on feminine psychology and her emphasis on life-span growth and self-actualization. Carl G. Jung (1875–1961) was a theoretical innovator in adult development and aging. Melanie Klein (1882–1960), who developed *object relations the-*

ory, was a rival of Anna Freud, and emphasized the first 2 years of life, particularly the importance of the mother.

Normative Developmental Psychology

Until the 1940s, much of developmental psychology was descriptive and normative. Arnold Gesell (1880–1961) was important in promoting this approach. Although his mentor, G. Stanley Hall, had tried to develop normative data on children, it was the work of Gesell that proved of lasting value. Gesell collected voluminous data on infants and children, particularly on their physical and motor development. Moreover, he organized the information to make it useful and available to parents.

The effect of his work was to encourage parents to relax and to trust more in nature. In the tradition of Rousseau, the natural unfolding of the child was more important than any interference on the part of parents or educators. Thus, he became a spokesman for the maturation position. Many of Gesell's developmental norms are still in use today.

The Testing Movement

There had been many early attempts to develop measures of intelligence, notably by Francis Galton (1822–1911), but they proved unproductive. However, Alfred Binet, in Paris, tried a new approach and the tests were almost immediately successful. Binet published scales in 1905, 1908, and 1911, the year of his death, each scale more sophisticated than the last.

An American, and former student of G. Stanley Hall, Henry H. Goddard (1866–1957) brought a version of Binet's scale to the United States. After trying it on a number of children, both normal and disabled, he declared the measure a success and immediately began sending copies of his translated version around the country.

Another former student of G. Stanley Hall, Lewis M. Terman (1877–1956), also an American, developed the most widely used version of the Binet–Simon scales, eventually referred to as the Stanford–Binet, which became the standard against which all measures of intelligence were compared. Terman also initiated the first longitudinal study of development, beginning in 1921. His sample, selected for being gifted in intelligence, continues to be followed today. Later longitudinal studies included the Harvard Growth Study (1922), the Berkeley Growth Study (1928), and the Fels Institute Study of Human Development (1929).

Lev Vygotsky (1896–1934) and Contextualism

Although Vygotsky has been dead for more than six decades, he is sometimes referred to as the most important contemporary developmentalist. His ideas are particularly suited for the contextualist theoretical framework which has became popular in recent years. Born and raised in Russia, Vygotsky was a Marxist who believed in the importance of the social and historical context to development. At the same time, he had an appreciation of the internal features of development. This ability to consolidate these two diverse positions has led some to see his work as forming the basis for an integrative theory of development.

Although he is often compared to Piaget, Vygotsky differed from him in substantial ways. For instance, he placed much more emphasis on the role of the parent and teacher in cognitive development. He emphasized the function of speech, particularly as an aid to the child's development. His "zone of proximal development," a construct describing the ability of children to perform beyond their current level, has been found particularly useful for teachers.

Learning Theory

John Watson (1878–1958), the father of behaviorism, ushered in a movement that differed in important ways from classical developmental psychology. Learning became the central issue for study. Hence, a model based on Locke rather than Rousseau became the standard. In his famous "Little Albert" experiment (1920), Watson attempted to show how a child's emotional development could be understood in terms of learning. Later, Mary Cover Jones (1896–1987), with Watson's guidance, conducted a study of a three-year-old boy to demonstrate how undesirable fears could be eliminated, and by so doing, began the field of behavior modification.

After his departure from academic psychology, Watson continued to write about child development, and his work became popular among parents. He was instrumental in promoting a scientific basis for child care. Eventually, he was replaced as the leader of the child-care movement by less rigid and more child-oriented specialists such as Benjamin Spock.

Influences were still felt from outside of learning theory. Kurt Lewin (1890–1947), for instance, was more interested in motivation and conflict than learning. He conducted some well-designed field studies which had a practical impact on changing developmental psychology. Still, the focus of psychological research at this time was on learning, although some of it strayed from Watson's thinking.

One variation included the research of a group at Yale University under the intellectual leadership of Clark Hull (1884–1952). This group began a program of research that tried to combine learning theory and psychoanalytic theory. A member of the group, Robert Sears (1908–1989), applied learning principles to an understanding of the socialization of children. His work, with others, resulted in the book *Patterns of Child Rearing* (Sears, Maccoby, & Levin, 1957), a frequently cited assessment of child-rearing practices and outcomes. While the group was ultimately unsuccessful in uniting learning theory and psychoanalysis, they succeeded in moving developmental psychology away from a descriptive science to an empirically testable one. By the 1950s and 1960s in America, developmental psychology was dominated by these learning theory approaches.

Notable among more recent learning theorists was B. F. Skinner (1904–1990), a strict behaviorist, who stressed the role of operant learning. He and his followers performed many experiments demonstrating the role of reinforcement in everyday development. Skinner's work led to widespread use of behavior modification techniques, particularly among autistic children and the developmentally disabled. A highly influential contemporary behaviorist, Albert Bandura (1925–   ) has focused more on social learning than Skinner. He has emphasized the importance of modeling, and has conducted many experiments demonstrating how socialization takes place, including the development of aggression, altruism, and sex roles. More recently he has focused on issues of health psychology.

The Genetic Epistemology of Jean Piaget (1896–1980)

The impact of Jean Piaget's theory on U.S. developmental psychology can hardly be overestimated. Although he contributed a chapter to the first *Handbook of Child Psychology* (1931), his early work was largely ignored in the United States. By the 1950s, however, a revival of his work began. His stage theory soon became the centerpiece for American developmental psychology, attaining its most important role in the 1970s. His theory was not only essential for most psychologists, it became essential for educators as well.

Piaget saw the child as a scientist, actively constructing increasingly more complex views of the world. At each stage of development, the child is constrained by the cognitive structures available. Piaget was criticized for his methodology and his apparent unwillingness to address the approaches of other prominent developmentalists. Although the era of his greatest prominence has passed, his theory still continues to have an impact on a broad range of developmental issues.

Life-Span Psychology

Initially, most developmental psychology focused on the child and adolescent. However, there were some early attempts to investigate the entire life span. In 1777, Johann Tetens (1736–1807), a German physicist and philosopher, published a book which addressed many life-span issues still of concern today. Friedrich Carus (1770–1808) had a view of development that was similar to that of Tetens. He wrote that aging was not simply about loss and decline, but was an occasion for growth and perfectibility. Adolphe Quetelet (1796–1874) was probably the first to collect data on physical and psychological variables across the life span. Francis Galton (1822–1911), inspired by Quetelet, established an "anthropometric laboratory" in London in 1884, where he collected measurements on more than 9,000 people. His data constituted an early cross-sectional view of selected physical and psychological characteristics across the life span.

The work of these pioneers in life-span development was largely ignored. It was not until the 1920s and 1930s, with the publication of several textbooks on development, that life-span approaches became prominent again. There was additional interest in later developmental periods when several longitudinal studies began to come of age. Robert Havighurst (1900–1991) and Bernice Neugarten (1916–   ), at the University of Chicago, were active researchers on development in the middle and later years. Later, the University of West Virginia became an important site for research in life-span development.

Centers of Research

The Iowa Child Welfare Research Station was founded after World War I through the efforts of an Iowa housewife, Cora Bussey Hillis. She argued that if useful research could be conducted in order to understand animals, equally effective research should be directed to an understanding of the child. The Iowa Station was the first of many child development research centers to be established in the United States. Beginning in the 1920s, a number of institutes were established through the efforts of Lawrence K. Frank, initially with money provided by the Laura Spelman Rockefeller Memorial Fund.

Organizations and Journals

There are literally hundreds of organizations which are concerned with issues of human development. Many developmental psychologists belong to the American Psychological Association (APA), which includes divisions devoted to Developmental Psychology; Adult Development and Aging; and Child, Youth and Family Services. The APA publishes several relevant journals, including *Developmental Psychology* and *Psychology and Aging*. The American Psychological Society is also the organizational home for many American developmental psychologists. Increasingly, however, developmentalists are found in specialty organizations. One prominent developmental organization is the Society for Research in Child Development, begun in 1933, with its own journal, *Child Development*, and a monograph series.

The Future

Theorists no longer seem to be working on a "grand theory" of development; they are content with offering miniature theories. Greater attention has been paid to all ages of development so that the phrase "life-span development" more accurately reflects the science. As developmental psychologists have become more aware of the importance of context in development, they have become more vocal advocates for improving that context, particularly arguing for changes in government policy. There is increased awareness that values matter in development, and that science cannot provide those values. Although developmental psychology has traditionally emphasized research, a new subspecialty called applied developmental psychology, has emerged.

Bibliography

Aries, P. (1962). *Centuries of childhood.* New York: Random House. A view of children through history.

Borstelmann, L. J. (1983). Children before psychology: Ideas about children from antiquity to the late 1800s. In P. H. Mussen (Ed.), *Handbook of child psychology: Vol. 1. History, theory, and methods* (4th ed., pp. 1–40). New York: Wiley.

Cairns, R. B. (1997). The making of developmental psychology. In W. Damon (Ed.), *Handbook of child psychology* (5th ed., pp. 25–105). New York: Wiley. A comprehensive history of developmental psychology.

Charles, D. C. (1970). Historical antecedents of life-span developmental psychology. In L. R. Goulet & P. B. Baltes (Eds.), *Life-span developmental psychology: Research and theory.* New York: Academic Press.

Dixon, R. A., & Lerner, R. M. (1988). A history of systems in developmental psychology. In M. H. Bornstein & M. E. Lamb (Eds.), *Developmental psychology: An advanced textbook* (pp. 3–50). Hillsdale, NJ: Erlbaum.

Eckardt, G., Bringman, W. G., & Spring, L. (Eds.). (1985). *Contributions to a history of developmental psychology.* Berlin: Morton. Contains several important essays on European contributors to developmental psychology.

Hilgard, E. R. (1987). *Psychology in America.* New York: Harcourt Brace. The chapter on developmental psychology is spiced with relevant personal anecdotes and remembrances.

Kessen, W. (1965). *The child.* New York: Wiley. An excellent source for original readings.

Lerner, R. M. (1983). *Developmental psychology: Historical and philosophical perspectives.* Hillsdale, NJ: Erlbaum. Particularly useful for its emphasis on life-span development.

Parke, R. D., Ornstein, P. A., Rieser, J. J., & Zahn-Waxler, C. (Eds.). (1994). *A century of developmental psychology.* Washington, DC: American Psychological Association. (Original work published 1992.) A collection of excellent historical articles including some useful overview material.

Ross, D. (1972). *G. Stanley Hall: The psychologist as prophet.* Chicago: University of Chicago Press. A rich biography of the father of American developmental psychology.

Sears, R. R. (1975). Your ancients revisited: A history of child development. In E. M. Hetherington (Ed.), *Review of child development research* (Vol. 5, pp. 1–73). Chicago: University of Chicago Press. A history by one of the important contributors to the field.

Senn, M .J .E. (1975). Insights on the child development movement in the United States. *Monographs of the Society for Research in Child Development,* 40 (Serial No. 161).

John D. Hogan

Theories

Human beings, and their families, communities, and societies develop; they show systematic and successive changes over time. These changes are interdependent. Changes within one level of organization, for example, developmental changes in personality or cognition within the individual, are reciprocally related to developmental changes within other levels, for example, changes in caregiving patterns or spousal relationships within the familial level of organization (Lewis & Rosenblum, 1974).

Moreover, the reciprocal changes among levels of organization are both products and producers of the reciprocal changes within levels. For example, over time, parents' manner of behavior and of rearing influence children's personality and cognitive functioning and development; in turn, the interactions between personality and cognition constitute an emergent characteristic of human individuality that affects parental behaviors and the quality of family life.

These interrelations illustrate the integration of changes within and among the multiple levels of organization comprising the ecology of human life. Human development within this ecology involves organized and successive changes—that is, systematic changes—in the structure and function of interlevel relations over time. In other words, the human development system involves the integration, or "fusion" (Tobach & Greenberg, 1984), of changing relations among the multiple levels of organization that comprise the ecology of human behavior and development. These levels include biology, culture, and history.

Given that human development is the outcome of changes in this developmental system, then, for individual ontogeny, the essential process of development involves changing relations between the developing person and his or her changing context. Similarly, for any unit of analysis with the system (for example, for the family, studied over its life cycle, or the classroom, studied over the course of a school year), the same developmental process exists. In other words, development involves changing relations between that unit and variables from the other levels of organization within the human development system. Accordingly, the concept of development is a relational one. Development is a concept denoting systemic changes—that is, organized, successive, multilevel, and integrated changes—across the course of life of an individual (or other unit of analysis).

A focus on process, and particularly on the process involved in the changing relations between individuals and their contexts, is the predominant conceptual frame for research in the study of human development in the early twenty-first century. Previously, theories about human development often involved causal splits between nature and nurture (Gottlieb, 1997; Overton, 1998). These theories emphasized either predetermined organismic bases of development, for instance, as in attachment theory (Bowlby, 1969), ethological theory (Lorenz, 1965), behavioral genetics (Plomin, 1986), psychoanalytic theory (Freud, 1949), and neopsychoanalytic theory (A. Freud, 1969; Erikson, 1959), or environmental, reductionistic, and mechanistic bases of behavior and behavior change (Bijou & Baer, 1961).

Other theories stressed more of an interaction between organismic and environmental sources of development (Piaget, 1970). Nevertheless, there remained in the discipline a presupposition that there were two distinct sources of development, that is, that there was a split between organism and environment. As such, it was the role of theory to explain the contributions of these two separate domains of reality to human development (Overton, 1998).

The stress in contemporary theories, however, is on a "healing" of the nature/nurture split (Gottlieb, 1997), and on accounting for how the integrated developmental system functions, that is, for understanding probabalistic epigenesis. Gottlieb defined this process as being

> characterized by an increase of complexity or organization—that is, the emergence of new structural and functional properties and competencies—at all levels of analysis (molecular, subcellular, cellular, organismic) as a consequence of horizontal and vertical coactions among its parts, including organism-environment coactions. (1997, p. 90)

As such, the forefront of contemporary developmental theory and research is represented by theories of process, of how structures function and how functions are structured over time. For example, most contemporary research about human development is associated with theoretical ideas stressing that the dynamics of individual-context relations provide the bases of behavior and developmental change. Indeed, even models that try to separate biological or, more particularly, genetic, influences on an individual's development from contextual ones are at pains to (retro)fit their approach into a more dynamic systems perspective (Ford & Lerner, 1992; Thelen & Smith, 1994).

Four Dimensions

Thus, in emphasizing that systematic and successive change (that is, development) is associated with alterations in the dynamic relations among structures from multiple levels of organization, the scope of contemporary developmental theory and research is not limited by a unidimensional portrayal of the developing person (for example, the person seen from the vantage point of only cognitions, or emotions, or stimulus-response connections, or genetic imperatives). Contemporary developmental theory consists of four interrelated dimensions.

Change and Relative Plasticity. Contemporary theories stress that the focus of developmental understanding must be on systematic change (Ford & Lerner, 1992). This focus is required because of the belief that the potential for change exists across the life span (Baltes, 1987). Although it is also assumed that systematic change is not limitless (for example, it is constrained by both past developments and by contemporary contextual conditions), contemporary theories stress that "relative plasticity" exists across life— although the magnitude of this plasticity may vary across ontogeny.

There are important implications of relative plasticity for the application of developmental science. For instance, the presence of relative plasticity legitimates a proactive search across the life span for characteristics of people and of their contexts that, together, can influence the design of policies and programs promoting positive development (Fisher & Lerner, 1994).

Relationism and the Integration of Levels of Organization. Contemporary theories stress that the bases for change, and for both plasticity and constraints in development, lie in the relations that exist among the multiple levels of organization that comprise the substance of human life (Ford & Lerner, 1992; Schneirla, 1957; Tobach, 1981). These levels range from the inner biological level, through the individual psychological level and the proximal social relational level (involving dyads, peer groups, and nuclear families), to the sociocultural level (including key macro-institutions such as educational, governmental, and economic systems) and the natural and designed physical ecologies of human development (Bronfenbrenner, 1979; Riegel, 1975). These levels are structurally and functionally integrated, thus requiring a systems view of the levels involved in human development (Ford & Lerner, 1992; Sameroff, 1983; Thelen & Smith, 1994).

Developmental contextualism is one instance of such a developmental systems perspective. Developmental contextualism promotes a relational unit of analysis as a requisite for developmental analysis: Variables associated with any level of organization exist (are structured) in relation to variables from other levels; the qualitative and quantitative dimensions of the function of any variable are shaped as well by the relations that variable has with variables from other levels. Unilevel units of analysis (or the components of, or elements in, a relation) are not an adequate target of developmental analysis; rather, the relation itself—the interlevel linkage—should be the focus of such analysis (Riegel, 1975).

Relationism and integration have a clear implication for unilevel theories of development. At best, such theories are severely limited, and inevitably provide a non-veridical depiction of development, because of their focus on what are essentially main effects embedded in higher-order interactions (Walsten, 1990); at worst, such theories are neither valid nor useful. Accordingly neither biogenic theories, for example, genetic reductionistic conceptions such as behavioral genetics or sociobiology (Freedman, 1979; Plomin, 1986); psychogenic theories, for example, behavioristic or functional analysis models (Bijou & Baer, 1961); nor sociogenic theories, for example, "social mold" conceptions of socialization (Homans, 1961; Hartup, 1978) provide adequate theoretical frames for understanding human development. Simply, neither nature nor nurture theories provide adequate conceptualizations of human development (Gottlieb, 1997). For instance, theories that stress critical periods of development (Bowlby, 1969; Erikson, 1959; Lorenz, 1965), that is, periods of ontogeny constrained by biology (for example, by genetics or by maturation) are seen from the perspective of theories that stress relationism and integration as conceptually flawed (and empirically counterfactual).

Moreover, many nature/nurture interaction theories also fall short in this regard; theories of this type often treat nature and nurture variables as separable entities and view their connection in manners analogous to the interaction term in an analysis of variance (Bijou & Baer, 1961; Erikson, 1959; Plomin, 1986; Walsten, 1990). The cutting edge of contemporary theory moves beyond the simplistic division of sources of development into nature-related and nurture-related variables or processes; instead the multiple levels of organization that exist within the ecology of human development are seen as part of an inextricably fused developmental system.

Historical Embeddedness and Temporality. The relational units of analysis of concern in contemporary theories are understood as change units. The change component of these units derives from the ideas that all of the above-noted levels of organization involved in human development are embedded in history, that is, they are integrated with historical change (Elder, Modell, & Parke, 1993). Relationism and integration mean that no level of organization functions as a consequence of its own, isolated activity (Tobach, 1981). Each level functions as a consequence of its fusion (its structural integration) with other levels. History is a level of organization that is fused with all other levels. This linkage means that change is a necessary, an inevitable, feature of variables from all levels of organization (Baltes, 1987); in addition, it means that the structure, as well as the function, of variables changes over time.

Indeed, at the biological level of organization, one prime set of structural changes across history is subsumed under the theory of evolution; evolution can be applied also to functional changes (Darwin, 1872; Gottlieb, 1997). In turn, at more macro levels of organization many of the historically linked changes in social and cultural institutions or products are evaluated in the context of discussions of the concept of progress (Nisbet, 1980). The continuity of change that constitutes history can lead to both intra-individual (or, more generally, intralevel) continuity or discontinuity in development—depending on the rate, scope, and particular substantive component of the developmental system at which change is measured (Brim & Kagan, 1980). Thus, continuity at one level of analysis may be coupled with discontinuity at another level; quantitative continuity or discontinuity may be coupled with qualitative continuity or discontinuity within and across levels; and continuity or discontinuity can exist in regard to both the processes involved in (or the "explanations" of) developmental change and in the features, depictions, or outcomes (that is, the "descriptions") of these processes.

These patterns of within-person change pertinent to continuity and discontinuity can result in either constancy or variation in the rates at which different individuals develop in regard to a particular substantive domain of development. Thus, any pattern of intra-individual change can be combined with any instance of inter-individual differences in within-person change, that is, with any pattern of stability or instability. In other words, continuity-discontinuity is a dimension of intra-individual change and is distinct from, and independent of, stability-instability—which involves between-person change and is, therefore, a group, and not an individual, concept (Baltes, 1987; Lerner, 1986).

In sum, since historical change is continuous, temporality is infused in all levels of organization. This infusion may be associated with different patterns of continuity and discontinuity across people. The potential array of such patterns has implications for understanding the importance of human diversity.

The Limits of Generalizability, Diversity, and Individual Differences. The temporality of the changing relations among levels of organization means that changes that are seen within one historical period (or time of measurement), and/or with one set of instances of variables from the multiple levels of the ecology of human development, may not be seen at other points in time (Baltes, 1987; Bronfenbrenner, 1979). What is seen in one data set is only an instance of what does or what could exist. Accordingly, contemporary theories focus on diversity—of people, of relations, of settings, and of times of measurement.

Individual differences within and across all levels of organization are seen as having core, substantive significance in the understanding of human development (Baltes, 1987; Lerner, 1998). Diversity is the exemplary illustration of the presence of relative plasticity in human development. Diversity is also the best evidence that exists of the potential for change in the states and conditions of human life (Brim & Kagan, 1980).

Moreover, the individual structural and functional characteristics of a person constitute an important source of his or her development. The individuality of each person promotes variation in the fusions he or she has with the levels of organization within which the person is embedded. For instance, the distinct actions or physical features of a person promote differential actions (or reactions) in others toward him or her. These differential actions, which constitute feedback to the person, shape at least in part further change in the person's characteristics of individuality (Lerner, 1986; Schneirla, 1957). For example, the changing match, congruence, or goodness-of-fit between the developmental characteristics of the person and of his or her context provide a basis for consonance or dissonance in the ecological milieu of the person; the dynamic nature of this interaction constitutes a source of variation in positive and negative outcomes of developmental change (Thomas & Chess, 1977).

Methodological Implications

The temporality involved in contemporary theories of human development necessitates change-sensitive measures of structure and function and change-sensitive (that is, longitudinal) designs (Baltes, 1987; Brim & Kagan, 1980). The key question vis-à-vis temporality in such research is not whether change occurs; rather, the question is whether the changes that do occur make a difference for a given developmental outcome.

Moreover, given that the study of these changes will involve appraisal of both quantitative and qualitative features of change, which may occur at multiple levels of organization, there is a need to use both quantitative and qualitative data collection and analysis methods. In essence, then, the concepts of historical embeddedness and temporality indicate that a program of developmental research adequate to address the relational, integrated, embedded, and temporal changes involved in human life must involve multiple occasions, methods, levels, variables, and cohorts (Schaie, 1965).

Empirical appraisals of cross-time variation and covariation are more veridical with the character of change phenomena. Moreover, such analyses would afford examination of whether changes are consistent with theoretical propositions about developmental pro-

cesses. In other words, to study any process and, more basically, to study any change phenomenon, cross-temporal (multi-occasion) data must be gathered, and it would be both theoretically interesting and important and empirically useful to recast many extant cross-sectional data as longitudinal investigations.

Indeed, change-sensitive (that is, longitudinal) designs must be used in research that is intended to appraise adequately the alterations over time that are associated with individual behavior across the life span. As noted, these designs must involve the use of measures that are developed to be able to detect change; however, it is typically the case that measures of traits are not developed to be sensitive to developmental change. Furthermore, multivariate measurement models must be used to appraise the several individual and contextual levels integrated within and across developmental periods.

However, a dynamic, systems theory, such as developmental contextualism, would move the study of human development beyond just the point of promoting multivariate-longitudinal designs involving change-sensitive measures. In addition, developmental contextualism would lead scholars to design research studies that involve

1. dynamic (fused) relations among levels of organization (Ford & Lerner, 1992; Tobach & Greenberg, 1984) involved in the ecology of human development;
2. the appraisal of levels ranging from the inner-biological, and individual-psychological, to the physical ecological, the sociocultural, and the historical, and concepts that stress the ways in which levels interrelate, or are fused—such as the "goodness of fit" notion (Thomas & Chess, 1977)—may be particularly helpful;
3. the individual differences (the diversity) that derive from variation (for example, in the timing) of the interactions among levels; and
4. as necessary, a "co-learning" model for the design of research (and intervention) programs, which would rely on the contributions of individuals themselves to further knowledge about the issues, assets, and risks affecting their lives.

Such research thus diminishes problems of "alienation" between researchers and participants (Riegel, 1975) and suggests that any quantitative appraisal of human development rests on a qualitative understanding of their life spaces and meaning systems. Since such understanding is shaped at least in part by the participants' input, research, and especially programs derived from such information, is more likely to be efficacious for the participants.

Thus, developmental contextualism underscores the need for policies and programs that are derived from research to be diversity sensitive and to take a change-oriented, multilevel, integrated, and developmental systems approach (Ford & Lerner, 1992). The integrated nature of this system means that change can be effected by entering the system at any one of several levels or at several levels simultaneously—depending on the precise circumstances within which one is working and on the availability of multidisciplinary and multiprofessional resources.

Conclusions

Theoretical views such as developmental contextualism not only provide an agenda for a developmental, dynamic, and systems approach to research about human development but also allow for the promotion of positive developmental trajectories in people. When actualized, developmental systems, along with policies and programs, can ensure a continuous social support system across the life course. Such a system would be a network encompassing the familial, community, institutional, and cultural components of the ecology that impacts a person's behavior and development across his or her life (Bronfenbrenner, 1979).

There is growing recognition that traditional and artificial distinctions between science and service and between knowledge generation and knowledge application and practice need to be reconceptualized. Scholars, practitioners, and policy makers are increasingly recognizing the important role that developmental science can play in stemming the tide of insults to the quality of life caused by poverty, premature births, school failure, child abuse, crime, adolescent pregnancy, substance abuse, unemployment, welfare dependency, discrimination, ethnic conflict, and inadequate health and social resources.

Research designs that examine topics of immediate social concern, that consider both normative and atypical developmental pathways as means of promoting and enhancing human welfare, that take into account the contextual nature of development and employ ecologically valid means of assessing functioning, and that are sensitive to the ethical dimensions of action research are required if science is to make a difference in the life of the community. Without such research, the knowledge produced by developmental scientists risks being ignored or misused by practitioners, educators, policy makers, and the public itself.

[*See also* Behavioral Genetics; *and* Psychoanalysis.]

Acknowledgments. The preparation of this chapter was supported in part by a grant from the W. T. Grant Foundation.

Bibliography

Baltes, P. B. (1987). Theoretical propositions of life-span developmental psychology: On the dynamics between growth and decline. *Developmental Psychology, 23,* 611–626.

Bijou, S. W., & Baer, D. M. (Ed.). (1961). *Child development: A systematic and empirical theory.* New York: Appleton-Century-Crofts.

Bowlby, J. (1969). *Attachment and loss: Vol. 1. Attachment.* New York: Basic Books.

Brim, O. G., Jr., & Kagan, J. (Ed.). (1980). *Constancy and change in human development.* Cambridge, MA: Harvard University Press.

Bronfenbrenner, U. (1979). *The ecology of human development.* Cambridge, MA: Harvard University Press.

Cairns, R. B. (1998). The making of developmental psychology. In W. Damon (Series Ed.) & R. M. Lerner (Vol. Ed.), *The handbook of child psychology: Vol. 1. Theoretical models of human development.* (5th ed., pp. 25–106). New York: Wiley.

Darwin, C. (1872). *The expression of emotion in men and animals.* London: J. Murray.

Elder, G. H., Jr., Modell, J., & Parke, R. D. (1993). Studying children in a changing world. In G. H. J. Elder, J. Modell, & R. D. Parke (Eds.), *Children in time and place: Developmental and historical insights* (pp. 3–21). New York: Cambridge University Press.

Erikson, E. H. (1959). Identity and the life-cycle. *Psychological Issues, 1,* 18–164.

Fisher, C. B., & Lerner, R. M. (Eds.). (1994). *Applied developmental psychology.* New York: McGraw-Hill.

Ford, D. L., & Lerner, R. M. (1992). *Developmental systems theory: An integrative approach.* Newbury Park, CA: Sage.

Freedman, D. G. (1979). *Human sociobiology: A holistic approach.* New York: Free Press.

Freud, A. (1969). Adolescence as a developmental disturbance. In G. Caplan & S. Lebovier (Eds.), *Adolescence* (pp. 5–10). New York: Basic Books.

Freud, S. (1949). *Outline of psychoanalysis.* New York: Norton.

Gottlieb, G. (1997). *Synthesizing nature-nurture: Prenatal roots of instinctive behavior.* Mahwah, NJ: Erlbaum.

Hartup, W. W. (1978). Perspectives on child and family interaction: Past, present, and future. In R. M. Lerner & G. B. Spanier (Eds.), *Child influences on marital and family interaction: A life-span perspective* (pp. 23–45). New York: Academic Press.

Homans, G. C. (1961). *Social behavior: Its elementary forms.* New York: Harcourt, Brace, & World.

Lerner, R. M. (1986). *Concepts and theories of human development* (2nd ed.). New York: Random House.

Lerner, R. M. (1998). Theories of human development: Contemporary perspectives. In W. Damon (Series Ed.) & R. M. Lerner (Vol. Ed.). *The handbook of child psychology: Vol. 1. Theoretical models of human development.* (5th ed., pp. 1–24). New York: Wiley.

Lewin, K. (1943). Psychology and the process of group living. *Journal of Social Psychology, 17,* 113–131.

Lewis, M., & Rosenblum, L. A. (Ed.). (1974). *The effect of the infant on its caregivers.* New York: Wiley.

Lewontin, R. C., Rose, S., & Kamin, L. J. (1984). *Not in our genes: Biology, ideology, and human nature.* New York: Pantheon.

Lorenz, K. (1965). *Evolution and modification of behavior.* Chicago: University of Chicago Press.

Nisbet, R. A. (1980). *History of the idea of progress.* New York: Basic Books.

Overton, W. F. (1998). Developmental psychology: Philosophy, concepts, and methodology. In W. Damon (Series Ed.) & R. M. Lerner (Vol. Ed.), *The handbook of child psychology: Vol. 1. Theoretical models of human development* (5th ed., pp. 107–189). New York: Wiley.

Piaget, J. (1970). Piaget's theory. In P. H. Mussen (Ed.), *Carmichael's manual of child psychology* (pp. 703–732). New York: Wiley.

Plomin, R. (1986). *Development, genetics, and psychology.* Hillsdale, NJ: Erlbaum.

Riegel, K. F. (1975). Toward a dialectical theory of development. *Human Development, 18,* 50–64.

Sameroff, A. J. (1983). Developmental systems: Contexts and evolution. In W. Kessen (Ed.), *Handbook of child psychology: Vol. 1. History, theory, and methods* (pp. 237–294). New York: Wiley.

Schaie, K. W. (1965). A general model for the study of developmental problems. *Psychological Bulletin, 64,* 92–107.

Schneirla, T. C. (1957). The concept of development in comparative psychology. In D. B. Harris (Ed.), *The concept of development* (pp. 78–108). Minneapolis, MN: University of Minnesota Press.

Thelen, E., & Smith, L. B. (1994). *A dynamic systems approach to the development of cognition and action.* Cambridge, MA: MIT Press.

Thomas, A., & Chess, S. (1977). *Temperament and development.* New York: Brunner/Mazel.

Tobach, E. (1981). Evolutionary aspects of the activity of the organism and its development. In R. M. Lerner & N. A. Busch-Rossnagel (Eds.), *Individuals as producers of their development: A life-span perspective* (pp. 37–68). New York: Academic.

Tobach, E., & Greenberg, G. (1984). The significance of T. C. Schneirla's contribution to the concept of levels of integration. In G. Greenberg & E. Tobach (Eds.), *Behavioral evolution and integrative levels* (pp. 1–7). Hillsdale, NJ: Erlbaum.

Walsten, D. (1990). Insensitivity of the analysis of variance to heredity-environment interaction. *Behavioral and Brain Sciences, 13,* 109–120.

Richard M. Lerner and Marcella E. Korn

Research Methods

The topic of research methods in developmental psychology encompasses an array of methodological and statistical issues that arise when attempting to study development, or change in behavior as a function of time. To organize ideas about research methods, it is useful to distinguish among three domains—the design of developmental research, measurement issues that are of particular relevance in developmental work, and the statistical models and methods that characterize research efforts in the field.

Developmental Research Designs

The topic of developmental research designs has been broached many times during the past 75 years. As Wohlwill (1973) argued, the most basic aim of developmental science is to study change in behavior (B) as a function of time (T), or $B = f(T)$. Hence, developmental research designs should promote the modeling of change in behavior across time. Time can, however, be measured in many ways (Schroots & Birren, 1990), and different ways of indexing time have important implications for representing and understanding behavioral change. Because researchers are typically interested in the ontogenetic development of behaviors, the most common index of time is chronological age, or time since birth. Under this approach, the goal of developmental psychology is the determination of the relationship between a behavior of interest and the chronological age of participants, often symbolized as $B = f(A)$, reflecting the assumption that behavior (B) is a specifiable function of age (A). But, Schroots and Birren offered many other indicators of psychological age or time that are related to chronological age but that may govern, or at least better track, developmental change, so chronological age should be considered only an approximation of the optimal time dimension along which behavioral development should be charted.

One option that must be faced when designing a developmental study is whether the same individuals or different individuals will be measured at the multiple ages. Most researchers recognize the benefits of assessing the same individuals at the several times of measurement, as this allows the direct determination of age changes, or the age-related change in a given behavior by each individual (Baltes & Nesselroade, 1979). Of course, this approach can slow the progress of research if the aim of the investigation is to portray behavioral change across a considerable age span. To tackle this issue, Bell (1953) presented a method of approximating long-term age changes by means of shorter term study of several samples. This could be accomplished by assessing multiple groups of subjects belonging to different birth cohorts across more restricted age spans and then organizing the partially overlapping trends as a function of chronological age. This notion was formalized by Schaie (1965) as a general developmental model that recognized the potential influences on behavior of the chronological age (A) and birth cohort (C) of the individual as well as the historical moment or period (P) at which measurements are taken. The resulting conception was organized around the potential effects on behavior of age, period, and cohort, signified as $B = f(A, P, C)$, and the interpretation of these effects on behavior, as will be discussed below.

Clear distinctions among three simple developmental

designs are possible, based on considerations of age, period, and cohort effects. The most commonly used simple developmental design is the cross-sectional design, in which all measurements are obtained at a single time or period of measurement. Two or more samples of participants who differ in chronological age are obtained, and empirical results are arrayed as a function of the chronological age of the samples of participants. But, year of birth, or birth cohort, is perfectly correlated with, and therefore perfectly confounded with, chronological age in a cross-sectional design, so cohort effects are viable alternative explanations for any age-related trends in data.

Furthermore, because the performance of different samples is compared, cross-sectional designs can provide, at best, information on age-related differences, or age differences, as opposed to assessing directly changes with age. Several assumptions must be met in order to have confidence that age differences from a cross-sectional design represent trends that would likely result from individuals changing or developing across the age span of the study. Chief among these is the assumption that comparable sampling of participants was conducted for each of the samples. Even unintended differences in sampling may distort trends, yielding mean aging trends that no individual person would exhibit. For example, consider drawing random samples of students in school in grades 6, 8, 10, and 12. Students who drop out of school tend to perform at lower levels on many variables (for example, school achievement) than do students who remain in school through the completion of high school. Thus, a random sample of sixth graders would likely be more representative of all 11-year-olds than would a random sample of twelfth graders selected to be representative of all 17-year-olds, given the progressive dropout of students during junior and senior high schools. ˒

Even if one could verify equal representativeness of sampling at each age level, a cross-sectional design cannot yield information about the stability of individual differences from age to age, because different individuals are assessed at each time of measurement. Given the importance of understanding both the general developmental trend for any behavior of interest as well as individual differences around this trend, the inability to study individual differences in change is an important shortcoming of the cross-sectional design.

A second common design is the longitudinal design, in which all measurements are obtained from a single sample of participants, persons who are usually of a single birth cohort. This single sample is then observed at two or more times of measurement. Results from longitudinal studies are often arrayed as a function of the chronological age of the sample at the several times of measurement. But, historical time or period is perfectly correlated with, and hence completely con-

founded with, chronological age of participants at the different times of measurement, so historical period effects are alternative explanations of any purported age-related trends in data.

The longitudinal design has one major advantage over the cross-sectional design: the longitudinal design allows the researcher to study age changes, as changes in behavior by individuals are assessed directly by tracking the same subjects at two or more ages. This allows the modeling of individual differences about the developmental trend in addition to charting the mean developmental trend. Unfortunately, the typical longitudinal design also must confront at least two important methodological problems. The first of these involves retesting effects. Simply testing subjects a second time on a particular test often leads to some change in scores. In most longitudinal studies, participants are assessed at three or more times of measurement, increasing the likelihood that retesting will confound results of age changes. For example, Nesselroade and Baltes (1974) presented evidence that retesting effects explained approximately one half of the mean age changes on several dimensions of mental ability. The second problem concerns sample representativeness and the presence of the differential dropout of participants across time. Often, participants willing to commit to participation in a longitudinal design are not representative of the population at large, and later dropping out of a longitudinal study is usually nonrandom. Both of these problems limit the generalizations that may be made from longitudinal studies.

The time-lag design is a third simple developmental design, although it is rarely used. In the time-lag design, measurements are obtained from participants all of whom are the same age, but who are tested at different points in historical time. That is, one could study 10-year-olds in 2010, 2020, and so on. In a time-lag design, cohort and period are perfectly confounded. Further, because age is held constant, the time-lag design is most useful for tracking secular trends. Because developmental psychology has a primary goal of studying age-related trends and because age is held constant in this design, the time-lag design has less direct relevance for the field than do the other two simple designs, but timely applications of the time-lag design should not be overlooked.

Returning to the general developmental model proposed by Schaie (1965), three more complex developmental designs are possible within this framework. These are (a) the cohort-sequential design, obtained by the factorial crossing of cohort and age; (b) the time-sequential design, arising from the factorial crossing of period (or time of measurement) and age; and the cross-sequential design, defined by the factorial crossing of cohort and period (or time). Although Schaie initially contended that the effects of age, cohort, and period could be identified separately, subsequent commentators (for example, Mason & Fienberg, 1985) have concluded that the influences of age, cohort, and period cannot be disentangled in a simple mathematical way. The lack of separate identification of these effects is portended by the dependence among age, period, and cohort in any of the three designs discussed by Schaie. For example, consider the cohort-sequential design, in which cohort and age are crossed factorially. In this design, the time of measurement (or period) is fixed by the need to assess a given cohort at a particular chronological age (for example, children born in 2000 and assessed at 10 years of age must be assessed in the year 2010). Thus, one cannot vary factorially and independently all three factors of age, period, and cohort in a single design; once levels of two of these factors are fixed, the levels of the third are fixed as well.

Because effects of the three factors of age, period, and cohort cannot be estimated separately, the choice of a design should be dictated by theory regarding which factors will have important influences on change. For example, the effects in a cohort-sequential design, in which cohort and age are crossed, are interpreted most simply under the assumption that period (or historical time) has no influence on the behavior of interest. If this assumption is accurate, the cohort-sequential design yields age trends for each of several cohorts, enabling the researcher to study the form of general age trends and how these are moderated by cohort. Similar conditions hold for the two remaining designs: the time-sequential design offering clear interpretations if cohort effects are negligible, and the cross-sequential design yielding unconfounded interpretations if age effects are assumed to be zero. Given these considerations, the cross-sequential design appears to be the least adequate of the three complex designs, as age effects must be assumed to be zero, and the cohort-sequential design is the most optimal, because both age and cohort are explicitly included in the design. Ironically, the cross-sequential design has been the most widely used of the designs (for example, Nesselroade & Baltes, 1974), and the cohort-sequential design has arguably been the least used of the designs. The reasons for the differential use of designs are clear, as the cohort-sequential design takes a longer number of years to complete and yields developmental functions across a smaller number of age levels. Still, the cohort-sequential design deserves wider use in the future to corroborate and place on firmer empirical footing the findings generated by other designs.

Measurement Issues

Measurement involves the assignment of numbers to observations (for example, persons) to represent the magnitude of a particular characteristic for each observation. Thus, one may use a ruler to assign numbers on any of a set of numerical units—for example, inches, feet, or centimeters—to represent the height of each of a set of individuals. Here, the measuring device is the ruler, the characteristic of interest is height, and a direct ratio mapping exists between the length on the measuring scale and the numbers to be assigned to observations.

Measurement is a crucial, if undervalued, aspect of all research endeavors in psychology, with profound implications for representing relations among variables and hence for the theories designed to account for these phenomena. Nowhere is the importance of measurement more obvious than in developmental psychology. When attempting to study the relation of behavior to age, as $B = f(A)$, measurement is paramount, for one must ensure that the units of a measurement scale are comparable across the age span and that one is assessing the same characteristic at all ages for the function related behavior and age to have any interpretation. Researchers frequently assume that their measurements embody desiderata such as comparability of units across age levels but rarely are these assumptions tested directly.

Scales of measurement are often discussed in terms of the well-known classification into nominal, ordinal, interval, and ratio scales. Numbers on a nominal scale serve only to identify the class into which a person falls and do not imply an ordering of individuals on any continuum. In contrast, numbers on the remaining three scales provide an ordering of individuals: an ordering with unequal intervals using an ordinal scale, with equal intervals on the interval scale, and with both equal intervals and a nonarbitrary zero point with a ratio scale.

Cross-cutting the preceding classification, at least partially, is the distinction between qualitative and quantitative variables. A nominal scale clearly represents qualitative differences among persons, but the relations between the three remaining scale types and the qualitative-quantitative distinction are less clear. For example, an ordinal scale might represent an ordered categorical or qualitative variable, with numbers representing different, qualitatively distinct, and hierarchically ordered stages. Or, the ordinal scale may represent an initial, unrefined attempt to assess a quantitative continuum. The confusion between scale types and the qualitative-quantitative distinction has been muddied by researchers in certain domains (for example, moral development, ego development) who have argued for the viability of qualitative, hierarchically ordered stages in the particular domain, but these same researchers have provided instruments with scoring options that yield scores that seemingly fall on interval scales, suggesting the presence of a quantitative dimension. Complications of this sort continue to concern the field of developmental psychology.

Early longitudinal studies, such as the Berkeley Growth Study by Bayley (1956; Bayley & Jones, 1937) employed measures from multiple domains, and many of the variables had either ratio or at least interval status. For example, Bayley (1956) displayed charts of growth in height and weight, which are usually assumed to meet the stipulations of a ratio scale. These scales enabled the fitting of informative age functions to data but were of greater utility in portraying physical growth than psychological development. For psychological development, Bayley developed an interesting approach to constructing derived scales for psychological variables (for example, her 16-D scale was normed to the mean and standard deviation exhibited by a sample of 16-year-olds) that would allow one to study changes in both mean and variance across age levels. However, the idea never took hold, and measurement concerns have a less central role than in the past. Most contemporary work uses measures designed for use with participants in fairly restricted age ranges, circumventing problems of comparability across extended age ranges and, in the process, hindering the study of developmental changes across these broader age levels. Moreover, the only measures that tend to be used across a wide range of ages during the developmental period from infancy through adolescence are measures of intelligence. These measures typically provide an IQ, which is normed in a nondevelopmental fashion—to yield a mean of 100 and standard deviation of 15 in the population at each age level. Hence, modeling the mean developmental trend is hazardous or impossible given the measurement properties of most measures used in current research.

One dependent variable that may provide a common metric across age levels and is widely used in studies of cognitive processes is reaction time, a variable that appears clearly to have ratio scale properties. In aging work, several meta-analyses have been performed on the general slowing hypothesis. Under general slowing, the rate of mental processes may slow (Birren, 1965) or information may be lost in a consistent fashion (Myerson, Hale, Wagstaff, Poon, & Smith, 1990) during the aging period. Regardless of the basis for the effect, various mathematical and statistical models have been fit to reaction time data to represent the extent and consistency of the slowing. Some work has been done to model the speeding up of processing, represented by reductions in reaction time, during childhood and adolescence. The basis of the speeding up of processing during the developmental period, however, is treated as a quantitative improvement in performance, and this is clearly a problematic assumption, as it may be for slowing during aging.

For example, in the domain of numerical processing (for example, addition, subtraction), children appear to proceed through a series of qualitatively distinct stages, representing different strategies for solving problems of a given type. Regardless of whether strategy choice continues unabated throughout life or a person finally adopts his or her optimal strategy and uses this strategy consistently, the qualitative advances in strategies may underlie the quantitative improvements in reaction time (Widaman, 1991). Thus, researchers may misconstrue the research problem as the understanding of the form of the function relating the quantitative reaction time variable to age, whereas the important developmental finding is the qualitative changes producing the quantitative improvements in performance. This is but one example of the measurement problems arising in developmental contexts. Future advances in both substantive theory and measurement theory may lead the way to clearer thinking about such problems—studying the measures of behavior that matter the most, rather than studying measures of behavior that are easiest to amass.

Statistical Models and Procedures

During the 1950s and 1960s, Wohlwill (1973) detected a clear "invasion of the experimentalists" into developmental psychology. This invasion took the form of researchers trained in experimental studies of mature persons, usually college students, opting to design studies that included multiple age groups, to test whether similar results would be found at all points on the age continuum. This invasion had both strengths and weaknesses. For example, the rigor of developmental research was perhaps improved, and research topics certainly were expanded in interesting directions, but, the results generated often had less relevance to traditional issues that defined the field than did typical research results.

Experimentalism has become firmly ensconced as one approach to developmental science. Statistical methodologists, however, have brought to the field the most modern analytic techniques available. Nevertheless, the standard methods of statistics—including correlation, regression, and the analysis of variance (ANOVA)—continue to be the most commonly used in developmental studies and will likely be the standard for some time to come.

Before discussing the newer methods of representing and analyzing developmental data, some comments should be made about the kinds of questions traditionally framed within developmental theories. The standard techniques of ANOVA and correlation and regression analysis are frequently used in developmental research and are often used as intended, but these techniques are subject to misuse and may fail to capture certain important aspects of developmental data. For example, ANOVA, designed to analyze mean differences across levels of qualitative independent variables, is used to test developmental changes as a function of age in many contexts. However, when used with longitudinal, repeated measures data, researchers cannot model the pattern of individual differences over time, as these are relegated to the within-group covariance matrices, which are frequently ignored and almost always unreported in research publications.

With correlation/regression methods, crucial tests of differences across groups often are not conducted, leaving the research literature in disarray. For example, when investigating gender differences in development, researchers commonly test whether correlations or regression weights differ significantly from zero, and they do this separately for samples of males and females. If a correlation or regression weight is significant for one group and not for the other, this is construed as evidence of a difference in the development of the genders. The crucial tests of the difference between the correlations (or regression weights) for the two groups, however, might reveal nonsignificance, suggesting a lack of difference across genders in developmental processes. Tests of the significance of the difference between independent correlations are often viewed as unpowerful, however, failure to utilize the proper tests results in a research literature that is open to many, conflicting interpretations.

Regardless of their inadequacies and potential misuse, ANOVA and correlation and regression analysis have helped frame statistically the important questions asked in developmental research. ANOVA emphasizes the understanding of the mean developmental trend, and correlation and regression analysis are used to study individual differences about the mean trend. Indeed, correlational measures were the mainstay for investigations of the differentiation of abilities and other processes during childhood and adolescence. The invasion of the statistical methodologists may be seen as an attempt to introduce new methods of analysis that correct problems in both ANOVA and correlation/regression analysis and that represent more adequately developmental processes and developmental change.

In a special issue of *Child Development* published in early 1987, several researchers promoted the utility of structural equation modeling (SEM) for developmental psychology, although others offered rational concerns about how the techniques would be used and interpretations would be drawn. Despite misgivings, the manner in which SEM can structure ideas and results cannot be discounted. Indeed, ways of addressing many key problems—including the distinctions between state and trait constructs as well as the proper causal lag in longitudinal studies—are uniquely applied with SEM. These benefits have been so clearly realized that applications of SEM in developmental research are becoming quite common.

One way of using SEM informatively in developmental research is multiple-group confirmatory factor analysis (CFA) to study the factorial invariance of a set of measures (Widaman & Reise, 1997). Using this multiple-group CFA approach, the investigator can test whether a consistent relation holds between the underlying factors and their observed indicators across age levels. Factorial invariance of this type is evidence that the same theoretical constructs are assessed at the different age levels. Moreover, researchers may then investigate differences in mean level and variance on the latent variables identified, as well as the structural relations among the latent variables. In the future, applications of item response theory methods, which are related to CFA models (Reise, Widaman, & Pugh, 1993), offer hope of establishing the comparability of the metric of measured variables across age levels, a problem that continues to plague the field.

Another application of SEM that has special relevance to developmental research is the specification of growth curve models. Under this approach, data from multiple times of measurement are the primary measured variables, and the latent variables that are specified represent both initial level at the first time of measurement and growth since the first time of measurement. Because individual differences in both level and growth are identified in this manner, variance on these latent variables may be predicted from other variables in the model. In this way, the investigator may find the key explanatory variables that account for individual differences in initial level and subsequent growth in a particular behavior of interest. Contributions in this vein continue to mount, and fruitful approaches for dealing with planned or unplanned missing data, a common woe in longitudinal studies, are being developed.

Yet another approach to the identification of level and growth factors within longitudinal data is a generic approach often identified as hierarchical linear modeling (HLM) (Bryk & Raudenbush, 1987, 1992). HLM recognizes the hierarchical structure of data. For example, children are nested within families, families are nested within socioeconomic strata, and so forth. In a longitudinal study, measurements at different ages are nested within individuals, so initial level and growth can be represented in HLM models, along with predictors of both initial level and subsequent growth. Whether SEM or HLM models are able to fit easily or well growth data in which individuals may have different intercepts, growth rates, and asymptotes is a topic for future research.

Another statistical model that will be of increasing importance for developmental psychology goes by the name of survival analysis (Willett & Singer, 1997). Here, an important transition or event—such as dying or dropping out of school—is the outcome variable.

The survival model represents the likelihood or probability of the event as a function of age, and covariates may be added that affect the likelihood of occurrence. Although survival modeling is rare in developmental research, applications of the method are almost certain to increase in the future.

Advances have been made in representing qualitative developmental advances as well. For example, Collins and Cliff (1990) discussed a longitudinal extension to the Guttman scale for representing unitary, cumulative development. In 1997, Collins and colleagues (Collins, Graham, Rousculp, & Hansen, 1997) developed computer programs and analytic procedures for latent class analysis and latent transition analysis (LTA). LTA is useful for representing the unidirectional changes that characterize certain domains of behavior, such as stages of drug use or stages of arithmetic competence. LTA yields probabilities of making the transition from one level or stage to another more advanced stage and can test assumptions of lack of regressions to earlier levels or stages. Moreover, covariates can be included that explain individual differences in probabilities of stage transition.

One common requirement of all of the preceding new methods of analysis is the need for large sample sizes. This is perhaps the single largest stumbling block to widespread, confident use of these methods, as the standards in the field—given the temporal and monetary expenses associated with longitudinal studies—are for sample sizes that are not optimal for the application of sophisticated methods of analysis. With the elegant methods of analysis that have been and are being developed, the field of developmental psychology will be well equipped to understand growth, stability, and decline across the life span in unprecedented ways if a solid commitment is made to collection of adequate measurements on samples of adequate size.

Summary

The research methods used in developmental psychology are undergoing tremendous change, abetted by the invasion of the statistical methodologists. Continuing advances in the design of studies, the construction of measures and their proper scoring, and the methods used to analyze data promise exciting advances in the substantive understanding of the growth and development of individuals across the life span.

Bibliography

Baltes, P. B., & Nesselroade, J. R. (1979). History and rationale of longitudinal research. In J. R. Nesselroade & P. B. Baltes (Eds.), *Longitudinal research in the study of behavior and development* (pp. 1–39). New York: Academic Press.

Bayley, N. (1956). Individual patterns of development. *Child Development, 27,* 45–74.

Bayley, N., & Jones, H. E. (1937). Environmental correlates of mental and motor development: A cumulative study from infancy to six years. *Child Development, 8,* 329–341.

Bell, R. Q. (1953). Convergence: An accelerated longitudinal approach. *Child Development, 24,* 145–152.

Birren, J. E. (1965). Age changes in speed of behavior: Its central nature and physiological correlates. In A. T. Welford & J. E. Birren (Eds.), *Behavior, aging, and the nervous system* (pp. 191–216). Springfield, IL: Charles C. Thomas.

Bryk, A. S., & Raudenbush, S. W. (1987). Application of hierarchical linear models to assessing change. *Psychological Bulletin, 101,* 147–158.

Bryk, A. S., & Raudenbush, S. W. (1992). *Hierarchical linear models: Applications and data analysis methods.* Newbury Park, CA: Sage.

Collins, L. M., & Cliff, N. (1990). Using the longitudinal Guttman simplex as a basis for measuring growth. *Psychological Bulletin, 108,* 128–134.

Collins, L. M., Graham, J. W., Rousculp, S. S., & Hansen, W. B. (1997). Heavy caffeine use and the beginning of the substance use onset process: An illustration of latent transition analysis. In K. J. Bryant, M. Windle, & S. G. West (Eds.), *The science of prevention: Methodological advances from alcohol and substance abuse research* (pp. 79–99). Washington, DC: American Psychological Association.

Mason, W. M., & Fienberg, S. E. (Eds.). (1985). *Cohort analysis in social research: Beyond the identification problem.* New York: Springer-Verlag.

Myerson, J., Hale, S., Wagstaff, D., Poon, L. W., & Smith, G. A. (1990). The information-loss model: A mathematical theory of age-related cognitive slowing. *Psychological Review, 97,* 475–487.

Nesselroade, J. R., & Baltes, P. B. (1974). Adolescent personality development and historical change: 1970–1972. *Monographs of the Society for Research in Child Development, 39* (1, Ser. No. 154).

Reise, S. P., Widaman, K. F., & Pugh, R. H. (1993). Confirmatory factor analysis and item response theory: Two approaches for exploring measurement invariance. *Psychological Bulletin, 114,* 552–566.

Schaie, K. W. (1965). A general model for the study of developmental problems. *Psychological Bulletin, 64,* 92–107.

Schroots, J. J. F., & Birren, J. E. (1990). Concepts of time and aging in science. In J. E. Birren & K. W. Schaie (Eds.), *Handbook of the psychology of aging* (3rd ed., pp. 45–64). San Diego: Academic Press.

Widaman, K. F. (1991). Qualitative transitions amid quantitative development: A challenge for measuring and representing change. In L. M. Collins & J. L. Horn (Eds.), *Best methods for the analysis of change: Recent advances, unanswered questions, future directions* (pp. 204–217). Washington, DC: American Psychological Association.

Widaman, K. F., & Reise, S. P. (1997). Exploring the measurement invariance of psychological instruments: Applications in the substance use domain. In K. J. Bryant, M. Windle, & S. G. West (Eds.), *The science of prevention: Methodological advances from alcohol and substance abuse research* (pp. 281–324). Washington, DC: American Psychological Association.

Willett, J. B., & Singer, J. D. (1997). Using discrete-time survival analysis to study event occurrence across the life course. In I. H. Gotlib & B. Wheaton (Eds.), *Stress and adversity over the life course: Trajectories and turning points* (pp. 273–294). New York: Cambridge University Press.

Wohlwill, J. F. (1973). *The study of behavioral development.* New York: Academic Press.

Keith F. Widaman

DEVELOPMENTAL SCIENCE. A common characteristic of scientific progress in empirical disciplines is increasing specialization. In natural sciences, when specialization has reached a certain stage, the engaged researchers recognize that the important next step for further understanding of the structures and processes with which they are concerned is in integration with neighboring disciplines. An important step forward for understanding and explaining the function and development of the physical world was taken when specialization in physics and chemistry as distinctly different disciplines was followed by integration in the interface of the two and the establishment of a new field: physical chemistry. During the last decades of the twentieth century, the most important scientific progress has taken place in the interface, first, of chemistry and biology, and later of chemistry, physics, and biology, all highly specialized fields. The characteristic iterative process of specialization and integration can be seen in the contributions to scientific progress that have been awarded Nobel prizes during the postwar period.

A prerequisite for this iterative process has been the fact that subdisciplines in natural sciences function within the same common general model of nature. Since the end of the seventeenth century, the Newtonian model of the physical world served two interrelated general purposes: (a) it offered a common theoretical framework for planning and implementation of empirical research on specific problems; and (b) it offered a common conceptual space for effective communication among researchers concerned with problems at very different levels of the total universe.

An Emerging Scientific Discipline

The way that the total system of mental, biological, behavioral, and social factors functions in a specific situation is the result of a developmental process, starting at conception. From the beginning, constitutional factors form the potentialities and set the restrictions for nested developmental processes of maturation and experiences. The characteristic features of these processes are determined in a continuous interaction among mental, biological, and behavioral person-bound factors and social, cultural, and physical characteristics of the environment.

The overriding goal for scientific psychology is to contribute to the understanding and explanation of why individuals think, feel, act, and react as they do in real life, and to understanding and explaining the developmental background to the current functioning of individuals at different stages of the life course. For effective research toward this goal, the view of individual functioning and development briefly summarized here has two consequences. First, knowledge from a number of specialized scientific disciplines must be considered. The total space of phenomena involved in the processes of lifelong individual development forms a clearly defined and delimited domain for scientific discovery, which constitutes a scientific discipline of its own: developmental science (Magnusson & Cairns, 1996). Accordingly, developmental science refers to "a fresh synthesis that has been generated to guide research in the social, psychological, and biobehavioral disciplines" (Carolina Consortium on Human Development, 1996, p. 1). This domain is located in the interface of developmental psychology, developmental biology, physiology, neurospsychology, social psychology, sociology, anthropology, and neighboring disciplines. Indications of the relevance of this proposition appear at an increasing pace. Under the auspices of the Royal Swedish Academy of Sciences, which is responsible for most of the Nobel prizes, and funded by the Nobel Foundation, a symposium was held in 1994 that clearly demonstrated the motives for the new discipline (Magnusson, 1996). The establishment of the Center for Developmental Science at the University of North Carolina in Chapel Hill (Cairns, Elder, & Costello, 1996), and the newly established scientific journal, *Applied Developmental Science*, are among other manifestations of this development.

Second, for research in this new field to be effective, it needs a common theoretical framework, serving the same purposes as the common theoretical framework in natural sciences. Such a theoretical perspective has to consider the proposition that the individual functions and develops as an integrated whole, and is part of an integrated person-environment system, that is, it must take on a holistic perspective (Magnusson, 1995).

A Holistic Perspective. A modern holistic view emphasizes an approach to the individual and the person-environment system as organized wholes, functioning as integrated totalities. The individual develops as an integrated, complex, and dynamic organism, and the individual is an active, purposeful part of an integrated, complex, and dynamic person-environment system. At each level, the totality derives its characteristic features and properties from the interaction among the elements involved, not from the effect of each isolated part on the totality. Each aspect of the structures and processes that are operating (perceptions, plans, values, goals, motives, biological factors, conduct, etc.), as well as each aspect of the environment, takes on meaning from the role it plays in the total functioning of the individual.

Two comments are pertinent here. First, the role and functioning of a holistic model is not to offer a specific hypothesis or an explanation for all problems. The Newtonian model did not answer all questions in natural sciences about the structure and functioning of the physical world, but it served the two purposes summarized earlier. The same role would be played by a holistic model of individual functioning and development. Second, the holistic, integrated model for individual functioning and individual development does not imply that the entire system of an individual must be studied in every research endeavor. Acceptance of a common model of nature for research in natural sciences has never implied that the whole universe should be investigated in every study.

The Modern Holistic Model. A holistic view, that is, making the individual the organizing principle for individual functioning and development, is not a new idea in scientific psychology. During the first part of the twentieth century, some of the most distinguished psychologists, among them Gordon Allport, Alfred Binet, Wilhelm Stern, Egon Brunswik, and Kurt Lewin strongly argued, from different perspectives, for a holistic position. However, for a long time, the propositions put forward had little if any impact on empirical psychological research. A main reason for this state of affairs was that the traditional holistic model lacked specific content about the functioning and interplay of basic psychological, biological, and social elements operating in the processes of the integrated organism. What occurred between the stimulus and the response was regarded as unknown and inaccessible for scientific inquiry; it was concealed in the black box.

However, later in the twentieth century, the holistic perspective was enriched in a way that not only emphasized the old claim for the necessity of a holistic approach to psychological inquiry, but also helped turn such an approach into a solid theoretical foundation for planning, implementing, and interpreting empirical research on specific problems.

The new scenery is the result of influences from four main interrelated sources.

1. For a long time, a consequence of the postwar dominance of stimulus-response models was the neglect of mental processes. However, since the 1960s, research on information processing, memory, and decision making has made dramatic progress, and has contributed essential knowledge to the understanding and explanation of individual development and functioning.

2. During the last decades of the twentieth century in biological and medical sciences developments have helped fill the empty holistic model with new content from three main interrelated directions.

- The first contribution concerns detailed knowledge about the brain, how it develops from conception over the life span in a process of interaction between constitutional factors and context factors, and how it functions at each stage of development, as an active organ, selecting, interpreting, and integrating information from the environment. The rapid development of research on brain functioning and its role for understanding mental processes has helped bridge the gap between biological and psychological models that had obstructed a deeper understanding and explanation of mental and behavioral processes (Barinaga, 1997).
- The second contribution lies in new insights into the role of internal biological structures and processes in the total functioning and development of individuals. Research into the role of biochemicals in the developmental processes of individuals, and in the individual's way of dealing with current situational-environmental conditions is developing at an increasing pace (Susman, 1993).
- Third, research in molecular biology, fostered by the discovery of DNA, has opened up new perspectives for understanding the mechanisms behind genetic factors in developmental processes.

3. The third important source for the application of a holistic perspective in psychological research lies in the general modern models that have been developed in the natural sciences for the study of dynamic, complex processes. In psychology, the most influential of these models has been the general systems theory (Thelen, 1989). The modern models for dynamic complex processes are important for research on developmental phenomena in several interrelated respects.

- The models emphasize the holistic, integrated nature of dynamic, complex processes. At all levels, the systems involved in the total person-environment system are undivided in function.
- The models emphasize the interactive, often nonlinear character of the processes within the organism and in the organism's interaction with the environment.
- The interactive character of dynamic processes means that the models highlight the concept of context. The role of context is important for understanding individual development at all levels of the total system, from the cellular level to the individual's interaction with the environment. In most developmental research, the concept of context has been used to denote the environment in which an individual grows up and functions (Lerner & Kauffman, 1985). The de-

velopmental science perspective draws the attention to a broader view of the role of context.

- The models provide a theoretical basis for the development of effective methodological tools for the investigation of the interactive, dynamic processes underlying individual functioning and development. The basis for the claim that the processes of individual development are accessible to systematic, scientific inquiry is that these processes are not random: They occur in a specific way within organized structures and are guided by lawful principles. In natural sciences the formulation of the new models has led to a strong methodological development. It is important for further real progress in psychological research that we create methodological tools appropriate to the nature of the phenomena of primary concern in developmental science.

4. The fourth main source lies in the revival of longitudinal research. Inadequacies of the piecemeal or variable-oriented approach to the study of developmental issues become obvious in well-planned longitudinal studies that track individuals over time and contexts. Such a design is necessary for understanding developmental processes for a number of reasons. One is that operating factors necessarily shift over time, both with respect to which factors operate, their distinct character per se, and their significance and role in the total integrated interactive processes of the individual. It is only the organism that remains distinct and identifiable.

The Holistic Perspective in the Mainstream of Life Sciences Research. The definition of developmental science as a well-defined field for scientific inquiry rests on the holistic view of individual functioning and development. This view is in line with developments in other disciplines concerned with dynamic, complex processes, for example, meteorology, ecology, chemistry, and biology.

The contributions from cognitive research, research in biology and medicine, modern models for dynamic complex processes, and longitudinal research have enriched the old holistic view of individual development in a way that makes it a fruitful theoretical framework for planning, implementing, and interpreting empirical research in the field of developmental science. The modern holistic view offers us a stable platform for further scientific progress in developmental science, enabling us to fall into step with what happens in other scientific disciplines in life sciences.

The Role of Psychology in Developmental Science

The proposition that research on individual development constitutes a field of research with its special demands on theory, methodology, and research strategy, does not mean that psychology loses its identity as a scientific discipline. Physics, chemistry, and biology did not lose their special merits as a result of new developments in the interfaces among them. Rather, by contributing essential knowledge to the field of developmental science, psychology strengthens its position as an active partner in the mainstream of scientific progress in the life sciences.

[*Many of the people mentioned in this article are the subjects of independent biographical entries.*]

Bibliography

Barinaga, M. (1997). Visual system provides clues to how the brain perceives. *Science, 275,* 1583–1585.

Cairns, R. B., Elder, G. H., Jr., & Costello, E. J. (1996). *Developmental science.* Cambridge, England: Cambridge University Press.

Carolina Consortium on Human Development. (1996). Developmental science: Toward a unified framework. In R. B. Cairns, G. H. Elder, Jr., & E. J. Costello (Eds.), *Developmental Science* (pp. 1–6). Cambridge, England: Cambridge University Press.

Lerner, R. M., & Kauffman, M. B. (1985). The concept of development in contextualism. *Developmental Review, 5,* 309–333.

Magnusson, D. (1995). Individual development: A holistic integrated model. In P. Moen, G. H. Elder, Jr., & K. Lüscher (Eds.), *Linking lives and contexts: Perspectives on the ecology of human development* (pp. 19–60). Washington, DC: American Psychological Association.

Magnusson, D. (Ed.). (1996). *The life-span development of individuals: Behavioral, neurobiological, psychosocial perspectives. A synthesis.* Cambridge, England: Cambridge University Press.

Magnusson, D., & Cairns, R. B. (1996). Developmental science: Toward a unified framework. In R. B. Cairns, G. H. Elder, Jr., & E. J. Costello (Eds.), *Developmental science* (pp. 7–30). Cambridge, England: Cambridge University Press.

Susman, E. J. (1993). Psychological, contextual, and psychobiological interactions: A developmental perspective on conduct disorder. *Development and Psychopathology, 5,* 181–189.

Thelen, E. (1989). Self-organization in developmental processes: Can systems approaches work? In M. R. Gunnar & E. Thelen (Eds.), *Systems theory and development* (pp. 77–117). Hillsdale, NJ: Erlbaum.

David Magnusson

DEWEY, JOHN (1859–1952), American philosopher, educator, and psychologist. A native of Burlington, Vermont, Dewey graduated from the University of Vermont in 1879. In 1882, after three years as a high school teacher, he began graduate work in philosophy at Johns

Hopkins University, where he studied the "new" physiological psychology with G. Stanley Hall (1844–1924) and logic with Charles S. Peirce (1839–1914). Given his interest in Charles Darwin, G. W. F. Hegel, and liberal Congregational theology, however, Dewey gravitated to the third member of the department, George S. Morris (1840–1889), whose "dynamic idealism" was inspired by Hegel. On completion of his doctorate in 1884, Dewey was hired as an instructor at the University of Michigan. Except for a brief appointment at the University of Wisconsin, he remained at the University of Michigan for the next 10 years. In 1886, he married Harriet Alice Chipman (1858–1927). Their daughter Jane would later write that Alice was instrumental in awakening in Dewey a critical attitude toward religious dogma and social injustice. Alice Chipman Dewey died in 1927. In 1946, Dewey married Roberta Lowitz Grant (1904–1970), and in 1948 they adopted two young children. Dewey died on 1 June 1952 at his home in New York City.

Dewey's earliest articles on psychology attempted to reconcile the idealism of Morris with the new experimental psychology of Hall. The full-frontal attacks on dualism that would be a central feature of his later work were already present during this period. He rejected the theories of the British empiricists on the grounds that they treated the elements of sensation as prior to experience rather than as products of reflection upon it. Psychology must start with experience, he argued, and it is only afterwards that the relations between subject and object can be isolated. The task of the psychologist is to show how these relations arise out of consciousness.

In his *Psychology* (1886), the first textbook for the "new" psychology published by an American, Dewey continued his efforts to reconcile Hegelian idealism with experimental psychology. Both Hall and William James criticized Dewey's approach, however, because of its attempt to rescue idealism and its reliance on "soul" as a psychological concept. Although Dewey's text was widely adopted, it was soon supplanted by others, including James's own *Principles of Psychology* (1890).

Dewey's revisions of his *Psychology* exhibited his steady movement away from idealism and toward an evolutionary naturalism that emphasized the adjustment of the individual within its environment. This was a part of the growing momentum toward what would later be known as functional psychology.

In 1894, Dewey accepted a position at the new University of Chicago as head of the department of philosophy, which included psychology and pedagogy. His plans for an educational laboratory, which would be to education as a scientific laboratory was to scientific practice, were realized when the "Laboratory School," also known as the "Dewey School," opened its doors in

1896. Dewey used his laboratory to refine his functional psychology, his ethical theory, and his concept of democracy, all of which he saw as intimately connected to his educational research.

Dewey later wrote that William James's *Principles of Psychology* exerted a major influence on his work during this period. Like James, Dewey now rejected the idea of a substantive consciousness or ego. He argued instead that consciousness is a "stream" of overlapping interests, memories, and habits. From the first, Dewey's psychology had been organic and evolutionary. Now, as ethics supplanted religion in his thought, it became increasingly naturalistic and social. His opposition to mind-body dualism remained, but its basis shifted from idealism to an instrumentalist form of pragmatism. "Mental entities" were now treated as tools, products, and byproducts employed by the organism to effect adjustment.

Although William James's essays from the 1880s had exhibited functionalist themes, it is Dewey's essay "The Reflex Arc Concept in Psychology" (1896) that is generally recognized as the official debut of functionalism in psychology. Instead of attempting to describe basic elements of thought, the laws of their combination, and their neurophysiological correlates, as E. B. Titchener (1867–1927) was doing as a part of his structuralist/introspectionist program at Cornell, Dewey focused on the behavior of the organism as a whole as it adapts itself to changing environmental conditions and as it reconstructs those conditions to meet its changing needs. His "Reflex Arc" essay held that stimulus and response are not separate but a coordination, and that a stimulus is not external to the organism but one of its states. It may be fair to say that Dewey was absorbing structuralism rather than rejecting it out of hand. He was prepared to recognize "elements" and "laws" of thought, but only as provisional working tools utilized by the adjusting organism, and not as existing prior to inquiry, as the structuralists claimed.

In 1942, the editors of *The Psychological Review* asked "seventy prominent psychologists" to rank the top five essays published in the journal during its first 49 years. Dewey's "Reflex Arc" essay was ranked first (H. Langfeld, *Psychological Review*, 1943, 50, 143–155).

"Psychology and Social Practice," Dewey's presidential address at the 1899 meeting of the American Psychological Association, and a companion piece, "Psychology and Philosophic Method" (1899), exhibit still further developments in his understanding of psychology and its relation to philosophy. In these essays, Dewey attacked attempts to construct a science of the psyche isolated from its social conditions.

Thirteen years earlier, in 1886, Dewey the idealist had argued that philosophy is the science of absolute self-consciousness, and that psychology is the science of the manifestation of absolute self-consciousness in the consciousness of individuals. He had consequently characterized psychology as the completed method of philosophy. By 1899, however, as a result of his reading of William James, his collaboration with the Chicago philosopher-sociologist George Herbert Mead (1863–1931), and his educational research, Dewey the pragmatist had jettisoned the notion of absolute self-consciousness. He had come to view psychology as the social science that studies what he called "sociable" (or socializable) individuals and the ways in which conscious value and meaning are and can be introduced into human experience. His interest now centered on the reconstruction of the habits and character of social individuals and the reform of cultural institutions. His psychology now had profound implications for the philosophy of science, education, and democracy.

In 1904, following disagreements with President William R. Harper (1856–1906) concerning support for his laboratory school, Dewey resigned his position at the University of Chicago. He quickly accepted a position at Columbia University, where he taught regularly until his appointment as Professor Emeritus of Philosophy in Residence in 1930. He entered full retirement in 1939. During these years, Dewey traveled and lectured widely. He spent 2 years in Japan and China and visited schools in the Soviet Union, Mexico, and Turkey. In 1937, at the age of 78, he served as chair of the "Trotsky Commission" hearings in Mexico City, which gave the exiled Trotsky a public venue for defending himself against trumped-up charges brought by Stalin in Moscow.

Although all of Dewey's major works during this period have significant implications for psychology, the only work he devoted specifically to the subject was *Human Nature and Conduct* (1922). Responding to what he regarded as the conservatism of the political left (which assumed an "acquisitive instinct"), the political right (which glorified social Darwinism), and evangelical Christianity (which emphasized original sin), Dewey rejected the term "instinct" because of its implication of something well organized. In its place he proposed the term "impulse," by which he understood something loose and undirected. When impulses are directed and informed, however, they become the basis of habitual behavior. Conflict of habits releases impulses, and this requires the modification of habits.

Dewey thus emphasized the plasticity of habits and their centrality in learning and the formation of character. He therefore rejected the idea that innate qualities are indicators of a fixed intelligence. He was particularly critical of the tendency of psychoanalysis to transform, as he thought, social results into psychic causes. He continued to stress his rejection of a substantial mind, soul, or psyche that precedes action. He

thought that such a conception tends to isolate humans from nature and individuals from one another.

Dewey's treatment of instincts and habits was attacked by some, such as William McDougall (1871–1938) who argued that Dewey's rejection of a fixed taxonomy of instincts had undercut the possibility of systematic psychology and that he had failed to provide adequate criteria for distinguishing active from passive habits.

In "Conduct and Experience" (1930), Dewey recapitulated many of the psychological themes that he had developed during the 34 years since the "Reflex Arc" essay. He attacked both introspectionism and behaviorism, which he regarded as extremes of psychological theory. Introspectionists, such as Wilhelm Wundt (1832–1920), cast their net too widely, he argued, by failing to recognize that classification always involves interpretation. Transaction between organism and environment is the primary fact of experience, and differentiation of the structural features of experience, including differentiation into subject and object, follows selective abstraction. Behaviorists, on the other hand, such as John B. Watson (1878–1958), cast their net too narrowly by claiming that immediate stimulus-response features of behavior exhaust experience. Behavioral acts are always nested within a life career, or what Dewey termed "conduct." Avoiding both extremes, he argued that the subject matter of psychology is "the behavior of the organism so far as that is characterized by changes taking place in an activity that is serial and continuous in reference to changes in an environment that persists although changing in detail." Put another way, "psychology is concerned with the life-career of individualized activities" (Dewey, *The Later Works*, Vol. 5, p. 224).

Remarkably, Dewey took little notice of the work of his contemporary, Sigmund Freud (1856–1939). The stark contrast between their views, nevertheless, helps put Dewey's work in perspective. Freud argued for fixed psychic structures, emphasized the central role of sexual drives in the formation of personality, held that liberation is possible only through analysis of the past, and set out an authoritarian social psychology. Dewey, on the other hand, argued for the plasticity of the organism, rejected the notion of fixed instincts and drives, emphasized the consequences of conscious habit formation for future growth, and set out a democratic social psychology.

Among Dewey's most significant contributions to psychology, then, were his devastating arguments against subject-object dualism; his stress on the plasticity of habits, especially those of young children; and his insistence that there can be no psychology of the individual apart from environmental factors, including those that involve education and ethics.

Bibliography

Works by Dewey

Dewey, J. (1967–1990). *The collected works of John Dewey, 1882–1953.* Edited by J. A. Boydston. Carbondale and Edwardsville, IL: Southern Illinois University Press. The standard edition of the works of John Dewey. Published in three series as *The Early Works* (EW), *The Middle Works* (MW), and *The Later Works* (LW). Contains each of Dewey's works mentioned or cited in this article.

Works about Dewey

Allport, G. W. (1939). Dewey's individual and social psychology. In P. A. Schilpp and L. E. Hahn (Eds.), *The philosophy of John Dewey* (3rd rev. ed., pp. 265–290). La Salle, IL: Open Court Press.

Dykhuizen, G. (1973). *The life and mind of John Dewey.* Carbondale, IL: Southern Illinois University Press.

Hickman, L. A. (1990). *John Dewey's pragmatic technology.* Bloomington, IN: Indiana University Press.

Phillips, D. C. (1971). James, Dewey, and the reflex arc. *Journal of the History of Ideas, 32,* 555–568.

Rockefeller, S. C. (1991). *John Dewey: Religious faith and democratic humanism.* New York: Columbia University Press.

Schneider, H. W. (1970). Dewey's psychology. In J. A. Boydston (Ed.), *Guide to the works of John Dewey* (pp. 1–14). Carbondale, IL: Southern Illinois University Press. Although now out of print, this excellent collection of essays on Dewey's work can be found in many libraries.

Westbrook, R. B. (1991). *John Dewey and American democracy.* Ithaca, NY: Cornell University Press.

Larry A. Hickman

DIABETES is a chronic medical condition that affects 16 million people in the United States, half of whom are unaware that they have the disease according to the National Diabetes Data Group (*Diabetes in America,* 1995). Each year more than 169,000 deaths are attributed directly to diabetes and many more deaths occur as a result of its complications (NIDDK, *Diabetes Statistics,* NIH Publication No. 96-3926, 1995). Furthermore, the financial burden of diabetes in terms of health care costs, lost wages, and lost productivity is estimated at 92 billion dollars annually (American Diabetes Association, 1993). While there is no cure for diabetes, it can be treated. The importance of behavioral factors for the effective management of diabetes makes it a topic of interest to psychologists.

Description and Classification

Diabetes mellitus is a term that refers to a group of heterogeneous disorders that are characterized by a defect in insulin secretion or action. Insulin is a hormone secreted by the pancreas that is necessary in order for most cells of the body to be able to take up and utilize glucose as energy. The absence of adequate insulin action results in a chronically elevated level of glucose in the bloodstream known as hyperglycemia, the major diagnostic criterion for diabetes. Early signs of diabetes include frequent urination (a result of hyperglycemia), constant thirst due to water loss, and glycosuria or sugar in the urine. In fact, the word diabetes means "passing through" and mellitus means "sweet" so the name of the disease actually refers to one of its common symptoms, sweet urine. Other symptoms of diabetes include weight loss and fatigue, which can result from the body's need to break down protein, fat, and glycogen (a form of carbohydrate stored in muscle) for energy. There are two major types of diabetes mellitus: Type 1 and Type 2 diabetes.

Type 1 or insulin-dependent diabetes mellitus (IDDM), has an estimated prevalence of 500,000 to 1 million and an annual incidence of 30,000 in the United States. IDDM is nearly twice as prevalent in Whites as compared to Blacks or Hispanic Americans and is rare among Asian Americans (National Diabetes Data Group, *Diabetes in America,* 1995). The onset of IDDM usually occurs during childhood or early adolescence, which is why it is sometimes called "juvenile diabetes." However, the distinguishing feature of Type 1 diabetes is the complete or near complete absence of endogenous insulin secretion, necessitating that persons with IDDM take daily insulin injections to survive. Without insulin, the body is forced to break down protein and fat for energy, producing byproducts called ketones, which are weak acids. Left untreated, the eventual outcome of this process, known as ketoacidosis, is coma and finally death. The mechanism by which insulin is depleted in IDDM is now widely understood to be the gradual destruction of the insulin-secreting pancreatic beta cells by the body's own immune system. The etiology of the disease is not entirely clear, although it appears that as yet unidentified environmental factors may be at least as important as genetic variables.

The most common form of diabetes is Type 2 or non-insulin-dependent diabetes mellitus. Type 2 diabetes accounts for 90 to 95% of all diagnosed cases of diabetes in the United States with approximately 595,000 new cases being diagnosed annually. Compared with Whites, the prevalence of Type 2 diabetes is about two times greater in Blacks and two to three times greater in Hispanic Americans. Asian Americans also show greater rates of Type 2 diabetes as do Native Americans, though rates vary widely by tribe. The Pima Indians have the highest prevalence rate of Type 2 diabetes in the world at 50% (National Diabetes Data Group, 1995). Typically the onset of Type 2 diabetes occurs in adulthood and its prevalence increases with age. So as the average life expectancy continues to rise, Type 2 diabetes will become increasingly common. Unlike Type 1 diabetes, insulin secretion is not absolutely compromised in Type 2 diabetes, which means that insulin taking is not strictly necessary for these patients. The nature of the defect in Type 2 diabetes appears to be heterogeneous, so that for some patients the primary problem is reduced insulin secretion, while for other patients insulin resistance or the body's lack of response to insulin may be primary. The etiology of Type 2 diabetes seems to involve a very strong genetic component, but environment is also important as evidenced by the strong relationship between obesity and Type 2 diabetes.

Diabetes is associated with a variety of potential complications, some of them related to acute changes in blood glucose and others that develop over time. As mentioned previously, a lack of insulin will cause extremely high blood glucose levels and may result in ketoacidosis in Type 1 patients. A blood sugar level that is too low, or hypoglycemia, can also result in an acute crisis. Early signs of hypoglycemia include trembling, sweating, and headache, and if left untreated confusion, seizures, and even a loss of consciousness can occur. Most of the complications of diabetes, however, are long-term ones. Specifically, people with diabetes are 25 times more likely to develop blindness, 17 times more likely to get kidney disease, 30 to 40 times more likely to undergo a major amputation and twice as likely to develop coronary artery disease as compared to people without diabetes. Since complications have been linked to chronic hyperglycemia, the best way to delay or even prevent the long-term complications of diabetes is by maintaining good metabolic control. Therefore, treatments that help control high blood sugar are of vital importance in reducing the morbidity and mortality associated with diabetes.

Treatments

All patients with Type 1 diabetes must take several injections of insulin daily. In order to give themselves the appropriate dose they must repeatedly measure their blood sugar level by pricking their finger and analyzing the blood with a portable glucose meter. Now the option of using an insulin pump, a device that delivers a measured dose of insulin through a catheter, is available. The pump may be more convenient than having to carry around syringes and vials of insulin. Insulin is not required in Type 2 diabetes, but certain patients with Type 2 diabetes may still need to use insulin for adequate glycemic control.

There are several different types of drugs that can be taken orally to help lower blood glucose in Type 2 diabetes. Sulfonylureas are probably the most common group of drugs used to treat diabetes and work primarily by stimulating insulin release from pancreatic beta cells. Metformin belongs to the class of drugs known as biguanides, and it works by reducing glucose production by the liver and increasing peripheral uptake of glucose. Alpha-glucosidase inhibitors are compounds that reduce the breakdown and therefore absorption of carbohydrate so that the rise in blood glucose after a meal is attenuated. Finally, thiazolidinediones (such as troglitazone) are new groups of drugs that work by reducing insulin resistance. While oral agents can significantly improve glycemic control in people with Type 2 diabetes, they also have some risks, including side effects and an increased chance of having a hypoglycemic episode.

In the past, people with diabetes were instructed to eat a high-fat, low-carbohydrate diet since carbohydrate results in a higher postmeal increase in blood glucose. However, it is now known that a high-fat diet increases the risk for heart disease. Therefore, the current recommendation is to eat a balanced diet rich in complex carbohydrates and fiber with no more than 30% of calories from fat. This type of balanced diet has been shown to maintain or improve metabolic control in Type 2 diabetes patients. Careful attention to the timing and size of meals is also important, particularly for Type 1 diabetes. Skipping meals could lead to hypoglycemia in persons with Type 1 diabetes or in persons with Type 2 diabetes who are on oral agents. Eating too much, on the other hand, can result in hyperglycemia unless the insulin dose is adjusted properly. Overeating is a particular problem for patients with Type 2 diabetes because the majority of this group are overweight. In these patients, a reduced-calorie diet designed to produce weight loss can help improve their glycemic control.

Regular physical activity can be very beneficial in diabetes since it improves insulin sensitivity and therefore reduces insulin requirements. This is of great benefit to people with Type 2 diabetes since insulin resistance is one of the main defects of their illness. Also, regular exercise can promote weight loss, which also significantly reduces insulin resistance. People with Type 1 diabetes must pay attention to any changes in their level of physical activity so that they can adjust their insulin dose accordingly.

Psychological and Behavioral Issues

Noncompliance with diabetes self-care has been identified as a behavior that can interfere with successful treatment. Examples of noncompliance could include not taking medications, improperly administering insulin, or not following the diabetes diet. It appears that some form of noncompliance is present in a large proportion of diabetes patients and that compliance is a multidimensional concept. This means that the level of adherence to the many different behaviors that constitute a diabetes regimen are independent of one another. For example, it has been found that the failure to take insulin is extremely rare among children with Type 1 diabetes, but that failure to follow the diet is much more common. This may be because not taking insulin can have serious immediate consequences whereas dietary indiscretions may not. In general, it seems that modifications like diet and exercise are harder to maintain than taking pills or insulin.

A good deal of attention has been focused on how to enhance adherence to the diabetes regimen. The developmental stage of the patient must be considered when determining how to maximize compliance. For example, in children the family plays a big role in both administering care and encouraging self-care, so a stable family environment must be fostered. Adolescents often show very high rates of noncompliance due to a desire to fit in with their peers and for them a combination of education and peer social skills training has shown to be helpful. Education about diabetes and about how to manage it properly is important, but alone it will not improve compliance. Combining education with reminders, behavior-cueing, social support, and the use of contingency contracts seems to result in improved compliance. A relatively recent innovation in diabetes care is home glucose monitoring, which allows the patient to get frequent accurate feedback about his or her level of control. Some research has found that increased compliance with glucose monitoring can result in better diabetes control. However, this has not always been found, maybe because some people simply check blood sugar without making adjustments in care in response to the sugar values.

The term *compliance* implies a passive patient who does as he or she is told, and this is unfortunate because the patients with the best outcomes are those who form a partnership with their doctor in determining their care. For this reason, many psychologists prefer to use the term *adherence* rather than compliance. Mutual agreement on the care regimen predicts compliance and better glycemic control, possibly because the patient feels more involved and in charge of his or her health. Also, it is obvious that even perfect compliance with a poorly planned regimen will not be beneficial, therefore, both doctor and patient must work together and exchange information about how well a treatment is working. With this type of cooperation, adherence and therefore glycemic control can be enhanced.

Stress may play a role in both the etiology and the treatment of diabetes. The main way that stress impacts diabetes is by triggering the body's so-called fight or flight response, which mobilizes the body's energy resources. One component of this response is an increase in blood glucose. Normally, the excess glucose is readily taken up into the cells for use as energy, but in diabetes, due to ineffective insulin action, the glucose just accumulates in the bloodstream. Therefore, in people who

are at risk for diabetes, stress may trigger the onset of the disease. In fact, some researchers have found an association between major life changes and the onset of Type 1 diabetes. Similarly, anecdotal reports of a highly stressful event preceding the onset of Type 2 diabetes are common. While these observations suggest that stress may contribute to the development of diabetes, it is important to point out that stress by itself cannot cause diabetes in the absence of a preexisting genetic vulnerability.

In persons who have diabetes, stress has the ability to worsen their condition. It is well known that physical stressors such as illness or surgery result in increases in blood glucose. Research has shown that for many people with diabetes psychological stressors can also be associated with exacerbations of hyperglycemia. The hyperglycemic effect of stress could be due to its physiological effects, but stress may also indirectly cause a worsening of diabetes by reducing compliance. So, while under stress, people may be more likely to skip their daily exercise, go off their diet, or otherwise neglect aspects of their diabetes care regimen.

A few studies have attempted to determine if behavioral interventions such as progressive muscle relaxation can reduce stress and therefore improve glycemic control in people with diabetes. While the results are mixed, it appears that for some people relaxation training does result in improvements in their diabetes. One study found that improvements in glycemic control after relaxation training could be predicted by a high score on a measure of trait anxiety. Therefore, it may be that only diabetes patients with certain personality characteristics benefit from stress management.

People with diabetes have a higher prevalence rate of depression than the general population. The fact that both Type 2 diabetes and depression are more prevalent in older people may in part account for this. Depression may also result from the psychological impact of having diabetes itself, so, people with diabetes may have disabling complications from their disease or feel overwhelmed by the complex task of managing their illness from day to day. Depression is often found to be more common among people with medical illnesses, and it is not yet clear whether the rate of depression in diabetes is actually higher than the rate in other chronically ill populations. Depression, however, may be particularly relevant to diabetes because of certain physiological effects associated with it.

Several stress hormones that oppose the action of insulin are elevated during a period of clinical depression. It has been shown that even in people without diabetes, depression causes insulin resistance. Since people with diabetes already have problems with glucose metabolism, depression may cause a worsening of their diabetes. Depression could also have an impact on diabetes control by reducing self-care behaviors. Some of the symptoms of depression can include fatigue, inactivity, and changes in appetite. It is conceivable that these depressive symptoms could negatively impact patient adherence to the diabetes regimen. Therefore, the accurate diagnosis and treatment of depression in diabetes could be very important in maintaining good metabolic control.

Conclusion

Diabetes is a serious chronic illness with tremendous personal and social impact. Although it is a medical condition, optimal treatment of diabetes demands the consideration of behavioral and psychological issues. These issues include, but are not limited to, increasing adherence to diabetes self-care behaviors, minimizing the impact of stress, and recognizing and treating depression in diabetes. Psychological research has played an important role in helping to understand diabetes and will undoubtedly continue to contribute toward the greater goal of achieving the best possible quality of life for people with diabetes.

[*See also* Nutrition.]

Bibliography

Davidson, M. B. (1991). *Diabetes mellitus: Diagnosis and treatment*. New York: Churchill Livingstone.

Geringer, E. S. (1990). Affective disorders and diabetes mellitus. In C. S. Holmes (Ed.), *Neuropsychological and behavioral aspects of diabetes*. New York: Springer-Verlag.

Haire-Joshu, D. (1996). *Management of diabetes mellitus: Perspectives of care across the lifespan*. St. Louis, MO: Mosby-Year Book. Considers diabetes treatment from a developmental perspective.

Johnson, S. B. (1990). Adherence behaviors and health status in childhood diabetes. In C. S. Holmes (Ed.), *Neuropsychological and behavioral aspects of diabetes*. New York: Springer-Verlag.

Kaplan, R. M., Sallis, J. F., & Patterson, T. L. (1993). *Health and human behavior*. New York: McGraw-Hill. A general introduction to the field of health psychology with a chapter on diabetes.

National Diabetes Data Group, National Institutes of Health, National Institute of Diabetes and Digestive and Kidney Diseases (1995). *Diabetes in America* (2nd ed.). NIH Publication No. 95-1468. A detailed and comprehensive volume incorporating the latest scientific research on diabetes epidemiology, complications, and treatment. Includes a chapter on psychosocial aspects of diabetes.

Surwit, R. S., & Schneider, M. S. (1993). Role of stress in the etiology and treatment of diabetes mellitus. *Psychosomatic Medicine, 55*, 380–393.

Watkins, P. J., Drury, P. L., & Howell, S. L. (1996). *Diabetes and its management* (5th ed.). Oxford, England: Blackwell. A good clinical overview of diabetes and its treatment.

Priti I. Parekh and Richard S. Surwit

DIAGNOSTIC AND STATISTICAL MANUAL OF MENTAL DISORDERS. Mental disorders are clinically significant impairments in one or more areas of psychological functioning, including (but not limited to) thinking, feeling, eating, sleeping, and other important components of behavior (Wakefield, 1992). The *Diagnostic and Statistical Manual of Mental Disorders* (DSM) is a nomenclature of mental disorders developed by the American Psychiatric Association (*DSM–IV*, 1994). What is included within and excluded from the *DSM* and how these mental disorders are diagnosed are of substantial importance, as many social, clinical, forensic, and scientific decisions are informed by this text. Persons within society seeking guidance with respect to whether a behavior pattern is or is not a mental disorder, will usually turn to the *DSM*, and there have been many difficult, controversial decisions (e.g., whether or not certain instances of homosexuality, serial rape, or premenstrual syndrome should be considered to be a mental disorder). The substantial impact of the *DSM* on social and clinical decisions is often bemoaned, even by the authors of the manual (Pincus, Frances, Davis, First, & Widiger, 1992). This is because scientific support for many of the *DSM* diagnoses is often less than it might be given the social and clinical importance of the diagnoses. The manual is reasonably consistent with current scientific research, but none of the diagnostic criteria sets are infallible. There continue to be important questions regarding the validity of all the disorders listed in the manual (Pincus et al., 1992).

A common, uniform diagnostic nomenclature is a necessity within clinical practice. Communication among clinicians regarding etiology, pathology, and treatment of psychopathology is exceedingly difficult in the absence of a common language. Prior to the development of a standard nomenclature, hospitals, clinics, and even individual clinicians were using a wide variety of inconsistent diagnoses. Therefore, in 1917 the American Medico-Psychological Association (which in 1921 became the American Psychiatric Association) developed a list of 22 disorders for use within hospital settings (Grob, 1991). The list was adopted by most hospitals until 1935, when a revised and expanded version was included within the second edition of the American Medical Association's (AMA) classification of diseases.

The AMA's classification, however, was not adopted unanimously by all social agencies, in part because it was confined to conditions of importance within inpatient settings. Its limitations became particularly evident during World War II, with the occurrence of many acute disorders that were not recognized within the AMA classification. By the end of World War II, the Army, Navy, and Veterans Administration had all developed their own classification systems (Blashfield, 1984; Grob, 1991).

There was also a need internationally for a common language of psychopathology. The diversity of nomenclatures within the United States paled in comparison to the diversity around the world. Therefore, in 1948, the World Health Organization (WHO) included a section devoted to the diagnosis of mental disorders in the sixth edition of the *International Classification of Diseases* (*ICD–6*). The *ICD–6*, however, also failed to be adequate for clinicians treating the casualties of World War II. Notably absent were many of the personality and adjustment disorders that were frequently being seen in veterans' hospitals. In 1952 the American Psychiatric Association developed a version of the *ICD–6*, which became the first edition of the *DSM*, for the application of *ICD–6* within the United States (Blashfield, 1984; Grob, 1991).

Although the mental disorders section of *ICD–7* was essentially identical to *ICD–6*, the authors of *ICD–8* anticipated substantial revisions to *ICD–7*. The American Psychiatric Association (APA) therefore determined that it would be advisable to revise *DSM–I* in coordination with *ICD–8*. It was important to revise the *DSM* so it was compatible with the *ICD*. But it was also important to influence the *ICD* revision to increase *its* consistency with the *DSM* (Frances, Pincus, Widiger, Davis, & First, 1990). Coordination with the *ICD* is essential for international communication and for meaningful membership and participation within the WHO.

The impetus for *DSM–III* was the development of *ICD–9*. By this time, however, the diagnosis of mental disorders was receiving substantial criticism (Blashfield, 1984). One fundamental concern was the unreliability of clinicians' diagnoses. If a patient's symptomatology received different diagnoses from different clinicians, there was unlikely to be much validity to the diagnoses (e.g., if two clinicians provide different diagnoses, at least one of them is likely to be wrong). *DSM–II* had not been particularly helpful in addressing this problem (Blashfield, 1984; Spitzer, Williams, & Skodol, 1980). The diagnostic criteria provided within the manual consisted of only brief, narrative descriptions of each disorder. There was no indication of which of the descriptors were necessary and which were optional, and there was no guidance as to how to interpret or apply the criteria in clinical practice. Many researchers, therefore, developed their own diagnostic criteria for the disorders included within the *DSM–II*. They indicated empirically that the reliability of mental disorder diagnoses can be obtained if ambiguities within the criteria set are removed and interviewers systematically assessed and adhered to the criteria sets. The most influential of these efforts were the research criteria for 16 mental disorders developed by Feighner et al. (1972).

DSM–III, therefore, included relatively more explicit, specific diagnostic criteria for each disorder (Spitzer et al., 1980). Another innovation of *DSM–III* was the inclusion of more systematic and detailed information in the text discussion of each disorder concerning the associated features, course, complications, impairment, prevalence, differential diagnosis, sex ratio, familial pattern, and other information relevant to the diagnosis of the disorder. A third innovation was the inclusion of a multiaxial diagnostic system. Most of the mental disorders were diagnosed on Axis I. Axis II was reserved in *DSM–III* for personality disorders (and for specific developmental disorders), to ensure that clinicians not overlook the possible presence of a personality disorder when their attention is focused primarily upon a more acute, immediate condition. Axis III was for physical disorders, Axis IV for severity of psychosocial stressors, and Axis V for an assessment of the highest level of adaptive functioning during the past year (Spitzer et al., 1980). These additional axes were included to facilitate a recognition that an informative clinical assessment is not confined simply to the determination of which mental disorder is present.

DSM–III proved to be enormously successful, although it was not without substantial controversy. One of the major issues at the time was the proposed removal from the manual of particular psychodynamic concepts (e.g., neurosis) (Blashfield, 1984; Spitzer et al., 1980). Some felt that their removal reflected a political struggle between opposing theoretical perspectives (i.e., neurochemical versus psychodynamic psychiatry). Most of the original (Feighner et al., 1972) researchers were biologically oriented and some were indeed critical of psychodynamic theory and treatment. However, the decreasing impact of the psychodynamic concepts was also simply a valid reflection of the status of the scientific research.

However, the development of specific, explicit criteria also had limitations. It is much easier to provide general descriptions of mental disorders than it is to develop unambiguous diagnostic criteria. There is insufficient knowledge regarding most mental disorders for diagnostic boundaries to be defined so precisely that no diagnostic errors will occur (Clark, Watson, & Reynolds, 1995). Explicit, specific criteria are preferable to vague, general criteria because the source of errors are more readily identified. The authors of *DSM–III*, however, often had to develop specific inclusion and exclusion criteria in the absence of sufficient knowledge regarding the likely effects and even validity of these criteria (Widiger, Frances, Pincus, Davis, & First, 1991). For example, even before *DSM–III* was published in 1980, the authors recognized that the exclusion of the diagnosis of panic disorder in the presence of a major depressive disorder was a mistake (i.e., panic disorder can occur during the course of a major depressive disorder).

The American Psychiatric Association therefore authorized the development of a revision of *DSM–III* to correct the more obvious errors. This revision was not coordinated with a forthcoming revision of the *ICD*, and was to be completed by 1985. By the time *DSM–III–R* was published in 1987, however, the WHO had begun work on the development of *ICD–10*. The year after *DSM–III–R* was published (Frances et al., 1990), work began on the development of *DSM–IV*, in collaboration with *ICD–10*. The authors of *DSM–IV* were also given an additional mandate to provide more explicit documentation of the scientific support for any revisions to the nomenclature (Frances et al., 1990). *DSM–III*, and perhaps to an even greater extent *DSM–III–R*, included a number of controversial diagnoses which may have lacked sufficient empirical support. Four diagnoses approved for inclusion by the authors of *DSM–III–R* were overturned by the board of trustees of the American Psychiatric Association, three of the diagnoses being included in an appendix to *DSM–III–R* (i.e., late luteal phase dysphoric disorder, self-defeating personality disorder, and sadistic personality disorder) and one was deleted entirely (i.e., paraphiliac rapism).

The authors of *DSM–IV* therefore developed a more explicit process by which decisions were made, emphasizing a systematic and comprehensive obtainment, review, and documentation of scientific, empirical support. This process included extensive reviews of the published literature, reanalyses of existing data sets, and field trials (Widiger et al., 1991). Only a few new diagnoses were given an official recognition in *DSM–IV* (e.g., acute stress disorder), many controversial proposals were placed within an appendix to the manual for proposals needing further research (e.g., premenstrual dysphoric disorder, factitious disorder by proxy, and dissociative trance disorder), and a few disorders that had been included in *DSM–III–R* that lacked sufficient empirical support were deleted (e.g., idiosyncratic alcohol intoxication).

Some degree of dispute and controversy with respect to the *DSM*, however, is perhaps unavoidable. *DSM–IV* is useful in providing a common language for mental health clinicians, but clinicians can vary widely with respect to their clinical perspectives and theoretical orientations, and it is difficult to develop a scientifically validated classification that is equally suitable for every theoretical perspective (Frances et al., 1990). Theoretical perspectives (Kaslow, 1996), professional organizations (Schacht & Nathan, 1977), and social interest groups (Caplan, 1995) have often felt inadequately represented or considered in the development of the *DSM*.

An additional difficulty is the pressure for the manual to be optimal for use across a wide diversity of settings (e.g., private practice, inpatient, and forensic settings) and needs (e.g., decisions concerning treatment, hospitalization, criminal responsibility, disability claims, insurance reimbursement, and research). No single manual is likely to be optimal for all settings and needs, and the ideal balance among these conflicting demands

is hard to determine (Frances et al., 1990; Pincus et al., 1992). One approach is to develop variations on the manual for different needs, as the *ICD–10* has done for research settings, and the American Psychiatric Association has done for primary care physicians. The *DSM–IV* is in fact itself a variation on the *ICD–10* for application within the United States. The coordination of *DSM–IV* with *ICD–10*, however, also provides a substantial constraint on its flexibility. For example, body dysmorphic disorder and hypochondriasis are recognized within the United States as being quite distinct conditions, but *DSM–IV* must provide the same code number for these two disorders because the *ICD–10* makes no distinction between them. However, viable alternatives to the *DSM–IV* are being developed, including, for example, a dimensional classification of personality disorders (Costa & Widiger, 1994) and a classification of relational pathology (Kaslow, 1996).

[*See also* International Classification of Diseases.]

Bibliography

American Psychiatric Association. (1994). *Diagnostic and statistical manual of mental disorders* (4th ed.). Washington, DC: Author.

Blashfield, R. K. (1984). *The classification of psychopathology. Neo-Kraepelinian and quantitative approaches.* New York: Plenum Press. Scientific and historical overview of the diagnosis of psychopathology.

Caplan, P. J. (1995). *They say you're crazy. How the world's most powerful psychiatrists decide who's normal.* Reading, MA: Addison-Wesley. Feminist critique of the *DSM–IV*.

Clark, L. A., Watson, D., & Reynolds, S. (1995). Diagnosis and classification of psychopathology: Challenges to the current system and future directions. *Annual Review of Psychology, 46,* 121–153. Scientific review of the diagnosis of mental disorders.

Costa, P. T., & Widiger, T. A. (Eds.). (1994). *Personality disorders and the five-factor model of personality.* Washington, DC: American Psychological Association. Alternative dimensional model for the diagnosis of personality disorders.

Feighner, J. P., Robins, E., Guze, S. B., Woodruff, R. A., Winokur, G., & Munoz, R. (1972). Diagnostic criteria for use in psychiatric research. *Archives of General Psychiatry, 26,* 57–63. Widely cited, influential study that had major impact on development of *DSM–III*.

Frances, A., Pincus, H. A., Widiger, T. A., Davis, W. W., & First, M. B. (1990). *DSM–IV*: Work in progress. *American Journal of Psychiatry, 147,* 1439–1448. Overview of the rationale and issues in the development of *DSM–IV*.

Grob, G. N. (1991). Origins of *DSM–I*: A study in appearance and reality. *American Journal of Psychiatry, 148,* 421–431. Overview of psychiatric diagnosis prior to the first edition of the *DSM*.

Kaslow, F. W. (Ed.). (1996). *Handbook of relational diagnosis and dysfunctional family patterns.* New York: Wiley. Alternative classification of dysfunctional or pathologic marital and family relationships.

Pincus, H., Frances, A., Davis, W., First, M., & Widiger, T. (1992). *DSM–IV* and new diagnostic categories: Holding the line on proliferation. *American Journal of Psychiatry, 149,* 112–117. Discussion of the empirical support and rationale for the inclusion or exclusion of diagnoses from the *DSM*.

Schacht, T. E., & Nathan, P. E. (1977). But is it good for the psychologists? Appraisal and status of *DSM–III*. *American Psychologist, 32,* 1017–1025. Critique of *DSM–III* by representatives of the American Psychological Association.

Spitzer, R. L., Williams, J. B. W., & Skodol, A. E. (1980). DSM–III: the major achievements and an overview. *American Journal of Psychiatry, 137,* 151–164. Description and rationale for the major features and innovations of *DSM–III*.

Wakefield, J. C. (1992). The concept of mental disorder. On the boundary between biological facts and social values. *American Psychologist, 47,* 373–388. Discussion of the concept of a mental disorder.

Widiger, T., Frances, A., Pincus, H., Davis, W., & First, M. (1991). Toward an empirical classification for *DSM–IV*. *Journal of Abnormal Psychology, 100,* 280–288. Description and rationale of the scientific process for the development of *DSM–IV*.

Thomas A. Widiger

DIETING lies at the heart of a controversy that has polarized many health professionals and has put the eating disorders and obesity fields at odds with one another. For example, French, Jeffery, and Murray (1999) conclude that "many specific weight control strategies are effective and produce weight control effects in a dose-response fashion with duration." Conversely, Polivy (1996), in a review of the literature on dieting as a remedy for overweight, concludes that dieting may be more dangerous than the problem it seeks to solve, problems blamed on overweight may be caused by dieting, and the pursuit of ever more rigorous dieting has predictable and quite negative consequences.

Professionals concerned with the epidemic of obesity and its serious health and psychosocial consequences see dieting as a solution. Those concerned with eating disorders see dieting as primary pathology. This debate generates extreme arguments, with passions often prevailing over science. The purpose of this chapter is to discuss the consequences of dieting and to identify in whom, under what conditions, and for what purposes dieting is helpful or harmful.

Prevalence and Distribution in the Population

Estimates on the prevalence of dieting vary depending on how the term is defined, or even whether the word *diet* is used. In the paper by French and colleagues mentioned above, the percentage of people who said they were "dieting" ranged from 17 to 28%, while 82% reported engaging in intentional behaviors for the purpose of weight control. It appears that approximately three quarters of women and two thirds of men engage in specific behaviors for the purpose of weight control, and about 50% of women and 33% of men would label what they do as a "diet." It is widely assumed that Black and Hispanic women, while having the highest prevalence of obesity, are less preoccupied with weight than are whites, and therefore diet less. Recent reports suggest that social class differences, rather than race, may explain these results.

To the degree that dieting holds the potential for harm, rates in children are frightening. At the age when proper nutrition is essential for development and when body image is being formed, food restriction and body image discontent are common. Surveys of girls 9 to 18 years of age find as many as 70% restricting food intake. Girls, and to a lesser extent boys, report concern with appearance and dieting as early as the third grade. Reports have now appeared showing cases of failure to thrive in infants of parents who restrict the child's intake in hopes of preventing obesity.

A number of behaviors can be subsumed under the term *dieting*. These range from practices as debilitating as nearly total calorie restriction to those as reasonable as making modest reductions in dietary fat. The field is moving beyond the global concept of dieting to examine specific behaviors and attitudes.

The Social Origins of Dieting

In most industrialized countries, particularly the United States, extreme importance is attached to physical appearance. This, combined with highly unrealistic ideals for what constitutes desirable weight and shape, creates what has been called normative discontent. Most people internalize: (a) the unrealistic standard for a thin and sculpted body; (b) the belief that personal effort, if sufficient, can provide the ideal body; and (c) the notion that an imperfect body reflects an imperfect person. The predictable response is an attempt to control the behaviors that govern weight.

When dieting fails to deliver the perfect body, the appropriate but atypical response is to adjust goals to be more realistic, abandon arbitrary and destructive social norms, and accept the body weight that follows from a sensible eating and exercise plan. The more typical response is self-blame and more rigid dieting. The internal attribution for failure is supported by diet advertisements promising miracle results, promotions for exercise equipment and health clubs, pictures of fashion models, and multiple other messages.

Theoretical Predictions on the Effects of Dieting

The classic work of Keys and colleagues, described in *The Biology of Human Starvation*, showed the profound biological and psychological effects of severe, prolonged food restriction. Normal-weight males were starved to approximately 75% of their baseline weight. Even after refeeding and restoration of the lost weight, there were reports of the men eating very large amounts, to the point of being ill.

This work has been interpreted to show that caloric restriction, especially when severe, creates a psychological and perhaps biological climate in which compulsive, driven eating is likely. The concept of dietary restraint, developed originally from studies by Nisbett, Herman, Polivy and others, was designed to explain this psychological process. In typical studies on restrained eating, restrained eaters (dieters) are compared to nondieters on food intake after a challenge in the laboratory such as having a high-calorie milkshake, consuming alcohol, or being subjected to stress. Dieters consistently eat more under these circumstances (counterregulation), while nondieters are more likely to regulate and eat less.

When dieters are challenged, they become disinhibited, a "what the heck" phenomenon occurs, and eating increases. In the case of the milkshake experiments, experimenters have manipulated both real and perceived caloric content. What subjects believe they have eaten better predicts disinhibition than does actual caloric content, so there are clearly psychological effects of energy restriction.

From this theoretical perspective, dieting is doomed to fail because it creates a psychological environment in which control over eating is fragile and easily disturbed, and the response to perturbances is overeating. This creates the need for further dieting, which may become more severe as this cycle continues. Some people become chronic dieters, with success at restriction being punctuated by overeating. When the overeating becomes sufficiently serious in magnitude and duration, binge eating disorder can be diagnosed, and when individuals compensate for the binges with some form of purging (vomiting, diuretics, laxatives, or excessive exercise), bulimia nervosa is present.

There is no unifying biological theory in this area. Many have speculated that the body interprets caloric restriction as a threat and responds with protective mechanisms such as decreased satiety, lower metabolic rate, increased lipoprotein lipase activity, and so forth. These and other mechanisms would serve to replenish energy stores.

While this general biological scheme is appealing from a survival perspective, it says little about for whom energy restriction would be threatening. An obese person, for example, might have far more energy stored than is necessary for survival, and vast amounts of weight could be lost before threat occurs. A person with anorexia nervosa could risk death with continued restriction, so the threat is immediate.

In this context, the concept of "set point" may be helpful. It is possible that the body defends a natural biological weight (the set point), much as a thermostat protects a building from temperature variation. Energy restriction would prompt the most aggressive countermeasures in persons most below their set points. This also is an appealing concept, one which is supported by animal studies and, to a lesser extent, studies on humans. Many humans maintain a remarkably stable weight, but others gain and then maintain, keep gaining, show large fluctuations, or lose weight after a period of being overweight. Whether there is a set point has not been established. Currently, there is no means for identifying an individual's set point, and only some of the conditions under which a set point might be altered (e.g., brain lesions) have been identified.

Empirical Examinations of Dieting

It is common lore that 95% of diets fail. In fact, no long-term population study has been done to see what the success rate might be, but the rate is likely to be much higher. *Consumer Reports*, for example, reported that 25% of individuals surveyed had lost weight and kept it off for a year or more. Furthermore, if the question were asked, "What percentage of people who eat differently in order to control weight or improve health achieve some degree of success?" a much more positive picture might emerge. This is speculation, however. From existing data, it is not possible to declare dieting a success or a failure.

As mentioned above, there is an abundant literature on restrained eating showing that individuals who are dieting are likely to overeat, at least for the short term, when initial challenge eating takes place. Studies however, are done primarily in laboratory settings and most have not examined eating beyond a few hours.

Cross-sectional studies of adults dieting in an attempt to control weight show moderate levels of success. Such a study by Williamson, Serdula, Anda, Levy, and Byers (1992), with 21,673 adults found a median length of dieting and reported weight losses to be 4 weeks and 8 pounds in women and 6 weeks and 10 pounds in men. There is growing agreement that weight losses as small as 5 to 10% of initial body weight may have beneficial health consequences, so the average person in this survey might be considered successful. Whether these losses are maintained and whether the long-term effects of such efforts are helpful is not known.

Several recent prospective studies provide a more detailed examination of dieting. Ogden and Wardle (in press) studied 23 dieters and 18 nondieters for a 6-week period of caloric restriction. Rating scales were completed three times per week and interviews were conducted weekly to assess mood, cognitive, and motivational states. The authors found "surprisingly few differential changes over the period of the diet," that the dieters increased in body satisfaction, and that "even a small weight loss seemed to provide encouragement for the dieters."

French, Jeffery, and Murray (1999) did annual assessments over 4 years on 1,120 adults who volunteered for a weight-gain-prevention program. The most common behaviors employed were increased exercise, decreased fat intake, reduced food quantity, and reduced calories. Global reports of dieting did not predict weight change, but there was a dose-dependent relationship between the duration of specific weight-control strategies used over the four years and changes in behavior and weight. Subjects who reported no caloric restriction gained 5 pounds over the 4 years, compared to 0.59 pounds for those engaging in caloric reduction for 49 weeks or more.

Nondieting Approaches to Obesity

Those who claim that diets nearly always fail and that obese individuals subject themselves to inevitable cycles of weight loss and regain have proposed alternatives to traditional approaches. These generally focus on eating a healthy diet (but not restricting calories), body acceptance, self-esteem enhancement, and attitude change to separate weight from self-image. The theory is that the cessation of chaotic eating and the removal of a restriction mentality will leave the person free to do what is natural—eat a healthy diet and lose weight in a reasonable fashion.

The nondieting approach has been discussed in the scientific literature and even written into popular books, but has been evaluated only recently. In studies where overweight people (in some cases binge eaters) have been assigned to traditional weight-loss treatment versus a nondieting approach, the results have been consistent. Both approaches appear to have similar effects on binge eating and psychological measures, although the nondieting approach will sometimes have stronger effects on issues specifically targeted by the program, such as body acceptance. Weight losses are the same or greater using the traditional approach.

The utility of nondieting approaches must be questioned in light of existing findings. While enhancing self-esteem and body acceptance is desirable and would be a worthy goal when there is no possibility of weight loss, obesity is a significant health risk and is left untouched by these approaches. One would not let smokers, for example, assume that because smoking is difficult to stop there is no hope, and then help people

accept their identity as smokers and protect their self-esteem in the face of the antismoking sentiment in society. Of course, it is important to consider more than health risk in obese persons because of the serious psychological and social effects it produces, so some measure of body acceptance and self-esteem enhancement is important. Not treating the obesity is difficult to justify.

Conditions Under Which Dieting Is Likely to Be Harmful or Beneficial

There seems little utility in asking whether dieting is harmful or beneficial because the term can represent many different combinations of behaviors. Some can lead to weight loss or prevention of weight gain while others can lead to eating disorders. Furthermore, the behaviors can be employed in the service of various pursuits, some healthier than others.

Certainly dieting can be pathological. When severe caloric restriction occurs in pursuit of unrealistic beauty ideals, the potential for harm far outweighs the gain, particularly in nonoverweight persons. Damaged self-esteem, body image disturbance, binge eating, weight cycling, bulimia nervosa, and anorexia nervosa are among the outcomes. Excessive exercise, laxatives, diuretics, and untested weight loss remedies (e.g., many herbal products) join severe caloric restriction on the list of practices that can have harmful consequences.

Cross-sectional and prospective studies on weight control efforts in overweight people seeking to lose weight and individuals hoping to prevent weight gain have shown modestly beneficial results. This stands in contrast to the oft-repeated but not tested claim that nearly all diets fail. Experiences from the general population might be more positive than those from clinical samples, in which morbid obesity, binge eating, and psychopathology are overrepresented.

Most weight control practices can be readily grouped into healthy and unhealthy categories. Some behaviors, such as purging, are unhealthy in any amount, whereas behaviors such as caloric restriction and exercise may be healthy or not, depending on the amount. Success at weight control is associated with the use of healthy practices. Reducing fat in the diet, making modest calorie reductions, reducing food quantity if high initially, and increasing physical activity offer the most hope.

There is also a person X behavior interaction that must be considered. Individuals who stand to benefit from weight loss and for whom there is some hope that behaviors such as caloric restriction and exercise will be successful are justified in dieting if safe practices are used. If a body-weight set point exists, and if an individual is at or below this point even though objectively overweight, weight loss may be difficult, but one can only speculate that this is the case.

Some dieting practices are safe and moderately effective, while others are not. Attempts to lose weight are indicated in some individuals and not others. Discovering the specific practices that are safe and effective, identifying those most likely to benefit, and understanding the conditions under which the practices are most likely to succeed will lead down a more productive path than will asking whether dieting is good or bad.

[*See also* Eating Disorders.]

Bibliography

Brownell, K. D., & Fairburn, C. G. (Eds.). (1995). *Eating disorders and obesity: A comprehensive handbook.* New York: Guilford Press. A detailed handbook covering all aspects of body-weight regulation, dieting, and the treatment of obesity disorders and obesity.

Brownell, K. D., & Rodin, J. (1994). The dieting maelstrom: Is it possible and advisable to lose weight? *American Psychologist, 49,* 781–791. A review and conceptual paper on the beneficial and harmful effects of dieting.

French, S. A., & Jeffery, R. W. (1994). Consequences of dieting to lose weight: Effects on physical and mental health. *Health Psychology, 13,* 195–212. One of the few papers to deal with both medical and psychological consequences of dieting.

French, S. A., Jeffery, R. W., & Murray, D. (1999). Is dieting good for you?: Prevalence, duration, and associated weight and behavior change for specific weight loss strategies over four years in U.S. adults. *International Journal of Obesity, 33,* 320–327. A large, prospective study of dieting and its long-term effects on adult men and women.

Neumark-Sztainer, D., Jeffery, R. W., French, S. A. (1997). Self-reported dieting: How should we ask? What does it mean? Associations between dieting and reported energy intake. *International Journal of Eating Disorders, 22,* 437–449. A study showing how phrasing of questions about dieting has substantial impact on self-reports of behavior.

Ogden, J., & Wardle, J. (in press). Emotional, cognitive and motivational consequences of dieting. *International Journal of Eating Disorders.* A small but thorough six-week study comparing individuals dieting to those not dieting on a variety of measures of mood, motivation, and cognition.

Polivy, J. (1996). Psychological consequences of food restriction. *Journal of the American Dietetic Association, 96,* 589–594.

Polivy, J. (1998). The effects of behavioral inhibition: Integrating internal cues, cognition, behavior, and affect. *Psychological Inquiry, 9,* 181–204. A review and theoretical article discussing the negative effects of inhibiting behavior, including food intake.

Wadden, T. A., Steen, S. A., Wingate, B. J., & Foster, G. D. (1996). Psychosocial consequences of weight reduction: How much weight loss is enough? *American Journal of Clinical Nutrition, 63* (Suppl.), 461S–465S. A paper discussing whether a minimum weight loss is necessary to achieve psychological benefits.

Williamson, D. F., Serdula, M. K., Anda, R. F., Levy, A., & Byers, T. (1992). Weight-loss attempts in adults: Goals, duration, and rate of weight loss. *American Journal of Public Health, 82,* 1251–1257. A cross-sectional, population-based study of dieting practices and results in 21,673 adults.

Kelly D. Brownell

DIFFERENTIAL AGING is a term in psychological gerontology describing the aging process as multidimensional within individuals (intra-individual change) and across individuals (interindividual differences). This term implies that aging must be studied in a multifaceted manner, examining age differences by comparing age groups, age changes over time by studying the same individuals longitudinally, and variations within age groups by examining individual differences in psychological performance (Baltes, Reese, & Nesselroade, 1977; Thomae, 1979).

The term *differential aging* stands in sharp contrast to the erroneous conceptions of aging as a uniform process of decline. Although it is true that the natural and inevitable outcome of the aging process is death of the organism, this fact does not rule out diverse avenues toward death including the possibility of growth in psychological functions even at the end of life. A corollary of the term *differential aging* is the premise that chronological age is not necessarily a good index of an individual's level of functioning. Gerontologists have long argued for the necessity of distinguishing among the biological, psychological, and social clocks that are assumed to tick at different rates within and across individuals.

Individual differences in the rate of aging have also been established. Rather than people becoming more alike as they get older, there is evidence that people become "more different." Support for this position has emerged from analyses of measures of variability in which it is shown that the majority of studies in gerontology, particularly longitudinal ones, show evidence of increasing variability over time (Nelson & Dannefer, 1992). Theoretical explanations of this diversity among older adults focus on the effects of varying experiences that individuals accumulate over their lives and relate to models in life-span developmental psychology that emphasize the importance of person-context transactions as influences on development (Lerner, 1995). Such transactions affect the rate of aging within and across individuals as they are exposed to and select environments that differentially affect their physical, psychological, and social characteristics. Another factor that may account for heightened variability among older populations in the rate and timing of aging is that of secondary aging, or disease processes that become more prevalent in later life. Pathological aging, when it occurs, adds to the diversity of patterns of change within and across individuals.

Differential Aging in the Relationship between Physical and Psychological Functioning

An interesting question is the interrelationship between physical (Schneider & Rowe, 1996) and psychological aging. The multiple threshold model (Whitbourne, 1996) postulates a reciprocal relationship between the aging of the physical systems and the individual's identity or self-conception throughout the years of adulthood. The term *multiple* in this model refers to the multidimensionality of the aging process and the fact that it involves potentially every system in the body. Changes occur within these systems at varying rates over time, both as a function of genetic predisposition and as a function of interactions with the environment. The term *threshold* in this model refers to the point at which the individual becomes aware of having experienced an age-related change in an area of functioning. Before this threshold is reached, the individual does not think of the self as "aging" or "old," or even as having the potential to be "aging" or "old." After the threshold is crossed, the individual becomes aware of having moved from the world of the middle-aged and young to the world of the elders. At this point, the individual recognizes the possibility of losing functions through aging (or disease) and begins to adapt to this possibility by incorporating this change into identity. Furthermore, as the threshold is crossed, the individual's objective adaptation to the environment may be altered as the age change impinges on daily activities. Even if the individual is not aware of the actual change, he or she may be made aware as the result of altered performance on familiar tasks.

The differential nature of the model is represented by the proposition that there is no single threshold leading to the view of the self as aging. The individual may feel "old" in one domain of functioning, but feel "not old," "middle-aged," or possibly "young" in other domains. Whether a threshold is crossed, it is theorized, depends in part on whether a particular area of functioning has been affected by the aging process, but also on the importance to the individual of the domain. Mobility may not be as important to an individual whose major source of pleasure is derived from sedentary activities. In the multiple threshold model, it is assumed that changes in areas important to the individual's adaptation and sense of competence will have greater potential for affecting identity than changes in relatively unimportant areas. Changes in life-sustaining functions may, however, supersede changes in nonvital functions.

Not only are changes in important functions likely to have a greater impact on adaptation and identity, it is assumed further that the functions that are most central to identity will be watched for most carefully by the individual. Thus, the model becomes reciprocal in the sense that the individual's identity can affect the way that age changes are anticipated. Heightened vigilance to age-related changes in central aspects of identity results in the individual's greater sensitivity to noticing early signs of age-related changes in some areas but not others. As a result of the increased vigilance and sensitivity, the impact of changes in these areas can be predicted to be even higher than they might otherwise be. The individual may become more motivated to adopt compensatory strategies in anticipation of age-related changes and avoid activities that may exacerbate the aging process in that area. Heightened sensitivity may also lead the individual to be more likely to react negatively to signs that loss has occurred. If such negative reactions occur, the individual may give up in despair over the inevitability and inexorable progression of the aging process. Such reactions are the complementary process in the reciprocal relationship between physical and psychological aging.

As applied to interindividual variations in the rate of aging, the second aspect of differential aging, the multiple threshold model, regards interindividual variations as a function of actions that individuals engage in to regulate the rate of their own aging. There are a number of preventive and compensatory mechanisms that individuals can take advantage of across a wide area of functions. For example, in the case of aerobic capacity, it is well known that regular activity can help to offset the aging process, even if this activity is begun quite late in life. By contrast, individuals can also choose to hasten the rate of their aging process by adopting harmful health habits, such as cigarette smoking or a sedentary life style. The decision to engage in protective or risky activities may reflect social as well as psychological factors. Individuals with higher levels of affluence are able to take advantage of certain preventative or compensatory steps (such as joining a health club) that are not available to those from less fortunate circumstances. Education and occupational background are further contributing factors, as individuals from higher socioeconomic levels are more likely to be aware of strategies they need to employ to moderate the rate of their own aging. For whatever reasons, the choices that individuals make with regard to these behaviors may be seen as a major factor influencing individual differences in the rate of aging in addition to differential genetic predispositions for diseases within specific organ systems.

As it is assumed to operate in the actual lives of individuals, the multiple threshold model is not seen as a series of linear, unconnected processes. Instead, the processes are highly interconnected. Crossing a threshold in one area (appearance) may reset the threshold for functioning in another area (aerobic capacity). Each new threshold has the potential to alter the individual's identity which, in turn, can alter the individual's vigilance regarding future age-related changes in other areas of functioning and the behaviors relevant to the threshold just crossed.

Research based on the multiple threshold model provides support for the notion that individuals are in fact differentially sensitive to the aging process and its effects on their functioning (Whitbourne, 1996). Middle-aged adults are more aware of the effects of aging on the appearance of the face and body in contrast to older adults, who are more sensitive to the effects of aging on mobility and balance. There are also gender differences in aging thresholds, with men more likely to cross thresholds related to physical strength and women to physical appearance. Further testing on larger age samples of adults will provide greater specificity regarding the nature of these aging thresholds as well as refinements in the specified relationships among aging processes, identity, coping, and adaptation.

Differential Aging of Intelligence

As the result of greater awareness of intra- and inter-individual variations in patterns of intellectual aging, the search for consistent patterns of age effects on intelligence that characterized early investigations, has been replaced in the past few decades with a more differential picture. Following the realization of a discrepancy between the findings of cross-sectional and longitudinal studies on intelligence, with cross-sectional studies showing a more exaggerated pattern of negative age effects than longitudinal studies, researchers in the mid-1960s first became aware of the need to develop a more refined conception of aging and intelligence. Horn and Donaldson (1980), who postulated the existence of two broad types of abilities, fluid and crystallized intelligence, based their theory on observations of differential patterns of age differences for verbal compared to nonverbal subscales of intelligence. Subsequent investigations by Schaie (1983) and Baltes (1993) have provided ample evidence of interindividual and intra-individual variations in the aging of intelligence. It is now generally accepted that fluid abilities show a pronounced decline in adulthood, but that crystallized intelligence is maintained well into old age. However, these overall patterns mask the variations associated with health status, socioeconomic background, personality, and degree of activity in one's life style.

The multiple threshold model may also have some applicability to intellectual changes in later life. The findings of one of Schaie's studies on intelligence suggests that individuals who have adjusted their identities in response to changes in intellectual performance may hold certain advantages in maintaining their abilities into the future (Schaie, Willis, & O'Hanlon, 1994). In the 1984 testing, respondents in the Seattle Longitudinal Study were asked to compare their current performance with their scores seven years earlier. By comparing these self-assessments with the actual performance changes, it was possible to categorize the respondents into three groups: the "optimists" (those who overestimated positive changes), "pessimists" (who overestimated negative changes), and "realists" (whose ratings were accurate). The findings revealed that the pessimists declined the least or even gained compared to the optimists, who declined the most. Thus, the incorporation of changes in performance into identity seemed to have a protective effect on actual ability, perhaps by moderating future activity.

Implications

As shown in these two examples presented here, from theories and data in the area of physical and intellectual aging, the term *differential aging* provides a useful heuristic for conceptualizing the complex and multifaceted nature of development in the later years. Within the life of one individual, the aging process occurs at varying rates, both through factors that are outside of the individual's control and through actions that the individual has the power to take to alter the rate of aging. The interaction of the individual's identity with these physical changes suggests reciprocal relationships in these developmental processes that further contribute to the variation within individuals in the rate of their own aging. The individual's appraisal of cognitive abilities may also influence the course and progression of the multiple dimensions that constitute intelligence. Across individuals, variations in the rate of physical and intellectual aging may be seen as increasing over the years of adulthood and old age as the result of variations in aging processes and, again, in the compensatory and preventative actions that individuals engage in as a response to these changes.

These examples have demonstrated not only the value of the concept of differential aging as an explanatory vehicle, but also suggest the necessity of developing research strategies for the study of aging that incorporate reciprocal multidimensional assumptions, methods, and analytical strategies. It is not sufficient to document the existence of age differences or changes over time employing standard analytical methods. With the increasing availability of sophisticated structural modeling programs current scholars have the opportunity to translate the principle of differential aging into operational terms. Research based on the notion of differential aging will not only reflect more accurately the nature of the aging process but can also provide the basis for more effective interventions to improve the lives of older individuals.

Bibliography

Baltes, P. B. (1993). The aging mind: Potential and limits. *Gerontologist, 33,* 580–594.

Baltes, P. B., Reese, H. W., & Nesselroade, J. R. (Eds.). (1977). *Life-span developmental psychology: Introduction to research methods.* Hillsdale, NJ: Erlbaum.

Horn, J. L., & Donaldson, G. (1980). Cognitive development in adulthood. In J. Kagan & O. G. Brim, Jr. (Eds.), *Constancy and change in development.* Cambridge, MA: Harvard University Press.

Lerner, R. M. (1995). Developing individuals within changing contexts: Implications of developmental contextualism for human development, research, policy, and programs. In T. J. Kindermann & J. Valsiner (Eds.), *Development of person-context relations* (pp. 13–37). Hillsdale, NJ: Erlbaum.

Nelson, E. A., & Dannefer, D. (1992). Aged heterogeneity: Fact or fiction? The fate of diversity in gerontological research. *Gerontologist, 32,* 17–23.

Schaie, K. W. (1983). The Seattle Longitudinal Study: A 21-year exploration of psychometric intelligence in adulthood. In K. W. Schaie (Ed.), *Longitudinal studies of adult psychological development* (pp. 64–135). New York: Guilford Press.

Schaie, K. W., Willis, S. L., & O'Hanlon, A. M. (1994). Perceived intellectual performance change over seven years. *Journals of Gerontology: Psychological Sciences, 49,* pp. 108–118.

Schneider, E. L., & Rowe, J. W. (Eds.). (1996). *Handbook of the biology of aging* (4th ed.). San Diego, CA: Academic Press.

Thomae, H. (1979). The concept of development and life-span developmental psychology. In P. B. Baltes & O. G. Brim, Jr. (Eds.), *Life-span development and behavior* (Vol. 2, pp. 281–312). New York: Academic Press.

Whitbourne, S. K. (1996). *The aging individual: Physical and psychological perspectives.* New York: Springer.

Susan Krauss Whitbourne

DIFFERENTIAL PSYCHOLOGY. The concept of individual differences and its romantic counterconcept of uniqueness refer to anything that marks a person as a distinct human being. This may run from superficial properties such as a flattering hat or one's bodily characteristics to basic psychological qualities such as instincts, motives, and dispositions. The set of possible characteristics includes attitudes, values, ideologies, interests, emotions, capacities, skills, socio-economical status, gender, height, and so forth. Differential psychology, therefore, is concerned with individual differences in the broadest sense of the word, and its focus traditionally has been description and taxonomy.

Stability and Individuality

All definitions of individual differences and personality assume the relevance of individuality and stability. Descriptions of personality should emphasize individual variations from person to person but only to the extent that those individualizing features exhibit continuity over time. Without such continuity, the study of personality is impossible.

A first listing of virtually all differential characteristics was constructed by Gordon Allport and Henry Odbert (1936). They collected 17,953 descriptive words from an English dictionary, each suggesting an individual-difference variable. The history of philosophy and psychology has tried to separate the wheat from the chaff, by distinguishing temporal and stable characteristics, good and bad, appearance and reality, superficiality and depth. The delineation of individual differences has been documented in textbooks under such rubrics as character, temperament, personality, and intelligence.

The issues captured by those rubrics are repeatedly discussed in the *Journal of Personality,* the *Journal of Research in Personality,* the *European Journal of Personality* (publication medium of the European Association of Personality Psychology), the *Journal of Personality Assessment* (medium of the Society for Personality Assessment), the *Journal of Personality and Social Psychology, Personality and Individual Differences* (International Society for the Study of Individual Differences), and the *Personality and Social Psychology Bulletin* (Society for Personality and Social Psychology).

Character

Since time immemorial people have tried to catch the characteristic features of humans in a word or striking expression. Such a word or expression functions *pars pro toto,* because it stands for a complex of traits and features, habits and inclinations, partially inborn, partially learned. We use a single word but mean a story, a life story or personal paradigm: it is about the mark someone sets on all his or her actions. The best-known antique "psychological" system is that of Theophrastus. His 30 characters had mainly suggestive, edifying meaning. They convey aspects of the morals of the time and were provided to give observers the opportunity to become better people.

Psychological types of all kinds have been put forward throughout history (Roback, 1927). Plato's categorization into those who are developed well intellectually, those in whom passion and competition play an important role, and those who are mainly led by lust and desire, is an early example. In the writings of Theophrastus, Plato, and many others, a major aim is to point out the societal importance of the scarce psychological resources of high moral and educated nature. In order to be useful, character descriptions should be easily recognized and understood, and they should have a generalized form. Since the term *character* was largely replaced by *personality*, the moral aspect has faded into the background of differential psychology.

Temperament

Among personality psychologists, it is widely accepted that the gist of personality is temperamental. The history of temperamental thinking closely paralleled that of characterology but had, instead of a moral, a medical emphasis. Prototemperamental thinking like that of Empedocles, Hippocrates, and, half a millennium later, Galen, emphasized the medical function of their elementary principles, the meaning of which was colored by mythological thinking. Though Galen made some reference to character, those references were at best fragmentary; the four humors, blood, phlegm, black bile and yellow bile, "were foremost the determinants of illness, constitution, and physiognomy" (Stelmack & Stalikas, 1991). No psychological, let alone dispositional, meaning was involved. Quite the contrary, temperament, consisting of mixtures of those four humors, could change by the minute. About one-and-a-half millennia later, when the medical function was taken over by a moralistic function, under the influence of Thomism, temperaments came to be conceived of as having a stable form. Behaviors were seen as resonating physical processes and characteristics of the nerve tissue.

Temperament is usually distinguished from personality, in that the first emphasizes formal (Strelau, 1987) or stylistic aspects (Thomas & Chess, 1977), and the second emphasizes the content of traits and behavior. Historically, character, less personality, may have emphasized the description of individualizing features instead of focusing on generalization and abstraction of behavior. Ultimately, however, in all domains of individual differences, the emphasis is on recurrent patterns, stable structures, paradigms, or typical tales, and therefore on form and style.

Personality

Allport (1937, pp. 25–26) discussed the etymology of the concept *personality* by referring to the Latin *per sonare*, meaning "to sound through," that is, to sound through the mouthpiece of a mask as used by actors in Greek theater. This "verbal" meaning is hardly recognized nowadays and has been replaced by the mask concept of personality through the noun *persona*. The mask concept is about appearance, which is controlled by a variety of expressive means. A partial reading of the common sense understanding of personality conveys this conception: a person who "has" personality is one who makes a strong, lasting, good impression.

The study of personality is often understood as the approach to "unmask," to uncover the hidden reality concealed by the mask. Psychologists do not listen to the content of what the voice conveys through the mask, but they rather listen to how the person talks and to characteristics of the voice. Also here, formal and stylistic features are emphasized in studying behavior for its recurrent pattern. This is the way to find out about the person behind the mask. Listening to the content, and therefore listening to the person, would mean communicating with that person as a unique individual. The unique person is someone to talk with, not to try to describe and to study. Uniqueness is thus not an object of scientific investigation but rather a presupposition.

Personality is not an unequivocal concept. For example, does one refer to structure or dynamics? Dynamics are excluded from this discussion because individual differences do not form the primary focus for dynamic conceptions. In a theoretical analysis, Alston (1976) proposes a distinction between disposition and goal as conceptual alternatives. The trait conception has fared by its emphasis on response predisposition (frequency of response or typical behavior). Alternatively, Wallace (1966) formulated the abilities conception of personality, which emphasizes response capability or performance under maximal conditions. This alternative conception expresses efficiency of performance and stresses the importance of stimulus conditions for behavior.

Intelligence

Sir Francis Galton was the first who attempted to measure intelligence, referred to as "natural ability" covering "those qualities of intellect and disposition, which urge and qualify a man to perform acts that lead to reputation" (Galton, 1869, p. 37). Galton conceived of intelligence as a single, underlying, pervasive, mental power, for which he developed the mental test largely consisting of the psychophysical measures typical of the beginnings of psychological experimentation: how well can a person distinguish between small differences in weights, smells, lengths of lines, and so forth. These measures did not prove useful in predicting achievement outcomes. Instead of the sensory skills tested by Galton, the French psychologist Alfred Binet focused on higher-order skills such as "comprehension, judgment, reasoning, and invention" (Binet & Simon, 1916/1973, p. 40). In 1905, Binet and Simon constructed the first "Metrical Scale of Intelligence," which did prove useful in predicting academic achievement.

The emphasis on single, pervasive constructs was

reinforced by the psychometric method of the time, namely Charles Spearman's two-factor method. Spearman's model matched most of the theorizing on personality and abilities of that period. Spearman (1904) thus sustained the search for a single, unitary construct of ability, and he envisaged the general factor g of mental ability and eventually identified group factors, such as verbal ability, numerical ability, and speed, each peculiar to one specific (s factor) test. This became the basis of a hierarchical view of intelligence, group factors being subordinate to the general factor g.

The hierarchical view of ability has been conditioned by those who favored a multifactor view of abilities, a view reinforced by findings from factor analysis. After the first few decades of the twentieth century, there was a shift toward common factors, supported by Lewis L. Thurstone's psychometric model (Thurstone, 1938) in which a certain number of "factors" or components are supposed to be common to a given number of variables. Thurstone identified seven independent abilities, termed primary mental abilities, such as verbal comprehension, verbal fluency, and perceptual speed. The growth of separate abilities escalated in J. P. Guilford's (1959) "Structure of Intellect Model," representing 120 distinct abilities displayed in a cube.

The main problem with Thurstone's analyses was that subsequent research showed the primary abilities being correlated, so that it became logical to search for second-order factors. Horn and Cattell (1966) distinguished "fluid" intelligence and "crystallized" intelligence as second-order factors of primary importance. Fluid intelligence is reasoning ability that develops independently from schooling, while crystallized intelligence reflects scholastic and cultural knowledge acquisition.

Basic Personality Factors

The contemporary search for basic factors of personality started during the first three or four decades of this century when there was an emphasis on broad, unitary constructs that had a bearing upon the total personality. A first factor of a unitary nature was provided in Webb's (1915) conception of character. Webb, working under Spearman's guidance, performed a first "attempt at an exact study of character." His conception of personality was twofold: intelligence on the one hand and character, defined as "the sum of all personal qualities which are not distinctly intellectual" (1915, p. 2), on the other hand. Webb listed a large number of "mental qualities," both intellective and nonintellective, in a rating scale for schoolteachers. Using a prototype of factor analysis, he found support for the general factor of intelligence, g, and he found evidence for a second factor of wide generality, prominent on the character side of mental activity. Webb conceived of the latter factor as persistence of motives or will (w) (1915, p. 60).

With the shift toward Thurstone's common factors approach also for personality, the search started for a larger number of independent factors. In order to summarize the interrelationships among 60 trait variables, for example, Thurstone (1934) reported five common factors to account for the trait information. These five independent factors form an interesting foretaste of a model of personality traits over which there is a growing universal acceptance, particularly regarding its coverage of the field of individual differences. The rationale of the model, stating that important individual differences are represented in language, was given by Cattell (1943), who tried to summarize the lexicon of trait terms. It took about half a century of research for this model, the so-called Big Five model of traits, to gain the status of an effective, crossculturally reproducible, organizing framework of individual differences. The model also evoked criticisms, especially over the exact number and nature of basic traits. The contemporary understanding is that extraversion (E) and neuroticism (N) are beyond dispute. Of E and N, N has acquired the strongest position in the early personality literature, not only because of its easily identifiable and distinct nature but also because of its direct clinical relevance. Thurstone and Thurstone's (1930) "A Personality Schedule," compiled mostly from work by others, including Woodworth (1920), was the first "Neurotic Inventory" discussed in some length.

Allport and Odbert (1936) and Cattell (1943, 1945) were the pioneers who tried to identify all relevant traits of personality. But it took a few decades before this descriptive approach provided the Big Five as a rather solid framework, consisting of the dimensions extraversion, agreeableness, conscientiousness, emotional stability (or neuroticism), and intellectual autonomy or openness to experience. The model came about through the use of correlational procedures, the most frequently used methods in individual differences research. The main figure responsible for the breakthrough of both the approach and of the model was Lewis Goldberg (1990). The Big Five movement probably received its strongest impetus from the team of Costa and McCrea (1992), whose Five Factor model and the corresponding assessment instrument, the NEO-PI, find their origin in the psycholexical school. The model has internationally been accepted as the best working hypothesis for personality-taxonomic work in the near future.

The Big Five model has undergone a metamorphosis through a fine-grained representational configuration (Hofstee, De Raad, & Goldberg, 1992) that shows a maximum of 90 distinct facets within the five-dimensional system. Because of its explicit coverage of the trait domain, the latter model, the so-called

Abridged Big Five Circumplex (AB5C), provides an excellent starting point for the development of personality assessment instruments. The FFPI (Five Factor Personality Inventory, Hendriks, 1997), which is the first that is based on this faceted model, marks the beginning of a new generation of personality assessment instruments in which systematic coverage of the various facets of the trait domain is realized. The earlier mentioned NEO-PI is another faceted Big Five assessment instrument in case.

[*See also* Individual Differences.]

Bibliography

Allport, G. W. (1937). *Personality: A psychological interpretation.* New York: Holt.

Allport, G. W., & Odbert, H. S. (1936). Trait-names: A psycho-lexical study. *Psychological Monographs, 47,* no. 211.

Alston, W. P. (1976). Traits, consistency and conceptual alternatives for personality theory. In R. Harré (Ed.), *Personality* (pp. 63–97). Oxford: Blackwell.

Binet, A., & Simon, T. (1916/1973). *The development of intelligence in children* (The Binet-Simon Scale). New York: The Arno Press.

Cattell, R. B. (1943). The description of personality: Basic traits resolved into clusters. *Journal of Abnormal and Social Psychology, 38,* 476–507.

Cattell, R. B. (1945). The description of personality: Principles and findings in a factor analysis. *American Journal of Psychology, 58,* 69–90.

Costa, P. T. Jr., & McCrae, R. R. (1992). *Revised NEO Personality Inventory and NEO Five Factor Inventory: Professional manual.* Englewood Cliffs, NJ: Prentice Hall.

Cronbach, L. J. (1949). *Essentials of psychological testing.* New York: Harper.

Galton, F. (1869). *Heredity genius: An inquiry into its laws and consequences.* London: Macmillan.

Goldberg, L. R. (1990). An alternative "description of personality": The Big-Five Factor structure. *Journal of Personality and Social Psychology, 59,* 1216–1229.

Guilford, J. P. (1959). Three faces of intellect. *American Psychologist, 14,* 469–479.

Hendriks, A. A. J. (1997). *The construction of the Five-Factor Personality Inventory (FFPI).* Unpublished doctoral dissertation, University of Groningen, The Netherlands.

Hofstee, W. K. B., De Raad, B., & Goldberg, L. R. (1992). Integration of the Big Five and circumplex approaches to trait structure. *Journal of Personality and Social Psychology, 63,* 146–163.

Horn, J. L., & Cattell, R. B. (1966). Refinement and test of the theory of fluid and crystallised intelligence. *Journal of Educational Psychology, 57,* 253–270.

Roback, A. A. (1927). *The psychology of character, with a survey of personality in general.* London: Routledge and Kegan Paul.

Spearman, C. (1904). General intelligence objectively determined and measured. *American Journal of Psychology, 15,* 201–293.

Stelmack, R. M., & Stalikas, A. (1991). Galen and the humour theory of temperament. *Personality and Individual Differences, 12,* 255–263.

Strelau, J. (1987). The concept of temperament in personality research. *European Journal of Personality, 1,* 107–117.

Thomas, A., & Chess, S. (1977). *Temperament and development.* New York: Brunner/Mazel.

Thurstone, L. L. (1934). The vectors of mind. *Psychological Review, 41,* 1–32.

Thurstone, L. L. (1938). *Primary mental abilities.* Chicago: University of Chicago Press.

Thurstone, L. L., & Thurstone, T. G. (1930). A neurotic inventory. *Journal of Social Psychology, 1,* 3–30.

Wallace, J. (1966). An abilities conception of personality: Some implications for personality measurement. *American Psychologist, 21,* 132–138.

Webb, E. (1915). *Character and intelligence: An attempt at an exact study of character.* Cambridge: Cambridge University Press.

Woodworth, R. S. (1920). *Personal Data Sheet.* Chicago: Stoelting.

Boele De Raad

DIRECT OBSERVATION refers to a collection of techniques used by behavioral scientists to assess human behavior and the many factors that control it using systematic visual inspection procedures. Direct observation is most likely the oldest form of assessment. For example, Nietzel, Bernstein, and Milich (1998) argued that the capacity to systematically observe and evaluate behavior would have predated all other forms of psychological assessment that require language, written communication, or instrumentation.

Contemporary direct observation techniques have their origins in empiricism, a scientific philosophy in which it is argued that careful examination of relationships among observable events yields the best understanding of cause-effect relationships (James, Mulaik, & Brett, 1983). Empiricism exerted a profound influence on the behavioral sciences and promoted the development of behaviorism, a philosophy of behavior in which it is argued that the most effective way to study and learn about human behavior is to combine careful observation with experimentation (Bongar & Butler [Eds.], 1995; Freedheim, Kessler, Messer, Peterson, & Strup [Eds.], 1992). In turn, behavioral scientists and clinicians who endorsed the behaviorist position significantly contributed to the development and use of direct observation systems as a way to assess human behavior in basic and applied research (Suen & Ary, 1989).

Direct observation is used for a wide variety of research and clinical purposes. Additionally, many types of direct observation systems have been developed.

These systems are similar to the extent that they all emphasize the importance of carefully defining, recording, and quantifying behavior. They also share a fundamental goal of identifying and evaluating relationships between behavior and factors that control it. They differ, however, in three main ways: (1) how behavior will be sampled, (2) where behavior will be observed, and (3) who will observe the behavior.

Common Goals: Establishing Operational Definitions and Identifying Relationships among Behavior and Controlling Factors

The principal objective in direct observation is to empirically assess behavior and the many factors that control it. In order to accomplish this, the behavioral scientist must initially generate precise operational definitions of key behaviors, labeled target behaviors, and situational events that exert an influence on the target behaviors. These latter situational variables are sometimes labeled controlling factors. The process of generating operational definitions of target behaviors and controlling factors is referred to as a topographical analysis.

There are many ways that behaviors and situations can be measured. In order to simplify this complexity, one can sort target behaviors into three main categories: cognitive-verbal behaviors, emotional-physiological behaviors, and overt-motor behaviors. Although these different components of behavior could be evaluated in many different ways, most direct observation systems emphasize the measurement of: (a) the magnitude or intensity of responding, (b) the frequency of responding, and/or (c) the duration of responding.

Situational controlling factors can be divided into two main categories: social/interpersonal events and nonsocial/environmental events. Social/interpersonal events refer to controlling factors that involve interactions with other people or groups of people. Nonsocial/environmental events refer to controlling factors that exist in the environment outside of social interactions. Examples of these latter types of controlling factors include temperature, noise levels, season of the year, lighting levels, and the structure of the built environment. Similar to the dimensions that are used to evaluate behavior, the magnitude, frequency, and duration of social/interpersonal and nonsocial/environmental controlling factors are routinely measured in direct observation systems.

Once target behaviors and controlling factors have been operationally defined, behavioral scientists using direct observation systems will often carefully examine relationships among these sets of variables in order to determine the function of a behavior. The term *functional analysis* has been used to describe this second common purpose of direct observation systems (Haynes

& O'Brien, 1990) and it is most effectively accomplished using experimentation, conditional probability analysis, or time series analyses (Schundt, 1985; Watson & Gresham, 1998).

Differentiating Element I: How Behavior Is Sampled and Where Behavior Is Observed

Because behavior occurs in a continuous stream and because it cannot be observed at all times in all locations, behavioral scientists using direct observation must design strategies for sampling behavior. In designing sampling procedures, the behavioral scientist must consider how behavior will be sampled and where it will be sampled. The overarching goal in selecting the method and location of sampling is to generate information that is most representative of target behaviors and controlling factors. It is also often important to collect data that generalize to true world environments.

Method of Sampling. There are four types of sampling strategies that are commonly used in direct observation: event sampling, duration sampling, interval sampling, and time sampling. Event sampling involves noting and recording the occurrence of a carefully specified behavior whenever it is observed. A frequency measure is then calculated by summing the number of times the behavior occurs within a relevant time interval (for example, number of occurrences per minute, hour, day, week) and/or context (for example, number of occurrences in a particular setting such as a classroom or simulated social interaction). In duration sampling, the amount of time that elapses between the beginning and end of a target behavior is measured. Event and duration sampling are most readily accomplished when the target behavior has clear beginning and end points. Additionally, these sampling methods are well suited for evaluating behaviors that do not occur at high frequencies.

Interval sampling refers to a procedure where discrete and time-limited observation periods are used to sample behavior. These intervals typically range from several seconds to hours. If the target behavior reaches a prespecified criterion, usually based on the proportion of the interval during which the behavior is observed, the entire interval is coded as an occurrence of the target behavior. A summary measure of the number of intervals in which the target behavior reached the prespecified criterion is then generated. Interval sampling is most useful when the target behavior occurs at a high frequency or when the beginning and end of the target behavior are not easily discernible.

Time sampling combines elements of event, duration, and interval sampling. In time sampling, the observer records the time at beginning and end of a target behavior whenever it occurs. Frequency information is derived by counting the number of times the behavior occurs across a relevant time frame. Duration is derived by calculating the average time that elapses between the beginning and end of the target behavior. Interval information can be obtained by dividing the observation periods into discrete intervals and calculating the number of intervals that met the prespecified criterion of target behavior occurrence. In many cases, time sampling is aided by hand-held computerized coding devices that will automatically time stamp the beginning and end of an observed behavior when the observer enters specific codes on a keyboard. The availability of such automated devices has increased the accessibility of time sampling in observational research and applications.

Settings Where Direct Observation Can Be Conducted. Direct observation can occur in naturalistic settings or analogue settings. Observation in naturalistic settings occurs when the target behavior is evaluated in everyday, social, occupational, or domestic settings. Naturalistic observation provides the most ecologically valid type of assessment information. This means that the collected information more closely approximates "real life" behavior in "real world" situations.

Because direct observation can be very difficult to use in naturalistic settings, behavioral scientists frequently conduct assessments in analogue settings. An analogue setting is a controlled environment that is specifically designed to make it easier for the observers to measure target behaviors, controlling factors, and the relationships among them. Analogue settings can range from highly controlled laboratory settings to "quasi-naturalistic" settings such as a structured living environment or office.

Differentiating Elements II: Types of Observers

Observational data can be coded by human judges and/or technological devices. Human judges include: nonparticipant observers, participant observers, and self-observers. Nonparticipant observers are specifically trained to conduct observations of target behaviors exhibited by a person or groups of persons. They have no other relationship with the persons under scrutiny aside from this function. Typically, nonparticipant observers include paid research technicians and students working in a research setting. Participant observers are trained to carry out direct observation of a person or persons with whom they maintain an ongoing relationship outside of their function as an observer. Participant observers may include family members, health care providers, coworkers, teachers, and peers.

The third type of observer is the self. Self-monitoring is a technique where the target person is trained to conduct systematic observations of his or her own be-

havior. This strategy has the advantage of allowing behavioral scientists to evaluate behaviors that are only accessible to the person being observed. Examples of these types of behaviors include thoughts, emotional reactions, and covert activities that would be suppressed in the presence of nonparticipant or participant observers.

Technological device coding involves the use of mechanical or electronic instruments to record the occurrence of target behaviors and controlling factors. Commonly used technological devices include audiotape recorders, videotape recorders, keyboard-stroke detectors, motion sensors, speech analyzers, and psychophysiological recording equipment. Technological devices have become more readily available to behavioral scientists within the recent past. As a result, they are being increasingly used to collect information on a wide variety of target behaviors in the workplace (for example, work productivity, telephone use), community (for example, car speed), clinical settings (for example, behavioral responses to stressors), and home (for example, television use, computer use).

Psychophysiological recording systems are a special type of technological observation system. In psychophysiological assessment, mechanical and electronic recording devices are used to measure physiological responses that are not visible to external observers. Commonly used psychophysiological measures include cardiovascular measures (heart rate, blood pressure, blood flow), central nervous system activity (electroencephalogram, evoked potentials), and peripheral nervous system activity (skin conductance, hand temperature, muscle tension).

Psychometric Issues

The reliability and validity of observational data are dependent upon the quality of the recording system. Specifically, valid and reliable observational data can be collected when there are well-trained observers and/or appropriately calibrated technological devices recording clearly specified target behaviors and controlling factors in an appropriate setting. Alternatively, problems with reliability and validity most commonly arise when (a) target behaviors and controlling factors have not been adequately operationalized, (b) observers have not been adequately trained and monitored for continued accuracy, (c) technological devices have not been properly calibrated and routinely checked for accuracy, and (d) the observational setting is not conducive to target behavior occurrence or accurate observation of behavior.

An additional psychometric issue related to observation is reactivity. Reactivity effects occur when the person or persons under scrutiny modify their behavior in the presence of observers. In some cases, reactivity effects can lead to behavioral suppression (for example, participants may suppress behaviors that they perceive to be socially undesirable) or behavioral intensification (for example, socially desirable behaviors may occur at a higher rate of frequency, intensity, or duration). Reactivity effects associated with direct observation can be lessened when the salience and intrusiveness of an observational system are minimized.

Conclusion

The primary goals of direct observation are to provide precise, quantifiable, information about behavior, controlling factors, and the relationships among them. Direct observation systems can use several methods for sampling behavior in settings that range from naturalistic settings to analogue settings. Different types of human observers or technological devices can record the occurrence of target behaviors and controlling factors. The reliability and validity of direct observation varies with the integrity of the methods used to collect data. Enhanced levels of reliability and validity are expected when carefully defined behaviors and controlling factors are recorded by properly trained observers or correctly calibrated technical devices in settings that promote target behavior occurrence and unobstructed observation.

Bibliography

Craighead, W. E., Craighead, L. W., & Ilardi, S. S. (1995). Behavior therapies in historical perspective. In B. M. Bongar & L. E. Butler (Eds.). *Comprehensive textbook of psychotherapy: Theory and practice* (Vol. 1, pp. 64–83). New York: Oxford University Press.

Fishman, D. B., & Franks, C. M. (1992). Evolution and differentiation within behavior therapy: A theoretical and epistemological review. In D. K. Freedheim, H. J. Freudenberger, J. W. Kessler, S. B. Messer, D. R. Peterson, H. H. Strup, & P. L. Wachtel (Eds.), *History of psychotherapy: A century of change* (pp. 159–196). Washington, DC: American Psychological Association.

Gresham, F. M., & Lambros, K. M. (1998). Behavioral and functional assessment. In W. S. Watson & F. M. Gresham (Eds.), *Handbook of child behavior therapy* (pp. 3–22). New York: Plenum Press.

Haynes, S. N., & O'Brien, W. H. (1990). Functional analysis in behavior therapy. *Clinical Psychology Review, 10,* 649–668.

James, L. R., Mulaik, S. A., & Brett, J. M. (1983). *Causal analysis: Assumptions, models, and data.* Beverly Hills, CA: Sage.

Nietzel, M. T., Bernstein, D. A., & Milich, R. (1998). *Introduction to clinical psychology* (5th ed.). Upper Saddle River, NJ: Prentice Hall.

Schlundt, D. G. (1985). An observational methodology for functional analysis. *Bulletin for the Society of Psychologists in Addictive Behaviors, 4,* 234–239.

Suen, H. K., & Ary, D. (1989). *Analyzing quantitative behavioral observation data.* Hillsdale, NJ: Erlbaum.

William H. O'Brien and Stephen N. Haynes

DISCIPLINE involves values, power, and beliefs about people and institutions. Within hierarchical relationships (parent-child, teacher-student), society defines the adult as having the legitimate power, or discipline, to control or influence the child. The American Psychological Association opposes the use of corporal punishment in all institutions, public or private, where children are cared for or educated. It maintains that effective use of punishment is difficult, rare, and fraught with unintended consequences, for example, displacement or imitation (APA, 1975, p. 632).

Discipline Goals, Strategies, and Situations

Kelman (1958, 1961) distinguishes among three discipline goals: compliance, identification, and internalization. Compliance occurs when the individual behaves to get a reward or avoid a punishment. Identification is achieved when the individual acts appropriately as long as a valued model is salient. Internalization is inferred when the behavior endures across a variety of settings without external constraints or inducements. Discipline goals are value and situationally sensitive. For example, compliance is probably a sufficient goal for raising your hand for recognition in school; however, valuing and living a healthy life (internalization) is preferable to simple avoidance of illicit drug use when monitored.

Research on discipline strategies primarily is based upon behavioral principles of control as operationalized by B. F. Skinner (1953). Skinner focused on reinforcements and the acquisition and maintenance of behavior, noting that individuals are more predictably (and better) controlled by reinforcement schedules than by punishments. Modern theories of behaviorism evoke covert processes (for example, mediation) with overt behavior and reinforcements to promote the ultimate goal of self-regulation, defined in part as self-reinforcement for self-defined goals. Current recommendations for effective use of reinforcements are consistent with Skinnerian principles and modern elaborations: Reinforcements are more effective to the extent that they are specific to the targeted behavior, informative, and subtle. Modern theorists stress in particular the subtlety factor. Subtle reinforcements, defined by the minimal sufficiency principle of social control, are hypothesized to promote internalization goals because they do not make external (compliance) reasons salient.

Discipline strategies reportedly used by adults and

children predictably differ by interpersonal conflict situation. Gordon (1970) defines these situations by the needs they arouse and identifies three levels of "problem ownership." In self-owned problems, the protagonist feels personally challenged, threatened, irritated, or angry. In other-owned problems, he does not feel responsible for the problem but may feel sympathetic. In shared problems, self and other are both involved in thwarting each other's needs.

Research on parent discipline, classroom management, and peer relations has found a distinct discipline profile associated with each level of problem ownership. Self-owned problems involve short-term control/desist goals. Self-owned problems impose attributions that the offending individual is behaving intentionally and with personal control (and therefore choice). These attributions elicit anger and salient punishment strategies that interfere with internalization goals.

Other-owned problems promote long-term mental hygiene goals. Other-owned problems involve attributions that the problem individual is not behaving with control or intention; rather, he is a "victim." Victim attributions elicit pity and long-term supportive strategies meant to foster internalization. Finally, shared problems promote specific and immediate behavioral substitution goals. Shared problems involve attributions that, whether or not there is personal control, the offending individual's behavior is unintentional. Discipline strategies are primarily contigent-reward focused.

Models of Parent Discipline

Five domains of parent behavior are considered essential in the promotion of children's mental health: verbal interaction between mother and child, affective relationship between parent and child, discipline and control strategies, expectations for achievement, and parent beliefs and attributions about their children. Discipline strategies can serve as a proxy for each domain because they are based in an affective relationship and communication pattern that convey parent understandings, beliefs, and expectations about their children. Parent discipline is defined by parent control of and affect toward their children. Parent control and affect are independent; a parent may discipline out of concern or hostility. Primarily, research focuses on general trends rather than situational differences in three styles of parent control (laissez-faire, authoritarian, authoritative).

One extreme of parent control is laissez-faire or permissive management. Permissive parents provide little structure, control, or instruction; their policy is non-interference. The burden is on the child to seek parent involvement. The lack of structure inherent in this approach is not associated with positive child outcomes.

Authoritarian control anchors the dimension at the opposite extreme. Authoritarian control is dogmatic and obedience focused. Authoritarian parents control their children independent of present or emerging capabilities; thus these parents may have unrealistically high or low expectations for their children. Coercive authority may involve rewards and punishments, but it does not involve explanation of parent reasoning. Rationales for parent demands are of the "because I said so" genre. Ironically, this approach creates the conditions for its continued coercive presence because external reasons for behavior are salient. It also is inefficient: power derived from rewards and punishments requires continuous monitoring.

In contrast, authoritative control is reciprocal: The parent recognizes the influence of the developing child on the appropriateness of parent control. These parents explain the reasons for their "firm yet flexible" rules. Children's self-control, rather than parent control, is the goal. Self-control is learned through parental instruction and supports that are enacted when needed and removed when superfluous. In this manner, authoritative parents "co-regulate" the development of their children's self-regulation. The authoritative model of parent control is associated with child mental health (autonomy, healthy risk-taking) and school achievement.

Models of Classroom Management and School Discipline

Current recommendations for teacher management involve combinations of instructional pacing and group-level strategies to minimize disruption, individual behavior modification strategies to instill or maintain behavior, and instruction in and opportunities for student goal-setting, self-evaluation, and self-control. Recommended task requirements, feedback, and reward structures also are designed to promote student self-reflection rather than social comparison. Students progressively assume more responsibility for self-control. Modern calls for classroom management include features of authoritative parenting.

Similarly, recommendations for school administrators include systems based upon behavioral principles and self-control strategies to coordinate classroom management across grades and teachers. These publications stress behavior modificaton that targets substitution and focus on positive relationships between educators and students.

In practice, however, much of classroom and school-based discipline targets the form and schedule of punishment. This is especially the case with schoolwide management packages. For example, certain transgressions (for example, tardiness) are "tolerated" to some maximum number and then finally punished. In "three-strikes-you're-out" policies, transgressions accrue independent of the culpability associated with each offense (for example, individual fighting provoked or otherwise). In "zero-tolerance" policies, a single incidence of certain behaviors compel expulsion (for example, gang activity), which guarantees that appropriate substitute behavior cannot be influenced by the school—self-owned problem "solving" at the school level that seems especially egregious.

Congruence Between Management at Home and School

Overlap between home and school discipline results in at least four considerations. First, parents respond to school events through their own management style; children's reports of mistakes at school can lead to quite different responses at home (for example, instruction, punishment). Second, incongruence between home and school norms can lead to misunderstandings that are difficult to clarify. For example, the child of authoritative parents who asks questions to better understand and value the rules may be viewed as challenging rather than respecting authority. Third, parent discipline styles and the level of self-regulation they promote can be ahead or behind classroom practices, particularly in expectations for individual responsibility and autonomy. Conformity can be seen as immaturity rather than good behavior. Fourth, students can have difficulty with discipline policies that are more primitive than their attributional knowledge of personal and cultural rules for social behavior. It *does* matter why you were fighting, why you joined a gang. A critical feature of these discrepencies is the extent to which the child is able to interpret and meet differing expectations and rules. Some discipline goals and strategies promote this flexibility, others thwart it.

Conclusions

Discipline is about power; it is also about learning. In what appears to be the most successful approach to discipline, authoritative management at home and/or school, power is shared and learning is reciprocal. As the child develops strategies, skills, and dispositions, the authoritative adult "co-regulates"—adjusts expectations, removes unnecessary supports, and provides new opportunities to challenge and promote the child's development of self-regulation. Co-regulation also promotes the internalization of goals we wish a child to seek. In this manner, self-regulation is inherently social and learned.

[*See also* Punishment.]

Bibliography

American Psychological Association (1975). Proceedings for the year 1974: Minutes of the annual meeting of the Council of Representatives. *American Psychologist, 30,* 620–651.

Bandura, A. (1997). *Self-efficacy: The exercise of control.* New York: Freeman.

Baumrind, D. (1987). A developmental perspective on adolescent risk-taking in contemporary America. In C. Irwin, Jr. (Ed.), *Adolescent social behavior and health* (pp. 93–125). San Francisco: Jossey-Bass.

Eisenberger, R., & Cameron, J. (1997). Detrimental effects of reward: Reality or myth? *American Psychologist, 52,* 1153–1166.

Gordon, T. (1970). *P.E.T. Parent effectiveness training: The tested way to raise responsible children.* New York: Wyden.

Hess, R., & Holloway, S. (1984). Family and school as educational institutions. In R. D. Parker (Ed.), *Review of child development research: Vol. 7. The family* (pp. 179–222). Chicago: University of Chicago Press.

Higgins, E., Ruble, D., & Hartup, W. (Eds.). (1985). *Social cognition and social development: A sociological perspective.* Cambridge: Cambridge University Press.

Kelman, H. C. (1958). Compliance, identification, and internalization: Three processes of opinion change. *Journal of Conflict Resolution, 2,* 51–60.

McCaslin, M., & Good, T. (1996). The informal curriculum. In D. Berliner and R. Calfee (Eds.), *The handbook of educational psychology* (pp. 622–670). New York: Macmillan.

Schaefer, E. (1959). A circumplex model for maternal behavior. *Journal of Abnormal and Social Psychology, 59,* 226–235.

Skinner, B. F. (1953). *Science and human behavior.* New York: Macmillan.

Mary McCaslin and Helen Infanti

DISCRIMINATION. Understanding the concept of discrimination has been a steadfast pursuit among social scientists for the past several decades. While knowledge of this complex phenomenon has substantially increased because of these efforts, the dynamic nature of our society necessitates ongoing efforts toward not only describing the nature and consequences of discrimination but also developing effective strategies for eliminated the negative impact of discrimination. Although complex, the concept of discrimination has had unique consistency across many attempts at a conceptual definition. As Jones writes, "discrimination is . . . actionable" (1998, p. 10). This focus on behaviors or actions that are derived, in part from negative (or positive) attitudes toward an individual or a group represents a key feature of most contemporary definition of discrimination. While these definitions are somewhat consistent, the different types, consequences, and remedies for discrimination are quite varied.

Types, Levels, and Targets of Discrimination

Clearly, discriminatory acts and behaviors take on many different forms. Attempts to describe and classify the different types of discrimination have focused on three key issues: whether discriminatory behavior is overt or subtle; whether discrimination occurs at the individual, institutional, or societal level; and, whether discriminatory actions vary based on the characteristics of the target group.

Early on, attention focused on "classic" or traditional forms of discrimination. This involved both overt forms of discrimination in which the target (person or group), the action, and the intention of the actor were clear and identifiable. Overt discrimination was viewed as the result of "old-fashioned" forms of racism (or sexism, and so forth) that involve the desire to establish and maintain superiority through the differential use of power based on group (for example, race, sex, nationality) membership. The emergence of civil rights legislation and other legal statutes banning discrimination based on race (then sex and later, other specific groups) attention shifted toward identifying new or "modern" forms of discrimination. Dovidio and Gaertner (1998) developed the concept of "aversive racism" to describe a subtle and unintentional form of bias that is based on a conflict between egalitarian individual values and negative attitudes toward specific groups. This concept is quite similar to the notions of ambivalent racism, (Katz, Wackenhat, & Hass, 1986), symbolic racism (Sears, 1988) and modern racism (McConahay, 1986). Each of these concepts attempts to describe the catalyst for what scholars characterized as discriminatory actions that are covert rather than overt, unconscious rather than conscious, and denied rather than acknowledged. Thus, a key issue in understanding the different types of discrimination is whether these biased actions involve intentional inequity that is based on group membership (or what Pettigrew labels as "direct discrimination") versus actions that are hidden ("indirect") and thus, more difficult to detect (Pettigrew & Taylor, 1992).

As to whether discrimination is subtle compared to overt, the level at which the behavior occurs has been studied as a key aspect of discrimination. Typically, there are three different levels at which discrimination can occur: individual, institutional, and structural. Researchers have studied individual attitudes and demonstrated their ability to explain or predict later discriminatory actions by these individuals (Jones, 1998). Another aspect of work that focuses on individual-level factors, involves whether individuals are able to detect discriminatory actions based on the type of information available to them and whether or not they are the targets of discrimination (Rutte, Diekmann, Polzer, Crosby, & Messick, 1994). This work represents a very intriguing view on the issue of micro- versus macro-indices of discrimination. One may argue that an outgrowth of the shift in discrimination from overt to subtle has not only been in researcher's efforts to develop different ways to measure discrimination but also in the different skills that an individual needs in order to detect discrimination even when they themselves are the target.

Macro-level factors such as institutional and structural discrimination have traditionally received less attention than their micro-level counterparts. Most conceptualizations of institutional discrimination focus on the role that social structures play in allocating different opportunities and consequences based on group membership. A widely studied example of institutional discrimination is occupational segregation. This concept captures the disproportionate over-representation of women and minorities in low-paying, low-status occupations compared to men and nonminorities. One explanation for the persistence of this type of discrimination is the impact of institutional barriers such as the "dual labor market" (Morrison, White, & Van Velsor, 1987). While most majority group members are employed in the "primary labor market," women and minorities have been shown to dominate the "secondary labor market," The notion of different labor markets based on demographic factors such as race and sex helps to explain issues such as pay inequity, differences in mobility and advancement, and other workplace disparities. The dual labor market as an impermeable barrier for career advancement is a well-studied example of macro-level forms of discrimination, particularly within the work setting.

Other examples of macro-level or structural types of discrimination can be found in studies of biases that exist within the social structures such as the legal system. For example, evidence shows racial disparities in conviction rates, severity of sentencing, and public perception of guilt versus innocence (Nickerson, Mayo, & Smith, 1986). Notions about the structural aspects of discrimination have also been introduced through other concepts such as "environmental racism." Similar to work examining disparities within the legal system, this research argues that exposure to toxic substances is related to group differences such as social class and race. For example, exposure to lead poisoning in youth and toxic waste disposal have been shown to occur more frequently in poor and minority communities than in White and affluent communities (Needleman, Riess, Tobin, Biesecker, & Greenhouse, 1996).

In addition to characterizing the different types and levels of discrimination, previous research has explored discrimination based on a specific target group. The two most widely groups studied have been African Americans and women; however, other groups have received some attention (for example, elderly, social class, sexual orientation). The most frequently studied setting for sex discrimination is the workplace, where the concept of the "glass ceiling" defines the invisible barrier that prevents many women and minorities from advancing into senior and executive management positions within organizations (Morrison, White, & Van Velsor, 1987). Thus, a number of studies have shown that women perceive and experience more discrimination in the workplace than men as manifested by disparities in job opportunities, pay, career mobility, work-family conflict, and exposure to sexual harassment at work (Nieva & Gutek, 1980).

Research examining discrimination based on sex is not limited to the workplace. For example, a wide variety of research on women in educational settings found that a "chilly climate" on college campuses often discourages young women from pursuing nontraditional careers such as math, science, and engineering (Pettigrew, 1998). Previous studies have shown that women are often excluded as research subjects in tests of new drugs, medical treatments, and surgical techniques, whereas men are routinely included. Similar evidence of sex-based discrimination has been shown to occur for women in government and public service sectors, consumer marketing, the political arena, and the military (Lawn-Day & Ballard, 1996). Women of color can be targets of both sex and race discrimination, although less research has addressed this intersection.

There is emerging literature on discrimination targeted toward other racial and ethnic groups. Evidence exists for discrimination in the workplace of Latinas and Asians. Work by James Jackson and his colleagues focuses on the international dimensions of discrimination and demonstrates that the forms and targets of discriminatory behavior and actions represent a global phenomenon (Jackson, Brown, & Kirby, 1998).

Other targets of discrimination are emerging as important areas of investigation. For example, Birt and Dion (1987) showed that gay men and lesbians perceived discriminatory treatment based on sexual orientation, resulting in higher militancy and lower life and community satisfaction. The Age Discrimination in Employment Act of 1967 (and amended in 1986) outlawed the differential treatment of workers based on age. This legislation protects individuals in the workplace age 40 and older, covering issues, such as hiring, firing, promotion, training, compensation, and retirement. As a result, there has been an increase in the attention paid to issues of age discrimination in the workplace. For example, Perry, Kulik, and Bourhis (1996) argue that both personal and contextual factors inhibit the use of older persons and can often facilitate the negative impact of stereotypes of these individuals in work settings.

Consequences of Discrimination

Clearly discrimination, which varies by the type level and targeted group, has consequences that are profound and frequently negative. Missed opportunities and limited access can create barriers to success and serve as a significant source of stress. Discrimination can lead to lower levels of physical and psychological well being and impair individuals, families, and communities. A number of studies demonstrate that the targets of discrimination experience stress particularly in occupational settings. Jerome Taylor (Taylor & Jackson, 1990) has shown that individuals who have experienced racial discrimination are at greater risk of social maladjustment compared to other groups. These individuals report low marital satisfaction and feelings of aggression and report less warmth toward others, even within their same racial/ethnic group. Other consequences include low self-esteem, frequent depression, and low ego maturity.

Another area of study that illustrates the consequences of discrimination focuses on issues related to access such as education and housing. The notion of limited access as a consequence of discrimination in other aspects of daily life has been studied by Lucas (1996). He has shown that consumer behavior and marketers' assumptions concerning spending, needs, and preferences are often based on race and gender. There are also data that shows patterns of discrimination in terms of access to capital, bank lending, and investment. According to this research, minority communities received less mortgage credit for every dollar deposited in banks compared to their White counterparts (Shearer, 1992). Even controlling for income disparities between different communities, profound differences by race and ethnic background were reported (Nesiba, 1996). Clearly issues related to access represent one of the most profound yet hard to detect consequences of long-term discrimination.

Remedies for Discrimination

While the types, levels, and consequences of discrimination have been researched, there are now efforts in research to develop strategies to eliminate discrimination in its various forms as well as its consequences. The classic individual-level approach that has been widely studied as a strategy for eliminating discrimination on racial group membership is the contact hypothesis (Cook, 1985). This construct specifies the conditions under which positive interactions between previously advantaged and previously disadvantaged groups can and should exist in order to decrease discrimination and achieve equality. However, after extensive research, a number of limitations and shortcomings of this theory have been delineated. In fact, some research shows that if cooperative interactions as facilitated by intergroup contact fail, conflict (and discriminatory actions) will actually escalate. It seems, therefore, that increased contact may have a limited positive impact on attitudes toward members of disadvantaged groups and does not necessarily assure that discrimination (particularly macro-level format) will be eliminated.

With the infusion of cognitive models such as categorization and social identity theory, attempts to reduce discrimination have been focused on the process of altering an individual's category representations based on group membership. Recategorization, decategorization, indivduation, and personalization are all techniques for reducing discrimination by changing one's cognitive representation of group membership. For example, recategorization requires that a superordinate group membership is created, and, thus, discrimination against "others" is reduced because individuals are seen as part of the same group. Providing more personalized interaction that is less category based has been shown to have some impact, although limited.

It appears that when an individual is made aware of inconsistencies or contradictions in his or her values, attitudes, self-conceptions, and behaviors, a sufficient state of dissatisfaction is created that can, under some circumstances, lead to attitude and behavior change. This approach is heavily dependent on theories such as cognitive dissonance as a mechanism for creating an individual-level change in discriminatory behavior as well as negative attitudes. Many have speculated that in the face of apparent inconsistencies, individuals are motivated to protect their self-concept, which is seen as egalitarian, nonprejudiced and nondiscriminatory (Murrell, Dietz-Uhler, Dovidio, Gaertner, and Drout, 1994). Thus, being faced with discrepancies between what they "believe they would do" and what they "should do," most people will increase the amount of effort they put forth in controlling their discriminatory acts in the future. While this perspective has conceptual appeal, extensive empirical validation remains elusive.

Despite a frequent focus on individual-level strategies to end discrimination in its various forms, a widely studied macro-level strategy for reducing discrimination involves antidiscriminatory efforts, most notably, affirmative action. This legislation, outlined by the Civil Rights Act of 1964 (and the subsequent Executive Order No. 11246), banned discrimination based on race and later discrimination based on sex, religion, and national origin. Social scientists have studied individual and social perceptions of affirmative action as well as the overall impact and effectiveness of these programs and policies (Murrell & Jones, 1996). Despite the enormous amount of public attention paid to this issue, there is a lack of definitive research that clearly demonstrates the impact of policies and programs like affirmative action as an effective remedy for eliminating discrimination. Notwithstanding, advancements by women and minorities have been attributed, at least in part, to these antidiscriminatory efforts (Murrell & Jones, 1996).

At the beginning of the 1990s, attention turned to diversity initiatives as a remedy for discrimination in the workplace and educational settings. Diversity initiatives may have an important impact on increasing access to opportunities for women and minorities in the workplace and educational settings. In the early stages, diversity initiatives focused primarily on race and sex. This focus has broadened and includes age, sexual orientation, people with disabilities, religion, national origin, and professional expertise. Other work highlights the notion of "valuing" diversity, a perspective that emphasizes interpersonal communication and economic equality. While programs and initiatives aimed in increasing diversity are themselves, quite diverse, there are a number of common attributes. Most contemporary diversity efforts include dimensions such as broadened recruitment efforts, standard selection methods, skills straining, enhancement of the environment, and career development. Similar to the evaluation of affirmative action as an antidiscriminatory effort, the impact of diversity is still under exploration by social scientists and organizational scholars.

Looking Toward the Future

Clearly, the factors that underlie and help to prevent discrimination are complex and dynamic ones. While most research has focused on better understanding the different forms and consequences of discrimination, there are efforts in developing strategies for preventing discrimination in a number of settings. The nature and impact of discrimination touches each member of a society both directly and indirectly. Understanding and preventing the negative consequences of these acts requires increased research across a number of settings and levels of analyses.

Many legal scholars have noted the problems in contemporary approaches to remedy past discrimination such as the increased demand set forth by legal standards of "strict scrutiny." Issues such as burden of proof, isolation of cause, and evidence of intentionality pose threats to our ability to detect the existence and demonstrate the impact of emergent forms of discrimination within society. In addition, as group conflict theory asserts, competition for shared resources contributes to bias and discrimination. Thus, as shared resources become more scarce, the incidents of intergroup discrimination will increase particularly in subtle or indirect form. While our ability to understand and classify different types, levels, and consequences of discrimination may have increased somewhat over the past several decades, our ability to detect more subtle forms of discrimination and their impact, as well as our ability to predict the factors that exacerbate this behavior, has not.

Another topic that represents a priority for future

work relates to global dimensions of discrimination in key areas such as social justice and employment. Contemporary researchers (for example, Jackson, Brown, & Kirby, 1997) challenge the largely U.S.-specific focus that previous work on discrimination has taken. Their work examines actions toward people across nationalities, religions, race, cultures, and social class. These researchers argue that more attention to cross-national (and cross-cultural) studies should be given in order to understand better the concept of discrimination. By examining discrimination in comparative studies, we can better understand this concept in diverse settings, economic systems, historical contexts, and social structures.

There is also need to study the complex and dynamic nature of how discrimination varies by the specific target group. Much of the previous work has focused on the factors that define discrimination, what forms discrimination may take, and strategies for reducing its occurrence. This work almost exclusively takes the perspective of the empowered or majority group in terms of the definitions of group membership, nature of power and status within our society, and desired outcomes for intergroup interactions. However, the nature and meaning of group membership, particularly multiple group memberships, must play a critical role in understanding the type, severity, consequences, and remedies for discrimination. While scholars write about the social construction of categories such as race and gender, theoretical paradigms that explore the meaning and identity of these groups continue to contribute new perspectives to our understanding of the concept of discrimination.

[*See also* Ageism; Employment Discrimination; Heterosexism; Homophobia; Prejudice; Racism; Sexism; *and* Stereotypes.]

Bibliography

Birt, M., & Dion, K. L. (1987). Relative deprivation theory and responses to discrimination in a gay male and lesbian sample. *British Journal of Social Psychology, 26,* 139–145.

Cook, S. W. (1985). Experimenting on social issues: The case of school desegregation. *American Psychologist, 40,* 452–460.

Dovidio, J. F., & Gaertner, S. L. (1998). On the nature of contemporary prejudice: The causes, consequences and challenges of aversive racism. In J. Eberhardt & S. Fiske (Eds.), *Confronting racism: The problem and the response* (pp. 3–32). Newbury, CA: Sage.

Jackson, J. S., Brown, K. T., & Kirby, D. C. (1998). International perspectives on prejudice and racism. In J. Eberhardt & S. Fiske (Eds.), *Confronting racism: The problem and the response* (pp. 101–135). Newbury, CA: Sage.

Jones, J. M. (1998). The essential power of racism: Commentary and conclusion? In J. Eberhardt & S. Fiske (Eds.), *Confronting racism: The problem and the response* (pp. 280–294). Newbury, CA: Sage.

Katz, I., Wackenhut, J., & Hass, R. G. (1986). Racial ambivalence, value duality, and behavior. In J. F. Dovidio & S. L. Gaertner (Eds.), *Prejudice, discrimination, and racism* (pp. 35–60). Orlando, FL: Academic Press.

Kohn, M. L. (1987). Cross-national research as an analytic strategy: American Sociological Association 1987 presidential address. *American Sociological Review, 52,* 713–731.

Krieger, L. H. (1995). The content of our categories: A cognitive bias approach to discrimination and equal opportunity. *Stanford Law Review, 47,* 1161–1248.

Lawn-Day, G. A., & Ballard, S. (1996). Speaking out: Perceptions of women managers in the public service. *Review of Public Personnel Administration, 56* (Winter), 41–58.

Lucas, A. (1996). Race matters. *Sales & Marketing, 148* (9), 50–62.

McConahay, J. B. (1986). Modern racism, ambivalence and the modern racism scale. In J. F. Dovidio & S. L. Gaertner (Eds.), *Prejudice, discrimination, and racism* (pp. 91–125). Orlando, FL: Academic Press.

Murrell, A. J., Dietz-Uhler, B. L., Dovidio, J. F., Gaertner, S. L., & Drout, C. (1994). Aversive racism and resistance to affirmative action: Perceptions of justice are not necessarily color-blind. *Basic and Applied Social Psychology, 15,* 71–86.

Murrell, A. J., & Jones, R. (1996). Assessing affirmative action: Past, present, and future. *Journal of Social Issues, 52* (4), 77–92.

Needleman, H. L., Riess, J. A., Tobin, M. J., Biesecker, G. E., & Greenhouse, J. B. (1996). Bone lead levels and delinquent behavior. *Journal of the American Medical Association, 275,* 363–369.

Nesiba, R. F. (1996). Racial discrimination in residential lending markets: Why empirical researchers always see it and economic theorists never do. *Journal of Economic Issues, 30* (1), 51–77.

Nickerson, S., Mayo, C., & Smith, A. (1986). Racism in the courtroom. In J. F. Dovidio & S. L. Gaertner (Eds.), *Prejudice, discrimination and racism* (pp. 255–278). Orlando, FL: Academic Press.

Nieva, V. F. & Gutek, B. A. (1980). Sex effects on evaluation. *Academy of Management Review, 5,* 267–276.

Perry, E., Kulik, C., & Bourhis, A. (1996). Moderating effects of personal and contextual factors in age discrimination. *Journal of Applied Psychology, 81* (6), 628–647.

Pettigrew, T. F. (1998). Prejudice and discrimination on the college campus. In J. Eberhardt & S. Fiske (Eds.), *Confronting racism: The problem and the response* (pp. 263–279). Newbury, CA: Sage.

Pettigrew, T. F., & Taylor, M. (1992). Discrimination. In E. F. Borgatta & M. L. Borgatta (Eds.), *The encyclopedia of sociology* (Vol. 1, pp. 498–503). New York: Macmillan.

Ruggiero, K. M., and Major, B. M. (1998). Group status and attributions to discrimination: Are low-or high-status group members more likely to blame their failure on discrimination? *Personality and Social Psychology, 24* (8), 821–838.

Rutte, C. G., Diekmann, K. A., Polzer, J. T., Crosby, F. J., & Messick, D. M. (1994). Organizing information and the detection of gender discrimination. *Psychological Science, 5,* 226–231.

Sears, D. O. (1988). Symbolic racism. In P. A. Katz & D. A. Taylor (Eds.), *Eliminating racism: Profiles in controversy* (pp. 53–84). New York: Plenum Press.

Audrey J. Murrell

DISENGAGEMENT THEORY. *See* Social Gerontological Theories.

DISHABITUATION. *See* Habituation.

DISRUPTIVE BEHAVIOR DISORDERS, now generally out of usage, applies to those patterns of behavior in which there is a pervasive and sustained disregard for authority or lack of regard for the feelings or well being of others (American Psychiatric Association, 1994). The category "disruptive behavior disorders" did not appear in the *Diagnostic and Statistical Manual* (*DSM*) classification until *DSM–III–R* (1987), where it refers to attentional, conduct, and oppositional disorders. Each revision of the *DSM* reflects substantive changes in the selection criteria for the disruptive behavior disorders. These changes represent refinements in the diagnostic criteria and subtypes resulting from new data about the validity and reliability of the criteria for disruptive behavior disorders.

In *DSM–IV* (1994), the category "attention-deficit and disruptive behavior disorders" refers to a range of behavior problems including attention-deficit/hyperactivity disorder (ADHD), conduct disorder (CD), and oppositional defiant disorder (ODD). The two most common disruptive behavior disorders are conduct disorder and oppositional defiant disorder.

Conduct disorder is characterized by repetitive and persistent violation of age-appropriate norms and disregard for the basic rights of others. *DSM–IV* (1994) groups the behaviors of this disorder in four categories: aggressive conduct, nonagressive conduct, deceitfulness or theft, and serious violation of rules. Although ODD includes some of the features observed in conduct disorder (for example, disobedience and opposition to authority figures), it does not include the persistent pattern of the more serious forms of behavior in which either the basic rights of others or age-appropriate societal norms or rules are violated. Diagnosis of ODD is based on eight criteria, most of which are manifestations of suspicion of and hostility toward authority figures. When an individual's pattern of behavior meets the criteria for both conduct disorder and oppositional defiant disorder, the diagnosis of CD takes precedence and ODD is not diagnosed.

No definitive cause of disruptive behavior disorders has been identified. Some studies show both genetic and environmental components. There is increasing sentiment from a developmental perspective that explanations of disruptive behavior disorders need to be couched in terms of multiple influences among phenomena at many levels of analysis, from genes to national culture (Costello & Angold, 1993). Some studies suggest that risk factors for disruptive behavior disorders include learning difficulties, school failure, perinatal complications, and violence in the home. Protective factors are thought to include a positive relationship with grandparents and ability to express feelings (Grizenko & Pawliuk, 1994).

The onset of CD tends to be in late childhood or early adolescence; diagnoses have been made as early as age 5 but rarely after 16 years of age. Oppositional defiant disorder, which develops earlier than CD, may lead to the development of conduct disorder (Loeber, Lahey, & Thomas, 1991). Conduct disorder is relatively persistent over time, although specific behaviors may vary from year to year (Lahey, Applegate, Barkley, & Garfinkel, 1994). Early onset increases risk for adult antisocial personality disorder, while later onset and milder symptoms usually results in academic and occupational adjustment in adulthood. Onset of ODD is usually slow, occurring over a number of months or years. Typically, the disorder is evident before 8 years of age and rarely emerges after early adolescence.

[*See also* Attention-Deficit/Hyperactivity Disorder; Conduct Disorder; *and* Oppositional Defiant Disorder.]

Bibliography

American Psychiatric Association. (1987). *Diagnostic and statistical manual of mental disorders* (3rd rev. ed.). Washington, DC: Author.

American Psychiatric Association. (1994). *Diagnostic and statistical manual of mental disorders* (4th ed.). Washington, DC: Author.

Costello, E., & Angold, A. (1993). Toward a developmental epidemiology of the disruptive behavior disorders. *Development and Psychopathology, 5,* 91–101.

Grizenko, N., & Pawliuk, N. (1994). Risk and protective factors for disruptive behavior disorders in children. *American Journal of Orthopsychiatry, 64* (4), 534–544.

Lahey, B. B., Applegate, B., Barkley, R., & Garfinkel, B. (1994). *DSM–IV* field trials for oppositional defiant disorder and conduct disorder in children and adolescents. *American Journal of Psychiatry, 151,* 1163–1171.

Loeber, R., Lahey, B. B., & Thomas, C. (1991). Diagnostic conundrum of oppositional defiant disorder and conduct disorder. *Journal of Consulting and Clinical Psychology, 100,* 379–390.

Mary E. Walsh and Natasha M. Howard

DISSOCIATIVE DISORDERS. The *Diagnostic and Statistical Manual of Mental Disorders* (*DSM–IV*; 1994) defines dissociative disorders as disruptions "in the usually integrated functions of consciousness, memory, identity, or perception of the environment" (p. 477). This succinct definition does not begin to describe the fascinating history of conditions that include people unable to remember even who they are or who experience themselves as embodying different identities.

This article will focus on dissociative disorders in adults, although there is an incipient but growing literature on dissociative disorders in children and adolescents. Dissociative *symptoms* can occur in many neurological (e.g., "seizure disorders") and psychiatric conditions (e.g., panic attacks), or as the result of ingesting some psychoactive substances. However, a diagnosis of dissociative *disorders* requires that the dissociative symptoms be a central presenting problem, produce clinically significant distress and/or maladjustment, and not be produced by neuropathies or the effect of a substance. Finally, dissociative *phenomena* are not necessarily pathological and can occur in everyday life and in special but benign contexts, such as hypnosis or meditation.

The term *dissociation* is used inconsistently in the clinical literature. It is used sometimes as an explanatory construct (e.g., "To tolerate that trauma, X dissociated from it"), and sometimes as a descriptive construct for incongruity between two or more indicators of information (e.g., "She honestly believes she is not anxious, but her skin conductance shows otherwise"), psychogenic amnesia (e.g., "Y cannot remember her name even though she has no neurological damage"), or a state of consciousness characterized by experiential detachment from the self or the environment (e.g., "During the rape I observed my body from above").

Perhaps the clearest understanding of dissociative phenomena can be attained by describing psychological processes in which dissociation occurs. Dissociative alterations in the sense of the self include experiences in which individuals feel estranged from themselves, or experience dreamlike or unreal states. Individuals who cannot experience any emotions, although their behaviors imply intense emotions, are good examples. *Depersonalization* is a term often used for these type of experiences. Dissociation of physical sensations usually entails a lack of awareness of interoceptive or exteroceptive stimulation not explainable by sensory damage or receptor fatigue. Lack of physical sensations in a physiologically intact hand is a good example.

Dissociative alterations in the sense of the environment involve experiencing estrangement from the environment, or perceiving it as dreamlike or unreal. An example is experiencing events as if they occurred in a fog. A more extreme example would be losing awareness of the environment, either because the mind seems to go blank, or because of being so involved in an internal event that one seems temporarily incapable of regaining awareness of the surrounding environment. *Derealization* is a term commonly used for such phenomena.

Dissociation in the sense of agency involves experiencing lack of control of voluntary muscles in the body, either as paralysis or uncontrollable movements. Pathological dissociation of physical sensations or sense of agency are the province of some somatoform disorders, which are not part of the dissociative disorders category in the *DSM–IV* classification.

Dissociative alterations of memory include the inability to remember important personal information, which cannot be explained by ordinary forgetfulness or neurological conditions, as in the case of soldiers who may not remember what happened during a battle in which they participated. Even though conscious recollection may be absent, the information that cannot be recalled may still affect behavior (a deficit of explicit, but not of implicit, memory). A different alteration consists in the recollection of an event as if the person had watched it rather than experienced it (impersonal recollection, or lack of episodic memory).

Finally, at the level of identity, there are two typical dissociative variants. In one, the person experiences two or more different identities that concurrently or alternatively inhabit his or her physical body; in the other, a person sometimes experiences that his or her usual identity is displaced by another identity, as in experiences of spirit possession.

History

Either as alterations of consciousness or mixed with complaints of lack of somatic sensation or control, references to dissociative phenomena go back to pharaonic Egypt and have been observed in preindustrial societies. The systematic study of dissociation began in earnest in the latter part of the nineteenth century. The development of modern psychological theories of mental illness overlaps considerably with attempts by Jean-Martin Charcot, Pierre Janet, Edouard Claparède, Josef Breuer, Sigmund Freud, and William James, among others, to explain what was then termed *hysteria*. The hysterical patients that so puzzled those authors typically suffered from a number of somatization and dissociative symptoms.

Charcot, an eminent neurologist in the latter part

of the nineteenth century, provided a psychological explanation for the display of hysterical patients including those who, after exposure to patients with epilepsy, developed hysteroepilepsy, or what might now be called *pseudoseizures*. Along with these displays, hysterical patients also exhibited other alterations of consciousness, such as amnesia, restriction of awareness, dreamlike states, and alterations of identity.

The credit for a comprehensive psychological theory of dissociative disorders and phenomena has to go to Pierre Janet, who provided a theory about normal and abnormal psychological "automatisms," similar to current notions of cognitive-emotional-behavioral schemata. In Janet's account, predisposed individuals exposed to intense emotions may experience alterations of consciousness, and the events experienced at the time will not be integrated with the usual stream of consciousness, but will have an independent life outside the awareness and/or control of the person. In the case of repeated or chronic dissociative phenomena, such independent units can become alternate identities.

Janet's theories and observations became well-known and influential in Europe and the United States. However, the overwhelming impact of psychoanalytic theory and the success of Eugen Bleuler's proposed category of schizophrenia in the earlier part of the century soon drowned most vestiges of Janet's theory. The eminent North American psychologist Ernest Hilgard rediscovered Janet's ideas through his influential neo-dissociation theory in the 1970s. Hilgard's casting of Janet's theory in modern cognitive terms, and various studies showing a higher prevalence than once thought of dissociative disorders, and of traumatic events and their dissociative sequelae have all produced an interest in dissociation unseen since the end of the nineteenth century. At the close of the twentieth century, there is an organization, a journal, and evaluation instruments exclusively devoted to the study of dissociation.

In the 1990s, a controversy arose over the possibility that dissociative disorders, especially dissociative identity disorder, are caused by overzealous therapists using inappropriately suggestive techniques. Nonetheless, systematic studies on whether the condition is only diagnosed by therapists who use suggestive techniques or hold an apriori belief in the validity of dissociative identity disorder, have failed to support the iatrogenic explanation for the condition. This does not deny, of course, that some therapists working with dissociative patients have made exaggerated or unfounded pronouncements, and that in this, as in other conditions, incompetent therapists can have an iatrogenic effect. A number of recent clinical guidelines have advocated caution in the diagnosis and treatment of individuals with dissociative disorders to avoid reinforcing symptoms and possibly false recollections.

The classification of dissociative disorders in North America began in the early part of the twentieth century. Various editions of the *Statistical Manual* (1918–1942), a predecessor of the *Diagnostic and Statistical Manual of Mental Disorders* (Washington, DC), included hysteria within its purview. In *DSM–I* (1952), the psychoneurotic disorders included the categories of dissociative reaction (depersonalization, dissociated personality, fugue, amnesia, and others) and conversion reaction (anesthesia, paralysis, and diskinesis). *DSM–II* (1968) characterized these phenomena as hysterical neuroses, either of a dissociative or conversion type. *DSM–III* (1980) and *DSM–III–R* (1987) brought two major changes: First, detailed descriptions were provided for psychogenic amnesia, psychogenic fugue, multiple personality disorder, depersonalization disorder, and dissociative disorder not otherwise specified (DDNOS); and second, conversion phenomena were separated from the category of dissociative disorders and included as a subcategory of the somatoform disorders. Notwithstanding this separation, research has shown considerable symptom and traumatic history overlap between dissociative and conversion disorders, thus some authors have advocated the relocation of conversion under the dissociation umbrella. In the latest edition of the *International Classification of Diseases* (WHO, 1992, Geneva, Switzerland), the most widely used clinical taxonomy in some countries, conversion disorders have remained part of the dissociative disorders.

DSM–IV (1994) modifications included relabeling multiple personality disorder as *dissociative identity disorder*, changes in the criteria for dissociative amnesia and fugue, and greater discussion of the cross-cultural variation of dissociation. A proposal for a secondary dissociative disorder due to a medical condition was not accepted into the *DSM–IV*, although there is some evidence that seizure disorder and other medical conditions are associated with dissociative symptoms.

The *DSM–IV* included the new diagnosis of acute stress disorder, which was originally proposed as a dissociative disorder, but became a subcategory of the anxiety disorders. Its criteria include dissociative and anxiety symptoms. Individuals with posttraumatic stress disorder also commonly exhibit dissociation. The symptom overlap and traumatic etiology of the dissociative and posttraumatic disorders suggest that further study is needed before a final determination as to the correct placement of these conditions can be made.

Descriptions of the Dissociative Disorders

The remainder of this article will focus on the dissociative disorders categorized in *DSM–IV*. There have been some studies, most of them in the North American continent, that have evaluated the prevalence of dissociative disorders in various samples. Among clinical or traumatized groups, there is a wide range, from 10% comorbidity among individuals with obsessive-compulsive disorder (a similar figure to that found in some studies with nonclinical populations), to 88% among women reporting sexual abuse. Individuals with a dissociative disorder, especially those with severe conditions, typically have a history of other diagnoses, partly because of a misunderstanding of their condition, and partly because many also have other Axis I and Axis II conditions. The usefulness of a dissociative diagnosis in these individuals depends on a good match with diagnostic criteria and on a good response to treatment that deals with their dissociative symptoms.

The most frequent comorbidity of the dissociative disorders is with the following conditions: depression and affective lability; anxiety, either as panic attacks or generalized; conversion and somatization; sexual dysfunction (not surprising considering that many of these individuals have an independently corroborated history of early sexual abuse); and, less frequently, substance abuse and eating disorders. Individuals with dissociative identity disorder also often fulfill criteria for borderline and avoidant personality disorders. Many, if not most, of these individuals have a recent or remote history of trauma. Nonetheless, a history of abuse cannot be considered a sufficient cause for these disorders because many individuals with a history of abuse do not develop them.

Dissociative Amnesia. Dissociative amnesia is defined as one or more instances of inability to remember important personal information, which cannot be explained by ordinary forgetfulness, developmental amnesia for the first years of life, or an organic condition. In dissociative amnesia, the individual loses explicit memory for personal experience, although implicit memory for general knowledge, skills, habits and conditioned responses is usually unimpaired.

Episodes of dissociative amnesia can be generalized, localized, or selective. In generalized amnesia, the individual is unable to remember all or most of his or her personal information. In localized amnesia, the individual cannot remember certain periods of time. In selective amnesia, memories related to particular issues or persons cannot be recalled. The vast majority of dissociative amnesias are of a selective nature, organized according to emotional rather than temporal parameters. As with the other dissociative disorders, a common precipitating factor is severe stress or trauma. Reported triggers for amnesia episodes include combat, legal or financial problems, natural disasters, serious crime, and sexual and physical abuse.

There has been acrimonious debate on the validity of amnesia for early sexual or physical abuse when there has been later recovery of such memories. Although not absent of methodological shortcomings, there are now dozens of published studies and legal cases that consistently show that, at some point, a substantial minority of individuals have not recalled instances of early abuse that were later recalled, and in some cases, independently corroborated. Besides early abuse, instances of amnesia following other types of trauma, such as war or disasters, have been documented for over a century. It should be borne in mind, however, that the considerable support for the validity of some recalled memories does not preclude the possibility that other memories may be partially or completely false. The evidence suggests that memories of abuse "recovered" in or out of therapy have about the same validity as memories maintained all along. Every case should be judged on its own merits, considering both the reality of dissociative amnesia and the reconstructive and fallible nature of memory.

A differential diagnosis for dissociative amnesia should include malingering, neurological conditions that involve amnesia such as transient global amnesia, seizure disorders, and head injury, and the effect of psychoactive substances. Dissociative fugue is a superordinate diagnosis to dissociative amnesia.

Dissociative Fugue. The definition of dissociative fugue includes sudden and unexpected travel away from home or work accompanied by generalized amnesia, and confusion about personal identity or the development of a new identity. A typical example involves an individual who, after enduring severe stress or trauma, leaves home and becomes confused as to his or her whereabouts and identity. There are many descriptions of dissociative amnesia and fugue in the literature about war, but more recently, fugue has been described in cases of sexual or physical abuse. The differential diagnosis includes malingering, poriomania in complex partial seizure episodes, and other organic conditions such as drug-related fugues. Dissociative identity disorder (DID) is a superordinate diagnosis to dissociative fugue.

Dissociative Identity Disorder. This condition used to be called *multiple personality disorder* in previous editions of the *DSM*, and is considered the most severe of these disorders. The name was changed to indicate that the problem is not a multiplicity of personalities, but the inability to forge a coherent and consistent identity. The core of this condition is the presence of two or more distinct identities, each with a characteristic way of perceiving, thinking, feeling, and relating to the environment and the self, associated with dissociative amnesia for previous or current events. At least two of these identities or personality states recurrently control the person's behavior. It is important to point out that there is no need to reinforce these individuals' experience of different identities by treating them as if they were indeed different people, but there is no evidence that ignoring their experience has therapeutic value either. Most therapists use individual psychotherapy with hypnosis as an adjunct with these individuals, but there are no comparative data on the efficacy of different therapeutic approaches.

The validity of this disorder has been seriously questioned, with some critics arguing that the apparent explosion in its diagnosis is the result of therapist reinforcement of the symptoms or, at the very least, of a joint delusion between the therapist and the patient. However, many of the critiques have carried little evidential weight (e.g., single cases of presumed therapeutic incompetence, or the argument that because a clinician has not encountered such individuals, the diagnosis lacks validity). As mentioned previously, studies have failed to support an iatrogenic explanation for the condition. On the other hand, recently developed assessment tools show that this and other dissociative disorders can be evaluated reliably. Also, initial survey and experimental studies indicate that these individuals show a consistent profile of symptoms and phenomena, and perform in projective, memory, and psychophysiological tests in a way that is consistent with the validity of the diagnosis and inconsistent with malingering or mere role-playing. Nonetheless, our understanding of this condition is very limited and demands further investigation.

The lack of evidence for an iatrogenic explanation for DID does not preclude a role for culture in the shaping and epidemiology of this and other disorders. Although there is growing evidence that this disorder is found in other countries besides the United States, cultures still provide information on what are the expected "idioms of distress" given certain conditions, and interpret discontinuities in experience as being caused by, for instance, psychological problems or spiritual forces.

There is no other psychiatric or neurological condition that closely resembles DID, but there is some surface resemblance between DID and some forms of psychosis. Individuals with DID typically have other dissociative symptoms such as fugues and depersonalization, and may be polysymptomatic with affective, anxiety, personality, and other disorders.

Depersonalization. Depersonalization disorder is defined as chronic and recurrent experiences of feeling detached from one's thoughts, feelings, or sensations, or experiencing that they are somehow unreal or dreamlike. These episodes are not accompanied by the failures in reality testing typical of psychosis.

It is important to distinguish depersonalization *disorder*, which involves recurrent episodes of depersonalization as the central problem, from depersonalization *symptoms*, which are common as secondary symptoms in other disorders including panic attacks, or as transient reactions to severe stress, trauma, or intoxication. Common features of depersonalization episodes include alterations in the sense of self such as experiencing the body as an object, a precipitating event such as stress or a psychoactive substance, a sense of unreality, and sensory alterations such as diminished experience of colors or sounds. A related phenomenon, derealization, refers to a sense of unreality or estrangement from the environment. Although depersonalization and derealization are described as different phenomena, they usually occur together.

Differential diagnosis includes dissociative and other psychiatric conditions where depersonalization is a secondary symptom, and neurological conditions that are frequently accompanied by depersonalization episodes such as temporal lobe epilepsy.

Dissociative Disorders Not Otherwise Specified. Some studies have found that most individuals with dissociative disorders do not clearly fit the criteria for the disorders described here. A number of dissociative disorders not otherwise specified (DDNOS) are described in the *DSM–IV*, including identity alterations that do not fulfill all criteria for DID, derealization without depersonalization in adults, loss of consciousness in the absence of a neurological condition, and dissociative states in individuals subjected to intense forms of coercion.

Particular mention must be made of dissociative trance disorder, a condition that was deemed to deserve further study by the *DSM–IV* task force. This condition includes pathological forms of *trance*, defined as episodes of unawareness, unresponsiveness, or lack of control over one's behaviors, and of *spirit possession*, defined as alterations of identity and consciousness interpreted as the displacement of the usual identity by that of a putative external entity, often accompanied by reports of amnesia. It is important to mention that this diagnosis refers only to forms of trance or possession that produce serious distress or maladjustment and are not part of culturally sanctioned rituals. Dissociative presentations in many nonindustrialized cultures seem to fit the criteria for this diagnosis better than the criteria for the other dissociative diagnoses.

[*See also* Amnesia; *and* Dissociative Identity Disorder.]

Bibliography

American Psychiatric Association. (1994). *Diagnostic and statistical manual of mental disorders* (4th ed.). Washington, DC: Author. The currently accepted diagnostic criteria and related information for dissociative disorders and other conditions.

Cardeña, E. (1997). Dissociative disorders: Phantoms of the self. In S. M. Turner & M. Hersen (Eds.). *Adult psychopathology and diagnosis* (pp. 384–408). New York: Wiley. A concise overview of diagnostic, epidemiological, and cultural issues in the dissociative disorders.

Ellenberger, H. F. (1970). *The discovery of the unconscious. The history and evolution of dynamic psychiatry.* New York: Basic Books. A classical study of the history of dynamic psychiatry, with extensive coverage of the theoretical and clinical contributions by Janet, Freud, and others.

Gleaves, D. H., May, M. C., & Cardeña, E. (2000). An examination of the diagnostic validity of Dissociative Identity Disorder. *Clinical Psychology Review.* A thorough analysis of the empirical evidence for the validity of DID according to three widely recognized guidelines to evaluate diagnostic validity.

Good, M. I. (1993). The concept of an organic dissociative disorder: What is the evidence? *Harvard Review of Psychiatry, 1,* 145–157. An authoritative overview of the various neurological conditions, including those brought about by legal and controlled psychoactive substances, associated with dissociative symptoms; an important reference for the differential diagnosis of the dissociative disorders.

Kihlstrom, J. F. (1994). One hundred years of hysteria. In S. J. Lynn & J. W. Rhue (Eds.), *Dissociation: Clinical and theoretical perspectives* (pp. 365–394). New York: Guilford Press. An historical overview of the classification of dissociative disorders, and a strong argument for the reintegration of conversion and similar phenomena into the dissociative disorders fold.

Lynn, S. J., & Rhue, J. W. (Eds.). (1994). *Dissociation: Clinical and theoretical perspectives.* New York: Guilford Press. An anthology of theoretical and empirical issues in dissociation, including clinical assessment, and ongoing controversies in the field, written by many of the most influential authors in the field.

Michelson, L. K., & Ray, W. J. (Eds.). (1996). *Handbook of dissociation: Theoretical, empirical, and clinical perspectives.* New York: Plenum Press. A massive anthology of recent works on dissociation, with an emphasis on clinical evaluation and treatment.

Nijenhuis, E. R., Spinhoven, P., Vanderlinden, J., van Dyck, R., & van der Hart, O. (1998). Somatoform dissociative symptoms as related to animal defensive reactions to predatory imminence and injury. *Journal of Abnormal Psychology, 107,* 63–73. Initial support for what may be the most elaborate evolutionary explanation for some somatoform dissociative symptoms such as freezing and analgesia.

Putnam, F. W. (1997). *Dissociation in children and adolescents: A developmental perspective.* New York: Guilford Press. Written by the most influential researcher on dissociative identity disorder and developmental aspects of dissociation, this book provides an excellent overview of the present and future study of dissociation in children and adolescents.

Spanos, N. (1996). *Multiple identities and false memories.* Washington, DC: American Psychological Association. One of the last contributions by the most formidable critic of dissociative theories for dissociative identity disorder and related phenomena. Spanos proposed, instead, a sociocognitive explanatory model based on role enactment and sociocultural forces.

Spiegel, D. (Ed.). (1997). *Repressed memories.* Washington, DC: American Psychiatric Press. A brief but substantial anthology of clinical and/or research experts on the evidence and rationale for and against "repressed memories" and clinically meaningful pseudomemories.

Spiegel, D., & Cardeña, E. (1991). Disintegrated experience: The dissociative disorders revisited. *Journal of Abnormal Psychology, 100,* 366–378. An influential article that gives a rationale for the criteria changes for the *DSM–IV,* and evaluates the relationship between traumatic events and dissociation.

Swica, Y., Lewis, D. O., & Lewis, M. (1996). Child abuse and dissociative identity disorder/multiple personality disorder. The documentation of childhood maltreatment and the corroboration of symptoms. *Child and adolescent psychiatric clinics of North America, 5,* 431–447. One of a number of studies showing independent corroboration for reports by dissociative individuals of early abuse and symptomatology.

Waller, N. G., Putnam, F. W., & Carlson, E. B. (1996). Types of dissociation and dissociative types: A taxometric analysis of dissociative experiences. *Psychological Methods, 3,* 300–321. An innovative analysis in which the authors provide evidence for distinct types of dissociation, only one of which seems to be characteristic of patients with dissociative conditions.

van der Hart, O., & Horst, R. (1989). The dissociation theory of Pierre Janet. *Journal of Traumatic Stress, 2,* 397–412. A succinct and lucid exposition of Janet's main ideas about dissociation and dissociative psychopathology.

Etzel A. Cardeña

DISSOCIATIVE IDENTITY DISORDER. A complex and complicated dissociative disorder characterized by disturbances of memory and identity, dissociative identity disorder (DID) was previously referred to as multiple personality disorder. Society's view of this disorder has largely been shaped by the popular press, TV, and movies in which separate personalities are seen to switch in an all-or-nothing fashion with clear amnesia about the other identities. In reality, this disorder is more complex and less clear-cut than commonly portrayed. There may even be periods in which symptoms are not expressed. In-depth discussions of DID are available (Kluft, 1995, 1996; Putnam, 1989; Ross, 1997), on which the current discussion draws.

In this disorder, relatively consistent but alternating subjectively separate identities are manifested in a single individual who may display memory disruptions or amnesia for autobiographical material. These identities may have characteristics such as being controlling, self-destructive, or using a vocabulary which differs from the primary identity. A given identity may deny knowledge of other identities as well as show amnesia for autobiographical information. This amnesia may be experienced as not remembering significant portions of one's past, not knowing how one acquired various objects in one's house, or having people describe one's behavior or interactions with others in ways that are not remembered. Similar manifestations of the disorder have been reported in North America, Europe, and Asia.

The *Diagnostic and Statistical Manual of Mental Disorders* (DSM–IV; American Psychiatric Association, 1994) characterizes dissociation as a "disruption in the usually integrated functions of consciousness, memory, identity, or perception of the environment." Thus, the disorder is characterized by a failure to integrate identity, memory, and consciousness which may lead to confusion and internal struggle over the nature of one's identity. In this sense, the disorder represents not the development of multiple personalities but the lack of development of one coherent personality with a singular identity. It is commonly assumed that this lack of development results from the experiencing of traumatic events such as sexual, physical, or psychological assault, especially in childhood. However, the experience of trauma in itself does not necessarily lead to DID. Thus, it is possible that critical environmental events (e.g., trauma) in conjunction with other factors (e.g., critical period in which attachment to a caregiver is being developed, a specific vulnerability on the part of the child, etc.) leads to DID. However, no clear etiology has been identified.

DSM–IV lists four diagnostic criteria for dissociative identity disorder. First, the presence of two or more distinct identities or personality states (each with its own relatively enduring pattern of perceiving, relating to, and thinking about the environment and self). Second, at least two of these identities or personality states recurrently take control of the person's behavior. Third, there is an inability to recall important personal information that is too extensive to be explained by ordinary forgetfulness. And fourth, the disturbance is not due to the direct physiological effects of a substance (e.g., blackouts or chaotic behavior during alcohol intoxication) or a general medical condition (e.g., complex partial seizures). It should also be noted that children who have imaginary playmates or other such fantasy activity are not suffering from DID.

During the late 1800s and early 1900s a number of respected scientists and clinicians including Pierre Janet, Sigmund Freud, William James, and Morton Prince described cases in which there were pronounced shifts in identity, memory, and consciousness consistent with current DID diagnosis. Following this initial interest, the study of dissociative processes was largely ignored until the 1980s. At this time, the study of dissociation began to regain prominence, and the dissociative disorders category was added to the *Diagnostic and Statistical Manual of Mental Disorders*. This twentieth-century gap in the study of dissociative disorders has resulted in fewer epidemiological and etiological studies than for most other psychopathological disorders.

Epidemiology

Although dissociative processes such as "spacing out" while listening to a boring talk or driving are common experiences in almost all individuals (Ray, 1996), psychopathological dissociative symptoms are much less common. In one study of over 1,000 individuals in a large Canadian city, it was concluded that as many as 3% of the population had a dissociative disorder, although other studies have placed this number closer to 1%. In terms of psychiatric populations, it has been reported that 3 to 8% of psychiatric inpatients have previously undiagnosed dissociative identity disorder. This is consistent with the report that most DID patients have spent many years in the mental health system with nondissociative disorder diagnoses before being given a DID diagnosis.

Current statistics report that male and female children show signs of DID in equal numbers whereas in adults, more females than males, by about 9 to 1, are hospitalized with DID. The adult data may be skewed because of differences between male and female behavior and help-seeking patterns. It has been suggested that whereas females utilize the health-care system, male DID patients do not and may also have more negative interactions with the criminal justice system. However, the data is lacking to support or refute this speculation. In terms of the characteristic manifestations of the disorder or prior sexual abuse history, it is reported that males and females appear similar. Assessment instruments such as the Structured Clinical Interview for *DSM–IV* disorders (SCID–D; Steinberg, 1996) and the Dissociative Disorders Interview Schedule (DDIS; Ross, 1997) should aid reliability and validity studies in future years.

Etiology

There exist a variety of suggestions concerning the etiology of DID with most experts suggesting that there are multiple routes for the development of the disorder. The most common pathway suggested is that of severe, chronic childhood trauma in which the child cannot escape or control the situation. This model suggests that in order to cope, the child dissociates the experience. This may occur by watching the experience in a detached manner to the extent of even imagining it is happening to someone else. Chronic neglect has been suggested as another pathway to dissociative disorders. In this situation, a substance abusing, depressed, or otherwise unavailable caregiver does not offer the child needed physical and emotional attention. Whether these pathways work independently or through other processes such as attachment mechanisms is not known at this time.

An important neurological question is the relationship between dissociative processes and other neurological disorders, especially temporal lobe epilepsy (see Zahn, Moraga, & Ray, 1997 for a review). While the appearance of dissociative phenomena among individuals with temporal lobe epilepsy has been well documented, the data do not support a seizure disorder model as a primary mechanism for dissociation. Thus, although it is clear that individuals with temporal lobe epilepsy can show dissociative symptoms, it does not appear that the presence of dissociative symptoms suggests temporal lobe epilepsy.

Treatment

The treatment of dissociative disorders has been approached from a variety of perspectives including cognitive, psychodynamic, psychopharmacological, and inpatient using a variety of techniques including hypnosis (see Michelson & Ray, 1996 for a description of these techniques). Although there are a variety of approaches, there appear to be some common themes that cut across therapeutic approaches: (1) the initial establishment of safety in the therapeutic relationship; (2) allowing experiences and memories to come forth on the part of the patient rather than instituting a "search" for "forgotten" events. Because dissociative defenses are seen to help individuals separate themselves from experiencing traumatic events (Speigel, 1991), it follows that most therapeutic approaches emphasize in some manner understanding and putting into perspective a variety of levels of prior history including traumatic experiences. The underlying goal of the therapy work is an integration of current functioning with a personal history. Current functioning is worked on in terms of developing new behaviors and coping skills. As with any therapy, a social network and support group needs to be established. Although Kluft (Kluft, 1996; Ross, 1997, for a bibliography) has described a variety of case study therapy reports, there currently exist few if any studies of the effectiveness of different therapeutic interventions with DID.

[See also Dissociative Disorders.]

Bibliography

American Psychiatric Association. (1994). *Diagnostic and statistical manual of mental disorders* (4th ed.). Washington, DC: Author.

Kluft, R. P. (1996). Dissociative identity disorder. In G. Baggard (Ed.), *Treatments of psychiatric disorders*. Washington, DC: American Psychiatric Press, pp. 1599–1632.

Kluft, R. P. (1996). Dissociative identity disorder. In L. Michelson & W. Ray (Eds.), *Handbook of dissociation* (pp. 337–366). New York: Plenum.

Michelson, L., & Ray, W. (Eds.). (1996). *Handbook of dissociation*. New York: Plenum.

Putnam, F. W. (1989). *Diagnosis and treatment of multiple personality disorder*. New York: Guilford Press.

Ray, W. J. (1996). Dissociation in normal populations. In L. Michelson & W. Ray (Eds.), *Handbook of dissociation* (pp. 51–66). New York: Plenum.

Ross, C. (1997). *Dissociative identity disorder: Diagnosis, clinical features, and treatment of multiple personality* (2nd ed.). New York: Wiley.

Spiegel, D. (1991). Dissociation and trauma. In A. Tasman & S. Goldfinger (Eds.), *American psychiatric press review of psychiatry* (Vol. 10). Washington, DC: American Psychiatric Press.

Steinberg, M. (1994). *Structured clinical interview for DSM-IV dissociative disorders–Revised* (SCID-D-R). Washington, DC: American Psychiatric Press.

Zahn, T., Moraga, R., & Ray, W. (1996). Psychophysiological assessment of dissociative disorders. In L. Michelson & W. Ray (Eds.), *Handbook of dissociation* (pp. 269–287). New York: Plenum.

William J. Ray

DIVORCE. Since 1960, as marriage has become a more optional, less permanent institution in Western industrialized nations, the divorce rate has more than doubled. Although there has been a modest decrease in the divorce rate since the late 1970s, almost one half of marriages in the United States end in divorce, and one million children a year experience their parents' divorce. Following divorce, most children reside in a mother-headed household. Although father-headed households are the most rapidly increasing type of household in the United States, and although there has been an increase in joint legal custody, 84% of children reside with their mothers following divorce and see their fathers intermittently or not at all. This usually is a temporary situation since 75% of men and 66% of women remarry. However, divorce occurs more rapidly and frequently in remarriages than in first marriages, especially if children are involved. Thus, more adults and children are encountering multiple marital transitions and rearrangements in family structure, roles, and relationships. Although the changes and stresses accompanying divorce may put adults and children at risk for developing psychological, behavioral, and health disorders, it also may give them an opportunity to escape from conflictual, unsatisfactory, deleterious family relationships, to find more fulfilling relationships, and in the case of some women, to attain a greater sense of individuation, competence, and achievement.

Who Divorces?

Divorce rates are higher in couples who marry young, are poor, uneducated, urban, and African American.

The role of poverty and education is not quite as simple as this statement would indicate, because highly educated, economically independent women and couples in which the wife's income exceeds that of the husband also are more likely to divorce. African Americans not only are more likely to divorce, but are also more likely to separate without legal divorce and are less likely to remarry. Hence, compared to non-Hispanic Whites, African American spouses and children spend more time in a single-parent family or in one with a cohabiting partner or other family members such as a grandparent.

Both parents and children in families in which divorce will later occur show more problems in adjustment long before the divorce than do those who will remain in nondivorced families. This may be attributed to dysfunctional relationships and stresses in an unhappy marriage. However, it has been proposed that there is a divorce-prone personality. Some adults have characteristics, such as being neurotic, depressed, alcoholic or antisocial, that increase their probability of marital instability and of troubled relationships within and outside the family, of displaying inept parenting, and of encountering stressful life events.

In marital interactions, couples who will later divorce in comparison to those who will not exhibit contempt, denial, withdrawal, reciprocated aggression, more negative attributions about their spouse's behavior, dysfunctional beliefs about relationships, and generally poor problem-solving and conflict-resolution skills. They also are more erratic, irritable, and inept in parenting prior to the divorce than are parents whose marriages will not later be disrupted. The characteristics and social interactions of such individuals not only place them at risk for multiple marital transitions, but contribute to problems in family relations and children's adjustment following divorce.

Adjustment of Adults Following Divorce

Most adults, even those adults who have initiated divorce, encounter notable changes and stresses in their lives following a marital dissolution that may compromise their psychological and physical well-being. Both divorced men and women complain about loneliness, a sense of failure and being externally controlled, diminished self-worth, emotional lability, difficulty forming significant new intimate relationships, and anxiety about the unknowns and rapid alterations in their lives. Custodial parents express concerns about child rearing and task overload, noncustodial parents about alienation from, and loss of, their children. Although men show modest declines in retainable income following divorce, women show a substantial economic decrement, which has been estimated to be from 19% to as much as 35% in various studies. For divorced women,

this is associated with multiple occupational and residential changes. These changes are often to less desirable, more disordered neighborhoods with fewer resources, inadequate schools, and deviant peer groups, which makes raising competent children more difficult. However, the economic decrement for women following divorce has diminished as education and employment of women have increased, and as more aggressive legal means of enforcing support awards by spouses have been pursued.

Parents and children in divorced families encounter more stressful life events than do those in nondivorced families, and the more negative changes they experience, the more problems in adjustment they exhibit. Increased rates of psychopathology such as depression, alcoholism, and antisocial behavior and elevated rates of suicide, violence, homicide, and automobile accidents occur in adults following divorce. Furthermore, a breakdown in the immune system associated with an increased incidence of physical illness and morbidity from diseases also is found.

There is evidence that marriage is more strongly associated with the well-being of men than women. Perhaps that is why men remarry more rapidly. Even controlling for initial health and health habits, marriage is a stronger predictor of survival for men and friendship for women. Divorced fathers who do not reside with their children may be at special risk for engaging in impulsive and health-compromising behavior. However, there is a substantial subset of women who show notable benefits from divorce and report a sense of increased individuation, achievement, competence, and relief from no longer having to deal with a nonsupportive or undermining spouse in childrearing. Over time both divorced men and women become less depressed, anxious, and likely to engage in risky behavior, and this recovery is facilitated by the formation of new intimate relationships.

Adjustment of Children Following Divorce

Children exposed to divorce, on the average, show more antisocial, psychological, social, emotional, and academic problems than those whose parents have never divorced, especially compared to children in harmonious nondivorced families. These problems decrease over the first few years following divorce as children adjust to their new family situation. However, adolescence may trigger new problems in adjustment for adolescents in divorced, single-parent or remarried households. In adolescence there is about a twofold increase in the rates of school dropout, teenaged pregnancy, delinquency, and total behavior problems in the offspring of divorced parents over that found among adolescents in nondivorced families. Problems continue or increase in young adulthood and are reflected in lower socioeconomic status and educational attainment, more unemployment and welfare dependency, higher divorce rates, and more difficult or distant relationships with parents, especially with fathers. The average children from divorced families show more problems than those in nondivorced families and a twofold increase in certain specific problem behaviors, which must be viewed with concern. However, there is considerable overlap in the adjustment of children in the two types of families. Most children are resilient in the long-term response to their parents' divorce and emerge as reasonably competent, well-functioning individuals.

There is considerable diversity in children's responses to divorce and living in a single-parent family. The most important factors protecting against adverse outcomes of divorce include the personal factors of intelligence, an easy temperament, high academic achievement, self-worth, ego strength, and an internal locus of control. Important is a harmonious, supportive family environment with an authoritative residential parent who is high in warmth, responsiveness, control, and monitoring, and low conflict between the divorcing parents. Helpful are extrafamilial factors such as a close relationship with an adult, for example, with a teacher or a parent of a friend, positive relations with nondelinquent peers, and an authoritative school environment. For girls, a supportive relationship with a female sibling or a noncustodial mother may help to mitigate some of the adverse effects of divorce. For boys, the involvement of an authoritative custodial or noncustodial father or a caring stepfather plays an especially important protective function.

The most important single protective factor is the quality of the relationship with the residential custodial parent. If the parent can remain responsive, supportive, and authoritative, it can to a considerable extent moderate the adverse effects not only of divorce, but of some of its concomitant risks such as parental depression, poverty, infrequent contact with the noncustodial parent, and conflict between the divorced parents. It frequently has been found that family functioning, rather than family structure or type, is more important to the adjustment of children.

Finally, probably the most frequently asked question about divorce is whether couples in conflictual, unhappy marriages should stay together for the sake of the children. This depends to a large extent on the conditions before and after divorce. If children have not been aware of family problems or exposed to conflict before divorce and move into a more stressful environment with inept parenting following divorce, problems in their adjustment increase. If they move from a conflictual family environment to a more harmonious family situation with an authoritative custodial parent, problems decrease. However, children who have a difficult temperament, high levels of behavior problems,

multiple problems in multiple domains such as the family, peer group, school, or neighborhood prior to the divorce are most likely to have difficulty in adjusting after their parents' divorce.

Relations of Custodial Parents and Children

Although both joint legal custody and physical custody have become more common in recent years, even when joint custody is awarded, most children reside almost full time with their mothers. Divorced mothers, especially in the early years following divorce, are lower in warmth, responsiveness, control, and monitoring; that is, they are less authoritative parents than those in nondivorced families. Children following divorce also often exhibit anxious, angry, resistant, and noncompliant behavior toward their parents. Mothers and sons are especially likely to become involved in coercive exchanges of irritable, aggressive behavior. Problems between mothers and sons are more intense and long lasting than those between mothers and daughters, who often develop close companionable relationships. However, conflict in the relationship between mothers and daughters may emerge in adolescence as these girls often become more precociously sexually active. Children in divorced families grow up faster and spend less time under adult supervision, are more active in family decision making, and more vulnerable to the influences of peers. About one quarter of adolescent girls and one third of adolescent boys in divorced homes in comparison to about one tenth in nondivorced families become disengaged from their families, spending little time in shared activities or in the home. If this disengagement is accompanied by the involvement and supervision of another caring adult, it may be a good solution to a difficult family situation; if it is associated with involvement with an antisocial peer group, it can have adverse consequences on the achievement and conduct of these adolescents.

Custodial fathers experience many of the same problems in parenting and the isolation and interference with work and social life experienced by custodial mothers. However, fathers have greater economic resources to gain assistance in household tasks and child care, better housing, schools, and neighborhoods. Custodial fathers do not have the difficulties in control and discipline characteristic of custodial mothers. However, they report more problems in monitoring their children's health, activities, schoolwork, and behavior. Fathers who seek custody of their children are more capable parents and have more positive relations with their children than those who assent to custody because of maternal incompetence or disinterest.

Children can thrive in either a mother-custody or father-custody home, and there is little evidence of the superiority measured in terms of child adjustment of joint custody over sole custody in a well-functioning, single-parent household. Some research findings have indicated that children may fare better in the custody of a parent of the same sex, and that boys may be especially disadvantaged by the lack of a close relationship with a caring man, but again, the quality of the home environment appears more important than parental gender.

Noncustodial Parents

Contact with noncustodial parents diminishes rapidly after divorce. Only about one quarter of noncustodial fathers see their children once a week or more, and one quarter do not see their children at all or only a few times a year by one year following divorce. Noncustodial mothers maintain about twice as much contact with their children as do noncustodial fathers and are more likely to rearrange their living situation to accommodate their children's visits. Noncustodial mothers are more likely than noncustodial fathers to try to sustain an active parenting role, monitoring their children's activities, giving them instrumental help in such things as homework, serving as confidants and advisors, and providing support in times of stress. Noncustodial fathers are more likely to assume a recreational, companion role than the role of monitor, disciplinarian, or teacher.

Sheer amount of contact with the noncustodial parent is not associated with child adjustment. It is the quality of the contact that counts. Contact with a warm, supportive, authoritative parent under conditions of low conflict promotes the well-being of children with some evidence that contact with a same-sex noncustodial parent is most advantageous. Parents are most likely to maintain contact if interparental conflict is low, if they feel they have some control about decisions in their children's lives, and if proximity is close. African American fathers are more likely to maintain contact than are non-Hispanic White fathers, and Hispanic fathers are least likely.

No-Fault Divorce, Joint Custody, and Divorce Mediation

No-fault divorce, joint custody, and divorce mediation were advanced to minimize conflict during and after the divorce process, and/or to promote contact of the child with both parents. All have been partially successful in their goals. No-fault divorce laws have reduced the prolonged, acrimonious disputes, blaming, and vindictive and demeaning evidence gathering common under fault divorce laws. However, it also has allowed people to divorce who were going through temporary perturbations in what might have been a salvageable marriage. Even with no-fault divorce, marital dissolution is seldom a happy cooperative endeavor, and is more often painful and rancorous. Community

property laws have helped, but not solved, the inequities to women in divorce, but financial distributions and support and child custody remain the areas of most dissension in divorce.

Joint legal custody was promoted as a way to involve both parents in the responsibility, care, and welfare of their children and reduce conflict over custody. It has been successful in those regards. Contact with both parents and child support by fathers is more sustained, and returns to court to resolve disagreements are less frequent under joint custody. However, for the 25% of parents who have intensely conflictual relationships, the continued contact in joint custody may lead to greater exposure and enmeshment of children in parental dissension.

Although divorce mediation does not have notable effects on the long-term adjustment of children, it has reduced returns to court, and fathers, but not mothers, are more satisfied with mediated than with nonmediated divorces.

Legislators continue to be concerned about the high rates of marital dissolution. Some states have initiated fault divorce laws or have promoted the option of covenant divorces requiring demonstration of fault in divorce. Making divorces more acrimonious, or locking parents and children into unhappy, conflictual marriage is not an appropriate solution to divorce. Promoting satisfying stable marriages through support, workplace policies that reduce the conflicting requirements of families and jobs, affordable child care, and premarital and marital counseling and education programs may be more effective in limiting marital dissolution.

[See also Couples Therapy; Family Therapy; and Marriage.]

Bibliography

Emery, R. E. (1988). Marriage, divorce, and children's adjustment. Newbury Park, CA: Sage. This book presents a history of divorce and a review of the research on family relations and children's adjustment in divorced families, as well as interventions and legal policies dealing with divorce; a new edition of this book is expected in 1999.

Gottman, J. M. (1994). What predicts divorce: The relationships between marital processes and marital outcomes. Hillsdale, NJ: Erlbaum. This book is suitable for a research audience. It presents the results of one of the most meticulous studies of marital relations and divorce, and discusses conflict-resolution style, cognitive factors, and physiological responses that predict marital happiness and marital dissolution.

Hetherington, E. M., & Clingempeel, W. G. (1992). Coping with marital transitions: A family systems perspective. Monographs of the Society for Research in Child Development, 55 (Serial Nos. 2–3). This monograph takes a family systems approach to studying the marital, parent-child, and sibling relationships and their effects on the adjustment of adolescents in nondivorced, divorced mother-custody, and stepfather families.

Hetherington, E. M., & Stanley-Hagan, M. (1995). Parenting in divorced and remarried families. In M. Bornstein (Ed.), *Handbook of parenting* (pp. 233–255). Hillsdale, NJ: Erlbaum. In this chapter the relationships and parenting of custodial, noncustodial, and stepparents and their influence on child development are discussed. Differences in relationships of boys and girls with mothers and fathers are presented.

Maccoby, E. E., & Mnookin, R. H. (1992). *Dividing the child: Social and legal dilemmas of custody.* Cambridge, MA: Harvard University Press. This book presents the results of a large California study evaluating the challenges and outcomes associated with sole father or mother physical custody and joint physical custody. As it was written by a psychologist and a lawyer, it gives a unique interdisciplinary perspective on the issues.

McClanahan, S., & Sandefur, G. (1994). *Growing up with a single parent: What hurts, what helps?* Cambridge, MA: Harvard University Press. These authors use databases of several large-scale surveys to evaluate the effects of growing up in a single-parent family on educational and economic attainment, idleness and inactivity, and early child rearing. Risk and protective factors, and gender and racial differences are discussed.

Simons, R. L. (1996). *Understanding differences between divorced and intact families: Stresses, interaction, and child outcome.* Thousand Oaks, CA: Sage. This book examines the effects of divorce on family functioning, and parent–child adjustment in divorced and nondivorced families.

Veroff, J., Douvan, E., & Hatchett, S. (1995). *Marital instability.* Greenwich CT: Greenwood Press. This is one of the few comparative studies of the socioeconomic factors and interactional styles associated with marital satisfaction or divorce in African American and White couples. The authors discuss the role of cultural factors in modifying the meanings of interactions and styles of behavior and their consequences for marital well-being and stability in the two racial groups.

E. Mavis Hetherington and Margaret M. Stanley-Hagan

DIX, DOROTHEA LYNDE (1802–1887), American teacher, humanitarian reformer, and Superintendent of Women Nurses during the Civil War. Though Dorothea Dix had three careers, she is remembered primarily as an impassioned advocate for humane living accommodations and a therapeutic climate for the insane poor.

Dorothea Dix was born in Hampden, Maine, 4 April 1802. Following a turbulent and unhappy childhood she opened a private school for small children in Worcester, Massachusetts. Later in Boston, she ran a private school during the day and a charity school during the evenings. As a teacher, Dix was an active researcher and scholar, publishing books designed to involve parents in the education of their children. Her best known book, *Conversations on Common Things* (Boston, 1824), is a treasury of information on geography, history, word origins, and natural science.

Dix's career as a reformer was launched in 1841 following a visit to the East Cambridge, Massachusetts jail. There she found the mentally ill housed with hardened criminals in unfurnished, frigid, damp quarters. The deplorable conditions of the East Cambridge facility prompted Dix to travel throughout the state of Massachusetts to visit jails, prisons, and almshouses. As in Cambridge, she encountered insane persons living in unconscionable conditions; confined or chained in cages, boxes, sheds, and cellars, and often living in accumulations of their own filth. Following her travels she prepared a petition to the Massachusetts legislature documenting her observations and asking for funds for a new hospital to provide comfortable accommodations for the incurably insane and a therapeutic climate for those deemed curable. Her petition resulted in a major addition to the existing hospital at Worcester. Following success in Massachusetts, Dix thrust herself into a political-social arena reserved exclusively for men in Victorian society. She campaigned tirelessly on behalf of the insane throughout the United States and in foreign countries such as Canada, England, Italy, Scotland, Russia, and Turkey. Helen Marshall, in her biography *Dorothea Dix: Forgotten Samaritan* (New York, 1937), underscores Dix's capacity to raise money, shape public opinion, and shepherd legislation by pointing out that Dix was instrumental in founding 32 hospitals in the United States and several in foreign countries.

At the outbreak of the Civil War the 58-year-old Dix volunteered her services to the government and was named Superintendent of Women Nurses. She helped organize the medical infrastructure needed to accommodate wounded and dying soldiers. However, Dix's career as an independent reformer had been a poor training ground for daily work in a military-medical bureaucracy. She irritated physicians with her insistence on sobriety and sanitation and she was overly rigid and restrictive in her selection criteria for nurses. She performed a valuable service at the end of the war by assisting veterans with pensions and helping families secure records on soldiers missing in action.

In her later years, Dix returned to her work as a reformer traveling the country to raise money, inspect facilities, and consult with lawmakers and professionals. In her final years she was aware of the deterioration of the hospitals she had helped found. Never properly funded, her hospitals fell victim to neglect and became as custodial as the jails and almshouses they had replaced. She died at the age of 85 on 17 July 1887.

Gwendolyn Stevens and Sheldon Gardner in *The*

Women of Psychology (Cambridge, 1982) suggest that Dix became the "soul and conscience of psychology in its earliest days" and helped sensitize early psychologists to problems that existed outside the restricted atmosphere of the laboratory. Dix's work is also an invaluable study for professionals who must deal with political systems to apply psychological principles to social problems. Dix's intellectual contributions are often overlooked, but it is clear that her humanitarian mission was guided by the earlier values of the scholar-teacher. Her knowledge of history and statistics are evident in her petitions to lawmakers, and she embraced an informed view of mental illness, regarding it as a disease of the brain and as a product of civilization. She pointed to religious excitement, unemployment, and personal loss as proximate causes of insanity. Dix had expertise in astronomy and botany. The careful observation associated with these disciplines served as a model for her reform work. She argued that what she stated for fact she must see for herself. Her emphasis on institutionalization for the mentally disturbed has proven to be untenable, but her methods and her pioneering quest for benevolence, justice, and an informed social-political conscience continue to be relevant to our unsolved problems.

Bibliography

Works by Dix

Dix, D. L. (1845). *Remarks on prisons and prison discipline in the United States* (2nd ed.). Philadelphia: Joseph Kite. A discussion of penal philosophies and defense of a utilitarian theory of punishment and humane living accommodations for prisoners.

Rothman, D. J. (Ed.). (1971). *Poverty U.S.A.: The historical record.* New York: Arno Press/The New York Times. Includes a collection of ten of Dix's memorials to legislatures.

Snyder, C. M. (1975). *The lady and the president: The letters of Dorothea Dix and Millard Fillmore.* Lexington, KY: University of Kentucky Press.

Works about Dix

Gollaher, D. (1995). *Voice for the mad: The life of Dorothea Dix.* New York: Free Press. A scholarly, appreciative, and critical treatment of Dix's life and work including numerous arguable interpretations of her values and motives.

Tiffany, F. (1891). *Life of Dorothea Lynde Dix.* Boston: Houghton Mifflin. First major biography of Dix; a chronology of her work and sentimental celebration of her life.

Viney, W. (1996). Dorothea Dix: An intellectual conscience for psychology. In G. A. Kimble, C. A. Boneau, & M. Wertheimer (Eds.), *Portraits of pioneers in psychology* (Vol. 2, pp. 15–31). Washington DC: American Psychological Association. A brief biography that examines Dix's reform work in the context of the philosophical values she embraced as a teacher.

Wilson, D. C. (1975). *Stranger and traveler: The story of Dorothea Dix, American reformer.* Boston: Little, Brown. A sympathetic and dramatic celebration of Dix's life and work written by a novelist and playwright.

Wayne Viney

DOCTORAL DEGREE. The highest academic degree awarded by universities in North America is the doctor of philosophy (Ph.D.) degree, a research degree. According to the Council of Graduate Schools (1990, p. 1), "The doctor of philosophy program is designed to prepare a student to become a scholar, that is, to discover, integrate, and apply knowledge, as well as communicate and disseminate it." Other doctorates—such as doctor of education (Ed.D.), doctor of jurisprudence (J.D.), and doctor of medicine (M.D.)—are intended to train professionals or emphasize applied research.

The first earned doctorates in America were doctor of philosophy degrees awarded by Yale University in 1861. The first such degree in psychology was awarded by Harvard University in 1878. A century later nearly 3,000 doctorates were awarded annually in psychology, reflecting the discipline's growth as a science and a profession (Bartlett, 1994). Much of that growth occurred after World War II, but its earliest roots took hold in American universities during the late nineteenth century, with psychology's evolution from a discipline of philosophy into one of experimental science. With that change came the earliest research laboratories (Cadwallader, 1992) and the first psychological clinic in which the new science of psychology could be applied to everyday problems (Benjamin, 1996). For all students of that day, the emphasis in doctoral education was on the science of psychology, for which the Ph.D. degree was appropriate recognition of scholarly achievement in research. To this day, that remains the predominant degree of choice among university graduate programs, even those preparing students for the professional practice of psychology.

The wisdom of this academic model as preparation for a licensed profession, as psychology became by the mid-twentieth century, was seriously challenged during the 1960s in the face of increasing public need for psychological services and what some regarded as lack of sufficient attention in university graduate departments to the knowledge, skills, and attitudes essential to professional practice. This resulted in debates about pedagogical issues that differentiate graduate education in research from that required for the practice of a profession, the genesis of professional schools in psychology, and the adoption of the professional doctor of psychology (Psy.D.) degree (Peterson, 1997). The first

Psy.D. degree was awarded in 1971 by the University of Illinois, and within the next two decades more than 30 Psy.D. degree programs were established. By the mid-1990s, approximately 4,000 doctorates in psychology were awarded annually, about 20% being Psy.D. degrees, almost all of which were awarded by professional schools of psychology (APA Research Office, 1995). A few professional schools also award the Ph.D. degree, and, over the years, the doctor of education (Ed.D.) degree has been awarded to a small percentage of graduates whose psychology doctoral programs were located within university colleges of education.

A remaining challenge for the discipline of psychology is to clarify for the public its doctoral degree structure in relation to other professions and learned disciplines as guided by policy of the Council of Graduate Schools.

Bibliography

American Psychological Association Research Office. (1995). *Numbers and percentages of Ph.D.s and Psy.D.s awarded in psychology by professional schools of psychology: 1995.* Washington, DC: Author.

Bartlett, N. (1994). Octopuses and students. *History of Psychology Newsletter, 26,* 2, 37–51.

Benjamin, L. T., Jr. (1996). Lightner Witmer's legacy to American psychology. *American Psychologist, 51,* 3, 235–236.

Cadwallader, T. C. (1992). The historical roots of the American Psychological Association. In R. B. Evans, V. S. Sexton, & T. C. Cadwallader (Eds.), *100 years of the American Psychological Association: A historical perspective* (pp. 3–41). Washington, DC: American Psychological Association.

Council of Graduate Schools. (1990). *The doctor of philosophy degree: A policy statement.* Washington, DC: Author.

Peterson, D. R. (1997). *Educating professional psychologists: History and guiding conception.* Washington, DC: American Psychological Association.

Paul D. Nelson

DOCTOR OF PSYCHOLOGY DEGREE. The doctor of psychology (Psy.D.) degree is awarded to psychologists whose education is designed to prepare them for careers of professional practice. With considerable variation in content and emphasis, the programs that lead to the degree include the basic scientific knowledge relevant to professional psychology, training in the six professional competency areas (relationship, assessment, intervention, research and evaluation, consultation and education, and management and supervision) identified by the National Council of Schools and Programs of Professional Psychology (NCSPP), supervised practicum experiences, and an internship. Dissertation requirements usually have an applied focus and range from relatively small, clinically oriented doctoral projects to products of the level and scope that might be found in Ph.D. programs. A typical program requires five years of graduate study beyond the baccalaureate degree.

The first formal proposal for a professional degree in psychology was advanced by Loyal Crane in 1925. The proposal was not cordially received in the academic community. Only two "Ps.D." programs, both in Canada and both short lived, were attempted. The scientist-practitioner model leading to the Ph.D. degree, established at the Boulder, Colorado, conference on clinical training in 1949, remains the most common design for the education of professional psychologists. The "Boulder model," as it came to be called, prepares graduates as researchers as well as clinicians, in the belief that each form of activity enhances the other.

By the middle of the 1960s, however, critics expressed discontent with some clinical programs in academic departments, which were seen as overemphasizing research at the expense of education for practice, the career the majority of graduates entered even at that time. After deliberation, an American Psychological Association (APA) committee recommended establishment of practitioner programs leading to the Psy.D. degree. In 1968, the Department of Psychology at the Urbana–Champaign campus of the University of Illinois inaugurated the first Psy.D. program in the United States.

Five years later, the concept of explicit education for the practice of psychology and the use of the Psy.D. degree were endorsed at the conference in Vail, Colorado. In the years that followed, additional Psy.D. programs were developed in universities and professional schools throughout the United States, although the initial program at the University of Illinois was discontinued in 1980. Throughout the 1980s there was still debate as to whether the Ph.D. or Psy.D. was the preferred degree for professional programs, but by the mid-1990s the consensus designation was the Psy.D. Also, some regional accrediting bodies asked professional programs to move to the Psy.D. from the Ph.D. By early 1997, at least 45 professional education programs were in operation, the great majority awarding the Psy.D. Approximately half of these were in universities, half were in free-standing professional schools, and 33 had been approved by the APA Committee on Accreditation. Almost all of these programs belong to the NCSPP, which, over a period of 20 years, has developed an explicit model for professional psychology education.

Bibliography

Peterson, D. R. (1997). *Educating professional psychologists: History and guiding conception.* Washington, DC: American Psychological Association.

Peterson, R. L., Peterson, D. R., & Abrams, J. (Eds.). (in press). *Standards for education in professional psychology: Reflection and integration.* Washington, DC: American Psychological Association & National Council of Schools of Professional Psychology.

Peterson, R. L., Peterson, D. R., Abrams, J. C., & Stricker, G. (1997). The National Council of Schools and Programs of Professional Psychology educational model. *Professional Psychology: Research and Practice, 28,* 373–386.

Roger L. Peterson

DOCTOR-PATIENT RELATIONSHIP. Until the last quarter of the twentieth century in the United States, the doctor-patient relationship could best be described as paternalistic. Major medical decisions, often involving the use of increasingly sophisticated technology, were made by the physician (who was usually male). It was believed that such decisions were made with beneficent intent, but they did not involve open discussion or participation by the patient or the family. The major advantage of such a relationship was that the patient and his or her family were spared from making difficult and complex decisions and put their trust in the physician, with whom they often had a long-standing relationship. The major disadvantage, though it was not perceived to be so at the time, was that patients were deprived of the opportunity to make decisions reflecting their own cultural, gender, racial, and socioeconomic factors, which might not be shared or understood by the physician.

Balint and Shelton (1996) suggested several trends that resulted in the questioning of this paternalistic model: (a) the steady growth of the concept of individual freedom, begun with the American and French revolutions; (b) the ongoing scientific developments in medicine resulting in the physician's ability to cure as well as care, but creating the dilemma of how aggressive treatment should be if cure is not likely, and (c) the development of the National Health Service in Great Britain, and Medicaid and Medicare in the United States, leading to the possibility of universal access to care and increasingly involving the government in decisions regarding the use of societal resources for medical care. The medical horrors of physicians under the Nazi regime in World War II and the recognition of examples of medical experimentation in the United States where patients' rights were clearly violated, raised issues of patient autonomy and rights in medical decision making. The civil rights movement and the women's movement further strengthened the move toward more individual autonomy. The explosion of the information age with toll free numbers for patients to request information about a specific disease, treatment, clinical trials, and local community resources, along with access to the Internet, allows patients to become well informed about their disease and treatment from both the traditional and the alternative/unconventional/complementary approaches. The transition from the fee-for-service (retrospective) to the managed care (prospective) health care system has altered the role of physicians by giving them less control over societal resources, and thus, has also lessened the power of physicians in their relationship with patients.

Models have been developed that give the patient more power in a relationship that has increasingly begun to be viewed as a partnership (Szasz & Hollender, 1956). Descriptions of this partnership emphasize patient autonomy, or independent choice (Quill & Brody, 1996). Patients and families are often asked to make medical decisions on the basis of information and statistics presented by the physician, as free as possible from a clear recommendation by the physician, which might influence the decision. Many physicians believe that this is the best way to respect patients' rights, as well as to provide further protection for themselves.

Increasingly, criticisms of this approach have been raised because patients are asked to make complex decisions without medical guidance, and physicians resort to the provision of information rather than careful consideration of the best course of action. Thus, a new model is being proposed, combining components of both the paternalism and autonomy approaches. Quill and Brody (1996) called this *enhanced autonomy* because their model suggests that autonomous decisions actually require the input or recommendation by the physician after a dialogue with the patient in which the physician has informed the patient of options and explored the patient's values. This is a relationship model, rather than a physician-or patient-dominated model, and includes consideration of the family as an important factor in patient care. Such a model allows the physician to support and guide the patient's decisions while also expressing an expert recommendation. This model is more demanding of the physician than the paternalistic or autonomous models because the physician's discourse with the patient and family must take into account the latter's values, their life stories, and their ability to hear information ("bad news"; see Girgis & Sanson-Fisher, 1995) at key points in an illness.

Recognizing this two-way interaction, Charles, Gafni, and Whelan (1999) term this a shared decision-making model. They have suggested the analogy that shared decision making takes "two to tango" (Charles, Gafni, & Whelan, 1997). The physician must know what "dance" the patient prefers and the required steps. Sometimes it is more important for the physician to lead (e.g., when technical information is given), while at other times, the patient must lead (e.g., when expressing preferences for treatment.

The complexity of this model can be seen from several studies showing that almost all patients do indeed want all the information, good or bad, about their illness, but fewer want to participate in decision making (e.g., Blanchard, Labreque, Ruckdeschel, & Blanchard, 1988). Predictors of cancer patient preference for participation in decision making have been found to be age (with younger patients desiring greater involvement) and education (with better-educated patients preferring greater involvement). It is not clear whether those with serious illness desire a higher degree of participation in decision making. Patients who asked more questions, expressed more concerns, and were more anxious have been found to receive more information from physicians than those who asked fewer questions, expressed fewer concerns, and showed less anxiety (R. L. Stewart, 1991).

Outcomes of the Doctor-Patient Relationship

Patient-physician discussions have long been seen as the way in which much of the caring and curing of medical care is conveyed. However, it was not until the 1960s that investigators began studying communication processes in the interactions between patients and providers and relating those to outcome measures, particularly satisfaction either with total care or with aspects of the provider's behavior. Studies vary considerably in the degree of patient satisfaction found, due to a variety of instruments being used and different diseases being studied. An average of 40 to 50% of patients are found to be noncompliant/nonadherent, and many studies have found that patients do not recall what is said to them, especially when receiving a potentially life-threatening diagnosis (see Ong, de Haes, Hoos, & Lammes, 1995).

Hall, Roter, and Katz (1988) published a meta-analysis of 41 studies examining correlates of physician behaviors in encounters with patient outcomes. Results showed that satisfaction had the most consistent relationship with provider behavior. Satisfaction was most predicted by the amount of information provided by physicians. Satisfaction was related to greater technical and interpersonal competence by the physician, more partnership building, more immediate and positive nonverbal behavior, more social conversation, more positive talk, less negative talk (excluding negative voice quality), and more communication overall. Only question asking showed no relationship to satisfaction. Thus, it seems that satisfaction reflects both task and socioemotional physician behaviors. Task behaviors were seen as those serving the instrumental goals of the medical visit: information giving, question asking, and

technical competence. Socioemotional behaviors were those in the expressive realm: partnership building, social conversation, positive and negative talk, and interpersonal competence.

Compliance was found to have a comparatively weak relationship to provider behavior. Analyses showed that compliance was associated with more information given, fewer questions asked overall (but more questions asked about compliance), more positive talk, and less negative talk. Compliance seemed to increase when providers took a more dominant role in the interaction. Not surprisingly, recall/understanding was best predicted by information giving and was also significantly predicted by less question asking, more partnership building, and more positive talk.

Patients of a higher social class received both more information and more communication overall. They also received higher quality care (both technical and interpersonal) and more positive talk. Female patients received more information and total communication than male patients did. Female patients also received more positive talk and more partnership-building behaviors. Other research has shown that women ask for more information and receive more health care services (tests, prescriptions, appointments); thus, the greater amount of information could be a response to more questions being addressed. Older patients received more information, more total communication, and asked more questions concerning drugs; they also elicited more courtesy and more laughter than younger patients. Perhaps this is one reason why older patients have consistently been found to be more satisfied, although this may also reflect different expectations of the interaction.

It appears from this meta-analysis that patients' task-relevant behaviors of recall and compliance are primarily related to physicians' task behaviors, whereas satisfaction is related to provider's task and socioemotional behaviors. This countered the then-prevailing view that patients were rather poor judges of physicians' task behaviors, and instead, relied on socioemotional behaviors when evaluating quality of care. It would seem that task behaviors by physicians trigger socioemotional attributions by patients, but socioemotional behaviors by themselves do not result in patients' task behaviors (recall, compliance). More recently, Lewis (1994) made the appropriate suggestion that perhaps the distinction drawn between task and socioemotional behaviors is too dichotomous as communication skills can be seen as a technical skill. The best physicians thus have been found to exhibit both technical skills (including communication) and interpersonal skills (politeness, sensitivity and perceptiveness, patient rapport, kindness, humaneness, compassion, and empathy; see DiMatteo, 1995).

Patient dissatisfaction with care has been reported to be connected to health-related litigation, changing health care providers, disenrollment from prepaid health plans, and nonadherence to a physician's recommendations (Marshall, Hays, & Mazel, 1996). Little is known about the typically found positive relationship between satisfaction and health status. Marshall et al. examined health status and satisfaction with health care using data obtained at baseline and at 12 months for 952 participants in the Medical Outcomes Study. General satisfaction was found to be related to mental, but not physical, health in cross-sectional analyses. Longitudinal analyses showed the same pattern. Baseline satisfaction with care was linked to subsequent mental health; initial mental health was linked to subsequent satisfaction with care. Both the cross-sectional and longitudinal findings were found for patients with significant depressive symptoms and for those with other health problems. Thus, it is possible that dissatisfaction with care may reflect general dissatisfaction, or a tendency to experience depressive symptoms. What was not measured in that study was the possible relationship to satisfaction of objective measures of health status such as disability days, blood glucose levels, or cholesterol.

M. A. Stewart (1995) reviewed randomized controlled trials and analytic studies with health as an outcome variable. She reported that studies focusing on history taking found physician education regarding patients' understanding and concerns regarding the problem, and the impact of the problem on function, affected the patients' emotional status. Patient education affected physical health, level of function, blood glucose level, and blood pressure.

An analysis of studies examining discussions of the management plan found that patient education had an impact on emotional and physical status, and physician education (e.g., patient encouraged to ask questions) impacted patients' emotional status. Several intervention studies targeting either physician communication skills or patient information-asking skills reported positive impacts on patient health outcomes. These findings support the theoretical model of partnership discussed earlier. Patients do better or are more satisfied when they are participants in their own care and decision making. They should be encouraged to ask questions and be given emotional support and, when possible, written information. Agreement between patient and physician regarding the nature of the problem and the direction of management is an effective interaction that may have an impact on health outcome.

Future Challenges

Several key challenges are apparent that will shape the future physician-patient relationship. Balint and Shelton (1996) point to the ongoing and increasing tension between the needs or preferences of a particular patient, the role of the physician as patient advocate, and the use of societal resources. The role of the physician in end-of-life care as goals of treatment move from cure to care is increasingly being explored, due in large part to the hospice movement. Finally, the use of complementary and alternative methods continues to expand, resulting in a mounting need for education of the physician about such methods, and research investigations to study the contributions of these methods.

Bibliography

Balint, J., & Shelton, W. (1996). Regaining the initiative: Forging a new model of the patient-physician relationship. *Journal of the American Medical Association, 275,* 887–891.

Blanchard, C. G., Labregue, M. S., Rucksdeschel, J. C., & Blanchard, E. B. (1988). Information and decision-making preferences of hospitalized adult cancer patients. *Social Science & Medicine, 27,* 1139–1145.

Charles, C., Gafni, A., & Whelan, T. (1997). Shared decision-making in the medical encounter: What does it mean? (Or, it takes at least two to tango). *Social Science & Medicine, 44,* 681–692.

Charles, C., Gafni, A., & Whelan, T. (1999). Decision-making in the physician-patient encounter: Revisiting the shared treatment decision-making model. *Social Science & Medicine, 49,* 651–661.

DiMatteo, M. R. (1995). Health psychology research: The interpersonal challenges. In G. G. Brannigan & M. R. Merrens (Eds.), *The social psychologists: Research adventures* (pp. 207–220). New York: McGraw-Hill. Presents an account of the author's work in medical settings examining the nature and significance of the physician-patient interaction and the author's personal reflections.

Girgis, A., & Sanson-Fisher, R. W. (1995). Breaking bad news: Consensus guidelines for medical practitioners. *Journal of Clinical Oncology, 13,* 2449–2456. Discusses the advantages and disadvantages of breaking bad news based on three disclosure models and presents suggested guidelines.

Hall, J. A, Roter, D. L., & Katz, N. R. (1988). Meta-analysis of correlates of provider behavior in medical encounters. *Medical Care, 26,* 657–675.

Kaplan, S. H., Greenfield, S., & Ware, J. E. (1989). Assessing the effects of physician-patient interactions on the outcomes of chronic disease. *Medical Care, 27,* S110–S127. Data are presented for four clinical trials of chronically ill patients. Better health measured physiologically, behaviorally, or subjectively was related to specific aspects of the doctor-patient relationship. Interventions to improve the relationship and results are discussed.

Lewis, J. R. (1994). Patient views on quality care in general practice: Literature review. *Social Science & Medicine, 39,* 655–670. Examines research on patient satisfaction and the factors that influence patient attitudes regarding quality in general practice. Data are used from the United States and other sources; conclusions are focused on general practice in the United Kingdom.

Marshall, G. N., Hays, R. D., & Mazel, R. (1996). Health status and satisfaction with care: Results from the Medical Outcomes Study. *Journal of Consulting and Clinical Psychology, 64,* 380–390.

Ong, L. M. L., deHaes, J. C. M., Hoos, A. M., & Lammes, F. B. (1995). Doctor-patient communication: A review of the literature. *Social Science & Medicine, 40,* 903–918. A comprehensive review of doctor-patient communication addressing the purposes, interaction analysis systems, specific communicative behaviors, and the impact of communicative behaviors on outcomes.

Quill, T., & Brody, H. (1996). Physician recommendations and patient autonomy: Finding a balance between physician power and patient choice. *Annals of Internal Medicine, 125,* 763–769.

Roter, D. L., & Hall, J. A. (1993). *Doctors talking with patients/patients talking with doctors: Improving communication in medical visits.* Westport, CT: Auburn House. The authors, experienced researchers in this field, focused primarily on physician-patient communication in the outpatient setting. They addressed principles for communication, reviewed research of factors related to communication between patient and doctor, examined how communication processes are related to compliance or treatment outcome, and reviewed the randomized trials aimed at improving physician-patient communication. They stressed the importance of the physician-patient relationship as a partnership, with clear implications for medical care and treatment outcomes.

Stewart, M. A. (1995). Effective physician-patient communication and health outcomes. *Canadian Medical Association Journal, 152,* 1423–1433. This is a thorough review of 21 randomized and analytic studies of physician-patient communication in which patient health was an outcome variable. The author concluded that most studies did demonstrate a correlation between effective communication and positive health outcomes.

Stewart, R. L. (1991). Information giving in medical consultations: The influence of patients' communicative styles and personal characteristics. *Social Science & Medicine, 32,* 541–548.

Stoeckle, J. D. (Ed.). (1987). *Encounters between patients and doctors: An anthology.* Cambridge, MA: MIT Press. These classic readings were gathered by one of the leading advocates of primary care in the United States and emphasize the importance of the doctor-patient relationship in medical care. Articles cover ground rules for the relationship, dynamics of the exchange, the nature of the communication, barriers to communication, case studies, and suggestions for a good relationship.

Szasz, T. S., & Hollender, M. H. (1956). A contribution to the philosophy of medicine: The basic models of the doctor-patient relationship. *Archives of Internal Medicine, 97,* 585–592.

Christina G. Blanchard

DOGMATISM. *See* Authoritarianism; *and* Rigidity.

DOLEŽAL, JAN (1902–1965), Czech psychologist. Born in Vnorovy (Moravia) on 30 March 1902, Doležal was an important contributor to Czech applied and experimental psychology (cf. Hoskovec, 1992, p. 122) and a skillful organizer. He served first as codirector, and then as director, of the Psychotechnological Institute in Prague. In 1937 he became an unpaid assistant professor (docent) at Prague's Charles University, keeping the position as director of the Central Psychotechnological Institute, which was transformed in 1938 into the broader-based Institute of Human Work. The new Institute had two divisions: applied and research oriented. The former had sections on employee selection, ergonomics, and vocational education and training. The research division dealt with issues on the physiology, psychology, and sociology of human work. Doležal facilitated the survival of the Institute and some of its personnel during World War II. After the war he shifted to an academic career, and became associate professor of experimental and applied psychology in 1947, and was promoted to full professor in 1956. In addition, he served as head of the university's Department of Psychology and director of the university's research-oriented Psychological Institute (Bureš, Hoskovec, & Štikar, 1985).

Doležal's career began in the early 1920s with his studies at Charles University, but he soon transferred to the University of Leipzig where he received a doctorate in psychology. His dissertation, dealing with work motion (cranking), was based on research carried out at the Psychotechnological Institute of the Technological University (Technische Hochschule) in Dresden (Doležal, 1930). He wrote a monograph on the psychology and psychotechnology of efficiency in Czech, which appeared in the first volume of the *Encyclopedia of Efficiency* (Doležal, 1934). It was followed, years later and under profoundly altered sociopolitical conditions, by a chapter on the psychology of work, contained in *The Uses of Psychology in a Socialist Social Practice* (Doležal, 1959).

Doležal's major publication was *The Science of Human Work* (Doležal, 1948). The English translation of the Introduction to this work (Doležal, 1948/1997) was included in a volume documenting psychological thought of Czech authors who had studied or taught at Charles University during the 650 years of its existence. In this work, Doležal stressed that, although the ways of life of subhuman organisms are biologically determined, the development of humankind is characterized by a progressive decrease in its dependence on nature. Humans construct their own physical, cultural, and economic environment, adapting nature to their needs. In this process, work plays a central role. By means of physical work, people modify their external environment and thus affect the possibilities of biological existence. It is through psychological activities that humans create the cultural values, including morality, which in turn affect their behavior.

In addition to his outstanding organizational talent, Doležal was an innovative designer of psychological tests and apparatuses, some of which are held in a permanent collection housed in the department of psychology at Charles University (Hoskovec & Štikar, 1994). In one version of an instrument designed to measure the latency of reactions to stimuli (Doležal, Břicháček, & Fischer, 1965), the stimulus was the stopping, at random intervals, of the movement of a rotating arm. Doležal died in Prague on 12 January 1965.

Bibliography

Works by Doležal

Doležal, J. (1930). *Über die Bewegungsform bei der Arbeit an Drehkurbeln* [On the form of movement in work with turning cranks]. Munich: Beck.

Doležal, J. (1934). Psychology and psychotechnology of efficiency. In *Encyclopedia of efficiency* (pp. 214–313). Prague: Sfinx.

Doležal, J. (1948). *Věda o práci* [The science of human work]. Prague: VŠPS [Political and Social University].

Doležal, J. (1959). Psychology of work. In *The uses of psychology in socialist social practice* (pp. 31–36). Bratislava: Slovak Academy of Sciences.

Doležal, J. (1997). The science of human work. In J. Brožek & J. Hoskovec (Eds.), *Psychological ideas and society: Charles University, 1348–1998* (pp. 103–105). Prague: Charles University. (Original work published 1948)

Doležal, J., Břicháček, V., & Fischer, P. (1965). New type of electrochronograph. *Československá Psychologie, 9,* 304–308.

Works about Doležal

Bureš, Z., Hoskovec, J., & Štikar, J. (1985). Twenty years from the death of Prof. J. Doležal. *Psychologie y Ekonomicke Praxi, 20,* 37–39.

Hoskovec, J. (1992). Czechoslovak experimental psychology. In *The secrets of experimental psychology* (pp. 121–132). Prague: Academia.

Hoskovec, J., & Štikar, J. (1994). Historische Geräte in der Psychologie [Historical apparatuses in psychology]. *Psychologie und Geschichte, 5,* 286–292.

Josef Brožek and Jiří Hoskovec

DOMESTIC VIOLENCE, by legislation and statute law, is generally defined as an intentional abuse or physical assault committed by a past or present spouse, intimate partner, or family or household member against another spouse, intimate partner, or family or household member, regardless of age or gender. The issue of child abuse, spousal abuse, intimate partner abuse, and elder abuse are now integral and fundamental components of most domestic violence legislation (Miller, 1998). There are few statistics universally agreed on. In fact, while some academics argue that domestic violence is a serious social problem, others continue to question its true gravity (Swisher, 1996).

Regardless of the rhetoric, the *Bureau of Justice Statistics Sourcebook* data demonstrate that abuse suffered by children and women in the home is a greater problem for them than is violence in the streets. These data also offer little doubt that while domestic violence does cross all socioeconomic and educational strata, it is not classless. Indisputably, numerous National Institute of Justice studies show that the difference in numbers of domestic violence abuse is proportional to the wealth and education of the victim. Families with incomes of less than $7,500 have higher rates of aggravated assault than families with incomes of more than $50,000. Data from the *Bureau of Justice Statistics Sourcebook* and other National Institute of Justice studies demonstrate that although domestic violence occurs in all racial, socioeconomic, and educational groups, it is more prevalent among people in poverty with little education. This does not mean that domestic violence is confined to the underclass, but that it is simply more prevalent there. This is also not intended to dispute the proposition that domestic violence does indeed permeate all racial, socioeconomic, and educational tiers.

There are little empirical scientific data to deny that, overwhelmingly, the majority of severe spousal abuse in our homes is inflicted on women by men. Bureau of Justice Statistics data demonstrate that in America a woman is more likely to be physically assaulted, raped, or murdered by a current or former male partner than any other assailant. The August 5, 1998, issue of the *Journal of the American Medical Association* estimates that between 700,000 and 1.1 million women each year seek care at hospital emergency rooms for acute injuries incurred from abuse by a present or former husband, boyfriend, or intimate partner. In violence between men and women, because of the greater physical and emotional injuries suffered by women, there can be little argument that men are the abusers and women the predominant victims of severe injuries (Straus & Gelles, 1990). Women are seven to ten times more likely to be injured in acts of intimate violence than are men. The November 1998 Research in Brief, *Prevalence, Incidence, and Consequences of Violence Against Women: Findings From the National Violence Against Women Survey,* sponsored by the National Institute of Justice, reports that of women who were raped and/or physically assaulted since the age of 18, three quarters were victimized by a current or former husband, cohabiting partner, date, or boyfriend. Women are significantly more likely to be killed by intimates, such as husbands and boyfriends, compared to men. However, reams of data in the *Bureau of Justice Statistics Sourcebook* also demonstrate that when the victim is weaker than the perpetrator, abuse can and often does occur regardless of age or gender.

In *Violence in Families: Assessing Prevention and Treatment Programs*, the editors in the executive summary report that "running through discussions of child maltreatment, domestic violence [spousal/intimate partner abuse], and elder abuse is the idea of unequal power in the relationship between the abuser and victim." Recent government data reveal that as many as 3 million children in the United States are annually reported to child protective agencies as alleged victims of maltreatment and at least one third of these cases are confirmed. There are 210,000 incidents of child sexual abuse that occur every year (Wallace, 1996, p. 37). Data from the *Bureau of Justice Statistics Sourcebook* demonstrate that when physical abuse and not sexual abuse is examined, the majority of child abuse is by female care givers. This high rate of abuse includes abuse by single mothers. When child abuse occurs in a two-parent household the abuse is equally shared between women and men. The July 1994 Justice Department special report, *Murder in Families*, examined 8,000 homicides in 75 large urban counties and found that one third of family murders involved a female as the murderer. In sibling murders, females were 15% of the murderers, and in the murder of their parents 18%; in the murder of a spouse, 41%, and in the murder of children, 55% of the killers were the mother of the child. In 1992, a congressional committee reported an estimate that as many as 1.5 million elder Americans suffer from physical, psychological, or financial abuse. *The National Elder Abuse Incidence Study 1998* reports that 47% of the abusers of the elderly are women. Data demonstrate that this form of behavior, domestic violence, is displayed more by men than women. However, data also demonstrate that this behavior *is not exclusive to men only*. Data by government and private agencies can and should be carefully examined to expose bias and discover truths.

Domestic violence is an aberrant, sometimes pathological, and profoundly complicated form of social, economic, and institutional power and control behavior, regardless of the age or gender of the abuser or victim. There are now hundreds of studies, both public and private, that demonstrate, in varying degrees, that the majority of abusers are people who display one or more of the following behaviors:

1. Grew up in a violent home or environment
2. Have chronic alcohol and drug abuse problems
3. Lack interpersonal skills
4. Have low socioeconomic and/or educational status

5. Have high levels of anger and exhibit hostile behaviors that may be caused by a variety of antisocial behavioral and personality disorders, such as passive dependent/compulsive behavior and borderline personality.

In the past few decades, domestic violence has emerged as a major social, health, and law enforcement issue. Contemporary intervention programs include both public and private child and adult protective services, battered women's shelters, batterers programs, specific criminal justice laws and programs, victim-witness advocates focused on spousal abuse in health and criminal justice agencies, and child advocacy centers. Too often the victims of domestic violence discover that many of these intervention efforts consist of multifaceted, competing, and independent agencies, each with diverse policies and strategies, and they are often unconcerned or unaware of other agencies' goals. Many of these diverse agencies' successes or failures remain largely undocumented and unanalyzed, and their efforts remain uncoordinated (Chalk & King, 1998).

Violence in our homes between family members has long been considered a private family matter rather than a criminal matter. We as a society, and more specifically the civil and criminal justice systems, social service providers, health officials, and researchers, are just beginning to understand the causes and research the long-term consequences of domestic violence. Because of the fragmentation of services, the lack of cooperation between service providers, and problems with the study designs and methodology of researchers, it has been difficult if not impossible to determine the effectiveness of the interventions. Presently, there is little disagreement that reactive policies (civil, criminal justice system, and court mandated battering programs) rather than preventive strategies (proactive education and early health-care intervention) predominate (Chalk & King, 1998).

Over the last 20 years major changes have been made by the criminal justice system. Every state now allows for warrantless arrest by law enforcement officers in misdemeanor domestic violence cases. There is general agreement in law enforcement that their intervention in domestic violence is necessary to solve the problem. Law enforcement's role should be to rigorously enforce existing law, provide emergency intervention to stop the violence, and restore the peace. Law enforcement should further provide the victim with information regarding what other agencies are available for further assistance.

In all 50 states, civil protective or restraining orders designed to augment criminal prosecution are also available for victims of domestic abuse. It is the intent of these policies that sanctions against abusers will act as a deterrent by demonstrating that criminal sanctions would occur if abusers violated a restraining order or abused a family member. It was further anticipated that these criminal sanctions would create a deterrent affect not only on the abuser and prevent the abuser from repeating the act, but that they would also deter others in society who might have a desire to commit the same type of criminal behavior. The July 1998 National Institute of Justice Research in Brief, *Preventing Crime: What Works, What Doesn't, What's Promising*, reports that studies demonstrate that arresting abusers reduces repeat domestic abuse by employed suspects as well as people who "have roots in the community." The arrest of abusers who have a history of criminal behavior, or unemployed suspects, seems to have had less success, and, in fact, the arrest process may cause higher rates of repeat offense. Batterer intervention programs were established in the late 1970s, as rape crisis centers, women's shelters, and feminists called attention to the victimization of women because of spousal abuse. The use of batterer intervention programs or court imposed sanctions is increasingly becoming a condition of probation in many jurisdictions. It is here, in battering intervention, that the origins, causes, and proper interventions of domestic violence are most intensely debated. There is general agreement that there are three theoretical categories. Although few batterers programs claim to promulgate a single theory, there is little disagreement that the majority have profeminist affiliation, and hence almost all such programs favor the feminist educational approach designed for male clients only (Healy & Smith, 1998).

In *Family Violence: Legal, Medical, and Social Perspectives*, Harvey Wallace writes that most researchers agree that there are three categories of domestic violence theories of spousal abuse that locate the cause, and hence the cure, differently: (1) the psychiatric classifications that examine and analyze the abuser's personality traits and mental status; (2) the social-psychological classifications that examine and analyze external factors that affect families, such as individual stress, family stress, and the typology of family interaction; and (3) the sociocultural classifications that focus on the social and familial interaction between men and women and the cultural acceptance of the role of violence in society. All major evaluations have produced data that demonstrate that the majority of men who successfully complete a structured educational program do not abuse their partner during the 6 to 18 months following completion. Favorable evaluations supporting the use of batterers programs also demonstrate their imperfections. Studies report that it is not unusual for one third to one half of the men to drop out after the first session. In one recent evaluation, over 500 men initially contacted the program over a 12-month period. Of these, only 283 completed the intake process, and of that number, only 153 completed the program. In the final analysis, only 20% of those who contacted the program completed it successfully. Most researchers concur that the majority of these studies are inconclusive because of methodological problems. Studies that are methodologically sound have produced only modest results (Edleson, 1995).

There are many controversies that continue to contentiously rage among feminists, scholars, academics, and other professionals concerning the definition, causal factors, and proper remedy of domestic violence. However, one proposition that creates little debate is that this form of abusive behavior requires additional research before we determine all of its ramifications. Another proposition that causes little to no disagreement is that however domestic violence manifests itself, it is aberrant and unacceptable behavior. Psychologists in hospitals, clinics, and a myriad of agencies both public and private already provide clinical and counseling services to people who display these forms of behavior. They also provide numerous services for the victims of abuse. As counselors, clinicians, and researchers, psychologists have much to contribute to a clearer understanding of personality and behavioral typologies and characteristics of abuses. Often, members of the medical profession are the first to come into contact with victims of domestic violence. They must understand and recognize not only the physical, emotional, and psychological symptoms of the victims, because of the criminalization of domestic violence they must now appreciate how their role can relate to both the civil and criminal justice system and prepare themselves for that eventuality.

To end this multilayered, complex, and contentious dilemma, the identification of abuse and treatment interventions must not continue to take precedence over preventive strategies. Proper progress will not be made until there is a national collective method of implementation that all researchers, the civil and criminal justice systems, and service providers are willing to accept.

[*See also* Child Abuse and Neglect; Family Violence; *and* Violence and Aggression.]

Bibliography

Chalk, R., & King, P. A. (Eds.). (1998). *Violence in families.* Washington, DC: National Academy Press.

Edleson, J. L. (1995). *Do batterers' programs work?* Available Web site: http://www.mincava.umn.edu/papers/battrx.htm

Healy, K. M., & Smith, C. (1998). *Batterer programs: What criminal justice agencies need to know.* Available Web site: http://www.ncjrs.org/txtfiles/171683.txt

Miller, N. (1998). *Domestic violence legislation affecting police and prosecutor responsibilities in the United States. Infer-*

ences from a 50-state review of state statutory codes. Available Web site: http://www.ilj.org/dv/DVVAW.HTM

Straus, M. A., & Gelles, R. J. (1990). *Physical violence in American families.* New Brunswick, NJ: Transaction Books.

Swisher, K. L. (Ed.). (1996). *Domestic violence.* San Diego, CA: Greenhaven Press.

Wallace, H. (1996). *Family violence: Legal, medical, and social perspectives.* Boston: Allyn & Bacon.

Richard L. Davis

DONDERS, FRANCISCUS CORNELIS (1818–1889), Dutch physiologist and ophthalmologist. Born in Tilburg, he attended a village school and a monastery before entering a military medical school and beginning study of medicine at the University of Utrecht in 1835. Five years later he sat for his examination for doctor of medicine in Leyden and received the degree. Donders worked for several years as a military medical officer and began teaching and contributing to medical journals. In 1847, he was appointed professor extraordinary on the medical faculty at the University of Utrecht. His interest in physiological optics led him to the practice of ophthalmology. In 1852 he became ordinary professor at Utrecht and in 1858 opened a charity hospital that served as a research and educational institution attracting international attention and educating students who became outstanding practitioners. He accepted the professorship in physiology at Utrecht in 1862 but continued also as director of the hospital until 1883. Required to retire at age 80, he died soon thereafter.

Donders was a close friend and collaborator with many of the mid-nineteenth-century international set of physiologists who were forging ahead in establishing experimental physiology and medical science. He edited the *Nederlandsch Lancet* and with A. von Graefe served as coeditor of the *Archiv für Opthalmalogie* from 1855. His publications (numbering more than 340) covered a broad range of topics and included clinical observations, laboratory studies, theoretical explanations of physiological phenomena, and practical applications. His most influential investigations focused on theory and applied aspects of the physiology and pathology of the eye, from which came prescriptions on how to employ corrective glasses for farsightedness, nearsightedness, and astigmatism. The culmination of that work, *On the Anomalies of Accommodation and Refraction of the Eye* (1864), was published in London (translated by W. D. Moore) and widely recognized as a stellar contribution. Elected a foreign member of the Royal Society of London in 1866, he was also active as officer of and presider over scientific societies and assemblies, both in his own country and abroad.

Donders's contributions to experimental psychology included work done on color sense and color blindness, eye movements, and vowel sounds. He proposed a chemical-based theory of color vision and advanced a principle of visual fixation, known as "Donders's law," that continued to stimulate research in the 1990s. His prominence in the history of psychology, however, is largely based on his presentation of a procedure known as the subtractive method for studying "mental chronometry." He identified three types of reaction times to presented stimuli: simple reaction, discrimination-plus-choice reaction, and discrimination. Demonstrating that the time required to make each type of response can be measured, he proposed that the duration of mental processes for making discriminations between different stimuli could be determined by subtracting the simple reaction time from the discrimination reaction times. The enduring nature of his contribution is evident in the surge of scholarship that began in the 1960s on choice behavior, information processing, and reaction time, where Donders's 1868 paper is cited as the classic seminal work. In August 1968 the Donders Centenary Symposium on Reaction-Time, held at Eindhoven, Netherlands, attracted an international group of researchers whose works attest to the currency of Donders's innovation.

Bibliography

Bowman, W. (1891). In memoriam F. C. Donders. *Proceedings of the Royal Society, 49,* vii–xxiv.

Goodman, E. S. (1971). Citation analysis as a tool in historical study: A case study based on F. C. Donders and mental reaction times. *Journal of the History of the Behavioral Sciences. 7,* 187–191. Employs a quantitative method to assess use and recognition of Donders's pioneering work on reaction time by modern investigators.

Koster, W. D. (Ed.). (1969). *Attention and performance II.* Amsterdam: North Holland. Proceedings of the Donders Centenary Symposium, which includes a translation of Donders's 1868 classic paper on measurement of reaction times.

ter Laage, R.J.C.V. (1971). Donders, Franciscus Cornelis. In C. C. Gillespie (Ed.), *Dictionary of scientific biography* (Vol. 4, pp. 162–164). New York: Charles Schribner's Sons.

Pfeiffer, R. L. (1936). Frans Cornelis Donders, Dutch physiologist and ophthalmologist. *Bulletin of the New York Academy of Medicine, 12,* 566–581.

Elizabeth Scarborough

DOWN SYNDROME is a chromosomal disorder that affects the biopsychosocial functioning of approximately 300,000 U.S. citizens. Down syndrome ranks second to fragile X syndrome as the most frequent genetic cause of mental retardation. Although recognized by Edouard Seguin, a French physician and educator, as early as 1846, the first written description of the disorder was published in 1866 by John Langdon Down, a British physician from whom the syndrome derives its name. Jerome LeJeune, a French geneticist, and his colleagues established the genetic basis of Down syndrome in 1959.

Epidemiology

The incidence of Down syndrome has been estimated to be 1 in 700 to 1 in 1,000 live births. Down syndrome is evident prenatally and may be detected through chromosomal analysis derived from either chorionic villus sampling (at 8–10 weeks gestation) or amniocentesis (at 14–17 weeks gestation). Although less conclusive, low levels of maternal serum alpha-fetoprotein measured in the second trimester of pregnancy have been associated with the presence of a Down syndrome fetus. If prenatal diagnosis is not conducted, Down syndrome is generally determined soon after birth because health professionals are very familiar with its physical characteristics. Boys outnumber girls 1.3 to 1.0, and the disorder occurs in all racial and ethnic groups.

Ninety-five percent of Down syndrome is due to trisomy of chromosome 21. Trisomy results from nondisjunction or a failure of the two chromosomes of pair 21 to separate during meiosis prior to ovulation. In Down syndrome the nondisjunction is almost always maternal in origin (95% of cases), and is significantly related to increased maternal age. Five percent of Down syndrome results from translocation in which a portion of chromosome 21 attaches to another chromosome or from mosaicism due to an error in cell division soon after conception.

Clinical Characteristics

Affected individuals share, to varying degrees, a set of physical stigmata. The most common features of Down syndrome include microcephaly (small head), flattened face with a recessed bridge of the nose, upward slanting eyes, small ears and mouth, large tongue, short, broad hands and feet, stubby fingers, broad neck, stocky appearance, and loose skin folds at the nape of the neck. Down syndrome has a large number of associated medical problems including congenital gastrointestinal and cardiac abnormalities, obesity, diabetes, hypothyroidism, eye problems such as myopia, strabismus, nystagmus, and cataracts, mild to moderate conductive hearing loss secondary to chronic middle ear infections, sleep apnea, hair loss, and low muscle tone. Infants and young children with Down syndrome are also at increased risk for acute leukemia as compared to the general population.

There has been considerable study of the neuroanatomical aspects of Down syndrome. Research shows that the cortex and cerebellum are markedly reduced in overall size relative to matched controls. Moreover, there is an immaturity of brain development evident in both neurons and their synaptic connections. Comparative studies of people with Down syndrome and matched controls reveal underdevelopment of cerebellar, limbic, and frontal regions especially. A particularly interesting aspect of the disorder is the propensity for people with Down syndrome to manifest neurological abnormalities associated with Alzheimer's dementia. Investigators have suggested that the premature aging and neurological anomalies evident in Down syndrome might present a model for the study of Alzheimer's disease. Several longitudinal studies are currently underway to characterize the cognitive and behavioral changes that occur in older adults with Down syndrome, and to differentiate between precocious but normal aging and Alzheimer's disease.

Intellectual and Adaptive Functioning

Most people with Down syndrome function within the mild to moderate range of mental retardation on standardized intelligence tests. Some function in the borderline or low-average ranges, and only a few have severe mental retardation. They demonstrate greater deficits in verbal-linguistic skills relative to visuospatial skills. Delayed language acquisition has been linked to deceleration of overall intellectual development in longitudinal studies of infants and young children with Down syndrome. People with Down syndrome mosaicism typically have higher IQs, by 12 to 15 points on average, than people with trisomy 21. Performance on measures of adaptive behavior is generally commensurate with intellectual ability.

Developmental Aspects

Children with Down syndrome attain early developmental milestones at much later ages than typically developing children. In particular, children with Down syndrome have significantly delayed gross motor development, which has come to represent a cardinal behavioral feature of the syndrome. Independent sitting is usually attained at 1 year of age, whereas independent walking is not achieved until an average age of 2 years. Slow progress is also noted in early language development, particularly in language production.

Early clinical descriptions of people with Down syndrome propagated a behavioral stereotype that has not been supported by empirical study. For example, the stereotype suggested that people with Down syndrome are highly sociable. Studies of sociability suggest that people with Down syndrome are not universally more sociable. Rather, sociability seems to be both age and gender dependent with young, particularly female, children being the most sociable. Similarly, there is inconsistent support for the belief that people with Down syndrome have a characteristically easy temperament. Although many people with Down syndrome are perceived as having an "easy temperament," there is also a restless, aggressive, and difficult to manage subgroup.

Studies of mother-child interactions reveal that children with Down syndrome generate fewer positive social signals, exhibit delayed responsiveness, and demonstrate less predictable responses than do typically developing children. In the absence of clear and frequent signals from their children, mothers of children with Down syndrome may be more likely than mothers of typically developing children to adopt a controlling and directive interactive style during naturalistic play. These studies demonstrate the interrelatedness of child characteristics and parental behavior, contribute greatly to professionals' understanding of delayed language and concept development, and suggest intervention techniques to enhance the quality of early interactions.

Adults with Down syndrome may reside in family homes, small-group homes in the community, or in situations of independent or semi-independent living. The majority of Down syndrome adults work in paid employment settings with some degree of support (e.g., supervision, training, or transportation). People with Down syndrome show interest in sexual expression and, therefore, sex education is an important issue. Although men with Down syndrome are sterile, women with Down syndrome are typically fertile and may deliver children with or without Down syndrome.

People with Down syndrome have a greater early mortality rate as compared to people of similar ages from the general population and to people with comparable levels of mental retardation due to other causes. Congenital heart disease contributes greatly to the increased early mortality rate, as do respiratory tract infections, leukemia, and congenital gastrointestinal tract anomalies. Children are at marked risk for early death. For example, a population-based study showed that children with Down syndrome between the ages of 1 and 9 years are approximately 17 times more likely to die than matched controls. Improved medical management of respiratory infection and congenital heart disease in young children with Down syndrome has significantly increased life expectancy. However, the average life expectancy for people with Down syndrome is still less than the general population. For example, 44% of people with Down syndrome are alive at age 60 as compared to 78% of the general population.

Psychological Disorders

Like other people with mental retardation, people with Down syndrome are susceptible to the full range of mental disorders evident in nonretarded people. Research has shown increased rates of conduct problems (e.g., oppositional behavior) during childhood, and greater risk for depression and dementia, perhaps of the Alzheimer's type, in adulthood. Depression may not be diagnosed because the family may attribute the depressive symptoms to Down syndrome, or misinterpret changes in cognitive and behavioral functioning as dementia. Researchers are working to establish new measures to facilitate accurate differential diagnosis.

Family Issues

The presence of a person with mental retardation can have a profound effect on all facets of family functioning. Although not a frequent focus of study in family research, there is a suggestion that families of people with Down syndrome may be better functioning than families with non-Down syndrome retarded children. Further research is necessary to determine the factors that account for greater adaptation among these families.

Prevention and Intervention

Down syndrome is incurable. The only current preventive strategy is termination of pregnancy, an option that is being used and may be affecting incidence rates. Infants and young children with Down syndrome are routinely involved in early intervention programs aimed at maximizing their developmental potential. Such participation has been shown to mitigate, to some degree, the developmental deceleration in intelligence described previously. School-age children and adolescents with Down syndrome benefit from academic curricula that embed reading, writing, and arithmetic skills within teaching of daily living and personal-social skills. The ability to care for oneself, maintain good interpersonal relationships, and exhibit appropriate work habits and behaviors is crucial to successful transition from school to work and from home to community living.

[See also Mental Retardation.]

Bibliography

Cicchetti, D., & Beeghly, M. (Eds.). (1990). *Children with Down syndrome*. Cambridge, England: Cambridge University Press.

Down syndrome prevalence at birth: United States, 1983–1990. (1994). *Morbidity and Mortality Weekly Report, 43,* 617–622.

Jernigan, T. L., & Bellugi, U. (1994). Neuroanatomical distinctions between Williams and Down syndromes. In S. H. Broman & J. Grafman (Eds.), *Atypical cognitive deficits in developmental disorders* (pp. 57–66). Hillsdale, NJ: Erlbaum.

Mundy, P., Kasari, C., Sigman, M., & Ruskin, E. (1995). Nonverbal communication and early language acquisition in children with Down syndrome and in normally developing children. *Journal of Speech and Hearing Research, 38,* 157–167.

Pueschel, S. M. (Ed.). (1988). *The young person with Down syndrome: Transition from adolescence to adulthood.* Baltimore, MD: Paul H. Brookes.

Pueschel, S. M., & Pueschel, J. K. (Eds.). (1992). *Biomedical concerns in persons with Down syndrome.* Baltimore, MD: Paul H. Brookes.

Rozien, N. J. (1997). Down syndrome. In M. L. Batshaw (Ed.), *Children with disabilities* (4th ed., pp. 361–376). Baltimore, MD: Paul H. Brookes.

Zigman, W., Silverman, W., & Wisniewski, H. M. (1996). Aging and Alzheimer's disease in Down syndrome: Clinical and pathological changes. *Mental Retardation and Developmental Disabilities Research Reviews, 2,* 73–79.

William E. MacLean, Jr.

DREAMS. [*This entry comprises three articles: a definition and description of the physiology of dreaming; a broad overview of the psychological theories of and research on dreaming; and a survey of various cross-cultural perspectives about the causes and significance of dreams and altered states of consciousness. See also the many independent entries that relate to or affect dreams*; Amnesia; Anger; Brain; Brain Imaging Techniques; Cognition; Consciousness and Unconsciousness; Daydreams; Emotion; Experimental Psychology; Fantasy; Fear and Terror; Hallucinations; Memory; Nightmares; Night Terrors; Psychoanalysis, *article on* Theories; Sleep; *and the biographies of Freud and Wundt.*]

Physiology

Modern sleep science and folk psychology concur in defining dreaming as a mental state which occurs in sleep and which is characterized by a rich panoply of sensory, motor, emotional, and cognitive experiences. When we dream we see, feel, and move through an entirely fabricated world that seems real despite the physical impossibility of some of the imagined events and despite the bizarre improbability of many others. Except for rare and evanescent instances of awareness of our true state (called lucidity), we are duped into believing ourselves awake. And, despite the vivid intensity of this virtual reality we have difficulty remembering our dreams unless we awaken promptly from REM sleep; even then, we may be aware that much content cannot be retrieved from memory.

A dream theory must thus account for the following formal aspects of cognition: (1) vivid imagery, especially vision and movement; (2) intense emotion, especially fear, elation, and anger; (3) delusional acceptance of dreams as real and as occurring as if in waking; (4) discontinuity and incongruity of plot times, places, and persons; and (5) the amnesia for most of these subjective experiences. [*See* Memory.] These five features suggest an analogy between dreaming and delirium, a clinical condition caused by organic brain dysfunction. [*See* Organic Mental Disorder.]

History of Dream Theory

Following eons of attribution of dreaming to extracorporeal agencies, such as the winged gods of the Greeks and the Christians' angels, thinkers of the eighteenth-century Enlightenment boldly proposed an entirely endogenous source of dreams; dreams could arise, they said, from the altered brain activity of sleep. But this theory was quickly eroded by the mysticism of the Romantic movement in the late eighteenth and early nineteenth centuries and found no solid empirical base until the mid-twentieth century.

With the birth of experimental psychology in the second half of the nineteenth century, the brain physiology thesis was enunciated again. The most explicit hypothesis was advanced by Wilhelm Wundt, who held that some brain functions were enhanced (i.e., those subserving visual image generation and emotion) while others were impaired (i.e., those subserving recent memory and self-reflective awareness). Following Wundt, Sigmund Freud at first lauded the brain physiology approach, but for lack of data, he later repudiated this thesis in favor of his psychoanalytic hypothesis that the bizarre features of dreaming were the result of the disguise and censorship of unacceptable unconscious wishes. Freud thus likened dreaming to neurosis rather than delirium.

Physiology of Dreaming

Only after Hans Berger's discovery of brain waves in 1928, and the subdivision of sleep into two distinct phases by Eugene Aserinsky and Nathaniel Kleitman in 1953, was a truly experimental approach to dream psychology possible. Although most of sleep was characterized by electroencephalogram (EEG) evidence of brain deactivation, or non-rapid eye movement sleep (NREM), periods of wakelike EEG activation and rapid eye movements (REMs) recurred at 90- to 100-minute intervals and occupied as much as 25% of sleep. It is the work that sprang from this discovery that established the strong correlation between REM sleep and dreaming, a correlation that has spawned current models relating the formal psychology of dreaming to its origins in the brain. Although dreamlike mentation has been shown to occur in many states including quiet waking, sleep onset, and even in NREM sleep, it is REM sleep that provides by far the most favorable physiological conditions for dreaming. For this reason, it is war-

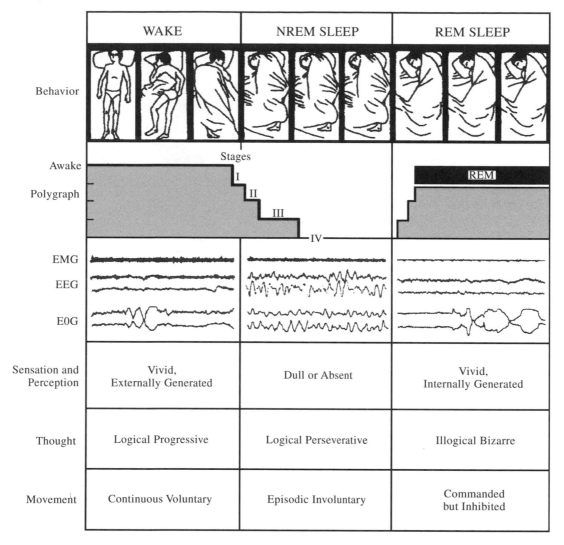

	WAKE	NREM SLEEP	REM SLEEP
Behavior			
Awake Polygraph	Stages I, II, III, IV		REM
EMG			
EEG			
E0G			
Sensation and Perception	Vivid, Externally Generated	Dull or Absent	Vivid, Internally Generated
Thought	Logical Progressive	Logical Perseverative	Illogical Bizarre
Movement	Continuous Voluntary	Episodic Involuntary	Commanded but Inhibited

DREAMS: Physiology. Figure 1. Behavioral states in humans. Body position changes during waking and at the time of phase changes in the sleep cycle. Removal of facilitation (during stages 1–4 of NREM sleep) and addition of inhibition (during REM sleep) account for immobility during sleep. In dreams, we imagine that we move, but no movement occurs. Tracings of electrical activity are shown in ~ 20 second sample records. The amplitude of the electromyogram (EMG) is highest in waking, intermediate in NREM sleep, and lowest in REM sleep. The electroencephalogram (EEG) and electrooculogram (EOG) are activated in waking and REM sleep and inactivated in NREM sleep.

ranted to scrutinize REM sleep neurophysiology for clues to the brain mechanisms of dreaming.

Cellular and Molecular Neurophysiology of REM

Because REM sleep is a brain state shared by all mammals, it is possible to conduct experiments in animals that reveal deep neurophysiological mechanisms of relevance to dream theory. Following Michael Jouvet's localization 1962, of the REM-sleep generator to the pontine brain stem and the simultaneous description of the chemical specificity of several brain-stem cell groups, the neuronal activity of that region (as well as many others) was described. Neurons containing the chemicals norepinephrine and serotonin were found to be active in waking but inactive in REM, while neurons containing acetylcholine were more active in REM than in waking. Both groups were relatively quiescent in NREM. These data were utilized to create two complementary models (see Figure 1).

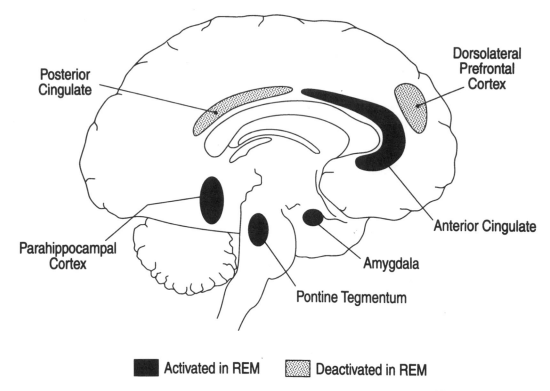

Activated in REM   **Deactivated in REM**

DREAMS: Physiology. Figure 2. Convergent findings on relative regional brain activation and deactivation in REM compared with waking. Schematic sagittal view of the human brain showing those areas of relative activation and deactivation in REM sleep compared to waking and/or NREM sleep. The depicted areas in this figure are representative portions of larger CNS areas subserving similar functions (e.g., limbic-related cortex, ascending activation pathways, and multimodal association cortex).

The first model, reciprocal interaction, ascribes REM to a decline of noradrenergic and serotonergic modulation and to the complementary increase in cholinergic neuromodulation of the brain. Neuromodulation determines the mode of information processing that the brain uses in response to different chemicals. In the reciprocal interaction model, waking consciousness (with its characteristic capacity for attention, analytic thought, and memory) is seen as dependent on the strong noradrenergic and serotonergic modulation of the brain that is lost in REM sleep dreaming (when all three of these wake-state characteristics are impaired). This model led to important chemical tests culminating in the experimental induction of REM (and of dreaming in human subjects) using cholinergic agonist drugs.

Like waking, REM sleep is a state of electrical activation of the brain. But in contrast to waking, both external inputs and motor outputs are blocked, while internal stimuli are generated by a cholinergic process and then processed by the aminergically demodulated forebrain as if the information arose in the outside world. This set of concepts gave rise to a second model: the activation-synthesis hypothesis of dreaming. Activation-synthesis ascribes the incongruity and discontinuity of dream cognition to both the chaotic nature of the cholinergic autostimulation process while the failure to recognize dreaming as different from waking is caused by the cognitive deficits resulting from aminergic demodulation.

To understand these concepts it is helpful to recognize that most psychoactive drugs used to alter mental state act via these same neuromodulatory systems. For example, stimulants (e.g., amphetamines) mimic aminergic neuromodulation, and the antidepressants (e.g., Prozac) enhance it by blocking the breakdown or reuptake of norepinephrine and/or serotonin.

The Human Brain and REM Sleep Dreaming

Recent positron emission tomography (PET) imaging studies of the human brain in REM have richly elaborated the physiological dream theory, besides showing the predicted activation of the pontine brain stem, a selective regional activation of the limbic forebrain, especially the amygdala, which are known to be mediators of emotion, especially fear and anxiety, and these are the most common dream emotions. Neuropsychological investigations have simultaneously revealed that when these regions are damaged by stroke lesions, there is a global loss of dreaming. [See Brain Imaging Techniques.]

Taken together, these two complementary data sources indicate that the distinctive character of dreaming, particularly the emotional intensification and the cognitive bizarreness, may derive from direct and preferential activation of the limbic brain by cholinergic inputs from the brain stem. The failure of memory and of directed and critical thought could then be due to the inability of the dreaming brain to control and integrate the emotional activation. This deficit process is evidenced in one PET study by a relative deactivation of the prefrontal cortex in REM compared to waking. This observation also helps explain the loss of self-reflective awareness and the delusion that we are awake when we dream because the dorsolateral prefrontal cortex is the seat of working memory and directed thoughts. As for the visual imagery of dreams, it is significant that both PET studies find as much activation of the medial occipital cortex in REM as in waking and that stroke lesions of this region render dreaming less vivid.

These approaches and extensions of them, which use pharmacological probes to assess neuromodulator receptor activation, can now be further exploited. They could then quantify the regional differentiation of brain chemistry associated with the shift in neuromodulatory balance from aminergic dominance in waking to cholinergic dreaming in REM. Other hypotheses, such as the prediction of frontal activation in REM when dreamers become aware that they are dreaming, may also be testable using imaging technology. The great promise of this physiological approach to dreaming is to provide a unified model of normal and abnormal states of consciousness.

Bibliography

Aserinsky, E., & Kleitman, N. (1953). Regularly occurring periods of ocular motility and concomitant phenomena during sleep. *Science, 118,* 361–375.

Berger, H. (1930). Über das Elektrencephalogram des Menschen. Zweite Mitteilung. *J. Psych. Neur., 40,* 160–179.

Hobson, J. A. (1988). *The dreaming brain.* New York: Basic Books.

Hobson, J. A. (1989). *Sleep.* New York: Scientific American Library.

Hobson, J. A. (1998). *Consciousness.* New York: Scientific American Library.

Hobson, J. A. (1999). *The chemistry of conscious states.* Cambridge, MA: MIT Press.

Hobson, J. A. (1999b). Sleep and dreaming. In R. Y. Moore & E. M. Stricker (Eds.), *Fundamental neuroscience.* San Diego, CA: Academic Press.

Jouvet, M. (1962). Recherche sur les structures nerveuses et les mechanismes responsables des differentes phases du sommeil physiologique. *Archives Italiennes de Biologie, 100,* 125–206.

Allan Hobson

Theories and Research

Dreams occur during a state of sleep from which one must first awaken before being able to describe them. In the course of the transition from sleep to waking, features of the dream are forgotten and a substantial part of the dream is transformed and distorted. To make matters worse, the reported events in the dream, or its content, have little relation to the physical or mental stimuli impinging on the dreaming sleeper and few dream events seem ever to have occurred, or could ever occur, in real life. This situation means that most of the powerful research tools of experimental psychology cannot be used effectively to study dreaming. The mere act of presenting the stimulus alters the sleeping state of the subject, as does the act of making a response. If the dreamer does respond to the stimulus, the response may have such a remote relation to the stimulus that a complex judgment is required to distinguish it from other imaginal events in the dream. Further, the time required before the subject returns to a state where a second stimulus can be delivered may allow only four data samples a night, so that even when useful data can be obtained, the cost of running such studies is prohibitive.

Under these circumstances assumptions about how the dream is produced and what it means are strongly dependent on theories about waking cognitive events and processes. In cultures where the belief in communication with the supernatural is strong, people believe that dreams are messages from the spirit world. Starting with the Greek Enlightenment there were efforts to find a nonsupernatural explanation for the dream. Hippocrates suggested that the dream might provide early diagnostic evidence for disease, and Plato remarked that the dream was evidence of primitive or beastlike characteristics in each of us. This conception reappears in nineteenth-century German poetry, and Freud used it to account for hysterical behavior in otherwise circumspect young women. The opposition of rigid conformity and sexual freedom was a powerful issue in the late nineteenth-century Victorian and Viennese middle class. Freud's famous work, *The Interpretation of Dreams* (1900/1953), is based on the assumption that the parts of the mind that represent social strictures (i.e., the superego), and one's *sexuality* (the libido), play out this conflict during sleep when the ego, the most rational part of the mind, is taking a rest. The dream represents the imaginal characteristics of this conflict. Freud seemed confident that every detail in a dream narrative could be interpreted in a way that was consonant with his theory. His consummate skill in inventing plausible explanations of the relationships between events in his patients' dreams, their waking lives, and his theory of neurosis is so remarkable that his scientific stature has been likened by some to that of the physicist Einstein. Some of Freud's colleagues felt that his account was too narrowly sexual. The Swiss psychologist Carl Jung proposed that many of the objects in dreams were universal symbols that could be taken as evidence for mind-brain biological inheritance of some symbols. The Austrian psychiatrist Alfred Adler asserted that feelings of interpersonal inferiority were also played out in the dream.

One hundred years after Freud wrote his masterpiece there is little scientific evidence to support his theory of the interpretation of dream images (Foulkes, 1985), nor is there any evidence that dreams convey messages from other minds. Lacking such evidence, one must ask why psychoanalysts or for that matter anyone continues to interpret dreams with such confidence. Part of the answer is that dreams are interpreted in the context of a substantial amount of information about the dreamer, her or his past behavior, desires, and life situation, and the dream interpretations are constrained by this information. Interpretations are also constrained by the theoretical assumptions and like experience of the interpreter. Freudian analysts tend to give more sexual interpretations than Adlerians, who in turn give more weight to feelings of interpersonal inferiority. As one can imagine, the interpretation of a dream depends on the joint contribution of many sources of information, only one of which is the dream itself. How these different sources of information are integrated to produce an interpretation is undoubtedly quite complex, and the extent to which the interpretation has to do with the dream itself is unknown. Although interpretations of a dream by different interpreters generally have little in common, interpreters nevertheless tend to feel remarkably confident about the accuracy of their interpretations. Perhaps this assurance is the reason why the interpretation process itself has not been systematically studied.

In the practice of psychotherapy, therapists and analysts say that they are aware of the relationships described by the dream well before the dream is reported. They use the dream less for obtaining information about the patient than for attributing the source of the information to the dreamer. Because people do not feel responsible for the dreams they produce, they can describe embarrassing relationships without taking responsibility for them. The therapist makes the interpretation but says to the patient, in effect, "You said it." Because the interpretation is attributed to the patient's dream, the patient may be more willing to accept it than if it were attributed only to the therapist's interpretation of his or her waking behavior.

The epic discovery in 1953 by Nathaniel Aserinsky, a doctoral degree student in physiology, and his mentor, Kleitman, the father of modern sleep research, marked the beginning of scientific study of dreaming as a neurocognitive process. Studying the electroencephalograph (EEG) and electrooculographs (EOGs) of the sleeper through the entire night, they noticed irregular periods of about 90 minutes in which the slow waves of early sleep returned to a wakelike pattern accompanied by rapid eye movements (REMs) under the closed lids. They called this REM sleep to distinguish it from several other stages of non-REM (NREM) sleep. Aserinsky assumed, as anyone else might have done under the same circumstances, that the sleeper was watching her or his dreams. Therefore, he systematically wakened subjects in REM and NREM sleep and found that long, visually vivid dreams were reported consistently from REM sleep and only rarely from NREM sleep, where the reports were much more thoughtlike. Antrobus (1983) found that 94% of REM reports are more dreamlike than NREM reports matched by sleeper and time of night. The strength of this relationship was that it enabled the scientist to know with remarkable accuracy *when* the sleeper was dreaming. Thus, it became possible to look for physiological and neurophysiological processes that distinguish dreaming from nondreaming—without waking the sleeper for a report.

A single REM period often extends for over 30 minutes, during which time dreaming occurs continuously. Because a dream has no discrete beginning and end, research shifted from the study of the dream to the study of *dreaming* as a process over time. Because they were able to locate dreaming in time, Hoelscher, Klinger, and Barta (1981) were able to show experimentally that sleepers were more likely to incorporate into their dreams verbal stimuli that described personal concerns than stimuli without personal relevance.

Although they cannot report their dreams, subhuman species have provided substantial information about REM dreaming. For example, Jouvet and Michel (1959) demonstrated that when the normal REM sleep inhibition of efferent motor pathways was surgically inhibited in a cat, the animal would motorically act out its dream—hissing and attacking—apparently hallucinating its enemies.

One major line of early research concerned the consequences of dreaming and sleep deprivation. The initial finding that deprivation of REM sleep was followed on subsequent nights by the "makeup" time, almost to the minute, of the lost REM sleep, implied that dreaming sleep was absolutely essential for waking equilibrium, indeed, for survival (Dement, 1960). Interpretation of this and subsequent studies raised the obvious questions of mind versus body and efforts were made to assign processes to either one or the other. Dreaming, or dreaming sleep, was regarded as a compensatory process whose function is to "make up for" cognitive and motivational deficits in waking, including maturation and maintenance of the central nervous system, consolidation of memory, representation of repressed information, and the modulation of motivational systems (for an excellent review of this work, see Ellman & Weinstein, 1991).

Other investigators looked for psychophysiological parallelism across REM sleep and waking (Kerr, 1993). Neural systems that are genetically selected and then trained to carry out a specific process in the waking state should perform the same function in REM sleep. The REMs themselves were assumed to be part of a scanning or tracking process similar to that of waking saccades. An initial study by Roffwarg, Dement, Muzio, & Fisher (1962) supported the parallelism position but was discarded because of methodological problems. Several other studies found little or no supporting evidence. Weitzman (1982) once noticed a sleeper producing such a regular, extended sequence of right-left saccades that even though he was not studying dreaming he awakened him for a report. The sleeper said he was looking out of a window in a subway car and watching the posts in the tunnel as they went by. Anecdotes such as this kept the original hypothesis alive, and Herman (1992) eventually reported evidence for a limited relationship between eye movements and imaginal looking in the dream. Gardner, Grossman, Roffwarg, and Weiner (1975) found that periodic gross body movements also occur throughout REM sleep and are also weakly associated with imagined body movements in the dream.

Some evidence was clearly opposed to the parallelism model. Johnson found that skin potential and conductance measures that are characteristic of highly emotional states in waking are even more dramatic in Stage 4 of NREM sleep, where the sleeper is truly dead to the world. Stage 4 is a state in which some children have night terrors and awaken screaming. Prior to awakening, their EEG shows no sign of disturbance. Johnson suggested that the labile skin potential indices may occur in sleep because the processes that normally dampen them in the waking state have become too weak to maintain the appropriate modulation. Because night terrors tend to occur about an hour after falling asleep, waking the child after a half-hour of sleep will usually maintain the modulatory process and avoid the night terror.

The primary contradiction to psychophysiological parallelism within REM sleep, of course, is that the mind-brain is actively producing imagery and thought, and the EEG looks very much like that of the waking state; and yet, aside from occasional muscle twitches and REMs, the body looks as though it is in a coma! This is why the Europeans call it paradoxical sleep. The solution to this paradox was provided by Hobson and McCarley (1977) after extensive study of the brain-stem processes that controlled sleep and sleep states in the cat. In 1949, Moruzzi and Magoun located a region in the brain stem, the reticular activating system, that controlled the waking and sleep state of the entire brain. Hobson and McCarley found that during REM sleep most of this region was activated in turn by brain-stem nuclei in the locus coeruleus. But the nuclei that control REM sleep also broadly inhibit both sensory input from the sensory projection regions of the brain and motor commands issued by the brain. Only the cardiac, pulmonary, and oculomotor system are excluded from inhibition.

Although the Hobson and McCarley model is based on the behavior and brain neurophysiology of cats—who cannot report their dreams—it is compelling enough to account for the paradoxical relation between dreaming in humans as the product of an active brain state in the presence of motor flaccidity that is normally associated with an inactive brain.

Inhibition in this context means elevated sensory and neural thresholds. If a stimulus is sufficiently strong one can always waken a person from REM sleep. And in a nightmare, the dreamer's attempt to run can result in a brief twitch or jerk of the leg—which may terminate the REM period.

A second equally plausible component in their model has strong implications for theories of the meaning of dreams as well as for the parallelism models described above, but it is not supported by empirical research on dreaming. They observed during REM sleep a sequence of high-voltage spike bursts in the brachium conjunctivum, a branch connecting the cerebellum to the pons in the brain stem. The bursts were called PGO spikes because they start in the *p*ons and travel up through the lateral *g*eniculate nucleus of the thalamus to the *o*ccipital region of the cerebral cortex. During REM sleep, bursts of REMs are always accompanied by these PGO spikes. The possible implication of these spikes for the understanding of dreaming was enormous. The large voltage of the spikes relative to that of surrounding neurons suggested that they might account for the sudden changes of scene that make the dream seem bizarre. Furthermore, they claimed that the spike originated in the pons rather than in the cortex and argued that the absence of cortical participation in PGO spikes implied that the cortex could not be the source of or control REMs! The dream-producing cortex, Reinsel, Antrobus and Wollman (1992) argued, must receive information about REMs *after* they have occurred and must then "synthesize," that is, make sense of the information. Because the PGO spikes originate in the pontine brain stem, which has no cognitive memory, they argued that the PGO source was random and therefore that the source of the dream was also random, i.e., neural noise. However, they show no support for the PGO synthesis model.

The argument appeared to represent a double blow to the Freudian interpersonal theorists for whom dreams were initiated by basic biological and social conflicts. First, the occurrence of dreaming was determined by a biological 90-minute REM cycle, regardless of an individual's conflicts. If the source of the content of the dream was truly random, then personal conflictual material would be irrelevant.

Although subsequent research has not supported the REM synthesis model of dreaming, the model has spawned research in which brain neurophysiology rather than peripheral-physiological measures and models are used to build neurocognitive models of dreaming. One argument against the REM synthesis model is that while REMs occur during only a portion of any given REM period, reported dreaming occurs throughout the REM period. Therefore dreaming is partially *independent* of whether REMs are present.

If PGO spikes are not the origin of the dream, what is? The question implies a unitary mind-brain whose activity is determined only by external input. But the mind-brain is a quasi-modular system whose modules continuously send messages back and forth to one another. The question is, which modules participate in the construction of dreaming?

In waking perception, the primary visual cortex produces line and visual textures, the next layers produce edges and corners, and the parietal regions interpret the information as the shapes of objects. Other regions interpret the location of the object relative to the individual, the left temporal cortex names the object, and the frontal cortex helps to determine how to respond to it. But Braun et al. (1998), using a sensitive brain imaging technique during the early hours of sleep, have shown that while many of the visual and spatial cortical modules are active in REM sleep, the striate cortex is unexpectedly inactive. As expected the left temporal cortex is inactive, which accounts for why dreamers tend to name their visual images only after they awaken. Their description of the dreaming brain is a set of modules that are dissociated from other modules that are normally active in the waking state. Together with the evidence that the sensory and kinesthetic input to the brain is strongly attenuated in REM

sleep, this conception helps to understand how dreaming differs from waking imagery and thought. For example, if the visual system produces a face and the face is unfamiliar, and the dream setting is one's kitchen, the frontal cortex may interpret this as high risk—there's an unexpected stranger in the kitchen!—and the motor system may give orders to run fast. But the motor commands are inhibited in REM sleep and the sensory motor system gets no feedback that it is moving. The dreamer concludes that she is paralyzed or stuck. The oculomotor system sends commands to look where she is going, but the moved eyes are unable to elicit a new image on their retina. This scenario illustrates that the mind-brain has the capability of producing elaborate dreams without input external to itself. When mind-brain modules are active they send information to each other. The dream need not have a single origin in brain space or time.

One of the most important findings of the Braun group is that the amygdala and limbic-related projection areas that respond to waking threat and create emotional experience, and the parahippocampal cortices that produce short-term memory process, are quite active in REM sleep. The participation of these areas may explain the emphasis of dreaming on personally relevant threats based on events from the prior day. These structures may construct the emotions and memories that we "interpret" when, upon awakening, we note associations between dreaming and waking events (Antrobus & Conroy, 1999).

Although the distribution of activation among different modules changes with the demands of a task in the waking state, the distribution of activation during sleep appears to be determined primarily by the brainstem reticular formation. Although this distribution appears to be independent of voluntary control, the paradoxical phenomenon of lucid dreaming, where the dreamer reports being awake while still dreaming, suggests that, with training, it can also be elicited voluntarily (LaBerge, 1985).

The most vivid and bizarre dreams occur in the late morning hours, especially on the weekend when one tends to sleep in. Antrobus, Kondo, Reinsel, and Fein (1995) showed that these late-morning vivid dreams are caused by the joint activation effects of the 90-minute REM-NREM sleep cycle and the rising edge of the 24-hour diurnal cycle. Because the reticular activating system activates the cortex in both cycles, the superimposition of the cycles should magnify the imagery and thought characteristics of the normal REM-NREM cycle. This model was supported when subjects who slept three hours past their normal waking time in the laboratory reported visually vivid and unusually dramatic dreams. Verbal imagery, which is rare in normal REM periods, was reported in late-morning REM dreams. This suggests that it is the distributed pattern of mind-brain activation that determines the imaginal characteristics of the dream.

Knowledge about the participation of different brain regions is immensely helpful in roughing out the main components of a theory of dreaming. But how the individual neural clusters act upon one another to create a stream of credibly integrated meaning cannot be determined by these relatively gross measures. Within the last 15 years, Rumelhart, Smolensky, McClelland, and Hinton (1986) have developed computational models of artificial neural networks that have begun to show us how information distributed across a large number of neural units can be combined in novel yet coherent ways. In demonstrating how a complete percept can be instantiated even though only a small fraction of the neurons that belong to the percept are initially activated, these models demonstrate how the brain might create an entire visual image even though no external sensory information was present (Antrobus, 1991). The active brain consists of a network of pattern-recognizing modules that can continuously transform even chaotic neural activity into coherent patterns of image, meaning, and desire. When this process is experienced during sleep, we call the sequence of coherent patterns our dream.

Bibliography

Antrobus, J. S. (1983). REM and NREM sleep reports: Comparison of word frequencies by cognitive classes. *Psychophysiology, 20,* 562–568.

Antrobus, J. S. (1991). Dreaming: Cognitive processes during cortical activation and high afferent thresholds. *Psychological Review, 98,* 96–121.

Antrobus, J. S., & Conroy, D. (1999). Dissociated neurocognitive processes in dreaming sleep. *Sleep and Hypnosis, 2,* 105–111.

Antrobus, J., Kondo, T., Reinsel, R., & Fein, G. (1995). Summation of REM and diurnal cortical activation. *Consciousness and Cognition, 4,* 275–299.

Aserinsky, E., & Kleitman, N. (1953). Regularly occurring periods of ocular motility occurring during sleep. *Science, 118,* 273–274.

Braun, A. R., Balkin, T. J., Wesensten, N. L., Gwadry, F., Carson, R. E., Varga, M., Baldwin, P., Belenky, G., & Herscovitch, P. (1998). Dissociated pattern of activity in visual cortices and their projections during human rapid eye movement sleep. *Science, 279,* 91–95.

Dement, W. C. (1960). The effect of dream deprivation. *Science, 131,* 1705–1707.

Ellman, S. J., & Weinstein, L. N. (1991). REM sleep and dream formation: A theoretical integration. In S. Ellman & J. S. Antrobus (Eds.), *The mind in sleep* (2nd ed., pp. 466–488). New York: Wiley.

Foulkes, D. (1985). *Dreaming: A cognitive-psychological analysis.* Hillsdale, NJ: Erlbaum.

Freud, S. (1953). The interpretation of dreams. In J. Strachey (Ed. & Trans.), *The standard edition of the complete psychological works of Sigmund Freud* (Vols. 4–5). London: Hogarth Press. (Original work published 1900)

Gardiner, R., Grossman, W., Roffwarg, H., & Weinewr, H. (1975). The relationship of small limb movements during REM sleep to dreamed limb action. *Psychosomatic Medicine, 37,* 147–159.

Herman, J. H. (1992). Transmutative and reproductive properties of dreams: Evidence for cortical modulation of brain-stem generators. In J. Antrobus & M. Bertini (Eds.). *The neuropsychology of sleep and dreaming* (pp. 251–264). Hillsdale, NJ: Erlbaum.

Hinton, G. E., Dayan, P., Frey, B. J., & Neal, R. M. (1995). The "wake-sleep" algorithm for unsupervised neural networks. *Science, 268,* 1158–1161.

Hobson, J. A., & McCarley, R. W. (1977). The brain as a dream state generator: An activation-synthesis hypothesis of the dream process. *American Journal of Psychiatry, 134,* 1335–1348.

Hoelscher, T. J., Klinger, E., & Barta, S. G. (1981). Incorporation of concern- and nonconcern-related verbal stimuli into dream content. *Journal of Abnormal Psychology, 90,* 88–91.

Jouvet, M., & Michel, F. (1959). Correlations electromyographiques du sommeil chez le chat decortique et mesencephalique chronique. *Compte Rendu Sociologie et Biologie (Paris) 153,* 422–425.

Kerr, N. (1993). Mental imagery, dreams, and perception. In C. Carvallero & D. Foulkes. (Eds.), *Dreaming as cognition.* Hemel Hempstead, Hertfordshire, U.K.: Simon & Schuster/Harvester Wheatsheaf.

LaBerge, S. (1985). *Lucid dreaming.* Los Angeles: Jeremy Tarcher.

Moruzzi, G., Magoun, H. W. (1949). Brainstem reticular formation and activation of the electroencephalogram. *Electroencephalography and Clinical Neurophysiology, 1,* 455–473.

Reinsel, R., Antrobus, J., & Wollman, M. (1992a). Bizarreness in sleep and waking mentation. In J. Antrobus & M. Bertini (Eds.), *The neuropsychology of dreaming sleep* (pp. 157–186). Hillsdale, NJ: Erlbaum.

Roffwarg, I., Dement, W., Muzio, J., & Fisher, C. (1962). Dream imagery: Relationship to rapid eye movements of sleep. *Archives of General Psychiatry, 7,* 235–258.

Rumelhart, D. E., Smolensky, P., McClelland, J. L., & Hinton, G. E. (1986). Schemata and sequential thought processes in PDP models. In D. E. Rumelhart & J. L. McClelland (Eds.). *Parallel distributed processing, 2* (pp. 7–57). Cambridge, MA: MIT Press.

Weitzman, E. D. (1982). Personal communication.

John S. Antrobus

Cross-Cultural Perspectives

Since the development of systematic research on different phases of sleep by Aserinsky and Kleitman in the 1950s, it has been known that not only all humans but indeed all mammals dream several times a night and in specific sleep stages. Dreaming is primarily associated with rapid eye movement (REM) sleep. Human societies vary widely in the attention they pay to dreams, the degree to which they cultivate memory of dreams, whether or not dreams are shared, how much specialized practice of dream interpretation exists, what catalogue of dream symbols there may be, and so forth.

In the contemporary United States, it appears, dreams are generally dismissed as unimportant. This is part of a Western philosophical tradition that can be traced back to Aristotle. However, there also exists a contrary trend: there are dream groups and people who keep dream diaries. Specialized interest in dreams exists, specifically in connection with certain forms of psychotherapy, particularly in the Freudian and Jungian traditions. There are also popular dream books, some purporting to be of ancient or medieval origins, which are sometimes used as aids to gambling, predicting the future, or for other forms of divination. While we understand that dreams are intimate, private productions of individuals, it is clear that their content, experience, use, and interpretation are decisively influenced by the culture in which the dreamer lives.

Dreaming in Traditional Societies

In contrast to the devaluation of dreams in Western rationalist philosophies, dreams are assigned a special status in many traditional societies, including those to which our own is heir. Dreams are reported and interpreted in the Bible, as, for example, in the story of Joseph and his brothers and Joseph's adventures in Egypt. There are traditions of dream interpretations in Greek and Roman classical antiquity as well as in the Middle Ages. Other classical traditions, such as that of the Upanishads of India, also accord importance to dreams.

Anthropologists and others have long collected and reported dreams and theories of dreaming from traditional societies in all parts of the world. In one of the earliest comparative studies of dreams, J. S. Lincoln (1935) collected dreams from eight Native American groups. He distinguished between individual, unsought dreams, and what he termed "culture-pattern dreams." The latter category of dreams have major symbolic significance for the individual and often for the society as well. They may be considered to be supernatural revelations and reaffirm traditional understandings or launch innovations in both religious and political institutions. The manifest content of dreams is rarely taken literally; instead there may be rules for the interpretation of dreams and various dream elements may be assigned symbolic meaning. It is important to note that there is no universal consensus on what specific elements mean. For example, Tedlock (1987) notes how the same dream of being given food might be assigned opposite interpretations among two Native American groups. Among the Quiché Maya of Guatemala it is thought to be a good dream, while among the Zuni of New Mexico, it would be interpreted as predicting death.

Theories of dreaming vary widely and are part of a larger understanding of events and experiences, of cosmology and the relations between human beings and other beings in the universe. In Haitian folk belief, dreams are important sources of information about reasons for "bad luck" (illness, job loss, or other critical events), and they are to be interpreted by a specialist, who finds messages from spirits or dead ancestors in the dreams. The very experience of having (or remembering) many dreams is understood as a sign of supernatural calls for rituals, sacrifices, initiations, or other actions. Some actions may take place within the dream itself.

Since the individual is often thought of as consisting of various components, often translated as "souls," the question arises as to what part of the person does the dreaming. In Haitian folk belief, the dream is the experience of one of two "souls." With regard to the Mekeo of New Guinea, Stephen (1995) speaks of the "dream-self," which leaves the body and has the experiences of the dream. Where dreams are calls to ritual actions among Haitians, for the Mekeo they are primarily omens, often announcing the death of someone. Among these people, the very act of dreaming may be considered dangerous.

In studying dreams cross-culturally, many contextual questions may be asked: Are the events of dreams thought to be real, that is, equal in some way to actions of the waking individual? If so, how must they affect the actions to be taken by the individual? How do the experiences of the dreamer relate to the dreamer's self? Are they predictive? Do they require action? Are the accounts to be shared with others or to be kept secret? Are dreams a means of communication with the dead, with ancestors, with supernatural beings? Are dreams guides to dealing with life situations? Are dreams used for problem solving? Are there specialists in the interpretation of dreams and do they play a significant role in the group—perhaps as diagnosticians or healers?

Some examples may be helpful. Among the people of the Colombian village of Arimatima, we are told that many dream symbols refer to the death of relatives. At the same time, to dream of the death of one's mother, of dead people, graves, and so forth, is a prediction of happiness, and to dream of other people's death portends wealth. A somewhat similar view of dream symbols is held by the Pokoman of Guatemala. Here it is also believed that dreams are the real actions of the soul.

Among some people, dream sharing is considered of great importance. Among the Alorese of Indonesia a household may be roused one or more times at night when some member wishes to share a dream. Dream sharing also is of importance among the Mekeo of New Guinea, where dreams are intimately involved with magic.

It has often been noted that, as narratives, myths and dreams share certain characteristics. In some societies, for example among the Hopi people of the American Southwest, as studied by Dorothy Eggan (1966), myths are used in the construction of "dream stories," which consist of the remembered content of a dream together with the dreamer's associations to it. The relationship between myths and dreams may be a reciprocal one, that is, mythic material may be used in the construction of dreams, and elements from the dreams of some individuals may be accepted into the mythic repertoire of a community. This is the case among Haitian participants in the Vodou religion. Here, too, at least some dreams are treated as equal to waking actions, as accounts of actions by the spirits or ancestors, warning of dangers and so forth.

It is known that life experiences ("day residues") find their way into dreams. In addition, elements of concern in daily life enter into the manifest content of dreams. In some societies, action taken by the dreamer in a dream may be thought of as dealing with a given situation, particularly one involving supernaturals. Such actions are then thought of as equivalent in reality status to waking actions.

The Social Uses of Dreams

As noted, the interpretation of dreams may be used by specialist in assisting individuals in the resolution of problems, including the healing of illnesses. In Haiti, as in the other African American regions of the Caribbean and Latin America, dreams may be interpreted as calling for initiation into religious groups (Vodou, Santería, Xangô, etc.). Among the Iroquois, dreams used to be interpreted as "the wishes of the soul" and called for the accomplishment of actions that the dream proposed. It was thought that if these actions were not carried out, the dreamer would suffer. Since, however, the wishes of the soul were not always clear, diagnostic and interpretive procedures had to be enacted.

Among North American Indian groups, a guardian spirit was sought by adolescent boys through the "vision quest." This involved isolation, fasting, and other elements of sensory deprivation. It is difficult to distinguish whether these visions were indeed dreams or waking dreams (visions, hallucinations). Among the Ojibwa a series of four night dreams was required to become a medicine man or conjurer. It is clear that in these cases preparation and anticipation were able to influence the content of the dreams or visions and the achievement of the desired goal. The quest and the dream were part of the socialization of young men, giving them the kind of confidence they required in their mature lives. The North American vision quest is

part of a worldwide complex which d'Andrade has referred to as "the use of dreams to seek and control supernatural power" (1961, p. 326).

In situations of rapid social change, dreams have often played an important role in the development of leaders, their innovations, and their revelations of new social programs. This is partly related to the creative imagination that dreams give play to, and partly to the authority dreams have where they are interpreted as supernatural messages. The cargo cults of Melanesia and New Guinea offer a number of examples of such dream inspirations.

While dreams occur spontaneously, and most are not remembered, interpreted, or consciously controlled by the dreamer, it is clear that there are cultural styles of dreaming and that persons can learn to control their dreams. "Lucid dreaming" is a process whereby the individual is aware of dreaming and controls the course of the dream. This is a learned skill and is often associated with shamanism. More generally, as is particularly clear with regard to "culture-pattern dreams," both the content and the very experience of dreams is influenced by what people believe about dreams and by their experience of daily life. The experience of the dream is often transformed by the very act of recording or telling it, putting it into words and often partially analyzing it in the process, according to prevailing beliefs.

Group Studies

The study of individuals' dreams by anthropologists has often been influenced by psychoanalytic approaches and has been conducted as part of life history research, or, more rarely, of psychotherapy. As such, the analysis of symbols and interpretation has played an important role. G. Devereux, both anthropologist and psychoanalyst, worked as a therapist with a Plains Indian veteran. He notes that in people of that cultural tradition, profuse dreaming may be seen not as a sign of anxiety, as in some other groups, but as part of the tradition of the vision quest. By contrast, some social science studies of dreams from given populations have focused instead on the manifest content of dreams and considered the relationship between it and some aspects of the sample population's situation. For example, in studies of groups in conflict situations, anxiety over being attacked appears clearly. In the 1930s, L. Sharp collected a large number of dreams among the Yir Yoront, a group of Australian Aborigines. Analyzing this sample more than 30 years later, D. Schneider (1965) found that in the majority of dreams with themes of aggression it was the dreamer who was the victim, expressing a fear of being attacked rather than a wish to harm others. Similarly, in a study of Jewish and Arab children in Israel and on the West Bank, during the years 1980–1984, Y. Bilu (1994) found that these children expressed in their dreams the themes of the ongoing conflict. Again, the children tended to dream of themselves as victims rather than perpetrators of aggression. Such dreams were more frequent among the Arab children than among the Jewish children.

Dreams and dreaming offer fertile sources of information about psychological development and adaptation; cultural differences and similarities; the use of intrapersonal and interpersonal dimensions to control the environment; human creativity and innovation; means of self-expression and communication; and many more aspects of psychological functioning.

Bibliography

Bilu, Y. (1994). The other as nightmare: The Israeli Arab encounter in children's dreams. In I. S. Lustick (Ed.) *Religion, culture and psychology in Arab-Israeli relations.* New York: Garland.

Bourguignon, Erika (1972). Dreams and altered states of consciousness in anthropological research. In F. L. K. Hsu (Ed.). *Psychological anthropology* (2nd ed., pp. 404–434). Cambridge, MA: Schenkman.

D'Andrade, R. G. (1961). Anthropological studies of dreams. In F. L. K. Hsu (Ed.). *Psychological anthropology.* Homewood, IL: Dorsey.

Devereux, G. (1951). *Reality and dream.* New York: International Universities Press.

Eggan, D. (1966). Hopi dreams in cultural perspective. In G. G. von Grunebaum and R. Caillois (Eds.). *The dream in human society.* Berkeley and Los Angeles: University of California Press.

Lincoln, J. S. (1935). *The dream in primitive cultures.* Baltimore, Maryland: Williams and Wilkins.

O'Nell, C. W. (1976). *Dreams, culture and the individual.* San Francisco: Chandler and Sharp.

Schneider, D., & Sharp, L. (1969). The dream life of a primitive people: The dreams of the Yir Yoront of Australia. Anthropological Studies Number 1. W. Goodenough (Ed.). American Anthropological Assoc. Ann Arbor, MI: University Microfilms.

Stephen, M. (1995). *A'aissa's gifts: A study of magic and the self.* Berkeley: University of California Press.

Tedlock, B. (Ed.). (1987). *Dreaming: Anthropological and psychological interpretations.* Cambridge: Cambridge University Press.

Tedlock, B. (1994). The evidence from dreaming. In P. K. Bock (Ed.). *Handbook of psychological anthropology* (pp. 279–296). Westport, CT: Greenwood.

Erika Bourguignon

DREVER, JAMES (1873–1950), Scottish psychologist. Drever was born on the island of Shapinsay, one of the Orkney Islands, off the coast of Scotland. He received his doctorate from Edinburgh University. Much of his early work was in education; however, in 1918 his focus shifted to psychology with his appointment as department head and lecturer in Psychology at Edinburgh University. In 1931, a chair in psychology was established to which he was appointed, thus becoming the first professor of psychology at Edinburgh University. In his 27 years at Edinburgh, Drever played a major role in the development and recognition of the psychology department as a first-rate academic program.

Drever wrote books and articles covering a diverse range of topics. These included his *Instinct In Man* (1916), *The Psychology of Everyday Life* (1921), *The Psychology of Industry* (1921), *A First Laboratory Guide in Psychology* (with Mary Collins, 1926), and *A Dictionary of Psychology* (1952), published after his death.

Drever was also extremely active in the community. In 1925, he established a clinic to address juvenile delinquency in the local community. The clinic was a multidisciplinary collaboration of volunteers from the psychology department and experts in other fields. The success of this clinic lead to the development of other child guidance clinics across the country. Drever is also credited with developing a battery of psychological selection tests for apprentice printers. Once again, the success of this venture was such that its use spread to organizations in other areas of Scotland and England.

Drever was also instrumental in developing methods that aided in the instruction of children with special needs. One outcome of these endeavors was the development of a test to assess the abilities of both deaf and hearing children for the purposes of instruction and vocational guidance. This test was used extensively throughout Great Britain and its empire. He also served as chairman of the Royal Blind Asylum and School in Edinburgh, where he was instrumental in developing improvements in the teaching and care of blind children. Drever's contributions to the training of the blind also extended to his involvement in the establishment of a training center for blind war veterans that later became the Scottish National Institute for Blinded Ex-Servicemen.

Drever held a number of important and influential positions in professional associations. These included president of the British Psychological Society, president of the Psychology Section of the British Association for the Advancement of Science, member of the National Advisory Council for Scotland on Physical Training, editor of the *British Journal of Psychology Monographs*, and assistant editor of the *British Journal of Psychology*.

In all of the endeavors with which he has been associated, Drever is credited with having a significant and positive influence on the policies and quality of work provided by these enterprises. The significance of his contributions to psychology, both in its development as a science and as an educator of future psychologists, has been acknowledged by his peers (e.g., Collins, 1951, *The Psychological Review*). Furthermore, although much of his work was done in his native Scotland, the far-reaching effects of Drever's contributions to psychology and society are aptly demonstrated by his being knighted by the king of Norway in 1938.

Bibliography

Collins, M. (1951). James Drever: 1873–1950. *The Psychological Review, 58* (1), 1–4.

Drever, J. (1932). James Drever. In C. Murchison (Ed.), *A history of psychology in autobiography* (Vol. 2) (pp. 17–34). Worcester, MA: Clark University Press.

Watson, R. I. (1974). James Drever. In *Eminent contributers to psychology: A bibliography of primary references* (Vol. 1). New York: Springer. Contains list of many of Drever's more noted books and articles.

Anthony R. Paquin

DRIVE. One of the central aspects of Freud's concept of mind is that it can be motivated or activated both by external stimulation from the environment or endogenous stimuli, which he termed drive. Freud conceptualized drives as what cause or motivate the mental apparatus to act. For Freud, drives function in accordance with the pleasure principle that dictates that human beings seek maximal pleasure by reducing drive tension through their action. Freud identified two separate drives, libido and aggression, which he attributed to somatic sources. Over the course and evolution of psychoanalytic theory, Freud's original definition of drive as motivation has remained, though the governing principles of how drives are directed has changed a great deal. Ronald Fairbairn (1952) suggested that drives are directed toward contact with others as primary sources of motivation. Fairbairn also suggested that the pleasure principle is not the primary source of motivation and that human beings seek contact with others as an inherent and primary source of motivation.

The Freudian Concept of Drive

For Freud, drives have a somatic source but create a psychic effect or result. Freud wrote that drives are "on the frontier between the mental and the somatic . . . a measure of the demand made upon the mind for work, in consequence of its connection with the body" (1915, p. 122). In other words, drive is a mythological concept used to understand the relationship between psyche and soma. In "The New Introductory Lectures on Psycho-Analysis," Freud was explicit about the mythological nature of the drive concept. He wrote:

> The theory of drives is what might be called our mythology. The drives are like mythical creatures, magnificent in their indefiniteness. In our work we cannot disregard them for a moment, yet we are never sure that we have a clear view of them. (1933, p. 95)

Libido and aggression each have a somatic source. The sources for libido are what Freud termed the erogenous zones. Freud identified the erogenous zones as the genitals, anus, and mouth. In "Three Essays on Sexuality" (1905), Freud used his observations from childhood and the nature of sexual perversions to provide support for the notion that the erogenous zones provide sexual stimulation. He also noted that other sources of stimulation include sensations such as sound, smell, touch, and sight. He asserted that the sexual wishes and activities of both children and perverts are related to the unconscious fantasies and wishes of adult neurotic patients. In other words, Freud's support for the libido theory came primarily from distinctly psychoanalytic data, that is, the elucidation of unconscious fantasy which he associated with the erogenous zones.

Prior to 1920, Freud's theory of drive revolved more exclusively around the concept of libido. After 1920, Freud elucidated the notion of aggression or the death instinct as another primary drive. The aggressive drive was seen as a death drive that all living matter demonstrates. The aim of aggression is death and the destruction of the self or the object (Freud, 1920, 1924). In "Beyond the Pleasure Principle," Freud wrote that the death drive is omnipresent in all living matter, including cellular activity. It is not related, however, to any specific body parts or process as he had suggested with libido.

The life and death drives are separate and in biological opposition to one another. But as Brenner (1982) suggested, the distinction between the two drives is seen more accurately as a psychological polarity, that is, in the minds of human beings more than a biological opposition. Brenner pointed out that life and death, organic and inorganic, are not chemically distinct or distinctly separable from each other. Contemporary molecular biology finds little support for the idea that there is a discontinuity between living and not living. Instead, there is a continuum between physical and chemical systems we refer to as inorganic and those that we refer to as living animals and plants. On the contrary, there is a gradual change in chemical properties from one system to the next that originates with the inorganic and progresses to living matter.

For Freud, the aims of drives are what he terms objects. Thus there is nothing inherent in the wish for contact with objects that motivate us. Instead, drives are the force that impels activity and objects are the aims of these drives. British object relations theory viewed this as a rather impersonal or mechanistic depiction of human nature. In fact, Morris Eagle (1984) argued that there is nothing inherent in drive theory that argues that the aim of a drive be an experience with another human being. Eagle cites René Spitz's (1960) research on the deleterious effects of maternal deprivation as a stark example of the power and perhaps the reductionism of drive theory. Spitz found that infants who experienced more maternal deprivation were much less likely to thrive than infants who did not experience such deprivation. Spitz explained his research findings as the results of a lack of opportunity for reduction in drive tension among the maternally deprived infants. Object relations theorists of various kinds would be much more likely to see the deleterious effects of maternal deprivation as explained more by the loss of contact with the mother than the loss of the opportunity for drive tension. Obviously, these explanations are not mutually exclusive.

Within Freudian theory, the aims differ for the two drives. Freud (1905) delineated the variety of libidinal aims of childhood that are bound to the erogenous zones. Libidinal excitement and pleasure are genetically determined through constitutional factors. Post-Freudian analysis has paid a great deal of attention to the importance of experience in determining which objects are chosen to reduce drive tensions. Even for Freud, the final organization of libidinal aims is altered through experience up until puberty.

The aim of aggression is the destruction of whatever is the object of the drive (Freud, 1920, 1930). The equating of destruction and death is a psychical one that exists in the fantasy life and imagination of the individual. The aim follows from Freud's belief in the universality of the death instinct and has been questioned by many analysts such as Leo Stone (1979). He argued that while there is a great deal of evidence for the importance of destructive wishes in mental life, the aims of aggression are so variable and change so much through the life cycle as to raise questions about the notion of aggression as a drive.

The aims of both the libidinal and aggressive drive are influenced by experiential factors but were not well delineated by Freud. In fact, one of the greatest sources of controversy in psychoanalysis involves Freud's assertion that sexual and aggressive drives are most influenced by unconscious fantasy as he minimized the importance of actual event, including trauma. Freud was always bothered by the obscurity of the neurophysiology of drives. It was always Freud's hope that neurophysiological and neurochemical data would eventually be able to inform the psychological inferences that are generated by the psychoanalytic study of the mind.

Fairbairn's Revision of the Drive Concept and Object Relations Theory

In one of the most revolutionary and challenging revisions of Freudian theory, Ronald Fairbairn (1952) suggested that there is a drive that he called object relating. This statement has implications for understanding a number of dimensions related to classical Freudian theory, posing questions especially about the nature of the pleasure principle, the centerpin of human motivation.

Fairbairn suggested that the drive for object relating was at the center of human motivation. Fairbairn reconfigured the central developmental conflicts of the child, moving anxiety to the background and dependency conflicts to the foreground. For Fairbairn, pleasure is an accompaniment of object relating, in contrast to the notion of the pleasure principle as the main source of motivation for human behavior. If pleasure is the accompaniment of object relating, then pleasure is an outcome of object relating, not the primary source of motivation. In fact, Fairbairn took his argument one step further. He suggested that when the pleasure principle is the primary source of motivation, severe psychopathology is implied. Thus the pleasure principle is seen as a breakdown product of an overly frustrating, depriving, or impinging early environment. If the dependency needs of the child are met relatively reliably, then pleasure accompanies the natural pull toward objects.

Fairbairn (1952) also challenged the notion of an aggressive drive inherent to human functioning. He viewed aggression as secondary to environmental failure. In other words, aggression is the result of frustration with other persons, not a primary drive in and of itself. This idea, that aggression is secondary to environmental failure was a central feature of a later analyst, Heinz Kohut (1971), in the development of his theory of self-psychology. Kohut argued that aggression results from empathic failures from parental figures, leading to compensatory psychological structures, chiefly narcissistic character structure. The narcissistic personality results from massive attempts to insulate and protect the individual from environmental failure. Other analysts such as Harry Guntrip (1971), another British object relations theorist, termed this kind of insulation the schizoid citadel, which protects the schizoid individual from revisiting hurtful experiences from others. Its purpose is to ensure that the individual will not be hurt again. Thus the aggressive drive is secondary to frustration with objects. Arnold Modell (1975) in the United States elaborated a similar view of schizoid phenomena in his depiction of what he termed self-sufficiency as a defense against needing others.

Donald Winnicott (1971) was a kind of bridge theorist who retained the notion of Freud's belief in the libidinal and aggressive drives, while adding a belief in the inherent pull for object relating as a drive. However, Winnicott broadened the view of aggression to include a variety of forms of assertion, including motility itself. In other words, Winnicott viewed the aggressive drive as an inherent destructive force as well as that which impels us as children to assert ourselves in the environment, to explore our surroundings and the object world itself.

Contemporary relational models (for example, Mitchell, 1988) have developed in much more detail the problems with the drive model of Freud's. These theorists have raised questions about the notion of a monadic concept of mind with its accompanying beliefs in an encapsulated infantile neurosis forged by aggressive and libidinal drives. Instead, they have elaborated the ways in which objects reciprocally influence each other through the life cycle. Nevertheless, psychoanalysis continues to struggle with the concept of motivation. While many analysts question the notion of the pleasure principle as a comprehensive explanatory organizing principle for describing human motivation, there is still the problem of explaining seemingly irrational human behavior, including the ubiquitousness of aggressive and destructive forces.

[See also Motivation.]

Bibliography

Brenner, C. (1982). *The mind in conflict*. New York: International Universities Press.

Eagle, M. (1984). *Recent developments in psychoanalysis*. New York: McGraw-Hill.

Fairbairn, R. (1952). *Psychoanalytic studies in personality*. London: Routledge.

Freud, S. (1905). Three essays on the theory of sexuality. *Standard Edition* (Vol. 7, 125–245).

Freud, S. (1915). Instincts and their vicissitudes. *Standard edition* (Vol. 14, 109–140).

Freud, S. (1920). Beyond the pleasure principle. *Standard Edition* (Vol. 18, pp. 1–64).

Freud, S. (1924). The dissolution of the Oedipus complex. *Standard edition* (Vol. 19, pp. 173–179).

Freud, S. (1930). Civilization and its contents. *Standard edition* (Vol. 21, pp. 57–145).

Freud, S. (1933). New introductory lectures on psychoanalysis. *Standard edition* (Vol. 22, pp. 1–182).

Guntrip, H. (1971). *Psychoanalytic theory, therapy, and the self*. New York: Basic Books.

Kohut, H. (1971). *The analysis of the self*. New York: International Universities Press.

Modell, A. (1975). Self-sufficiency as a defense against affect. *International Journal of Psycho-analysis*.

Spitz, R. (1959). *A genetic field theory of ego formation*. New York: International Universities Press.

Stone, L. (1979). Remarks on certain unique conditions of human aggression. *Journal of the American Psychoanalytical Association*, 27, 27–64.

Winnicott, D. (1971). *Playing and reality*. Middlesex, UK: Penguin.

Steven H. Cooper

DRIVING AND HIGHWAY SAFETY. There are three interconnecting elements in the highway-vehicle system: the vehicle's dynamics and technology; the roadway environment, including road characteristics, signage, and hazards arising primarily from traffic and pedestrians; and the driver, whose strengths and limitations in such information processing activities as attention, perception, judgment, and response affect his or her own safety and that of other people.

Task Analysis

The driver balances two competing and conflicting goals: to travel to a destination in a timely fashion (productivity); and to travel to a destination without losing control of the vehicle, being involved in a collision, or getting speeding citations or other moving violations (safety). The conflict between these goals is inherent in the role of *speed*, which, while benefiting productivity, greatly compromises safety (Evans, 1991). In the United States, around 40,000 lives are lost annually in vehicle accidents, most involving excess speed (Evans, 1996), and perhaps half a million lives are lost in this fashion worldwide.

In order to accomplish the two goals of productivity and safety, the driver must perform a two-axis vehicle-tracking task, while performing a series of side tasks. The two axes of tracking involve speed control and lateral control. Speed control involves maintaining a relatively constant speed on clear roads, a relatively constant headway or relative speed in heavy traffic, and appropriate braking behavior in response to events ahead. Lateral (steering) control is accomplished by orienting the direction of the vehicle (aimpoint) with the direction of the highway, a goal that will achieve smooth steering in the lane center.

Breakdown in either lateral or speed (headway) tracking compromises safety. Accidents due to loss of lateral control most frequently occur with the youngest drivers at very high speeds, such that the "bandwidth" of the lateral tracking task exceeds human information processing capabilities. Failures of headway control are typically responsible for the more frequent collisions, and these are associated with three causal factors described below: visibility and attention, response time, and risky decision making.

Visibility and Attention

Near continuous visibility of the highway tracking input is necessary to assure proper guidance and hazard detection. Driving at night or in bad weather can produce unsafe conditions. But effective overhead lighting has been responsible for some substantial decreases in these types of accident. In the same manner, reflective road markings provide effective feedback of lane position, clearly an aid to safe driving. In addition to external visibility, a second source of compromise of tracking input arises from the diversion of *visual attention* to the variety of side tasks or competing activities: scanning outside for signs, dealing with radios, glancing at the speedometer, or evaluating navigational information. The loss of visual input from the roadway caused by such behavior can be substantial, involving head-down glances as long as 10 seconds for some map-related tasks. While tracking visibility is most seriously degraded by competing visual tasks, nonvisual tasks, such as listening to a conversation, or cellular phone use, can also compete with the processing of related visual channels involved in driver safety.

Response Time

A second contribution to accidents is prolonged response time (RT) to unexpected events on the roadway, such that the time *required* to stop or swerve before contacting a hazard is greater than the time *available* before the hazard is contacted. This RT can be decomposed into three driver-related components: Hazard detection time, maneuver selection time, and maneuver execution time. The first two, determined by human information processing capabilities, have been estimated to be approximately 2.5 seconds, with a range as long as 4 seconds. Detection time is inversely influenced by visibility and is also strongly influenced by the cognitive factor of *expectancy*. Thus unexpected events, such as a stalled car in the lane ahead at night, may double the hazard RT, relative to expected events. The time to select the appropriate maneuver (brake or swerve) will depend upon skill and experience, as well as local traffic conditions. Finally, the time to execute the maneuver will depend both upon the severity of the correction (braking or swerving) and *vehicle inertia*, which is increased by vehicle weight.

The previous analysis reveals the critical role of speed in hazard response. At higher speeds, a given driver's RT will cover a greater distance, thus decreasing the time available for responding to a given hazard ahead. Higher speeds will also increase vehicle inertia, increasing the maneuver time. Finally, higher speeds will increase the damage on impact, or the likelihood of control loss, should a lateral maneuver be selected. The speed at which to drive is heavily governed by the judgment of the driver.

Risky Decision Making

Some of the most important decisions a driver can make are those involving safe behavior (or alternatively, those that might increase or decrease risk), of which the prime decision is choice of vehicle speed (on an open highway) or vehicle headway (on a crowded one). Despite the hazards of speeding, highway safety data point to the prevalence of speeding behavior. Most people drive over the speed limit, and on busy freeways, most people drive with a headway of only 1.3 seconds, in spite of the mean driver RT of 2.5 seconds (i.e., the time that would be expected to respond, if the driver in front came to a sudden halt).

Why do people speed? First, perceptual factors cause people to underestimate the speed at which they are driving, and hence, drivers accelerate to compensate. For example, quiet vehicles, or those traveling at night diminish auditory and visual feedback of speed. Vehicles in which the driver is higher above the roadway provide feedback of slower speed. Second, drivers may *underestimate* the risk of fast, or unsafe driving, because the probability of unsafe consequences of such behavior are not appreciated. For example, the tendency to drive with less than allowable headway may result from the driver's lack of any expectation that the vehicle ahead will suddenly stop, or that the crossing car at the intersection will run the red light. Third, drivers may intentionally violate the standards of safety, choosing to ignore the known risks. This may be done for reasons of productivity (e.g., to make an appointment on time), or thrill seeking.

Driving Impairments: Fatigue, Alcohol, and Age

Driving at night is around ten times as hazardous per mile driven as daytime driving. While part of the hazard is related to visibility factors, a major contributor is the fact that the night driver will often be both more fatigued, after driving all day, and will be driving during the low arousal portion of the circadian rhythm cycle. These factors compromise driver ability to detect unexpected, low salience events (the unexpected roadway hazard, or the departure of one's own vehicle from the lane).

Alcohol impairs a variety of information processing characteristics related to response speed, attention allocation (i.e., task management), and judgment. The heavy role of alcohol as a cause in approximately 50% of fatal accidents has been well documented.

The effects of age on accident risk follows a U-shaped function, with a high accident rate for younger and older drivers, but for different reasons. For the youngest drivers (age 16), the lack of perceptual-motor skill is a primary source, accounting for the relatively high proportion of loss-of-control accidents. For slightly older drivers (i.e., 17–24, particularly males), the primary factors are speeding and the increased risk of driving at night, and under the influence of alcohol (i.e., while impaired). Above age 60, the cause is associated with longer RT, poorer visual capabilities, and poorer attentional skills. However, older drivers partially compensate for these skill losses by reducing risk exposure, e.g., driving more slowly and driving less at night than younger drivers.

Remediations to Safety Concerns

Enforcement has been perhaps the most effective way of ensuring safe driving. Lower speed limits, coupled with enforcement have substantially reduced fatal accidents per mile traveled, as have laws regarding seatbelt usage, and driving under the influence of alcohol. An increase in the minimum driving age to 18, as in Europe and New Jersey, reduces the frequency of accidents for the first-year driver. Proper enforcement of these, and other safety-inducing laws increases driver compliance though social pressures appear to be even more effective in inducing compliance (Evans, 1991). For example, the strong social stigma against driving under the influence of alcohol, developing in the last decade in the United States, appears to be responsible for the substantial reduction in alcohol-related fatalities.

Remediations to roadway design can also induce safer behavior. Standardization of roadway layouts and sign placement can reduce the likelihood of unexpected events and decrease visual search time. Divided highways reduce the risks associated with lane violations.

Driver training, surprisingly, has had relatively little effect on driving safety. This failure may reflect the fact that neither of the two environments selected for such training—the classroom and "behind the wheel"—represent ideal environments for learning the skills necessary for safe driving. The increased use of driving simulators can address these shortcomings.

Technological advances have been introduced with the goal of improved driver safety. They include headlight dimmers, antilock brakes, and high mounted brake lights, or head-up displays designed to keep the driver's eyes on the highway. Some features are designed to reduce the lethal nature of a collision (air bags, seatbelts, car seats for infants and children), while others, such as high mounted brakelights or antilock brakes are designed to support more effective driver response. A criticism of such devices is that they may produce *risk homeostasis:* when a device is introduced to improve safety, drivers may adjust their own behavior to maintain safety at a constant level, but improve productivity. For example, drivers might drive faster in bad weather, knowing that they have antilock brakes. However, analysis reveals that such homeostasis is not inevitable. In only a few cases is safety actually compromised. In some cases its benefits may not be realized (e.g., driver education), but in others the benefits of safety-related technology are as great, or even greater than were anticipated (Evans, 1991).

Automation, such as cruise control, electronic navigation systems, or headway sensors, is a technology that in some form replaces or simplifies the driving task. While benefits of such techniques are self-evident, there may be two potential costs to safety related to human factors: increased head-down time (attention diversion to the automated devices), and possible *complacency* or overtrust, compromising safety should the automation fail to perform as expected.

Bibliography

Evans, L. (1991). *Traffic safety and the driver.* New York: Van Nostrand Reinhold.

Evans, L. (1996). A crash course in traffic safety. In *1997 Medical and Health Annual.* Chicago: Encyclopedia Britannica.

Green, P. (1995). Automotive techniques. In J. Weimer (Ed.), *Research techniques in human engineering* (pp. 165–201). San Diego, CA: Academic Press.

Wickens, C. D., Gordon, S., & Liu, Y. (1998). *An introduction to human factors engineering.* New York: Addison Wesley Longman.

Christopher D. Wickens

DRUG ABUSE. People have been using psychoactive drugs in virtually all cultures and across all eras (Siegel, 1991). Concern about psychoactive substance use arises when the behavior is seen as causing or potentially causing adverse consequences for the user or society. The cardinal feature of psychoactive substance use disorders is continued use despite the possibility of negative consequences. While many explanations have been offered (e.g., negative and positive reinforcement), to date, no theory adequately explains compulsive drug use (Institute of Medicine, 1996; Milby, Schumacher, & Stainback, 1997).

Dependence and Tolerance

Two salient features of substance use disorders are tolerance and dependence. Dependence is a pattern of compulsive drug seeking that comes to dominate one's activities and for some drugs can include physiological withdrawal symptoms upon cessation of use (American Psychiatric Association, 1994; Schuckit, 1995). The core symptoms need not occur with the same frequency or intensity within or between drug classes (for some drugs, e.g., hallucinogens or cannabis, withdrawal symptoms are not evident or less salient) and all symptoms need not be present for dependence to be diagnosed (American Psychiatric Association, 1994; Schuckit, 1995). Severity of dependence has been conceptualized as on a continuum (American Psychiatric Association, 1994).

The second salient feature of substance use disorders is acquired (chronic) tolerance; with repeated use, more of the substance is needed to achieve the same effect(s) (American Psychiatric Association, 1994; Schuckit, 1995). High tolerance levels allow people to consume higher doses of drugs, which increase the likelihood that withdrawal symptoms will occur upon cessation. The time-course and magnitude of the development of tolerance varies across drug classes (for some drugs—cocaine, nicotine—tolerance develops rapidly and for other drugs is slower—cannabis, alcohol).

Diagnosis

An accurate diagnosis is important for an initial understanding of the problem behavior as well as for treatment planning. The fourth edition of the *Diagnostic and Statistical Manual of Mental Disorders* (American Psychiatric Association, 1994) identifies eleven drug classes associated with abuse or dependence: alcohol; amphetamines; caffeine; cannabis; cocaine; hallucinogens; inhalants; nicotine; opioids; phencyclidines; and sedatives, hypnotics or anxiolytics. Substance dependence also can be specified as with or without physiological dependence (i.e., tolerance or withdrawal). The *DSM–IV* criteria for a substance dependence diagnosis requires evidence of a maladaptive pattern of use as manifested by 3 or more of 7 criteria (e.g., substantial tolerance; unsuccessful efforts to cut down) occurring in the same 12-month time period (American Psychiatric Association, 1994, p. 181). A substance abuse diagnosis involves a maladaptive pattern of use that does not meet dependence criteria, but is manifested by one or more of four criteria (e.g., continued use resulting in inability to fulfill obligations) occurring in the same 12-month time period (American Psychiatric Association, 1994, pp. 182–183).

Psychiatric Comorbidity

There is consensus that the prevalence of psychiatric disorders among drug abusers in treatment is high (7–65%) compared to rates in population studies (Institute of Medicine, 1996; Milby, Schumacher, & Stainback, 1997; National Institute on Alcohol Abuse and Alcoholism, 1997; Onken, Blaine, Genser, & Horton, 1997). While studies show that the two most common psychiatric problems associated with drug abuse are affective and personality disorders, anxiety disorders also occur frequently (Institute of Medicine, 1996; Milby et al., 1997; Onken et al., 1997). There are several treatment implications for drug abusers with comorbid diagnosis compared to those with only a drug dependence diagnosis. Generally, they need more intensive or longer treatment, are more disabled and prone to suicide, have higher rates of homelessness and more legal and medical problems and longer hospital stays, and have higher rates of relapse and poorer treatment outcomes (Institute of Medicine, 1996; National Institute on Alcohol Abuse and Alcoholism, 1997; Onken et al., 1997). Consequently, diagnostic formulations should document the extent and nature of the drug problem and also establish whether other psychiatric disorders are present, and, if so, whether the drug problem is primary or secondary. While there are no empirical guidelines about how to treat comorbid drug abusers, the field is moving toward an integrated approach (i.e., simultaneous mental health and drug services by the same program; Onken et al., 1997) that may produce improved outcomes.

Multiple Drug Abuse

For drug abusers who use or abuse other drugs, it is important to gather a profile of their psychoactive substance use. The following are important when assessing multiple drug use (National Institute on Alcohol Abuse and Alcoholism, 1997; Schuckit, 1995): (a) pharmacological synergism (i.e., multiplicative effect of similarly acting drugs taken concurrently); (b) cross-tolerance (i.e., decreased effect of drugs due to heavy use of pharmacologically similar drugs); (c) drug use patterns may change over treatment (e.g., increased drinking with cessation from opioid use); and (d) more than 80% of drug abusers report smoking cigarettes (Sobell, Toneatto, & Sobell, 1994).

The Development and Course of Drug Abuse

A recent U.S. survey on drug abuse (Substance Abuse and Mental Health Administration, 1997b) revealed that 6% of individuals 12 or more years old used illicit drugs in the month prior to the interview. In 1996, next to cigarettes and alcohol (32% and 65%, respectively), marijuana (8%) was the third most used psychoactive substance in the past year, and the most widely used illicit substance—77% of current drug users used marijuana or hashish (Institute of Medicine, 1996; Substance Abuse and Mental Health Administration, 1997c).

U.S. survey rates of lifetime (that is, ever used) psychoactive substance use (Substance Abuse and Mental Health Administration, 1997b) range from a low for heroin (1%), crack (2%), and PCP (3%) to higher rates for inhalants (6%), hallucinogens (10%), and cocaine (10%), to a third reporting ever using marijuana (33%). Compared to lifetime rates for licit drugs (alcohol, 83%; cigarettes, 72%), these rates are very low (Substance Abuse and Mental Health Administration, 1997b). Thus, except for marijuana, most illicit psychoactive substance use and abuse does not involve a sizable percentage of the population.

Because of differing definitions, the number of individuals who abuse drugs is more difficult to determine. U.S. surveys have revealed very low rates of heroin use (past month = 0.1%; past year = 0.2%) compared to other illicit drugs (Substance Abuse and Mental Health Administration, 1997a). Among heavier (that is, 12 or more days per year) cocaine and marijuana users, 26% and 41%, respectively, reported 3 or more problems, which is suggestive of dependence (Substance Abuse and Mental Health Administration, 1997a). In contrast to illicit drugs, about 5% reported current heavy alcohol use, and of those 31% reported 3 or more problems (Substance Abuse and Mental Health Administration, 1997a).

In the 1990s, there was a leveling off of illicit drug use over the past decade (Substance Abuse and Mental Health Administration, 1997a; Substance Abuse and Mental Health Administration, 1997c), except for increased marijuana use among 12- to 17-year-olds. Further, while cocaine abuse decreased, heroin abuse increased, suggesting that drug use and abuse rates change as a function of availability, costs, and legal sanctions (Institute of Medicine, 1996; Milby et al., 1997).

Etiology and Genetic Vulnerability

Although a genetic vulnerability to drug dependence has been suggested, for many reasons, "it is difficult to marshal evidence regarding genetic determinants as they relate to drugs other than alcohol" (Lowinson, Ruiz, Millman, & Langrod, 1992, p. 46). Although there is some agreement that genetics is involved in drug abuse, there is no consensus as to what might be inherited (Institute of Medicine, 1996). Further, it appears that the etiology of drug dependence will be multifactorial as "no single variable or set of variables explains drug use by an individual" (Institute of Medicine, 1996, p. 117). A salient factor associated with drug use and abuse, particularly among adolescents, is peer environment (Institute of Medicine, 1996). Sociocultural factors (e.g., neighborhood crime, availability) have also been linked to drug abuse rates (Milby et al., 1997). Alternatively, two factors (social support, lack of availability) associated with low rates of illicit drug use are also associated with recovery (Institute of Medicine, 1996; Lowinson, Luis, Millman, & Langrod, 1992; Sobell & Sobell, 1998).

Because different drugs have different pharmacological actions and legal sanctions, no single clinical picture of drug dependence can be formed. What can be said is that individuals with drug problems will show impairment from very mild symptoms and no consequences to severe symptoms and serious consequences (Institute of Medicine, 1996).

Other factors comprising a general clinical picture of drug abuse include: (1) a significant incidence of psychiatric comorbidity; a vast majority also smoke cigarettes; (2) most substance abusers never seek treatment; and (3) drug abusers who change without treatment generally have less severe drug histories than those in treatment.

While substance abuse problems can be scaled along a severity continuum, mild substance abuse does not predict the development of more severe problems. Evidence for progressivity is strongest for nicotine where most individuals who smoke only a few cigarettes are likely to progress toward heavier use (Schuckit, 1995). Evidence for progressivity of other drug problems has been studied little.

A considerable amount of illicit drug initiation including cigarette smoking starts in the early teens. Although there has been much speculation and assertion about cigarettes and marijuana being "gateway" drugs to more serious illicit use, evidence for this is lacking (Peele & Brodsky, 1997). Evidence shows that while most individuals who have used heroin, LSD, and cocaine have used marijuana, "most marijuana users never use another illegal drug" (Zimmer & Morgan, 1995, p. 14.). Further, while experimentation with many drugs is the "statistical norm" among young people, most such individuals do not become chronic users (Milby et al., 1997). Lastly, if variables associated with progressivity could be identified, then intervention and prevention strategies associated with those variables could be developed and evaluated.

Substance abuse is a recalcitrant clinical disorder characterized by high relapse rates six months post-treatment (Institute of Medicine, 1996; Lowinson et al., 1992; Milby et al., 1997). Unfortunately, this characterization has given the disorder a reputation as being difficult to treat and seldom "cured." The high likelihood of recurrence has led to the development of relapse prevention procedures (Lowinson et al., 1992; Milby et al., 1997). Not only do men outnumber women in drug use and abuse (Institute of Medicine, 1996; Substance Abuse and Mental Health Administration, 1997c), but use and abuse are inversely related to age (Substance Abuse and Mental Health Administration, 1997a).

Even though epidemiological studies provide information on ethnic and racial differences in relation to drug use and abuse, the methods for categorizing respondents' backgrounds have been rudimentary. Consequently, data on ethnic differences must be interpreted with caution. A few notable findings show that drug use is higher among the unemployed (Institute of Medicine, 1996; Substance Abuse and Mental Health Administration, 1997a). Also, illicit drug use is highly correlated with educational status (Substance Abuse and Mental Health Administration, 1997a). Several studies also show that among those under twenty-five there are no sizable ethnic/racial differences in use rates (Institute of Medicine, 1996; Substance Abuse and Mental Health Administration, 1997c), particularly when social and environmental conditions are controlled (Milby et al., 1997).

The vast majority of individuals with substance abuse problems do not seek treatment or use self-help groups (Substance Abuse and Mental Health Administration, 1997a). Substance abusers who recover without formal interventions tend to have milder problems compared to those in treatment (Sobell, Cunningham, & Sobell, 1996; Sobell & Sobell). Studies of drug abusers who have changed on their own have found that a large percentage of such recoveries are associated with a cognitive appraisal process (i.e., weighing the pros and cons of changing; Sobell & Sobell). Factors that have helped maintain natural recoveries include social support and moving away from areas where drugs are sold.

Assessment

A careful and continuing assessment is an important part of the treatment process for drug abusers. Good assessments have several clinical benefits: (a) provide a basis for treatment planning and goal setting; (b) help formulate diagnoses; (c) feedback or advice can be given to clients about their past use; such advice can enhance or strengthen motivation for change (Miller & Rollnick, 1991; Sobell et al., 1994); and (d) help evaluate whether treatments are working and if not, what the next step(s) should be (i.e., stepped care; Sobell & Sobell, in press).

Clinicians must rely on their clients' self-reports for most of the assessment and treatment information (Sobell et al., 1994). Contrary to folklore, several studies show that drug abusers' self-reports are generally accurate if they are interviewed when (1) drug and alcohol free, (2) in a clinical or research setting, and (3) given assurances of confidentiality (Milby et al., 1997; Sobell et al., 1994).

The following assessment instruments were selected to (a) be user friendly for clients (e.g., easy, relevant), (b) require minimal time and resources, (c) be psychometrically sound, (d) be free, and (e) if possible, provide meaningful feedback to clients.

Drug Use History. Although no single drug use instrument has been adopted by the drug field, typically a structured interview is used that captures various information (for example, years used, frequency) about different drug classes (Sobell et al., 1994).

Self-Monitoring. Self-monitoring requires clients to record aspects of their drug use or urges (for example, amount, frequency) over treatment. Self-monitoring can (1) be used to identify situations that pose a high-risk of drug use, (2) provide feedback about changes in drug use, and (3) give clients an opportunity to talk about their use with their therapist during treatment (Sobell et al., 1994).

Alcohol and Other Drug Timeline Followback (TLFB) Calendar. The TLFB calendar, originally developed for gathering retrospective estimates of daily alcohol consumption (American Psychiatric Association, in press; Sobell et al., 1994), has been extended to gathering information about frequency of other drug use. The TLFB can be used in treatment as an advice-feedback tool to analyze clients' drug use and to increase their motivation to change (Sobell et al., 1994).

Addiction Severity Index (ASI). The ASI is a structured interview that uses 147 questions to assess problems in seven areas of substance use (American Psychiatric Association, in press). It must be administered by a trained interviewer and takes about 30 to 45 minutes.

Drug Abuse Screening Test (DAST). The DAST is a brief, self-administered measure of drug consequences that occurred in the last year (American Psychiatric Association, in press; Sobell et al., 1994).

Motivation, Treatment, and Prevention

There has been an increasing recognition of the importance of assessing the extent to which clients believe change is necessary (Miller & Rollnick, 1991). Motivation can be conceptualized as a state of readiness to change that may fluctuate over time and can be influenced by several variables (Sobell et al., 1994). Even when clients are convinced of the importance of changing, other factors can interfere with one's intent to change (Milby et al., 1997). The most important issue is that treatment of clients who are not strongly committed to changing their drug use should initially focus on increasing their motivation rather than on methods for changing.

Two major treatment options exist for drug abuse—pharmacotherapy and psychosocial therapy or a combination of these options. The major programs that offer such treatment options include therapeutic communities (TCs), methadone maintenance (MM), drug-free outpatient programs, and chemical dependency (CD) programs (Institute of Medicine, 1996; Lowinson et al., 1992; Milby et al., 1997). The first major drug treatment program in the United States was Synanon, a residential therapeutic community, staffed by ex-addicts and employing confrontation and peer pressure to produce change. Synanon gave rise to other long-term residential programs.

While several pharmacotherapies exist for drug abuse, methadone, an opiate agonist, has received the most attention. Methadone has been embraced as an inexpensive and effective treatment for heroin dependence. Maintenance on an agonist drug (that is, blocks euphoric drug effects) like methadone has several short- and long-term advantages (for example, stabilizes an abuser's life, reduced drug use; Institute of Medicine, 1996; Schuckit, 1995). Other major pharmacological agents for treating heroin dependence include naltrexone, LAAM, and buprenorphine (Institute of Medicine, 1996; Schuckit, 1995).

In contrast to methadone programs, drug free outpatient programs were developed to treat non-opioid abusers. The treatment objective of these programs is abstinence and initially such programs did not include pharmacotherapy (hence, the label "drug free"). Today, outpatient programs serve most drug abusers, offering counseling and other services. Contingency management has also been used with drug abusers for many years. The objective has been to produce a change in drug use or target behaviors or to structure an environment favorable for new behaviors through the use of contingent reinforcement, for example, methadone (Institute of Medicine, 1996). Lastly, chemical dependency programs are short-term inpatient programs that follow a 12-step model like Narcotics Anonymous.

Several large scale treatment research studies have shown modest effects for drug treatment (Hubbard, Craddock, Flynn, Anderson, & Etheridge, 1997; Institute of Medicine, 1996). Also, although not evaluated in a controlled trial, length of time in treatment has been shown to be an important predictor of successful outcomes (that is, longer stays result in better outcomes; Hubbard et al., 1997; Institute of Medicine, 1996).

Over the past decade there has been increased interest in prevention programs, especially school-based programs (Institute of Medicine, 1996). Although their major goal has been to reduce the incidence and prevalence of drug use, the effectiveness of such programs is questionable with some programs showing no preventative effects on substance use (Institute of Medicine, 1996). For example, programs like D.A.R.E. (Drug Abuse Resistance Education) have repeatedly shown only short-term (1 year or less) effects on use, knowledge, and attitudes (Institute of Medicine, 1996).

While drug prevention programs for adolescents have an intuitive appeal for reducing use, research has not supported these efforts. Although the Institute of Medicine (1996) has recommended additional prevention research efforts, it has emphasized efforts beyond the school (for example, family, media) and interventions aimed at high risk groups.

[See also Addictive Personality; Cocaine; Drugs; Hallucinogens; Marijuana; and Opiates.]

Bibliography

American Psychiatric Association. (1994). *Diagnostic and statistical manual of mental disorders* (4th ed). Washington, DC: American Psychiatric Association.

American Psychiatric Association. (in press). *Handbook of psychiatric measures*. Washington, DC: American Psychiatric Association. Concise summary of assessment, process, and treatment outcome measures recommended for use by the American Psychiatric Association.

Hubbard, R. L., Craddock, S. G., Flynn, P. M., Anderson, J., & Etheridge, R. M. (1997). Overview of one-year follow-up outcomes in the Drug Abuse Treatment Outcome Study (DATOS). *Psychology of Addictive Behaviors, 11*, 261–278.

Institute of Medicine. (1996). *Pathways of addiction: Opportunities in drug abuse research*. Washington, DC: National Academy Press.

Lowinson, J. H., Ruiz, R., Millman, R. B., & Langrod, J. G. (Eds.). (1992). Substance abuse: A comprehensive textbook (2nd ed.). Baltimore, MD: Williams & Wilkins. A comprehensive textbook with 80 chapters addressing substance abuse and its background, determinants, evaluation, treatment, special populations, and policy issues.

Milby, J. B., Schumacher, J. E., & Stainback, R. D. (1997). Substance use-related disorders: Drugs. In S. M. Turner & M. Hersen (Eds.), *Adult psychopathology and diagnosis* (3rd ed.) (pp. 159–202). New York: Wiley.

Miller, W. R., & Rollnick, S. (1991). *Motivational interviewing: Preparing people to change addictive behavior*. New York: Guilford Press. An excellent clinical presentation with examples of how to do motivational interviewing with substance abusers.

National Institute on Alcohol Abuse and Alcoholism. (1997). Alcoholism and co-occurring disorders. *Alcohol Health & Research World, 20*, Issue 2.

Onken, L. S., Blaine, J. D., Genser, S., & Horton, A. M. (Eds.). (1997). *Treatment of drug-dependent individuals with comorbid mental disorders* (NIDA Research Monograph 172). Rockville, MD: National Institute on Drug Abuse. A special monograph addressing various aspects of psychiatric comorbidity.

Peele, S., & Brodsky, A. (1997). How alcohol came to be scapegoated for drug abuse. *Addiction Research, 5*, 419–425.

Schuckit, M. A. (1995). *Drug and alcohol abuse: A clinical guide to diagnosis and treatment* (4th ed.). New York: Plenum Medical Book Company. In-depth clinical guide to the diagnosis and treatment of most psychoactive substances.

Siegel, R. K. (1991). *Intoxication: Life in pursuit of artificial paradise*. New York: E. P. Dutton.

Sobell, L. C., Cunningham, J. A., & Sobell, M. B. (1996). Recovery from alcohol problems with and without treatment: Prevalence in two population surveys. *American Journal of Public Health, 86*, 966–972.

Sobell, L. C., Toneatto, T., & Sobell, M. B. (1994). Behavioral assessment and treatment planning for alcohol, tobacco, and other drug problems: Current status with an emphasis on clinical applications. *Behavior Therapy, 25*, 533–580.

Sobell, M. B., & Sobell, L. C. (1998). Guiding self-change. In W. R. Miller & N. Heather (Eds.), *Treating addictive be-

haviors (2nd ed.) New York: Plenum Press. The book that this chapter appears in contains several other up-to-date summaries of treatment research.

Sobell, M B., & Sobell, L. C. (1999). Stepped care for alcohol problems: An efficient method for planning and delivering clinical services. In J. A. Tucker, D. A. Donovan, & G. A. Marlatt (Eds.), *Changing addictive behavior: Bridging clinical and public health strategies* (pp. 331–343). New York: Guilford Press.

Substance Abuse and Mental Health Administration. (1997a). *National household survey on drug abuse: Main findings 1995.* Rockville, MD: U.S. Department of Health and Human Services.

Substance Abuse and Mental Health Administration. (1997b). *National household survey on drug abuse: Population estimates 1996.* Rockville, MD: U.S. Department of Health and Human Services.

Substance Abuse and Mental Health Administration. (1997c). *Preliminary results from the 1996 national household survey on drug abuse.* Rockville, MD: U.S. Department of Health and Human Services.

Zimmer, L., & Morgan, J. P. (1995). *Exposing marijuana myths: A review of the scientific evidence.* New York: Open Society Institute.

Linda C. Sobell and Mark B. Sobell

DRUGS. Psychologists are interested in the study of drugs for a variety of reasons. Because some drugs can have profound effects on psychological processes, scientists have considered the possibility that the altered psychological states produced by these drugs might provide a method for analyzing normal psychological processes. The general idea is that different drugs might selectively alter different basic psychological functions, allowing greater insight into what those basic functions consist of and how they interact under normal circumstances. The set of drugs that have significant effects on psychological processes such as thinking, perception, and emotion are referred to as psychoactive drugs. As neuropharmacologists have learned more about the biochemical processes in the brain that are influenced by these drugs, the possibility seems to be just within reach that specific psychological processes such as mood or memory might be linked to specific biochemical processes, thus giving us not only a greater understanding of brain-behavior relationships but opening the door to the development of more effective and more specific drugs for treating mental dysfunctions. We will see, however, that such clear and specific links between basic psychological functions and specific neurochemicals have continued to remain, like a mirage on the desert or the end of the rainbow, just out of our grasp. We do not yet have useful chemical models to understand such problems as psychological depression, addiction, schizophrenia, or memory loss in Alzheimer's disease, in spite of years of extensive research and in contrast to popularly presented "explanations" of these disorders.

Another reason why psychologists are interested in psychoactive drugs is that several types of drugs play a practical role in the management of mental disorders, such as obsessive-compulsive disorder, depression, or schizophrenia. A psychologist who is trying to help someone contend with such a disorder needs to be familiar with the potential benefits of these drugs and also with their limitations. Although most psychologists are not legally able to prescribe these drugs, it is quite common for a patient to be taking psychoactive medications prescribed by a medical doctor while at the same time working with a psychologist who is taking a cognitive, behavioral, or intrapsychic approach to dealing with the same problem. Comparisons between drug therapy and psychotherapy, as well as the effects of combining drug therapy and psychotherapy, have provided a number of interesting opportunities for research. The branch of medicine called psychiatry, once dominated by psychodynamic approaches to psychotherapy, now often seems to be focused on the specialty of psychopharmacology, the study of the uses of psychoactive drugs. In fact, many psychiatrists are concerned that in modern health-care systems they have been relegated to the role of prescribers of medicine, leaving "talk" therapy to less expensive providers, including psyehologists or perhaps social workers. Partly due to the shortage of psychiatrists, especially in rural or poor urban settings, a large proportion of the prescriptions for psychoactive medications are written by general practitioners who may have little or no training in dealing with mental disorders. For this and other reasons, some clinical psychologists have been calling for legislation allowing specially trained psychologists to prescribe psychoactive medications.

Since drug-taking behavior sometimes becomes compulsive, excessive, and/or dangerous to the point that serious problems are caused in the user's professional, social, or personal life, understanding such behavior and how to control or eliminate it has become a focus of a great deal of psychological research and a common issue in therapy. Although much of the research and therapy has focused on compulsive use of individual substances, such as alcohol or cocaine, there is also considerable interest in looking for commonalities among compulsive users of any of these substances. The term *addiction* is often applied to compulsive substance use.

Pharmacological concepts that are related to addiction and are significant for many psychoactive drugs include tolerance, physical dependence, and psychological dependence. Tolerance refers to the decreased effect of a drug resulting from its repeated use. Sometimes it is possible to overcome the effects of tolerance by increasing the dose, but it is important to remember that all drugs produce multiple effects, and tolerance does not occur equally for all the various effects of a drug, so increasing a dose often results in increased unpleasant or dangerous side effects. Physical dependence is defined by the presence of a withdrawal syndrome when the use of a drug is terminated. When this occurs, it is usually after tolerance has developed, and so the two concepts are usually related to each other. As an example, the use of a CNS depressant as a sleeping pill may work well for the first night or two. However, after several nights of repeated use, tolerance may develop to the effects of many types of sleeping pills, which may lead the user to increase the dose and continue using the drug. If the person then tries to stop using the sleeping pills, he or she may experience a strong rebound insomnia on the first night. If the dose has been increased to very high levels and continued for some time, a more dramatic withdrawal syndrome may appear, including hallucinations and delusions, and in some cases *grand mal* seizures.

Psychological dependence is defined in strictly behavioral terms as an increased tendency to use a substance, resulting from experience with it. Dependence is often accompanied by descriptions of craving the substance, and becomes clinically significant when the use becomes so compulsive that obtaining and using the substance interfere with other important functions at home or work, or when use continues in spite of repeated negative consequences. It is important that psychological dependence can become very powerful even in the absence of clear evidence of either tolerance or physical dependence, although often all three occur together. The American Psychiatric Association's *Diagnostic and Statistical Manual of Mental Disorders*, fourth edition (*DSM–IV*), which describes a wide variety of mental disorders, distinguishes between substance abuse disorder, characterized primarily in terms of psychological dependence (compulsive use, repeated use in spite of negative consequences) and substance dependence disorder, which for most substances includes evidence of tolerance and the appearance of withdrawal symptoms.

Categories of Psychoactive Drugs

Drugs are commonly grouped into large categories defined by their most prominent effects. For example, we distinguish between the central nervous system (CNS) stimulants, which produce wakefulness and enhanced alertness, and the CNS depressants, which produce sedation and drowsiness.

Stimulants. Stimulants are drugs that keep you awake, may make you feel jittery or nervous, and can increase effort—leading to their widespread use for many years in athletic competitions. The most familiar stimulant, caffeine, produces relatively mild effects compared to other members of this class. Nevertheless, excessive use of caffeine can lead to insomnia, anxiety, and outbursts of anger. Tolerance develops with repeated use, and the withdrawal syndrome includes headaches, drowsiness, and a lack of energy. Caffeine is a natural constituent of coffee and tea, and is also found in many soft drinks and in some over-the-counter medications.

Cocaine is a powerful CNS stimulant. It is produced by the *coca* bush, the leaves of which have been chewed for thousands of years in the Andes mountains. The pure drug has been used medically (it is a local anesthetic) and recreationally for over 100 years, and some users have experienced addiction to it. Cocaine produces a profound sense of energy and well-being, lasting about 30 minutes. Following the brief "high" there may be a rebound effect, including mild psychological depression. With repeated use tolerance develops quickly, and use of higher doses may result in a paranoid psychotic state. Withdrawal after such high-dose use results in profound psychological depression and lack of energy. Cocaine hydrochloride may be converted into "crack" or "rock" cocaine, which may be heated and "smoked" (the cocaine vapors are inhaled). This produces a very rapid effect on the brain.

Ephedrine is derived from a Chinese herbal tea. The pure ingredient has been sold over the counter for many years as a treatment for asthma. Ephedrine is also a CNS stimulant, perhaps slightly more powerful than caffeine, and it is also sold in convenience stores and truck stops as an "alertness" drug. There has been some concern in recent years about overuse and abuse of ephedrine.

Amphetamine is a synthetic drug derived from ephedrine and has a similar chemical structure. Although its original use was in treating asthma, it proved to be a powerful CNS stimulant. It has been used to treat a rare sleep disorder called narcolepsy, as an appetite suppressant, as a short-term treatment for mild depression, and it was the first drug discovered by accident to increase attention and (surprisingly) reduce hyperactivity in attention-deficit/hyperactivity disorder (ADHD). Amphetamine has also been used recreationally and to enhance athletic performance. A slight modification of the amphetamine molecule results in methamphetamine, which is even more potent in its CNS effects than amphetamine. This drug has been abused by users who inject it intravenously, or inhale the vapors ("smoke" it) in a form known on the streets as "ice" or "crystal meth." Excessive use of this drug produces affects like those of high doses of cocaine, but the effects of methamphetamine last for several hours.

Methylphenidate (brand name Ritalin) is an amphetaminelike stimulant that is widely used to treat ADHD in children. It is considered to be a slightly milder stimulant than amphetamine and appears to work equally well.

Depressants. These drugs produce sedation and drowsiness under many circumstances; at other times they might diminish inhibitions and appear to "release" behavior from its normal controls. Alcohol and several other types of substances are thought of as general depressants of the CNS. Some CNS depressants are prescribed as sedatives, sleeping pills, or to reduce the frequency of epileptic seizures.

Alcohol is one of the most commonly used (and misused) of the psychoactive drugs. Some may ask whether it is appropriate to consider alcohol a drug, since it has so many roles in human societies. When one is discussing whether to serve red or white wine with dinner, we are looking at it as a food or beverage item. But when one is discussing how many glasses of wine one can drink before reaching the minimum blood alcohol concentration (BAC) to be considered legally drunk, then viewing alcohol as a drug that varies in dose and whose effect depends upon dose is more appropriate.

Since alcohol has behavioral effects so similar to the other depressant drugs, it is logical for us to consider it a drug in the current context. At low doses (up to a BAC of about 0.10%), alcohol produces a sense of relaxation and a lessening of inhibitions that may lead to increased social interactions and recklessness. At higher BACs the generalized depressant action of the substance becomes more obvious: slowed reaction times, slurred speech, staggering when walking, and other clear signs of impairment. At still higher doses the user may become unconscious and difficult to arouse, and at BACs of around 0.60 there is a chance that respiration will cease, leading to death. Tolerance of many of these effects develops, and prolonged use of high doses can lead to a withdrawal syndrome that includes restlessness, tremors, hallucinations, and sometimes dangerous *grand mal* seizures. Addiction occurs in some users, and the worldwide problem of alcoholism is well-studied among psychologists interested in why it develops and how it can best be treated.

There is a wide variety of other depressant drugs, including the benzodiazepines, a reference to their common chemical structure. The benzodiazepines include prescription drugs used as sleeping pills, such as Halcion, and others used as antianxiety agents, such as Xanax. The benzodiazepine known as Rohypnol is not legally sold in the United States, but is available in many other countries. Because it has been secretly combined with alcohol to produce a profound state of intoxication, it became known as a "date-rape" drug.

Psychotherapeutic Drugs. Both Ritalin, the stimulant used to treat ADHD, and the benzodiazepine antianxiety agents would be considered psychotherapeutic agents. Two major classes of drugs within this group are the antipsychotics and the antidepressants.

Antipsychotics were once referred to as tranquilizers, but they are not general CNS depressants. Some may produce drowsiness but others do not, and CNS depression is not responsible for their effectiveness in treating schizophrenia and other forms of psychotic behavior. The main thing they do is to decrease the frequency of "crazy talk" and erratic behaviors.

Antidepressants include several basic types, but recently the selective serotonin reuptake inhibitors, such as Prozac, have become by far the most widely used. The antidepressant drugs are able to reduce the severity and duration of major depressive episodes, but they are not a cure for depression.

Lithium is also prescribed fairly widely, as it is the drug of choice for treating bipolar disorder (once known as manic-depressive disorder).

Narcotic Analgesics (Opioids). The classic drug in this group is morphine, derived from the opium poppy. The primary medical use has been for the relief of severe pain, but these drugs also produce a dreamy, relaxed feeling of contentment and well-being. Heroin is a more potent derivative of morphine, and there is a wide variety of synthetic compounds that have opiate-like effects. Although these drugs can induce sleep in higher doses, they are distinguished from the general CNS depressants in that there is no slurring of speech or staggering gait associated with intoxication. The withdrawal syndrome is also different, characterized by diarrhea, muscle cramps, and a runny nose. While very unpleasant, withdrawal from narcotics is much less dangerous than withdrawal from alcohol or the other general CNS depressants. One thing the narcotics do have in common with CNS depressants is the depression of respiration, and accidental overdose deaths often occur as a result of combining narcotics with alcohol.

Nicotine. This is the major psychoactive ingredient in tobacco. It has the properties of a mild CNS stimulant, although cigarette smokers often say that smoking relaxes them. Nicotine does enhance one's ability to pay attention to a specific task, and one withdrawal sign is drowsiness and fatigue. Powerful addiction to nicotine apparently occurs in a majority or regular tobacco users because attempting to quit tobacco, even in the face of clear health warnings, usually results in relapse within a few days or weeks. Those who keep trying to quit are often successful, but usually only after several attempts.

Hallucinogens. This group includes a wide variety of plant-derived and synthetic substances. Mescaline, derived from a cactus, and LSD, a synthetic, are two well-known examples. These drugs alter perception (especially visual perception) and enhance emotional responsiveness so that images are distorted in ways that may be interpreted as very interesting or very frightening. Most often the user is aware that the drug-induced experience does not represent "reality," and knows that the experience is due to the drug. They are often able to describe the experience to others, either at the time it is occurring or later. That is less true for another type of hallucinogen, PCP, which often produces distortions of the perception of one's own body and which also is a dissociative anesthetic, meaning that even while a person appears to be awake he or she may not respond to extreme pain. Users of PCP are often uncommunicative during the experience and often cannot remember much at a later time.

Marijuana. This is a common name for smokable material from the *Cannabis* plant. Various preparations of cannabis have been smoked, drunk, or eaten for thousands of years for both medical and recreational purposes. Smoking cannabis produces an initial sense of lightheadedness and euphoria, often accompanied by hilarity. Later the user typically feels relaxed and may be less active. At low doses these effects resemble the effects of low doses of CNS depressants. At very high doses, users often experience hallucinations and the drug is sometimes considered an hallucinogen. At the most commonly used doses withdrawal symptoms are not seen and addiction is less frequent than with nicotine, the CNS stimulants or depressants, or the opiates.

How Psychoactive Drugs Work in the Brain

Much has been learned about the actions of these drugs on neurochemical systems in the brain, and the pace of discovery seems to accelerate with each decade. We know, for example, that within the brain, receptor structures exist that are selectively affected by the opiates, and there are natural opiatelike substances produced in the brain that are presumably the normal activators of those receptors. We are not entirely sure what functions these endorphins normally support in the brain, but one of them is likely to be the psychological control of pain.

For other types of drugs, the method of action on the brain also seems fairly clear, for example, all of the effective antipsychotic drugs block receptors in the brain for a neurotransmitter substance called dopamine. In one region of the brain, we know that dopamine is released by neurons and that the release of dopamine is critical for the maintenance of normal muscle tone. Permanent loss of dopamine from the area results in tremors and rigidity and eventually to paralysis. The dopamine blockers that reduce psychotic behavior can also produce tremors and rigidity in some patients. One word of caution, however. Although we believe that antipsychotic drugs act to reduce psychosis because of their action at dopamine receptors, we can find little or no consistent evidence of dopamine imbalance or malfunction in psychotic patients. In other words, knowing that these drugs block dopamine receptors does not explain why blocking dopamine receptors diminishes psychotic behavior, nor does it prove that some abnormal dopamine function is responsible for psychosis. Likewise with the selective serotonin reuptake inhibitors. Their grouping name signifies that we know something about the neurochemical effect of these drugs—they selectively block the reuptake into neurons of serotonin that has just been released. However, other antidepressant drugs that work equally well do not selectively block serotonin reuptake. Some selectively block the reuptake of norepinephrine, another of the brain's neurotransmitters. Thus, a conclusion that depression is caused by a serotonin deficiency or imbalance is not warranted by the data.

More remains to be learned about the actions of these and other drugs on the brain's neurotransmitter chemicals and their receptors. At stake are potential improvements in the chemical treatment of depression, bipolar disorder, psychosis, and other disorders, as well as potential chemical treatments for addiction.

[*See also* Depressants, Sedatives, and Hypnotics; Drug Abuse; *and* Drugs and Intelligence. *Also, many illicit drugs are the subjects of independent entries.*]

Bibliography

American Psychiatric Association. (1994). *Diagnostic and statistical manual of mental disorders* (4th ed.). Washington, DC: Author.

Feldman, R. S., Meyer, J. S., & Quenzer, L. F. (1997). *Principles of neuropsychopharmacology*. Sunderland, MA: Sinauer. A thorough description of brain function and how drugs act in the brain.

Gitlin, M. J. (1996). *The psychotherapist's guide to psychopharmacology* (2nd ed.). New York: Free Press.

Ray, O. S., & Ksir C. (1999). *Drugs, society and human behavior* (8th ed.). New York: McGraw-Hill. A review of the history, pharmacology, and psychology of psychoactive drugs and their use.

Charles Ksir

DRUGS AND INTELLIGENCE. Psychologists define intelligence in many ways. The characteristics of intelligence include the ability to learn from experience, to respond quickly to novel stimuli, and to solve problems. [*See* Thinking, *article on* Problem Solving.] Intelligence may also be defined as the highest level of neural integration in the brain that is expressed by the action of knowing, perceiving, and conceiving. Each of these characteristics of intelligence can be influenced by drugs that alter brain function. In short, most psychotropic drugs alter one's ability to demonstrate the characteristics of intelligence.

Recent developments have contributed to our interest in the manipulation of intelligence by drugs. One important development has been the untangling of the mystery of the anatomy of the brain and the recognition of the role of its individual elements in intelligence, particularly the neurotransmitter pathways. Neural pathways form the communication lines between different brain regions. It is at their points of communication with each other that nearly all of the important drug-brain interactions occur; these points of communication are called synapses. Within these synapses are specific proteins that act as recognition sites, or receptors, for the different drugs. The brain has many such pathways that communicate by releasing specific chemicals, called neurotransmitters. These neurotransmitters are made by the brain from nutrients in the diet. Indeed, the balance of dietary nutrients, or their imbalance, can influence brain function and intelligence by altering the production of the neurotransmitter molecules. [See Determinants of Intelligence, article on Nutrition and Intelligence.] For example, the neurotransmitter serotonin is important for controlling mood. Some recreational drugs, such as amphetamines and cocaine, can temporarily relieve the symptoms of depression because they enhance the release of serotonin as well as other neurotransmitters. In contrast, psychedelic drugs induce hallucinations by interfering with the actions of serotonin neurons.

Hallucinogens

Little reliable information is available on the effects of hallucinogens, such as PCP (phencyclidine piperidine HCl, or angel dust), bufotenin, DMT (N,N-dimethyltryptamine), ecstasy (3,4-methylenedioxy-methamphetamine), LSD (lysergic acid diethylamide), mescaline (from peyote, i.e., the cactus Lophophora williamsii) or psilocybin (from the mushroom Psilocybe mexicana), on intelligence (Judd, 1987). In most cases, the actions of these drugs on the brain are so profound that normal intellectual processes are significantly impaired until the drugs leave the brain. Therefore, it is very difficult to determine the effects of hallucinogens on intelligence.

The consequences of the long-term use of most hallucinogens has never been completely determined. Scientists believe that prolonged and daily use of PCP can produce short-term memory deficits; in addition, some individuals have reported significant speech difficulties one year later. The permanent pathological effects of the drug ecstasy on the brain are better understood; however, its long-term effects on intelligence are not. In primates, a single low dose of ecstasy irreversibly destroyed most of the neurons that produce serotonin. Surprisingly, humans and nonhuman primates given ecstasy do not demonstrate significant changes in learning and memory abilities, mood, or sleeping habits, i.e., those brain functions that are thought to require serotonin neurons. The consequences of ecstasy use may only be appreciated as these people become older and their brain's ability to compensate is diminished.

Long-term, daily marijuana use impairs short-term memory, particularly those events that occur during or immediately after its use. However, the ability to retrieve information that is already in long-term memory is not altered by marijuana intoxication. However, marijuana intoxication impairs the consolidation process, i.e., the transformation of short-term memories to long-term storage. This action of marijuana would have a significant impact on most measures of intelligence. Some users often compare the effects of marijuana to those of alcohol (to be discussed later); however, the effects of marijuana on brain function are quite different from those of alcohol intoxication. In contrast to marijuana, which does not depress central nervous system function, alcohol does have this effect and therefore prevents normal information processing of any kind from occurring. Both alcohol and marijuana intoxication can prevent the user from engaging in complicated mental or verbal tasks. The impairment in short-term memory produced by marijuana may also underlie changes in time-sense, which has been reported by recreational users, i.e., the user feels that time is accelerated.

Stimulants

Drugs that stimulate the brain tend to enhance attention, an important aspect of intelligence. The best-studied stimulants are caffeine, amphetamine, cocaine, and nicotine. Caffeine has many beneficial effects. Primarily, it enhances mental clarity and lessens fatigue. Caffeine is most effective in improving performance that has deteriorated due to excessive stress or fatigue. However, it has much less benefit on well-rested individuals. Interestingly, caffeine has a more pronounced benefit on the performance abilities of highly impulsive people as compared to less impulsive people. [See Impulsivity.] It also increases vigilance and prevents the decline in attentional ability, which is frequently seen after meals. Caffeine also enhances the ability of subjects to simultaneously pay attention and respond to two different stimuli. The performance of women engaged in intelligence-related tasks are most enhanced by low doses of caffeine during the first five days of their menstrual cycle, suggesting an interaction with the body's hormones. [See Endocrine Systems.] Overall, caffeine does not actually improve intelligence; it only enhances the ability to focus one's attention.

Amphetamine enhances performance in many different behavioral tasks that require learning and memory or increased vigilance (Judd, 1987). The brain's utilization of its primary energy source, glucose, is greatly increased by amphetamine. In addition, the electrical activity measured at the scalp, one's EEG, is enhanced, and this is correlated with improved performance. Amphetamine's effects on cognitive function may be related to its actions outside the brain that are completely unrelated to its actions within the brain that cause excitation and euphoria. For example, peripheral administration of amphetamine, i.e., taking a pill or receiving an injection, enhances memory. In contrast, injection of amphetamine directly into the brain does not. This may be due to its ability to quickly increase blood glucose levels.

Cocaine is a powerful brain stimulant and enhances the performance of laboratory animals in tasks that require memory or vigilance. In one study on humans, cocaine use disrupted learning; in another, it increased the reaction time of subjects who were sleep deprived but not of those who were well rested. The similarities between the actions of cocaine and amphetamine in the brain may underlie their similar effects on intelligence. It is important to recognize that in these experimental studies very low doses of amphetamine and cocaine, well below the doses typically taken by humans, were given only once or twice to naive rats. Repeated exposure to high doses of either drug actually impairs performance on these same tasks.

Studies on humans have suggested that nicotine influences overall performance by increasing subjects' speed of response in selected tasks, enhancing their ability to focus quickly on relevant visual information, and improving overall attention and information processing, rather than by enhancing any particular memory process within the brain (Heishman et al., 1994). Making a clear determination about the enhancing effects of nicotine on intelligence is problematic, however, because these studies have all assessed performance under abstinence conditions. Therefore, positive effects might simply be due to the amelioration of withdrawal-associated deficits. Indeed, this caveat could potentially apply to the results of many stimulant drugs that enhance intelligence in controlled laboratory studies.

Depressants

In contrast to stimulants, the depressants, drugs that depress the function of the brain, such as opiates (heroin and morphine), alcohol, barbiturates, and the anxiolytics (drugs that reduce anxiety, such as Valium and related drugs), tend to impair performance on intelligence tasks. Opiate use interferes with learning and memory, while drugs that block the actions of opiates in the brain actually improve memory abilities and enhance attention. Overall, higher cognitive functions

have not been affected by low doses of opiates, but they have been impaired at high doses. The timing of the administration of the opiate was also important, i.e., whether it was taken before or after the subject attempted to perform the task.

Alcohol and the barbiturates depress the activity of neurons within the brain. They produce such profound changes in brain function that the determination of intellectual abilities is very difficult. Both types of drugs tend to release behavior that had been previously suppressed by punishment. Assuming that these drugs are not used repeatedly, intellectual ability after their use is usually not permanently impaired. However, following chronic use, disorders of memory and critical cognitive processes that underlie intelligence have been associated with the degeneration of specific brain regions.

Valium (which is Latin for "be strong and well") and its related drugs have a similar major side effect: drowsiness. Their primary effects on intellectual ability are probably related to this drowsiness. Recent studies have found that specific attentional abilities are impaired, such as tracking eye-movements, i.e., the ability to follow the movements of an object with the eyes, particularly when driving a car. This tracking impairment is also seen with alcohol. A typical dose of Valium impairs lane tracking, lane changing, and stopping ability for up to 3.5 hours. These drugs may also impair function in brain regions that are important for learning and memory and produce a temporary amnesia.

Drugs That Influence Creativity

Studies of the effects of drugs on creativity, an important expression of intelligence, are not hampered by problems of generalization to our species from laboratory animals; most of the artistic products judged to have aesthetic value to humans were created by humans. Some drugs may enhance creativity, not through their actions on some unknown brain structure, but through their ability to release the user from the constraints of another problem, either mental or physical, e.g., the relief from physical or mental pain or anguish, anxiety or depression, or severe personal problems. An excellent example of a recreational drug used in this way is alcohol. The creative genius of many artists, such as Thomas Wolfe, Dylan Thomas, and F. Scott Fitzgerald, may have been released by the ability of alcohol to relieve physical and emotional pain and anxiety. Valium and its related drugs have provided immeasurable relief from anxiety for many lesser artists.

Caffeine, chocolate, and amphetamine have probably allowed many businesspeople and artists to remain alert during a period of fatigue so that a specific creative task could be completed. Hallucinogens have often been used to enhance creativity, especially LSD and peyote (Leavitt, 1982). These drugs generate an altered state of consciousness somewhat similar to dreaming that the users claim may lead to enhanced creative abilities. The following were "invented" while their creators were dreaming: the story of Dr. Jekyll and Mr. Hyde, by Robert Louis Stevenson; the model of the atom, by Bohr; the nature of the benzene ring, by Kekule; the sewing machine, by Howe; and various musical scores, as claimed by Mozart and Robert Schumann. In contrast, a few authors who have claimed benefit from recreational drug use include Alan Watts (*As a Man Thinketh*), Ken Kesey (*One Flew Over the Cuckoo's Nest*), and William Burroughs (*Naked Lunch*). Individuals who choose to live an unconventional life, such as artists, may also choose to try unconventional experiences, such as those produced by hallucinogens (Masters & Houston, 1968).

Conclusions

Any drug that influences brain function must have an effect on some aspect of intelligence. The nature of this effect depends on the particular neurotransmitter system that is affected within the brain. The effects of some drugs are so profound that any attempt to measure intelligence is impossible. In general, although some drugs may temporarily improve performance, most tend to impair, rather than enhance, overall intelligence.

Whether drugs can truly enhance any aspect of intelligence is unknown; indeed, it may not be possible to enhance intelligence. First, the brain may already be functioning at its peak level of performance; it may be impossible to improve on millions of years of evolution by the administration of a single drug. Second, the systems of the brain function in subtle balance with each other; the gross manipulation of any neural systems by a drug usually imbalances the interplay of the systems. Therefore, although a single measure of intelligence may be enhanced by a drug, other cognitive functions that contribute to one's overall intelligence may become severely impaired.

[*See also* Alcoholism; Amnesia; Attention; Brain; Cocaine; Creativity; Depressants, Sedatives, and Hypnotics; Depression; Drugs; Hallucinations; Hallocinogens; Information Processing Theories; Intelligence; Learning; Marijuana; Memory; Mood; Stimulants; Synapse; *and* Thinking, *article on* Problem Solving.]

Bibliography

Feldman, R. S., Meyer, J. S., & Quenzer, L. F. (1997). *Principles of neuropsychopharmacology.* Sunderland, MA: Sinauer. A thorough introduction to the basics of brain chemistry and the specific effects of psychoactive drugs on brain function and behavior.

Hardman, J. G., & Limbird, L. E. (1996). *Goodman and Gilman's: The pharmacological basis of therapeutics* (9th ed.). New York: Pergamon. An excellent resource book on all aspects of drug effects upon the body.

Heishman, S. J., Taylor, R. C., & Henningfield, J. E. (1994). Nicotine and smoking: A review of effects on human performance. *Experimental and Clinical Psychopharmacology, 16,* 345–395.

Iversen, S. D. (Ed.). (1985). Psychopharmacology of cognition. *Psychopharmacology: Recent advances and future prospects* (pp. 125–130). New York: Oxford University Press.

Judd, L. L., Squire, L. R., Butters, N., Salmon, D. P., & Paller, K. A. (1987). Effects of psychotropic drugs on cognition and memory in normal humans and animals. In H. Y. Meltzer (Ed.), *Psychopharmacology: The third generation of progress.* New York: Raven Press. This book is an excellent reference source for many aspects of psychopharmacology.

Leavitt, F. (1982). *Drugs and behavior* (2nd ed., pp. 348–482). New York: Wiley.

Masters, R., & Houston, J. (1968). *Psychedelic art.* New York: Grove.

Wenk, G. L., & Olton, D. S. (1989). Cognitive enhancers: potential strategies and experimental results. *Progress in Neuro-Psychopharmacology and Biological Psychiatry, 13* (Suppl.), S117–S139.

Gary L. Wenk

DRUG THERAPY. *See* Psychopharmacology, *article on* Pharmacotherapy.

DSM. *See* Diagnostic and Statistical Manual of Mental Disorders.

DUNCKER, KARL (1903–1940), German American psychologist. An experimental psychologist in the Gestalt tradition, Duncker made lasting contributions to perception, the psychology of problem solving, and other areas in psychology. Born 2 February 1903, in Leipzig, Germany, he studied with Gestalt theorists Wolfgang Köhler and Max Wertheimer at the University of Berlin. He earned his master's degree from Clark University in Worcester, Massachusetts in 1926 with a thesis on productive thinking, and his doctorate from Berlin University in 1929 with a dissertation on the perception of induced motion, then remained at Berlin as Köhler's assistant, conducting further studies of productive thinking, learning, and perception. Dismissed from Berlin by the Nazis, Duncker moved to England and worked in Sir Frederic Bartlett's psychology laboratory at Cambridge. After a stay in Kreuzlingen, Switzerland, at Ludwig Binswanger's clinic, for treatment of a severe depression, Duncker became an instructor at Swarthmore College in 1938. He continued scholarly work until his self-inflicted death on 23 February 1940. [*See the biographies of Köhler, Wertheimer, and Bartlett.*]

Duncker's contributions cover a wide range of areas in psychology, from influential experimental work to articles on theoretical and philosophical psychology. Best known are his works on the psychology of productive thinking and his experiments on apparent motion, but he also published studies on pain, motivation, an effect of past experience on taste perception, and systematic psychology. He also collaborated on two books intended to assist American students in learning to read psychological material in German.

Duncker's works on productive thinking, still frequently cited by cognitive psychologists late in the twentieth century, asked participants to "think aloud" while trying to solve standard problems that Duncker posed to them. The resulting verbal protocols reinforced the Gestalt distinction between what Duncker called "organic" solutions that analyze the problem "from above" and "mechanical" approaches that analyze the problem "from below." The former are meaningful and involve insight and understanding; they qualify as "productive thinking." The latter are senseless and "blind," using rote memorization; they are purely "reproductive" and, while they can occasionally generate solutions, do not really involve "thinking." Still influential in cognitive psychology are Duncker's conceptions of the structure and dynamics of productive problem-solving processes; the use of verbal protocols; his distinction between insightful learning and "simple finding" or automatic retrieval; and "functional fixedness" or the interference (generated by realizing that the item can be used in a particular way in one problem context) in using an item differently in another problem context.

Duncker's work on apparent motion established that when there is relative displacement between an object and its surround, the motion is typically perceptually attributed to the object and not the framework. This "induced motion" extended earlier Gestalt work on the perception of movement.

Other contributions included demonstrating paradoxical relief from one source of pain by intentional exposure to a second source of pain; the influence of social suggestion and prestige on children's food preferences; and the effect of the color of chocolate (white or brown) on its apparent flavor, and theoretical writings that developed the Gestalt position on motivation, epistemology, and phenomenology, and that criticized behaviorism and ethical relativism.

Bibliography

Duncker, K. (1926). A qualitative experimental and theoretical study of productive thinking (solving of comprehensible problems). *Pedagogical Seminary, 33*, 642–708.

Duncker, K. (1929). Über induzierte Bewegung (Ein Beitrag zur Theorie optisch wahrgenommener Bewegung) [Induced motion (A contribution to the theory of optically perceived motion)]. *Psychologische Forschung, 12*, 180–259.

Duncker, K. (1967). Induced motion. In W. D. Ellis (Ed.), *A source book of Gestalt psychology* (pp. 161–172). New York: Humanities Press. (Original work published 1938.) This is a condensed English language translation of Duncker (1929).

Duncker, K. (1935). *Zur Psychologie des produktiven Denkens* [The psychology of productive thinking]. Berlin: Springer. English version: Duncker, K. (1945). On problem solving. (L. S. Lees, Trans.). *Psychological Monographs, 58*, Whole No. 270. (Original work published 1935)

Duncker, K., & Watt, D. B. (1929). *Exercises for the rapid reading of scientific German texts (with interlinear translation of difficult words)*. Ann Arbor, MI: Edwards.

Duncker, K., & Watt, D. B. (1930). *A German-English dictionary of psychological terms*. Ann Arbor, MI: Edwards.

King, D. B., Cox, M., & Wertheimer, M. (1998). Karl Duncker: Productive problems with beautiful solutions. In G. A. Kimble, & M. Wertheimer (Eds.), *Portraits of pioneers in psychology* (Vol. 3, pp. 163–179). Washington, DC: American Psychological Association and Mahwah, NJ: Erlbaum. Provides biographical material on Duncker and lists Duncker's publications.

Michael Wertheimer

DUNLAP, KNIGHT (1875–1949), American psychologist. Dunlap received his bachelor's degree (1899) and master's degree (1900) from the University of California at Berkeley where his mentor was George M. Stratton, an experimental psychologist who had studied with Wilhelm Wundt. Dunlap completed his doctorate in psychology at Harvard University in 1903 under Hugo Münsterberg, whom he admired and whose interest in the practical applications of psychology influenced him. In 1906, following a brief and unhappy experience as an instructor at Berkeley, Dunlap was named an instructor in psychology at Johns Hopkins University, where he eventually rose to the rank of professor of experimental psychology. John B. Watson, the founder of behaviorism, joined Dunlap at Johns Hopkins in 1908. Their relationship was cordial and mutually beneficial. Undoubtedly, Dunlap's reappraisal of introspection had a stimulating effect on Watson and therefore played a role in the creation of behaviorism. Dunlap was appointed chairman in 1920 and became instrumental in resurrecting Hopkins's moribund doctoral psychology program. His philosophy of graduate education combined methodological rigor with training in practical skills. Dunlap remained at Johns Hopkins until 1936, when he accepted an offer to develop a graduate psychology program at UCLA, where he remained until his retirement in 1946.

Dunlap's pioneering and highly influential analyses of imagery, consciousness, instinct, and habit assure him an important niche in the history of American psychology. He opposed the use of introspection to categorize consciousness into images or ideas, but he believed that conscious awareness could be studied as an objective response. In his critique of instincts, Dunlap argued that William McDougall's widely cited instinctive explanations of behavior were vitalistic and teleological. However, he did acknowledge that innate, biological factors were important determinants of behavior, and he proposed that the science of psychology be based upon a collaboration between psychology and biology. In this regard, he developed a neuropsychological model that correlated consciousness with integrated patterns or systems of neural-motor circuits. Dunlap's analysis of habit is noteworthy for its anticipation of contemporary interest in the impact that cognitive and motivational factors have on learning. Utilizing his insight that certain habits may be weakened through repetition, he developed the "negative practice" therapeutic technique for eliminating such maladaptive behaviors as stuttering and tics.

After first proposing the term "scientific psychology" to designate his approach, Dunlap ultimately settled on the name "response psychology." Given its emphasis upon practical applications, commitment to the physiological correlates of behavior, and inclusion of both behavioral and cognitive processes, response psychology may be viewed as an evolutionary development of the functionalist school of psychology. Dunlap never systematically tested the postulates of response psychology but instead presented theoretical arguments for his position in books and articles. His experimental research encompassed investigations of word association, psychomotor skills, color vision, reaction time, auditory perception, and the nystagmatic reflex. A creative developer of laboratory apparatus, Dunlap's inventions include the Johns Hopkins's chronoscope, the Dunlap tapping table, and the Dunlap chair for vestibular research. He also was among the first to demonstrate practice effects in intelligence testing.

Although frequently portrayed as a proto-behaviorist, Dunlap actually believed that the inherent oversimplifications of behaviorism, especially the denial of cognitive processes, had impeded the progress of scientific psychology. Watson's elimination of mental events and his extreme environmentalism far exceeded Dunlap's proposals for the reconceptualizations of the mental and biological determinants of behavior. Dunlap refused to accept the behavioristic elimination of the mind, and it is this adamant insistence upon taking mental processes into account that distinguishes him from Watson and demonstrates his relevance for contemporary psychology. It is ironic that Watson's generous but unintentionally misleading statements about Dunlap's contributions to the development of behaviorism may have deflected attention away from the latter's focus on cognitive processes and may have thereby distorted psychologists' perceptions of Dunlap's actual views on the nature of psychology.

Dunlap had an eclectic range of interests. He authored books on physiological psychology, the psychology of religion, social psychology, general psychology, eugenics, and personal adjustment. The first editor of the *Journal of Comparative Psychology*, he also served as an editor of *Comparative Psychology Monographs*, *Mental Measurements Monographs*, and *Child Development*. Dunlap was also an influential leader of such national and regional organizations as the American Psychological Association, the Western Psychological Association, the National Institute for Psychology, and the National Research Council. His 1922 presidential address to the American Psychological Association argued against the then dominant "group mind" concept and proposed that social psychology become an experimental discipline. Dunlap's papers are housed at the Archives of the History of American Psychology, University of Akron, Ohio.

Bibliography

Works by Dunlap

Dunlap, K. (1912). The case against introspection. *Psychological Review, 10,* 404–413. Published shortly before John B. Watson's classic 1913 article "Psychology as the Behaviorist Views It." Dunlap's critique of consciousness, although less radical than Watson's, was still quite influential.

Dunlap, K. (1919). Are there any instincts? *Journal of Abnormal Psychology, 14,* 307–311. This paper has been described as the pioneering anti-instinct article in American psychology.

Dunlap, K. (1920). *Mysticism, Freudianism, and scientific psychology.* St. Louis, MO: C. V. Mosby. Dunlap compares psychoanalysis to a mystical-religious movement.

Dunlap, K. (1930). Response psychology. In C. Murchison (Ed.), *Psychologies of 1930* (pp. 309–323). Worcester, MA: Clark University Press. The final formal presentation of Dunlap's theoretical system.

Dunlap, K. (1932). [Autobiography]. In C. Murchison (Ed.), *A history of psychology in autobiography: Vol. 2.* (pp. 35–61). Worcester, MA: Clark University Press.

Dunlap, K. (1932). *Habits, their making and unmaking.* New York: Liveright. Dunlap's definitive presentation of negative practice.

Works about Dunlap

Dorcus, R. M. (1950). Knight Dunlap (1875–1949). *The American Journal of Psychology, 63,* 114–119. Obituary that contains useful information about Dunlap's life.

Kornfeld, A. D. (1991). Contributions to the history of psychology: LXXVI. Achievement, eminence, and histories of psychology: the case of Knight Dunlap. *Psychological Reports, 68,* 368–370. Outlines Dunlap's major accomplishments and speculates about the reasons for his current position of relative obscurity.

Pauly, P. J. (1986). G. Stanley Hall and his successors: A history of the first half-century of psychology at Johns Hopkins. In S. H. Hulse & B. F. Green, Jr. (Eds.), *One hundred years of psychological research in America: G. Stanley Hall and the Johns Hopkins tradition* (pp. 21–51). Baltimore, MD: The Johns Hopkins University Press. Includes an account of Dunlap's stewardship as chair at Johns Hopkins and the causes for his move to UCLA.

Alfred D. Kornfeld

DURKHEIM, ÉMILE (1858–1917), French sociologist. Emile Durkheim was one of the founders of sociology as an academic discipline. Born in Epinal, he went to Paris to study philosophy at the École Normale Supérieure. He taught pedagogy, sociology, and philosophy first at the University of Bordeaux (1887–1902) and then at the newly constituted Sorbonne in Paris until his death.

His dissertation, *The Division of Labor in Society* (1893/1984), was his first major work. In it, he drew on historical and comparative studies of law and morality to argue that labor specialization was giving rise to a new, "organic" type of social solidarity in modern societies that was replacing the older, "mechanical" form. He explicated the empirical methods of this and his subsequent sociological works in *The Rules of Sociological Method* (1895/1982), in which he drew a sharp distinction between sociology and psychology. Where psychology studied individual mental representations, he argued, the goal of sociology was to study the collective representations that bind people to their respective societies.

Of all his works, perhaps Durkheim's *Suicide* (1897/1951) had the greatest impact on psychology. In it, he demonstrated the importance of sociological factors, specifically social integration and regulation, to explain suicide rates of social groups. Social integration had to do with moral relationships and regulation with economic relationships. An excess or deficiency of either could lead to higher suicide rates. Thus, there were four types of suicide: First, egoistic suicide, typified by the suicide of lonely old bachelors, was the result of a lack of social integration. Second, altruistic suicide, typified by the sacrifice of a soldier to save his comrades, resulted from an excess of social integration. To the extent that Protestants commit suicide more often than Catholics, and Catholics more often than Jews, Durkheim thought that these different religions offered their congregations different degrees of social integration. Third, anomic suicide reflected a lack of social regulation and was most prevalent during economic crises. Fourth, fatalistic suicide, at least in Durkheim's time, was relatively rare, as it is due to excessive social regulation characteristic of a high degree of specialization in labor that even industrialized societies had not yet achieved. Mixed forms of suicide were also possible, especially egoistic–anomic suicide. It must be stressed that these categories were meant to explain suicide rates and not individual suicides. These rates, Durkheim argued, could not be explained in terms of a combination of psychological factors, such as rates of mental illness (see Schmaus, 1994, ch. 7, for a more detailed interpretation).

After publishing *Suicide*, Durkheim founded and edited the journal *L'Année sociologique* (1898–1913). His last major work, *The Elementary Forms of Religious Life* (1912/1995), investigated the social causes and functions of religious belief and ritual, especially in so-called primitive societies. The main interest of this work for psychologists is Durkheim's account of the religious, and hence social, origins of our basic categories of thought, including space, time, causality, substance, genus, and personhood. This highly influential work initiated a tradition of anthropological research into the social and cultural aspects of cognition.

[*See also* Anthropology; Religious Experience; *and* Suicide.]

Bibliography

Works by Durkheim

Durkheim, É. (1951). *Suicide: A study of sociology* (J. A. Spaulding & G. Simpson, Trans.). New York: Free Press. (Original work published 1897.) Unfortunately, this translation is not reliable, even in its translation of Durkheim's definitions of key terms.

Durkheim, É. (1982). *The rules of sociological method and selected texts on sociology and its method* (Introduction by S. Lukes, Ed.; W. D. Halls, Trans.). New York: Free Press. (Original work published 1895.) This edition contains a useful collection of Durkheim's shorter writings on method, including essays on the relation of sociology to psychology and the other social sciences. Lukes's introduction, however, questions the value of the *Rules* for interpreting Durkheim's other works, an interpretation that was challenged by Schmaus (1994).

Durkheim, É. (1984). *The division of labor in society* (Translation of Durkheim's second, 1902 edition by W. D. Halls). New York: Free Press, (Original work published 1893.) For the first edition introduction, see the translation by G. Simpson, 1933, Macmillan, New York.

Durkheim, É. (1995). *The elementary forms of religious life* (K. Fields, Trans.). New York: Free Press. (Original work published 1912.) This is much superior to the older 1915 translation by J. W. Swain.

Works about Durkheim

Lukes, S. (1985). *Émile Durkheim: His life and work* (rev. ed.) Stanford, CA: Stanford University Press. This is a slightly revised version of the original 1973 work, which is still the standard intellectual biography of Durkheim, although some of Luke's interpretations have been superseded by more recent scholarship.

Schmaus, W. (1994). *Durkheim's philosophy of science and the sociology of knowledge: Creating an intellectual niche.* Chicago: University of Chicago Press. This work provides a fresh interpretation of Durkheim's major empirical works in light of a careful analysis of the unity of his views on method in the social sciences.

Warren Schmaus

DUTY TO REPORT. *See* Mandated Reporting.

DUTY TO WARN. *See* Violence Risk Assessment.

DYSLEXIA. The prevalence of dyslexia, or severe reading disability, is estimated to be 4% of school-aged children in the United States. Lower prevalence figures may be found in other countries where stricter diagnostic criteria are used or the nature of the native language is unique (e.g., phonetically regular/irregular). The prevalence of dyslexia has also been difficult to establish because the number of individuals with dyslexia has been compiled with other learning disorders such as mathematical and written language disorders. Males typically outnumber females by a ratio of 3–5:1. A bias toward identification of males, possibly because of more males than females exhibiting external behaviors associated with academic frustration, may account for at least some of this large gender specific inclination in diagnosis.

Dyslexia is typically not diagnosed until the beginning of formal schooling when reading instruction begins. Some individuals are not diagnosed with dyslexia until adulthood. In children with high IQs, a reading disability may not be recognized in the early grades because their reading achievement is usually average in comparison to their chronological age peers. Identification may occur when education becomes more demanding and independent as in the later middle or high school or even college years, where it is harder to compensate for reading weaknesses.

Early identification of dyslexia is thought to have the best outcome because early intervention can be implemented. Dyslexia persists throughout life, although with good early intervention some adults are able to compensate using learning strategies for their difficulties with reading. Comorbidity for dyslexia and attention-deficit/hyperactivity disorder (ADHD), mathematics disabilities, spelling and written expression disabilities have been commonly reported.

The diagnosis of dyslexia is typically accomplished through school district evaluations. A discrepancy model is used by most school districts to identify children with reading disabilities as well as other learning disabilities. The model is based on the definition of reading performance that is 1.5–2 standard deviations below their expected performance based on their IQ score, which must be in the average range. A regression formula is also used by some states to diagnose dyslexia. Many of these children are identified during the preschool years as having language delays or attention difficulties that may accompany dyslexia. Children who are identified as learning disabled are required by law (PL 94-142) to be served by the public school systems special education programs. Federal and state funds are provided for these programs, which are available in elementary school through college, and services may continue to be provided through graduate education.

Studies have shown that children with dyslexia progress in reading skills at the same rate as normal readers, but the level of mastery is consistently slower than same age peers and normal readers. Dyslexia is believed to be a language-based disorder in which the ability to engage in phonological processing is impaired thus impacting fluent reading. Often children have difficulty making the orthographic-phonological connections between written letters and their sounds. Remediation for dyslexia is usually focused on improving phonological awareness and increasing reading rate and comprehension. The service delivery model most often in schools is to have the children spend part of their day in a resource room to remediate reading skills, or children may receive these same remedial services in the regular classroom. Direct instruction of phonics, building sight-word vocabulary, and learning strategies are taught to students. Programs may also include study skills, counseling, cognitive-behavioral therapy, and behavior management. Some children with dyslexia are able to compensate for their disability, and they do not require special education for their entire school career. Other students require accommodations through college, and their disability continues to effect them in their jobs. Jobs that require a large amount of reading and writing can be difficult for adults with dyslexia. They may require more time to complete the same amount of work as their colleagues.

Neurobiological correlates of dyslexia are being explored through brain structure studies conducted through postmortem examination and the use of neuroimaging and electrophysiological techniques. There is evidence that individuals who have dyslexia are more likely to have symmetry or reversed asymmetry of the left posterior central language area. Language is lateralized (dominant in one hemisphere) to the left hemisphere of the brain in the majority of people, and this asymmetry in function is believed to be linked to the structural asymmetry of the language cortex. Postmortem studies have also provided evidence that leftward asymmetry is found in about 65% of normal brains and that there is greater potential for reversed asymmetry when an individual has dyslexia. The planum temporale, an area of the temporal lobe of the brain, has been implicated in language functions. It has been found in some magnetic resonance imaging (MRI) studies and postmortem studies to be symmetrical or asymmetrical favoring the right side in dyslexic individuals. Galaburda and colleagues (*Annals of Neurology*, 1985, *18*, 222–233) found an increased amount of focal dysplasia in dyslexics in the left planum temporale. Other cerebral anomalies have been found in the left hemisphere in dyslexics by Leonard and colleagues (*Archives of Neurology*, 1993, *50*, 461–469). Disorganization in subcortical areas related to the lateral geniculate nucleus of the thalamus has also been found in autopsy studies by Livingstone and associates (*Neurobiology*, 1991, *88*, 7943–7947).

Studies such as these suggest that there is cerebral reorganization in individuals with dyslexia not found in those without dyslexia. Positron emission tomography (PET), functional magnetic resonance imaging (fMRI), and regional cerebral blood flow (rCBF) studies have shown different patterns of neural activity during reading for normal readers and individuals with dyslexia. Differences in metabolic function have been found in the frontal and temporal regions of the brain's hemispheres. Adults with dyslexia have shown symmetrical activity in the brain favoring the left side. Electrophysiological studies of individuals with dyslexia have shown slower interhemispheric transaction times. Dyslexics also showed a larger number of errors on letter-matching tasks suggesting that the corpus callosum, which may facilitate communication between the hemispheres, may be impaired in dyslexia.

There is indication of a genetic link to dyslexia. Twin studies such as those done by DeFries and Alarcon (1996) have provided evidence that there most likely is a heritable component. Sibling studies of individuals with dyslexia using linkage analysis has allowed researchers to screen for gene loci. Significant markers have been found in families with a history of dyslexia on chromosomes 15 and 6 in studies by Pennington (*Journal of Child Neurology*, 1995, *10*, S69–S77). These chromosomal markers are now being tested in twin pairs where at least one twin is dyslexic.

There have been many advances made in understanding the neurobiological basis of dyslexia in the last decade. Information of genetics, brain morphology, and brain electrophysiology found in dyslexia may eventually assist in the early identification of individuals with dyslexia so intervention can begin in the early stages of reading instruction. Interventions for reading disabilities have also become more sophisticated and detailed as we learn more about how reading skills are acquired. By uncovering the components that are used in learning to read, testing can become more specific for the different components of reading, and intervention then may become more effective.

[*See also* Learning Disabilities.]

Bibliography

American Psychiatric Association. (1994). *Diagnostic and statistical manual of mental disorders* (4th ed.). Washington, D.C.: Author. Includes the diagnostic criteria for psychiatric disorders used by clinicians and researchers.

DeFries, J. C. & Alarcon, M. (1996). Genetics of specific reading disability. *Mental Retardation and Developmental Disabilities Research Reviews, 2*, 467–473.

Fleischner, J. E. (1994). Educational management of students with learning disabilities. *Journal of Child Neurology, 10*, S81–S85. Includes educational programming information concerning students diagnosed with learning disabilities.

Frith, U. (1997). Brain, mind, and behavior in dyslexia. In Hulme, C., & Snowling, M. (Eds.), *Dyslexia Biology Cognition and Intervention* (pp. 1–20). London: Whurr Publishers Ltd. Discussion of the role of brain function in determining the characteristics of dyslexia.

Galaburda, A. M., Sherman, G. F., Rosen, G. D., Aboitiz, F., & Geschwind, N. (1985). Developmental dyslexia: Four consecutive patients with cortical anomalies. *Annals of Neurology, 18*, 222–233. This is a study looking at cerebral asymmetry in adults with dyslexia.

Leonard, C. M., Voeller, K. K. S., Lombardino, L. J., Morris, M. K., Hynd, G. W., Alexander, A. W., Anderson, H. G., Garofalakis, M., Honeyman, J. C., Mao, J., Agee, F., & Staab, E. V. (1993). Anomalous cerebral structure in dyslexia revealed with magnetic resonance imaging. *Archives of Neurology, 50*, 461–469.

Livingstone, M. S., Rosen, G. D., Drislane, F. W., & Galaburda, A. M. (1991). Physiological and anatomical evidence for a magnocellular defect in developmental dyslexia. *Neurobiology, 88,* 7943–7947. An autopsy study that presents evidence of subcortical disorganization in dyslexic adults.

Lyon, G. R. (1995). Toward a definition of dyslexia. *Annals of Dyslexia, 45,* 3–27.

Pennington, B. F. (1995). Genetics of learning disabilities. *Journal of Child Neurology, 10,* S69–S77. Overview of the research uncovering a genetic link in learning disabilities.

Riccio, C. A., & Hynd, G. W. (1996). Neuroanatomical and neurophysiological aspects of dyslexia. *Topics in Language Disorders, 16 (2),* 1–13. Review of autopsy studies, neuroimaging, functional imaging, and electrophysiological studies of dyslexia.

Kathleen H. Nielsen and George W. Hynd

DYSTHYMIA. *See* Depression.

E

EAR. *See* Hearing.

EARLY CHILDHOOD. [*This entry provides a general survey of the theories, research, and findings that have informed our knowledge about cognitive and mental development during early childhood. For discussions dealing with other stages of development, see* Infancy; Middle Childhood; *and* Adolescence.]

Twenty years ago Rochel Gelman (*Annual Review of Psychology,* 1978) could accurately claim that our knowledge of children's thinking focused primarily on school-age children. Early childhood—from infancy through the preschool years—represented merely an impoverished ground floor from which the staircase of cognitive development began. In the ensuing years, younger children have been intensively investigated, thereby revealing step upon step of early cognitive achievements. Indeed, the current picture of accumulating early competencies can leave the impression that the achievements of later childhood are more anticlimactic than fundamental. This impression should be resisted; Paul Baltes, a noted life-span psychologist, reminds us that cognitive development is a life-long process filled with crucial gains and losses. Nonetheless, early developments are of legitimate special interest.

Early cognition is fascinating in its own right: How do infants and children, who are so seemingly different from adults, construe the world, think, and learn? Early cognition is crucial developmentally: What conceptions, capacities, and mechanisms constitute the infrastructure on which later knowledge and learning must build? And early abilities raise fundamental questions about human nature: What conceptions and capacities are innate? In what ways are basic cognitive competencies dependent on individual, social, and cultural experiences?

Piaget's Theory

Jean Piaget's proposals, more than any others, helped shape a "traditional account" of cognitive development. Piaget described two major periods within early childhood (see, for example, Piaget & Inhelder, 1969). First, in the "sensorimotor" period, infants are without representational thoughts, ideas, memories, or symbolic reasoning. They are cognitively active, but their interactions with and learnings about the world are in terms of perceptions and actions. Much as an adult "knows how" to walk without thinking about or conceiving of walking, infants "cognize" in the sense of at first reflexively and then more deliberately acting on the world. They do so initially via sucking, looking, grasping, and reaching; and then somewhat later via locomoting, searching for objects, and even imitating others' actions. The transition from the sensorimotor world of the infant to the "preoperational" period of the toddler and preschooler is marked by the onset of symbolic abilities, evident in part in children's acquisition and use of language. But, according to Piaget, in these early childhood years symbolic thought remains quite limited; it is preoperational rather than operational. Specifically, in this period children's symbols and concepts are centered on, or captured by, their own unique point of view—hence young children's thinking is systematically egocentric. Similarly, young children's thinking is similarly centered on the apparent, surface, perceptual features of objects and events, as opposed to more abstract, deeper qualities. Consequently, preoperational children deem anything that moves as alive, judge amount in terms of the changing length of a row of markers instead of their invariant number, and largely fail to appreciate causal connections between occurrences.

Cognition about Objects and Numbers

Most contemporary researchers no longer subscribe to this deficit view of early childhood, as initially *non*symbolic and then later *pre*operational. One area of cognition that has helped reconfigure our views of young children concerns their understanding of physical objects.

Consider the basic understanding that objects exist independent of oneself and thus continue to exist "out there" when out of sight or touch. Piaget concluded that this object concept was acquired late in infancy as an endproduct of sensorimotor developments such as the child's grasping and reaching for objects. Before that time, when an object is hidden, even if the infant sees it hidden and clearly wants it, he or she will not search for the object. It is as if the object ceases to exist. In the past ten years, the claim that young infants fail to understand object permanence has been systematically overturned, in part due to new findings from research using different methods, such as preferential looking tasks. Given a choice, infants prefer to look at some displays over others and in the right circumstances look longer at novel rather than familiar events. Infants as young as 3 and 4 months systematically look longer at physically anomalous displays than at physically possible ones. For example, they will look longer at a solid panel apparently moving right through a box hidden behind it, than they do when the panel stops on contact with the hidden box. This suggests that young infants are puzzled when the panel does not stop on expected contact with the box and thus believe the box continues to exist even when hidden from view. Extended findings of this sort, especially from the laboratories of Renée Baillargeon and Liz Spelke, show that quite young infants appreciate object existence, object continuity and solidity, as well as certain aspects of objects' movements (Baillargeon, 1993).

There is much for young children to learn about the physical world, based on but extending beyond initial understandings of objects' existence, appearances, and movements. For example, what about objects' material composition or the nature of their insides? Chairs are not only solid objects, they may be wood, or steel, or plastic; the gears inside a watch or muscles inside a frog may be largely unobservable but particularly important for explaining how they function. If asked to report the inside of objects, even 3-year-olds offer systematically different answers for animate and inanimate things (blood, bones, and muscles versus cotton, gears, and wood). Preschoolers judge that nonobvious insides are more essential to an object's identity and function than are outsides (the white and yolk of an egg versus its shell). Furthermore, young children

know that material objects (for example, a paper cup) that are ground up into tiny bits are no longer the same object (not a cup) but are still the same material (paper).

Regarding numbers, "threeness" or "fourness" is not a property of a single object as would be "red" or "round," and, indeed, physical features such as color or shape are irrelevant to numerosity. Moreover, the same item can be "three" or "four" or whatever, depending on where and how one counts the set. Yet even infants discriminate numerosities, as demonstrated in studies using habituation tasks. In such studies, infants are given trials viewing different sets of objects. Each set has the same number (for example, two objects) but the objects are constantly varied (for example, a ball and a spoon, then a toy car and pencil). After multiple trials, infants habituate; they look less and less at each succeeding set. But their looking increases significantly if they are now shown a set with a different number (for example, three objects, or one). Dishabituation thus shows attention to number in the preceding trials. A variety of studies demonstrates this early appreciation of object number in 3- and 4-month-olds and even in newborns. More controversial is the proposal that infants add and subtract, that is, that they are sensitive to the exact changes in numerosity that result when an item is added or taken away from an initial set (as argued by Wynn, 1991).

Infant attention to numerosities sets the stage for a considerable early developing competence with number in the toddler and preschool years, at least if number skills are assessed in relation to small sets of objects that the child counts. Number words are often acquired before the age of 2 years (with "two" typically the first acquired). Principled counting—where children use stable strings of number names, attempt to count all objects once and only once, and understand that the last number counted represents the cardinal value of the set—develops quickly and is evident even in the counting of many 2- and 3-year-olds when counting small sets (Gelman, 1993). Young children engage not only in number extraction—typically via counting—but in several forms of number reasoning as well. They can judge that four is more than three, or that if three dolls each have a hat there will be the same number of hats as dolls. Infant discrimination of numerosities thus leads to a preschool counting-based conception of number (Sophian, 1996).

Young children's attention to and knowledge about numbers, or objects' insides, help to contradict claims that young children's concepts are focused on the perceptual, static, and manifest characteristics of phenomena whereas only older children are concerned with conceptual, dynamic, and inferred characteristics. Young children's conceptions of persons, or their social cognition, contradicts such traditional accounts as well.

Social Cognition

Cognition about the social world includes conceptions about self and other, social roles, social interactions, social groups, and human behavior. It has been proposed that an understanding of the social world relies on an underlying mentalistic construal of persons, or a "theory of mind." Adults, for example, often construe persons' external observable actions and interactions in terms of their internal mental states, their beliefs, desires, intentions, and feelings.

Understanding persons mentalistically is evident in everyday reasoning. For example: Why did Jill go to the gym? She wanted to lose weight and thought that exercise would help. This example illustrates a basic belief-desire reasoning about persons: people engage in actions because they believe those actions will satisfy their desires. By 3 or 4 years, if given information about a person's beliefs and desires, then children can sensibly predict their actions, emotions, or statements. By 3 years, children can distinguish beliefs and desires, as mental entities and states, from physical objects and events. For example, if told about a boy who has a dog and another one who is thinking about a dog, young children correctly judge which dog can be seen, touched, and petted (Wellman, 1990).

Young children do not understand about all mental states equally or all at the same time. In particular, before about four years, they seem to have difficulty with mental states such as beliefs, that are representational. For example, if 4- and 5-year-olds are shown a distinctive candy box that actually contains pencils, they can correctly predict a naïve viewer of the box will believe it contains candy, not pencils. Success on this and other false-belief tasks seems to require the child to know that the target person represents the world as one way when in fact it is different. Younger children, typically 3-year-olds, fail such tasks; they say the naïve person will think the candy box indeed contains pencils, failing to separate beliefs and reality. This developmental difference from 2 to 4 or 5 years is also evident in young children's everyday conversations using such terms as *want*, *think*, and *know*. Thus, many researchers now propose that there is a major reorganization in children's mentalistic construal of persons from ages 2 to 5 as children acquire a representational theory of mind (Astington, 1993).

To be clear, it is not that before 4 or 5 years, children lack appreciation of any mental states—even 2-year-olds understand something of such mental states as desires, emotions, and perceptions. Thus, two-year-olds are able to understand that desires are subjective; for example, they are able to state that while to them a particular cookie is desirable and yummy, someone else could not like it and feel it was "yucky." Similarly, they understand that people can have very different percep-

tual experiences—you see a couch on your side of a closed door but I see a refrigerator on my side. In these ways, young children evidence a mentalistic construal of persons as well as a nonegocentric understanding of others.

Infants evidence initial understandings of persons. In the period from 8 to 14 months, infants are described as newly showing a sense of subjectivity, intentional understanding, or even an implicit theory of mind. Empirically, infants at this age begin to follow others' eye gaze and to direct their attention to objects by showing and pointing. They also engage in social referencing, where they use the mother's emotional expression about an ambiguous situation as a guide to their own evaluation and interaction within that situation. Thus, by about their first birthday, infants come to see persons as organisms who have experiences about the world (see, for example, the review by Moore & Corkum, 1994).

Young children's rapidly developing understanding of certain basic aspects of the physical world and contrasting aspects of the social world contribute to a characterization of cognitive development as domain specific. In certain core domains of understanding but not necessarily in other areas, young children can evidence coherent, systematic conceptions and reasoning. Young children's causal reasoning adds further support to such a view. Early in childhood, children reason about persons and about objects causally but also in very distinctive fashions—people act because of desires, intentions, and reasons; objects move because of contact and mechanical forces.

Causal Reasoning

Belief-desire reasoning (Jill went to the gym because . . .), as already described, is an important form of psychological causal reasoning. Psychological causes are also routinely cited in young children's explanations of human behavior. If preschool children are asked to explain simple human actions (for example, Jane is looking for her kitty), they, like adults, predominantly advance belief-desire explanations (she wants her kitty, she thinks the kitty is missing). Similarly, 3-, 4-, and 5-year-olds often can comprehend the psychological causality depicted in appropriately simple stories, where personified characters want certain goals, possess certain beliefs, use the information in their beliefs to execute plans to overcome obstacles to their goals, and are happy or sad or angry when they have attained or failed to attain these goals.

In contrast, young children reason about physical occurrences in different fashions, in terms of physical mechanisms such as contact and force. For example, Merry Bullock and her colleagues examined physical causal reasoning with a domino-like device (Bullock, Gelman, & Baillargeon, 1982): a stuffed rabbit was perched on a platform at the end of a line of blocks; a device with a rod preceded the first block; when the rod was pushed it toppled the first block that then toppled the others, eventually knocking the rabbit off. Young children were asked to predict the effect of potential changes to the device. Causally relevant changes included using a rod too short to hit the first block, or removing intermediate blocks. Irrelevant modifications included changing the material of the initial rod (from wood to glass). Three-year-olds were about 80% and four-year-olds about 90% correct at these predictions, demonstrating considerable reasoning about physical causation.

Again, infants display some early appreciations. For example, infants have been shown films or demonstrations of either one object colliding with and launching a second, or contrasting anomalous events such as a first object making contact with a second one that begins to move only after a considerable delay. Patterns of habituation and dishabituation to these displays indicate that infants were attending to the physical causal interactions of the objects by one year or perhaps even 6 months of age. Infants also seem to distinguish the sorts of causal forces that might apply to people versus objects. Within the first year, infants will imitate the actions of persons but not similar activities of mechanical objects. At 7 months, infants appear surprised if objects begin moving without some external force causing them to do so but not if people begin to move spontaneously.

In part, these sorts of findings undermine general stage theories of cognitive development such as Piaget's. At times, young children's thinking can indeed be egocentric, a-causal, and logically insensible. But for some topics and problems—including many central to understanding of people, bounded physical objects, and small counting numbers—young children's understanding and reasoning is notably coherent, causal, and sensible. Consequently, various domain-specific accounts of early cognitive development have been advanced. Some of these accounts invoke more general learning mechanisms that, when applied to people versus objects, yield different sorts of understanding. Other accounts invoke more neurological and modular proposals about cognition. Analogous to Noam Chomsky's proposals that language acquisition is served by a specially dedicated innate language acquisition device, it is possible that special mental modules and innate representations underlie early knowledge and reasoning about physical objects versus intentional human agents (Wellman & Gelman, 1998).

Understanding of people, physical objects, and number are probably not the only core domains of early knowledge. Language competence provides an obvious additional candidate. [See Language.] More controversial is the proposal that young children may rapidly acquire a naïve biological understanding as well, focused on entities such as plants and animals and phenomena such as growth, illness, and inheritance. At the very least, young children recognize that surface appearances and similarities are less important than underlying, essential ones for plants and animals as well as for persons. For example, in a series of studies Susan Gelman has exploited cases where perceptual appearance and underlying biological identity differ (Gelman & Markman, 1986). In an illustrative task, children see a picture of a pink flamingo and a black bat and hear that the flamingo has a pink heart whereas the bat has a red heart. Then they are asked to judge the heart color of a third animal, a black bird closely resembling the bat in appearance. Even 3-year-olds predict the blackbird would have a pink heart like the flamingo, overriding perceptual similarities and instead reasoning on the basis of nonobvious conceptual features and biological category memberships.

Information Processing

Beyond young children's conceptions and knowledge, the story of early cognitive development must also include their developing capacities and procedures for information processing. Memory is representative here. Young children remember enormous amounts of information. Consider word learning. By first grade, children are estimated to know 10,000 or more words. In the years from 2 to 4, children can acquire as many as 30 to 40 new words a week.

Memory comes in many forms—intentional versus incidental, short-term and long-term, episodic or semantic. [See Memory.] Developmentally, a key distinction concerns recognition memory versus recall. Processes of recognition operate early in life. Habituation procedures—where infants are presented a picture or display repeatedly and their looking gradually decreases as the picture becomes increasingly familiar—demonstrate recognition memory in young infants, even preterm infants. Recognition quickly attains adultlike levels. Three- and four-year-olds, like adults, are often 80 to 100% correct when shown scores, even hundreds, of pictures and then later required to recognize the old ones mixed in with new ones (Bjorklund & Schneider, 1998).

Processing a stimulus to the extent of later recognizing it as familiar indicates a rudimentary but important capacity for attending to and learning about the world. Indeed, habituation offers a measure of overall infant information processing. Beginning at about age four or five years, traditional IQ tests show considerable stability in children's overall cognitive performance. First-graders' IQs predict their IQs at age 16 quite accurately, although of course there is much variability with some children having large increases or decreases as they grow older. However, traditional tests developed for infants and young children fail to show such stability. Scores on intelligence tests (for example, the Stanford–Binet) or developmental assessments (for example, Bayley scales) at ages 1, 2, or 3 years are essentially unrelated to IQ scores a few years later. But, the rates at which infants habituate to familiar stimuli has proven to be quite predictive of later IQ. Infants who habituate more rapidly to a picture, and dishabituate more when a novel picture is then shown, reliably test higher on IQ tests at 5 and 6 years (Bornstein & Sigman, 1986).

At what age can children not only recognize items but recall them, that is, when can they mentally represent an item or event to themselves after it is perceptually absent? Preschoolers come to do this often, of course, when they verbally recall past experiences. In research using nonverbal methods that rely on delayed imitation, even one-year-olds consistently recall prior experiences. Eleven- and 13-month-olds who are shown a novel sequential action (placing a bar across a support, hanging a bell on the bar, and striking the bell with a mallet) will actively reenact the sequence even a week later, demonstrating recall for the prior event (Bauer, 1996). Some forms of delayed imitation may be evident even earlier in life.

In most conceptual analyses, genuine instances of recall require and manifest representational thought—active mental representation of prior experiences. However, as noted earlier, Piaget claimed that such representational cognition was unavailable in infancy and only appeared at about 18 months with the transition from sensorimotor to symbolic thought. As Jean Mandler (1992) has argued, however, several sorts of new evidence, including delayed imitation recall capacities and object permanence understandings for hidden objects, suggest that representational thought is an early contributor to the infant's ability to know and interact with the world, rather than a later outcome of such interactions. From very early in life infants actively represent the world, not just perceive it and act on it.

Much memory is incidental or automatic—children's everyday perceptions, conversations, actions, and explorations engage their multiple information processes, yielding the storage in memory of various sorts of information (words, life events, associations). But memory can also be more deliberate and strategic, for example, when children set themselves the goal of remembering information and then adopt certain effortful strategies to help themselves do so. Intentional memory strategies, such as rehearsing a list of items or organizing a group of words into larger categories of items to enhance recall, first systematically appear in the early school years at 6 to 8 years of age. That such memory strategies first appear at school age makes sense in that school experiences increase the demands on children to remember deliberately (for ex-

ample, acquiring reading vocabulary, addition facts, and so forth) and such demands may encourage deliberate attempts to memorize and remember. However, younger children's failure to use rehearsal, organization, and the like, does not mean that they are nonstrategic. Well before their third birthday, young children evidence deliberate, strategic remembering. Suppose a child sees a doll hidden in one of several locations and has to remember its location over a 3- to 4-minute delay. Toddlers and preschoolers engage in several strategies to help themselves remember, such as deliberately attending to the location during the delay interval, pointing at it periodically, and naming it. They do so more when asked to remember than when asked to simply wait, indicating these activities are generated to specifically aid remembering (DeLoache & Brown, 1983). And of course young children engage in a variety of social remembering strategies as well, asking parents to help find something, asking what a word means, and requesting someone to remind them.

Young children's strategic efforts at remembering clearly evidence problem solving skills as well as various memory processes. According to Piaget, and others since, even 9- to 12-month-old infants solve certain simple problems, for example using one object (such as a stick or cloth) to rake in a target object so that the target can then be grabbed and played with. Developing problem-solving skills are also apparent in young children's attempts to gain needed attention from others, to cooperate with or persuade others to get what one wants, to learn words, to count objects, and to learn to use tools such as spoons, doors, and light switches. Indeed, why do young humans so quickly come to certain understandings about objects, about number, about people, about animals? At least part of the answer must be that this knowledge is achieved in, and is useful for, the acquisition of certain desired goals and outcomes, that is, for solving certain everyday problems of early life. Problem solving evidences and requires burgeoning abilities to deliberately regulate behavior, to plan ahead, to reason about physical and about social situations, causes and constraints.

Conclusions

Increased understanding of early cognitive development has depended on the creation and utilization of ingenious methods to reveal very young children's knowledge, learning, and skill. A typical description of the methodological successes of this research is that investigators have simplified tasks by stripping away unnecessary processing demands, removing complexity, and often utilizing nonverbal or less verbal methods and measures—preferential looking, habituation, imitation, search, and simple judgments tasks. These descriptions are partly correct, but, in addition, investigators have keyed in on young children's domains of special competence and interest. Beyond simplification in a domain-neutral task-demands sense, investigators have simplified their research in the sense of accommodating more precisely to infants' and children's core understandings.

Young children are often incompetent and ignorant as well. Current theoretical questions of great import thus concern how to characterize early partial knowledge and the extent to which early childhood limitations reveal serious constraints on the nature of the early knowledge that young children possess.

Bibliography

Astington, J. (1993). *The child's discovery of the mind.* Cambridge, MA: Harvard University Press. Discussion and review of children's early theory of mind, or social cognition.

Baillargeon, R. (1993). The object concept revisited: New directions in the investigation of infants' physical knowledge. In C. E. Granrud (Ed.), *Visual perception and cognition in infancy.* Hillsdale, NJ: Erlbaum. Compelling review of recent research on infants' early understanding of physical objects, by one of the premier researchers in that area.

Bauer, P. J. (1996). What do infants recall of their lives? *American Psychologist, 51,* 29–41.

Bjorkland, D. F., & Schneider, W. (1997). Memory. In D. Kuhn & R. Siegler (Eds.), *Cognition, perception, and language: Vol. 2. Handbook of child psychology* (5th ed.). New York: Wiley. Comprehensive review of the development of memory processes. The first half of this article focuses on early childhood.

Bornstein, M. H., & Sigman, M. D. (1986). Continuity in mental development from infancy. *Child Development, 57,* 251–274. A careful review of the predictive relation between infant habituation measures and IQ scores in later life.

Bullock, M., Gelman, R., & Baillargeon, R. (1982). The development of causal reasoning. In W. J. Friedman (Ed.), *The developmental psychology of time.* New York: Academic Press. An early, now classic, paper arguing and demonstrating that young children are often remarkably good at causal understanding of simple physical-mechanical events.

DeLoache, J. S., & Brown, A. L. (1983). Very young children's memory in location of objects in a large-scale environment. *Child Development, 54,* 888–897.

Gelman, R. (1993). A rational-constructivist account of early learning about numbers and objects. In D. Medin (Ed.), *Learning and motivation* (Vol. 30). Academic Press: New York.

Gelman, S. A., & Markman, E. M. (1986). Categories and induction in young children. *Cognition, 23,* 183–209.

Hirschfeld, L. A., & Gelman, S. A. (1994). *Mapping the mind: Domain specificity in cognition and culture.* New York: Cambridge University Press. An edited volume presenting various domain-specific approaches to understanding cognition and cognitive development.

Legerstee, M. (1992). A review of the animate-inanimate distinction in infancy. *Early Development and Parenting, 1,* 59–67. A discussion of research indicating ways that infants distinguish animate persons from inanimate physical objects.

Mandler, J. M. (1992). How to build a baby. II. Conceptual primitives. *Psychological Review, 99,* 587–604. Discussion and analysis of theories and data pertaining to when children first think and reason symbolically.

Moore, L., & Corkum, V. (1994). Social understanding at the end of the first year of life. *Developmental Review, 14,* 349–372.

Piaget, J., & Inhelder, B. (1969). *The psychology of the child.* New York: Basic Books. A clear presentation of Piaget's ideas, in his own words.

Siegler, R. S. (1997). *Children's thinking* (3rd ed.). Englewood Cliffs, NJ: Prentice Hall. Textbook treatment of cognitive development, with good coverage of early childhood. Includes chapter-length expositions of Piaget's theory, memory development, conceptual development, problem solving, and academic skills.

Sophian, C. (1996). Young children's numerical cognition: What develops? In R. Vasta (Ed.) *Annals of Child Development* (Vol. 12). London: Jessica Kingley Publisher. Review of infants', toddlers', and preschoolers' understanding of number.

Wellman, H. M. (1990). *The child's theory of mind.* Cambridge, MA: MIT Press.

Wellman, H. M., & Gelman, S. A. (1998). Knowledge acquisition in foundational domains. In D. Kuhn & R. Siegler (Eds.), *Cognition, perception, and language. Vol. 2. Handbook of child psychology* (5th ed.). New York: Wiley. Focused coverage of infants' and preschoolers' understanding of physical phenomena, persons (theory of mind), and biological phenomena.

Henry M. Wellman

EASTERN PSYCHOLOGICAL ASSOCIATION. *See* Regional Psychological Associations.

EASTERN RELIGIONS AND PHILOSOPHIES. With the publication of William James's Gifford lectures in 1902, a dialogue between Asian religion and philosophy and psychology was initiated within the Western world. In the 1870s, the Theosophical Society was founded in New York, and its initial focus on Hinduism soon took in Buddhism. This discourse was encouraged through the integrative commentaries on Buddhism psychology, Sanskrit translations of Hindu texts, and during the 1930s through the popular discussions of Zen Buddhism by Suzuki. Asian religion and philosophy consider many of the key issues in psychology, including the relationship between body and mind, the nature of perception, consciousness, personality, and the meaning of suffering and illness. In considering the psychological contributions inherent within Asian cultures, it is important to understand that Asian religions do not have a notion of formal religion in the Christian, Jewish, or Islamic sense. In Hinduism and Buddhism, soteriology, or a doctrine of salvation, includes insight through practices such as meditation and personal devotion, as well as, a sense of duty.

In Hinduism, the Veda, the liturgical hymns to the deities, starts with the four Samhitās ("collections"), including the Rgveda Samhita (Veda of Chants), and concluded with the Atharvaveda Samhita. The Atharvaveda is psychologically crucial as the manual of charms to undo evil, counteract illness, and harm enemies. Vedic religion was elaborated into the ritual and sacrificial religion of the Brāhmanas, based on the power inherent in mantra. In the Upanisads Vedic, polytheism was demythologized, and all action was seen to lead to a cycle of reincarnations (samsāra).

Buddhism may be classified into three great "vehicles" (yāna). The Hinayāna, or "Lesser Vehicle," emphasized the gradual process of individual salvation (arāhat), and included the Theravada and Sarvāstivada schools. The Mahāyāna, or "Great Vehicle," added new elements. Multiple Buddhas may be worshipped, including Avalokitesvara, "Lord Who Looks Down," a savior for suffering human beings. There is no clear code of discipline, but the emphasis is on the saving of other human beings. Right conduct became a matter of the spontaneous expression of a person's awareness. In this sense, the Indian Mahāyāna toned down the Theravada emphasis on renunciation, to emphasize the ethical value on everyday life. The Chinese Mahāyāna, too, emphasized the moral obligations of loyalty to family and state. The Vajrayāna (Diamond Vehicle), or Mantrayāna (Sacred Sounds Vehicle), Esoteric Buddhism, or Tantric Buddhism, began in India. Tibetan Buddhism was introduced from India in the late Mahāyāna and Vajrayāna forms. Salvation could be accomplished quickly, even in the present life, using texts called tantras, and written in obscure language. The four divisions include the Yoga Tantra and Anuttarayoga Tantra, in which the person is assigned to one of several Buddha families according to the predominant consciousness (lust, hatred, delusion, or avarice) of the individual's personality.

One of the Buddha's contemporaries founded Jainism, which spread to northern and central India. Living substance (jiva) permeates animals; and inanimate substance (ajiva) includes space, time, and matter. Karma flows into and clogs the jiva, causing the bondage of life. Disciplined conduct can stop this inflow and lead to liberation.

Confucianism is a social ethic that exists among Chinese and East Asian societies. There is considerable overlap with Taoism. Orthodox Confucianism focused on the creation of a system that fashioned society and empire; whereas Taoism represented more personal and metaphysical preoccupations. According to ancient Chinese cosmology, the world was governed by the circulation of the sun and the celestial vault. Tao means the "way" or the "rule of conduct." Yin is cold, passive, feminine; yang warm, active, masculine. The five elements or "five phases" (water, fire, wood, metal, and earth) represented the main cosmic forces. All phenomena, including the human body and behavior, can be classified under one or another of the five phases. The body is a microcosm, the head round like Heaven, the feet square like the Earth, the 360 joints represented the days of the Chinese year, the eyes the sun and moon, the five viscera (lungs, heart, spleen, liver, and kidneys) the Five Elements and the Five Sacred Mountains. Each person hides within a primordial breath, needed to maintain life.

Zen Buddhism in Japan is derived from the Chinese Ch'an Buddhist School, and was introduced into Japan during the 1100s. The two main influences were the Rinzai and Dogen Kigen schools.

Shinto, introduced in Japan around the sixth century, means "the way of kami" (the polytheistic principle of life, mystical, or divine power), as opposed to Buddhism, or Butsudo, "the way of the Buddha." Later, Shinto kami were viewed as protectors of Buddhism and were thought to be incarnations of Buddhas and bodhisattvas.

The Southeast Asian Cross-roads

Southeast Asia has been a crossroads for all the Asian religions. Mainland Southeast Asia was a mixture of Austro-Asiatic, Austronesian, and Tibeto-Burman language families. The tribes of protohistoric Southeast Asia developed "cadastral" cults—the local religions—based on common experience. What people knew best was that the world was inhabited by spirits, and so were they, which was what made them alive. If one of these vital spirits left the body for too long, the person would become ill and die.

Mainland Southeast Asia, especially Burma, Thailand, Cambodia, Laos, and southern Vietnam, was Indianized. Theravada and Mahayana Buddhism and Brahmanism never dislodged the beliefs in spirits. In northern Vietnam, the "triple religion" of Mahāyāna Buddhism, Confucianism, and Taoism was grafted onto proto-Indochinese ancestor cult. Central to the family cult was ancestor worship. In southern Vietnam, the Cham accepted Islam. In insular Southeast Asia, the Sarvāstivadin and Mulasarvāstivadin sects of Theravada Buddhism arrived in Indonesia. This area has been characterized during the twentieth century by Hindu-Buddhist religious movements in colonial Java and Bali, by Christian movements in the Philippines, and by Muslim movements throughout the region.

Dharma

There is no Asian equivalent of the Western term *religion*. The closest one gets is the Hindu term *dharma*, from the Sanskrit *dhr* ("support, uphold"). Dharma means the personal actions that engender or maintain divine law, and which keep the universe from falling into disarray. By the time the *Brāhmanas* were composed around 800 BCE, the priests' rituals were thought to shape the well-being of people, and dharma became linked to karman. Thus, dharma came to mean how a person fits in with the natural and social world.

Body and Mind

Western psychologists sometimes have difficulty coming to grips with Hindu views of body and mind. Sāmkhya and the Upanisads distinguish matter ("prakrti"), which is the objective world including the impermanent human body and mind, and spirit ("purusa"), which is the world without limitations of time or space, and which survives the death of the gross body. This subtle body has the psychological states described by Western philosophy, the sense organs ("indriyas") around which everyday consciousness exists, the inner sense ("manas"), the ego ("ahamkāra"), and awareness, representations and ideas ("buddhi") (Bhattacharyya, 1987).

As for Buddhism, the empirical self consists of five categories, or skandhas, analyzed into components, or dharmas. First, bodily processes (rupa) are constituted by the dharmas of ear, eye, nose, tongue, and skin, and the corresponding dharmas of color, sound, odor, flavor, and resistance. Second is the group comprising the processes involved in feeling ("vedana"). Third are the processes constituting perception. Fourth, conscious and unconscious impulses to action ("sankharas") reveal the dharmas constituting perception and feeling. These comprise mental activity present in consciousness (such as feeling, perception, will, immediate sensation, desire, understanding, memory, attention, concentration); constituents of virtue (for example, equanimity, nongreed, compassion, and mindfulness); and constituents of vice (doubt, anger, hypocrisy, envy, hatred, and pride). Nowhere is there a self to be found.

In ancient Buddhist metaphysics, the anatomical structures of the body are similar to those used by Cambodian traditional healers today (Eisenbruch, 1992). According to Theravadin Buddhist notions, the body consists of 33 elements, 21 earth elements derived from the father, and 12 water elements from the mother. Earth comes from the father and connotes the solid tissues, such as hair on the outside of the body. Water, the other main element, comes from the mother, and makes up tissues such as the gall bladder.

Self and Soul

Western thought has been influenced by Plato's theory of reality of Forms—that there was a soul, not dissolved like the material body, and which ruled and gave life to it. According to Hindu tradition, rebirth has no effect on the eternal self ("ātman") for, after death, the individual self ("jiva") is the transmigrating entity. Depending on karma from the previous life, the jiva on leaving the body may go the way of the gods, to the heavens, with final liberation. It may go the way of the ancestors, to the moon, with return to earth in the form of rain that attaches to a plant, converted into semen when eaten by an animal, and thus bringing new life to the individual self; or it may be reborn on earth or in hell as an insect, small animal, or plant. Self and consciousness itself is transmigrated. The Buddhist theory of rebirth is clear that there is no enduring entity that moves from one existence to another. At the same time, there is no self ("anātman"). So how can there be cycles of rebirth if there is no self? According to Theravada, there is a chain of discrete events (for example, the transformation of fresh milk into curds).

Having dealt with transmigration, now for the question what is self. A first impression of Theravadin Buddhist doctrine of *anatta* is that there is literally no self. The Abhidhamma teaching showed self to be a transient stream of bits of sensation, consciousness, feeling, activity, impulses, and bodily processes. The fundamental elements, or dhammas, are elemental forces, not substances. The Law of Dependent Origination mandates that there is non self (Koller, 1985). With the evolution of Buddhist schools, the Abhidhamma doctrine of non self changed too. The Mahayana Buddhists noted a connection between the empirical person—in which self was unreal—and an enlightened one, who has achieved *tathata*, which translates more or less as "suchness" or "such as it is." In defining self, little room is left to maneuver when one has to obey the Law of Dependent Origination. In contrast to Indian self through renunciation from society, the Confucian concept of self-development is communal. The self is a developing part of a continuing family lineage, and "reālized neither in the transcendental ātman of Hindu thought with no earthly ties, nor in an individual ego" (DeVos, Marsella, & Hsu, 1985). Hsu (1985) describes the Chinese distinction between *ta wo* or "greater self," which encompassed the concerns for wider society, from *hsiao wo* or "smaller self," which focuses on concerns about the person and the family. He contrasts the kinship-centered Chinese kinship definition of self, in which all Chinese sons are tied to their first human group, with the Japanese case, in which noninheriting sons must find their human network elsewhere. The Chinese are tied psychologically to their kinship base, while Japanese noninheriting sons cut off their relationship with their origin, including the obligations to the ancestors.

The Nature of Perception and Consciousness

Nyaya philosophy centers on how people know an object. In ordinary perception, contact is established between the senses and their objects. In extra-ordinary perception, people see things in the past or future, or hidden things, in the course of disciplined meditation. The objects of valid knowledge depend on the relation between a knowing subject and the objects themselves, which include the self, the body, the senses, mental imperfections, suffering, and freedom from suffering (Koller, 1985). To understand the Buddhist approach to perception, one must see how it fits into the wheel of suffering ("dhukka"). Old age and death depend on birth, and clinging to life depends on desire; desires upon perception; perception upon sense perceptions, which would not be possible without the six sense organs. The sense organs depend on the mind and body ("nama-rupa"), which depend on consciousness; consciousness depends upon the impulses for action. All of these phases can belong to the self only upon the presence of ignorance, which in turn depends on the preceding factors in the cycle. Perception sits in the wheel of suffering. In Hindu belief, there are four states of consciousness. *Jāgrat*, the first, is the normal waking consciousness. *Svapna* is the experience of reality as the product of the person's projections rather than as random. *Susupti* is the divine wisdom of the liberated person. *Turiya* is ineffable (Needleman et al., 1987). Buddhist consciousness has three components. *Citta* is the receptive intellectual thinking ("cit"), from the Pali word *citta*, which is defined as both heart and mind. *Mano* is purposive minding and represents the intellectual functioning of the consciousness. *Viññana* is the sensory and perceptive aspects of consciousness. It was used in early Buddhism to mean the part of a person that survived after the death of the body and is more or less equivalent to the Western concept of the soul.

Popular Religion

Popular religion is the key to understanding the psychology of formal religion. Popular Hinduism includes "pure divinities," which are *avatāras* of Visnu and Siva—and "impure divinities" such as lineage, caste, and village deities. Cultic ritual aims to improve the worshiper's life by avoiding illness and maintaining the family and include sacrifice ("yajña"); ancestral ceremonies ("srāddha"); life cycle rituals ("samskāra"); meditational or ascetic practices ("tapas"); worship of deities ("pujā"); pilgrimage ("yātra"); personal vows ("vrata"); healing and exorcism ("cikitsā") (Courtright, 1987). The role of religious healing rituals is most important.

From its beginnings, Buddhism has included rituals that are intended to protect against danger and to exorcise evil. Protective, exorcistic rituals are closely associated with texts called *parittas*. The Tibetan lamas practice Tantric meditation, to the extent of controlling physiological breathing, that is, temporarily interrupting the cycle of life and rebirth. These masters can also perform other magical healing and protective rituals. In Japanese Buddhism, people participate in mass cult Buddhist practices involving folk beliefs. The Buddha's birth, enlightenment, and death are celebrated in Therāvadin countries on one day, in Mahayana countries on different days.

In Southeast Asia, people often disregard the Buddhist teaching, maintaining that attachment to rituals as a quick fix for the relief of suffering stands in the path of salvation. In real life, people seek relief now. It is striking that the *arahat*, the term denoting one of the most archaic icons of Theravadin Buddhism, also signifies someone with magical powers capable of protecting against illness (Tambiah, 1984). Officially, the Taoist doctrine minimized the role of spirits but, in reality, mass movements of Taoism, such as the Way of the Heavenly Masters, developed and continue to the present. Communal Taoism died out during the Sung dynasty and was replaced by ritual secrecy and esoterism (Lagerwey, 1987). Popular religion, as fusion of the three doctrines, is known as "worshipping the deities" ("pai-shen"). It is loosely structured, focusing on cults of local deities, to promote health and long life; expel evil spirits; and release from suffering. Some anthropomorphic deities ("shen") cure illness (Cohen, 1987).

The worship of ancestors and ancestral spirits is a fulcrum of Asian popular religions. Failure to propitiate leads to suffering and illness. Hindus and Buddhists observe annual rituals with offerings to the ancestors. The Chinese have formal rituals in a lineage cult and a domestic rituals at home. The yin portion of the soul, if not propitiated, can become a demonic apparition ("kuei") and cause illness; the yang portion of the soul, associated with the benevolent spirits of the ancestors ("shen") will protect the descendants and their families (Ahern, 1973). Cambodians believe that violation of the code of conduct of the family or of the Buddhist teachings can provoke an ancestral spirit to withdraw its protection and sometimes induce "ancestral spirit madness" or even physical illnesses such as tuberculosis (Eisenbruch, 1992).

Demons are the next ingredient of popular religion. The Vedas described demons in two groups. In one, the deities, such as *apsaras* live in the sky, and are usually benevolent. In the other, such as *asuras*, they are subterranean, and malevolent. The *pretas* are spirits of the ancestors; *bhutas* are evil spirits associated with the dead; *rāksasas*, *pisācas*, and *yātudhānas* are associated with ghoulish appearance. The Hindu demons were adopted by Buddhism. The Buddha's doctrine led the person to a mental state where they were no longer prone to the perceptions and threats of the evil spirits. Finally, there is magic. The Veda, especially the Atharvaveda, is replete with magic ("māyā") used to neutralize evil forces ("santi"), and the *āngirasah*, employed to attack individuals. In the period after the Veda, magic in Hindu tradition is derived mainly from Siva. *Māyā* gives a person the power to deceive the enemy. The Hindu Yoga Sutras and the Buddhist Tantra provide extensive classification of magical powers. Chinese popular religion includes magic to do with shamanism ("wu-shu"), and with spirits.

Conclusion

For the psychologist, Asian religions are intriguing for they show the importance of soteriology, a doctrine of salvation. People need to be saved morally, which implies that there is some psychological need as well. Indian systems explain the problem as stemming from ignorance (*avidyā*). Whereas in Western religions, salvation occurs in this life, in Hindu and Buddhist tradition it can occur in the next.

Bibliography

Collins, S. (1982). *Selfless persons*. Cambridge: Cambridge University Press. An explanation of the Buddhist concept of *anatta*, or "not-self," related to its Brahmanical background.

de Silva, P. (1979). *An introduction to Buddhist psychology*. Thetford, Norfolk: The Macmillan Press. A review of the basic features of Buddhist psychology; the psychology of cognition, motivation and emotion; personality; the relation between Buddhist and Western therapeutic systems; and health and sickness in Buddhist perspective.

DeVos, G. A., Marsella, A. J., & Hsu, F. L. K. (1985). Introduction: Approaches to culture and self. In A. J. Marsella, G. A. DeVos, & F. L. K. Hsu (Eds.), *Culture and self: Asian and Western perspectives* (pp. 2–23). New York and London: Tavistock Publications. This book is about ethnocultural variations in the constitution, experience, and conceptualization of the self. The Western concepts of self are compared with those developed in Hindu, Confucian, Japanese, and Maoist thought.

Eisenbruch, M. (1992). The ritual space of patients and traditional healers in Cambodia. *Bulletin de l'École Française d'Extrême-Orient, 79* (2), 283–316. A detailed account of the relationship between the Buddhist, Brahamic, and local folk cosmologies, explanatory models, and ritual healing systems for mental, physical and spiritual disorders.

Eliade, M. (Ed.). *The encyclopedia of religion*. New York: Macmillan Publishing Company. An authoritative text presenting a comprehensive overview of Asian religious traditions. This text includes discussion of Taoism (Baldrian), Indian philosophies (Bhattacharyya), Chinese religion (Cohen), Hindu cultic worship (Courtright), Buddhism in the West (Ellwood), Indian religions (Gonda), Hinduism (Hiltebeitel), Taoism (Lagerwey), Hindu Dharma (Mahony), Shinto (Naofusa), Buddhist ethics (Reynolds), meditation (Underwood), and Vijñāna (Wayman).

Hsu, F. L. K. (1985). The self in cross-cultural perspective. In A. J. Marsella, G. A. DeVos, & F. L. K. Hsu (Eds.), *Culture and self: Asian and Western perspectives* (pp. 24–55). New York and London: Tavistock Publications.

James, W. (1902). *The varieties of religious experience: A study in human nature*. Cambridge, MA: Harvard University Press. The seminal work.

Johansson, R. E. A. (1983). Defence mechanisms according to psychoanalysis and the Pāli Nikāyas. In N. Katz (Ed.), *Buddhist and western psychology* (pp. 11–24). Boulder, Colorado: Prajñā Press.

Koller, J. M. (1985). *Oriental philosophies* (2nd ed.). Basingstoke, Hampshire: Macmillan.

Nakamura, H. (1964). *Ways of thinking of Eastern peoples: India-China-Tibet-Japan*. Honolulu: East-West Center Press. A classic description of thought patterns of four Asian groups as revealed in their languages, logic, and cultural products.

Swearer, D. K. (1995). *The Buddhist world of Southeast Asia*. Albany: State University of New York Press. A holistic analysis that includes Buddhism as popular tradition—inclusive syncretism; as civil religion—political legitimation and national integration; and modernization—the dynamic of tradition and change.

Tambiah, S. J. (1984). *The Buddhist saints of the forest and the cult of amulets: A study in charisma, hagiography, sectarianism, and millenial Buddhism*. Cambridge: Cambridge University Press. A study showing the links between formal Buddhist and folk beliefs.

Maurice Eisenbruch

EATING DISORDERS. The classical disorders of eating are anorexia nervosa and bulimia nervosa, the first characterized by starvation and low weight, the second by binge eating followed by purging. More recently the syndrome of binge eating disorder has been described, in which individuals binge eat but do not compensate for the extra calories by purging. Less common eating disorders include ruminative disorder and pica, the former in which food is regurgitated and chewed again, and the latter in which nonnutritive substances such as clay, are eaten. While cases of apparent disordered eating have been described for centuries, the earliest accounts focused on dramatic cases of self-starvation or voracious eating. These cases were viewed as medical oddities, or sometimes as miraculous when individuals were observed to eat nothing for extended periods of time and survive. It is likely that some of these early cases were associated with brain injury, brain tumor, or a severe endocrine disorder.

The term *bulimia* was first used in ancient Greece deriving from *buos* meaning ox, and *limos* meaning hunger, denoting a state in which an individual was as hungry as an ox. Case descriptions in the European literature from the 1600s onward describe individuals with voracious appetites, sometimes combined with vomiting, with the patients eating huge amounts of food and often inappropriate items such as cats, dogs, snakes, grass, and dirt. Sometimes the bulimia would be associated with emaciation and sometimes with obesity.

The first well-documented case of what is today known as anorexia nervosa was described by Richard Morton, a British physician, in 1689 in his treatise *Phthisiologia: Sue exercitationes de Phthisi*. He described two cases, one a young woman aged 18 years, and the other a 16-year-old man. In both cases the disorder was judged to have arisen from disturbed emotions, and none of the then known causes of weight loss were present. Morton described severe weight loss in both cases, with amenorrhea in the female who eventually died, while the male apparently made a partial recovery. The term *anorexia nervosa* was first used by Sir William Gull in a paper entitled "*Anorexia nervosa*" (*Lancet*, 516–517, 1888). Gull first termed the disease *apepsia hysteria* in a lecture on the subject in 1873; however, he then followed the terminology coined by a French physician Lasegue, in a paper published in 1873, namely *anorexia hysterica*. Case reports from this era document the marked weight loss characterizing the disorder, with amenorrhea in the female, often combined with denial of being thin and a feeling of well-being. There is little mention in these reports of the now cardinal feature of the syndrome, namely the pursuit of thinness and fear of becoming fat. Two other elements now seen in more than half of all cases of anorexia nervosa are rarely mentioned, namely binge eating and purging by inducing vomiting.

The modern syndrome of bulimia nervosa first emerged with sporadic reports of binge eating and self-induced vomiting in cases of anorexia nervosa during the first half of the twentieth century. However, it was not until the 1940s that the first cases of bulimia nervosa separate from anorexia nervosa appeared in the medical literature. Among these are the detailed study of Ellen West, a patient with binge eating, self-induced vomiting, and laxative abuse, by German psychiatrist Ludwig Bingswanger (1944). This case appeared in translation as the "Case of Ellen West" in *Existence* (May & Ellenburger, 1958). The emergence of bulimia nervosa as a disorder distinct from anorexia nervosa coincided with an increasing concern about weight and shape in young women, as exemplars of female beauty (e.g., models and beauty contestants) became ever thinner. Clinics throughout the Western world noted an upsurge in the number of patients with bulimia nervosa during the latter half of the 1970s. The syndrome in its modern form, distinguished from anorexia nervosa, was first described by Russell (1979) in a paper entitled "Bulimia nervosa: An ominous variant of anorexia nervosa" (*Psychological Medicine*, 9, 429–448).

As the study of bulimia nervosa progressed and the elements of the syndrome were refined, it became apparent that a related eating disorder existed in which individuals binged but did not purge. This syndrome at first termed *nonpurging bulimia nervosa*, was eventually termed binge eating disorder. Unlike patients with bulimia nervosa who tend to be of normal weight, those with binge eating disorder tend to be overweight, indeed the frequency of the disorder increases with increasing weight. Although descriptions of binge eating without purging usually associated with obesity had appeared in the medical literature sporadically in the latter half of the twentieth century, the disorder was codified in the fourth edition of *Diagnostic and Statistical Manual of Mental Disorders* (DSM–IV; APA, 1994) as a disorder requiring further study.

Causes of the Eating Disorders

In discussing the causes of the eating disorders it must be recognized that there is much that is not known about this subject. Nonetheless, it is generally agreed that both inherited and environmental factors play a part in the etiology of these disorders. In the case of anorexia nervosa, twin studies reveal that an identical twin has eight times the risk of developing the disorder compared to a nonidentical twin if their twin pair has the disorder, strongly suggesting a genetic basis for anorexia nervosa. Twin studies in bulimia nervosa also suggest that inherited factors may account for some half of the variance in the cause of the disorder. The nature of the inheritance in these disorders is debatable, but it seems likely that it differs between anorexia nervosa and bulimia nervosa. The relatively high comorbidity between anorexia nervosa and obsessive-compulsive disorder, together with the many food obsessions and compulsions seen in most cases of anorexia nervosa, has led some to suggest that there may be a commonly inherited factor between these two disorders. Some studies suggest that anorexics have high levels of brain serotonin, a hormone with diverse functions both in the central nervous system and throughout the body, including the control of feeding. High levels of serotonin are associated with behavioral inhibition, as seen in the anorexic inhibition of eating, and general social inhibition. On the other hand, studies suggest that patients with bulimia nervosa have low levels of central nervous system serotonin, which in turn would be associated with impulsivity and a diminished sense of satiety, both characteristic of bulimia nervosa. Hence, it is possible that a neurochemical abnormality affecting central nervous system serotonin may be involved in both anorexia nervosa and bulimia nervosa, and may form one feature of the inheritance of these disorders. It is also possible, however, that the disturbed eating behavior seen in both anorexia nervosa and bulimia nervosa is responsible for the alterations in serotonin function.

Difficulty in regulating feeling states may also play a part in the genesis of eating disorders. Some 50% of individuals with an eating disorder will develop a serious episode of depression during their lifetime. Family studies suggest that the genetic predisposition to an eating disorder and to depression are inherited separately. Nonetheless, this propensity toward depression may explain why the most frequently reported antecedent to a binge is a negative feeling state often arising from an unsatisfactory interpersonal interaction.

One of the strongest environmental influences contributing to the apparent increase in the number of cases of eating disorder in the last quarter of the twentieth century is the changing attitude concerning ideal weight and body shape, a change that particularly affects women. The shift away from a fuller body shape toward a thinner profile occurred in the mid-1960s sparked by the portrayal of ever thinner models in the media. In addition, since there is evidence that overweight persons are selected against when applying for a job or a promotion, the increase in the number of women joining the workforce may have reinforced the trend toward thinness in women. Concurrent with these trends was an impressive increase in the number of diet articles appearing in women's magazines. It is believed that these trends led to the increase in dieting observed among women, a behavior that appears to set off the chain of events leading to an eating disorder, which would particularly affect the predisposed individual. Longitudinal studies suggest that dieting markedly increases the risk of developing an eating disorder. A reduction in caloric intake leads to hunger and ultimately to loss of control over eating and the consumption of large quantities of food to make up for the physiologic and psychological deprivation. This pattern constitutes binge eating. In the bulimic, purging usually begins a few months after the onset of binge eating. For unknown reasons some individuals do not purge and hence, develop binge eating disorder. The response to dieting is different in the anorexic, since many of these patients lose large amounts of weight without binge eating or purging.

Family influences are also important in the genesis of the eating disorders. It is now believed that such influences are usually directed toward a specific child and not to every child in the family. The most important influence appears to be of mothers on their daughters, particularly during adolescence. Hence, maternal concerns about their daughters' weight and shape, often based on maternal concerns about their own weight and shape, have been shown in several studies to be an important influence in the development of an eating disorder. Peer influences that involve teasing about weight and shape or rejection because of "fatness" may also play a part in influencing young women to begin strenuous dieting. Mothers with eating disorders may also influence the development of their offspring. Clinical studies suggest that eating disordered mothers have difficulty feeding their offspring, interact more negatively with their offspring over food than noneating disordered mothers, and because of their fears about fatness may underfeed their infant.

The Relationship Between the Disorders

The exact relationship of the three classical eating disorders to one another is uncertain. The three disorders can be regarded as a continuum, from anorexia at one end of the spectrum, to binge eating disorder at the other. Weight varies from low in anorexia nervosa through overweight and obesity in binge eating disorder, with a fairly normal weight distribution in bulimia nervosa. Binge eating also varies along the continuum, with about half of all anorexics binge eating, often with small binges, and all those with bulimia nervosa and binge eating disorder, binge eating. The degree of dietary restriction and weight and shape concerns are highest in anorexia nervosa, somewhat less in bulimia nervosa, and less or nonexistent in binge eating disorder. Finally, anorexia nervosa tends to turn into bulimia nervosa over the years. Nonetheless, the continuum hypothesis is not entirely satisfactory. Anorexia nervosa characterized by extreme dietary restriction and no binge eating, at least in its early stages, seems distinctly different from the other two eating disorders. Some researchers believe that anorexia nervosa is related to obsessive-compulsive disorder, while the remaining eating disorders are not. Hence, frank obsessive-compulsive disorder is seen in a higher percentage of cases of anorexia nervosa than the other eating disorders. Moreover, as indicated earlier, patients with anorexia nervosa demonstrate many obsessions and compulsions regarding food. Finally, recent work suggests that fluoxetine (Prozac) may be helpful to the anorexic in maintaining weight once it is restored. This is important since fluoxetine is useful in the treatment of obsessive-compulsive disorder.

The Course of the Eating Disorders

The eating disorders usually begin in adolescence, although the full-blown disorder is often preceded by many years in which the individual demonstrates low self-esteem, excessive concerns about weight and shape, and attempts to diet. Anorexia nervosa presents as a full-blown syndrome at two peak ages, 14 and 18. Hence, the majority of cases of anorexia nervosa present for treatment in adolescence. Anorexia nervosa is the most chronic of all the eating disorders. The disorder often progresses from pure dietary restriction with marked weight loss, to binge eating and purging combined with low weight, and to a slow diminution in the severity of weight loss and frequency of binge eating and purging over many years. Between 5 and 15% of patients with this disorder die from complications, including suicide and various medical complications consequent upon organ damage due to malnutrition. Bulimia nervosa is also considered to be a chronic disorder. The mean age of onset for the full syndrome is 19 years, and the disorder continues with waxing and waning of the symptoms of binge eating and purging over the years. The average age of presentation for treatment is in the mid- to late 20s. The long-term outcome of this disorder is not known at present. Binge eating disorder onsets at the same age as bulimia nervosa. Because there is little compensation for the excess calories consumed in binges, individuals with this disorder tend to gain weight over the years, usually presenting for treatment in their forties in the context of a weight loss program. These individuals are at risk to develop the disorders associated with obesity, including: high blood pressure, diabetes, high cholesterol levels, heart disease, gall bladder disease, osteoarthritis, some cancers, sleep apnea, and the psychological consequences of societal discrimination. All the eating disorders are associated with other psychological disorders at frequencies higher than those found in noneating disordered individuals. Among these problems are depression, anxiety disorders including social phobia, and drug and alcohol abuse and dependence.

In addition to the full-blown syndromes of anorexia nervosa, bulimia nervosa, and binge eating disorder, many individuals demonstrate less severe forms of these disorders. Epidemiological studies suggest that the major syndromes of anorexia nervosa, bulimia nervosa, and binge eating disorder probably occur in some 2 to 3% of the population, while a further 3 to 4% suffer from a less severe form of these syndromes.

Rumination Disorder and Pica

These two disorders appear to have little in common with the classical eating disorders described above, nor are they related to one another. The cause of the disorders is also unclear.

Rumination Disorder. Rumination spans the life cycle from infancy to old age. The syndrome consists of regurgitating food and either chewing and swallowing it, or spitting it out. The disorder is most frequently seen in the mentally retarded, with some surveys suggesting that between 6 and 8% of severely retarded individuals in institutions ruminate. The disorder is also seen, although less frequently, in infancy. The etiology of the disorder is unknown, although environments which offer little stimulation, e.g., institutions, or infants relatively neglected by their mothers, appear conducive to the development of the disorder, which appears to be inherently reinforcing. Infants, for example, curl their tongues back to regurgitate milk already swallowed, hence prolonging the taste of milk in their mouth. Rumination disorder may lead to death both in the mentally retarded due to aspiration of food, and in infancy due to starvation. Other complications of rumination in the adult include dental decay, aspiration pneumonia, anemia, and increased susceptibility to infection due to malnutrition.

The most frequently used treatment for rumination disorder is aversive therapy, although in infancy, very high levels of attention have been reported in uncontrolled studies to produce positive effects. The first controlled studies of rumination in infancy used electric shock contingent on abdominal movements preceding the infant spitting up milk with rapid cessation of the problem. Such therapy should be used only in situations which pose evident danger to the patient, and should be supervised by a committee with representation from outside the institution in which the treatment is taking place. A less aversive procedure, using a drop of lemon juice placed on the infant's tongue contingent on the mouthing movements preceding regurgitation, was also demonstrated to rapidly eliminate the problem. Such treatment may be life saving in infancy. Similar treatment approaches have been used in the mentally retarded with success, including less aversive procedures such as having the individual brush his or her teeth for two minutes with an antiseptic solution, following each episode of rumination. Other types of therapy such as increased attention to the individual or enriching institutional environments may hold promise in the treatment of this disorder.

Pica. Pica is a relatively rare eating disorder in which nonnutritive substances such as clay, chalk, or starch, are consumed, and appears to be diminishing in prevalence. The etiology is unknown, although various theories ranging from deficiencies in iron or zinc, through a lack of a stimulating environment have been suggested. Pica is associated with iron deficiency. It is not clear, however, whether pica causes the deficiency or is caused by it. Some of the substances ingested in pica may bind to iron preventing its absorption, and the ingested substances may substitute for food, leading to a deficiency in iron intake. Pica is particularly prevalent in pregnant women and children. Like rumination, the disorder is not uncommon in the institutionalized mentally retarded. The ingestion of starch or clay during pregnancy particularly affects rural Blacks, a culture in which such practices may be more acceptable than in other cultures. Complications of pica include: swallowing foreign objects sometimes necessitating surgical removal, lead poisoning from ingesting paint, and infections due to malnutrition.

Treatment for the disorder falls into two classes. In cases in which a nutritional deficiency, such as iron, is found, supplementation with the deficient mineral has been demonstrated to lead to either diminution or cessation of the behavior. In mentally retarded individuals with no such nutritional deficiency, aversive therapy similar to that used in rumination disorder may be useful.

Overview

The earliest eating disorder to be described in a recognizable manner was anorexia nervosa, although the characteristic drive for thinness seen in most cases today, was either lacking or overlooked. Hence, cultural changes over time may influence the presentation of the disorder. Bulimia nervosa was only separated from anorexia nervosa as a distinct entity in 1979 as the disorder became more prevalent with the rising concern about weight and shape, leading women to extreme forms of dieting. Binge eating disorder was then separated from bulimia nervosa, although the syndrome was only tentatively recognized in the late 1990s. Inherited factors—possibly deficient neurochemical systems—interact with environmental factors, particularly societal views concerning the ideal shape for women, and familial and peer influences, leading to the development of weight and shape concerns in adolescents. This in turn may lead to excessive dieting and eventually to the full-blown development of one or other of the eating disorders. These eating disorders are common problems in our society and appeared to have increased in prevalence over the last quarter of the twentieth century. Fortunately, a number of relatively successful treatments have been developed over the same period of time providing hope to the large number of individuals afflicted with these disorders.

[See also Anorexia; Bulimia; and Dieting.]

Bibliography

American Psychiatric Association. (1994). *Diagnostic and statistical manual of mental disorders* (4th ed.). Washington, DC: Author.

Bruce, B., & Agras, W. S. (1992). Binge eating in females: A population-based investigation. *International Journal of Eating Disorders, 12*, 365–373. A study of the prevalence of binge eating disorder.

Fairburn, C. G., & Beglin, S. J. (1990). Studies of the epidemiology of bulimia nervosa. *American Journal of Psychiatry, 147*, 401–408. A comprehensive review of studies of the prevalence of bulimia nervosa.

Halmi, K., Eckert, E., Marchi, P., Sampugnaro, V., Apple, R., & Cohen, J. (1991). Comorbidity of psychiatric di-

agnoses in anorexia nervosa. *Archives of General Psychiatry, 48*, 712–718. A ten-year follow-up study examining the relationship between anorexia nervosa and other psychopathology.

Kaplan, A. S., & Garfinkel, P. E. (Eds.). (1993). *Medical issues in the eating disorders*. New York: Brunner/Mazel. A review of medical complications and biologic underpinnings of the eating disorders.

Kaye, W. H. (1992). Neurotransmitter abnormalities in anorexia nervosa and bulimia. In G. H. Anderson & S. H. Kennedy (Eds.), *The biology of feast and famine* (pp. 105–134). New York: Academic Press. A review of central nervous system control of eating in anorexia and bulimia.

Kendler, K. S., MacLean C., Neale, M., Kessler, R., Heath, A., & Eaves, L. (1991). The genetic epidemiology of bulimia nervosa. *American Journal of Psychiatry, 148*, 1627–1637. An important twin study examining the genetic influences on the development of bulimia.

Liebowitz, S. F., & Shor-Posner, G. (1986). Brain serotonin and eating behavior. *Appetite, 7*, 1–14. A review of the role of serotonin in modulating eating behavior.

Polivy, J., & Herman, C. P. (1985). Dieting and bingeing: A causal analysis. *American Psychologist, 40*, 193–201. An important paper relating dieting to the development of binge eating.

Stein, D. M., & Laasko, W. (1988). Bulimia: A historical perspective. *International Journal of Eating Disorders, 7*, 201–210. A review of early descriptions of bulimia nervosa.

Striegel-Moore, R. H., Silberstein, L. R., & Rodin, J. (1986). Toward an understanding of risk factors for bulimia. *American Psychologist, 41*, 246–263. A classic paper discussing potential risk factors for bulimia.

Strober, M., Lampert, C., Morrell, W., Burroughs, J., & Jacobs, C. (1990). A controlled family study of anorexia nervosa: Evidence of familial aggregation and lack of shared transmission with affective disorder. *International Journal of Eating Disorders, 9*, 239–253. An important study demonstrating that anorexia nervosa runs in families.

Vandereycken, W., & Van Deth, R. (1989). Who was the first to describe anorexia nervosa: Gull or Lasegue? *Psychological Medicine, 19*, 837–845. A historical account of the origins of the term anorexia nervosa.

Weight-Control Information Network. 1 Win Way, Bethesda, MD 20892-3665. A goverment-sponsored organization providing free information on the eating disorders and obesity. A useful resource.

Yanovski, S. Z. (1993). Binge eating disorder: Current knowledge and future directions. *Obesity Research, 1*, 306–324. An excellent overview of the new syndrome of binge eating disorder.

W. Stewart Agras

EBBINGHAUS, HERMANN (1850–1909), German experimental psychologist. Although he is most famous for his pioneering research on human memory, Herman Ebbinghaus's accomplishments also include his painstaking work as the founding editor of a major research journal, his development of an original method for assessing intelligence, and his highly readable German and English textbooks on general psychology. His memory research was especially significant because it demonstrated that it was indeed possible to apply experimental research methods to issues concerning higher mental functions—an idea rejected by much of the conventional wisdom of his day (Rodi, 1987). His work on memory also stands as a model for excellence, ingenuity, and dedication to psychological research.

Traditional German and English biographies of Ebbinghaus are readily available (Jaensch, 1908; Shakow, 1930; Woodworth, 1909); however, since the 1985 centennial of Ebbinghaus's classic book *On Memory* (Über das Gedächtnis), a series of archival studies on his life has been published. These have focused on his formative childhood and school years (Abresch, 1987), his travels to France and England (Bringmann & Bringmann, 1986a), the details of his memory research (Schuster-Tyroller, 1987), the work of his laboratory (Gundlach, 1986a), his academic career at Berlin University (Sprung & Sprung, 1987), and his plans to accept a professorship in the United States (Bringmann & Bringmann, 1986b).

According to Gundlach (1986b), Ebbinghaus's publication record includes 7 books or monographs, 12 research articles, 103 short book reviews, 11 letters to the editor, and a number of obituaries and conference reports—all for a total of 3,874 pages. Ebbinghaus's private papers are housed at the Institute for the History of Modern Psychology at Passau University in Germany. A smaller collection from his scientific estate is preserved at Graz University in Austria. Finally, a video about the life and work of Ebbinghaus is available from the Institute for Modern Film in Gottingen, Germany (Bringmann, Schuster-Tyroller, & Kalkofen, 1986).

Eugen Hermann Ludwig Ebbinghaus was born on 24 January 1850, into a respected and well-to-do family in Barmen, which was a prosperous manufacturing center near Bonn in the Rhine province of the kingdom of Prussia. After completing his basic education at the Gymnasium (German high school) in his hometown, he spent six years at the Prussian universities of Bonn, Halle, and Berlin studying ancient history, classical philology, archeology, and Greek philosophy. During the Franco-Prussian War of 1870–1871, he volunteered to serve on active duty as a trooper with a regiment of lancers. Afterward he completed his formal education at Bonn University where he received his doctorate in philosophy on 16 August 1873. During these two years, from 1871 to 1873, he studied psychology and anthropology under Neo-Kantian philosopher Jurgen Bona Meyer (1829–1897). An examination of his academic transcripts suggests that Ebbinghaus may well have planned to become a classics teacher at the high school level.

The Memory Project

Ebbinghaus's initial interests in memory can be traced to his first doctoral dissertation (his theoretical dissertation), on Hartmann's philosophy of the unconscious (1873), which was directed by his only psychology teacher. During an extended stay in England from 1875 to 1877, Ebbinghaus broadened his knowledge of modern psychology by immersing himself in second-hand copies of the classic books available on psychophysics, physiological psychology, and the nascent field of experimental psychology. More important, Ebbinghaus carried out his first memory studies while working as a teacher, first at a "Gentleman's Academy" in Seaford, a small community in Sussex on the southeast channel coast of England, and then later at the Royal Grammar School in Guildford near London. His first memory project involved a 14-year-old boy at Seaford whose digit span Ebbinghaus studied for about 2 months. For his second investigation, Ebbinghaus used himself as his only research subject, studying the process of rote memorization using English poems and prose. As a result of this work Ebbinghaus concluded that the *meaning* of the subject matter he was rotely memorizing affected his success.

After spending nearly 2 years in English, where he perfected his knowledge of English, Ebbinghaus lived from 1877 to 1878 in Paris, where he acquired almost native fluency in French. He supported himself by giving German lessons to the children of the aristocracy and made use of the rich library resources in Paris to further expand his psychological horizons. It was also in Paris that he became familiar with Greek and Roman writings on memory techniques. Ebbinghaus returned to Germany in the fall of 1878 to serve as French tutor to Prince Waldemar at the German Imperial Court. This prestigious appointment ended in the spring of 1879, when the young prince suddenly died from diphtheria.

Ebbinghaus began his formal memory research in the spring of 1879, with an investigation of the effects of repetition on rote memorization. To reduce the distracting effect of semantic meaning, he developed his own series of "meaningless syllables." Specifically, these "artificial words" (often referred to as "nonsense syllables") were constructed by placing a vowel or dipthong between two consonants of the German alphabet. After generating a large pool of these items, Ebbinghaus randomly created lists of these new "words," which he then memorized, all the while carefully recording the number of repetitions through a list that was necessary to enable perfect recall. In the spring of 1880, Ebbinghaus submitted a handwritten report of his method and statistical results as his second dissertation (his research dissertation) to the Philosophical Faculty of Berlin University. His manuscript was evaluated by Hermann von Helmholtz (1821–1894) and Eduard Zeller (1814–1908), an eminent historian of philosophy. Helmholtz primarily focused on the methodological contributions of the work, while Zeller gave the project a "satisfactory" grade but suggested that Ebbinghaus needed to publish more in order to have a successful academic career.

Between 1883 and 1885, Ebbinghaus replicated and expanded his memory project somewhat before publishing it as a small book titled *On Memory* in the fall of 1885. Although the psychology textbooks he later wrote did, of course, contain a great deal of information about the topic of memory, he did not continue his memory research; and, apart from a brief letter to an English journal protesting inappropriate conclusions drawn from his work, he did not publish any subsequent articles on memory. In Germany, the Ebbinghaus tradition of memory research was followed up primarily by Georg Elias Müller (1850–1934) and some of Müller's early assistants and students.

Following an enthusiastic review of Ebbinghaus's memory book by William James (1842–1910), American psychologists became fascinated with the topic of memory. Following Ebbinghaus's lead, American research focused on learning individual nonsense syllables or a series of nonsense syllables and also included the construction of mechanical, and then later electrical, equipment for the presentation of the items to be committed to memory (McPherson, 1987). More recently, however, this approach to the study of memory has increasingly come under attack by cognitive psychologists who argue for the relevance of context and meaning to memory. For example, Neisser has argued that "orthodox psychology" in the tradition of Ebbinghaus has produced few useful results after more than a hundred years of empirical memory studies. Neisser also noted that the same group of scholars has consistently avoided the "naturalistic study of memory," which appears to have far more important applications than the traditional laboratory studies of memory found in the Ebbinghaus tradition (1982, p. 3).

Professional Career

The acceptance of his second dissertation qualified Ebbinghaus for appointment to an untenured and unsalaried position as instructor of philosophy at Berlin University. After the 1885 publication of his memory book, Ebbinghaus was promoted to a salaried professorship but remained untenured. In the fall of 1894, he received an appointment as a full professor at Breslau University in provincial Silesia, which was located close to the Russian-Polish border. Ebbinghaus remained at Breslau until 1910 when he moved to Halle-Wittenberg University, which was about midway between Leipzig and Berlin. There he taught for the remaining years of his life as a full professor. An examination of his teaching record shows that Ebbinghaus founded and equipped experimental laboratories wherever he taught. These facilities, however, were primarily used for teaching and demonstration purposes and were rarely used by Ebbinghaus and his few doctoral students for the production of publishable research. Ebbinghaus was clearly an expert classroom teacher who taught a heavy load of philosophy and psychology courses to thousands of undergraduates, but only to a relatively small number of advanced students.

Ebbinghaus's major accomplishment during his later Berlin period was the 1892 establishment, with Arthur Konig, of the *Journal for Psychology and Sensory Physiology* (Zeitschrift für Psychologie und Physiologie der Sinnesorgane), which he edited for a total of 16 years. His coeditors for the journal were the most eminent contributors to German psychology outside the Wundtian school and included Sigmund Exner, Herman von Helmholtz, William T. Preyer, Johannes von Kries, Georg E. Müller, Carl G. Stumpf, and others. Ebbinghaus was a very demanding editor who readily rejected weaker manuscripts by eminent scholars.

Shortly after beginning his work at Breslau University, Ebbinghaus became involved in an ambitious project concerned with the influence of fatigue on school achievement (McPherson, 1987). Ebbinghaus proposed to measure the effect of fatigue with his famous completion test that required school children to supply omitted words in prose texts. This procedure was later adapted for use by Binet and then by Terman for inclusion in their respective intelligence scales.

Although Ebbinghaus published relatively little, he kept himself fully informed about current developments in psychology and related subjects through his extensive multilingual reading. He accumulated a vast collection of reprints, which he read, annotated, and excerpted. A major consequence of these efforts was his popular lectures on psychology, which he also offered to public school teachers in Breslau. During his years in Breslau, Ebbinghaus published the first half of his *Principles of Psychology* (Grundzüge der Psychologie, 1897). The second volume of this work, which was published in 1902, contains Ebbinghaus's later reflections about the nature of human memory and forgetting. A shorter version of this textbook was published in 1908 in German and in English under the title *Psychology: An Elementary Textbook* (Abriß der Psychologie). Both textbooks were impressive successes in Germany and abroad, in part because of their clear and readable style.

As a person, Ebbinghaus was a self-confident and assertive individual who enjoyed his academic status and the privileges accorded to a tenured university professor. His friends in Berlin included many of the younger intellectuals and faculty members such as Lou Andreas-Salomé (1861–1937), who was to become a well-known psychoanalyst; the sociologist Ferdinand Tönnies (1855–1936); Hermann Diels (1848–1922), a scholar of pre-Socratic philosophy; the Indologist Paul Deussen (1845–1919); the philosopher Paul Rée (1849–1901); the Danish literary historian Georg Brandes (1842–1947); and the younger military historian Hans Delbrück (1848–1929).

Ebbinghaus was a good son to his father, and throughout his life he was concerned with the well-being of his brother, his two sisters, and a paternal aunt who helped finance his rather expensive education far more generously than his ultrareligious and parsimonious mother.

In scientific controversies, Ebbinghaus did not suffer fools gladly, and he also found it difficult to forgive or forget old disagreements. His few doctoral students report that he was demanding, especially in his seminar courses in experimental psychology. He acknowledged that this new science was a difficult and sometimes even a boring subject but insisted that only serious and ambitious students be admitted to his laboratory courses. In addition to being a gifted classroom professor, he was an exceptional public speaker who enjoyed participating in the discussions held at psychology meetings in Germany and abroad.

Ebbinghaus was only 59 years old when he died from pneumonia on 26 February 1909, while serving at the University of Halle. Because of his creative and tenacious methical research on memory, Ebbinghaus is traditionally regarded by psychology's historians as one of the giants in the field. While his methodology has survived more than 100 years in psychology, his other achievements, while noteworthy, are mainly of interest to historians.

When Ebbinghaus was invited to join the faculty at Cornell University in New York, he declined the position for personal reasons, including his commitment to his family in Germany. The position instead went to Edward B. Titchener, who developed structuralism, one of psychology's earliest classical schools of thought. It is interesting to speculate on what might have happened if Ebbinghaus had followed the invitation and gone to Cornell instead of Titchener (who counted E. G. Boring, the famous historian of psychology, as one of his students). It seems possible that Ebbinghaus, who by 1894 was thoroughly bored with the rote memorization of meaningless syllables, might instead have encouraged a more applied psychology than either Titchener or Boring, and the development of American psychology could easily have been quite different.

Bibliography

Works by Ebbinghaus

Ebbinghaus, H. (1885). *Über das Gedächtnis* [On memory]. Leipzig: Duncker & Humblot. Ebbinghaus's classic work on human memory.

Ebbinghaus, H. (1908). *Abriß der psychologie* [Psychology: An elementary textbook]. Leipzig: Feit. Ebbinghaus's shorter version of his two-volume *Principles of psychology*. Also translated as *Summary of psychology*.

Ebbinghaus, H. (1897–1902). *Grundzüge der psychologie* [Principles of psychology] (Vols. 1 & 2). Leipzig: Feit. Ebbinghaus's two-volume textbook on psychology. The book contains Ebbinghaus's mature thinking on memory.

Works about Ebbinghaus

Abresch, J. (1987). *Hermann Ebbinghaus: Kindheit und Jugend in Wupperthal* [Hermann Ebbinghaus: Childhood and adolescence in Wupperthal]. In W. Traxel (Ed.), *Ebbinghaus Studien II* (pp. 71–87). Passau, Germany: Passavia. Archival study of Ebbinghaus's early life in Germany.

Bringmann, W., & Bringmann, N. (1986a). Hermann Ebbinghaus 1875–1879: The missing years. In W. Traxel & H. Gundlach (Eds.), *Ebbinghaus Studien I* (pp. 59–10). Passau, Germany: Passavia. Archival reconstruction of Ebbinghaus's foreign travels and the genesis of his memory research.

Bringmann, W., & Bringmann, N. (1986b). Hermann Ebbinghaus and Cornell University. In W. Traxel & H. Gundlach (Eds.), *Ebbinghaus Studien I* (pp. 101–116). Passau, Germany: Passavia. Contextual analysis of Ebbinghaus's unsuccessful call to a professorship at Cornell University.

Bringmann, W., Schuster-Tyroller, G., & Kalkofen, H. (1986). *Passauer Hermann Ebbinghaus Symposium*. Gottingen: Institute für den Wissenschaftlichen Film. Video about 1985 Ebbinghaus symposium and exhibit.

Gundlach, H. (1986a). Apparative Moglichkeiten und Begrenzu ngen des Werkes Ebbinghaus' [The equipment and the limitations of Ebbinghaus's work]. In W. Traxel & H. Gundlach (Eds.), *Ebbinghaus Studien I* (pp. 117–166). Passau, Germany: Passavia. Critical assessment of Ebbinghaus's limited laboratories and equipment in Germany.

Gundlach, H. (1986b). Hermann Ebbinghaus—Eine kommentierte bibliographie [Hermann Ebbinghaus: An annotated bibliography]. In W. Traxel & Horst Gundlach (Eds.), *Ebbinghaus Studien I* (pp. 181–213). Passau, Germany: Passavia. Comprehensive list of Ebbinghaus's publications.

Jaensch, E. (1908). Hermann Ebbinghaus. *Zeitschrift für Psychologie*, 51, 1–8. A brief German biography of Ebbinghaus.

McPherson, M. (1987). The Ebbinghaus combination method: Its origins and later influences on psychometrics, 1897–1985. In W. Traxel (Ed.), *Ebbinghaus Studien II* (pp. 131–144). Passau, Germany: Passavia. Careful analysis of the Ebbinghaus completion type of intelligence test.

Neisser, U. (1982). *Memory observed*. San Francisco: Freeman. A collection of accounts of memory as applied to natural tasks, in contrast to laboratory research tasks.

Postman, L. (1965). Hermann Ebbinghaus. *American Psychologist, 23*, 149–157. A discussion of Ebbinghaus's research methods and their impact.

Rodi, F. (1987). Die Ebbinghaus-Dilthey Kontgroverse. Biographical Hintergrund und sachlicher Ertrag [The Ebbinghaus-Dilthey controversy and its outcome]. In W. Traxel (Ed.), *Ebbinghaus Studien II* (pp. 145–154). Passau, Germany: Passavia. Detailed discussion of the conflict between Dilthey and Ebbinghaus about the nature of modern psychology.

Shakow, D. (1930). Hermann Ebbinghaus. *American Journal of Psychology, 42*, 505–518. A biography of Ebbinghaus. Includes a bibliography of his works.

Schuster-Tyroller, G. (1987). Hermann Ebbinghaus als Experimentator—zur Methodologie seiner Gedachtnisuntersuchungen [Hermann Ebbinghaus as experimentalist and the methodology of his memory investigation]. In W. Traxel (Ed.), *Ebbinghaus Studien II* (pp. 41–58). Passau, Germany: Passavia. Review of Ebbinghaus's research methods.

Sprung, L., & Sprung, H. (1987). Ebbinghaus an der Berliner Universität—Ein akademisches Schicksal eines zu fruh geborenen. [Ebbinghaus at Berlin University: The academic fate of an early psychologist]. In W. Traxel (Ed.), *Ebbinghaus Studien II* (pp. 89–106). Passau, Germany: Passavia. Archival analysis of the ups and downs of Ebbinghaus's career at Berlin University.

Traxel, W. (Ed.). (1987). *Ebbinghaus Studien II*. Passau, Germany: Passavia. A collection of studies on Ebbinghaus.

Woodworth, R. S. (1909). Hermann Ebbinghaus. *Journal of Philosophy, 6*, 253–256. A brief biographical sketch of Ebbinghaus. Contains a bibliography of Ebbinghaus's work.

Wolfgang G. Bringmann and Charles E. Early

ECLECTIC PSYCHOTHERAPY. All psychotherapies are eclectic in a very broad sense. They all build on prior theory and research and, at least at the time of their inception, are innovative amalgamations of old and new principles. However, eclectic psychotherapy has also evolved as a separate and identifiable approach to treatment that embodies its own unique perspectives and identity.

Frederick C. Thorne (1967) was among the first and most vocal advocates of establishing eclecticism as a formal approach to psychotherapy. Thorne expressed concern that the treatment typically provided was more often a reflection of the theory in which the therapist had been schooled than of the client's need. In turn, each theory advocated the use of some procedures and proscribed against the use of many that were advocated by other approaches. Thorne asserted that the techniques associated with most psychotherapy theories worked with some, but not all, people and observed that, like any skilled technician, a psychotherapist should have available the widest array of tools and procedures possible in order to address the specific and unique needs of each individual. He advocated understanding the effects and applying the procedures of treatment independently of their founding theories, and suggested that a structured and systematic eclectic practitioner would be advantaged because of the ability to use any and all of those procedures that might be helpful in a particular circumstance.

Lazarus (1967) is credited with distinguishing among various types of eclecticism. His distinction between technical and theoretical eclecticism has been widely adopted in the field. In his framework, technical eclectics are those who combine the procedures and techniques from different treatment models without regard to their spawning theories, whereas theoretical eclectics are those who attempt to integrate two or more theories at a conceptual level. Lazarus favored a technical eclectic approach, applying procedures in a systematic manner that is governed by empirically derived decision rules. His multimodal therapy is an example of this type of eclecticism.

Norcross (1986) offered an even finer distinction of eclectic models than Lazarus, with many categories incorporated as defining terms in the field. He observed that although most practicing clinicians see themselves as eclectic, the preponderance of them are unsystematic and inconsistent in their approach. These haphazard eclectics alter their treatment methods based upon their private inclinations of the moment, following no identifiable or consistent principles or guidelines. Their stance may vacillate between theoretical and technical eclecticism, and the rules that guide treatment application are neither articulated nor replicable.

Others follow a form of common factors eclecticism in which they believe that there is a core set of procedures and concepts that account for change in all psychotherapies; the specific and unique interventions posed by these different theories are seen as superfluous. Those who use these latter models differ from the technical and theoretical eclectics by the relative lack of systematic and explicit rules of application. The healing powers are in the qualities of the helping relationship. Norcross suggested that such applications are usually unreplicable and observed that they may become excuses for practice rather than guides for it.

Some writers have taken a slightly different perspective, attempting to integrate among treatment models at multiple levels simultaneously. Some, for example, propose a model of integration that bridges various approaches at both the level of specific techniques and the level of using theory-relevant strategies. Transtheoretical therapy, for example, emphasizes the importance of fitting the stage of client readiness to the aims and strategies used. Similarly, systematic treatment selection emphasizes that effective treatments must match an array of initial client states and traits with variables that characterize both treatment types and therapists. This latter model proposes that a client's initial problems, circumstances, and personal qualities may each serve as indicators or contraindicators for matching with a specific dimension of treatment. These treatment dimensions include: the treatment setting, modality, and format; the particular qualities of the clinician-client relationship that best enhance change (e.g., common relationship factors, client-therapist matching factors, etc.); and the specific strategies and techniques to be used.

Collectively, these and other eclectic approaches reflect differences in the level of organization and abstraction at which integration is advocated. Some models integrate approaches at the level of theory; others integrate treatment at the level of a superordinant treatment strategy; and still others advocate for integration at the level of specific techniques and procedures. The advocates of these various approaches remain united in their emphasis on the importance of treatments that are not constrained by the narrow range of interventions prescribed and proscribed by any one theory or treatment model. They also are united in their desire to expand the theoretical and practical armamentarium of the clinician by extracting and using useful interventions, irrespective of where they are found.

The field of eclectic psychotherapy is still a work in progress; at the end of the twentieth century none of the methods of integrating the different treatment models has emerged as superior or more efficient than any other. However, research has largely been confined to understanding the influence of specific client-treatment or client-therapist matching dimensions on effective treatment processes and outcomes. This aptitude-treatment interaction (ATI) research has confirmed the central assumption that particular families of interventions are differentially effective as a function of client standing on a number of (largely) nondiagnostic qualities.

There remain a number of issues facing this field of study that must be addressed in future research. The principle and greatest obstacles to defining the most productive matches between clients and interventions are the large samples and complex research designs required to test the many possible permutations of client, therapist, therapy model, and problem that might constitute effective matches. Among the less oppressive problems that must be addressed in future research are

a variety of issues related to the selection and training of psychotherapists to increase the range of their effectiveness, and to encourage them to think beyond the limits of narrow theories.

[See also Attitudes; Cognitive Styles; Integrative Psychotherapy; Multimodal Therapy; Psychotherapy, *article on* Approaches; Training; Treatment; *and* Working Alliance.]

Bibliography

Beutler, L. E., & Clarkin, J. (1990). *Systematic treatment selection: Toward targeted therapeutic interventions.* New York: Brunner/Mazel.

Bongar, B., & Beutler, L. E. (Eds.). (1995). *Comprehensive handbook of psychotherapy.* New York: Oxford University Press.

Goldfried, M. R. (Ed.). (1982). *Converging themes in psychotherapy.* New York: Springer.

Lazarus, A. A. (1967). *Psychological Bulletin, 21,* 415–416.

Norcross, J. C. (Ed.). (1986). *Handbook of eclectic psychotherapy.* New York: Brunner/Mazel.

Norcross, J. C., & Goldfried, M. R. (Eds.). (1992). *Handbook of psychotherapy integration.* New York: Basic Books.

Striker, G., & Gold, J. R. (Eds.). (1993). *Comprehensive handbook of psychotherapy integration.* New York: Plenum Press.

Thorne, F. C. (1967). The structure of integrative psychology. *Journal of Clinical Psychology, 23,* 3–11.

Larry E. Beutler

ECOLOGICAL SYSTEMS THEORY. Ecological models encompass an evolving body of theory and research concerned with the processes and conditions that govern the course of human development in the actual environments in which human beings live. Since its first comprehensive statement by Bronfenbrenner in 1979, ecological theory has itself undergone substantial new development both in the evolution of basic constructs and of corresponding research designs. Whereas the original formulation was devoted primarily to a more differentiated conceptualization of the environment as a context of development in terms of successively nested systems ranging from *micro-* to *macro-* (Bronfenbrenner, 1979), the present, still evolving paradigm, now referred to as the *bioecological model*, accords equal importance to the role in development of the biopsychological characteristics of the individual person. The primary focus of the new formulation, however, is on what Bronfenbrenner calls *proximal processes*, defined both conceptually and operationally as the mechanisms that produce development.

Finally, whereas the original model dealt almost exclusively with the formative years, the bioecological model treats development as a process that continues both through the life course and across successive generations, thus according importance to historical continuity and change as forces indirectly affecting human development through their impact on proximal processes.

The Defining Properties of the Bioecological Model

These are stated in the form of two propositions:

Proposition I. Human development takes place throughout life through processes of progressively more complex reciprocal interaction between an active, evolving biopsychological human organism and the persons, objects, and symbols in its immediate external environment. To be effective, the interaction must occur on a fairly regular basis over extended periods of *time.* Such enduring forms of interaction in the immediate environment are referred to as *proximal processes.* (Bronfenbrenner & Morris, 1998, p. 996)

Examples of proximal processes are found in such ongoing behaviors as feeding or comforting an infant, playing with a young child, child-child activities, group or solitary play, reading, problem solving, caring for others, acquiring new knowledge and know-how, or planning or engaging in other intellectual, physical, social, or artistic activities that become increasingly complex over time. In sum, proximal processes are posited as the primary engines of development.

A second defining property identifies the fourfold source of these dynamic forces.

Proposition II. The form, power, content, and direction of the proximal processes effecting development vary systematically as a joint function of the characteristics of the developing *person*; the *environment*—both immediate and more remote—in which the processes are taking place; the nature of the *developmental outcomes* under consideration; and the social continuities and changes occurring over *time* through the life course and the historical period during which the person has lived.

Propositions I and II are theoretically interdependent and subject to empirical test. An operational research design that permits their simultaneous investigation is referred to as a *Process-Person-Context-Time model* (PPCT).

Note that characteristics of the person actually appear twice in the bioecological model: first as one of the four elements influencing the "form, power, content, and direction of the proximal process," and then again as *developmental outcomes.* The last are qualities of the developing person that emerge over time as the result of the joint, interactive, mutually reinforcing effects of the four principal antecedent components of the model. In short, in the bioecological model, the characteristics of the person function both as an indirect producer and as a product of development.

Proposition I also has a corollary that pertains to proximal processes involving other persons.

Corollary 1. The developmental power of proximal processes is substantially enhanced when they occur within the context of a relationship between persons who have developed a strong emotional attachment to each other.

The establishment of a close affectional tie between parent and child during the formative years is especially critical. It enables parents better to withstand the inevitable stresses and strains involved in child rearing while at the same time leading them to be more responsive to the child's needs and bids for attention, thereby initiating and sustaining mutually rewarding interactions. As a result of such participation in proximal processes over time, the young develop the capacity for self-control, and the ability to defer immediate gratification in the interest of pursuing and achieving longer-range goals. The process through which this transition is achieved is called *internalization.*

The Model Applied. Given the recency of the foregoing theoretical formulations, full-scale implementations of the PPCT design are hardly to be expected. Nevertheless, a close approximation appeared in a research monograph published more than three decades ago. The author, Cecil Mary Drillien (1964), was a physician and professor of child life and health at the University of Edinburgh Medical School. The work is the product of what Bronfenbrenner calls a "latent paradigm"; that is, a theoretical model that is not explicitly stated, but is implicit in the research design used for analyzing the data.

Figure 1 depicts both the model and the research findings. The data are drawn from Drillien's longitudinal study of factors affecting the development of children of low birth weight compared to those of normal weight. The figure shows the impact of the quality of mother-infant interaction at age 2 on the number of observed problem behaviors at age 4 as a joint function of birth weight and social class. Mother-infant interaction was assessed in terms of the extent to which, over time, the mother was responsive to the state and behavior of the infant. The graph does not appear in Drillien's monograph, but was constructed from data reported in various tables in that volume.

As can be seen, a *proximal process*, in this instance maternal responsiveness across time, emerges as the most powerful predictor of developmental outcome. In all instances, the proximal process appears to reduce substantially the degree of behavioral disturbance exhibited by the child.

Herein lies the main justification for distinguishing

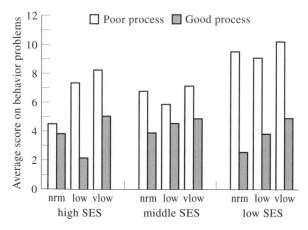

nrm = normal birthweight; low = between normal and 5.5 lbs; vlow = 5.5 lbs or less

ECOLOGICAL SYSTEMS THEORY. Figure 1. Effect of mother's responsiveness on problem behavior at age 4 by birthweight and social class.

between proximal processes and the environments in which they occur; namely, the former turn out to be the more potent force in furthering developmental growth. Furthermore, as stipulated in Proposition II, the power of the *Process* varies systematically as a function of the environmental *Context* (in this instance, social class) and of the characteristics of the *Person* (in this case, weight at birth). The Process appears to have made its greatest impact on young children growing up in the most disadvantaged environment (the lowest socioeconomic level); but, within that environment, it is those who at birth were of normal weight who benefited most. Moreover, it was in this same disadvantaged Context that, under high levels of maternal responsiveness, birth weight showed its most consistent and strongest effect, with the number of behavior problems steadily rising as birth weight fell. Finally, across the board, maternal responsiveness had the general effect of decreasing or buffering against environmental differences in developmental outcome. Thus, at high levels of maternal responsiveness, social class differences in problem behavior became much smaller.

It is noteworthy that application of the same PPCT design, using as the outcome measure the number of problem behaviors when the infants were only two years old, revealed a somewhat similar but much more attenuated pattern. This finding is nicely consistent with the stipulation of Proposition I that to be effective proximal processes must occur "over extended periods of time."

The approximation of the bioecological model reflected in the research design employed by Drillien over three decades ago falls short of today's explicitly stated theoretical formulation. For example, whereas Proposition I defines proximal processes as bidirectional, Drillien's measure of process was based only on the mother's responsiveness to changes in the state and behavior of the infant. No data were reported that would permit calculating a complementary measure of the infant's responsiveness to changes in the state and behavior of the mother. This means that the operational measure available in Drillien's research tapped only one side of the contemporary definition of proximal process. For that reason, it appears likely that, to the extent the infant's contribution to reciprocal interaction does carry weight (as stipulated in Proposition I), Drillien's results may represent an underestimate of the true power of proximal processes as drivers of human development.

Developmental Science in the Discovery Mode

The obtained findings also illustrate an important distinguishing characteristic of research designs appropriate to the bioecological model. Their main purpose is not the usual one of testing for statistical significance. Rather, the design must provide for carrying out an equally essential and necessarily prior stage of the scientific process: hypotheses of sufficient explanatory power and precision must be developed to warrant their being subjected to empirical test. In short, we are dealing with science in the *discovery mode* rather than in the *mode of verification*. From its very beginnings, the bioecological model, through its successive reformulations, represents a sustained effort to meet this scientific need.

Given its stated purpose, an appropriate design strategy for developmental science in the discovery mode is one that involves a series of progressively more differentiated formulations and corresponding data analyses, with the results at each successive step setting the stage for the next round. In short, the research designs employed must be primarily generative rather than confirmatory versus disconfirming. In this generative process, implications derived from the theoretical model play a more prominent role than those drawn from research findings, but the latter are also critical. Their importance is best conveyed by specifying a key feature of the corresponding research design; namely, it must provide a structured framework for displaying the emergent research findings in a way that reveals more precisely the pattern of the interdependencies that in fact obtain among the available measures for the constructs involved.

Of primary scientific interest are not results already anticipated in the existing conceptual model, but those features that point to more differentiated and precise theoretical formulations. These can then be evaluated in light of the newly obtained information, and, if deemed scientifically promising, can be incorporated in the research design for a next step. In sum, the proposed strategy for developmental investigations in the discovery mode involves an iterative process of successive confrontations between theory and data leading toward the ultimate goal of being able to formulate hypotheses that both merit and are susceptible to scientific assessment in the verification mode.

Some Concrete Examples. To be sure, the process here described, or something like it, is what scientists have always done. Where the bioecological model goes further is to define that process explicitly, in the belief that doing so will result in progressively more powerful and precise research designs that, in turn, will advance scientific theory and knowledge. For example, employing the sequential procedure described above ultimately led to the following working hypothesis:

> The greater developmental impact of proximal processes on children growing up in disadvantaged or disorganized environments is to be expected mainly for outcomes reflecting developmental *dysfunction*. By contrast, for outcomes reflecting developmental *competence*, proximal processes are posited as likely to have greater impact in more advantaged and stable environments.

For the successive reformulations, research designs, and findings leading to this working hypothesis see Bronfenbrenner and Morris (1998, pp. 1001–1005). The term "dysfunction" refers to the recurrent manifestation of difficulties on the part of the developing person in maintaining control and integration of behavior across a variety of situations, whereas "competence" is defined as the further development of abilities—whether intellectual, physical, socioemotional, or combinations of them. For instance, acquiring the ability to care for a young infant involves all three.

By treating the above working hypothesis as a point of departure, Bronfenbrenner and Ceci (1994) pursued the strategy of the discovery mode to the next stage by suggesting a new theoretical model, and corresponding research designs, for analyzing the interactive contribution of genetics and environment in human development.

A Bioecological Model of the Nature/Nurture Concept

The theoretical argument is set forth in a series of working hypotheses (Bronfenbrenner & Ceci, 1994).

> *Hypothesis 1.* Proximal processes raise levels of effective developmental functioning, and thereby increase the proportion of individual differences attributable to actualized genetic potential for such outcomes. This means that heritability (h^2) will be higher when proximal processes are strong and lower when such processes are weak. (p. 572)

> *Hypothesis 2.* Proximal processes actualize genetic potentials both for enhancing functional competence and for reducing degrees of dysfunction. Operationally, this

means that as the level of proximal process is increased, indexes of competence will rise, those of dysfunction will fall, and the value of h^2 will become greater in both instances.

> a. The power of proximal processes to actualize genetic potentials for developmental competence (as assessed by an increase in h^2) will be greater in advantaged and stable environments than in those that are disadvantaged and disorganized.

> b. The power of proximal processes to buffer genetic potentials for developmental dysfunction will be greater in disadvantaged and disorganized environments than in those that are advantaged and stable. (p. 578)

> *Hypothesis 3.* If persons are exposed over extended periods of time to settings that provide developmental resources and encourage engagement in proximal processes to a degree not experienced in the other settings in their lives, then the power of proximal processes to actualize genetic potentials for developmental competence will be greater for those living in more disadvantaged and disorganized environments. (p. 579)

In a literature review, Bronfenbrenner and Ceci found indirect evidence consistent with these tentative formulations. For example, both Scarr-Salapatek (1971) and Fischbein (1980) report results in accord with the expectation, based on the bioecological model, that values of h^2 for IQ would be highest in the most advantaged social-class groups and lowest in the most disadvantaged. Also, a number of investigations permit an indirect test of the hypothesized reverse pattern for outcomes of developmental dysfunction (Jenkins & Smith, 1990; Rutter & Rutter, 1992).

From Research to Policy and Practice

In addition to proposing possible new answers for old questions, bioecological theory and research have provided models for analyzing the nature and sources of major social problems in ways that provide a basis for designing programs and social policies for addressing these problems. For example, in their early form, ecological models played an important role in the conceptualization and design of Head Start by expanding the primary focus of intervention beyond the child to encompass the child's family (Zigler & Valentine, 1979). More recently, Bronfenbrenner and his colleagues (Bronfenbrenner, McClelland, Wethington, Moen, & Ceci, 1996) have documented convergent social changes taking place in economically developed nations, and especially in the United States, that are progressively undermining the development of competence and character in successive generations. A summary of the findings appears in Table 1. Concurrently, several research articles based on the bioecological model trace the origin of these trends, analyze their

ECOLOGICAL SYSTEMS THEORY. Table 1. Summary of selected findings.

1. Annual surveys over the past two decades reveal growing cynicism and disillusionment among American youth, reflected in a loss of faith in others, in their government, in the basic institutions of their society, and in themselves.
2. In the United States far greater percentages of youth and women are victims of homicide, with rates more than ten times as high as those for any other developed country.
3. The young are not only likely to be the victims of murder, they are also more likely to commit it. Youth and young adults (ages 18–25) now account for the majority of those arrested for homicide.
4. The percentage of Americans in prison is four times higher than in other developed countries, and the number is rising rapidly.
5. Despite recent gains made by youth from Black families, American high school students are still far behind those from other developed countries in academic achievement. This includes the top 10% of students in each nation. The trend already threatens our productivity and capacity to compete economically in the future.
6. The United States stands in first place in the percentage of children growing up in single-parent families, which now includes over a quarter of all America's children under 6 years of age.
7. Families with children under 6, particularly single-parent mothers, are those who most seek—and desperately need—a job. But they also have the highest unemployment rates. The proportion of Black mothers working full time is much higher than that for White mothers (in 1994, 76 vs. 29%).
8. The percentage of U.S. children living in poverty today is twice as high as that for any other developed nation.
9. Among developed nations, the incomes of rich versus poor families are farthest apart in the United States. We are rapidly becoming a two-class society.
10. Two thirds of children in poverty live in families with a working adult. Less than one third of poor families with a young child rely solely on welfare.

From Bronfenbrenner et al., (1996), *The State of Americans: This Generation and the Next.* New York: The Free Press.

We are indebted to our colleagues who, as coauthors of chapters of the volume *The State of Americans: This Generation and the Next*, provided these findings. They include Steven J. Ceci, Helen Hembrooke, Peter McClelland, Phyllis Moen, Elaine Wethington, and Tara L. White.

implications for the future, and suggest basic principles for designing practices and policies that could reduce, and ultimately reverse, the prevailing course. The general thrust of this ongoing work is perhaps best conveyed in the following excerpt from a chapter in the fifth edition of the *Handbook of Child Psychology* (Bronfenbrenner & Morris, 1998).

At a more general level, the research evidence reveals growing chaos in the lives of families, in child care settings, schools, peer groups, youth programs, neighborhoods, workplaces, and other everyday environments in which human beings live their lives. Such chaos, in turn, interrupts and undermines the formation and stability of relationships and activities that are essential for psychological growth. Moreover, many of the conditions leading to that chaos are often the unforeseen products of policy decisions made both in the private and in the public sector. Today, in both of these arenas, we are considering profound economic and social changes, some of which threaten to raise the degree of chaos to even higher and less psychologically tolerable levels. The most likely and earliest observed consequences of such a rise would be reflected in still higher levels of youth crime and violence, teenage pregnancy, and single parenthood, as well as in reduced school achievement, and, ultimately, a decline in the quality of our nation's human capital.

Thus, we have arrived at a point where the concerns of basic developmental science are converging with the most critical problems we face as a nation. That convergence confronts us, both as scientists and as citizens, with new challenges and opportunities. (Bronfenbrenner & Morris, 1998, p. 1022).

Bibliography

Bronfenbrenner, U. (1979). *The ecology of human development: Experiments by nature and design.* Cambridge, MA: Harvard University Press.

Bronfenbrenner, U., & Ceci, S. J. (1994). Nature-nurture reconceptualized: A bioecological model. *Psychological Review, 101,* 568–586.

Bronfenbrenner, U., McClelland, P., Wethington, E., Moen, P., & Ceci, S. J. (1996). *The state of Americans: This generation and the next.* New York: Free Press.

Bronfenbrenner, U., & Morris, P. A. (1998). The ecology of developmental processes. In W. Damon (Series Ed.) & R. M. Lerner (Vol. Ed.), *Handbook of child psychology: Vol. 1. Theory.* (5th ed., pp. 993–1028). New York: Wiley.

Drillien, C. M. (1964). *Growth and development of the prematurely born infant.* Edinburgh & London: E. & S. Livingston.

Fischbein, S. (1980). IQ and social class. *Intelligence, 4,* 51–63.

Jenkins, J. M., & Smith, M. A. (1990). Factors protecting children living in disharmonious homes: Maternal reports. *Journal of the American Academy of Child and Adolescent Psychiatry, 29,* 60–69.

Rutter, M., & Rutter, M. (1992). *Developing minds: Challenge and continuity across the life span.* New York: Penguin Books.

Scarr-Salapatek, S. (1971). Race, social class, and IQ. *Science, 174,* 1285–1295.

Zigler, E., & Valentine, J. (1979). *Project Head Start: A legacy of the war on poverty.* New York: Free Press.

Urie Bronfenbrenner

ECSTASY. *See* Mysticism; Peak Experiences; *and* Religious Experience, *article on* Religious Experiences and Practices.

ECT. *See* Electroconvulsive Therapy; *and* Elementary Cognitive Tasks.

ECUADOR. As in other Latin American countries, psychology in Ecuador was influenced by philosophy, medicine, and education. In Ecuador, education was especially important and has continued to remain so. Ecuador is one of the Andean nations and has been isolated from many of the international influences that were significant in other Latin American countries such as Argentina, Mexico, Brazil, and Chile.

There are a number of universities that have developed faculties of psychology. The principal ones are the Central University of Ecuador and the Catholic University in Quito; the University of Guayaquil, the Catholic University of Santiago, and the University of Vicente Rocafuerte in Guayaquil; the University of Cuenca in Cuenca; and the University of Loja in Loja. The formation of the professional psychologists is either in the area of educational or clinical psychology and the faculties tend to specialize in one or the other, although in some faculties industrial organizational psychology, and sport psychology have developed. In the last few years there has been a move to internationalize the approach to psychology with the adoption of new methods of professional development. The 6 years of study that train the student at pregraduate level in educational or clinical psychology is changing to one which is similar to other Latin American countries.

In terms of the theoretical bases, the concepts of classical conditioning as developed by Pavlov have been of considerable importance, leading to a number of research projects and the publication of several books. A second influence has been Freudian psychoanalysis, which has been strongly associated with psychological assessment, including projective techniques such as the Rorschach Inkblot Test.

The influence of the dualism and the Thomist school of philosophy, which dominated much of the nineteenth and twentieth centuries, gave rise to the emphasis on psychometric testing in psychology. These were always very important in Ecuador and continue to be so today. They are relevant in the psychological diagnosis as is applied to clinical treatment, which in Ecuador has traditionally been through the application of projective techniques. The work of three of the pioneers of Ecuadorian psychology, Julio Endera, Jorge Escudero, and Agustín Cueva, was important in the development of these techniques of psychological diagnosis, and the general progress of psychology from the 1930s.

There are few journals of psychology published in Ecuador. The oldest is the *Archivos de Criminología, Neuropsiquiatría y Disciplinas Conexas* [Archives of Criminology, Neuropsychiatry and Related Disciplines] in which the first articles relating to psychology appeared. Later there followed *Archivos Ecuatorianos de Orientación* [Ecuadorian Archives of Counseling], and *Anales de Psicología* [Annals of Psychology].

There is a great interest in applied psychology, especially in the areas of clinical and psychotherapy, in addition to the established areas of education and counseling.

Rubén Ardila

EDUCATIONAL COUNSELING enjoys a long tradition in psychology. As a method of enhancing human development, educational counseling shares a common philosophical base with vocational counseling and other school- or college-based psychoeducational interventions. At a broad level, each of these interventions is aimed at maximizing students' options for achieving personal and vocational success in life and for contributing productively to society. They may best be viewed as complementary methods that differ in their specific goals and processes. Educational counseling, in particular, focuses on helping students to surmount obstacles (for example, attitudinal, affective, or skill-based problems) that impede their academic progress. The goals of educational counseling, however, are not only remedial; they also include prevention of academic problems and optimal development of scholastic potential and educational/life planning skills, even in currently well-functioning students.

Like other forms of counseling, educational counseling typically involves individualized or small-group activities, administered by a counselor or psychologist. Such activities have also been adapted for delivery in larger group, classroom, and community-level outreach settings. Among the psychological specialties, counseling psychologists have been the primary purveyors of educational counseling at the college level, and educational and counseling psychologists have been the major contributors to the knowledge base on academic development and adjustment from which educational counseling methods derive. School counselors offer educational counseling services in school settings. University-based psychologists who are housed in colleges of education often assist in the training of school counselors. Additionally, school psychologists offer counseling-related services (for example, educational assessment) in school settings.

History

The impetus for educational counseling grew partly from the vocational guidance movement of the early

1900s, when social reformers in the United States, such as Frank Parsons, sought to assist students and workers to identify and plan for appropriate vocational options. Other key influences on the early development of educational and vocational counseling included advances in the psychometric movement and the study of individual differences as well as the economic depression of the 1930s and the later return of veterans from World War II, which dramatically increased the demand for educational/vocational guidance and counseling services (Whiteley, 1984). Educational counseling has continued to expand and develop as a form of counseling, owing partly to advances in the study of academic, career, and cognitive development; refinement and testing of specific intervention methods; and economic and political concerns about the role of schools in preparing students to enter the workplace.

A great many psychologists have contributed, directly or indirectly, to progress in educational counseling. To cite a few key developments and innovators: Francis Robinson, in *Effective Study* (New York, 1970), developed an influential study method, termed SQ3R, in the 1940s. E. G. Williamson and Edward Bordin (1941) offered an early discussion of methodological issues in educational-vocational research, describing various criteria by which the outcomes of educational counseling might be assessed (for example, academic achievement, educational choice). They also admonished evaluation researchers to discover "what counseling techniques (and conditions) will produce what types of results with what types of students?" (This differential outcome question predated a similar methodological shift by psychotherapy researchers in the 1960s.) Several vocational theorists, such as John Holland, have included educational development themes within their theories, and practical applications of these theories have subsequently been made to problems of educational choice and achievement. A spate of researchers have also designed, and explored the effects of, specific counseling techniques aimed, for example, at improving decisional skills, reducing test anxiety, or enhancing study habits (for example, see reviews by Myers, 1986; Russell & Petrie, 1992).

Central Techniques and Practices

Counseling psychologists have, historically, embraced an "educational-developmental" role as part of their mission (Gelso & Fretz, 1992), including efforts to assist students to adjust to academic demands and to relate their studies to future vocational goals. The tendency has been to view education as a part of the larger career development process inasmuch as the development of students' talents, interests, and values during the school years is likely to affect their later range of vocational options, as well as their success in pursuing

preferred options. This interface between educational and career development helps explain why the goals and methods of educational counseling overlap with those of vocational/career counseling.

Broadly speaking, both educational and career counseling focus on issues of decision making and "role effectiveness" (Myers, 1986). In the case of educational counseling, this entails helping students to plan their studies, to develop effective decision-making skills, and to maximize use of their academic skills. In career counseling, the thrust is on assisting persons to decide on potentially satisfying vocational options and to adjust successfully to the work environment. Naturally, given the differences between students' and workers' roles, contexts, and life experiences, educational and career counseling differ in their specific targets and techniques. For instance, educational counseling deals with problems, such as test anxiety or study skill deficits, that pertain to role effectiveness in scholastic settings, whereas career counseling may involve analogous issues that impair the role effectiveness of adult workers, such as job-related stress or sub-par work skills.

Research Findings

Psychologists have studied a wide range of factors relating to academic adjustment, motivation, and success, a partial list of which includes aptitude and ability, study and time management skills, test anxiety, self-efficacy (for example, beliefs about one's scholastic capabilities), social support, family dynamics, and performance attributions, or beliefs about the causes of one's academic successes and failures (Russell & Petrie, 1992; Spielberger & Vagg, 1995). A number of theories have been developed, helping to organize research findings, identify key determinants of academic choices and attainments, and suggest potentially useful counseling or instructional strategies (Bandura, 1993; Eccles, 1987; Lent, Brown, & Hackett, 1994). There has also been a wealth of studies examining the effectiveness of a variety of specific educational counseling methods.

Reviews of the educational counseling literature suggest several general conclusions (Myers, 1986; Russell & Petrie, 1992). First, the preponderance of evidence lends overall support to the practice of educational counseling. Second, the technical adequacy of research on educational counseling has improved dramatically in recent years. Third, there is a decided preference in the current literature for employing cognitive and behaviorally based methods, that is, techniques that are directed at changing maladaptive beliefs or behaviors, and for studying the effects of structured, skills-focused interventions in a group or class format.

While it is useful to know that educational counseling has generally been found to be effective, psychologists are much more concerned with the sorts of differential effectiveness questions posed by Williamson and Bordin (1941). Thus, much research has examined such issues as which specific techniques are most helpful for certain types of educational problems and individuals, and how their effects are achieved. Some selected findings will be summarized briefly here. Cognitive-behavioral methods have been shown to reduce reliably test anxiety, a condition that inhibits exam performance for many students. Systematic desensitization has been the most frequently studied of the cognitive-behavioral methods for anxiety reduction, though a number of other treatment variants have also proved useful.

Apart from test anxiety, many students express concerns about their abilities to study efficiently, manage their time, or earn satisfactory grades. Study counseling programs, designed to address such problems, are frequently employed by school counselors, counseling psychologists, and other student personnel workers. A variety of these programs, administered either individually or in group or classroom formats, have been found to enhance students' study habits and attitudes. In instances where test anxiety coexists with deficient study skills, multicomponent counseling programs that treat both problems are generally more effective in improving students' grades than are programs that treat only test anxiety or study skills alone.

Substandard scholastic performance may also stem from a variety of factors—such as limitations in students' subject-specific skills or cognitive processing capabilities, or in the quality of the educational experiences to which students have been exposed—that are not always tractable via short-term counseling methods. Thus, depending on the extent and origin of students' performance deficits, more extensive remedial experiences, such as academic tutoring or special education placements, may be necessary in addition to (or apart from) counseling interventions.

Finally, counseling for educational choice and decision making draws largely from the same pool of methods used in vocational counseling, which have been shown to be effective in individual, group, and classroom formats (Swanson, 1995). Psychologists have at their disposal a variety of procedures and measures, derived from several theoretical positions, that are aimed at imparting effective decisional skills and assisting students to explore educational choice options in relation to their interests, skills, and other self-attributes.

Future Directions

Future innovations in educational counseling seem likely to emerge from several current lines of research and theory on academic choice, interest, and perfor-

mance processes, such as inquiry on performance attributions, parental expectations, gender role socialization, goal setting, ability conceptions, and sources of self-efficacy (Bandura, 1993; Eccles, 1987; Lent, Brown, & Hackett, 1994). Particularly promising are analyses that sketch the theoretical mechanisms responsible for academic choice and performance, and that suggest new intervention ingredients or means for restructuring commonly offered ingredients. Some of this work offers intriguing possibilities for enhancing school performance or decision making, though it has not as yet made the transition from the laboratory to the counseling office. Research is especially necessary to build more effective preventive or remedial programs for particular groups of students, such as those who are at-risk for academic failure or dropout, students with learning disabilities, and children from lower socioeconomic strata.

Bibliography

Bandura, A. (1993). Perceived self-efficacy in cognitive development and functioning. *Educational Psychologist, 28,* 117–148.

Eccles, J. S. (1987). Gender roles and women's achievement-related decisions. *Psychology of Women Quarterly, 11,* 135–172. Proposes a model of educational and occupational choice that highlights the role of personal expectations and gender role socialization.

Gelso, C. J., & Fretz, B. R. (1992). *Counseling psychology.* Fort Worth, TX: Harcourt Brace.

Lent, R. W., Brown, S. D., & Hackett, G. (1994). Toward a unifying social cognitive theory of career and academic interest, choice, and performance [Monograph]. *Journal of Vocational Behavior, 45,* 79–122. Presents a theory of academic and career development, derived primarily from A. Bandura's general social cognitive theory.

Myers, R. A. (1986). Research on educational and vocational counseling. In S. L. Garfield & A. E. Bergin (Eds.), *Handbook of psychotherapy and behavior change* (3rd ed., pp. 715–738). New York: Wiley.

Russell, R. K., & Petrie, T. A. (1992). Academic adjustment of college students: Assessment and counseling. In S. D. Brown & R. W. Lent (Eds.), *Handbook of counseling psychology* (2nd ed., pp. 485–511). New York: Wiley.

Spielberger, C. D., & Vagg, P. R. (Eds.). (1995). *Test anxiety: Theory, assessment, and treatment.* Washington, DC: Taylor & Francis.

Swanson, J. L. (1995). The process and outcome of career counseling. In W. B. Walsh & S. H. Osipow (Eds.), *Handbook of vocational psychology* (2nd ed., pp. 217–259). Mahwah, NJ: Erlbaum.

Whiteley, J. M. (1984). A historical perspective on the development of counseling psychology as a profession. In S. D. Brown & R. W. Lent (Eds.), *Handbook of counseling psychology* (pp. 3–55). New York: Wiley.

Williamson, E. G., & Bordin, E. S. (1941). The evaluation

of vocational and educational counseling: A critique of the methodology of experiments. *Educational and Psychological Measurement*, *1*, 5–24. A pivotal early treatise on the methodology of studies of educational and vocational counseling.

Robert W. Lent

EDUCATIONAL PSYCHOLOGY. [*This entry surveys assessment methods in education, including assessments of students, teachers, and administrators. It will not cover general intelligence, aptitude, and motivation. It considers methods and purposes as well as changes from preschool to college, concluding with issues of endurance and value.*]

Student Assessment

Educational psychologists have been major players in the measurement of student performance, virtually defining a national achievement curriculum. The keystone is the standardized test. Alternatives have appeared under labels like authentic or performance-based assessment, along with packages for placement in special programs (learning handicapped, emotionally distressed, gifted, English-language learners).

Linking these assessments are criteria and methods to establish validity and reliability and an overarching system of constructs and standards. Validity assures that an assessment measures a well-defined construct. For example, a reading test should test "reading." Reliability refers to the trustworthiness of an instrument. Groups of judges rating student compositions must agree among themselves.

Several tensions trouble the field of student assessment, reflecting the importance of schooling for the individual and the society. Most significant is locus of control, pitting the classroom teacher against more distant authorities (the school district, the state, or even the federal government). In developed countries, centralized testing often determines admission to secondary and postsecondary schooling. Local control of U.S. schools is a long-standing tradition. This tradition has been challenged, however, as states and the federal government provide increased funding for public education and concomitant demands for accountability. Some teachers have resisted pressure to "teach to the test," offering alternative methods of their own devising.

Multiple-Choice Methods

The standardized achievement test is, without doubt, the most important creation of educational psychologists. It impacts most individuals throughout their life.

From kindergartners' school readiness to examinations for entry to graduate programs, individuals are judged by marks on an answer sheet.

Test development begins with construct definition, typically in terms of behavioral objectives. For example, identify the topic sentence in a paragraph or calculate the sum of four 2-digit numbers in column format. Writing and revising items is the next step. The item stem poses the question, and the choices provide answers. One is correct and the others reflect degrees of wrongness. Plausible alternatives increase item difficulty. Scripted instructions determine test administration, including time allocations, scoring information, and interpretation. Publishers conduct extensive trial runs, ensuring users of test reliability and providing normative data like averages and percentiles. They also offer scoring services. The teacher does little more than distribute booklets, read instructions, and package booklets for shipment.

Test development is only part of a larger enterprise. Test theorists and publishers rely on psychometric methods to transform scores from "percentage correct" to normative indicators like grade level equivalent, percentile, and normal curve equivalent. These indicators provide test users with general measures that compare individuals with a larger population. Classical psychometrics began with the normal "bell-shaped" curve but now employ a wide range of techniques, including factor analysis, item-response theory, generalizability design and analysis.

Criterion-referenced methods appeared in the 1950s as an alternative to normative indicators, the focus on whether students meet absolute and predefined standards. Standard setting begins with professional judgment about performance levels, or what constitutes adequate and exceptional achievement. Tests remain the same, but scores are interpreted differently.

Standardized tests serve various purposes in schools. They compare students and schools. For example, students with high test scores are admitted to prestigious universities or may be identified in third grade as gifted. Parents search out schools with high achievement scores. School improvement and program effectiveness are gauged by standardized measures; a few points up or down can leave educators celebrating or depressed.

Tests influence other facets of schooling. In the elementary grades, teachers monitor reading and mathematics achievement by curriculum-embedded, end-of-unit tests that mirror standardized instruments. Test batteries accompany high school and college textbooks, allowing instructors the convenience of cut-and-paste examinations, and publishers provide do-it-yourself manuals for constructing tests.

Performance-Based Assessment

Standardized tests have had critics from the outset. Criticisms are that tests are low-level, and differences due to socioeconomic status, ethnicity, and language background signify test bias. Not until the 1970s did alternatives emerge. Movements like whole language, hands-on math, and discovery-based science militated against standardization and externally mandated tests, stressing instead the teacher's role in adapting instruction to student needs, and the validity of portfolios, exhibitions, and projects.

Performance is the distinctive feature that sets these methods apart from multiple-choice tests. The techniques span a wide range. At one end are on-demand writing tests; students have an hour or less to write a composition on a predetermined prompt, with no resources, no questions, no chance to revise. At the other extreme are free-form portfolios, collections assembled over weeks or months to demonstrate learning. Individual students decide what to put in the folder and may even judge the quality of the collection.

How are performance samples evaluated? Olympic games like diving and gymnastics serve as metaphors. Judges confer about the characteristics of a quality performance and then evaluate each participant on rating scales or rubrics for specific performance (analytic ratings) and for overall quality (holistic ratings). Psychometric techniques apply to some of these judgments; interrater agreement provides an index of consistency, for instance. Performance-based methods possess considerable face validity; students must directly "do" what they have learned, rather than simply select a correct answer. Trustworthiness is more problematic. Although raters can learn to make consistent judgments, students may look very different depending on the task.

Performance-based methods sprang from practice rather than policy, from classrooms rather than state houses, from teachers rather than publishers. They require human judgment and are expensive. Nonetheless, substantial efforts are underway to adapt these methods for large-scale assessment. On-demand writing tests are now commonplace. Several states complement multiple-choice tests with projects and portfolios, and Vermont relies entirely on these approaches. The demand for high standards provides continuing impetus for the use of performance assessment, the argument being that there is no substitute for demonstrating competence in complex and demanding tasks. For teachers, the connection to classroom practice is compelling, as is the opportunity to gauge student interest and motivation.

Current assessment practice varies from the primary grades through graduate school. Young students are just learning the school game, and standardized tests reflect early home preparation more than individual potential; performance assessments, therefore, are more appropriate. From the late elementary grades through entrance to postsecondary education, multiple-choice tests reach a peak. Afterward, performance samples, such as application letters, thesis papers, and dissertations, become critical.

Assessment for Categorical Placement

This topic does not fit under the previous headings but has become increasingly important because of government funding of categorical programs like special education. Regulations govern assessment practices, but psychologists play important roles in setting local policy and actual implementation. Government funding for disadvantaged students depends on family characteristics like poverty more than achievement. Assessment is important as part of the debate about program effectiveness accountability, that is, whether the investment is justified by student learning.

Categorical programs depend heavily on assessment for selection of students, determination of appropriate services, and exit to regular education. For these assessments, professionals (often psychologists) employ regulated (and expensive) clinical methods, combining teacher recommendations, standardized instruments, interviews and observations, and family consultations.

Teacher Assessment

Only in recent decades has the evaluation of teachers emerged as a significant research topic. Assessment methods vary within levels of teacher development: admission to preservice programs, initial licensure, and induction leading to tenure. The trend is to use standardized procedures for entry-level decisions (e.g., admission to training programs) and performance-based methods for professional advancement decisions (e.g, tenure).

Because of concerns about applicant quality, college students planning to enter teaching must now demonstrate basic skills in many states. The multiple-choice tests resemble those given to high school students, with the same advantages and limitations. High failure rates by underrepresented minorities mean that many potential teacher candidates are denied access to the field. The tests have been challenged as biased and unrelated to teaching potential; the counterargument is that every teacher should possess a minimum level of competence.

Following preservice preparation and during the first few years of service, teachers are in turn licensed and then inducted into tenure positions. During these steps, which most states regulate heavily, candidates undergo serious and sustained evaluation. Prior to 1990, the National Teacher Examination (NTE), a multiple-choice test covering teaching practices and content knowledge, often served for licensure. The NTE was criticized as lacking validity because it did not assess "real teaching." In the late 1980s, Educational Testing Service introduced Praxis, a combination of computer-based tests of basic skills, paper-pencil exercises of subject-matter knowledge, and performance-based observations. Praxis has greater face validity and appears more closely linked to practice.

Professional preparation in teaching is "thin" compared with other fields. You can track the progress of doctors, nurses, lawyers, and accountants by certificates on office walls. Once a teacher has acquired tenure, however, opportunities for professional development are scarce and go unrecognized. In 1987, the National Board for Professional Teaching Standards was formed to develop and promote methods for assessing excellent teaching. Teachers desiring to move beyond initial licensure can now apply for an intensive experience composed of ten performance exercises; the teacher prepares six at the local school, and four are administered during a one-day session in an assessment center. The classroom exercises include instructional videotapes and student work samples, which the candidate must analyze and interpret. At the assessment center, the candidate reviews prescribed lesson materials and designs sample lessons. Panels of expert teachers rate each portfolio and award certificates of accomplishment. The standards are high, and pass rates have been modest. Some states now give certificated teachers pay incentives, but the movement has yet to catch on.

Two final issues warrant brief mention. The first is reliance on student achievement as an indicator of teaching effectiveness. Teacher associations like the National Education Association and the American Federation of Teachers oppose this policy, arguing that student scores reflect many factors the teacher cannot control. States increasingly hold schools responsible for achievement standards. Although the focus is the school, teachers share incentive payments for exceptional schoolwide performance and must deal with the consequences of low scores.

The second issue centers around teacher knowledge of assessment procedures. Externally mandated tests receive most attention, but teachers also rely on their own observations and classroom assessments to judge student learning. How trustworthy are teacher judgments? How knowledgeable are they about standardized tests? Surveys show that teachers receive little preparation in assessment concepts and methods and typically rely on intuition and prepackaged methods. Some educators have proposed the concept of "assessment as inquiry" to support classroom-based methods like portfolios and exhibitions, but with little effect on practice thus far.

Administrator Assessment

Teacher evaluation has not captured the same attention as student assessment but even less attention has been given to assessment of principals and superintendents. One might think that school leaders should be required to demonstrate their knowledge and skill, both to enter their positions and as part of continuing professional development. In fact, work in this area is sparse, with few contributions by psychologists. The research foundations are limited but are emerging around leadership concepts and practical needs.

Administrators typically attend more to budgets and personnel matters than to teaching and student learning, except when schools stand out as exceptional or in dire straits. Research suggests that effective schools are correlated with strong administrative leadership; unfortunately, less is known about how to assess or support leadership. The criterion for effectiveness has typically been standardized student performance. Analogous to an assembly-line model, the administrator's task is to increase the output. Newer models stress human relations and organizational integrity but much remains to be done.

What Has Endured and What Is Valuable?

Standardized multiple-choice tests will remain most likely primary indicators of student achievement. Performance-based methods for large-scale accountability, a closer link between classroom assessment and local reporting of student achievement, and clinical strategies like the best of those found in categorical programs all offer alternative assessment models for the future. The new methods have stimulated public debate about the outcomes of schooling and about the trustworthiness of methods for judging the quality of educational programs. Equity issues are a significant element in these debates. Assessment data show that U.S. schools are doing reasonably well for students in affluent neighborhoods but are failing families in the inner cities and poor rural areas. Indicators can serve to blame victims or to guide improvements. We have much yet to learn about methods for supporting the second strategy.

Bibliography

American Educational Research Association, American Psychological Association, & National Education Association. (1985). *Standards for educational and psychological testing*. Washington, DC: Author.

American Federation of Teachers, National Council on Measurement in Education, & National Education Association. (1990). Standards for teacher competence in educational assessment of students. *Educational Measurement: Issues and Practice*, 9 (4), 30–32.

Berliner, D. A., & Calfee, R. C. (Eds.). (1996). *Handbook of educational psychology*. New York: Macmillan. Part 2 of the *Handbook* includes chapters on individual differences among students, emphasizing a broad span of assessment concepts and practices in the achievement domain, along with motivation, attitudes, and aptitudes, ranging from preschool through adulthood. Chapter 23 describes methods for teacher evaluation from selection through licensing and induction and on to professional certification, including descriptions of NBPTS and Praxis.

Bloom, B. S., Hastings, J. T., & Madaus, G. F. (1971). *Handbook of formative and summative evaluation of student learning*. New York: McGraw-Hill. A classic presentation of a broad range of testing and assessment methods based on behavioral principles that undergirded the design of standardized tests, as well as many classroom and textbook assessments from the 1960s up through the present time.

Camilli, G., & Shepard, L. A. (1994). *Methods for identifying biased test items*. Thousand Oaks, CA: Sage. Describes in readable prose (except for a few technical asides) the concepts and methods underlying standardized tests, along with techniques for addressing problems of group bias.

Candoli, I. C., Cullen, K., & Stufflebeam, D. L. (Eds.). (1997). *Superintendent performance evaluation: Current practice and directions for improvement*. Boston, MA: Kluwer. Part of a series that uses the *Personnel evaluation standards* as a foundation.

Glaser, R., & Linn, R. (1997). *Assessment in transition*. Stanford, CA: National Academy of Education. The focus of this paperback is the *National Assessment of Educational Progress*, the "nation's report card." But the book also covers a broad range of issues in the assessment of student achievement in nontechnical language and sets the stage for discussions of state and national policy about how to find out how students are doing in our schools.

Herman, J. L., Aschbacher, P. R., & Winters, L. (1992). *A practical guide to alternative assessment*. Alexandria, VA: Association for Supervision and Curriculum Development.

Joint Committee on Standards for Educational Evaluation. (1981). *Standards for evaluations of educational programs, projects, and materials*. New York: McGraw-Hill. Several organizations have established standards for educational assessment practices. Implementation of the standards is voluntary in most instances, but the quality of the recommendations is uniformly high.

Linn, R. L. (Ed.). (1989). *Educational Measurement* (3rd ed.). New York: Macmillan. The technical foundations for measuring student achievement, based largely on multiple-choice tests. Although the techniques have broader applications, most of the examples assume "right-wrong" answers. The handbook covers validity and reliability, methods for scaling achievement, along with special chapters on cognitive psychology and measurement, computers and testing, and practical applications of test scores.

Mitchell, J. V., Jr., Wise, S. L., & Plake, B. S. (Eds.). *Assessment of teaching: Purposes, practices, and implications for the profession*. Hillsdale, NJ: Erlbaum. Describes a wide range of methods for assessing teaching knowledge and practice for selection and tenure decisions at local level, grounded in concept that improving education depends on improving teaching.

Nettles, M. T., & Nettles, A. L. (Eds.). (1995). *Equity and excellence in educational testing and assessment*. Boston, MA: Kluwer.

Office of Technology Assessment. (1992). *Testing in American schools: Asking the right questions*. (OTA-SET-519). Washington DC: U.S. Government Printing Office. An up-to-date history of standardized testing.

Phye, G. D. (Ed.). (1997). *Handbook of classroom assessment: Learning, adjustment, and achievement*. San Diego, CA: Academic Press.

Richardson, V. (Ed.). *Handbook of research on teaching* (4th ed.). New York: Macmillan. This series offers an important historical perspective on evaluation of teachers and teachers' evaluations of students. The first edition discusses various methods for studying teaching but does not connect these with evaluation per se. The second edition contains a chapter on assessment of teacher competence as well as a chapter on observation as a method for teacher evaluation. The third edition includes a chapter on the "measurement of teaching," which describes relations between teacher activities and student performance on standardized tests.

Shinkfield, A. J., & Stufflebeam, D. L. (Eds.). (1995). *Teacher evaluation: Guide to effective practice*. Boston, MA: Kluwer Academic Publishers. Offers a review of current research along with practical suggestions.

Stiggins, R. J. (1994). *Student-centered classroom assessment*. New York: Merrill.

Wiggins, G. P. (1993). *Assessing student performance*. San Francisco: Jossey-Bass.

Robert C. Calfee

EDUCATIONAL TESTING SERVICE. The world's largest private measurement institution, and a leader in educational research, Educational Testing Service (ETS) and its for-profit subsidiary, Chauncey Group International, develop and administer achievement, occupational, and admission tests for clients in education, government, and business. ETS annually administers more than 9 million tests in the United States and 180 countries, including the Scholastic Aptitude Test (SAT), the Graduate Record Examinations (GRE), the Graduate Management Admission Test (GMAT), the Test of English as a Foreign Language (TOEFL), and the National Assessment of Educational Progress (NAEP).

The American Council on Education, the Carnegie Foundation for the Advancement of Teaching, and the College Board created ETS in December 1947 by consolidating their testing operations. The founding organizations believed that this restructuring would facilitate research and development.

The ETS's Board of Trustees held its first meeting on 20 December 1947 and elected James B. Conant chair, and appointed Henry Chauncey, director of the College Board, president of ETS. Business operations began 1 January 1948, with a staff complement of 233 employees.

Some of ETS's early contributions to the field include Ledyard Tucker's improved equating models in 1948; Norman Frederiksen and Ben Schrader's 1951 comparative study of the progress of veterans and nonveterans in college, *Adjustment to College*; and Robert Abelson's 1952 study, *Sex Differences in Predictability of College Grades*, which examined high school grades and standardized tests as predictors of college grades for men and women. In 1954, ETS initiated a series of studies for the U.S. Navy on the relationship between test scores and performance on mechanical jobs for both men and women. In 1955, William Mollenkopf conducted an early ETS study with sociological implications entitled *Relationships of School, Parent and Community Characteristics to Performance on Aptitude and Achievement Tests*.

In 1960, Glen Stice conducted ETS's first study of factors leading high school students to drop out, *Talent Losses Before High School Graduation*. ETS researchers, led by Al Beaton, also developed survey instruments and conducted the statistical analysis for James Coleman's influential 1965 report, *Equality of Educational Opportunity*. In 1968, T. Anne Cleary and Thomas Hilton presented a method for investigating bias on individual test items, focusing on Black and White students in *An Investigation of Item Bias*. In 1969, Sam Ball and Gerry Bogatz led a team of ETS researchers to confirm the educational effectiveness of PBS's *Sesame Street* television programs.

During the 1970s, some of ETS's contributions included: Walter Emmerich and Virginia Shipman's 1971 study, *Disadvantaged Children and Their First School Experiences*, which examined child development based on data from ETS's Head Start study; William Angoff's 1972 delta-plot method for determining bias in test items; and in 1976, Garlie Forehand and Marjorie Ragosta's U.S. Department of Health, Education, and Welfare guide to help formerly segregated schools integrate effectively, entitled *A Handbook for Integrated Schooling*.

In 1980, Frederic Lord published his seminal work on item response theory, *Applications of Item Response Theory to Practical Testing Problems*. In 1981, Samuel Messick expanded the concept of validity to include the social consequences of testing in his report, *Evidence and Ethics in the Evaluation of Tests*. In 1982, ETS researchers led by Neil Dorans and Paul Holland began to develop differential item functioning (DIF) procedures; by 1987 all ETS test questions were screened for DIF. Warren Willingham and other ETS researchers examined the comparability of scores achieved under special conditions in their 1988 report, *Testing Handicapped People*.

During the 1990s, ETS's contributions included: Luis Laosa's longitudinal study on the impact of migration on Puerto Rican elementary schoolchildren; Beatriz Chu Clewell and Molly Joy's 1990 assessment of the impact of magnet schools on education in *Choice in Montclair, New Jersey*; and Marjorie Ragosta's 1990 study, *Standardized Testing of Deaf Students: Problems and Solutions*. Neil Dorans and Alicia Schmitt investigated applications of DIF to contructed response questions in their 1991 report, *Constructed Response and Differential Item Functioning*. In 1995, Irwin Kirsch and a team of ETS researchers produced a series of reports on adult literacy for the Department of Education. In 1996, Warren Willingham and ETS President Nancy Cole completed work on a comprehensive analysis of gender-related issues in testing in *Gender and Fair Assessment*.

ETS headquarters are in Princeton, New Jersey. Approximately 2,400 people comprise the permanent ETS staff, which includes more than 1,000 professionals. Professional training and expertise are concentrated in education, psychology, statistics, and psychometrics. The Educational Testing Service Network (ETS Net) is a World Wide Web (http://www.ets.org) gateway to information about college and graduate school admissions and placement tests, with links to AP, GRE, GMAT, SAT, The Praxis Series, and TOEFL sites, as well as other educational resources. ETS Net provides sample test questions, test preparation, and test registration. It also contains information on ETS research initiatives, teacher certification, college planning, financial aid, and links to college and university sites.

[*See also* Testing.]

Elizabeth Blasco

EDWARDS, JONATHAN (1703–1757), empiricist, Puritan divine, and early psychologist of religion. Edwards was born in East Windsor, Connecticut, the only son of 11 children. His father and maternal grandfather were Congregationalist ministers. A child prodigy, he entered Yale University in 1716 at the age of 13, where his Christian faith was both challenged and tempered by encounters with the ideas of John Locke and Sir Isaac Newton. From Locke he understood that nothing is in the mind that was not first in the senses. This made him a thoroughgoing empiricist, as he came to believe that God could be known only through what we experience through sensations. From Newtonian physics he derived a naturalistic conception of the universe, which he understood was at odds with traditional Christian belief but somehow had to be tempered to it. His answer was to develop a theology based on a rational explanation of sensory experience, an early precursor of the modern scientific outlook in psychology.

After receiving a master's degree in 1820, Edwards entered a period of reflection that led to an intense religious experience in which he believed that he talked to Christ and realized that religion was an affair of the heart. At 20 he was called to a series of parishes in New York and Connecticut, before returning to Yale as a tutor. He was soon called to his grandfather's church in Northampton, Massachusetts, as assistant pastor in 1729, a position he held for the next 23 years and one that eventually cast him as the most important spiritual and political influence in western Massachusetts. He also married Sarah Pierrepont, whom he had known at Yale, and they subsequently produced 12 children.

By the early 1730s, Edwards emerged as the New England leader of the Great Awakening, a charismatic wave of religious enthusiasm that swept through the colonies and west to the Mississippi, beginning in the 1720s. Combining reason and sensation with revivalism, he gave vivid, rational descriptions of the fires of hell to his parishioners, but delivered in an unadorned monotone. Such sermons led to various conditions of dissociation in his audience, members of which would faint, shriek, jerk in the aisles, speak in tongues, and engage in the laying on of hands. An epidemic of spontaneous trance states soon spread beyond the church to surrounding towns. Edwards published his observations of these phenomena in *A Faithful Narrative of the Surprising Work of God* (1737), the first systematic treatise in the New World that used a rational and empirical approach to the delineation of different states of religious consciousness.

In 1741, Edwards published *The Distinguishing Marks of a Work of the Spirit of God*, in which he outlined the various signs that confirmed whether such experiences were genuine or counterfeit. In the more extensive *Treatise on Religious Affections* (1746), he elaborated on the development of the spiritual side of the human personality and enumerated a series of signs by which spiritual experiences could be recognized as genuine because of their enduring fruits.

In 1750, after 23 years of leading his congregation, a bitter struggle broke out over interpretation of doctrine and he was summarily dismissed. He retired with his family to the wilderness village of Stockbridge, where he was charged with bringing Christianity to Native Americans. Under these conditions he worked as a solitary scholar for 7 years. His most enduring work from this period was *The Freedom of the Will* (1754), a tract that appropriated the powers of the will under the faculty of reason.

In 1757, Edwards became president of the College of New Jersey, later renamed Princeton University. In 1758, ever a believer in the new science, Edwards submitted to the new treatment of inoculation against smallpox, but died from the procedure after having held his new office for only 2 months.

Bibliography

Hatch, N., & Stout, H. S. (Eds.). (1988). *Jonathan Edwards and the American experience*. New York: Oxford University Press.

Lesser, M. X. (1994). *Jonathan Edwards: An annotated bibliography, 1979–1993*. Westport, CT: Greenwood.

Miller, P. (1949). *Jonathan Edwards*. New York: William Sloan Associates.

Stout, H. S. (Gen. Ed.). (1957–). *The works of Jonathan Edwards*. New Haven, CT: Yale University Press. The definitive edition in progress of Edwards's works; includes the treatises cited in this article.

Eugene Taylor

EFFECT SIZE ELIMINATION. *See* Data Analysis.

EGO. The concept of ego, and the associated ego psychology framework, represent important perspectives within psychoanalytic theory. Ego psychology theories extend classical psychoanalytic drive theory by combining a biological and psychological view of individual development with concepts referring to the complex influences of sociocultural dimensions on individual functioning. The scope of psychoanalysis is thereby broadened from the study of unconscious events and psychopathology to explorations of adaptive processes within a matrix of interpersonal, familial, and sociocultural forces. (Hauser & Safyer, 1995) As used in contemporary psychoanalytic theoretical and clinical discussions, the concept of ego includes cognitive processes (e.g., synthetic functions), defenses (e.g., supression, sublimation, anticipation), and various executive functions (e.g., planning, reflecting about self and others).

Freud's conceptualization of the ego can be understood in terms of the three phases through which his definition evolved (Rappaport, 1959). In the first phase, the ego was defined with the least precision, as the term was used interchangeably with one's own person or the self. Despite this ambiguity, one aspect of ego processes was already apparent—the defensive functions of the ego. In this first phase, the ego was conceptualized as preventing painful memories from entering awareness. In the second phase, Freud's interest in ego functions transiently receded, as he now more fully addressed drives, their vicissitudes, and various manifestations of drives (derivitives; Freud, 1915a, 1915b). Nonetheless, Freud distinguished the central aspects of ego functioning: secondary process, (conscious rational ideas and beliefs) reality principle, and repression. The final phase began with Freud's introduction of the structural model, delineating the ego as a coherent system, which—together with the id (impulse, nonrational ideas), and superego (conscience) systems—is a component of the tripartite personality organization. In this most comprehensive formulation, ego processes refer to many connections among current perceptions, ideals, moral principles, and conflicts engendered by impulses. The work of the ego is now understood as being dedicated to fostering and sustaining harmonious relations between ego functions and the two other major psychic structures (the id and the superego). In this third model of the ego, Freud laid the groundwork for the current recognition of the ego representing the individual as an active agent with his or her own independent interests, rather than passively responding to other psychological forces (e.g, conflicts, moral precepts, responses to others) (Rappaport, 1959).

Significant later theoretical, empirical, and clinical writings incorporate and clarify several concepts derived from these earlier models of ego functioning. Their additions to the ego construct have led to contemporary ego psychology advancing from mechanistic ideas, with limited recognition of context, to incorporating major new knowledge about such important issues as attachment, interpersonal relationships, mastery, resilience, coherence, and identity. Meaningful links from ego psychology to current ideas about adolescence, adult development, and adaptation can now be conceptualized.

Measuring Ego and Ego Development

Given the richness of the ego construct, and the multiplicity of phenomena referred to by this term and by ego development, generating meaningful operational definitions of these concepts for systematic empirical studies is a daunting challenge. Fortunately, several researchers have undertaken programs of research devoted to investigating specific questions and hypotheses regarding ego functions and ego development. Clearly, the domain of ego psychology is too vast to be studied through any single program of empirical studies. Selected constructs relevant to ego psychology, personality theory, and developmental psychology are the target of continuing empirical research.

Ego Development. Ego defenses and ego develop-

ment are related, yet the many complex facets of this relationship have not yet been fully articulated (Hauser, 1993). An illustration of the interplay between these two realms is through two prevailing models of ego development. One view focuses on the ego as representing the collection of ego mechanisms, while the other calls attention to the centrality of a single ego-process, comprising integrative activities (e.g, of thoughts and feelings, of past and present ideas) in its definition of ego development (Hauser, 1979).

Bellak and his colleagues (1973) contributed empirical studies assuming the "collection" model. Viewed in this way, ego development refers to the unfolding of multiple functions, including adaptive strengths, cognitive processes, defenses, and perceptions of others, linked with self-representations (object relations) (Hauser & Daffner, 1980). The second model of ego development points to integrative processes and the individual's overall frame of reference. This view has been elaborated, together with a closely linked assessment technique, by Loevinger and her colleagues (e.g., Loevinger, 1976; Hy & Loevinger, 1996). For over 20 years a series of studies have applied this theoretical approach and psychometrically rigorous assessment technique to investigate ego development in children, adolescents, and adults, and with respect to psychological and sociocultural variables (e.g., Cohn, 1991; Westenberg, Blasi, & Cohn, 1998; Hauser, 1976, 1993; Loevinger, 1979a, 1979b). Our increasing knowledge of connections among individual behavior, individual experience, and ego development based on these research program invaluably adds to diagnostic and longitudinal studies of varied psychopathology and development arrests (Hauser & Safyer, 1995; Hauser, 1991, 1999). An example of such studies are the ongoing longitudinal investigations of adolescent and adult development (repeated measurement over 20 years), which clarify links among family processes, attachment, and ego development (see Hauser, 1991; Hauser, 1999; Hauser, Gerber, & Allen, 1998)

Loevinger's model of ego development assumes that each person has a customary orientation to the self and the world and that there is a continuum (ego development) along which these frames of reference can be arrayed. "In general, ego development is marked by a more differentiated perception of one's self, of the social world, and the relations of one's feelings and thoughts to those of others" (Candee, 1974, p. 621). In this assessment of ego development, specific ego processes (e.g., defense mechanisms and aspects of cognition) cannot be distinguished from one another since they are considered aspects of one integrated structure of the developing ego (Loevinger, 1979b). Loevinger conceives of the ego as a relatively stable structure, maintaining its coherence through initially screening out information that would disrupt homeostasis. Yet this definition does not assume that the ego is without periods of disequilibrium. Qualitative changes gradually occur in ego development as the individual continues to confront phenomena incompatible with his or her current framework of meaning. Consequently, inconsistencies in experience have the potential to trigger periods of disequilibrium, thereby facilitating possible shifts to higher levels of ego development (Loevinger, 1976; Loevinger & Wessler, 1970).

Future Perspective

Arguably, we are witnessing major advances in more precise conceptualizations and empirical research on ego processes and ego development. Two overarching principles are relevant for a future agenda targeting a better understanding of theoretical and empirical connections between ego psychology and the field of general psychology. First, ego constructs—inspired by psychoanalytic data and theory—must be even more explicitly integrated with the insights, theories, and empirical approaches of neighboring disciplines (Holzman & Aronson, 1992). These disciplines include those investigating stress, contextual dimensions (e.g., family, school, and neighborhood), coping, and individual development. The second principle is that to promote even fuller understandings of the interface between ego psychology and other areas of personality and developmental psychology, we must continue to launch theoretically driven, systematic empirical programs of research.

[*See also* Id; Psychoanalysis, *article on* Theories; *and* Superego.]

Bibliography

Bellak, L., Hurvich, M., & Gediman, H. K. (1973). *Ego functions in schizophrenics, neurotics, and normals: A systematic study of the conceptual, diagnostic, and therapeutic aspect.* New York: Wiley.

Candee, D. (1994). Ego developmental aspects of new left ideology. *Journal of Personality and Social Psychology, 30,* 620–630.

Cohn, L. (1991). Sex differences in the course of personality development: A meta-analysis. *Psychological Bulletin, 109,* 252–266.

Freud, S. (1915a). Instincts and their vicissitudes. In J. Strachey (Ed. and Trans.). *The standard edition of the complete psychological works of Sigmund Freud* (Vol. 14, pp. 117–140). London: Hogarth Press.

Freud, S. (1915b). Repression. In J. Strachey (Ed. and Trans.), *The standard edition of the complete psychological works of Sigmund Freud* (Vol. 14, pp. 146–158). London: Hogarth Press.

Hartmann, H. (1939a). *Ego psychology and the problem of adaptation.* New York: International Universities Press.

Hartmann, H. (1939b). Psychoanalysis and the concept of health. *International Journal of Psychoanalysis, 20,* 308–321.

Hauser, S. T. (1976). Loevinger's model and measure of ego development: A critical review. *Psychological Bulletin, 83,* 928–955.

Hauser, S. T. (1993). Loevinger's model and measure of ego development: A critical review II. *Psychological Inquiry, 4,* 23–29.

Hauser, S. T. (1999). Understanding resilent outcomes: Adolescent lives across time and generations. *Journal of Research on Adolescence, 9*(1), 1–24.

Hauser, S. T., & Daffner, K. (1980). Ego functions and development: Empirical research and clinical relevance. *McLean Hospital Journal, 5,* 87–109.

Hauser, S. T., Gerber, E. B., & Allen, J. P. (1998). Ego development and attachment: Converging platforms for understanding close relationships. In P. M. Westenberg, A. Blasi, & L. D. Cohn (Eds.), *Personality Development* (pp. 203–217).

Hauser, S. T., Powers, S., & Noam, G. (1991). *Adolescents and their families: Paths of ego development.* New York: Free Press.

Hauser, S. T., & Safyer, A. W. (1995). The contributions of ego psychology to developmental psychopathology. In D. Cicchetti & D. Cohen (Eds.), *Handbook of developmental psychopathology* (Vol. 1, pp. 555–581). New York: Wiley.

Holzman, P. S., & Aronson, G. (1992). Psychoanalysis and its neighboring sciences. *Journal of the American Psychoanalytic Association, 40,* 63–88.

Hy, L. X., & Loevinger, J. (1996). *Measuring ego development* (2nd ed.) Mahwah, NJ: Erlbaum.

Loevinger, J. (1976). *Ego development: Conceptions and theories.* San Francisco: Jossey-Bass.

Loevinger, J. (1979a). Construct validity of the sentence completion test of ego development. *Applied Psychological Measurement, 3*(3), 281–311.

Loevinger, J. (1979b). *Scientific ways in the study of ego development.* Worcester, MA: Clark University Press.

Loevinger, J., & Wessler, R. (1970). *Measuring ego development* (Vol. 1). San Francisco: Jossey-Bass.

Rappaport, D. (1959). An historical survey of psychoanalytical ego psychology. *Introduction to Psychological Issues, 1,* 5–17.

Westenberg, P. M., Blasi, A., & Cohn, L. D. (1998). *Personality development: Theoretical, empirical, and clinical investigations of Loevinger's conception of ego development.* Mahwah, NJ: Erlbaum.

Stuart T. Hauser

EGO PSYCHOLOGY THEORY was the final model of the mind in Sigmund Freud's evolving thought. Two overarching themes define this theory: (1) conflict between three intrapsychic agencies, the id, the ego, and the superego, and (2) adaptation to the realities of the environment. The ego, the id, and the superego are viewed as the principal structures of the mind, so the term *structural theory* is often used in association with ego psychology. In this model, aggression and sexuality

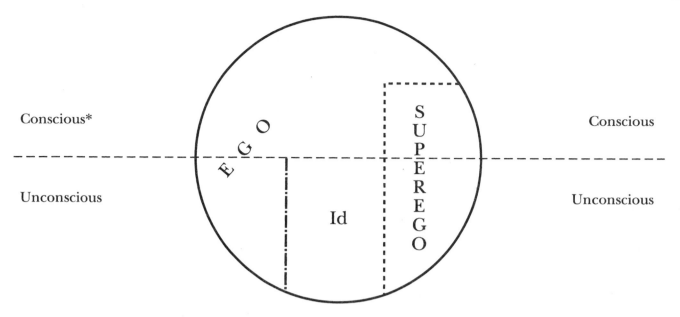

EGO PSYCHOLOGY THEORY. Figure 1. Illustration of the relationship between the ego, id, and superego and Freud's earlier topographic model of consciousness versus unconsciousness. The preconscious has been deleted for the sake of simplicity. (From Gabbard, 1994, p. 31. Copyright 1994 by American Psychiatric Press.)

are striving for expression and discharge. The three agencies battle among themselves to control these drives, and the conflict produces anxiety. This anxiety was referred to as signal anxiety by Freud (1926) because it signals the ego that a defense mechanism is required. The defensive response is instrumental in neurotic symptom formation, in that the defense leads to a compromise between two or more intrapsychic agencies. Neurotic symptoms are regarded as compromise formations that both defend against a wish arising from the id and gratify that wish in some disguised form.

Figure 1 illustrates the relationship between the ego, id, and superego and Freud's earlier topographic model of consciousness versus unconsciousness. The ego is the executive organ of the psyche and is responsible for a variety of functions, such as the capacity to distinguish the real from the unreal, judgment, impulse control, and cognitive processes. It is also the domain of the defense mechanisms, most of which are unconscious. Unlike the ego, the id is entirely unconscious and seeks to discharge tension arising from the drives of sexuality and aggression. The superego, like the ego, is partly conscious and partly unconscious. It is the agency involving moral conscience, ideals, and values.

The ego ideal is generally considered a component of the superego that prescribes what one should do and how one should behave. By contrast, the superego proscribes certain behaviors, thoughts, and feelings that are regarded as unacceptable.

Freud's tripartite structural theory evolved out of his concerns over the failures of the topographic model in the clinical setting. His attempts at directly accessing repressed unconscious memories met with formidable resistances by his patients. He soon recognized that the defense mechanisms responsible for the resistance were themselves unconscious. When he shifted to a more ego-psychological frame of reference in his classic paper "The Ego and the Id" (1923), he was acknowledging that he had been mistaken when he thought that repression caused anxiety. Instead, he was postulating that an unconscious wish that was threatening to the individual signaled a danger to the ego, which in turn creates anxiety. The danger could be related to the body (castration anxiety), one's moral values (guilt), the loss of a significant person (separation anxiety), or simply the loss of love from a meaningful person. The anxiety signals the ego to initiate a defense that allows compromised expression of the drive.

Inherent in the shift from the topographic to the structural model was an emphasis in clinical practice on analysis of the ego rather than the id. In other words, unconscious mental content took a backseat to a focus on analyzing conflict and defense. Instrumental in this shift was *The Ego and the Mechanisms of Defence* (1946) by Freud's daughter Anna. In her view, the analysis of a patient's characteristic defense mechanisms revealed much about the patient's character.

In recent years a vast literature on defense mechanisms has developed (Vaillant, 1992). Specific defense mechanisms have been associated with particular disorders, and extensive empirical research has supported the validity of defense as a basic ego-psychological construct. Defense mechanisms have been placed on a hierarchy, from immature defenses like projection and denial, to mature defenses like sublimation and humor. Positive associations between the maturity of defenses and mental health have been validated in prospective longitudinal studies (Vaillant, 1992). This linkage is independent of gender, social class, and education.

Ego psychology is also defined by its orientation toward the environment and adaptation. Hartmann (1939) was a key figure in this transition from a purely intrapsychic psychology to one that included adaptation to the environment. In his view, human behavior was not entirely explainable by intrapsychic conflict and fantasy. He noted that each child is born with certain primary autonomous ego functions, such as perception, memory, thought, and motility (motor behavior), that are in the conflict-free sphere of the ego. Environmental responses from family members and others act in concert with those structures to shape the individual. Another component of Hartmann's theory was a revision of the concept of motivation so that it was broader than simply lust and destructiveness. He argued for the concept of neutralization, which provided a model of energy that supported certain aspects of the ego that were independent of drive pressures. Thus, a "neutralized libido" leads to modifications of aspects of the sexual drive, such as friendliness and affection. Similarly, self-assertion and healthy competitiveness are regarded as forms of neutralized aggression.

Hartmann also suggested that certain defenses originally arising as the outgrowth of conflict might become secondarily autonomous through the neutralization of the sexual and aggressive energies associated with them. He and other ego psychologists were influential in the broadening of psychoanalysis beyond the study of psychopathology to a general theory of personality.

Erik Erikson (1956) also played a role in extending ego psychology to include social themes, adding identity concerns to the ego-psychological lexicon. In addition, to complement Freud's psychosexual stages based on libidinal zones (e.g., oral, anal, and phallic), he constructed a series of well-known developmental struggles, such as basic trust versus mistrust in infancy, and autonomy versus shame and doubt in the toddler years.

Modern structural theory has increasingly evolved beyond ego psychology so that it is now less dependent on Freud's model of conflict among the three psychic agencies. The id has been increasingly deemphasized, and theorists such as Arlow and Brenner (1964) have stressed that certain aspects of Freud's conceptual model are not necessary to understand conflict as it appears in the clinical setting. Instead, they have emphasized the importance of unconscious fantasy and compromise formation.

Bibliography

Arlow, J. A., & Brenner, C. (1964). *Psychoanalytic concepts and the structural theory*. New York: International Universities Press.

Erikson, E. H. (1956). The problem of ego identity. *Journal of the American Psychoanalytic Association, 4*, 56–121.

Freud, A. (1946). *The ego and the mechanisms of defense* (C. Baines, Trans.). New York: International Universities Press.

Freud, S. (1959). Inhibitions, symptoms, and anxieties. In J. Strachey (Ed. and Trans.), *The standard edition of the complete psychological works of Sigmund Freud* (Vol. 20, pp. 75–175). London: Hogarth Press. (Original work published 1926)

Freud, S. (1961). The ego and the id. In J. Strachey (Ed. and Trans.), *The standard edition of the complete psychological works of Sigmund Freud* (Vol. 19, pp. 1–66). London: Hogarth Press. (Original work published 1923)

Gabbard, G. O. (1994). *Psychodynamic psychiatry in clinical practice: The DSM–IV edition*. Washington, DC: American Psychiatric Press.

Hartmann, H. (1958). *Ego psychology and the problem of adaptation* (D. Rapaport, Trans.). New York: International Universities Press. (Original work published 1939)

Vaillant, G. E. (1992). *Ego mechanisms of defense: A guide for clinicians and researchers*. Washington, DC: American Psychiatric Press.

Glen O. Gabbard

EHRENFELS, CHRISTIAN VON (1859–1932), Austrian philosopher. In 1890 von Ehrenfels published an influential paper on Gestalt qualities that has come to be viewed as a precursor to the later Gestalt school of psychology. Born in Rodaun, near Vienna, to a family of Austrian nobility, he studied philosophy with Franz Brentano at the University of Vienna and with Alexius von Meinong at the University of Graz, obtaining his doctorate in philosophy from Graz in 1885, with a dissertation on size relations of numbers. He completed a *habilitation* thesis on feeling and willing in 1888 at the University of Vienna, and taught there as a lecturer from 1889 to 1896. Called to Prague as an associate professor in 1896, he became full professor there in 1900, retired in 1930, and died 7 September 1932. Max Wertheimer, a founder of Gestalt psychology, took several courses from von Ehrenfels around the turn of the century.

His more than one hundred publications dealt with a broad range of topics: monism and dualism, ethics, esthetics, epistemology, theory of values, eugenics, sexuality, religion, Darwinism, Kant, music, the theory of prime numbers, philosophy of mathematics, and what he called *cosmogony*. His 1890 paper on Gestalt qualities (properties that later Gestalt theorists called "Ehrenfels qualities") had a major impact on subsequent psychology. When the paper was published, there was widespread dissatisfaction with the piecemeal elementism of the dominant theoretical perspectives in psychology. Wilhelm Wundt had proposed a principle of "creative synthesis" to explain why psychological wholes may have properties that are not discernible in their constituent parts in isolation. In 1886 Ernst Mach, in his influential book *Analysis of Sensations and the Relation of the Physical to the Psychical* (Jena, Germany) argued that sensations are the basis of all science, and that these sensations include "space forms" and "time forms" that are not dependent upon the quality of their constituent elements. A circle can be altered in size or color without losing its circularity, and a melody can be transposed into a different key so that all the notes in it are different without the form of the melody being lost. Von Ehrenfels took the next step: these form qualities are not simply combinations of summed elemental qualities, but are new elements in their own right, over and above the qualities of the parts that make up the whole. Such Gestalt qualities are ubiquitous in all perception. A square, for example, has as elements four equally long straight lines plus four right angles—but also its "squareness." This squareness is an immediately experienced additional element. Von Ehrenfels proposed a criterion for Gestalt qualities: an independent one must exist if it remains unchanged when qualities of the whole's constituent elements are changed.

Meinong, Hans Cornelius, Stephan Witasek, and Vittorio Benussi soon published variants of von Ehrenfels's theory. But the next major step occurred two decades later, when the Gestalt school argued that the Ehrenfels qualities are not added elements but are primary, and that properties of constituent parts are determined by their place, role, and function within the whole of which they are parts.

Bibliography

Boring, E. G. (1950). *A history of experimental psychology* (2nd ed.). New York: Appleton-Century-Crofts. Boring's classic is among the many textbooks on the history of psychology that discuss von Ehrenfels.

Ehrenfels, C. v. (1890). Über Gestaltqualitäten [On Gestalt qualities]. *Vierteljahrsschrift für wissenschaftliche Philosphie, 14*, 249–292. For a brief English account of von Ehrenfels's position on the topic, see his 1937 paper "On Gestalt-qualities," *Psychological Review, 44*, 521–524.

Köhler, W. (1947). *Gestalt psychology.* New York: Liveright. One of the numerous works by Köhler in which "Ehrenfels qualities" are mentioned.

Weinhandl, F. (Ed.). (1960). *Gestalthaftes Sehen: Ergebnisse und Aufgaben der Morphologie: Zum hundertjährigen Geburtstag von Christian von Ehrenfels.* Darmstadt, Germany: Wissenschaftliche Buchgesellschaft. Festschrift for von Ehrenfels; includes biographical material, appreciations, and reprints of several of his works on Gestalt qualities.

Wertheimer, M. (1974). The problem of perceptual structure. In E. C. Carterette & M. P. Friedman (Eds.), *Handbook of perception* (Vol. 1, pp. 75–91). New York: Academic Press. Discusses the transition from elementism via form qualities as new elements to the Gestalt view of form qualities as primary.

Michael Wertheimer

EIDETIC IMAGERY. Theorists of visual perception have been grappling for centuries to understand the different kinds of visual images human beings experience. At one extreme is the perception we have of a scene now before our eyes; at the other are pure fantasies that we have constructed from imagination alone. Between these extremes are perceptions that outlast the termination of stimulation, and memories of scenes we once saw. The boundaries between self-produced cognitions and percepts arising from current stimulation are often blurry, and the boundaries among the different forms of imagery, memory, and fantasy are even blurrier.

One form of visual imagery, termed *eidetic imagery* by the earlier researchers working in Germany late in the nineteenth century, has occupied an unusual place in this listing, partly because it has been confused with all of these other cognitions at one time or another, and partly because only a small number people have it. However, research since 1960 has provided a consistent and distinctive description of its properties. Eidetic imagery is defined by the reports of some children (and a very few adults) who say they *can continue to see a visual representation of prior, but no longer present, visual stimulation* (such as a picture). In most cases, people with eidetic imagery report that the image is in front of them, usually where the stimulus picture had been that gave rise to it. They continue to see the picture, even though they know it is no longer there. When reporting eidetic images, all eidetic children use the present tense (e.g., "I see a tree"); after their image fades, if they continue to describe the picture, they switch to past tenses. In contrast, when non-eidetic individuals are asked to describe the stimulus after it is removed, they invariably use a past tense (e.g., "I saw a tree," or "There was a tree"). Furthermore, reports of the content of eidetic images are made fluently, as if the child is looking at something while describing it. The fluency of the report lasts as long as the child says the image is visible. In contrast, reports from memory (whether from non-eidetic children, or eidetic children after their images have faded) may start out fluently, but then hesitations arise, consistent with fluency of retrieval from nonvisual memory. Most children and adults with eidetic imagery can maintain their images for a minute or two, with some holding them for many minutes. All children and adults with eidetic imagery indicate that an eidetic image ends by its different parts fading away one by one, rather than all at once. Children say they can terminate their images at will by blinking, or by trying to move them to another surface. If a second picture is presented while an eidetic child is still reporting the presence of an image of a first picture, most eidetic children report that the two images are superimposed. They can usually tell which is which (as long as the two pictures are each coherent and different from each other), but they see both together. For specially constructed stimuli that create a cohesive pattern when two pictures are superimposed that is not predictable from independent viewing of either stimulus alone, some, but not all, eidetic children report the new image in their superimposed eidetic image. Some eidetic children report reversals of Necker cubes in their image of the two-dimensional stimulus, indicating that eidetic images can be three dimensional if the stimulus is appropriate. Most eidetic children report eidetic images in one eye alone after looking at the stimulus with that eye. All such children can do this with either eye. However, transferring an eidetic image from one eye to the other (e.g., examining the stimulus with one eye and then viewing the now empty surface with the other eye) can only be done sporadically, presumably because of the inevitable opening and closing of eyes that routinely terminates eidetic images. Eidetic children fail to form eidetic images under two conditions: (a) insufficient time to examine parts of the picture, and (b) if they name parts of the picture while it is still on view.

Eidetic imagery is not a photographic memory. It is now well known that even when we are looking at a scene in front of our eyes, our perception of the scene is not photographic: it is not simply a reproduction of the energy patterns at the receptor surfaces. While what we perceive may be closely related to the stimulus structure, as perceivers we select and organize among the components of stimulation to achieve our percepts. Similarly, eidetic imagery is not photographic. Rather, like all perception and memory, eidetic images are constructed and organized selectively based on experience. Specifically, when eidetic and non-eidetic children describe the same picture from memory, no difference in accuracy is found. This finding obtains whether the eidetic child can still "see" the eidetic image, or is reporting from memory. The reports of the images of eidetic children are as likely to omit present elements as are the reports of memories of the same stimulus. Similarly, if the picture is likely to be described from memory with an added element, based on normal expectancies, the same addition is likely to be found in the eidetic reports.

The type of imagery most similar to eidetic imagery is after-images, which nearly everyone experiences: we can continue to see a relatively intense stimulus after its termination. After-images have been extensively investigated. They result from differential adaptation of retinal receptor cells along the boundaries of the stimulus, so that when the retina is then exposed to a neutral surface, the "mirror" image of the previous stimulus pattern is perceived. A stimulus will produce an after-image only if there are no eye movements during the exposure: If the eye moves, there is no differential adaptation and no after-image.

The easiest test to differentiate eidetic images from after-images involves eye movements. To get an eidetic image of a stimulus, the person's eyes must scan it. In contrast, any scanning of the stimulus prevents an after-image from forming. Whereas most eidetic children also experience after-images, they do so only if they do not scan their eyes during stimulus exposure.

A description of the standard elicitation procedures for eidetic imagery can be found in Haber and Haber (1988). Experimental procedures to demonstrate the nature and properties of eidetic imagery, and to differentiate eidetic imagery from other forms of cognitions, are described in detail in Leask, Haber, and Haber (1969) and Haber (1979a, 1979b).

Eidetic imagery has been identified in 2 to 10% of children between the ages of 6 and 12. In contrast, nearly all studies fail to find younger children or adults with eidetic imagery. These results are based on a sampling of over 10,000 individuals by 15 independent laboratories in the United States, Europe, and in a number of countries in which children of these ages are not taught to read.

All attempts to find cognitive, intellectual, emotional, schooling, or experience correlates of eidetic imagery have failed, especially attempts to show that eidetic imagery is a more concrete and less abstract way to represent stimulation. Although only a small number of children possess eidetic imagery, those children are not intellectually slower (or faster) than non-eidetic children, they are not different in their emotional or social maturity, and they do not differ in their exposure to literacy training.

To summarize, eidetic imagery is well defined and well documented, but not at all well understood. Why, like perfect pitch, is it found in such a small segment of people? Why, unlike perfect pitch, does the ability appear primarily in children but only very rarely in adults? On the other hand, unlike many forms of visual imagery that occur independently from concurrent stimulation, eidetic imagery has been uniquely defined using rigorous and replicable experimental procedures.

[*See also* Imagination.]

Bibliography

Haber, R. N. (1979a). Eidetic imagery still lives, thanks to twenty-nine exorcists. *The Behavioral and Brain Sciences*, 2, 619–629.

Haber, R. N. (1979b). Twenty years of haunting eidetic imagery: Where's the ghost? *The Behavioral and Brain Sciences*, 2, 583–618.

Haber, R. N., & Haber, L. R. (1988). The characteristics of eidetic imagery. In L. K. Obler & D. Fein (Eds.), *The exceptional brain: Neuropsychology of talent and special abilities* (pp. 218–241). New York: Guilford Press.

Leask, J., Haber, R. N., & Haber, R. B. (1969). Eidetic imagery in children: 2. Longitudinal and experimental results. *Psychonomic Monograph Supplements*, 3, 25–48.

Ralph Norman Haber and Lyn Haber

ELDER ABUSE AND NEGLECT. First identified as a social problem by the British in 1975, and within a year or so by Americans and Canadians, elder abuse has become recognized as a worldwide phenomenon. Although still "underreported, underresearched, and little understood" (Bennett et al., 1997), mistreatment of older people in domestic settings has gained international attention as countries grapple with issues of human rights, gender equality, domestic violence, and population aging.

Theories and Definitions

After 20 years of study, elder abuse emerges as a multifaceted concept that cannot be described in a single statement or encompassed by one theory. As with other forms of family violence, the phenomenon can be viewed from many perspectives: psychological, situational, ecological, and political, and according to various theories, including symbolic interactionism, social exchange, social learning, and feminist models. Although the psychological basis for explaining child and spouse abuse was renounced early on in favor of sociopsychological and sociocultural factors, studies now show that among perpetrators who are the most aggressive, the percentage of men who have alcohol problems and/or personality disorders is much higher than that found in the general or maritally discordant populations (O'Leary, 1993). So too, it is difficult to dismiss the relatively large proportion of elders' abusers who have histories of mental illness and/or substance abuse. Until more information is available, an intraindividual explanation for physical and psychological mistreatment in particular appears to be reasonable.

Problems of defining elder abuse have plagued researchers and policymakers alike. Hudson's taxonomy (1991) is helpful in understanding the complexity of the concept. Beginning with "violence involving older adults" as the overarching theme, the schema classifies the concept in terms of the relationship between victim and perpetrator: self-mistreatment, elder mistreatment, and crime by strangers. Elder mistreatment can involve either a personal/social or professional/business relationship. It can be an act of commission (abuse) or omission (neglect), intentional or unintentional, and involve several types of behavior. While many manifestations and symptoms are associated with elder mistreatment (e.g., hitting, burning, humiliating, and threatening), the generally agreed-on basic types are physical abuse, psychological abuse (also known as emotional abuse or verbal aggression), financial abuse or exploitation, and neglect.

Some researchers are now questioning the utility of the legal and professional definitions, suggesting that the older person's perception of the particular behavior may be the salient factor for identification and intervention. Others have noted the importance of cultural values, attitudes, and traditions in defining what is acceptable or unacceptable behavior within the family.

Demographic Incidence

Scientific literature reports few prevalence studies on elder abuse. Although carried out in different countries with diverse methodologies, the results are surprisingly similar. Pillemer and Finkelhor surveyed over 2,000 noninstitutionalized elders (65 years and older) in the metropolitan Boston area using an approach adapted from national domestic violence surveys (1988). They found that 3.2% had experienced physical abuse, verbal aggression, and/or neglect since they had reached 65 years of age. Partner abuse was more prevalent (58%) than abuse by adult children (24%); the proportion of victims was roughly equally divided between males and females; and economic status and age were not related to the risk of abuse.

The Pillemer and Finkelhor survey, to which financial abuse was added, was repeated in Canada with a nationally representative sample of persons who could respond on the telephone (Podnieks, 1992). Four percent of elder Canadians were abused; most prevalent was financial abuse (2.5%), then verbal, physical, and neglect. A Finnish team (Kivelä, Köngäs-Saviaro, Kesti,

Pahkala, & Ijäs, 1992) distributed questionnaires, part of a larger mental health study, to all elderly residents of a semiindustrialized town, which included a question on physical, psychological, economic, and sexual abuse and neglect. Almost 6% (5.7%) acknowledged being mistreated in one or more ways since their retirement. A fourth study, conducted as part of a larger omnibus survey in Great Britain, revealed that 5% of elders had been verbally abused and 20% physically and/or financially abused (Ogg & Bennett, 1992). Finally, using definitions similar to the Pillemer and Finkelhor survey, a Netherlands team (Comijs et al., 1998) assessed a population-based sample of 1,797 older people living independently in Amsterdam and found a one-year prevalence rate of 5.6%.

So far, the United States is the only country to have a fully developed system for receiving incident reports of abuse, neglect, and exploitation. Adult protective services agencies are operated by individual states; however, there is little consistency in definitions, eligibility criteria, or administrative structures. In 1986, an estimated 117,000 reports were made to state agencies. By 1996, the number reached 290,000, an increase of 147.9%. The prototypical victim was a woman, 76 years of age, poor, and suffering from physical and/or mental impairment. Like other forms of domestic abuse that show higher rates of reporting for non-Whites than Whites, attributed to bias in the reporting systems, elder African Americans and Hispanics are overrepresented in the report data.

Risk Factors

Causal factors remain equivocal, but characteristics associated with elder abuse cases are victim-perpetrator dependency, perpetrator deviance, victim disability, and poor victim-perpetrator relationship. Substance abuse and social isolation are also contributing features. Poverty, job status, loss of family support, and the intergenerational transmission of violence, which are closely associated with child and partner abuse, do not appear to be important risk factors for elder abuse; neither is caregiver stress.

An analysis of abuse cases by type of mistreatment showed different characteristics were associated with each type (Wolf & Pillemer, 1989). The perpetrators of physical and psychological abuse were apt to have a history of psychopathology and to be dependent on the victim for financial resources. The victims were likely to be in poor emotional health but relatively independent in their activities of daily living. Since this type of abuse involved family members who were most intimately related and emotionally connected, the violence may be attributed to long-standing, pathological family dynamics or interpersonal relationships that became more highly charged because of illness or financial need. Victims of neglect tended to be widowed, very old, cognitively and physically impaired, and with few social contacts.

In sharp contrast to the cases of physical and/or psychological abuse, those involving neglect appeared to be very much related to the dependency needs of the victim. Neither psychological problems nor financial dependency were significant factors in the lives of these perpetrators. For them, the victims were a source of stress. Financial abuse presented still another profile. Factors related to the physical and mental states of the victims seemed to be relatively unimportant. However, victims were generally unmarried with few social contacts. Rather than interpersonal pathology or victim dependency, the risk factors appeared to be perpetrator greed and victim loneliness.

Consequences

Because of the difficulties in trying to separate the impact of the abuse and/or neglect on the elder victim's health from the effects of aging and disease processes, researchers have shied away from examining the issue. However, one team matched a sample of elders from one of the National Institute on Aging's EPESE sites (Established Populations for Epidemiologic Studies of the Elderly) with adult protective services agency reports of abuse over a multiyear period (Lachs et al., 1998). The mortality rates of three groups within the sample were tracked: those who had been physically abused and/or neglected; those who had been investigated for self-neglect; and the remainder of the cohort. In the first few years, no difference in mortality rates was found. At the end of the 13-year follow-up period from cohort inception, only 9% of the group who had been seen for elder mistreatment were still alive, compared to 17% of the self-neglect group and 40% of the noninvestigated group.

Although clinical experience and case reports have documented the severe emotional distress experienced by older persons as a result of mistreatment, again, few empirical studies have been reported. Exceptions are several case comparison investigations that found depression in higher proportions among abused elders than nonabused elders. Because these studies were cross-sectional, it cannot be said with certainty that the depression resulted from the mistreatment. Other psychological states, such as loss of self-esteem, learned helplessness, alienation, guilt, shame, fear, and denial have all been proposed as effects of mistreatment, but no research can be cited. Some suggest that the withdrawal, vigilance, distrust, and dysphoria of elder abuse victims may be symptoms of posttraumatic stress disorder.

Except for the work on care-giver stress, the consequences of aggressive behavior on the perpetrator have been unexplored. Increased levels of depression, anxiety, helplessness, hopelessness, emotional exhaustion, low morale, distress, feelings of isolation, guilt, and anger have been associated with providing care to dependent, frail older people. Research on violence in care-giving relationships with Alzheimer's disease patients has shown that depression distinguishes between nonabusive and abusive caregivers. Once again, however, the studies are cross-sectional and unable to explain the pathway that leads from the care recipient's aggressive behavior to care-giver burden, depression, and abuse.

A high level of tolerance for aggressive behavior has been identified in families in which the abusers are adult children who suffer from emotional distress, mental illness, or alcoholism. One author found an "undeniable sense of parental protectiveness [that] overshadowed interactions between these parents and their adult children" (Greenberg, McKibben, & Raymond, 1990, p. 81). Anetzberger reports that "prolonged and profound intimacy between the abusive adult offspring and their elder" (1987, p. 94) is characteristic of these relationships. The consequences of these behaviors may be the entrapment of the parent and child (victim and abuser) in a "web of interdependency."

Service Delivery

As noted above, the United States has a network of state adult protective services agencies. These public agencies or their private designates are charged with the responsibility of receiving reports of suspected cases of elder mistreatment, screening for their potential seriousness, conducting a comprehensive assessment if indicated, and developing a care plan. As soon as the immediate situation is addressed, the case is generally turned over to other community agencies for ongoing case management and service delivery.

When elder abuse was thought to be primarily a result of care-giver stress, reducing the dependency of the victim on the care giver was the primary goal of treatment. Skilled home nursing, personal care, homemaker and chore services, respite care, Meals on Wheels, day care, friendly visitors, and emergency shelter have been offered to assist the care giver. The realization that the financial and emotional dependency of the perpetrator on the victim is an important risk factor, especially in cases of physical and psychological abuse, has suggested another set of interventions: mental health services, alcohol and drug treatment, vocational counseling, job placement, housing assistance, and financial support for the perpetrator.

Response by Psychologists

The emotional issues, psychopathology, and poor family dynamics associated with cases of elder mistreatment call out to psychologists for intervention. As mental health professionals, psychologists can help victims and perpetrators around care-giving issues, alcohol and drug related problems, depression, codependency, and matters of power and control. However, adult protective services agencies have not only had difficulty in accessing mental health services, but perpetrators are generally unwilling to accept help or absent themselves from the situation. Very few cases reach the courts, most often because the victims do not want to press charges. Even victims refuse services; for example, in almost one fourth of Massachusetts cases, victims declined offers of assistance.

A broader role for psychology in this aspect of family violence is needed. Psychologists, like physicians, social workers, and others caring for older persons, must be familiar with the state adult protective services and elder abuse legislation, the procedure for reporting, and community resources. Through mental health consultation to elder abuse case workers and treatment for families, substance abuse counseling, assertiveness training for victims, and support groups for care givers, psychologists can play an important role in prevention and treatment. Moreover, as researchers of the causes and consequences of abuse and neglect and as designers and evaluators of treatment and preventive modalities, psychologists can make a profound contribution to the field.

Bibliography

Anetzberger, G. J. (1987). *The etiology of elder abuse by adult offspring.* Springfield, IL: Charles C Thomas.

Bennett, G., Kingston, P., & Bridget, B. (1997). *The dimensions of elder abuse: Perspectives for practitioners.* Hampshire, England: Macmillan Press.

Comijs, H. C., Pot, A. M., Smit, J. H. & Jonker, C. (1998). Elder abuse in the community: Prevalence and consequences. *Journal of the American Geriatrics Society, 46,* 885–888.

Hudson, M. (1991). Elder mistreatment: A taxonomy with definitions by Delphi. *Journal of Elder Abuse and Neglect, 3*(2), 1–20.

Greenberg, J. R., McKibben, M., & Raymond, J. (1990). Dependent adult children and elder abuse. *Journal of Elder Abuse and Neglect. 2*(1/2), 73–86.

Kivelä, S. L., Köngäs-Saviaro, P., Kesti, E., Pahkala, K., & Ijäs, M. (1992). Abuse in old age: Epidemiological data from Finland. *Journal of Elder Abuse and Neglect, 4*(3), 1–18.

Lachs, M., Williams, C. S., O'Brien, S., Pillemer, K. A., & Charlson, M. E. (1998). The mortality of elder mistreatment. *Journal of the American Medical Association, 280*(5), 428–432.

Ogg, J., & Bennett, G. (1992). Elder abuse in Britain. *British Medical Journal, 305,* 998–999.

O'Leary, K. D. (1993). Through a psychological lens: Personality traits, personality disorders, and levels of violence. In R. J. Gelles & D. R. Loeske (Eds.), *Current controversies on family violence* (pp. 7–30). Newbury Park, CA: Sage.

Pillemer, K., & Finkelhor, D. (1988). The prevalence of elder abuse: A random sample survey. *Gerontologist*, 28(1), 51–57.

Podnieks, E. (1992). National survey on the abuse of the elderly in Canada. *Journal of Elder Abuse and Neglect*, 4(1/2), 5–58.

Wolf, R. S., & Pillemer, K. (1989). *Helping elderly victims: The reality of elder abuse*. New York: Columbia University Press.

Rosalie S. Wolf

ELDER CARE. The dramatic increase in the proportion of older people in the population in the twentieth century poses a major challenge to society for providing elder care. In 1900, only 4% of the population of the United States was 65 years of age or older. Currently, 13.5% of the population is over 65, and that figure is projected to increase to 22% by the year 2030. While most older people live independently, a significant minority (about 16% of people 65 or older) require regular and ongoing assistance with activities of daily living. The need for care increases with advancing age, so that by age 85, 45% of people living in the community need some assistance with activities of daily living (ADLs). This trend is particularly important because people age 85 and older are increasing at a faster rate than other age groups in the population. The result is unprecedented numbers of people needing help but without adequate resources available to address these needs.

A guiding principle of old-age care is to help people stay in their own homes as long as possible or in the least restrictive alternative. This principle has grown from a concern with the negative consequences associated with institutional life, particularly the loss of personal control and increased dependency. Home care is also promoted at a policy level because of the belief that it can be arranged more cheaply than institutional care, although a definitive empirical test of the costs of alternative approaches remains to be conducted. Although institutional care is typically uninspired and, on occasion, tragically deficient, innovative models are being developed that provide new strategies for dealing with care. A major obstacle to developing and sustaining better models of elder care in the United States is that Medicare does not reimburse for chronic care needs in community or institutional settings. As a result, older people and their families often have to struggle to get adequate help to stay out of an institution, while institutionalization is associated with costs that are catastrophic for all but the wealthiest. The result is a paradoxical system that delays institutionalization by making it too expensive for many people, yet which provides little of the help that might prolong continued residence in the community.

Family Care

Families remain the main source of assistance to their older relatives, but they often have diminished resources for providing care. Smaller family size combined with women's increasing involvement in the workplace and lower economic resources of younger generations make it increasingly difficult for some families to provide assistance to their older relatives on a sustained basis.

When an older person needs care, usually one family member assumes primary responsibility for providing assistance. Strong social norms govern who assumes the role. If the care recipient is married, his or her spouse will almost always take on the main care giving role. If no spouse is available, adult children, especially daughters, will assume responsibility. If there are no children, or children are unavailable, then siblings, grandchildren, or even nonrelatives will help out. Using data from a national survey identified through Medicare records, Stone, Cafferata, and Sangl (1987) found the following proportions of primary care givers: 31% wives, 18% husbands, 29% daughters, 6% sons, and 17% other relationships (including nonrelatives). Adult children are frequently secondary care givers, that is, they provide some help to a parent or sibling but do not take on the main responsibility (Stone, Cafferata, & Sangl, 1987). Adult children who provide care are typically older themselves. Stone and her colleagues report that 13% of care giving daughters and 9% of sons are over 65 themselves. Despite media attention to the problems of the "sandwich generation," the number of middle-age children who find themselves occupying multiple roles of parent and caregiver to their own parents is relatively small.

Research on family caregiving has generally been guided by stress theory (e.g., Aneshensel, Pearlin, Mullan, Zarit, & Whitlatch, 1995), although family-systems approaches have also been used (e.g., Niederehe & Frugé, 1984). It has generally been found that care givers' experiences of strain and emotional distress are associated with exposure to higher levels of primary (disability-related) and secondary (spillover effects) stressors, but there are also considerable individual differences in the psychological impact of stressors (Aneshensel, Pearlin, Mullan, Zarit, & Whitlach, 1995). Caring for someone with dementia or mental illness is generally more stressful than assisting a physically disabled but otherwise intact elder. Care givers' health may also suffer, although reports of health effects are less consistent than for psychological distress.

Several factors mediate the relationship of stressors and psychological outcomes, including the use of active and cognitive coping strategies (e.g., Aneshensel, Pearlin, Mullan, Zarit, & Whitlach, 1995) and receiving social support (Aneshensel, Pearlin, Mullan, Zarit, & Whitlach, 1995). The amount of help families receive from either formal or informal sources is often small, and so the beneficial effects of social support are sometimes not found (Pruchno, Kleban, Michaels, & Dempsey, 1990). Families sometimes disagree over care arrangements, resulting in greater emotional distress for the primary care giver.

Although placement in a nursing home or other long-term care facility is often viewed as the termination of care giving, families continue to be involved with their relative and to experience strains related to institutional care (Zarit & Whitlatch, 1992). Strains are associated with visiting and helping relatives with ADLs, as well as concerns about the quality of care and the continued ability to pay for care. An added factor is that spouse caregivers find themselves in an ambiguous role, not widowed yet having lost the social and emotional benefits associated with marriage. A significant minority of caregivers still experience pronounced feelings of emotional distress as long as 4 years after placement (Aneshensel Pearlin, Mullan, Zarit, & Whitlach, 1995).

A variety of clinical strategies have been proposed for working with distressed family care givers. Individual treatment has generally been found to be more effective than support groups and no-treatment control conditions (Knight, Lutzky, & Macofsky-Urban, 1993). A particular promising approach combines therapy with the primary care giver and one or more sessions with the extended family. This treatment reduces the primary care giver's feelings of distress and may also delay nursing home placement (Whitlatch, Zarit, Goodwin, & von Eye, 1995).

Community Service Programs

A network of age-based community service programs has been developed to support older people to remain in their homes and to supplement the efforts provided by families and provide relief to them. Many services are authorized under provisions of the Older Americans Act. Costs are paid from a variety of sources, including federal, state, and local government funds, charitable donations, and by older people or their families.

Senior centers and nutrition programs target the well-elderly, that is, people living independently and requiring little or no help. Senior centers typically provide social and recreational activities for older people and usually do not have sufficient staff to accommodate people with significant disabilities. Like senior centers, nutrition programs are designed for people who are at least partly independent and can travel to a communal meals site, though homebound elders can obtain home-delivered meals. Transportation services for medical and mental health appointments as well as for other services is generally available, but coverage is often limited in rural areas.

For people who need assistance with everyday tasks, home health programs provide nurses to assist with health care in the home or nursing assistants to help with the activities of daily living, such as dressing or bathing. One of the major sources of assistance to family care givers is respite services, such as in-home respite, adult day services, and overnight respite. Adult day-service programs may be organized on a medical or social model. Some programs provide specialized care for dementia patients, while others integrate cognitively impaired and intact people into the same program, or exclude cognitively impaired people altogether. Families often prefer hiring a home health aid to care for a relative at home, but aids are sometimes poorly trained or unreliable, and services are sometimes provided in a rigid and overly bureaucratic manner (MaloneBeach, Zarit, & Spore, 1992). Overnight respite remains relatively rare in the United States, although in the United Kingdom it has long been a cornerstone of efforts to support elders and their families.

Controlled trials of respite have had varying effects in lowering stress on family care givers, in part because the amount of help provided has been relatively small (e.g., Lawton, Brody, & Saperstein, 1989). When adequate amounts of help are provided on a regular basis, care givers' subjective appraisals of stress and depressive symptoms decrease (Zarit, Stephens, Townsend, & Greene, 1998).

The availability of services as well as funding mechanisms vary considerably from one community to another. To deal with these complexities, programs have been developed to help older people and their families identify and obtain the services they need. Called case management, care management, or similar terms, these programs assess an older client's needs and eligibility for a variety of services. Evaluation of case management programs suggest that they are moderately successful in increasing the appropriate use of services, and may be able to delay or decrease nursing-home placement in at least some cases (Greene, Lovely, Miller, & Ondrich, 1995). Funding remains a major issue, with most of the costs of community care for a chronically disabled person likely to be paid privately.

A major concern to policy makers is how to increase help to families without allowing formal services to replace informal care altogether. Noelker and Bass (1989) have described four patterns of care: (1) family only; (2) formal help that complements (i.e., gives help with different tasks than) the family; (3) formal help that supplements (i.e., gives help with the same tasks as) the family; and (4) formal help only. Little is known about the implications of these different patterns or under what circumstances formal help replaces family assistance.

Specialized Housing for Older People

Many different housing options are available for older people. Some types, such as retirement communities, are designed to enhance the lives of well-elderly or people who require little or no regular assistance. These settings do not usually provide care to older residents who become disabled while living there. The exception is Continuing Care Retirement Communities (CCRCs), which provide a full range of housing, from independent living to nursing home care. CCRCs require a large entrance fee, although subsequent care needs are covered by a monthly fee.

A wide range of settings provide care for people with chronic physical, cognitive, and emotional disabilities, including retirement homes, board and care homes, personal care, and assisted living. Most facilities have congregate meals available, as well as social activities. Some provide assistance with the activities of daily living as well as therapeutic services.

For people with significant disabilities, nursing homes remain the most widely available option. Nursing homes are chronically underfunded and are periodically subjected to intense scrutiny by the government or media because of reports of abuse or neglect. Fortunately, most nursing-home care meets the basic requirements for health and well-being. The model of care, however, emphasizes dependency rather than supporting areas of competence. Organized on a medical model as mini-hospitals, nursing homes treat residents as helpless and dependent. Care routines are organized according to what Parmelee and Lawton (1990) call the "autonomy-security dialectic," that is, stressing safety and security over promoting autonomous behavior by residents. Interactions between staff and patients often reinforce dependent behavior while ignoring or even punishing competent performance, a pattern that Baltes (1996) has called "dependency-support scripts."

Despite high rates of mental health problems among residents, most patients receive little or no mental health treatment. Clinical interventions, including assessment, treatment, and consultation with staff and families, can reduce problems associated with institutional care.

Alternative models have been proposed to create settings that support autonomy and independence. Assisted living facilities attempt to normalize the relationship of staff and residents by providing care in home-like settings and utilizing a variety of social, therapeutic, and environmental strategies for supporting the maintenance of remaining abilities. Within nursing homes, special care units (SCUs) are designed specifically for people with dementia. SCUs combine therapeutic goals to support independent functioning and environmental design to control wandering and other problem behaviors. To date, evaluations of the effectiveness of assisted living and SCUs are limited.

Conclusions

The continued growth of the older population will place increasing pressure on families and on the formal care system to provide adequate assistance. Promising interventions have been developed that lower stress on families and which support the optimal functioning of elders. More work is needed, however, to extend the limited knowledge base for optimal approaches for assisting elders and their families, or for structuring specialized housing that maximizes remaining abilities rather than contributing to residents' dependencies.

[*See also* Retirement.]

Bibliography

Aneshensel, C. S., Pearlin, L. I., Mullan, J. T., Zarit, S. H., & Whitlatch, C. J. (1995). *Profiles in caregiving: The unexpected career.* New York: Academic Press.

Baltes, M. M. (1996). *The many faces of dependency in old age.* New York: Cambridge University Press.

Greene, V. L., Lovely, M. E., Miller, M. D., & Ondrich, J. I. (1995). Reducing nursing home use through community long-term care: An optimization analysis. *Journal of Gerontology: Social Sciences, 50B,* S259–S268.

Knight, B. G., Lutzky, S. M., & Macofsky-Urban, F. (1993). A meta-analytic review of interventions for caregivers distress: Recommendations for future research. *Gerontologist, 33,* 240–248.

Lawton, M. P., Brody, E. M., & Saperstein, A. (1989). A controlled study of respite service for caregivers of Alzheimer's patients. *Gerontologist, 29,* 8–16.

MaloneBeach, E. E., Zarit, S. H., & Spore, D. L. (1992). Caregivers' perceptions of case management and community-based services: Barriers to service use. *Journal of Applied Gerontology, 11*(2), 146–159.

Niederehe, G., & Frugé, E. (1984). Dementia and family dynamics: Clinical research issues. *Journal of Geriatric Psychiatry, 17,* 21–56.

Noelker, L. S., & Bass, D. M. (1989). Home care for elderly persons: Linkages between formal and informal caregivers. *Journals of Gerontology: Social Sciences, 44,* S63–S70.

Parmelee, P. A., & Lawton, M. P. (1990). The design of special environments for the aged. In J. E. Birren & K. W. Schaie (Eds.), *Handbook of the psychology of aging* (3rd ed., pp. 464–488). San Diego, CA: Academic Press.

Pruchno, R. A., Kleban, M. H., Michaels, E., & Dempsey, N. P. (1990). Mental and physical health of caregiving spouses: Development of a causal model. *Journal of Gerontology, 45,* P192–P199.

Stone, R., Cafferata, G. L., & Sangl, J. (1987). Caregivers of the frail elderly: A national profile. *Gerontologist, 27,* 616–626.

Whitlatch, C. J., Zarit, S. H., Goodwin, P. E., & von Eye, A.

(1995). Influence of the success of psychoeducational interventions on the course of family care. *Clinical Gerontologist*, *16*, 117–130.

Williamson, G. M., & Schulz, R. (1990). Relationship, orientation, quality of prior relationship, and distress among caregivers of Alzheimer's patients. *Psychology and Aging*, *5*, 502–509.

Zarit, S. H. (1996). Interventions with family caregivers. In S. H. Zarit & B. Knight (Eds.), *A guide to psychotherapy and aging* (pp. 139–162). Washington, DC: American Psychological Association.

Zarit, S. H., Stephens, M. A. P., Townsend, A., & Greene, R. (1998). Stress reduction for family caregivers: Effects of adult day care use. *Journal of Gerontology: Social Sciences*, *53B*, S267–S277.

Zarit, S. H., & Whitlatch, C. J. (1992). Institutional placement: Phases of the transition. *Gerontologist*, *32*, 665–672.

Steven H. Zarit

ELECTROCONVULSIVE THERAPY. The Hungarian psychiatrist L. J. Meduna (Meduna & Friedman, *Journal of the American Medical Association*, 1939, *112*, 501–506) first proposed, in 1935, the use of induced convulsive seizures in the treatment of schizophrenia, based on a venerable but erroneous observation that epilepsy and schizophrenia were mutually incompatible disorders. He reasoned, somewhat loosely, that epileptic seizures somehow prevented the development of schizophrenia, and hence that artificially produced convulsive seizures might have therapeutic effects for schizophrenic patients.

The earliest attempts to induce convulsive seizures in this group of patients employed injections into the bloodstream of toxic chemicals, such as camphor in oil or a synthetic version thereof known in the United States as Metrazol, and the inhalation of an etherlike substance called Indoklon. Various difficulties were encountered with these methods of seizure induction, not the least being that some patients did not lose consciousness prior to onset of the seizure and experienced feelings of impending death, leading to extreme reluctance to submit to a second treatment (Kalinowski, in S. Arieti [Ed.], New York, 1959).

The preferred and now standard mode of achieving seizure was introduced by the Italian physicians Ugo Cerletti and Lucio Bini in 1938 (*American Journal of Psychiatry*, 1938, *94*, Suppl., 107–113). Their standard technique, the basics of which remain in use today, was to apply, via electrodes placed in the temporal region of both sides of the head, "wall socket" alternating current (AC) at between 70 and 150 volts for 0.1 to 1.0 seconds. Electrical energy is thus transmitted through the brain, causing massive firing of the brain's circuitry.

Meanwhile, and pointing up the serendipitous nature of the discovery of electroconvulsive therapy (ECT), it was gradually learned that ECT was far more effective in producing recovery from severe mood disorder episodes than as an intervention for schizophrenia. The maximally effective therapeutic range thus includes major depression, especially where psychotic features are present, and bipolar disorder, including manic as well as depressive episodes. Occasionally, other types of mental disorder are also observed to be responsive. The mechanism of therapeutic action has never been adequately determined. Today, ECT tends to be employed only after other measures, for example, drugs, have failed, or where a suicidal emergency precludes the use of slower acting methods.

The more elaborate versions of contemporary ECT delivery machines permit deliberate presetting for virtually all pertinent parameters of the electrical stimulus, including duration, AC waveform, graduated intensity buildup, pulsating versus constant flow, and so on. The most important modification, perhaps, has been the now common use of a low-energy stimulus in the range of 5 to 40 joules of electrical energy. The consequent reduction of current density is believed to minimize the usually short-term, posttreatment cognitive disturbances that are frequently upsetting to patients and their families. Normally, ECT is given three times weekly.

It is also believed by many practitioners that nondominant side (that is, right for right-handed persons) unilateral placement of the electrodes—in contrast to the standard bilateral placement—further reduces the likelihood of memory and other cognitive disruptions, without diminished therapeutic effectiveness. Available research does seem to indicate lessened cognitive dysfunction with unilateral placement, but is more equivocal on the question of relative therapeutic efficacy (Janick et al., Baltimore, 1993).

Another important modification of earlier practice is that of premedicating patients who are about to undergo ECT. Two types of brief-acting premedication are generally used, a barbiturate to induce sedation, and a curarelike drug (succinylcholine) to block violent muscle activation in response to nervous system seizure. The latter measure has virtually eliminated the injuries, such as vertebral fractures, that were once a fairly common consequence of ECT. Unfortunately, both these types of medication can enhance other risks, such as cardiac arrest, during ECT administration. Accordingly, the presence of adequate resuscitation resources, including anesthesia personnel and oxygenation equipment, are now widely considered to be essential aspects of the procedure. The contemporary mortality rate per course (usually under ten treatments) of ECT is approximately 1 in 10,000 and compares favorably with the mortality rates of untreated patients having diagnoses comparable to those considered highly responsive to ECT.

Despite the apparent relative safety of modern ECT, it continues to evoke aversive reactions among many members of the public, including many members of the mental health professions. In November 1982 the citizens of Berkeley, California voted to ban the use of ECT within that city, an action that was later judicially overturned. In fact, there remains some concern about possible long-term cognitive impairment in some patients treated with ECT (Breggin, New York, 1979). In 1985, a Consensus Development Conference on the use of ECT sponsored by the National Institute of Mental Health (NIMH) essentially concluded that the benefits of ECT far outweighed its risks (NIMH, Bethesda, MD, 1985).

Most practitioners do not consider ECT a "cure" for the underlying depressive or bipolar disorder. It is employed primarily as a means of interrupting the current episode of mood derangement, and there is some evidence that its employment reduces the interval between the present and the next episode, relative to episodes that terminate spontaneously. Accordingly, ECT is usually followed up by the prophylactic administration of mood-regulating drugs.

Bibliography

American Psychiatric Association. (1990). *The practice of electroconvulsive therapy: Recommendations, treatment, training, and privileging: A task force report of the American Psychiatric Association.* Washington, DC: Author. Reviews the pertinent research relating to efficacy and safety, and states the guidelines adopted by the American Psychiatric Association in regard to the use of ECT.

Coffey, C. E. (1993). *The clinical science of electroconvulsive therapy.* Washington, DC: American Psychiatric Press. A monograph with emphasis on the more technical aspects of ECT.

Fink, M. (1979). *Convulsive therapy: Theory and practice.* New York: Raven Press. Although now somewhat dated, this book was for many years the "bible" of ECT practitioners. It remains a valuable resource.

Robert C. Carson

ELECTROPHYSIOLOGY. *See* Cognitive Electrophysiology.

ELEMENTARY COGNITIVE TASKS. Successful performance on conventional psychometric tests of mental ability, such as an IQ test, typically involves various cognitive processes, which include attention, discrimination, learning, memory, recall, recognition, generalization, judgment, inference, inductive and deductive reasoning, and verbal, spatial, and numerical problem solving. An individual's total score on a complex test, which results from the combined action of a number of such processes, does not reveal which particular ones were involved or to what extent various ones may account for individual differences in test scores. To research these theoretically important questions analytically, cognitive psychologists have used elementary cognitive tasks (ECTs).

ECTs are a class of cognitive tasks, each of which is intended to measure some much smaller number of cognitive processes than is involved in typical psychometric tests. The simple performance requirements of the ECT are explained to the subject and practice trials insure that subjects understand and can execute the task requirements. The ECT is usually so simple that all subjects can perform the task with few, if any, errors. Typically, errors are counted but do not enter into the principal score. The measure of interest is not the correctness of response (since everyone can perform the task), but the response time in performing the test averaged over a large number of trials. Most ECTs are so simple that the response times, measured in milliseconds (ms), are typically less than 2,000 ms and often less than 1,000. Modern research on ECTs uses microcomputers. The subject views a monitor screen; following a "ready" signal, the reaction stimulus appears and the subject responds by pressing a key on a keyboard or a specially devised response console. The response time is the time interval between the onset of the reaction stimulus and the subject's response (e.g., pressing a key).

The ECTs most frequently used in research are:

- Simple response time to the onset of a single visual (or auditory) stimulus to measure the speed of the stimulus apprehension
- Choice or discrimination response time, when there are two or more alternative responses, only one of which is cued
- The oddity problem, responding to the "odd-man-out" among three or more alternatives
- Identifying whether a pair of letters (or words) are either physically or semantically the same or different, to measure speed of access to verbal codes in long-term memory
- A visual scan of a series of letters (or numbers) in search of a previously targeted letter (or number)
- Memory scan, identifying whether a single presented number (or letter) was or was not a member of a previously presented set, as a measure of speed in accessing short-term memory
- Sentence verification, indicating whether or not a statement agrees with a pictorial representation (e.g., "The star is above the circle")

. • Inspection time, the duration (in milliseconds) of the response time required for the subject to make a simple correct visual or auditory discrimination on some specified percentage of the trials.

With a sufficient number of trials, each of these ECTs yields highly reliable measures of speed of information processing. The various ECTs are moderately correlated with each other and, taken singly, are also correlated with conventional estimates of psychometric *g*, such as IQ, mostly in the range of −.20 to −.40. The size of the correlation is generally a positive function of the complexity of the particular ECT. Composite scores based on a number of different ECTs have considerably larger correlations with IQ, but seldom larger than about −.60. ECTs and mental chronometry are recommended not as a replacement for standard psychometric tests, but as analytic tools for studying the nature of individual differences in information processing.

Bibliography

Jensen, A. R. (1982). Reaction time and psychometric *g*. In H. J. Eysenck (Ed.), *A model for intelligence* (pp. 93–132). New York: Springer.

Jensen, A. R. (1985). Methodological and statistical techniques for the chronometric study of mental abilities. In C. R. Reynolds & V. L. Willson (Eds.), *Methodological and statistical advances in the study of individual differences* (pp. 51–116). New York: Plenum Press. Describes a variety of elementary cognitive tasks most commonly used in contemporary research on individual differences in the speed of information processing.

Jensen, A. R. (1992). Understanding *g* in terms of information processing. *Educational Psychology Review, 4,* 271–308.

Jensen, A. R. (1994). Reaction time. In R. J. Corsini (Ed.), *Encyclopedia of psychology* (Vol. 3, 2nd ed., pp. 282–285). New York: Wiley.

Vernon, P. A. (Ed.). (1987). *Speed of information-processing and intelligence.* Norwood, NJ: Ablex. This multiauthored work provides a survey of diverse methods, empirical findings, and theories in this field.

Arthur R. Jensen

ELEMENTARY EDUCATION. Over the twentieth century, psychology has had a varied influence on American education both in the areas of measurement and learning. Some of the major areas for which the psychology of learning has had an impact on American education are teacher training, curricula, and instructional innovations. Historical developments in the marriage of psychology and elementary education are described as part of an ongoing attempt to apply theory and research to the important and challenging issues of educating young children.

Early Applications of Psychology

Psychology in America often starts with a discussion of William James, and so too does the application of psychology to elementary education. James's impact on education is for the most part indirect, through his text *Principles of Psychology*, which influenced educational psychologists like Edward L. Thorndike and John Dewey. James more directly focused on education in his *Talks with Teachers* in 1891. He believed that psychology was relevant to education but often doubted there were sufficient data to support its direct application. In spite of his doubts, James suggested that psychological ideas about memory and associations supported more recitation and hands-on learning, both major shifts from the didactic instruction common in elementary education at the time. Joseph Mayer Rice and Dewey later reiterated this call for more active learning. James, however, was no champion of teachers and his interest in making applications of psychology to education was shallow. He had little respect for teachers and typically did not enjoy his contact with them (Berliner, 1993).

Joseph Mayer Rice, a physician turned journalist, was the first to conduct applied research in classrooms. Rice visited schools across the country and what he described was often memorization and boredom. Although he did describe good schools with inspiring teachers, he felt they developed in spite of the system, which supported didactic instruction. In an observational study of spelling instruction in 1895, Rice found no correlation between mindless drill instruction in spelling and math and students' achievement on tests of spelling and math (Rice, 1914). As a result, Rice severely questioned educational practices of the day and promoted applying empirical classroom research to identify effective instructional practice. Rice, however, was at least 20 years ahead of his time, and school administrators' belief in faculty psychology (the grounding for mindless drill) caused his ideas to fall on deaf ears.

During this same time, G. Stanley Hall began his studies of children and what they knew, ultimately giving rise to developmental psychology and the study of individual differences. Both fields later had a variety of effects on elementary education. Perhaps one of the most profound effects Hall had was on the students he trained, including Louis Terman, Raymond Cattell, and John Dewey. Terman and Cattell were central to studying human abilities, particularly intelligence. Dewey, on the other hand, focused on the educational process.

Changing Schools

Early in his career, Dewey, like Rice before him, argued against didactic instruction and the notion that children's minds are empty vessels to be filled with information. He believed that it was important for students to respond and participate actively in learning activities; in particular, he felt that knowledge was useful only to the degree the learner was able to use it in solving problems (Dewey, 1929). Dewey also argued that knowledge was interpreted depending on the context, and, therefore, learning needed to be contextualized in naturalistic problems (Berliner, 1993).

Dewey was a strong believer in the use of the scientific method to develop pedagogy and study its impact on children. He believed it was necessary to study psychology in the classroom because the complexity of classroom instruction could mitigate or alter the findings of psychology (Dewey, 1929). Like Rice before him, Dewey called for an applied scientific study of teaching. He started a school to further this goal of empirical research on teaching and promote his more active and engaging curricula and pedagogy. Through this study, Dewey became interested in the effects of students' interest and motivation in learning activities (Berliner, 1993), perhaps the earliest recognition of task value and intrinsic motivation in classroom research.

Dewey did not engage in extensive study of any of these topics but, instead, evolved into more of a philosopher than a psychologist. He challenged both education and psychology to consider education within a broader context. Teachers, he believed, lived at the crossroads of psychology, politics, and social practice. To address educational issues, it was necessary to consider the social, political, and policy issues imbedded in them (Dewey, 1929). At the same time, he challenged the reformers as well, criticizing the progressive education movement for not evaluating the impact of their principles on students. Without such scientific self-evaluation, Dewey felt the progressives were just as dogmatic and anti-intellectual as traditional educators (Smith & Smith, 1994). Although his career was primarily known for his philosophy, Dewey continued to press for applications of science and psychology in education.

Edward Thorndike was a peer of Dewey's and is often called the father of educational psychology. Like Dewey, Thorndike strongly supported the application of the scientific method evolving in psychology, and he himself was a leader in studying the psychology of learning as related to education. Perhaps the first major impact that Thorndike had on education was his research with Robert Woodworth that debunked the mental discipline notion of learning. Their studies changed the idea that school subjects were only to strengthen the faculties of the mind (like perseverance, neatness, and memory), arguing instead that school subjects should develop skills and knowledge that are useful and applied. The research became central to

the move to more utilitarian notions of curricula in schools.

Thorndike's conceptions of school subjects as having an applied and useful purpose became an overarching goal as he began to look more closely at applying psychology to teaching and learning. His research was at least in part due to his observations of his own children's school experiences. For example he noted his 11-year-old son had spelling words like "marasmus" and "phthisic." This observation, and undoubtedly some parental anger, motivated Thorndike to go into a study of word frequency as a means to identify words most commonly used in children's literature, textbooks, newspapers, correspondence, and other sources. From his word study, Thorndike developed a list of 10,000 common words, which he used to make spelling books and vocabulary lists. The thought was that spelling and vocabulary should focus on the words children are most likely to encounter and build up from there.

Thorndike's word lists also came into play in perhaps one of his most enduring impacts on education, the Thorndike dictionary. He responded to seeing his children struggle to use dictionaries where words were often defined using more difficult (less frequent) vocabulary, for example, *bear* defined as a carnivorous, quadruped (Thorndike, 1991). Thorndike, again, applied his psychological research and logic to redesign the dictionary. The words in the Thorndike dictionary were defined using only easier words than the object word, to make the definitions understandable. The definitions for words were in order of use, so the reader would encounter more frequent uses before the more esoteric ones. He also added pictures to the dictionary for the first time and used the object word in an example sentence to clarify further the definition through context. The Thorndike dictionary was revolutionary in its time and became a classic.

Thorndike also looked at mathematics and reading instruction in public schools and voiced concern for needed changes. For example, in mathematics Thorndike pushed for meaningful, real-world word problems and less emphasis on straight computation. In reading, Thorndike's observations were insightful as well. He argued that reading is reasoning and that reading instruction should be more than just "word calling"; reading instruction should involve students in reading interesting and thought-provoking stories. In his study of good and poor readers in sixth grade, Thorndike found that some readers knew when they were comprehending or not comprehending what they read, whereas poor readers often did not. Finally, Thorndike, like many of those who followed, argued that schooling should teach students by beginning with their existing knowledge or skills and building upon those, understanding that education must "take its lead from human nature as individually expressed" and lead the student to increased knowledge.

Thorndike's view of education, however, was overly mechanistic; he believed that it could be studied solely in the laboratory. This translated to a disdain of applied research in schools. He also recommended that teacher preparation should require no time observing or working in schools, instead preservice teachers should "read all they could about education in order to learn what was happening in the schools" (Berliner, 1993, p. 61).

Perhaps the lack of direct connection to schools and applied research was both Thorndike's and educational psychology's fatal weakness. Although the issues psychological research raised and psychologists' recommendations for change seemed appropriate, their impact on schools and the processes of education were minimal. Psychologists were likely to be perceived by teachers and the public as more interested in understanding and describing learning rather than in applied issues in classroom instruction (Berliner, 1993). Most educational psychologists during the first half of the twentieth century did not get actively involved in classroom practice or educational policy issues. As a result, by mid-century educational psychology was notably detached from schools.

Behavioral Movement in Schools

During the 1950s and 1960s, educational psychology became reconnected with school learning as an applied area of research of behavioral theories of learning. In 1954, B. F. Skinner visited his daughter's fourth-grade classroom and became very interested in applying his research to teaching humans. He was convinced that learning could be very effective with appropriate analysis of behaviors, active responding, shaping, and judicious use of reinforcement schedules. Skinner thought the greatest problem of classrooms was the infrequency of reinforcement for student behavior and the excessive use of aversive control (Skinner, 1954). Skinner believed that immediate positive reinforcement of correct responses would greatly promote learning. He also felt that through the use of the principles of behavior analysis and shaping, one would be able to see "learning take place" (Skinner, 1954, p. 86).

Skinner also recognized the real limitations to implementing these principles in a classroom with one teacher and thirty students, so he developed a teaching machine. The teaching machine presented small pieces of information to students, gave them response opportunities, and provided immediate reinforcement. By 1954, he was demonstrating a simple learning machine that presented spelling and arithmetic activities; this was clearly the precursor to modern instructional technology and web-based learning.

Although Skinner's teaching machines did not have a great impact at the time, his focus on behavior analysis did. One long-lasting result is the conceptualization of behavioral or instructional objectives as explicit statements of the focus of an instructional episode. Robert Mager and others became great proponents of objectives, and many teachers trained in the late 1960s and early 1970s still cringe at memories of writing objectives to the point of monotony. Unfortunately, the connection of the objective to the instruction and assessment was often lost in the training.

Skinner believed that one of the most difficult problems in learning in schools was that all students were held to learning at the same rate, proceeding at the same pace through instruction. He called this "the greatest source of inefficiency in the classroom." He believed that slow learners suffered disastrous consequences by being pressured to progress at a faster pace than their own ability to learn permitted. He thought this produced gaps in learning that had profound cumulative effects on the slower learners. Unfortunately, his solution was for schools to use teaching machines.

The idea of differential learning rates took hold in the learning community, and John Carroll and Benjamin Bloom worked to apply it to school learning. Carroll developed his model for school learning where each individual's aptitude resulted in differential learning rates, and the amount of time allowed for learning (opportunity to learn) needed to vary according to the learning rate of the student (Carroll, 1989). Carroll also called for educational psychologists to become more focused on solving learning problems encountered in school, reinvigorating the relationship of psychology to education. Benjamin Bloom expanded on Carroll's model to include the quality of instruction along with the opportunity to learn and student aptitude in what became mastery learning. Both Carroll and Bloom believed strongly that any student could learn if given sufficient time and conditions for learning (Bloom, 1976). For the most part, programmatic research on mastery learning showed achievement advantages for students in mastery learning. Various forms of mastery learning spread through the nation's schools and for a time were well accepted. Eventually, however, teachers complained of the inflexibility of the model. Perhaps the most long-lasting impact is that the concept of mastering content and opportunity to learn are now foundational concepts in education and teacher training.

Open Education Movement

Other models of classroom instruction took their theoretical base from developmental psychology, rather than learning theory. Perhaps the most prominent being the open classroom, which was loosely based on Piagetian theory, although some have criticized open education as an inappropriate reading of Piaget's ideas of education. Open education involved children in unstructured self-exploration of the learning environment. Children initiated learning activities based on curiosity and interest. Research did find more positive attitudes among students in open classrooms, but in all large well-designed studies, students in traditional classrooms achieved significantly higher than those in open classrooms. Over time, too, teachers became disenchanted with the lack of structure in classrooms, finding it difficult to manage a classroom where twenty-five students were all doing different things.

Increased Federal Government Involvement

In the 1960s, there was rapidly increasing federal government involvement in education brought about by two major historical events: the launching of Sputnik starting off the space race and the sociopolitical movement against poverty launching President Lyndon B. Johnson's Great Society Programs. These events focused the public and politicians on improving schools and, in particular, using schools as a vehicle to raise people out of poverty. This opened the door for approaches like mastery learning that promoted success of all students. It also focused financial resources on curricular and programmatic development to address school learning. The most notable curricular developments were in math and science. These advances typically involved content experts more than educational psychologists and provided schools with laboratory-based science curricula and new math curricula. The programmatic developments revitalized the study of learning and instruction in schools and revitalized application of psychology to education.

As part of the Great Society Programs' attempt to combat poverty through education, the Head Start preschool program was developed to better prepare low-income children for school. Although the short-term effects of the program were positive, after one or two years of elementary school, the Head Start children lost any achievement advantages. As a result researchers and politicians called for programmatic efforts for students in elementary school to "follow through" on the successes of Head Start for low-income students. The result was a large federally funded study implemented nationwide called the Follow Through Planned Variation Study. The mission was for research institutes and universities to develop programs based on current theory and research in learning, development, and sociology. Thirty programs received federal funding and their approaches ranged from parent education to redesigned elementary education. The education models were equally varied, being based on humanistic psychology, child development, and behavioral theories of learning. As a result, the instruction ranged from discovery learning to programmed learning to teacher-directed instruction and combinations of the three. Taken as whole the instructional models represented nearly all aspects of psychology that could be applied to issues of classroom learning for elementary-age children (Stanford Research Institute, 1972).

A nationwide evaluation of these models was to determine the effectiveness of the programs as contrasted to traditional instruction and to investigate the instructional processes that led to achievement outcomes. In general, the findings supported teacher-directed models that actively engaged students in academic activities and interactions with the teacher. The three programs that were most closely tied to current learning theory produced positive effects on students' achievement. Programs that were loosely based on humanistic or developmental theories had achievement that was no better than traditional instruction, and, in particular, open unstructured models where children determined what they would study produced poorer achievement than traditional instruction. Some of the effective models continue to be used in schools today.

Concurrently, with the Follow Through study, a number of educational psychologists became interested in determining what processes or behaviors resulted in more effective classroom instruction, called teacher effectiveness research. Led by Nate Gage, Barak Rosenshine, Jere Brophy, and David Berliner, researchers used experimental and correlational studies to determine what made teachers effective. The research culminated in synthesis studies that delineated the behaviors and processes of effective teachers in a teacher-directed style of instruction with an academic focus, frequent student participation guided by the teacher, and positive and corrective feedback to student responses (Rosenshine & Stevens, 1986). Teaching functions have become integrated in textbooks for preservice teachers and many school districts have given training workshops to develop classroom teachers' skills in these behaviors.

Cognitive Psychology's Impact on Instruction

During the 1970s, learning theory underwent an evolution from behavioral to cognitive theory, where learning was considered a more active process involving learner input and interpretation, a more complex process than what can be described through reinforcement mechanisms. Many of these developments were due in part to increased federal funding for basic research in reading, math, and science learning. Cognitive psychology suggested that teacher-student and student-student interaction served important learning functions as learners made connections between new information and their prior knowledge (Wittrock, 1986). Instructional models based on cognitive theory stressed student interactions guided by the teacher, such as reciprocal teaching (Palincsar & Brown, 1984), cooperative learning (Stevens, Slavin, & Farnish, 1991) and cognitive apprenticeship (Collins, Brown, & Newman, 1989). Research evaluating more interactive models of instruction has been generally positive although effective implementation requires intensive training of teachers (Rosenshine & Meister, 1994).

Beyond innovations in instructional processes, cognitive psychology has changed the content of what is taught. In both reading and writing, there is a stronger focus on strategic instruction. In part, strategies were derived from cognitive research on students who developed proficiency in reading comprehension and writing. Similarly, cognitive research in math has acted as a catalyst for problem-solving strategies and problem-based learning (Schoenfeld, 1985). Effective instruction still is viewed as teacher structured, actively engaging and interactive, but our increased understanding of different instructional tasks has helped increase our understanding of how to vary instruction to meet the demands of less structured kinds of learning.

Summary

Historically, the relationship between educational psychology and elementary education has been mixed. At times, educational psychology research has been at best tangentially related to educational practice. Yet, over time two important concepts emerge from educational psychology that have gradually shifted the way we think about learning in elementary school. All of the predominant research has focused on (a) students' opportunity to learn and master material, and (b) changing instruction to engage students more actively in learning.

Elementary education will continue to benefit from advances in educational psychology so long as educational psychology focuses on solving ecologically-pertinent questions that have implications for educational policy. Certainly, there has been a growth in that direction with researchers working in collaboration with teachers in classrooms and engaging in meaningful dialogue with administrators and policy makers concerning issues of learning in schools. The evolution of the relationship between educational psychology and elementary education to the point of collaboration and dialogue certainly bodes well for future applied research that both adds to our knowledge and has an impact on education practice.

[*Many of the people mentioned in this article are the subjects of independent biographical entries.*]

Bibliography

Berliner, D. C. (1993). The 100-year journey of educational psychology: From interest, to disdain, to respect for practice. In A. Anastasi, D. Berliner, F. Landy, K. Salzinger, & H. Strupp (Eds.) *Exploring applied psychology: Origins and critical analyses.* Washington, DC: American Psychological Association.

Bloom, B. S. (1976). *Human characteristics and school learning.* New York: McGraw-Hill.

Carroll, J. B. (1989). The Carroll Model: A 25-year retrospective and prospective view. *Educational Researcher, 18,* 26–31.

Collins, A., Brown, J. S., & Newman, S. E. (1989). Cognitive apprenticeship: Teaching the craft of reading, writing, and mathematics. In L. Resnick (Ed.), *Learning, knowing, and instruction: Essays in honor of Robert Glaser* (pp. 453–494). Hillsdale, NJ: Erlbaum.

Dewey, J. (1929). *The sources of a science of education.* New York: Liveright.

Palincsar, A. S., & Brown, A. L. (1984). Reciprocal teaching of comprehension-fostering and monitoring activities. *Cognition and Instruction, 1,* 117–175.

Rice, J. M. (1914). *Scientific management in education.* New York: Hinds, Noble, and Eldredge.

Rosenshine, B. V., & Meister, C. (1994). Reciprocal teaching: A review of the research. *Review of Educational Research, 64,* 479–530.

Rosenshine, B. V., & Stevens, R. J. (1986). Teaching functions. In M. C. Wittrock (Ed.), *The handbook of research on teaching* (3rd ed.). New York: Macmillan.

Schoenfeld, A. H. (1985). *Mathematical problem solving.* New York: Academic Press.

Skinner, B. F. (1954). The science of learning and the art of teaching. *Harvard Educational Review, 24,* 86–97.

Smith, L. G., & Smith, J. K. (1994). *Lives in education: A narrative of people and ideas.* New York: St. Martin's Press.

Stanford Research Institute. (1972). *Follow Through Program sponsors.* (SRI project No. URU-7370.) Washington, DC: Department of Health, Education, and Welfare. (ERIC Document Reproduction Service No. ED 080 494.)

Stevens, R. J., Slavin, R. E., & Farnish, A. The effects of cooperative learning and direct instruction in reading comprehension strategies on main idea identification. *Journal of Educational Psychology, 83,* 8–16.

Thorndike, R. L., (1991). Edward L. Thorndike: A professional and personal appreciation. In G. Kimble, M. Wertheimer, & C. White (Eds.), *Portraits of pioneers in psychology* (pp. 139–151). Washington, DC: American Psychological Association.

Wittrock, M. C. (1986). Students' thought processes. In M. C. Wittrock (Ed.), *Handbook of research on teaching* (pp. 297–314). New York: Macmillan.

Robert J. Stevens and Jennifer R. Duffy

ELLIS, HENRY HAVELOCK (1859–1939), English physician and sexologist. Born in Croydon, England and trained as a physician, Ellis dedicated most of his career to writing on subjects as diverse as literary criticism, philosophy, criminality, eugenics, psychology of sex, color sense, sex differences, drug effects, and genius. Although he was a prolific author on psychological matters, Ellis remains a relatively unknown figure in the history of psychology, an obscurity due in large part to the fact that he neither trained in psychology nor held an academic position. Only recently have scholars examined the influence of Ellis on psychology, particularly his approach to the study of sexual deviance.

Most of Ellis's wide-ranging studies share a theoretical reliance on evolutionary theory. Drawing upon the work of Darwin and other evolutionists, Ellis selected among these writings, produced his own version of social and biological evolution, and then extended it to explain various psychological processes. Among the evolutionary tenets in his work are notions of variation, inheritance of characteristics, latency (the quiescence of an inherited trait for one or more generations followed by its reappearance), recapitulation (individual development recapitulates development of the race), natural and sexual selection, and the social evolution of customs and habits.

The application of evolutionary notions to human psychology is evident in Ellis's *Man and Woman: A Study of Human Secondary Sex Characteristics* (London, 1894) which arguably was the first systematic text published on empirical studies of the psychology of sex difference. In addition to asserting the necessity for conducting empirical studies of sex difference, Ellis also sought to distinguish "natural" or biologically based sex differences from "artificial" or socially induced differences, an aspiration which remains central to contemporary sex difference studies. He also distinguished between sex differences that are primary, secondary, and "tertiary" (characteristics such as intelligence and metabolism). He utilized an evolutionary criterion to assess differences in numerous characteristics including head size, affectability, intellectual impulses, and the variability of these characteristics. This evolutionary measure relied upon the idea of recapitulation in that Ellis classified the various characteristics as resembling either the human child or the savage: on this scale characteristics more resembling the human child represented a progressed degree of evolution. Ellis concluded that women were more akin to the child prototype, and hence, not only were they the more advanced sex but men were evolving after the female type. Especially in his later writings, however, Ellis warned that social progress and the realization of women's fuller participation in society might impede the manifestation of natural traits. He thus held that such social experiments would only be beneficial if they were consistent with biological evolution.

Ellis's better known work on the psychology of sex appeared in his multivolume *Studies on the Psychology of Sex* which began with the *Study of Sexual Inversion,* (London, 1897). Evolutionary theory was employed to argue that sexuality and reproduction were separate phenomena; to establish what constituted "normal" sexual expression; and to explain types of sexual deviance, especially "inversion" or homosexuality. Sexual inversion was, according to Ellis, an organic variation of evolved characters, yet he believed that homosexuality was not a disease, as many of his contemporary sexologists claimed. By naturalizing homosexuality and by similarly justifying various sexual activities (including masturbation) as natural, higher-order acts, Ellis conveyed a sentiment of tolerance and open-mindedness.

Ellis's legacy, then, resides in his elaborate typologies, distinctions between natural and social, and in taking an open-minded attitude toward sex. Ellis is distinctive in his idiosyncratic meshing of liberal politics with scientific determinism and a philosophy of enlightenment with a dutiful reverence toward the hard empirical facts of nature. His works and ideas not only influenced psychologists who would later undertake empirical studies of sex and sex differences but also lay readers who were informed by his popular books and articles.

Bibliography

Brome, V. (1979). *Havelock Ellis: Philosopher of sex*. London: Routledge & Kegan Paul.

Calder-Marshall, A. (1959). *Havelock Ellis: Sage of sex*. London: Hart & Davis.

Grosskurth, P. (1980). *Havelock Ellis: A biography*. New York: Alfred A. Knopf.

Peterson, H. (1928). *Havelock Ellis: Philosopher of love*. London: George, Allen, & Unwin.

Jill Morawski

EMIC-ETIC THEORY. *See* Cross-Cultural Psychology, *article on* Theories and Methods of Study.

EMOTION. [*This entry comprises three articles: a broad overview and description of the term, including a brief history of the study of emotion in the field of psychology and a survey of the various kinds of emotion; a review of the principal theories of emotion, including those from various subdisciplines of psychology; and a discussion of the methods used to research and measure emotion and mood.*]

An Overview

Psychology has witnessed a renaissance of interest in emotion. Emotion is now a central theme in neuroscience, development, personality, psychopathology, and culture. Although researchers approach emotion with different measures and theoretical backgrounds, most agree in defining emotions as brief, rapid responses involving physiological, experiential, and behavioral activity that help humans respond to survival-related problems and opportunities. Emotions are briefer and have more specific causes than moods.

History of the Study of Emotion in Psychology

Emotion was a central interest to theorists who pioneered the science of psychology. In *The Expression of Emotions in Man and Animals* (1872/1988), Charles Darwin provided evidence of universality, continuity across different species, and explanations of why particular expressions are shown for particular emotions. In his 1884 essay "What is an emotion?" William James advanced two propositions that are the impetus of research and argument to this day: Each emotion is defined by specific physiological responses; and the experience of emotion follows rather than precedes the behavioral response of emotion.

The scientific study of emotion, however, would wait until the late 1960s to begin to emerge as a subdiscipline of psychology in its own right. Behaviorists who dominated psychological research during the 1930s, 1940s, and 1950s were skeptical of studying seemingly unobservable emotions that would prove difficult to measure with means other than introspection. The cognitive revolution in psychology of the 1960s, 1970s, and 1980s gave priority to cognitive and informational explanations over motivational and emotional explanations of human behavior.

The renaissance of interest in emotion has several origins. The theorizing of Sylvan Tomkins in the early 1960s directed a generation of researchers to consider the biological bases of emotion and the role of expression in emotional experience. Schachter and Singer's two-factor theory of emotion of 1962, which held that emotion is the result of the context-determined labeling of physiological arousal, had appeal because it seemed counterintuitive. Cognitively oriented theorists such as Herbert Simon posited that emotions serve functions within information processing systems. The study of stress and coping led researchers to consider different kinds of stress in the form of specific emotions. Finally, the cross-cultural studies of Paul Ekman and Izard, first published in 1969, demonstrated that facial expressions of emotion were universal, challenging the prevailing view that emotions, like the sounds of language, were culturally specific.

Questions, Issues, and Tensions in the Study of Emotion

The study of emotion is guided by a set of interrelated questions whose answers vary according to the theoretical perspective of the researcher. First, what is an emotion? How do emotions differ and resemble each other and other psychological entities, such as sensations and moods? Is it most productive to develop theories about emotion in general, or about specific emotions or classes of emotions, such as the self-conscious, approach-related, or positive emotions? Are some emotions more basic than others, in the sense that more basic emotions are simpler, irreducible, and biologically based?

Second, what are the causes of emotions? To understand the proximal causes of emotion, researchers have examined how cognitive appraisals, expressive behavior, and physiological response contribute to the intensity and quality of emotional experience. Other researchers have considered the more distal processes that account for the content of emotion, addressing which aspects of emotion might be closed systems, predetermined by genetic code and biological maturation, and which aspects of emotion are open systems totally written by learning and culture, and which aspects are partially open.

Finally, why do humans have emotions? What functions do emotions serve? What adaptive problems do they solve? Theorists since the classical philosophers have often assumed that emotions disrupt rational, adaptive behavior. More recently, theorists, inspired by evolutionary theory, have argued that emotions solve specific problems essential to human survival, such as forming attachments, fleeing predators, or allocating collective resources. Researchers have likewise considered the functions of the different emotional responses, asserting that the facial, postural, and vocal display of emotion communicates important information to others, the physiology of emotion helps prepare individuals for quick action, and the experience of emotion serves to organize cognitive processes. These three general questions—what emotions are, what causes them, and what their functions are—motivate the different research traditions described in the ensuing sections.

Research on Different Aspects of Emotion

Research on different aspects of emotion has focused on how emotion is communicated, how it is registered in the autonomic and central nervous systems, and how it relates to cognitive appraisal, language, and judgment.

Communication. Information about what emotions are being experienced is conveyed by a person's facial expression, gaze activity, posture, gesture, voice, and spoken word. The research on the communication of emotion has centered on three related questions. First, is the experience of different emotions encoded or communicated in distinct behaviors? Second, do individuals accurately decode or interpret other individuals' emotions from their expressive behavior? Third, can individuals disguise their emotional reactions or fabricate emotions they are not experiencing, and if so, what is the nature of that emotional experience?

Most studies have focused on people's abilities to interpret emotional expression. The initial studies of Paul Ekman and also of Carroll Izard presented photographs of theoretically derived facial expressions of emotion to individuals in different literate cultures and had those indviduals judge the emotion shown. Ekman also did such studies with people who had little exposure to Western culture—the Fore of New Guinea. In those studies and dozens that followed, individuals from different cultures accurately identified facial displays of anger, disgust, fear, happiness, sadness, and surprise, in some studies shame and contempt, and more recently embarrassment and amusement. In one of the only cross-cultural studies of emotional expression (rather than recognition), Ekman found that American and Japanese students displayed similar emotional behavior when alone, but showed much different, culturally proscribed emotional displays when in the presence of an authority figure.

Subsequent research has focused on the nature of emotion perception and the functions of facial expressions within social interactions. Studies have ascertained that the perception of facial expressions is categorical, and that people may be biologically prepared to respond to certain expressions in adaptive ways. For example, when people are presented with facial displays of anger, even at subliminal levels, they respond with fear. Studies of parent-child interactions have found that facial expressions reward children for certain behaviors and discourage them from more dangerous behaviors, such as approaching a visual cliff.

Other researchers have investigated the acoustic properties of different emotions, motivated by the assumption that emotion is encoded in distinct acoustic properties that are reliably decoded by observers. Although the research is less extensive, findings indicate that different emotions are signaled by distinct acoustic properties, such as rise time and pitch, and that the acoustic signals of emotion play an important role in social interactions, for example, those between parent and child.

Autonomic Nervous System. William James argued that each emotion, from anger to aesthetic rapture, is defined by a distinct pattern of ANS activity, evident in changes in heart rate, breathing patterns, sweating, and other responses, that supports adaptive action. Walter Cannon and Carl Lange countered that emotions could not be associated with discrete ANS responses, which are too diffuse and slow to account for rapid and differentiated emotional responses.

To this day, the question of whether emotions involve discrete ANS responses is hotly contested. Studies have documented some emotion-specific ANS responses when people move emotion-related facial muscles or relive emotional experiences. For example, fear, anger, and sadness, compared to disgust, are associated with increased heart rate elevation, and anger is associated with increased blood flow to the hands, compared to fear. Critics have noted that these studies do not differentiate the ANS activity of certain emotions. Other studies have documented specific ANS responses associated with other emotions. The increased capillary blood flow in the cheeks associated with blushing and embarrassment differs from fear-related ANS activity, while parasympathetically mediated crying associated with sadness differs from nonemotional crying. Sympathetically mediated piloerection, the contractions of muscles surrounding the hair follicles on the neck, is another little explored ANS response related to specific emotions. More recent work by Stephen Porges has documented the role of parasympathetic ANS activity in stress responses and emotional communication.

Central Nervous System. Researchers examining central nervous system (CNS) activity have been motivated by such questions as: What is the CNS activity associated with each emotion? As emotions unfold, are different CNS structures and processes involved? Using such techniques as EEG, which measures electrical activity on the surface of the scalp, PET and functional MRI, which are slower in resolution than EEG but allow researchers to examine more specific brain sites, researchers have begun to make progress in understanding the CNS activity associated with emotion.

One of the first systematic attempts to examine emotion and the central nervous system was undertaken by Richard Davidson and his colleagues. Motivated by an approach-withdrawal framework, they have shown that approach-related emotions, such as happiness, correlate with relative left hemispheric activity, whereas withdrawal-related emotions, such as disgust, correlate with relative right hemispheric activity.

Other researchers have attempted to identify more specific CNS structures or systems that relate to emotion. Jaak Panksepp has posited that specific CNS structures and neurotransmitter systems relate to emotion systems related to play, expectancy, flight, and fight. Recent evidence by Joseph LeDoux compellingly demonstrates that the amygdala, a portion of the midbrain, provides an immediate emotional evaluation of stimuli, which is integrated with other kinds of information about the stimulus.

Cognitive Appraisal. Consistent with the formulations of Aristotle and Sartre, certain researchers have defined emotions as the products of appraisals of environmental events relevant to the individual's goals and well-being. Rapid, automatic appraisals of environmental events are believed to be the proximal causes of emotional experience. Although it is difficult to measure appraisal processes directly, the study of emotion-related appraisal is a central area in emotion research.

Richard Lazarus's theory of appraisal posits that each emotion is defined by a discrete "core relational theme," which is the specific appraisal of the individual's interaction with the environment that produces an emotion. For example, anger is produced by the appraisal that a demeaning offense has occurred against me or that which is mine. Dimensional appraisal theorists such as Ira Roseman, Klaus Scherer, Craig Smith, and Phoebe Ellsworth have proposed specific patterns of appraisal that differentiate the emotions, such as the valence, causal agency, effort, and certainty of the event. The advantage of a dimensional approach is that it can account for similarities in emotions and the transitions between them.

Language and Representation. Poets, therapists, and romantic partners all struggle to put emotions into words. The study of the language and representation of emotion reveals that people represent emotions with specific words, metaphors (e.g., emotion as a natural force), and complex narratives.

Studies of the words people use to describe emotions have addressed basic questions in emotion research. For example, members of different cultures classify emotion words into categories that resemble the categories for which there are facial expressions of emotion, suggesting that the organization of the emotion lexicon corresponds to the biological constituents of emotion. In contrast, reviews of the emotion lexicons of different cultures find variation in the emotions that are represented lexically as well as the number of emotion words (English has about 2,000, whereas the Ifaluk of Micronesia have 56). Certain distinctions made in English, between fear and shame for example, reportedly are not made in other languages; conversely, emotions represented by single words in other languages, such as the Czech *listost*, defined as the sudden realization of tragic circumstances, are not found in single English words.

Other researchers have studied how the representation of emotion is learned and influences emotional response. For example, mothers tend to talk about all emotions except anger to their girls more than their boys, which may account for why women appear to talk more about emotional events. Other researchers have addressed how the labeling of emotional experience changes the emotion, which has intrigued psychologists from Sigmund Freud and William James and is relevant to clinical treatment and certain psychological disorders, such as alexythymia, which is defined by a pronounced absence of emotion words. Evidence indicates that the labeling and written representation of stressful experiences gives structure and coherence to the experience and reduces the likelihood of health-related problems.

Judgment, Perception, and Memory. The widespread assumption that emotions influence judgment, memories, and perception has motivated research on the effects of emotions on cognitive processes. Evidence indicates that emotions influence the content of cognitive processes: Positive and negative emotions influence memories from the past, levels of optimism, and personal satisfaction in valence-specific ways. Emotions also exert more specific influences on cognition: Anger but not sadness leads people to accentuate the injustice of others' actions. Finally, emotions influence the style of information processing: Anger and happiness lead to more automatic, heuristic, and less careful judgments, whereas sadness and fear are associated with more controlled, systematic, and careful judgments.

Research on Specific Emotions

Whereas certain researchers focus on the general properties of emotions, others focus on specific emotions. The same questions motivate such research: What are the defining properties, causes, and functions of specific emotions? The conceptual focus, however, is on single emotions or conceptually related families of emotions.

For example, several investigators have examined the forms and functions of the so-called self-conscious emotions, which include shame, embarrassment, guilt, and pride. Early emotion theorists defined these emotions as slight variations of the same emotion. Recent empirical work however, suggests that although embarrassment, shame, and guilt all remediate previous social transgressions, these three emotions have different antecedents, appraisals, and experiential properties, and in the case of embarrassment and shame, different facial displays. Other similarly motivated research has ascertained distinctions between jealousy and envy. More recently, theorists have speculated about possible differences between such little-studied positive emotions as amusement, contentment, relief, and sensory pleasure. Finally, other researchers have focused on variations within a category of emotion, as in Paul Rozin's study of the different kinds of disgust about death, gore, and moral violations, and their variations of the facial expression of disgust.

Related Topics in the Field of Emotion

Research on the aspects of different emotions has inspired researchers to look at how emotions emerge in the course of development and relate to individual differences and psychopathology.

Development. Emotions play a critical role in development. Consistent with the influential theorizing of John Bowlby, from the first day of the child's life emotional exchanges between parent and child contribute to the development of attachments. Parents' emotional displays are an essential source of information about the environment for the child. Learning how to regulate emotions appropriately, and to respond with embarrassment and shame following social transgressions, are important components of socialization.

Developmental psychologists have addressed several important questions regarding emotion. One of the first is the order in which children first display and understand emotions. Typically, researchers relate the emergence of specific emotions, such as fear or embarrassment, to the emergence of related abilities, such as motoric development or self-consciousness. Developmental psychologists have also advanced the understanding of certain functions of emotional expression in attachment processes. Finally, developmental psychologists have examined the processes by which young children develop the understanding of emotions and learn to talk about their emotions in social interactions, such as family conflict.

Individual Differences. Consistent with early theorizing about emotion and personality, researchers have made important discoveries concerning how and why individuals vary in the intensity and quality of the emotional experience. First, individual differences in emotion emerge in the first months of life and are quite stable during development. Second, basic dimensions of adult personality, in particular neuroticism and extraversion, consistently relate to the tendency to report and display increased negative and positive emotion, respectively. Third, the life histories of individuals prone to different emotions differ profoundly. For example, people prone to anger are less successful in love and work, whereas people prone to happiness are more successful. Finally, researchers are now investigating the distal etiological causes of individual differences in emotion, such as levels of serotonin or family coflict, and proximal causes such as individual variation in emotion thresholds or environmental events.

Psychopathology. The notion that deviation in emotional response contributes to psychological maladjustment dates to the ancient philosophers and is evident in the frequent reference to emotion in the *Diagnostic and Statistical Manual of Mental Disorders*. It is only recently that this general notion has generated systematic research.

Some researchers have identified specific emotions to which people with certain disorders are prone. Depression is characterized by high levels of negative emotion and low levels of positive emotion. Generalized anxiety disorder relates to excessive fear, and social phobia to excessive embarrassment and shame. Antisocial or externalizing disorder in young children has been linked to excessive anger and reduced embarrassment, which inhibits antisocial behavior. Researchers are now documenting the emotional correlates of other disorders, such as borderline disorder.

Other researchers have examined the interaction of the different emotion response systems within different psychopathologies. For example, contrary to claims that schizophrenia is defined by flat affect, studies show that schizophrenics tend to report comparable levels of emotion in response to emotionally evocative stimuli, but show little of the reported emotion in the face.

Finally, other researchers have documented how coping responses to emotional experiences may contribute to psychological adjustment. For example, women may be twice as prone to major episodes of depression as men because they are more likely to ruminate than distract themselves in response to negative events, which prolongs and heightens the distress to the extent that it can lead to depression. Individuals who dissociate from the distress of losing a spouse actually experience less anxiety and depression in the course of bereavement.

Bibliography

American Psychiatric Association. (1994). *Diagnostic and statistical manual of mental disorders* (4th ed.). Washington, DC: Author.

Calhoun, C., & Solomon, R. C. (Eds.). (1984). *What is an emotion: Readings in philosophical psychology.* New York: Oxford University Press.

Clark, M. S. (Ed.). (1990). *Emotion.* Newbury Park, CA: Sage.

Darwin, C. (1872). *The expression of emotions in man and animals* (3rd ed.). New York: Oxford University Press, 1988.

Ekman, P. (Ed.). (1982). *Emotion in the human face* (2nd ed.). New York: Cambridge University Press.

Ekman, P., & Davidson, R. J. (Eds.). (1994). *The nature of emotion.* New York: Oxford University Press.

Frijda, N. (1986). *The emotions.* Cambridge, England: Cambridge University Press.

Harris, P. (1989). *Children and emotion: The development of psychological understanding.* Oxford, England: Basil Blackwell.

Izard, C. E. (1977). *Human emotions.* New York: Plenum Press.

Kemper, T. D. (Ed.). (1990). *Research agendas in the sociology of emotions.* Albany, NY: State University of New York Press.

Lazarus, R. S. (1991). *Emotion and adaptation.* New York: Oxford University Press.

Lewis, M., & Haviland, J. M. (Eds.). (1993). *The handbook of emotions.* New York: Guilford Press.

Lutz, C. A., & Abu-Lughod, L. (Eds.). (1990). *Language and the politics of emotion.* New York: Cambridge University Press.

Markus, H., & Kitayama, S. (Eds.). (1994). *Culture and the emotions.* Washington, DC: American Psychological Association.

Plutchik, R., & Kellerman, H. (Eds.). (1980). *Emotion: Theory, research, and experience.* Orlando, FL: Academic Press.

Scherer, K., & Ekman, P. (Eds.). (1984) *Approaches to emotion.* Hillsdale, NJ: Erlbaum.

Tangney, J. P. & Fischer, K. W. (Eds). (1995). *Self-conscious emotions: The psychology of shame, guilt, embarrassment, and pride.* New York: Guilford Press.

Dacher Keltner and Paul Ekman

Theories

In the field of emotions, theories have been numerous and, until recently, better known than empirical findings. In the second half of the twentieth century, with new conceptions and new research, those have become testable and related to theories in other areas of psychology, particularly in development, cognition, and biological psychology.

The history of theories of emotions remains fascinating because thinkers have offered insights into profound issues, in terms recognizable within folk psychology and aimed at self-understanding. What is more, because emotions are important in different ways, theorists have explored different aspects of them. So, rather than merely competing with each other, theories can be thought of as illuminating different facets of life.

The Philosophical and Literary Background

Plato devoted one of his best-known books, *The Symposium* (385 BCE), to love. Each guest at a party made a speech on love, and these included the wonderful idea of Aristophanes that human beings were once more powerful than now; each had two heads, four arms, four legs, and so on. Because they were so arrogant, these beings were sliced in half by the gods, the result being human beings much as we are now—afflicted by love, seeking our lost halves. In typical fashion, the dialogue is concluded by Plato's protagonist Socrates giving the correct answer: One has to start with earthly loves but must transform these into something resistant to worldly corruption, into love of truth. In this dialogue we see articulated two central issues in understanding human emotions: the enormous pull of interconnectedness in love and the intuition that cultural pursuits such as philosophy and psychology start from a warm and important relationship with someone, such as a teacher.

Plato's most famous student, Aristotle, is usually credited with the first analyses of emotions. Emotions, he said, are types of judgment. They are evaluations of events, and they are "all those feelings that so change [people] as to affect their judgments, and that are also attended by pain or pleasure" (circa 330 BCE).

Aristotle's functionalist approach is a forerunner of modern cognitive psychology, and his idea of emotions as evaluations has influenced much subsequent thinking. For instance, both Aquinas and Spinoza wrote extensively about emotions in this tradition. Even Descartes, who started his 1649 book, *Passions of the Soul*, by saying that he discarded the ideas of the ancients is recognizably Aristotelian. In this book he laid the foundations for the analyses of stimuli, and of both simple and complex response patterns that are recognizable today in ethological ideas of species-typical action patterns that used to be called instincts, and that in current biological psychology are thought to be the bases of distinct emotions in humans and other mammals. These are trustful infant attachment to a care giver, affectionate maternal behavior, fearful escape from predators, angry confrontation with rivals in dominance hierarchies, and so forth.

Aristotle's analyses were also the foundations for the Hellenistic ethical schools of Epicureanism and Stoicism as seen in the writings of Lucretius, Seneca, and Marcus Aurelius, which can be understood as forerunners of cognitive-behavioral therapies (Nussbaum, 1994). Then, as now, the fundamental insight is that although we cannot directly alter our emotions, because they are types of evaluations, we can change our emotions if we can change the thoughts that lead to these evaluations. It was Epicureanism, with its emphasis on being sensitive to our simple and natural propensities, that influenced the founding fathers of the American Constitution with the idea of a right to the pursuit of happiness. And Roman Stoicism blended easily with Christianity, and passed on to our own day the idea of being wary of certain worldly goals such as wealth and power, because the emotions of anger, contempt, envy, and pride that these goals often engender are destructive to the individual and society.

Alongside the philosophical background is the literary one. World literature takes emotions as given but problematic. From the Hebrew story of the creation comes the idea of human eagerness for knowledge—including sexual knowledge—and the consequent founding of self-conscious human society on the emotion of shame. In the tragedies of Aeschylus and Sophocles occurs the idea that we humans must act despite never being able to know enough to foresee the outcomes of our actions; nevertheless, we must take responsibility for them and suffer their emotional consequences. And, as Aristotle pointed out, if we join the audience at the theater, we too experience emotions—pity for the protagonist, fear for ourselves.

There is not space here to follow literary treatments of emotions, for instance, in the great novels of the nineteenth century—Jane Austen on the gradual revelation of oneself to another whom one loves, Gustave Flaubert on the transformation of boredom into sexual excitement, George Eliot on the personal and interpersonal effects of being alive to one's emotions, Henry James on the effects of envy and jealousy—as well as the modernist and postmodernist novels of this century.

But the insights of great philosophers and writers continue as central to understanding our own psychology.

Emotions as Human Universals

Modern research on emotions starts with Charles Darwin (1872), who proposed that emotions are human universals derived in part from our evolutionary past and in part from our development as infants. He sought to show that human beings were not perfect, as would be required if our species were a special and divine creation. Just as there are imperfections of human anatomy, such as the appendix that is now without function, so there are imperfections of behavior, notably emotional expressions. Although in our evolutionary past, expressions, like our hair standing on end in anger or the baring of a canine tooth in a sneer, were functional, they are no longer functional in modern humans. And whereas in infancy, as Darwin argued, crying protected the eyes during screaming, in adulthood tears are still shed although now they seem to have no use.

Nowadays all but radical social-constructionists accept that emotions have an evolutionary basis. Some emotions and moods, such as happiness, love, sadness, anxiety, anger, and shame have been taken up into many human cultures. The wide variability of emotions of sexual love, anger, anxiety, shame, and many other emotions in the East and West, and in industrial and nonindustrial societies, can be understood in terms of human emotional propensities that are elaborated into culturally functional patterns. So, according to a recent American survey, love in marriage is the state most closely associated with happiness, and this love has culturally specific attributes: the basis for contracting a lifelong partnership, expanding the individual self to include another, justification for severing existing ties. Sadness in grief is enabled and ritualized in many cultures in funerals and the social support that surrounds bereavement. Vengeful destructive anger has long been a motivator of personal and international aggression in many societies, and it has in turn been a source of social honor; it has also become recently a daily staple of our TV screens in the form of the proper response to wrongdoing.

If some of Darwin's arguments seem forced today, his conclusion that some emotional expressions take place whether or not they are of any use is not. For example, hostile contempt, by which other people are treated as nonhuman, has been shown by John Gottman (1993) to be the most destructive emotion in marriage; and it has socially corrosive effects through racial prejudice and in episodes such as the Holocaust or ethnic cleansing in Bosnia. Ethologists call the effect pseudospeciation: treating others as members of a different species. One can imagine that it had a place in former eras, perhaps as nomadic humans dispersed across unpeopled spaces or separated themselves from other hominid species. But most commentators see no place for it in the modern world.

Emotions as Monitors of Bodily Events

It was William James who introduced the idea of emotions as monitors of our selves (1884). He argued that if we see a bear in the woods, the folk-psychological idea—that we become afraid and therefore run—is wrong. We see the bear and run; then our fear is the perception of our bodies as we run.

James's theory is known as the peripheral theory: emotions as perceptions of the periphery (the body), to be distinguished from central theories in which emotions derive from the brain. Stanley Schachter and Jerome Singer (1962) joined peripheral and central ideas by proposing that a peripheral change, induced, for instance, by the injection of adrenaline, caused arousal that could be labeled according to the current social situation. If the situation were happy, then people injected with adrenaline but ignorant of the effects of the injection would feel more happy than those given a placebo. If the social situation were angry, then injected individuals would feel more angry than those given a placebo. Replications of the effect have not been entirely successful, but Schachter and Singer's idea persists in a host of misattribution experiments, in which moods are induced but misattributed, and effects on social judgments found. It also continues in the theory of George Mandler, that emotion occurs with arousal at the failure of an expectancy, together with a cognitive labeling of the arousal (1984).

The idea of peripheral feedback was taken up by Sylvan Tomkins (1995), one of the first to propose a clear function for emotions: It is emotions that give the "oomph" to life. We have various motivations, such as hunger, thirst, sex, and exploration, but these do not determine our urges. The determinant is an emotion, which amplifies some specific motivation by means of feedback from the periphery. One of Tomkins's examples is sexual arousal: We have the capacity of sexual motivation all the time, but when this is accompanied by arousal of the genitalia it is amplified and becomes the urgency of sexual excitement.

Although other kinds of bodily feedback are important, Tomkins argued that it is the face that provides the most crucial feedback, so when we smile this amplifies happiness, and when our face droops, or we cry, we feel sad. According to Tomkins, an emotion is an affect program. It has a neural basis, it involves feedback from the body and it has a conscious feeling to it. The program tends to be set off as a package, with each aspect entraining the other parts. This idea fits easily with the idea of species-specific action patterns.

Tomkins's theories prompted research on facial expressions of the kind that Darwin described. Influenced by Tomkins, Paul Ekman and Carroll Izard both provided evidence of a small number of basic emotions, each with a distinctive facial expression that is a human universal, seen in infants as well as cross-culturally. Among Ekman's experiments is a study of actors and scientists who posed facial expressions characteristic of specific emotions, and accompanying each such expression there occurred a somewhat distinctive bodily response recorded by polygraph (Ekman, Levenson, & Friesen, 1983).

The conclusions of Ekman and Izard have been questioned (e.g., by Russell & Fernandez-Dols, 1997). It is not denied that there is some universal basis of facial expressions, but there are several theories, not just the theory of facial affect programs, that could account for them, including Russell's idea of orthogonal dimensions of pleasure-distress and arousal-relaxation.

Appraisal and Cognitive Theories of Emotions

In the same year that Tomkins first proposed his theory, ideas of Aristotle and Aquinas were introduced into modern research by Magda Arnold (e.g., Arnold & Gasson, 1954) and they form the bases of "appraisal theory." Emotions are those psychological states that relate the outer world of events to the inner world of desires—an emotion is an evaluation, or appraisal, of an event in terms of goals. The theoretical move made by Schachter and Singer involved linking bodily arousal to just such appraisals. Appraisal theory also connects to Tomkins's idea of amplification, because, according to Nico Frijda (1986), an emotion elicited by appraising an event in relation to a goal (which he calls a concern) is an "action-readiness," which sets priority among concerns and hence determines urgency.

Appraisal theorists today show that specific emotions are each determined by specific features of an appraisal, for example, an event that blocks a goal and that damages self-esteem is likely to elicit anger. So, as Richard Lazarus put it (1991), the primary appraisal of the event is made in terms of the goal affected by it. Then a secondary appraisal is made of what to do about the event, of how to cope with it: Anger becomes more likely if the goal could be reinstated. This line of research also led to the investigation of coping with events and the emotions they elicit and has become important in the psychology of health.

Emotions and Emotional Disorders

Research on emotional disorders can be thought of as starting with Sigmund Freud, whose innovation was to take what people said about their emotional lives seriously. Although Freud did not propose a theory of emotions, he launched a psychology based on human beings having multiple desires—goals. From this, it is a short step to modern cognitive theories of the role of emotions in the management of goals, as described in the previous section.

First, Freud hypothesized that an emotional trauma could be responsible for later anxiety and depressive disorders (Freud & Breuer, 1895). Although the terms of his hypotheses have been modified, it is clear from the evidence of psychiatric epidemiology that traumatic events early in life not only increase the risk of adult anxiety and depressive disorder, but that severely stressful events and difficulties in adulthood are the immediate causes of most episodes of depression.

Second, Freud emphasized the importance of relationships with parents. It was John Bowlby (1971) who combined this idea with the idea from ethology, of baby animals becoming imprinted on their mothers, to produce the theory of attachment as a biologically given program in which an infant stays close to its mother, particularly in circumstances of danger. Following this came the idea of socioemotional development, which has achieved a level of importance in developmental psychology to rival theories of cognitive development.

Third, Freud instituted a form of psychotherapy. Although his work is a touchstone to which subsequent therapies in one way or another refer, it had much in common with the schools of Epicurean and Stoic thought, in the idea of self-knowledge, and also had much in common with Spinoza's theory that to understand and accept our emotions is to be liberated from the bondage that some of them can impose.

Emotions as Bases of Personality

Although Freud's theories of personality development are less accepted today than previously, the idea that enduring traits of personality derive from the interplay of genetics and early experience remains important. *Temperament* is the term used to describe genetically given aspects of emotional responsiveness, for instance, in reacting to novelty either calmly or with arousal and anger (Campos, Barrett, Lamb, Goldsmith, & Stenberg, 1983). A genetic predisposition plus a particular experience of upbringing then builds a foundation of personality. For instance, according to attachment theory, people with secure attachment to a care giver at the age of 1 subsequently form trusting relationships in life. Those who are anxiously avoidant of their care-giver tend to be more distrustful later. Those who are ambivalent—both anxious and angry at their care-giver—remain preoccupied with relationships and are likely to have a stormy love life in adulthood.

Taking Tomkins's type of theory, each individual tends to base his or her life around a script in relation to some specific emotion or to some emotional issue. In commitment scripts, an individual narrows options in the world through commitment to a specific relationship, such as marriage, or to a cause. In an affect management script the object is to control negative emotions, so scripts might be based around alcohol, sex, travel, or watching TV, all of which can preoccupy and reduce negative feelings. Or, taking a more empirically based theory, individuals who are very shy or very aggressive in childhood base their appraisals of events on their preferred emotional style and show high continuity of the avoidant or the angry trait into adulthood in ways that profoundly affect their life chances (Caspi, Elder, & Bem, 1987).

Personality currently tends to be seen in terms of the "Big Five" personality traits: neuroticism, extroversion, openness, agreeableness, and concienciousness. In the definitions of these traits, all but the last have explicitly emotional ingredients. Theories such as that of Tomkins are equipped to explain the continuities of such traits through socioemotional schemas built in early life so that life's multiplicity of events are appraised predominantly in just one particular way to yield a characteristic emotion, rather than appraised in different ways to yield a range of emotions. So, for an anxious person, almost all novel events are appraised as dangerous and hence are fear producing. Therefore, a fearful schema is built that minimizes novelty and danger. For someone aggressive, events tend to be appraised as frustrating, and a preferred response pattern of angry aggression is primed and constantly ready.

An extension of such ideas provides a basis for understanding some aspects of emotional disorders. Internalizing disorders of childhood are those of anxiety and sadness; externalizing disorders are those of anger. There is strong evidence of continuity: When people have internalizing patterns in early childhood, then, if they suffer disorder later, for instance in response to a severe loss, the later disorder is likely to be an anxiety or depressive disorder. By contrast, those with externalizing disorders in childhood will have tendencies to delinquency in adolescence and sociopathic or substance abuse disorders in adulthood (Oatley & Jenkins, 1996, from which further references to the issues discussed in this article may also be found).

Two Recent Theoretical Trends

Among interesting modern theoretical movements are ideas that emotions, rather than being disruptors of behavior, are the very center of rational life in the social world. Antonio Damasio, for instance, has shown that people with frontal lobe damage are impaired both in their emotions and in their ability to make ordinary arrangements with others (1994).

The idea of emotional intelligence (Salovey & Mayer, 1990), based on modern evidence, is of being aware of one's own appraisals and others' emotional expressions, of being able to mange one's own emotions to-

gether with being sensitive to emotions of others, and of being able to use emotion to motivate oneself. Unlike models of conventional intelligence, which have tended to emphasize genetically fixed factors, emotional intelligence can be cultivated and helped through reflection on one's own life and the insights of writers on emotions.

Bibliography

Aristotle. (1954). *Rhetoric and poetics* (W. R. Roberts, Trans). New York: Random House. (Original work circa 330 BCE)

Arnold, M. B., & Gasson, J. A. (1954). Feelings and emotions as dynamic factors in personality integration. In M. B. Arnold & J. A. Gasson (Eds.), *The human person* (pp. 294–313). New York: Ronald.

Bowlby, J. (1971). *Attachment and loss: Vol. 1. Attachment.* London: Hogarth Press (reprinted by Penguin, 1978).

Campos, J. J., Barrett, K. C., Lamb, M. E., Goldsmith, H. H., & Stenberg, C. (1983). Socioemotional development. In M. M. Haith & J. J. Campos (Eds.), *Handbook of child psychology* (pp. 783–915). New York: Wiley.

Caspi, A., Elder, G. H., & Bem, D. J. (1987). Moving against the world: Life course patterns of explosive children. *Developmental Psychology, 23,* 308–313.

Damasio, A. R. (1994). *Descartes' error.* New York: Putnam.

Darwin, C. (1965). *The expression of the emotions in man and animals.* Chicago: University of Chicago Press. (Original work published 1872)

Descartes, R. (1911). Passions of the soul. In E. L. Haldane & G. R. Ross (Eds.), *The philosophical works of Descartes.* New York: Dover. (Original work published 1649)

Ekman, P., Levenson, R. W., & Friesen, W. V. (1983). Autonomic nervous system activity distinguishes among emotions. *Science, 221,* 1208–1210.

Freud, S., & Breuer, J. (1974). *The Pelican Freud Library: Vol. 3. Studies of hysteria* (J. Strachey, A. Strachey, & A. Richards, Eds.) London: Penguin. (Original work published 1895)

Frijda, N. H. (1986). *The emotions.* Cambridge, England: Cambridge University Press.

Gottman, J. M. (1993). The roles of conflict engagement, escalation, and avoidance in marital interaction: A longitudinal view of five types of couples. *Journal of Consulting and Clinical Psychology, 61,* 6–15.

James, W. (1884). What is an emotion? *Mind, 9,* 188–205.

Lazarus, R. S. (1991). *Emotion and adaptation.* New York: Oxford University Press.

Mandler, G. (1984). *Mind and body: Psychology of emotions and stress.* New York: Norton.

Nussbaum, M. C. (1994). *The therapy of desire: Theory and practice in Hellenistic ethics.* Princeton, NJ: Princeton University Press.

Oatley, K., & Jenkins, J. M. (1996). *Understanding emotions.* Oxford: Blackwell.

Plato. (1955). *The symposium* (W. Hamilton, Ed. & Trans.).

Harmondsworth, England: Penguin. (Original work published 385 BCE)

Russell, J. A., & Fernandez-Dols, J. M. (1997). What does a facial expression mean? In J. A. Russell & J. M. Fernandez-Dols (Eds.), *The psychology of facial expression* (pp. 3–30). New York: Cambridge University Press.

Salovey, P., & Mayer, J. M. (1990). Emotional intelligence. *Imagination, Cognition, and Personality, 9,* 185–211.

Schachter, S., & Singer, J. (1962). Cognitive, social, and physiological determinants of emotional state. *Psychological Review, 69,* 379–399.

Tomkins, S. S. (1995). *Exploring affect: The selected writings of Sylvan S. Tomkins* (E. V. Demos, Ed.). New York: Cambridge University Press.

Keith Oatley

Methods of Study

In recent years, interest in emotion has grown within psychology, along with methodological advances in emotion measurement. Emotions are complex processes, the understanding of which requires multiple measures and entails potentially numerous methodological problems.

When emotions are elicited, changes ensue among behavioral/expressive, physiological, and subjective systems of the body. The fact that emotional responses are so diverse is both a blessing and a curse; it allows for several routes of access to emotion but also creates difficulty in measurement, by either forcing a choice of which measure to obtain or creating the complexity of collecting and analyzing multimodal responses.

Unfortunately, there is often ambiguity about the type of emotional process under investigation. The term *emotion* has often been used interchangeably with *mood,* but these words are not synonyms. Emotions are very brief states that arise in response to important changes in a person's perceived environment. Though brief, emotions often register in consciousness before they are over. Moods, by contrast, arise much more subtly, can endure for much longer periods of time, and tend to occupy the background of consciousness. They may or may not be characterized by expressive changes, but moods do have physiological and experiential effects. The reader is referred to other sources for more in-depth discussion of the relationship between emotion and mood (see Ekman 1994). Although the present chapter focuses on emotions, many of the measurement issues apply to the study of mood, especially those regarding subjective experience. [*See* Affect; Mood; *and the overview article on* Emotion.]

Emotion Elicitation

One of the most difficult methodological issues is how to reliably elicit emotions. One cannot assume that any elicitor—however well planned or piloted—guarantees an emotional response of any kind, let alone the particular response sought by the investigator. There is no elicitor that evokes the same emotion for everyone.

Ultimately the choice of elicitor depends on the researcher's questions: Does one want to measure a particular type or set of emotions or emotions generally, regardless of what type? Is the interest in intra- or interpersonal contexts, or naturally occurring or controlled situations? Several types of elicitors have been employed with varying degrees of success.

Films. Films are popular for eliciting emotion in the laboratory. It is not easy to establish ahead of time which emotions are likely to be elicited by a film, and the self-reports often used to determine the emotions films elicit are vulnerable to demand characteristics (e.g., the tendency of people to report experiencing emotions that are expected of them rather than what they are truly feeling). Even though it is impossible to create any film that reliably elicits the same emotion in everyone, it is possible to find stimuli that have greater tendency to elicit some emotions than others.

The benefits of films include standardization in emotion induction; ease of use; and the ability to show them to either individuals or groups. The drawbacks include: extensive piloting may be required to develop reliable film segments; with the exception of emotions like disgust, sometimes it is difficult to elicit emotions beyond mild to moderate intensity; and certain emotions, such as anger, are very difficult to elicit by film.

Still slides of emotional scenes are similar to films, involving the same advantages plus the possible added benefit of involving less time in presentation. Slides have many of the same drawbacks of films, plus the added possibility of eliciting less intense emotional reactions than films. We are not aware of studies comparing films and slides, however.

Emotional Stories or Statements. Individuals can read prepared statements of emotional content or brief scenarios describing emotional situations. Like film viewing, this method allows for standardization of induction procedures, can be used with individuals as well as groups, and requires confirmatory studies that demonstrate that the stories do, indeed, elicit emotion. Statements and stories are less likely to produce observable emotional behavior than film viewing, although they do elicit reports of emotional experience. Another drawback of this method is that the emotions induced are likely to be of mild to moderate intensity, at best.

Imagery Techniques. Imagery techniques of various types usually involve either imagining oneself in an emotional situation or recalling and reliving past emotional events. The primary benefit of imagery is that one can draw on intense, personally-relevant situations. This technique can be used to study single individuals but not groups. The major drawback is that people vary in the extent to which they can successfully recall, relive, or imagine an emotional event. This technique is also less likely to elicit facial expressions of emotion than film viewing or other techniques, and it requires a coach to lead the imagery exercise.

Hypnosis has been used frequently in research on mood and memory, and it is also an imagery technique. The primary benefit is creating realistic emotional experiences in some people. The drawbacks are that hypnotic imagery requires a trained practitioner to administer hypnotic suggestions and works well only on highly hypnotizable people, who comprise about 10% of the population.

Voluntary Facial Movement. Another laboratory technique for emotion induction involves instructing subjects to voluntarily move their faces to produce facial expressions of emotion. Two general approaches have been taken: posing and directed facial action. Posing simply involves telling the subjects to either put on an expression that is known by common vernacular, such as a smile or frown. A variation on this theme is to tell people, "Put on a happy or sad or angry face." The posing approach is easy to use and it is standardized. There are some drawbacks, however. A given request, such as frown, can elicit several types of facial poses, ranging from a brow furrow to downturned lip corners; it is also not clear whether posing is sufficient to create an emotional experience in all or most people.

Directed facial action (DFA) is a quite different approach to voluntary facial movement in which subjects are instructed to move certain facial muscles. Although the muscular movement instructions produce facial configurations that are representative of certain emotions, no verbal reference to emotions or to lay expression terms are given during the instruction period. Given its anatomical basis, DFA overcomes the first drawback of standard posing methods—heterogeneity in expression is greatly reduced when muscular instructions are given rather than lay expression terms. Although DFA was developed with the intention of studying emotion-specific physiological patterns that are associated with facial expressions of emotion—and not necessarily emotional experience per se—the facial configurations often create emotional experiences. The drawback of DFA is that it requires a trained coach as well as participants who can contract their facial muscles voluntarily to produce high-quality expressions.

Interpersonal Interaction. Interpersonal contexts form the basis of our most intense emotions—the challenge is to capture such intensity in the laboratory. Marital interactions create personally significant emotions but involve the complexity of studying two individuals in conversation. Other interpersonal situations, such as when two strangers are assigned to discuss a topic, are less likely to evoke personally significant emotion.

Naturally Occurring Emotion in Daily Life. Mood researchers have often looked to people's real-life experiences as a source of variation in emotional state. Both minor events (such as final exams for students) and major life events (such as bereavement) have been studied. Such events create strong, personally significant emotion, but they are very difficult to study by means other than self-report. If one's primary interest is in tracking variations in subjective experience of emotion or mood, then studying life events may be worthwhile. Daily events are not useful if one aims to measure the expression and physiology of emotion.

Measuring the Emotional Response

There is no agreement on which aspect of the response might serve as a gold standard for the occurrence of emotion. Furthermore, there may be individual differences in which response system is most sensitive for a given person. Given these caveats, it is incumbent on the investigator to use multiple measures, with the constraints that some will be used for verification and some as dependent variables. Also, there are practical limitations on what one can obtain without exhausting participants.

Physiological Measures. The physiological measures used in emotion research have aimed to tap activity in three particular systems: the autonomic nervous system, the central nervous system, and the endocrine system.

Autonomic Indices. The autonomic nervous system (ANS) has been the most widely studied physiological system in emotion research. The most common ANS measures are heart rate and skin conduction, but some studies have measured several additional channels, including but not limited to skin temperature, respiratory depth, pulse transit time to ear or finger, and beat-by-beat blood pressure. Measures vary in the extent to which they serve as indicators of sympathetic versus parasympathetic changes (heart rate, for example, reflects both). A relatively new approach to measuring sympathetic reactivity is impedance cardiography, which provides measures of cardiac output and total peripheral resistance.

Important methodological issues to consider when measuring the ANS include: choice of baseline, whether a marker will be used (such as facial expression) to dictate which epochs of data should be studied, and controlling for the influence of factors that might bias the data such as movement, drugs, and general health status. (For further discussion of ANS measurement, see Levenson, 1988).

Central Nervous System (CNS). The oldest method

of CNS measurement is electroencephalography (EEG), in which surface electrodes placed on the scalp (usually via a skull cap) detect the electrical activity of neurons in underlying brain areas. The spatial resolution of EEG is limited, allowing the discussion of activation in general regions of the brain (e.g., frontal, occipital, parietal, or temporal lobes) and/or the right versus left hemispheres only. EEG has good temporal resolution, however, making it possible to link electrical changes in general brain areas to exposure to emotional stimuli. Methodological issues involved in EEG research include: the choice of a reference point, movement artifact, issues of baseline measurement, and the parsing of data in relation to extrinsic emotion variables.

Positron emission tomography (PET) is a CNS imaging technique. The participant is injected with a radioactive isotope (usually glucose) and the activity of regions of the brain is measured by detecting where the radioactive glucose is being metabolized. PET offers good spatial resolution and may provide a useful index of brain function while the person is experiencing particular states. There are drawbacks: PET requires injection with a radioactive isotope, which is fairly benign but not risk free; the temporal resolution of PET is poor, thus metabolic brain changes are not easily linked to exposure to emotional stimuli; it is very expensive; and PET can only be done at institutions that have a cyclotron (which are rare and require highly trained medical personnel).

Magnetic resonance imaging (MRI), another CNS imaging technique, offers good spatial resolution. In contrast to PET, there is no risk for subjects except the discomfort of being in the confined and noisy environment of an MRI machine. It, too, is costly, but MRI is becoming more widely available and is more accessible than PET. The standard MRI simply looks at structure and is not very useful for studying brain changes during emotion, but functional MRI allows for the study of changes in brain activity and thus promises to be a safe alternative to PET.

Endocrine. Neuroendocrine systems have also been studied in relation to emotions and moods. The most common systems studied are the noradrenergic and the adrenocorticoid systems, given their involvement in ANS activation and the stress response. Each of these systems is sensitive to changes in emotional states, although it may be methodologically difficult to access such changes. The problems are with resolution and route of access. If these neurochemicals are assessed through urine it is difficult to determine how long one should one wait after emotion induction to get a sample that might reflect that state. Timing is still an issue with blood samples, and there is the added stress of venipuncture, which could serve as an emotion induction in and of itself.

Behavioral/Expressive Measures. Measures of facial expression and vocal behavior comprise the major indices of the expressive component of emotion.

Facial Expression. The most frequently measured expressive system in emotion research is the face. Different types of facial measurement include: observer judgments, componential coding schemes, and electrophysiological recording.

Naive observers viewing videotapes or on-line behavior can make judgments of the extent to which they see certain emotions in a target face. Although this method seems easy, drawbacks include: naive judges may miss several subtle expressions; morphological characteristics of the target's face, independent of changes in facial muscular activity, might bias emotion judgments; and it is difficult to determine where in a segment of behavior the rated emotions actually occurred.

By contrast, in componential coding schemes highly-trained "coders" follow a prescribed set of procedures for detecting certain facial actions. The two most widely used systems are the Facial Action Coding System (FACS), developed by Paul Ekman and Wallace Friesen in 1978, and the Maximally discriminative facial movement coding system (MAX), developed by Carroll Izard in 1979. Izard's MAX is theoretically derived, coding just those facial configurations that he theorized correspond to universally recognized facial expressions of emotion. Although more economical than FACS, such a system cannot discover behaviors that were not posited in advance.

By contrast, FACS is a comprehensive measurement system that is anatomically based; it measures all movements that are observable in the face. As a comprehensive system, FACS is not limited to those behaviors that are theoretically related to emotion, and it allows for the discovery of new configurations of movements that might be relevant to extrinsic variables of interest.

Facial expressions of emotion have also been measured electrophysiologically through facial electromyography (EMG). Facial EMG measures electrical potentials from facial muscles in order to infer muscular contraction via the placement of surface electrodes on the skin of the face. The advantages of EMG include detection of muscular activity that is not observable to the naked eye. Problems include: The placement of electrodes calls subjects' attention to the fact that their faces are being measured, which may increase self-conscious behavior; although in recent years there have been considerable advances refining EMG signals, there remains a problem with cross-talk (whereby adjacent muscular contractions interfere with one another), which may misrepresent the "picture" of movement on the face.

Vocal Behavior. The autonomic arousal that accompanies emotion can cause measurable changes in voice production. Observers can rate the emotion they hear in audio tapes that have been filtered to remove intelligible speech. Componential measurement involves analysis of the characteristics of the vocal waveform. Patterns of change in vocal intensity (loudness), frequency (pitch), and quality (phonation type), as well as other features have been studied. To date, the evidence for distinctive patterning is not as refined as it is for the face. (For more detailed information, see Scherer, 1988.)

Subjective Experience. Measures of the subjective component of emotion are perhaps the most prevalent. Although it may seem that there could be nothing easier than asking people what they are feeling, subjective measurement is complicated and fraught with problems. There are social psychological problems such as presentation bias, social desirability, and demand characteristics as well as methodological problems, such as how the choice of time frame and response scales influences the information obtained from a given self-report.

Oral Versus Written Reports. Reports of one's emotional experience can be obtained via either oral query or written emotion report. Oral reports may benefit from the rapport developed between an interviewer and interviewee, and therefore may yield more honest reports. However, the social contact between the interviewer and interviewee might also increase self-consciousness and demand characteristics, leading to bias in what is reported. Written reports overcome some but not all self-consciousness in that research participants do not spontaneously reveal their feelings to another person, but rather write them down. The increased anonymity of a written report might also reduce social desirability effects. The problem with written responses is that participants may be less motivated to be accurate when they are not immediately held accountable for what they are reporting.

Open Versus Closed Response Options. Open response categories simply pose a question to the participant, for example, "What did you feel while watching the film?" Closed questions provide participants with a list of words or scales by which to rate their emotional experience. Open responses do not restrict subjective report, affording individuals the option of expressing their feelings verbally in whatever manner is most appropriate for them. However, categorizing open-ended responses can be painstaking and time-consuming. There is also the risk that participants will not write anything down. Providing them with response scales by which to rate their experience remedies these two problems but creates its own: Participants might report having felt emotions simply because those words appeared on the page in front of them, and the preset categories or dimensions on which they must rate their experience may produce a distorted picture of that experience by forcing participants to convey their experience in a particular way. Ideally, response scales allow for a range of emotionality without being too cumbersome to complete.

Temporal Issues. A major problem concerns when to obtain self-reports. Retrospective reports are commonly used, but they involve problems of: memory recall bias (e.g., recency effects); memory reconstruction; and the problem of representing an entire emotional experience in a single report, as many emotions can occur in a very brief period of time, so a single report may be biased toward the most intense emotion felt. On-line reporting remedies this last problem but interrupts the flow of emotional experience.

Some techniques strike a balance between retrospective and on-line procedures. In Levenson and Gottman's video-recall technique, people watch a videotape of their marital interaction session and then report on what they remembered feeling during that interaction. The participants use dials to rate the degree of positive and negative emotion they remember having felt during the session and use the video replay as a cue to aid memory. The dial technique allows for the continuous retrospective reporting of emotion, but for only positive-negative emotion distinctions. Erika Rosenberg and Paul Ekman developed a recall procedure called cued-review for use in film-viewing situations. Cued-review involves the viewing of a previously seen stimulus film, during which time people complete multiple emotion reports according to when they remembered having felt an emotion during the initial film-viewing period. The detailed reports provide finer-grained distinctions among positive and negative emotions than does video-recall with dials.

Further Issues

Emotion researchers also need to be concerned with data analysis issues concerning how to compare, correlate, or combine multiple indices of emotions in order to address their hypotheses. As many emotions can be elicited during a brief period of time, one may either study point-to-point correspondences or combine several responses in a given time period. Each approach has its pros and cons, the full discussion of which is beyond the scope of this article (see Levenson, 1988, which discusses these issues in some detail.

Bibliography

Ekman, P. (1994). Moods, emotions, and traits. In P. Ekman & R. J. Davidson (Eds.), *The nature of emotion: Fundamental questions* (pp. 56–58). New York: Oxford University Press.

Ekman, P., Levenson, R. W., & Friesen, W. V. (1983). Autonomic nervous system activity distinguishes between emotions. *Science, 221,* 1208–1210.

Gross, J. J., & Levenson, R. W. (1995). Emotion elicitation using films. *Cognition and Emotion, 9,* 87–108.

Levenson, R. W. (1988). Emotion and the autonomic nervous system: A prospectus for research on autonomic specificity. In H. Wagner & A. Manstead (Eds.), *Handbook of social psychophysiology.* New York: Wiley.

Scherer, K. R. (1988). Vocal correlates of emotional arousal and affective disturbance. In H. Wagner & A. Manstead (Eds.), *Handbook of social psychophysiology.* New York: Wiley.

Erika L. Rosenberg and Paul Ekman

EMOTIONAL LEARNING. Our experiences consist of awareness of our stimulus environment as well as our emotional responses evoked by stimulation. Many emotional responses evoked by pleasant or unpleasant experiences are unlearned. However, our experiences also alter our subsequent emotional responses to specific stimulation and, additionally, emotions can influence our explicit memories of emotionally arousing events. These influences of emotion clearly have adaptive consequences. In his book *The Expression of Emotions in Man and Animals* (1872), Charles Darwin noted the similarities of emotional expression in man and animals and argued that emotions evolved because they compel organisms toward adaptive behaviors that increase their chances for survival.

There has been considerable controversy concerning the bases of our emotional states. In 1884, William James proposed that emotions are the conscious awareness of certain "peripheral" bodily responses (an idea independently proposed by the Danish physiologist C. G. Lange). In contrast, the research of Walter Cannon in 1927 and Philip Bard in 1934 suggested that emotions are the direct result of brain processes (critically involving the hypothalamus), and that bodily responses are but the consequences of the centrally activated emotions. An important experiment by Schacter and Singer in 1962 helped clarify the issue. They found that the emotional reaction produced by an injection of the adrenal hormone epinephrine (adrenaline) depended on the subjects' cognitive interpretation of the situation. Although there is still no generally accepted theory of emotion today, there is a broad consensus that emotional reactions require both cognitive processes, based on activation of the central nervous system as well as peripheral nervous system responses.

As our past experiences modify our responses to emotionally arousing stimulation in several ways, the term *emotional learning* (or *emotional memory*) can have several different meanings. Findings of research on emotional learning in human subjects indicate that emotionally related, learned judgments can be made without conscious awareness. In 1980, Robert Zajonc found that subjects develop affective preferences for stimuli they have seen before even when they have no explicit memory of the stimuli. Studies of amnesic patients confirm the development of this "mere exposure effect" in the absence of explicit memory. For example, amnesic patients developed preferences for Korean melodies despite the fact that they had weak explicit memory of having heard them (Johnson, Kim, & Risse, 1985).

Experiments with animals indicate that "emotional memory" can be readily induced through the formation of a classically conditioned (Pavlovian) stimulus-reinforcement association, that is, a neutral stimulus associated with a stimulus that induces that an emotional reaction may elicit an emotional response. Extensive research indicates that such learning involves a region of the brain in the medial temporal region called the amygdaloid complex (AC) (Davis, 1992; LeDoux, 1995). In 1956, Lawrence Weiskrantz reported that lesions of the AC impaired monkeys' ability to learn stimulus-reinforcement associations. Subsequent research investigating the effects of AC lesions on Pavlovian aversive conditioning in rats has suggested that the AC may be a critical link in the formation of nonconscious "emotional memory" circuits (LeDoux, 1995). Lesions of the AC in rats, the basolateral nucleus in particular, impair acquisition and retention of several forms of Pavlovian aversive conditioning. However, as the AC is also critical for the expression of unlearned responses typically used as indexes of fear (e.g. "freezing" responses; see Blanchard & Blanchard, 1972), it is difficult to dissociate AC involvement in putative emotional memory circuits from its involvement in the expression of fear-based responses (Cahill, Weinberger, Roozendaal, & McGaugh, 1999).

The term *emotional memory* also refers to conscious ("declarative") memory of emotionally arousing experiences. Many investigators have commented on the strong and detailed nature of conscious memories of emotionally arousing events. In a remarkably prescient discussion, Stratton observed that a person may recall "in almost photographic detail the total situation at the moment of shock" (1919). It is this vivid nature of emotionally influenced memory which inspired Brown and Kulik in 1977 to coin the term "flashbulb memory." Although conscious memories of emotionally arousing events are not perfect "pictures" of the event and are not indelibly etched in the brain, there is substantial evidence that such memories are, in comparison with those of nonarousing events, more accurate and less susceptible to decay (see Christianson, 1992).

Emotional arousal thus appears to play an important role in selectively preserving memories of significant events. This influence of emotional arousal on lasting memory clearly has adaptive value. In 1890, William James noted that "if we remembered everything, we should on most occasions be as ill off as if we remembered nothing" and concluded that "selection is the very keel on which our mental ship is built." There is, as Seymour Kety commented in 1970, an "obvious adaptive advantage in a mechanism that consolidates . . . only those experiences that are significant."

Studies of the neurobiological systems activated by emotionally arousing experiences have provided important insights into how emotion influences long-term memory. Research on this issue was stimulated by the finding that long-term memory storage can be enhanced by administration of stimulant drugs immediately after learning (McGaugh & Herz, 1972). It is now well established that stress-related hormones, including epinephrine (adrenaline) and corticosterone (or cortisol in humans) are released from the adrenal gland (the adrenal medulla and the adrenal cortex, respectively) following emotionally arousing stimulation. Additionally, low doses of these hormones administered to animals after training enhance long-term memory (McGaugh & Gold, 1989). Such findings suggest that these endogenously released hormones regulate the storage of experiences that induce their release by activating brain systems involved in modulating memory storage.

Corticosterone freely enters the brain and can thus directly affect brain activity. Epinephrine passes the blood-brain barrier poorly, if at all. Several lines of evidence suggest that epinephrine influences memory by activating peripheral adrenergic receptors located on nerves (e.g., the vagus) that project to the brain (Williams & McGaugh, 1993). The influence may involve brain stem nuclei, such as the locus coeruleus and the nucleus raphe, which project diffusely throughout the forebrain. Other evidence suggests that epinephrine may influence memory, at least in part through its well-known effects on blood glucose levels (Gold, 1995). In any case, the effects of epinephrine on memory involves activation of β-adrenergic receptors. In animals, the β-adrenergic receptor antagonist propranolol blocks the memory-enhancing effects of epinephrine and, in human subjects, propranolol blocks the enhancing effects of emotional arousal on long-term memory (McGaugh, Cahill, & Roozendaal, 1996; Cahill et al., 1994).

Extensive evidence indicates that many drugs and stress hormones affect memory through influences involving the AC. In animals, lesions of the AC (particularly the basolateral nucleus) block drug and stress hormone influences on memory storage. Additionally, long-term memory can be enhanced by microinfusing drugs and stress hormones directly into the AC after learning (McGaugh, Cahill, & Roozendaal, 1996). These effects appear to require activation of β-adrenergic receptors within the AC, as they all blocked by β-adrenergic antagonists. Findings of studies using human subjects also indicate that the amygdala is involved in emotionally influenced memory. For example, in humans with lesions of the AC, the enhancing effect of emotional arousal on long-term memory is impaired (Babinsky et al., 1993; Cahill, Babinsky, Markowitsch, & McGaugh, 1995).

Modern brain-imaging techniques (such as positron emission tomography, or PET) allow us to examine directly the activity in specific regions of the human brain. To date, only a handful of studies have used human-brain-imaging techniques to examine "emotional learning." One PET study examined AC participation in emotional versus unemotional learning situations (Cahill et al., 1996). Subjects in this study received two PET scans: one while viewing a series of relatively emotionally arousing (aversive) film clips, and another (on a separate day) while viewing a series of similar but relatively nonemotionally arousing film clips. Three weeks later, memory for both the emotional and neutral films was tested. The results showed that activity in the right AC correlated very highly with recall of the emotional films, yet did not correlate with recall of the neutral films. Thus, the right AC appeared to be selectively involved with memory formation for the emotional material.

Another recent PET study (Reiman et al., 1997) found that the AC became active while subjects viewed (and presumably stored memories about) emotional material, but was not active when subjects recalled previously learned emotional material. Both of these PET studies are consistent with the view derived from animal experiments that the AC is especially important for storing memories of emotionally arousing events in humans. Analogous to the hippocampus, the AC does not appear to be involved in the retrieval of long-term declarative memory once it is formed. It seems likely that AC activity serves to modulate the storage of information in other brain regions, and that the AC is not the locus of emotionally influenced, conscious memory traces.

Attempts to understand basic mechanisms of emotionally influenced memory have led to new developments in understanding clinical disorders associated with emotionally stressful events. In considering the potential implications of the evidence for endogenous, hormone-based memory modulation systems, Roger Pitman proposed in 1989 that an overactivation of such normally adaptive systems after a highly traumatic event may underlie the pathogenesis of anxiety-based disorders, such as posttraumatic stress disorder (PTSD). This proposal raised the possibility that it may be possible to prevent PTSD with pharmacological blockade of stress hormone modulation of memory soon after a trauma is experienced.

A final meaning of the term *emotional memory* concerns memory of the personal feelings (as opposed to the facts or details) associated with an emotional experience. It is a common experience that memory of feelings associated with an event often seems to last long after memory of the facts of the event has all but disappeared. Sir Fredric Bartlett, in his classic 1932 book *Remembering*, argued that the primary memory of an experience is often affective in nature (for example, "I remember I liked it" or "I remember it was awful"), and that memory retrieval in this case is a process of reconstructing events to justify this affective memory. This important aspect of "emotional memory," the conscious memory of feelings associated with an event remains an important and largely unexplored area for neurobiologists interested in "emotional learning."

[*See also* Learning; *and* Motivation.]

Bibliography

Babinsky, R., Calabrese, P., Durwen, H. F., Markowitsch, H. J., Brechtelsbauer, D., Heuser, L., & Gehlen, W. (1993). The possible contribution of the amygdala to memory. *Behavioral Neurology, 6,* 167–170.

Bard, P. (1934). Central nervous system mechanisms for emotional behavior patterns in animals. *Research Publications, Association for Research into Nervous and Mental Disorders, 19,* 190–218.

Bartlett, Sir Frederic. (1932). *Remembering: A study in experimental and social psychology.* Cambridge, England: Cambridge University Press.

Blanchard, D. C., & Blanchard, R. J. (1972). Innate and conditioned reactions to threat in rats with amygdaloid lesions. *Journal of Comparative and Physiological Psychology, 81,* 281–290.

Brown, K., & Kulik, J. (1977). Flashbulb memories. *Cognition, 5,* 73–99.

Cahill, L., Babinsky, R., Markowitsch, H., & McGaugh, J. L. (1995). The amygdala and emotional memory. *Nature, 377,* 295–296.

Cahill, L., Haier, R. J., Fallon, J., Alkire, M., Tang, C., Keator, D., Wu, J., & McGaugh, J. L. (1996). Amygdala activity at encoding correlated with long-term, free recall of emotional information. *Proceedings, National Academy of Sciences, 93,* 8016–8021.

Cahill, L., Prins, B., Weber, M., & McGaugh, J. L. (1994). β-adrenergic activation and memory for emotional events. *Nature, 371,* 702–704.

Cahill, L., Weinberger, N. M., Roozendaahl, B., & McGaugh, J. L. (1999). Is the amygdala a locus of "conditioned fear"? *Neuron, 23,* 227–228.

Cannon, W. (1927). The James-Lange theory of emotions: A critical examination and an alternative theory. *American Journal of Psychology, 39,* 106–124.

Christianson, S-A. (1992). *The handbook of emotion and memory: Research and theory.* Hillsdale, NJ: Erlbaum.

Darwin, C. (1872/1965). *The expression of emotions in man and animals.* Chicago: University of Chicago Press.

Davis, M. (1992). The role of the amygdala in fear and anxiety. *Annual Review of Neuroscience, 15,* 353–375.

Gold, P. E. (1995). The role of glucose in regulating brain and cognition. *American Journal of Clinical Nutrition, 61,* 598?–599?.

James, W. (1890). *Principles of psychology,* New York: Holt.

James, W. (1884). What is an emotion? *Mind, 9,* 188–205.

Johnson, M., Kim, J., & Risse, G. (1985). Do alcoholic Korsakoff's syndrome patients acquire affective reactions? *Journal of Experimental Psychology: Learning, Memory, and Cognition, 11,* 22–36.

Kety, S. (1970). The biogenic amines in the central nervous system: Their possible role in arousal, emotion, and learning. In F. O. Schmitt (Ed.), *The neurosciences* (pp. 324–336). New York: Rockefeller University Press.

LeDoux, J. E. (1995). Emotion: Clues from the brain. *Annual Review of Psychology, 46,* 209–235.

McGaugh, J. L., Cahill, L., & Roozendaal, B. (1996). Involvement of the amygdala in memory storage: Interaction with other brain systems. *Proceedings, National Academy of Sciences, 93,* 13508–13514.

McGaugh, J. L., & Gold, P. E. (1989). Hormonal modulation of memory. In R. B. Brush & S. Levine (Eds.), *Psychoendocrinology,* New York: Academic Press, pp. 305–339.

McGaugh, J. L., & Herz, M. J. (1972). *Memory consolidation.* San Francisco: Albion.

Pitman, R. K. (1989). Posttraumatic stress disorder, hormones, and memory. *Biological Psychiatry, 26,* 221–223.

Reiman, E. M., Lane, R. D., Ahern, G. L., Schwartz, G. E., Davidson, R. J., Friston, K. J., Yun, L. S., & Chen, K. (1997) Neuroanatomical correlates of externally and internally generated human emotion. *American Journal of Psychology, 154,* 918–925.

Schacter, S., & Singer, J. E. (1962). Cognitive, social, and physiological determinants of emotional state. *Psychological Review, 69,* 379–399.

Stratton, G. M. (1919). Retroactive hypermnesia and the other emotional effects on memory. *Psychological Review, 26,* 474–486.

Weiskrantz, L. (1956). Behavioral changes associated with ablation of the amygdaloid complex in monkeys. *Journal of Comparative and Physiological Psychology, 49,* 381–391.

Williams, C. L., & McGaugh, J. L. (1993). Reversible lesions of the nucleus of the solitary tract attenuate the memory-modulatory effects of posttraining epinephrine. *Behavioral Neuroscience, 107,* 955–962.

Zajonc, R. B. (1980). Feeling and thinking: Preferences need no inferences. *American Psychologist, 35,* 151–175.

Larry Cahill and James L. McGaugh

EMPATHIC ACCURACY. Empathic accuracy emerged as an important research topic in the 1990s. It is the most recent of four areas of study within the accuracy tradition of interpersonal perception research (Ickes, 1997). This tradition began over 50 years ago with the study of accuracy in judging other people's personality traits. It later expanded to include the study of accuracy in judging others' attitudes, values, and self-conceptions, the study of accuracy in inferring others' emotional states, and the study of accuracy in inferring the specific content of others' thoughts and feelings (i.e., empathic accuracy).

As early as 1957, the American clinical psychologist Carl Rogers called attention to the importance of accurate empathy in the therapist-client relationship. His work suggested that an ideal measure of empathic accuracy would be one that (a) could be used to track the accuracy of the therapist's inferences over the course of the client-therapist interaction, and (b) would be objective in defining accuracy in terms of the degree to which the perceiver's inferences matched the client's actual reported thoughts and feelings. During the next four decades, many attempts to develop such a measure were made by researchers in areas such as clinical and counseling psychology, communication studies, marriage and family studies, psychiatry, and personality and social psychology.

Two of the most promising measurement approaches were introduced in the early 1990s by William Ickes, Linda Stinson, Victor Bissonnette, and Stella Garcia (1990) and by Robert Levenson and Anna Ruef (1992). The approach developed by Ickes and his colleagues assesses how accurately perceivers can infer, "on-line," the specific content of other peoples' successive thoughts and feelings. The approach developed by Levenson and Ruef assesses how accurately perceivers can infer "on-line" the valence and intensity of other peoples' changing emotional states. In both approaches, perceivers attempt to infer aspects of a target person's actual subjective experience while viewing a videotape of the target person in conversation with either a therapist or another interaction partner. Accuracy is objectively defined in terms of the degree to which the perceiver's inference matches the target's actual subjective experience, and the accuracy scores for individual inferences can be differentially aggregated to assess changes across time or to create a single, more global index.

In 1992, Levenson and Ruef found evidence that a perceiver's accuracy in inferring a target's negative emotional states was related to the degree of physiological synchrony between the perceiver and the target. They interpreted this finding as supporting their more general argument that emotional contagion may mediate the accuracy of one's inferences about another person's emotional states. This argument was supported by evidence that the perceivers' own facial expressions of emotion were positively correlated with both (a) their level of empathic accuracy, and (b) at least one measure of their level of physiological synchrony with the target.

Applying the measurement procedure developed by Ickes and his colleagues in a clinically relevant context, Marangoni, Garcia, Ickes, and Teng (1995) found evidence that empathic accuracy improved with increasing exposure to a target person and could be further enhanced through the provision of immediate, veridical feedback about the person's actual thoughts and feelings. They also found evidence that although targets differed substantially in their overall "readability," perceivers nonetheless displayed impressive cross-target consistency in their empathic accuracy, with some perceivers being consistently good, others consistently average, and still others consistently poor at reading different target persons' thoughts and feelings.

Trying to develop a psychological profile of the "good" perceiver has proved difficult, however. Surveying the available research conducted since 1955, Davis and Kraus concluded in 1997 that self-report measures of social sensitivity have consistently failed to predict individual differences in accuracy on various social inference tasks. A plausible reason for this failure is that individuals cannot provide valid self-report data because they lack the requisite metaknowledge regarding their own empathic ability (Davis & Kraus, 1997). Moreover, contrary to the social stereotype regarding the presumed superiority of "women's intuition," a review of the relevant literature did not find that women, on average, have more *ability* than men to accurately infer the specific content of other people's thoughts and feelings. Instead, the findings suggested that situational factors can evoke more *motivation* in women to do well on empathic inference tasks, and that women will outperform men when this differential motivation is engaged (Graham & Ickes, 1997).

The role of empathic accuracy in close relationships has received increasing research attention. As common sense suggests, friends are reliably more accurate than strangers in "reading" the content of each other's thoughts and feelings (Colvin, Vogt, & Ickes, 1997). However, satisfaction and stability in close relationships are not always enhanced by high levels of empathic accuracy. Under certain circumstances, motivated inaccuracy appears to be adaptive in helping individuals preserve their close relationships in situations in which accurate knowledge of the partner's thoughts and feelings would have a highly threatening and destabilizing effect (Simpson, Ickes, & Blackstone, 1995). And, surprisingly perhaps, empathic accuracy in marital relationships may actually decline after the honeymoon period is over, as the spouses devote less effort to monitoring each other's specific words and actions and instead increasingly rely on more general cognitive representations of each other (Bissonnette, Rusbult, & Kilpatrick, 1997; Thomas, Fletcher, & Lange, 1997).

Although the research on empathic accuracy is still in its infancy, the topic has already proved to be of considerable theoretical and applied interest. As a fundamental dimension of social intelligence, empathic accuracy is of interest to communication researchers, evolutionary theorists, clinical and counseling psychologists, developmental and social psychologists, and psychiatrists and social workers. From an applied perspective, it is of interest not only to clinical practitioners but also to professionals in fields such as education, diplomacy, bargaining and negotiation, personnel management, and direct sales and marketing.

[*See also* Empathy.]

Bibliography

Bissonnette, V. L., Rusbult, C. E., & Kilpatrick, S. D. Empathic accuracy and marital conflict resolution. In W. Ickes (Ed.), *Empathic accuracy* (pp. 251–281). New York: Guilford Press.

Colvin, C. R., Ickes, W., & Vogt, D. (1997). Why do friends understand each other better than strangers do? In W. Ickes (Ed.), *Empathic accuracy* (pp. 169–193). New York: Guilford Press.

Davis, M. H., & Kraus, L. A. (1997). Personality and empathic accuracy. In W. Ickes (Ed.), *Empathic accuracy* (pp. 144–168). New York: Guilford Press.

Ickes, W. (Ed.). (1997). *Empathic accuracy.* New York: Guilford Press.

Ickes, W., Stinson, L., Bissonnette, V., & Garcia, S. (1990). Naturalistic social cognition: Empathic accuracy in mixed-sex dyads. *Journal of Personality and Social Psychology, 59,* 730–742.

Levenson, R. W., & Ruef, A. M. (1992). Empathy: A physiological substrate. *Journal of Personality and Social Psychology, 63,* 234–246.

Marangoni, C., Garcia, S., Ickes, W., & Teng, G. (1995). Empathic accuracy in a clinically relevant setting. *Journal of Personality and Social Psychology, 68,* 854–869.

Rogers, C. R. (1957). The necessary and sufficient conditions of therapeutic personality change. *Journal of Consulting Psychology, 21,* 95–103.

Simpson, J. A., Ickes, W., & Blackstone, T. (1995). When the head protests the heart: Empathic accuracy in dating relationships. *Journal of Personality and Social Psychology, 69,* 629–641.

Thomas, G., Fletcher, G. J. O., & Lange, C. (1997). On-line empathic accuracy in marital interaction. *Journal of Personality and Social Psychology, 72,* 839–850.

William Ickes

EMPATHY has been defined in many ways, in different decades, and in different subdisciplines of psychology. In the 1950s and 1960s, empathy meant the ability to understand others' mental states. More recently, empathy has been defined as an emotional reaction to the comprehension of another's emotional state or condition that is the same or very similar to the other's state or condition (e.g., a girl observes a peer crying and reacts by feeling sad). Thus, empathy involves not only some minimal recognition and understanding of another's emotional state (or what the other person is likely to be feeling given the situation), but also the affective experience of the other person's actual or inferred emotional state.

Empathy is similar to, and often may be the origin of, other related emotional reactions. Especially after the early years of life, empathy is likely to turn into either sympathy or personal distress (or both). Sympathy is an emotional reaction based on the apprehension of another's emotional state or condition; it involves feelings of compassion, sorrow, or concern for another person rather than feeling merely the same emotion as the other individual. Sympathy involves an other-orientation and the motivation to assist the needy or distressed person, whereas empathy by itself does not. [*See* Sympathy.]

Empathy may also engender personal distress, an aversive, self-focused emotional reaction to another's emotional state or condition, such as anxiety, distress, or discomfort. Personal distress is hypothesized to result from empathic overarousal and to lead to the egoistic motive of alleviating one's own distress. Thus, people experiencing personal distress are expected to try to escape contact with the emotion-eliciting individual and to help that person only if doing so is the easiest way to reduce one's own distress. In real-life interactions and in much of the existing research, it is difficult to differentiate among empathy, sympathy, and personal distress.

Theories of Vicarious Emotional Responding

Based on a social learning perspective, theorists such as Aronfreed and Hoffman have suggested that empathy is acquired early in life through conditioning or association, that is, by repeated pairing of the young child's positive affect or pain with another person's expression of the corresponding feelings. In contrast, some psychoanalytic theorists have suggested that empathy emerges in early infant-caretaker interactions as the caretaker's moods are communicated to the infant by touch, tone of voice, and facial expressions.

Martin Hoffman has emphasized both the cognitive and affective aspects of empathy, and the link of empathic emotion with prosocial action. In his view, empathic distress, defined as experiencing another's painful emotional state, develops early in infancy as a consequence of either built-in, biological tendencies toward empathy or early classical conditioning. For example, cues of pain or displeasure from another or from another's situation may evoke associations with the observer's own past pain, resulting in an empathic affective reaction.

Hoffman has argued that infants are capable of experiencing empathic distress before they can clearly differentiate themselves from others. Consequently, they are often unclear about who is feeling the emotion that they witness and may behave as if what has happened to another person is happening to them. Once infants can cognitively differentiate between themselves from others, their empathic distress may be transformed, at least in part, to concern for the victim. However, although toddlers are aware of others as separate individuals, they view the world for some time from their own perspective and do not understand that other people have their own thoughts, preferences, and feelings. Thus, their empathy- or sympathy-based helping is often inappropriate because toddlers attribute their own feelings to others.

According to Hoffman, at about the age of 2 or 3, children begin to view others as distinct physical entities with their own emotions and thoughts, so they are better able to determine the source of another's distress and engage in sensitive helping behavior. However, young children's vicarious emotional responses are restricted to another's immediate, transitory, and situation-specific distress. Because of their greater cognitive maturity and awareness of their own and others' continuing existence, older children begin reacting to others' general conditions (including deprivation, oppression, illnesses, and incompetence), as well as to another's immediate distress.

Some aspects of Hoffman's theory have received support, such as the shift from helping behaviors based on an egocentric view of the world to those based on an understanding of others' emotions, thoughts, and needs. Moreover, the role of developmental advances in cognitive perspective-taking skills in empathy has received some support, as has the relation of self-related processes (i.e., the recognition of the self) to empathy and prosocial behavior. Although some of the theory is speculative and difficult to test, it has provided a basis for developmental studies of empathy.

Development of Vicarious Emotional Responding

In the first days of life, infants cry in response to the cries of other infants, a behavior that Hoffman believes is a precursor to empathic responding (although others question whether this is true). Although 6- to 12-month-olds show little reaction to the distress of others, children between 12 and 18 months of age sometimes react to others' negative emotion with agitation or sustained attention. By 18 months of age, toddlers occasionally try to comfort others in distress, and some children's prosocial actions appear to be based on empathic reactions. By 2 to 3 years of age, it is not unusual for children to demonstrate behaviors that seem to reflect empathy and genuine sympathy. By ages 4 to 5, children sometimes report or display emotions akin to empathy, sympathy, and personal distress, and markers of their empathic sadness or sympathy tend to be associated with prosocial behavior. By ages 11 to 12, individual differences in self-reports of empathy are relatively stable.

Children's reports of increasing sympathy or empathic sadness during the elementary and junior high school years may be real or due to increases with age in the desire to appear sympathetic to others and to oneself. Facial reactions indicative of empathic sadness, sympathy, or distress sometimes decrease with age (particularly for boys), perhaps because of the general tendency to inhibit facial displays of negative emotion more with age. However, some forms of prosocial behavior do increase with age, a finding that suggests that empathy may increase in frequency in childhood.

Gender Differences in Empathy and Related Responses

A common gender stereotype is that females are more caring and emotionally responsive than males. However, the degree to which males and females have been found to differ in empathy varies with the method used to assess empathy. For self-report measures of empathy, especially questionnaire measures, there are large differences favoring girls and women. In self-reports of emotional reactions in experimental settings in which study participants are exposed to empathy-inducing stimuli, a modest difference favoring females has been found. However, no consistent gender differences have been found when physiological or unobtrusive observations of nonverbal (e.g., facial) behavior have been obtained, although females occasionally exhibit slightly more empathy or sympathy facially when exposed to needy or distressed individuals.

Differences in findings for different measures may reflect, in part, the degree to which the intent of the measure is obvious and respondents can control their responses. Gender differences are greatest when what is being assessed is clear and respondents have conscious control over their responses, as in self-report measures. Gender differences in empathy generally disappear when demand characteristics are subtle and respondents have less conscious control over their responses, as when physiological responses are the measure of empathy. Thus, when gender stereotypes are activated and individuals can control their responses, they may try to project a stereotype-consistent image. Moreover, females more than males may want to believe that they are empathic and sympathetic and, consequently, may tend to interpret their emotional reactions in empathy-inducing contexts as empathy or sympathy, even when they are in personal distress.

Gender differences in observed empathy-related behavior may also reflect the tendency for girls to perform more prosocial behaviors than boys. This finding, along with the gender difference in self-report data, suggests that girls may be slightly more empathic than men. It also is possible that females experience more sympathy rather than empathy than males.

Empathy, Aggression, and Prosocial Development

Numerous theorists have suggested that people who tend to experience another's pain or distress are likely to refrain from aggression because of the discomfort induced by their empathic response to the victim's emotional (or imagined) reactions. There is some empirical support for this notion, although the association between aggression and empathy appears to be modest and contingent on whether empathy is measured by self-report. When empathy has been assessed with picture-story measures (in which children are told stories about hypothetical children in emotion-eliciting situations and are then asked how they themselves feel), empathy has been negatively related to elementary children's aggression, but not preschoolers'. When empathy has been assessed with questionnaire measures, there is also a negative association between empathy and aggression/acting-out behaviors. For example, Cohen and Strayer (1996) found that empathy was lower among conduct-disordered than comparison youth. Moreover, low maternal empathy has been linked to child abuse. In contrast, the relation of aggression to adolescents' and adults' reports of empathy in experimental contexts and to facial reactions indicative of children's empathy has been weak and nonsignificant. Thus, it appears that there is a modest relation between empathy and aggression, albeit primarily for self-report measures of empathy.

There also is evidence that empathy is related to prosocial behaviors such as helping and sharing, as well as higher level reasoning about prosocial moral dilemmas. However, it is likely that sympathy is more closely related to prosocial behavior than is pure empathy.

Origins of Empathy

In studies of twins, there is evidence that genetic factors partially account for individual differences in empathy-related responding. For example, Carolyn Zahn-Waxler and her colleagues (1992) noted a significant genetic component for empathic concern, prosocial actions, and unresponsive-indifferent reactions to others' distress at both 14 and 20 months of age. However, the sizes of the heritability estimates were modest (generally in the .20s), so socialization is also likely to influence the development of empathy-related responding.

Children with a secure attachment to their parent and who experience supportive parenting appear to be relatively empathic, although the findings are not always consistent. Parental empathy (rather than sympathy) has not been found to be related to children's empathy, although parental abuse appears to be negatively related to children's empathy. However, parental warmth may be insufficient in itself to foster empathy in children. Parental practices that involve appropriate discipline or restrictiveness may foster empathy. For example, parents' demands for their children's responsible behavior (i.e., the parent's tendency to point out responsibilities or say which behavior is expected in a given context) have been associated with elementary-school children's self-reported empathy. However, research on the socialization of empathy per se, rather than sympathy, is limited.

Acknowledgments. Work on this entry was supported by a grant from the National Institutes of Mental Health (1 R01 HH55052) and a Research Scientist Development and Research Scientist Awards from the National Institute of Mental Health (K05 M801321).

Bibliography

Batson, C. D. (1991). *The altruism question: Toward a social-psychological answer.* Hillsdale, NJ: Erlbaum.

Cohen, D., & Strayer, J. (1996). Empathy in conduct-disordered and comparison youth. *Developmental Psychology, 32,* 988–998.

Davis, M. H. (1994). *Empathy: A social psychological approach.* Madison, WI: Brown & Benchmark.

Eisenberg, N. (1992). *The caring child.* Cambridge, MA: Harvard University Press.

Eisenberg, N., Carlo, G., Murphy, B., & Van Court, P. (1995). Prosocial development in late adolescence: A longitudinal study. *Child Development, 66,* 911–936.

Eisenberg, N., & Fabes, R. A. (1998). Prosocial development. In W. Damon (Series Ed.) & N. Eisenberg (Vol. Ed.), *Handbook of child psychology: Vol. 3. Social, emotional, and personality development* (5th ed., pp. 701–778). New York: Wiley.

Eisenberg, N., & Mussen, P. (1989). *The roots of prosocial behavior in children.* Cambridge, England: Cambridge University Press.

Eisenberg, N., & Strayer, J. (1987). *Empathy and its development.* Cambridge, England: Cambridge University Press.

Hoffman, M. L. (1982). Development of prosocial motivation: Empathy and guilt. In N. Eisenberg (Ed.), *The development of prosocial behavior* (pp. 281–313). New York: Academic Press.

Miller, P., & Eisenberg, N. (1988). The relation of empathy to aggression and externalizing/antisocial behavior. *Psychological Bulletin, 103,* 324–344.

Miller, P. A., Eisenberg, N., Fabes, R. A., & Shell, R. (1996). Relations of moral reasoning and vicarious emotion to young children's prosocial behavior toward peers and adults. *Developmental Psychology, 32,* 210–219.

Radke-Yarrow, M., Zahn-Waxler, C., & Chapman, M. (1983). *Prosocial dispositions and behavior.* In P. Mussen (Series Ed.) and E. M. Hetherington (Vol. Ed.), *Handbook of child psychology: Vol. 4. Socialization, personality, and social development* (pp. 469–545). New York: Wiley.

Zahn-Waxler, C., Radke-Yarrow, M., Wagner, E., & Chapman, M. (1992). Development of concern for others. *Developmental Psychology, 28,* 126–136.

Nancy Eisenberg

EMPIRICISM. *See* Philosophy, *article on* Philosophy of Science.

EMPLOYEE ASSISTANCE PROGRAMS. About 10% of the U.S. workforce suffers from some type of chemical dependency, and the costs of chemical dependency amount to billions of dollars annually. Chemically dependent employees are four times more likely to be involved in accidents and use sick leave three times more often than other workers. Alcohol and drug abuse affects personnel at all levels in the organization, from rank-and-file employees to top management executives. Employee assistance programs (EAPs) are job-based programs that help employees with personal or job-related problems that impair job performance. EAPs are the most popular vehicle for mental health and substance abuse counseling in the workplace. A nationally representative survey of U.S. work sites conducted in 1993 found that 33% of all work sites had some type of EAP, and the average cost of an EAP was $22 to $27 per employee (French, Zarkin, Bray, Hartwell, T.D. 1997).

History of Employee Assistance Programs

EAPs have their roots in occupational alcohol programs, which were started in the 1940s by Alcoholics Anonymous. These programs offered an alternative to dismissing employees whose job performance had severely deteriorated due to alcohol abuse. First-line supervisors were trained to recognize alcohol-related problems and to refer the worker for treatment. These programs grew from about 50 in the early 1950s to 500 by 1970. In the early 1970s, occupational alcoholism programs gave way to broader-based, employee assistance programs. EAPs did not rely as heavily on supervisor identification model and focused more on impaired work performance as the criterion for early identification. Thus, EAPs avoided the stigma associated with alcoholism by focusing on returning employee work performance to acceptable levels.

Central Practices and Services

EAP services range from screening, assessment and referral of employees to community resources through direct clinical treatment by psychologists and/or other mental health professionals. At minimum, EAPs offer assessment and substance abuse and personal counseling to workers and their families. In the past decade, however, EAPs have been asked to deal with more varied and serious workplace problems, such as job stress, workplace violence, sexual harassment, attention deficit disorder (ADD), posttraumatic stress disorder (PTSD), and financial problems. These new problems require more than short-term counseling and signal a more prominent role for psychologists who have specialized training in psychosocial disorders, the clinical skills to conduct long-term therapy, the administration skills for case management, and methodology skills to evaluate program effectiveness.

Structure of Employee Assistance Programs

EAPs can be either internal or external to the organization. Large firms (over 10,000 employees) tend to sponsor in-house programs, whereas smaller firms, singly or in consortia, tend to contract with external agencies, such as consulting firms and hospitals. About 80% of all U.S. work sites utilize external EAPs. It is easier to main confidentiality in external EAPs and they tend to offer a greater variety of counselors, but they often lack knowledge about the internal workings of the organization they serve. Internal EAPs usually offer a broader range of services, such as consultations with supervisors (internal = 88% vs. external = 58%), constructive confrontations (internal = 63% vs. external = 30%), follow-up with employees' supervisors (internal = 65% vs. external = 40%), and involvement in health promotion activities (internal = 86% vs. external = 36%). The staff of EAPs can include a wide range of health professionals, including psychiatric social workers, psychiatric nurses, alcohol abuse counselors, and clinical/counseling psychologists. Alcohol abuse counselors often are recovered alcoholics who have been state certified as alcohol counselors or alcohol and drug counselors.

Key Assumptions and Theories

The primary assumption of the EAP is that it is more cost-effective to rehabilitate a formerly competent employee than to hire and train a replacement. Employee replacement costs have been estimated at $7,000 for a salaried worker, over $10,000 for a midlevel employee, and more than $40,000 for a senior executive. (National Institute on Drug Abuse, 1992).

Employees enter an EAP in one of two ways: The first is self-referral, in which the employee initiates contact with the EAP and obtains counseling independent of supervisory awareness. The second is supervisory referral, which occurs in response to declining job performance. The employee is confronted by the supervisor and informed of company disciplinary actions that may be taken unless the employee agrees to seek confidential assistance through the EAP. Constructive confrontation has been the predominate strategy for dealing with alcoholics in the work setting. The confrontation is between the supervisor and the employee, and the focus is on poor work performance, not problem drinking. The constructive element of the strategy is the provision of EAP services to the worker while still employed. The constructive confrontation strategy utilizes social controls within the work organization rather than creating a "deviant" role for the worker. Constructive confrontation has been successful because (a) the focus is on work performance, not the employee's personal behavior, which is a legitimate concern for employers; (b) it is more difficult for the alcoholic to use denial mechanisms in view of documented evidence of impaired work performance; and (c) the threat of disciplinary actions, even job loss, is a powerful motivating factor for employees.

Effectiveness of Employee Assistance Programs

Many studies since the 1970s have attested to the benefits of EAPs for rehabilitating employees and reducing health care costs. Roman and Blum (1996) reviewed the literature and concluded that EAPs are effective in rehabilitating workers with chemical dependencies, and seem to be cost-effective for organizations. However, they also noted that many of the studies were subject to criticism on methodological grounds (e.g., no random assignment to experimental and control groups).

Based on accumulated research and experience, an effective EAP has these key ingredients: commitment and support from top management; a written set of policies and procedures outlining the purpose of the EAP and how it functions in the organization; close cooperation with local union(s); training of supervisors on their role in problem identification; education of employees and promotion of EAP services to foster widespread utilization throughout the company; a continuum of care, including referral to community agencies and follow-up; an explicit policy on confidentiality of employee information; and coverage of EAP services by company health insurance benefits.

Several organizations provide current information and assistance about EAPs and substance abuse prevention. The Employee Assistance Society of North America (EASNA) is an international group that was formed to provide a standard of care for EAPs through accreditation, peer review, and staff development; a step-by-step guide to accreditation is available on the Internet (http://www.ccsa.wiseeasn.html). The National Clearinghouse for Alcohol and Drug Information's Web page (http://www.health.org/aboutn.htm) is the information service of the Center for Substance Abuse Prevention of the U.S. Department of Health and Human Services, and is the world's largest resource for current information and materials concerning substance abuse prevention. The National Institute for Alcoholism and Alcohol Abuse's (NIAAA) Web site (http://www.niaaa.nih.gov) is the most complete Web site on alcohol abuse, and contains information on publications, videos, and a complete list of assessment and screening instruments.

Bibliography

Berridge, J., Cooper, C. L., & Highley-Marchington, C. (1997). *Employee assistance programmes and workplace counseling.* Chichester, England: Wiley. The most recent review of the nature, theory, and practice of EAPs in the United States and Great Britain, with a special emphasis on the role of EAPs in combating stress at work.

Dickman, F. (1988). *Employee assistance programs: A basic text.* Springfield, IL: Charles C Thomas.

French, M. T., Zarkin, C. A., Bray, J. W., & Hartwell, T. D. (1997). Costs of employee assistance programs: Findings from a national study. *American Journal of Health Promotion, 11,* 219–222.

National Institute on Drug Abuse. (1992). *How drug abuse takes profit out of business* (Publication No. 574). Rockville, MD: National Clearinghouse In Alcohol and Drug Information.

Roman, P., & Blum, T. (1996). Alcohol: A review of the impact of worksite interventions on health and behavioral outcomes. *Journal of Health Promotion, 11,* 136–149.

Trice, H. M., & Roman, P. (1972). *Spirits and demons at work: Alcohol and other drugs on the job.* Ithaca, NY: Cornell University Press. Another of the classic works in this field, this scholarly book describes the problem of substance abuse at the workplace and identifies job-based risk factors, job behaviors reactions of supervisors, and key elements of the constructive confrontation strategy.

Wrich, J. (1980). *The employee assistance program.* Center City, MN: Hazelden Educational Foundation. This is a classic book on employee assistance programs and provides all of the fundamentals of EAP practice. (The 1984 revised edition may be more accessible at public libraries than the original version.)

Lawrence R. Murphy

EMPLOYEE TRAINING is a systematic approach to learning and development to improve individual team or organizational effectiveness. A systematic approach refers to the fact that the employee training is intentional; it is being conducted to meet some perceived need. Learning and development concerns the building of expertise as a function of these systematic training efforts. Learning outcomes include changes in knowledge, skills, and/or attitudes. The issue of improvement focuses on the extent to which the learning that results from training leads to meaningful changes in work performance. Therefore, a critical issue is the extent to which the knowledge, skills, and/or attitudes gained in training are transferred to the job and improve individual effectiveness. Finally, employee training can also be viewed from a broader, more macro perspective, as a mechanism for enhancing work team and organizational effectiveness. In this way, training is seen as integral to facilitating larger-scale organizational change and development issues.

Businesses are spending an increasing amount of money on training their own workforce in order to increase competitiveness and to improve services. Psychologists play various roles relevant to improving the quality and effectiveness of employee training. These include:

1. The development of theoretical perspectives and models of what is meant by learning and transfer;
2. The derivation of testable models and the conduct of empirical research on the factors that impact learning during training and the transfer of training to the job;
3. The identification, design, delivery, evaluation, and improvement of training programs;
4. The study of key issues beyond individual training to broader issues of team training and organizational change and development.

The Learning Process

Learning is typically defined as a relatively permanent change in knowledge, skill, or attitudes produced by some type of experience. Training transfer is usually defined as the degree to which trainees effectively apply the knowledge, skills, and attitudes gained in training to a job. Applied psychologists have tended to view learning and transfer as conceptually distinct constructs, with learning during training seen as a direct precursor (necessary, but not sufficient) to transfer. In contrast, researchers in cognitive and instructional psychology often conceptualize learning and transfer as two ends of the same continuum. Proponents of this perspective argue that the effectiveness of learning is revealed and measured by the level of retention and transfer shown. It is clear that the psychological processes underlying transfer and learning are largely inseparable. From an organizational training perspective, though, there remains value in discussing separately the acquisition or building of expertise and the application of that expertise to the job.

Acquisition and Building Expertise. Psychologists are quite interested in identifying and understanding the changes that occur as an employee moves from novice through competence and then on to expert status. Expertise is defined as the achievement of consistent, superior performance through the development of specialized mental processes acquired through experience and training. To investigate the dynamic issues underlying this movement toward expertise, researchers have taken a multidimensional perspective to learning. Three key learning outcomes are changes in cognition, skills, and attitudes.

Cognition refers to the quantity and type of knowledge obtained as a function of various experiences, such as training. Evaluations of training effectiveness have tended to examine whether the trainees have achieved a certain level of declarative knowledge. Declarative knowledge is the acquisition of facts as measured by multiple-choice or free-recall methods. Recent advances in research on expertise have led to the examination of procedural knowledge, knowledge organization, and metacognitive strategies as key knowledge-acquisition outcomes.

As individuals move beyond novice levels and gain knowledge and experience, declarative knowledge can become proceduralized. This means that an individual's expanding knowledge about situations, responses, and outcomes leads to the development of context-specific rules for diagnosis, action, and monitoring. Proceduralized knowledge is often described as a set of conditional-action rules of the form "if condition A, then action B" (e.g., if I pull this lever, then the plane will go in this direction).

As knowledge becomes highly proceduralized, the learner begins to develop meaningful structures for organizing that knowledge. The term mental model has been used to describe how well people organize their knowledge. Mental models serve as frameworks that trainees use to describe functions and forms of tasks, explain and observe the integration of tasks, and anticipate future task requirements. Trainees are believed to possess separate models for multiple functions on the job. For example, a military pilot may possess distinct mental models for preflight briefings, takeoffs, landings, tactical engagements, and aircrew coordination. Mental models provide a context for the interpretation of events; they not only organize existing information, but also influence the acquisition of new knowledge.

Metacognitive strategies involve the capability of a learner to self-monitor and self-regulate activities. These capabilities allow individuals to take actions that lead to improved knowledge and skill acquisition, retention, and application to the job. Indicators of metacognitive processes include the ability to select alternative learning strategies, monitor the use of strategies, and revise or select a different strategy if the current approach is not successful. For example, experts are more likely to know that they have understood task relevant information, are more likely to discontinue a problem-solving strategy that would ultimately prove unsuccessful and are more accurate about judging the difficulty of new problems.

Skill-based learning refers to the development of technical or motor skills. The development of expertise from initial skill acquisition to skill compilation and automaticity requires more than just practice and experience. The transition from declarative to procedural knowledge sets the stage for initial skill development as procedural knowledge enables the reproduction of modeled behaviors. The compilation of skills occurs with the development of highly organized mental models that comes from experience beyond initial successes at reproducing certain behaviors. Performance at the compilation phase is characterized by faster, less error-prone performance and by the integration of discrete task steps into a single act. With subsequent practice, experience, and feedback, individuals can obtain a level of automaticity at which they not only can perform tasks quickly but also are able to maintain parallel rather than successive processing of activities. Automaticity enables task accomplishment with minimal conscious monitoring. Cognitive resources are then available for concurrent performance on additional tasks or for attending to peripheral demands of the task (e.g, situational pressures).

Models of learning that focus solely on knowledge and skill acquisition are incomplete. Individuals come to training programs with various attitudes, beliefs, and motivations based on individual characteristics, past experiences, and social influences. These affective reactions are internal states that influence the choice of personal action. While attitudes arise from some complex set of beliefs and feelings of liking and disliking, the important issue for training is what action these reactions support. For example, if a trainee's attitudes toward the value of safe behaviors in the workplace have undergone some change as a function of training, then learning has occurred. The key issue is how changes in attitudes lead to changes in behaviors on the job.

Applying Expertise to the Job. The systematic acquisition of knowledge, skills, and attitudes is an important but imperfect indicator of learning. Acquisition performance during training may indicate only temporary rather than a permanent change in the individual. The main objective of training is to enhance performance in the transfer or work setting. Demonstrating transfer requires clear linkages between the expected changes during training and observable changes in behaviors in the work setting. Expected outcomes of the transfer process include the generalization of trained skills to the job, the maintenance or long-term

retention of training, and the adaptability of trained responses to new tasks and situations.

Generalization concerns the extent to which attained skills and behaviors are exhibited in the transfer setting and are applied to situations and conditions beyond those incorporated into the training program. Generalization involves more than mimicking trained responses to particular events that occurred during training; it requires trainees to exhibit behaviors in response to stimuli that is similar but nonidentical to that presented in training (different settings, people, and situations).

Maintenance or long-term retention is defined as the length of time that trained skills and behaviors continue to be used effectively on the job. It is clear that people who exhibit similar levels of skill proficiency immediately after training can differ substantially in long-term retention. Performance at the end of training is not a sufficient predictor of long-term retention.

An emerging literature in cognitive psychology contends that another key indicator of learning is the extent to which an individual can adapt to novel or changing situational demands. Adaptability is evidenced when the trainee responds successfully to changes in the nature of the trained task. Adapting one's knowledge and skills to novel tasks requires an understanding of the deeper principles underlying the task, executive-level capabilities to recognize and identify changed situations, and knowledge of whether or not the existing repertoire of procedures can be applied. In training for adaptive expertise, it is critical to encourage active and mindful learning during training.

Factors That Affect Learning and Transfer

Much research has been conducted to examine the factors that might affect knowledge and skill acquisition during training and the transfer of those skills and knowledge to the job. A number of training effectiveness models have been developed. Three categories of variables identified as having an impact on acquisition and transfer include the incorporation of learning principles and learning strategies into training design, the impact of individual differences, such as the motivation and abilities of the trainees, and the influence of various characteristics of the work environment.

Learning Principles and Strategies. Traditionally, research has centered on the four learning principles: (1) identical elements; (2) the teaching of general principles; (3) stimulus variability; and (4) various conditions of practice. Identical elements contends that retention is enhanced when there is psychological and physical fidelity between the training context and the job setting. Physical fidelity involves matching the training context as closely as possible to the actual work environment (surroundings, tasks, and equipment). Psychological fidelity is the degree to which trainees attach similar meanings to objects and events in the training and organizational context. To enhance psychological fidelity, training exercises can be developed that necessitate the same responses and decision-making processes that the trainee should use in the work setting, given similar job pressures and stresses.

Teaching through general principles maintains that learning and transfer are facilitated when trainees are taught not just applicable skills but also the general rules and theoretical principles that underlie the training content. Retention is enhanced when the principles underlying a specific content or behavior to be learned are understood or coded along with new behaviors.

Stimulus variability is based on the notion that transfer is enhanced when the variety of situations that trainees will face on the job are incorporated into the training program. Providing several examples of a content to be learned strengthens the trainee's knowledge structure so that the trainee is more likely to see the applicability of a concept in a new situation.

Conditions of practice include a number of specific design issues, including whole or part training, feedback, and overlearning. Whole or part training concerns the relative efficiency of practice with all the steps involved in a performance event as opposed to practice one step at a time. Evidence suggests that the whole method is advantageous for enhancing learning when the training material is high in task organization but low in task complexity.

Feedback or knowledge of results refers to information provided to trainees about their progress in training. Feedback is a critical element in achieving learning, with the timing and specificity of feedback the critical variables in determining its effects. Overlearning is the process of providing trainees with practice far beyond the point at which the task has been performed successfully. Overlearning impacts retention and can lead to skill compilation and automaticity.

The learning principles provide a structured strategy for designing training programs and building expertise. Researchers have begun to examine learning environments that facilitate learning and transfer by taking into account individual needs and preferences. Three such strategies include inductive learning, learner control, and error management.

The typical learning strategy is to explicitly instruct learners on the complete task and its concepts, rules, and strategies. With inductive approaches to learning, such as discovery learning, individuals must explore and experiment with the task to infer and learn the rules, principles, and strategies for effective performance. The approach emphasizes the importance of hypothesis testing and problem solving by the learner that is guided by an instructor. For example, an instruc-

tor can provide the general strategy to troubleshooting an electrical problem and then have the trainee discover the specific steps to take.

Training is often designed to maximize control over the learning process by the instructor. Recent attention has been given to enhancing the learner's control of their own learning process. Learner control refers to the extent to which trainees have the opportunity to select the method, timing, practice, and/or feedback of training. With greater control, learners can more actively tailor the training to meet their own changing needs. It is hypothesized that this method for engaging learners leads them to a deeper understanding of the task (its procedural knowledge and mental models). Effective use of metacognitive strategies is a critical component to the learner being more in control of their own learning.

The behavioral approach to learning has emphasized the need to shape correct responses, minimize incorrect responses, and reinforce the correct responses to build skills. Error-based learning strategies highlight the advantages of designing an experience in which trainees learn from mistakes. Errors can gain learner's attention because they signal unexpected events and can alert learners of incorrect assumptions that are being made. In this way, making progress as well as mistakes can lead to a more comprehensive mental model of a task.

Individual Differences. Trainee characteristics such as ability, skill, experience, personality, and motivational factors are important predictors of performance in a training-and-transfer environment. Ability, experience, and skill factors have been examined to understand trainability or the extent to which certain types of trainees (e.g., those with high levels of previous experience) benefit more from training than others. For example, researchers have examined issues of aptitude/treatment interaction, or the extent to which certain types of trainees (e.g., high-ability trainees) perform better with one type of training method (e.g., self-paced), while other types of trainees (e.g., low-ability trainees) perform better with another type of method (e.g., instructor-led training). Indicators of abilities include scholastic aptitude, spatial aptitude, verbal reasoning, reasoning ability, and analytic ability.

A variety of personality and motivational factors have been examined for their impact on training effectiveness. Personality factors that have been found to be predictors of learning in training settings include the dimensions of conscientiousness, openness to experience, and extraversion. Thus, individuals who are outgoing have a strong sense of purpose and a willingness to take risks seem to do better in training, especially when training is a new experience. Work-related attitudes, such as job involvement and career-related attitudes, have also been found to have an influence on trainee motivation to learn and subsequent learning in the training environment.

Research has examined motivational determinants more directly. Social cognitive theory posits reciprocal determinism among the trainee's knowledge, the environment, and behavior. That is, individuals regulate their behavior based on their prior beliefs about their ability to accomplish a task (self-efficacy) and their beliefs about the environmental consequences of their behavior (outcome expectancies). Training success is maximized when trainees believe that they have the capability to learn the training material and that they perceive that desirable outcomes are attained as a result of completing a training program satisfactorily.

Work Environment Characteristics. The work context that surrounds the employee is critical for effective transfer. This context can provide opportunities to apply training or obstacles to successful transfer. Key factors that have been studied for their impact on learning and transfer include situational constraints, work-group climate and factors in the larger organizational system.

Investigators have examined situational constraints to performance on the job, including the lack of job-related information, tools and equipment, materials and supplies, budgetary support, services and help from others, and time availability. These factors can place limits on how much of what is trained can be successfully applied to the job. A key constraint that has direct relevance for training transfer is the opportunity to use or apply the knowledge and skills gained in training on the job. Lack of the opportunity to immediately apply trained skills not only reduces subsequent motivation to enhance skill development but can also lead to rapid skill decay. Research has found that factors such as supervisory attitudes toward a trainee, the supportiveness of the work group, and the individual's level of self-efficacy can impact the quantity and quality of opportunities that trainees obtain to use trained skills on the job.

Work-group climate is a multidimensional construct which includes issues such as supervisory and co-worker support for training, an openness by the work group to innovation and going beyond the status quo, and a tolerance for mistakes made as part of learning. The more favorable the work climate, the more likely the trainee will attempt to apply the knowledge and skills gained in training to the job. Once applied, the level of support impacts transfer outcomes of generalization, maintenance, and adaptability. For example, research shows that pretraining discussions with supervisors and subsequent posttraining mentoring contributes to the transfer of skills to the job.

Training programs are embedded within a larger or-ganizational system. This system conveys information regarding the importance of training and development relevant to other uses of organizational resources. Also conveyed is information as to what individual behaviors are rewarded and whether learning and improvement lead to desired outcomes, such as promotions. Similarly, organizational policies and procedures that impact what happens on a daily basis on the job can facilitate or hinder effective transfer. The bottom line is whether employees feel that there is commitment through all levels of the organization in support of training, workplace development, and continuous learning efforts. Without that commitment, trainees may feel little need to acquire and transfer trained knowledge and skills.

Systematic Approach to the Design and Delivery of Training

Numerous researchers and practitioners have stressed the need for training to be based on a systematic and organized framework. Training activities must be carefully planned and developed to meet the needs of individual employees, teams, departments, and/or organizational functions. A well-established framework for organizing the important steps of training is the instructional systems design model. Based on this model, psychologists can be involved in the development of a systematic approach to employee training programs in one or more of the following ways: analysis of training needs; design and planning of the training program; delivery or implementation of training; and evaluation and improvement of training.

Training Needs. A thorough assessment of training needs forms the foundation of any training endeavor. Training needs analysis is typically described as consisting of three interrelated components: (1) organizational analysis; (2) operations analysis; and (3) person analysis. Organizational analysis involves the examination of the entire organization to determine where training is needed. This analysis typically examines whether the existing goals of the organization might be better met by increasing employee knowledge and skills or changing existing attitudes.

Given an organizational need for training, an operations analysis can be conducted. An operations analysis concentrates on the jobs that are to be part of the training effort. It focuses on what tasks employees must perform, what knowledge and skills are required to complete those tasks, and what standards of performance are expected. Based on this comprehensive analysis of the job, the required content of a training program can be identified. A person analysis assesses whether individuals are performing to expected levels. This analysis determines if there is a gap between standards of performance for a job and the actual level of performance of the employees. An analysis can then be done to determine if the cause of the performance "gap" is due to inadequate knowledge, skills, or experience with the task. An action plan for each individual can then be developed that might include training activities, goal setting, job rotation, or other developmental actions that might be needed to meet or exceed job expectations.

Training Design. Training needs assessment provides information about where, what, and who needs to be trained. The next step is determining how to design training environments and experiences that enhance acquisition and transfer. Program design is the process of developing a plan of instruction for each training program to be offered. Developing a plan of instruction requires the identification of training content, training objectives, and specific lesson plans.

A plan of instruction requires some prioritization of information from the training needs assessment. The content of training should be based on the important tasks or knowledge and skills identified. Then decisions have to be made about how much effort (time and resources) will be devoted to training each component (task, knowledge, and skill) that is part of the training program. Once the content is specified, training objectives can be written and the sequencing for training can be determined. Training objectives constitute the formal description of what a trainee should be able to do once training is completed. The next step is to sequence the training objectives in such a way as to enhance learning activities in the training program. The key to sequencing is to ensure that the prerequisite knowledge and skills have been acquired prior to the introduction of advanced material. Once objectives are sequenced, lesson plans can be developed. For each objective, the specific facts, concepts, principles and skills needed to build competency in an area can be identified. The methods of instruction (lecture, discussion, demonstration, and practice), testing procedures to use, and how much training time is needed to accomplish each training objective must be identified.

Training Method and Delivery. Training methods can be divided into nonexperiential and experiential techniques. Nonexperiential training methods are knowledge-oriented and include such techniques as lecture, group discussion, and audiovisual presentation.

Experiential techniques focus more on building trainee skills and include work simulations, behavioral modeling, and on-the-job training. Work simulations allow trainees to perform outside the work context but with high levels of physical (e.g., the equipment used on the job) and psychological (e.g., noise level and time pressures) fidelity. Behavioral modeling is based on the principles of social learning theory, which contends that we learn most through focused observation of ourselves and others and through the reinforcements we obtain as a consequence of our behaviors or actions.

Behavioral modeling involves trainees watching a model display the set of key behaviors to be learned (e.g., how to be assertive), role-playing so that trainees can practice the key behaviors, and feedback and social reinforcement for successful behavioral rehearsal. With on-the-job training, an experienced worker or mentor provides instruction in the actual work context and supports the application of required knowledge and skills to be effective. For example, police cadets are often paired with an experienced officer on the job to refine the skills gained in the formal training program.

While the majority of training is face-to-face classroom instruction, there are a number of emerging training delivery platforms. A platform that allows for training across multiple sites at one time is distance learning. Through audio and data links, trainees from various sites can access and interact with an instructor from a distant location. Another platform is the development of work simulations through virtual reality training. Trainees can view a three-dimensional world of the kinds of situations they might typically face on the job. Objects in this simulated world can be touched, looked at, and repositioned. The learner (e.g., astronaut) is immersed in the training experience (such as correcting the Hubble telescope) where mistakes can be made without real-world consequences.

Other platforms, such as computer-based instruction (CBT), intelligent tutoring systems, and Web-based training allow for more self-paced instruction and learner control. With CBT, trainees interact with instructional materials on CD-ROM that allow for intensive drill and practice with knowledge-based tests and immediate feedback. CBT can embed branching patterns (e.g., different levels of difficulty to learn training material) based on responses to questions to allow for some individualized learning or provide simulations that place trainees in scenarios in which they must use problem-solving skills (e.g., troubleshooting a mechanical malfunction on a jet engine).

Intelligent tutoring systems are computer-based programs that strive to completely individualize instruction. Through various methods, there is a diagnosis of the trainees' current level of understanding or performance and the selection of the appropriate intervention that can transform a trainee toward more expert performance. The difference between CBT and intelligent tutoring systems lies in the use of artificial intelligence programming techniques to emulate the properties of tutors in one-on-one instruction.

The growth of the World Wide Web has triggered an interest in Web-based training delivered via the Internet or corporate intranet. Information is sorted and transmitted as requested by trainees at remote sites as accessed by Web browsers. Web-based instruction allows for just-in-time training delivery, with trainees accessing the material when needed. Learners can also control how much information to attend to through the use of hyperlinks to additional material, practice exercises, and feedback. Web-based systems also have the potential for sharing intellectual capital by linking people across locations through chat rooms and e-mails to discuss training and support each other's learning.

In addition to these training platforms, organizations are moving away from traditional classroom training and embracing experienced-centered learning that emphasizes learning from job-related activities. One of the most practiced job-oriented learning experiences is job rotation, where employees are provided a series of job assignments in various parts of the organization. Another approach has been called action learning, where groups of participants work to solve real organizational problems or develop new and innovative approaches and reflect on how the learning can be generalized throughout the organization. This is in contrast with recent efforts at adventure learning, where a group of employees are exposed to difficult and unfamiliar physical and mental challenges in an outdoor environment in order to build problem-solving and team-building skills that will hopefully be transferred back to the job setting.

Training Evaluation. A key characteristic of a systematic approach to training is the emphasis on the continuous use of evaluative feedback to adapt the program to better meet its stated objectives. The evaluation process can aid in identifying, collecting, and providing information to make a variety of instructional decisions. Evaluation information can be collected prior to or during training program implementation to make immediate instructional improvement in the design, development, and delivery stages. This formative evaluation process is typically conceived of as an iterative process of tryout, measurement, and revision of instructional components by program developers.

Other efforts focus on posttraining evaluation for decision-making and marketing purposes. This summative evaluation process is conducted to determine instructional effectiveness after the program has been implemented and stabilized. Information collected at this point is used by decision makers to determine whether training objectives have been met, whether trainees are applying the knowledge and skills gained in training to the job, and whether the program should be continued or perhaps expanded to other locations or trainees. The evaluation information can also be used to select new training course content, revise the emphasis placed on different aspects of the current course content, and modify instructional objectives and activities to improve learning and transfer to the job.

A key evaluation question is whether any changes found in performance on the job can be attributed to the training. Research methods and experimental and quasi-experimental designs can be used to systematically examine this issue. One useful design for determining the success of training is the pretest, posttest, experimental design, which compares the acquisition and transfer of knowledge and skills for a group of trainees with a control group that has not had access to the training program.

Beyond Individual Effectiveness

Businesses are spending an increasing amount of money on training and development of their own workforce as people are seen as the primary source of enduring competitive advantage. In addition, the increasing scope and complexity of the changes occurring in the workplace, such as team-based work systems, the focus on quality and customer service, and the infusion of new technology all require a highly trained workforce that is prepared to deal with the changing realities of the workplace. Training is now viewed not only as an important factor in improving individual effectiveness but also from a broader perspective as a key lever for improving team and organizational effectiveness.

From a research perspective, the emerging literature in organizational psychology on multiple levels of analysis issues mirrors the applied interests in moving beyond the examination of factors impacting individual effectiveness. A levels perspective, an extension of the general systems paradigm, posits that events should be viewed within their larger contexts (e.g., individuals are part of groups of workers) and that the levels are interrelated (organizational issues can impact work team effectiveness). Organizational researchers typically have used the terms *organizational, team,* and *individual* to denote the hierarchical ordering of levels. While there are a number of training models that focus on factors impacting the success of training in improving individual effectiveness on the job, few models exist on training from a broader perspective at the team and organizational levels.

Team Training and Effectiveness. Work organizations have embraced new initiatives, such as just-in-time inventory control, total quality management, and advanced computer-based systems. These types of initiatives have led to more integrated approaches to work that require the increased coordination of efforts. Many organizations have adopted team-based work systems as a way of meeting these increasing integration needs, with training as a critical component in improving the work team effectiveness.

Recent efforts have investigated the knowledge and skills that distinguish between effective and ineffective teams. Based on this type of information, training interventions can be developed to build team skills for enhancing work team effectiveness. In particular, team researchers have differentiated between task-work and teamwork skills. Task work refers to the individual performing the tasks required for their job. Individuals must be competent in their role if they are to become effective team players. One approach for increasing co-ordination is cross-training, in which individuals learn multiple jobs. This not only increases flexibility in the workgroup (e.g., if a team member is absent from work), but also provides teams with a greater appreciation of the demands of each job and the need for co-ordinated efforts.

Teamwork skills are those related to functioning effectively as a team member—skills such as communication, coordination, cooperation, morale, adaptability, decision making, and situational awareness. Training teamwork skills can advance the ability of teams to dynamically adapt to the demands of the situation, often without explicit instruction from leaders or supervisors. For example, work with airline cockpit crews indicates that training on key skills such as how to be assertive helps to reduce team conflicts and decreases the likelihood of crews experiencing avoidable accidents.

Organizational Learning and Effectiveness. The success of new initiatives in work settings, such as team-based work systems and total quality management, relies on the expertise of individuals and the co-ordinated efforts of team members. Organizations have begun to acknowledge the importance of learning and creating a knowledge base as a key strategic weapon for improving competitiveness and for delivering effective services. Consequently, organizations have become more interested in how to build learning capabilities in the workforce on an ongoing basis. This organizational learning cycle has been labeled continuous learning.

The goal of continuous learning is to encourage everyone in the organization—employees, line managers, supervisors, and technical personnel—to become actively engaged in expanding their skills and improving organizational effectiveness. Learning becomes an everyday part of the job rather than being confined to formal training sessions in the classroom. Employees can learn skills of others in their work unit (cross-training), teach other employees in areas of expertise, and learn from one another on a day-to-day basis. Thus, while learning and development are clearly rooted in individuals, organizations can attempt to create the context for a positive learning environment. A positive learning environment occurs when individuals know how their job fits with the larger systems, individuals are assigned tasks that stretch and challenge them, mistakes are tolerated during learning, constraints to learning are minimized, new ideas are valued and encouraged, and polices and procedures support the effective use of training.

The backbone of any effort to develop a continuous learning orientation is the development of problem-solving skills. Problem-solving skills include the ability to identify the gap between the aims of an improvement effort and the current reality of the system, the analysis of the root causes of the gap, the identification of improvement options, the choice of which option has the greatest potential to add value to the organization, and the evaluation of the effectiveness of the improvement effort. There are a number of methods or techniques to facilitate this problem-solving process, including the use of brainstorming, the nominal group technique, and multivoting, all of which identify and prioritize gaps. Methods for diagnosing problems and conducting root cause analysis include the use of flow charts of a work process, force-field analysis, and cause-and-effect diagrams.

Bibliography

Historical Perspective on Workplace Training

Campbell, J. P. (1971). Personnel training and development. *Annual Review of Psychology, 22,* 565–602.

McGehee, W., & Thayer, P. W. (1961). *Training in business and industry.* New York: Wiley.

Works on the Learning Process

Anderson, J. R. (1983). *The architecture of cognition.* Cambridge, MA: Harvard University Press.

Bandura, A. (1986). *Social foundations of thought and action: A social cognitive theory.* Englewood Cliffs, NJ: Prentice Hall.

Kraiger, K., Ford, J. K., & Salas, E. (1993). Application of cognitive, skill-based, and affective theories of learning outocmes to new methods of training evaluation [Monograph]. *Journal of Applied Psychology, 78,* 311–328.

Weiss, H. N. M. (1990). Learning theory and industrial and organizational psychology. In M. D. Dunnette & L. M. Hough (Eds.), *Handbook of industrial and organizational psychology* (2nd ed., Vol. 1, pp. 171–221). Palo Alto, CA: Consulting Psychologists Press.

Works on Factors Impacting Learning and Transfer

Baldwin, T., & Ford, J. K. (1988). Transfer of training: A review and directions for future research. *Personnel Psychology, 41,* 63–105.

Noe, R. A. (1986). Trainee attributes: Neglected influences on training effectiveness. *Academy of Management Review, 11,* 736–749.

Schmidt, R. A., & Bjork, R. A. (1992). New conceptualizations of practice: Common principles in three paradigms suggest new concepts for training. *Psychological Science, 3,* 207–217.

Works on a Systematic Approach to Training

Gagne, R. M., Briggs, L. J., & Wager, W. W. (1992). *Principles of instructional design* (4th ed.). New York: Harcourt Brace Jovanovich.

Goldstein, I. (1993). *Training in organizations* (3rd ed.). Pacific Grove, CA: Brooks Cole.

Beyond Individual Effectiveness

Rousseau, D. M. (1985). Issues of levels in organizational research: Multilevel and cross-level perspectives. In L. L. Cummings & B. M. Staw (Eds.), *Research in organizational behavior* (Vol. 7, pp. 1–38). Greenwich, CT: JAI.

Senge, P. M. (1991). *The fifth discipline: The art and practice of the learning organization.* New York: Doubleday.

Swezey, R. W., & Salas, E. (1992). *Teams: Their training and performance.* Norwood, NJ: Ablex.

Tannenbaum, S. I. (1997). Enhancing continuous learning: Diagnostic findings from multiple companies. *Human Resource Management, 36,* 437–452.

J. Kevin Ford

EMPLOYMENT DISCRIMINATION is adverse treatment of an employee in which the employee's race, color, national origin, sex, age, religion, psychological or physical disability, previous opposition to apparent discrimination, or participation in discrimination claims, is a motivating factor resulting in restricted employment opportunities or limited career advancement. Prohibited adverse actions include both discrete decisions, such as nonhire, nonpromotion, discipline or discharge, and acquiescence in the face of harassing comments or conduct about protected groups. Four theories of discrimination are distinguished: (a) intentionally less favorable treatment than that afforded to similarly situated individuals who are not members of a protected group; (b) facially neutral systemic practices that fall more harshly on a protected group and that are not justified by business necessity; (c) a hostile or abusive workplace atmosphere that unreasonably interferes with an employee's work performance or employment opportunities (e.g., sexual harassment); and (d) denial of reasonable accommodation or special consideration for an employee's religious observances or for a physical or psychological disability (Goodman-Delahunty, 1999).

Stereotyping and Discrimination

Hostility to outside groups is a culturally learned phenomenon. Employer perceptions and attitudes about the abilities of various groups in society (ethnic, racial, gender, age, etc.) can cause negative stereotyping. Use of cultural or gender differences as a basis for categorizing and defining intergroup boundaries diminishes the salience of multicultural shared values. As sociolegal constraints against discrimination became more widespread, racism, sexism, and other forms of prejudice became more subtle. Contemporary research on prejudice demonstrates how normal cognitive and motivational processes can contribute to the development, maintenance, and perpetuation of discrimination through processes of social categorization, negative stereotyping, and priming (Rudman & Borgida, 1995; Tyler, Boeckmann, Smith, & Huo, 1997).

Conditions that generate negative stereotyping based on membership in a protected class include: (a) the target protected group constitutes a disproportionately low ratio of the work team, usually 15% or less of the total group, leading to role encapsulation; (b) the target is in a nontraditional occupation; and (c) the evaluative criteria are ambiguous or subjective, and individuating information is scarce, perhaps limited to brief encounters between the evaluator and employee. In such circumstances, successes of women and minorities in other protected groups may be attributed to external factors such as luck, rather than the skill or expertise of the employee. Employers may resort to determinations based on the perceived "fit" between stereotypes and the job type or task. Ambiguous evaluation criteria that permit the use of subjective factors can enable aversive racism (Dovidio & Gaertner, 1986). Examples of negative stereotypes are, for instance, that clientele prefer not to be served by racial minorities, or that it is inappropriate to discuss finances with women.

Comments or conduct by coworkers based on sex role expectations, sexual, racial, disability, or age-biased stereotypes may comprise actionable harassment or a hostile workplace. A workplace environment in which sexually oriented materials are present, or in which employees are perceived as sex partners or sex objects, rather than in terms of their occupational role and worth, is sexualized and can foster discriminatory sexual harassment through sex role spillover. Local organizational norms and what is tolerated by management may encourage sexual harassment. For example, when male employees and management share sexualized views of women, men with a proclivity to harass become disinhibited (O'Donohue, 1997).

Factors that inhibit harassment in the workplace include: (a) unbiased attitudes of top management personnel who serve as role models and establish policies and who counteract negative stereotypes, because people look to authority figures to define "outsiders"; (b) use of cooperative work teams to promote the interdependence of diverse groups and diminish the salience of intergroup boundaries; (c) an increased ratio of protected group members at the work site; (d) clearly defined and appropriate nondiscriminatory norms; and (e) disincentives, such as discipline, for violating nondiscriminatory norms (Eberhardt & Fiske, 1998; Fishbein, 1996; Jackson & Ruderman, 1996).

Psychologists may testify as expert witnesses in employment cases, drawing on research on stereotyping to describe the mental antecedents of prejudice, or how social influence, social roles, and group dynamics can foster prejudice or inhibit it. To establish that stereotyping is discriminatory, there must be evidence that (a) discriminatory comments or behavior occurred that included stereotypes, and (b) those stereotypes were relied upon in making the employment decision that adversely affected an individual employee or group of employees in a protected class (*Price Waterhouse v. Hopkins*, 1989).

Statistically Based Evidence of Differential Hiring and Promotion Practices

Circumstantial proof of discriminatory patterns and practices that disproportionately impact a protected group of employees can be demonstrated by statistical evidence. Statistical evidence typically compares the composition of the workforce with the pool of applicants or relevant labor market. Facially neutral practices with a substantially greater impact on a protected group comprise systemic disparate impact discrimination, such as glass-ceiling cases, where women and minority-group members are overrepresented in low-level positions.

Psychologists can identify specific objective or subjective employer practices that cause the significant disparities, such as employer reliance on biased tests or other selection devices, and can also identify less discriminatory alternatives to achieve job-related objectives. Three statistical methods to assess the impact of hiring or promotional criteria are the policy-capturing or regression models, the survey model, and psychometric analysis (Schwartz & Goodman, 1992). Multiple regression analysis computes mathematical equations that combine several factors to provide the best possible prediction of the employment decision in issue, expressed in correlations or proportion of variance accounted for by job-relevant qualifications (e.g., education, age, most recent occupation, etc.). Significant relationships between employment decisions like hiring and illegitimate factors like race or gender when relevant factors are controlled for, may establish intentional discrimination. Decision-making models may also prove that innocent factors (career choices personality factors, employee interest) produced some portion of the apparent glass-ceiling phenomenon.

Survey analysis gathers data to determine the impact of permissible (employee interest in promotion) and impermissible (negative stereotypes) factors that cause an adverse impact. For example, current and former employees may be surveyed about management attitudes to promotions of male versus female or majority versus minority individuals, and about employee interest in promotion, to determine whether disparities in the work force are caused by perceived discriminatory attitudes or employee interest. To contest liability, psychologists may offer relevant analyses challenging the raw data, labor market, or statistical methods and techniques. They may demonstrate, for example, that factors other than the challenged practice can account for the disparity, or may provide expertise about the validity of personnel tests to establish that the practice is job related and justified by business necessity.

Psychometric analysis is most useful when a specific employment practice (e.g., a psychological test, structured interview, education, or experience requirements) is at issue. Validation studies examine the extent to which a test instrument or other selection procedure is job related. Three psychometric methods of validation are criterion-related validity, content validity, or construct validity. Criterion validity studies are preferred as they most clearly examine whether an employment practice is predictive of successful performance of important elements of a job. Psychologists can evaluate whether employers are using a test the way the publisher planned it and whether the validation methods meet professional standards (Haney & Hurtado, 1994). Most typically, industrial/organizational psychologists provide expertise on psychometric analysis and statistical proofs.

[*See also* Discrimination.]

Bibliography

Dovidio, J. F., & Gaertner, S. L. (1986). (Eds). *Prejudice, discrimination, and racism*. San Diego, CA: Academic Press.

Eberhardt, L., & Fiske, S. T. (Eds.). (1998). *Confronting racism: The problem and the response*. Thousand Oaks, CA: Sage.

Fishbein, H. (1996). *Peer prejudice and discrimination*. Boulder, CO: Westview Press.

Goodman-Delahunty, J. (1999). Civil law: Employment and discrimination. In R. Roesch, S. D. Hart, & J. P. Ogloff (Eds.), *Psychology and law: The state of the discipline* (pp. 277–337). New York: Plenum Press.

Haney, C., & Hurtado, A. (1994). *Standardized error: Testing, diversity and discrimination in the workplace*. New York: Kluwer.

Jackson, S., & Ruderman, M. (Eds.). (1996). *Diversity in work teams*. Washington, DC: American Psychological Association.

O'Donohue, W. (Ed.). (1997). *Sexual harassment: Theory, research and treatment*. Boston, MA: Allyn & Bacon.

Rudman, R. A., & Borgida, E. (1995). The afterglow of construct accessibility: The behavioral consequences of priming men to view women as sexual objects. *Journal of Experimental Social Psychology, 31*, 493–517.

Schwartz, D. J., & Goodman, J. (1992). Expert testimony on decision processes in employment cases. *Law and Human Behavior, 16* (3), 337–355.

Tyler, T. R., Boeckmann, R. J., Smith, H. J., & Huo, Y. J. (1997). *Social justice in a diverse society*. Boulder, CO: Westview.

Jane Goodman-Delahunty

EMPOWERMENT. The concept and practice of empowerment has many different interpretations and has been an elusive construct in psychological, political, and community contexts. Empowerment has been viewed as both a process and an outcome. As a fluid process that moves individuals, communities, and organizations along a continuum, empowerment has an end point wherein individual, community, and organizational systems are perceived as having reached a state of actualized power. However, the lack of agreement on the conceptualization of empowerment at micro and macro levels of practice and process makes measurement of this construct even more elusive. In a very general sense, the term refers to one's capacity to acquire understanding and control over personal, social, and political forces in order to improve life situations.

Empowerment is the antithesis to powerlessness. It is easy to define in its absence. It is often seen as a political process, suggesting a societal redistribution of power and advancement of equity among stakeholders. In *Pedagogy of the Oppressed* (1970), Paulo Freire (a Brazilian educator) applied empowerment principles to his internationally renowned work to address the illiteracy problem among Brazilian peasants. His approach first defines community powerlessness as a prevailing state of mind in which the individual assumes the role of "object," controlled by random impulses of the environment, as opposed to "subject," exerting significant influence on the factors that affect one's life and community. In the context of this definition, the individual is alienated from genuine participation in the construction of social reality. For Freire, powerlessness results from the passive acceptance of oppressive cultures. It further combines an attitude of self-blame, a sense of generalized distrust, feelings of alienation from sources of social influence, experiences of disenfranchisement and economic vulnerability, and a sense of hopelessness in the sociopolitical struggle.

Previous work by Braithwaite advocated for community organization and development as an antecedent to community empowerment. However, poverty of the spirit and resources remains the antecedent risk factor for preventable disease. Poverty and powerlessness create circumstances in people's lives that predispose them to high levels of social dysfunction, the highest indices of morbidity and mortality, the lowest access to primary care, and little or no access to primary prevention programs.

Social epidemiologic research has well documented that lower socioeconomic status is negatively correlated with increased morbidity and mortality, from such risks as poor sanitation, hazardous work environments, malnutrition, poor education, unemployment, and minority status. Recent studies have begun to assess the underlying susceptibility to disease from the risk of lack of control and disempowerment as confounders of specific risk factors. Except for slavery, the most contemporary and blatant example of disempowerment in this context is the infamous Tuskegee syphilis experiment (1932–1972), when racism (a confounder) was perpetrated against African American men from Macon County, Alabama, resulting in egregious abuse as uniformed research subjects by the U.S. Public Health Service.

Individual empowerment has been used in therapeutic environments in an effort to assist clients in changing self-defeating behaviors to more adaptive and health promoting ones. In health promotion and therapy, empowerment is often defined as "a process of assisting others to assert control over factors which affect their health." It has been used synonymously with such measures as coping skills, mutual support, social support systems, personal efficacy, competence, locus of control, self-esteem, and self-sufficiency. Individual empowerment is positively correlated with self-efficacy, positive self-esteem, and self-concept or personal competence. The psychological effects of empowerment enable one to actualize a sense of full citizenship participation, and mastery, control, and proficiency over life's obstacles. Historically, such actualizations have been marginalized for ethnic minorities, women, the illiterate, physically challenged, poor, uninsured, unemployed, and other disenfranchised populations.

Community empowerment grew from roots in social action ideology and advances the plight of disenfranchised groups to gain control of resources affecting their quality of life. According to many health psychologists and behavioral scientists actively involved in the conduct of empowerment research, increasing citizen participation in community activities typically leads to improved neighborhoods, a stronger sense of community, and personal and political efficacy. Community empowerment and its relationship to civil rights, justice, political and social structures, and quality-of-life issues have been the focus of study in such disciplines as philosophy, religion, political science, sociology, education, and psychology. While considerable research documents the effects of lack of control or powerlessness in causing disease, empowerment is health enhancing. The literature in social epidemiology and community psychology addresses the relationship between the lack of control over one's life as a risk factor stemming from an overburden of life demands without the adequate resources to meet those demands. Several models for community empowerment exist, such as social action, social planning, national campaigns, single-issue advocacy, and community organization. These models transcend hierarchical, patriarchal, coercive, or violent conceptualizations of power and challenge the assumption that power is a zero-sum commodity (the premise that increasing the power of one community, organization, or individual implies decreasing the power of another).

The object of organizational empowerment is to maximize the effectiveness of the members of the organization relative to decision-making processes for the mutual benefit of meeting personal and organizational goals. Given that information is power, organizational empowerment places a premium on communication, information sharing, and shared leadership. In this context, the management style typically embraces concepts of mutually defined goals wherein members develop and buy in to a collective vision for the organization. Organizations that practice genuine empowerment principles can be viewed as open systems, where any organizational member (irrespective of status) can affect organizational change for improvement and capacity building.

Philosophically and pragmatically, to embrace empowerment means that one refrains from "blaming the victim" for his or her disadvantaged status and focuses attention on structural impediments and systemic reasons for the presence of negative forces in the environment. With regard to addressing equity among community stakeholders, "victim blaming" and "deficit model" approaches are no longer acceptable explanations for the ills that plague disenfranchised citizens.

[See also Power.]

Bibliography

Braithwaite, R. L. (1992). Coalition partnerships for health promotion and empowerment. In R. L. Braithwaite and S. E. Taylor (Eds.), *Health issues in the black community* (pp. 321–334). San Francisco: Jossey-Bass.

Braithwaite, R. L. & Lythcott, N. (1989). Community empowerment as a strategy for health promotion for Black and other minority populations. *Journal of the American Medical Association, 261*, 282–283.

Chavis, D., & Wandersman, A. (1990). Sense of community in the urban environment: A catalyst for participation and community development. *American Journal of Community Psychology, 18*(1), 55–81.

Fawcett, S. B., Seekins, T., Whang, P. O., Muiu, C., and Suarez de Balcazar, Y. (1984). Creating and using social technologies for community empowerment. In J. Rappaport, C. Swift, and R. Hess (Eds.), *Studies in empowerment* (pp. 145–171). New York: Haworth Press.

Florin, P., & Wandersman, A. (1990). An introduction to citizen participation, voluntary organizations, and community organization: Insights for empowerment through research. *American Journal of Community Psychology, 18*(1), 41–54.

Freire, P. (1970). *Pedagogy of the oppressed*. New York: Seabury Press.

Israel, B. A., Checkoway, B., Schulz, A., & Zimmerman, M.
(1994). Health education and community empowerment: Conceptualizing and measuring perceptions of individual, organizational, and community control. *Health Education Quarterly, 21*(2), 149–170.

McKnight, J. L. (1985). Health and empowerment. *Canadian Journal of Public Health, 76*, 37–38.

Neighbors, H. W., Braithwaite, R. L., & Thompson, E. (1995). Health promotion and African-Americans: From personal empowerment to community action. *American Journal of Health Promotion, 9*(4), 281–287.

Rappaport, J. (1987). Terms of empowerment/exemplars of prevention: Toward a theory for community psychology. *American Journal of Community Psychology, 15*, 121–144.

Ryan, W. (1971). *Blaming the victim*. New York: Random House.

Wallerstein, N. (1992). Powerlessness, empowerment, and health: Implications for health promotion programs. *American Journal of Health Promotion, 6*, 197–205.

Ronald L. Braithwaite

ENCODING. *See* Memory, *article on* Coding Processes.

ENCOPRESIS. Having bowel movements in the clothing or in other inappropriate places is a common childhood problem. It is estimated that between 5 and 8% of children have this problem. Fecal incontinence can occur for a wide variety of reasons, such as illness or other organic conditions or as a result of psychological or behavioral factors. Encopresis, by definition, refers to cases in which the problem has no basis that is primarily organic or due to illness. The official diagnostic criteria specified by the *Diagnostic and Statistical Manual of Mental Disorders* (American Psychiatric Association, 1994) further state that the inappropriate fecal soiling, which may be voluntary or involuntary, must occur at least once per month for three months in a child who is 4 years of age or developmentally the equivalent of this age before diagnosis may be made.

Walker (1978) has identified three catagories of encopresis: (1) manipulative soiling, (2) soiling due to diarrhea, and (3) constipation-based soiling (sometimes referred to as overflow incontinence). Manipulative soiling refers to cases in which the child uses soiling as a means to control the environment. For example, a child might have a soiling accident at school when he or she is not prepared for a class test. The soiling makes it necessary for the parent to remove the child from school in order to change clothes. Although many mental health workers believe this to be a frequent cause of soiling, it is really relatively rare. Soiling due to diarrhea occurs when excessive stress in the life of the child produces loose bowel movements that the child is unable to control. This is somewhat more common than manipulative soiling but is still not the most common reason for encopresis. Approximately 85 to 90% of cases of encopresis result from constipation (Levine, 1975).

It may seem paradoxical to state that fecal soiling accidents are caused by constipation. However, an understanding of the process involved makes the relationship clear. Children may become constipated for many reasons. Some individuals seem to have inherited a tendency to become constipated more easily than others. Unfortunate dietary choices undoubtedly play a very significant role in the majority of cases. If the child becomes dehydrated while playing or withholds stools rather than interrupting play for necessary toileting, constipation may result. Similarly, inattention to teaching the child proper toileting habits often plays a role. Emotional factors such as depression tend to reduce motility of the bowel, which may precipitate constipation. These, as well as many other factors, may produce the original condition of constipation in the child. The fact that the child is constipated generally goes unrecognized because the child does not report it to the parent, and the parent may not notice that the child is not using the toilet for bowel movements with sufficient frequency. In time, the constipation becomes chronic and produces a condition known as psychogenic megacolon, in which the colon becomes excessively enlarged and distended. The distended and impacted colon is unable to move fecal material through the body via normal peristaltic action. When the child ingests food, the stomach converts the food to liquid form, which then moves through the intestine. Eventually the food reaches the point of impaction, where it forms a pool. This liquid material seeps around the impacted mass and leaks out of the anal opening. This produces a stain in the child's underclothing. Since this leakage is a passive process, not accompanied by the normal contractions of defecation, the child correctly reports that he or she was not aware that the soiling was occurring. Parents often think their child is not trying to control the bowel, but from this description it is obvious that the bowel cannot be controlled under the circumstances. To further complicate the problem, after a period of time, the chronic constipation obliterates the sensation of the need to have a bowel movement. Thus efforts to help the child are met with protests that he or she does not feel the need to use the toilet.

Emotional and psychological characteristics of encopretic children have been studied. Contrary to popular belief, most encopretic children are not emotionally disturbed. Rather, they have had the misfortune to develop chronic constipation. The following statements summarize the literature in this area. Most encopretic children are not emotionally disturbed. Most emotionally disturbed children are not encopretic. However, there is a slightly higher rate of encopresis in emotionally disturbed children compared with children who are not emotionally disturbed. This higher rate of incidence is probably due to emotional or family problems interfering with establishing and maintaining good dietary and toilet habits. No profile of unique or unusual personality characteristics has ever been established for encopretic children. Other than suffering some embarrassment and loss of self-esteem due to their problem, encopretic children are like all other children (Walker, 1995).

Treatment of encopresis depends on the specific etiology. If the problem results from efforts to manipulate the environment, psychotherapy to improve the child's coping skills and family therapy to deal with related factors will generally be effective. If the cause of soiling is stress-induced diarrhea, stress management skills, along with medication for symptomatic relief, are effective. Constipation-based encopresis is best treated with a program involving, first, elimination of the underlying constipation by enemas, laxatives, and dietary changes, and second, reestablishing bowel control by rewarding regular bowel movements and toileting hygiene. Numerous programs for accomplishing this have appeared in the literature (Houts & Abramson, 1990; Walker, Milling, & Bonner, 1988). Appropriate treatment for encopresis is effective in over 90% of cases. Some difficult cases may require biofeedback or medical intervention such as surgery. These two treatments, however, are much more likely when there is an organic etiology for the problem, in which cases, as noted, the diagnosis is not encopresis.

Bibliography

American Psychiatric Association. (1994). *Diagnostic and statistical manual of mental disorders* (4th ed.). Washington, DC: Author.

Houts, A. C., & Abramson, H. (1990). Assessment and treatment for functional childhood enuresis and encopresis: Toward a partnership between health psychologists and physicians. In S. B. Morgan & T. M. Okwumabua (Eds.), *Child and adolescent disorders: Developmental and health psychology perspectives* (pp. 47–103). Hillsdale, NJ: Erlbaum.

Levine, M. D. (1975). Children with encopresis: A descriptive analysis. *Pediatrics, 56*(3), 412–416.

Walker, C. E. (1978). Toilet training, enuresis, and encopresis. In P. Magrab (Ed.), *Psychological management of pediatric problems* (Vol. 1, pp. 129–189). Baltimore: University Park Press.

Walker, C. E. (1995). Elimination disorders: Enuresis and encopresis. In M. Roberts (Ed.), *Handbook of pediatric psychology* (2nd ed., pp. 537–558). New York: Guilford Press.

Walker, C. E., Milling, L. M., & Bonner B. L. (1988). Incontinence disorders: Enuresis and encopresis. In D. K. Routh (Ed.), *Handbook of pediatric psychology* (pp. 363–397). New York: Guilford Press.

C. Eugene Walker

ENCULTURATION. *See* Acculturation.

ENDOCRINE SYSTEMS. Endocrinology is the study of hormones, and hormones are chemical messengers that activate cellular processes. There are three types of chemical messengers: autocrine, paracrine, and endocrine. Autocrine messengers are produced by the same cells in which they act. Paracrine messengers act upon cells nearby those that produce and release them, for example, neurotransmitters. Endocrine signals are produced at some distance in the body from where they act. Hormones generally are endocrine signals but can, in specific circumstances, play the part of autocrine and paracrine messengers.

Types of Hormones

A partial list of hormones is found in Table 1. Peripheral target hormones of the thyroid, adrenals, and gonads are formed and released in response to pituitary hormones, which are in turn released in response to hormones from the hypothalamus. Hormones of the posterior pituitary gland are produced by neurons residing in the hypothalamus that send long axons to form synaptic endings in the posterior pituitary gland; the posterior pituitary hormones are released in response to the activation of these neurons by nerve impulses. These two components—the anterior and posterior pituitary hormones—constitute the neuroendocrine system, described in more detail below.

Hormones from the adrenal medulla, principally adrenaline, are released by direct nerve stimulation from the autonomic nervous system. They play a major role in mobilizing energy stores during the "fight or flight" response and they cause peripheral vasoconstriction and increase heart rate and blood pressure.

Hormones of the pancreas, thyroid, and cells within the gut are involved with metabolism; they are regulated for the most part by a combination of nervous and hormonal agents. Insulin and glucagon from the pancreas regulate glucose homeostasis. Parathyroid hormone and calcitonin control calcium and mineral balance. Hormones of the gut are involved in regulating satiety. The renin-angiotensin system of the kidney and liver regulates the production of aldosterone from the adrenal cortex, which, in turn, promotes retention of sodium by the kidney and regulates salt appetite via the brain.

Neuroendocrinology

Neuroendocrinology studies the relationships between the endocrine system and the brain, including all of the hormone systems mentioned above that are regulated by innervation from the autonomic nervous system. Part of neuroendocrinology deals with regulation of hormone release, whereas another aspect concerns the actions of hormones to produce changes in brain function and behavior.

Regulation of hormone secretion involves both neural control of the hypothalamic neurons that produce hormones as well as hormone feedback. Negative feedback acts like a thermostat and turns down hormone secretion. Postive feedback, which operates in controlling ovulation, primes the neuroendocrine system to produce a large bolus of luteinizing hormone, which is the stimulus for ovulation. Nerve cells in the hypothalamus produce hormones, called releasing factors, which are released into a portal blood supply and travel to the anterior pituitary gland where they trigger the release of trophic hormones such as adrenocorticotrophic hormone (ACTH), thyroid stimulating hormone (TSH), luteinizing hormone (LH), follicle stimulating hormone (FSH), prolactin and growth hormone (see Table 1). These hormones, in turn, regulate endocrine responses—for example, ACTH stimulates cortisol secretion by the adrenal cortex; TSH, thyroid hormone secretion; and LH stimulates sex hormone production.

Other hypothalamic neurons produce the hormones vasopressin and oxytocin and release these hormones at nerve terminals located in the posterior lobe of the pituitary gland. Brain activity stimulates the secretion of these hormones. For example, oxytocin and prolactin release are stimulated by suckling, and the sight and sound of an infant can stimulate "milk let-down" in the mother; ACTH secretion is driven by stressful experiences and by an internal clock in the brain that is entrained by the light-dark cycle; and LH and FSH secretion are influenced by season of the year in some animals and by sexual activity in many species.

As far as hormone actions are concerned, the brain controls the endocrine system through the hypothalamus and pituitary gland, and the secretions of the gonads, adrenals, and thyroid act upon tissues throughout the body, and on the brain and pituitary, to produce a wide variety of effects. Some hormone effects occur during development and are generally long-lasting and even permanent for the life of the individual. Other hormone actions take place in the mature nervous system and are usually reversible. Still other hormone actions in adult life are related to permanent changes in brain function associated with disease processes or with aging.

ENDOCRINE SYSTEMS. Table 1. Hormones

Hypothalamic Hormones	Anterior Pituitary Hormones
Hypotrophin releasing factor	Adrenocorticotrophic hormone (ACTH)
Thyroid hormone releasing factor	Thyroid stimulating hormone (TSH)
Luteinizing hormone releasing factor	Luteinizing hormone (LH)
Somatostatin, growth hormone releasing factor	Follicle stimulating hormone (FSH)
Dopamine	Growth hormone (GH)
	Prolactin

Peripheral Target Hormones	Posterior Pituitary Hormones
Cortisol (ACTH)	Oxytocin
Thyroid hormone (TSH)	Vasopressin
Testosterone (LH)	
Estradiol (LH)	
Progesterone (LH)	
Somatomedins (GH)	

Some Other Hormones

Renin
Angiotensin
Aldosterone
Parathyroid hormone
Insulin
Glucagon
Calcitonin
Melatonin
Adrenaline

Mechanism of Hormone Action

Steroid hormones and thyroid hormone act on cells throughout the body via intracellular receptors that regulate gene expression. Such intracellular receptors are found heterogeneously distributed in many organs and tissue of the body, and they are also found in the brain, with each hormone having a unique regional pattern of localization across brain regions. The hypothalamus and amygdala have receptors for sex hormones, with both sexes expressing receptors for androgens, estrogens, and progestins, although, because of sexual differentiation, there are somewhat different amounts of these receptors expressed in male and female brains. The hippocampus and amygdala have receptors for adrenal steroids, whereas thyroid hormone receptors are widely distributed throughout the nervous system, particularly in the forebrain and cerebellum.

Effects mediated by intracellular receptors are generally slow in onset over minutes to hours and long lasting because alterations in gene expression produce effects on cells that can last for hours and days, or longer. Steroid hormones also produce rapid effects on the membranes of many brain cells via cell surface receptors that are like the receptors for neurotransmitters. These actions are rapid in onset and short in duration; however, the precise nature of the receptors for these rapid effects is in most cases largely unknown.

Actions of hormones that are amino acid derivatives, like epinephrine, or peptides, like corticotrophin releasing hormone, or proteins like ACTH and the gonadotrophins involves cell surface receptors that are linked to intracellular second messenger systems, like cyclic AMP or phospholipase C. The activation of these intracellular second messenger systems results in phosphorylation of enzymes, ion channels, and gene-regulatory proteins, which become more or less potent in doing their jobs when they are in the phosphorylated state.

Developmental Action of Hormones

Thyroid hormone and sex hormones act early in life to regulate development and differentiation of the brain, whereas the activity of the stress hormone axis is programmed by early experiences via mechanisms that may depend to some degree on the actions of glucocorticoid hormones.

Both excesses and deficiencies of thyroid hormone secretion are associated with altered brain development. Extremes in thyroid hormone secretion lead to major deficiencies in cognitive function (e.g., cretinism), whereas smaller deviations in thyroid hormone secretion are linked to more subtle individual variations in brain function and cognitive activity.

Sex hormones play an important role in development and sexual differentiation. Testosterone secretion during mid gestation in the human male and then again during the first two years of postnatal life alters brain development and affects cognitive function as well as reproductive function. Other mammals have comparable periods of testosterone production in early development. In genetic females, the lack of testosterone leads to the female behavioral and body phenotype. Likewise, the absence of androgen receptors in the testicular feminizing mutation leads to a feminine phenotype. Exposure of genetic females to androgens early in development produces a masculine phenotype. Sexual differentiation of the brain involves subtle sex differences in a variety of brain structures, ranging from the hypothalamus (which governs reproduction along with many other processes) to the hippocampus and cerebral cortex (which subserve cognitive function). Though less well studied, the human brain undergoes functional and structural sexual differentiation that are similar to those found in lower animals. This includes subtle effects upon cognitive function. For example, sex differences are found in the strategies used for spatial learning and memory, with males using the more global spatial cues and females relying upon the local contextual cues.

Stress and stress hormones play a role in brain development. Early experience has a profound role in shaping the reactivity of the stress hormone axis and the secretion not only of ACTH and glucocorticoids but also the activity of the autonomic nervous system. Prenatal stress and certain types of aversive experience in infant rodents (e.g., several hours of separation from the mother) increase reactivity of the stress hormone axis for the lifetime of the individual. In contrast, handling of newborn rat pups, which is a much briefer form of separation of the pup from the mother, produces a life-long reduction in activity of the stress hormone axis. Actions of glucocorticoid and thyroid hormones play a role in these effects. There is growing evidence for rodents that elevated stress hormone activity over a life time increases the rate of brain aging, whereas a life-time of reduced stress hormone activity reduces the rate of brain aging.

Activational Effects of Hormones

Whereas the actions of hormones on the embryonic and neonatal brain are confined to windows of early development and also, later on, in the peripubertal period, most of the same hormone produce reversible effects on brain structure and function throughout the life of the mature nervous system. Sex hormones activate reproductive organs as well as reproductive behaviors, including defense of territory, courtship, and mating, and they regulate neuroendocrine function to ensure successful reproduction; however, reflecting sexual differentiation of the brain and secondary sex characteristics of the body, the activational effects of sex hormones in adult life are often gender specific.

Thyroid hormone actions maintain normal neuronal excitability and promote a normal range of nerve cell structure and function; excesses or insufficiencies of thyroid hormone have adverse effects on brain function and cognition, which are largely reversible. Among these effects are an exacerbation of depressive illness by the hyperthyroid state.

There are two types of adrenal steroids—mineralocorticoids and glucocorticoids—which regulate salt intake and food intake, respectively, and also modulate metabolic and cognitive function during the diurnal cycle of activity and rest. Adrenal steroids act to maintain homeostasis, and glucocorticoids do so in part by opposing, or containing, the actions of other neural systems that are activated by stress and also by promoting adaptation of the brain to repeatedly stressful experiences. Containment effects of glucocorticoids oppose stress-induced activity of the noradrenergic arousal system and the hypothalamic system that releases ACTH from the pituitary.

Primary targets of stress hormones are the hippocampal formation and also the amygdala. Repeated stress causes atrophy of hippocampal pyramidal neurons and inhibits the replacement of neurons of the dentate gyrus by ongoing neurogenesis. Adrenal steroid hormones produce biphasic effects on cognitive function, enhancing episodic and declarative memory at low to moderate levels but inhibiting these same functions at high levels or after acute stress. Along with adrenal steroids, the sympathetic nervous system participates in creating the powerful memories associated with traumatic events, in which the amygdala plays an important role. Glucocorticoid hormones act in both the amygdala and hippocampus to promote consolidation of fear-related memory traces.

Hormone Action in Pathophysiology and Disease

Hormones participate in many disease processes, in some cases as protectors and in other cases as promoters of abnormal function. Estrogens enhance normal declarative and episodic memory in estrogen-deficient women, and estrogen replacement therapy appears to reduce the risk of Alzheimer's disease in postmenopausal women. Estrogens also have antidepressant effects. They modulate pain mechanisms, and they regulate the neural pathways involved in movement, with the result that estrogens enhance performance of fine motor skills and enhance reaction times in a driving simulation test in women. Androgen effects are less well studied in these regards. Adrenal steroids exacerbate neural damage from strokes and seizures and mediate damaging effects of severe and prolonged stress, and this leads to a consideration of stress.

The Physiology and Pathophysiology of Stress

Stress is an aspect of neuroendocrinology that has far reaching implications for health and disease. Stress may be defined as a threat, real or implied, to the psychological or physiological integrity of an individual. Because psychological and physiological systems are linked through the brain, the behavioral and physiological consequences of stress reflect two sides of the same coin. Developmental process, experiences, genetic factors, and the actions of hormones on the brain, however, combine to produce large differences among individuals in how they react to stress.

Stress involves a stressor and a stress response. A stressor may be physical, such as trauma or injury, or physical exertion, particularly when the body is being forced to operate beyond its capacity. Physical stressors include environmental factors like noise, overcrowding, excessive heat or cold. Stressors also include primarily psychological experiences such as traumatic life events as well as daily hassles in the family and workplace, but these stressors have real physiological consequences such as increased blood pressure and altered metabolism. Job stress, both physical and mental, is among the most important stressors that exacerbate disease.

Stress responses include both behavior and the responses of physiological systems, particularly the autonomic nervous system and the adrenocortical system. Behavioral responses to stress may get the individual out of trouble, but they may also exacerbate the consequences of stress. In the latter category are behaviors that confront and exacerbate the stressful circumstances, as well as self-damaging behaviors like smoking, drinking, and driving an automobile recklessly.

Physiological stress responses include primarily the activation of the autonomic nervous system and the hypothalamo-pituitary-adrenal (HPA) axis. There are two important features of the physiological stress response. The first is turning it on in amounts that are adequate to the challenge; the second is turning it off when it is no longer needed. The physiological mediators of the stress response, namely, the catecholamines of the sympathetic nervous system and the glucocorticoids from the adrenal cortex, initiate cellular events that promote adaptive changes in cells and tissues throughout the body that in turn protect the organism and promote survival.

Physiological stress responses produce not only protective and adaptive changes, but they also can promote disease processes, particularly when the stress response is stimulated frequently or when it does not shut off or habituate when it is not needed. The price of adapation, involving wear and tear on the body and promotion of pathophysiological changes, has been called "allostatic load." Allostasis, meaning achieving stability through change, refers to the process of physiological adaptation, and allostatic load refers to a gradual process of incremental change. Examples of allostatic load include the exacerbation of atherosclerosis by psychosocial stress, stress-induced acceleration of abdominal obesity, hypertension and coronary heart disease resulting from job strain, bone calcium loss in depressive illness and as a result of intensive athletic training, atrophy and damage to nerve cells in the hippocampus with accompanying memory impairment.

The brain and behavior play an important role in determining what is stressful, and the brain is a target of stress. The brain interprets what is stressful on the basis of past experience of the individual and then determines the behavioral response—whether to flee or to fight or to engage in displacement behaviors such as smoking and drinking that are themselves harmful. The brain is also a target of stress, which increases activity of systems that subserve fear (the amygdala) and impairs systems that subserve declarative, episodic, spatial, and contextual memory (the hippocampus). One of the most important aspects of stress that is related to disease is the sense of control. Learned helplessness is a condition that has been described in animals and humans and represents one type of coping mechanism. Less extreme, the lack of control on the job has been shown to have adverse health consequences, affecting rates of cardiovascular disease. Interventions that have increased the sense of control and reduced time pressures have increased physical and mental health.

Hormone Effects Related to Aging

The vulnerability of many systems of the body to stress is influenced by experiences early in life. In animal models, unpredictable prenatal stress causes increased emotionality and increased reactivity of the HPA axis and autonomic nervous system and these effects last throughout the lifespan. Postnatal handling in rats, a mild stress involving brief daily separation from the mother, counteracts the effects of prenatal stress and results in reduced emotionality and reduced reactivity reactivity of the HPA axis and autonomic nervous system and these effects also last throughout the life span. The vulnerability of the hippocampus to age-related loss of function parallels these effects—prenatal stress increasing and postnatal handling decreasing the rate of brain aging.

Age-related decline of gonadal function reduces the beneficial and protective actions of these hormones on brain function. At the same time, age-related increases in adrenal steroid activity promotes age-related changes in brain cells that can culminate in neuronal damage or cell death. Life-long patterns of adrenocortical function, determined by early experience, contribute to rates of brain aging, at least in experimental animals.

Conclusion

Hormones are mediators of change, acting in large part by regulating the activity of enzymes and ion channels and, in part, by modulating expression of the genetic code. They provide an interface between structure and function of the brain and other organs and tissues and experiences of the individual, including the regular changes in season of the year and day and night, as well as traumatic and stressful events. Hormone action during development and in adult life participates in the processes that determine individual differences in physiology, behavior and cognitive function, and helps, along with the genetic endowment, to determine the risk for a variety of diseases.

Bibliography

Adkins-Regan, E. (1981). Early organizational effects of hormones. In N. T. Adler (Ed.), *Neuroendocrinology of reproduction* (pp. 159–228). New York: Plenum Press.

Conn, P. M., & Melmud, S. (Eds.). (1997). *Endocrinology: Basic and clinical principles.* Totowa, NJ: Humana Press.

Kimura, D. (1992). Sex differences in the brain. *Scientific American, 267,* 119–125.

McEwen, B. S. (1991). Non-genomic and genomic effects of steroids on neural activity. *Trends in Pharmacological Sciences, 12,* 141–147.

McEwen, B. S. (1994). Endocrine effects on the brain and their relationship to behavior. In G. Siegel (Ed.), *Basic neurochemistry: Molecular, cellular and medical aspects* (5th ed., pp. 1003–1023). New York: Raven Press.

McEwen, B. S. (1995). In F. E. Bloom & D. J. Kupfer (Eds.), *Neuroendocrine interactions in psychopharmacology: The fourth generation of progress* (pp. 705–718). New York: Raven Press.

McEwen, B. S. (1998). Protective and damaging effects of stress mediators. *New England Journal of Medicine, 338,* 171–179.

McEwen, B. S., Albeck, D., Cameron, H., Chao, H., Gould, E., Hastings, N., Kuroda, Y., Luine, V., Magarinos, A. M., McKittrick, C. R., Orchinik, M., Pavlides, C., Vaher, P., Watanabe, Y., & Weiland, N. (1995). Stress and the brain: A paradoxical role for adrenal steroids. *Vitamins and Hormones, 51,* 371–402.

McEwen, B. S., Gould, E., Orchinik, M., Weiland, N. G., & Woolley, C. S. (1995). Oestrogens and the structural and functional plasticity of neurons: Implications for memory, ageing, and neurodegenerative processes. *Ciba Foundation Symposium 191,* 52–73.

McEwen, B. S., Sakai, R., Spencer, R. (1993). Adrenal steroid effects on the brain: Versatile hormones with good and bad effects. In J. Schulkin (Ed.), *Hormonally induced changes in mind and brain* (pp. 157–189). San Diego: Academic Press.

McEwen, B. S., & Sapolsky, R. M. (1995). Stress and cognitive function. *Current Opinion in Neurobiology, 5,* 205–216.

McGaugh, J. L., Cahill, L., & Roozendaal, B. (1996). Involvement of the amygdala in memory storage: Interaction with other brain systems. *Proceedings of the National Academy of Sciences USA 93,* 13,508–13,514.

Meaney, M. J., Tannenbaum, B., Francis, D., Bhatnagar, S., Shanks, N., Viau, V., O'Donnell, D., & Plotsky, P. M. (1994). Early environmental programming hypothalamic-pituitary-adrenal responses to stress. *Seminars in the Neurosciences 6,* 247–259.

Purifoy, F. (1981). Endocrine-environment interaction in human variability. *Annual Review of Anthropology 10,* 141–162.

Sapolsky, R. (1992). *Stress, the aging brain, and the mechanisms of neuron death.* Cambridge: MIT Press.

Tallal, P., & McEwen, B. S. (Eds.). (1991). Special issue: Neuroendocrine effects on brain development and cognition. *Psychoneuroendocrinology 16,* 1–3.

Bruce S. McEwen

ENDORPHINS. Morphine can produce powerful analgesia and intensely pleasurable sensations. In the early 1970s, this opiate drug was found to act at specialized receptors in the brain and in peripheral tissues. This finding fueled a search for substances, produced within the body, that not only attached to those receptors, but that also precipitated similar pain-killing and euphoric effects. As reported in *Nature* (1975, *258,* 577–580), Hughes, Smith, Kosterlitz, and other researchers at St. Andrew's University in Scotland isolated the first two of these substances from the brain tisssue of pigs.

In the ensuing years, additional endogenous opioid (opiatelike) compounds were discovered. The term *endorphin,* meaning "the morphine within" is often used generically to refer to all substances produced in the body that have opioid properties. However, endorphins are actually classified within three families or categories: enkephalins, endorphins, and dynorphins. These families are structurally similar, but differ in terms of their distribution within the nervous system and their genetic and biochemical precursors. Although regulatory (e.g., temperature, cardiovascular, and respiration) and other functions have been proposed for endorphins, their involvement in "natural" pain control and pleasure systems has received the most research attention

Endorphins and Analgesia

It is well established that analgesia can be elicited, without administration of exogenous opiates or other drugs, by a wide variety of aversive environmental stimuli. A common test for the involvement of endorphins in the production of this stimulation- or stress-induced analgesia (SIA) assesses the extent to which drugs (e.g., naloxone or naltrexone) that antagonize or block the pain-killing effects of exogenous opiates have similar effects on SIA. The literature on SIA refers to naloxone- or naltrexone-sensitive SIA as opioid mediated and SIA that is insensitive to these drugs as nonopioid mediated. Shock, centrifugal rotation, cold swims, food deprivation, restraint, and exposure to innate predators are among the events shown to produce a naloxone- or naltrexone-reversible SIA in rats. Furthermore, opioid-mediated analgesia can be produced by conditioned stimuli (CSs) that are associated with shock or other aversive stimuli following training with Pavlovian procedures.

Evidence for opioid mediation of SIA has not been obtained consistently or under all conditions. Several generalizations have been offered in an attempt to identify factors that produce opioid and nonopioid forms of SIA. According to the severity hypothesis (M. Fanselow, *Behavioral Neuroscience*, 1984, 98, 79–95), opioid mediation of SIA is confined to relatively weak (e.g., low intensity, short duration) aversive stimulation. Nonopioid analgesia becomes more likely as the severity of aversive stimulation increases. Alternatively, J. Grau (*Behavioral Neuroscience*, 1987, 101, 272–288) interpreted SIA within the sometimes opponent process (SOP) model of animal memory proposed in 1981 by the American learning theorist A. Wagner. According to the SOP model, when a painful stimulus first occurs, it is represented in the "A1 state" of working memory before gradually decaying into the A2 memory state. Furthermore, Pavlovian CSs that are associated with painful stimuli activate the memory of those aversive events directly into the A2 state, bypassing the A1 state. According to Grau, memories of aversive stimuli evoke nonopioid SIA when they reside in the A1 state, and evoke opioid-mediated SIA when they reside in the A2 state. A third view, offered by L. Watkins and collaborators (*Brain Research*, 1982, 243, 119–132), also proposes that the opioid form of conditioned analgesia is elicited by Pavlovian CSs that signal shock. In contrast, only shock that is confined to certain bodily locations, such as the hind paws, evokes an unconditioned, nonopioid analgesia.

Endorphins and Pleasure

Endorphins have been linked to the production of pleasurable sensations such as those accompanying sexual activity and food intake. It is also claimed that endorphins underlie the occurrence of certain behavioral addictions in humans, based on mechanisms similar to those that support opiate drug addiction. For example, intense physical exercise is often reported to produce euphoria (e.g., runner's "high") that is subject to both tolerance (reduced euphoria with repeated stimulation) and to the unpleasant consequences of withdrawal should the opportunity to maintain the addictive behavioral regimen be denied. These phenomena are viewed by some as the manifestation of addiction to endorphins. Furthermore, mood disorders such as depression have been attributed to impaired endorphin system functioning. Unfortunately, evidence for such claims has often been anecdotal or based on studies that lack the controls necessary for unambiguous interpretation of the findings.

More direct evidence for the involvement of endorphins in pleasure systems has been provided by experiments with animal subjects. Rats learn to perform responses (e.g., lever pressing) that deliver small quantites of endorphins directly to the ventricles of the brain. Thus, these intracerebroventricular (ICV) infusions reinforce or reward conditioned responses that enable rats to self-administer endogenous opioids. Intracerebroventricular administration of β-endorphin (a specific subtype of endogenous opioid) also supports "place conditioning" in rats. In place conditioning the rewarding or reinforcing effects of opioids are demonstrated to the extent that animals prefer a place where the effects of the opioids were experienced relative to a place that is not associated with those effects.

Intracerebroventricular infusion of opioids also stimulates food intake, whereas administration of opiate antagonists has been shown to reduce feeding and drinking. Rather than influencing hunger or satiety, S. J. Cooper and T. C. Kirkham suggest that endorphins mediate the palatability or reward value of food. This suggestion is based, in part, on findings that preference for highly palatable tastes is enhanced by administration of opioid peptides and reduced by opiate antagonists, whereas these treatments have little effect on responding for neutral or nonpreferred tastes.

Research has also been directed toward specification of the brain areas involved with the rewarding effects of endorphins. There is much evidence that the dopamine pathways in the mesolimbic system of the brain mediate the rewarding properties of not only opiates, but of other drugs of abuse, such as cocaine and amphetamine. According to Spangel, Herz, and Shippenberg (*Proceedings of the National Academy of Sciences of the United States of America*, 1992, 89, 2046–2050) the role of endogenous opiates in reward and motivation is based on their ability to modulate the activation of this dopamine reward circuit.

Bibliography

Akil, H., Bronstein, D., & Mansour, A. (1988). Overview of the endogenous opioid systems: Anatomical, biochemical, and functional issues. In R. J. Rodgers & S. J. Cooper (Eds.), *Endorphins, opiates, and behavioral processes* (pp. 1–23). New York: Wiley.

Cooper, S. J., & Kirkham, T. C. (1993). Opioid mechanisms in the control of food consumption and taste preferences. In A. Herz (Ed.), *Handbook of experimental pharmacology* (Vol. 104/II, pp. 239–262). Berlin: Springer.

Hawkes, C. H. (1992). Endorphins: The basis of pleasure? *Journal of Neurology, Neurosurgery, & Psychiatry, 55,* 247–250.

Olson, G. A., Olson, R. D., & Kastin, A. J. (1996). Endogenous opiates: 1995. *Peptides, 17,* 1421–1466.

Pert, C. B., & Snyder, S. H. (1973). Opiate receptor: Demonstration in nervous tissue. *Science, 179,* 1011–1014.

Tseng, L. F. (Ed.). (1995). *The pharmacology of opioid peptides.* Harwood Academic.

Wagner, A. R. (1981). SOP: A model of automatic memory processing animal behavior. In N. Spear & R. Miller (Eds.), *Information processing in animals: Memory mechanisms* (pp. 5–47). Hillsdale, NJ: Erlbaum.

Terry L. Davidson

ENDSTAGE RENAL DISEASE. Chronic renal failure, or, in other words, the gradual deterioration of kidney function, can be caused by many diseases and conditions. Some of these diseases are localized only in the kidneys, while others are generalized and also attack other organs or systems. Some of these diseases are hereditary while others are acquired. Whatever the cause of chronic renal failure, the outcome is always bad, that is, death.

During the 1960s, machines were introduced to replace the functioning of the kidneys. The term *end stage renal disease* (ESRD) was introduced to describe that final and terminal phase in which replacement therapy was required to sustain life. The introduction of replacement therapy, or as one should now say, replacement therapies, was a major breakthrough in medicine. For the first time, machines could replace the functions of a vital and complicated internal organ. It also fired the excitement and imagination of the behavior scientists. Here was a group of patients "alive after they should have been dead" and having machine-dependent life.

Every year, about 50 to 60 people per 1 million reach ESRD and require replacement therapy—tens of thousands of people survive by renal replacement therapies. Basically, there are three modes of replacement. The oldest and still the most common in most countries is hemodialysis. In this treatment, the patient is "hooked" to a machine, the blood circulates through the machine, and the waste products, as well as excess fluids, are taken out, that is, dialyzed. The early machines were big and inefficient, and patients had to have dialysis 24 to 26 hours a week. The whole process has since become much more efficient. Dialysis hours

per week have been reduced to about 12 and the problems of severe anemia that accompanied dialysis have been solved. Still, patients are severely restricted in fluid intake as well as in protein and potassium intake. Most important of all, their lives depend on being connected to the machine three times a week, forever.

The second mode of replacement therapy is peritoneal dialysis, and the most common form of this is the continuous ambulatory peritoneal dialysis (CAPD). The basic idea in this treatment is that the peritoneum—a kind of curtain inside the abdomen—can do the dialysis of waste products, like the membranes in the machines of hemodialysis. Thus, fluids are introduced into the abdomen and later taken out, and so on. Broadly speaking, in CAPD the patients are not machine dependent and are less restricted in their diet, but are highly exposed to infection.

The third replacement therapy is kidney transplantation, with more than 90% being cadaver transplant and the rest involving living, usually related, donors. Great progress has also been made in this replacement, especially with the introduction of cyclosporine, which decreases, though it does not abolish, the problem of rejection.

Many people are alive by virtue of one or another of the renal replacement therapies. For example, in Japan the prevalence of ESRD treatment is more than 700 per 1 million; in the United States it is more than 600 per 1 million, and in Germany more than 500 per 1 million. Yet from the very beginning, these treatments have raised a host of problems that have not become less acute. Only two areas, resources and their allocation, and patients' psychological condition, are briefly reviewed here.

Allocation of Resources

From the beginning of hemodialysis in the early 1960s, resources were not sufficient, and behavior scientists were involved in a selection process. One of the early solutions was to determine the patient's "value to society." This was unacceptable to many, and a "first come, first served" policy was adopted. However, contrary to some events in medicine that are acute (e.g., one can state exactly the day and hour when a myocardial infarct occurred), chronic renal failure and ESRD is often a question of weeks and months. Thus, a patient can be taken on dialysis weeks earlier and at times months later. A third policy has been to allocate the limited facilities to patients with the best chances to survive. Thus, patients with life-threatening diseases, for example, cancer or severe heart disease, were excluded, as well as the elderly. An effort was made to exclude patients who would shorten their survival by their behavior. Some of the very early studies have a reportedly high rate of suicide in dialysis patients, and many studies describe severe compliance problems with the strict diet. Therefore, the idea was to exclude these patients. It is possible, although very costly, to predict patients' compliance as well as psychological and psychiatric complications. However, no study succeeded in predicting patients' survival by their pre-ESRD-treatment behavior or personality.

The resources have increased dramatically over the years, at least in the developed countries, and the basic, impossible question of who should be given a chance to live has disappeared. Yet some resource allocation problems are still very acute.

Patients' Psychological Condition

Many studies have described the psychological problems of ESRD patients. Though not specific to ESRD, these problems are more extreme than in other chronic diseases. One should mention the loss of control because life is machine dependent, the severe body image problems caused by transplantation, the bloating up because of peritoneal dialysis or of having to accommodate the machine. One should also mention the very strict diet in hemodialysis and the constant threat of infection in CAPD and that of rejection in transplantation. This is a population that has had many losses—loss of control and freedom, vigor, looks, and often potency, loss of income, and often social status. Therefore, it is not surprising that it was often stated that about 25% of patients are moderately to severely depressed.

In the earlier years, studies concentrated on psychological reaction and psychiatric complications. Later, the focus shifted to quality of life (QOL), though the definition and/or assessment of this concept is no easier. Hundreds of papers were published about the QOL of ESRD patients but still little is known about the factors that influence it.

There is no doubt that comorbidity, especially diabetes, which is so common in ESRD, decreases QOL. Some, but not all, reported poorer QOL in women than in men, and some reported lower QOL in the elderly. It seems that patients with higher education and higher incomes have better QOL. On the other hand, in the United States, Whites seem to have poorer QOL than Blacks.

The question of whether the QOL is influenced by the mode of treatment is crucial. There has not been even one study that has randomized the patients between the modes of treatment or between the three major modes of treatment—hemodialysis, CAPD, and transplantation. Furthermore, only a few longitudinal studies have followed up patients as they transferred from one mode of treatment to another. The typical study is a cross-sectional one, often of a not very large group and often not controlling for case mix and for comorbidity. Nonetheless, the general impression is that transplanted patients are happier than dialysis patients. However, it seems that the superiority of transplanta-

tion is only minimal when case mix is controlled. At the same time, many dialysis patients wish to have transplantation. One could claim that their expectations are not realistic, yet there is not even one study of transplanted patients wishing to go back to dialysis.

One additional issue should be addressed, and that is the dissociation between the medical condition of the patients and their QOL. Nowadays, hemodialysis is shorter and better than it was in the 1960s, but not the QOL of the patients. That can be explained possibly by differences in case mix and/or comorbidity. There is no such simple explanation for the limited effects of erythropoietin. There is no doubt that this drug solved the problem of anemia and improved the physical functioning and vigor of the patients. However, this was not followed by improved rates of employment, and only little, if any, improvement was found in patients' psychological conditions.

In summary, one could say that it is now more than 30 years since ESRD and its therapies have graduated from experimental treatments to accepted medical treatment. Many thousands of papers have been written, and some of the excitement of machine-dependent life has died. The medical, surgical, and technical aspects have vastly improved, with no concomitant improvement in patients' QOL. Furthermore, the problems of allocation of resources, which modes of therapy are better and for whom, and what factors enhance or reduce patients' QOL are as acute today as they were in the early days of ESRD.

Bibliography

Abram, H. S., Moore, G. I., & Westervelt, F. B. (1971). Suicidal behavior in chronic dialysis patients. *American Journal of Psychiatry, 127,* 1199–1202.

De-Nour Kaplan, A., & Czaczkes, J. W. (1976). The influence of patients' personality on adjustment to chronic disease. *Journal of Nervous and Mental Disease, 162,* 323–333.

Evans, R. W. (1991). Recombinant human erythropoietin and the quality of life of endstage renal disease patients: A comparative analysis. *American Journal of Kidney Disease, 18,* 62–70.

Evans, R. W. (1985). The quality of life of patients with endstage renal disease. *New England Journal of Medicine, 312,* 553–559.

Gokal, R. (1993). Quality of life of patients undergoing renal replacement therapy. *Kidney International, 40,* 23S–27S.

Hart, L. G., & Evans R. W. (1987). The functional status of ESRD patients as measured by the sickness impact profile. *Journal of Chronic Disease, 40,* 117S–130S.

Kurtin, P., Nissenson, A. R. (1993). Variation in endstage renal disease outcomes: What we know, what we should know, and how do we find it out. *Journal of American Social Nephrology, 3,* 1738–1747.

Laupacis, A., Wong, C., Churchill, D., and the Canadian erythropoietin study group (1991). The use of generic and specific quality of life measures in hemodialysis patients treated with erythropoietin. *Controlled Clinical Trial, 12,* 168S–179S.

Levenson, J. L., Glocheskis (1991). Psychological factors affecting endstage renal disease: A review. *Psychosomatics, 32,* 382–389.

Simmons, R. G., Anderson C. R., Abress, L. K. (1990). Quality of life and rehabilitation differences among four endstage renal disease therapy groups. *Scandinavian Urology and Nephrology 131* (Suppl.), 7–22.

USRDS Annual Data Report. (1993). Prevalence and cost of ESRD therapy. *American Journal of Kidney Disease, 22,* 22–29.

A. Kaplan-DeNour

ENEMY IMAGE. When people look at other political groups, they assess them. What kind of group is it? More importantly, what are its motivations toward my group? Is it threatening or does it offer the opportunity to achieve some goal? As these questions are answered, people classify other groups into images. Images are similar to stereotypes. They are bundles of knowledge about, and feelings toward, groups commonly found in a person's environment.

The image concept has been used in political psychology as an analytical device for many years (Boulding, 1956; Finlay, Holsti & Fagen, 1967; White, 1968; Jervis, 1976). It is now the foundation of a general theory of political psychology called image theory. Drawing on studies of cognition, political psychologists have argued that people must organize and simplify their political environments as they do any other environment. The world is too complex to be understood in its entirety, so we simplify it by organizing it into cognitive categories, or images. Images are used to filter information, make sense of the actions of others, and guide the perceiver in determining a course of action.

In political psychology the image concept is most frequently used to examine perceptions of other countries in international politics. In that context it is argued that images of types of states, such as enemies and allies, are the cognitive organizing devices that serve as information filters. The image of the enemy is not necessarily restricted to international politics, however, and there is increasing interest in using that image and others to analyze conflict in the domestic politics of multiethnic and multinational states. Indeed, the concept of the enemy image may even be useful in analyses of gang violence and competition.

What is the enemy image? The enemy image, in its ideal-typical form, is an image of a country that is highly threatening, relatively equal to the perceiver's state in capability and cultural sophistication, mono-lithic in decision making (that is, a small elite makes decisions), and highly rational to the point of being able to generate and orchestrate multiple complex conspiracies (R. W. Cottam, 1977; R. K. Herrmann, 1985). Emotions associated with the enemy image include fear, distrust, anger, and, when the image is very intense and salient, hatred. Most Americans saw the Soviet Union in these terms during the Cold War as well as Hilter's Germany during World War II. Countries perceived as inferior in capability and/or culture are not, by definition, perceived as enemies, even if their intentions are considered hostile. Thus, neither Saddam Hussein's Iraq, nor Fidel Castro's Cuba, fits the image. Instead, they would belong to variants of what is referred to as the colonial image.

When a country, or any political group, is perceived as an enemy, it is assumed to have the above characteristics and intentions toward the perceiver's country. Interactions with the country are then largely determined on the basis of the characteristics associated with the image, rather than the true characteristics of the country in question. Information about a country that is consistent with the preexisting image is accepted as correct, while inconsistent information is rejected. Particular policy alternatives are also part of the image. The appeasement of an enemy, for example, is generally considered to be a foolish course of action.

There are different views regarding the origin of the image. Vamik Volkan (1988) examines the enemy image from a psychoanalytic perspective and believes that enemies are psychologically necessary. The enemy image is a natural outgrowth of human psychological development, beginning with stranger anxiety in young children. Others rely on social cognitive psychology and argue that the enemy image exists only when it is useful in organizing one's environment (M. L. Cottam, 1986, 1992; Herrmann, Voss, Schooler, & Ciarrochi, 1997). If the international world regularly contains countries that fit the enemy image, people will be socialized to use the image and will be resistant to information indicating that that image is inappropriate for countries so perceived. The logic of this argument is supported by social identity theory, which has increasingly been used as another psychological foundation for the study of images (Druckman, 1994). The human propensity to form in-groups and out-groups would make the emergence of an enemy image very possible whenever intense threat is perceived to emanate from another country or group. Thus, the image is likely to emerge in the world views of observers of political arenas, but it is not inevitable.

The impact of the enemy image on behavioral predispositions is of central concern to political psychologists. Once a country or group is perceived through the enemy image, what policies are favored in dealing with the enemy? Clearly, since the enemy is equal in capabilities and cultural sophistication and is also highly rational, it is a formidable opponent. Because it is equal in capabilities and cultural sophistication, the odds are even that if it is challenged directly it cannot be defeated. Given its aggressive intentions, it also cannot be changed. Therefore, a policy of containment is logical. Containment involves avoiding direct confrontation, never permitting oneself the luxury of trusting the enemy, and preventing it from increasing its opportunities to attack or hurt you. This was the policy followed by the United States during the Cold War as one administration after another entered office with an enemy image of the Soviet Union.

Not all situations are simply bilateral, however. Image dynamics and policy predispositions change when an enemy is perceived as interfering in another country. If that other country is perceived through a childlike "colonial" image, as in many Americans' perceptions of countries and people in Latin America, the assumption is that they are inferior in terms of culture and capability, simple, inefficient, often corrupt, and generally in need of strong guidance by the perceiver's country. Given the calculating rationality and aggressive intentions accorded the enemy, the country seen as a colonial could never withstand the enemy's evil and clever machinations. In this kind of perceptual scenario, which occurred with great frequency during the Cold War, immediate action is necessary to prevent the colonial country from falling under the influence of the enemy. Rapid intervention is called for, using quick-acting instruments such as military or paramilitary forces. If time allows, a covert operation would be favored to eliminate local "agents" or sympathizers helping the enemy infiltrate the country in question.

Some studies of the impact of the enemy image on behavior have focused on variations in policy preferences when individuals in policy-making positions differ in the extent to which they perceive another country as fitting the enemy image. Generally, the less extreme the image, that is, the farther a person's enemy image of another actor is from the ideal-typical, the more willing the person is to take risks in negotiations with the enemy (Shimko, 1991). To date, studies of the enemy image and individual variations therein have focused only on the extremity of the image and have not examined other personality factors that would affect the policy preferences. This is a ripe area for theoretical cross-fertilization in political psychology.

Images do change. There have been several studies of the process of change in the American enemy image of the Soviet Union. The Soviet Union was increasingly perceived as less and less appropriately belonging to the enemy image after Mikhail Gorbachev came to power (Silverstein & Holt, 1989; M. L. Cottam, 1992). When the Soviet Union was no longer seen as an enemy, the Cold War was over. But images may change in a more

hostile direction as well. The logic of containment as a policy for dealing with an enemy was quite clear in the case of the U.S.-Soviet standoff during the Cold War. Interaction with an enemy group can remain at low emotional intensity levels more easily in interstate relations than in conflicts among enemy groups within a single country, which may occur in multiethnic states. Often in such situations, as Bosnia illustrates, people see themselves in terms of in-groups and out-groups but may live together without violence for years. When circumstances change and the perceived threat from the other groups increases, enemy images emerge. When people live cheek-to-jowl with those they fear and hate, the emotional intensity and sense of the proximity of a conflict over a group's very existence is much greater than in interstate conflicts, such as the Cold War. Thus, such conflicts can easily be overwhelmed by the emotional properties associated with enemies. With fear, hatred, and rage driving the response to an out-group now perceived as an enemy, and with actual acts of violence being committed the image itself shifts, and the group is increasingly seen not as an equal, but as a barbarian. Once this threshold is crossed, genocide is a serious possibility.

[See also International Relations; Peace; and War and Conflict.]

Bibliography

Boulding, K. (1956). *The image*. Ann Arbor, MI: University of Michigan Press. One of the earliest treatments of the concept of images.

Cottam, M. L. (1986). *Cognitive limitations and foreign policy decision making*. Boulder, CO: Westview Press. Contains a review of the cognitive psychology on which image theory rests.

Cottam, M. L. (1992). Contending dramas in American foreign policy. In M. L. Cottam & C.-y. Shih (Eds.), *Contending dramas: A cognitive approach to international organization*. New York: Praeger.

Cottam, R. W. (1977). *Foreign policy motivation: A general theory and a case study*. Pittsburgh, PA: University of Pittsburgh Press. This is the original presentation of image theory and its political psychological framework of analysis.

Druckman, D. (1994). Nationalism, patriotism, and group loyalty: A social psychological perspective. *Mershon International Studies Review, 38*, 43–68. A thorough review of the uses of social psychology in analyses of political group behavior.

Finlay, D., Holsti, O., & Fagen, R. (1967). *Enemies in politics*. Chicago, IL: Rand-McNally. Contains a case study of the enemy image of John Foster Dulles in the early years of the Cold War.

Herrmann, R. K. (1985). *Perceptions and behavior in Soviet foreign policy*. Pittsburgh, PA: University of Pittsburgh Press. An application of image theory in a non-

American case. Explores the Soviets' enemy image of the United States.

Herrman, R. K., Voss, J. F., Schooler, T., & Ciarrochi, J. (1997). Images in international relations: An experimental test of cognitive schemata. *International Studies Quarterly, 41,* 403–434.

Jervis, R. (1976). *Perception and misperception in international politics.* Princeton, NJ: Princeton University Press.

Shimko, K. (1991). *Images and arms control: Perceptions of the Soviet Union in the Reagan administration.* Ann Arbor, MI: University of Michigan Press.

Silverstein, B., & Holt, R. R. (1989). Research on enemy images: Present status and future prospects. *Journal of Social Issues, 45,* 159–175. Examines the diminution of the American enemy image of the Soviet Union.

Volkan, V. (1988). *The need to have enemies and allies.* Northvale, NJ: Aronson.

White, R. (1968). *Nobody wanted war: Misperception in Vietnam and other wars.* Garden City, NY: Doubleday.

Martha Cottam

ENGINEERING PSYCHOLOGY. *See* Human Factors Psychology.

ENGLAND. The study of historical and philosophical psychology in England has been marginalized over the last 30 years or so. This is because there has been a strong move to make psychology a truly scientific field of study. However, more recently it has been argued that psychology may be a very different science (Valentine, 1998) and that history and philosophy provide a necessary social and historical perspective to present-day psychological enquiry. Therefore, it seems we have come full circle, for the origins of modern-day English (and also British) psychology began, as we shall see, from a strong empirical philosophical base in the seventeenth century. Furthermore, up until the present, the development of English psychology has often benefited from historical analysis, as we periodically assess the merits and demerits of the key figures in psychology, such as Galton, Spearman, Burt, and, more recently, Eysenck.

The Philosophical Genesis of English Psychology

It was John Locke (1622–1704) who laid the foundations of empirical philosophy, which emphasized the role of experience in gaining knowledge for human beings. His position was strongly opposed to that of Descartes's notion of ideas being innate entities. Rather, the human mind, according to Locke, is like a blank sheet on which ideas first appear through our sensory system. For Locke, ideas or concepts are linked in a logical fashion and are part of a network of associations. The association of ideas is at the heart of Locke's philosophical position, which provided English psychology with a sound base from which to develop.

George Berkeley (1685–1753) overlaps Locke somewhat, strengthening the role of sensation as a key factor in explaining the nature of thinking. He provided a valuable source of ideas for investigating the field of perception for future English psychology, in which other areas, such as attention and visual and auditory perception, continue to be investigated.

Although David Hume (1711–1776) was a Scot, he had a profound influence on English psychology, as he probed more deeply into the validity of knowledge through experience. To Hume, there were two main sources of knowledge: first, through impressions (sensations), and secondly, through ideas that arise from what we perceive and how we organize what we perceive in the act of thinking. Unlike Berkeley, Hume reformulated Locke's view of human understanding by proposing so-called laws of association, which were implicit in Locke's original thinking on the subject. Hume, in effect, laid the basis for associationist psychological enquiry, setting the scene for a distinguished number of associationists to follow in his footsteps. The first of these was Hartley (1705–1757), a physician who provided a particular brand of associationism, which emphasized the physiological basis for explaining human behavior. Much of his ideas on the importance of vibrations that impinge on our senses, although somewhat sketchy in detail, were remarkably prescient of later twentieth-century neurological theory of brain behavior.

Like Hartley before him, James Mill (1773–1836) was a strong advocate of associationism in explaining human behavior. However, Mill's approach to human behavior was essentially one of classifying and analyzing mental phenomena. He interpreted behavior from the standpoint of philosophical associationism and was not comfortable explaining feelings through scientific observation and experimental approaches. Mill marks the zenith of English associationism.

John Stuart Mill (1806–1873), the son of James Mill, widened the concept of associationism to embrace a more chemical explanation of the mind. For J. S. Mill, association was not a mixture of components, but more like a compound bearing little resemblance to its original ingredients. At the end of the present century, chemical interpretations of mental states have once again emerged as neurochemistry, which is currently having a significant impact on explaining defects in brain functioning and its effect on behavior.

Establishing a Scientific Psychology

Alexander Bain (1818–1903), another Scot, made psychology a more scientific discipline in both in Scotland

and England. His training as a physiologist in Aberdeen enabled him to pioneer the link between physiology and psychology, which in turn influenced English psychology by becoming more scientific in its outlook. Bain's contribution marks a transition in the history of British psychology, forming a link between the dominant empirical philosophical tradition and the movement to make psychology a science. However, a number of Bain's contemporaries, such as James Ward (1843–1925) and Francis Galton (1822–1911), were to establish beyond any doubt that in England psychological enquiry would be characterized by strong scientific credentials. English psychology would be molded by the combined influences of Ward's idealistic philosophy and Darwin's evolutionary theory as interpreted by Galton.

Galton, the most important of Bain's contemporaries, left an indelible mark on English psychology with his work on individual differences and the use of statistics in measuring behavior. Darwin's theory of evolution was the catalyst which lead Galton to study the inheritance of abilities and especially the nature of genius. His first book on the subject, *Hereditary Genius* (1869), and his later publications on the development of human faculties were to prove a landmark not only in England, but in the United States, France, and Germany. His contribution to the field of individual differences was to have a major impact on American work in this area, mainly through that of James McKeen Cattell.

James Ward, the other of Bain's key contemporaries, worked at Cambridge, and together with his student George Stout (1860–1944), was to establish a philosophical tradition for English psychology which would replace associationism with philosophical idealism. Ward's views were influenced by the Scottish philosopher Thomas Reid and the German school of philosophy represented by Leibnitz and Immanuel Kant. While Ward and Stout were undoubtedly well disposed to the establishment of a scientific and experimental psychology in England, their philosophical position was to strongly influence English theoretical psychology, some would say even having a retarding effect on the advancement of scientific psychology until the start of World War II (Misiak & Sexton, 1966).

As we enter the next millennium the fact that English psychology is once again reflecting on its philosophical and historical traditions raises issues about the significance of the historical and philosophical roots of the subject. While Galton was the most influential and original of the late nineteenth-century figures to be responsible for the establishment of psychology as a scientific discipline in England, three other persons—Herbert Spencer, James Sully, and William H. R. Rivers—must also be seen as having played an important part in the development of the "new scientific psychology." Spencer (1820–1903), the author of *Principles of Psy-*

chology (1855) introduced evolutionism into English psychology, while Sully (1842–1923), a professor at University College, London, wrote *Outlines of Psychology* (1884), the first textbook of psychology to be published in the English language. In 1886, he published a simplified version of this text, entitled *The Teachers' Handbook of Psychology*. Sully will also be remembered for founding an experimental laboratory at University College, London, and pioneering the cause of child psychology as a field of psychological study.

William H. R. Rivers (1864–1922) played an important role in the development of experimental psychology in England. He originally trained as a physician and turned to psychology later in life. He injected an enduring sense of experimentalism into psychology, establishing the first and now famous experimental psychology laboratory in Cambridge in 1897. Rivers can be regarded as the first truly experimental psychologist of the English school.

The Twentieth Century

Unlike American psychology, the rise of psychology in England was slow. This was mainly attributable to the cautious and conservative attitudes of English universities, which did not consider psychology a serious discipline in the curriculum. The strong and continuing influence of philosophical psychology also contributed to the lack of progress in the subject. This was reflected especially in the older universities like Oxford and Cambridge, where there was a strong distrust (mainly by philosophers and theologians) of a subject that tried to approach the study of mental processes from a purely scientific point of view.

By the turn of the century the new scientific psychology had been launched along more experimental lines, much of it influenced by the German tradition. This tradition was reflected in the work of Sully, Rivers, William McDougall, and Charles Spearman, who either studied or were well acquainted with the famous German centers of experimental psychology. Galton's work, however, is representative of a key indigenous British influence, namely that of Darwinism. Galton's work on individual differences and his use of statistics to measure behavior meant that the stage was set for intensifying the drive to bring English psychology closer into the wider scientific community. Preparation for this had already begun with the work of Rivers, for he saw the need to train future psychologists to continue the experimental tradition, which he had initiated. He trained a cadre of future British experimental psychologists during his time at the Cambridge laboratory, among the most famous of whom was Charles S. Myers (1873–1947).

In 1912, Myers was appointed director of the Cambridge laboratory. He is remembered for his book *The Text-book of Experimental Psychology*, published in 1909 and considered to be the first text of its kind in the field. Myers laid great stress on psychophysical methods but was also aware of the importance of introspection in experimental psychology. He had great insight and a sense of clarity about his subject and was among the most able and balanced minds that have contributed to English psychology (Hearnshaw, 1964). His connection with Cambridge terminated with World War I, but not before he had firmly established the Cambridge laboratory on new premises.

Charles E. Spearman (1863–1945) is one of the great pioneers of English psychology, and he is often considered, along with Galton, to be a main protagonist of the correlational tradition, embracing statistical and measurement psychology. Spearman was trained in the German psychological tradition, having studied under Wundt in Leipzig, where he obtained his doctorate in 1904. He later studied physiology, also in Germany. In 1906 he returned to England and took a teaching appointment at University College, London, where he stayed until 1931. His best-known contributions are to statistics and the study of human abilities as part of a wider understanding of human intelligence. He enriched the correlational tradition by laying the fundamentals for factor analysis. In 1904, he published his ideas on a two-factor theory of intelligence. Spearman distinguished between a general ability factor, g, and a special abilities factor, s. His theory was to form the basis of much speculation, but it also provided English psychology with a basis for mental measurement.

A contemporary of Spearman was Karl Pearson (1857–1936), who also worked at University College, London, where he eventually occupied the chair of eugenics endowed earlier by Galton. Pearson was an ardent devotee of science and scientific method. His main contribution to English psychology was in the field of statistics. It is to Pearson that we owe the sustained use of correlation in psychology, and also the first-time use of terms such as *normal distribution, standard deviation,* and *chi squared* or *goodness of fit.* Pearson was to provide countless psychologists and other scientists with many of the tools of statistical analysis worldwide.

During this time, other figures made a mark on the rise of scientific psychology. One such figure was Lloyd Morgan (1852–1936), known for his seminal work on comparative psychology, especially in the area of methodology. Another was Henry Maudsley (1835–1918), the first person in England to attempt to unite normal and abnormal psychology. He was only partially successful, but he will be mainly remembered for his work on insanity, his theory of imagination, and his advocacy of a multidisciplinary approach to mental problems.

William McDougall (1871–1938) was another key figure during these formative years. He spent the first 20 years of his professional life at University College,

London, being appointed in 1900 as a part reader in the Psychology Department. After 1920, he crossed the Atlantic to the United States and worked at Harvard University and then Duke University, where he was to make a profound impact on psychology. His main influence on English psychology was in the field of physiological psychology, for he posed significant questions about the physiological basis of attention and consciousness, among other areas. His book *Introduction to Social Psychology* (1908) was to become a watershed for the future development of psychology. His wider conception of psychology as a social science, however, was yet to be appreciated by the international community. In his early years, McDougall had been influenced somewhat by the work of Sir Charles Sherrington (1857–1952), and it is to this high-profile contributor to English psychology that we now turn.

The contribution which Sherrington made to the scientific development of English psychology is immensely important, as he strengthened the link between physiology and psychology at the start of the twentieth century. Most of his productive life was spent as professor of physiology at the universities of Liverpool and Oxford, respectively. His dictum that "behavior is rooted in integration" sums up his position concerning the neural functioning that lies at the heart of any scientific psychology. The implication of his fine and elegant work on neuromuscular action, his coining of the terms *synapse* and *proprioreceptors,* and the discovery of neuromuscular feedback mechanisms are key landmarks in the development of physiological psychology. However, Sherrington was more skeptical about the part the brain played in explaining the notion of mind, and in this area he remained a dualist. Sherrington's contributions to psychology extend through to the interwar years.

The Interwar Years

By 1939, there were only six chairs of psychology in the whole of Britain and 30 university teachers of the subject. The principal interests of English psychology centered around its applications to education, mental health, and industrial and occupational problems. Animal psychology did not develop very significantly and was overshadowed by the growth of Nikolaas Tinbergen's ethology at Oxford. While the contribution of key figures such as Spearman, Sherrington, and Myers continued to be felt in their fields of psychology, the subject was not taken seriously by most universities.

There are a number of reasons for this. First was the conservatism of English universities toward new disciplines and methodologies. Second was the skepticism and even hostility of some philosophers toward the recognition of a new subject that dared to study the mind from a scientific point of view. A sense developed among philosophers, especially Alexander

(1859–1938), professor of philosophy at Manchester University, that psychology should be concerned with actions and not content. However, the long drawn-out philosophical debate that ensued was to retard considerably the development of psychology in England.

During this period, the theoretical position of English psychology was to be shaped by McDougall's hornic system, the reemergence of the doctrine of instinct, and the focus on a factor-analytical theory of intelligence and cognition. These ideas provided psychology with a framework for a comprehensive theory of personality, and that provided a rich substratum for the development of educational psychology. While developments in social psychology, personality, research methodology, learning, and behaviorism were gaining ground in America, none of these fields of study were getting any substantive attention in England.

There were, however, pockets of expertise and specialization in different parts of the country that were contributing significantly to the development of the subject. Sir Frederic Bartlett (1886–1969), who later succeeded Charles Myers as director at the Cambridge Laboratory, contributed to experimental psychology in the fields of thinking, memory, and imaging. He was also interested in the industrial applications of psychology, and his work on skilled performance laid the foundations for further developments in this field at Cambridge. Many future holders of British chairs of psychology were to be filled by persons who had studied under Bartlett. Between the wars, James MacCurdy (1886–1947), a Canadian by birth, had a substantial influence on psychology at Cambridge University. His main contribution was in the field of psychopathology, in which he attempted to integrate psychology with physiology through the concept of patterns.

While Oxford University remained aloof to scientific psychology, it was the motivation of William Brown (1881–1951), a physician, which was partly responsible for the creation in 1936 of the now famous Oxford Institute of Experimental Psychology. Brown became its first director, but a chair of experimental psychology was not established until 1947. At University College, London, the so-called London School, initiated by Spearman with its interests in human abilities and the structure of personality, enjoyed wide recognition not only throughout Britain, but also in America and continental Europe. In 1930, Spearman was succeeded by Cyril Burt (1883–1971), who maintained the same interests as Spearman for the 20 years he was the director.

The interwar years also saw specific developments within educational psychology. The interest of earlier figures, such as Mills, Bain, Adams, Nunn, Ballard, and McDougall regarding the relationship between psychology and its possible application to education were later taken up by three famous workers, namely, Burt, Godfrey Thomson, and Charles Valentine. Burt's written work was extensive and varied, covering areas such testing, juvenile delinquency, and factorial statistics. He was successful in selling educational psychology to the teacher training establishment, as well as popularizing educational psychology through the press and professional journals. His main interest was in the psychology of individual differences, claiming that these differences owed more to nature than to nurture. Although after his death his standing was severely shaken by accusations that he based much of his arguments regarding individual differences on fraudulent data, his reputation has recently been restored.

Godfrey H. Thomson (1881–1955) was the director of Moray House for over 25 years, supervising and developing the Moray House tests, which were used in many parts of the English educational system. The third interwar figure was Charles W. Valentine (1879–1964), who will be remembered as the founder the prestigious *British Journal of Educational Psychology*, in 1931. Valentine also wrote extensively in the field of early childhood and on the principles of educational psychology for those training to be teachers.

While other fields in psychology, such as social psychology, industrial psychology, comparative studies, physiological psychology, and clinical applications, were also being pursued in this interim period, compared to the intensity that existed within educational psychology, the interwar years for these areas were not particularly productive.

Renaissance in English Psychology

The effect of World War II and the period up to the present day has seen exciting developments in several fields of English psychology, the culmination of which is a discipline characterized by a greater degree of integration across areas of psychology, and with other disciplines like medicine and the social sciences. Furthermore, as we enter the next millennium, there is a growing awareness on the part of English (as well as British) psychologists that psychology is becoming part of a more global discipline. Let us trace the course of English psychology during the last 50 years or so by examining a number of key developments embracing professional and organizational influences, as well as changes in academic and intellectual direction, which have affected psychologists and others, such as teachers, those in the caring professions, social scientists, and commercial and industrial managers.

Professional and Organizational Influences. Before World War II, psychology as a profession was a muted affair, even though the mainly academic British Psychological Society was founded in 1901. The beginnings of applied psychology dates from 1918, when a committee set up on the Health of Munition Workers, in which issues of health and occupation related to these workers, formed the basis of research to improve their working conditions. The work of Craik (1914–1945) and Bartlett during the interwar years was mainly responsible for developing occupational psychology. This was done with the help of funding from the Medical Research Council. Furthermore, it is from C. S. Myers's work at the private National Institute of Industrial Psychology that industrial psychology as a profession can trace its origins. During World War II, psychologists such P. E. Vernon and A. Rodgers were actively engaged with the armed forces reinforcing previous developments in occupational psychology.

Earlier, we discussed the dominant position of educational psychology and its established place as respected profession during the interwar years. Cyril Burt is mainly seen as the driving force behind this development, but Susan Isaacs and Charles Valentine also played key roles. After the World War II, the scene was set for the establishment of another professional body, namely clinical psychology. Here, Hans Eysenck (1916–1997) built on the foundations laid by Henry Maudsley during the interwar years. As professor of psychiatry at the Institute of Psychiatry at the University of London, the German-born Eysenck not only contributed to a fine intellectual tradition focusing on personality, but also put the training of clinical psychologists on a firm footing with the help of Mary Davidson and Grace Rawlings. Eysenck will also be associated with the creation of an empirically tested and scientifically based psychotherapy, now called cognitive-behavioral therapy, that replaced psychodynamic dogma.

With the rapid expansion of higher education in the early 1960s and the upgrading of polytechnics to universities at the end of the 1980s, the number of psychology departments has mushroomed. The job aspirations for clinical and educational psychologists qualifying from these institutions is generally met by the National Health Service and the State Educational System, respectively. Those students who qualify in occupational, industrial, and organizational psychology find jobs mostly in the private sector. There has also been an increase in the numbers qualifying in social psychology, psychotherapy, and health psychology over the last 20 years. These trends provide a new cadre of professionals who we hope will be equipped to deal with society's mental and social pressures.

The professional status and activities of psychologists are handled by the British Psychology Society, founded in 1901. The society started as an academic organization, which admitted anyone interested in the subject. However, since the end of World War II, members are admitted on the basis of having qualifications in psychology. There are graded forms of membership (e.g., member and fellow) based on the applicant having higher qualifications and proven contributions

of high caliber to the subject. The British Psychological Society was incorporated under the Companies Act in 1941, and further incorporated by royal charter in 1965. This means that the society is required not only to promote the advancement of psychology as a study in its own right, but to ensure that it applies its knowledge and research, where appropriate, to the community at large. In 1987, the charter was amended to require the society to maintain a code of conduct for the guidance of its members and to draw up a register of chartered psychologists. At the end of 1990s, the number of society members is over 30,000, making it the second largest psychological society in the world.

This is an impressive and encouraging achievement when viewed against the faltering attempts during the earlier years of this century to give the field of psychology a higher academic and professional profile. However, the society is proving to be a dynamic and forward looking body of professionals who are currently discussing the development of the profession as we enter the next millennium (Lunt, 1998). Through conferences and colloquia, a vision is being drawn which is optimistic and expansionist, building on the gradual development of psychology since 1901, and especially since 1945. The society is determined to strengthen its scientific and professional standing, and to foster excellence in basic and applied research that will be reflected in sound praxis in all areas of psychology.

Academic and Intellectual Directions. By the close of World War II, psychometrics, neurophysiology, and cognitive psychology (i.e., memory and thinking) were still well-established academic and intellectual traditions in English psychology, and (with modifications) they continue to be so. Psychometerics formed the dominant theme of most of educational psychology until the late 1950s, when its overall value and relevance for schooling began to be questioned. However, psychometrics continued to have an academic direction when the field was developed to determine personality differences. An example of this application would be the employment of factor analysis to tests of personality, in which Hans Eysenck's work on neuroticism and intraversion is well known. However, with the change in successive government policies favoring a return to more pupil testing in primary and secondary schools, psychometrics is once again playing a higher profile in education. Nevertheless, it is unlikely that it will return to the preeminent status that it enjoyed during the interwar years.

The work of Sherrington in neurophysiology, discussed earlier, and that of neurologists like Hughlings-Jackson (1835–1911), Sir David Ferrier (1842–1928), and Sir Henry Head (1861–1940) laid a firm foundations of what was to become the most intensive development within psychology by end of the twentieth century, namely, that of neuropsychology. At Cambridge, O. L. Zangwill developed innovative methodology to study the link between brain damage and deficits in brain functioning. Weiskrantz and his associates, with their investigations into the impairment of the visual system and brain functioning, coupled with research by Warrington, Baddeley and Coltheart on aphasia and amnesia, have provided valuable data for clinical applications, as in dyslexia, and provides new and exciting insights into the complex functioning of the brain as an organ. This surge in neuropsychological research is also reflected by the work of J. A. Gray, which currently links personality dimensions (akin to Eysenck's work in this field) with the role of the hypothalamus.

Human cognition is also an extremely active field of research in current English psychology. A short survey by the author, of psychological research carried out at English universities over a period of 25 years (prior to 1998) appearing in the prestigious *British Journal of Psychology*, showed that over half of the articles reported research into cognitive psychology. A further breakdown of these contributions showed that almost two thirds reported research on memory or memory-related behavior. Other areas of cognitive psychology in this survey included work on thinking processes, visual and auditory perception, language development, reading, and psychomotor research, including the behavioral effects of being right- or left-handed. The work of Donald Broadbent, the director of the Applied Psychology Unit in Cambridge for 16 years, and workers such as Gregory, Poulton and Conrad, are regarded as the key figures in furthering the development of cognitive psychology in the later part of the twentieth century. Broadbent's seminal work on attention, memory, and information processing laid the foundations for the current research being carried out on "working memory," on which Alan Baddeley, the current director of the Cambridge Applied Psychology Unit, is a leading authority.

The renaissance in English psychology also embraces areas of psychology that had been neglected prior to the 1950s. For instance, in developmental psychology, the work of J. S. Bruner as visiting professor at Oxford University in the mid-1970s and early 1980s, and, more recently, Bryant at the same university, has given genetic psychology a more constructivist stance. In social psychology there is renewed activity in interpersonal relationships, development of social skills, and social interaction in general. The influence of Oxford-based Michael Argyle is seminal in these fields; his research has provided English social psychology with a well-defined tradition in this area. Henri Tajfel, who was based in Bristol, also invigorated social psychology in England by his work on sociolinguistics and the dynamics of group cohesiveness.

As we come to the close of the twentieth century, the pragmatic and applied tradition of British and English psychology is taking a new and exciting intellectual direction, one characterized by integration of certain psychological specializations. For instance, some workers in cognitive and occupational psychology are collaborating with their counterparts in clinical and health psychology to investigate growing concerns about job stress and anxiety. As one of the "trail blazers" in the trend toward great interdisciplinary integration, the Cambridge Applied Psychology Unit, is fully involved in stimulating the new field of cognitive neuropsychiatry. This may lead to treatments of patients with certain cognitive deficits, which reflect research collaboration between neurologists, cognitive psychologists, and psychiatrists. English psychology is also continuing to contribute to the wider scientific arena within Britain. Research into many fields of psychology, such as aging and stress at work, are reported at the annual meetings of the British Association for the Advancement of Science. An interesting part of the psychology section of the annual conference is devoted to young persons about to leave school for university and the world work and who might wish to know more about the subject.

Persual of the proceedings of the British Psychological Society conferences and *The Psychologist*, the society's monthly bulletin, shows that since the late 1980s English psychologists have not been slow to reflect on the state of their subject. For instance, within educational psychology there is growing doubt about what role the subject has in the preservice and in-service training of teachers in the light of government policy on teacher accreditation and training, which gives more professional control to schools than was the case before 1988. Tony Gale, former professor of psychology at the University of Southampton and who gave the annual C. S. Myers Lecture in 1996, raised the issue of making British psychology more responsive to its growing popularity among university students and its consequent expansion within the United Kingdom.

Gale spoke about the need for the reconstruction of British psychology, by removing barriers such as the distinction between basic and applied research, the gulf between the university and wider community, and between professionals and academics. It is these and other hurdles that impede the development of psychology as a well-integrated, effective, and relevant discipline.

In effect, Gale is reinforcing the theme of integration and the cross-fertilization of ideas and views already beginning to take place across many fields in psychology, as we have seen, and which is part of the present renaissance within English psychology. The next step would be for English psychologists to pool their expertise and intellectual and academic traditions to be part of a wider international body of psychological theory and practice.

[*See also* British Association for the Advancement of

Science; British Psychological Society; Northern Ireland; Republic of Ireland; Scotland; *and* Wales.]

Bibliography

Baddely, A., & May, A. (1994). Fifty years of the MRC Applied Psychology Unit. *Psychologist, 7*(11), 513–514.

Broadbent, D. (1994). Psychology in Great Britain. In *Encyclopedia of Psychology* (pp. 190–193). Chichester, England: Wiley. A very useful discussion about three key traditions in the development of British psychology.

Fuller, R., Noonan-Walsh, P., & McGinley, P. (Eds.). (1997). *A century of psychology: Progress, paradigms and prospects for the new millennium.* London: Routledge. A good set of contributions which analyze past, present, and future issues within British psychology.

Gale, T. (1997). The reconstruction of British psychology. Paper given at the C. S. Myers Lecture, 1996. *Psychologists 10*(1), 11–15.

Gray, J. (1997). Hans Eysenck—Obituary 1916–1997. *Psychologist. 10*(11), 510.

Hearnshaw, L. S. (1964). *A short history of British psychology.* London: Methuen. An excellent and detailed account of the history of British psychology, especially the contributions of English psychologists to the development of the subject in Britain.

Lunt, I. (1997). *Psychology and education: A century of challenge for educational psychology.* In R. Fuller, P. Noonan-Walsh, P. McGinley (Eds.). *A century of psychology: Progress, paradigms and prospects for the new millennium.* (pp. 123–138). London: Routledge.

Lunt, I. (1998). The development of psychology as profession. *Psychologist, 11*(1), 27–28.

Misiak, H., & Sexton, V. S. (1996). *History of psychology.* New York: Grune & Stratton.

Newman, C. (1988). *Evolution and revolution, charter guide. Occasional paper no. 2.* Leicester, England: British Psychological Society.

O'Neil, W. M. (1982). *The beginnings of modern psychology.* Sussex, England: Harvester Press.

Valentine, E. (1998). Out of the margins. *The Psychologist, 11*(4), 167–168.

Elwyn Thomas

ENURESIS is classified under Axis I in the *Diagnostic and Statistical Manual of Mental Disorders (DSM–IV*; American Psychiatric Association, 1994) as an elimination disorder usually first evident in infancy, childhood, or adolescence. Four diagnostic criteria must be met: (1) repeated voiding of urine, either involuntary or intentional, into clothing or bedding; (2) a frequency of twice a week for a minimum of three consecutive months or evidence of impairment in important areas of functioning, such as social, or evidence of clinically significant distress; (3) a chronological or equivalent developmental level of 5 years; and (4) the behavior is not caused exclusively by a substance such as a diuretic or a general medical condition such as diabetes.

There are three subtypes of enuresis: nocturnal, voiding during the night; diurnal, voiding during the day; and a combination of the two. Enuresis is classified as primary if continence has never been achieved or secondary if the enuresis developed after continence had been achieved and maintained. The primary versus secondary distinction does not appear to have prognostic validity (Doleys, 1977). Primary enuresis represents 85% of all cases.

Enuresis can effect a child's self-esteem, result in peer social ostracism, and create anger and resentment in parents. These problems become worse as the child ages. Parental punishment and rejection are not uncommon. The problems associated with daytime wettings appear to be more severe because parents are more likely to regard it as an act of disobedience and thus may be more extreme in both their reactions and measures employed in responding to it (Berg, 1979). Perhaps the major difference between the two is simply that diurnal enuresis is more easily detected by individuals outside the family and hence is more embarrassing for both the child and parents. However, nocturnal enuresis may result in a loss of opportunities for camp or sleepovers with friends. Urinary tract infections are sometimes present.

The overall prevalence of enuresis at age 5 is 7% for males and 3% for females, whereas it is 3% and 2%, respectively, at age 10 (Erickson, 1987). The disorder occurs in about 1% of adults.

Diurnal Enuresis

At age 2, 50% of U.S. children have achieved daytime continence, and by age 4, 90% have done so. Surprisingly little has been written on diurnal enuresis, whereas there is a vast literature on the nocturnal type. Forsythe and Redmond (1974) studied over 1,000 nocturnal enuretics and found that 28% also had daytime wetting problems. Diurnal enuresis also has been found to be associated with encopresis. Successful treatment has been behaviorally based (Azrin & Foxx, 1974; Foxx, 1986).

Nocturnal Enuresis

Approximately 12 to 15% of nocturnal enuretics stop bed-wetting each year, although there are no valid predictors for selecting which children will become dry without treatment (Doleys, 1977). Also, there appears to be a hereditary predisposition toward enuresis. Most enuretic children have a parent who was enuretic, and concordance is higher in monozygotic twins than in dizygotic twins.

No definitive etiologic factor has been identified, although several have been suggested. They include allergies, smaller functional bladder capacities, urine production exceeding bladder capacity during sleep, abnormal sleep patterns, a lack of antidiuretic hormone secretion, gaining attention, urinary tract infections, and coexisting mental and other developmental disorders. When a enuretic child has emotional problems, they are often the outcome of enuresis rather than its cause. There is not strong evidence supporting enuresis as a sleep arousal disorder.

There have been a number of treatments recommended and attempted. Short-term psychotherapy has been shown to be no more effective than no treatment. Well-controlled studies have failed to demonstrate either the relationship between bladder capacity and enuresis or the utility of urine-retention control training (Christophersen & Edwards, 1992).

Imipramine, a tricylic antidepressant, has been the drug most commonly used to treat enuresis. Although effective in about 60% of cases, it has serious side effects and high relapse rates. Desmopressin has been used to control high urine output during sleep and was successful in up to 70% of cases. However, it also has high relapse rates, side effects, and is costly.

The most successful treatment has been behavioral, beginning with the bell and pad (urine alarm) procedure (Mowrer & Mowrer, 1938) and continuing with dry-bed training (Azrin, Sneed, & Foxx, 1974). Success with urine-alarm-based programs has ranged between 70 and 90%, with treatment lasting 5–12 weeks. Relapse is common (46% of cases), but reinstituted training typically produces a complete cure (Christophersen & Edwards, 1992). The Mowrers attributed programmatic success to classical conditioning, whereas most researchers now suggest that avoidance learning is responsible.

[*See also* Sleep Disorders.]

Bibliography

American Psychiatric Association. (1994). *Diagnostic and statistical manual of mental disorders* (4th ed.), Washington, DC: Author.

Azrin, N. H., & Foxx, R. M. (1974). *Toilet training in less than a day.* New York: Simon & Schuster.

Azrin, N. H., Sneed, T. J., & Foxx, R. M. (1974). Dry-bed training: Rapid elimination of childhood enuresis. *Behaviour Research and Therapy, 12,* 147–156.

Berg, I. (1979). Day wetting in children. *Journal of Child Psychology and Psychiatry, 20,* 167–173.

Christophersen, E. R., & Edwards, K. J. (1992). Treatment of elimination disorders: State of the art 1991. *Applied and Preventive Psychology, 1,* 15–22.

Doleys, D. M. (1977). Behavioral treatments for nocturnal enuresis in children: A review of the recent literature. *Psychological Bulletin, 84,* 30–54.

Erickson, M. T. (1992). *Behavior disorders of children and adolescents: Assessment, etiology, and intervention* (2nd ed.). Englewood Cliffs, NJ: Prentice Hall.

Forsythe, W. I., & Redmond, A. (1974). Enuresis and spontaneous cure rate: Study of 1,129 enuretics. *Archives of Diseases in Childhood, 49,* 259–263.

Foxx, R. M. (1986). The successful treatment of diurnal and nocturnal enuresis and encopresis. *Child and Family Behavior Therapy, 7,* 39–47.

Mowrer, O. H., & Mowrer, W. M. (1938). Enuresis: A method for its study and treatment. *American Journal of Orthopsychiatry, 8,* 436–459.

Richard M. Foxx

ENVIRONMENTAL DESIGN RESEARCH. The field of environmental psychology originated, in part, from a desire among psychologists to generate information that would help improve the quality of the designed environment. To meet this goal, psychologists joined design professionals and other social scientists to develop a perspective and conduct research that differ substantially from mainstream psychology. This growing body of work is often called *environment-behavior studies* or more inclusively *environmental design research.*

The perspective of environmental design research is necessarily interdisciplinary: relevant material is drawn from many fields and collaboration among members of different disciplines is pursued. Links are made to geography, human ecology, psychology, anthropology, sociology, history, urban planning, urban design, architecture, and landscape architecture.

Attention is given not only to the individual and intrapersonal phenomena, but also to groups, communities, and organizations and to a wide range of behavior and experience. The places studied are indoors and outdoors, and vary in scale from rooms or parts of rooms to buildings and discrete outdoor spaces to neighborhoods and even entire cities. Researchers often focus on categories of places, such as offices, schools, hospitals, housing for the elderly (Howell, 1980), housing for single parents (Sprague, 1991), urban plazas or other outdoor spaces (Carr, Francis, Rivlin, & Stone, 1992; Wekerle & Whitzman, 1994; Whyte, 1980), and farmers' markets (Sommer, 1983), or on categories of people including the elderly, children, teenagers, or people who do wage work at home.

Human behavior and experience may be viewed not only in physical and social contexts, but also in cultural, political, and historic ones. The physical environment is not seen as determining certain behaviors and attitudes, but as supporting or constraining them. Furthermore, the relationship between people and environments is fluid and reciprocal; each changes and each influences the other. Because the focus is on people pursuing activities in environments, a variety of naturalistic research methods, rather than controlled experiments, is needed. Many environmental design researchers seek types of publications and ways of presenting information that will reach professionals and students in design and planning fields.

Several Key Concepts

Environmental design researchers often examine a variety of everyday activities, experiences, and attitudes to determine how particular environments meet the needs of occupants. Such research may draw upon several concepts that have been developed to shed light on people-environment relationships from a behavioral perspective. Many of these concepts refer to the spatial and physical dimensions of behavior or to environmental knowledge and attitudes.

One of the earliest spatiophysical dimensions was noted by Henry Osmond who distinguished sociopetal space that tends to push people apart, from sociopetal space that encourages social interaction. A row of chairs all facing in the same direction, as in an airport, for example, creates a sociopetal space, whereas chairs placed in a circle facing inward, creates a sociofugal space. Additional physical characteristics of hard surfaces, fixed furniture, resistance to change, and a stark, institutional atmosphere can also discourage interaction (Sommer, 1983).

The concepts of privacy, personal space, and territoriality are all used to understand person–environment relationships and to make recommendations for design. Privacy is a process by which individuals and groups make themselves available for interaction with others; personal space and territoriality can then be viewed as mechanisms for achieving degrees of privacy (Altman, 1975). Personal space is person-centered, moving with the person, and is not delimited by any visible boundary, whereas a territory is a fixed, visibly marked region that may be associated with a person, a household, or a group of people.

The activity of decorating or modifying a territory, called *personalization*, enables people to express feelings of self, group, and cultural identity in the built environment and to accommodate their lifestyle. As a consequence, they may develop feelings of attachment and responsibility for their surroundings, particularly in residential settings (Cooper Marcus & Sarkissian, 1986; Newman, 1972). The degree and permanence of the markers vary with the kind of territory. Primary territories, including homes or bedrooms, are occupied for longer time periods, are more central to people's lives, can be more fully personalized than secondary territories that are more accessible to other people, but are still subject to some degree of control (Altman, 1975). A space in a public place, such as a seat on a bus or a table in a restaurant, can also be marked with a coat or other personal belongings, but only temporarily.

The connections between place and self-identity or place and group identity can be quite strong, as suggested by the concepts of place identity and place attachment. Places come to serve as repositories of memories as well as representations of one's self and one's group. Home and neighborhood figure prominently: changing one's dwelling either by moving or by significant modifications may reflect and encourage personal growth (Cooper Marcus, 1995).

Conceiving of spaces as part of a sociospatial hierarchy is very useful in conducting environmental design research and in making design recommendations. Newman (1972) observed that the clear delineation of a hierarchy of zones with real and symbolic barriers encouraged residents in public housing to use and to appropriate the private and semiprivate spaces, and was a clear indication to outsiders of where they could enter. Sprague (1991) used a nested, four-zone hierarchy of person, household, community, and neighborhood to compare the spatial arrangements and patterns of use evident in various cases of conventional and special needs housing.

People's use of an environment is facilitated by their understanding of its spatial organization; this understanding in turn is facilitated by cognitive images that often take on the characteristics of a mental map. Analysis of the mental maps that people drew of cities suggested to Lynch (1960) five elements in the urban environment that people use to structure their images: paths, edges, landmarks, nodes, and districts. Paths are routes people travel along; edges are boundaries between parts of city or town that act as boundaries; landmarks are significant buildings, monuments, or discrete and notable locations; nodes are points of intensive activity; and districts are areas that have a distinctive character. The elements of some cities, such as New York, make their layout more legible, or more easily learned and remembered than the elements of other cities, such as Los Angeles. Orientation and way finding in smaller scale settings, such as buildings, is influenced by other features that include physical cues that distinguish spaces from each other and visual access from one space to another.

Visual access plays a role in other environmental behaviors as well. Being able to see into a public or semipublic space before entering it allows more freedom of choice as to whether or not to enter, and may increase the use of the space (Howell, 1980; Whyte, 1980). Visual access to spaces outside the private dwelling often increases people's sense of responsibility for the spaces and provides a greater degree of safety (Newman, 1972). In other cases, people's ongoing surveillance of a shared space may feel intrusive to other occupants, as in the lobbies of housing for the elderly (Howell, 1980).

Research Methods

A rich variety of research methods is available to environmental design researchers. The conventional tools of standardized questionnaires for surveys or personal interviews, as well as focused interviews with groups or individuals, can all be developed to address environmental topics. Other specialized techniques, which may involve visual cues and responses, can be incorporated or used independently.

Photographs or slides may be used in questions on preferences or sorting tasks. Respondents can also be given cameras to take pictures on assigned topics in their own homes or neighborhoods. In cognitive mapping, respondents are asked to draw a quick sketch map of a city or an area as they would describe the place to a visitor. Respondents' maps can be compared with researchers' observations of the significant features of the location to determine what physical elements are used to form mental images and to see how images differ among groups (Lynch, 1960).

Respondents can also be shown floor plans of buildings or base maps of their communities and asked to indicate the routes they take, places where they feel safe or unsafe, places where they feel at home, or the boundaries of their neighborhoods. In exploring people's ideals of a home, a school, or other types of places, researchers may ask respondents to draw a picture of their ideal house or school, as well as the one they currently occupy. Respondents may also draw and describe previous homes and neighborhoods or places they loved best or visited when they wished to be alone.

Such drawings may be part of an environmental autobiography in which respondents recall and describe the various places they have lived and what those places felt like. To explore people's emotional bonds with their homes further, Cooper Marcus (1995) developed a Gestalt role-playing technique in which respondents "speak" to their homes about their feelings toward them and then take the role of the home and respond. Such dialogues may arouse deep emotions and surprising insights, leading to renovations, decisions to move, or recognition of the features desired in a new home.

Emotional, cognitive, and attitudinal factors are important, but so are the actual activities that take place in designed environments. These can be described in self-reports, but they can also be documented in more detail and more reliably through various kinds of on-site observations. Observers may make notes, possibly on base maps or diagrams of the setting, or they may use precoded checklists as in behavior mapping. This is a systematic technique for recording the precise location, activity, props, number, and characteristics of participants of ongoing activities and any other significant conditions (such as the weather in outdoor observa-

tions). The categories of information and the appropriate coding are defined in advance and observers are trained to conduct the observations at prescribed times. Time-lapse photography can also be used to record behavior over time. Whyte's (1980) analysis of the data from such films of urban plazas helped him determine the physical and social features that attract users; this information helped shape revisions to the New York City zoning ordinance.

Base plans of the setting can also be used to draw the location, size, and type of furniture, and to note other physical features pertinent to the research project. Howell's (1980) documentation of the size and type of furniture of elderly residents led to design recommendations for accommodating such furniture in the future. Additional observations can be noted, on plans or with photographs, of the evidence of people's past activities, such as paths made across a lawn, litter or toys left outside, or decorations on a door (Zeisel, 1981). Both recording ongoing activities and recording such physical traces indicate how an environment is used and adapted, and may indicate advantages and problems with particular features. The observations may also generate questions that require further investigation. Zeisel's observation of open containers of food on the window ledges of a veteran's residence led him to discover that residents enjoyed their own snacks apart from the regular meals provided in the common dining room.

Documentation of the physical features and traces in a setting can take place on a tour led by persons familiar with it. Frequent users of an environment can point out significant design, management, or other features. Information collected from tours of public places conducted with women in Toronto, called *safety audits*, contributed to design guidelines for increasing public safety for all (Wekerle, 1994).

Visual and written documents, records, and other archival material provide additional sources of useful information to environmental design researchers. Architectural floor plans of a building or site plans of the grounds can be analyzed from a behavioral point of view to note physical design characteristics that may have an impact on patterns of use (Zeisel, 1981). Records kept by institutions, for example, on crime, vandalism, maintenance problems, or complaints, may reveal variations in problems by location or time. Newman (1972) used crime reports kept by the New York City Housing Authority to analyze differences in type and frequency of crime among housing developments with different physical and social features. Information from newspapers, books, and magazines can add historical and cultural dimensions to contemporary environments, conditions, or attitudes. Photographs of chairs and people in different postures contributed to Cranz's (1998) understanding of the cultural influences on chair design and use in contemporary Western society.

Kinds of Work

Much environmental design research is directed to those people who make decisions about the design, use, and management of built environments: architects, interior designers, landscape architects, planners, urban designers, facility managers, policy makers, clients of design or planning projects, and students in the design and planning fields, as well as everyday building occupants. Two kinds of studies particular to environmental design research are analyses of user needs and postoccupancy evaluations.

An analysis of user needs may be conducted as part of the programming process prior to the design of an environment. During this process the spatial, physical, and environmental requirements that the building must meet are determined by the architect and the client. Information about the users and their needs will suggest particular requirements to be met and will help inform subsequent design choices. The information on needs can be taken from a review of existing research, or research can be conducted specifically to determine the needs of the future occupants (Sommer, 1983).

In participatory design and planning, occupants are directly involved in the programming and design process, usually in a series of meetings and hands-on workshops, which may include tours of similar sites, generation of rough plans, and manipulation of take-apart models (Sanoff, 1989). In a fully collaborative process, professionals engage in a dialogue with occupants, and the knowledge of each person is valued and shared (Schneekloth & Shibley, 1995).

Postoccupancy evaluation determines how a designed environment does and does not meet occupants' needs. The researcher may compare environments of a similar type, or may determine how one building meets the intentions of the architect and the needs outlined in the architectural program. Evaluation research may also be generative, providing information and ideas that can be used in different ways in future planning and design, thus overlapping with user-needs analysis (Wener, 1989).

In addition to technical research reports directed to architects and other professionals who have commissioned the research or to granting agencies, environmental design researchers also write various kinds of design guidelines to explain the ways and reasons why particular environments work or don't work, and how they can best be designed in the future. Sometimes research has been done specifically to help generate the guidelines (Howell, 1980; Newman, 1972; Sprague, 1991; Wekerle & Whitzman, 1994; Whyte, 1980), and sometimes a wider body of existing work is drawn upon and presented as the basis for discussion and guidance

(Carr et al., 1992; Cooper Marcus & Sarkissian, 1986). Publications may also include techniques that can be used for evaluating environments of that type (Howell, 1980; Wekerle & Whitzman, 1994). Other books focus on research methods (Zeisel, 1981), the practice of participatory design and planning (Schneekloth & Shibley, 1995), or a combination of both (Sommer, 1983). If research is to reach the everyday occupants of environments and enable them to make choices about environments, design features, or ways of living, more popularized books are appropriate such as those by Cooper Marcus (1995) and Cranz (1998).

An Evolving Field

Some tension exists within environmental design research between the values and needs of designers and those of social scientists. Whereas designers emphasize types of places and their design features, social scientists emphasize human behavior and experience. Designers need information they can understand easily and translate fairly quickly into design decisions. Social scientists are trained to conduct rigorous and time-consuming research, and to present findings in a manner particular to their disciplines. As the field of environmental design has evolved, researchers have increasingly conducted studies on types of places, which accommodates designers' needs, and have learned to make research findings and their implications more accessible to design audiences.

These developments reflect a strengthening of the normative stance of environmental design research. Not only is research more clearly directed toward ways of improving the built environment, but researchers may also serve as advocates for the occupants of the environments they study. In outlining the human dimensions of public urban space, Carr et al. (1992) explored and presented a series of user rights as well as needs; improving the equity of access to public space is a key theme in their work. The aim of Schneekloth and Shibley's (1995) practice of participatory planning is to reveal and question the underlying meanings of a place and then to facilitate, with the occupants, its desired social and physical transformation.

Recommendations for change may be directed not only at physical features of the designed environment, but also at patterns of use and belief and how they might best evolve. In addition to making recommendations for understanding human physiology and changing furniture design to improve people's health and well-being, Cranz (1998) suggested the adoption of postures and movements in the workplace and in the home that are radically different from those presently acceptable in Western society. As researchers explore how much the environment is a consequence of human actions and not only an antecedent to them, the significance of cultural and historic influences in shaping the physical environment and our relationship to it is clarified. It is becoming increasingly clear that in order to make substantial changes in the design of environments to improve our well-being, cultural changes must also occur.

[*See also* Environmental Psychology.]

Bibliography

Altman, I. (1975). *The environment and social behavior*. Monterey, CA: Brooks/Cole.

Carr, S., Francis, M. Rivlin, L., & Stone, A. (1992). *Public space for public life*. Cambridge, England: Cambridge University Press.

Cooper Marcus, C. (1995). *House as a mirror of self*. Berkeley, CA: Conari Press.

Cooper Marcus, C., & Sarkissian, W. (1986). *Housing as if people mattered*. Berkeley: University of California Press.

Cranz, G. (1998). *The chair: Rethinking the body, culture and design*. New York: Norton.

Howell, S. (1980). *Designing for aging*. Cambridge, MA: MIT Press.

Lynch, K. (1960). *The image of the city*. Cambridge, MA: MIT Press.

Newman, O. (1972). *Defensible space*. New York: Macmillan.

Sanoff, H. (1989). Facility programming. In H. Zube & G. T. Moore (Eds.), *Advances in environment, behavior and design* (Vol. 2, pp. 239–286). New York: Plenum Press.

Schneekloth, L. H., & Shibley, R. G. (1995). *Placemaking: The art and practice of building communities*. New York: Wiley.

Sommer, R. (1983). *Social design: Creating buildings with people in mind*. Englewood Cliffs, NJ: Prentice Hall.

Sprague, J. F. (1991) *More than housing: Lifeboats for women and children*. Boston: Butterworth Architecture.

Wekerle, G., & Whitzman, C. (1994). *Safe cities: Guidelines for planning, management and design*. New York: Van Nostrand Reinhold.

Wener, R. (1989). Advances in the evaluation of the environment. In H. Zube & G. T. Moore (Eds.), *Advances in environment, behavior and design* (Vol. 2, pp. 287–313). New York: Plenum Press.

Whyte, W. H. (1980). *The social life of small urban spaces*. New York: Conservation Foundation.

Zeisel, J. (1981). *Inquiry by design: Tools for environment–behavior research*. Monterey, CA: Brooks/Cole.

Karen A. Franck

ENVIRONMENTAL PSYCHOLOGY examines the dynamic transactions between people and their everyday, sociophysical environments. Whereas many areas of psychological research (e.g., those rooted in theories of learning, perception, and social influence) are fundamentally concerned with relationships between environmental factors, intrapersonal processes, and behavior, environmental psychology is distinctive in several respects.

First, environmental psychology gives greater attention to molar units of the environment, such as people's homes, neighborhoods, and work and community settings than other areas of psychology, which have focused more exclusively on micro-level stimuli and events.

Second, in keeping with Kurt Lewin's "action research" orientation (1946), research in environmental psychology integrates the scientific goals of analyzing and explaining the nature of people-environment transactions with the more practical goal of enhancing—and even optimizing—people's relationships with their everyday environments through more effective urban planning and environmental design.

Third, because of its dual emphasis on analyzing and improving the quality of people's relationships with their environments, environmental psychology brings a multidisciplinary approach to the study of environment and behavior, incorporating the perspectives of architecture, urban planning, psychology, anthropology, sociology, geography, and other fields.

The multidisciplinary orientation of environmental psychology has contributed to its innovative and eclectic qualities, but has also resulted in a more diffuse and less easily circumscribed identity for the field as a whole. Environmental psychology cannot be neatly categorized as a singular paradigm or research tradition. Rather, it encompasses a disparate set of research areas and perspectives, spanning multiple disciplines, which are linked by a common focus on people's relationships with their sociophysical surroundings. Although environmental psychology can be viewed as a branch of psychological research, it is more accurately characterized as part of a multidisciplinary field addressing environment and behavior and combining the conceptual and methodological perspectives of several disciplines. Thus, the terms *environmental psychology* and *environment-behavior studies* are used synonymously here in recognition of the multidisciplinary orientation of the field.

Social and Academic Origins of Environmental Psychology

The emergence of environmental psychology as a scientific field during the late 1960s can be traced to both social events and academic developments. On the social level, the environmental crisis of the 1960s raised public awareness about the adverse health and social impact of overpopulation, environmental pollution, interracial tensions, and urban conflict. During the 1970s and 1980s, the widely publicized technological disasters in the community of Love Canal, New York, and those that occurred at the Three Mile Island and Chernobyl nuclear power plants (in Pennsylvania and Ukraine, respectively) reinforced the public's concern about environmental problems. At the same time, dramatic examples of "dysfunctional architecture," exemplified by the 1972 demolition of the Pruitt Igoe low-income housing project in St. Louis, Missouri (built in 1956 and containing 2,870 dwelling units in 33 eleven-story buildings), highlighted the failure of many residential and neighborhood environments to support the behavioral and social needs of their occupants.

Within academic circles, scientific analyses of population density, air pollution, energy conservation, and racial conflict prompted the development of broader-gauged theories and methodologies for studying the transactions between people and their everyday environments. In psychology, researchers turned their attention to the molar, sociophysical environment and its influence on cognition, social behavior, life-span development, and well-being. During the late 1960s and early 1970s, these developments in psychology, and similar concerns about the behavioral impacts of large-scale environments in sociology, anthropology, geography, and urban planning, led to the formation of new academic journals, professional organizations, and graduate training programs focusing on environment and behavior.

Scientific Foundations and Contributions of Environmental Psychology

The scientific foundations of environmental psychology are rooted in both the behavioral sciences, as well as the design and planning professions. Architects and urban planners, for example, played a major role in establishing the Environmental Design Research Association (EDRA), the largest and longest-standing professional organization in the environment and behavior field. Design and planning professionals also played key roles in establishing additional, international organizations to promote environmental design research, that is, the International Association for People-Environment Studies (IAPS), based in Europe; People and Physical Environment Research (PAPER), based in Australia and New Zealand; and the Man-Environment Research Association (MERA) of Japan.

The first EDRA conference was organized in 1969 by two architects, Henry Sanoff of the School of Design at North Carolina State University and Sidney Cohn of the Department of City and Regional Planning at the University of North Carolina, Chapel Hill. Since its inception, EDRA has held yearly conferences focusing on environmental design research and has published their proceedings, from 1970 to the present time. A key goal of EDRA is to foster the design of environments that effectively support users' needs, through greater collaboration between design professionals and behavioral scientists. The membership of EDRA, like those of IAPS,

PAPER, and MERA, includes researchers and practitioners from the fields of architecture, facilities management, urban planning, psychology, sociology, anthropology, geography, and natural resources management.

The influence of the design and planning professions on the directions of environmental psychology is reflected in the derivation of behaviorally based guidelines for improving the fit between occupants' needs and activities on the one hand, and the physical and social attributes of their environments (e.g., homes, workplaces, and public spaces) on the other. In their landmark volume *A Pattern Language* (1977), Christopher Alexander, Sara Ishikawa, Murray Silverstein and others presented 253 guidelines, derived from psychological, social, and aesthetic principles, for optimizing the comfort, attractiveness, and overall quality of physical environments. Similarly, Clara Cooper Marcus and Wendy Sarkissian (1986) offered 254 site-design guidelines for enhancing the quality of residential environments. Also, Stephen Carr, Mark Francis, Leanne Rivlin, and Andrew Stone (1992) outlined several criteria for the design of effective public spaces.

Another long-standing concern of environmental design research has been the development of postoccupancy evaluation (POE) strategies for determining how well buildings and other designed environments work or support the needs and activities of their users (Preiser, 1989; Zeisel, 1981). POE is closely related to predesign research (PDR), which is conducted prior to the design and construction of built environments to ensure that occupants' needs are considered by design professionals and incorporated into their plans for future developments (Bechtel, 1997).

The directions of environmental psychology also have been shaped by theoretical and methodological perspectives drawn from the behavioral sciences. During the 1970s, the Division of Population and Environmental Psychology was established within the American Psychological Association. Also, the Environmental Section of the Canadian Psychological Association, and the Environment and Technology, and Community and Urban Sociology, sections of the American Sociological Association were formed. An edited text, *Environmental Psychology*, was published (Proshansky, Ittelson, & Rivlin, 1970), and doctoral training programs in environmental psychology, environment-behavior studies, and social ecology were established at the City University of New York, the University of Wisconsin, Milwaukee, and the University of California, Irvine, respectively. Major reference works and monograph series were published, including the *Handbook of Environmental Psychology* (Stokols & Altman, 1987), *Human Behavior and Environment—Advances in Theory and Research* (Altman & Wohlwill, 1976), *Advances in Environmental Psychology* (Baum, Singer, & Valins, 1978); *Advances in Environ-*

ment, Behavior, and Design (Zube & Moore, 1991). Also, periodic chapters summarizing developments in environmental psychology have been published in the *Annual Review of Psychology* since 1973. At the same time, several journals focusing on environment-behavior studies were established, including *Environment and Behavior* (Sage Publications), the *Journal of Environmental Psychology* (Academic Press), and the *Journal of Architecture and Planning Research* (Locke Science Publishing Company).

Over the past three decades, a number of topics have received extensive theoretical and empirical attention among environment-behavior researchers. The role of physical space in regulating social behavior was one topic widely studied by sociologists, anthropologists, and psychologists during the early phase of environment-behavior research. For example, the effects of spatial proximity on the development of neighbors' friendships, their political attitudes, and consumer behavior were documented in a study of graduate student housing at MIT conducted by Leon Festinger, Stanley Schachter, and Kurt Back (1950). Edward Hall's anthropological research (1966) later demonstrated important cross-cultural differences in how people use space in social situations. His work was extended by Robert Sommer's experimental studies of personal space (1969), and Irwin Altman's theoretical model of the relationships between privacy, personal space, territoriality, and crowding (1975). Sommer's and Altman's studies were rooted in social psychology, whereas Oscar Newman's (1973) theory of defensible space offered a sociological inquiry into those features of housing design that either facilitate or constrain residents' surveillance and control over their apartment buildings and neighborhoods.

A major influence on the course of environment-behavior research was Roger Barker's (1968) theory of behavior settings, that is, systemically organized environmental units that occur at particular times and places and consist of both physical components and a behavioral program. The behavior-setting concept provided a more molar and dynamic unit of environmental analysis than the micro-level stimuli and short-term situations emphasized in earlier psychological theories. Through a series of programmatic studies, Barker and his colleagues charted the diversity and distribution of behavior settings in whole communities and identified systemic processes (such as under- and overstaffing) that regulate the stability and growth of particular settings (Barker & Schoggen, 1973; Wicker, 1979). In a separate research program, Rudolph Moos (1976) presented a theoretical analysis of the social climate within organizational and institutional environments. He also developed a battery of questionnaires designed to measure the dimensions of social climate and their influence on psychological and social outcomes in res-

idential, educational, and occupational settings.

The increasing emphasis on multiple levels and molar units of environmental analysis, clearly evident in Barker's work, was reflected in several other programs of environment-behavior research. In the areas of perceptual and cognitive psychology, distinctions were drawn between environmental and object perception (Ittelson, 1973), and between fundamental and macrospatial cognition (Moore & Golledge, 1976). Also, sketch maps, way finding, and photographic-recognition tasks were devised to measure the image-ability of urban environments (Lynch, 1960; Milgram & Jodelet, 1976). This research on environmental cognition extended earlier studies that had examined perceptual and cognitive processes associated with discrete stimuli and objects, but not in relation to larger-scale physical settings. Similarly, Urie Bronfenbrenner (1979) presented an ecological theory of human development highlighting the developmental significance of large-scale environments, that is, the microsystem, mesosystem, exosystem, and macrosystem, while Powell Lawton and Lucile Nahemow (1973) contributed an ecological analysis of environmental competence in older adults. In addition, Kenneth Craik (1976) offered a conceptualization of environmental dispositions, or people's response tendencies toward urban and natural environments, which took their place alongside the traditional trait constructs of personality psychology.

At least three other areas of inquiry have generated sustained research programs and cumulative scientific contributions to the study of environment and behavior. First, environmental assessment studies contributed new methodological tools, including perceived environmental quality indices (Craik & Zube, 1976) and environmental simulation techniques (Appleyard & Craik, 1978; Marans & Stokols, 1993). These methods have been used to evaluate people's reactions to existing or imagined settings, such as residential, recreational, and health-care environments. Also, behavioral mapping protocols (Ittelson, Rivlin, & Proshansky, 1976) and behavior-setting surveys (Barker & Schoggen, 1973) were developed for recording individuals' and group's activity patterns within buildings, public parks, and whole communities.

Second, in their pioneering studies of environmental stress, David Glass and Jerome Singer (1972) revealed the behavioral aftereffects of exposure to unpredictable and uncontrollable noise. They also extended Lazarus's prior analysis (1966) of psychological stress (arising from perceived environmental threats) to the study of "urban stressors." These and subsequent stress studies have employed a variety of observational, self-report, and physiological probes to measure people's reactions to such environmental demands as aircraft noise in residential communities, traffic congestion on urban roads, technological disasters, and prolonged periods of overtime work in occupational settings (Baum & Fleming, 1993; Evans, Bullinger, & Hygge, 1998; Frankenhaeuser, 1980; Stokols, Novaco, Stokols, & Campbell, 1978). As an antidote for environmental stressors, "restorative environments," such as wilderness and garden areas, have been conceptualized as places that alleviate stress by affording opportunities for spontaneous, as well as voluntary, attention and for "getting away" from one's normal routine (Kaplan & Kaplan, 1989; Korpela & Hartig, 1996; Ulrich, 1984).

Finally, studies of environmentally protective behavior have applied psychological theories to the analysis of resource shortages, pollution, and conservation. For example, Peter Everett (1974) and his colleagues at Pennsylvania State University developed token reinforcement strategies for modifying travel behavior. These procedures were found to be effective in several field experiments as a means of increasing community levels of bus ridership. Also, cash rebates, social praise, and feedback about the consequences of environmentally supportive behavior have proven effective in changing patterns of household energy consumption, waste disposal, and recycling (Scott Geller, Richard Winett, & Peter Everett, 1982). More recently, Paul Stern (1992) contributed an important analysis of the behavioral underpinnings of global environmental change.

Future Directions of Environmental Psychology

The scientific developments outlined above suggest that over the past three decades environmental psychological research has yielded several new conceptual and methodological tools for expanding our knowledge of people-environment transactions. Environmental psychology is a distinctive area of behavioral research, owing to its emphasis on: (1) the influence of physical and social features of large-scale, everyday environments on human behavior and well-being; (2) the dynamic, reciprocal transactions that occur among individuals, groups, and their sociophysical surroundings; (3) the behavioral and psychological influence of both natural and built environments; (4) the behavioral consequences of both objective and subjective (perceived) qualities of the environment; (5) the multidisciplinary and interdisciplinary nature of the field; and (6) the dual emphasis on basic research and theory development, as well as community problem-solving and environmental design, reflecting the "action-research" orientation of the field (Lewin, 1946).

Looking toward the future, it appears that the basic and applied research directions of the field will be strongly influenced by at least five major social concerns that have arisen in recent decades and are likely to become even more salient during the twenty-first century: (1) toxic contamination of environments and rapid changes in the global ecosystem; (2) the spread of violence at regional and international levels; (3) the pervasive impact of information technologies on work and family life; (4) escalating costs of health-care delivery and the growing importance of disease prevention and health promotion strategies; and (5) processes of social aging in the United States and other regions of the world (Stokols, 1995). In the coming decades, environmental psychologists will continue to play an active and influential role in developing innovative theoretical and empirical analyses of these community problems, and in formulating effective environmental design and public policy strategies for ameliorating and resolving them.

[See also Environmental Design Research.]

Bibiography

Appleyard, D. A., & Craik, K. H. (1978). The Berkeley Environmental Simulation Laboratory and its research program. *International Review of Applied Psychology*, 27, 53–55.

Baum, A., & Fleming, I. (1993). Implications of psychological research on stress and technological accidents. *American Psychologist*, 48, 665–672.

Bronfenbrenner, U. (1979). *The ecology of human development*. Cambridge, MA: Harvard University Press.

Carr, S., Francis, M., Rivlin, L., & Stone, A. (1992). *Public space*. New York: Cambridge University Press.

Cooper Marcus, C., & Sarkissian, W. (1986). *Housing as if people mattered*. Berkeley, CA: University of California Press.

Craik, K. H. (1976). The personality research paradigm in environmental psychology. In S. Wapner, S. Cohen, & B. Kaplan (Eds.), *Experiencing the environment* (pp. 55–80). New York: Plenum Press.

Craik, K. H., & Zube, E. H. (Eds.). (1976). *Perceiving environmental quality: Research and applications*. New York: Plenum Press.

Evans, G. W., Bullinger, M., & Hygee, S. (1998). Chronic noise exposure and physiological response: A prospective study of children living under environmental stress. *Psychological Science*, 9, 75–77.

Everett, P. B., Hayward, S., & Meyers, A. W. (1974). The effects of a token reinforcement procedure on bus ridership. *Journal of Applied Behavioral Analysis*, 7, 1–10.

Festinger, L., Schachter, S., & Back, K. (1950). *Social pressures in informal groups*. New York: Harper.

Frankenhaeuser, M. (1980). Psychoneuroendocrine approaches to the study of stressful person environment transactions. In H. Selve (Ed.), *Selye's guide to stress research* (Vol. 1, pp. 46–70). New York: Van Nostrand Reinhold.

Ittelson, W. H., Rivlin, L. G., & Proshansky, H. M. (1976). The use of behavioral maps in environmental psychology. In H. M. Proshansky, W. H. Ittelson, & L. G. Rivlin (Eds.), *Environmental psychology: People and their physical* settings (2nd ed., pp. 340–351). New York: Holt, Rinehart, & Winston.

Kaplan, R., & Kaplan, S. (1989). *The experience of nature: A psychological perspective.* New York: Cambridge University Press.

Korpela, K., & Hartig, T. (1996). Restorative qualities of favorite places. *Journal of Environmental Psychology, 16,* 221–233.

Lawton, M. P., & Nahemow, L. (1973). Ecology and the aging process. In E. Eisdorfer & M. P. Lawton (Eds.), *Psychology of adult development and aging* (pp. 619–674). Washington, DC: American Psychological Association.

Lewin, K. (1946). Action research and social problems. *Journal of Social Issues, 2,* 34–36.

Marans, R. W., & Stokols, D. (1993). *Environmental simulation: Research and policy issues.* New York: Plenum Press.

Milgram, S., & Jodelet, D. (1976). Psychological maps of Paris. In H. M. Proshansky, W. H. Ittelson, & L. G. Rivlin (Eds.), *Environmental psychology* (2nd ed., pp. 104–124). New York: Holt, Rinehart, & Winston,

Preiser, W. F. E. (Ed.). (1989). *Building evaluation.* New York: Plenum Press.

Stern, P. C. (1992). Psychological dimensions of global environmental change. *Annual Review of Psychology, 43,* 269–302.

Stokols, D. (1995). The paradox of environmental psychology. *American Psychologist, 50,* 821–837.

Stokols, D., Novaco, R. W., Stokols, J., & Campbell, J. (1978). Traffic congestion, type-A behavior, and stress. *Journal of Applied Psychology, 63,* 467–480.

Ulrich, R. S. (1984). View through a window may influence recovery from surgery. *Science, 224,* 420–421.

Wicker, A. W. (1979). *An introduction to ecological psychology.* New York: Cambridge University Press.

Zeisel, J. (1981). *Inquiry by design: Tools for environment-behavior research.* New York: Cambridge University Press.

*Major Publications and Reference Works
in Environmental Psychology*

Alexander, C., Ishikawa, S., Silverstein, M., Jacobson, M., Fiksdahl-King, I., & Angel, S. (1977). *A pattern language.* New York: Oxford University Press.

Altman, I. (1975). *Environment and social behavior: Privacy, personal space, territory, and crowding.* Monterey, CA: Brooks/Cole.

Altman, I., & Wohlwill, J. F. (Eds.). (1976). *Human behavior and environment: Advances in theory and research* Vol. 1. New York: Plenum Press.

Barker, R. G. (1968). *Ecological psychology: Concepts and methods for studying the environment of human behavior.* Stanford, CA: Stanford University Press.

Barker, R. G., & Schoggen, P. (1973). *Qualities of community life.* San Francisco: Jossey-Bass.

Baum, A., Singer, J. E., & Valins, S. (Eds.). (1978). *Advances in environmental psychology: Vol. 1. The urban environment.* Hillsdale, NJ: Erlbaum.

Bechtel, R. B. (1997). *Environment and behavior: An introduction.* Thousand Oaks, CA: Sage Publications.

Bronfenbrenner, U. (1979). *The ecology of human development.* Cambridge, MA: Harvard University Press.

Glass, D. C., & Singer, J. E. (1972). *Urban stress.* New York: Academic Press.

Hall, E. T. (1966). *The hidden dimension.* Garden City, NY: Doubleday.

Ittelson, W. H. (1973). *Environment and cognition.* New York: Seminar Press.

Lazarus, R. (1966). *Psychological stress and the coping process.* New York: McGraw-Hill.

Lynch, K. (1960). *The image of the city.* Cambridge, MA: MIT Press.

Moore, G. T., & Golledge, R. G. (Eds.). (1976). *Environmental knowing.* Stroudsburg, PA: Dowden, Hutchinson, & Ross.

Moos, R. H. (1976). *The human context: Environmental determinants of behavior.* New York: Wiley.

Newman, O. (1973). *Defensible space: Crime prevention through urban design.* New York: Macmillan.

Proshansky, H. M., Ittelson, W. H., & Rivlin, L. (Eds.). (1976). *Environmental psychology: People and their physical settings* (2nd ed.). New York: Holt, Rinehart, & Winston.

Sommer, R. (1969). *Personal space: The behavioral basis of design.* Englewood Cliffs, NJ: Prentice Hall.

Stokols, D., & Altman, I. (Eds.). (1987). *Handbook of environmental psychology* (Vols. 1–2). New York: Wiley.

Zube, E. H., & Moore, G. T. (Eds.). (1991). *Advances in environment, behavior, and design* (Vol. 3). New York: Plenum Press.

*Academic Journals in the Environment
and Behavior Field*

Environment and Behavior. Sage, Thousand Oaks, CA. Available Web site: http://www.sagepub.co.uk/journals/details/jo163.html

Journal of Architectural and Planning Research. Locke Science Publishing Company, Chicago, IL. Available Web site: http://archone.tamu.edu/Press/japr2.html

Journal of Environmental Psychology. Academic Press Ltd., London, England. Available Web site: http://www.hbuk.co.uk/ap/journals/ps/

People and Physical Environment Research. Department of Architecture, University of Sydney, New South Wales, Australia. Available Web site: http://www.arch.su.edu.au/deptarch/publications/paper.html

Daniel Stokols

ENVY. *See* Jealousy and Envy.

EPIDEMIOLOGY is the study of the spatial, temporal, social, and ecological distribution of symptoms, illness, disease, disability, and other health-related states or events in human populations. Typically, epidemiologists measure the characteristics of individuals from samples of populations and use statistical methods to partial out the effects of specific variables on health outcomes and to extrapolate from random or representative samples to a larger population.

The goal of epidemiological research may be descriptive (to characterize the nature and prevalence of a problem) or substantive (to identify causal factors or assess the effectiveness of interventions). Descriptive epidemiology can establish the incidence (the rate of new cases) and prevalence (the rate of active cases) of a disease or disorder. Substantive epidemiology is designed to identify risk factors that increase the likelihood that an individual or group will contract a health problem, and protective factors that reduce risk.

These goals of epidemiological research may be closely related. For example, mapping the geographic distribution of occurrences of a disease may reveal an association with a specific location, which in turn may suggest a specific local causal factor. The influence of a potential cause then may be tested by examining the effect of exposure to that factor on the likelihood of contracting the disease. Statistical analyses are used to quantify associations (often in terms of the relative risk or odds of an adverse outcome) and to adjust for the effects of factors that confound relationships (distort or nullify the extent of true associations). Factors contributing to the cause and influencing the course of disorders may be studied with longitudinal studies of cohorts that allow stronger conclusions about the direction of causality among correlated variables based on their temporal priority. Through such studies, epidemiology can contribute directly to knowledge of basic mechanisms of pathology and recovery. Epidemiological studies also are used to identify health service needs and patterns of utilization related to different arrangements of the health care system.

Clinical epidemiology examines groups of patients in treatment settings. This allows the study of disorders that are uncommon in the general population but may be concentrated in specialized clinics. However, studies based on clinical populations may confound factors related to help seeking with those intrinsic to a disorder (the result of this confounding is termed "Berkson's bias"). Clinical epidemiology includes the design and conduct of clinical trials to evaluate the effectiveness of diagnostic and treatment modalities. Randomized controlled trials, in which subjects are randomly assigned to treatment or control (or other treatment) groups without the subjects' or investigators' knowledge, are considered the gold standard of such approaches. Clinical practice and decision making based on systematic appraisal of research data is termed "evidence-based medicine."

Epidemiological research on psychiatric and psychological disorders has faced special problems in establishing the reliability and validity of diagnoses based entirely on clusters of symptoms and behaviors, in the absence of discrete biological markers. Three generations of studies in psychiatric epidemiology can be distinguished in recent history: (1) an early period associated with asylum or hospital-based studies of major mental disorders and with the use of institutional records or key informants to ascertain diagnosis (1900–1950); (2) population surveys utilizing self-report scales of generalized distress or clinical assessments based on nonoperationalized diagnostic criteria (1950–1980); (3) clinical and population surveys using standardized highly structured interviews designed to collect data sufficient to make specific diagnoses according to operationalized criteria (1980–).

The advent of the *Diagnostic and Statistical Manual of Mental Disorders* (American Psychiatric Association) in 1980 was associated with an effort to improve the reliability of psychiatric diagnosis and to conduct large-scale population surveys. Determining the prevalence of specific disorders should give a better estimate of the actual service needs of the population as well as advancing research in psychopathology. This led to the development of the U.S. National Institute of Mental Health Diagnostic Interview Schedule (DIS), which allows trained lay interviewers to collect data sufficient to make diagnoses according to *DSM–III* criteria. The DIS was used with some 20,000 respondents in the U.S. Epidemiological Catchment Area Study from 1980 to 1984.

In the 1990s, the structure of the DIS was adapted to produce the Composite International Diagnostic Interview (CIDI) for the World Health Organization. The CIDI includes items to address the criteria of *DSM–IV* and the 10th edition of the *International Classification of Disease* (ICD–10). In addition to instruments like the DIS and the CIDI, there are structured instruments designed for the use of clinicians including the Structured Clinical Interview for *DSM–IV* (SCID) and the Schedules for Clinical Assessment in Neuropsychiatry (SCAN) for *ICD–10*, which evolved out of the earlier Present State Examination (PSE). The availability of translated versions of these standardized instruments has allowed large surveys in many countries permitting systematic cross-national comparisons for many psychiatric disorders. The development of structured diagnostic interviews in psychiatry has been adapted to other areas in medicine such as functional gastrointestinal syndromes and rheumatological disorders. Other epidemiological instruments have been developed to assess level of functioning, disability, quality of life, and needs for specific services.

The recent emphasis on increasing diagnostic reliability and specificity with structured instruments has raised concern about a lack of attention to the validity of diagnostic constructs. This has prompted reconsideration of dimensional approaches to psychological distress that allow for a continuum of levels of severity and that do not impose a priori diagnostic categories or cutpoints.

Genetic epidemiology involves the use of survey methods in concert with genetic techniques to identify the familial distribution, heritability, and manifestations of genetic variations. Although many neurological conditions have been localized in this way, the study of psychiatric disorders has been limited by the fact that the genetic contribution to most involves multiple genes interacting in a complex fashion with varying environmental circumstances. Genetic epidemiology can be used not only to identify the genetic contribution to disorders but equally to establish the contributions of familial (shared) and individual environmental experiences.

[*See also* Psychiatry.]

Bibliography

Eaton, W. W., & Kessler, L. G. (Eds.). (1985). *Epidemiological field methods in psychiatry: The NIMH epidemiological catchment area program.* Orlando, FL: Academic Press.

Mezzich, J. E., Jorge, M. R., & Salloum, I. M. (Eds.). (1994). *Psychiatric epidemiology: Assessment, concepts, and methods.* Baltimore: Johns Hopkins University Press.

Sackett, D. L., Haynes, R. B., Guyatt, G. H., & Tugwell, P. (1991). *Clinical epidemiology: A basic science for clinical medicine.* Boston: Little, Brown.

Streiner, D. L., & Norman, G. R. (1996). *PDQ epidemiology.* St. Louis: Mosby.

Tansella, M., de Girolamo, G., & Sartorius, N. (1992). *Annotated bibliography of psychiatric epidemiology.* London: Gaskell.

Tsuang, M. D., Tohen, M., & Zahner, G. E. P. (Eds.). (1995). *Textbook in psychiatric epidemiology,* New York: Wiley.

Laurence J. Kirmayer

EPILEPSY is a complex disorder that has long intrigued investigators of human behavior. Epilepsy is not a disease, but rather a disorder characterized by a tendency for recurrent seizures. The impact of epilepsy goes well beyond the direct effects of seizures and includes many factors which may lead to disability and impaired quality of life. Seizures result from unprovoked cerebral discharges that may be manifested as alterations in sensation, motor functions, and/or consciousness. Behavioral changes resulting from seizures have many forms, ranging from brief lapses of consciousness to full convulsions. Other seizures are characterized by unusual behavioral manifestations and stereotypic motor movements. The confusing terminology used to describe seizures in the past has been replaced by a formal classification system.

Approximately 1 to 2% of the population is affected by epilepsy, making it one of the most common neurological conditions. In the United States alone, more than two million individuals have epilepsy and hundreds of thousands develop epilepsy every year. Rates of epilepsy are slightly higher in men than in women. The condition develops most commonly among individuals under 20 years of age. Increased rates are also seen in those over 60 years. Many epileptic syndromes are associated with specific age groups, such as the neonatal seizures, infantile spasms, and febrile convulsions observed in young children. When developing in adults, epilepsy is often seen as a consequence of brain tumors, stroke, or traumatic brain injury. Epilepsy occurs at higher rates in individuals who are mentally-retarded or have some form of developmental disability. Some studies have indicated higher rates of epilepsy in minority populations, though this may reflect a confound of socioeconomic factors rather than ethnicity.

The diagnosis of epilepsy is made by obtaining a comprehensive medical history in conjunction with electroencephalography (EEG). The history includes a medical background and details about the seizures, including the changes behavior seen before, during, and after them. The EEG provides a method for documenting the underlying electrical brain activity associated with the seizures. Many seizures are characterized by specific patterns of electrical abnormality. Abnormal electrical discharges can also be detected when patients are not having seizures. Many patients require comprehensive monitoring with simultaneous EEG and video recording for proper diagnosis. This enables physicians to observe the correspondence between behavioral changes and underlying abnormal brain activity.

Many forms of epilepsy have an identifiable cause, such as the presence of a tumor or some other identifiable brain lesion. Other forms may be the result of genetic or systemic factors, such as the lack of a certain enzyme. Many cases previously labeled as idiopathic epilepsy are now found to be associated with a subtle underlying brain abnormality. The increased detection of these abnormalities has been a result of advances in structural brain-imaging techniques such as magnetic resonance imaging (MRI). Functional brain-imaging methods, such as positron emission tomography (PET), single photon emission computerized tomography (SPECT) and functional MRI (fMRI) have also advanced our ability to localize and understand the brain and the behavioral abnormalities associated with epilepsy.

Anticonvulsant drugs provide the most common and effective form of treatment. These act by altering the potential for abnormal cerebral discharge. Their goal is to reduce seizure activity and to improve quality of life. The number of drugs available to treat epilepsy has more than doubled over the past ten years. While many patients may require more than one anticonvulsant drug for optimal seizure control, the goal is to limit the number of drugs to reduce possible side effects. Approximately 30% of those treated do not respond adequately to drug management. Many of these individuals benefit from treatment with epilepsy surgery, which involves removing the abnormal portion of the brain that has been found, through extensive presurgical testing, to be causing the seizures. Alternative methods for treating epilepsy are available, though their efficacy remains less established. Individuals with some forms of epilepsy may benefit from changes in diet. Some have shown a reduction in seizures after surgical implantation of a special electrical device that is used to stimulate the vagal nerve. Others exhibit a reduction in seizure frequency after receiving focused behavioral treatment.

While many individuals with epilepsy lead normal, healthy lives, many studies have found increased rates of psychopathology in patients with epilepsy. Higher rates of psychosis, depression, anxiety, personality disorders, and sexual dysfunction have all been reported. Questions remain as to whether the rates of psychiatric disturbance are higher in individuals with epilepsy in comparison to populations with other chronic medical conditions. Some studies have reported up to a sevenfold increase in the rate of psychosis in patients with epilepsy, although these studies are typically conducted on patients appearing at specialized centers for treatment of the most severe forms of epilepsy. Questions about the rates of psychopathology in epilepsy need to be addressed through formal epidemiologic studies using accepted methods for diagnosing seizures and diagnosing the presence of psychiatric disturbance.

There are a number of striking parallels between behaviors resulting from seizures and symptoms associated with various psychiatric conditions. For example, some of the hallucinations and perceptual alterations resulting from temporal lobe seizures are very similar to some of the symptoms experienced by patients with schizophrenia. These observations suggest that the cerebral mechanisms underlying epilepsy might provide a valuable model for understanding the biology of schizophrenia and other psychiatric illnesses. Epilepsy has been used as an analog for understanding the neural substrate of aggression and the cyclical disorders of mood and behavior. Controversies exist over whether some forms of aggressive behavior may actually represent the effects of "subclinical" seizures.

Epilepsy is often thought to affect mood and personality. Some investigators have reported that patients with temporal lobe seizures are prone to changes in personality reflecting increased electrical activity in the limbic region. This may be manifested by increased writing behavior, higher levels of emotionality, and changes in sexual behavior. Depression is commonly experienced as a result of biological factors and as a psychological reaction to chronic illness. Individuals with epilepsy commonly experience "learned helplessness" resulting from their response to a condition characterized by an intermittent and abrupt loss of control. Other patients are known to exhibit recurring seizures without any underlying brain abnormality. These "nonepileptic" seizures are often the result of complex psychological factors that may include conversion reaction or attempts to obtain secondary gain. Psychotherapy appears to be the most effective method for treating nonepileptic seizures.

A number of cognitive abnormalities have been documented in patients with epilepsy. Results from early studies showed decreased levels of intellectual functioning in patients with generalized seizures or with frequent seizure activity. Increased rates of learning and behavioral problems are commonly seen in children with epilepsy. Many individuals with epilepsy experience mild impairments in memory and attention that may be a result of the seizures, an underlying brain abnormality, or the side effects associated with anticonvulsant medications. Patients with seizures arising from focal brain regions may exhibit specific patterns of cognitive dysfunction. For example, it is well known that patients with left temporal lobe seizures exhibit relatively specific impairments in verbal memory while their recall of spatial information is less affected. Neuropsychological testing provides the most sensitive and reliable means of identifying these cognitive abnormalities. Studies of patients undergoing surgical procedures such as temporal lobe resection and callosotomy have played major roles in the development of neuroanatomic theories of memory functioning and hemispheric specialization. Information from these studies has contributed significantly to the body of knowledge on brain-behavior relationships.

Many people with epilepsy experience a unique form of stigma resulting from the intermittent nature of their symptoms. Throughout history, those with epilepsy have been labeled holy or possessed as a result of changes in behavior during seizures. In other societies, these individuals were considered "insane" and were placed in asylums. Currently, social attitudes toward epilepsy and disability vary across ethnic and cultural groups. The effects of epilepsy include academic underachievement, chronic emotional distress, and social isolation. There is a significant economic impact on society, which includes not only the high costs of diagnosing and treating epilepsy but the loss of productivity from a significant portion of the population. Despite information showing that seizures do not affect overall job performance, people with epilepsy have higher rates of unemployment and restrictions in their earning power as a result of their condition. Issues of discrimination can be addressed through patient advocacy and changes in public policy pertaining to epilepsy.

Bibliography

Bear, D., & Fedio, P. (1977). Quantitative analysis of inter-ictal behavior in temporal lobe epilepsy. *Archives of Neurology, 34*, 454–467.

Engel, J., & Pedley, T. A. (Eds). (1998). *Epilepsy: A comprehensive textbook*. Philadelphia: Lippincott-Raven.

Gazzaniga, M. S. (1970). *The bisected brain*. New York: Appleton-Century-Crofts.

Hauser, W. A., & Hesdorffer, D. C. (1990). *Epilepsy: Frequency, causes, and consequences*. New York: Demos.

Hermann, B. P., & Whitmann, S. (1984). Behavioral and personality correlates of epilepsy: A review, methodological critique, and conceptual model. *Psychological Bulletin, 95*, 451–497.

Milner, B. (1972). Disorders of learning and memory after temporal lobe lesions in man. *Clinical Neurosurgery, 19*, 421–446.

Novelly, R. A. (1992). The debt of neuropsychology to the epilepsies. *American Psychologist, 47*, 1126–1129.

Penfield, W., & Rasmussen, T. (1952). *The cerebral cortex of man*. New York: Macmillan.

Temkin, O. (1971). *The falling sickness*. Baltimore: Johns Hopkins University Press.

Trimble, M. R. (1991). *The psychoses of epilepsy*. New York: Raven Press.

William B. Barr

EPISTEMOLOGY is the discipline concerned with the nature of knowledge, its origins, the conceptual assumptions or grounds out of which knowledge arises and is possible at all, methods of attaining knowledge, and the status of knowledge as real knowledge, that is, a concern for its trustworthiness. Epistemology, along with metaphysics and ethics, has been one of the fundamental and defining disciplines within Western philosophy. The most basic epistemological question is whether it is possible to achieve certain knowledge. Certain knowledge, it is generally understood, would be knowledge of what really is; it would be true for all persons and in all circumstances.

Epistemology and Psychologism

Psychologism is the term used to describe the position that questions of the nature knowledge and the processes by which it is acquired can be reduced to questions of the actual workings of the human mind, or even to the workings of the brain. Thus, epistemological questions will ultimately be answered by the accrual of scientific knowledge about the workings of the mind or brain. Knowledge contingent on the workings of the mind or the brain would not qualify as certain knowledge. Hence, psychologism is a skeptical position.

Among the most influential critics of psychologism in the twentieth century were Edmund Husserl (1859–1938), Gottlob Frege (1848–1925), and Ludwig Wittgenstein (1889–1951). The fundamental argument against psychologism begins with the recognition that the workings of the human mind or the human brain are contingent phenomena, subject to personal idiosyncracies as well as such environmental and biological conditions as might affect human beings in their contingent, limited, and imperfect state. Therefore, psychologism must regard all knowledge as contingent, obviating the possibility of certainty in any field of inquiry. To accept any psychologistic account of knowledge is to reject the possibility of knowing anything to be true in the strong sense, that is, true in all circumstances. Science would not escape these same limitations on certainty. This same problem of contingent versus noncontingent knowledge lies at the heart of the current confrontation of modernism and postmodernism in psychology.

The Interdependence of Ontology and Epistemology

Epistemology began with the Greek thinkers of the sixth century BCE. Philosophy was able to develop because of the shared assumption among the pre-Socratic Greek cosmologists that there was a rationality to the universe which could be understood by the exercise of the powers of the mind. The same project continued in the classical period in the thought of Socrates, Plato, and Aristotle. Epistemology, grounded in reason and rational order, was integral to Western philosophy and the subsequent pursuit of knowledge.

It is important to note the intimate connection between ontology, which addresses the question of what really is, and epistemology, which examines how or whether what is real can be known. Any claim regarding the fundamental nature of reality requires justification for the claim, and the justification must be as fundamental as the claim—it must be a truth claim. At the same time, every ontological claim will constrain the nature of the knowledge claims used to defend it. Thus, ontology and epistemology have always been inextricably linked, as much in psychology as in philosophy.

Greek philosophy from the pre-Socratic period through the classical period is often characterized by the division of reality into Being and Becoming. The realm of Being is taken to be a noncontingent realm composed of realities independent of the natural processes of change, eternal, perfect, and unambiguously real. On the other hand, the realm of Becoming is taken to be a contingent realm composed of things in the experienced world, which are subject to the processes of nature and change, temporal, imperfect, only real in some sense, and made real by Being.

Knowledge of noncontingent realities (such as Platonic forms, Being, or the absolute) must be noncontingent—knowledge that can be taken as true across contexts and across time. Such knowledge seemed to the Greeks to be available only through reason and not through the fallible senses or contingent experience. Thus, to postulate the existence of noncontingent realities is to postulate noncontingent knowledge, and to legitimate certain methods, generally reason and logic, as the means of attaining such knowledge. The contingent world known by experience is real, but in a way radically different from noncontingent and necessary truths.

The distinction between the contingent and the noncontingent, and between the two types of knowledge and methods for knowing required by each, produced an important distinction in Greek philosophy—that between knowledge (episteme) on the one hand and mere opinion on the other. For Aristotle especially, "scientific" knowledge included causal principles behind things and events. This same concern for causal principles has been preserved in the prescription that genuinely scientific explanations will be in terms of true and general laws. Mere descriptions of the facts of experience, and explanations in terms of the merely contingent and transient, are designated "mere opinion," while explanations grounded in noncontingent general laws are the hallmark of scientific knowledge. However, out of concern for scientific credibility, contemporary thinking in psychology seeks a type of noncontingent explanation through contingent means—empirical observation.

Epistemology and Explanation

From Greek times to the present, philosophers as well as scientists have inquired as to what constitutes adequate or genuine explanation. In the *Meno*, Plato distinguished "true belief" from knowledge. Persons may hold true beliefs about some state of affairs such that they are able to reach right conclusions and render proper answers to questions. Such beliefs may accrue from experience. However, according to Plato and Aristotle, genuine knowledge (episteme), requires knowledge of the grounds for the belief and the conclusion to which it leads. Traditionally, genuine knowledge of a phenomenon has been assumed to entail knowledge of the principles or the reality underlying it. In other words, explanation must reflect what is genuinely the case, and it must reflect true and adequate grounds for itself.

Knowledge of a thing sufficient to render an adequate explanation must be knowledge of the essential nature of the thing. This requires a formalist epistemology, one in which truth claims are ultimately defensible. Aristotle coined the term *first philosophy* to describe the project of metaphysics, the project of understanding and describing a thing in terms of its absolute and necessary qualities. Although Aristotle

also recognized other sciences, practical and political, and granted that the several sciences were to be valued for their contribution to knowledge, first philosophy was in some sense privileged because it could arrive at the more secure grounds of knowledge, as in the axioms of mathematics. This privileging of knowledge as first philosophy continued through the centuries and is manifest in much contemporary scientific thinking and theorizing. The best and adequate explanation of a phenomenon will be given in terms of knowledge of the necessary and fundamental.

In contemporary psychology, this same epistemological concern is seen in the preference for causal explanation and prediction over "mere" description. However, it is prudent to understand that concern for real knowledge over true beliefs does not necessarily map neatly onto concern for causal (scientific) explanation and prediction over description. Causal explanation and prediction by themselves do not have epistemological authority, since they are concerned with and can often arise out of the merely contingent, as when they are based on observations and sensory experience rather than noncontingent foundations. Thus, the question of the contingency versus noncontingency of knowledge is really at the heart of the question of true belief versus knowledge.

Skepticism

While it has been commonly held that genuine knowledge makes truth claims, there has been no shortage of positions skeptical of any such claims. Skepticism has existed as individual doubt and as intellectual movements. As early as the fifth century BCE, skeptics argued against the possibility of arriving at truth through rationality. Skepticism, however, has always been vulnerable to self-refutation, since it cannot both be true in its assumptions and correct in its conclusions.

Although the first skeptics aimed their arguments at the limitations of reason, it did not take long for knowledge gained through experience to be challenged as well. Skeptics held that since experience is constantly changing, knowledge gained through observation or experience is inevitably transitory. Furthermore, since the senses themselves are demonstrably fallible, knowledge gained through observation and experience is fallible. In response to skepticism, it could be argued that demonstrations that a method of acquiring knowledge (reason or experience) is fallible do not establish that the method will *necessarily* fail to reveal genuine knowledge. However, because of the inherently contingent and transitory nature of experience, it would appear unlikely that one could, relying only on experience as the source of knowledge, ever break through mere appearances to the real and attain more than true belief.

In addition to simply defending reason, traditional rebuttals of skepticism have appealed to a record of successes in adapting knowledge in the accomplishment of specific purposes, that is, our knowledge seems to work. Other support for the validity of knowledge revolves around correspondences of, for example, the natural world to the principles of abstract mathematics. If all knowledge claims are suspect, these correspondences and successes lack explanation.

Universals and Particulars

An important epistemological question that particularly occupied medieval philosophers was whether universals really exist or whether only particular instances are real. To a universalist view, universals have existence, and therefore knowledge must be grounded in the universals which make the particulars what they are, and thus render them understandable. Universalist views tend to be rationalist because the universals and knowledge of them are accessible through the exercise of the rational powers. Particulars are then understood through a process of deduction from the knowledge of the universals. To a nominalist (particularist) view, since only particulars are real, knowledge must begin with experience of particulars. Such views tend to be empiricist, emphasizing the importance of sensory experience and observation. Based on knowledge of particulars, it is possible to generalize knowledge and create abstractions through induction. However, nominalists remind us that the abstractions are simply products of mental processes and have no ontological status of their own.

In psychology, deduction and induction are usually discussed as parts of the scientific process. However, the deeper question underlying the contrast between deduction and induction is that of the possible grounding for genuine knowledge. Because of the contingent nature of particulars, knowledge based purely on induction seems unlikely to produce more than contingent knowledge, lacking certainty. On the other hand, deduction is a source of certain knowledge only if universals are real, and can be truly known through rational powers.

William of Ockham (1285–1347) articulated the nominalist argument in terms of what has come to be called "Ockham's Razor," often interpreted as the forebear of the "Law of Parsimony." Since the purest knowledge comes from experience of the world of particulars, abstractions are mental creations and should not be taken to be more real than the particulars from which they are derived, and thus should be used judiciously in explanations. They may be used, however, and seem to be required for noncontingent knowledge. St. Thomas Aquinas (1225–1274) had earlier argued that even if universals are products of the mind, they may be valid nonetheless.

Certainty and the Privatization of Knowledge

During the centuries following Ockham, confidence in rationalism waned. In the seventeenth century, however, rationalism experienced a revival of sorts in the work of René Descartes (1596–1650). Descartes, in a sense, shifted the grounds of epistemology from the "other world" of forms and ideals to the individual mind. In an attempt to save knowledge from skepticism, he effected a major reconceptualization of knowledge itself. Real knowledge consisted of clear ideas. Of these ideas, certainty was possible, and certainty was defined as that which could not be (reasonably) doubted.

The certainty pursued by Descartes required a privileged perspective from which to reason. This was achieved through the method of systematic doubt. Descartes doubted everything that could be doubted until he arrived at something he could not reasonably doubt—that he was doubting, and thus, that he existed. From this unassailable truth he then deduced other truths, including the existence of God. Descartes's method and his philosophy did not go unchallenged by his contemporaries. His work, however, had a major defining influence on modern epistemology. It marks the beginning of the modern period in philosophy.

Several important implications of Descartes's work have direct relevance for psychology. Whether Descartes himself intended it or not, his work had the effect of grounding certainty and knowledge in the individual mind. An individual mind was capable of achieving certainty by critically examining its own operations. This represented a departure from more ancient thinking, in which knowledge might require dialogue or enlightenment from another realm. Furthermore, that which could be directly and best known (clear ideas) was the contents of one's own mind. Descartes's philosophy thus provides support for epistemologies based on intuitive knowledge, or on that which can be known by disciplined reflection.

Descartes's distinction between mind and "extended matter" provided the foundation for a sharp distinction, drawn by later thinkers, between the inner subjective world and the outer objective world, paralleling the bifurcation of mind and body. It has been an important tenet of epistemological thinking that mind (the mental) and world (the physical) constitute separate and irreconcilable ontological realms. This dualist ontology is the foundation of much of the contemporary criticism leveled at "Cartesianism," although it may not adequately reflect Descartes's own position on the subject.

Granting this dualistic perspective, the acquisition of knowledge requires some way of getting what is outside the mind into it, or, conversely, of getting the ideas of the mind arrayed outward as organizing principles for making sense of the world. When reality is divided into the inner and the outer, the problem of "other minds" presents itself. If the mind is subjective and interior, and its own contents are all it can directly know, then from the perspective of any mind all other minds are unknowable. Because they are immaterial, they cannot be the objects of any other's experience. Since they are others' minds, they are not directly knowable by any but those others. How then can one mind be confident that other minds exist at all? This and other issues have been at the center of concern for the public validation of knowledge and the role of intersubjectivity in knowledge and meaning.

For Descartes, knowledge is based in truths that can be known intuitively. These truths, perhaps exemplified best by mathematical axioms, are sometimes referred to as innate ideas. These truths are not, nor can they be, given by experience. But from such truths other knowledge can be properly and safely deduced. Innate ideas are not contingent, and thus constitute a firm grounding for knowledge. Innate ideas are not to be thought of as fully formed bits of information. They are ideas or principles that can be immediately perceived as true by rational beings.

Rationalism and Empiricism

Perhaps no epistemological issue has influenced psychology as directly as rationalism versus empiricism. The difference between (Continental) rationalism and (British) empiricism is captured succinctly, if oversimply, in the contrast between Descartes's contention that the two principal sources of knowledge are intuition and deduction, and the suggestion of Thomas Hobbes (1588–1679) that the two sources are observation (or experience) and deduction. Neither classical rationalists nor empiricists deny the existence nor the importance of reason. The disagreement centers around the foundation of knowledge. On this issue, the two positions are irreconcilable.

Classical empiricism, in the work of John Locke (1632–1704), George Berkeley (1685–1753), and David Hume (1711–1776), is a radicalization of the empiricism of Aristotle and other classical and medieval thinkers. It holds that all knowledge comes originally from sensory experience. Thus all knowledge is contingent. Empiricism is also psychologistic, since knowledge is produced by the senses and the combining, separating, and abstracting functions of the mind. To hold that all knowledge comes from experience is to hold that there are severe limitations on knowledge because there are severe limitations on experience. Furthermore, many things we know or claim to know, such as the self, causes, and other abstractions, cannot be directly experienced. Thus, modern empiricism, particularly in the work of David Hume, is often seen as the beginning of modern skepticism and epistemological and moral relativism.

Classical empiricism has been extremely influential in psychology as the philosophical grounding for behaviorism and many other related approaches. Empiricism has also been influential as a foundation for empirical scientific methods. However, it is arguable whether the use of so-called empirical methods requires any prior commitment to the epistemology of classical empiricism.

Modern rationalism is often traced to the work of Descartes, but has been, in one form or another, the major epistemological position throughout the Western philosophical tradition. Rationalism was given perhaps its most complete and comprehensive form in the work of Immanuel Kant (1724–1804). Kant undertook a response to, among other things, the work of Hume and the implications that followed from the assumption that all knowledge is grounded in experience, and the contention that causality and identity, as well as moral principles, were artifacts of habitual modes of thought. The concern of classical rationalism is for the noncontingent foundations of knowledge. It is argued that certain preconditions must exist for knowledge, including knowledge gained from experience, to be possible at all. Rationalism suggests that there must be some universal and a priori grounds for knowledge, perception, cognition, and ethics. Kant postulated the existence of "pure intuitions of time and space" as the necessary preconditions for all experience, and the "pure categories of the understanding" as the necessary preconditions of all knowledge. These function as innate organizing principles without which neither experience nor knowledge could be formed.

For Kant, ethics required an epistemology in which there were noncontingent grounds for ethical principles and comportment. He formulated the "categorical imperative" as the central element of all morality. Ethical systems derived from Kantian forms of rationalism are deontological, that is, nonrelativistic, absolute, and principle based. Rationalism has been influential in psychology as well, though often unacknowledged. Its influence can be discerned in the work of personality theorists such as Sigmund Freud, Carl Jung, Alfred Adler, and George Kelly, in developmental theories such as that of Jean Piaget, and to a certain extent in Gestalt psychology and modern cognitive theories.

The epistemological issue of rationalism versus empiricism is substantive and central to psychology. It cannot be resolved by psychology (unless psychologism is true) because the issue itself forms the ground out of which any psychology must arise. Furthermore, the two positions are irreconcilable since they represent alternative claims about the originative grounds and status of knowledge, and differing claims about the nature of explanation in any psychology.

Epistemology and Science

Psychology's primary methodological commitment has been to a version of scientific method adopted in the late nineteenth century, influenced by an intellectual movement known as positivism. The hope has been that a commitment to this scientific method is a sufficient response to epistemological concerns. Logical positivism combined a confidence in formal logic, a fairly radical empiricism, and psychologism. Logical positivists held that only that which could be framed and validated in observational terms could count as scientific knowledge.

The positivists strongly influenced the development of psychology in the first half of the twentieth century and continued to be influential long after their tenets had been more or less abandoned in philosophy and the other sciences. Nevertheless, this methodological and epistemological perspective is still taken by some to be essential to the project of any scientific psychology. Indeed, the tenets of logical positivism are sometimes taken to be science itself. The legacy of logical positivism is perhaps most evident in the model of scientific explanation formulated by Carl Hempel (1905–1997), the so-called nomological-deductive model.

When science is taken to be an epistemology—a response to questions of the origin and quality of knowledge—several issues become important. The problem of verification centers around the ability of the methods of science to validate theories or hypotheses, and therefore to settle questions of truth. Though not widely acknowledged in psychology, it has been widely understood in philosophy that all theories are underdetermined by data. The Duhme-Quine thesis points to this by noting that any theory can, given sufficient alteration, be shown to be compatible with any body of data. Karl Popper (1902–1994) drew attention to the difficulty in verifying universal laws by means of finite observations. Such verification would require an infinite number of observations. Popper's "falsificationist" criterion was part of his larger critique of many of the assumptions of logical positivism. It is a common fallacy to assume that when a theory cannot be falsified it is somehow verified by default. It is also a genuine question whether scientific method can, in principle, arrange any crucial test of a theory sufficient to falsify it. If not, falsification is also refuted.

Imre Lakatos (1922–1974) proposed a modification of falsificationism, suggesting that it can take place only with limited "programmes of research." Thomas Kuhn (1922–1996) and others in the so-called *Weltanschauung* perspective have argued that social forces influence scientific theories, questions, and methods, and that scientific progress takes place within paradigms, but also in dramatic and revolutionary paradigm shifts. Other philosophers of science, notably Paul Feyerabend

(1924–1994), have been more critical of theories that emphasize smooth paradigmatic advance, arguing that a type of "anarchy" is the best guarantee that science will achieve its ends.

Given the currency of various views of the nature of science, each one making some different epistemological assumptions, science itself is not a sufficient response to epistemological questions. Hans-Georg Gadamer (1900–) has argued that no method can provide an adequate epistemology because prior understandings of truth (epistemological assumptions) will underlie the development and deployment of any method.

Explanation and Understanding

The late nineteenth and early twentieth century saw the emergence of a post-Kantian tradition which emphasized the difficulty in applying the same methods and epistemological criteria in understanding the human world as may be applied to the natural world. This is sometimes referred to as the *Verstehen* tradition, after the German word meaning "understanding." Wilhelm Dilthey (1822–1911) made an important distinction between the natural sciences and the *Geisteswissenschaften*, often translated as "human sciences." While the natural world could be accounted for by causal explanations, human beings must be "understood." This understanding is a more sympathetic and intersubjective understanding, a respect for the subjectivity of the subject of study, and a recognition that, in important ways, human beings are not part of the natural world. Two different epistemologies are thus required by two different ontologies. This tradition is importantly related to the phenomenological and hermeneutic traditions descending from the work of Edmund Husserl (1859–1938), and it is an influential precursor to the contemporary "human science" tradition in psychology. Likewise, this historical concern for "understanding" is manifest as a broader interest in qualitative research methods. A fundamental claim of these positions is that traditional explanation and scientific methods impose constructs on human phenomena, while understanding requires allowing knowledge to emerge from the phenomena themselves.

Pragmatism

One response to the modern loss of confidence in method and in noncontingent knowledge is pragmatism. Pragmatism entered contemporary psychology through the writings of William James (1842–1910) and Charles Peirce (1839–1914). It is an epistemology because it is a response to questions of truth and meaning. For pragmatism, the meaning and truth of propositions, theories, or practices are found in the examination of their consequences. Relevant consequences include the experiential, observable, conceptual, as well as the moral. As a response to the perceived failure of method and the loss of faith in the noncontingent, pragmatism has taken many forms, some incompatible with each other, ranging from strict empiricism, wherein only observable consequences count as knowledge, to complete relativism, wherein anything that works for an individual can be assigned the status of "truth."

Pragmatism is an incomplete and thus unsatisfactory solution to the epistemological questions, which lead many to embrace it because criteria are always necessary for the evaluation of consequences. Thus, in its more facile forms, pragmatism simply begs the question. In its more sophisticated forms, as for James and Pierce, it harkens back to traditional epistemologies.

Knowledge in the Postmodern Age

The last half of the twentieth century has seen the development of a number of philosophical positions loosely allied in their opposition to traditional epistemological and ontological perspectives. Likewise, there has been a decided decline in confidence in any method of achieving absolute truth. Two traditions have been markedly influential in this development: the "ordinary language" movement in philosophy, taking its lead chiefly from the later philosophy of Ludwig Wittgenstein (1889–1951), and the phenomenological movement following the work of Edmund Husserl.

Much work in modern analytical philosophy is dedicated to the problem of the relation of propositions, understood as knowledge claims, to actual states of affairs. This overarching project has some commonality with the work of the logical positivists, and in its modern manifestations, at least in the social sciences, it has been in part aimed at preserving traditional positivistic conception of science. The central tenet of this approach is that a proposition is true if what it asserts is actually the case. The central problem that continues to present difficulties for this linguistic or propositional approach to epistemology is that of verification. A related and important issue is whether human knowledge is ever of the world itself, or merely of propositions.

Perhaps the most optimistic approach to the verification problem was the "logical atomism" developed in the work of Bertrand Russell and in the early work of Ludwig Wittgenstein. This doctrine held that every true statement could be reduced to some sort of empirical experience that validated it. Although the doctrine proved to be untenable, the search for a solution to the verification problem continues in softer versions of positivism and other contemporary philosophical approaches. The issue central to all these approaches was articulated by Wilhelm Leibniz, who distinguished between truths of reason, which do not rest on verification through experience, such as A = A, and truths of fact. Truths of fact can be established by correspon-

dence, which in turn rests on experience with the world. If experience is insufficient to verify some belief or proposition, the fallback position is to equate truth with suitability as a basis for a course of action, i.e., pragmatism.

All attempts to verify propositions through experience ultimately rest on inductive processes. Substantial attention has been devoted to the possibility of achieving genuine knowledge inductively. "Gettier problems," from the work of Edmund Gettier, are demonstrations that it is possible to have justified true beliefs but without genuine knowledge, that is, one may be correct to believe "that p," based on one's experience, and it may indeed be the case "that p." However, it may be that p is the case for reasons other than those given by experience and on which the belief is based. There may be other factors that make p the case, or it may be incidently the case. Experience could not establish one's belief in proposition p as knowledge rather than as mere coincidence.

Other lines of analysis have been developed to expose the limits of induction. One such approach, known as "Goodman's paradox" from the work of Nelson Goodman, holds that induction from experience can never produce genuine knowledge. It may be the case that all observations up to the present (t_1) verify that p is true of the world; however, it may also be the case that at a future time (t_2) the nature of the world may be such that p is no longer true, and our observations will be different. Thus, past and present observations cannot constitute a foundation for noncontingent knowledge. Other contemporary thinkers have argued that decisions about the knowledge status of ideas or propositions derived from experience, i.e., their truth, will always be made on grounds of believability not derivable from experience itself. This argument is similar to Plato's much older argument, developed in the *Meno*, concerning the dependence of knowledge on conceptually a priori knowledge.

Another line of analysis relevant to the criterion problem concerns "possession" of knowledge. It is held that to possess knowledge, a thinker must find certain inferences compelling while the inferences are not based on information. Such inferences will depend necessarily on the perceptions and relationship of the possessor with the environment, not on purely sensory information. Since humans uniquely can make such inferences, only humans can be said to possess knowledge. Human knowledge, since it is derived from relations with the world, is always "about something": To know is to know about something. Such "aboutness" is a defining characteristic of human knowledge. This argument harkens back to earlier work on intentionality in the work of Franz Brentano. The analytical philosopher John Searle articulated a similar position, arguing that knowledge claims come from "aspects" of experience, but since there is more to experience than aspects, and since the aspects are derived from resources apart from experience, experience can give aspects but not certain knowledge.

This work on the limitations of knowledge derived from experience poses significant problems for any project of verification of knowledge by means of experience. The problem of verification arises from the claim that knowledge is really always of propositions rather than of the world. The response of some in this position has been to abandon the idea that knowledge is innately propositional. These thinkers, notably J. L. Austin and G. E. Moore, moved toward a position on knowledge reminiscent of the Common Sense philosophy of Thomas Reid—that knowledge of the world is tied to experience, not of the sort that verifies propositions but of a more immediate, direct sort.

Another more radical version of the linguistic approach to knowledge and truth has emerged from the difficulties intrinsic to the work on propositional knowledge and verification. The primary epistemological contribution of the various perspectives descendant from the so-called ordinary language movement is that the analysis of knowledge is integrally bound up with the analysis of language. It is argued that since meaning is achieved through an essentially discursive process by persons situated in cultural contexts, knowledge thus achieved is likewise situated. This general thesis about knowledge and language has been adopted in psychology in various movements, including social constructionism, discursive psychology, and a number of other narrative approaches.

Although Husserl is in the minds of many as the last of the classical rationalists, his conclusions are radical enough to cast the issue of knowledge in a new light. Husserl's phenomenology, and the phenomenological psychology that descends from it, pursued a form of essential, or apodictic, knowledge through a method of reduction in which the merely contingent is suspended and consciousness achieves a pure seeing of its objects in terms of their intentional meaning. Husserl's work inspired others to take different directions. The modern hermeneutic movement, exemplified in the work of Martin Heidegger (1889–1976), Maurice Merleau-Ponty (1907–1961), Paul Ricoeur (1913–) Jurgen Habermas (1924–), and Hans-Georg Gadamer (1900–), has been influential in psychology in the last half of the twentieth century. Existentialism, exemplified in the work of Jean-Paul Sartre (1905–1980), is closely related to hermeneutics, and has influenced psychology as well.

Existentialism, most obviously in its Sartrean form, is characterized by a radical subjectivism, leading to a radical view of human freedom and a subjectivist epistemology. Such a view surrenders hope of noncontingent knowledge and inclines toward epistemological relativism and even solipsism. Although, on a hermeneutic view, knowledge is contextual, interpretive, and always instantiated in language, the hermeneutic movement has been less inclined than existentialism to move in the direction of subjectivity. Indeed, in its approach to the question of knowledge, it seeks to transcend the traditional categories of contingent and noncontingent. Habermas seeks to retain a grounding for knowledge in a modified rationality, while Gadamer proposes to anchor truth in "effective historical consciousness." Merleau-Ponty emphasizes the role of the lived body in the project of knowing and understanding. Heidegger argues that the proper response to epistemological questions will be possible only after a richer hermeneutic understanding of being itself.

In contrast to conventional approaches to knowing, Heidegger offers an analysis of various "modes of engagement." The type of knowledge traditionally sought in philosophy and epistemology emphasizes a reflective mode of involvement with the world, which preserves the traditional subject-objective dichotomy. This he terms the "present at hand" mode. However, Heidegger suggests that knowledge can also be understood in terms of a more natural, unreflective, and intimate mode of engagement with the world, the "ready to hand," in which the subject-object dichotomy is entirely in the background and knowledge takes the form of projects and performances that have meaning in the interpretive world, where human beings exist. This approach to knowledge is neither rationalist nor empiricist.

The postmodern movement has spawned a number of other positions related to the traditions mentioned here, including critical theory and many feminist theories, all sharing epistemological commitments. Some of these depart more and some less radically from traditional epistemological concerns. All attempt some new understanding of knowledge in terms of human actions rather than the products of mental activity or sensory input. It remains to be demonstrated whether postmodern approaches to knowledge can evade the problems that have pursued epistemology through the centuries while making possible some standard of knowledge which permits both science and meaning in human life.

The Importance of Epistemology for Psychology

Human beings are distinguished from other living beings by virtue of an enlarged capacity for knowledge as well as the types of knowledge of which they are capable. Any attempt to study and understand human beings must take these singular and defining human characteristics into account. Any satisfactorily comprehensive theory of human functioning must offer some account of the nature of human knowledge as well as its origins. The link between knowledge and behavior is one of the most important and enduring psychological questions. Furthermore, psychological theories will necessarily offer differing explanations of human behavior and human potential, depending on whether it is presumed that persons acquire knowledge passively and only from experience or whether they possess active and a priori powers of knowing. Epistemology is a watershed issue for theorizing about human beings.

Some branches of psychology set out to map the processes by which knowledge, however defined, is acquired and how it affects behavior. While some models of learning and cognition are never meant to be more than working models of the processes of knowing, never claiming to make ontological claims about knowledge, there are epistemological assumptions and implications imbedded in every such model, however modest its claims.

Epistemology is relevant not only to the question of how human beings can know generally, but also to the question of the validity of claims of knowledge made by scientists. Science, and all scientific methods, are grounded in epistemological commitments and make epistemological claims. Science distinguishes itself as science by virtue of its claim about the trustworthiness of scientific knowledge compared to other kinds of knowledge. The status of psychology as science finally rests on the adequacy and validity of its epistemological commitments.

[*See also* Epistemology of Practice; Philosophy, *article on* Philosophy of Science; Psychology, *articles on* Classical Antiquity, Middle Ages, Renaissance through the Enlightenment, *and* Nineteenth Century Through Freud.]

Bibliography

Baynes, K., Bohman, J., & McCarthy, T. (1987). *After philosophy: End or transformation?* Cambridge, MA: MIT Press. The leading figures in recent, postmodern philosophy treat the crisis in contemporary epistemology.

Bem, S., & deJong, H. B. (1997). *Theoretical issues in psychology: An introduction.* Thousand Oaks, CA: Sage. An introductory treatment of philosophical issues, with substantial coverage of epistemology, written from a moderate postmodern perspective.

Bernstein, R. J. (1983). *Beyond objectivism and relativism: Science, hermeneutics, and praxis.* Philadelphia: University of Pennsylvania Press. A careful yet accessible analysis of the issues entailed in the confrontation between classical and more recent hermeneutical traditions, with due coverage given to science.

Dancy, J. & Sosa, E. (Eds.). (1992). *A companion to episte-mology.* Cambridge, MA: Blackwell. Perhaps the best single resource for someone interested in the history of epistemology, its leading figures and issues.

Gadamer, H-G. (1982). *Truth and method.* New York: Crossroad. Essential work for understanding the hermeneutic perspective on method. It is a demanding work for those not familiar with hermeneutic philosophy.

Hamlyn, D. W. (1967). Epistemology, History of. In P. Edwards (Ed.), *An encyclopedia of philosophy* (Vol. 3). New York: Macmillan. A very good, brief, but insightful history of epistemology from the ancient Greeks to modern movements from a traditional perspective.

Hempel, C. G. (1965). *Aspects of scientific explanation.* New York: Free Press.

James, W. (1975/1907). *Pragmatism: A new name for some old ways of thinking.* Cambridge, MA: Harvard University Press.

Kenny, A. (Ed.). (1997). *The Oxford illustrated history of Western philosophy.* New York: Oxford University Press. Covers epistemology in proportion to its considerable importance to Western philosophy; readable, and offers interesting historical information.

Lakatos, I., & Musgrave, A. (Eds.). (1982). *Criticism and the growth of knowledge.* Cambridge, England: Cambridge University Press. This volume is a good condensed introduction to the major perspectives on the philosophy of science that centers on falsfiability and the possibility of truth claims. It concentrates more particularly on the work of Kuhn and Lakatos.

Merleau-Ponty, M. (1962). *The phenomenology of perception.* London: Routledge. This phenomenological treatment of perception and knowledge is generally more accessible to psychologists than some other writing in the same tradition.

Popper, K. R. (1959). *The logic of scientific discovery.* New York: Basic Books.

Robinson, D. N. (1995). *An intellectual history of psychology* (3rd ed.). Madison, WI: University of Wisconsin Press.

Slife, B. D., & Williams, R. N. (1995). *What's behind the research: Discovering hidden assumptions in the behavioral sciences.* Thousand Oaks, CA: Sage. Written as a primer in philosophical issues in psychology, it aims at the nonprofessional. Chapters on science and ways of knowing are particularly relevant to epistemology.

Richard N. Williams

EPISTEMOLOGY OF PRACTICE refers to an interdisciplinary theoretical and philosophical discussion across a wide variety of professions concerning the nature of practical knowledge (knowing what to do and how to do it in the real world), and its relationship to theoretical or scientific knowledge (knowing the conceptual principles that explain the nature, structure, and functioning of the world). In their seminal work on this topic, Argyris and Schön (1974) observed that the relationship of scientific theory to professional practice became a point of considerable tension within those professions that sought to incorporate their free-standing professional schools (e.g., psychology, nursing, engineering, education, business and management, dentistry, medicine, architecture, etc.) into the modern American university. In exchange for the legitimacy offered, the university exacted a commitment to the epistemological and academic primacy of the liberal arts and sciences in the training programs or admissions requirements of these professions.

In psychology, this could be seen after World War II in the development of the new training programs in clinical psychology. The Boulder-Model maintained that practitioners were to be trained first and foremost as scientists and that a high level of professional competence would result. Practitioner knowledge was seen as applied science. Science, conceptualized in classical logical positivist terms, would reveal what caused people to have psychological problems, and it would also demonstrate what caused those problems to be ameliorated. Practitioners armed with this knowledge would prevent the problem by removing from the world the antecedent causal conditions, or treat the problem by introducing those variables shown to produce change into a clinical situation. It was a model of brilliant clarity and simplicity that also served to assert the hegemony of scientific knowledge over practical knowledge.

The model directly challenged clinical practitioners who often looked to their own accumulated clinical experience, or that of their colleagues in clinical psychiatry and social work, as creating a relatively autonomous base of experience on which to formulate theories of practice. Scientists rejected this clinical knowledge base as anecdotal, riddled with subjective biases, and as offering causal assertions supported by unsystematic uncontrolled observations. Practitioners countered by asserting a kind of epistemological privilege that exempted their theories from verification via the scientific method. They claimed that clinical practice was based on intuition, empathic understanding, wisdom, and a kind of artistic virtuosity that set it apart from scientific scrutiny. In 1954, Paul Meehl attempted to resolve the controversy by statistically comparing actuarial and clinical predictions. He showed that simple multiple regression equations consistently outperformed seasoned clinicians in predicting a variety of clinical outcome criteria. He was startled to discover that rather than settling the matter, his literature review and analysis only fanned the flames of dissension between scientists and practitioners.

The Vail Conference on clinical training in psychology encouraged a more practice-based approach to the training of clinical psychologists. Donald Peterson, who was a leader in the development of the doctor of psychology degree (Psy.D.) movement, offered an alternative conceptualization of the profession's knowledge base that he referred to as disciplined inquiry (Peterson,

1968). By describing the way various theories are applied to and tested against clinical experience in a systematic and objective fashion, Peterson began the process of demystifying clinical wisdom, intuition, and the art of practice, and he did this without reducing clinical problem-solving to applied science or rejecting the value of scientific psychology, per se.

In 1974, Chris Argryis and Donald Schön, examining the issue of practitioner knowledge across a wide variety of professions, argued that practitioner knowledge is generated from a pragmatic reflection-in-action. The practitioner engaged in a real-life problem develops a relationship with those in need of help, gathers information, conceptually reformulates the problem in such a way as to generate novel possible solutions, and then proceeds to evaluate the solutions until a feasible one emerges. The test of the adequacy of the practitioner's problem formulation and solutions is whether or not the problem is solved to the satisfaction of the parties involved. Good theories and good practitioners get the job done.

The formulation of the problem and the testing of solutions are analogous, but not identical, to the development and testing of scientific theories. Practitioners are forced to consider a situation in all its complexity in order to find a specific solution to a specific problem in a specific historical-social-political context. The conceptualization of the problem must stay fluid, flexible, and tentative until a solution is found. On the other hand, the scientist's goal is to find a way to restrict a problem to a very limited and clearly defined set of variables that hopefully will be causally relevant across a wide variety of situations and social contexts.

Differences such as these, led Murray Levine (1974), William Runyon, (1982), Dennis Bromley (1986), Lisa Hoshamond (1992), and Daniel Fishman (1999) to suggest that case study research conducted in a comprehensive and systematic fashion was the proper way to establish a quasi-judicial case-law knowledge base for professional practice in psychology. This view had been advocated 50 years earlier by Gordon Allport and Henry Murray, but it lost favor during the heyday of behaviorism and positivism.

Working out of a Continental philosophical tradition of epistemology and ontology, Donald Polkinghorne (1988) reached a similar but more radical conclusion by considering the narrative nature of all psychological phenomena. Relying on a hermeneutic approach to human behavior originating in the German Idealism of Immanuel Kant, G. W. F. Hegel, Martin Heidegger, and more recently Hans Georg Gadamer and Jurgen Habermas, Polkinghorne argued that both professional practice and basic research in psychology are primarily about interpreting the meaning of our own and other's experiences. Clinical knowledge is an intersubjective, self-reflexive, contextual process of finding and making meaning in the world. It is not in conflict with scientific knowledge because, on the hermeneutic account, all psychological knowledge is concerned with this sort of understanding of our world (*Verstehen*), and not about explaining the universal laws of nature.

In all accounts of the epistemology of practice there is an either explicit or implicit recognition that professional practice is a thoroughly value-laden enterprise (Miller, 1992). For Aristotle, any action in the world required not only theoretical or scientific knowledge, but what he called *phronēsis*, "practical wisdom." Professional practice is a moral undertaking that attempts to make at least one small corner of the world a better place to live. Consequently, the warrant for such practical knowledge claims may lie in part in the moral principles that serve as a foundation for practice.

[*See also* Epistemology.]

Bibliography

Argyris, C., & Schön, D. A. (1974). *Theory in practice: Increasing professional effectiveness*. San Francisco: Jossey-Bass.

Bromley, D. B. (1986). *The case-study method in psychology and related disciplines*. Chichester, England: Wiley.

Fishman, D. (1999). *The case for a pragmatic psychology*. New York: New York University Press.

Hoshmond, L. T. (1992). Clinical inquiry as scientific training. *The Counseling Psychologist, 19*, 431–453.

Levine, M. (1974). Scientific method and the adversary model: Some preliminary thoughts. *American Psychologist, 29*, 661–677.

Meehl, P. (1954). *Clinical vs. statistical prediction: A theoretical analysis and review of the evidence*. Minneapolis: University of Minnesota Press.

Miller, R. B. (Ed.). (1992). *The restoration of dialogue: Readings in the philosophy of clinical psychology*. Washington, DC: American Psychological Association.

Peterson, D. R. (1968). *The clinical study of social behavior*. New York: Appleton-Century-Crofts.

Polkinghorne, D. E. (1983). *Methodology for the human sciences: Systems of inquiry*. Albany, NY: State University of New York Press.

Runyon, W. McK. (1982). *Life histories and psychobiography: Explorations in theory and method*. New York: Oxford University Press.

Ronald B. Miller

EQUIVALENCE. *See* Bias and Equivalence.

ERGONOMICS. *See* Human Factors Psychology.

ERIKSON, ERIK H. (1902–1994), American psychologist and personality theorist. Erik Erikson's theory of personality development is one of the most influential bodies of work in psychological theory of the twentieth century. Erikson based his work initially on the psychoanalytic theory of Freud, but eventually moved far beyond it as he formulated his own developmental approach to personality. Erikson's contributions to psychology, particularly to the study of personality, can be divided into four major areas: (a) his emphasis on the importance of the entire life cycle in personality change; (b) the psychosocial origins of personality; (c) the centrality of self-identity in personality development; and (d) the importance of life histories for personality study.

The Life Cycle Approach to Personality Development

Erikson's theory charted changes in personality over the entire life cycle, rather than focusing on the early childhood years as critical to all later personality functioning. As a result, his work has had a major influence on the field of developmental psychology, spurring the trend away from a narrow consideration of child development toward studying life span developmental psychology.

Erikson proposed eight stages of human development, each with its own normative crisis, by which he meant not a debilitating conflict, but rather a period of heightened vulnerability and potential. Erikson's life cycle approach placed him among the stage theorists in developmental psychology. He viewed human development as occurring in orderly stages, each with its own special characteristics and its own particular age relationship. The stages always occur in a particular order and cannot be skipped. His stages illustrate what Erikson termed the *epigenetic principle*. Briefly stated, this principle proposes that critical elements of human personality have a ground plan from which they grow, similar to the physical growth principle by which the undifferentiated cells of embryos develop in orderly ways into organ systems. Thus, all human beings will face the normative crisis of trust versus mistrust in the period of infancy. The resolution of this crisis leaves the infant with an abiding sense of either trust or mistrust that will become part of later personality functioning. Each stage builds upon what has gone before and carries elements of itself into future stages. Erikson's eight stages of personality development are listed in Table 1.

The Psychosocial Origins of Personality

Like many of Freud's followers, Erikson believed that too much emphasis had been placed on psychosexual development in Freud's psychoanalytic account of personality formation. Erikson's theory is called a psycho-

ERIK H. ERIKSON. Table 1. Erikson's eight stages of the life cycle

Normative Crisis	Age	Major Characteristics
Trust vs. Mistrust	0–1	Primary social interaction with mothering caretaker; oral concerns; trust or mistrust in life-sustaining care, including feeding.
Autonomy vs. Shame and Doubt	1–2	Primary social interaction with parents; toilet training; beginnings of autonomous will.
Initiative vs. Guilt	3–5	Primary social interaction with nuclear family; beginnings of oedipal feelings; development of conscience to govern initiative.
Industry vs. Inferiority	6–puberty	Primary social interaction outside home among peers and teachers; school-age assessment of task ability.
Identity vs. Role Confusion	Adolescence	Primary social interaction with peers, culminating in heterosexual friendship; psychological moratorium from adult commitments; identity crisis; consolidation of resolutions of previous four stages into coherent sense of self.
Intimacy vs. Isolation	Early adulthood	Primary social interaction in intimate relationship (usually opposite sex); adult role commitments accepted, including commitment to another person.
Generativity vs. Stagnation	Middle adulthood	Primary social concern in establishing and guiding succeeding generation; productivity and creativity.
Ego Integrity vs. Despair	Late adulthood	Primary social concern is reflective: coming to terms with one's place in the nearly complete life cycle, and with one's relationships with others.

Source. Hopkins (1983, p. 74), adapted from Erikson (1968). Copyright 1983 by J. R. Hopkins; permission granted by author.

social theory of personality to reflect the shift of emphasis away from psychosexuality and toward social and cultural influences on human personality development.

Each stage of development in Erikson's model emphasizes a particular social network. In the first three stages, the parents and the nuclear family form the most critical social network. In the fourth stage, peer groups and authority figures outside the home, particularly in the schools, take on greater significance. In adolescence, peer groups, particularly friends and dating partners, become a social focus; in early adulthood, romantic partners achieve prominence in their influence on personality. In middle adulthood, as the shift toward generativity takes place, future generations become the focus for interaction. Finally, in old age, social interaction becomes more reflective, and more restricted to close members of the family. In each of these

stages, reciprocity with others is a key to personality development. Erikson's cultural and anthropological studies, with the Sioux and Yurok Indians, with poor families in Pennsylvania, and his writings on ethnic groups within America, reflect his concern with the psychosocial underpinnings of personality.

The Importance of Self-Identity

In his life cycle scheme, Erikson viewed identity as a central construct, and set the decisive period for its normative crisis in adolescence, moving beyond Freud's focus on early childhood as the critical time for personality development. Erikson is sometimes called "the father of the identity crisis." Historians of psychology refer to this branch of personality study as *ego psychology*, and Erikson was one of the first, as well as one of the most influential, of the ego psychologists. Many contemporary themes in personality research that involve the self in various guises—self-actualization, self-concept, self-efficacy, self-esteem, self-monitoring, and so on—can be traced in part to Erikson's concept of self-identity.

The Importance of Life Histories

Erikson believed that the best source of information about personality development was individual life histories. His works include liberal notes from his clinical cases, as well as personality profiles of historical figures, including British critic and playwright George Bernard Shaw, philosopher-psychologist William James, Nazi dictator Adolf Hitler, and Russian novelist and playwright Maxim Gorky. He also wrote two full-length psychobiographies, about religious reformer Martin Luther and Hindu leader and social reformer Mohandas Gandhi, which have been influential in several academic disciplines as well as popular with the general public. The book about Gandhi won a Pulitzer Prize. His case studies of historical figures were highly influential in the development of the new interdisciplinary fields of psychohistory and psychobiography.

Erikson's Life History

In order to appreciate Erikson's work fully, one needs to understand some important fragments of his own life history. As originator of the term *identity crisis*, he knew a great deal about the phenomenon firsthand. Erikson was born 15 June 1902 near Frankfurt, Germany, where his mother had gone after the breakup of her first marriage. Erikson had been led to believe throughout childhood that his stepfather, pediatrician Theodore Homburger, whose surname he had been given, was his biological father. He did not learn about the circumstances of his parentage until his adolescence: that period of the life cycle where he located identity as the normative crisis. In actuality, his birth had resulted from an extramarital liaison of his mother's, but he was known as Erik Homburger until shortly before he emigrated to the United States in the early 1930s, when he adopted the surname Erikson, literally "son of Erik."

After graduation from his German high school, Erikson decided that he would be an artist. Like many other young people before and since his time, Erikson became alienated from his family and from the context in which he grew up. He wandered for a year or so around Europe, and then enrolled in an art school in Karlsruhe, Germany. At this point, when he was in his mid-20s, Erikson was summoned by his friend Peter Blos (who himself became an important figure in psychoanalytic psychology) to Vienna, to teach in a progressive school for English and American children whose parents were studying with Freud.

During Erikson's Vienna years, 1927 to 1933, he made a number of decisive turns in his life history. He came to the attention of Anna Freud, Sigmund Freud's daughter, who was then developing her own specialty within psychoanalysis as an analyst of children. She invited Erikson to come into a training analysis with her, conducted almost every day for three years. In addition, Erikson participated in a more general child-analysis seminar led by Anna Freud, with such teachers as August Aichhorn, Edward Bibring, Helene Deutsch, Paul Federn, Heinz Hartmann, and Ernst Kris, all of whom were important figures in the history of psychoanalysis. It was also in Vienna that Erikson met and married Joan Serson, a dancer and artist who was in analysis with Ludwig Jekels, one of Freud's early followers. Joan Erikson was to be his intellectual partner and editor throughout the rest of his life.

The Nazi menace that had gathered in Europe by 1933 prompted many psychoanalysts to leave for America. After trying vainly to acquire Danish citizenship and settle in Copenhagen, Erikson and his wife settled in the United States. Remarkably, within ten years, Erikson had received appointments at premier universities and medical research centers at Harvard, Yale, and Berkeley. As Boston's only child analyst in the early 1930s, Erikson's services were widely sought. He also met Henry A. Murray, one of the most important American personality theorists of the time. Through Murray, Erikson became associated with the Harvard Psychological Clinic, and also enrolled briefly at Harvard as a doctoral candidate in psychology. But Erikson was never one for the discipline required for formal educational certification, and he soon left the program. In fact, he had no earned degrees beyond his high school diploma. Between 1934 and 1936, he studied Harvard undergraduates at the psychological clinic. He was to use many of the insights gathered in this work as he developed his views about the identity crisis of adolescence.

Erikson spent the decade of the 1940s (1939–1950) in California; he was a training analyst working primarily with children in San Francisco, and became associated with the Institute for Child Welfare at the University of California, Berkeley. It was also during this decade that he became an American citizen. In 1950, he resigned his professorship at Berkeley and became a member of the senior staff at the Austen Riggs Center in Stockbridge, Massachusetts, where he remained for the next decade (1950–1960). He also worked periodically in Pittsburgh during this period at the University of Pittsburgh's Western Psychiatric Institute and at the Arsenal Health Center. There his cases included poor mothers and their children, many of them recent immigrants.

In 1960, Erikson was invited back to Harvard as professor of human development, where he remained until his retirement in 1970. In 1987, the Erik Erikson Center was established in Cambridge, associated with Cambridge Hospital and the Harvard Medical School. Erikson, one of the last of the great synthesizers of theory in psychology, the academic stepson who had only a high school diploma, died 12 May 1994, in Harwich, Massachusetts.

Bibliography

Works by Erikson

Erikson, E. H. (1950). *Childhood and society*. New York: Norton. Erikson's theoretical revision of Freud's psychoanalytic theory, in which emphasis is placed on social and cultural, rather than sexual, contributions to personality development. This work also outlines Erikson's eight stages of the life cycle.

Erikson, E. H. (1958). *Young man Luther: A study in psychoanalysis and history*. New York: Norton. Erikson's psychobiographical analysis of religious reformer Martin Luther.

Erikson, E. H. (1964). *Insight and responsibility*. New York: Norton. A collection of six lectures that deal with issues such as ethical implications of psychoanalysis, the nature of clinical evidence, and the generational and historical transmission of values.

Erikson, E. H. (1968). *Identity: Youth and crisis*. New York: Norton. Erikson's theoretical emphasis on identity as a major issue in personality development. In this work, he traced the epigenesis of identity over the life cycle and presented case studies of identity formation and confusion.

Erikson, E. H. (1969). *Gandhi's truth*. New York: Norton. Erikson's psychobiographical analysis of Hindu leader and social reformer Mohandas Gandhi.

Schlein, S. (Ed.). (1987). *Erik H. Erikson: A way of looking at things*. New York: Norton. A collection of Erikson's papers published between 1930 and 1980, including reflections on such figures as Anna Freud, Peter Blos, Ruth Benedict, Laurence K. Frank, Paul Tillich, and Robert P. Knight. There is also a complete bibliography of Erikson's writings from 1930 to 1985.

Works about Erikson

Coles, R. (1970). *Erik H. Erikson: The growth of his work*. Boston: Little, Brown. Traces the philosophical and historical roots of Erikson's work and provides an intellectual biography of Erikson.

Evans, R. I. (1967). *Dialogue with Erik Erikson*. New York: Harper & Row. Edited transcripts of a series of interviews with Erikson about the eight stages of the life cycle, cross-cultural and psychohistorical analysis, and the overall impact of psychoanalysis.

Hopkins, J. R. (1983). *Adolescence: The transitional years*. San Diego, CA: Academic Press.

J. Roy Hopkins

ESTES, WILLIAM KAYE (1919–   ), experimental and mathematical psychologist. Estes was born to George Downs Estes and Mona Kaye Estes in Minneapolis, Minnesota, on 17 June 1919. He married Katherine C. Walker in 1942. He received both his bachelor's degree (in 1940) and his doctorate (in 1943) from the University of Minnesota, where he worked with B. F. Skinner. After serving in the Army Air Force during World War II, he began teaching at Indiana University in 1946, where he became Research Professor of Psychology. In 1962, he joined the faculty at Stanford University. In 1968, he moved to Rockefeller University, and in 1979, he went to Harvard University. Finally, in 1999, Estes returned to Indiana University.

Estes is the single individual most responsible for founding the field of mathematical psychology. The method he pioneered involves translating theoretical assumptions and interpretations into a quantitative form, which allows for the deduction of implications that can be assessed by examining observable data and which leads to an appreciation of the interrelationships among the various theoretical elements. Although this method had been frequently employed in the physical sciences, it had been rarely employed in psychology when Estes introduced it in 1950 to the study of learning and memory with his landmark article "Toward a Statistical Theory of Learning." In over 50 dedicated years of painstaking, rigorous research, Estes demonstrated how experimental observations of animal or human behavior can be compared quantitatively and precisely to the predictions of a formal mathematical or computer simulation model describing internal mental processes and states that are not directly observable themselves.

Employing this method, Estes had a profound impact on the field through numerous groundbreaking theoretical and empirical studies on a wide range of topics in learning, memory, perception, choice, and categorization. His elegant models reflect brilliant insights into fundamental psychological mechanisms underlying behavior, formulated both in terms of associations among mental representations of events and in terms of cognitive operations on information. For example, according to his stimulus sampling theory, a given situation can be described for an individual in terms of a population of stimulus elements, each of which is conditioned to one of the possible response alternatives. Only a sample of these elements affects the individual's behavior at any given instant, with a random process governing which stimulus elements are sampled and with conditioning or extinction occurring only to the sampled elements. Elaborations of this theory enabled Estes to account for spontaneous recovery from extinction, for spacing effects in learning, and for the learning and matching of probabilities. For another example, according to his perturbation model of memory, the representations of successive stimulus items are not associated or linked directly, but rather associative links occur between each item representation and a control element representing the current environmental context. A reverberatory loop connects each item representation and the control element, with a periodic recurrent reactivation of the items' representations and with a difference in reactivation times reflecting the difference in item input times. Rapid forgetting of order information is explained by random timing perturbations that lead to interchanges in the relative timing of successive item representations. With this theory and elaborations of it, Estes was able to account for a wide range of phenomena in short-term memory and in long-term memory.

Estes's monumental contributions are not limited to theoretical and empirical studies. He also made substantial contributions to experimental methodology. For example, with B. F. Skinner, he introduced the popular conditioned emotional response technique, which is an alternative to the Pavlovian paradigm for studying conditioning. Also, with H. A. Taylor, he introduced the prevalent detection method, which is used to separate effects of perception from effects of memory in tachistoscopic recognition. In addition, he contributed to the understanding and use of statistical methods in psychology.

From 1958 to 1962, Estes was associate editor of the *Journal of Experimental Psychology*; from 1963 to 1968, he was editor of the *Journal of Comparative and Physiological Psychology*; from 1977 to 1982, he was editor of the *Psychological Review*; and from 1990 to 1994, he was the first editor of *Psychological Science*. In addition, from 1975 to 1978, he edited the six-volume *Handbook of Learning and Cognitive Processes* (Hillsdale, NJ).

Estes made immense contributions as a leader of many professional organizations in the field. He was one of the founders of the Psychonomic Society and was chair of the governing board in 1972, the year when the society's journals were started. He was also chair of the organizing group of the Society for Mathematical Psychology and was chair of the society in 1984. Estes helped shape national science policy in his roles as member and chair of numerous committees and commissions of the National Research Council and grant panels of the National Institutes of Health, the National Institute of General Medical Sciences, and the National Science Foundation.

Bibliography

Works by Estes

Estes, W. K. (1944). An experimental study of punishment. *Psychological Monographs, 57* (3). Doctoral dissertation under the guidance of B. F. Skinner.

Estes, W. K. (1950). Toward a statistical theory of learning. *Psychological Review, 57*, 94–107. Article in which Estes introduced stimulus sampling theory and introduced

mathematical modeling to the field of learning and memory.

Estes, W. K. (1972). An associative basis for coding and organization in memory. In A. W. Melton & E. Martin (Eds.), *Coding processes in human memory* (pp. 161–190). Washington, DC: V. H. Winston. Chapter in which Estes introduced the perturbation model of memory.

Estes, W. K. (1982). *Models of learning, memory, and choice: Selected papers*. New York: Praeger. Volume in the Centennial Psychology Series, which reprints many of Estes most important papers along with his commentary and includes an autobiographical chapter and complete bibliography of his publications to that date.

Estes, W. K. (1989). William K. Estes. In G. Lindzey (Ed.), *A history of psychology in autobiography* (Vol. 8, pp. 94–124). Stanford, CA: Stanford University Press. Autobiographical chapter.

Estes, W. K. (1991). *Statistical models in behavioral research*. Hillsdale, NJ: Erlbaum. Advanced textbook on statistical methods in psychology, in which Estes illuminates the models that underlie the statistical methods.

Estes, W. K. (1994). *Classification and cognition*. New York: Oxford University Press. Volume by Estes based on the Fifth Paul M. Fitts Lectures, which he delivered at the University of Michigan; this volume summarizes his influential array model of categorization.

Estes, W. K. (1997). Processes of memory loss, recovery, and distortion. *Psychological Review, 104*, 148–169. Article in which Estes shows how his perturbation model of short-term memory can be extended to cover memory processes in general.

Estes, W. K., & Skinner, B. F. (1941). Some quantitative properties of anxiety. *Journal of Experimental Psychology, 29*, 390–400. Article introducing the conditioned emotional response technique.

Estes, W. K., & Taylor, H. A. (1964). A detection method and probabilistic models for assessing information processing from brief visual displays. *Proceedings of the National Academy of Sciences, 52*, 446–454. Article introducing the detection method.

Works about Estes

Healy, A. F. (1992). William K. Estes. *American Psychologist, 47*, 855–857. Biography of Estes published at the time of his receipt of the American Psychological Foundation Gold Medal Award.

Healy, A. F., Kosslyn, S. M., & Shiffrin, R. M. (Eds.). (1992). *From learning theory to connectionist theory: Essays in honor of William K. Estes* (Vol. 1). Hillsdale, NJ: Erlbaum.

Healy, A. F., Kosslyn, S. M., & Shiffrin, R. M. (Eds.). (1992). *From learning processes to cognitive processes: Essays in honor of William K. Estes* (Vol. 2). Hillsdale, NJ: Erlbaum. Two-volume festschrift honoring the illustrious career of Estes by some of his many former students, postdoctoral fellows, and colleagues. Most chapters include fond reminiscences and affectionate personal comments about Estes. Volume 1 emphasizes mathematical psychology; Volume 2 emphasizes cognitive psychology.

Alice F. Healy

ETHICS. [*This entry comprises four articles. The first article provides an overview of ethics in the field of psychology. The three companion articles provide broad profiles of the ethical issues that pertain to research in psychology (especially with regard to experimentation with human and nonhuman subjects), clinical practice in psychology, and publication in the field of psychology. See also* Confidentiality; *and* Informed Consent.]

An Overview

One of the elements that makes professions distinctive is the duty to abide by standards, primarily those embodied in the profession's ethics code. Ethics in psychology represents two important aspects: striving to the highest standards in the profession and identifying those behaviors that deserve sanction. The first aspect, aspirational ethics, is closest to one of the definitions of "ethics," which is synonymous with "moral philosophy." The second aspect of ethics is concerned with enforcement of a code and generally thought of as stating the minimal expectations. A person who does not behave according to even minimal standards is subject to being investigated and being found to have behaved unethically. A psychologist can deserve sanction for committing a forbidden act, as well as for failing to engage in a required behavior.

History of the APA Ethics Code

The primary ethics document in psychology is the ethics code of the American Psychological Association (APA) found in the Ethical Principles of Psychologists and Code of Conduct (APA, 1992). While the Ethics Committee was formed in 1938 and began informal resolution of ethical problems brought to its attention, the first formal code, Ethical Standards of Psychologists (APA 1953), was not adopted until 1952. That first code was distinctive in that it was developed using the critical incident method. Incidents illustrating ethical situations were solicited from APA members and then developed into ethical rules. That code is still the longest of all APA codes at 171 pages, with 310 rule elements. The APA Ethics Code is available on the APA Web site at http//www.apa.org/ethics. Most revisions have made only modest changes to content, and only the 1959 and 1992 revisions altered the format substantially.

Two changes are of historical importance. An emergency revision of the APA Ethics Code was made by APA to produce the "1989 amended" Ethical Principles of Psychologists (1990) as part of a negotiation to end an investigation by the Bureau of Competition of the Federal Trade Commission (FTC) (Consent Order, 1993). The investigation related primarily to advertising and referral fees and was initiated despite major liberalization in the late 1970s of advertising provisions in the APA Code.

An important factor in the revision that led to adoption of the 1992 APA Ethics Code was a court decision (*White v. the North Carolina State Board*, 1990) that found some provisions in the 1981 Ethics Code to be unconstitutionally vague in one state. A fundamental legal principle in enforcing ethics codes is that the rules must provide fair notice to the professional as to what behavior will lead to a sanction. This led to a clearer conceptualization of the aspirational as opposed to the enforceable ethics provisions in the APA code. Descriptions of the history of the APA Code may be found in *Ethics for Psychologists* (Canter, Bennet, Jones, & Nagg, 1994) and *Ethics in Psychology* (Koocher & Keith-Spiegel, 1998).

Other Ethics Codes and Standards

In addition to the APA Ethics Code, there are a number of other codes that are relevant. The Canadian Psychological Association (CPA) adopted its own code in 1986, revised in 1991. The CPA code has used a very different style from the APA code, by incorporating a decision-making process into the code itself and structuring the code by relating each general principle to the more specific provisions. The Association of State and Provincial Psychology Boards (ASPPB) adopted a model code of conduct in 1990. It has been used by a number of state licensure boards but substantially addresses only those areas needed in regulating licensed psychologists.

Of course, ethics codes do not address all the information needed by psychologists in order to do a good job. The 1992 Ethics Code encourages psychologists to "consider other professional materials" when the code alone is not sufficient, and lists as "most helpful in this regard" the many "guidelines and standards that have been adopted or endorsed by professional psychological organizations." The code lists guidelines, such as APA's *General Guidelines for Providers of Psychological Services* (1987). Several new guidelines have been adopted since, and some of those listed have been formally rescinded, are being revised, or are otherwise out of date. It is important to recognize that "such guidelines . . . , whether adopted by the American Psychological Association (APA) or its Divisions, are not enforceable as such by this Ethics Code, but are of educative value to psychologists, courts, and professional bodies." There is often substantial concern by psychologists that in fact, courts or others, may use guidelines as if they are standards. In addition to ethics codes and guidelines, there are also laws that must be considered by psychologists.

The 1992 APA Ethics Code

The 1992 Ethics Code (APA 1992) became effective in December 1992. The Ethics Code contains four basic sections. The Introduction provides an overview and comments on applying the code in relationship to other professional standards and to the law. It also comments on the use of the code as a disciplinary standard by the APA and by other groups. For example, it notes that the code may be adopted by licensure boards and may otherwise be applied to psychologists who are not members of APA. The Preamble and General Principles state aspirational goals covering a wide range of ethical concerns.

The Standards provide the enforceable rules. The standards are divided into seven groups. Groups one (General Standards), three (Advertising and Other Public Statements), and five (Confidentiality) apply to all psychologists. The other groups (Evaluation, Assessment, or Intervention; Therapy; Teaching, Training Supervision, Research, and Publishing; and Forensic Activities) apply more to some groups of psychologists than others, but it is important for all psychologists to consider the entire code when applying it to actual situations. For example, a clinician doing research on clinical problems must comply with the sections regarding research. A researcher considering problems of confidentiality must consider the confidentiality provisions in the general section as well as in the research section.

The 1992 Ethics Code introduced a number of important features. For the first time in an APA code, aspirational statements were differentiated from those that were to be enforceable. The enforceable statements are also more specific, and for both reasons provisions were more likely to withstand legal challenge. Statements were also organized into functional groups and limited to single behavior "unitary" concepts. New provisions provided explicit guidance regarding sexual involvement with former clients (Standard 4.07) and with certain students (Standard 1.19), barter (Standard 1.18), informed consent to therapy (Standard 4.02), withholding records for nonpayment (Standard 5.11), and forensic services (Standards 7.01–7.06). There were also modified provisions regarding advertising (Standards 3.01–3.03) as well as referrals and fees (Standard 1.27), testimonials (Standard 3.05), and in-person solicitation (Standard 3.06). These were believed to be acceptable to the FTC in place of provisions that were rescinded in the 1989 revision.

Decision Making

Psychologists are constantly confronted with situations in which ethical choices must be made, and several models have been developed that provide guidance (see, for example, Canter et al., 1994; Haas & Malouf, 1989; Kitchener, 1984; and Koocher & Keith-Spiegel, 1998). Important elements of most models include identifying the ethical aspects of the problem; identifying relevant ethical and other standards; determining relevant facts and collecting additional information as needed; identifying options and selecting an action plan; taking the action; and evaluating the results. Models also emphasize strongly the importance of consultation with experts throughout the process. It is generally recommended that psychologists document the process used, factors considered, action taken, and outcome observed. Good ethics education during graduate training and regular continuing education later help psychologist identify ethical challenges before they become problems. Also, being prepared to handle a range of situations is a benefit because many situations that pose ethical problems require immediate action and a formal system cannot be used at the time.

Simple rules or tests are helpful for situations in which action must occur quickly and also for reviewing a tentative action decision. For example, a psychologist may ask, "Is the planned action ethical, practical, and reasonable?" or "Am I acting in a responsible and accountable manner?" A method cited by Haas and Malouf (1989) is for the psychologist to imagine him or herself in a "clean, well-lit room" in order to gauge the acceptability of a planned action taken with the full understanding of colleagues.

How Are Professional Codes Enforced?

Professional codes are enforced in a variety of ways. The most direct method is for an association that adopts the code to conduct an enforcement program. A second way is for an authority, such as a state, to incorporate into licensure legislation a profession's ethics code, in which case, the code, with the force of law, is enforced by the licensure board and/or professional discipline agency of the state. A third method is for a code to be stated as a basis for action regarding professionals working in various settings, such as a hospital medical staff or a university. In that case, action might be taken against a professional on the staff of the facility if the professional violated provisions of his or her profession. A fourth type of enforcement is indirect and includes processes such as malpractice or other civil litigation. Here the code is used as a statement of professional standards. The plaintiff may argue that the code shows that the professional did not perform properly, just as the defendant may use it to demonstrate that appropriate procedures were used.

It is important to recognize that other systems within which the psychologist works may also enforce rules other than a professional ethics code. For example, university or governmental research ethics review bodies may use federal regulations regarding the conduct of research, and these may be similar to or even identical to the requirements of a particular ethics code. Also, a professional may be found guilty of the criminal action of insurance fraud due to violating a law regarding such behavior. This would be true whether or not there was an ethics code provision prohibiting the same behavior.

A concern is often raised as to the possibility of conflict between different codes, but this does not occur as frequently as it appears. Most often, one code simply requires a higher standard and does not require that the other code not be upheld. On the other hand, there are often conflicts between an ethics code and legal requirements.

APA Complaint Procedures

The APA Ethics Committee Rules and Procedures (1996) govern the process for conducting ethics investigations of members. These rules are periodically revised and the changes can have a substantial effect on investigations. For example, the 1996 Rules revision (APA, 1996) resulted in new APA student affiliates being subject to jurisdiction of the ethics committee, limited to review of activities not under the scrutiny of the student's graduate program and of affiliates who join with this understanding. Also, that revision changed the time limit for a member filing a complaint against another member from one to three years. Beginning with the 1992 rules revision (APA, 1992b), the rules include a brief overview that is likely to be included in the future and to be helpful when reviewing future revisions. Interested individuals should ensure that they have the current rules, which may be obtained from APA or are available on the APA Web site, http://www.apa.org/ethics.

The APA ethics program experienced a substantial increase in activity beginning about 1986. Between 1985 and 1997, 249 members lost their membership due to unethical behavior. However, this represented action against a very small percentage of APA members. For example, the APA Ethics Committee annual report covering 1997 (Ethics Committee, 1998) indicated that complaints were filed against only 0.14% of members. Most of the serious complaints involve sexual misconduct (110 of the 183 members who lost membership during 1990–1997) and insurance fraud (22 of 183). Of complaints that were received from complainants in 1993–1995, the most frequent complaints were regarding child custody evaluations and confidentiality.

The APA procedures for a number of years have provided for two types of investigations. One is called "show cause" proceedings and provides for review of an APA member's loss of licensure, conviction of a felony, or loss of membership in a state psychological association due to unethical conduct. Because another authoritative body has sanctioned the member, the burden is on the member to convince APA that he or she should not be expelled. (The term comes from the member being given an opportunity to "show cause" why the member should not be expelled.)

The other type of investigation involves a review of alleged unethical conduct. This type of investigation usually begins by an individual filing a complaint and may also be started by the committee acting on its own, called a *sua sponte* review. In these investigations, the burden is on the committee to prove the charges. The complaint is judged by the ethics code in effect at the time the behavior occurred.

In both types of investigations, members are not allowed to resign membership in APA (directly or by nonpayment of dues) while under scrutiny of the committee. There are time limits for filing complaints; nonmembers have 5 years in which to file a complaint, and APA members have 3 years. The time limit can be waived for serious matters, but no more than 10 years after the alleged events occurred. This 10-year limit also holds for APA opening show cause investigations, except that the limit is 20 years for an offense involving a minor.

Bibliography

American Psychological Association. (1953). *Ethical standards of psychologists.* Washington, DC: Author.

American Psychological Association. (1959). Ethical standards of psychologists. *American Psychologist, 14*(6), 279–282.

American Psychological Association. (1987). General guidelines for providers of psychological services. *American Psychologist, 42,* 712–723.

American Psychological Association. (1990). Ethical principles of psychologists (amended 2 June 1989). *American Psychologist, 45,* 390–395.

American Psychological Association. (1992a). Ethical principles of psychologists and code of conduct. *American Psychologist, 47,* 1597–1611.

American Psychological Association, Ethics Committee. (1992b). Rules and procedures. *American Psychologist, 47,* 1612–1628.

American Psychological Association, Ethics Committee. (1996). Rules and procedures. *American Psychologist, 51,* 529–548.

American Psychological Association, Ethics Committee. (1998). Report of the Ethics Committee, 1997. *American Psychologist, 53,* 969–980.

Association of State and Provincial Psychology Boards. (1991). *Code of conduct.* Montgomery, AL: Author.

Canadian Psychological Association. (1991). *Canadian code of ethics for psychologists* (Rev. ed.) Ottawa, ON: Author.

Canter, M. B., Bennet, B. E., Jones, S. E., and Nagy, T. F. (1994). *Ethics for psychologists: A commentary on the APA Ethics Code.* Washington, DC: American Psychological Association.

Federal Trade Commission (FTC). (1993). Consent order. *Federal Register, 58*(3), 557.

Haas, L., & Malouf, J. (1989). *Keeping up the good work: A practitioner's guide to mental health ethics.* Sarasota, FL: Professional Resource Exchange.

Kitchener, K. (1984). Intuition, critical evaluation and ethical principles: The foundation for ethical decisions in counseling psychology. *The Counseling Psychologist, 12* (3), 43–55.

Koocher, G., & Keith-Spiegel, P. (1998). *Ethics in psychology: Professional standards and cases* (2nd ed.). New York: Oxford University Press.

White v. the North Carolina State Board of Examiners of Practicing Psychologists, 8810SC1137 North Carolina Court of Appeals, Wake County No. 86-CVS-8131 (Feb. 6, 1990).

Stanley E. Jones

Ethics in Research

The ethics of psychological research is not just about following rules but also about promoting value and benefit for all participants. Well-meaning investigators, researching worthy topics, mindful of government regulations and the American Psychological Association's code of ethics, may still overlook the concerns of subjects (I use *subject* rather than *participant* to remind the reader that persons being studied typically have less power than the researcher and must be accorded the protections that render inequality mutually acceptable) and others to the detriment of all. An important element of research competence is understanding of the perspective of the subjects. Harmful or disrespectful research often follows from ignorance of context and of individual sensitivities and from failure to analyze and plan. Legal and professional guidelines for researchers are general in scope and typically written with certain cultures (such as literate members of western society) or species (such as laboratory animals) in mind. They serve their intended purpose only when interpreted appropriately to the context, culture, or ecology of the subjects. For example, the researcher seeking to respect subjects may not realize that some cultures consider eye contact rude, or consider written and signed informed consent meaningless or even insulting (Marshall, 1992). Similarly, the researcher who immediately replaces wet bedding of animal subjects is likely to become as stressed as the animals if that species is one that immediately marks any new bedding with urine. Ethical research practice requires knowledge of principles of research ethics and their sensitive application with special attention to the culture or ecology of the particular subject population.

This broad overview of research ethics assumes familiarity with the details of the relevant codes and laws, review of which is recommended via the publications or Web sites listed in the bibliography. Human research guidelines emanating from the American Psychological Association and federal law express general goals, such as competence of investigator and respect for subjects' welfare and autonomy. They express ethical requirements very simply (for example, they list the elements of informed consent) and leave the subtleties of interpretation to the researcher. Guidelines for animal research emphasize knowledge of the species and minimizing of discomfort, illness, and pain. Some have criticized the failure of APA and government guidelines to require ethical decision making or harm/benefit analysis in animal research (Orlans, 1997).

Institutional Review Boards (IRBs) or human subjects ethics committees and Institutional Animal Care and Use Committees (IACUCs) are mandated by law to be established within each organization that conducts research and receives federal funding. The purpose of these committees is to review all proposals for human research to ascertain that the plan or "protocol" has adequately considered the ethical dimensions of the project and complies with relevant regulations. Many journals require proof of committee approval prior to accepting research articles. However, it is the responsibility of the scientist, not ethics committees, to apply ethical and legal principles appropriately. In some cases, this means interpreting the spirit or intent, rather than the letter, of the law or code, then presenting this interpretation (with citation of supporting scientific literature) to one's institutional ethics committee or editor. There is a growing scientific literature on research ethics, such as the journals *Ethics & Behavior, Science and Engineering Ethics,* and *IRB: A Review of Human Research*; the role of personal opinion and discretion now plays no greater role in judgment of what is ethical than in judgment of what is valid science.

In psychological research on humans, key concerns are respect of privacy and autonomy, maximizing benefit and minimizing risk, and giving potential subjects an adequate basis for deciding whether to participate. However, many subjective factors complicate matters: a range of cultural, developmental, socioeconomic, and individual psychological variables influence privacy needs, the perception of risk and benefit, and the way in which individuals communicate and make decisions, as well as the degree of trust, rapport, and comprehension that accompanies their relationship with the researcher. Researchers must resist the temptation to assume that subjects will necessarily respond as though they held, understood, or valued the same cultural perspectives as the researcher. Most dictionaries define culture as a system of values, morals, norms, experiences, beliefs, concepts, and language. The following is a useful heuristic for researchers seeking to understand the implications of culture for research ethics:

	Subject Knows	Subject Doesn't Know
Researcher Knows	Shared culture, or understanding of subject's culture & beliefs	What the subject doesn't know about the researcher's culture & beliefs
Researcher Doesn't Know	What the researcher doesn't know about the subject's culture & beliefs	Shared ignorance

When there is much shared culture, traditional informed consent procedures may be highly appropriate. The researcher explains the research; the subject largely understands and may ask some questions, and after appropriate discussion of these matters, agrees to participate or declines. Where shared culture does not exist, the researcher should compensate by learning about the subject's culture and relevant beliefs and adjusting procedures accordingly.

There is often the illusion of shared culture when, in fact, neither knows much about the other's beliefs or culture. For example, most psychologists regard certain kinds of self-disclosure and openness about personal matters as basic to mental health and social maturity. Hence, it would be natural (but thoughtless and unsophisticated) to conduct an experimental intervention involving self-disclosure without realizing that subjects from some traditional cultural backgrounds may consider such behavior as shameful, involving loss of face and disgrace to family. Failure to recognize where cultural differences may exist and to seek to understand the relevant culture and beliefs of subjects can result in many procedural errors, including inadequate assurances of confidentiality, inadequate informed consent, exposure of subjects to serious risk, and research methods or instructions that subjects will find offensive and puzzling. Subjects may disclose information harmful to themselves, misunderstand instructions, experience guilt, disrespect and lie to the researcher, refuse to participate or sabotage the project, or even precipitate public protest against the research.

An important part of research planning and pilot testing is to learn how various segments of the research population would respond to the intended procedure. If unacceptable to some critical segments of the research population, a more culturally sensitive version of the procedure needs to be designed. In addition, the informed consent should be carefully crafted to communicate effectively with the target population, so that potential subjects have an opportunity to come to terms with the procedure or decline to participate.

The cell of "shared ignorance" involves the unexpected risks and the benefits foregone when the researcher lacks understanding of the subjects and the subjects know too little to protect themselves. For example, unknowing researchers have stumbled upon possible child abuse because subjects did not understand the implications of their disclosures, leaving the researcher in confusion about the legal and ethical obligations that follow from such an ambiguous disclosure. The ethical researcher uses a variety of techniques to enlarge the window of shared knowledge, learning more about the culture and vulnerabilities of the subjects, and the research risks and benefits that could ensue.

Discovering Vulnerabilities and Risks

Predicting and preventing risks requires understanding possible vulnerabilities of subjects. Those who are especially vulnerable in research include persons who:

- do not share the researcher's values or culture.
- are poor, uneducated, or otherwise have little power in society.
- are weakened, physically, economically, politically, or emotionally.
- are located in an institution (workplace, school, prison) that may compromise their autonomy, coerce their participation, or make harmful use of their data.
- may be damaged by subjects' revelations (for example, relatives, co-workers).
- may be engaged in illegal activities.
- are visible public figures.
- are scapegoats or targets of prejudice.
- are too young or too old to avoid coercion or exercise autonomy.

All animals are vulnerable because of power inequality between scientist and animal.

Information about vulnerabilities and ways to do sensitive research may be gained through: consultation with relevant ethnographic literature, personal experience with the populations, use of surrogate subjects, focus groups drawn from relevant gatekeepers and stakeholders in the research, or community consultation. The aim of each of these methods is to learn how informed subjects are likely to respond to the intended research. For example:

- Would they approve of any uses of placebo conditions or concealment?
- What risks or fears (warranted or otherwise) are likely to arise?
- What issues of privacy and confidentiality are important to subjects?
- What benefits do subjects and other stakeholders expect to receive from the research?
- Are the intended uses or dissemination of the results acceptable to the stakeholders?
- What communication processes are acceptable to use to recruit, inform, and involve subjects?
- Will the intended informed consent procedure be attended to, comprehended, believed, and produce competent decisions in the target population?

Surrogate subjects are drawn from the research population, "walked through" the research procedure with detailed explanation, and asked to comment on issues such as the above.

Focus groups meet in a comfortable private place, where food and drink are provided. The focus group leader describes the project and what it seeks to achieve; participants comment and ask questions. Depending on whether the focus group participants are surrogate subjects, scientists who have studied the subject population, or gatekeepers of the subject community (ministers, teachers, politicians, union representatives, informal leaders), the perspectives they offer will differ; multiple perspectives should be sought. Focus groups can move much information into the cell of shared culture and understanding and out of the other cells of the diagram above. Bowser and Sieber (1992) describe focus group procedures used to develop effective approaches in recruiting and interviewing youthful crack cocaine users about safe sex practices and knowledge about AIDS; a carefully developed underground "grapevine" then served to inform and recruit participants, and some focus group members who shared subjects' culture became research assistants.

Community consultation involves equal status meetings between researchers and self-appointed representatives of the group to be studied. This concept was developed when members of the San Francisco gay community refused to participate in clinical trials of emerging treatments for HIV infection unless they were involved as equals in the design of the research (Melton, Levine, Koocher, Rosenthal, & Thompson, 1988).

Other *gatekeepers* and *stakeholders* include any persons who have a stake in assuring that the research is ethical, legal, or valid and who are likely to offer additional useful ethical perspectives if consulted. In addition to the groups already mentioned, these may include representatives of the research institution (including legal counsel, research administrators, and any others having relevant expertise or authority), the funder, representatives of scientific associations, and nonscientific representatives such as relevant human or animal rights advocates.

Researchers often justify risk and inconvenience to subjects on grounds that the research will benefit science and society yet make no provision for such benefits. Those who "grab data and run" with no regard for benefiting stakeholders of research are unwelcome in that setting again and spoil the reputation of science for others who follow. There are many ways to benefit the subjects of research and many of the stakeholders, even if the initial data are scientifically unexciting. The resulting goodwill with subjects and gatekeepers means that the door will be open to continued fine-tuning of the project.

Providing Benefits

Many kinds of benefits may ensue from a research project. The recipients of benefits may include all stakeholders: subjects, their community (family, workplace, and so forth), the researcher and research team, the research institution, funder, and science. The kinds of benefits each might receive include: good relationships, knowledge, material resources, opportunities to give or receive training, opportunities to do good and earn the esteem of others, empowerment, and scientific success (Sieber, 1992).

Discovering Meanings of Privacy, Confidentiality, and Anonymity

Privacy is about persons; it refers to the ability to control the access that others have to one's self. Although researchers know when someone has invaded their privacy, this is a poor basis for deciding when subjects would want to restrict access to themselves. Age, culture, status, education, and circumstances largely determine the degree of access that individuals wish to grant and the controls they exercise over access (Laufer & Wolfe, 1977). For example, personal questions about matters such as love and friendship may be eagerly answered by those who are happy with their relationships or for whom relationships are not salient, but may cause humiliation and pain to those who have recently experienced rejection. Powerful adults may refuse to answer a question that feels invasive; a less powerful adult may lie to the researcher; while a young child may reveal much and feel very upset. Conversely, very young children have little sense of social embarrassment and may comfortably answer questions that would embarrass an older child.

Many methods have been developed to respect the privacy of subjects and to guard the integrity of research against the subterfuges of subjects seeking to protect their privacy. (See Boruch & Cecil, 1977, for a comprehensive review of methods.) For example, a researcher who discovers the names of persons with HIV infection and tries to interview them by phone might expect a hostile "Where did you get my name?" and refusal to participate. However, a researcher seeking such sensitive medical history data might employ physicians to serve as "brokers" compiling the needed data, with explicit permission of the subjects, and removing any identifiers that would enable the researcher or anyone else to deduce the names of the subjects. Simply removing names might not prevent *deductive disclosure*; for example, license, Social Security, or phone numbers, or other demographic information could enable one to trace back to the name of an individual. *Anonymous* data contain no information that might permit deductive disclosure.

An individual's right to privacy in research is legally protected by their right to refuse to participate; hence, informed consent is an important way to respect privacy. The law says little about privacy and social research, except that the Buckley Amendment prohibits access to children's school records without parental consent, the Hatch Act prohibits asking children questions about religion, sex, or family life without parental permission, and the National Research Act requires parental permission for research on children. Various state laws also pertain.

Confidentiality is about data and is an extension of the concept of privacy. It refers to whatever agreement persons enter into about how access to information will be controlled. Confidentiality agreements are part of informed consent agreements. Subjects may willingly share personal information under a believable confidentiality agreement. Unfortunately, researchers may glibly promise to prevent any access by others without ensuring that there is no possibility of data theft, subpoena, or snooping. Research that could be subject to subpoena should be protected by a certificate of confidentiality, which may be obtained from the Office for Protection from Research Risk (National Institutes of Health). Other protections of sensitive data include substituting numbers for names and storing the unique identifiers and associated numbers elsewhere, under lock.

Many ways of assuring confidentiality of data have been used (Boruch & Cecil, 1979). For example, various methods of randomized response or error inoculation provide a strategy for asking questions such as "Have you cheated on your income tax?" so that no one can know who has given an incriminating answer. The simplest variant is for subjects to roll a hidden die before answering. If the die comes up, say, two, the subject is to answer untruthfully. The researcher knows that one response in six is false and can use simple algebra to determine the proportion of subjects who have cheated on their taxes (Fox & Tracy, 1986).

Voluntary Informed Consent

Voluntary informed consent is two-way communication about the conditions of research participation between subjects and researcher, not simply a consent form. *Voluntary* means without threat or undue inducement. *Informed* means that the subject is told what a reasonable person in that situation would need to know to decide whether to participate. At a minimum, subjects should be informed about the research purpose and procedures, any foreseeable risks, benefits, alternatives to participation, confidentiality agreements, compensation for harm, and whom to contact with questions or complaints; subjects should be assured that any participation is voluntary with right to withdraw at any time and should be given a copy of the written consent statement. *Consent* means an explicit agreement to participate. The literature in cognitive, social, and educational psychology describes ways to create readability, comprehension, trust, personalization of information, and decision-making ability, and should be used to create effective informed consent. A written statement is usually presented along with a verbal statement and discussion, and when the information is complex for the subject population, the researcher may also employ a videotape, simulation, or group discussion to engage subjects in fuller exploration and understanding of the research.

Debriefing is important both to enhance the subject's understanding of the research experience and to give the researcher a chance to learn subjects' perceptions of the research. At a minimum, the researcher should describe the purpose and importance of the study, what is known about the problem studied, and what variables were employed. A written layperson's version of the literature on which the study was based can be provided immediately, and the findings sent to subjects and other stakeholders when available. Thoughtful sharing of findings and solicitation of comments from subjects and other stakeholders is beneficial to all concerned.

Deception and Concealment

Deception or concealment may be justified when they are the only feasible ways to achieve stimulus control, study responses to low-frequency events, avoid serious risk to subjects, or obtain data that would otherwise be unobtainable due to subjects' defensiveness, embarrassment, or fear of reprisal. Research on responses to aggression, for example, might be studied by having an actor (disguised as another research participant) make aggressive statements to the subject. *Role* deception means that the subject is misled as to the real identity of another. *Device* deception means that a device is presented as being something it is not. *Implicit* deception means that the subject is tacitly led to assume something that is not so. An unjustifiable rationale for using deception is to trick people into participation they would find unacceptable. Some forms of deception are harmful and wrongful especially when immoral or highly private behavior is strongly induced (Sieber 1982, 1983a) and are indefensible. In such cases, alternative approaches not requiring deception should be employed (for example, simulation and role-playing).

Other alternatives include obtaining informed consent to deceive or conceal. For example, subjects may be asked if they would participate in one of several studies in which some of the studies might involve deception and others not, or in a study in which they might be assigned to a placebo or control condition. Subjects may waive their right to be informed. Less benign are studies in which subjects may consent to participate but are misinformed about the nature of the study or are observed without consent and with implicit deception.

When using a "consent to concealment" method, it is easy to dehoax subjects about what has really happened. Not so with false informing or implicit deception, for having been deceived once, subjects would tend not to believe a researcher who finally tells the truth. It is still harder to desensitize subjects, that is, to return them to a state of mind at least as positive and constructive as when they entered the research (Sieber, 1983b).

In summary, ethical research requires more than the following of rules. It calls for sensitive application of psychological knowledge of human (or animal) nature and creative problem solving as well.

Bibliography

Boruch, R. F., & Cecil, J. S. (1979). *Assuring the confidentiality of social research data.* Philadelphia: University of Pennsylvania Press. This is the single most comprehensive source of methods and procedures that researchers may employ to assure the confidentiality of research information.

Bowser, B. P., & Sieber, J. E. (1992). AIDS prevention research: Old problems and new solutions. In C. M. Renzetti & R. Lee (Eds.), *Researching sensitive topics.* Newbury Park, CA: Sage.

Canadian Council on Animal Care (1989). *Ethics of animal investigation* (Rev. ed.). Ottawa, Canada. This thoughtful document includes a scale of categories of invasiveness in animal experiments, ranging from use of tissue culture, eggs, or protozoa and of short-term, skillful restraint and observation of animals to procedures that cause severe pain to conscious animals.

Fox, J. A., & Tracy, P. E. (1986). *Randomized response: A method for sensitive surveys.* Newbury Park, CA: Sage. This is a comprehensive presentation and critique of variants of the randomized response method.

Guide for the care and use of laboratory animals. (1996). Washington, DC: National Research Council, Institute for Laboratory Animal Resources. This guide sets forth standards for animal research by U.S. Public Health Service grantees. It offers standards that are widely influential among researchers and IACUCs worldwide, but which are less concerned with ethics and animal welfare than are national standards in countries such as Great Britain, Germany, Switzerland, Denmark, and Australia.

Laufer, R. S., & Wolfe, M. (1977). Privacy as a concept and a social issue: A multidimensional developmental theory. *Journal of Social Issues, 33,* 44–87. This thoughtful essay illustrates the importance of understanding privacy from the subject's perspective, and understanding the role of culture, power, and developmental factors in understanding what constitutes a threat to privacy, and how individuals succeed or fail in regulating others' access to them.

Marshall, P. A. (1992). Research ethics in applied anthropology. *IRB: A Review of Human Subjects Research, 14,* (6), Nov.–Dec., 1–5. This article discusses some complexities of applying ethical guidelines or research regulations to cultures other than mainstream American culture. For example, the principle of respect for subjects is interpreted in Western ethics and research regulations to mean respecting individual autonomy and obtaining informed consent; this fails to recognize that some communal cultures would require consent of the leader and may not place any value on the written word or signatures.

Melton, G. B., Levine, R. J., Koocher, G. P., Rosenthal, R., &

Thompson, W. C. (1988). Community consultation in socially sensitive research: Lessons from clinical trials on treatments for AIDS. *American Psychologist, 43,* 573–581.

Orlans, B. (1997). Ethical decision making about animal experiments. *Ethics and Behavior, 7* (2), 163–171. This article appears in a special issue on "Ethical Issues in the Use of Animals in Research." It compares the criteria on which American and several other Western nations' Institutional Animal Care and Use Committees (IACUC) evaluate the acceptability of research protocols. Orlans discusses the ethical criteria that should enter into evaluation, urges the use of pain and distress scales in these evaluations, and suggests ways to make IACUCs more balanced in viewpoint.

Sales, B., & Folkman, S. (Eds.). (2000). *Ethics in the conduct of research with human participants.* Washington, DC: APA. This is a guide for researchers in interpreting and applying ethical principles to research on humans. It offers comprehensive discussion of ethical principles, research planning, recruitment, informed consent, privacy and confidentiality, authorship and intellectual property, training, identifying conflicts of interest, and resolving ethical dilemmas.

Sieber, J. E. (1982). Deception in social research I: Kinds of deception and the wrongs they may involve. *IRB: A Review Of Human Subjects Research, 4,* 1–2, 12. Deception ranges from benign and tactful acts to harmful and wrongful acts. This article taxonomizes kinds of deception along this dimension.

Sieber, J. E. (1983a). Deception in social research II: Factors influencing the magnitude of potential for harm or wrong. *IRB: A Review of Human Subjects Research, 6,* 1–3, 12. The magnitude of harm done by deception is shown to vary with a range of associated circumstances.

Sieber, J. E. (1983b). Deception in social research III: The nature and limits of debriefing. *IRB: A Review Of Human Subjects Research, 6,* 1–2, 4. Debriefing and desensitizing do not always achieve their objectives.

Sieber, J. E. (1992). *Planning ethically responsible research.* Newbury Park, CA: Sage. This is a succinct guide for researchers and institutional review boards (IRBs) on translating federal regulations and ethical principles of research into ethical methods and procedures.

Smith, J. A., & Boyd, K. M. (Eds.). (1991). *Lives in balance.* London: Oxford University Press. This is the report of a working group convened by the institute of Medical Ethics in the United Kingdom. It presents a scheme in which costs (severity and duration of pain or distress and number and species of animals used) and benefits (likely social, educational, scientific value of the research) are identified and rated as low, medium and high, forming the basis for cost/benefit assessment of proposals.

Joan E. Sieber

Ethics in Practice

Some ethics problems in psychology are not difficult to identify; they involve gross violations of patients' rights or exploitation of vulnerable individuals. Other ethics problems are more subtle, involving issues that require psychologists to balance self-interest or convenience against the well being of their patients or the ideals of the profession. The specific temptations that they must avoid and the specific ideals to which they should aspire are given in the "Ethical Principles of Psychologists and Code of Conduct" (1992) and in the formal and informal curricula to which all psychologists are exposed over the course of their professional training. Psychology deals with problems that matter greatly to individuals and society (e.g., child abuse, violence, divorce, childrearing, suicide, and sexuality) so both the technical and ethical correctness of psychologists' choices are significant.

Professionals have special knowledge and skills, but possessing these does not in and of itself determine what is right or moral. Society grants professions access to status, power, and resources (income) and in return expects that professions will regulate themselves and act in ways that benefit society. Psychologists owe a special duty to persons in a professional relationship, known in legal terms as a fiduciary obligation. It denotes the special duty to care for the welfare of those who have become one's clients or patients.

Ethics as a Means of Regulating Conduct

In order to do what is right, the practitioner must first understand what is right. Ethics, along with law and etiquette, provide principles and standards that help to determine whether an action is right, good, or proper. Ethics focuses on the ideals of human behavior and according to many moral philosophers is distinguished by three main features: (1) it is based on principles, (2) the principles have universality (e.g., they could be applied generally to all similar persons), and (3) appropriate behavior may be deduced from the principles by moral reasoning. Professional ethics in practice is a combination of ethics, law, and etiquette.

Much of ethical philosophy is concerned with the basis on which acts are considered ethical. One method of moral justification—teleology or utilitarianism—justifies an action as ethical if it results in the creation of more good than harm. Jeremy Bentham articulates this viewpoint in An Introduction to the Principles of Morals and Legislation (New York, 1863/1948). An alternative justification, deontology, focuses on the essence of the act itself, particularly as it is based on respect for persons. This approach is most closely associated with Immanuel Kant's theories, as William Frankena describes in his Ethics (2nd ed., New Jersey, 1973). In actual practice, professional ethics involves a mixed deontological-teleological framework. The minimal ethical obligations are termed "mandatory obligations," and the ideals or maximal obligations are termed "aspirational." The psychology code divides aspirational obligations into six

ethical principles and focuses on the mandatory obligations in its 102 standards.

Considerable research in moral development has shown that over the course of their education and professional training, psychologists (like other professionals) engage in principled reasoning. However, as J. Rest and D. Narvaez describe in Moral Development in the Professions: Psychology and Applied Ethics (Hillsdale, NJ, 1994), this is only one of the elements necessary to act ethically. It is necessary for the professional to: (1) recognize that a moral issue is at stake, (2) give priority to acting ethically, (3) understand the ethical principles at stake, and; (4) have the skills necessary to implement the proper action. Thus ethics is both a cognitive and behavioral aspect of professional practice. Once an ethical dilemma has arisen, a process of decision making must be undertaken to determine the best action under the circumstances. There are several approaches to ethical decision making, such as those described by Leonard Haas and John Malouf in Keeping Up the Good Work: A Practitioners' Guide to Mental Health Ethics (1995); M. Canter, B. Bennett, S. Jones, and T. Nagy in Ethics for Psychologists: A commentary on the APA Ethics Code (1994); and D. Marsh and R. Magee in Ethical and Legal Issues in Professional Practice with Families (1997).

Psychology and Ethics. Psychology is both a learned profession and a healing art. Thus, in common with other healing arts, its central ideals concern the promotion of human welfare and the alleviation of suffering. Psychology also is based in science, so that its approaches to healing and treatment should be based on valid evidence. Psychology is an independent profession, not subject to the supervision of any other profession. Therefore, psychologists must maintain and monitor their own standards. As members of a scientific discipline, psychologists are obliged to use only valid scientific evidence and to be accurate and honest in their representations. Psychologists function not only as mental health practitioners but as teachers, researchers, and public advocates. Many of the principles of psychology ethics are applicable to all psychologists, regardless of their field of specialization. Others (for example, the need to uphold privacy and confidentially) are particularly applicable to those psychologists who deliver professional services.

The development of ethical standards in organized psychology is unique. In 1948, a committee of psychologists convened by the American Psychological Association undertook an empirical assessment of ethical problems in the field. By survey and questionnaire, critical incidents in ethics were solicited from psychologists and codified into psychology's first ethics code (Ethical Standards of Psychologists, Washington, D.C., 1953). Subsequently, the association indicated that the code should periodically be revised in order to reflect changing realities in the field.

The six principles of the ethics codes are themselves not "enforceable," since they are aspirational. However, the 102 standards, covering eight areas of practice, are clear-cut rules for appropriate conduct that can be enforced (that is, penalties may be imposed for violations). All in one way or another have implications for the practicing psychologist. The code's six principles are as follows:

1. *Competence.* This principle focuses on the need for psychologists to provide services and use techniques in which they are qualified by education, training, or, experience. It underscores psychologists' obligations to exercise good judgement in areas of emerging practice and to undertake continuing education for professional competence.

2. *Integrity.* This principle underscores the need for honesty and accuracy in describing services, fees, products, and so forth. It also focuses on psychologists' obligation to be aware of their own values, belief systems, needs, and limitations. It implies a variety of standards in the area of informed consent and reminds psychologists to avoid potentially harmful dual relationships.

3. *Professional and scientific responsibility.* This principle underscores the need to remain accountable for ones' decisions as a psychologist, regardless of whether one is an employee or a supervisor. It also focuses on the interrelationship of all members of the profession, in that psychologists have a responsibility to uphold the reputation of the discipline and the public's trust in psychology and psychologists. It is the basis for standards regarding confronting colleagues' improper behavior.

4. *Respect for people's rights and dignity.* This principle gives rise to standards in the area of privacy and confidentiality. It reminds psychologists of their inherently powerful position and their need to understand cultural and other differences between themselves and consumers of their service.

5. *Concern for others' welfare.* This principle underscores the obligation to avoid exploitation and to contribute to the welfare of those with whom psychologists interact, not limited to patients but including students, supervisors, and research participants.

6. *Social responsibility.* This principle focuses on psychologists' obligations to improve the community and society in which they work and live. It also implies contributing professional time pro bono (from *pro bono publico*, for the benefit of the public).

Inculcating Ethical Principles

No matter how good the ethics enforcement mechanism, prevention of ethics infractions and the maintaining of high ethical standards in the profession at large is a more effective means of protecting the public than is apprehending offenders.

Prevention begins with the profession attracting those who aspire to its highest ideals and with training experiences that reinforce their commitment to high standards of practice. In 1981, mandatory ethics education was instituted for all programs that received accreditation from the American Psychological Association as professional psychology training programs (clinical, counseling, school, and industrial/organization psychology). Psychology was the first mental health profession to make formal ethics instruction mandatory. Ethics instruction is also provided at all psychology internship training sites, in addition to the informal professional socialization that occurs continuously during the years of training.

Many of the ordinary ethics problems that practitioners encounter involve misunderstandings and failures to appreciate conflicts of interest, as P. Keith-Spiegel notes in the article, "Violation of ethical principles: Ignorance or poor professional judgment versus willful disregard" (*Professional Psychology*, 1977, 8, 288–296). Publication of professional journal articles such as the regular ethics feature in the journal *Professional Psychology* and continuing education in ethics (now required in several states) serve to educate practicing psychologists about current dilemmas.

Enforcement of Ethics Standards

The American Psychological Association maintains an Office of Ethics, staffed by a full-time psychologist and ethics associates. Complaints are heard by a volunteer ethics committee composed of nine psychologists and one layperson. The ethics office receives an average of 110 formal complaints against members each year, and of these 66 to 75% are opened as formal cases; in 1996, "complaints were filed against approximately 0.11% of the membership," the committee reported (Report of the Ethics Committee, 1996. *American Psychologist*, 1997, 52, 897–905). The ethics committee both responds to complaints against psychologists and answers educational questions from the membership and the public at large. Psychology is a licensed mental health profession in all 50 states. Therefore, psychologists' practice is subject to the oversight and enforcement of state boards of psychology. All of these state boards incorporate the Ethical Principles of Psychologists and Code of Conduct into the statutes that govern the practice of psychology. Therefore, ethics violations may be the basis for complaints to state licensing boards. There are also state psychological associations in every state, and each has a volunteer ethics committee, which responds to complaints against members. Licensing boards regulate licensed psychologists and pursue those complaints against individuals practicing psychology without a license, while state associations focus on the behavior of their members. Finally, other psychological entities such as local psychological associations, the

American Boards of Professional Psychology, or specific psychological societies, maintain ethics committees.

It is also noteworthy that ethics violations can form the basis of legal complaints. Thus, courts can shape the ethics code of a profession by legal decisions. For example, the famous Tarasoff decision (*Tarasoff v. Board of Regents of the University of California*) made an impact on the ethical standards of all mental health professions when the court found a "duty to protect" incumbent on mental health practitioners.

Problems in Professional Psychology Ethics

There are certain common problems that are enduring issues in professional ethics, but the field is not static. New techniques, theories, research evidence, technology, and service delivery systems pose new problems and require new ways of interpreting the fundamental ethical principles. Some examples of both enduring and emerging areas of ethical concern follow:

Sex and boundaries. A persistent problem in psychology, as in other mental health professions, is the sexual exploitation of patients. This is considered a boundary violation, in that it blurs or transgresses the boundary between the therapist/patient relationship and the relationship of romantic or sexual partners. It is also considered a dual relationship in that the romantic and therapeutic relationships occur at the same time. The code of ethics prohibits sexual intimacy with patients as well as potentially injurious dual relationships (for example, treatment of friends or business associates). The problem has persisted, however, perhaps showing the difficulty of effectively controlling personal needs in a close relationship such as psychotherapy, as K. Pope, J. Sonne, and J. Holroyd suggest in *Sexual Feelings in Psychotherapy* (Washington, D.C., 1993).

Competence. Another area of persisting ethical concern is the maintenance of competence. All professions have a "half life" in which the knowledge accumulated during the training years becomes obsolete or irrelevant. Psychology is no exception to this trend and it is incumbent on a psychologist to maintain knowledge of current practices.

Finances. Clarity about fees and propriety in the collection of fees is an important area of psychological practice. Psychologists sometimes turn their past-due accounts over to collection agencies, and this can be the cause of considerable distress for possibly vulnerable patients if handled poorly.

Testing and assessment. Competence in psychological testing is one of the hallmarks of the professional psychologist. Increasing sophistication of psychological tests and increasing reliance by employers, courts, and others on psychological screening makes the use and misuse of psychological testing an area of considerable ethical conflict. Psychologists must use valid tests, interpret them competently, be clear with those whom they test about the purposes of the assessment and clear with those who use the results about the limits of such findings.

Confronting colleagues. Psychologists are obliged to limit their practices and get help when faced with alcohol and drug problems, depression, or other stresses that interfere with effective functioning. Although the current ethics code calls for self-awareness of one's limitations as a practitioner, this is not always easy to achieve, and confrontation by colleagues may be necessary. Psychologists, like other mental health professionals, have difficulty calling possible problems to the attention of their colleagues; the problem of impairment in the profession is one of continued concern, as R. Kilburg, P. Nathan, and R. Thoreson note in *Professionals in Distress* (Washington, D.C., 1986).

Duty to protect. A relatively new legal obligation that has in turn required clarification of psychologists' ethical obligations is the duty to protect. Courts have decided, based on the Tarasoff decision, that psychologists are obligated to attempt to protect those who may be harmed by the actions of their patients. This duty has long included mandatory reporting of possible child abuse, and now extends to reporting of domestic violence and reporting of threats of harm to specific others. The ethical obligation to uphold the law and the potentially conflicting ethical obligation to protect patient privacy can make this a complex area for psychologists.

Managed care. Managed care depends heavily on "utilization review" (to prevent overtreatment), "provider profiling" (to identify those who provide treatment consistent with the organization's rules) and "treatment guidelines" (which mandate specific interventions for specific problems). All of these cost-containment strategies can affect the traditional boundaries of the psychologist-patient relationship. For example, session limits raise an ethical conflict in that psychologists are obliged to maintain an established psychologist-patient relationship until the treatment is completed, a referral is made or it is clear that the patient will no longer benefit from the service. Otherwise, there is risk of abandonment. On the other hand, psychologists who continue to treat without reimbursement may jeopardize their practices. This may occur either because they no longer receive enough income to keep their offices open or because the managed care entity removes them from its panel of providers for "excessive" treatment.

Privacy and confidentiality. There are increasing threats to the privacy of psychotherapy patients, in that utilization reviewers, insurance companies, and other third-party payers insist on knowing details of the treatment. The rapid spread of electronic means of record keeping and billing also poses threats to privacy. Psychologists must on the one hand be accurate informing patients about the limits of privacy and confidentiality and on the other hand strive to protect the interests of their patients to the extent possible, obtain reimbursement, and provide a safe therapeutic environment in which private matters can be discussed.

Electronic service delivery. The rise of technologies such as the Internet poses the question of whether psychologists can deliver psychological services via video or computer with integrity. This is an emerging area of ethical concern in that it is unknown whether the techniques useable in face-to-face treatment are generalizable to electronic vehicles of treatment delivery.

Expert testimony. Increasingly, courts are relying on psychologists to provide expert testimony on the mental state of criminal defendants, the parental fitness of child custody disputants, mental disability of claimants, and other issues. This has increased psychologists' obligation to be clear about their roles and the limits of their expertise. This is particularly an ethical problem for psychologists who make a transition from providing treatment services to a parent to becoming expert witnesses for that parent in a custody evaluation (the current ethics code strongly advises against such a dual role).

The "professional estate" of the psychologist. The issue of how records are to be disposed of and practices dealt with following the psychologist's retirement, death, or disability has not been addressed extensively in the professional literature. This is another issue that combines legal problems and ethical obligations.

Group, marital, and family therapies. Most of the principles of professional psychology ethics were developed with the assumption that treatment involved one patient or client working with one therapist. The unique needs of group, couples, and family therapy particularly in regard to confidentiality, privileged communication, and possibly conflicting needs of different participants may require elaborations of the ethics code to clarify the ethical issues in multiperson therapies. Family therapists in particular have been actively writing about the unique ethical conflicts raised by treating several members of the same family at the same time. Group therapists have often dealt with the problem of confidentiality (i.e., group members are not bound by the ethical or legal restrictions on the therapist) by having group members sign agreements at the beginning of treatment to maintain each others' confidentiality.

Bibliography

American Psychological Association. (1953). *Ethical standards of psychologists.* Washington, DC: American Psychological Association. Original compilation of critical incidents and ethics principles comprising the first psychology ethics code. Out of print but possibly available at libraries.

American Psychological Association. (1985). *Standards for educational and psychological testing.* Washington, DC: American Psychological Association. Technical standards for test developers, test administrators, and test users.

American Psychological Association. (1992). Ethical principles of psychologists and code of conduct. *American Psychologist, 47* (12), 1597–1611.

Beauchamp, T. L., & Childress, J. F. (1989). *Principles of biomedical ethics* (3rd ed.). New York: Oxford University Press. Excellent overview of basic principles forming the foundation for ethical principles in medicine as well as mental health. Provides classic case examples as well.

Bennett, B. E., Bryant, B. K., Vandenbos, G. R., & Greenwood, A. (1990). *Professional liability and risk management.* Washington, DC: American Psychological Association. Explores ethics, guidelines for limiting liability exposure, and practice management suggestions.

Bersoff, D. N. (Ed.). (1995). *Ethical conflicts in psychology.* Washington DC: American Psychological Association. Compilation and brief discussion of excerpts from over 100 articles, legal cases, statutes, and policy documents covering the broad range of professional, scientific, and academic psychology.

Canter, M. B., Bennett, B. E., Jones, S. E., & Nagy, F. T. (1994). *Ethics for psychologists: A commentary on the APA Ethics Code.* Washington, DC: American Psychological Association. Written by the members of the committee which revised the APA ethical principles; reviews the overall process of ethical decision making and describes the history of the APA ethics code, examines the ethics code in some detail, and includes a section on the regulation of psychology.

Edye, L. D., Robertson, G. J., & Krug, S. E. (1993). *Responsible test use: Case studies for assessing human behavior.* Washington, DC: American Psychological Association. Developed by a working group of representatives from the American Psychological Association, American Counseling Association, American Speech Language Hearing Association, and National Association of School Psychologists; case book on principles of test use.

Haas, L. J., & Malouf, J. L. (1995). *Keeping up the good work: A practitioners' guide to mental health ethics* (2nd ed.). Sarasota, FL: Professional Resource Press. Covers issues faced by psychiatry, social work, and nursing in addition to psychology; describes ethical approaches to a variety of common problems in practice; and provides a guide to ethical decision making; includes ethics codes of the four core mental health disciplines.

Kalichman, S. C. (1993). *Mandated reporting of suspected child abuse: Ethics, law, and policy.* Washington, DC: American Psychological Association. Explores the evolution of laws mandating the reporting of suspected child abuse and the ethical dilemma between reporting and maintaining confidentiality and trust and reviews cases of mandated reporting by practicing clinicians and offers guidelines for managing difficult cases.

Kilburg, R. R., Nathan, P. E., & Thoreson, R. W. (1986). *Professionals in distress: Issues, syndromes and solutions in psychology.* Washington, DC: American Psychological Association. Covers impairment, distress, rehabilitation, confrontation of impaired colleagues.

Marsh, D. T., & Magee, R. D. (1997). *Ethical and legal issues in professional practice with families.* New York: Wiley. Covers ethical issues in multi-person therapies, specifically family therapy, domestic violence, and recovered memories of abuse.

Monahan, J. (1980). *Who is the client? The ethics of psychological intervention in the criminal justice system.* Washington, DC: American Psychological Association. Somewhat dated but useful review of legal, ethical, and philosophical issues facing psychologists who work in corrections, criminal justice, and police activities.

Pope, K. S., Sonne, J. L., & Holroyd, J. (1993). *Sexual feelings in psychotherapy: Explorations for therapists in training.* Washington, DC: American Psychological Association.

Van de Creek, L., & Knapp, S. (1993). *Tarasoff and beyond: Legal and clinical considerations in the treatment of life-endangering patients* (Rev. ed.) Sarasota, FL: Professional Resource Press.

Windt, P. Y., Appleby, P. C., Battin, M. P., Francis, L. P., & Landesman, B. M. (1989). *Ethical issues in the professions.* Upper Saddle River, NJ: Prentice Hall. Excerpts from moral philosophy literature on issues in various professions; good broad overview of issues in profession ethics.

Leonard J. Haas

Ethics in Publication

[This entry is extracted from the *Publication Manual of the American Psychological Association*, 4th ed., 1994, pp. 292–298.]

The "Ethical Principles of Psychologists and Code of Conduct" of the American Psychological Association (*American Psychologist*, 1992) includes six ethical standards related to scholarly publishing. These standards are reprinted in Table 1 and are described in this entry in greater detail. They reflect basic ethical principles that underlie all scholarly writing and publication. These longstanding ethical principles are designed to achieve two goals:

1. To ensure the accuracy of scientific and scholarly knowledge, and
2. To protect intellectual property rights.

Two of these standards (reporting of results and sharing data) deal with accuracy, three relate to property rights (plagiarism, publication credit, and professional reviewers), and one concerns both quality of knowledge and its ownership (duplicate publication of data).

Reporting of Results

The essence of the scientific method involves observations that can be repeated and verified by others. Hence, psychologists do not make up data or modify their results to support a hypothesis. Errors of omission also are prohibited. Psychologists do not omit trouble-some observations from their reports so as to present a more convincing story.

Careful preparation of manuscripts for publication is essential, but errors can still occur. It is the author's responsibility to make such errors public if they are discovered after publication. The first step is to inform the publisher. Journals publish correction notices that bring errors to the attention of future users of the information. Book publishers correct subsequent printings of the book.

Plagiarism

Quotation marks should be used to indicate the exact words of another. Summarizing a passage or rearranging the order of a sentence and changing some of the words is paraphrasing. Each time a source is paraphrased, a credit for the source needs to be included in the text. The following paragraph is an example of how one might appropriately paraphrase some of the foregoing material in this section:

> As stated in the *Publication Manual of the American Psychological Association* (1994), the ethical principles of scientific publication are designed to ensure the integrity of scientific knowledge and to protect the intellectual property rights of others. As the *Publication Manual* explains, authors are expected to correct the record if they discover errors in their publications; they are also expected to give credit to others for their prior work when it is quoted or paraphrased.

The key element of this principle is that an author does not present the work of another as if it were his or her own work. This can extend to ideas as well as written words. If an author models a study after one done by someone else, the originating author should be given credit. If the rationale for a study was suggested in the Discussion section of someone else's article, that person should be given credit. Given the free exchange of ideas, which is very important to the health of psychology, an author may not know where an idea for a study originated. If the author does know, however, the author should acknowledge the source; this includes personal communications.

Publication Credit

Authorship is reserved for persons who receive primary credit and hold primary responsibility for a published work. Authorship encompasses, therefore, not only those who do the actual writing but also those who have made substantial scientific contributions to a study. Substantial professional contributions to a journal article may include formulating the problem or hypothesis, structuring the experimental design, organizing and conducting the statistical analysis, interpreting the results, or writing a major portion of the paper.

ETHICS: Ethics in Publication. Table 1. Ethical standards for the reporting and publishing of scientific information

---

The following ethical standards are extracted from the "Ethical Principles of Psychologists and Code of Conduct," which appeared in the December 1992 issue of the *American Psychologist* (Vol. 47, pp. 1597–1611). Standards 6.21–6.26 deal with the reporting and publishing of scientific information.

6.21 Reporting of Results

(a) Psychologists do not fabricate data or falsify results in their publications.

(b) If psychologists discover significant errors in their published data, they take reasonable steps to correct such errors in a correction, retraction, erratum, or other appropriate publication means.

6.22 Plagiarism

Psychologists do not present substantial portions or elements of another's work or data as their own, even if the other work or data source is cited occasionally.

6.23 Publication Credit

(a) Psychologists take responsibility and credit, including authorship credit, only for work they have actually performed or to which they have contributed.

(b) Principal authorship and other publication credits accurately reflect the relative scientific or professional contributions of the individuals involved, regardless of their relative status. Mere possession of an institutional position, such as Department Chair [or Laboratory Director], does not justify authorship credit. Minor contributions to the research or to the writing for publications are appropriately acknowledged, such as in footnotes or in an introductory statement.

(c) A student is usually listed as principal author on any multiple-authored article that is substantially based on the student's dissertation or thesis.

6.24 Duplicate Publication of Data

Psychologists do not publish, as original data, data that have been previously published. This does not preclude republishing data when they are accompanied by proper acknowledgment.

6.25 Sharing Data

After research results are published, psychologists do not withhold the data on which their conclusions are based from other competent professionals who seek to verify the substantive claims through reanalysis and who intend to use such data only for that purpose, provided that the confidentiality of the participants can be protected and unless legal rights concerning proprietary data preclude their release.

6.26 Professional Reviewers

Psychologists who review material submitted for publication, grant, or other research proposal review respect the confidentiality of and the proprietary rights in such information of those who submitted it.

Those who so contribute are listed in the byline. Lesser contributions, which do not constitute authorship, may be acknowledged in a note. These contributions may include such supportive functions as designing or building the apparatus, suggesting or advising about the statistical analysis, collecting or entering the data, modifying or structuring a computer program, and recruiting participants or obtaining animals. Conducting routine observations or diagnoses for use in studies does not constitute authorship. Combinations of these (and other) tasks, however, may justify authorship. As early as practicable in a research project, the collaborators should decide on which tasks are necessary for

the project's completion, how the work will be divided, which tasks or combination of tasks merits authorship credit, and on what level credit should be given (for example, first author, second author).

Authors are responsible for determining authorship and for specifying the order in which two or more authors' names appear in the byline. The general rule is that the name of the principal contributor should appear first, with subsequent names in order of decreasing contribution. If authors played equal roles in the research and publication of their study, they may wish to note so in a footnote. Collaborators may need to reassess authorship credit and order if major changes are necessary in the course of the project (and its publication). This is especially true in faculty-student collaborations, when students may need intensive supervision or additional analyses may need to be conducted beyond the scope of a student's thesis or dissertation.

Authors are also responsible for the factual accuracy of their contributions. Authors not only receive credit for the published work, they take responsibility for the opinions and statements included in the work. The corresponding author (the author who serves as the main contact with the journal editor or book publisher) should always obtain a person's consent before including that person's name in a byline or in a note. Each author listed in the byline of a journal article should review the entire manuscript before it is submitted.

Duplicate Publication of Data

Data that have already been published once are not published again as if they were new and original. Duplicate publication distorts the knowledge base by making it appear there is more information available than really exists. It also wastes scarce resources (for example, journal pages and the time and efforts of editors and reviewers). Duplicate publication can also lead to copyright violations. An author cannot assign the copyright to more than one publisher.

This standard means that an author must not submit to a scientific journal a manuscript describing work that has been published in whole or in substantial part elsewhere. Journals serve as the archival record for a discipline. A major aspect of their worth is that they publish new, original knowledge. Duplicate publication would pollute their worth.

This policy does not necessarily exclude from consideration by journals manuscripts that have been previously published in abstracted form (for example, in the proceedings of an annual meeting) or in a periodical with limited circulation or availability (for example, in a report by a university department or by a government agency). This policy does exclude the same or overlapping material that has appeared in a publication that has been offered for public sale, such as conference proceedings or a book chapter; such a publication does not meet the criterion of "limited circulation." Publication of a Brief Report in most journals is with the understanding that an extended report will not be published elsewhere; the Brief Report is the archival record for the work. Problems of duplicate publication may also arise if material is first published through the mass media.

The prohibition of duplicate publication also means that the same manuscript must not be submitted to more than one publisher at the same time. If a manuscript is rejected by one journal, an author may then submit it to another.

Whether the publication of two or more reports based on the same or on closely related research constitutes duplicate publication is often a matter of editorial judgment. Any prior publication should be noted and referenced in the manuscript, and the author should inform the journal editor of the existence of any similar manuscripts that have already been published or accepted for publication or that may be submitted for concurrent consideration to the same journal or elsewhere. The editor can then make an informed judgment as to whether the submitted manuscript includes sufficient new information to warrant consideration.

The author is obligated to present work parsimoniously and as completely as possible within the space constraints of journal publications. Data that can be meaningfully combined within a single publication should be presented together to enhance effective communication. Piecemeal, or fragmented, publication of several reports of the results from a single study is undesirable unless there is a clear benefit to scientific communication. An author who wishes to divide the report of a study into more than one article should inform the editor and provide such information as the editor requests. Whether the publication of two or more reports based on the same or on closely related research constitutes fragmented publication is a matter of editorial judgment.

The prohibition of piecemeal publication does not preclude subsequent reanalysis of published data in light of new theories or methodologies if the reanalysis is clearly labeled as such. There may be times, especially in the instances of large-scale or multidisciplinary projects, when it is both necessary and appropriate to publish multiple reports. Multidisciplinary projects often address diverse topics, and publishing in a single journal may be inappropriate. Repeated publication from a longitudinal study is often appropriate because the data from different times make unique scientific contributions; useful knowledge should be made available to others as soon as possible.

As multiple reports from large-scale or longitudinal studies are made, the author is obligated to cite prior reports on the project to help the reader evaluate the work accurately. For example, in the early years of a longitudinal study one might cite all previous publications from it. For a well-known or very-long-term longitudinal study, one might cite the original publication, a more recent summary, and earlier articles that focused on the same or related scientific questions addressed in the current report. Often it is not necessary to repeat the description of the design and methods of a longitudinal or large-scale project in its entirety. The author may refer the reader to an earlier publication for this detailed information. It is important, however, to provide sufficient information so that the reader can evaluate the current report. It is also important to make clear the degree of sample overlap in multiple reports from large studies. Again, authors should inform and consult with the editor.

As indicated earlier, journals serve as an archival record for a discipline. The majority of books, however, often serve different purposes, one of which is the compilation, synthesis, and dissemination of the new information that has been published in journals. Therefore, journal articles are revised sometimes for publication as book chapters. The author has a responsibility to reveal to the reader that all or portions of the new work were previously published and to cite and reference the source. If copyright is owned by a publisher or by another person, copyright must be acknowledged, and permission to adapt or reprint must be obtained. For example, this entry is reprinted with minor modifications from the fourth edition of the *Publication Manual of the American Psychological Association* (Washington, D.C., 1994) by permission of the copyright holder, the American Psychological Association.

Data Verification

To permit competent professionals to confirm the results and analyses, authors are expected to retain raw data for a minimum of 5 years after publication of the research. Other information related to the research (for example, instructions, treatment manuals, software, and details of procedures) should be kept for the same period. This information is necessary if others are to attempt replication. Authors are expected to comply promptly and in a spirit of cooperation with such requests. Sometimes there may be special concerns that must be addressed, such as confidentiality of the participants and proprietary or other concerns of the sponsor of the research. Generally, the costs of complying with the request should be borne by the requestor.

Prior to publication, researchers must make their data available to the editor at any time during the review and production process if questions arise with respect to the accuracy of the report. Otherwise, the submitted manuscript can be rejected.

Professional Reviewers

Editorial review of a journal or book manuscript requires that the editors and reviewers circulate and discuss the manuscript. When submitting a manuscript to an APA journal, an author implicitly consents to the handling necessary for review of the manuscript. Editors and reviewers, however, may not, without the author's explicit permission, quote from a manuscript or circulate copies for any purposes other than that of editorial review. If a reviewer consults with a colleague about some aspects of the manuscript, the reviewer should inform the editor. Editors and reviewers may not use the material from an unpublished manuscript to advance their own or others' work without the author's consent. Editors and reviewers should also avoid con-

flict of interest, or its appearance, by declining to evaluate the manuscripts of colleagues.

Electronic Publishing

It is too soon to know what additional or alternative ethical guidelines, if any, will be needed as more and more scientific information is disseminated electronically. Such basic issues as copyright have not yet been agreed upon. Therefore, it is not clear how intellectual property rights will be maintained when scientific writing is distributed electronically. Word-processing procedures that allow one to combine electronic files may contribute to increased plagiarism. The free and easy interchange of ideas available through networks—a desirable property of electronic communication—may make it more difficult, in turn, to determine authorship. Research results may be disseminated electronically without careful peer review, which under the current publication system is thought to serve as a filter to enhance the quality of scientific knowledge. How will electronically disseminated information be recalled or corrected, if found to be in error? Where will the archival record exist, given the ease with which the electronic form can be modified? These are but a very few of the challenges facing scientific "publication" in light of the rapidly changing technology.

Bibliography

Fine, M. A., & Kurdek, L. A. (1993). Reflections on determining authorship credit and authorship order on faculty-student collaborations. *American Psychologist, 48,* 1141–1147.

Frankel, M. S. (1993). Professional societies and responsible research conduct. In *Responsible science: Ensuring the integrity of the research process* (Vol. 2, pp. 26–49). Washington, DC: National Academy Press.

LaFollette, M. C. (1992). *Stealing into print: Fraud, plagiarism, and misconduct in scientific publishing.* Berkeley: University of California Press.

ETHNIC AND RACIAL IDENTITY. [*This entry comprises two articles:* Ethnic Identity *and* Racial Identity. *For a general discussion of identity, see* Identity.]

Ethnic Identity

Ethnic identity is a dynamic, multidimensional construct that refers to one's identity, or sense of self, in ethnic terms, that is, in terms of a subgroup within a larger context that claims a common ancestry and shares one or more of the following elements: culture, race, religion, language, kinship, or place of origin. Ethnic identity is not a fixed categorization, but rather a fluid and dynamic understanding of self and group that changes with age, time, and context. An ethnic identity is constructed and modified as people become aware of other groups and of the ethnic differences between themselves and others and attempt to understand the meaning of their ethnicity within the larger setting. It is a central defining characteristic of many individuals, particularly those who are members of minority or lower-status groups.

Although at one time ethnic identity was expected to become less important due to mass communication and globalization, it became in fact more salient throughout the twentieth century as a consequence of complex social and historical forces, among them the persistence of intergroup prejudice and the increased movement of immigrants and refugees. There has been a related surge of interest in the topic from various social science disciplines, including sociology, anthropology, and psychology. Within psychology, the topic has been explored by social, cross-cultural, and developmental psychologists. Generally, sociologists and anthropologists have focused on group level processes, while psychologists have emphasized individual and interpersonal processes. However, the boundaries between disciplines have become increasing blurred as insights from one are incorporated into others.

Components of Ethnic Identity

There is general agreement that ethnic identity is a multidimensional construct, but there is little consensus on exactly what it includes. Most approaches recognize one or more of the following elements, described with their usual means of assessment.

1. Ethnic self-identification refers to one's self-label as an ethnic group member. Self-identification has been assessed by asking respondents to answer open-ended questions about their ethnic identification, to select one or more labels from a given list, or to generate their own list of self-labels from which researchers can determine whether and how prominently ethnicity is mentioned. Studies with children have used dolls or pictures to determine their ability to identify or label themselves and their ethnic group.

2. Affective components include feelings of belonging to the ethnic group and the attitudes and evaluations associated with ethnicity. Questionnaires have assessed affective components such as pride, affirmation, and positive feelings toward one's group, or preferences for ethnically related items, such as food or language usage. The sense of belonging to a group has been studied through direct questions, such as the desire to belong to or to leave the group, as well as through ratings of similarity to a variety of descriptors associated with the group. Measures for children have tapped preference for own-group or other-group with pictures or dolls.

3. Cognitive components include knowledge about the group, such as its history and traditions, together with one's understanding of ethnicity and its implications for oneself. Knowledge about the group has been assessed with questions about its customs, history, or famous people. Understandings about ethnicity have typically been studied through interviews, including questions assessing the extent to which one has thought about one's ethnicity.

4. Value orientations associated with ethnicity provide a worldview and define relationships between the self and others. Individualism, collectivism, and familism are the most frequently studied cultural values, but other values, such as gender roles and attitudes toward authority, have also been examined. Questionnaires have usually been used to assess values.

5. Processes of change in components of ethnic identity over time and with increasing age have also been studied, most often through interviews.

Comprehensive questionnaires that tap several components have been developed for specific groups (e.g., for Latinos, by Felix-Ortiz, 1994; for Asians, by Suinn, Ahuna, & Khoo, 1992) or for use with any ethnic group (Phinney, 1992).

These aspects of ethnic identity have been emphasized to a different extent and in varying combinations across the fields of sociology, anthropology, social psychology, cross-cultural psychology, and developmental psychology.

Sociological and Anthropological Approaches to Ethnic Identity

In the United States, initial interest in ethnic identity came from sociologists who studied the self-identification patterns of immigrants to the United States. Stonequist (1935) emphasized the problems of the immigrant caught between two cultures and never fitting in. It was assumed that in order to become part of their new society, immigrants would have to give up their old identities, based on their culture of origin, and become American. Research primarily with European immigrants examined the ways in which they became assimilated into the American mainstream and the extent to which they retained or did not retain an identification with their culture of origin. More recent research has extended this topic to immigrants from non-European backgrounds. The sociologist Mary Waters (1990) pointed out that the process is quite different in the United States for European and non-European groups. For descendants of immigrants from Europe, an ethnic identification can be chosen voluntarily; identification entails no social costs and provides enjoyment for those who choose to associate with an ethnic culture. Because of intermarriage and assimilation, many Americans from European backgrounds cease to identify themselves as members of an ethnic group after one or more generations in the United States and think of themselves only as Americans.

For those who are racially identifiable there may be relatively little choice, in that an ethnic label is likely to be imposed by others. However, within any one group a variety of labels is available. People of African descent can call themselves Black or African American; those of Latin American origin use labels such as Hispanic, Latino, or, for those of Mexican descent, Mexican American or Chicano. These labels are associated with different meanings for the individual. The actual labels used vary historically, as well, as is seen in the change from colored to Negro to Black to African American. For biethnic or biracial individuals, the choice of a label has changed from a time when a single non-White ancestor could determine one's group membership as non-White, to the current situation, in which self-identification is a complex interaction of appearance, choice, the particular setting, and the available social categories.

Sociologists and anthropologists have also looked at ethnic identity in a larger context. Sociologists and anthropologists such as Lola Romanucci-Ross and George DeVos (1995) and E. Roosens (1989) have shown that ethnic identity is embedded in social and historical processes worldwide. They provide case studies and analyses of the ways in which the identities of a wide range of ethnic groups throughout the world have evolved and changed in response to the social, political, and economic constraints and opportunities afforded by particular contexts.

Social Psychological Approaches

Most social psychological research on ethnic identity is based on social identity theory (SIT), as proposed by the British social psychologist Henri Tajfel (Tajfel & Turner, 1986). Social identity theory emphasizes that the social groups to which people belong, such as religious, occupational, or political groups, form an important basis for their identity. According to the theory, the basic need to maintain a positive sense of self underlies the tendency to evaluate positively the groups one belongs to. Much early research tested the theory using artificially created groups, the minimal group paradigm.

Tajfel also speculated about the specific identity problems that some ethnic groups face as a result of negative stereotypes of their group within society. He suggested that an affirmation of one's ethnicity is a way of dealing with the denigration of one's group by others and thus preserving self-esteem. Therefore, the affirmation of one's ethnicity is likely to be stronger and more salient among groups which have faced greater discrimination. In fact, ethnic identity varies across ethnic groups in the United States. African Americans generally show the strongest sense of affirmation and belonging to their group, followed by other ethnic minorities. European Americans consistently show lower salience and affirmation of their ethnicity. For racially distinct groups within the United States, ethnic identity is likely to remain salient as long as intergroup discrimination exists and European Americans predominate in positions of power.

Affirmation of one's ethnic identity is also generally assumed to be associated with positive self-evaluation with psychological well-being. Most measures of ethnic identity show consistent but low correlations with self-esteem, although some components, such as the positive evaluation of one's group, show a stronger correlation than others. Furthermore, the relationship between ethnic identity and attitudes toward self varies across ethnic groups and individuals. The relationship is likely to be stronger among individuals for whom ethnicity is highly salient, including members of most minority groups than among members of the majority group.

Social psychological research has examined the ways in which ethnic identity is negotiated at the individual level within the changing social contexts of both the ethnic group and the larger society. The various influences that individuals have been exposed to, together with the group's history and current social context, interact in complex ways to determine the expression of ethnicity, with individuals building on prior attitudes, understandings, and experiences to construct a way of being ethnic in each situation.

Ethnic identity varies in the short term over differing contexts, with strong ethnic feelings emerging in settings where ethnicity is highly salient, such as family gatherings or traditional celebrations, and receding in settings that deemphasize ethnicity. An unresolved question is whether ethnic identity is likely to be stronger or more salient for a very small subgroup within a setting, for example, a few minority students in a predominantly White school, or for a large group within a setting, such as a school that is predominantly Hispanic. In the former case, salience may result from minority status; in the latter, it may be an outcome of cultural dominance at the local level together with minority status as the societal level.

Acculturation and Cross-Cultural Approaches to Ethnic Identity

Acculturation has been described as the changes that occur when one cultural group comes into extended firsthand contact with another. Cross-cultural psychologists have explored the acculturation process of subgroups such as immigrants, refugees, indigenous peoples, and other minorities within a larger society. Early assimilationist views were based on the assumption that as members of such groups became acculturated and identified increasingly as members of the new society, their identity as ethnic group members would decline. Acculturation was viewed as a linear process in which closer ties with the new culture inevitably meant the loss of ties to the culture of origin. However, conceptualizations by cross-cultural psychologist John Berry and others emphasize that acculturation includes two independent dimensions, involvement with both the ethnic culture and the larger society. By dichotomizing and crossing these two dimensions, one can define four possible types of acculturation: biculturalism (involvement both with cultures), assimilation (involvement only with the larger society), separation (involvement only with the ethnic culture), or marginalization (involvement with neither). [*See also* Acculturation; Cultural Disintegration; *and* Marginalization.]

These types of acculturation may differ with regard to behaviors, attitudes, and identification. Research with immigrants has generally shown that over subsequent generations, behaviors such as food, language, and customs change to resemble those of the host society. On the other hand, ethnic identification and the affective components of ethnic identity, including feelings of belonging and pride in one's ethnic group, can be extremely persistent, remaining strong over many generations even though traditional ethnic practices and knowledge about the group decline. This aspect of ethnic identity has been termed ethnic loyalty or symbolic ethnicity. Such loyalty can be the basis for a bicultural identity, in which one identifies both as ethnic and as part of the larger society. A variety of forms of bicultural identity have been defined by LaFromboise and others (1994).

Language is one of the most complicated behaviors associated with ethnicity. It is frequently used as the primary indicator of acculturation. Some writers, such as Howard Giles and his colleagues (1977), suggest that language proficiency and use are core components of one's ethnic identity, intimately tied to one's sense of self as a group member. Among immigrants, research suggests a strong link between ethnic identity and language retention. However, many ethnic group members maintain a strong self-identification with their group even though the use of an ethnic language has declined or disappeared.

Cross-cultural psychologists have also explored the cultural values held by different ethnic and cultural groups and the relationship of such values to ethnic identity. The most widely studied values are individualism and collectivism. Researchers have shown that collectivism, the subordination of the self to one's group, is correlated with ethnic identity, whereas individualism, the emphasis of individual over group goals, is not. Both collectivism and ethnic identity are higher among ethnic minority groups than among European Americans.

Developmental Approaches

The study of ethnic identity by developmental psychologists has drawn from cognitive developmental theory, social identity theory, and the psychosocial theory of Erik Erikson (1968).

Cognitive developmental theory emphasizes the increasing cognitive competence of the child as a basis for understanding changes in ethnic identity with age. Frances Aboud (1987) has shown that young children typically learn their ethnic self-label between the ages of four and seven years, although the age varies with the particular group and contact with other groups. Around age eight to ten, following the learning of their ethnic group label, children develop an understanding of ethnic constancy (the fact that their ethnicity stays the same over time and in spite of superficial changes, such as clothing). They acquire knowledge about their ethnic culture through the process of enculturation as described by Martha Bernal and George Knight (1993).

Cognitive development influences the way in which children understand ethnicity. Young children understand it in literal and concrete terms, defined by food, customs, and often language. With increasing cognitive competence, children begin to develop a group consciousness and to understand ethnicity in terms of norms of behavior. Adolescents and adults are able to understand ethnicity in more abstract terms, as changing over time, and shaped by social and historical forces.

Children's feelings about their ethnicity are influenced from an early age by the family, community, and larger society. When families provide strong positive images of their ethnicity, children's early feelings about their ethnic group are likely to be positive. Warm, authoritative parenting contributes to children's affirmation of ethnicity. A vital ethnic community also provides a context in which individuals form a positive sense of their group. However, as social identity theory suggests, children are influenced as well by messages from the larger society. When negative messages become internalized, children may hold conflicting feelings about their ethnicity, including wanting to belong to another group. Confronting and dealing with such negative attitudes is part of the process of ethnic identity formation.

The psychosocial approach of Erik Erikson (1968) focuses on ego identity formation as a pivotal process of development that occurs primarily during adolescence. A stable sense of self is achieved through exploring and questioning attitudes and identifications in domains such as occupation, religion, and gender roles, and making commitments to roles and values that will serve as a guide to the future. Marcia defined four identity statuses on the basis of the presence or absence of exploration and commitment, foreclosure, diffusion, moratorium, and identity achievement (see Marcia et al., 1993).

Using Erikson and Marcia as a basis, Phinney (1989) developed a stage model of ethnic identity formation that has parallels to models of racial identity and minority identity development. Prior to adolescence, the child is assumed to have a foreclosed ethnic identity, that is, an identity derived from others rather than personally examined. Depending on prior socialization, it may include positive or negative attitudes toward one's group. With the onset of adolescence, as part of the task of identity formation, most minority youth enter a moratorium or exploration phase. The experience of discrimination may also motivate ethnic exploration. Adolescents begin questioning previously accepted views of ethnicity and trying to understand the meaning of being a member of an ethnic group within a larger society, often by learning about the history and traditions of their group. Such attempts ideally lead to an achieved ethnic identity, characterized by clarity about oneself as ethnic. This sense of self is assumed to be a source of personal strength and positive self-evaluation. Reexamination of the meaning of ethnicity can continue throughout life, depending on one's experiences. A related process model has been developed for white identity by Helms (1990). Phinney's Multigroup Ethnic Identity Measure (1992) is a questionnaire that measures both cognitive components of ethnic identity (exploration) and affective components (affirmation and sense of belonging); it can be used with any ethnic group.

The process of ethnic exploration and commitment has implications for attitudes toward oneself and other ethnic groups, but the process varies depending on group membership. For minorities, a foreclosed ethnic identity may include a preference for the dominant majority group. For the dominant group, foreclosure may involve feelings of racial superiority and negative stereotypes of other groups. During the moratorium phase, minority adolescents are often intensely involved in their own group, and strong in-group attitudes may be associated with negative feelings toward other groups. For the dominant group, the moratorium leads to growing awareness of racism and of the privilege resulting from their position of dominance. With the commitment that defines an achieved ethnic identity comes a secure, confident, and stable sense of self as an ethnic group member and a realistic assessment of one's group in the larger context. A broader understanding of one's own and other groups is expected to lead to more positive and accepting views of all groups. However, historical evidence suggests that this process is thwarted when political, economic, and social forces limit opportunities for individuals to express their identity as group members or to interact in positive ways with members of other groups.

Bibliography

Aboud, F. (1987). The development of ethnic self-identification and attitudes. In J. Phinney & M. Rotheram (Ed.), *Children's ethnic socialization: Pluralism and development* (pp. 32–55). Newbury Park, CA: Sage. A review of ethnic identity development in children.

Bernal, M., & Knight, G. (Eds.). (1993). *Ethnic identity: Formation and transmission among Hispanics and other minorities.* Albany, NY: State University of New York Press. A useful source of research and thinking on ethnic identity. It contains chapters by Bernal and colleagues, Aboud, Phinney, Berry, Hurtado and colleagues, and others.

Berry, J. (1990). Psychology of acculturation. In J. Berman (Ed.), *Nebraska symposium on motivation* (Vol. 37, pp. 201–234). Lincoln: University of Nebraska Press.

Erikson, E. (1968). *Identity: Youth and crisis.* New York: Norton.

Felix-Ortiz, M. (1994). A multidimensional measure of cultural identity for Latino and Latina adolescents. *Hispanic Journal of Behavioral Sciences, 16,* 99–116. A questionnaire measure of Latino cultural identity, including self-identification, knowledge, preferences, and behaviors.

Giles, H., Bourhis, R., & Taylor, D. (1977). *Towards a theory of language in ethnic group relations.* In H. Giles (Ed.), *Language, ethnicity, and intergroup relations.* London: Academic Press.

Helms, J. (1990). *Black and White racial identity: Theory, research, and practice.* New York: Greenwood.

LaFromboise, T., Coleman, H., & Gerton, J. (1993). Psychological impact of biculturalism: Evidence and theory. *Psychological Bulletin, 114,* 395–412. Explores various types of bicultural identity.

Liebkind, K. (1992). Ethnic identity: Challenging the boundaries of social psychology. In G. Breakwell (Ed.), *Social psychology of identity and the self concept.* London: Surrey University Press. A European perspective on ethnic identity.

Marcia, J., Waterman, A., Matteson, D., Archer, S., & Orlofsky, J. (1993). *Ego identity: A handbook of psychosocial research.* New York: Springer-Verlag.

Phinney, J. (1989). Stages of ethnic identity development in minority group adolescents. *Journal of Early Adolescence, 9,* 34–49. An interview study that provides evidence for developmental stages.

Phinney, J. (1990). Ethnic identity in adolescents and adults: A review of research. *Psychological Bulletin, 108,* 499–514.

Phinney, J. (1992). The Multigroup Ethnic Identity Measure: A new scale for use with diverse groups. *Journal of Adolescent Research, 7,* 156–176. A questionnaire measure designed for use with any ethnic group. The measure includes affective and cognitive developmental components of ethnic identity.

Phinney, J., & Rosenthal, D. (1992). Ethnic identity formation in adolescence: Process, context, and outcome. In G. Adams, T. Gulotta, & R. Montemayor (Eds.), *Identity formation during adolescence* (pp. 145–172). Newbury Park, CA: Sage.

Romanucci-Ross, L., & DeVos, G. (1995). *Ethnic identity: Creation, conflict, and accommodation.* Walnut Creek, CA: AltaMira Press.

Roosens, E. (1989). *Creating ethnicity.* Newbury Park, CA: Sage.

Stonequist, E. (1935). The problem of the marginal man. *American Journal of Sociology, 41,* 1–12.

Suinn, R., Ahuna, C., & Khoo, G. (1992). The Suinn-Lew Asian self-identity acculturation scale: Concurrent and factorial validation. *Educational and Psychological Measurement, 52,* 1041–1046. A questionnaire measure for Asian Americans that includes self-identification, preferences, and behaviors.

Tajfel, H., & Turner, J. (1986). The social identity theory of intergroup behavior. In S. Worchel & W. Austin (Ed.), *Psychology of intergroup relations* (pp. 7–24). Chicago: Nelson-Hall.

Waters, M. (1990). *Ethnic options: Choosing identities in America.* Berkeley, CA: University of California Press. A sociological examination of ethnic identity primarily among European Americans.

Jean S. Phinney

Racial Identity

Janet Helms, a prominent researcher of racial identity, describes racial identity as a sense of collective or group identity tied to one's perception that he or she is a member of a group that shares a cultural heritage (Helms, 1990). Two of the earliest research programs on racial identity were initiated in the 1930s. Ruth and Eugene Horowitz and, separately, Kenneth and Mamie Clark reported evidence that many African American children expressed a preference for White stimulus figures (e.g., dolls and photographs) over Black ones. Although Dr. Curtis Banks later demonstrated that true empirical evidence for White preference among African Americans was indeed lacking, these two research programs influenced the thinking even into the 1960s, possibly because the conclusions were so consistent with the pervasive theme of Black self-hatred prominent in the writings of social scientists during the same period.

The years between 1968 and 1975 have been described as the Black consciousness phase of the African American social movement. During this period, the study of racial identity progressed in a different direction. Social scientists (especially African American social scientists) became interested in strategies for differentiating intragroup differences among African Americans. At one end of the continuum, a growing cadre of African Americans were emerging who were, perhaps unfortunately, labeled as Black militants because they rejected the negative images of African Americans set forth by the larger society in favor of more positive self-definitions. These individuals also expressed a pride in their racial group membership. They stood in stark contrast to other African Americans who were viewed as more traditional because they believed they could improve their social position through integration and acceptance from the dominant society. Eventually the term *racial identity* was used to describe the extent or manner of identification with one's racial heritage and the sense of group identity with others who share a common racial heritage.

Years earlier, W. E. B. Du Bois had used the term *double consciousness* to describe the dynamics of being both American and of African descent. DuBois explained that African Americans had dual selves—both American and African—that, at times, could be antagonistic or inconsistent with each other. DuBois further proposed that each African American must determine how to combine these two selves in the identity process. Despite this common developmental task, it would be inaccurate to assume that every African American resolves this duality in the same manner. Rather, it is clear that considerable within-group variability still exists about what it means to be African American. Racial identity remains one way of understanding this variability.

The study of racial identity differs from the study of ethnic identity in at least one important respect. Many of the existing theories of ethnic identity are intentionally broad in order to explain the impact of culture and history on ethnic identity among various groups. However, despite common themes in identity development, the experiences of various racial and cultural groups are not identical. Rather, important ethnic group differences in the identity process are evident. Racial identity is used here primarily to describe the idiosyncratic experiences unique to African Americans as a result of the rich African heritage as well as the unique legacy of slavery, oppression, and colonialism.

Models of Racial Identity

Numerous models of racial identity have emerged. In *Black and White Racial Identity* (1990), Helms described eleven different models. Four alternative models are described below that illustrate the diversity in how racial identity is conceptualized. These four are the nigrescence models, African self-consciousness theory, optimal theory, and the multidimensional model of racial identity.

The French term, *nigrescence*, is used to describe the first set of models. Nigrescence type models developed by Thomas Parham, Janet Helms, William Cross, Jake Milliones, and others describe a developmental process that many African Americans undergo to rid themselves of negative images of "blackness" internalized via social interactions, the media, and other socialization experiences. Generally, the models suggest a progression from a way of thinking labeled by the theorists as "Negro" (a state in which the person has internalized the negative perceptions of the dominant society about blackness) to "black" (a state characterized by greater appreciation of one's racial group).

Janet Helms also points out that many of the various nigrescence models incorporate three separate identities when describing racial identity. These include personal identity (generic personality characteristics evident in all humans, such as self esteem, anxiety, and concern for others), reference group orientation (the degree to which one's own thoughts and behaviors are consistent with the values of a particular social group), and ascribed identity (affiliation with a particular racial group). Helms describes that, as an individual progresses toward a psychologically healthy racial identity, personal identity moves from negative to positive, and reference group orientation moves from a reliance on a White/Euro-American orientation to a Black, bicultural, and ultimately pluralistic reference group orientation. Ascribed identity moves from identifying with whites to identifying with Blacks or pan-Africans.

The stage model proposed by William Cross, Thomas Parham, and Janet Helms is a good example of the nigrescence models. In the first stage, preencounter, the individual, viewing the world from a white frame of reference, endorses a white normative standard and devalues his or her own blackness. Initially, these scholars proposed that an external negative event, such as a racist incident, triggers movement into the second stage, encounter. That event is assumed to be so powerful that it shatters the person's worldview and signals a need to change one's thinking about self and others of the same racial heritage. More recently, Thomas Parham has argued that a variety of encounter experiences could serve as a catalyst for recognizing the inadequacy of one's former frame of reference, including even a positive experience within the African American community. The third stage, immersion/emersion, is a period of transition or metamorphosis in which the person is consumed with replacing vestiges of the former Euro-American perspective with a new frame of reference more consistent with the emerging allegiance to one's own racial heritage. It is not uncommon for individuals in this stage to be quite involved in activities or organizations to improve the quality of life for African Americans. Individuals who progress to the fourth stage, Internalization, emerge from the state of withdrawal characteristic of the immersion/emersion stage to become less reactionary and psychologically more open. The enhanced self-confidence about blackness in the internalization stage enables the person to adopt a more pluralistic, nonracist worldview.

Thomas Parham and Janet Helms developed the Racial Identity Attitude Scale, which has preencounter, encounter, immersion/emersion, and internalization subscales. The design of the scale provides some additional information about their conceptualization of the racial identity process. Specifically, rather than assigning people to a single stage based on their responses, respondents receive scores on each of the subscales. This suggests that individuals may simultaneously possess attitudes associated with various stages. For example, even though an individual's worldview may be becoming more consistent with the internalization stage than some of the earlier stages, she or he may still display some attitudes in certain areas that are more consistent with encounter or immersion/emersion thinking.

Recently, Thomas Parham has proposed some revision of the theory. Specifically, he has proposed that (1) it is not inevitable that every African American starts at the *preencounter* stage, (2) that racial identity is a lifelong process and recycling through the stages is not uncommon, and (3) *internalization* may not be the only healthy resolution of racial identity.

Strengthening one's capacity for confronting the negative attitudes and experiences that African Americans encounter in the dominant culture is a major component of the nigrescence or stage models of racial identity. However, other perspectives of racial identity place less emphasis on interactions with the dominant society and focus more on the internalization of positive African philosophical beliefs and values. Kobi Kambon's social theory is an example of an African-centered approach to racial identity. The theory includes a biogenetic or predispositional component, African self-extension orientation, and a conscious expression of African spirit, African self-consciousness. African self-consciousness is particularly relevant for understanding racial identity because the level of African self-consciousness is assumed to be influenced by social-environmental forces. Four important values/behaviors are associated with the healthy expression of African self-consciousness. These include: (a) a recognition of oneself as African and an adoption of a worldview consistent with that membership, (b) a worldview that the survival of people of African descent is a high priority, (c) respect for and involvement in activities that perpetuate the survival of African life and cultural institutions, and (d) recognition of the need to resist any anti-African forces (e.g., oppression) that threaten the development and survival of African people. Other principles from African heritage are also components of the theory. These include communality, interdependence, corporate responsibility, and collective survival.

Optimal theory is a third theoretical approach to racial identity. Linda James Myers is the author of this theory. It is rooted in a conceptual system that dates back to the wisdom and traditions of ancient Africa

(Myers & Higgins, 1998). Individuals are assumed to differ in the extent to which they endorse two opposing worldviews with important value differences—optimal and suboptimal. An optimal worldview (more consistent with an African-centered philosophy) bases self-worth on internal factors, such as honesty, integrity, trustworthiness, and compassion. Great value is placed on the acquisition of peace, happiness, and positive interpersonal relationships.

A suboptimal worldview causes people to base their self-worth on external factors, such as material possessions and social standing. The more a person's inner beliefs are consistent with a suboptimal worldview, the greater the role that factors such as gender and race play in his or her self-perception because of the link between such factors and social standing.

The optimal and suboptimal worldviews also differ in how they perceive the spiritual to be connected to the material. An optimal worldview does not separate the spiritual from the material. However, a suboptimal worldview segments the material, sensory, and spiritual components of reality. Moreover, in a suboptimal system the material world is the basis for evaluating self-worth. Consequently, an optimal worldview is associated with a more favorable racial identity because the individual is less concerned with measuring up to the ideals of the dominant society that emphasize materialism and external characteristics.

Based on scientific evidence that human life began in Africa, Myers argues that all races can trace their ancestry to Africa. Therefore, this worldview is seen as applicable to all races. Moreover, even white males can be oppressed if they endorse a suboptimal worldview because they, too, are subject to the insecurity associated with the need to bolster self-worth through domination, control, and exploitation.

Optimal theory describes a sequence of seven phases that are somewhat similar to the identity development stages described above. The individual has no awareness of being in the first phase (Phase 0, infancy). During phases 1 (individuation), 2 (dissonance), and 3 (immersion), individuals move from a view of self that is passed down to them by their family through a period in which they explore aspects of the self that may be devalued by others and immerse themselves in the culture of the devalued group while rejecting the dominant group. During phases 4 (internalization), 5 (integration), and 6 (transformation), the individual gains acceptance of that part of the self that was previously devalued, begins to endorse a worldview that is based on positive values, connection to one's ancestors, and an enhanced spiritual awareness.

Robert Sellers and his colleagues proposed the most recent of the four models of racial identity—the Multidimensional Model of Racial Identity (MMRI). One unique feature of this model is the assertion that racial identity has both situational and stable features. For example, this team demonstrated that race is more salient in certain social settings (e.g., when the individual is the only African American in a situation in which racial themes are present) than in more race-neutral situations (e.g., when everyone present is the same race or racial themes are relatively absent from the situation). The four dimensions of the MMRI model are salience (relevance of race during a particular situation), centrality (the extent to which race is an integral component of how one defines oneself), regard (affective judgment and evaluation of one's racial group), and ideology. According to the model, four alternative ideological philosophies are common among African Americans. These philosophies are nationalist, oppressed minority, assimilationist, and humanist.

Measures of Racial Identity

A number of paper-and-pencil measures of adult racial identity have emerged. The diversity among them is another indicator of the various ways that racial identity is conceptualized. Kathy Burlew, Shana Bellow, and Marilyn Lovett recently identified four types or categories of racial identity measures. These include: (1) identity formation, especially process measures, (2) cultural connectedness (e.g., a perception that one belongs to the same group as other African Americans and an endorsement of African American traditions and values, (3) multicultural experiences (attitudes, experiences, and perceptions regarding other groups, primarily Whites), and (4) multidimensional measures that include more than one of the other three types in the same scale.

The most appropriate manner of measuring racial identity in children is still an unresolved issue. Dolls or other figures were used in some of the earliest studies. This methodology was used in perhaps the most well-known, albeit dated, work on racial identity among children—the doll studies by Kenneth and Marie Clark. In these studies, a child was presented with both a Black and a White doll. The experimenter asked the child to respond to a series of questions by selecting the doll they preferred. For example, the child was told: "Give me the doll that is a nice doll," or "Give me the doll that is a nice color." Later, the Clarks designed a coloring test. Children supposedly indicated their racial preference by how they responded to instructions to color a boy or girl as "you would like little boys (or girls) to be."

The Horowitzes used photographs of African American and White children in something they called the Show Me Test. Children were asked to select the child that they preferred as a companion for a variety of situations. Some of the situations were: "Show me all those you want to come to your party," or "Show me all those you like." These types of measures have received considerable criticism by those who question whether children's responses to these items are a true indication of their attitudes about their race. Consequently, the measures are seldom used today. However, findings by Darlene and Derek Hopson and Sharon-ann Gopaul-McNicol based on the doll test received national attention when the studies were presented at the Convention of the American Psychological Association as recently as 1987.

The Preschool Racial Attitude Measure was first developed by John E. Williams and Roberson in 1968 and revised in 1975. Here, African American children are presented with stories and asked to decide whether the picture of either the light (supposedly White) or the dark (supposedly African American) child best fits the story. Some of the stories portray the character in a positive manner and others portray the character in a negative manner. African American children are presumed to demonstrate more positive racial identity by either selecting the African American picture for positive stories or failing to select the African American child for negative stories.

Recently, several scholars have developed paper-and-pencil measures for children. Faye Belgrave has developed both the Afrocentric Values and the Racial Identity scales. Also, Maxine Clark developed the Children's Racial Attitude and Preference Test.

The Impact of Racial Identity

Many view a strong racial identity as an undesirable characteristic. This may be due in part to the fact that they may have been introduced to the term *racial identity* by social scientists trying to explain what some thought was a separatist or militant ideology. However, empirical research has revealed that racial identity has numerous positive consequences for African Americans, including less vulnerability to maladjustment, less psychological distress, greater levels of self-actualization, less alcohol consumption, more antidrug attitudes, and greater levels of marital satisfaction. Moreover, the evidence is mounting that racial identity has implications for counseling and therapy. For example, Thomas Parham and Janet Helms have demonstrated that individuals high in preencounter attitudes prefer a White therapist; those high in either encounter or immersion/emersion attitudes prefer an African American therapist; and the race of the therapist is not as important to those with high internalization attitudes.

The strong evidence that racial identity has positive benefits for development has prompted many parents to be concerned with the development of a positive racial identity in their children. There are signs of racial awareness in African American children as early as age three. Moreover, other evidence suggests that some children become aware of the positive and negative images ascribed to their race at a young age as well. Dar-

lene Powell-Hopson and Derek Hopson demonstrated the efficacy of interventions designed to counteract the negative stereotypes sometimes associated with African Americans. These results reinforce the importance of racial socialization in the home and the community.

Racial socialization refers to the activities of parents and the community to influence the attitudes of their children about race. Some common socialization activities include exposure to African American achievers, Black history, and Black cultural values (e.g., religious practices, customs, and strong extended family ties). A growing number of African American families are aware of or participate in a Kwanzaa celebration developed by Dr. Maulana Karenga to reinforce ties to strong African-based cultural values. Also, rites-of-passage programs that prepare adolescents for adulthood are available in many communities.

Many assume that racial identity would have little salience for Whites. Indeed, the emphasis of racial identity theories has been on explaining the African American experience. Nevertheless, in *Black and White Racial Identity*, Janet Helms argues that Whites undergo a process of racial identity as well. A major task in the process of White racial identity is to develop a healthy identity about what it means to be White that is not grounded in social notions of racial superiority.

Bibliography

Baldwin, J. A., & Bell, Y. R. (1985). The African self-consciousness scale: An Afrocentric personality questionnaire. *Western Journal of Black Studies, 9*, 61–68.

Banks, J. (1981). *Multiethnic education: Theory and practice.* Boston: Allyn and Bacon.

Brown, A. (1979). Conscious prototypes: A profile analysis of the developmental stages of consciousness. Unpublished doctoral dissertation, University of Pittsburgh.

Cross, W. (1971). The Negro-to-black conversion experience: Toward a psychology of liberation. *Black World, 20*, 13–26.

Denton, E. (1986). A methodological refinement and validational analysis of the developmental inventory of consciousness (DIB-C). Unpublished doctoral dissertation, University of Pittsburgh.

Helms. J. E. (Ed.). (1990). *Black and White racial identity: Theory, research, and practice.* New York: Greenwood.

Milliones, J. (1973). Construction of the developmental inventory of consciousness. Unpublished doctoral dissertation, University of Pittsburgh.

Myers, L. J. (1988). Understanding an Afrocentric worldview: Introduction to an optimal psychology. Dubuque, IA: Kendall.

Parham, T., & Helms, J. (1981). The influence of black students' racial identity attitudes on preferences for counselors' race. *Journal of Counseling Psychology, 28*, 143–146.

Sellers, R., Chavous, T., & Cooke, D. (1997). Racial ideology and racial centrality as predictors of African-American college student's academic performance. *Journal of Black Psychology, 24,* 8–27.

Thomas, C. S. (1971). *Boys no more.* Beverly Hills, CA: Glencoe Press.

Ann Kathleen Burlew

ETHNOCENTRISM suggests a belief that one's group is dominant and represents the standard against which all others are judged. It signifies the supremacy of one's own people and their ways of doing things. The phrase suggests an overestimated preference for one's own group and concomitant undervalued assessment or aversion of other groups (Cornell & Hartmann, 1998; LeVine & Campbell, 1972). The term describes a particular phenomenon, promotes a theory of attitude development, and introduces links with several important social psychological constructs. Ethnocentrism suggests that negative attitudes toward others originates from a need to preserve positive self-judgments by projecting one's own negative traits on to others. It is unclear whether or not fervent liking for one's own group is consistently associated with a firm disdain of other groups. Ethnocentrism represents a common aspect of ethnic identity but is seen as less virulent than is the view of inherent, biologically based inferiority and superiority that is generally attached to racism. It has been suggested that the difference between usage of ethnicity and race in the social sciences has to do with the observation that ethnicity denotes less the implication of some essential and unchangeable difference (Cornell & Hartmann, 1998).

The role of ethnocentrism in the life of ethnic groups incorporates both social and psychological functions and is inseparably related to the distinctive strategies of adaptive processes when in contact with other groups. Ethnocentrism is a phenomenon present among every ethnic group and has long attracted the attention of social scientists interested in the interaction and mutual influence among ethnic groups. As an aspect of the person's self concept, social identity is derived from membership in a group together with the value and emotional importance attached to it. The term *ethnocentrism* describes a particular phenomenon that is inherently linked to the formation of attitudes. It is closely associated with an individual's thinking concerning one's group of origin and reference group membership. The conceptualization of ethnocentrism suggests that negative attitudes toward other groups arise from a need to maintain and protect self-esteem by projecting one's own unflattering characteristics on to others. Accordingly, ethnocentrism spawns a particular ethnic identity or orientation to one's reference group and assumed quality of self-esteem. Basic theory

about normal development and available empirical data, however, suggest significant variations in one's orientation to reference group membership as a function of developmental status (that is, being a young child, adolescent, or adult).

Developmental Perspectives and Ethnocentrism

The expression and experience of ethnocentrism varies in significant ways as a function of developmental status. Young children learn about their social environment, and develop a sense of self and reference group orientation. Ethnocentrism has been linked to several constructs of importance for one's reference group orientation (for example, race consciousness, race awareness, racial and ethnic attitudes, and racial preference). Racial awareness has been documented in the literature for over half a century and has been observed for children as young as 3 years (Clark & Clark, 1939; Horowitz, 1939). Although the published studies did not consider the unique developmental status in the thinking of young children, much of the work, nevertheless, was ecologically sensitive in its demonstration of the link between children's racial identity and the character of the social context particularly for children of color.

The acquisition of attitudes has been described as an identificatory process discernible in children as early as 2 years of age since young children have a tendency to imitate their parents (for example, adoption of parental roles). In the later preschool years, the roles become incorporated into children's own value systems and perceptual ideals. Empirical findings demonstrate that normative cognitive development and broadening social experiences are involved in the more general development of ethnocentrism expressed as one's reference group orientation. More recent developmental research findings suggest that the patterns of reference group orientation and ethnic identity are expressions of ethnocentrism when considered for young preschool children, middle childhood youth (that is, 6- to 12-year-olds), and adolescents. They are different from the mature and differentiated attitudes, preferences, values and beliefs expressed by adults. The implications of developmental stage for the interpretation of constructs associated with ethnocentrism have been extensively reviewed (Spencer 1985; Spencer & Markstrom-Adams, 1990; Swanson, 1994). In sum, a developmentally sensitive interpretation of children's reference group orientation findings (for example, race awareness, racial attitudes, race consciousness, racial preference) suggest that young children generally may demonstrate White (European) oriented or Eurocentric valuing beliefs. A lack of Afrocentered values for African American youth, however, does not necessarily mean own-group rejection or self-hatred. A developmental interpretation suggests that social cognitive abilities and developmental status may impact reference group orientation and children's awareness of society's evaluative judgments concerning in-groups and out-groups. It does not mean necessarily that the out-group has internalized the negative perceptions of the group's status into one's own self-evaluative judgments. Instead, information gleaned from the social context may represent a young child's increasing knowledge of social stereotypes. For young "out-group" children, the level of normal cognitive egocentrism may protect the psyche from internalizing negative values concerning the self which are associated with societal ethnocentrism. In sum, young children's own level of cognitive egocentrism prevents the exposure to ethnocentrism and opposing value systems from resulting in cognitive dissonance and psychological discomfort (Spencer, 1985; Spencer & Markstrom-Adams, 1990; Swanson, 1994). However, there are important changes with the transition into middle childhood or the latency years. Data indicate a shift from extreme Eurocentric responses to neutral or Afrocentric response patterns for African American youngsters (Spencer, 1982; Spencer & Markstrom-Adams, 1990). Developmental theorizing suggests an important role of social cognition (Alejandro-Wright, 1985; Semaj, 1985; Spencer & Markstrom-Adams, 1990) and parenting. The broadening role of social context for more general ethnocentrism is evident in adolescence: racial socialization matters (Stevenson, 1995).

The most fundamental psychological developmental task of adolescence is achieving a sense of identity. The development of a clear sense of self stems from several sources given the broadening contexts of adolescent socialization and development. These sources include social identities based on gender, class, and ethnic group membership. Ethnic group membership and ethnic identity themes are important in societies that are heterogeneous in composition and have a history of significant intergroup tensions (for example, the experiences of Native Americans and African Americans in nineteenth- and twentieth-century America). Parental involvement in the racial socialization of its children varies significantly and has important implications for ethnocentrism (Swanson, 1994). Adolescents are vulnerable since all aspects of social identity processes undergo abrupt revisions during the unavoidable and rapid physical, physiological processes and psychological changes. What is known is that ethnic identity becomes increasingly ethnocentric during the adolescent and young adult years.

Empirical Approaches to Ethnocentrism

A major focus of ethnocentrism has been with adult subjects considered within limiting contexts (for example, college-age students). However, the outcomes and underlying theoretical assumptions have often been applied to the experiences of children. Accordingly, nor-

mative developmental processes were seldom considered and integrated into the conduct of research; young children's ethnic and racial attitudes were assessed and findings interpreted from an adult perspective.

Identity is frequently confused with ethnicity. Most early studies singularly assessed children's racial attitudes and preferences without a concomitant assessment of self concept (Spencer 1985, 1988; Spencer & Markstrom-Adams, 1990). In addition, efforts to understand normative developmental processes in contexts imbued with negative imagery were often based upon faulty assumptions about deficit family contexts in which minority youths were reared. Thus, early ethnocentric literature utilized a deficit and deficiency orientation for explaining minority youth behavioral patterns. There continues to be an inattention to cultural biases and social stereotyping about minority status that results in a lack of critical attention to societal context as a risk factor and source of chronic life course stress for visible minorities. Ecological context analyses and the more recent phenomenological variant of ecological systems theory (Spencer, 1995) provide alternative conceptual interpretations of ethnocentrism studies.

Contemporary "whiteness studies," have begun to theorize about the impact of ethnocentrism on the psychological well-being and identity processes of Whites. Traditionally, the literature has always assumed minority psychopathology and problem outcomes, on the one hand; Whites' or majority group members' psychological status and assumed health were considered the standard. The recent burgeoning of "White identity" theorizing and research efforts, however, suggest new speculations about White privilege, psychopathology, and vulnerability (Fine, Weiss, Powell, & Wong, 1997; Helms, 1990).

Conclusions

The internal factors that support ethnocentrism are linked to contextual factors, developmental status, economic and social variables, gender- and sex-role expectations and stereotypes. These internalized attributes are often regarded as social-perceptual coping strategies that may help group members maintain positive group identity in the process of functioning with other, particularly dominant, group members. These strategies, while perhaps protective for minority group members functioning in a larger and dominant culture, do not account for the role of ethnocentrism among majority group members that often exacerbate perceptions of privilege and power in intergroup interactions.

Bibliography

Alejandro-Wright, M. N. (1985). The child's conception of racial classification: A socio-cognitive developmental model. In M. B. Spencer, G. K. Brookins, & W. R. Allen (Eds.), *Beginnings: Social and affective development of Black children* (pp. 185–200). Mahwah, NJ: Erlbaum.

Clark, K. B., & Clark, M. P. (1939). The development of consciousness of self and the emergence of racial identity in Negro preschool children. *Journal of Social Psychology, 10,* 591–599.

Cornell, S., & Hartmann, D. (1998). *Ethnicity and race.* Thousand Oaks, CA: Pine Forge Press.

Fine, M., Weiss, L., Powell, L. C., & Wong, L. M. (Eds.). (1997). *Off white: Readings on race, power, and society.* New York: Routledge (1997).

Helms, J. (Ed.). (1990). *Black and White racial identity: Theory, research, and practice.* New York: Greenwood Press.

Horowitz, R. E. (1939). Racial aspects of self-identification in nursery school children. *Journal of Psychology, 7,* 91–99.

Levine, R., & Campbell, D. (1992). *Ethnocentrism: Theories of conflict, ethnic attitudes, and group behavior.* New York: Wiley.

Semaj, L. T. (1985). Afrikanity, cognition, and extended self-identity. In M. B. Spencer, J. K. Brookins, & W. R. Allen (Eds.), *Beginnings: The social and affective development of Black children* (pp. 173–184). Hillsdale, NJ: Erlbaum.

Spencer, M. B. (1982). Personal and group identity of Black children: An alternative synthesis. *Genetic Psychology Monographs, 106,* 59–84.

Spencer, M. B. (1985). Racial variation in achievement prediction: The school as a conduit for macrostructural cultural tension. In H. McAdoo & J. McAdoo (Eds.), *Black children.* Beverly Hills, CA: Russell Sage Foundation Press.

Spencer, M. B. (1988). Self-concept development. In D. T. Slaughter (Ed.), *Perspectives in Black child development: New directions in child development* (pp. 59–72). San Francisco, CA: Jossey-Bass Press.

Spencer, M. B. (1995). Old issues and new theorizing about African-American youth: A phenomenological variant of ecological systems theory. In R. L. Taylor (Ed.), *Black youth: Perspectives on their status in the United States* (pp. 37–70). Westport, CT: Praeger.

Spencer, M. B., & Markstrom-Adams, C. (1990). Identity processes among racial and ethnic minority children in America. *Child Development, 61*(2), 290–310.

Stevenson, H. C. (1995). Relationship of racial socialization to racial identity for adolescents. *Journal of Black Psychology, 21* (1), 49–70.

Swanson, D. P. (1994). *Self-efficacy and racial identity: Effects of psychosocial processes on academic and behavioral problems.* Unpublished dissertation, Emory University, Atlanta, GA.

Margaret Beale Spencer and Dena Phillips Swanson

ETHNOCULTURAL PSYCHOTHERAPY refers to psychotherapy that is intended to enhance therapeutic effectiveness by responding to and incorporating pertinent elements of the client's ethnic and cultural background. This responsiveness may include awareness of the cultural values and experiential background of clients and the development of intervention strategies that are effective, given their background. The assumptions of ethnocultural psychotherapy are that culture has a profound effect on attitudes, emotions, and behaviors and that failure to consider culture can be an impediment to effective treatment. Related concepts include multicultural therapy and culturally competent psychotherapy.

History

Because the United States has many distinct ethnic and cultural groups, ethnocultural psychotherapy was largely developed in the United States. For a number of decades, the practice of Western psychotherapies in the United States has been criticized for being culturally biased and ineffective with clients with non-Western backgrounds or cultures. While few rigorous studies have examined the outcome of psychotherapy with members of different ethnic groups, the available evidence suggests that ethnic minority clients tend to prematurely terminate treatment or fail to show the positive treatment outcomes often found among mainstream clients. Therapists who encounter clients from different cultures may not understand the meaning of the client's behaviors and symptoms and may have a more difficult time establishing rapport, credibility, and a therapeutic alliance. Western treatment practices may also be at variance with the cultural patterns of clients. Thus, psychotherapeutic treatments developed for clients in one culture may be less effective with clients from different cultures. For example, Western psychotherapies often focus on the person and attempt to promote the growth, independence, and individuation of the person. Clients from non-Western cultures, such as the Chinese, may find the treatment emphasis on independence and individuation as being inappropriate because they come from more collectivistic societies that encourage interdependence rather than independence. It should be noted that members of a particular ethnic group may not share all of the same cultural values. Individual differences are important to consider in ethnocultural psychotherapy because the intent of the therapy is to respond to the cultural values of the particular client.

Another ethnocultural consideration is the experiences of the different groups in a multicultural society. Most societies have many different cultural groups, such as the African Americans, Asian Americans, Latinos, Native Americans, as well as mainstream European Americans in the United States. All of the groups vary not only in cultural backgrounds and histories, but also in patterns of intergroup relations. Some groups have been subjected to racism, prejudice, and discrimination. Given this history, therapists and clients from different cultures may have stereotypes, prejudices, and misinformation about each other. In psychodynamic terms, transference on the part of clients and countertransference on the part of therapists may occur because of the history of intergroup relations. Ethnocultural therapy must therefore take into account possible transference and countertransference phenomena due to intergroup relations as well as cultural differences between therapists and clients.

Ethnocultural therapy does not assume that all clients need to have totally different kinds of treatment depending on their cultures. Some tactics in treatment may work well with clients regardless of culture, and more research needs to be devoted to the therapeutic conditions that promote favorable treatment outcomes regardless of culture and those that have culture-specific effects. However, the more frequent problem in therapy is the application of treatment without due consideration of the cultural or experiential backgrounds of clients.

In one sense, all therapies are ethnocultural in that they are developed in a particular cultural setting and are likely to be culturally compatible with clients from that setting. Problems occur when the client's cultural background differs markedly from the cultural orientation of the treatment.

Ethnocultural Therapy

There is no single method in ethnocultural therapy because the precise treatment method may depend on the particular culture of the client and the theoretical orientation of the therapist. Moreover, clients within an ethnic group may exhibit considerable individual differences. Many advocates of ethnocultural psychotherapy focus on the processes rather than the methods involved in the treatment. Three processes have been popularly discussed, namely, therapist attitudes and beliefs, knowledge, and skills (D. Sue, Ivey, & Pedersen, 1996).

Therapists should be aware of their own culture and cultural biases toward their clients that may occur. They should also be knowledgeable about the culture of their clients and the sociopolitical influences that impinge on the lives of their clients. For example, knowledge of how clients conceptualize their mental health problems, goals for treatment, and preferred means for solving problems is important to ascertain. The knowledge can be acquired in many ways: immersion in the culture of the client, learning through readings, exposure to and consultation with experts in the culture. Finally, therapists should realize that helping styles may be culturally limited and use those techniques that are culturally consistent with their clients. In this way rapport, communication, and therapeutic alliance between therapists and clients can be facilitated.

Because ethnocultural therapy is process oriented, therapists may use a variety of psychotherapeutic orientations and modify them to be more culturally responsive or use new, non-Western tactics with their clients. This does not imply that therapists need to simply employ cultural interventions that are used in the clients' cultures. For example, a client who comes from a culture that uses spiritual healing does not necessarily mean that the therapist should use such techniques. Therapists should decide on how to treat clients based on, among other considerations, a working knowledge of their own and their clients' cultures. The important point is the use of treatment strategies that are effective, which necessarily involves consideration of the cultural background of clients.

Little rigorous outcome research has been conducted on the effects of ethnocultural psychotherapy. As previously mentioned, there is no single method used in therapy. Available research suggests that interventions that consider cultural factors promote better treatment outcomes than those that do not (S. Sue, Zane, & Young, 1994).

Bibliography

Aponte, J. F., Rivers, R. Y., & Wohl, J. (Eds.). (1995). *Psychological interventions and cultural diversity*. Boston: Allyn & Bacon. Includes the contributions of many cross-cultural and ethnic experts who discuss issues concerning psychotherapeutic interventions and research for various ethnic minority groups.

Jones, J. M. (1997). *Prejudice and racism*. San Francisco: McGraw-Hill. Provides an analysis of race relations and the effects of racism.

Pope-Davis, D. B., & Coleman, H. L. K. (Eds.). (1997). *Multicultural counseling competencies*. Thousand Oaks, CA: Sage. Examines psychotherapy, training, and supervision issues when working with culturally diverse clients.

Ridley, C. R. (1995). *Overcoming unintentional racism in counseling and therapy*. Thousand Oaks, CA: Sage. Discusses how racism, prejudice, and discrimination have significant effects on the psychotherapeutic process.

Rogler, L. H., Malgady, R. G., & Rodriguez, O. (1989). *Hispanics and mental health: A framework for research*. Malabar, FL: Krieger. Examines the importance of cultural considerations, the client's experience of disturbance, help-seeking behaviors, treatment, and adjustment.

Sue, D. W., Ivey, A. E., & Pedersen, P. B. (1996). *A theory of multicultural counseling and therapy*. San Francisco: Brooks/Cole. Provides a theory of multicultural counseling and commentaries from a number of multicultural experts on the proposed theory.

Sue, S., & Zane, N. (1987). The role of culture and cultural techniques in psychotherapy: A critique and reformulation. *American Psychologist, 42*, 37–45. Examines how therapists can use cultural techniques to achieve position-treatment outcomes with culturally diverse clients.

Sue, S., Zane, N., & Young, K. (1994). Research on psychotherapy with culturally diverse populations. In A. E. Bergin & S. L. Garfield (Eds.), *Handbook of psychotherapy and behavior change* (4th ed., pp. 783–820). New York: Wiley. Presents an analysis of the research findings on psychotherapy with African Americans, Asian Americans, Native Americans, and Hispanic Americans.

Stanley Sue

ETHNOGRAPHY is concerned with the description of natural human communities. The collective product of this endeavor, the ethnographic record, stands today as sociocultural anthropology's foremost contribution to our knowledge of human behavior. For psychology, the primary value of ethnography consists of the information it provides about the worldwide range of variation in behavioral traits, the sociocultural contexts within which the behavior takes place, and the implications of that information for theory and research.

Historically, ethnography grew out of an already established genre, the accounts of exotic peoples written by travelers, missionaries, and colonial officials. Continuing in this vein, early-twentieth-century field-workers in anthropology often romanticized the cultural setting and—to use a current term—emphasized its "otherness." Many of the early efforts were somewhat unstructured, but as the discipline of anthropology became professionalized in the second quarter of the century, the ways of describing cultures came to be relatively standardized. During this classical phase, descriptions were frequently organized around a set of macro-categories classifiable as the techno-economic sphere (relation of humans to nature), the social-organizational (relation of humans to each other), and the magico-religious or ideational (relation of humans to the expressive world). (Most textbooks in anthropology continue to organize their substantive materials along these lines.) Beginning in the 1950s and 1960s, however, ethnographers began focusing on a "problem orientation," in which their investigations were confined primarily to specific elements of the sociocultural system, and they often accorded to those elements a much more detailed scrutiny and analysis than had the writers of the classical phase. In recent years, as the more specific studies have continued, ethnographers have also turned to the urban-industrial world and the investigation of special-interest groups such as tourists, occupational specialists such as psychiatrists, and social deviants such as narcotic addicts. In all approaches, the common thread has been the reliance on fieldwork, that is, on close and direct contact with the people under study.

For each of the delineated phases, there are definable strengths and weaknesses. In the early period, prior to the advent of worldwide culture contact and the inevitable losses of tradition it entailed, researchers could still capture and portray many of the customs most different from Western norms. But in gathering information almost solely by means of the informal technique of participant observation, these early ethnographers were susceptible to a "romantic bias," a tendency to exaggerate positive characteristics and downplay negative traits (Rohner, DeWalt, & Ness, 1973). A corrective to the bias, through the use of cross-validating methods, was seldom employed or even envisioned in the years when ethnography was a new field of inquiry. Subsequently, in the classical era, the trend toward standardization in ethnographic description was facilitated by more self-conscious efforts to provide documentation in the form of censuses and genealogies, property schedules, and maps and house plans. With standardization came greater ease of cross-cultural comparison, for it assumed the existence of transcultural categories (technological, social-structural, magico-religious, and so on) that were to some degree commensurable. But as to any conception that the great ethnographies were complete and fully accurate, both critical reflection and the results of follow-up research pointed to the problematic character of the fieldwork process, and prompted general acknowledgment of the partial and fallible nature of all ethnographic undertakings.

Some of the specialized investigations that followed the classical phase did produce exhaustive and systematic descriptive materials on narrow sociocultural topics, while others made use of new techniques and instruments to generate types of data previously unavailable cross-culturally. In more recent years a number of investigators, attempting to apprehend epistemological issues surrounding the ethnographic enterprise, have turned to a "hermeneutic" or interpretive approach. Pioneered by Clifford Geertz (1973), this approach, termed "thick description," emphasizes the necessity of contextualizing events in the process of building understanding. Relying on both local social discourse and his or her own intimate knowledge of the setting, the ethnographer eventually arrives at a description of the totality of "meanings" of people's lives, their behavior, and institutions.

A related development has focused on the writing of ethnography and on the recognition that the authorial presentation of "facts" is shaped by the generic conventions of ethnographic writing. This movement has led to a critique of the ethnographic monograph as a semiliterary rather than scientific product, and to various forms of experimental writing that attempt to incorporate more nearly authentic representations of the ethnographic scene. The contract between these latter approaches and the positivist program in behavioral science is marked. Nevertheless, all of the genres in the modern era can and do produce penetrating and informative monographs on a multitude of topics.

The Human Relations Area Files and Ethnographic Codes

A valuable sampling from the ethnographic record can be found in the Human Relations Area Files (HRAF), an archive consisting of reproductions of the texts on almost 400 societies (of more than 2,000 in the world), with the information on each distributed into more than 700 topical categories constructed to cover the range of sociocultural phenomena (e.g., blood feuding, child training, cremation, elopement, kinship, malnutrition, monotheism, political movements, recreation, spinsters, subsistence, and transvestism). Altogether, almost one million pages of ethnography have been processed for the HRAF through its standardized classification system. This indexed system, available on paper slips, microfilm, and/or electronic files in over 300 educational and research institutions, makes possible cross-cultural surveys of the information on a given topic, or rapid inspection of the information on specific societies, geographical areas, and social types (for example, hunter-gatherers, agriculturalists, and peasants). Additionally, the HRAF's archive facilitates the testing of hypotheses about the relationships among sociocultural variables, some with psychological implications (for example, whether unpredictability of resources is associated with frequency of warfare).

Although many of the most extreme customs described in the literature can no longer be studied in vivo because they are now culturally extinct, their established existence at particular times and places is indicative of the various "strong treatments" to which people are capable of subjecting themselves, treatments that for ethical reasons cannot be experimentally imposed on individuals. But such cultural loss reminds us that the rapid and unremitting cultural change in much of the world over the past century means that any cultural description would necessarily hold only for the specific spatiotemporal nexus it was reported to occupy, and that contemporary conditions may be far different. For example, a group like the !Kung Bushmen of the Kalahari Desert, who as a result of anthropological study in the 1960s became emblematic of the foraging way of life, had by the 1990s been drawn increasingly into the cash economy and become smallholders who made a living by herding, farming, craft production, and some hunting and gathering. The continuance of some foraging by the !Kung typifies the way in which sociocultural change tends to be partial and demonstrates how earlier descriptive materials, while requiring updating and checking, can remain applicable.

In addition to the systematized textual reproduction with which the HRAF is involved, another major effort has been the attempt to codify cultural characteristics of a large world sample of societies. The most ambitious undertaking is the *Ethnographic Atlas* of George P. Murdock (1967), which presents coded data on more than 1,000 societies. Among the variables included in the atlas are family organization (extended and nuclear), kin-group types (patrilineal and matrilineal), settlement patterns (bands, villages), norms of premarital sexual behavior, and games. Codes on other cultural attributes have also been developed (especially for a carefully chosen world sample of 186 societies), for example, for adolescence, child-training practices, the status of women, and theories of illness. (The periodical *Ethnology* published numerous codes between 1962 and 1984, and *Cross-Cultural Research* [before 1993, *Behavior Science Research*] continues to do so.) Research based on these codes has produced many outcomes with implications for psychological inquiry, for example, Alice Schlegel and Herbert Barry III's finding (1991) that adolescence is not a special life stage confined to preadults in the Western world, but rather that it is a constant in the human life cycle.

Methodology and Measurement

Methodology is among the concerns of a relatively small minority of sociocultural anthropologists, but these researchers have worked to raise the standards of ethnographic data-gathering. One periodical, the journal *Field Methods* (formerly *Cultural Anthropology Methods*), contains useful methodological contributions, including discussions of text-management programs for handling field notes, integration of textual and statistical methods, computer simulation of ethnographic analyses, and computer-readable orthographies and fonts for the alphabets of a variety of languages. For some types of structured data collection, a few ethnographers have begun to use pocket-sized microcomputers in directly recording information and even the training of informants for direct data entry.

Attention has been devoted to the development of techniques for systematic behavioral observations in naturalistic settings. Most are variants of those used in psychological research, but with modifications appropriate to fieldwork conditions. Adequate interobserver reliability has been achieved for some formats among all types of techniques. The subject matter has ranged from daily activities (child care, housekeeping, recreation, subsistence) to social behavior (aggression, nurturance) to direction of gazing (at males, females, adults, children). To cite a single finding, in *Intimate Fathers* (1991), Barry S. Hewlett showed that Aka Pygmy fathers spend 47% of their day holding or within arm's reach of their infants. The level of paternal care by the Aka far exceeds that reported for any other society.

A continuing comparative project, focused on estimates of time use, has thus far published information systematically gathered and coded on 13 societies (Johnson & Johnson, 1987). Each individual study presents data (on disk) both in their original format, as coded by the field investigator, and in a standardized format that readily allows cross-cultural comparisons. Accompanying each data set is a standard set of supporting information, including background cultural data (on economic organization, social structure, etc.).

A model of "culture as consensus," introduced by A. Kimball Romney, Susan C. Weller, and William H. Batchelder (1986), is based on the theoretical idea of culture as shared knowledge and meaning systems. The procedure, which enables the assessment of cultural statements with small numbers of individuals, measures patterns of agreement and is a form of reliability theory wherein the universe is one of subjects (rather than of items), and data are coded as given (rather than as correct or incorrect). Subjects provide responses to a series of questions, and from these data one is able not only to estimate how much each individual knows but also to arrive at a composite picture of what, collectively, the subjects "know." In this way one arrives at a set of precisely measured cultural statements and also an assessment of the degree of correspondence between any given individual's knowledge and the collective cultural knowledge.

These recent contributions promise to improve the quality of the ethnographic record in its continuing cumulation. Ethnography takes on added importance for psychology at the opening of the twenty-first century as the flow of peoples across geographic and political boundaries increases and new ethnic enclaves and cultural forms appear almost everywhere.

Bibliography

Durrenberger, E. P. (1996). Ethnography. In D. Levinson & M. Ember (Eds.), *Encyclopedia of cultural anthropology* (Vol. 2, pp. 416–422). New York: Henry Holt. Discusses approaches to ethnography and epistemological and methodological issues associated with the enterprise.

Geertz, C. (1973). *The interpretation of cultures.* New York: Basic Books. The *Locus classicus* of the interpretive social-science alternative to the positivist social sciences.

Goodenough, W. H. (1980). Ethnographic field techniques. In H. C. Triandis & J. W. Berry (Eds.), *Handbook of cross-cultural psychology* (Vol. 2, pp. 29–55). Boston: Allyn & Bacon. A how-to introduction to ethnographic work, based on the people (who is who), the physical arrangements (what is where), activities (what is happening), and talk (what is on people's minds).

Hays, T. E. (Ed.). (1992). *Ethnographic presents: Pioneering anthropologists in the New Guinea highlands.* Berkeley, CA: University of California Press. A collection of essays by ethnographers on their experiences in one of the last "pristine" cultural areas of the world.

Hewlett, B. (1991). *Intimate fathers.* Ann Arbor. MI: University of Michigan Press.

Jessor, R., Colby, A., & Shweder, R. A. (Eds.). (1996). *Ethnography and human development.* Chicago: University of Chicago Press. Essays attempting to integrate qualitative and quantitative approaches in order to illuminate the development of youths at risk.

Johnson, A., & Johnson, O. R. (1987). *Time allocation among the Machiguenga of Shimaa.* New Haven, CT: HRAF Press.

Keiser, R. L. (1969). *The vice lords: Warriors of the streets.* New York: Holt, Rinehart, & Winston. One of the first anthropological accounts of an urban subgroup in the United States.

Malinowski, B. (1967). *A diary in the strict sense of the term.* New York: Harcourt, Brace & World. The posthumously published diaries of one of the great ethnographers, Bronislaw Malinowski, provide a demystifying account of his inner experiences while carrying out fieldwork.

Marcus, G. E., & Fischer, M. J. (1986). *Anthropology as cultural critique.* Chicago: University of Chicago Press. Celebrates the demise of canonical ethnographies and the rise of self-consciously experimental texts, which the authors hope will lead to more complex representations of the "other."

Munroe, R. H., & Munroe, R. L. (1994). Field observations of behavior as a cross-cultural method. In P. K. Bock (Ed.), *Handbook of psychological anthropology* (pp. 255–277). Westport, CT: Greenwood. Introduction to the use of systematic naturalistic observations in the study of family life, child life, and socialization. Includes procedural notes and several examples of forms for recording observations.

Murdock, G. P. (1967). *Ethnographic atlas.* Pittsburgh, PA: University of Pittsburgh Press.

Richardson, M. (1990). *Cry lonesome and other accounts of the anthropologist's project.* Albany, NY: State University of New York Press. An attempt at "an ethnography of the anthropologist."

Rohner, R. P., DeWalt, B. R., & Ness, R. C. (1973). Ethnographer bias in cross-cultural research. *Behavior Science Notes, 8,* 275–317.

Romney, A. K., Weller, S., & Batchelder, W. (1986). Culture as consensus. *American Anthropologist, 88,* 313–338.

Sanjek, R. (Ed.). (1990). *Fieldnotes: The makings of anthropology.* A collection of useful discussions about what anthropologists write before they write ethnographies—field notes.

Schlegel, A., & Barry, H., III. (1991) *Adolescence: An anthropological inquiry.* New York: Free Press.

Weller, S. C., & Romney, A. K. (1988). *Systematic data collection.* Newbury Park, CA: Sage. Introduces consensus theory and other structured data-collection techniques.

Robert L. Munroe

ETHNOPEDAGOGY refers to the way in which ethnicity (culture, ethnology, human diversity) is taught. It includes the study and practice of teaching about cultural and ethnic groups—their origins, values, patterns of thinking, styles of communication, customs and behaviors, and related topics. Among its goals are the development of cross-cultural awareness, cultural sensitivity, and a methodology for the effective teaching of these interrelated issues. It draws heavily on concepts and research associated with cross-cultural psychology, cultural and social anthropology, and sociology.

Development of the Concept

Ethnopedagogy is a new term, not previously defined in the literature. However, it encompasses a variety of activities formerly and currently addressed in various ways by the disciplines mentioned above. Its origins can be found in a number of complementary terms, including the two from which it is formed: ethnology (the description and study of similarities and differences within and between cultural or ethnic groups) and pedagogy (the art or science of teaching). In general, it refers to the application of knowledge to the teaching of culture and ethnicity.

Areas of Interest and Application

In practice, ethnopedagogy and the techniques associated with it can be applied to a broad range of subject areas. These include the teaching of courses such as cross-cultural psychology, cultural anthropology, society and culture, cross-cultural human development, and others in which culture, ethnicity, and diversity are a major focus.

Other rapidly growing areas of interest include cross-cultural and diversity training for individuals planning to study or work in other cultures, students involved in international exchange programs, counseling and clinical programs preparing professionals to interact with clients of diverse cultural backgrounds, and employees working for multinational corporations or in culturally diverse workplaces.

Teaching Strategies and Methodologies

The way in which culture, ethnicity, and diversity are taught will vary depending, in part, on one's familiarity with and understanding of cultural similarities and differences, the availability of materials and teaching resources, the context in which the teaching and learning occurs, and the background and needs of those being taught. Therefore, what follows is not meant to be an all-inclusive inventory of teaching strategies and methodologies. Instead, it consists largely of techniques found by the author to have been particularly effective in his own teaching of culture, ethnicity, and diversity in a variety of circumstances over a period of nearly three decades.

Simulation Games. Experience has shown that active participation by learners in real-life situations results in the greater understanding of cultural and ethnic concepts. Simulation games like Barnga, in which participants experience the effects of cross-cultural interaction, culture shock, and lack of common communication patterns is particularly effective (available from Intercultural Press, Yarmouth, ME). Other simulations include BaFá BaFá, with its focus on misperceptions of the intercultural experience (available from Simulation Training Systems, Del Mar, CA), Ecotonos, which analyzes and compares decision-making in monocultural and multicultural groups (available from Intercultural Press, Yarmouth, ME).

Films and Videos. Carefully selected educational films and popular videos can be an effective method for providing interesting and often insightful adventures into all aspects of culture, including the portrayal of stereotypes (followed by discussions of how they are learned and how they can be unlearned), cultural differences in verbal and nonverbal patterns of communication, and issues related to discrimination, ethnocentrism, acculturation, and other relevant topics. A valuable resource providing advice on finding, selecting, and effectively using video and film materials in teaching about culture, diversity, and ethnicity is Ellen Summerfield's *Crossing Cultures Through Film* (1993). Some examples of films include *Becoming American, A Class Divided, City of Joy, Dim Sum, Iron and Silk, The Joy Luck Club, Valuing Diversity,* and *Zorba the Greek.*

Student Panels. In academic settings, cultural issues and topics presented by students, faculty visitors to the classroom professionals in business, medicine, and other areas generally provoke great interest and discussion. For example, a panel might consist of international students from campus comparing and contrasting their views on child rearing, family life, dating and marriage customs, and educational experiences in their home cultures and their host culture, as well as difficulties in adapting to a new culture. Another panel might be made up of local students who have completed a study abroad program and offer their insights into living and studying in another culture.

Exercises and Activities. Cultural awareness and the understanding of similarities and differences in ethnicity and diversity can be enhanced by the use of a wide range of creative exercises and activities (see the bibliography for several suggested resources). Other pedagogical approaches include having individuals spend some time tutoring minorities (Native Americans, Southeast Asians, recent European immigrants), discussing cultural topics with e-mail "pals" in other countries (see Gardiner's article in *Cross-Cultural Psychology Bulletin*), completing take-home exams that involve Internet assignments such as "cyber field trips" and "cultural scavenger hunts" (see chapter by Gardiner in *Teaching About Culture, Ethnicity, and Diversity,* by Singelis), preparation of research papers and presentations (adolescent rites of passages, cultural differences in birth practices, bicultural families, culture, and elder care), and a "Cross-Cultural Food Day," to which participants bring a food associated with a particular ethnic group (often their own), discuss its preparation and role in the culture, and share with others in the group.

One final suggestion for integrating a variety of ethnopedagocial models into the classroom is to team-teach courses with those individuals in related disciplines who also deal with cultural topics, such as teachers of foreign languages, English as a Second Language, and intercultural communication.

Concluding Comments

Although use of the term *enthnopedagogy* is new to the literature, attempts to teach about culture, ethnicity, and diversity are not. As the world becomes increasingly multicultural, issues related to these topics will become even more important, as will the need for integrated approaches to learning and understanding about the role culture plays in the everyday lives of individuals throughout the world.

[*See also* Multicultural Education.]

Bibliography

Gardiner, H. W. (1995). Plug in, dial up, and log on. *Cross-Cultural Psychology Bulletin, 29*(3), 10–14. Discusses the design and implementation of a computer component matching American students with students in 23 countries, allowing them to exchange ideas via electronic mail; considers advantages and disadvantages of the approach.

Gardiner, H. W., Mutter, J. D., & Kosmitzki, C. (1998). *Lives across cultures: Cross-cultural human development.* Needham Heights, MA: Allyn & Bacon. Brings a cross-cultural dimension to the study of human development across the life-span and includes an extensive collection of successful ethnopedagogical aids.

Gordon, E. W. (1995). Culture and the sciences of pedagogy. *Teachers College Record, 97*(1), 32–46. Discusses the intersection between the pedagogical sciences and culture and advocates pedagogical training for teachers that includes awareness of the cultural contexts in which knowledge exists.

Kohls, L. R., & Knight, J. M. (1994). *Developing intercultural awareness: A cross-cultural training handbook* (2nd ed.). Yarmouth, ME: Intercultural Press. Includes case studies, simulation games, and exercises on values, communication, and related topics.

Kruger, A. C., & Tomasello, M. (1996). Cultural learning and learning culture. In D. R. Olson & N. Torrance (Eds.), *The handbook of education and human development:* *New models of learning, teaching and schooling* (pp. 369–387). Oxford, England: Blackwell. Discusses the importance of culture learning and suggests methods by which it can be accomplished.

Singelis, T. (1998). *Teaching about culture, ethnicity, and diversity: Exercises and planned activities.* Thousand Oaks, CA: Sage. Provides a variety of useful pedagogical strategies for teaching about culture, ethnicity, and diversity.

Summerfield, E. (1993). *Crossing cultures through film.* Yarmouth, ME: Intercultural Press. Discusses films and videos having a cross-cultural perspective and provides suggestions for their effective use.

Harry W. Gardiner

ETHNOPSYCHOLOGY. *See* Cross-Cultural Psychology; *and* Cultural Psychology.

ETHNOPSYCHOPHARMACOLOGY. *See* Psychopharmacology.

ETHOLOGY, the objective study of animal behavior in naturalistic perspective, has had productive interactions with comparative psychology since the middle of the twentieth century. Both disciplines had their roots in nineteenth-century Darwinian biology. As ethology developed over the past 70 years, it was nurtured by a set of European zoologists, whose primary research focused on insects, fish, and birds. In particular, during the 1940s and 1950s, the Austrian zoologist Konrad Lorenz and the Dutch zoologist Nikolaas Tinbergen provided a theoretical framework for examining and analyzing behavior. They turned what had been a loosely organized field involving the observation of behavior in its natural context into a coherent discipline with a clearly defined set of questions and a cluster of core concepts. They also provided a set of exemplars: experimental studies of behavior in field and laboratory situations that demonstrated the potential of the approach.

In 1950, a clear statement of Lorenz's position appeared for the first time in English. This paper, resulting from a symposium sponsored by the Society for Experimental Biology in the United States, served to introduce Lorenz's ideas to an American audience. An expanded version of the ethological program was presented in Tinbergen's *The Study of Instinct,* published in 1951. In short order, an influential critique of the ethological approach was published by the American comparative psychologist Daniel Lehrman (1953). Before considering the critique and its aftermath, however, we must outline the essential elements of the theoretical approach presented by Lorenz and Tinbergen.

The Four Questions

Ethologists have emphasized the breadth of their approach by discussing four types of questions that have to be answered before a particular bit of behavior is truly understood. We might illustrate this by referring to Lorenz's studies of imprinting, the process through which a young animal (in his studies, a bird) learns to recognize its mother and to demonstrate appropriate attachment.

The first question has to do with immediate causation—that is, how do the state of the organism and the features of its environment result in the emergence of a particular pattern of behavior? For example, in the case of imprinting, ethologists have devoted many experimental hours to defining the "optimal" sensory characteristics of the imprinting stimulus. The second question concerns development. Other studies have been devoted to determining the precise age in the young bird's life at which imprinting is likely to occur and to recognizing the point at which a limiting age is reached—that is, an age at which imprinting on a parental figure is unlikely to occur even in the presence of an optimal stimulus. The third question involves function—in our illustrative case, what are the functional consequences of the young bird imprinting on a maternal figure? This might be answered by demonstrating the protection provided to the young bird as the result of maintaining close proximity to its parent. The bird at this early age might also be learning the characteristics of its species in a manner that will ensure selection of an appropriate mating partner during adult life. Fourth, there is the question of behavioral evolution: What was the evolutionary route that resulted in the appearance of imprinting in this particular species? Is it found in all other species in this genus or family, suggesting the presence of the characteristic in a common ancestor? These evolutionary questions are frequently the most difficult to answer, because the process occurred during remote periods of time and cannot be studied directly.

Core Concepts and a Research Strategy

As for all animal behaviorists, the starting point for classical ethologists involves the accurate description of behavior. Here, Lorenz drew on a distinction that had been introduced by the American zoologist C. O. Whitman and divided behavior into two categories. The term *appetitive behavior* was employed to describe the components of behavior that varied within an animal from day to day and between animals of the same species in identical situations, for example, when animals searching for food took different routes in the same environ-

ment. However, stereotypic aspects of behavior, particularly the terminal elements in a sequence of motivated behavior, were termed *consummatory behaviors*. These constant components of behavior, demonstrated by all members of a species when conditions were appropriate, were designated as *fixed action patterns* (FAPs).

Darwin's studies of facial expression in his classic work *The Expression of the Emotions in Man and Animals* (London, 1872) are a prime example of this critical step in behavioral analysis. Following Darwin's lead, Lorenz argued that behavioral FAPs as indicators of evolutionary heritage were as reliable as the structure of the hand or forepaw. Given Lorenz's interest in using behavior for phyletic reconstruction, mapping the FAPs of a species (or of a domain of behavior such as courtship in a particular species) became the first step in the study of behavior.

Next in the ethological analytic strategy was the experimental determination of the critical stimuli responsible for eliciting or releasing FAPs. For example, using captive graylag geese and artificial eggs of different sizes and shapes, Lorenz determined the optimal stimulus characteristics for an egg incubated by a goose in its nest. Lorenz found that he could literally build a better egg than that provided by nature, as judged by the vigor of retrieval behavior. The use of models for defining the critical dimensions of eliciting, or releasing, stimuli became a staple feature of ethological research.

Ethologists noted early on that behavior showed spontaneous variability even when it was emitted in a constant stimulus situation. The spontaneity of behavior was explained by Lorenz and Tinbergen in what was to become the most controversial aspect of the classical ethological framework. In particular, they suggested that spontaneous appetitive behavior patterns and subsequent consummatory FAPs were energized by the metabolic accumulation of action specific energy in motivational centers in the nervous system. Foraging for food and eating, seeking sexual partners and mating, patrolling one's territory and fighting were thought to be stimulated by the accumulation of action specific energy. The termination of these behavior patterns resulted, in turn, from the motor performance of the consummatory patterns in question. The motivational system presented by Lorenz and Tinbergen had much in common with drive systems proposed by Sigmund Freud and William McDougall, including a hydraulic metaphor that involved "pressure" building up in the system when consummatory behaviors remained unexpressed. For the ethologists, their motivational system explained many common phenomena. Vacuum activities—the appearance of consummatory sequences in the absence of any environmental stimulus, as when a kitten pounces on an imaginary prey—were "explained" by the accumulation of such high levels of action specific energy that performance of the relevant FAPs was inevitable. Similarly, the waxing of feeding behavior as a function of time since eating was attributed to the accumulation of energy, whereas a lack of interest in food immediately following a meal was linked with the dissipation of energy through performance of feeding-related FAPs. There was, however, a price to be paid for this facile explanation.

Comparative Psychology and the Classical Ethologists

For most of the twentieth century, comparative psychology constituted a relatively small component of animal psychology in the United States. Comparative psychology was concerned with naturalistic perspectives, species-characteristic behavior patterns, and species variation in behavior (Dewsbury, 1984). More broadly, however, animals were typically employed in American laboratories as convenient substitutes for human participants in providing data on the critical general laws of learning, and the white rat (or the Skinnerian pigeon) became the subject of choice (Beach, 1950). Given this background, it is not surprising that, when connections were made with the ethologists, it was a relatively small subset of American animal psychologists, the truly comparative psychologists, who led the way.

For some (e.g., Beach, 1960), the essential task was awakening psychologists to the crucial importance of studying animals in naturalistic perspective. Although terms were modified to suit the taste of American psychologists (for example, Frank A. Beach used "species-characteristic behavior" as a substitute for "instinctive behavior"), the emphasis was on the fascinating experimental phenomena revealed by ethological research in Europe. However, for others, the theoretical framework could not be bypassed.

In 1953 Daniel Lehrman published his classic paper "A Critique of Konrad Lorenz's Theory of Instinctive Behavior." The heart of Lehrman's critique was an attack on the too-casual use of "instinct" in the Lorenzian formulation and the failure (in Lehrman's view) of Lorenz to deal adequately with the complexities of developmental analysis. It was, in a sense, an old argument. After all, psychologist Zing-Yang Kuo (1922) had debated the instinct psychologists of his day along similar lines. But, focusing on Lorenz's own writings, Lehrman's arguments revealed how the use of terms such as *instinct* served to terminate prematurely the search for developmental understanding and pointed to the absence of a physiology that could be offered in support of Lorenz's energetic schemes.

There was also a political element to Lehrman's critique. Lorenz's use of instinct could be interpreted to mean "fixed" or "inevitable" when applied to humans. And the natural accumulation of an action specific ag-

gressive energy in animals that must have overt expression in the natural order of life might appear to have sinister implications in a world dealing with the aftermath of World War II. The existence in Lorenz's prewar bibliography of articles that provided biological justification for maintenance of racial purity (Kalikow, 1979) did not pass Lehrman's notice. Other comparative psychologists offered additional critiques of the instinct concept while recognizing the basic significance of the ethological approach (Beach, 1955; Hebb, 1953), and the English ethologist Robert Hinde (1960) published a powerful critique of energetic drive theories.

From these interactions between ethologists and comparative psychologists during the 1950s and 1960s a new synthesis emerged. It was, perhaps, best reflected in Robert Hinde's text of 1966, *Animal Behaviour: A Synthesis of Ethology and Comparative Psychology*. The newly emerging field of animal behavior drew on the developmental and learning perspectives, on technology, and on the methodological sophistication of American psychology while incorporating the breadth of species, naturalistic reference points, and evolutionary concerns of the ethologists. The appearance in the 1970s of books devoted to the analysis of species-characteristic learning processes, studied in both European ethological laboratories and American psychological laboratories, was visible testimony to the symbiotic benefits of these interactions (Hinde & Stevenson-Hinde, 1973; Seligman & Hager, 1972).

Sociobiology: Challenging the "Synthesis"

In the 1970s, however, a new approach to animal behavior emerged that was to change the research of both classical ethologists and comparative psychologists. The most enduring and powerful component of this new approach drew on the theoretical writings of William D. Hamilton (1964a,b). Hamilton provided a genetic analysis of social behavior based on the proportion of shared genes between social actors. In a short period of scientific time, these writings completely changed the study of animal societies from sociological descriptions of behavior in terms of age and sex roles to a new focus on the behavior of individuals competing and/or cooperating to maximize "inclusive fitness," as measured by success in promoting the appearance of one's genes in subsequent generations. This emphasis on individual genetic competition became the key concept incorporated in Edward O. Wilson's 1975 synthesis of animal behavior as "sociobiology." Wilson drew fire from both the ethologists and the comparative psychologists, in part because of his neglect of behavioral ontogenies and mechanisms and his focus on genetic outcomes. However, the situation was compounded by a diagram in the first chapter of Wilson's book. According to this schematic analysis, both comparative psychology and ethology were vigorous players in 1950. But by 1975 comparative psychology was portrayed as "absent," and ethology was much reduced in size. Indeed, according to Wilson's prediction, by the year 2000 even ethology would be reduced to a "sliver," joined with physiological psychology in linking the "important" disciplines of sociobiology and integrative neurophysiology.

Despite Wilson's dire predictions, there is an ever-changing field of animal behavior that receives information from and is enriched by the parent disciplines of zoology and psychology. Just as evolutionary biology provided the background for Hamilton's genetic analysis, so the cognitive revolution in psychology, emerging at about the same time as Hamilton's analysis, has reawakened interest in the animal mind. This conceptual transfer is routed from the parent discipline (psychology) through the subdiscipline (comparative psychology) to a common contemporary field of animal behavior.

[*Many of the people mentioned in this article are the subjects of independent biographical entries.*]

Bibliography

Beach, F. A. (1950). The snark was a boojum. *American Psychologist, 5,* 115–124.

Beach, F. A. (1955). The descent of instinct. *Psychological Review, 62,* 401–410.

Beach, F. A. (1960). Experimental investigations of species-specific behavior. *American Psychologist, 15,* 1–18.

Dewsbury, D. A. (1984). *Comparative psychology in the twentieth century.* Stroudsburg, PA: Hutchison Ross.

Hamilton, W. D. (1964a). The genetical evolution of social behaviour: I. *Journal of Theoretical Biology, 7,* 1–16.

Hamilton, W. D. (1964b). The genetical evolution of social behaviour. II. *Journal of Theoretical Biology, 7,* 17–52.

Hebb, D. O. (1953). Heredity and environment in mammalian behaviour. *British Journal of Animal Behaviour, 1,* 43–47.

Hinde, R. A. (1960). Energy models of motivation. *Symposia of the Society for Experimental Biology, 14,* 199–213.

Hinde, R. A. (1966). *Animal behaviour: A synthesis of ethology and comparative psychology.* New York: McGraw-Hill.

Hinde, R. A., & Stevenson-Hinde, J. (1973) *Constraints on learning: Limitations and predispositions.* New York: Academic Press.

Kalikow, T. J. (1979). Konrad Lorenz's "brown past": A reply to Alec Nisbett. *Journal of the History of Behavioral Science, 15,* 173–180.

Kuo, Z.-Y. (1922). How are instincts acquired? *Psychological Review, 29,* 344–365.

Lehrman, D. A. (1953). A critique of Konrad Lorenz's theory of instinctive behavior. *Quarterly Review of Biology, 28,* 337–363.

Lorenz, K. (1950). The comparative method in studying innate behavior patterns. *Symposia of the Society for Experimental Biology, 4,* 221–268.

Tinbergen, N. (1951). *The study of instinct.* London: Oxford University Press.

Wilson, E. O. (1975). *Sociobiology: The new synthesis.* Cambridge, MA: Harvard University Press.

Stephen E. Glickman and Mark R. Rosenzweig

ETIC-EMIC THEORY. *See* Cross-Cultural Psychology, *article on* Theories and Methods of Study.

EUROPEAN FEDERATION OF PROFESSIONAL PSYCHOLOGISTS' ASSOCIATIONS.

The EFPPA is a relatively young organization, founded in 1981. Its origins began in the late 1970s when there was movement among psychology associations in European nations including the European Community (now the European Union), to cooperate and to share information in a formal manner. At the time, representatives of twelve national psychology associations convened to draft a constitution and statutes. There were good reasons for European psychology associations to work together, both generally, and specifically in relation to developments in the European Community (e.g., the EC Directive 49/84) linked to harmonization of training and mobility of psychologists. The EFPPA was founded in Germany as a federation of national psychology associations, and the first general assembly was held in Heidelberg in 1981. Since 1982, general assemblies have been held every 2 years, and since 1991, in conjunction with biennial European Congresses of Psychology, which are arranged under the auspices of EFPPA. EFPPA is a federation of national psychology organizations that seeks to develop European policy and to promote psychology at the European level.

According to EFPPA statutes, only one association of psychologists may represent a country, and EFPPA tries to ensure that this is the most representative association in the country. EFPPA now has 30 member associations, including all the European Union member states, the other countries of western Europe, and a growing number of members from central and eastern Europe. Thus, EFPPA could be said to represent more than 100,000 psychologists. In general, member associations are concerned with promoting and improving psychology as a profession and as a discipline, particularly, though not exclusively, in clinical settings. EFPPA has a particular focus on professional issues, such as training and research associated with psychological practice, and other professional issues, such as ethics, codes of conduct, and professional regulation.

Psychologists in member associations include clinical practitioners as well as academic and research psychologists. One of EFPPA's goals is the integration of practice with research and the promotion of an integrated discipline of psychology in Europe.

The aims of EFPPA are broad and include: (a) promoting communication and cooperation among member associations in Europe; (b) promoting the application of psychology to improve the well-being of those whom psychologists serve; (c) promoting the discipline of psychology and its application, with particular reference to the professional training and professional status of psychologists; (d) supporting member associations in promoting the interests of psychology within their own countries; (e) facilitating contacts with international bodies of psychology; and (f) encouraging the development of professional psychology in all its different areas and subject matters. EFPPA was originally formed to facilitate collaboration, particularly in relation to developments in the education and training of psychologists and the increasing trends in different countries toward legal definitions and regulations for psychologists. Since its formation, EFPPA has engaged in a number of different activities in relation to the discipline and profession of psychology: (a) collection and dissemination of information; (b) development of policy and standards; (c) communication; (d) lobbying and political activity; and (e) congresses and conferences.

EFPPA has a unique potential for collecting and disseminating information on a wide range of areas in psychology, particularly through its task forces. EFPPA produces booklets and reports on professional issues in Europe, publishes a quarterly newsmagazine, is associated with the quarterly journal, the *European Psychologist*, publishes news and information on its Web site's home page, and arranges the biennial European Congress of Psychology. The congress aims to provide a forum for integration and interchange, and for psychologists from different areas to develop collaboration and shared understanding. It is also an occasion when many European organizations focusing on special topics may arrange satellite congresses or participate in symposia or keynote addresses in the congress itself.

An original objective of EFPPA has been to develop a more common framework for standards of training and professional practice of psychologists. "Optimal Standards for Training" was adopted by member associations in 1990; current booklets on regulation, education, and training provide a framework to build on. EFPPA now participates in a European Union–funded project to develop a European Framework for Psychologists Training, which will eventually lead to a European Diploma for Psychologists. Further objectives are to encourage and support individual member associa-

tions in their efforts to gain regulation of the profession in their own countries, and to investigate the possibility of a European law to regulate the profession as a whole. These objectives have been the focus of two task forces. In general, EFPPA attempts to monitor developments and lobbies for directives and legislation, both within and outside the European Community.

The EFPPA has several means of communication with its member associations and with others. These include regular circulars mailed to member associations from the secretariat, a home page on the World Wide Web, a quarterly magazine (*News from EFPPA*), and the biennial general assembly and European Congress of Psychology. In 1996, the first issue of *European Psychologist*, published in collaboration with the EFPPA, made its appearance. An annual meeting of the Presidents Council, which consists of presidents of its member associations provides an opportunity for wide-ranging and more informal exchange. EFPPA also has links to many other bodies of psychologists, in particular, the International Association of Applied Psychology and the International Union of Psychological Science.

During 1995–1999, EFPPA had task forces in the following areas: (a) clinical psychology, (b) European legal matters, (c) evaluation of psychology curricula, (d) forensic psychology, (e) health psychology, (f) organizational psychology, (g) psychology in education, (h) psychotherapy, (i) traffic psychology, (j) refugees and enforced migration, (k) disaster and crisis psychology, and (l) tests and testing. EFPPA has a standing committee on ethics. Task forces provide a valuable means of collecting information in particular areas from member associations, and their reports are useful resources both for members and others (EFPPA usually publishes reports in booklet form and as abbreviated reports in the *European Psychologist*).

The EFPPA is expanding in membership and activity. Several psychology associations from nonmember countries are preparing applications for membership in EFPPA. The implications of this growth reflect the expansion of Europe: more languages, more national interests and traditions, more possibilities for richness in diversity, and more emphasis on academic study. Many countries are actively seeking to learn new applications of the discipline, with new opportunities for psychologists to develop and use their skills.

Bibliography

EFPPA. (1990). *Optimal standards for training of professional psychology.* (Available from the EFPPA Secretariat, Galerij Agora, Bureau 421, Grusmarkt 105/18, B-1000 Brusich, Sweden. e-mail: efppa@skynet.bc. Web site: www.efppa.org.

EFPPA. (1995). *Information booklet on European Federation of Professional Psychologists' Associations.* (Available from the EFPPA Secretariat, Galerij Agora, Bureau 421, Grusmarkt 105/18, B-1000 Brusich, Sweden. e-mail: efppa@skynet.bc. Web site: www.efppa.org

EFPPA. (1995). *Statutes of EFPPA.* (Available from the EFPPA Secretariat, Galerij Agora, Bureau 421, Grusmarkt 105/18, B-1000 Brusich, Sweden. e-mail: efppa@skynet.bc. Web site: www.efppa.org

EFPPA. (1997). *Education and training in psychology in European countries.* (Available from the EFPPA Secretariat, Galerij Agora, Bureau 421, Grusmarkt 105/18, B-1000 Brusich, Sweden. e-mail: efppa@skynet.bc. Web site: www.efppa.org

EFPPA. (1997). *Inventory of regulations in psychology in Europe.* (Available from the EFPPA Secretariat, Galerij Agora, Bureau 421, Grusmarkt 105/18, B-1000 Brusich, Sweden. e-mail: efppa@skynet.bc. Web site: www.efppa.org

Lunt, I. (1996). The history and organization of the European Federation of Professional Psychologists' Associations. *European Psychologist, 1,* 60–64.

Ingrid Lunt

EUROPEAN SCIENCE FOUNDATION. The ESF is a multidisciplinary association more than 60 national research funding agencies and academies from more than 20 countries committed to the promotion of all branches of basic science. It was established in 1974 at the instigation of a group of senior scientists and the heads of Europe's principal research funding agencies who, for a number of years, had been discussing the need to form a network of European laboratories and scientific institutions. Their solution was to create a flexible, nongovernmental organization whose main task would be to facilitate cooperation in, and harmonization of, its members' scientific activities. Included among this founding group were Hubert Curien, then Director of Physics at France's Centre National de la Recherche Scientifique (CNRS) and later French Minister for Science, Friedrich Schneider, Secretary General of the German Max Planck Gesellschaft (MPG), and Sir Brian Flowers of the United Kingdom's Science Research Council (SRC).

The ESF came into being in Strasbourg, France, on 18 November 1974 when representatives of forty-two academies and research councils from fifteen European countries agreed to its establishment. The principal aims of ESF, set out in its first statute, are to advance cooperation in basic research, promote mobility of research workers, assist the free flow of information and ideas, and coordinate, where appropriate, the basic research activities supported by its member organizations. It was further envisaged that the Foundation would facilitate cooperation in the use of existing research facilities and in assessing and executing projects of major importance.

Sir Brian Flowers was elected as the first ESF president, Professor Olivier Reverdin of Switzerland and Professor Povl Riis of Denmark were elected vice presidents, and Dr. Friedrich Schneider of Germany was elected secretary general.

ESF's scientific activities were to be directed by a number of standing committees covering broad scientific disciplines. In ESF's first year of operation it was agreed that the already existing European Medical Research Councils and the European Science Research Councils (ESRC) should become ESF standing committees along with the newly created standing committee for the social sciences. These three committees were joined by a fourth in 1977 with the establishment of an ESF standing committee for the humanities. In 1994, two new committees for the life and environmental sciences and for the physical and engineering sciences were created from the old natural sciences committee (ESRC). In addition, ESF refocused its mission to include providing advice on research and science policy issues of strategic importance.

Since its establishment, ESF has launched and coordinated a large range of scientific activities in all the main disciplinary fields, from physics to the humanities. These activities have included workshops, conferences, networks, and programs, as well as summer schools, and in certain specific fields such as neuroscience, training grants to enable young European researchers to work in other countries and be introduced to new techniques. For the social sciences and the humanities, ESF has provided the only place where it has been possible to develop a European science policy.

The promotion of psychology within ESF's portfolio of scientific activities has been taken up principally by the standing committee for the social sciences, but it has also figured in scientific programs, networks, and conferences in the fields of the humanities and medical sciences. One of ESF's very first actions was to adopt as an additional activity the European Training Programme in Brain and Behaviour Research. ESF's interest in the development of this interdisciplinary field, which brought together scientists from disciplines as diverse as experimental psychology, neuroscience, and pharmacology, was to prove long lasting, culminating in the European Neuroscience Programme, which ran until 1996.

Another research area identified early on by the ESF as appropriate for development at a European level was second-language acquisition by adult immigrants. This program, which ran from 1981 to 1987, examined the ways in which adults acquire a language other than their mother tongue in everyday interactions with native speakers, and made a significant contribution to the European development of this research field.

In a similar fashion, a European network on longitudinal studies on individual development, led by Professor David Magnusson of the University of Stockholm, proved important in promoting more effective research. Running for 6 years from 1985, the network resulted in a series of influential textbooks on a variety of issues including transition mechanisms in child development, successful aging, and data quality and methodological problems in longitudinal research.

Other ESF initiatives involving psychologists have included three scientific networks on neural mechanisms of learning and memory, on code switching and language contact, and on written language and literacy. The first of these ran from 1988 to 1991 and fostered collaboration among psychologists, neuroscientists, and neurologists working in Europe on the experimental analysis of the neural mechanisms of memory processes viewed within the context of neural plasticity. The second network, from 1989 to 1992, focused on describing and explaining code-switching phenomena through comparison of a large number of varied contact situations. A third network on written language and literacy ran from 1991 to 1994 and tackled the complex cultural and psychological processes involved in writing and written language acquisition.

More recently, ESF has been examining human-computer interactions and the impact of environmental factors and degradation on cognitive functions. A five-year research program on learning in humans and machines has drawn on psychology, computer science, educational research, and sociology in an attempt to create a new discipline aimed at increasing understanding of learning processes and designing more effective tools for distance learning. As part of a wide-ranging initiative to draw up a future European research agenda in the field of environment and health, leading scientists have been looking at how cognitive functions can act both as mediators for health consequences and as potential end points of environmental influence in order to identify future research priorities and key questions.

In addition, a series of ESF research conferences on the development of sensory, motor, and cognitive capabilities in early infancy, with funding from the European Commission, has enabled young researchers to participate in high-level discussions at the frontiers of research development.

The European Science Foundation is based in Strasbourg, France; extensive information about the ESF is available through its World Wide Web site (http://www.esf.org).

Andrew Smith

EVALUATION RESEARCH. *See* Research Methods.

EVOLUTIONARY PSYCHOLOGY represents a synthesis of modern evolutionary theory with current formulations of psychological phenomena. The synthesis is based on a series of premises:

1. Manifest behavior depends on underlying psychological mechanisms, defined as information-processing devices instantiated in brain wet-ware.
2. Evolution by selection is the only known causal process capable of creating such complex organic mechanisms.
3. Evolved psychological mechanisms are functionally specialized to solve adaptive problems that recurred for human ancestors over the vast expanse of evolutionary history.
4. Human psychology consists of a large number of these functionally specialized and integrated evolved mechanisms, each sensitive to particular forms of contextual input. Each of these premises is described below.

Manifest Behavior Requires Underlying Psychological Mechanisms

No behavior can be produced without psychological mechanisms, and all theories within psychology imply the existence of such mechanisms. If a man responds to a public insult with violence but a woman does not; if a child cries to get its way but an adult does not; if a human gossips and a chimpanzee does not, it is because these different beings possess somewhat different psychological mechanisms. All psychological theories, even the most ardently environmental ones, imply the existence of psychological mechanisms. Even Skinner's theory of operant conditioning, for example, implies the existence of domain-general mechanisms that cause organisms to alter their behavioral output in accordance with the history of reinforcement that they have experienced. The next question is: What causal process is responsible for the origins of these psychological mechanisms?

Evolution by Selection Is the Central Causal Creator

Only three theories retain currency for the origins of complex organic mechanisms: Evolution by selection, creationism, and seeding theory. Creationism, the idea that a supreme deity fashioned current organic mechanisms in all their glorious diversity, is regarded as a matter of religious belief. It leads to no specific scientific predictions and cannot explain in a principled manner the specific organic forms that science has observed. Seeding theory—the idea that extraterrestrial organisms came down and planted the seeds of life on earth—begs the questions of the origins of the intelligent extraterrestrial beings and of the subsequent evolutionary process that produced humans from the initial seeds. Evolution by selection, in contrast, is a powerful and well-articulated theory that has successfully organized and explained thousands of diverse facts in a principled way. In one bold stroke, this theory united all living forms into one grand tree of descent, accounted for the origins of new species and the modification in organic structures over time, and explained the apparent purposive quality of the component parts of those structures, that is, that they seem "designed" to serve particular functions linked with survival and reproduction. Other causal processes in evolution, such as mutation, genetic drift, recombination, hitchhiking, and antagonistic pleiotropy are unlikely to produce complex functional organic mechanisms in the absence of selection.

Evolved Psychological Mechanisms Are Functionally Specialized

A central premise of evolutionary psychology is that the main nonarbitrary way to identify, describe, and understand psychological mechanisms is to articulate their functions—the specific adaptive problems they were designed to solve. Anatomists identify the liver, heart, and lungs as separate, although connected and integrated, mechanisms because they perform different functions (e.g., filter toxins, pump blood, and uptake oxygen). Understanding the nature of these mechanisms requires understanding their functions, that is, what they were designed to do or the manner in which they contributed to reproduction. Analogously, evolutionary psychologists suggest that the human mind consists of functionally specialized psychological mechanisms, each designed to solve a specific information-processing problem. For example, cheater-detection mechanisms function to solve the problem of free-riders in social exchange (Cosmides, 1989); mate-preference mechanisms function to solve the problem of selecting reproductively valuable mates (Buss, 1994); and kin-identification mechanisms function in part to solve the adaptive problem of allocating acts of altruism (Burnstein, Crandell, & Kitayama, 1994).

The adaptive problems that psychological mechanisms are designed to solve have several key features. First, they must have recurred over the long course of human evolutionary history. Since evolution is a slow process, there is no expectation that humans have evolved mechanisms to solve modern adaptive problems, such as avoiding electrical outlets that could cause death or fast food that could clog arteries. Second, adaptive problems are those whose solution contributed to successful reproduction, either directly or indirectly. Since differential reproduction is the engine of evolution by selection, only solutions that lead to an increment in reproduction, relative to alternative variants that happen to exist in the population at that time, could have evolved. Third, the manner in which an adaptive problem is solved defines the function of the mechanism.

The functional specialization of evolved psychological mechanisms means that they are highly sensitive to narrow slices of context. Even a complex mechanism like the eye is not designed to "see everything." In fact, the eye is functionally specialized to see only electromagnetic waves within a narrow range (the visual spectrum), and not waves outside that range, such as radio waves or X rays. Moreover, within the visual spectrum, the eye is further designed to register motion, edges, particular colors, depth, and so on. Contrary to most people's intuitions, the exquisite flexibility and context-sensitivity of human behavior comes from having a large number of these functionally specialized mechanisms, not from having a few general "plastic" psychological mechanisms.

Methods for Generating and Testing Evolutionary Psychological Hypotheses

Evolutionary psychologists use two methods for generating and testing hypotheses about evolved psychological mechanisms. The first is to start with an adaptive problem and generate hypotheses about an evolved psychological solution. As an example of this "top-down" method, consider the adaptive problem of paternity uncertainty. Because fertilization occurs internally within women, they are 100% certain that they are the mothers of their children. Putative fathers can never be sure, because another man might have inseminated his mate and hence fathered "his" child. Evolutionary psychologists have hypothesized that male sexual jealousy is a psychological mechanism that has evolved as one possible solution to the adaptive problem of paternity uncertainty (Daly, Wilson, & Weghorst, 1982). The prediction is that men's jealousy should focus heavily on cues to sexual infidelity. Women are also predicted to get jealous, but no woman has ever faced the adaptive problem of maternity uncertainty. From an ancestral woman's perspective, however, if her mate committed an infidelity she stood to lose her mate's investment, commitment, and resources—all of which could get channeled to rival women. Therefore, the prediction is that women's jealousy will focus more on cues to the long-term diversion of her partner's commitments, such as him becoming emotionally involved with another woman. It is important to recognize that, although jealousy has been studied extensively, no previous social science theories prior to the evolutionary one had ever predicted that the sexes would differ in the weighting given to the triggers of jealousy.

A variety of empirical studies were subsequently conducted to test the evolutionary psychological hypothesis. Consider the following scenario: *Imagine that your romantic partner became interested in someone else. What would upset or distress you more? (A) Your partner having sexual intercourse with that other person, or (B) your partner becoming emotionally involved with that other person.* In contrast to the dozens of previous studies that had yielded no sex differences in jealousy, this dilemma produced large sex differences. While both events are upsetting to both sexes, the majority of men (roughly 60%) indicated that they would be more distressed by sexual infidelity. In contrast, only 15% of the women indicated that they would be more distressed by sexual infidelity, with the overwhelming majority declaring greater distress about emotional infidelity (Buss, Larsen, Westen, & Semmelroth, 1992).

These gender differences have been replicated using physiological measures of distress as well. When imagining a partner's sexual infidelity, men show greater distress, as measured by increased electrodermal activity, electromyographic activity, and heart rate (Buss, Larsen, Westen, & Semmelroth, 1992). These sex differences have been replicated across cultures as diverse as Germany, the Netherlands, Korea, and Japan (Buunk, Angleitner, Oubaid, & Buss, 1996), and they have been pitted against alternative hypothesis designed post hoc to account for the gender difference (Buss, 2000). In sum, gender differences in the triggers of jealousy were discovered using the first method of evolutionary hypothesis generation—starting with an adaptive problem and making predictions about a possible evolved solution. Men who were sexually jealous presumably acted to prevent a partner's sexual infidelity, thus solving the adaptive problem of paternity uncertainty. Modern humans are the descendants of men who acted to prevent such infidelities, not the descendants of men who were indifferent to the sexual contact their partners had with other men.

The second method consists of starting with observed psychological phenomena and generating hypotheses about what adaptive problem they might have evolved to solve. As an example, evolutionary psychologists started with the observation that women and men seemed to be very selective in their choice of marriage partners (Symons, 1979). Mainstream nonevolutionary psychologists, of course, had also observed this phenomenon, but none had developed hypotheses about what functions it might have evolved to solve. Evolutionary psychologists predicted that women's mate preferences might have evolved to solve the problem of securing resourceful mates to invest in their children, whereas men's mate preferences might have evolved to solve the problem of selecting fertile mates. These predictions were then tested in a study involving 37 different cultures, ranging from the Zulu tribe in South Africa to coastal dwelling Australians (Buss, 1989). The results confirmed predictions generated from these hypotheses: In all 37 cultures, women expressed a greater preferences for mates who were high in status, ambition, industriousness, and financial prospects, whereas men expressed a greater preference for mates who were young and physically attractive, two known cues to a woman's fertility. In sum, the studies of mate preferences illustrate the second method of generating and testing evolutionary psychological hypothesis—starting with a known phenomenon and generating hypotheses about design features, based on hypothesized solutions to adaptive problems.

These two methods have been used to discover a host of interesting psychological phenomena, including: patterns of fears and phobia, particular mechanisms of color vision, universal adaptations to terrestrial living, beliefs and desires about the minds of other people, patterns of step-child abuse, causes of marital dissolution, shifts in mate preferences depending on temporal context, gender differences in sexual fantasy, patterns of mate guarding and mate retention, gender differences in risk-taking, superior spatial location memory in women, mechanisms of cheater detection in social exchange, patterns of sexual harassment, patterns of altruism and cooperation, and cross-cultural variations in patterns of food sharing (see Barkow et al., 1992, and Buss, 1999, for extensive summaries).

The Field of Psychology from an Evolutionary Perspective

Scientific success in uncovering the mysteries of life have been based on three critical foundations—mechanism, natural selection, and historicity (Williams, 1992). Since the cognitive revolution, psychologists have moved away from behaviorism's unworkable antimentalism, making it respectable to study information-processing mechanisms inside the head. Evolutionary psychology adds the importance of natural selection and historicity in the creation of those information-processing mechanisms. The previous neglect of natural selection has led psychologists to ignore the adaptive functions of mechanisms and therefore has hindered the quest to unravel the mystery of why these mechanisms exist at all, and more specifically why they exist in the particular forms that they do.

A critical task for this new psychological science will be the identification of the key adaptive problems that humans confronted repeatedly over evolutionary history. By identifying some of the problems most obviously and plausibly linked with survival and reproduction, we have barely scratched the surface. Most adaptive problems remain unexplored, most psychological solutions undiscovered. Evolutionary psychology provides the conceptual tools for emerging from the fragmented state of current psychological science. It provides the keys to unlocking the mysteries of where we came from, how we arrived at out current state, and the mechanisms of mind that define who we are.

Charles Darwin ended his classic book, *On the Origin of Species* (1859), with this prophesy: "In the distant future I see open fields for far more important researches. Psychology will be based on a new foundation, that of the necessary acquirement of each mental power and capacity by gradation." Evolutionary psychology, emerging more than 130 years after *Origin*, represents the fulfillment of Darwin's prophesy (Buss, 1999).

Societies and Research Institutions Focusing on Evolutionary Psychology

Several universities host centers and areas within departments devoted to the study of evolutionary psychology, including: the University of California at Santa Barbara (Center for Evolutionary Psychology), the University of Texas (the Individual Differences and Evolutionary Psychology Area within the Psychology Department), and the University of New Mexico at Albuquerque. The international society devoted to evolutionary psychology is the Human Behavior and Evolution Society (HBES), founded in 1989, and which hosts annual meetings that draw international scholars from psychology, anthropology, economics, sociology, biology, and psychiatry. The journal for HBES is the *Journal of Evolution and Human Behavior*.

Bibliography

Barkow, J., Cosmides, L., & Tooby, J. (Eds.). (1992). *The adapted mind: Evolutionary psychology and the generation of culture*. New York: Oxford University Press.

Burnstein, E., Crandall, C., & Kitayama, S. (1994). Some neo-Darwinian decision rules for altruism: Weighing cues for inclusive fitness as a function of the biological importance of the decision. *Journal of Personality and Social Psychology, 67*, 773–789.

Buss, D. M. (1989). Sex differences in human mate preferences: Evolutionary hypotheses tested in 37 cultures. *Behavioral and Brain Sciences, 12*, 1–49.

Buss, D. M. (1994). *The evolution of desire: Strategies of human mating*. New York: Basic Books.

Buss, D. M. (1999). *Evolutionary psychology: The new science of the mind*. Boston: Allyn & Bacon.

Buss, D. M. (2000). *The dangerous passion: Why jealousy is as necessary as love and sex*. New York: Free Press.

Buss, D. M., Larsen, R., Westen, D., & Semmelroth, J. (1992). Sex differences in jealousy: Evolution, physiology, and psychology. *Psychological Science, 3*, 251–255.

Buunk, B. P., Angleitner, A., Oubaid, V., & Buss, D. M. (1996). Sex differences in jealousy in evolutionary and cultural perspective: Tests from the Netherlands, Ger-

many, and the United States. *Psychological Science, 7*, 359–363.

Cosmides, L. (1989). The logic of social exchange: Has natural selection shaped how humans reason? *Cognition, 31*, 187–276.

Daly, M., Wilson, M., & Weghorst, S. J. (1982). Male sexual jealousy. *Ethology and Sociobiology, 3*, 11–27.

Darwin, C. (1859). *On the origin of species by means of natural selection*. London: Murray.

Symons, D. (1979). *The evolution of human sexuality*. New York: Oxford University Press.

Williams, G. C. (1992). *Natural selection*. New York: Oxford University Press.

David M. Buss

EXCEPTIONAL STUDENTS. *Exceptional* is an umbrella term covering a wide range of conditions and problems that refer to deviations or differences from normative developmental and social expectancies. These differences may be physical, sensory, cognitive, emotional, or behavioral, and may range from mild to severe. What is considered exceptional is defined, in part, by the social and political climate of the times, thus, definitions have varied historically. Classification systems developed by the American Psychiatric Association and the U.S. Office of Education are currently used to order the array of exceptional conditions (Keogh & MacMillan, 1996).

The public education system has been the major agency providing services to exceptional children and youth, although those with severe disabilities may be served in residential or hospital placements. Historically, services were limited to individuals with severe disabilities in physical/sensory functions. Compulsory school attendance laws forced recognition of the needs of a broader range of students with disabilities and led to increased numbers of special education programs, usually delivered in segregated classes or schools. Following the 1960s civil rights movement, legal challenges were mounted by parents and advocates, and major new legislation at the federal level emerged: the 1975 Education for All Handicapped Children Act, the 1991 Individuals with Disabilities Education Act (IDEA), and the 1994 Improving America's Schools Act (IASA). All have had major impact on services for children and youth with disabilities, and on the facilities that provide services for them.

IDEA requires that all children and youth with disabilities have access to a fair and appropriate public education in the least restrictive environment as determined on an individual basis. IDEA also contains procedural safeguards that protect the rights of children and families, including parent and student input into the Individual Education Plan (IEP). The guarantees in

IDEA have been maintained, broadened, and strengthened in subsequent legislation. Part H of IDEA (P. L. 94–142, the Education of the Handicapped Act Amendments of 1986, and the later amendments under P. L. 102–119) provides services for at-risk children or those with disabilities from birth through 2 years of age.

Child counts documenting the use of special services are taken by states on 1 December of each year, with data reported to, and integrated by, the U.S. Office of Special Education Programs (OSEP). In the 1994–1995 school year, a total of 5,545,198 children and youth, ages 3 to 21, received services under IDEA. Approximately 10% were 5 years old or younger. About 12% of elementary and secondary school students received special education services. Federal support for education and related services for children and youth with disabilities has increased steadily since 1975. In 1995, $2,322,915,000 was appropriated; allocation per child for 1995 was $418 (U.S. Dept. of Education, 1996).

Services by Categories

Current legislation identifies 12 categories of disabilities for children 6 to 21 years old. The percentage of students receiving services in each category is based on 1994–1995 figures provided by OSEP: specific learning disabilities (51.1%); speech or language impairments (20.8%); mental retardation (11.6%); serious emotional disturbance (8.7%); multiple disabilities (1.8%), hearing impairments (1.3%); orthopedic impairments (1.2%); other health impairments (2.2%); visual impairments (0.5%); autism (0.5%); deaf-blind (2.6%); and traumatic brain injury (0.1%) (U.S. Dept. of Education, 1996). Services are delivered in programs ranging from the regular class to home or hospital settings. In 1994–1995, 95% of exceptional children received services in regular school buildings; however, placement patterns differed according to exceptional conditions, and regular class placements were more common for elementary than for secondary students. Resource room programs are widely used for students with problems in speech and language and learning disabilities. Separate classrooms are more often used for children with mental retardation, autism, and multiple disabilities.

Preschool children who receive services under Part H of IDEA are not categorized by disability, but rather may be considered for special services as needed in settings ranging from regular classes to home or hospital. Intervention needs are framed within the Individual Family Service Plan (IFSP) rather than the IEP. In 1994, 47% of services for infants and toddlers were delivered in homes, 31% in early intervention classrooms, and 17% in outpatient facilities. The most frequent services included speech and language, physical and occupational therapy, and family counseling and special instruction.

Professional and Advocacy Groups

Major professional organizations and advocacy groups related to exceptionality include the American Association on Mental Retardation, the Association for Retarded Citizens, the Council for Exceptional Children, Division 33 of the American Psychological Association, the Learning Disabilities Association of America, and those targeting specific low-incidence conditions, such as the Autism Society of America, the Association for Children with Down Syndrome, and the Foundation for the Junior Blind. Most major organizations publish journals, newsletters, and monographs. The National Association for Gifted Students provides advocacy and information for exceptionally able and talented individuals. Gifted or talented students are not covered by IDEA, but a number of states and school districts provide special services for those students. Gifted or talented students with physical, sensory, or specific learning disabilities are termed *twice exceptional* and may be covered by IDEA.

Assessment and Identification

Identification and referral for services for children with exceptional needs may come from health professionals or parents; however, except for young children or those with severe physical or sensory disabilities, identification usually occurs after school entrance. Determining the need for special education services is typically a process of referral by regular classroom teachers and subsequent assessment by school psychologists and language specialists. Systemwide screening in the primary grades is relatively rare. Eligibility for services in categories of mental retardation, learning disabilities, and speech or language impairment involves estimation of ability level, a potential problem as some states have banned or restricted use of IQ tests. A discrepancy between expected achievement (ability) and actual performance remains a pivotal but controversial consideration for diagnosis of learning and language disorders (Gresham, MacMillan, & Bocian, 1996).

Alternative approaches to standardized testing such as curriculum-based assessment, pre-referral interventions, and dynamic assessment are increasingly used. Assessment of emotional or behavioral disorders typically involves case histories, parent or teacher symptom checklists, and measures of social adaptation. Potential problems arise from low concordance between school criteria for serious emotional disturbance (SED) and symptoms of clinical disorders derived from emotional or behavioral checklists. Children with attention deficit hyperactivity disorder (ADHD), for example, often do not qualify for special education services, but may be provided regular classroom adaptations under Section 504 of the 1973 Rehabilitation Act. This law prohibits discrimination against persons with disabilities, and defines disability more broadly than IDEA. Test bias and disproportionate representation of children from minority ethnic, cultural, or language backgrounds in special education programs remain controversial.

Intervention and Treatment

Comprehensive systems of care involving joint case management and treatment with medical and social services agencies outside the school are emerging (Short & Talley, 1997). A number of children and youth with emotional and/or behavioral disorders receive pharmacological treatment under medical supervision, but their use remains controversial. Many children with attention deficit disorder (ADD) and ADHD respond well to methylphenidate hydrochloride (Ritalin), improving on attentional and behavioral measures. Dosage and monitoring of effects are critical, as doses that improve attention and classroom behavior may impair classroom learning (Forness, Sweeney, & Toy, 1996). Psychotropic drugs are best used in therapeutic programs that combine psychosocial interventions with children and families. A number of treatment approaches from different disciplinary and professional perspectives have strong advocates, but lack solid evidence of efficacy and are considered controversial (Silver, 1987). These include diet regimens, patterning exercises, and perceptual-motor training.

Individual educational planning remains a hallmark of special education and related services. Objectives for each pupil's cognitive, academic, social, and emotional development are specified in the IEP and the progress toward goals is monitored periodically. The 1997 amendments to IDEA require formal reevaluation every three years. Instructional responses to special learning needs include: collaborative teaching, in which regular and special education teachers jointly plan and teach lessons; pre-referral interventions in which instruction is modified and tested before referral for formal assessment; and peer-mediated instruction using classmates with no disabilities as tutors. Basic skill instruction in reading has focused on early phonological awareness and training in executive functions such as self-monitoring of attention. These approaches have stronger empirical support than previously favored aptitude-treatment strategies that focused on isolated deficits in perceptual or linguistic skills (Forness, Kavale, Blum, & Lloyd, 1997). Computer-assisted instruction and other technologies designed to minimize disabilities have met with some success, but effective classroom software continues to lag behind technological advances. There is an increasing, but controversial, trend toward mainstreaming and full inclusion, meaning full-time placement of all children with disabilities in regular classrooms, and the elimination of special schools and classrooms or part-time placements in resource classrooms (Fuchs & Fuchs, 1994). Educators are supportive in principle, but uncertain about the implementation and effectiveness of inclusive models of service delivery.

Research

Research on children with disabilities has received major support from the National Institute of Child Health and Human Development (NICHD) and from OSEP. Research topics include basic research on neuropsychological, neurophysiological, and linguistic processes, and educationally oriented research addressing phonological awareness, curriculum-based assessment, peer-mediated instruction, social skills development, and cognitive strategy training including mnemonics, working-memory, and self-monitoring or evaluative strategies (Berninger, 1997). Behavioral approaches and single-subject research designs remain popular. Prevention strategies, such as classroom-wide interventions followed by targeted instructional strategies for nonresponders, have become the focus of research on pre-referral intervention. Meta-analyses of major interventions in special education and related services have been used to address efficacy questions (Forness et al., 1997). Contemporary scientific approaches and qualitative, ethnographic methods are increasingly used to address contextual effects; however, quantitative research continues to be the prevailing methodology.

Few large-scale efficacy studies of children with disabilities are in process at the end of the 1990s, and follow-up studies of special education graduates provide a somewhat dismal outcome picture (Blackorby & Wagner, 1996). The findings may reflect real inadequacies in special education programs, or they may be related to changing demographics of children who receive services. Sampling issues and practices present challenges and possible confounds. As more children are taught in inclusive settings, programs for students with mental retardation or serious emotional disturbance contain fewer, but more seriously impaired children. The use of the term *developmental delay* for children up to age 9 is useful in practice, but means a lack of sample specificity. There has also been an increase in the number of children with newly recognized morbidities, such as prenatal substance abuse, cancer survival, and fetal alcohol effects. Failure to recognize or detect comorbid conditions is a problem. Suspension or expulsion of children with histories of school violence complicate intervention efforts and threaten reliable tests of program efficacy. Recent amendments to IDEA provide for immediate placement of violent or aggressive children with disabilities in interim alternative placements for up to 45 days, but what constitutes appropriate alternative placements is often uncertain. Questions of who should be identified as exceptional and where and how they should be educated remain.

[*See also* Teachers.]

Bibliography

Berninger, V. W. (1997). Special issue on intervention. *Learning Disability Quarterly, 20,* 162–167.

Blackorby, J., & Wagner, M. (1996). Longitudinal post-school outcomes of youth with learning disabilities: Findings from the National Longitudinal Transition Study. *Exceptional Children, 62,* 399–423.

Forness, S. R., Kavale, K. A., Blum, I., & Lloyd, J. W. (1997). Mega-analysis of meta-analyses: What works in special education and related services. *Teaching Exceptional Children, 29,* 4–9.

Forness, S. R., Sweeney, D. P., & Toy, K. (1996). Psychopharmacologic medication: What teachers need to know. *Beyond Behavior, 7,* 4–11.

Fuchs, D., & Fuchs, L. S. (1994). Inclusive schools movement and the radicalization of special education reform. *Exceptional Children, 60,* 294–309.

Gresham, F. M., MacMillan, D. L., & Bocian, K. M. (1996). Learning disabilities, low achievement, and mild mental retardation: More alike than different? *Journal of Learning Disabilities, 29,* 570–581.

Keogh, B. K., & MacMillan, D. L. (1996). Exceptionality. In D. C. Berliner & R. C. Calfee (Eds.), *Handbook of educational psychology* (pp. 311–330). New York: Simon & Schuster.

Short, R. J., & Talley, R. C. (1997). Rethinking psychology and the schools: Implications for national policy. *American Psychologist, 52,* 234–240.

Silver, L. B. (1987). The "magic cure": A review of the current controversial approaches for treating learning disabilities. *Journal of Learning Disabilities, 20,* 498–504.

U.S. Department of Education. (1996). *Eighteenth annual report to Congress on the implementation of the Individuals with Disabilities Education Act.* Washington, DC: Author.

Barbara K. Keogh and Steven R. Forness

EXCHANGE RELATIONSHIP. *See* Interdependence, *article on* Interdependence Theory.

EXCITEMENT refers to the bodily condition of being roused, or figuratively, the experience of "shaking one's feathers." In nonmetaphoric terms, being roused or *a*roused manifests itself in heightened overt and covert activity. This manifestation is thought to characterize all vital emotions, and its experience is considered part of all strong feelings. Excitement, then, is deemed an essential component of acute pleasure and displeasure, sadness and happiness, love and hate, despair and elation, gaiety and dejection, rage and exultation, exhilaration and grief, frustration and triumph, merriment and fear, anger and joy, along with all other intensely experienced behaviors. Although sexual activities are usually not included in listings of emotions, they certainly have their place among excitement-linked behaviors.

As an accompaniment of emotions, the indicated state of bodily arousal or excitedness is independent of pleasantness or unpleasantness. Acute anger, for instance, is an unpleasant experience associated with great agitation. Similar levels of agitation are also found, however, in the pleasant experiences of triumph and exultation or in sexual engagements. The apparent hedonic neutrality of excitation is not necessarily invoked by the excitement concept. Increasingly, this concept is used to focus on the pleasurable experience of states of great excitedness. Excitement has come to denote the essentials of high-intensity, quality experiences worthy of pursuit. Excitement is to be sought and appreciated, which implies that the concept is partial to pleasure.

Excitement seeking has been directly linked, in fact, to the pleasure principle. Mood-management theories are based on the hedonistic premise that humans behave so as to attain good moods of the greatest possible intensity for the longest possible time. This premise entails the assumption that the experience of pleasurable excitement is the more intense, the greater the associated bodily excitation.

Alternative theories place less emphasis on pleasure maximization. Zuckerman (1979) suggested that humans, like other primates, are constitutionally prepared to cope with aversive conditions on a regular basis, but that modern life deprives them of opportunities. He focused on a need for stimulation, essentially an inclination to seek out challenges, as an individual difference variable in order to explain why some are more driven than others to jump from airplanes, climb cliffs, do drugs, or watch horror movies. In this frame, stimulation is attained for its excitatory quality and at times might be deemed noxious throughout. As a matter of course, however, challenging circumstances will terminate and their overcoming or elusion can be expected to foster some degree of pleasure.

The transition from challenge to pleasurable reactions has led to proposals that make the intensity of pleasure partly, if not entirely, dependent on the intensity of preceding displeasure. Apter (1992) invoked such a dependency. He distinguished zones of safety, danger, and trauma and proposed that (a) nonrisky behavior in the safety zone is unexciting; (b) risky behavior in the danger zone is exciting and enjoyable to the extent that trauma is avoided; and (c) risky behavior in the trauma zone, although exciting, causes harm and hence, if not fatal, displeasure. In this model, risky behaviors in the danger zone are more enjoyable the closer they are to the border of the trauma zone. Prior risk maximization amounts to ultimate pleasure maximization, provided that traumatic conditions are successfully eluded. Playing it safe, on the other hand, is the formula for boredom because of the lack of excitedness.

Apter (1992) has aggregated an impressive array of illustrations that seem to agree with his model. Car racing, roller coaster riding, rock climbing, hang gliding, bungee jumping, fugu eating, juvenile wilding, and erotic scarfing are all considered demonstrations of the practice of pushing danger to the trauma edge in order to attain the most intense experiences of excitement. Apter included coercive actions in this paradigm, suggesting that rape is often committed to intensify sexual excitement, that violent crime is, on occasion, perpetrated for the thrill of it, and that slaughter in combat can foster joyful excitement of the utmost intensity.

Implicit in the consideration of such extreme behaviors is that unproblematic achievements may satisfy needs and prove gratifying in a quiet way that is readily experienced as boredom. Reminiscent of Freud's observation that initially unrequited love has depth, whereas easy seduction does not, excitement and emotional intensity appear to depend on obstacles, competition, rivalry, even spite, as well as the possibility of failure. Experiences of triumph and exultation presuppose effort, striving, and struggling in the face of defeat and humiliation. A degree of aversion, anticipated or manifest, is thus considered prerequisite to gratifying excitement.

A more universal paradigm of emotional interdependencies that are exploitable for pleasure was proposed by Zillmann (1996). This paradigm applies to all emotions associated with increased excitation and specifies the bodily processes that mediate the intensification of particular emotions by the emotions that precede them. A theory of excitation transfer focuses on sympathetic activity in the autonomic nervous system. Such activity is common to all acute emotions and to all forms of sexual excitedness. Owing much to the functional interpretation that Walter B. Cannon provided in his well-known analysis of fight-and-flight reactions, transfer theory projects that sympathetic activation serves immediate energy mobilization by supplying brain and muscles with glucose. The mobilization is mediated by catecholamine release, mostly adrenaline and noradrenaline, into the systemic blood circulation. This being a sluggish humoral process, the instigated activity dissipates only slowly. It is its lingering presence that is considered to influence subsequent emotions. Specifically, the theory posits that humans are equipped with (a) a comparatively fast-acting cognitive apparatus that allows rapid adjustments to environmental changes, and (b) an excitatory system that is archaic in acting slowly and in rather undifferentiated fashion. The cognition-excitation time discrepancy in this adjustment creates what could be considered inappropriate reactions and emotional confusions.

Consider a woman who steps on a snake in the grass. The event is likely to instigate a strong excitatory reaction, along with evasive action. Consider further that it was a prank by her son who planted a rubber snake. Cognition reveals instantly that her fear is groundless. Excitation, however, is just manifesting itself, and she is likely to tremble for minutes after the shock. During this period of residual excitation from fear, she is bound to overexperience any emotion dictated by cognition. For instance, she might feel abused, get angry, and overreact aggressively. On the other hand, she might feel foolish at being angry and burst into hysterical laughter, exhibiting mirth to a degree that is entirely incommensurate with the safe sighting of a rubber snake.

Excitation transfer thus explains the extreme demonstrations of excitement seeking described by Apter (1992): Apprehension of trauma fosters sympathetic excitation, and residues thereof facilitate the experience of pleasurable excitement upon the apprehension's termination. Apprehension of trauma is but one excitatory precondition, however. Numerous nonthreatening conditions are also capable of evoking excitatory reactions of considerable intensity. Unexpected pleasant events and innocuous surprises can excite. So can stark sensory stimulation. Moreover, excitement may result from empathy with observed liked others or from witnessing the abusive treatment of parties deemed deserving of punishment. For instance, action-inviting music can excite, and so can merely witnessing others' sexual activities or exposure to the fictional portrayal of the slaughter of a serial killer. Residual excitation from all these sources can intensify subsequently experienced pleasurable excitement. It has been demonstrated, for instance, that sexual pleasure can be intensified by excitation from preceding anxiety or anger reactions, that intense enjoyment of drama hinges on the intensity of empathic distress that precedes satisfying resolutions, or that parachuting is most thrilling and gratifying for novices who experience more initial anxiety than hardened veterans of the sport. The excitement-augmenting stimulation may also accompany, rather than follow, the primary instigation of emotion. Embedding exciting sexual images in music videos, for instance, has been shown to elevate the appreciation of the accompanied music.

The experience of pleasurable excitement, then, presupposes two conditions: (a) cognition must foster an appraisal that the prevailing circumstances are safe and rewarding; and (b) sympathetic excitation must be pronounced in order to provide individuals with extero- and interoceptive feedback of being physically excited (e.g., heavy breathing, racing heart, or muscular tenseness). The experience-intensifying excitation may come from different sources, however, and give a global impression.

The mediation of excitation that fuels excitement involves gonadal hormones as well as adrenal catecholamines. The androgen testosterone proves particularly important. According to an analysis by Henry (1986), elevated testosterone levels are uniquely linked with elation that derives from successful social competition and the achievement of dominance. It has been shown that victory in both physical and mental competition leads to increased testosterone release, along with reduced release of the stress hormone cortisol. Defeat has the opposite consequence and results in a depression-like response pattern. The control and mastery of social and environmental circumstances, especially after an expenditure of effort, thus appears to be a potent contributor to pleasurable excitement. Confronting danger in a difficult climb and making it safely to the mountaintop may be exciting, but it would be more exciting if it were linked to victory over competitors: Getting there first promises an elating testosterone rush; getting there last might be depressing despite overcoming danger.

Henry's (1986) analysis includes endocrine processes in the brain. Of particular interest to excitement is the release of endorphins and related opioids. Elation, once achieved, is associated with low endorphin levels. Depressive displeasure is linked with increased endorphin release. These observations help explain why experiences of acute displeasure cannot be sustained for long periods and why, on occasion, they seem to yield euphoric sensations in their wake. In accordance with suggestions by Solomon (1980), it appears that endocrine regulation applies to hedonism in that prolonged experiences of displeasure initiate an opponent process, the release of endorphins, that eventually removes the displeasure and possibly fosters pleasure. The runner's high, which depends on the self-infliction of prolonged bodily torment, could be explained in this way. So might be the oddly pleasurable experience of having watched a tragic play. On the other hand, the symmetry of opponent-process theory projects that no state of intense pleasurable excitement can be sustained and must come to an end, if only because endorphin levels diminish. Findings concerning the release of neuropeptides during pleasurable excitement suggest, however, that a reversal into displeasure does not inevitably follow pleasure. Such regulation merely prevents intense pleasure from becoming painful, and restores the organism's capacity for new bouts of excitement.

Bibliography

Apter, M. J. (1992). *The dangerous edge: The psychology of excitement.* New York: Free Press.

Frijda, N. H. (1986). *The emotions.* Cambridge, England: Cambridge University Press.

Henry, J. P. (1986). Neuroendocrine patterns of emotional response. In R. Plutchik & H. Kellerman (Eds.), *Emotion:*

Theory, research, and experience: Vol. 3. Biological foundations of emotion (pp. 37–60). San Diego, CA: Academic Press.

Plutchik, R. (1980). A general psychoevolutionary theory of emotion. In R. Plutchik & H. Kellerman (Eds.), *Emotion: Theory, research, and experience: Vol. 1. Theories of emotion* (pp. 3–33). San Diego, CA: Academic Press.

Schachter, S. (1964). The interaction of cognitive and physiological determinants of emotional state. In L. Berkowitz (Ed.), *Advances in experimental social psychology* (Vol. 1, pp. 49–80). San Diego, CA: Academic Press.

Smith, G. P. (1973). Adrenal hormones and emotional behavior. In E. Stellar & J. M. Sprague (Eds.), *Progress in physiological psychology* (pp. 299–351). San Diego, CA: Academic Press.

Solomon, R. L. (1980). The opponent-process theory of acquired motivation: The costs of pleasure and the benefits of pain. *American Psychologist, 35,* 691–712.

Thayer, R. E. (1989). *The biopsychology of mood and arousal.* New York: Oxford University Press.

Zillmann, D. (1996). Sequential dependencies in emotional experience and behavior. In R. D. Kavanaugh, B. Zimmerberg, & S. Fein (Eds.), *Emotion: Interdisciplinary perspectives* (pp. 243–272). Hillsdale, NJ: Erlbaum.

Zillmann, D. (1998). *Connections between sexuality and aggression* (2nd ed.). Hillsdale, NJ: Erlbaum.

Zuckerman, M. (1979). *Sensation seeking: Beyond the optimal level of arousal.* Hillsdale, NJ: Erlbaum.

Dolf Zillmann

EXEMPLAR. *See* Schema.

EXERCISE AND PHYSICAL ACTIVITY. Regular physical activity, defined as any movement created by skeletal muscles that leads to energy expenditure, is an important contributor to health, functioning, and quality of life among people of all ages. The almost exclusive scientific and public health focus prior to the 1980s on vigorous forms of planned, structured exercise aimed at improving physical fitness has been broadened to include a growing appreciation of the benefits of more moderate intensity forms of physical activity on health. Among the established physical health benefits of regular physical activity are lower premature mortality rates for both younger and older adults; decreased risk of cardiovascular disease mortality, high blood pressure, colon cancer, non-insulin-dependent diabetes mellitus, and obesity; and development and maintenance of normal muscle strength, joint structure, joint function, and bone mass, which may play a role in the prevention or treatment of diseases such as osteoarthritis and osteoporosis.

There are a number of physiological mechanisms

through which regular physical activity may exert its protective effects against cardiovascular disease. They include effects on plasma lipoprotein profile, blood pressure, oxygenation of the heart muscle, blood clotting factors, body fat distribution, heart rhythm disturbances, and other factors directly influencing atherosclerotic plaque development.

Regular physical activity also has a positive impact on a variety of psychological outcomes in both clinical and nonclinical populations—mood, symptoms of depression and anxiety, perceived stress, and psychological well-being—factors that have been linked to improvement in health-related quality of life. In addition, the preservation of strength, endurance, and flexibility that accompanies an active lifestyle can promote continued independence, which has been identified as an important contributor to quality of life as people age. Moderate intensity forms of physical activity such as brisk walking appear to be equally effective compared to more vigorous activities in promoting psychological benefits.

The pathways through which regular physical activity promotes psychological benefits remain to be fully explored. Possible mechanisms include increases in core body temperature, which may decrease muscle tension and promote relaxation; physical activity–induced changes in brain neuroreceptor concentrations of monoamines or endogenous opiates; cognitive factors such as enhanced feelings of self-efficacy or mastery; social factors related to positive social interactions or support; and time away from daily stressors.

In addition to its many benefits, physical activity, particularly when it is excessive, can also produce adverse effects, including musculoskeletal injury, metabolic abnormalities, increased contact with environmental hazards (e.g., motor vehicles, uneven surfaces), and, under certain circumstances, serious cardiac events (i.e., heart attack, sudden death). In many cases, such adverse events can be avoided or minimized through gradual increases in physical activity frequency, intensity, and duration commensurate with an individual's capacity and health profile. Although during vigorous physical exertion an individual may be at somewhat higher risk for a cardiac event than at other periods throughout the day, the net impact of regular physical activity is to lower the overall risk of cardiac death.

Epidemiology and Determinants of Physical Activity Patterns

Despite current national recommendations encouraging regular physical activity, only 22% of U.S. adults engage in sustained leisure-time physical activity of any intensity on most days of the week. Another 24% or more of adults are, by self-report, completely sedentary during leisure time. Among the population subgroups that are at increased risk for being underactive are women, older adults, and groups that are less educated or have lower socioeconomic status. Only about half of U.S. youth between the ages of 12 and 21 participate regularly in vigorous physical activity. Youth participation in all types of physical activity shows a marked decline with age and school grade.

Among the most frequently reported correlates of physical inactivity are a perceived lack of time, issues related to lack of enjoyment, inconvenience, or other perceived barriers to being physically active, lack of confidence in one's ability to engage in regular physical activity (i.e., self-efficacy), lack of support from others, and perceptions concerning the costs relative to the benefits of engaging in regular physical activity. Such factors are potentially mutable with appropriate intervention. In addition, a growing number of studies indicate that physical activity determinants across several different domains (e.g., demographic, physiological, psychosocial, program-based) may interact to facilitate or impede sustained physical activity participation. For instance, evidence from a recent physical activity intervention study suggested that overweight persons assigned to a group-based physical activity program were at highest risk for nonadherence two years later (i.e., only 7.7% were adequately physically active by the second year). In contrast, persons with less than a completed high school education who were less stressed and less fit at baseline relative to other participants, and who were assigned to supervised home-based exercise programs of either high or lower intensity, had the greatest likelihood of successful adherence two years later (i.e., 69.2% were adequately physically active). Such results underscore the importance of continued efforts to understand the combined effects of different physical activity determinants.

Interventions to Promote Regular Physical Activity

In light of the substantial proportion of the population that is currently underactive, the development of interventions to promote regular physical activity across the population at large is essential. Applications of social learning theory and its derivatives that stress the reciprocal interaction of personal, behavioral, and environmental factors on physical activity patterns have met with some success. Such approaches have emphasized the use of goal setting, self-monitoring, regular feedback, ongoing levels of social support, external and self-reinforcement, stimulus-control techniques, and relapse prevention training and other cognitive decision-making strategies to promote early adoption as well as long-term maintenance of physical activity. When such strategies have been combined with a home-based format that allows an individual to choose when and where to exercise, sustained levels of physical activity participation among both women and men have been demonstrated for up to two years. Ongoing staff supervision and support was provided primarily through mediated channels (i.e., telephone and mail). Recent efforts to utilize behavioral approaches to reduce sedentary behavior among children have also shown promise.

Cognitive-behavioral approaches have been recently combined with models emphasizing processes and stages relevant to motivational readiness for change (e.g., the transtheoretical model) with promising, albeit preliminary, results. Instructional materials and messages are matched to the individual's stage of readiness to engage in physical activity (e.g., precontemplation, contemplation, preparation, action, maintenance).

These and similar conceptual approaches have been applied to physical activity interventions conducted in a variety of community settings, including worksites, health care settings, and schools, with mixed results. Given the newness of the physical activity intervention field relative to other risk factor areas (e.g., smoking cessation, weight control), it is likely that future research in this area will continue to build on successful strategies supplemented with increased audience segmentation and intervention tailoring, with more powerful interventions a likely result.

Given the importance of environmental and policy-related factors on physical activity participation levels, a focus on interventions aimed at environmental and policy change, in combination with individual-level approaches, is essential. The development of such approaches in the United States is in its infancy. However, the push toward reduced physical energy expenditure accompanying this century's modern technological age has imposed increasing limits on natural forms of physical activity, which will likely require policy- or societal-level interventions to counteract. Examples of potentially useful interventions at this level of impact include increased proximity of safe and attractive physical activity resources to homes and worksites; incentives for the development of alternative transportation systems that encourage walking and bicycling; health insurance–based incentives to promote regular physical activity; zoning and land use policies that protect and enhance recreational outdoor space; and building construction and facilities development policies that encourage activity throughout the day (e.g., accessible and attractive stairways). Such environmental and policy interventions can occur within specific community settings (e.g., worksites, schools, public buildings), across the community at large, or at county, state, regional, or national levels.

[See also Anxiety; Depression; Diabetes; Health Belief Model; Health Promotion; Health Psychology, article on Assessments and Interventions; Injury; Obesity; Quality of Life; Self-Concept and Self-Representation; Self-Effi-cacy; Social Learning Theory; Sport Psychology; Stress; and Wellness and Illness.]

Bibliography

Dishman, R. K. (1991). Increasing and maintaining exercise and physical activity. *Behavior Therapy, 22,* 345–378. Presents a critical review of 56 studies that used behavior modification or cognitive-behavioral modification strategies to increase physical activity in adult populations.

Epstein, L., Saelens, B. E., Myers, M. D., & Vito, D. (1997). Effects of decreasing sedentary behaviors on activity choice in obese children. *Health Psychology, 16,* 107–113. Methods of decreasing highly preferred sedentary behaviors were compared and the effects on subsequent activity choice studied in a sample of 34 obese children. The results suggest that reinforcing decreases in high-preference sedentary activity can decrease how much the targeted sedentary activities are liked and increase physical activity.

King, A. C., Blair, S. N., Bild, D. E., Dishman, R. K., Dubbert, P. M., Marcus, B. H., Oldridge, N. B., Paffenbarger, R. S., Jr., Powell, K. E., & Yeager, K. K. (1992). Determinants of physical activity and interventions in adults. *Medicine and Science in Sports and Exercise, 24* (Suppl. 6), S221–S236. Presents a summary of the known physical activity determinants and interventions that have been evaluated in adult populations.

King, A. C., Haskell, W. L., Young, D. R., Oka, R. K., & Stefanick, M. L. (1995). Long-term effects of varying intensities and formats of physical activity on participation rates, fitness, and lipoproteins in men and women aged 50–65 years. *Circulation, 91,* 2596–2604. Supervised home-based forms of physical activity were found to be particularly effective in promoting sustained two-year physical activity adherence, and improvements in physical fitness and HDL cholesterol among men and women aged 50 to 65 years relative to a group-based program. The results indicated that frequency of physical activity participation may be particularly important for achieving HDL cholesterol changes among older adults.

King, A. C., Jeffery R. W., Fridinger, F., Dusenbury, L., Provence, S., Hedlund, S., & Bartlett, K. J. (1995). Environmental and policy approaches to cardiovascular disease prevention through physical activity: Issues and opportunities. *Health Education Quarterly, 22,* 499–511. This article discusses the use of policy, regulatory, and environmental interventions in promoting regular physical activity.

King, A. C., Taylor, C. B., & Haskell, W. L. (1993). The effects of differing intensities and formats of twelve months of exercise training on psychological outcomes in older adults. *Health Psychology, 12,* 292–300. Regardless of program assignment to either moderate- or high-intensity forms of exercise, greater exercise participation was significantly related to less anxiety and fewer depressive symptoms across a one-year period independent of changes in fitness or body weight.

Telephone-supervised home-based exercise training of either higher or lower intensity was found to be particularly effective in reducing perceived stress levels relative to exercise training undertaken in a group format.

Pate, R. R., Pratt, M., Blair, S. N., Haskell, W. L., Macera, C. A., Bouchard, C., Buchner, D., Caspersen, C. J., Ettinger, W., Heath, G. W., King, A. C., Kriska, A., Leon, A. S., Marcus, B. H., Morris, J., Paffenbarger, R., Patrick, K., Pollock, M. L., Rippe, J. M., Sallis, J., & Wilmore, J. H. (1995). Physical activity and public health: A recommendation from the Centers for Disease Control and Prevention and the American College of Sports Medicine. *Journal of the American Medical Association, 273*, 402–407. Describes national recommendations for physical activity, which focus on moderate intensity activity in addition to the more vigorous forms of exercise described in previous U.S. recommendations.

U.S. Department of Health and Human Services. (1996). *Physical activity and health: A report of the Surgeon General.* Atlanta, GA: U.S. Department of Health and Human Services, Centers for Disease Control and Prevention, National Center for Chronic Disease Prevention and Health Promotion. A comprehensive review of the literature linking physical activity to health, as well as the current status of epidemiological and intervention research in this field.

Abby C. King

EXHIBITIONISM is one form of paraphiliac behavior. Paraphilias are described in the *Diagnostic and Statistical Manual* (4th ed.) of the American Psychiatric Association (1994) as characterized by "recurrent, intense, sexually arousing fantasies, sexual urges, or behavior generally involving (1) nonhuman objects, (2) the suffering or humiliation of one's self or one's partner, or (3) children or other nonconsenting persons that occur over a period of six months" (p. 523). The behavior urges or fantasies must cause significant distress or impair the individual in an area of functioning.

Exhibitionism involves the person exposing his genitals to an unsuspecting person. While specific etiology of exhibitionism is unknown, several theories have been proposed to explain the behavior. Psychodynamically oriented theorists see the behavior as a means by which to allay castration anxiety. Behavioral therapists view the behavior as a result of learning experiences, whereby certain behaviors are reinforced by sexual arousal that end in orgasm or by the impact the behavior has on the environment. The role of fantasy is considered crucial in the development of sexual behaviors. Fantasies to which a person masturbates are reinforced and may serve as a rehearsal for the sexual activities that the person ultimately engages in. A biological basis to the behavior has also been proposed implicating differences in hormonal levels in exhibitionists as compared to nonexhibitionists. As with most behaviors the theory, explaining the etiology of the behaviors should be comprehensive and include biological, social, and psychological factors.

Exhibitionism is a disorder diagnosed almost exclusively in males; however, it can occur in females. A large-scale study including more than 200 exhibitionists found the average age of the men was 28.9 years. These men reported that they first had urges to expose between the ages of 13 and 16. Two thirds of the men acknowledged that they had masturbated while exposing their genitals. When questioned as to what the nature of the desired sexual behavior was with the person they were exposing to, 62.4% reported a desire to touch the target person (victim) intimately, and 51.9% desired to have intercourse. When these men were questioned as to how they wanted the target person (victim) to respond, 35.1% reported that they wanted the target person to have intercourse with them, 0.5% wanted the victim to respond with fear, 14.1% with admiration, 4% with anger, 15.1% wanted the victim to show his or her private parts, 11.9% wanted any type of reaction, and 19.5% said no reaction was necessary at all. (Freund, Watson, & Rinze, 1988).

Exhibitionists may experience other forms of paraphilias. Abel, Becker, Cunningham-Rathner, Mittleman, and Rouleau (1988) interviewed several hundred sex offenders under a certificate of confidentiality. Of those exhibitionists interviewed, only 7% had one category of paraphiliac behavior. Twenty percent had two categories of paraphiliac behavior and 23% had at least three types of paraphilias. Consequently, it is imperative that when an exhibitionist is evaluated that he be assessed for other types of paraphilias as well as the exhibitionism.

Prior to developing a treatment program for the exhibitionist, it is important that a comprehensive assessment be conducted. The assessment should include information regarding the nature of the specific offense (available from police reports), victim characteristics, and any statements made by the victim. Since exhibitionists as well as other sexual offenders are apt to minimize or deny the extent of the sexual offense, it is critical that external sources of information be surveyed. It is also important to obtain a developmental history, legal history, and social and medical history. An extensive and detailed sexual history should be taken. This would include the age of onset of sexual fantasies, urges, and actual sexual behaviors, both paraphiliac and nonparaphiliac. Information pertaining to previous offenses and how particular victims were selected should be obtained. An assessment should be conducted of the individual's cognitive distortions, degree of empathy, specific skills, such as social skills and anger management. It also would be helpful to conduct psychophysiological assessment of both deviant and nondeviant arousal patterns.

While the exact prevalence of exhibitionism is unknown, a survey of college females indicated that 32% reported that they had been victims of exhibitionism. Exhibitionism is not a victimless crime in that almost all victims report that they are negatively impacted by the experience.

The exhibitionist rarely is self-motivated to receive treatment. In most cases, he enters treatment after he has been arrested and at the recommendation of the legal system. A variety of therapeutic modalities have been used to treat exhibitionists, including individual therapy, group therapy, behavior therapy, cognitive behavior therapy, hormonal treatment and psychotropic medications.

Behavioral approaches have included aversive conditioning, including covert sensitization, assisted covert sensitization, and aversive behavioral rehearsal (ABR). There are two forms of ABR; in vivo ABR (I-V-ABR) involves the therapist having the exhibitionist expose himself to people who know of him in a clinical setting under controlled conditions. The goal is to elicit and confront any fantasies and cognitive distortions that mediate the exhibitionistic behavior. Vicarious aversive behavior rehearsal (V-ABR) involves arranging for the exhibitionist to observe via videotape another exhibitionist being treated with I-V-ABR.

Biological treatments, including hormonal and psychotropic medications, have been used with some individuals who have paraphilias. Anti-androgenic medications have been widely used throughout the world since the late 1960s to treat sex offenders. Medroxyprogesterone acetate (MPA) and cyproterone acetate (CPA), both progesterone derivatives, have been the most extensively used. These medications appear to work best in those paraphiliac individuals with a high sexual drive and less well with those with a low sexual drive. More recently, other forms of pharmacological treatment have been utilized. Fluoxetine has been utilized successfully in the treatment of patients with voyeurism, exhibitionism, pedophilia, and frottage, and in persons who have committed rape (Perilstein, Lipper, & Friedman, 1991).

Serotoninergic medications have been used in the treatment of individuals who presented with sexual obsessions, addictions, and paraphilias. As opposed to the above-cited studies, Stein and his colleagues found the medications were ineffective in treating the paraphilias. Those authors hypothesize that compulsivity and impulsivity may be on a neurobiological spectrum in which obsessions and compulsions are at the compulsive end and paraphilias at the impulsive end. It is clear that further controlled research using larger sample sizes is warranted to evaluate further the efficacy of serotoninergic medication in treating individuals with paraphilias.

Relapse prevention utilizes a psychoeducational model that combines behavioral skills training with cognitive intervention techniques. More recently, a relapse prevention model has been described in treating sex offenders. This model involves assisting the individual in identifying high risk situations (those situations in which the individual might be more likely to expose himself), the development of coping skills, specific skills training for dealing with high risk situations, cognitive restructuring, teaching the individual how to cope with urges, enhancing empathy, and specific lifestyle interventions.

Marshall and colleagues (1991) compared two forms of treatment for exhibitionists. The first involved modifying deviant sexual preferences; the second involved enhancing relationship and interpersonal skills and improving awareness of relapse prevention issues. These authors report that exhibitionists can be treated effectively and conclude that those treatments that take a broad conceptualization of the problem (focus on social, cognitive, and interpersonal problems) as opposed to narrowly focusing on deviant sexual preferences have the best chance of success.

For the past two decades, the studies of paraphilias have come under more rigorous investigation. Given the "hidden" nature of these behaviors and the fact that individuals with paraphilias rarely present for treatment on their own, and the majority of those individuals are referred by the legal system, we still do not have extensive information on the extent of exhibitionism in our society. Further research needs to focus on attempting to identify early those individuals at risk for developing exhibitionistic behavior and intervening as soon as possible given that a percentage of exhibitionists will go on to engage in other forms of paraphiliac behavior. Further controlled research is also called for to investigate the success of the relapse prevention model in treating exhibitionists as well as for the research looking at psychopharmacological treatments in conjunction with cognitive behavioral treatments.

[*See also* Sexual Disorders.]

Bibliography

Abel, G. G., Becker, J. V., Cunningham-Rathner, J., Mittelman, M., & Rouleau, J. L. (1988). Multiple paraphiliac diagnoses among sex offenders. *Bulletin of the American Academy of Psychiatry and Law*, 16 (2), 153–168.

American Psychiatric Association. (1994). *Diagnostic and statistical manual of mental disorders* (4th ed.). Washington, DC: Author.

Cox, D. J., & Daitzman, R. (1979). Behavioral theory research and treatment of male exhibitionism. In M. Hersen, R. N. Eisler, & P. M. Miller (Eds.), *Progress in behavior modification*. (Vol. 7). New York: Academic Press.

Freund, K., Watson, R., & Rienzo, D. (1988). The value of self-reports in the study of voyeurism and exhibitionism. *Annals of Sex Research, 1*, 243–262.

Marshall, W. L., Eccles, A., & Barbaree, H. E. (1991). The treatment of exhibitionists: A focus on sexual deviance versus cognitive and relationship features. *Behavior Research and Therapy, 29* (2), 129–135.

Perilstein, R. D., Lipper, S., & Friedman, L. J. (1991). Three cases of paraphilias responsive to Fluoxetine treatment. *Journal of Clinical Psychiatry, 52*, 169–170.

Pithers, W. D., Martin, G. R., & Cunning, G. F. (1989). In D. R. Laws (Ed.), *Relapse prevention with sex offenders* (pp. 292–325). New York: Guilford Press.

Stein, D. J., Hollander, E., & Anthony, D. T. (1992). Serotoninergic medications for sexual obsessions, sexual addictions, and paraphilias. *Journal of Clinical Psychiatry, 53*, 267–271.

Wickramasekera, I. (1980). Aversive behavior rehearsal: A cognitive behavioral procedure. In R. D. J. Cox & R. J. Daitzman (Eds.), *Exhibitionism: Description and assessment and treatment* (pp. 123–149). New York: Garland Press.

Judith V. Becker

EXISTENTIALISM. "Existentialism," writes Maurice Friedman in *The Worlds of Existentialism*,

> is not a philosophy but a mood embracing a number of disparate philosophies; the differences among them are more basic than the temper which unites them. This temper can best be described as a reaction against the static, the abstract, the purely rational, the merely irrational, in favor of the dynamic and the concrete, personal involvement and "engagement," action, choice, and commitment, the distinction between "authentic" and "inauthentic" existence, and the actual situation of the existential subject as the starting point of thought. Beyond this the existentialists divide according to their views on such matters as phenomenological analysis, the existential subject, the intersubjective relation between selves, religion, and the implications of existentialism for psychotherapy.

Existentialism is a direction of movement toward particulars, but it is not and can never be an espousal of the particulars at the expense of all generality and abstraction. If that is recognized, a distinction must still be made between philosophers who are existentialist in the sense of analyzing existence according to general existential categories and others who are existentialist in the very different sense of pointing to the unique and concrete in existence that lies beyond all analysis.

Forerunners

While the forerunners of existentialism reach all the way back to Heraclitus and the Hebrew Bible, it is the nineteenth-century Danish theologian Søren Kierkegaard (1813–1855) who is the founder of the philosophy of existence proper, through his emphasis on the existential subject—the "Single One," whom Kierkegaard opposed to "the crowd" (= "untruth"). Kierkegaard saw the Single One as set in a direct relation with a transcendent God, but before this relationship can come into being a person must have discovered her true inwardness, and it is with all the passion of this inwardness that Kierkegaard clings to the "absurd" and attacks the "system."

The Russian novelist Fyodor Dostoevsky may also be considered a forerunner of twentieth-century existentialism through his awareness of *Angst*—the anguish and dread of human existence, his concern with the recovery of the human being's alienated freedom, his emphasis on the particular fact and the absurd, and his portrayal of the "man-god's" proclamation of self will in remarkable anticipation of Nietzsche and Sartre. Friedrich Nietzsche's teaching of "will to power," of "the death of God"—the loss of any absolute base for values, of the importance of the self, of man as a valuing animal, of the uniqueness of each person's way—all make him one of the foremost proto-existentialists.

Phenomenology

Although the leading phenomenologists—Wilhelm Dilthey and Edmund Husserl—were not themselves existentialists, and many existentialists are not, or are only very secondarily, phenomenologists, we cannot understand existentialism adequately without touching on phenomenology. Dilthey based his thought on the radical difference between the way of knowing practiced in the *Geisteswissenschaften*—the human studies such as philosophy, the social sciences, and psychology—and that practiced in the *Naturwissenschaften*—the natural sciences. In the former, one cannot be merely a detached scientific observer but must also participate oneself, for it is through one's participation that one discovers both the typical and the unique in the aspects of human life that one is studying. At the same time, one must suspend foregone conclusions and the search for causality that marks the natural scientist in favor of an open attempt to discover what offers itself.

The man who raised phenomenology from an approach to philosophy to a systematic philosophy was Edmund Husserl (1859–1938). By the method of "parenthesizing," or phenomenological reduction, he replaced the detached subject and independent object of older philosophy with a field of knowing in which phenomena are accepted as pure phenomena without their independent existence being questioned. The existential status of the world arises "from me as the transcendental Ego," Husserl wrote, and the exploration of the field of transcendental experience becomes equivalent to the phenomenological knowledge of the world.

It was inevitable that Husserl's existentialist successors would either: emphasize the direct experiential quality of his thought, as opposed to the idealist, like the French philosopher Maurice Merleau-Ponty; break with the transcendental ego altogether while retaining the method of phenomenology and the reality of intersubjectivity, like the French philosopher, novelist, and playwright Jean-Paul Sartre; or transform phenomenology from a method of knowledge into a "fundamental ontology," like the German philosopher Martin Heidegger.

Both Sartre and Heidegger accepted Husserl's motto "To the things themselves" as an obstacle to any attempt to find Being behind phenomena; only an existential analysis of the existent, the "ontic," would yield any knowledge of being. For Heidegger, this analysis was posited on his special use of *Dasein*—the person's "being there" in the world, thrown into a situation apart from which neither subject nor consciousness have any meaning. But while Sartre rejected Husserl's transcendental ego in favor of an impersonal consciousness which is nothing other than an emptiness or absence in the presence of the solid being of existents, Heidegger moved toward a concept of Being—the "ontological"—that was linked more with person than with consciousness—the person who becomes aware of herself as "there," "thrown," "in the world."

Karl Jaspers, under the influence of Kant, Kierkegaard, and Dilthey, but independent of Husserl, developed his own phenomenology of "limit situations," which had an important influence on Heidegger. Later, Jaspers explicitly rejected "ontology"—the study of Being—in favor of "the Encompassing," or "the Comprehensive"—a way of knowing that transcends the subject-object relationship even more radically than phenomenology by recognizing that we can never grasp the whole reality since we are a part of it. Martin Buber took the phenomenology of Dilthey over into the kind of knowing that is central to the "I-Thou" relation—one which emphasizes the incomparable uniqueness of what is known in mutual relationship.

The Existential Subject

Each existential thinker stresses becoming a real person, a Single One, an authentic human being, and each is opposed to those trends of the age that level, objectify, depersonalize, alienate, or divide the human person. Martin Heidegger's treatment of the existential subject, though lacking the religious counter-pole of Kierkegaard's, is like Kierkegaard's in his contrast between the authentic self and "*das Man*"—the "One," or the "They," who is lost in the anonymity of what others think. Through resolute anticipation of one's death as one's nonrelational, not-to-be-outstripped, ownmost reality, one is called back to authentic existence.

With Sartre, the existential subject becomes still more sharply defined: first, by cutting off from the self every link with Being or transcendence that would serve as a guide to value decisions; and second, through his dialectic between *pour soi*—the subjectivity of the self from within, and "for itself"—and *en-soi*—the self regarded objectively, whether by another or oneself, as "in itself," in the same sense that any definite object is.

Martin Buber finds the authentic self in the sharing of the I-Thou relationship, in the Single One, who is responsible to its interhuman Thou. One realizes one's unique direction ever anew in one's meeting with the concrete situation in which one finds oneself: "All real living is meeting."

Intersubjectivity

In Kierkegaard, the relationship between person and person tends to be secondary and inessential—an obstacle to becoming a Single One and to having an absolute relation to the Absolute. In contrast, the twentieth-century existentialists all recognize intersubjectivity in one form or another as essential to human existence. Yet even here a distinction must be made between such thinkers as Heidegger, Sartre, and Paul Tillich, for whom the intersubjective tends to remain a dimension of the self, and such thinkers as Martin Buber, Gabriel Marcel, Karl Jaspers, and Albert Camus, who in one way or another see the relationship between person and person as central to human existence.

Even between Heidegger and Sartre there are important differences. Heidegger's intersubjectivity remains the vague we of his "*Mitsein*" or "*Mitdasein*"—a being with others that expresses itself in solicitude but not in that sharp conflict between one particular person and another, which for Sartre enters into intersubjectivity.

Buber criticizes Heidegger's "solicitude" as monological. Heidegger's treatment of death as one's ownmost, ultimate, nonrelational reality does, in fact, show that *Mitsein* is not as basic for him as *Dasein*. On the other hand, Sartre's emphasis on conflict and particularity never take him beyond what Buber would call the "I-It" relation, in which I know the other only as a subject because I am aware of his looking at me as an object or because, in lovemaking, I am trying to possess his freedom and make it subject to my own. This also leaves Sartre short of the more rationalistic notion of *Kommunikation*, which is so central to the thinking of Karl Jaspers, and of the existence "for others," which Merleau-Ponty recognizes in his phenomenology.

Like Sartre, Albert Camus starts with Descartes's *cogito ergo sum*, yet he goes on to the dialogue between persons in which human beings really come to exist and sees both the interchange and the limitations of that dialogue as the key to real humanity. Gabriel Marcel arrives, like Buber, at a radical philosophy of I and Thou (*je et toi*), which he also understands, like Buber, as an approach to epistemology as well as to ethics and religion.

Atheist, Humanist, Religious, and Theological Existentialists

The distinction between atheist and theist existentialists, which Jean-Paul Sartre put forth in his famous essay "Existentialism Is a Humanism," obscures real differences and similarities of attitude, which are far more important even in terms of religion. Camus never ceased to speak of himself as an atheist, yet the latter Camus is closer in attitude to the theist Buber than he is to the atheist Sartre. Camus himself confirmed this by saying that he would not mind being called religious in Buber's sense of the I-Thou relationship.

As Heidegger's early thought represents a progression from phenomenology to "fundamental ontology," so his later thought represents a progression from "fundamental ontology" to metaphysics. Metaphysics, to Heidegger, begins by asking why there is anything instead of nothing, and ends with a mystical Nothingness and a wonder in the face of it reminiscent of the seventeenth-century Lutheran mystic Jacob Boehme's *Ungrund*. While Heidegger's goal—reaching the truth of Being—has not changed, his way to that goal is different. In *Being and Time*, Heidegger is exclusively occupied with an existential analysis of *Dasein*, whereas in his later thought he proceeds more directly to Being or Nothingness as such, even though it is a Being which he carefully guards from any confusion with the static or ideal Absolutes of traditional metaphysics.

Nietzsche, Sartre, Heidegger, and Buber all speak of the "death of God," but to each it means something essentially different. To Nietzsche it means the loss of a base for values that makes way for the will to power that creates new values and leads to the superman, or overman. For Sartre it means the necessity of inventing one's own values and choosing oneself as an image of the human for all persons. For Heidegger it means a void that cannot be filled by any overman, but the occasion, nonetheless, for a succession of new divine images arising out of the human being's clarifying thought about being. For Buber it means the "eclipse of God," which comes when God answers the human turning away—the predominance of the I-It relationship—by seeming to be absent himself.

Paul Tillich has said that existentialism provides the questions, the religious traditions the answers. Actually, an essential difference among the so-called religious existentialists is that some of them understand the "answers" in as thoroughly existentialist terms as the questions, while others follow an existentialist analysis of the human condition with an appeal to traditional theology as the only valid response to that situation. In fact, we must distinguish between religious existentialists, such as Martin Buber, the German-Jewish philosopher Franz Rosenzweig, the Russian Orthodox philosopher Nicolas Berdyaev, the Austrian Catholic thinker Ferdinand Ebner, and the French Catholic philosopher Gabriel Marcel, and existentialist theologians such as the German-American Protestant Paul Tillich, and the French Catholic Thomist Jacques Maritain.

Not only has Paul Tillich incorporated his existential analyses into his systematic theology, he had also attempted to use his existential approach as a specific proof of the superiority of Protestant Christianity to all other forms of religion. Tillich accepts Buber's I-Thou relationship with God, but ultimately wants to go beyond Buber's "eternal Thou" to "the God beyond God," the "ground of Being," which he sees as superior to both mysticism and theism. Buber, on the other hand, offers "the Absolute Person," the eternal Thou, who is not a person but becomes one only in relation with us. Tillich, in contrast, desires a *gnosis*—a knowledge which will give a more secure foundation to faith than that existential trust that knows meeting and presence but no continuity and security.

Existentialism and Hermeneutics

Existentialism has also had a significant impact on the postmodern emphasis on hermeneutics—the science of interpretation. Here we need only think of the writings of the French philosopher Paul Ricoeur, the impact of both Heidegger and Buber on Hans Georg Gadamer, Jurgen Habermas, Emmanuel Levinas, and through Levinas on Jacques Derridas, and Buber's central impact on the highly influential Russian literary theorist Mikhail Bakhtin and a number of other hermeneuts.

Existential Psychology and Psychotherapy

A number of existential thinkers have made significant contributions to psychology and psychotherapy—Kierkegaard with his concepts of *Angst* (anxiety or dread) and "sickness unto death" (the despairing will not to be oneself or the defiant will to be oneself); Jaspers with his concept of limit situations and his critique of the objectification of freedom by psychoanalysis; Buber with his concepts of distance and relation, confirmation, "imagining the real," existential guilt, and healing through meeting; Sartre with his concepts of bad faith, the lability of consciousness, freedom and choosing one's own project, existential analysis, and sex as the incarnation of subjectivity and the subjection of freedom to domination of the other; Tillich with his concepts of ontological anxiety and the courage to be.

Three explicitly existential psychotherapists are the Viennese neuropsychiatrist Viktor Frankl, founder of "logotherapy," and the two Swiss psychiatrists Ludwig Binswanger, founder of "existential analysis," and Medard Boss, founder of "*Daseinanalysis.*" In America, the spearhead of existential psychotherapy was Rollo May, who was strongly influenced by Kierkegaard and Heidegger, and to a lesser extent by Buber. Boss was strongly under the influence of Heidegger. Binswanger attempted to combine Heidegger's phenomenology ontology, which he called "world design," with Buber's categories of the interhuman as well as Kierkegaard's "sickness unto death."

Phenomenological analysis can certainly help in understanding, but it is not the same as direct communication between one person and another. Binswanger's analytic-synthetic "world-design" cannot capture the uniqueness and wholeness of a person, for these are only revealed in the dialogue between I and Thou. "The configuration of self and world or self to self is not existential," Paul Goodman has remarked. "It is interpretation just in the Freudian sense. Real existential psychotherapy would try to do as far as possible without interpretations and stick to particular situations." When Binswanger's analysis of the dead Ellen West as "Thou" takes the place of the meeting with a live Ellen West in therapy, the existential itself has been submerged in the waters of a new essentialism.

Also important for the development of existential psychotherapy is the movement of dialogical psychotherapy, based on Buber's philosophical anthropology and his healing through meeting. This movement began with Hans Trüb, who moved from Carl Jung's dialectical psychology to Buber's dialogical anthropology. It has been carried forward by Leslie H. Farber with his "psychology of the will," and after him by Maurice Friedman and Richard Hycner, codirectors of the Institute of Dialogical Psychotherapy in San Diego, by William Heard, California psychologist, and Ivan Boszormenyi-Nagy, M.D., and Barbara Krasner with their "contextual [intergenerational family] therapy." Because a number of existentialists have been influenced by Harry Stack Sullivan's interpersonal psychiatry, it is important to recognize that the "interpersonal" cannot be equated with Buber's concept of the "interhuman." Many interpersonal relations are really a mixture of direct I-Thou relationships and indirect I-It ones, and some are almost purely I-It.

Existentialism has also had an impact on the movement of humanistic psychology. Most Humanistic Psychologists emphasize the present and presentness, and are concerned with the dynamic and the concrete and with the self as the existential subject. Rollo May was a leading figure in both existential and humanistic psychology. Carl Rogers, another central figure in humanistic psychology, was decisively influenced by both Soren Kierkegaard and Martin Buber, and some of the most prominent Gestalt therapists have been strongly influenced by Buber's concept of the I-Thou relationship. On the other hand, both Viktor Frankl and Maurice Friedman have strongly criticized that emphasis on self-realization and self-actualization, which has been central for Rogers, Abraham Maslow, and many other humanistic psychologists, pointing out that self-realization is the by-product and not the goal.

[*See also* Hermeneutics; Humanistic Psychology; Phenomenological Psychology; *and* Phenomenology.]

Bibliography

Boszormenyi-Nagy, I. (1973/1984). *Invisible loyalties: Reciprocity in intergenerational family therapy.* New York: Harper & Row. (Reprinted by Brunner/Mazel) *Invisible Loyalties* and *Between Give and Take* are the two basic books needed to understand contextual therapy, an important intergenerational family therapy offshoot of existential and dialogical therapy.

Boszormenyi-Nagy, I., & Krasner, B. R. (1986). *Between give and take: A clinical guide to contextual therapy.* New York: Brunner/Mazel.

Buber, M. (1958). *I and thou* (2nd rev. ed.). New York: Scribner's. *I and Thou* is Buber's classic work, which stands at the head of his philosophy of dialogue, his philosophical anthropology, and the dialogical psychotherapy that has built on the foundation of these two.

Buber, M. (1965). *The knowledge of man: A philosophy of the interhuman* (Maurice Friedman, Ed., Maurice Friedman & Ronald Gregor Smith, Trans.). New York: Harper & Row. *The Knowledge of Man*, with an introductory essay by Maurice Friedman, is the mature expression of Buber's philosophical anthropology, and as such is the fountainhead for most of the theory and practice of dialogical psychotherapy. There is no single equivalent German original.

Farber, L. H. (1966). *The ways of the will: Essays toward a psychology and psychopathology of the will.* New York: Basic Books. *The Ways of the Will* is the basic presentation of Farber's existential-dialogical psychology of the will.

Friedman, M. S. (1985). *The healing dialogue in psychotherapy.* New York: Jason Aronson. *The Healing Dialogue in Psychotherapy* is the most important theoretical presentation of the movement of dialogical psychotherapy. The first part deals with schools of therapy, the second with topics, e.g., confirmation, dreams and the unconscious, existential guilt, the problematic of mutuality, inclusion, and touchstones of reality.

Friedman, M. S. (1991). *The worlds of existentialism: A critical reader* (3rd rev. ed.). Atlantic Highlands, NJ: Humanities Press International. *The Worlds of Existentialism* is the most important anthology of existential thinkers, both because of the scope of its coverage—from biblical and Greek forerunners to present-day philosophers—and because the existentialist authors are subsumed under issues, e.g. phenomenology, the existential subject, intersubjectivity, atheist, humanist, religious, and theological existentialists, and existential psychotherapists. It is also the best bibliographical source for literary figures, religious thinkers, psychologists, and existentialist philosophers (e.g., Heidegger, Jaspers, and Sartre). It also includes translations of material from Karl Jaspers and Hans Trüb not previously published in English translation.

Heard, W. G. (1993). *The healing between: A clinical guide to dialogical psychotherapy*. San Francisco: Jossey/Bass. Heard's *Healing Between* and Hycner's *Between Person and Person* (below) are the two best presentations of dialogical psychotherapy both in theory and in practice, including valuable case illustrations.

Heidegger, M. (1963). *Being and time* (John Macquarrie & Edward Robinson, Trans.). New York: Harper & Row. This is Heidegger's basic existentialist text—an exposition of what he called "fundamental ontology." Heidegger's later thought was concerned with a quasi-mystical disclosure of being that went beyond *Being and Time* in some decisive ways.

Hycner, Richard C. (1991). *Between person and person: Toward a dialogical psychotherapy*. Highland, NY: Center for Gestalt Development.

Jaspers, K. (1932). *Philosophie* (Vols. 1–3). Berlin: Springer Verlag. This is Jaspers's basic existential philosophy. The second volume deals with *Kommunikation*, the third with Jaspers's metaphysics of ciphers and the encompassing.

May, R., Angel, E., & Ellenberger, H. F. (Eds). (1958). *Existence: A new dimension in psychology and psychiatry*. New York: Basic Books. *Existence* is the classic presentation of essays (mostly translated from the German) on phenomenological and existential psychiatry and psychology.

Sartre, J.-P. (1956). *L'être et le neant* (Hazel E. Barnes, Trans.). New York: Philosophical Library. This is Sartre's basic existential philosophical work, based in important part on the phenomenology of Edmund Husserl. Later, Sartre's thought took on a dialectical and Marxist caste.

Maurice Friedman

EXISTENTIAL PSYCHOLOGY. *See* Existentialism; *and* Phenomenological Psychology.

EXPECTANCY EFFECTS refer to the situation in which expectations we hold for ourselves or for others come to serve as self-fulfilling prophecies, a concept introduced to the social sciences by Merton (1948). [*See* Self-Fulfilling Prophecy.]

Two Types of Expectancy Effects

The two main types of expectancy effects are intrapersonal expectancy effects and interpersonal expectancy effects. *Intrapersonal* expectancy effects, sometimes called *self-expectancy effects*, refer to the situation in which expectations we hold for our own behavior help to bring about that behavior. When athletic coaches tell their athletes, "you can do it," they are trying to bring about an intrapersonal expectancy effect or an intrapersonal self-fulfilling prophecy. Creating a more favorable self-expectancy is believed to improve actual performance. Another everyday example of an intrapersonal expectancy effect is the well-known placebo effect in which the patients' expectation that they will respond favorably to the treatment administered actually leads them to improve even though no real treatment has been administered. (*See* Placebo Effect in Research Design.)

*Inter*personal expectancy effects refer to the situation in which it is the expectation of one person for the behavior of a different person that actually helps to bring about that behavior. This phenomenon has been investigated experimentally since the late 1950s, both in the laboratory and in everyday life. One example of interpersonal expectancy effects in everyday life was described by Robert Rosenthal and Lenore Jacobson (*Pygmalion in the Classroom*, New York, 1968/1992). In the Pygmalion experiment, all of the teachers of an elementary school were told that a newly devised computer program was able to predict the intellectual development potential of children in their classroom. At the very beginning of the school year, a handful of children's names were selected completely at random and given to their teachers, who were told that those children would bloom intellectually in the academic year just begun. At the end of the school year those children whose names had been placed arbitrarily on the list of bloomers did, in fact, show greater intellectual gains than did the children in the control group.

Perhaps more surprising than these results from everyday life were the results showing that interpersonal expectancy effects could operate even in the controlled environs of a psychological experiment in such a way that psychological experimenters who expected a certain type of result were more likely to obtain that result because they expected it.

Research on Experimenter Expectancy Effects

The first experiments designed to investigate the effects of experimenters' expectations on the results of their research employed human research participants. Graduate students and advanced undergraduates in psychology were employed to collect data from introductory psychology students. The experimenters showed a series of photographs of faces to the research participants and asked participants to rate the degree of success or failure reflected in the photographs. Half the experimenters, chosen at random, were led to expect that the research participants would rate the photos as being of more successful people. The remaining half of the experimenters were given the opposite expectation.

EXPECTANCY EFFECTS. Table 1. Strategies for the control of experimenter expectancy effects

1. Increasing the number of experimenters:
      Decreases learning of influence techniques,
      Helps to maintain blindness,
      Minimizes effects of early data returns,
      Increases generality of results,
      Randomizes expectancies,
      Permits the method of collaborative disagreement,
      Permits statistical correction of expectancy effects.

2. Observing the behavior of experimenters:
      Sometimes reduces expectancy effects,
      Permits correction for unprogrammed behavior,
      Facilitates greater standardization of experimenter
         behavior.

3. Analyzing experiments for order effects:
      Permits inference about changes in experimenter
         behavior.

4. Analyzing experiments for computational errors:
      Permits inference about expectancy effects.

5. Developing selection procedures:
      Permits prediction of expectancy effects.

6. Developing training procedures:
      Permits prediction of expectancy effects.

7. Developing a new profession of psychological experimenter:
      Maximizes applicability of controls for expectancy effects
      Reduces motivational bases for expectancy effects

8. Maintaining blind contact:
      Minimizes expectancy effects (see Table 2).

9. Minimizing experimenter-subject contact:
      Minimizes expectancy effects (see Table 2).

10. Employing expectancy control groups:
      Permits assessment of expectancy effects.

EXPECTANCY EFFECTS. Table 2. Blind and minimized contact as controls for expectancy effects

Blind Contact
A. Sources of breakdown of blindness
   1. Principal investigator
   2. Subject (side effects)

B. Procedures facilitating maintenance of blindness
   1. The total-blind procedure
   2. Avoiding feedback from the principal investigator
   3. Avoiding feedback from the subject

Minimized Contact
A. Automated data collection systems
   1. Written instructions
   2. Tape-recorded instructions
   3. Filmed instructions
   4. Televised instructions
   5. Telephoned instructions
   6. Computer-based instructions

B. Restricting unintended cues to subjects and experimenters
   1. Interposing screen between subject and experimenter
   2. Contacting fewer subjects per experimenter
   3. Having subjects or machines record responses

Despite the fact that all experimenters were instructed to conduct a perfectly standard experiment, reading only the same printed instructions to all participants, those experimenters who had been led to expect ratings of faces as being more successful obtained such ratings from their randomly assigned participants. Those experimenters who had been led to expect results in the opposite direction tended to obtain results in the opposite direction. The idea that experimenters' expectations could actually affect participants' responses in the laboratory were at first so controversial that several replications, and eventually scores of replication experiments, were conducted, the combined evidence from which was quite robust (Rosenthal & Rubin, 1978).

If the results of those experiments employing human participants were surprising, the results of experiments employing animal subjects were even more so. In the first of those experiments, experimenters were told that their laboratory was collaborating with another laboratory that had been developing genetic strains of maze-bright and maze-dull rats. The task was explained as simply observing and recording the maze-learning performance of the maze-bright and maze-dull rats. Half the experimenters were told that they had been assigned rats that were maze-bright, whereas the remaining experimenters were told that they had been assigned rats that were maze-dull. None of the rats had really been bred for maze-brightness or maze-dullness, and experimenters were told what type of rats they had been assigned purely at random. Despite the fact that the only differences between the allegedly bright and dull rats were in the minds of the experimenters, those who believed that their rats were brighter obtained brighter performance from their rats than did the experimenters who believed that their rats were duller. Essentially, the same results were obtained in a replication of this experiment employing Skinner boxes instead of mazes.

Control of Experimenter Expectancy Effects

The cumulative evidence from nearly five hundred studies demonstrates the occurrence, magnitude, and importance of interpersonal expectancy effects. To the extent that these effects occur in everyday life, we have a substantive phenomenon of great importance that is discussed in other articles. To the extent that these effects occur among psychological experimenters, we have a methodological problem that must be addressed. Although it is not possible to give the details here of various procedures that have been proposed to help control the problems created by experimenter expectancy effects, Tables 1 and 2 give a brief overview; detailed resources are listed in the Bibliography.

[*See also* Artifact, *article on* Artifact in Research.]

Bibliography

Blanck, P. D. (Ed.). (1993). *Interpersonal expectations: Theory, research, and applications*. Cambridge, England: Cambridge University Press. Broad overview of substantive and methodological aspects of interpersonal self-fulfilling prophecies.

Eden, D. (1990). *Pygmalion in management: Productivity as a self-fulfilling prophecy*. Lexington, MA: Heath. Summary of scholarship bearing on interpersonal expectations in the organizational context.

Merton, R. K. (1948). The self-fulfilling prophecy. *Antioch Review, 8*, 193–210.

Rosenthal, R. (1976). *Experimenter effects in behavioral research* (enlarged ed.). New York: Irvington. (Original work published 1966.) Early research on interpersonal expectancy effects.

Rosenthal, R., & Rosnow, R. L. (Eds.). (1969). *Artifact in behavioral research*. San Diego, CA: Academic Press. Surveys a variety of methodological problems, including experimenter expectancy effects, and suggests relationships among some of these problems.

Rosenthal, R., & Rosnow, R. L. (1991). *Essentials of behavioral research: Methods and data analysis*. New York: McGraw-Hill. Includes an introduction to experimenter expectancy effects within the context of an advanced text on research methods.

Rosenthal, R., & Rubin, D. B. (1978). Interpersonal expectancy effects: The first 345 studies. *The Behavioral and Brain Sciences, 3*, 377–386. An early quantitative summary (meta-analysis) of the accumulated research on interpersonal expectancy effects.

Rosnow, R. L., & Rosenthal, R. (1997). *People studying people: Artifacts and ethics in behavioral research*. New York: Freeman. Fairly detailed but nontechnical introduction to experimenter expectancy effects and related sources of artifact in behavioral research.

Robert Rosenthal

EXPERIENTIAL PSYCHOTHERAPY. The phrase *experiential psychotherapy* is generally recognized as being introduced in the 1950s and 1960s to refer to the distinctive psychotherapeutic approach of Carl Whitaker, Thomas Malone, John Warkentin, and Richard Felder, four American psychiatrists. Since then, the phrase has been used to identify at least two dozen different psychotherapies, and an additional two dozen or so claim membership in a rather large and somewhat loose family of experiential psychotherapies.

Even though the family is not especially tightly knit or easily identified, perhaps the main kinship is in regard to what is and what is not relied upon as the way of helping to bring about psychotherapeutic change. In general, this family declines such common ways as the client's gaining insight and understanding, the development of a new and better way of thinking, modifying what the client's behavior is supposed to be contingent upon, or changing the group of which the client is a part.

Members of the experiential family share a trusted belief that psychotherapeutic change occurs mainly through "experiencing." At a rather loose and general level, this refers to discovering and accessing, facilitating and enhancing, opening up and carrying forward, what the person is experiencing, undergoing, and feeling, both on the surface and at a deeper level inside the person.

Beyond a shared belief in this rather loose and general, but perhaps distinctive avenue of bringing about psychotherapeutic change there is plenty of healthy diversity among family members. They differ a great deal in underlying philosophies and philosophies of science, in their specific meanings of experiencing, in their underlying theories of how a person comes about in the first place, in how a person develops and changes, in conceptions of personality structure, in what a person can become, and in their methods for psychotherapeutic change.

Where is the experiential family to be placed relative to other families of psychotherapy? If families are organized into psychoanalytic-psychodynamic, cognitive-behavioral, existential-humanistic, and eclectic-integrative, then the experiential family would probably fall under the existential-humanistic umbrella. If experiential psychotherapy is thought of as valuing experiencing as the avenue of change, and if its philosophy and theory are allowed to be a little flexible, the family can be stretched to include, for example, existential therapy, client-centered therapy, Gestalt therapy, and a few others.

What are some up-close, actual examples of the experiential psychotherapies? There are perhaps four rather different cornerstones.

One is the pioneering experiential psychotherapy of Whitaker, Warkentin, Malone, and Felder, with contributions by others such as Jourard and Moustakas. Psychotherapeutic change is understood as occurring mainly through the direct, clashing encountering-meeting of the whole self of the person and the whole self of the therapist. The whole self includes not only what the person or therapist is feeling, undergoing, or aware of on the surface, but especially the world of inner, deeper, ordinarily sealed off and withdrawn, hidden thoughts, feelings, and experiencings. Change is the product of the wholesale, unrestricted opening up, disclosing, and revealing of what is deeper inside both the therapist and patient. This is the encountering-meeting. Although the theory of psychotherapy may be relatively distinctive, this experiential psychotherapy is cast within a larger psychoanalytic-psychodynamic theory of human beings and personality.

A second cornerstone experiential psychotherapy evolved from the client-centered therapy of Carl Rogers, and is exemplified by the existential writings and the psychotherapeutic approach of Eugene Gendlin. In this approach, change occurs mainly through the progressively deeper exploration, carrying forward, and unfolding of internally felt meanings. Experiencing starts by clearing a space, selecting some personal problem, and directing attention to the ensuing inner-felt sense. By enveloping this sense with the sensitively right words and images there is a release, a "give," a palpable experiential shift in the concretely and bodily felt inner sense, or meaning.

A third cornerstone experiential psychotherapy is associated with the work of Laura Rice, Leslie Greenberg, Jeremy Safran, Robert Elliott, Fred Zimring, Shaké Toukmanian, and others. Therapy opens with the identification of a problematic concern and continues with an explicit focus on and processing of feeling-affective-emotional material. This processing is important because change is held as occurring largely through the contribution of processed feeling-affective-emotional material to the reorganization or reevaluation of the cognitive-perceptual framework, the cognitive structure or schema, frame of reference, or mode of information processing in regard to oneself, one's world, or the problem of concern.

The fourth cornerstone of experiential psychotherapy is from the philosophical, theoretical, and clinical writings of Alvin Mahrer. Each session opens with the identification of a scene of powerful feelings. By entering into and living in this scene, the actual moment of peak feeling serves as an entry into the inner world of deeper experiencing. Once a deeper potential for experiencing is discovered, the person is enabled to (a) welcome and appreciate the deeper potential for experiencing; (b) undergo the radical shift out of the ordinary continuing person and into the wholesale new person, who is the deeper experiencing; and (c) become a transformed, qualitatively new person, with the formerly deeper experiencing as an integral part of the new person. Each session is an opportunity for deep-seated transformation and for being free of whatever scene of bad feeling was front and center for that session.

Inside the field of psychotherapy, the experiential family has its own distinctive ways of working with dreams, infants and children, couples and groups, and patients labeled as psychotic. Outside the field of psychotherapy, the family's conceptualizations of personality structure, the origins of personality, infant and child development, how and why change occurs, and what people can become are largely borrowed from humanistic and psychodynamic theories. However, distinctively experiential conceptualizations are emerging from the philosophies and theories of Eugene Gendlin, Alvin Mahrer, and other existential-experiential writers.

Research on experiential psychotherapy is weak and is generally directed toward the study of in-session process work rather than assessment of outcome. Indeed, a review of research on experiential psychotherapy candidly concludes that "there is relatively little systematic research on the outcomes of experiential treatments" (Greenberg, Elliott, & Lietaer, 1994).

[See also Gestalt Therapy.]

Bibliography

Gendlin, E. T. (1962). *Experiencing and the creation of meaning*. New York: Free Press.

Gendlin, E. T. (1964). A theory of personality change. In P. Worchel & D. Byrne (Eds.), *Personality change* (pp. 100–148). New York: Wiley.

Greenberg, L. S., Rice, L. N., & Elliott, R. (1993). *Facilitating emotional change: The moment-by-moment process*. New York: Guilford Press.

Greenberg, L., Elliott, R., & Lietaer, G. (1994). Research on experiential psychotherapies. In A. E. Bergin & S. L. Garfield (Eds.), *Handbook of psychotherapy and behavior change* (pp. 509–539). New York: John Wiley and Sons.

Mahrer, A. R. (1989). *Experiencing: A humanistic theory of psychology and psychiatry*. Ottawa, Canada: University of Ottawa Press.

Mahrer, A. R. (1996). *The complete guide to experiential psychotherapy*. New York: Wiley.

Moustakas, C. (1973). *Children in play therapy*. New York: Basic Books.

Prouty, G. (1994). *Theoretical evolutions in person-centered/experiential therapy: Applications to schizophrenic and retarded psychoses*. Westport, CT: Praeger.

Rice, L. N., & Greenberg, L. S. (1990). Fundamental directions in experiential therapy: New directions in research. In G. Lietaer, J. Rombauts, & R. Van Balen (Eds.), *Client-centered and experiential psychotherapy in the nineties* (pp. 397–414). Leuven, Belgium: Leuven University Press.

Whitaker, C. A., & Malone, T. P. (1953). *The roots of psychotherapy*. New York: Blakiston.

Alvin R. Mahrer

EXPERIMENTAL DESIGN. *See* Research Methods.

EXPERIMENTAL NEUROSIS. Experimental neurosis is a laboratory-induced emotional reaction that was discovered in the context of animal conditioning experiments. The discovery was made in the laboratory of Ivan P. Pavlov (1849–1936), the Russian physiologist. Pavlov's research focused on digestion and responses such as salivation and secretion of various glands as a way of understanding neurological processes. This work led to the study of learning—specifically, how reflexive responses could be elicited by various stimuli unrelated to digestion.

Experimental neurosis emerged serendipitously in conditioning of dogs in two separate experiments in 1912 and 1913. These experiments, conducted by Mariya Yerofeyeva (1867–1925) and Nataliya Shenger-Krestovnikova (1875–1947), showed that under special circumstances, conditioning of animals was disrupted; the animals became visibly agitated and lost all of the responses that had been trained up to that point. For example, in one of the experiments a dog learned to salivate in the presence of a circle, which had been paired with food, but not in the presence of an ellipse, which had not been paired with food. The animal made the discrimination between a circle and ellipse, even after the ellipse was altered gradually to resemble the circle. With a difficult discrimination, the dog became very agitated, barked violently, and attacked the apparatus, and all simple discriminations that had been learned were lost. This disturbance of the conditioned reflex and the resulting emotional reactions were termed *experimentally induced neurosis* (Pavlov, *Conditioned Reflexes: An Investigation of the Physiological Activity of the Cerebral Cortex*, London, 1927) and later came to be called *experimental neurosis*. Other researchers extended the ways of inducing these reactions and the range of species in which the reactions were demonstrated, including goats, sheep, pigs, rabbits, cats, and dogs. The range of responses that characterized experimental neurosis was vast and, depending on the species, included irritability, aggression, regressive behavior, escape and avoidance, and disturbances in physiological activity, such as pulse, heart, and respiration rates.

Pavlov hypothesized that when in conflict, two processes of the brain, inhibition and excitation, led to a disruption of behavior. His views and those of others were extended to account for psychiatric disorders and emotional reactions in humans. Over the years, reservations have been expressed as to whether laboratory-induced reactions in animals bear any more than a superficial resemblance to human anxiety and fear. Nevertheless, investigation of experimental neurosis has had significant impact on the conceptualization of psychological disorders and their treatment. For example, Joseph Wolpe, a physician working in South Africa in the early 1950s, induced experimental neurosis in cats, devised procedures to eliminate these reactions, and then extended the procedures in such a way that they could be applied to treat anxiety in humans (Wolpe, *Psychotherapy by Reciprocal Inhibition*, Stanford, CA, 1958). This work culminated in the development of systematic desensitization, an effective treatment for anxiety.

Bibliography

Gantt, W. H. (1944). *Experimental basis for neurotic behavior: Origin and development of artificially produced disturbances of behavior in dogs*. New York: Hoeber. Gantt worked in Pavlov's laboratory for several years. In 1931 he returned to the United States, where he began a laboratory devoted to the study of conditioning. He systematically studied experimental neurosis for over a decade. This book traces that work and is an extensive treatise on the topic.

Kazdin, A. E. (1978). *History of behavior modification: Experimental foundations of contemporary research*. Baltimore: University Park Press. This book discusses experimental neurosis and its impact on research, psychopathology, and therapy.

Masserman, J. H. (1944). *Behavior and neurosis: An experimental psycho-analytic approach to psychobiologic principles*. Chicago: University of Chicago Press. Masserman, a psychiatrist, conducted research on experimental neurosis primarily with cats. He extended the concepts of conditioning and experimental neurosis to explain psychoanalytic theory and therapy. He also explored various techniques with cats that could be used to ameliorate experimental neuroses. This work is significant in showing the conceptual and empirical extensions of experimental neurosis to psychotherapy.

Alan E. Kazdin

EXPERIMENTAL PSYCHOLOGY. Edwin G. Boring, a historian of experimental psychology, claimed that "the application of the experimental method to the problem of mind is the great outstanding event in the history of the study of mind, an event to which no other is comparable." Producing a comparison by manipulating independent variables and observing their effects on dependent variables (measured behavior) defines the basic methodology of experimental psychology. This method allows the psychologist to determine causal relations between the manipulated and measured variables.

The Nineteenth Century

The birth of experimental psychology usually is cited as 1879, when Wilhelm Wundt opened his psychology laboratory at the University of Leipzig. Wundt, however, had many precursors who experimented on psychological phenomena. Important compatriots include Ernst Weber, who studied the sense of touch and Gustav

Fechner, who developed psychophysical methods. Hermann von Helmholtz made a variety of experimental contributions in sensory and neural physiology and is known for his books summarizing the psychology and physiology of vision and hearing.

In the United States, William James and his students at Harvard University scientifically studied psychology while Wundt was developing his laboratory. James had a psychological laboratory at Harvard that may have opened prior to Wundt's at Leipzig, although there is controversy about this possibility.

Wundt rates as founder of experimental psychology because of two legacies. The first relates to his written contributions to early psychological thought, which counted over 50,000 pages in 491 items. One of his books went through 15 editions, and Wundt founded the first journal devoted to experimental psychology, *Philosophische Studien*, in 1881.

The second legacy results from his teaching and advising. Wundt directed 186 doctoral dissertations, and the Leipzig laboratory was cosmopolitan, with students coming not only from Europe but also from Russia and the United States. Many of his students became major figures in the history of experimental psychology.

Although Wundt's importance should not be underestimated, many early figures in experimental psychology did not have direct ties to him. Some prominent ones include: Franciscus Donders (reaction time), Hermann Ebbinghaus (human memory), Ewald Hering (color vision), Oswald Külpe (perception), and Edward L. Thorndike (animal learning).

The laboratories of James and Wundt were quickly emulated. This was the case especially in North America, where over 40 psychological laboratories were established by the end of the nineteenth century.

Schools of Psychology

Around 1900, different approaches to experimental psychology cohered into schools of thought that dominated theory and research for nearly four decades. These schools are: structuralism, functionalism, behaviorism, and Gestalt psychology. Their research and theoretical disagreements provided an intellectually rich background for contemporary experimental psychology.

Structuralism. Edward B. Titchener studied with Wundt and later went to Cornell University. Titchener proclaimed that psychology's subject matter is mind with consciousness as the direct object of examination. Consciousness represented the sum of current mental processes, and the task of the experimenter involved selecting some point to obtain data. To obtain these data, structuralists used introspection as their primary method of investigation. Because introspection required well-trained observers to make accurate verbal reports of their conscious elements, structuralists studied the "generalized normal adult mind," ignoring behavior as

data and ignoring animals, children, and humans with limited verbal skills.

Titchener thought his approach was rigorous and experimental; however, the school ran into serious difficulties owing to heavy reliance on introspection. Introspective reports lack reliability across observers, and they lack validity because they cannot be independently corroborated. Thus, moot controversies arose between introspectionists in different laboratories, resulting in vigorous attacks against introspection, especially by the behaviorists and Gestalt psychologists. Structuralism as a school died when Titchener died, but its legacy was profound. Structuralism served as a target on which the other schools practiced their theories and methods.

Functionalism. If structuralism examined the *is* of mental life, then functionalism studied what mental life *is for*. Functionalism tried to apply Darwinian survival notions to psychology by minimizing introspection of consciousness and emphasizing how basic psychological processes fit into an organism's adaptation. Thereby, animals, children, and the demented became objects of study in contrast to structuralism.

The broader scope demanded methodology other than introspecton, and the functionalists were among the first to study animals in controlled circumstances. One aim involved studying how learning led to adaptation. Thorndike, among the first animal experimentalists, developed procedures now known as instrumental conditioning. Thorndike and his colleagues at Columbia University, James McKeen Cattell and Robert S. Woodworth, were a prominent group of functionalists, along with those at the University of Chicago, who included James Angell and Harvey Carr. One of Angell's students, John B. Watson, later rebelled against the remnants of mentalism in functionalism and founded a new school of thought.

Behaviorism. John B. Watson's agenda focused on ridding psychology of mentalistic concepts that he believed led to sloppy science:

> Psychology as the behaviorist sees it is a purely objective, experimental branch of natural science. Its theoretical goal is the prediction and control of behavior. Introspection forms no essential part of its methods nor is the scientific value of its data dependent on the readiness with which they lend themselves to interpretation in terms of consciousness. The behaviorist, in his efforts to get a unitary scheme of animal responses, recognizes no dividing lines between man and brute. ([1913]. Psychology as the behaviorist sees it. *Psychological Review, 20,* 158–177)

Watson's manifesto rested on the success of his early animal research. His dissertation, written in 1907, as well as other research he did at Chicago, concerned how rats learned mazes. These methodologically clever experiments had a major impact on experimental psychology that is still seen today. While still in graduate school, he conducted field studies on bird behavior, as well as research on a variety of animals. He accepted a position in the department of psychology at Johns Hopkins University in 1908.

In his 12 years at Hopkins, Watson's influence on psychology grew. He undertook famous studies on the classical conditioning of emotions in children, and he popularized the conditioning methods of Ivan Pavlov. Watson was fired in 1920 as a result of a marital scandal, and he had only occasional ties to academic psychology thereafter. Nevertheless, Watson had a substantial impact on experimental psychology. Because its main dependent variables are behaviors, experimental psychology today can be characterized as behavioristic

Gestalt Psychology. On the basis of perceptual phenomena such as apparent movement, the Gestalt psychologists developed theories contrary to the atomistic and analytic approaches of most experimentalists. The school began in Germany around 1912 under the aegis of Max Wertheimer and his students Wolfgang Köhler and Kurt Koffka. With the rise of Nazism, these psychologists came to the United States.

Gestalt roughly means "whole" or "form," and this notion appears in the creed of Gestalt psychology: the whole is different from the sum of its parts. Thus, breaking a percept into its components is a counterproductive way of understanding it. This idea was also applied to animal learning by emphasizing insight and intelligence rather than conditioned reflexes. Later, Kurt Lewin extended the notion to motivation and social behavior. Although the molar approach of the Gestaltists tempered the excesses of structuralism and behaviorism, their early impact was limited. Later, a Gestalt flavor appears in contemporary cognitive psychology.

Learning Theory

From the middle 1930s to the late 1950s, a major topic of concern of experimental psychologists was learning. Students of animal learning, such as Edwin Guthrie, Clark Hull, B. F. Skinner, Kenneth Spence, and Edward C. Tolman, dominated the literature of psychology and broadened the conditioning techniques of Pavlov, Thorndike, and Watson. Hull's influence extended to personality theory and social psychology, and Skinner's ideas were applied to teaching and the treatment of behavior disorders.

Contemporaneously, several experimentalists focused on human learning. Extending the general method used by Ebbinghaus, Arthur Melton and Benton Underwood studied the learning and memory of simple verbal items under controlled conditions.

Contemporary Experimental Psychology

Much of contemporary experimental psychology focuses on cognition leading to cognitive psychology and experimental psychology often being used as synonyms. Interest in cognition began with information processing theory. George Miller and Herbert Simon were the pioneers of this approach, in which data processing by digital computers provided a metaphor for cognition. Cognitive psychologists use experiments to test theories of the inner workings of the mind/brain in contrast to a behavioristic approach. This appealing method resulted in a reliance on experimentation to study language, social psychology, human factors, and industrial psychology. Furthermore, cognitive psychology has led to a dramatic increase in the use of physiological methods as tools for understanding. Thus, experimental psychologists may use magnetic resonance imaging or electroencephalography to study cognition.

The behavioristic heritage is not dead. Conditioning remains a focus of many experimental psychologists, and conditioning techniques are widely used to investigate the physiological substrates of behavior.

[*See also* Animal Learning and Behavior.]

Bibliography

Anderson, J. R. (1995). *Learning and memory.* New York: Wiley. Includes a survey of contemporary work on basic learning and conditioning phenomena, as well as an overview of research on memory.

Boring, E. G. (1950). *A history of experimental psychology* (2nd ed.). New York: Appleton-Century-Crofts. The standard reference work on the history of experimental psychology. A long, detailed work that is worth the effort.

Gardner, H. (1985). *The mind's new science: A history of the cognitive revolution.* New York: Basic Books. A readable history of the development of cognitive psychology and cognitive science.

Hearst, E. (Ed.). (1979). *The first century of experimental psychology.* Hillsdale, NJ: Erlbaum. Published on experimental psychology's centennial, the book contains excellent chapters on the schools of psychology, animal learning, and cognition. This is an advanced treatment.

Hilgard, E. R. (1987). *Psychology in America: A historical survey.* San Diego: Harcourt Brace Jovanovich. An interesting, advanced analysis of many of the issues discussed in this entry.

Hothersall, D. (1995). *History of psychology* (3rd ed.). New York: McGraw-Hill. A college-level textbook that has interesting vignettes of many figures in the history of experimental psychology.

Kantowitz, B. H., Roediger, H. R., & Elmes, D. G. (1997). *Experimental psychology: Understanding psychological research* (6th ed.). Minneapolis: West. A college textbook that includes a discussion of how to conduct valid experiments.

Sternberg, R. J. (1996). *Cognitive psychology.* Fort Worth, TX: Harcourt Brace.

David G. Elmes

EXPERIMENTATION. *See* Ethics, *article on* Ethics in Research.

EXPERTISE. *See* Thinking, *article on* Problem Solving.

EXPERT TESTIMONY. Psychologists testify as expert witnesses in legal settings on a variety of issues. The most frequent appearances are by clinicians who assist courts in making evaluations that involve judgments about mental health, such as competency to stand trial and custody decisions. Psychologists in nonclinical specialties also appear as expert witnesses. For example, psychologists testify on scientific findings concerning eyewitness accuracy and present survey results measuring potential jury prejudice in support of motions for a change of venue. Psychologists also testify on topics such as test construction and about employee recruitment and evaluation in cases involving allegations of employment discrimination.

Expert witnesses are permitted to offer scientific, technical, and other specialized information that will assist the trier of fact (Federal Rule of Evidence 702). Psychologists who are called upon to testify as experts should be prepared to demonstrate how their training, education, and experience have qualified them to provide relevant information that will aid in the resolution of the issues under consideration. Evidence of relevant expertise may include coursework and degrees, research and publications, and employment experience.

Unlike ordinary fact witnesses, experts are permitted to offer reports about behavior not involving the parties in the case at hand, give opinions, and derive their testimony from methods used by professionals in the expert's field. The admissibility and boundaries of permissible expert testimony are frequently matters of controversy, particularly in jury trials, in part due to concerns that experts will exert undue influence on the jury. For example, although the Federal Rules of Evidence (F.R.E.) permit experts to offer any helpful information, experts testifying about the mental state or condition of a defendant in a criminal trial are explicitly prohibited from offering an opinion on the so-called ultimate issue, that is, whether the defendant did or did not have the mental state or condition constituting an element of the crime charged or of a defense offered to that crime (F.R.E. 704 [b]). As a result, a psychologist in a federal court would be permitted to testify that the defendant was suffering from psychosis, but might be prohibited from giving an opinion on the defendant's ability to "appreciate the nature and quality or wrongfulness of his acts" (*U.S. v. Meader*, 914 F. Supp. 656 [1996]). There is little evidence that jurors are more

likely to be influenced by an expert opinion on the ultimate issue than by other case-specific testimony that has clear implications for the ultimate issue.

Courts have struggled with the expanding scope of expert testimony based on scientific evidence that parties have attempted to introduce in recent years. In *Daubert v. Merrell-Dow Pharmaceuticals* (113 S. Ct. 2786 [1993]), the U.S. Supreme Court focused attention on the role of judge as gatekeeper in determining what allegedly scientific evidence a jury should be permitted to hear. The Court held that federal judges must evaluate not only the expert's qualifications, but also the validity of the expert's methodology. The Court provided a nonexhaustive list of four factors that could be used in making these evaluations: (1) testability (or falsifiability) of the theory or technique; (2) whether the theory or technique has been subjected to peer review and publication; (3) the known or potential rate of error and the existence and maintenance of standards controlling the technique's operation; and (4) acceptance within a relevant scientific community. Although *Daubert* applies in all federal courts and has been followed in a number of state courts as well, some states follow the so-called Frye rule in evaluating scientific testimony. Under *Frye v. United States* (293 F. 1013 [D.C. Cir. 1923]), scientific testimony is admissible if the witness's tests and procedures have gained "general acceptance" within the relevant scientific or technical community. In *Kumho Tire Co. v. Carmichael* (560 U.S. 137 [1999]), the U.S. Supreme Court extended the reach of *Daubert* beyond scientific testimony to expert testimony based on technical and other specialized knowledge. The Court held that the trial court judge has a gatekeeping obligation to condition the admissibility of expert testimony on a determination of reliability, which may involve an application of the factors described in *Daubert*. Thus, psychologists offering clinical evaluations in federal courts or in states following *Daubert* may be subject to the factors outlined in *Daubert*.

Experts who agree to serve as witnesses may see themselves as serving in a number of potentially conflicting roles. They may see themselves as educators whose obligation is to provide the fact finder with information about their area of expertise. As representatives of their field, educators do not see themselves as representing a partisan position. An alternative role is as an advocate for a particular cause or position who presents evidence that favors only that position. Some experts are said to play a third role, that of a "hired gun." Hired guns do not merely offer testimony that supports a party when that position is consistent with their own analysis; they are willing to offer an opinion helpful to any party willing to pay for their services.

The ambiguity of these potentially conflicting roles may be one reason why fact finders are often suspicious of experts who are hired by the parties. Resourceful attorneys may be able to identify an expert whose views are sympathetic to the position of the attorney's client but are not well grounded. Moreover, the adversary system can sometimes bias even disinterested witnesses in favor of the side for whom they are testifying. Both jurors and judges seem to agree that court-appointed experts are a promising means of improving impartiality. Nevertheless, most judges, reluctant to interfere with the adversary system, rarely appoint experts. Attorneys also resist the use of court-appointed experts, preferring to maintain greater control by hiring their own experts.

Although courts depend on scientific experts to assist the trier of fact in resolving a variety of complex disputes, the relationship between experts and the legal system is sometimes uncomfortable for both. Judges and jurors express some dissatisfaction with lack of clarity in the testimony that experts present, complaining that some experts use unnecessarily technical language. Experts who wish to qualify their opinions find that attorneys press them to be less tentative or to express opinions that are outside their area of expertise. Experts also know that the attorneys who retain them use a variety of strategies to influence the expert to present testimony that is favorable to their client. These perceptions appear to discourage some experts from participating in legal proceedings, but it is not clear how much this affects the expert testimony that finds its way to court or the extent to which it would be changed by greater use of court-appointed experts.

One concern about expert testimony is that it will exert undue influence on the trier of fact. However, most research suggests that experts have a limited impact on fact finders and that lay persons do not accept the claims of experts uncritically. The testimony of a disinterested lay witness may be perceived as more persuasive than that of an expert who is paid by one of the parties. Expert testimony is most persuasive when it is case specific (e.g., based on the evaluation of an eyewitness versus based on a summary of general eyewitness research findings), provides a causal explanation (i.e., fact finders are told the reasons behind the expert's findings versus simply presented with the findings), and uses concrete examples (e.g., the majority of rapists watch for a victim and approach her with rape in mind) as opposed to abstract statements (e.g., the majority of rapes are planned in advance). Moreover, expert testimony on some topics can influence how fact finders evaluate other types of testimony. For example, expert testimony on the conditions under which eyewitness testimony is more or less trustworthy can sensitize the trier of fact to considerations that may affect the accuracy of an eyewitness identification.

Another concern regarding expert testimony is that fact finders may fail to understand or apply it accurately. For example, experts may use technical jargon or present complex quantitative information that challenge the fact finders' ability to absorb and comprehend the testimony. Fact finders may react in one of two ways. In some cases, they may discount the expert's message due to the lack of clarity, resulting in a reduction in the expert's influence. In other cases, they may turn to peripheral cues, like an expert's credentials or demeanor, to determine what weight the message should receive. We currently know little about how often and the conditions under which each of these reactions occurs. If either occurs, however, the fact finders' conclusions will not be influenced by the substantive information in the expert's testimony.

The adversarial nature of the legal system provides some potential checks on the influence of defective expert testimony. In theory, cross-examination and the opportunity to present an opposing witness can be relied upon to provide appropriate countervailing forces. It is unclear how effective such correctives actually are in counteracting the influence of an experienced witness. In particular, if the witness is presenting a position that is consistent with strong juror values, the adversarial process may fail to prevent unwarranted acceptance of the expert's testimony. The influence of evidence that contradicts the expert's testimony is likely to depend on a variety of factors. For instance, fact finders find eyewitness testimony to be quite compelling—perhaps even more compelling than they find many kinds of scientific evidence that are arguably more reliable.

When the contradictory evidence is an opposing expert's testimony, a common hypothesis is that the two experts will cancel each other out either because fact finders will infer that the lack of consensus means that science has little of probative value to say about the issue or because it will cause fact finders to dismiss both experts as obviously partisan. Fact finders may also rely on other strategies to evaluate conflicting expert opinions, such as taking the average of competing damages award estimates, or deferring to the expert who is more confident or better credentialed. Although there is some evidence to support these hypotheses, more systematic research is necessary.

Some legal scholars, scientists, and judges (e.g., Supreme Court Justice Stephen Breyer's concurrence in *General Electric Co. v. Joiner*, 118 S. Ct. 512, 520 [1997]) have identified court-appointed experts as a promising way to improve the caliber of expert information in the courtroom. Others have raised concerns that fact finders will unquestioningly accept the testimony of a court-appointed expert without giving it the degree of scrutiny they would afford evidence presented by the parties. What little research exists in this area suggests that fact finders are not unduly impressed by court-appointed expert testimony. Moreover, if a court-appointed expert is used, the parties are entitled to cross-examine the expert witness, just as they would the witness of an adversary, and to put their own rebuttal experts on the witness stand. However, issues of both cost and control may limit expansion of the use of court-appointed experts.

Although most work on the influence of expert testimony has focused on lay fact finders, cognitive limitations and leaps in inference are not the exclusive province of the jury. Thus, judges may be susceptible to some of the same limitations.

Expert testimony may also exert a strong influence on cases before trial, affecting the many cases in which parties settle or a defendant pleads guilty. For example, the identity of the expert hired by the opposing side or the report or testimony of an opposing expert at a deposition may influence an attorney's assessment of the risk in going to trial. At this time, there is little information about the role played by experts in the pretrial phase.

Bibliography

Brekke, N., & Borgida, E. (1988). Expert psychological testimony in rape trials: A social-cognitive analysis. *Journal of Personality and Social Psychology, 55,* 372–386.

Brodsky, S. L. (1991). *Testifying in court: Guidelines and maxims for the expert witness.* Washington, DC: American Psychological Association.

Cecil, J. S., & Willging, T. S. (1994). Accepting *Daubert's* invitation: Defining a role for court-appointed experts in assessing scientific validity. *Emory Law Journal, 43,* 995–1070.

Cutler, B. L., Penrod, S. D., & Dexter, H. R. (1989). The eyewitness, the expert psychologist, and the jury. *Law and Human Behavior, 13,* 311–332.

Diamond, S. S., & Casper, J. D. (1992). Blindfolding the jury to verdict consequences: Damages, experts, and the civil jury. *Law and Society Review, 26,* 513–563.

Faigman, D. L., Kaye, D. H., Saks, M. J., & Sanders, J. (1997). *Modern scientific evidence: The law and science of expert testimony* (Vol. 1–2). St. Paul, MN: West.

Golding, S. L. (Ed.). (1992). [Special issue]. *Law and Human Behavior, 16.*

Kovera, M. B., Levy, R. J., Borgida, E., & Penrod, S. D. (1994). Expert testimony in child sexual abuse cases: Effects of expert evidence type and cross-examination. *Law and Human Behavior, 18,* 653–674.

Raitz, A., Greene, E., Goodman, J., & Loftus, E. (1990). Determining damages: The influence of expert testimony on jurors' decision-making. *Law and Human Behavior, 14,* 385–395.

Schuller, R. A., & Hastings, P. A. (1996). Trials of battered women who kill: The impact of alternative forms of expert evidence. *Law and Human Behavior, 20,* 167–181.

Vidmar, N., & Laird, N. M. (1983). Adversary social roles: Their effects on witnesses' communication of evidence

and the assessments of adjudicators. *Journal of Personality and Social Psychology, 44,* 888–898.

Shari Diamond and Jason Schklar

EXPERT WITNESSES. *See* Expert Testimony.

EXPLICIT MEMORY. *See the overview article on* Memory.

EXPLORATORY DATA ANALYSIS (EDA) is a statistical tradition originated by John Tukey with the aim of understanding data in the broadest possible set of circumstances. EDA is primarily a bottom-up or data-driven approach that seeks to find patterns in data that suggest tentative hypotheses for subsequent assessment using traditional statistical methods which Tukey called confirmatory data analysis (CDA).

Tukey conceptualized EDA as a part of the continuum of data analysis that could be broken into three general stages. First, EDA deals with answering the question, What is going on here? in an attempt to learn from data even when the classical statistical assumptions do not hold. In a second stage, called rough confirmatory data analysis, researchers undertake the tasks of refining hypotheses and conducting rough tests, often using confidence intervals or other estimation techniques. In the final stage, called strict CDA, researchers test well-specified hypotheses following the decision-making approach to statistical tests. Some authors discuss the idea of working in the "exploratory mode." This reference to *mode* reflects the idea that it is not mathematical technique per se that makes an analysis EDA, but rather the set of assumptions and the range of valid conclusions that can follow from the work. For example, a factorial analysis of variance can be computed and interpreted in an exploratory mode if the hypotheses are not strictly held, if the goal is to get a rough understanding of the structure of the data, and if the conclusions are considered provisional with nothing tested or proven in the probabilistic sense. True EDA, however, would also employ the common tools of that tradition.

In their book *Understanding Robust and Exploratory Data Analysis* (1983), D. Hoaglin, F. Mosteller, and John Tukey argue that the tools of EDA are arranged around four themes: resistance, residuals, reexpression, and revelation. Resistance refers to the use of estimators that are not easily affected by small perturbations in the data. This arises from the recognition that data often come in unexpected forms, with aberrant individuals or subgroups that may mislead the summary from the bulk of the data. Accordingly, in EDA, the median is the most common measure of central tendency, even though its standard error is larger than that of the mean. This is because in the early stages of research a primary goal is to avoid being misled by outliers. After general patterns are well understood and the goal shifts to estimating and testing specific parameters, an emphasis on the efficiency of an estimate is more appropriate.

Residuals lie at the heart of EDA. Residuals are the deviations of observations from the value predicted by a tentative model. In both CDA and EDA, residuals are summarized to get a sense of overall fit. In EDA, however, residuals are also examined individually to see in what ways the model fits and does not fit the data. Here the goal is to find out which observations are well predicted and which are poorly fit. This matches the adage from the EDA tradition, that one must "impose structure to reveal structure." For example, it is common for those working with regression models to assume the underlying function is linear whether or not evidence has been collected to support this. The use of linear regression imposes a linear prediction structure and creates residuals that will have an observable nonlinear pattern if the data themselves are not linear in form. In EDA, residuals are used to modify tentative models until the form of the model fits the form of the data. This provides an accurate, yet tentative, model that can be tested in subsequent analyses on different data.

Reexpression is the term used in EDA for rescaling or transforming. Reexpression is a mainstay of EDA because data often are collected in forms based on convenience or habit rather than careful attention to scaling. Tukey's *Exploratory Data Analysis* (1977) and F. Mosteller's and John Tukey's *Data Analysis and Regression: A Second Course in Statistics* (1977) provide detailed discussions of the EDA view of data types and techniques for finding more easily interpreted scales through reexpression. Appropriate reexpression is preferred insofar as it leads to symmetric distributions that promote the interpretation of general linear models, improve comparison across groups, and reflect the structure of the sampling distributions. A number of reexpressions commonly used in EDA are also common in the psychological literature, including logarithmic, arcsine, and reciprocal transformations. Writing in volume 5 of *Memory and Cognition* (1977), H. Wainer argued that while many researchers assume that reaction time is the appropriate scale of measure, $1/$ (reaction time) = speed. Because speed is easily interpreted and often has a more symmetric distribution than reaction time, it is likely to be preferred on empirical grounds if no forceful theoretical reason for choosing between the two scales exists.

To promote the revelation of unexpected aspects of the data, EDA emphasizes the use of graphic representations of data and statistical summaries. To portray data, Tukey devised a number of plots that are now standard options in computing packages, including stem-and-leaf plots and the box plot. To portray statistical summaries, Tukey devised schematic plots for detecting patterns in time-series data, representing the predicted values in additive factorial models, plots for the comparison of empirical distributions with theoretical ones, and variations of residual plots. Tukey's work in EDA greatly influenced the development of statistical theories for graphic data analysis and data visualization.

Most psychological research programs emphasize the importance of theory-generated hypotheses and the application of strict statistical tests via confidence intervals, or p-values. This emphasis on the final analyses of data tend to leave the preliminary stages, where EDA is most valuable, overlooked and undervalued. However, statements of discontent with the sole use of statistical tests have led to increased interest in EDA. EDA supplements rather than supplants CDA, and exploratory data analysis is seen as a way to increase the breadth of appropriate questions and tools.

[*See also* Data Analysis.]

Bibliography

Behrens, J. T. (1997). Principles and procedures of exploratory data analysis. *Psychological Methods, 2,* 131–160. A review of EDA for psychologists, including reanalysis of psychological data from the EDA perspective.

Cleveland, W. S. (Ed.). (1988). *The collected works of John W. Tukey: Vol. 5. Graphics.* Belmont, CA: Wadsworth. A broad collection of Tukey's work in the theory and practice of graphic data analysis.

Cleveland, W. S. (1993). *Visualizing data.* Summit, NJ: Hobart Press. A reference regarding the application of graphics in EDA.

Hoaglin, D. C., Mosteller, F., & Tukey, J. (Eds.). (1983). *Understanding robust and exploratory data analysis.* New York: Wiley. A collection of essays addressing statistical aspects of EDA theory, robustness, and resistance.

Hoaglin, D. C., Mosteller, F., & Tukey, J. (Eds.). (1985). *Exploring data tables, trends, and shapes.* New York: Wiley. A collection of essays addressing statistical aspects of multiway tables of data, robust regression, and the shape of distributions.

Hoaglin, D. C., Mosteller, F., & Tukey, J. (Eds.). (1991). *Fundamentals of exploratory analysis of variance.* New York: Wiley.

Jones, L. V. (Ed.). (1986a). *The collected works of John W. Tukey: Vol. 3. Philosophy and principles of data analysis (1949–1964).* Belmont, CA: Wadsworth.

Jones, L. V. (Ed.). (1986b). *The collected works of John W. Tukey: Vol. 4. Philosophy and principles of data analysis*

(1965–1986). Belmont, CA: Wadsworth. A broad collection of Tukey's writing about the theory and practice of EDA.

Mosteller, F., & Tukey, J. W. (1977). *Data analysis and regression: A second course in statistics*. Reading, MA: Addison-Wesley. The second standard text of EDA, along with *Exploratory Data Analysis*. Numerous examples of working with data in the regression context. Computationally outdated, it still provides excellent guidance for working in exploratory and rough confirmatory modes.

Tukey, J. W. (1997). *Exploratory data analysis*. Reading, MA: Addison-Wesley. The canonical work on EDA that led to many current practices in data analysis. Designed as a work-as-you-go book, the use of hand computations are now outdated, although insights regarding data analysis in general remain valuable.

Wainer, H. (1977). *Memory and Cognition*, 5, 278–280.

John T. Behrens

EXTRASENSORY PRECEPTION. *See* Parapsychology.

EXTRAVERSION AND INTROVERSION. Extraversion-introversion (hereafter called extraversion, or E) is a broad personality trait that refers most generally to a person's overall orientation to the social world. People whose overall orientation falls closer to the extravert end of this trait continuum are especially sociable, outgoing, gregarious, spontaneous, talkative, and energetic. By contrast, those at the introverted end are described as relatively more withdrawn, retiring, reserved, inhibited, quiet, and deliberate. In a general sense, extraverts are more oriented to the external social world, whereas introverts are more oriented to the internal private world. In that individual differences in E are usually thought to assume a normal distribution in any given group or culture, many individuals may be placed in the middle of the continuum, showing a mixture of extraverted and introverted tendencies.

The Evolution of the Concept

The idea that some people are outgoing and sociable while others are more private and withdrawn is an extraordinarily common attribution of human individuality and appears to be well represented in many, if not most, of the world's languages. In addition, E has an impressive historical pedigree. In the ancient Greek typology of the four temperaments (attributed to Galen, around 200 CE), the cheerful sanguine type and the volatile choleric type are both generally extraverted, while the stoic phlegmatic and depressive melancholic types exhibit the introversion pole of this dimension. The distinction between extraversion and introversion

was reframed in the philosophical writings of Immanuel Kant in the eighteenth century and brought forward to modern times in the writings of such pioneers in psychological science as Wilhelm Wundt, Ivan Pavlov, Charles Spearman, and J. P. Guilford. Within modern psychology, the concept of E is most closely associated with the clinical writings of Carl Jung and the wide-ranging empirical work of Hans Eysenck.

In *Psychological Types* (1923/1971), Carl Jung couched the distinction between extraversion and introversion in terms of psychic energy. For the extravert, psychic energy tends to flow outward, in the direction of people and objects. The extravert is engaged by the outside world, is drawn to social activities and real-world pursuits, is strongly influenced by the social world and often seeks to have strong influence on it as well. By contrast, the introvert finds that psychic energy flows generally inward. The introvert turns away from social life and invests instead in the subjective world of private thought, feeling, and fantasy. Jung tended to view E as a bimodal trait: People tend to be either extraverted or introverted in the overall. Furthermore, the person who is extraverted in conscious daily life is likely to be introverted in the unconscious (e.g., in dreams), and vice versa.

Beginning with *Dimensions of Personality* (1947), Hans Eysenck sought to establish a rigorous scientific program for investigating the manifestations, origins, and consequences of E. He eschewed Jung's speculations about psychic energy and intrapsychic harmony in favor of an approach that emphasized precise measurement, careful laboratory experimentation, and neurophysiological explanations for individual differences in personality traits. Eysenck's factor analytic studies of self-report trait scales convinced him that extraversion (E) and neuroticism (N) were the two basic traits in all of personality, accounting for the most important individual differences seen in socio-emotional functioning. (Later, Eysenck added to the mix a third broad trait, called psychoticism.) Nonetheless, both Jung and Eysenck described extraverts as outgoing, sociable, and enthusiastic, but also somewhat impulsive and heedless. Introverts were seen as more quiet and withdrawn, but also more deliberate and contemplative.

Since the time of Jung's and Eysenck's original formulations, the concept of E has evolved in at least three different directions. First, the aspect of E having to do with energy level and social dominance has assumed more prominence in definitions of the construct. To that effect, some theorists prefer the label of "surgency" over "extraversion." Second, while both Jung and Eysenck viewed the extravert to be more impulsive than the introvert, the construct of impulsivity has migrated away from the center of E and, in some current conceptualizations, has found itself aligned with other groups of traits. Jeffrey Gray, for example, recast

Eysenck's two-dimensional trait space—bisected by the orthogonal dimensions of extraversion and neuroticism—in terms of two alternative dimensions, impulsivity and anxiety, each of which is positioned at 45-degree angles to E and N. In Gray's scheme, the highly impulsive individual is high on both E and N.

In another formulation, many contemporary trait theorists now divide up the universe of broad individual differences into five basic domains—the "Big Five" trait clusters, labeled by Paul Costa and Robert McCrae (1990) as extraversion, neuroticism, agreeableness, conscientiousness, and openness to experience. In this five-factor scheme, impulsiveness is viewed to be a facet of neuroticism rather than extraversion.

In a third change in the meaning of E, some theorists have found the empirical literature (described below) linking E to positive emotional experiences so impressive that they have argued that E itself is fundamentally a tendency to experience positive affect. David Watson and Auke Tellegen, for example, have reconceptualized the dimensions of E and N as positive affectivity and negative affectivity, respectively. While many psychologists are reluctant to reduce extraversion to a matter of emotional valence, a tendency toward positive emotionality has become a salient feature in current characterizations of E.

Correlates of Extraversion

Extraversion is arguably the most well-researched and scientifically well-established dimension of personality. Stimulated in large part by Eysenck's ambitious agenda for this trait, researchers have published hundreds of studies documenting associations between extraversion and a wide range of cognitive, emotional, and social variables. For example, extraverts talk more and sooner in a variety of social interactions than do introverts; they engage in more eye contact; they have larger friendship networks and more social support; they seek out social activities for leisure-time pursuits; they do more gambling; they engage in more sexual activity; and they are more likely to reside in households with other people rather than living alone. In the occupational realm, extraverts are more drawn to and tend to excel in occupations that involve dealing directly with other people, such as sales, marketing, personnel work, and teaching. By contrast, introverts tend to prefer jobs and professions in which they are more likely to work alone or in which social interaction is less sustained and intense, sharing interests with artists, mathematicians, engineers, researchers, and the like.

Laboratory research has also examined relations between E and various forms of cognitive performance. Extraverts and introverts show different cognitive strengths and weaknesses. For example, extroverts tend to show superior performance to introverts on tasks requiring divided attention, resistance to distraction, and resistance to interference. Relative to introverts, extraverted locomotive drivers show better detection of railway signal stimuli, extraverted post office trainees tend to perform better on speeded mail-sorting tasks, and extraverted television viewers show better short-term recall of television news broadcasts. Conversely, introverts tend to perform better on tasks requiring vigilance and careful attention to detail. Some evidence suggests that introverts show better long-term memory for words and superior performance under conditions of very low arousal, as when deprived of sleep. To the extent that differences are found in learning styles, extraverts tend to show a preference for speed over accuracy, whereas introverts focus more on accuracy over speed. Extraverts are "geared to respond" and introverts are "geared to inspect."

A significant body of research has found that E is positively associated with reports of feeling good about life. In other words, extraverts report greater levels of positive affect in everyday life than do introverts. E is consistently and positively associated with measures of subjective well-being. Typically, subjective well-being includes assessments of both positive and negative emotions. E tends to predict positive emotions, but tends to be unrelated to negative emotions. By contrast, the trait of neuroticism tends to be associated with measures of negative emotions but not positive emotions. Put simply, extraverts, compared to introverts, tend to report higher levels of positive affect but not necessarily lower levels of negative affect, and individuals high in N tend to report higher levels of negative affect but not necessarily lower levels of positive affect than individuals low in N.

Researchers have begun to examine possible reasons for the connection between E and positive affect. Among the explanations that have been offered include the possibilities that individuals high in E tend to ignore negative or punishing stimuli in their environment, recall past events in especially positive ways, enjoy higher levels of social skill and interpersonal competence, and receive more social support and experience more social reinforcement, compared to introverts. Despite the consistent associations displayed between positive feelings and E, evidence also suggests that under certain circumstances E can be linked to lower levels of well-being. For example, extraverts report lower levels of positive affect than do introverts when they are alone.

The Nature of Extraversion

In the last twenty years, a number of longitudinal studies have shown that interindividual differences in many personality traits tend to be relatively stable over time, especially during the adult years. Among the most impressive evidence is that garnered for the trait of extraversion. In one study, for instance, self-report assessments of E showed test-retest correlations of over +.70

across a 6- to 12-year span among individuals ranging in age from 17 to 85. In a 50-year longitudinal investigation, self-report and spouse ratings of personality descriptors indicative of E showed striking interindividual consistency. Cross-sectional studies suggest that older adults tend to be slightly more introverted as a group than younger adults. Still what appears to show substantial consistency is the relative rankings of individuals on the trait of E. Furthermore, as with many other traits, twin studies suggest that individual differences in E can be accounted for by genetic differences between people to a moderate extent, revealing heritability quotients in the +.40 to +.50 range.

Given the empirical evidence for heritability, many psychologists now suspect that E has a substantial biological substrate. In *The Biological Basis of Personality* (1967), Hans Eysenck proposed that individual differences in E are grounded in differences in arousal mediated by the brain's ascending reticular activation system. In a nutshell, he argued that introverts are dispositionally more aroused than extraverts. In that all people seek out an optimal level of cortical arousal, social stimulation moves introverts to that level more quickly than it does extraverts, causing introverts to inhibit social responding and avoid social situations that push them past the optimal arousal level. By contrast, extraverts seek out more and more stimulation; they are "stimulus hungry," and it therefore takes considerably more stimulation to get them to the optimal level of arousal.

Hundreds of studies, incorporating methodologies ranging from drug tests to EEG profiles, have tested hypotheses drawn from Eysenck's biological model. In the overall, results are mixed. There does appear to be reasonable empirical support for the general idea that extraverts prefer higher levels of stimulation than introverts and that introverts, compared to extraverts, are more physiologically reactive to sensory input at low-to-moderate levels of stimulation. But support for characteristic differences in resting levels of arousal for introverts versus extraverts is weak and inconsistent. Today, many researchers are skeptical about the viability of a concept of general cortical arousal, pointing out that while one region of the brain may appear underaroused other regions may be highly aroused at the same time.

Other researchers have begun to explore the possibility that individual differences in E may be mediated by what has been termed a *behavioral approach system* (BAS). As a functional system in the brain, the BAS is hypothesized to govern positive approach behaviors in response to incentives. Important components of the BAS may be dopamine pathways and electrical activity in the left anterior portion of the brain. A small but growing body of research evidence links dopaminergic activity and frontal-left brain activity to positive affect

and approach behaviors in some animals and humans. It has been proposed that individuals with a relatively strong BAS, being more sensitive and responsive to positive incentives, may be more likely to be highly extraverted and/or highly impulsive. Scientists have yet to flesh out an articulated picture of the BAS and have yet to offer compelling evidence linking the BAS to E. Nonetheless, this line of investigation would appear to offer many promising leads for future research on the origins and concomitants of extraversion-introversion.

Bibliography

Davidson, R. J. (1992). Emotion and affective style: Hemispheric substrates. *Psychological Science, 3,* 39–43. Davidson reviews recent research indicating that activation of the left-frontal regions of the cerebral cortex is associated with approach behavior and positive affect, which may link to individual differences in extraversion.

Eysenck, H. J. (1947). *Dimensions of personality.* London: Routledge & Kegan Paul. Eysenck introduces his trait-based theory of personality and specifies procedures for measuring extraversion and neuroticism.

Eysenck, H. J. (1967). *The biological basis of personality.* Springfield, IL: Charles C. Thomas. Eysenck lays out his theory of the biological bases of extraversion and neuroticism, underscoring the working of the brain's ascending reticular activating system in the mediation of arousal for extraversion.

Eysenck, H. J. (1973). *Eysenck on extraversion.* New York: Wiley. A collection of essays and research reports on the history of the extraversion concept, the relations between extraversion (and neuroticism) and a wide range of social and cognitive outcomes, and the biological bases of traits.

Geen, R. (1997). Psychophysiological approaches to personality. In R. Hogan, J. Johnson, and S. Briggs (Eds.), *Handbook of personality psychology* (pp. 387–414). San Diego, CA: Academic Press. Geen reviews the wealth of research on the psychophysiological underpinnings of extraversion and provides a balanced critique of Eysenck's arousal theory.

Gray, J. R. (1972). The psychophysiological nature of introversion-extraversion: A modification of Eysenck's theory. In V. D. Nebylitsin & J. Gray (Eds.), *Biological bases of individual differences* (pp. 182–205). New York: Academic Press. Gray presents his alternative conceptualization of traits related to extraversion and neuroticism by focusing on the activity of impulsivity and anxiety and linking these dimensions of neurophysiological functions.

Jung, C. G. (1971). *Psychological types.* Princeton: Princeton University Press. In this classic exposition of Jungian thought, Jung describes the trait of extraversion-introversion and provides examples of its manifestations in biography, literature, myth, and dreams.

Matthews, G., & Deary, I. (1998). *Personality traits.* Cambridge, England: Cambridge University Press. In this comprehensive and up-to-date survey of personality traits, the authors review a great many studies on extraversion and discuss the most important controversies and issues about the concept.

McCrae, R. R., & Costa, P. T., Jr. (1990). *Personality and adulthood.* New York: Guilford Press. McCrae and Costa describe the five-factor model of personality traits, of which E is one factor, and present data on the longitudinal stability of traits.

Watson, D., & Tellegen, A. (1985). Toward a consensual structure of mood. *Psychological Bulletin, 98,* 219–235. The authors make the argument that the trait structure defined by E and N parallels the structure of positive and negative affects, suggesting that E and N might be reconceptualized as traits of positive and negative affectivity, respectively.

Wilson, G. D. (1978). Introversion-extraversion. In H. London & J. E. Exner, Jr. (Eds.), *Dimensions of personality* (pp. 217–261). New York: Wiley. Wilson provides a comprehensive review of early research on E, most of it inspired by Eysenck's theory.

Dan P. McAdams

EYE. *See* Vision and Sight.

EYEWITNESS TESTIMONY is the act of reporting from memory about an event previously observed. In criminal cases, the justice system relies heavily on eyewitnesses to investigate crimes and to serve as trial witnesses to bring evidence against a defendant. In civil cases, eyewitnesses can be critical to reconstructing the details of previous events, such as accidents. Researchers in social and cognitive psychology have developed an extensive set of findings on the accuracy of eyewitness testimony, most of this work being done since the mid-1970s. The principal methods of research on eyewitness testimony involve staging live events (e.g., simulated crimes) for unsuspecting people or having people view material on video. Because the researchers created the event, they know the actual details and can thereby score the witness's recollections for accuracy. Control over the witnessed event allows for the systematic manipulation of various event and testing factors in order to study the conditions that cause accuracy and inaccuracy in eyewitness reports.

The scientific eyewitness literature borrows from both cognitive psychology and social psychology in order to account for many of the findings. Cognitive psychologists tend to study the roles of attention, perception, memory, and interference as factors affecting the accuracy of eyewitness testimony, whereas social psychologists tend to study the roles of witness beliefs and social influences on eyewitness testimony. Commonly, however, the phenomena observed in the experiments are both cognitive and social.

Eyewitness testimony research includes studies of the accuracy of witnesses' firsthand reports of memory for objects, actions, time, distance, and people. Memory for people has received a great deal of research attention because the identification of suspects from lineups (and photo spreads) is particularly powerful, direct evidence of guilt at criminal trials. Numerous general conclusions about the accuracy of eyewitness identifications can be derived from staged crime experiments. False identifications are surprisingly common in staged crime experiments. Rates of false identification can range from 5 to 95%, depending on various factors. Among those that affect the accuracy of eyewitnesses, a useful distinction has been made between factors that are beyond the control of the justice system (such as the cross-race factor) and those that are under the control of the justice system (such as instructions to an eyewitness prior to viewing a lineup). The former are called estimator variables and the latter are called system variables. System variables have proven particularly useful for linking eyewitness identification research to specific proposals for improving the accuracy of eyewitness evidence.

One of the most important factors determining the risk of mistaken identification is whether or not the actual perpetrator is in the lineup. When the perpetrator is in the lineup, the perpetrator is the person most commonly identified. When the actual perpetrator is not in the lineup, eyewitnesses often have great difficulty recognizing the perpetrator's absence. The process of identification from lineups seems to be one in which the eyewitness tends to select the person who looks most like the perpetrator relative to the other members of the lineup, a process called the relative judgment process.

When the perpetrator is not in the lineup, there is still someone who looks more like the perpetrator than do the other lineup members, and eyewitnesses tend to identify that person. The tendency to identify someone from a perpetrator-absent lineup is less pronounced if the eyewitness is explicitly warned that the perpetrator might or might not be in the lineup and is explicitly provided with the option of identifying no one. Failure to give this instruction is known as an instruction-biased lineup. Importantly, giving the warning does not have an appreciable effect on the rate of identifications of the culprit when the culprit is present, but only serves to protect innocent lineup members when the culprit is absent. In addition, false identifications increase if the suspect is the only one in the lineup who matches the general description of the culprit. Failure to use a lineup in which all members match the general description of the perpetrator is known as a structurally biased lineup. A lineup that is structurally fair serves to lower false identifications when the perpetrator is not present, but has little or no effect on the eyewitness's chances of selecting the perpetrator when the perpetrator is present.

Eyewitnesses making false identifications may express considerable confidence that the identified person is the culprit. There are conditions in which the confidence/accuracy correlation is higher and lower, but the overall correlation between confidence and accuracy in eyewitness identifications is a modest one. Some of the variables that drive up the confidence that an eyewitness holds in his or her identification are at odds with those that affect the accuracy of the identification. For instance, structurally biased lineups and biased instructions serve to increase the confidence of eyewitnesses even while increasing the frequency of false identifications. In addition, the confidence of an eyewitness who has made a false identification increases dramatically if the eyewitness is told that the person selected is the actual suspect in the case or is told that a cowitness identified the same person. These confidence-inflation effects are particularly problematic because the confidence of an eyewitness is the primary determinant of whether or not jurors will believe the eyewitness.

Other eyewitness identification phenomena that are relatively well established include "weapon focus," which is the tendency for eyewitnesses to focus on a weapon involved in a crime and thereby pay less attention to the perpetrator's face, and the cross-race effect, which is the tendency for people to have more difficulty identifying the faces of those of another race than those of one's own race.

Child eyewitnesses generally show the same pattern of mistakes as adult eyewitnesses, but their error rates are often higher. The younger the child, the more difficulty they have in recognizing the absence of the perpetrator in a lineup and the more suggestible they are regarding what they witnessed.

The scientific eyewitness literature has been instrumental in articulating the view in psychology that memories of an event can be changed after the event has been experienced. The work of Elizabeth Loftus using "postevent information" has received wide attention (1979). After witnessing an event, people are randomly assigned to receive information consistent or inconsistent with what they viewed, often in the form of a question. For example, an eyewitness might see a yield sign as part of a scene and later be asked a misleading question, such as whether a car that was stopped at a stop sign was blue or red. Later, when asked what kind of sign it was, those who were asked the misleading question tend to report that it was a stop sign. Some con-

troversy still exists as to whether these postevent information effects are actually affecting the original memory, whether they are a separate memory that competes for retrieval, or whether the effect is a form of social influence having little to do with memory per se. From a practical perspective of relevance to the courts, it matters little whether the effect is due to memory impairment or social influence because in either case the effect is one of changed testimony. From a theoretical perspective, however, the issue is of considerable import. Among other things, the phenomenon is relevant to the issue of whether long-term memory is permanent or whether later events can actually delete or change the original memories.

Research and theory on the creation of false memories have been particularly controversial when applied to claims about the recovery of repressed memories. People who claim that they were sexually abused as children but, due to repression, did not recall the abuse until adulthood are thought by many memory experts to be recalling false memories, a phenomenon dubbed the false memory syndrome. These memory experts note that false autobiographical memories can be created by suggestion, repeated imagination, belief in the concepts of repression and recovery of repressed memories, and hypnosis or hypnoticlike interventions. The issue of false memory syndrome remains controversial and has not been fully clarified.

Controversy exists over whether expert testimony on eyewitness issues should be admitted in criminal trials. Some states and some federal jurisdictions allow eyewitness researchers to give opinion testimony regarding the research on eyewitness accuracy while other states and federal jurisdictions do not. The use of forensic DNA tests in the 1990s using trial evidence from persons convicted by juries in the 1970s and 1980s has resulted in the exoneration of several dozen of these people. This has resulted in a new line of evidence that eyewitness evidence is fallible because, in the vast majority of these DNA exoneration cases, false eyewitness identification was the primary evidence leading to their wrongful conviction. An increasingly larger and more sophisticated body of scientific evidence on eyewitness accuracy, along with evidence from the recent DNA exoneration cases, has led to an increasing trend by courts to permit expert testimony on eyewitness issues.

[See also Children's Eyewitness Testimony.]

Bibliography

Bothwell, R. K., Deffenbacher, K. A., & Brigham, J. C. (1987). Correlation of eyewitness accuracy and confidence: Optimality hypothesis revisited. *Journal of Applied Psychology, 72*, 691–695. A meta-analysis of the cross-race identification effect.

Cutler, B. R., Penrod, S., & Dexter, H. R. (1990). Juror sensitivity to eyewitness identification evidence. *Law and Human Behavior, 14,* 185–191. A large study of factors that affect jurors' perceptions of the credibility of eyewitnesses.

Doris, J. (Ed.). (1991). *The suggestibility of children's recollections.* Washington, DC: American Psychological Association.

Lindsay, D. S., & Read, J. D. (1995). "Memory work" and recovered memories of childhood sexual abuse: Scientific evidence and public, professional, and personal issues. *Psychology, Public Policy, and Law, 1,* 846–909.

Loftus, E. F. (1979). *Eyewitness testimony.* Cambridge, MA: Harvard University Press.

Ross, D. F., Read, J. D., & Toglia, M. P. (Eds.). (1994). *Adult eyewitness testimony: Current trends and development* (pp. 223–244). New York: Cambridge University Press.

Sporer, S., Penrod, S., Read, D., & Cutler, B. L. (1995). Choosing, confidence, and accuracy: A meta-analysis of the confidence-accuracy relation in eyewitness identification studies. *Psychological Bulletin, 118,* 315–327.

Steblay, N. M. (1992). A meta-analytic review of the weapon focus effect. *Law and Human Behavior, 16,* 413–424.

Steblay, N. M. (1997). Social influence in eyewitness recall: A meta-analytic review of lineup instruction effects. *Law and Human Behavior, 21,* 283–298.

Wells, G. L. (1978). Applied eyewitness testimony research: System variables and estimator variables. *Journal of Personality and Social Psychology, 36,* 1546–1557. Introduces the distinction between system and estimator variables.

Wells, G. L. (1993). What do we know about eyewitness identification? *American Psychologist, 48,* 553–571. A review and perspective article on issues concerning identification evidence.

Wells, G. L., Small, M., Penrod, S., Malpass, R. S., Fulero, S. M., & Brimacombe, C. A. E. (in press). Eyewitness identification procedures: Recommendations for lineups and photospreads. *Law and Human Behavior.* A scientific review and position paper of the American Psychology-Law Society regarding how lineups and photo spreads should be conducted. Includes the first 40 DNA exoneration cases.

Gary Wells

EYSENCK, HANS JURGEN (1916–1997), naturalized British psychologist. Eysenck was one of Great Britain's most controversial psychologists. His work on personality, intelligence, crime, homosexuality, sport, parapsychology, and the causes of smoking-related diseases aroused impassioned debate and attacks, both verbal and physical. His greatest gift to psychology was his Personality Inventory, an original application of experimental and psychometric methods to a previously slippery construct that became the foundation of any study of personality for over a decade. He founded and subsequently edited the journals *Personality and Individual Differences* and *Behavior Research and Therapy.* He was a prodigious publisher in trade and academic outlets, publishing about 60 books and more than 1,000 scientific papers. At the time of his death, he was the most widely cited psychologist in the world.

As an empiricist, Eysenck had little patience with and withering rebuttals for those who posited unfounded claims. Often considered a devil's advocate who championed mind-stretching positions, he frequently espoused private opinions different from those of his public pronouncements. He goaded his students and the lay reader of his popular books into expanded realms of thinking through his gadfly manner.

Eysenck was adept with using the media; he became one of the world's most published popularizers of psychology through trade book publications that encouraged people to measure their own IQs, assess and describe their own personality constructs, and engage in thoughtful journeys of self-exploration. This skill brought him a degree of scorn and ridicule from his fellow psychologists. Some of his bestselling works include *Know Your Own IQ* (New York, 1962), *Uses and Abuses of Psychology* (London, 1953), *You and Neurosis* (London, 1977), *For Better, for Worse—A Guide to Happy Marriage* (London, 1983).

Born in Berlin, the only son of an economically stable but emotionally fractured family of actors, Eysenck was raised by his maternal grandmother. Following graduation from the Gymnasium and prior to enrolling at the University of Berlin, he left Berlin, where, as an aspiring physicist he would have been expected to become a member of the Nazi party. Following 2 years of study in France, he moved to London, where he took up the study of psychology by accident because the University of London would not accept his German school credits, except in the study of psychology.

Eysenck earned a first-class bachelor's degree from University College, London, where Cyril Burt was professor of psychology. Eysenck recounts in his aptly titled autobiography *Rebel with a Cause* (1990, rev. 1997) that because Burt could not read his handwritten examination protocols he earned his degree based on coursework. Posthumously, when Burt was charged with falsification of data, his former student loyally attempted to explain away the idiosyncracies of his former department head. He earned his doctorate at London University in 1941 and became professor of psychology in 1955. During his tenure, he founded the department of psychology at the Institute of Psychiatry, Maudsley Hospital, University of London. At the time of his death he was professor emeritus at the Institute of Psychiatry, University of London.

As an outspoken critic of psychoanalysis and other interpretive therapies, Eysenck advocated behavioral interventions that aim treatment at immediate problems rather than probing for hidden causes. He observed that "the symptoms of neurosis are indeed the disease itself, so that to cure the symptoms is to cure the disease." He espoused biological bases for pathologies, as well as for simple interpersonal differences, and as the primary explanatory variable for efficiency in learning. For example, he stated that since criminals had failed to develop conditioned moral and social responses, they could be cured by behavior therapy (*Crime and Personality*, 1964), and that smoking did not cause lung cancer, but that both conditions were symptoms of an underlying emotional disorder (*Smoking, Health, and Personality*, 1965). He provided forceful endorsement for the notion that intelligence is most strongly affected by variables of race (*Race, Intelligence, and Education*, 1971).

Eysenck's approach to the contribution of environmental variables to *g* (the presumed general factor in intelligence) softened as he grew older. His later work acknowledged the mediating effect of environmental forces on biological processes. For example, he acknowledged the importance of nutrition on the development of intelligence. In his autobiography, he also noted that Afrikaans-speaking Whites in South Africa once scored lower than English-speaking Whites on intelligence tests, but that the gap closed over time. "Whatever the reason for this change, it suggests that differences between groups may not necessarily be genetically caused and may be susceptible to change," he wrote (Eysenck, 1990, rev. 1997).

Known as challenging and demanding by fellow academics, in the British public's mind Eysenck was synonymous with all that comprised academic psychology. Sought out by journalists, he became an icon and explanatory voice for the science of psychology in Great Britain. Never at loss for an opinion about anything related to the psyche, Eysenck generated widespread public enthusiasm for exploring the human condition, which in turn led many to study applied human psychology. Very many contemporary practitioners and academics were spurred to study psychology based on Eysenck's earliest forays at bringing psychology to his public.

Bibliography

Eysenck, H. J. (Ed.). (1982). *A model for intelligence*. Berlin: Springer-Verlag.

Eysenck, H. J. (1995). *Genius: The natural history of creativity*. Cambridge, UK: Cambridge University Press.

Eysenck, H. J. (1990, rev. 1997). *Rebel with a cause: The autobiography of Hans Eysenck*. New Brunswick, NJ: Transaction.

Caven S. Mcloughlin

EYSENCK PERSONALITY QUESTIONNAIRE. Considered by his peers to be one of the greatest contributors to the field of clinical psychology during its first century, Hans J. Eysenck (1916–1997) was coauthor with Sybil B. G. Eysenck of the Eysenck Personality Questionnaire-Revised (EPQ-R). Eysenck was a prolific scholar, one of the most widely cited psychologists in the world, and author of over one thousand scientific papers. Controversial and provocative, he was particularly noted for his classic criticisms of psychotherapy efficacy and for his emphasis on the principles of quantification and measurement. An important legacy for generations of students and colleagues who were influenced by his work is a series of personality tests, several of which bear his name.

The original theory of specifying traits of personality into two major dimensions was postulated by Eysenck in the late 1940s; this conceptualization has stood the test of time. Two main factors, termed N (neuroticism) and E (extraversion) have formed the basis of Eysenck's personality model, later expanded to a third factor, termed P (psychoticism or toughmindedness). Other models have raised challenges and questions as to what additional dimensions lie beyond the Big Three trait factors. Nevertheless, Eysenck's personality framework remains fundamental to other theories and at least in the case of the first two factors, has been consistently replicated in research studies. The EPQ-R is the preeminent measure of Eysenck's personality dimensions.

Historically, Eysenck's trait quantification work began with the Maudsley Medical Questionnaire (assessment of N only) then the Maudsley Personality Inventory (N and E). Next followed the Eysenck Personality Inventory (N and E, as well as an L [Lie] scale to measure deception, an important factor for establishing the validity of self-report tests). The Eysenck Personality Questionnaire introduced the third factor (P), added to N, E, and L; the EPQ-R revised the P scale to address specific psychometric concerns and derived an Addiction scale. The exact relationships among the various Eysenck tests is not entirely clear. Considerable overlap exists, for example between the EPI and EPQ, including up to about 75% of the N and E scale items, but other modifications have been made that make different test version subscales not identical.

Different editions of the EPQ-R have been developed based on American versus United Kingdom normative samples. The item format for the one hundred questions requires simple yes/no answers. The administration time is approximately 30 minutes; the test is easily scored. A short form and a children's version are available. High scores on the EPQ-R E scale are interpreted as reflecting friendly sociability, with less emphasis on the impulsive rowdiness associated with earlier test versions. Findings with the Junior EPQ have generally shown E scores to increase with age. The N scale is a solid measure of nervous worrying that is predictive of emotional maladjustment. The P scale has been fraught with controversy both on psychometric grounds (low reliability and skewed normative distribution with resultant over-diagnosis of normals as "psychotics") and theoretical criticisms (challenging Eysenck's construct as questionably related to actual psychosis and more closely linked to aggression and empathy defects); this has partly led to terming the P scale by the attribute "tough-minded." The L scale attempts to measure "fake-good" tendencies, which is especially important for the N scale because some test respondents try to appear better or worse off emotionally.

Some technical aspects of the test are presented in the manual. Any scales that are supposed to measure stable personality characteristics must demonstrate consistency over a period of time. This psychometric attribute, termed *test-retest reliability*, has been found to be reasonable for the EPQ-R with subscale reliabilities ranging from 0.71 to 0.92 over a one-month period. Internal consistency is another important psychometric property and has been shown to be adequate for E, N, and L; the content of the P items is more heterogenous. Validity issues are critical to establishing whether the test is assessing what it purports to be measuring. The N scale has been successful in discriminating neurotic patients from normal controls. The L scale has demonstrated good sensitivity to detecting individuals who were instructed to try and fake their answers to look good. However, it is still possible for sophisticated respondents to notice these L-scale items because they are somewhat obvious; some psychologists believe the L scale actually measures its own trait, namely, the need for social approval.

The importance of the Eysenck tests rests on its worldwide use and broad applicability in varied though mainly research contexts. Surveys of North American clinical psychologists find that the test is not at all commonly used for psychodiagnosis. Hundreds of research studies, however, have relied upon the test to evaluate such diverse topics as personality trait predictors associated with the speed of medical surgery recovery, twin studies of the genetic predisposition to mental illness, correlations with behavioral health problems, mediating factors in psychopharmacology trials and relationship to cognitive performance on attention, memory and other neuropsychological tasks. Cross-cultural re-

search has produced translations into several languages, including versions in Japanese, Polish, Spanish, Hindi, German, Hungarian, and African (Zimbabwe). Studies have been conducted in every continent, providing a global picture of personality trait profiles ranging from peasant farmers in India, to churchgoers in Wales, anxious children in the United States, cancer patients in the Netherlands, teenagers in Mexico, and college students in Japan and Australia. The Eysenck test profiles of mental patients tend to show neurotic, introverted, and sometimes psychotic patterns, while prisoner groups are generally extraverted. People active in the work force show more stable (low N) scores with sales people in particular showing stable N patterns but with more extraverted traits. The Eysenck instruments have shown their greatest utility in scientific investigations of the importance of personality factors in everyday life.

[*See also the biography of Eysenck.*]

Bibliography

Bijnen, E. J., Van der Net, T. Z. J., & Poortinga, Y. H. (1986). On cross-cultural comparative studies with the Eysenck Personality Questionnaire. *Journal of Cross-cultural Psychology, 17,* 3–6.

Eysenck, H. J., & Eysenck, S. B. G. (1994). *Manual of the EPQ,* San Diego: Edits/Educational and Industrial Test of Services. The American edition of the tests can be obtained from Edits, P.O. Box 7234, San Diego, California USA 92167. Web site: www.edits.net. The British edition is published by Hodder & Stoughton Educational (England).

Eysenck, S. B. G., Eysenck, H. J., & Barrett, P. (1985). A revised version of the Psychoticism scale. *Personality and Individual Differences, 6,* 21–29.

Helmes, E. (1989). Evaluating the internal structure of the Eysenck Personality Questionnaire: Objective criteria. *Multivariate Behavioural Research, 24,* 353–364.

Richman, H., Sallee, F. R., & Folley, P. (1996). Personality differences between anxious and non-anxious children within a dimensional framework. *Journal of Anxiety Disorders, 10,* 149–162.

Zuckerman, M., Kuhlman, D. M., Joireman, J., Teta, P., & Kraft, M. (1993). A comparison of three structural models for personality: The big three, the big five and the alternative five. *Journal of Personality and Social Psychology, 65,* 757–768.

Joel O. Goldberg

F

FACIAL EXPRESSION. *See* Nonverbal Communication.

FACTOR ANALYSIS refers to a broad family of multivariate linear models designed to examine the interrelations among a set of continuously distributed manifest variables as a function of a smaller set of unobserved latent factors. This technique is often used to examine the common influences believed to give rise to a set of observed measures (measurement structure) or to reduce a larger set of measures to a smaller set of linear composites for use in subsequent analysis (data reduction). Spearman first introduced factor analysis as a method for understanding the common influences thought to underlie multiple measures of intelligence (1904), and Thurstone extended Spearman's model with the development of the common factor model (1935).

Factor analysis is based on the premise that the measured variables are a linear additive function of the unobserved latent factors, and that these factors give rise to the pattern of observed correlations among the measures. The fundamental equation for the factor model is:

$$y_j = \lambda_{j1}\xi_1 + \lambda_{j2}\xi_2 + \ldots + \lambda_{jm}\xi_m + \varepsilon_j$$

where y_j represents the jth of p continuously distributed variables measured on a sample of n independent subjects, λ_{jm} represents the factor loading (or partial regression coefficient) relating variable j to the mth factor ξ_m, and ε_j represents the influence that is unique to variable y_j and is independent of all ξs and all other εs. The variance of the observed measure is thus an additive combination of the variance associated with the set of underlying factors (the communality) and the variance associated with the unique factor (the uniqueness). The uniqueness can be further broken down into specific variance (the systematic variance unique to that particular measure) and random error variance.

The above equation represents the structure of the measured variables as a function of the underlying latent factors. Alternatively, the correlational structure among the measured variables can be derived from the equation in matrix terms such that

$$R = \Lambda\Phi\Lambda' + \Theta$$

where R is the $p \times p$ symmetric correlation matrix of p-measured variables, Λ is the $p \times m$ matrix of factor loadings λ, Φ is the $m \times m$ symmetric correlation matrix of the latent factors, and Θ is the $p \times p$ diagonal matrix of unique variances ε. If Φ is a diagonal matrix of ones (an identity matrix), then the factors are orthogonal, or uncorrelated. If, instead, Φ is a symmetric correlation matrix, then the factors are oblique, or correlated. The matrix of factor loadings Λ is called the factor pattern matrix, and the matrix of zero-order correlations between the measures and the factors is called the factor structure matrix. The factor pattern and factor structure matrices are equal only if the factors are orthogonal; if the factors are oblique the factor pattern matrix is usually consulted for purposes of interpretation.

There are two related approaches to the factor model, component analysis and common factor analysis. Component analysis is not a true factor analytic model because the resulting components are direct linear combinations of the measured variables. However, it is often considered with the common factor model, given several shared similarities. In component analysis, it is assumed that all variables are measured without error and that all observed variance among the measures is available for factoring. Thus, Θ is set to zero and the full correlation matrix R_f (containing values of ones on the diagonal) is factored. In contrast, the common factor model assumes that the observed variables are measured with error and that less than the observed variance is available for factoring. Thus, Θ is not constrained to zero and the reduced correlation matrix R_r (containing values less than one on the diagonal) is factored. The diagonal elements of R_r are communality estimates and represent the proportion of variance of each measured variable shared with the set of underlying factors.

Basic Steps in Factor Analysis

Once an appropriate sample and set of measures have been obtained, there are generally four major decision points when using factor analytic models: method of factor extraction, number of factors to extract, communality estimation, and factor rotation.

Factor Extraction. One method of factor extraction used for both the component and the common factor model is the method of principal factors. Principal factors is based on the computation of the eigenvalues and vectors (or characteristic roots and vectors) of the correlation matrix to maximize the variance of each successively extracted factor. Principal factoring can be applied either to the full correlation matrix R_f that results in principal components analysis, or to the reduced correlation matrix R_r that results in principal axis factoring. A more recently developed and commonly used technique for factoring R_r is maximum likelihood estimation, in which model parameters are estimated with the highest likelihood of having produced the observed correlation matrix. Additional extraction techniques include minimum residual analysis, alpha factoring, and image analysis.

Number of Factors. The next step is to determine the number of factors to be extracted. The Kaiser-Guttman Rule suggests that the number of factors should correspond to the number of eigenvalues of the full correlation matrix R_f that exceed one, although this criteria is criticized given the tendency to overextract factors. The scree plot is a graph of each eigenvalue plotted in descending order, and the number of factors is determined at the point where an appreciable "bend" occurs in the plot. The maximum likelihood goodness-of-fit test evaluates the magnitude of the residuals that exist in R after extracting a given number of factors, and it tests whether additional factors are necessary to meaningfully reduce the size of the residuals. Finally, cross-validation can be used in which two independent samples with two sets of measures from the same domain are examined simultaneously to evaluate the optimal number of factors to extract from each sample. Determining the appropriate number of factors to extract is often thought to be the most important decision in factor analysis.

Communality Estimation. For the common factor model, communality estimates must be obtained for placement on the diagonal of the reduced correlation matrix R_r. Methods for estimating communalities typically utilize an initial estimate that may then be iteratively updated during the computation of the factor solution. Initial estimates include the largest correlation of each variable with all other variables and the squared multiple correlation of each measure with all other measures. The method used for communality estimation becomes less important given larger numbers of measured variables.

Factor Rotation. The factors extracted from R_r can be rotated to aid in substantive interpretation. Factor rotation is possible because, for any one factor solution that fits the data to a specific degree, there will exist an infinite number of equally good solutions, each represented by a different factor loading matrix. Rotations can be orthogonal (e.g., varimax, quartimax, and equimax), in which the rotated factors are uncorrelated, or oblique (e.g., promax, direct oblimun, and orthoblique), in which the rotated factors are correlated. The goal of factor rotation is to achieve Thurstone's simple structure (1935), and the selection of an appropriate rotation is usually based on theory and the interpretability of the resulting solution.

Factor Score Estimation. Once the factor analysis is completed, factor scores can be estimated that represent the scores that would have been observed for an individual if the latent factors could be measured directly. The common factor model is considered indeterminate because there are more model parameters estimated than pieces of information observed. Thus, factor scores cannot be computed directly (as is possible in component analysis), but must be estimated using methods such as the regression method, the Bartlett method, the Anderson-Rubin approach, or simple unit weighting. Factor scores can then be used in subsequent analysis, such as multiple regression or MANOVA.

Variants of the Factor Model

The models described above are often termed exploratory factor analysis (EFA) and are applied when strong theory is lacking and the observed data are freely explored in search of meaningful patterns among the observations. In contrast, confirmatory factor analysis (CFA) provides formal statistical tests of a priori hypotheses about the specific factor structure thought to underlie the set of observed measures (Jöreskog, 1969). Unlike the EFA model, in which all measured variables relate to all latent factors, the CFA model imposes explicit restrictions on the factor pattern matrix so that the measured variables relate with some (or usually just one) latent factors but do not relate with others. Test statistics and goodness-of-fit indices evaluate the adequacy of these imposed restrictions as a function of the observed sample data. One type of structural equation model is a CFA model in which one or more of the latent factors are specified as dependent measures in a system of regression equations.

There are many techniques related to the factor model that share the general goal of examining similarities among observations. Correspondence analysis is a nonlinear principal-components analysis of raw categorical response data, or co-occurrence matrices of paired preferences. Profile analysis is used when a set of measures is gathered from multiple groups of individuals and the similarity of profiles of means is examined across the groups. Cluster analysis classifies previously unclassified observations into discrete groups based on two or more distance or similarity measures among the observations. Multidimensional scaling graphically maps a set of observed distance or similarity measures between pairs of items onto one or more underlying dimension, and multidimensional unfolding is a method for scaling individual preferences among a set of ranked stimuli.

Bibliography

Bollen, K. A. (1989). *Structural equations with latent variables*. New York: Wiley. The definitive advanced graduate-level text for matrix-based confirmatory factor analysis and structural equation modeling. Difficulty level is moderate to high. A revision from the same publisher is forthcoming.

Comrey, A. L., & Lee, H. B. (1992). *A first course in factor analysis* (2nd ed.). Hillsdale, NJ: Erlbaum. A comprehensive introduction to exploratory factor analysis with chapters addressing confirmatory factor analysis and structural equation modeling. Provides a detailed example of factor analysis as applied to the development of the Comrey Personality Scales.

Gorsuch, R. L. (1983). *Factor analysis* (2nd ed.). Hillsdale, NJ: Erlbaum. A widely used graduate-level introduction to exploratory factor analysis for the behavioral sciences. The text is moderately mathematical but is accessible to a variety of readers. Discusses both conceptual and practical issues in factor analysis as well as some discussion of computer programs.

Jöreskog, K. G. (1969). A general approach to confirmatory maximum likelihood factor analysis. *Psychometrika, 34,* 183–202.

Kim, J. O., & Mueller, C. W. (1978). *Factor analysis: Statistical methods and practical issues*. Beverly Hills, CA: Sage.

Kim, J. O., & Mueller, C. W. (1978). *Introduction to factor analysis: What it is and how to do it*. Beverly Hills, CA: Sage. Both Kim & Mueller guides provide a brief nontechnical introduction to the basic concepts and practical application of exploratory factor analysis. Also contains a short but useful glossary of factor analytic terms and frequently asked questions.

Loehlin, J. C. (1998). *Latent variable models: An introduction to factor, path, and structural analysis* (3rd ed.). Hillsdale, NJ: Erlbaum. An excellent graduate-level introductory text that addresses a wide variety of latent variable models, including exploratory factor analysis, confirmatory factor analysis, and structural equation models. Many applied examples and discussions of computer programs which greatly aid in practical understanding.

Mulaik, S. A. (1972). *The foundations of factor analysis*. New York: McGraw-Hill. A comprehensive advanced mathematical treatment of the factor analytic model from a rigorous matrix algebra approach. Provides several detailed chapters reviewing the basic mathematical foundations of factor analysis, including matrix algebra, composite variables, and partial correlation. A classic text in the general factor model.

Spearman, C. (1904). General intelligence, objectively determined and measured. *American Journal of Psychology, 15,* 201–293.

Thurstone, L. L. (1935). *The vectors of the mind*. Chicago: University Chicago Press.

Patrick J. Curran

FALSE MEMORY. False memories occur when people remember events differently from the way they happened or, in the most extreme case, remember events that never happened at all. These memory errors differ from the most studied types of memory errors, those involving forgetting. Forgetting is an error of omission, arising when a person tries to remember some bit of prior knowledge (a name, a fact, a previous occurrence), but it does not come to mind. False memories are errors of commission, because details, facts, or events come to mind, often vividly, but the remembrances fail to correspond to prior events.

The vicissitudes of memory were studied by European psychologists near the beginning of the twentieth century, especially by William Stern in Germany and Alfred Binet in France, but the first landmark study was by Frederic Bartlett, a British psychologist. In his famous book *Remembering* (1932), Bartlett emphasized the constructive nature of memory. He argued that recollection of experiences is a reconstructive process driven by schemas, or general organizational schemes. The basic idea is that specific experiences and their details may not be remembered, but overall themes are. When people try to recover memories, they are guided by these schemas or themes and fill in details that are consistent with the schemas, but that may actually be quite wrong.

A key concept to understanding false memories is recoding. People do not directly record experience as a faithful copy of the outside world, but rather recode it in terms of their knowledge of the world (their schemas). In one famous experiment, people looked at ambiguous shapes and were told to remember them. For two groups of people, the shapes were given different labels (such as, for one shape, either broom or rifle).

When these people were later asked to draw the shapes from memory, they tended to draw them to be consistent with the label. The ambiguous figure called a broom during the study was recalled as being more broomlike than it was originally. In this case, people recoded their visual experience in terms of language and then, apparently, remembered the recoded form. Such processes occur in virtually all types of remembering: People do not recollect the events of the world as they actually happened, but as they are recoded by the cognitive system.

The coherence or interrelatedness of presented information is another factor that can lead to false memories. When what one reads or hears strongly implies a fact or event, people can come to believe that the event occurred, even when it did not. For example, when a person hears, "The karate champion hit the cinder block," that person may later remember having heard that the karate champion *broke* the cinder block. Breaking the block may be implied, but is not stated and may not have occurred (the champion might have failed). As people perceive the world around them, they make inferences about what the events mean, and may later confuse their inferences (the champion broke the block) with what was actually stated (the champion hit the block). Again, we remember our recoded experiences, not the literal happenings of the outside world.

A number of factors aside from recoding lead to false memories. Interference processes are responsible for one large class of cases. One popularly studied situation involves eyewitness testimony, modeled after cases that might arise in legal settings. A person witnesses a traffic accident with a yield sign present. Later, the person reads a description of the accident in which most of the information is accurate, but a stop sign is mentioned rather than a yield sign (i.e., misleading information is provided). When people were later asked to recall or to recognize the original accident scene, they often remembered the sign as having been a stop sign rather than a yield sign, relative to recall or recognition in control conditions in which no misleading information had been given. Reading about the stop sign created interference, which caused people to remember the wrong sign when they tried to recollect the original scene. The critical point is that our memories for some events are not encapsulated in time and impervious to further manipulation, but can be changed by the processing of subsequent information.

Social factors can also affect remembering and cause false recollections. When people remember in groups, if one person recollects information that is wrong, others can incorporate the wrong information into their memories for the scene. As in the eyewitness paradigm, the misleading information provided by one person can distort the memories of others in the group. Even when people are highly confident that they are remembering

"the truth" of the original situation, experimental evidence shows that they can be wrong. In fact, some studies show little correlation between confidence and accuracy in memories. Many people who are cautious about their prowess in remembering may actually be more accurate than others who are perpetually sure that they are right.

Guessing and imagining can lead to false memories, too. If people are first tested in a situation in which they are told to guess about what might have happened (an instruction often given under conditions of hypnosis), they often produce wrong information. Later, when trying to remember accurately, they may recall events that they had produced while guessing. In a sense, these people have provided their own misinformation about the earlier events and now remember their self-created rendition of the events. Imagination can also lead to false memories. If people repeatedly imagine acting a certain way in a particular situation, they can come to believe that the events actually happened, especially when the imaginings fit plausibly with a person's prior experience.

These cases all fall under the rubric of what has been called *reality monitoring* or *source monitoring*: People confuse what actually happened (reality) with what they may have only inferred, imagined, or heard about. When people remember details provided later as having actually been present in the original event, they are combining information from two sources. In these cases, false memories arise due to a failure to monitor the sources of information.

Individual differences among people are also an important consideration. Some studies find that children seem especially prone to false recollections relative to young adults. Older adults may also be more susceptible than are young adults. One neuropsychological account of these differences emphasizes brain development, particularly frontal lobe functioning. Certain areas of the frontal lobes are believed to be critical in memory retrieval and in monitoring the source of information. Children's frontal lobes are still developing, and in older adults these areas atrophy, perhaps leading to the exaggerated proclivity to false recollections in these two groups. In addition, some individuals with severe frontal damage display rather dramatic false memories, including confabulation (recollections of wildly implausible events asserted as fact). The tie between frontal functioning and the arousal of false memories is still being actively investigated.

The issue of the truth or falsity of memories arises in many settings outside the psychology lab, particularly in legal cases. Three types of cases that hinge on accuracy of remembering will be discussed in turn. The first is the general issue of the accuracy of eyewitness memory of a crime, say with regard to identifying a suspect as the criminal. Such testimony carries great weight with juries—having a witness say, "That is the man. I'll never forget his face!"—seems very compelling. However, as discussed before, even highly confident witnesses can sometimes be completely wrong, so such eyewitness testimony must be regarded cautiously, unless corroborated by other evidence. In addition, because memories can be influenced by suggestion, the means of elicitation of the eyewitness memories must be examined carefully.

A second type of case involves the child witness. Some adults (teachers, day-care operators) have been accused of committing crimes of childhood sexual abuse based only on children's testimony. Of course, such crimes are horrific and perpetrators should be brought to justice. On the other hand, false accusations can ruin innocent people's lives. Because children seem quite susceptible to created memories through suggestive questioning techniques, it is again critical to ask how the memories were elicited and whether there is strong corroborating evidence from other sources.

A third type of case involves the issue of recovered memories after long delays in adults. In recent times, many cases have occurred in which adults seem to recover memories of having been physically or sexually abused as children, with such recoveries often occurring while they are undergoing therapy. They often accuse a parent, another relative, or a teacher of the abuse. The general idea behind such recoveries is that the original events were traumatic and hence repressed, or banished to an unconscious state, from which they are later recovered in therapy. A debate rages about the veracity of these recovered memories. Are they real? Or are they false memories aroused through suggestive questioning and through techniques such as hypnosis and imagination, which are known to lead to false memories? Some of these memories seem so improbable (ones involving cults practicing satanic ritual abuse, for which there is no evidence) or violate known facts about memory (recovering detailed accounts of abuse that supposedly happened before one year of age, a time about which people are known to consciously remember little or nothing), that there seems little doubt that they are false. But of course many other recovered memories are at least possible. Once again, the twin issues to raise in these cases are the techniques used to elicit the memories (Were they suggestive?) and the supporting evidence (Is there any?). In general, because the events happened so long ago, it is difficult to find evidence to corroborate or to disconfirm the memories.

The study of the vagaries of remembering has produced an interesting body of scientific information that is important for forensic purposes. Simply the claim that "I remember" should not, without converging evidence, be taken as an indicator that remembered events actually occurred. Much evidence exists that even detailed, highly confident recollections can be completely erroneous, hence simple recollection should not be routinely accepted as completely accurate.

[See also Repressed Memory.]

Bibliography

Bartlett, F. C. (1932). *Remembering: A study in experimental and social psychology.* Cambridge, England: Cambridge University Press.

Brewer, W. F. (1977). Memory for the pragmatic implications of sentences. *Memory and Cognition, 5,* 673–678.

Carmichael, L. L., Hogan, H. P., & Walter, A. A. (1932). An experimental study of the effect of language on reproduction of visually perceived form. *Journal of Experimental Psychology, 15,* 73–85.

Ceci, S. J., & Bruck, M. (1995). *Jeopardy in the courtroom: A scientific analysis of children's testimony.* Washington, DC: American Psychological Association.

Jacoby, L. L., Kelley, C., Brown, J., & Jasechko, J. (1989). Becoming famous overnight: Limits on the ability to avoid unconscious influences of the past. *Journal of Personality and Social Psychology, 56,* 326–338.

Johnson, M. K., & Raye, C. L. (1981). Reality monitoring. *Psychological Review, 88,* 67–85.

Loftus, E. F. (1993). The reality of repressed memories. *American Psychologist, 48,* 518–537.

Loftus, E. F., Miller, D. G., & Burns, H. J. (1978). Semantic integration of verbal information into a visual memory. *Journal of Experimental Psychology: Human Learning and Memory, 4,* 19–31.

Pendergrast, M. (1995). *Victims of memory: Incest accusations and shattered lives.* Hinesburg, VT: Upper Access.

Roediger, H. L., III. (1996). Memory illusions. *Journal of Memory and Language, 35,* 76–100.

Roediger, H. L., III, & McDermott, K. B. (2000). Distortions of memory. In E. Tulving & F. I. M. Craik (Eds.), *Oxford handbook of memory.* New York: Oxford University Press.

Schacter, D. L., Coyle, J. T., Fischbach, G. D., Mesulam, M. M., & Sullivan, L. E. (Eds.). (1995). *Memory distortion: How minds, brains, and societies reconstruct the past.* Cambridge, MA: Harvard University Press.

Henry L. Roediger III and David A. Gallo

FAMILY PSYCHOLOGY. [*This entry comprises three articles: an overview of the broad history of the field from its inception to the present; a survey of the principal theories that have determined the course of development of the field; and a general descriptive review of assessments and interventions used in or unique to the field. For a discussion related to family psychology, see* Family Therapy.]

History of the Field

Family psychology is a specialty within contemporary psychology. It has basic and applied aspects, covers treatment and prevention interventions, and is taught in graduate training programs, generally within clinical/child or counseling psychology. Although it has less of a formal and lengthy history than more well known and established specialties like clinical, counseling, or school psychology, it stands among the new specialties such as health and forensic psychology. Its name may indicate otherwise, but the specialty of family psychology covers a broad territory (L'Abate, 1985). Advances covering family and marital issues and processes research and interventions, as well as the core theoretical ideas of family psychology (contextualism and systems perspective) appear under the headings of many psychology content areas, including developmental, social, research design and methodology, environmental and community, gender, industrial/organizational, health, forensic, and, of course clinical, counseling, and school psychology (Crosbie-Burnett & Lewis, 1993; Liddle, 1987a).

One of the first tasks in family psychology's early history concerned its definition, in particular, its definition vis-à-vis the more widely recognized movement, field, and clinical specialty known as family therapy (Kaslow, 1991; L'Abate, 1992). The first issue of the *Journal of Family Psychology* included the following definition:

> Family psychology, using a systemic perspective, broadens psychology's traditional emphasis on the individual, and, while it retains a primary emphasis on marriage and the family, it uses the systemic view to focus on the nature and role of individuals in primary relationship structures, as well as, more broadly, the social ecology of the family—those networks in which the family interacts and resides. (Liddle, 1987a, p. 9)

Definitions of the specialty emphasized several themes: the systems perspective and the contextual tradition of family therapy (representing the clinical wing of family psychology); the theoretical perspectives of contextualism; reciprocal causality and influence; and an ongoing attempt to define the processes or mechanisms that mediate the relationship between different systems and levels of functioning (Kaslow, 1995; Liddle, 1987b). Family psychology embraced the newly forming tradition of conceptual complexity, which were taking place in many sectors of psychology and related sciences (Bell, 1968; Haynes, 1992; Kazdin & Kagan, 1994). One of the most important ways in which family psychology exemplified and, in its own way, developed along these complex lines, concerned the way it went beyond the literal meaning of the very term *family psychology*. Family psychology, like family therapy, invokes images of a particular conceptual or intervention unit—the family. Family psychology, embracing systems philosophy and contextualism at its core, surely includes family and marital processes in its theoretical, research, and clinical purviews, but it has moved beyond family as well (L'Abate, 1992; Parke, 1998). The emphasis is more on the notion of behavioral transactions that occur not only in the family, but between the family and other developmentally influential social systems (Bronfenbrenner, 1979). This broadened emphasis, in accord with Kazdin's (1997) recommendations for new kinds of conceptualization and intervention, has been the hallmark of contemporary family psychology interventions (Liddle, 1995; Markman, 1992; Tolan, Guerra, & Kendall, 1995). Peer group and other institutions of influence beyond the family are included in family psychology's conceptual framework, and today's interventions that could be said to reside in the family psychology tradition include assessment and intervention attention to multiple systems and levels of social influence, including peer, school, and community/neighborhood influences (Alexander, Holtzworth-Munroe, & Jameson, 1994; Henggeler et al., 1997; Liddle, 1998; Szapocznik & Coatsworth, in press).

Although the family, marriage, and systems theory and contextualism—theoretical notions that are core to family psychology—have been of interest to psychologists for some time, it was with the founding of the Division of Family Psychology in 1985 and 2 years later, its journal, the *Journal of Family Psychology* (JFP), that the family psychology specialty achieved a well-defined and differentiated identity within mainstream psychology. The division became a home for interests relevant to psychologists who wished to practice from a family therapy or systems perspective, for those who trained students in family systems ideas, research, and interventions, and for those concerned with carrying the standard of family and couple-related policy issues within the American Psychological Association (APA) as well as on the federal policy scene. The founding of JFP (first a divisional journal and now an APA journal) is an endorsement of the specialty's centrality in contemporary psychology, and can be considered another major event for the specialty. JFP became a context through which family psychology, as an identifiable and differentiated specialty within psychology, could define itself (Levant, 1992). The range of articles published in JFP has been broad, and has included basic normative and dysfunctional marital and family process research, research on diverse family structures and forms, research that informs social and public policy pertaining to families, and treatment outcome and process studies. Several other important developments have occurred in the dozen or so years since the founding of the Division of Family Psychology and the specialty's journal.

Training Programs and Accreditation

Ideas about training and supervision that are syntonic with systemic principles have been articulated (Ganahl, Ferguson, & L'Abate, 1985; Green, 1998; Liddle, Becker,

& Diamond, 1997). Complex, clearly specified doctoral level training models and programs have been advanced as well (Berger, 1988; Green, 1998). Programs such as these await the accreditation of family psychology as a formal specialty in the APA, a process that has begun and seems likely.

Family psychology ideas are now developed within conceptual models in and of themselves, but are also part of other evolving models of theory and practice. Many aspects of the family psychology research, theory, and clinical practice agenda of over a decade ago (Liddle, 1987b) have now been reached. Family psychology has proven to be a viable specialty within contemporary psychology. It has been an organizing influence for research on systemic theory and ideals within psychology; it has developed and rigorously tested new, family psychology theory-based (e.g., using developmental research as a guide to practice) preventive and treatment interventions; and it has been an active participant in legislation and health/mental health policy making.

Research

The research landscape changed dramatically in family psychology in the 1990s. Many of those changes became apparent at the first national conference on family psychology, sponsored by the APA Science Directorate in 1995 (Liddle, Santisteban, Levant, & Bray, in press). Long-term stable programs of basic and intervention (prevention and treatment) research exist (Szapocznik, Kurtines, Santisteban, & Rio, 1990). A strong interest in family and marital processes in both the applied and basic science areas can be found across federal, state, and foundation funding sources. More funding, from a wide variety of agencies (National Institute of Mental Health, National Institute on Drug Abuse, National Institute on Alcohol Abuse and Alcoholism, Center for Substance Abuse Treatment, Center for Substance Abuse Prevention, Centers for Disease Control, Department of Justice/Office of Juvenile Justice and Delinquency Prevention) specifically encouraging the evaluation of family-related intervention initiatives, is available now than ever before. The National Institute on Drug Abuse, for example, in an era in which the overall number of research centers is being reduced, recently funded a research center in the area of family-based treatments for adolescent substance abuse (Liddle, 1998). Family and couple interventions have been developed and tested with a wide variety of clinical problems and populations (Pinsof & Wynne, 1995). The technology of family psychology intervention science, as a subspecialty, has evolved a great deal as well (Bray, in press; Snyder, Cozzi, & Mangrum, in press). Complex interventions have been manualized and tested using state-of-the-science designs, measures, and statistical analyses. New studies, combining different research traditions (effectiveness, efficacy, and process studies)

are being conducted to test a new generation of interventions that are comprehensive in scope, target individual and family processes and family vis-à-vis extrafamilial interactional processes (Schoenwald & Henggeler, in press). In conclusion, advances on many fronts—scientific, clinical, theoretical, and organizational—are evident in family psychology. It continues to be defined as what has been called an emerging *and* an emerged discipline (Liddle, 1987b).

Bibliography

Alexander, J. F., Holtzworth-Munroe, A., & Jameson, P. B. (1994). The process and outcome of marital and family therapy: Research review and evaluation. In A. E. Bergin & S. I. Garfield (Eds.), *Handbook of psychotherapy and behavior change* (4th ed., pp. 595–630). New York: Wiley.

Bell, R. Q. (1968). A reinterpretation of the direction of effects in studies of socialization. *Psychological Review,* 75 (2), 81–95.

Berger, M. (1988). Academic psychology and family therapy training. In H. A. Liddle & D. C. Breunlin (Eds.), *Handbook of family therapy training and supervision* (pp. 303–315). New York: Guilford Press.

Bray, J. (in press). Methodological issues and innovations in family psychology intervention research. In H. A. Liddle, D. A. Santisteban, R. Levant, & J. Bray (Eds.), *Family psychology intervention science.* Washington, DC: American Psychological Association.

Bronfenbrenner, U. (1979). *The ecology of human development: Experiments by nature and design.* Cambridge, MA: Harvard University Press.

Crosbie-Burnett, M., & Lewis, E. (1993). Theoretical contributions from social and cognitive-behavioral psychology. In P. G. Boss, W. J. Doherty, R., LaRossa, W. R. Schumm, & S. K. Steinmetz (Eds.), *Sourcebook of family theories and methods: A contextual approach* (pp. 531–561). New York: Plenum Press.

Ganahl, G., Ferguson, L. R., & L'Abate, L. (1985). Training in family therapy. In L. L'Abate (Ed.), *The handbook of family psychology and therapy* (pp. 1281–1317). Homewood, IL: Dorsey Press.

Green, R. J. (1998). Training programs: Guidelines for multicultural transformation. In M. McGoldrick (Ed.), *Revisioning family therapy: Race, culture, and gender in clinical practice* (pp. 111–117). New York: Guilford Press.

Haynes, S. (1992). *Models of causality in psychopathology: Toward dynamic synthetic and nonlinear models of behavior disorders.* Needham Heights, MA: Allyn & Bacon.

Henggeler, S. W., Rowland, M. D., Pickrel, S. G., Miller, S. L., Cunningham, P. B., Santos, A. B., Schoenwald, S. K., Randall, J., & Edwards, J. E. (1997). Investigating family-based alternatives to institution-based mental health services for youth: Lessons learned from the pilot study of a randomized field trial. *Journal of Child Clinical Psychology, 26,* 226–233.

Kaslow, F. W. (1991). The art and science of family psychology: Retrospective and perspective. *American Psychologist. 46,* 621–626.

Kaslow, F. W. (Ed.). (1995). *Voices in family psychology.* Thousaud Oaks, CA: Sage.

Kazdin, A. E. (1997). A model for developing effective treatments: Progression and interplay of theory, research, and practice. *Journal of Clinical Child Psychology, 26,* 217–226.

Kazdin, A. E., & Kagan, J. (1994). Models of dysfunction in developmental psychopathology. *Clinical Psychology: Science and Practice, 1,* 35–52.

L'Abate, L. (1985). *The handbook of family psychology and therapy* (Vols. 1 & 2). Homewood, IL: Dorsey Press.

L'Abate, L. (1992). Family psychology and family therapy: Comparisons and contrasts. *American Journal of Family Therapy, 20,* 3–12.

Levant, R. F. (1992). The evolving field and its issues. *Journal of Family Psychology, 6,* 5–9.

Liddle, H. A. (1987a). Editor's introduction I. Family psychology: The journal, the field. *Journal of Family Psychology, 1,* 5–22.

Liddle, H. A. (1987b). Editor's introduction II. Family psychology: Tasks of an emerging (and emerged) discipline. *Journal of Family Psychology, 1,* 149–167.

Liddle H. A. (1995). Conceptual and clinical dimensions of a multidimensional, multisystems engagement strategy in family-based adolescent treatment. *Psychotherapy: Theory, Research and Practice, 32,* 39–58.

Liddle, H. A. (1998). *Multidimensional family therapy treatment manual for the Cannabis Youth Treatment Multisite Collaborative Project.* Rockville, MD: Center for Substance Abuse Treatment.

Liddle, H. A., Becker, D., & Diamond, G. M. (1997). Family therapy supervision. In C. E. Watkins (Ed.), *Handbook of psychotherapy supervision* (pp. 400–418). New York: Wiley.

Liddle, H. A., Santisteban, D. A., Levant, R., & Bray, J. (Eds.). (in press). *Family psychology intervention science.* Washington, DC: American Psychological Association.

Markman, H. J. (1992). Marital and family psychology: Burning issues. *Journal of Family Psychology, 5,* 264–275.

Parke, R. D. (1998). Editorial. *Journal of Family Psychology. 12,* 3–6.

Pinsof, W., & Wynne, L. (1995). The efficacy of marital and family therapy: An empirical overview, conclusions, and recommendations. *Journal of Marital and Family Therapy, 21,* 585–613.

Schoenwald, S., & Henggeler, S. (in press). Services research and family-based treatment. In H. A. Liddle, D. A. Santisteban, R. Levant, & J. Bray (Eds.), *Family psychology intervention science.* Washington, DC: American Psychological Association.

Snyder, D. K., Cozzi, J. C., & Mangrum, L. F. (in press). Conceptual issues in assessing couples and families. In H. A. Liddle, D. A. Santisteban, R. Levant, & J. Bray (Eds.), *Family psychology intervention science.* Washington, DC: American Psychological Association.

Szapocznik, J., & Coatsworth, J. D. (in press). An ecodevelopmental framework for organizing the influences on drug abuse: A developmental model of risk and protection. In M. Glantz & C. R. Hartel (Eds.), *Drug abuse: Origins and interventions.* Washington, DC: American Psychological Association.

Szapocznik, J., Kurtines W., Santisteban, D. A., & Rio, A. T. (1990). Interplay of advances between theory, research, and application in treatment interventions aimed at behavior problem children and adolescents. *Journal of Consulting and Clinical Psychology, 58,* 696–703.

Tolan, P. H., Guerra, N. G., & Kendall, P. C. (1995). A developmental-ecological perspective on antisocial behavior in children and adolescents: Toward a unified risk and intervention framework. *Journal of Consulting and Clinical Psychology, 63,* 579–584.

Howard A. Liddle

Theories of Family Dynamics

Family therapy has multiple origins and it is difficult to say exactly who conducted the first conjoint family treatment session. One early form of family intervention was the settlement house movement in the 1930s in which social workers attempted to keep impoverished families intact. Child guidance clinics, which originated in the early 1900s, included some attention to the role of parenting. However, in classical child therapy, parents were seen by the social worker, and a psychodynamically trained psychiatrist worked individually with the child. Parents were often seen as causing the child's difficulties, but could be harmful contaminants to individual therapy. Another early influence was the psychiatrist Nathan Ackerman, who noted that fathers' unemployment triggered family-wide distress emerging in the children's mental health problems.

In the early 1950s, a small group of investigators including Gregory Bateson (an anthropologist), Jay Haley (with an academic background in library science and communications), John Weakland (an engineer trained in anthropology) and Don Jackson (a psychiatrist and the only trained mental health professional in the group), were studying human and animal communication in several contexts. These early family therapists were often outsiders and either did not agree with or were not trained in conventional individual psychopathology or treatment. Bateson and colleagues observed that young adults with schizophrenia often exhibited acute symptom exacerbation immediately following a family visit. The interactions themselves included conflicting communication sequences termed *double binds.* For example, a mother would come to visit her adult son in the psychiatric unit. The son would stand at a respectful distance and say, "Hello, mother." She would respond by saying, "Don't you love your mother? Come and give me a hug." When he embraced her, she would physically stiffen, pull away, and say: "Son, you must act more grown up. You're not a baby anymore" (Nichols & Schwartz, 1998). These contradictory messages occurred within a relationship necessary for the patient's basic survival.

While double-binding communication is no longer seen as an etiological factor in schizophrenia, the concept was historically important in linking individual psychopathology to family interactions. Bateson introduced concepts from cybernetics to explain families as dynamic systems that maintained homeostasis.

Family therapy, particularly those models influenced by systems theory, reflected a paradigm shift in viewing symptoms as indicators of disturbed interpersonal interactions, rather than intrapsychic conflict. Kuhn (1962) noted that revolutions within disciplines are often initiated by individuals outside the mainstream. This was certainly the case in the early days of family therapy. Distinct schools of family therapy began emerging in the late 1960s and early 1970s.

Structural Family Therapy

Psychiatrist Salvadore Minuchin observed that teenagers' behavioral problems were associated with breakdowns in family structure. In his later work with anorectic teenagers, he emphasized that family boundaries and roles were often unclear. Structuralists emphasize that all families have roles—parent, child, spouse, and sibling—with accompanying responsibilities. Each role has a corresponding boundary, an area of authority and privacy. For example, the parental role is to care for and socialize children. Spouses model intimate relationships for children, but maintain a firm boundary around the couple so that marital needs can be met (Minuchin & Fishman, 1981).

One family pattern typically associated with distress is the cross-generational coalition. Such coalitions may feature children or grandparents functioning in spousal roles. In traditional two-parent families, such coalitions result in one parent having little authority over parenting or marital decisions. In extremely disorganized families, there are very few structural boundaries or roles. The household's composition may frequently change and include parents, grandparents, distant relatives, and friends. Because of the chaos, there is no one consistently fulfilling basic family roles (Minuchin & Fishman, 1981).

Minuchin's best-known work with psychosomatic families highlighted *enmeshment*, a pattern of overcloseness with few parent-child boundaries. The teenager with anorexia nervosa or uncontrolled diabetes was typically in a coalition with one parent, often the father. Although the adolescent was occupying the spousal role, family members denied any interpersonal distress or conflict.

The structural therapist is directive and creates boundaries and consolidates roles. Techniques such as enactment highlight the family's dysfunctional roles and boundaries, and are followed by directives for parents to work together. The adolescent would then be demoted from his or her parental or spousal role to a child's position. When there was strong denial of family differences, Minuchin would deliberately provoke conflict to explode the unity myth. One of Minuchin's best-known provocative interventions was the lunch session in which parents were directed to get their anorectic child to eat. The resulting parental failure and frustration forced members to overcome denial and face their distress.

Strategic Therapy

In the late 1960s, Haley, one of the original double-bind investigators, joined Minuchin at the Philadelphia Child's Guidance Clinic. Although Haley paid attention to family roles and how they change throughout the family life cycle, he emphasized power and control. Strategic therapists view psychological symptoms as serving an adaptive function while providing social power to the identified patient and other family members. Young adults who develop depression or schizophrenia are able to exempt themselves from normal responsibilities such as attending college, getting a job, or living on their own. Strategic therapists simultaneously assume that the young adult's incapacitation benefits one or both parents: his or her symptoms benevolently prevent marital discord from emerging. By being ill and unable to function, these individuals are keeping their family intact, and are also exercising power.

In the past decade, Haley's treatment approach has become extremely problem focused and almost theoretical. He pays little attention to insight or emotional experience. The essence of therapy is behavioral change. The therapist provides directives generally focusing on rituals or alterations in already fixed behavioral cycles that will occur outside the treatment session. With school-phobic children, the goal is regular school attendance. Similarly, for depressed young adults, the goal is to have them live and work independently. Haley's directives are based on psychiatrist Milton Erickson's hypnotic procedures. Erickson developed a form of hypnosis in which symptoms were accepted and skillfully redirected toward therapeutic goals. Haley described a couple in which the wife became upset because her husband frequently walked around the house with a thermometer in his mouth. The therapist agreed that the husband should be able to take his temperature whenever he wanted but with one small change: the husband should use a rectal thermometer (Haley, 1987).

Haley's emphasis on power is evident in the following therapeutic directive: A mother who felt she had "lost control" of her adolescent son came to therapy saying that she was seriously considering sending him to military school, but decided to attempt treatment first. The therapist agreed that military school might be effective but suggested that the boy first needed to understand what military school would be like. The therapist and mother developed a routine that included the boy making his bed, having his room inspected, standing at attention, and being respectful toward his mother. After several weeks, the boy's behavior had changed and military school was unnecessary. Haley believed that the mother had indeed lost control, and effective treatment required an acceptable rationale for her to take charge (Haley, 1987). Because directives are so highly individualized, strategic therapy is a difficult model to teach. In addition, there is often an implicit assumption that clients seeking treatment are not amenable to direct suggestions or advice, so directives must be carefully packaged to be accepted.

Historical and Psychodynamic Therapy

Whereas psychodynamic therapy describes how interactions with parents become internalized and influence adult functioning, family theorists contributed new constructs to traditional dynamic theory. Bowen's (1978) family-of-origin therapy emphasizes intergenerational history with two sets of counterbalancing forces: the emotional versus intellectual polarity, and the individual versus togetherness tension. Emotional functioning is visceral and immediate, whereas the intellectual dimension is cognitive and planful. Individuality emphasizes autonomy and personal identity, whereas togetherness reflects social connection. Maintaining personal goals and identity, particularly in the presence of emotional and social pressures to do otherwise, is termed *differentiation*. Poorly differentiated persons experience few boundaries between themselves and others and have strong emotional reactions to family members. Adults develop intimate relationships with others of similar levels of differentiation. With two relatively undifferentiated partners, dyadic tension will emerge as frequent, emotionally intense conflict. To reduce dyadic tension, a third person, usually a child, is brought into the interaction. One parent, or each parent alternately, may emotionally fuse with the child. When this fusion occurs, parent-child boundaries become indistinct, and the child becomes an extension of the parents' own interpersonal conflicts.

Framo (1982), influenced by Bowen (1978), incorporated object relations theory into his historical family therapy. Object relations theorists believe that children's early interactions with parents become internalized as unconscious representations of intimacy. These templates become reactivated in adolescence and early adulthood and are automatically projected onto significant others.

Historically oriented family therapy emphasizes the intellectual process of obtaining a thorough family history with attention to repetitive multigenerational themes. For example, husbands and fathers may have been irresponsible figures who were spontaneous and playful but not physically or emotionally available for wives and children. A married woman who can identify this multigenerational pattern may begin to understand her fears of depending on her husband and tendency to exclude him from decisions about the children. By pointing out these projections, she can begin to relate to her husband as an adult man in the here-and-now, rather than as an historical legacy. As this example illustrates, family-of-origin therapy focuses on individuals with other family members present, but less engaged with the therapist. Both Bowen (1978) and Framo (1982) encouraged adults to use their historical understanding of family dynamics to develop more satisfying relationships with their family of origin. Bowen also emphasized that family therapists should develop a thorough understanding of their own family dynamics. Therapists are encouraged to construct genograms (schematic family trees), and with the aid of a supervisor or coach, examine how their own family dynamics may influence how they conduct therapy. Family-of-origin therapy's key intervention is labeling or interpreting historical patterns. The history, supported by a genogram, tangibly supports the interpretation. In contrast to strategic therapy, family-of-origin therapy emphasizes theory and de-emphasizes technique and overt behavior change.

Behavioral Marital and Family Therapy

Although family therapy largely developed outside psychology's mainstream, behavioral models are an exception. Behavioral family treatment involves direct application of operant learning to modifying children's behavior. In contrast to systems-oriented approaches, the behavioral perspective does not view children's noncompliance as representing marital or intergenerational problems. The focus, instead, is modifying the child's behavior through consistent contingent rewards and punishments (Nichols & Schwartz, 1998).

After obtaining a description of the frequency and duration of the child's behavior and noting any environmental contingencies, the therapist instructs parents in behavioral management. Positive reinforcement, including tokens redeemable for long-term rewards or food for younger children, will increase desirable behavior. Undesirable behavior is primarily addressed through time-outs. The child is removed to an area of the home where there is no social interaction and remains there for a brief time period immediately after undesirable behavior. Response cost, in which tokens are taken away, may also be used for inappropriate conduct.

Behavioral parent training is an educational intervention that may occur in workshop settings. The emphasis is on parents acquiring skills to increase desirable, and decrease undesirable, behavior. Little attention is paid to the meaning of the child's behavior or its relation to marital or sibling discord (Nichols & Schwartz, 1998).

Behavioral therapists have made a significant contribution to the treatment of marital conflict. Marital therapy, historically, was practiced primarily by ministers and social workers in family service agencies. Although it has become included in family treatment, there has been significantly less theoretical and clinical understanding of distressed marriages as compared with child-focused family problems. One exception is application of social learning and operant principles to marital discord.

Stuart's (1980) social learning model is one of the best articulated and systematic approaches to marital conflict. Stuart attributed marital discord to few reinforcing exchanges between spouses and accompanying communication skill deficits. After an initial assessment, frequently including standardized self-report inventories, therapy moves into establishing contracts with specific, limited behaviors that each spouse would like the other to emit (e.g., bring me the morning newspaper, take me to lunch). If couples implement these contracts, there is usually increased positive affect in the relationship. In communication training, the therapist mediates and the couple is encouraged to discuss specific issues with the therapist functioning as a teacher. The therapist may interrupt the exchanges to encourage "I" statements ("I feel like . . ." rather than "You don't"), provide alternatives to terminal language ("You *never* ask me about my day"), and encourage specific affirmative, behavioral requests ("I would like to go to the movies with you tonight at six o'clock").

Compared to other marital and family approaches, behavioral treatments have particularly strong empirical support. Behaviorally specific treatment goals lend themselves to targeted outcome measures. In addition, many of these techniques were developed as part of ongoing university research programs.

Experiential Family Therapy

Experiential family therapists, including Carl Whitaker, Virginia Satir, and Walter Kempler, downplayed theory and emphasized genuine affective exchanges among family members. Experiential therapists focus on the individual within the family; they believe that personal growth produces healthier marriages and families. These therapists emphasized that family cohesiveness often suppresses authentic interaction and expression of feeling. The healthy family, from an experiential point of view, allows individual autonomy, frequently includes conflict, and operates from flexible patterns. As Whitaker and Bumberry (1988) noted, families may need scapegoats, but that role should never be affixed to one family member for any length of time.

Gender roles are particularly harmful. Both Whitaker and Kempler, a Gestalt therapist, noted that men have difficulty establishing intimate relationships and are frequently intellectualized and remote. Women typically enter marriage with the hope of establishing an emotional bond with their mate but are disappointed by "hopeless" men unable to invest emotionally in a relationship. Instead, men invest emotional energy in things: hobbies, careers, or sports. In one farm family, the husband was having an "affair" with his tractor. Women, having given up on their husbands, begin having "affairs" with their children for intimacy (Whitaker & Bumberry, 1988). These patterns are directly pointed out to family members (to the farm wife, "How long after you were married before you decided he loved the cows more than you?" Whitaker & Bumberry, 1988, pp. 21–22). Body language may also be directly interpreted by Gestalt therapists ("Your eyes tell me you've heard her say this before; it wears you down").

In contrast to strategic and behavioral therapists, experiential therapists provoke family members to feel, think, and act differently within sessions. Within a session, the therapist may work with one family member for a time before refocusing on the relationship. Emotional intensity and confrontation commonly occur. Kempler and Whitaker viewed families as fairly resilient; they can be verbally "knocked around." To grow, anxiety and discomfort are necessarily increased to disrupt stereotyped roles and modes of relating. Whereas flexibility and creativity are seen as healthy, experiential therapists view parents as needing to be in charge so that children experience a basic sense of security. Virginia Satir's warm, dynamic, yet challenging, personality was a major therapeutic force. Satir included *sculpting*, in which family members would physically act out their current and desired relationships with one another.

Experiential family therapy is difficult to articulate as a theory with constructs explaining pathology, change, and specific corresponding techniques. Although it may be a philosophy rather than a treatment model, experiential therapy does highlight the oppressive, nature of rigid family roles and the healthy forces of individual autonomy and creativity.

Communications Theory and Constructivist Family Therapy

Communications theory is a loose label describing therapies influenced by Bateson and the double-bind group. John Weakland, one of the double-bind theorists, was an early member of the Mental Research Institute

(MRI). Paul Watzlawick, trained in linguistics, and Richard Fisch, a psychiatrist, were also influential MRI therapists.

MRI therapists emphasize how clients categorize their experience with "frames." Typically, frames imply cause-effect sequences (e.g., "If my husband really cared about me, he would bring me flowers every week. Since I'm not receiving flowers, he is being emotionally cold toward me and I am considering divorce. There's no other option."). MRI therapists note that problems clients bring to treatment are often ordinary life difficulties labeled as outside the normal ebb and flow of daily existence (Fisch, Weakland, & Segal, 1982). Prior to seeking treatment, clients have usually attempted logical solutions to their problems. For example, a child receiving poor grades will often be grounded until academic performance improves. When poor grades continue, more periods of grounding are added. When the therapist is finally consulted, the child may be grounded for 5 years. Grounding is an example of a first-order change (Watzlawick, Weakland, & Fisch, 1974) because it follows from a logical interpretation of poor grades ("He's not trying hard enough"). MRI therapy centers around changing the implicit rules surrounding the problem, or second-order change. From the parents, the therapist might learn that poor grades are anything other than A's. The meaning of poor grades may be changed to C or below, or the therapist may describe how grounding is preventing the child from learning important lessons of managing a busy life: a temporarily difficult process that may briefly lead to poorer grades. The overall goal is change the current solution, which is seen as part of the problem. Grades have become a power struggle between parent and child and this battle is perpetuating poor academic performance.

MRI therapy is problem focused and emphasizes behavioral change as opposed to insight. However, the treatment focus is on client belief systems that maintain the problem. Although it is assumed that problems are supported by social interactions, the therapist may only work with one person rather than having conjoint marital or family sessions.

The Milan group translated Bateson's epistemological writing into family intervention. Four Italian psychiatrists, Selvini Palazzoli, Boscolo, Cecchin, and Prata (1978), developed their therapy by working with difficult clinical problems including schizophrenia and severe anorexia nervosa. They described young adults' psychopathology as stabilizing the family. However, family members were resistant to direct behavioral change because the identified patient was protecting family alliances, for example, between parent and grandparent. Treatment sessions involved cotherapists and a team observing behind a one-way mirror. The team developed hypotheses about the symptoms' family function and recommended a directive to disrupt this sequence. These directives were often paradoxical injunctions positively connoting the current family pattern. For example, if a depressed young man was not leaving the house, the therapist would emphasize the depressed adult's importance as mother's confidante. Mother was home alone because the father worked long hours. The therapists emphasized that if the depressed young man were not home, the father would have to make a difficult decision between his job and family.

MRI therapy influenced White and Epston's (1990) narrative approach and de Shazer's (1985) solution-focused treatment. These newer models emphasize how language constructs reality. Therapy clients rely on problem-saturated terminology to describe their lives (Nichols & Schwartz, 1998). This deficit focus prevents parents from seeing their problem child's positive attributes. Parents may describe their teenager as disrespectful and violating curfew; the same teenager may responsibly care for younger siblings and perform household chores. The problem-focused emphasis neglects the teenager's positive attributes, and his or her perceived irresponsibility eventually becomes self-fulfilling.

These therapists employ linguistic techniques to alter the problem's construction. White and Epston (1990) used externalizing language. Rather than accepting depression as an enduring state, they relabeled depression as an *outside force:* "How does depression affect your relationship with your husband? When have you kept depression from disrupting your life?" (Nichols & Schwartz, 1997). De Shazer (1985) altered problem-focused thinking by focusing on desirable aspects of clients' lives. At the end of the first session, he instructs clients: "Between now and the next time we meet, I would like you to observe . . . what happens in your family/life/marriage/relationship that you want to continue to have happen" (de Shazer, 1985, p. 137).

Current and Future Developments

The late 1980s and 1990s saw increased attention to larger social forces bearing on family life. It is somewhat ironic that family therapy's early attention to social context neglected the impact of gender roles, ethnicity, and economic forces on problems brought to treatment. Continued development of solution-focused and other brief therapy models were also encouraged through managed care's emphasis on efficient treatment.

As a field, family therapy has become more than just another mental health treatment. It is unlikely that the early founders could have predicted that their efforts would have resulted in a distinct mental health profession with specialized marital and family therapy graduate degree programs and independent licensure. For psychologists, this same period brought family therapy into the fold. Empirical articles on family treatment outcome began appearing in American Psychological Association journals, and a division of family psychology, with its own journal, was established. Psychologists are appreciating the broader perspective that family therapy brings to understanding human problems.

Bibliography

Bateson, G., Jackson, D. D., & Weakland, J. (1956). Toward a theory of schizophrenia. *Behavioral Sciences, 1,* 251–264.

Bowen, M. (1978). *Family therapy in clinical practice.* Northvale, NJ: Jason Aronson.

de Shazer, S. (1985). *Keys to solutions in brief therapy.* New York: Norton.

Fisch, R., Weakland, J. H., & Segal, L. (1982). *The tactics of change: Doing therapy briefly.* San Francisco: Jossey-Bass.

Framo, J. (1982). *Explorations in marital and family therapy.* New York: Springer.

Haley, J. (1987). *Problem-solving therapy* (2nd ed.). San Francisco: Jossey-Bass.

Kempler, W. (1981). *Experiential psychotherapy with couples.* New York: Brunner/Mazel.

Kuhn, T. (1962). *The structure of scientific revolutions.* Chicago: University of Chicago Press.

Minuchin, S., & Fishman, H. C. (1981). *Family therapy techniques.* Cambridge, MA: Harvard University Press.

Nichols, M. P., & Schwartz, R. C. (1998). *Family therapy: Concepts and methods* (4th ed.). Boston: Allyn & Bacon.

Satir, V. L. (1992). *Peoplemaking.* Palo Alto, CA: Science and Behavior Books.

Selvini Palazzoli, M., Boscolo, L., Cecchin, G., & Prata, G. (1978). *Paradox and counterparadox.* Northvale, NJ: Jason Aronson.

Stuart, R. B. (1980). *Helping couples change: A social learning approach to marital therapy.* New York: Guilford Press.

Watzlawick, P., Weakland, J., & Fisch, R. (1994). *Change: Principles of problem formation and problem resolution.* New York: Norton.

Whitaker, C. A., & Bumberry, W. M. (1988). *Dancing with the family: A symbolic experiential approach.* New York: Brunner/Mazel.

White, M., & Epston, D. (1990). *Narrative means to therapeutic ends.* New York: Norton.

H. Russell Searight

Assessments and Interventions

Family psychology is a specialty in psychology with basic and applied aspects (Stanton, 1975). It has revealed the deleterious consequences of dichotomous thinking about research and practice (Kaslow, 1991; Parke, 1998). Family psychology's applied branch developed rapidly in the 1990s. Evidence on several fronts suggests that we have a subspecialty within family psychology: family psychology intervention science (Liddle, Santisteban, Levant, & Bray, in press). The interventions within this subspecialty can be organized into preventive and treatment interventions. Family psychology interventions draw upon family systems ideas, particularly those of family therapy, but are not exclusively tied to them. Developmental psychology and developmental psychopathology, as well as the intersection of psychophysiological processes and cognitive and affective processes (Parke, 1998) are among the content foci that can now be included in the specialty called family psychology (L'Abate, 1992). These basic research areas continue to inform the intervention wing of family psychology, as a new generation of multicomponent and multisystem inverventions are being developed and tested in rigorously conducted studies (Alexander, Holtzworth-Munroe, & Jameson, 1994; Liddle 1995; Tolan, Guerra, & Kendall, 1995).

Given the mental health needs of children and adolescents today (Institute of Medicine, 1989) and the documented decline of our nation's youth, family psychology interventions, with their emphasis on taking into account and intervening into the natural ecology of children's and adolescents' lives, are in a strong position to enhance psychology's contribution to society. Family psychology is also in a unique position to contribute to treatment and prevention science. By design, family psychology's interventions are attempting to assess and intervene into the settings in which children and adolescents develop and in which dysfunction develops and expands (Vernberg, Routh, & Koocher, 1992). Attempts to change the processes of development and dysfunction in these natural ecologies have yielded knowledge about the development of dysfunction generally, as well as the processes of normative adaptation (Dishion & Andrews, 1995).

Advances in Intervention Science

The overall field of intervention science has made significant advances in the 1980s and 1990s. Prevention and treatment research is now conducted according to a more rigorous, well-developed set of standards than in earlier historical periods (Bryant, Windle, & West, 1997). Large-scale clinical trials have yielded technology guidelines (Carroll & Rounsaville, 1990; Docherty, 1984; Elkin, 1994). New methodological developments, for example, more and varied designs and statistical analyses, and therefore kinds of questions, have transformed the type and quality of studies being conducted. The variety of clinical research now being undertaken has changed as well. Process research studies complement large-scale outcome trials in an attempt to illuminate the processes or mechanisms by which change occurs (Greenberg & Pinsof, 1986). These studies address previous critiques of the lack of clinical relevance of clinical research. A well-organized, standard-defining set of activities aimed at the establishment and dissemination of empirically supported therapies has taken hold (Chambless, 1996). The empirically supported therapies movement has influenced public and professional discourse about therapy. The conversation, and sometimes debate, has included funders, payers, and consumers of services, those providing the services, and those training the service providers. Considerable professional attention has been devoted to the development of practice guidelines for a variety of clinical problems and disorders (American Academy of Child and Adolescent Psychiatry, 1997), and family interventions figure prominently in child and adolescent disorders such as attention-deficit/hyperactivity disorder (ADHD), conduct disorder, and substance abuse. Treatment manuals for a similar range of problems are more available than ever before (Center for Substance Abuse Treatment, 1998; National Institute on Drug Abuse, 1998). Many of these developments are embodied in the treatment development standards that are still evolving, some of which are closely associated with the managed care industry. Kazdin (1997) outlined a sequential schema for the field's development of child- and adolescent-focused treatments.

Family psychology intervention science matches up well to other specialties against an evaluative template of well-organized and programmatic treatment development activities. In the 1990s it was demonstrated that family-based treatment and family prevention studies can be done, and in a way that conforms to the rigorous standards of contemporary intervention science (Waldron, 1997; Weinberg, Rahdert, Colliver, & Glantz, 1998; Winters, Latimer, & Stinchfield, 1999).

Research Infrastructure

Funding opportunities have increased for family-focused intervention research. Federal agencies and foundations have demonstrated strong interest in funding family-oriented intervention research. The funding support has enabled many programmatic ventures in family psychology intervention science to continue and expand (Szapocznik, Kurtines, Santisteban, & Rio, 1990). The number and variety of family-oriented intervention studies continue to grow. A recent monograph reviewed some of the many areas in which considerable intervention research exists (Pinsof & Wynne, 1995). These reviews summarized family intervention research findings across a wide variety of content areas, including alcohol and drug abuse, conduct disorder, physical health problems, and major mental illness. Research training in family psychology intervention science exists, and prepares early career scholars with specialized research backgrounds for careers in family-oriented intervention research (Center for Treatment Research on Adolescent Drug Abuse, 1998).

Research Nature and Quality

Studies in the family-based intervention and prevention areas are conforming to contemporary standards of treatment and prevention intervention science. The studies are theory based, and theory of dysfunction and normative behavior guides intervention design and assessment. Basic research areas on particular aspects of development, such as social cognition or affect regulation, or the influence of peers on acquiring antisocial beliefs, informs intervention development. Intervention studies are evaluating the impact of interventions on clinically referred populations and samples including participants of varied ethnicity and race; in so doing, they address some of the limits of previous treatment and basic research about sample restrictiveness. The family psychology intervention science field is exemplary in its attempt to connect and use basic and applied science at every stage of its intervention, development, and evaluation development. The risk and protective factor framework, developmental psychopathology, and developmental psychology are primary content spheres used for contemporary intervention design, and that provide research leads. Family psychology intervention and prevention studies are using rigorous and creative designs, and, as a result of these designs and the use of state-of-the-science statistical methods, these studies are posing previously unasked questions. Efficacy, effectiveness, and process-of-therapy questions are now asked within single, large-scale clinical trials. Common exemplary design features also include attention to multiperson, multilevel, and multicontext assessments over multiple time points, including extended follow-up periods. Study instrumentation assesses symptom reduction as well as changes in prosocial or adaptive functioning, such as school attendance or grades. The extent of intervention specification must be considered high. This is impressive considering how interventions have changed over the past decade. Complex intervention models have been developed, many of which could be considered combination interventions, comprehensive in scope, and intended to address the range of functional and developmental impairments in the affected youth, family, and environment. And, critically, these interventions target areas known, on the basis of research, to be critical to the development of competence and prosocial behaviors. Although dissemination and utilization of the family psychology oriented treatment manuals must be considered at an early stage, manuals are increasingly available through many sources [e.g., commercial publishers' series on treatment manuals (Henggeler, Schoenwald, Borduin, Rowland, & Cunningham, 1998), and funding agencies such as the Center for Substance Abuse Treatment Cannabis Youth Treatment Initiative, and the National Institute on Drug Abuse]. These contemporary treatments are complex, theoretically based, principle driven, and frequently sequentially organized (interventions according to a sequence of change are detailed; Alexander, 1992; Liddle, Rowe, Dakof, & Lyke, 1998). Family psychology focused training and supervision models have been developed (Green, 1998; Liddle, Becker, & Diamond, 1997), and therapists can be taught to implement and adhere to those interventions. Furthermore, studies have begun to appear that confirm the link of adherence to well-developed, previously established, efficacious interventions to clinical outcomes (Henggeler et al., 1998). Family psychology interventions can be manualized and are being evaluated within the same kind of conformity to adherence standards as individual psychotherapy models (Hogue et al., 1998; Hogue, Rowe, Liddle, & Turner, 1994).

Challenges and Directions

Narrative and meta-analysis reviews of the family psychology intervention science literature summarize the available efficacy data. Although findings thus far have revealed family psychology interventions to be effective, and even effective when compared to nonfamily-oriented interventions (Stanton & Shadish, 1997), the matter of outcomes or of the clinical meaning and importance of outcomes is far from settled. As many constituencies and forces act upon the available outcome research data, the matter of how satisfied we should be with the levels of outcomes achieved is far from decided. The *how* questions—Are these interventions effective? What are the circumstances under which these interventions are effective?—are now supplemented with questions such as, Are these interventions effective enough? As researchers add more measures of prosocial change to their batteries while continuing use of symptom reduction measures, will the improvements in functioning and the remediations of impairment justify what some believe to be expensive and not very generalizable interventions? The topic of a model's transportability is one of the major research issues facing family psychology interventions. Surely this matter intersects with policy issues, policy makers, and program planners. Economic realities in the mental health care marketplace may influence programmers' willingness to adopt treatments, even treatments with proven efficacy. The continued development of process research, particularly those studies that can unlock the mysteries of why and how change occurs (Friedlander, 1998) has been an area of development closely allied to family psychology, and it will continue in its importance. This is particularly so as the new kinds of studies, partly due to funding-related reasons (clinical trial studies are being asked to do more in order to justify their large budgets), continue to develop along integrative lines.

That is, today's studies, like the therapy models many of them are attempting to evaluate, are becoming more integrative: combining different kinds of research designs, methodologies, and different genres of research into a single proposal/project. Just as these developments helped to break down ideological barriers in the therapy development realm, the same process is happening in therapy and intervention research studies. The treatment development movement, with its first systematic guidelines now being articulated (Kazdin, 1997; Linehan, 1996) will likely be the major organizing force for intervention science generally and for family psychology specifically. The ways in which a framework like Kazdin's can or needs to be adapted for family psychology researchers remains to be determined.

Bibliography

Alexander, J. F. (1992). An integrative model for treating the adolescent who is delinquent/acting-out. In W. Snyder & T. Ooms (Eds.), *Empowering families, helping adolescents: Family-centered treatment of adolescents with alcohol, drug abuse, and mental health problems* (pp. 101–109). Rockville, MD: U.S. Department of Health and Human Services.

Alexander, J. F., Holtzworth-Munroe, A., & Jameson, P. B. (1994). Research on the process and outcome of marriage and family therapy. In A. E. Bergin & S. L. Garfield (Eds.), *Handbook of psychotherapy and behavior change* (4th ed., pp. 595–630). New York: Wiley.

American Academy of Child and Adolescent Psychiatry. (1997). Practice parameters for the assessment and treatment of children and adolescents with substance use disorders. *Journal of the American Academy of Child and Adolescent Psychiatry, 36* (10), 140S–156S.

Bryant, K. J., Windle, M., & West, S. G. (Eds.). (1997). *The science of prevention: Methodological advances from alcohol and substance abuse research.* Washington, DC: American Psychological Association.

Carroll, K. M., & Rounsaville, B. J. (1990). Can a technology model of psychotherapy be applied to cocaine abuse treatment? In L. Onken & J. Blaine (Eds.), *Psychotherapy and counseling in the treatment of drug abuse* (NIDA Research Monograph 104, pp. 79–94). Washington, DC: U.S. Government Printing Office.

Center for Substance Abuse Treatment. (1998). *Adolescent substance abuse: Assessment and treatment* (Treatment Improvement Protocol Series [TIPS]). Rockville, MD: Author.

Center for Treatment Research on Adolescent Drug Abuse. (1998). *Research training program on family based interventions for adolescent drug abuse* (NIDA Grant No. T32-Da07297).

Chambless, D. L. (1996). In defense of dissemination of empirically supported psychological interventions. *Clinical Psychology: Science and Practice, 3,* 230–235.

Dishion, T. J., & Andrews, D. W. (1995). Preventing escalating in problem behaviors with high-risk young adolescents: Immediate and one-year outcomes. *Journal of Consulting and Clinical Psychology, 63,* 538–548.

Docherty, J. P. (1984). Implications of the technological model of psychotherapy. In J. B. W. Williams & R. L. Spitzer (Eds.), *Psychotherapy research: Where are we and where should we go?* New York: Guilford Press.

Elkin, I. (1994). The NIMH treatment of depression collaborative research program: Where we began and where we are. In A. E. Bergin (Ed.), *Handbook of psychotherapy and behavior change* (4th ed., pp. 114–139). New York: Wiley.

Friedlander, M. (1998). Family therapy process research. In M. Nichols & R. Schwartz, *Family therapy: Concepts and methods* (4th ed.). Needham Heights, MA: Allyn & Bacon.

Green, R. J. (1998). Training programs: Guidelines for multicultural transformation. In M. McGoldrick (Ed.), *Re-visioning family therapy: Race, culture, and gender in clinical practice* (pp. 111–117). New York: Guilford Press.

Greenberg, L. S., & Pinsof, W. M. (1986). Process research: Current trends and future perspectives. In L. S. Greenberg & W. M. Pinsof (Eds.), *The psychotherapeutic process: A research handbook* (pp. 3–20). New York: Guilford Press.

Henggeler, S. W., Schoenwald, S. K., Borduin, C. M., Rowland, M. D., & Cunningham, P. B. (1998). *Multisystemic treatment of antisocial behavior in children and adolescents.* New York: Guilford Press.

Hogue, A., Liddle, H. A., Rowe, C., Turner, R. M., Dakof, G. A., & Lapann, K. (1998). Treatment adherence and differentiation in individual versus family therapy for adolescent substance abuse. *Journal of Counseling Psychology, 45,* 104–114.

Hogue, A., Rowe, C., Liddle, H., & Turner, R. (1994). *Therapist Behavior Rating Scale (TBRS).* Philadelphia, PA: Temple University, Center for Research on Adolescent Drug Abuse.

Institute of Medicine. (1989). *Research on children and adolescents with mental, behavioral, and developmental disorders.* Washington, DC: National Academy Press.

Kaslow, F. W. (1991). The art and science of family psychology: Retrospective and perspective. *American Psychologist, 46,* 621–626.

Kazdin, A. E. (1997). A model for developing effective treatments: Progression and interplay of theory, research, and practice. *Journal of Clinical Child Psychology, 26,* 114–129.

L'Abate, L. (1992). Family psychology and family therapy: Comparisons and contrasts. *American Journal of Family Therapy, 20*(1), 3–12.

Liddle, H. A. (1995). Conceptual and clinical dimensions of a multidimensional, multisystems engagement strategy in family-based adolescent treatment. *Psychotherapy: Theory, Research and Practice, 32*(1), 39–58.

Liddle, H. A., Becker, D., & Diamond, G. M. (1997). Family therapy supervision. In C. E. Watkins (Ed.), *Handbook of psychotherapy supervision* (pp. 400–418). New York: Wiley.

Liddle, H. A., Rowe, C. L., Dakof, G. A., & Lyke, J. (1998). Translating parenting research into clinical interventions. *Clinical Child Psychology and Psychiatry, 3,* 419–422.

Liddle, H. A., Santisteban, D. A., Levant, R., & Bray, J. (Eds.). (in press). *Family psychology intervention science.* Washington, DC: American Psychological Association.

Linehan, M. M. (1996, August). *Development and dissemination of treatments for drug abuse.* Paper presented at the 104th annual convention of the American Psychological Association, Toronto, Canada.

National Institute on Drug Abuse. (1998). *Therapy manuals for drug addiction* [On-line]. Available: http:s/h/ www.nida.nih.gov/TxManuals.

Parke, R. D. (1998). Editorial. *Journal of Family Psychology, 12*(1), 3–6.

Pinsof, W., & Wynne, L. (1995). The efficacy of marital and family therapy: An empirical overview, conclusions, and recommendations. *Journal of Marital and Family Therapy, 21,* 585–613.

Stanton, M. D. (1975). Psychology and family therapy. *Professional Psychology, 6,* 45–49.

Stanton, M. D., & Shadish, W. R. (1997). Outcome, attrition, and family-couples treatment for drug abuse: A meta-analysis and review of the controlled, comparative studies. *Psychological Bulletin, 122,* 170–191.

Szapocznik, J., & Kurtines, W. M. (1993). Family psychology and cultural diversity: Opportunities for theory, research, and application. *American Psychologist, 48,* 400–407.

Szapocznik, J., Kurtines, W. M., Santisteban, D. A., & Rio, A. T. (1990). The interplay of advances among theory, research and application in treatment interventions aimed at behavior problem children and adolescents. *Journal of Consulting and Clinical Psychology, 58,* 696–703.

Tolan, P. H., Guerra, N. G., & Kendall, P. C. (1995). A developmental-ecological perspective on antisocial behavior in children and adolescents: Toward a unified risk and intervention framework. *Journal of Consulting and Clinical Psychology, 63,* 579–584.

Vernberg, E. M., Routh, D. K., & Koocher, G. P. (1992). The future of psychotherapy with children: Developmental psychotherapy. *Psychotherapy, 29,* 72–80.

Waldron, H. B. (1997). Adolescent substance abuse and family therapy outcome: A review of randomized trials. In T. H. Ollendick & R. J. Prinz (Eds.), *Advances in clinical child psychology* (Vol. 19, pp. 199–234). New York: Plenum Press.

Weinberg, N., Rahdert, E., Colliver, J. D., & Glantz, M. D. (1998). Adolescent substance abuse: A review of the past 10 years. *Journal of the American Academy of Child and Adolescent Psychiatry, 37* (3), 252–261.

Winters, K., Latimer, W. W., & Stinchfield, R. (1999). Adolescent treatment for alcohol and other drug use. In P. J. Ott & R. Tartar (Eds.), *Sourcebook on substance abuse: Etiology, epidemiology, assessment, and treatment* (pp. 350–361). Boston: Allyn & Bacon.

Howard A. Liddle

FAMILY THERAPY includes a large number of treatment forms with diverse conceptual principles, processes and structures, and clinical foci. Gurman, Kniskern, and Pinsof (1986, p. 565) define family therapy as "any psychotherapeutic endeavor that explicitly focuses on altering the interactions between or among family members and seeks to improve the functioning of the family as a unit, or its subsystems, and/or the functioning of individual members of the family." The field "is unified only in a belief that relationships are of at least as much importance in the behavior and experience of people as are unconscious intrapsychic events" (Gurman & Kniskern, 1981, p. 819).

These family and marriage interventions have been applied to the problems of individuals and discordant relationships, across every stage of the life cycle, and with an enormous variety of family structures (Walsh, 1993). Couples therapy and marital therapy are generally considered subtypes of family therapy (Jacobson & Gurman, 1995), although the historical origins of couple/marital therapy and family therapy are quite distinct (Broderick & Schrader, 1991).

Some family therapy approaches (for example, object relations therapy) reflect extensions of models of psychotherapy with individuals into the interpersonal realm, whereas others (for example, structural therapy and strategic therapy) evolved in less traditional contexts. Family therapy models vary enormously in terms of their typical length, past versus present orientation, and treatment goals. A significant number of population and disorder-specific (such as divorce and remarriage, abuse and violence, sexual dysfunction) methods have emerged since the 1980s.

Key Historical Developments

Present-day family therapy's origins can be traced to many professional disciplines: psychoanalysis, social casework, gynecological medicine and sexology, family life education, applied behaviorism, and others. Whereas the couple/marital therapy segment of the field grew partially out of the "marriage counseling" tradition of the 1920s and 1930s, the major catalyst in the evolution of modern family therapy was the clinical and research interest in the 1940s and 1950s in the multigenerational transmission processes of certain psychiatric disturbances, such as schizophrenia, soon followed by innovative work with child and adolescent-focused problems (Nichols & Schwartz, 1995). Psychiatrists were the most frequently visible early leaders in the field, but important contributions also came from clinical psychologists, communications analysts, social workers, anthropologists, and hypnotherapists. The majority of clinically oriented family and marriage research is conducted by psychologists. Virtually all the founding fathers and mothers of family therapy questioned the dominant individual (mostly psychoanalytic)

models of their day in terms of the development, maintenance, and treatment of clinical problems. The notion of circular causality challenged the time-honored perspective of linear causality.

In the 1960s, the first freestanding family therapy training institutes were established, and the field's first journal, *Family Process*, began publication. In the 1970s, the American Association for Marriage and Family Therapy (formerly the American Association of Marriage Counselors) became the official accrediting and credentialing body in the field, and the American Family Therapy Association (now Academy) was founded by many of the field's pioneers.

In the last two decades, four major evolving trends in the family therapy field increasingly have defined its identity. First, the professional literature of the field has expanded rapidly, and now includes more than three dozen journals published on all five continents and in a dozen languages. Second, research activity, especially on the part of family psychologists, has accelerated and has had a salient influence on training curricula and public health care policy. Third, contemporary social perspectives such as feminism and multiculturalism have widened the views of family life beyond those of traditional mental health theorists and clinicians. Finally, like the field of individual psychotherapy, family therapy has become increasingly integrative in terms of both the structure and the conceptualization of treatment.

Central Assumptions and Concepts

The key conceptual characteristic of the various family therapies is their emphasis on the context in which clinical problems arise. This encompassing systemic view potentially allows clinical attention to all levels of the organization of behavior, from the cellular to the unconscious to the conscious to the interpersonal to the community. Modern family systems theory includes a combination of core concepts from general systems theory (the study of the relationships between and among interacting components of a system that exists over time), cybernetics (the study of the regulatory mechanisms that operate in systems via feedback loops), and family development theory (the study of how families, their subunits, and individual members adapt to change while maintaining their systemic integrity over time). Psychodynamic (especially object relations theory) and social learning theory have also had profound influences on the clinical theorizing of family and couple therapists.

Family systems theory, applied to clinical situations, tends to be antireductionistic, leading therapists to try to understand symptoms and problem behaviors in their relational context. Objective "truth-seeking" is typically discouraged, and the observational constraints and limitations of particular theories ("the map is not the territory") are highlighted, leading to the valuing of multiple points of view. In family systems thinking, normality-abnormality is a relativistic notion, varying with prevailing cultural practices and the developmental exigencies of the family. Although clinical practices vary, the current organization of the family is usually emphasized ("the system is its own best explanation") in planning and carrying out treatment.

In addition to these overarching family systems principles, each of the major methods of family and couple therapy has evolved its own core organizing concepts. Some of these method-specific concepts and terms are identified in Table 1, along with major proponents of these "schools" of therapy.

The Practice of Family Therapy

Who participates in family therapy differs as a function of the presenting problem, the therapist's theoretical orientation, and her personal experience and skill. In cases with a designated or diagnosed "patient," that person is usually, although not always present (e.g., therapy focused on child behavior problems often includes only the parents, who are taught parenting skills). Since family therapy is as much a conceptual perspective as a set of well-defined techniques, it may even be conducted with only one family member (for example, MRI Brief Therapy, Bowen Family Systems Therapy). Family therapy is often limited to the nuclear family, but it may also be transgenerational, and it may be combined with other (such as individual) interventions. Generally, family therapists aim to include the smallest number of persons likely to be able to achieve particular therapeutic goals. Representatives of nonfamily systems (e.g., schools, health care providers), may also be included (Kaslow & Celano, 1995).

Most family therapy is conducted by a solo therapist, although cotherapist pairs and therapy teams including several observer-consultants are common in training settings. Family systems–oriented treatment typically ranges from as few as under ten (solution-focused therapy, MRI Brief Therapy) to as many as hundreds of sessions (Bowen Family Systems Therapy), with the great majority of family work lasting 10 to 20 sessions over less than 6 months (Gurman & Kniskern, 1981).

Goal Setting. All family therapists are concerned with interactional problem-maintaining cycles, though they vary widely in how they identify these cycles and how they intervene to change them. Paper-and-pencil self-report inventories and genograms are used regularly in certain family therapy approaches, and direct (therapist) observation is a common data-gathering method for the purpose of setting treatment goals. Nonetheless, the clinical interview is the primary method for establishing the goals of family therapy.

Although the usual treatment goals of family ther-

apies differ as a function of their views of symptom formation and symptom maintenance, most family systems–oriented clinicians endorse four major categories of therapeutic purposes: (1) reduction of "symptoms" or other problem behaviors, especially by changing interactions patterns that reinforce problem behavior; (2) increased family/couple resourcefulness, such as better communication and problem-solving skills, and enhanced adaptability and flexibility; (3) improvement of the family's/couple's capacity to fulfill the psychological needs of its members, such as attachment and intimacy; and (4) where appropriate, increased family ability to interact effectively with functionally meaningful larger social systems.

In some family treatment approaches (e.g., transgenerational family therapies, psychodynamic–psychoanalytic therapies), certain goals are thought to be essentially universal—that is, to be aimed for in all cases. On the other hand, certain family methods (for example, solution-focused therapy, MRI Brief Therapy) emphasize the setting of treatment goals that are unique to a given family, and almost never seek to achieve such universal ends.

Table 2 presents a sampling of common goals in the various approaches to family therapy.

Techniques. Given the very different historical origins of the major approaches to family therapy, it is not surprising that the variety of common systems-oriented treatment techniques is at least as large as the broad field of individual psychotherapy. Still, there are similarities among those family therapy "schools" that share a somewhat common heritage (strategic and Milan Systemic, for instance).

In the last several years, and in parallel with conceptual shifts in psychotherapy in general, technical eclecticism and theoretical integration have become influential sources of change in both clinical practice and training (Gurman, 1981; Pinsof, 1995). Moreover, as family therapy has generally become more accepted in mainstream health and mental health care treatment systems, its varied methods have been increasingly combined with both other psychosocial interventions (such as individual psychotherapy) and other sorts of intervention (such as psychopharmacological).

In general, and in contrast to much traditional individual psychotherapy, family therapy techniques emphasize behavior change more than enhanced insight or self-understanding. Indeed, meaningful behavior change is often seen as a precursor to, rather than a consequence of improved insight. Moreover, although family therapists usually believe that systemically important change may reverberate across different organizational levels of the family system, early treatment changes are typically sought at the observable, interactional level for pragmatic reasons.

Relatedly, family therapists are more likely than tra-

FAMILY THERAPY. Table 1. Core concepts of the major approaches to family and couple therapy

Therapeutic Approach (proponent)	Selected Core Concepts
Behavioral/cognitive-behavioral (Alexander, Jacobson, Patterson)	Functional analysis, social learning theory, communication and problem-solving
Bowen Family Systems (Bowen, Friedman, Kerr)	Differentiation of self, triangulation, emotional cutoffs
Experiential-humanistic (Greenberg and Johnson, Satir, Whitaker)	Communication styles (e.g., placater-blamer), psychotherapy of the absurd, attachment theory
Integrative (Gurman, Pinsof)	Multiple levels of experience, theoretical and technical eclecticism
MRI Brief Therapy (Jackson, Weakland, Watzlawick)	"Difficulties" vs. "problems," symptom as communication, first- and second-order change
Milan Systemic Therapy (Boscolo, Cecchin, Selvini-Palazzoli)	Therapeutic neutrality, "dirty games," counterparadox
Narrative (Epston, White)	Constructivism, "languaging," problem-saturated descriptions
Psychodynamic-psychoanalytic (Ackerman, Dicks, Scharff)	Object relations, projective identification, splitting
Psychoeducational (Anderson, Goldstein, McFarlane)	Biopsychosocial theory, stress-diathesis, expressed emotion
Solution-focused (de Shazar and Berg, O'Hanlon)	Focus on solutions vs. problems, disbelief in resistance
Strategic (Erickson, Haley, Madanes)	Power and control, family life cycle, function of problems
Structural (Aponte, Minuchin)	Boundaries, hierarchies, coalitions and alliances
Transgenerational (Boszormenyi-Nagy, Framo, Paul)	Invisible loyalties, ledgers and debts, family mourning

ditional individual psychotherapists to emphasize the importance of change-inducing and change-supporting interventions that occur away from the consultation room. In family therapy, change is usually sought in the natural relationships between and among family members more than between family members and the clinician.

Therapeutic techniques in family/couple therapy tend to consist of those oriented toward cognitive change and behavior change. Cognitively oriented techniques, whether of the direct (e.g., the cognitive therapist's identification and modification of "automatic thoughts" and "cognitive distortions,") or indirect (the "positive reframing" of the undesirable behavior of a family member) type, are geared toward shifting the meaning of relationship behaviors and the (usually negative) contributions associated with these meanings. Some attribution-focused interventions (e.g., those in cognitive-behavioral therapy) are assumed to reflect the reality of a patient's internal framework and dialogue, whereas others (e.g., strategic therapy and MRI Brief Therapy) are set forth for mere pragmatic reasons, that is, to promote problem-relevant change, without regard for the psychological "truthfulness" of their attributions.

Family therapy techniques that emphasize behavioral change can be differentiated on the basis of whether they (mostly implicitly) assume that family members lack the requisite skills or knowledge, or whether such capacities are already present in their repertoires but are being blocked from use. Action-oriented interventions,

FAMILY THERAPY. Table 2. Representative treatment goals in various family therapy approaches

Therapeutic Approach	Representative Treatment Goal
Behavioral/cognitive-behavioral	Improved communication/problem solving
Bowen Family Systems	Increased differentiation
Experiential-humanistic	Personal growth
Integrative	Greater interactional insight
MRI Brief	Second-order change
Milan Systemic	Changing symptom bearer's role
Narrative	Resolution of presenting problem
Psychodynamic-psychoanalytic	Disentangling interlocking pathologies
Psychoeducational	Relapse prevention
Solution-focused	Finding creative solutions
Strategic	Disruption of problem-maintaining sequences
Structural	Improved subsystem functioning
Transgenerational	Increased trust

FAMILY THERAPY. Table 3. Selected in-session and out-of-session family therapy techniques

Techniques Used in Session (therapy approach)	Techniques Used Out of Session (therapy approach)
Circular questioning (Milan Systemic)	Family management skills (psychoeducational)
Communication training (behavioral)	Letters, therapeutic (narrative)
Family sculpting (experiential)	Ordeal prescription (strategic)
Interpretation of unconscious processes (psychoanalytic)	Paradoxical injunctions (MRI)
Reframing (strategic)	Parent management training (behavioral)
Enactment (structural)	Pretending, prescription of (strategic)
Scaling/miracle/exceptions questions (solution-focused)	Rituals, prescription of (Milan Systemic) (e.g., invariant prescription)
Teaching the emotional functioning of systems (Bowen Family Systems)	Task assignment (structural)

appropriately, can be separated into those involving therapeutic directives which assume behavioral competence (as in much of structural family therapy) and those providing skill training (as in much of behavioral parent training), which assumes that new learning is necessary. Both categories of action-oriented interventions include specific methods that are called upon for in-session and out-of-session use.

Table 3 presents a sampling of commonly used family therapy techniques.

The Effectiveness of Family Therapy

There is an increasingly large body of empirical research supporting the effectiveness of family therapy (Gurman & Kniskern, 1981; Gurman, Kniskern, & Pinsof, 1986; Lebow & Gurman, 1995, 1996; Pinsof & Wynne, 1995). At the same time, several historically prominent treatment approaches have generated virtually no scientifically acceptable evidence of their efficacy. Thus Bowen Family Systems Therapy, symbolic-experiential therapy, Milan Systemic Therapy, MRI Brief Therapy, contextual therapy, narrative therapy, and solution-focused therapy maintain their influence in the field largely by virtue of their proponents' personal charisma and conceptual coherence. On the other hand, a reasonable accumulation of empirical support has been amassed for other treatment methods: cognitive-behavioral couple therapy, psychoeducational therapy, functional family therapy, emotionally focused couple therapy, behavioral parent training, insight-oriented marital therapy, and structural therapy.

Adult Disorders. Several disorders of adults are treated in family therapy.

Schizophrenia. Psychoeducational and behavioral methods, used in conjunction with medication, have been shown to be very helpful in reducing both symptoms and rehospitalization, at a greatly reduced cost compared to standard care. These methods emphasize interpersonal skills training and coping strategies.

Affective Disorders. Similar psychoeducational methods have shown promise in the treatment of patients with bipolar illness. In addition, behavioral marital therapy has reliably been shown to facilitate positive change in depressive symptomatology and marital satisfaction for couples whose relationships are significantly distressed.

Substance Abuse. Structural family therapy has demonstrated its ability to keep opiate addicts and their families in treatment longer than standard approaches and has been associated with decreased drug use and improved social functioning. A number of family-based models have been found to be useful in motivating alcoholics to enter treatment, although long-term outcomes have been only marginally better than traditional individual treatment.

Anxiety Disorders. Inclusion of an agoraphobic patient's spouse in treatment sessions appears to lower dropout rates and to increase the index patient's exposure practice. Spousal inclusion also helps reduce marital conflict, thereby facilitating change in the phobic partner.

Marital Discord. Compelling evidence exists that three conjoint couple therapy approaches are clinically effective. Behavioral marital therapy, the most extensively studied couple method, emphasizes communication and problem-solving skills training. Insight-oriented marital therapy addresses both individual and dyadic emotional processes. Emotionally focused couple therapy is the only validated couple approach rooted in attachment theory. Relatedly, sex therapy methods, while not historically connected to the family therapy movement, are decidedly interpersonal in focus and offer the treatments of choice for premature ejaculation, vaginismus, primary orgasmic dysfunction, and secondary erectile dysfunction.

Child and Adolescent Disorders. Family therapy is used successfully in treating some adolescent and childhood disorders.

Childhood Conduct Disorders. Behavioral parent training (also known as parent management training or social learning family therapy) is the most frequently investigated and validated treatment approach for conduct disorders of childhood. Of note, successful parental contingency management training also appears to increase marital satisfaction.

Delinquency and Drug Abuse. Three methods of family therapy have been found to be more effective than treatment-as-usual or individual psychotherapy: Functional family therapy, a variant of behavioral family therapy; structural family therapy; and multisystemic therapy, a variant and extension of the structural model. Taken together, these three approaches have reduced recidivism, drug use, and other forms of impulse control problems. They have helped therapists keep a larger proportion of cases in treatment than traditional forms of psychosocial intervention.

The Future of Family Therapy

Family therapy began as a clinical and conceptual movement directly opposed to the prevailing views of behavior pathology and behavior change. For a long time, family therapy remained, quite intentionally, outside the power and province of mainstream mental health practice. But family and couple therapy have been assimilated well into virtually every type of mental health delivery system. The field's iconoclastic tendencies have given way to the integrative trends in the broad domain of psychotherapy.

More recently as well, the earlier claims of family therapy's universal power have been appropriately tempered by more cautious and refined assessments of the helpfulness of these varied clinical methods. Family therapy is no longer viewed, even by most of its most vociferous and heralded heroes, as a panacea for life's difficulties. At the same time, the capacity of many family therapies to effect truly significant clinical change is beyond dispute, and some of its methods undoubtedly constitute the treatments of choice for specific problems. The major ethical responsibility of the family therapy field for the future is to continue to assess systematically the effectiveness of its clinical techniques and to improve the specificity with which particular strategies and methods are called upon for dealing with the wide array of clinical problems that regularly face workaday psychotherapists.

Bibliography

Broderick, C. B., & Schrader, S. S. (1991). The history of professional marriage and family therapy. In A. S. Gurman & D. P. Kniskern (Eds.), *Handbook of family therapy* (2nd ed., pp. 3–40). New York: Brunner /Mazel.

Gurman, A. S. (1981). Integrative marital therapy: Toward the development of an interpersonal approach. In S. Budman (Ed.), *Forms of brief therapy* (pp. 415–457). New York: Guilford Press.

Gurman, A. S., & Kniskern, D. P. (1981). Family therapy outcome research. In A. S. Gurman & D. P. Kniskern (Eds.), *Handbook of family therapy.* New York: Brunner/Mazel.

Gurman, A. S., Kniskern, D. P., & Pinsof, W. M. (1986). Research on the process and outcome of marital and family therapy. In S. L. Garfield & A. E. Bergin (Eds.), *Handbook of psychotherapy and behavior change* (3rd ed., pp. 565–624). New York: Wiley.

Jacobson, N. S., & Gurman, A. S. (Eds.). (1995). *Clinical handbook of couple therapy.* New York: Guilford Press.

Kaslow, N., & Celano, M. P. (1995). The family therapies. In A. S. Gurman & S. B. Messer (Eds.), *Essential psychotherapies* (pp. 343–402). New York: Guilford Press.

Lebow, J. L., & Gurman, A. S. (1995). Research assessing couple and family therapy. *Annual Review of Psychology, 46,* 27–57.

Lebow, J. L., & Gurman, A. S. (1996, January/February). Making a difference: A new research review offers good news to couples and family therapists. *Family Therapy Networker,* 69–76.

Nichols, M. P., & Schwartz, R. C. (1995). *Family therapy: concepts and methods* (3rd ed.). Boston: Allyn & Bacon.

Pinsof, W. M. (1995). *Integrative problem-centered therapy.* New York: Basic Books.

Pinsof, W. M., & Wynne, L. C. (Eds.). (1995). The effectiveness of marital and family therapy [Special issue]. *Journal of Marital and Family Therapy, 21* (4).

Walsh, F. (Ed.). (1993). *Normal family processes* (2nd ed.). New York: Guilford Press.

Alan S. Gurman

FAMILY VIOLENCE has existed for centuries and remains a daunting social problem today. Traditionally, much of what occurred within the home was considered the concern of the family, not the state. The women's movement focused attention on both domestic violence and child abuse, paving the way for new legislation and social action. Public concern with elder abuse is even more recent, arising primarily in light of a few widely reported cases. Family violence, which is associated with many societal ills (such as delinquency, depression, and substance abuse), occurs in all social classes and ethnicities, although poverty is one risk factor.

Definitions

Spousal or partner violence can range from mild physical aggression, such as pushing or slapping, to violent physical assault and homicide. It also includes spousal or partner rape. Child and elder maltreatment are divided into two categories: intentional acts of commission (abuse) or omission (neglect). *Physical abuse* is defined as nonaccidental acts of commission by an adult that leave signs of physical harm. Physical abuse can vary from overzealous spanking or hitting to acts that break bones or cause death. *Physical neglect* consists of failure to provide the proper or necessary care or support for a child or elder person's well-being. Acts of neglect include inadequate nutrition, abandonment, and refusal of needed medical care. *Sexual abuse* is defined as sexual interactions with a child or nonconsensual adult for purposes of sexual stimulation. Examples include rape, incest, sodomy, oral copulation, fondling, and exhibitionism. *Psychological or emotional maltreatment* is especially difficult to define. However, psychological maltreatment of children consists of acts of omission or commission that damage immediately or ultimately behavioral, cognitive, affective, or physical functioning. Examples of psychological maltreatment include acts of rejecting, terrorizing, isolating, exploiting, and promoting antisocial or illegal behavior (gang membership and drug use, for example).

Child Maltreatment

Reports of and responses to maltreatment of children have both changed over time.

Prevalence. Reports to Child Protective Services (CPS) provide one prevalence estimate of child maltreatment. Nationally, in 1997, CPS received nearly 3 million reports. However, on average, only 33% of these cases were "substantiated" (CPS determined that abuse had occurred), resulting in nearly one million substantiated child victims (approximately 55% reported for neglect, 24% for physical abuse, 13% for sexual abuse, 6% for emotional maltreatment, 2% for medical neglect, and 12% for "other" forms of maltreatment, including abandonment and congenital drug addiction). Between three and five children are killed each day in the United States as a result of child abuse. Since the late 1970s, reports of child maltreatment to CPS have skyrocketed; nationally, there was a 331% increase from 1976 to 1993. Mandatory reporting of suspected child abuse and heightened public awareness probably explain the increase, as opposed to increases in maltreatment itself. However, proportionally, reports to CPS of child sexual abuse declined in 1995 to 1997 compared to preceding years. It may be that growing concerns about false reports are leading people to be either more skeptical of abuse allegations or more hesitant to report their suspicions.

Random sample survey studies may provide better prevalence estimates than reports to CPS (because many incidents are not reported to the authorities), although random sample surveys are not without their problems as well. Surveys report mainly physical and sexual abuse. Based on parental self-report, survey studies indicate that about 700,000 children in the United States were subjected to severe violent behavior in 1985, but that these rates decreased somewhat in 1992. Although the lower rates reported for 1992 are encouraging, such statistics may still represent an underestimation because parents were hesitant to report abusive acts. When 10- to 16-year-olds themselves are interviewed, approximately 7.5% report at least one incident of physical assault by a family member. Nonfamily assaults (22%) were more frequent than family assaults.

Estimates of the prevalence of sexual abuse vary depending on how sexual abuse is defined (for example, if exhibitionism is included). Moreover, retrospective studies, which are common, suffer from cohort effects and respondents' memory biases and candor. According to community surveys 38 to 54% of women report experiencing at least one episode of sexual abuse before age 18; 12% report experiencing abuse before the age of 12. However, when 10- to 16-year-olds were interviewed, the lifetime rate of attempted or completed sexual victimization was 10.5%, considerably lower than that indicated in retrospective studies of adults. The retrospective nature of the adults' reports and the young age of some of the teenagers surveyed, as well as differences in cohorts' definitions of sexual abuse may account for the age-related differences noted.

Legal Response. Given widespread use of corporal punishment by parents, teachers, and clergy, it is possible that the *average* child of the past would be considered a child maltreatment victim today. Laws originally focused on nonparental assault or on orphaned or delinquent children. In 1875, however, a dramatic case of an adopted and abused child named Mary Ellen in New York led to greater state intervention. Under laws intended to protect animals (not children) from abuse by legal caretakers, attorneys were successful in having Mary Ellen removed from the home. Gradually, every state developed a CPS division for handling intrafamilial child maltreatment cases, to which any citizen could report suspected child abuse. Later, in the 1960s, C. Henry Kempe's paper on "the battered child syndrome," showing that some children's injuries would be nearly impossible through accidents, spurred establishment of mandatory reporting laws nationwide. Mandatory reporting laws differ from state to state but generally require professionals who work with children to report suspicions of child abuse to authorities.

Often CPS is the state's sole public agency for receiving and investigating reports of maltreatment of children within familial, foster care, and daycare settings. If a child is found to be in imminent danger, he or she may be immediately removed from home. Children who are left in abusive homes have a 40 to 70% chance of being reinjured and as much as a 5% chance of being killed. If services (such as substance abuse counseling) are deemed appropriate, they will be offered. If the child is removed or if needed services are refused, the case will be heard in juvenile court. Juvenile court can maintain custody of the child, place the child in foster care, and terminate parental rights, although it cannot directly punish parents.

Assaults on children can also be reported to the police. If extrafamilial abuse has occurred or intrafamilial abuse is severe, prosecution may be initiated within the criminal justice system. Penal codes in each state describe laws covering child abuse. Many more child maltreatment cases are handled by juvenile than criminal courts, but charges of child sexual abuse are particularly likely to result in criminal court action.

Especially in child sexual abuse cases, where physical evidence of assault is often lacking, children may be repeatedly interviewed by authorities or required to testify in juvenile or criminal court. Questions about how to conduct a forensic interview with children and about children's memory accuracy have sparked debate in recent years. [See Children's Eyewitness Testimony.] It has also been suggested that involvement in forensic interviews and prosecutions exacerbates the trauma caused by child abuse. In the short-term, involvement as victim/witnesses in the criminal court is associated with prolongment of emotional distress for a subset of children. The possibility of long-term effects into adulthood is just beginning to be studied. Several legal innovations, such as testimony via closed-circuit TV and joint interviews across CPS and police agencies, have been recommended to ease children's ordeals.

Spousal/Partner Abuse and Elder Maltreatment

Reports of maltreatment of adults are also significant.

Prevalence. Like estimates of child maltreatment, estimates of partner and elder maltreatment depend on whether official reports or random sample surveys are utilized. The latter suggest that only a fraction of all incidents of domestic violence or elder maltreatment are brought to the attention of authorities, with reports of elder maltreatment being especially low. One well-regarded random sample survey indicated that nonfatal partner abuse occurs in one out of every six households in the United States annually, with violent assaults occurring in 3% of households. Across studies, between 10 and 30% of women indicate they experienced some form of relationship violence. Incidents of spousal or intimate rape range from 1 to 10% of women reporting that their current husband or romantic partner attempted to force them to have sex. Marital rape appears to co-occur with other forms of domestic violence.

Regarding elder maltreatment, one study found that of 1,000 elderly persons, approximately 32 had been victims of some form of maltreatment. The abuse was most often perpetrated by a spouse, although elders'

adult children composed one fifth of the perpetrators. Male caregivers were more likely than female caregivers to perpetrate elder abuse. Among elders, cognitive or emotional difficulties, deterioration, and dementia are risk factors for abuse or neglect.

Legal Response. For domestic violence, legal response mainly involves the criminal justice system. Only relatively recently have police and legal professionals taken a firm stance in prosecuting perpetrators of domestic violence. Following horrific stories of domestic abuse and inadequate legal intervention (e.g., *Thurman v. City of Torrington, Conn.*), state and federal legislation was passed to ensure anyone who commits a violent act against another, regardless of their relationship, is prosecuted. For example, states no longer include spousal exceptions in their rape laws. Police are also now able to make arrests when they have probable cause to believe that a person committed a misdemeanor domestic violence crime. Furthermore, many states have enacted mandatory arrest laws for perpetrators of domestic violence and implemented mandatory overnight incarcerations or cooling-off periods so that the perpetrator is not released immediately after being arrested.

Currently, there is considerable debate about the effectiveness of mandatory arrests in preventing further domestic violence. The utility of mandatory arrests was dramatically shown in a Minneapolis study. When police arrested the perpetrator, the recidivism rate was only 10%, whereas when police either implemented a separation period by having one person leave or performed on-sight advice/mediation, the recidivism rate was 25%. Although these findings sparked a widespread campaign for mandatory arrest policies, the Minneapolis results have not always replicated. Also, when perpetrators are unemployed or when the violence is severe, mandatory arrests may be associated with an increase in subsequent domestic violence. Mandatory arrest effectiveness also appears to be influenced by ethnicity. Some recommend that police be given both special training to deal with domestic violence calls and "structured discretion" to make warrantless arrests when they believe that it will help resolve a current crisis and prevent further violence.

Other recent legal responses focus on interventions following initial police contact. These reforms include civil protection orders (restraining orders), special prosecution units, and treatment for batterers. However, these responses have met with mixed success. For instance, victims of domestic abuse often report that restraining orders do not help, and despite the existence of special prosecution units for domestic violence, rates of actual prosecution remain fairly low. Among those prosecuted, rates of recidivism are not generally affected, although there appears to be a reduction in recidivism when victims initiate and remain actively involved in the prosecution. At times, abused partners resort to violence: Years of enduring domestic violence has been used as a defense when the formerly abused partner kills the abuser, even when no immediate violence co-occurred.

For elder maltreatment, legal response has typically relied on civil litigation. Although both state and federal legislation have addressed problems of elder abuse and mandatory reporting laws exist, to date, much less is known about the effects of legal intervention. Furthermore, social service agencies remain in need of specific training on how to intervene in situations of elder abuse.

Given increasing public attention to family violence, prevalence estimates and legal interventions may continue to change. Prevention of family violence remains a crucial societal goal.

[*See also* Child Abuse and Neglect; Domestic Violence; *and* Violence and Aggression.]

Bibliography

Briere, J., Berliner, L., Bulkley, J., Jenny, C., & Reid, T. (1995). *The APSAC handbook on child maltreatment.* Newbury Park, CA: Sage.

Browne, A. (1993). Violence against women by male partners: Prevalence, outcomes, and policy implications. *American Psychologist, 48,* 1077–1087.

Buzawa, E. S., & Buzawa, C. G. (Eds.). (1996). *Do arrests and restraining orders work?* Thousand Oaks, CA: Sage.

Fagen, J., & Browne, A. (1994). Violence between spouses and intimates: Physical aggression between men and women in intimate relationships. In A. J. Reiss Jr. & J. A. Roth (Eds.), *Understanding and preventing violence: Vol. 3. Social influences* (pp. 115–292). Washington, DC: National Academy Press.

Garner, J., & Fagen, J. (1997). Victims of domestic violence. In R. C. Davis, A. J. Lurigio, & W. G. Skogan (Eds.), *Victims of crime* (pp. 53–85). Thousand Oaks, CA: Sage.

Goodman, G. S., Emery, R., & Haugaard, J. (1997). Developmental psychology and the law: Divorce, child maltreatment, foster care, and adoption. In W. Damon (Series Ed.) & I. Sigel & A. Renninger (Vol. Eds.), *Handbook of child psychology: Child psychology in practice* (pp. 775–874). New York: Wiley.

Kaplan, S. (Ed.). (1996). *Family violence: A clinical and legal guide.* Washington, DC: American Psychiatric Press.

Kapp, M. B. (1995). Elder mistreatment: Legal interventions and policy uncertainties. *Behavioral Sciences and the Law, 13,* 365–380.

Kempe, C. H., Silverman, F., Steele, B., Droegemueller, W., & Silver, H. (1962). Battered child syndrome. *Journal of the American Medical Association, 181,* 17–24.

Ohlin, L., & Tonry, M. (Eds.). (1989). *Family violence. Crime and justice: A review of research* (Vol. 11). Chicago: University of Chicago Press.

Schuller, R. A., & Hastings, P. A. (1996). Trials of battered women who kill: The impact of alternative forms of expert evidence. *Law and Human Behavior, 20,* 167–187.

Walker, L. E. A. (1996). Assessment of abusive family spousal relationships. In F. W. Kaslow (Ed.), *Handbook of relational diagnosis and dysfunctional family patterns* (pp. 338–356). New York: Wiley.

Gail S. Goodman and Jodi A. Quas

FANTASY. In everyday usage, fantasy is applied to inner experiences marked by vivid imagery, intense emotion, and a paucity of logic. Nocturnal dreams, when they delight or terrorize us, are readily labeled fantasy. Likewise, daydreams of blazing ambition, sizzling sensuality, or shattering revenge, are widely accepted as fantasy. Not all dreams and daydreams are so considered, however. Mundane dreams, when recalled at all, are commonly described as "just thinking." Brief, intrusive waking thoughts are considered mere distractions.

Psychology, too, lacks a clear, universal definition of fantasy, and the term describes only a range of mental experiences or processes. As in popular usage, the presence of vivid imagery and emotion, together with a relaxation or absence of logic, are key factors in its identification.

Clinical psychologists encounter fantasy in many contexts. A set of thoughts, feelings, and images about one's mother, spouse, or therapist is termed fantasy if deemed by a clinician as less than accurate. Early "memories," upon close examination in psychological treatment, may prove condensations or distortions of childhood experiences, hence fantasies. Reports of dreams and daydreams, whether as horrific symptoms (nightmares, flashbacks) or as insights and growth experiences, are readily integrated into psychological therapies. Made-up stories are deliberately elicited for diagnostic purposes, as in the well-known Thematic Apperception Test.

In working toward a better definition of fantasy, psychologist Eric Klinger noted those mental activities that lie well outside fantasy's boundaries; that is, thoughts directed toward completion of a task, or orientation to the environment, clearly are not fantasies. The remainder, those thoughts perceived by the experiencing person as *not* immediately useful or relevant, may be deemed fantasies. By this proposed definition, all human beings pass a considerable portion of their lives in fantastic thought, for it is the baseline to which mental life returns whenever immediate concerns may be relaxed.

History

At the threshold of the twentieth century, Sigmund Freud turned a harsh spotlight upon inner life, and upon fantasy in particular. He hypothesized nocturnal dreams to be fulfillments of desires, as were daydreams, and found all such fantasies tied to a primitive, irrational mode of thought termed *primary process*. This type of thought—distorted, condensed, rife with imagery and symbolism—he deemed largely unconscious. He contrasted primary process with *secondary process*: the mature, logical, problem-solving mode of thought. He also called attention to the irrational fantasies that arise in our dealings with other people, and how these create problems in relationships.

Despite the furor over Freud's theories and their dramatic impact upon clinical practice and society, the systematic study of fantasy found little place in American psychology before 1960. Behaviorism had so captivated the hearts and intellects of psychologists of that era that no place could be made for the study of private experience. That which could not be directly observed and measured, it was argued, must remain outside the realm of science.

In the 1950s, a spate of psychophysiological studies of rapid eye movement (REM) sleep and concomitant dreams stimulated a resurgence of interest in inner experience. Within several years, sleep and dream laboratories were in operation all over the country, and dreams were being routinely dissected and analyzed. Singer's (1966) book on daydreaming demonstrated the reality of an experimental approach even to this ubiquitous aspect of inner life, and began charting its parameters. Popular culture, at the time obsessed with Eastern philosophies and drug-induced enhancement of consciousness, eagerly embraced the new direction in psychology. Imagery, imagination, and creativity, once ostracized along with dreams and daydreams, became popular topics for psychological inquiry.

In subsequent decades, efforts have been made to integrate experimental findings in such diverse areas as dreams, daydreams, imaginative play, hallucination, and even hypnosis, in order to consider them under the broad umbrella of fantasy. Such efforts stress the continuity of inner life, and the possibility of identifying broad fantasy styles that transcend an individual's waking and sleeping fantasy productions. Dreams and waking fantasies are said to lie along a continuum, and to blend into one another at the borders of sleep. Klinger's (1971) work in this regard led to the parsimonious view that all fantasy, waking and sleeping, is expressive of "current concerns." Not all agree, of course, and some biologically oriented researchers insist that dreams, in particular, are essentially random side-effects of physiological processes.

Sick or Healthy?

Freud's identification of fantasy as a primitive mental process, associated with neurotic symptoms, reinforced a social bias against it. Americans, in particular, identify action, as opposed to fantasy, with health and suc-

cess. Daydreaming, already suspect in children, came to be viewed with direst concern as a likely precursor to psychosis. In adults, daydreaming was cause for ridicule, a demonstration of neurosis or inadequacy, as in Thurber's popular story about Walter Mitty. As for dreams, those were best left to poets and psychoanalysts.

Over the years, the search for causal links between fantasy and psychopathology has turned up little. Rather, findings suggest that individuals who freely access and accept their fantasies, waking and sleeping, are able to use them in creative and adaptive ways. Physicist Albert Einstein, examining his own manner of thinking and working, wrote of his remarkable conclusion that the gift of fantasy had meant more to him than his talent for absorbing knowledge.

Persons who interpret most life events from a single, narrow perspective, called *paranoid* or *delusional*, best demonstrate an utterly constricted fantasy life. It takes a bit of flexible, fantastic thought to explore alternative avenues of thought, empathize with other points of view, and creatively integrate new information. A chronic inability to use this normal mode of thought is suggestive of a threatened, fragile, inflexible personality.

Fear of fantasy appears deeply rooted in American culture, emerging anew whenever vivid, emotional, illogical images are presented to the public in new forms. This is one factor in the periodic uprising by psychologists, clerics, and other well-meaning groups against newspaper comic strips, comic books, movies, television, computer games, role-playing games, and the like.

[*See also* Daydreams; *and* Dreams.]

Bibliography

Klinger, E. (1971). *Structure and functions of fantasy.* New York: Wiley. Serious attempt at a comprehensive, unified theory of fantasy.

Singer, J. L. (1966). *Daydreaming.* New York: Random House.

Singer, J. L. (1975). *The inner world of daydreaming.* Describes and integrates seminal studies in the exploration of inner experience.

Starker, S. (1982). *Fantastic thought: Dreams, daydreams, hallucinations and hypnosis.* Englewood Cliffs, NJ: Prentice Hall. Explores the continuity of fantasy life and evidence for fantasy styles.

Starker, S. (1985). *F-states: The power of fantasy in human creativity.* Van Nuys, CA: Newcastle. Popularized account of the role of fantasy in creative thought.

Starker, S. (1989). *Evil influences: Crusades against the mass media.* New Brunswick, NJ: Transaction Books. Documents the social upheaval caused by fantasy in comics, novels, television, computer games, and other forms of media.

Steven Starker

FAR SENSES. *See* Hearing; *and* Vision and Sight.

FATHERING. Since the late 1800s, fatherhood has been of interest to at least some psychologists, and it has been the focus of considerable research, theory, and speculation since the late 1960s. As a result, a large literature has accumulated and substantial advances have been made in efforts to understand father-child relationships, paternal influences on child development, and the particular impact of father involvement on children and families (see Lamb, 1997, for detailed reviews).

A Brief History of Fatherhood

The established "history of fatherhood" is primarily a history of the more affluent and well-educated white men who colonized what became the United States. Little is known about Native American fathers or about the nature of fatherhood for Black men living under slavery and in the face of extraordinary hardship even after emancipation. Indeed, cultural and subcultural variations in fatherhood and its manifestations are only beginning to receive more than cursory attention from scholars (Hewlett, 1992; Lamb, 1987). One can discern four phases over the last two centuries of White American social history, however (Lamb, 1986; Pleck, 1984; Pleck & Pleck, 1997). In each of these, a different theme became prominent in writing about or to fathers, making other aspects of a complex, multifaceted role seem much less important by comparison.

The Moral Teacher or Guide. The earliest phase was one that extended from Puritan times through the Colonial period into early Republican times. During this lengthy period, the father's role was predominantly defined by responsibility for moral oversight and moral teaching. By popular consensus, fathers were deemed primarily responsible for ensuring that their children grew up with an appropriate sense of values, acquired primarily from the study of religious materials like the Bible. To the extent that a broader role was defined, fathers assumed responsibility for the education of children—not necessarily because education and literacy were valued in their own right but because children had to be literate to read the Scriptures.

The Breadwinner. Mothers and fathers had clearly shared the responsibility for provisioning before industrialization reduced the importance of both subsistence agriculture and home industry, forcing a separation between in- and out-of-home work. Industrialization prompted an important shift in the dominant conceptualization of the father's role as successful breadwinning became *the* criterion by which "good fathers" were appraised. The pursuit of economic self-sufficiency was even more burdensome for Black Americans, as men

left their families while pursuing jobs in distant northern cities (Griswold, 1993). For these families, the fathers' pursuit of paid work meant long periods of father absence. The emphasis on breadwinning endured from the mid-nineteenth century through the Great Depression.

The Sex-Role Model. Perhaps as a result of the disruption and dislocation brought about in rapid succession by the Great Depression, the New Deal, and World War II, the 1940s brought to prominence a new conceptualization of fatherhood, manifest primarily in a literature focused on the presumed or declared inadequacy of many fathers. Although breadwinning and moral guardianship remained important, focus shifted to the father's function as a sex-role model, especially for his sons. Many books and articles in the professional and popular literature focused on the need for strong sex-role models and the apparent failures of most men.

The New Nurturant Father. Around the mid-1970s, finally, a fourth stage emerged. For the first time, many writers and commentators emphasized that fathers could and should be nurturant parents, actively involved in the day-to-day care of their children. Active parenting was defined as the central component of fatherhood and was implicitly (sometimes even explicitly) portrayed as the yardstick by which "good fathers" might be assessed. As Griswold (1993) noted, fathers had been exhorted to be more involved in the care of their children since early in the century, but the 1970s marked a change in the relative and defining importance of such behavior. This concern with paternal participation in day-to-day child care prompted a focus on comparative analyses of the ways in which mothers and fathers cared for their children.

Summary. All four of the images or functions discerned by family historians remain important today, although the extent of their importance varies across cultural, ethnic, religious, and social class groupings. Fathers fill many roles, even if the relative importance of each varies from one cultural context to another, and thus fathering must be viewed in the context of the multiple activities that fathers undertake for and with their children (e.g., bread-winning, sex-role modeling, moral guidance, emotional support of mothers).

Components of Contemporary Father Involvement

Perhaps the most striking features of father involvement are (1) the diverse array of functions viewed as aspects of father involvement and (2) the vast individual and subcultural variability in the definition of and investment in these functions. Because the core features of mothering (nurturance and protection) are more universally recognized, moreover, much greater consensus exists about "good mothers" than about "good fathers." Committed fathers may perform in vastly different ways, whereas the same performances may be viewed as successful or unsuccessful depending on the implicit definitions held by those making the evaluations.

Economic provisioning, or bread-winning, is one feature of fatherhood that is almost universally viewed as central. A second feature is the psychosocial and emotional support of female partners (the mothers of the men's children) with special emphasis on the current partners (Cummings & O'Reilly, 1997; Parke & Buriel, 1998). Third is the nurturing and provision of care to young children. There continues to be widespread disagreement about the importance of this function, and even when it is evaluated positively, its importance may be seen to vary depending on the age and gender of the children. Even though (or perhaps because) this function approximates "mothering" in many respects, it is generally viewed today as secondary—less important than mothering by mothers and less important than the other functions of fatherhood. Fourth, there is moral and ethical guidance, viewed as a core feature of fatherhood within most religious traditions even though, in reality, most such guidance or socialization within the family is performed by mothers.

Although scholars do not question the fact that fathers have multiple roles and may influence their children in many ways (direct and indirect), the literature on paternal behavior is primarily concerned with interactions between fathers and children, and this limited focus is obvious in the next section. In particular, studies concerned with father involvement have focused narrowly on what fathers do with their children, rather than the other ways in which they contribute. The single-minded focus on quantitative and unidimensional conceptions of fatherhood and paternal involvement that dominated scholarship in the 1970s and 1980s has only yielded in the last several years to broader and more inclusive definitions of fatherhood.

Characteristics of Paternal Behavior

Assessing Levels of Paternal Involvement. For purposes of analysis, one can distinguish three components of paternal involvement (Lamb, Pleck, Charnov, & Levine, 1987). The first and most restrictive type of paternal involvement (*engagement* or *interaction*) involves time spent in actual one-on-one interaction with the child (whether feeding her, helping him with homework, or playing catch in the garden). Time spent in child-related housework or time spent in one room while the child is in an adjacent room is included in a second category of activity that implies parental *accessibility* to the child, rather than direct interaction.

Third, *responsibility* involves taking ultimate responsibility for ensuring the child's welfare and care. Responsibility involves making child-care and baby-sitting arrangements, ensuring that the child has clothes to wear, and making arrangements for care and nurturance when the child is sick. It involves more than "helping out" or "baby-sitting."

Extent of Paternal Involvement. In two-parent families in which mothers are unemployed, the average father spends about 20 to 25% as much time as the mother does in direct interaction or engagement with his children, and about a third as much time being accessible to his children (Lamb et al., 1987; Pleck, 1997). Many fathers assume essentially no responsibility (as previously defined) for their children's care or rearing, however.

In two-parent families with employed mothers, the levels of paternal compared with maternal engagement and accessibility are both substantially higher than in families with unemployed mothers. Lamb et al. (1987) reported figures for direct interaction and accessibility averaging 33 and 65%, respectively, whereas Pleck's (1997) later review reported that the averages had increased to 44 and 66%, respectively, by the early 1990s. So far as responsibility was concerned, however, there was initially no evidence that maternal employment had a major effect on the level of paternal involvement. Even when both mothers and fathers were employed 30 or more hours per week, the amount of responsibility assumed by fathers appeared as little as when mothers were unemployed. As noted below, however, the situation appears to have changed by the 1990s.

Child and family characteristics have much less effect on levels of paternal involvement than one might expect (Pleck, 1997). Both parents spend more time with their children when the children are younger. Fathers tend to spend more time with boys than with girls, regardless of the children's ages. There are no consistent regional, ethnic, or religious variations in the amount of time that parents, mothers or fathers, spend with their children.

Changes Over Time. There have been gradual changes in the extent of paternal involvement over the last quarter century. In his most comprehensive review, Pleck (1997) concluded that the average levels of father involvement, whether viewed in absolute or relative terms, had indeed increased. The average father spent approximately a third as much time as the average mother in direct interaction in the late 1970s, whereas that figure had increased to approximately 43% by the early 1990s. Likewise, whereas the average father was accessible to his children about half as much as the average mother in the earlier surveys, this figure has increased to almost two thirds of the time by the early 1990s.

Time use data do not yield good estimates of responsibility. According to O'Connell (1993), however, approximately 17% of the children who experienced some kind of nonmaternal care in the late 1970s obtained that care primarily from their fathers, whereas the comparable figure in 1993 was 23%, again reflecting a modest though real increase over time in the extent of paternal involvement.

Paternal Behavioral Styles. Both observational and survey data also suggest that mothers and fathers engage in rather different types of interaction with their children (Lamb, 1997). These studies have consistently shown that fathers tend to "specialize" in play, while mothers specialize in caretaking and nurturance, especially (but not only) in relation to infants.

Although mothers are associated with caretaking and fathers with play, we cannot assume that fathers are less capable than mothers of child care. A number of researchers have attempted to investigate the relative competencies of mothers and fathers with respect to caretaking and parenting functions, and the results of these studies are fairly clear (Lamb, 1997). First, they show that, in the newborn period, there are no differences in competence between mothers and fathers—both parents can do equally well (or equally poorly). Contrary to the notion of a maternal instinct, parenting skills are usually acquired "on the job" by both mothers and fathers. Mothers are "on the job" more than fathers are, however; not surprisingly, therefore, mothers become more sensitive to their children, more in tune with them, and more aware of each child's characteristics and needs. By virtue of their lack of experience, fathers become correspondingly less sensitive and come to feel less confidence in their parenting abilities. Fathers thus continue to defer to and cede responsibility to mothers, and mothers assume increasing responsibility.

Paternal Influences on Child Development

Over the last 40 years, more researchers have studied paternal influences on child development than have studied the determinants of paternal behavior (Lamb, 1997). In order to summarize and make sense of the voluminous literature on paternal influences, it is helpful to distinguish among three research traditions, noting how each has contributed in important ways to our understanding of paternal influences and roles.

Correlational Studies. Many of the earliest studies of paternal influences were designed to identify correlations between paternal and filial characteristics. The vast majority of these studies were focused on sex-role development, especially in sons, and the design of these early studies was quite simple: Researchers assessed masculinity in fathers and in sons, and then determined how strongly the two sets of scores were correlated. The quality of father-son relationships proved to be a crucial mediating variable. A similar conclusion was suggested by research on other aspects of psychosocial adjustment and on achievement: Paternal warmth or closeness appeared beneficial, whereas paternal masculinity appeared to be relatively unimportant.

Studies of Father Absence and Divorce. While "correlational" studies were burgeoning in the 1950s, other researchers tried to understand the father's role by studying families without fathers. As indicated by Hetherington and Stanley-Hagan (1997), boys growing up without fathers seemed to have "problems" in the areas of sex-role and gender-identity development, school performance, psychosocial adjustment, and perhaps in the control of aggression. The effects on girls were less thoroughly studied, and they appeared to be less dramatic and less consistent. Why do those differences exist and how should they be interpreted? Why do some boys appear to suffer deleterious consequences as a result of father absence, while others do not?

The results of studies conducted in the last two decades have underscored the many ways in which paternal absence influences children. First, children consistently do better following divorce when they are able to maintain meaningful relationships with both parents unless the levels of interparental conflict remain unusually high (Lamb, 1999; Lamb, Sternberg & Thompson, 1997). Second, there is the economic stress that frequently accompanies single motherhood, often also accompanied by emotional stress. Fourth, in many cases children of divorce are affected by the perceived, and often actual, abandonment by one of their parents (Thompson & Laible, 1999). Lastly, there are the effects of pre- and postdivorce marital conflict. This may be an especially important issue because there can be little doubt that children suffer when there is hostility or conflict in the family (Cummings & O'Reilly, 1997). Since most single-parent families are produced by divorce, and since divorce is often preceded and accompanied by periods of overt and covert spousal hostility, parental conflict may play a major role in explaining the problems of fatherless children.

In sum, the evidence suggests that father absence may be harmful not necessarily because a sex-role model is absent, but because many aspects of the father's role—economic, social, emotional—go unfilled or inappropriately filled in these families. Once again, the evidence suggests that recognition of the father's multiple roles as breadwinner, parent, and emotional partner is essential for understanding how fathers influence children's development.

Increased Paternal Involvement. Since 1980, several researchers have sought to identify the effects on children of increased paternal involvement. Children with highly involved fathers are characterized by increased cognitive competence, increased empathy, less sex-stereotyped beliefs, and a more internal locus of control (Pleck, 1997).

When parents assume less sex-stereotyped roles,

their children have less sex-stereotyped attitudes themselves about male and female roles. Second, these children may benefit from having two highly involved parents rather than just one. This assures them the diversity of stimulation that comes from interacting with people who have different behavioral styles. A third important issue has to do with the family context in which these children are raised, in that increased paternal involvement allowed both parents to feel much more fulfilled. One can speculate that the benefits obtained by children with highly involved fathers is largely attributable to the fact that high levels of paternal involvement created family contexts in which the parents felt good about their marriages and the child-care arrangements they had been able to work out.

The effects on children appear quite different when fathers are forced to become involved, perhaps by being laid off from work while their partners are able to obtain or maintain their employment. This constellation of factors appears to have adverse effects on children, just as the same degree of involvement has positive effects when the circumstances are more benign. The effects of increased involvement may thus have more to do with the context than with father involvement *per se*. It matters less who is at home than how that person feels about being at home, for the person's feelings will color the way he or she behaves with the children. Parental behavior is also influenced by the partner's feelings about the arrangement: Both parents' emotional states affect the family dynamics.

Bibliography

Cummings, E. M., & O'Reilly, A. W. (1997). Fathers in family context: Effects of marital quality on child adjustment. In M. E. Lamb (Ed.), *The role of the father in child development* (3rd ed., pp. 49–65). New York: Wiley.

Griswold, R. L. (1993). *Fatherhood in America*. New York: Basic Books.

Hetherington, E. M., & Stanley-Hagan, M. (1997). The effects of divorce on fathers and their children. In M. E. Lamb (Ed.), *The role of the father in child development* (3rd ed., pp. 191–211). New York: Wiley.

Hewlett, B. S. (Ed.) (1992). *Father-child relations: Cultural and biosocial contexts*. New York: Aldine de Gruyter.

Lamb, M. E. (1986). The changing roles of fathers. In M. E. Lamb (Ed.), *The father's role: Applied perspectives* (pp. 3–27). New York: Wiley.

Lamb, M. E. (Ed.). (1987). *The father's role: Cross-cultural perspectives*. Hillsdale, NJ: Erlbaum.

Lamb, M. E. (Ed.). (1997). *The role of the father in child development* (3rd ed.). New York: Wiley.

Lamb, M. E. (1999). Non-custodial fathers and their impact on the children of divorce. In R. A. Thompson & P. R. Amato (Eds.), *The post-divorce family: Research and policy issues* (pp. 105–125). Thousand Oaks, CA: Sage.

Lamb, M. E., Pleck, J. H., Charnov, E. L., & Levine, J. A. (1987). A biosocial perspective on paternal behavior and involvement. In J. B. Lancaster, J. Altmann, A. S. Rossi, & L. R. Sherrod (Eds.), *Parenting across the lifespan: Biosocial perspectives* (pp. 111–142). Hawthorne, NY: Aldine.

Lamb, M. E., Sternberg, K. J., & Thompson, R. A. (1997). The effects of divorce and custody arrangements on children's behavior, development, and adjustment. *Family and Conciliation Courts Review, 35*, 393–404.

O'Connell, M. (1993). *Where's papa? Fathers' role in child care*. Washington, DC: Population Reference Bureau.

Parke, R. D., & Buriel, R. (1998). Socialization in the family: Ethnic and ecological perspectives. In W. Damon & N. Eisenberg (Eds.), *Handbook of child psychology: Vol. 3. Social, emotional, and personality development* (5th ed., pp. 463–551). New York: Wiley.

Pleck, J. H. (1984). *Changing fatherhood*. Unpublished manuscript, Wellesley, MA: Wellesley College Center for Research on Women.

Pleck, J. H. (1997). Paternal involvement: Levels, sources, and consequences. In M. E. Lamb (Ed.), *The role of the father in child development* (3rd ed., pp. 66–103). New York: Wiley.

Pleck, E. H., & Pleck, J. H. (1997). Fatherhood ideals in the United States: Historical dimensions. In M. E. Lamb (Ed.), *The role of the father in child development* (3rd ed., pp. 33–48). New York: Wiley.

Thompson, R. A., & Laible, D. J. (1999). Noncustodial parents. In M. E. Lamb (Ed.), *Parenting and child development in "nontraditional" families* (pp. 103–123). Mahwah, NJ: Erlbaum.

Michael E. Lamb

FEAR AND TERROR. Fear is an emotion triggered by the detection of imminent threat; terror merely denotes extreme fear. Its psychobiological correlates constitute a system for defending against danger, and its qualitatively distinctive feel constitutes the conscious consequences of this system's activation. Although the stimuli that provoke fear vary widely across species, the neurobiological circuitry of defense is phylogenetically ancient, and similar among the vertebrates. Accordingly, scientists have often studied defensive behavior in rats to gain insight into how fear works in human beings.

To elucidate the circuitry of fear and defense, Ledoux (1996) and others used Pavlovian (i.e., classical) conditioning procedures to establish initially neutral cues (e.g., a tone) as conditioned stimuli by having them predict the unconditioned stimulus of electric shock. Then, employing lesion techniques, they discovered the pathways mediating fear responses to these conditioned stimuli. Thus, tone conditioned stimuli are detected by receptors in the ear, and this input is transmitted into the brain via the auditory nerve, which terminates in the auditory brain stem nuclei. Axons emerging from this region transmit the signal to the inferior colliculus of the midbrain whose axons then transmit it to the thalamus. Information about the conditioned stimulus emerging from the thalamus takes two routes that both lead to the amygdala, the key structure in the brain's defense system. The subcortical route transmits information about the threatening stimulus directly from the thalamus to the amygdala, entirely bypassing the cortex. This "quick and dirty" pathway provides rapid, coarse-grain information about the stimulus, whereas transmission through the other pathway takes about twice as long to reach the amygdala because it first passes through the cortex where it undergoes additional processing. Information about threat arriving via both subcortical and cortical routes converges at the lateral nucleus of the amygdala, and output exiting the central nucleus of the amygdala serves to initiate a range of defensive responses. These responses include activation of the sympathetic branch of the autonomic nervous system (e.g., increased heart rate, increased blood pressure), heightened propensity to startle, release of stress hormones (e.g., cortisol) into the bloodstream, and freezing.

Similar processes likely occur in human beings. Consider a hiker who encounters a coiled snakelike object in the woods. This visual stimulus is first processed by the thalamus, which rapidly transmits a crude representation of the object to the amygdala, thereby triggering defensive responses prior to the hiker's conscious awareness of the object's identity. Meanwhile, information about the coiled object travels from the thalamus to the cortex, where a detailed representation of the stimulus is created prior to its transmission to the amygdala. If the detailed input arriving via the cortical route indicates that the coiled object is a stick, not a snake, it will dampen firing of the amygdala, resulting in the waning of fear. On the other hand, if cortical processing identifies the object as a snake, the hiker's subjective feelings will be congruent with defensive responses preconsciously activated via the subcortical thalamic-amygdala route. The upshot is that defensive responses, such as startle and increased heart rate, can be initiated prior to the person's conscious awareness of the provocative stimulus. From an adaptive perspective, this makes sense: for the system to register a false alarm by rapidly responding to a stick as if it were a snake is better than waiting a potentially fatal length of time for cortical input to confirm the presence of danger.

Lesion studies have revealed the mediating circuits of fear and defense in rats, but such research cannot be conducted on human beings. Scientists, however, have recently begun to employ positron emission tomography (PET) methods to determine what regions of the brain exhibit enhanced activation when people experience states of experimentally induced fear. These studies are just beginning to be published, and hence most of what has been learned about the expression of fear in humans has been gleaned from other methods (e.g., measurement of peripheral autonomic responses such as heart rate).

In an influential interpretation of these data, Lang (1978) proposed that fear is composed of three loosely coupled response systems: somatic/visceral, motoric, and self-report. Detection of threat may result in autonomic arousal (e.g., increases in heart rate, skin conductance such as sweaty palms, and increased respiration), freezing or attempts to flee, and verbal reports of fear. Studying responses to fear-evocative stimuli among individuals afraid of snakes, Lang and others discovered that indices of fear do not always covary. Some people experienced increased heart rate, but approached the snake while denying subjective fear. Others exhibited behavioral avoidance and expressed great fear, yet displayed only small increases in physiologic indicators. Thus, the response profile of fear tended to vary across individuals and situations. Congruence across the three systems, however, tended to be greatest under the greatest degree of threat.

Cross-cultural researchers have shown that people throughout the world respond similarly to stimuli that frighten them, subject to the constraints of discordance noted by Lang (1978). Some scientists believe that the response systems that support fear and defense are therefore relatively hardwired, in that people do not have to learn to increase their heart rate, and so forth, under danger. A striking cultural universal, confirmed by Ekman et al. (1987) and others, is the facial expression for fear. People in diverse cultures, including preliterate ones, recognize this expression as a response to threat.

Evolution has furnished the response systems for defense, and thus the output side of fear is relatively hardwired. Although most fear-evoking cues have been established as such through learning, there are certain categories of stimuli capable of activating the defense system in the absence of previous aversive experiences. Even the input side of the fear equation may be partly hardwired. Thus, upon seeing a cat for the first time, a laboratory rat will exhibit characteristic defensive behavior. Young children will display fear in response to a sudden loud noise or to an object that rapidly approaches them. Moreover, stimuli that are discrepant from expectation commonly function as fear elicitors. Finally, many people express fear of heights, snakes, and other situations without ever having had aversive experiences with such stimuli. The frequency of these fears has led some scholars to suggest that people are biologically prepared to fear stimuli that have threatened the survival of the species throughout its evolutionary history.

Fear, as distinct from distress, emerges at about 6 months of age. Infants routinely display a fear of strangers that peaks at about 12 months. Other developmentally normal reactions are fears of strange, novel objects, separation from caretakers, and heights (visual depth cues), which emerge after the child has learned to crawl. The content of fear changes for children ranging from 2 to 6 years of age. Fears of animals, doctors, darkness, ghosts, monsters, and storms are common, but usually dissipate within a few months or years in the absence of treatment.

Not all fears wane in childhood. Some people retain their fears of animals and other objects into adulthood. The Epidemiologic Catchment Area survey revealed that approximately 60% of American adults acknowledge unreasonable fear of at least one object or situation at some point in their lives. Nearly half of these individuals reported fears of insects, snakes, mice, and bats; the second most common fear was that of heights.

An unreasonable fear only qualifies as a phobia if it produces marked distress, interferes with one's life, or both. About 11% of American adults suffer from a specific phobia of nonsocial situations such as animals, enclosed places, and heights. About twice as many women as men report specific phobias. Most people who have specific phobias, however, do not seek treatment. Instead, they commonly arrange their lives to avoid encounters with phobic stimuli.

According to the National Comorbidity Study, an epidemiologic investigation, about 13% of the American adult population suffers from social phobia. Social phobia refers to severe and persistent fear of interpersonal or performance situations in which embarrassment may occur. Many people with social phobia fear multiple public situations in which they may be negatively evaluated, including speaking in public, eating in public, blushing, sweating, or making fools of themselves in front of others. They may avoid social situations or endure them with dread, sometimes self-medicating their anxiety with alcohol.

Some people experience sudden bursts of terror that seem to come out of the blue, untriggered by any obvious external precipitant. These episodes, termed *panic attacks*, are characterized by a sudden increase in fear accompanied by many physiologic signs of arousal such as racing or pounding heart, breathlessness, dizziness, sweating, and trembling. People experiencing these attacks often fear that they are about to faint, have a heart attack, or lose control and "go crazy." Individuals with preexisting *anxiety sensitivity*—a set of beliefs about the potential harmfulness of bodily sensations (e.g., heart palpitations mean impending heart attack)—seem especially prone to develop panic attacks. Experience with inexplicable panic may worsen anxiety sensitivity such that they become fearfully hypervigilant about their own bodily sensations. A person who experiences repeated panic attacks and who develops a persistent dread of their recurrence qualifies for a diagnosis of panic disorder. Some theorists, such as Clark (1986), believe that panic is caused when individuals misinterpret a benign bodily sensation (e.g., heart palpitation) as a harbinger of imminent catastrophe (e.g., a heart attack), thereby provoking intense fear. Other theorists, such as Klein (1993), conceptualize panic as arising from a deranged suffocation alarm system, whereas others, such as Barlow (1988), view panic as simply the basic emotion of fear, albeit triggered at inappropriate times when no threat is present.

Many people with panic disorder begin to avoid situations in which they fear panic may strike, including crowded places (e.g., subways, shopping malls) or other situations in which rapid escape would prove difficult or embarrassing (e.g., classrooms, expressways, airplanes). If avoidance becomes widespread, panic disorder with agoraphobia is diagnosed. Although agoraphobia was once believed to be a fear of open or public places, people with agoraphobia do not fear these places *per se*. Rather they fear panicking in them. Accordingly, today many clinicians consider agoraphobia to be a fear of fear itself, rather than a fear of certain places. The National Comorbidity Study indicated that 3.5% and 1.5% of American adults qualify for diagnoses of panic disorder and panic disorder with agoraphobia, respectively, at some point in their lives.

Many scientists have identified commonalties in the psychobiology of fear and defense across settings and individuals. Kagan (1994), however, persuasively argued that *fear* probably denotes a family of related psychobiological states rather than a single state instantiated across species and contexts. For example, lesions in rats eliminate freezing responses to novel stimuli, but do not affect responses to shock. If fear were a unitary state, Kagan proposed, the entire defensive system ought to have been disabled by such lesions. That it was not strongly suggests that different contexts (e.g., novelty vs. pain) may evoke different states of fear. Klein (1993) expressed similar arguments concerning panic. Panic, he maintained, is psychobiologically distinguishable from fear states evoked by snakes, heights, and other external stimuli. Taken together, the arguments of these scholars suggest that further progress in our understanding of fear and terror will arise from careful analysis of the distinctive psychobiological states termed *fear* arising in diverse contexts.

Bibliography

Barlow, D. H. (1988). *Anxiety and its disorders*. New York: Guilford Press.

Clark, D. M. (1986). A cognitive approach to panic. *Behaviour Research and Therapy, 24*, 461–470.

Davey, G. C. L. (Ed.). (1997). *Phobias: A handbook of theory, research and treatment.* Chichester, UK: Wiley.

Eaton, W. W., Kessler, R. C., Wittchen, H. U., & Magee, W. J. (1994). Panic and panic disorder in the United States. *American Journal of Psychiatry, 151,* 413–420.

Ekman, P., Friesen, W. V., O'Sullivan, M., Chan, A., Dia-coyanni-Tarlatzis, I., Heider, K., Krause, R., LeCompte, W. A., Pitcairn, T., Ricci-Bitti, P. E., Scherer, K., Tomita, M., & Tzavaras, A. (1987). Universal and cultural differences in the judgments of facial expressions of emotions. *Journal of Personality and Social Psychology, 53,* 712–717.

Kagan, J. (1994). *Galen's prophecy.* New York: Basic Books.

Klein, D. F. (1993). False suffocation alarms, spontaneous panics, and related conditions: An integrative hypothesis. *Archives of General Psychiatry, 50,* 306–317.

Lang, P. J. (1978). Anxiety: Toward a psychophysiological definition. In H. S. Akiskal & W. L. Webb (Eds.), *Psychiatric diagnosis* (pp. 365–389). New York: Spectrum.

LeDoux, J. (1996). *The emotional brain.* New York: Simon & Schuster.

Marks, I. M. (1987). *Fears, phobias, and rituals.* New York: Oxford University Press.

McNally, R. J. (1994). *Panic disorder: A critical analysis.* New York: Guilford Press.

Richard J. McNally

FEAR OF FAILURE AND FEAR OF SUCCESS. *See* Achievement Motivation.

FECAL INCONTINENCE. *See* Encopresis.

FECHNER, GUSTAV THEODOR (1801–1887), German physicist, philosopher, psychophysicist. The centerpiece of Fechner's intellectual legacy is a two-volume work, *Elemente der Psychophysik* (Elements of Psychophysics [Leipzig] 1860). This work was important in two ways. First, it provided an experimental psychology in its infancy with objective and quantifiable methods, forming a basis for its claim to be a new science. Second, continuously since 1860, psychophysics has been psychology's most important methodology for the discovery of new facts about the sensitivity of organisms to physical stimuli.

Fechner made a second major contribution to psychology near the end of his life, *Vorschule der experimentellen Aesthetik* (Introduction to Experimental Aesthetics [Leipzig] 1876). In this work, which stands at the head of modern experimental aesthetics, Fechner extended the methods of psychophysics so that they could be used to measure the pleasingness of visual objects, and with them he searched for basic laws governing aesthetic experience.

Fechner's long life spans most of the nineteenth century, and the influences on his work are a lesson in the major philosophical and scientific dynamics of Germany during that period. Born in a small town, the son of an enlightened country pastor, Fechner was sent at the age of 17 to the University of Leipzig to study medicine because of his scientific bent. He qualified to practice medicine but considered himself unsuited to the profession and instead turned to a study of the romantic philosophy of nature that had captured his imagination. To qualify to lecture in philosophy, he wrote a thesis, "Praemissae ad Theoriam Organismi Generalem" (Premises Toward a General Theory of Organisms [Leipzig] 1823) in which he argued that the universe is a single unitary system (like a gigantic organism), that a single set of laws must therefore prevail throughout it, and that this law is amenable to mathematical expression. He also argued that the mental and the physical are just two manifestations of this single universal reality, and that mind and body are therefore processes that run in parallel with each other. From one point of view, this argument leads to a vision of the universe as alive and thoroughly spiritual. From the other point of view, it is objectively composed of matter and is precisely mathematically describable. With these ideas, Fechner, at the age of 22, had established the guiding thrust of his intellectual life and the foundation of his mature psychophysics.

Fechner, however, did not achieve the psychophysics directly through philosophy. He needed to earn a living and there were no lecturing positions open in the field, so instead he fell back on his considerable literary and linguistic talent and was employed to translate French scientific works into German. His first translation was of a textbook on physics by Jean Baptiste Biot. Fechner was stunned by the precision and rigor of Biot's work, and he saw that his own recent philosophical speculations lacked the clarity (and, to him, the beauty) of Biot's ideas. Although he did not lose sight of his basic philosophical convictions, he now set out doggedly to become a physicist through voluminous translating work and through studying independently the work of leading mathematicians such as Augustin Cauchy and Siméon Poisson. When the professor of physics at Leipzig became ill, Fechner was chosen as lecturer *pro tempore,* and by dint of prodigious work he both continued his translations and established himself as experimental physicist with a series of 135 experiments dealing with the verification of Ohm's law. These experiments showed Fechner to have incorporated the ideals of Biot, for they were characterized by precise measurement, experimental control, and objective reporting. With them Fechner gained the professorship of physics at Leipzig in 1833, the same year in which he married

Clara Volkmann, sister of the physiologist A. W. Volkmann. The next years were devoted to compiling texts on physics and chemistry, to editing a pharmaceutical journal, and to the thankless job of editing a household encyclopedia whose successive volumes marked a decline in Fechner's energy reserves.

Beginning in 1841, Fechner's long life was transected by a 3-year illness characterized by total incapacity, blindness, and inability to eat. He was forced to resign his position in physics and had given up all hope of recovery when suddenly his condition began to improve in a way that Fechner described as an ecstatic rebirth. The experience dramatically reconfirmed his belief in the spirituality of the universe and redirected his attention to the primary conundrum of his earlier philosophical work, the reconciliation of materialistic science with spiritualistic philosophy. During his career as physicist, Fechner had kept these ideas alive in minor humorous publications written under the pseudonym "Dr. Mises," a practice that he would continue through his lifetime. Fechner now authored wholly serious arguments for spirituality in works such as *Nanna, Oder Ueber das Seelenleben des Pflanzen* (Nanna, or Concerning the Mental Life of Plants [Leipzig] 1848) and *Zend-Avesta, oder ueber die Dinge des Himmels und des Jenseits* (Zend-Avesta, or Concerning Matters of Heaven and the Beyond [Leipzig] 1851) and was ridiculed by scientific contemporaries who thought he had become muddled. For his part, Fechner saw these critics as asleep in the arms of materialism, and he was determined to wake them up.

In fact, Fechner hit upon the methodological premise for his psychophysics while working on the unpopular *Zend-Avesta*, and announced his new principle of mathematical psychology in an addendum published with it. This principle made the functional relationship between mental and physical a logarithmic one, such that an absolute mental change accompanies a relative change in impinging physical stimuli. The physiologist E. H. Weber had observed such a relationship in particular sensory settings; Fechner generalized the relationship to apply to all mental and physical events and thought therewith to have the scientific answer to his philosophical puzzle. At this point, however, Fechner's formulaic statement was empirically empty because he had no way of measuring mental change.

The core of Fechner's problem was that the measurement of sensation is necessarily an indirect process because the sensations of a person are not accessible to an objective observer or measuring instrument. Human sensitivity, however, can be assessed by presenting a subject with a series of physical stimuli of varying magnitudes and asking the subject to report the presence or absence of sensation. In this way, an absolute threshold of sensitivity can be determined, namely a physical stimulus value above which (on average) reports of stimulus presence occur and below which reports of stimulus absence occur. Similarly, starting with physical stimuli above threshold, it is possible to determine the minimal difference between physical stimuli necessary for a subject to report sensing a difference. This value is known as the differential threshold or just noticeable difference (*j.n.d.*). Weber had found that in a given sensory domain the *j.n.d.* is a constant fraction of physical stimulus value. Fechner now seized on the general significance of the Weber fraction, arguing that if $\Delta S/S = K$ (Weber's law) for the *j.n.d.* then it could serve as the unit of measurement for a sensation where the zero point on the scale of measurement would be the absolute threshold. The measure of a sensation would be the number of *j.n.d.*'s a particular stimulus value lay above zero. Fechner's psychophysical law was written: $S = k \log R$, where S is the magnitude of sensation and R is the magnitude of the corresponding physical stimulus. Fechner, in fact, called this Weber's law, deferring to the seminal work of his teacher and friend.

Having grasped the methodological key to psychophysics, Fechner now spent nearly a decade amassing observations from his own original experiments and from the work of others, with the purpose of confirming the validity of his psychophysical law. In 1860 the *Elements of Psychophysics* appeared, the first volume providing the exact methodology and the scientific observations, the second volume arguing the philosophical premises. Fechner regarded the *Elements of Psychophysics* as a research progress report. The ultimate criteria of the success of the work lay, he said, in the degree to which it would provide testable ideas that would not have occurred otherwise, and in the degree to which its ideas ultimately would gain support in the exact investigations of the finest specialist scholars. The work succeeded brilliantly, particularly on the first criterion.

Fechner was not without political wisdom within the scientific forum. To maximize the likelihood of public acceptance for the *Elements of Psychophysics*, he took pains to show that his "exact science of the relationship between mind and body" could in fact be viewed *a-metaphysically*, that is, independently of any particular view of mind and body in the metaphysical sense. Further, he was careful to align his psychophysical law with other laws then accepted to govern the universe, insisting, for example, that the law of the conservation of energy is a law for the conservation of the universe, and that the mind is bound to feel, to think, or to will within the limitations of this law.

The *Elements of Psychophysics* immediately generated a great deal of interest and activity in the scientific community, and it was certainly not without critics at both the methodological and the philosophical level. Fechner eventually replied to the diverse scientific criticisms of men such as Hermann Helmholtz, Ernst Mach, Ewald Hering, Joseph L. R. Delboeuf, and Franz Brentano in *In Sachen der Psychophysik* (*On Psychophysical Matters* [Leipzig] 1877), introducing the book with these characteristic wry words: "The Tower of Babel was never finished because the workers could not agree on how they should build it; my psychological edifice will manage to survive because the workers cannot come to an agreement about how to knock it down."

In *A History of Experimental Psychology* (New York, 1929), Edward G. Boring described the way in which Fechner derived the psychophysical law for which he is famous. Boring also emphasized that Fechner's claim to greatness within psychology derives not so much from his grand generalizations as from accomplishing a new kind of measurement. The three methods that are Fechner's legacy (the method of just noticeable differences, the method of right and wrong cases, and the method of average error) are both experimental procedures and statistical treatments. Using them, psychology has taken measurement into fields of which Fechner had no inkling.

Even in Fechner's hands, the applicability of psychophysical measurement was exceedingly broad, as his *Aesthetics* of 1876 attests. Long interested in aesthetic matters, Fechner's talent for psychological analysis and his insistence on experiment as the pathway to understanding were nowhere shown more clearly than in his *Aesthetics*. Just as he had earlier conceived the universal relation between mind and body before he brought his empirical psychophysical arsenal into play, he now first constructed a general conceptual framework for aesthetics, arguing the principle of eudaemonism, in which the greatest good is defined as the greatest happiness for all organisms. He then suggested that increments of such universal happiness might be measured by individual feelings of pleasure and displeasure. Fechner called these aesthetic feelings, and the methods he invented for assessing them have reappeared in many variations within modern psychological measurement: the method of production (a number of subjects produce through drawing or otherwise the form most appealing to their taste), the method of application (the experimenter measures "found" forms that have been produced spontaneously and are actually in use), and the method of choice (many different people are asked to choose between comparable forms presented to them). Using the latter method, Fechner had earlier studied differential preferences for two pictures allegedly by Holbein; in the *Aesthetics*, he applied the same technique to a study of the Golden Mean, a ratio of length to side long thought to define the ideal rectangle.

Three years later, Fechner, then 78 years old, wrote a grand summary of his system of belief, *Die Tagesansicht gegenueber der Nachtansicht* (The Day View as Opposed to the Night View [Leipzig] 1879), wherein he integrated the physical, biological, psychological, moral, and religious implications of his spiritual view of the universe. Although this was the last time that Fechner would attempt to rouse a public asleep to spirituality, it is a nice irony that his last words were published posthumously. The psychologist Wilhelm Wundt, putting Fechner's papers in order after his death, discovered an extensive manuscript full of empirical observations. This was eventually published under the editorship of psychologist G. F. Lipps as *Kollektivmasslehre* (Doctrine of Group Measurement [Leipzig] 1879), a vast study of empirical frequency distributions prescient of the use of probability in psychological statistics.

[*Many of the people mentioned in this article are the subjects of independent biographical entries.*]

Bibliography

Brozek, J., & Gundlach H., (Eds.). (1987). *G. T. Fechner and Psychology. Passauer Schriften zur Psychologiegeschichte Nr. 6.* Proceedings of an international symposium on Gustav Fechner's contributions to psychology.

Fechner, G. T. (1966). *Elements of Psychophysics* (Vol. 1). (H. E. Adler, Trans., D. H. Howes & E. G. Boring, Eds.). New York: Holt, Rinehart & Winston. The only scientific work of Fechner to be translated into English.

Gundlach, H. (1987). Index Psychophysicus. *Passauer Schriften zur Psychologiegeschichte Nr. 7.* The authoritative bibliographical aid for the study of Fechnerian psychophysics, this index has a user's guide in English.

Heidelberger, M. (1986). Fechner's indeterminism: From freedom to laws of chance. In L. J. Daston, M. Heidelberger, & L. Krueger (Eds.), *The probabalistic revolution: Vol. 1. Ideas in history.* Cambridge, MA: Bradford Books/ MIT Press.

Lowry, R. (1971). *The evolution of psychological theory.* Chicago & New York: Aldine Atherton. Relates Fechner's psychophysics to the concept of conservation of energy.

Marshall, M. E. (1969). Gustav Fechner, Dr. Mises, and the Comparative Anatomy of Angels. *Journal of the History of the Behavioral Sciences, 5,* 39–58. Describes the historical and biographical context of Fechner's strictly literary work and lists the first editions of Dr. Mises.

Marshall, M. E. (1980). Biographical genre and biographical archetype: Five studies of Gustav Theodor Fechner. *Storia e Critica della Psicologia, 1,* 197–210.

Marshall, M. E. (1982). Physics, metaphysics, and Fechner's psychophysics. In W. R. Woodward & M. G. Ash (Eds.), *The problematic science* (pp. 65–87). New York: Praeger. Discusses the common presumptions of Fechner's physical and psychophysical science in the context of nineteenth-century atomism and in experimental work with electricity.

Woodward, W. R. (1972). Fechner's panpsychism. A scientific solution to the mind-body problem. *Journal of the History of the Behavioral Sciences, 8,* 367–386. Describes the response of the biologist Matthias Schleiden to Fechner's notion that plants have souls.

Marilyn E. Marshall

FEDERATION OF BEHAVIORAL, PSYCHOLOGI-CAL, AND COGNITIVE SCIENCES is an alliance of scientific societies that represents the interests of psychological scientists to the U.S. federal government and informs its members about relevant political developments. Discussion of an organization to represent behavioral science societies began in 1979 because of concern that the needs of subdisciplinary research specialties were not well addressed by the American Psychological Association. The organizational meeting of interested society presidents met in Chicago on 7 December 1980 at the invitation of Emanuel Donchin, president of the Society for Psychophysiological Research. Donchin was joined in the invitation by George Mandler, president of the Psychonomic Society, and James Davis, president of the Society for Experimental Social Psychology. The assembled presidents created the Federation of Behavioral, Psychological, and Cognitive Science.

The eight founding societies were the American Educational Research Association, American Psychological Association, National Conference on the Use of On-Line Computers in Psychology (now the Society for Computers in Psychology), the Cognitive Science Society, the Psychonomic Society, the Society of Experimental Social Psychology, the Society for Mathematical Psychology, and the Society for Psychophysiological Research. Member society dues support a central office in Washington, D.C., where an executive director oversees the staff. Governance is through a council appointed by member societies, and a council-elected executive committee. In 1981, a category of affiliate membership was established for university departments, regional associations, and related nonsocietal scientific groups.

With George Mandler as its first president, the federation was incorporated in Washington, D.C., on 4 March 1981 as a nonprofit corporation permitted under the federal tax code to advocate before government bodies. Within days, President Ronald Reagan sent appropriation cuts to Congress to eliminate federal support for behavioral and social science research. Most advocacy in the following two years was directed, in league with allied Washington groups, at saving behavioral and social science research.

Few legislators understood what they were poised to cut, and few scientists concerned themselves with federal politics. Alleviating this mutual lack of understanding has become the federation's mission. After the funding crisis of the 1980s passed, federation leader-

ship resolved that behavioral research would not again be endangered politically as the result of ignorance. The federation is now primarily an educational organization. It has a three-part mission: advocacy, science education, and communication.

As an advocate, the federation explains to policy makers the views of its scientists toward appropriation requests for research agencies, proposed public policy and regulatory changes, and structural changes at federal science agencies.

To educate about science, the federation, from its earliest days, has brought prominent behavioral and social scientists to Congress to explain their research and its relevance to national concerns. It publishes monographs and books based on these lectures. These are disseminated throughout the legislative and executive branches of government to assure that those who make policy and funding decisions about science have a good understanding of that science. The publications are also used in college classrooms.

A forum on research management is overseen by the federation. The forum is a working group of federal science program managers and university and industry science managers that seeks solutions to science management problems. The federation is also advised by a committee on animal research.

The federation's communication activity is directed at scientists. Through its newsletter, Internet site, action alerts, journal articles, book chapters, and meeting presentations, the federation seeks to increase scientists' understanding of their intimate, unavoidable ties to the political life of the country.

[*See also* Cognitive Psychology; Psychometric Society; Psychonomic Society; *and* Society for Research in Child Development.]

David H. Johnson

FEMININE CULTURES. *See* Masculine and Feminine Cultures.

FEMININITY. *See* Gender Identity.

FEMINISM. [*This entry comprises three articles*:
   Feminism and Philosophy
   Feminist Psychology
   Feminist Psychotherapy
The first article discusses the philosophical underpinnings of feminist psychology and psychotherapy. The second ar-

ticle presents a broad history of the field from its inception to the present. The third article describes and defines the feminist perspective of psychotherapy. For a discussion of the relationship of postmodern psychology to feminist critiques of psychology, see Postmodern Psychology.]

Feminism and Philosophy

Since the 1970s, feminist psychology has transformed the scientific study of sex, gender, and psychological differences between men and women. Feminist psychology is renowned for uncovering the biases in empirical studies of gender. It also is known for the execution of studies carefully designed to correct such biases. Finally, feminist psychology is credited with generating innovative studies of the experiences unique to women (experiences which had previously received little or no attention).

What is less known about contemporary feminist psychology, however, is this field's engagement with fundamental philosophical problems and tenets. In the reevaluation and remediation of empiricist methods and findings, many feminist psychologists returned to some perennial philosophical issues which the discipline had left unexamined for generations. These new philosophical inquiries include reappraisals of epistemology (theories of knowledge), assumptions about the nature of human kinds, the nature of knowing, and the ethics of knowledge production. The reappraisals had a synthetic effect in their encouragement of psychologists to contemplate the epistemological and metatheoretical bases of their work.

Feminist psychologists first engaged problems in the philosophy of science (epistemology) when they confronted notable biases on the part of presumably objective psychologists who were investigating gender differences. Influenced by the feminist movement emerging in the 1960s, these researchers initially believed that sexism in scientific work could be eliminated through a more conscientious adherence to the strictures of the empirical method. Their project was to remove sex-biased practices and ultimately realize genuinely objective, disinterested observation and assessment. This reserved but essentially empiricist stance, later called "feminist empiricism" by philosopher Sandra Harding (1986), was adopted by a considerable number of feminist psychologists. Other researchers doubted that such methodological correctives were sufficient; some suspected that certain biases are inherent in the investigator's gender. Thus, for instance, the American Psychological Association's Task Force on gender research claimed that sometimes male experimenters were not the most objective observers of certain gender-related phenomena. While these researchers transgressed a foundational assumption of empiricism (that all persons could be trained to observe), few of them extended

their caveats to take the more extreme position that observations always are dependent upon the status of the observer, a position that Harding called "standpoint feminism." To claim that the observer's status influences the knowledge-seeking process (whether the status attributes relate to gender, race, age, or some other factor), not only raises formidable methodological demands but also runs counter to the democratic ethos that pervades scientific work. For research psychologists, therefore, standpoint feminism poses a serious challenge to their methodological conventions and scientific ideology.

Concern with the ontology of the observer was heightened by feminist analysis of the totality of scientific epistemology. Modern science presumes not merely a separation of subject and object, observer and thing observed, but also values knowledge which is disinterested and detached and which enables precise control of the object. Feminist scholars have delineated the historical and structural connections between these epistemological ideals and masculine psychology (Bordo, 1987; Keller, 1985). They uncovered significant connections between the detachment and distance of the scientific gaze and the ego detachment of modern masculinity. The modern scientific objective to control and dominate nature likewise can be seen to parallel masculine identity. These analyses suggest that knowledge production itself is intrinsically gendered, and remediation of this situation requires substantial alterations in our theories of knowledge. It is not simply the observer's standpoint (gender) or practice (biased judgments) that permits the generation of invalid knowledge about women; the denigration of women also is a logical outcome of a gender-linked epistemology.

Whether researchers found a corrected empiricism to be a satisfactory remedy to gender bias in research or proceeded with an uneasy sense of the pervasiveness of the gender question in science, they remained engaged with projects to detect and describe biased practices. Their concerns dovetailed with accounts by philosophers of science of the "theory-ladenness" of observations and observational statements. These philosophers were developing an appreciation of the extents to which experiments and subsequent observation statements were prefigured or "overdetermined" by theoretical commitments to seeing the world in a certain way. Philosophical studies of science conducted in the 1960s and 1970s interrogated the power of theory and its various manifestations in scientific language, paradigms, experiential techniques, metaphors, and communities of practitioners. The presumed existence of gender as a fixed, dichotomous, and universal characteristic clearly exemplified the overdetermination of fact by theoretical premises. The predominance of male scientists and the cultural conditions of sexism were salient factors in making an androcentric climate of theorizing. Given such *a priori* commitments, scientific studies of gender effectively functioned to "construct" rather than "discover" gender.

Yet a third development in the philosophy of science influenced and eventually was led by feminist scholars. Historical and sociological studies have indicated the unremarkable nature of scientific practice. That is, science seems to consist of no special or unique practices that distinguish it in any crucial way from other human enterprises. Among its worldly properties is power and the play of politics. Science also is an extended and heterogeneous enterprise whose participants include corporations, government, and citizens as well as scientists. Psychological researchers have applied this more comprehensive view of scientific practice to understand, for instance, the many influences behind the rapid scientific articulation of the premenstrual syndrome despite the paucity of empirical mandates (Parlee, 1994).

These broad-based philosophical developments are important to the work of feminist philosophy, and have prompted some feminist philosophers to engage in the making of successor epistemologies. In response to that work, feminist psychologists have generated a variety of research programs which apply these philosophical developments to empirical studies of the psychological world. These projects are diverse in foci, although all of them share a notable sophistication regarding the philosophical premises of scientific practice. Four of the most visible revision projects are summarized below: categories of human nature, ways of knowing, object-subject relations, and ethics of knowledge production.

Related to epistemology and knowledge production are questions regarding the nature of the world. Whereas realists in psychology assume the existence of a material external world that can be known through scientific inquiry, nominalists are skeptical about our ability to know such a material world (although they usually agree that science can produce reliable, valid knowledge through its investigative procedures). In psychology, discussions about the nature of objects also extends to consideration of whether human kinds constitute fixed biological essences or are more malleable products of the environment and mentation. In other words, do human kinds represent stable categories of "nature" or plastic outcomes of "nurture." These questions are critical ones in the exploration of sex, gender, and psychological differences between men and women. Drawing upon these philosophical debates, feminist psychologists critically excavated the discipline's naive assumptions about the human kinds of gender, finding that psychological studies of sex and gender merely presumed that gender is a bipolar, dichotomous, transhistorical, universal, and symmetrical category of the world. Once the constructs of gender were found to stand on empirically inadequate presup-

positions scholars introduced more elaborate constructs and experimentation. Some have proposed theories in which gender is not taken to be an essential human kind but is constituted and occasionally reconfigured through sustained social interactions and institutional structures. Other researchers have proposed theoretical perspectives which understand gender to be fluid and mutable and have rejected the dualist presumption that gender entails only two categories, male and female. Such investigations are indicating that at least this particular human category must be understood as plural, asymmetric in its assignment of psychological attributes, and historically malleable rather than stable.

Interrogation of the categories of human nature comprise studies of the object of knowledge. Several other projects have extended epistemological work on the knowing subject, the observer of objects in the world. One project has entailed a critical reexamination of knowing, asking whether our dominant conceptions of knowing are themselves gendered in such a way that they represent the way men know. For example, Carol Gilligan's (1982) studies of moral reasoning indicate that men and women use different mental processes and evaluative goals in making moral judgments. Other researchers made related revisions to our knowledge about how knowers learn; they found that women are more relational in their strategies and objectives of learning than are men (Belenky, Clinchy, Goldberger, and Tarule, 1986). The proposition that men and women know the world differently by deploying different cognitive tools and strategies has received considerable empirical support and has fostered the generation of more complex theories of knowing. This work, however, is not consonant with the aforementioned projects which critically analyze the very categories of men and women, male and female. The theoretical dissonance has spawned numerous controversies.

Other research on knowing has attended not to the object of psychological inquiry—how the participant knows—but to the knowing of the psychological scientist herself. The interest in how and what the scientific knower knows or learns is directly connected to the early feminist apprehensions of how the observer's gender might prefigure or predetermine what he or she observed. Questions about the scientist's knowing also ensue from the epistemological critiques which challenge notions of objectivity and the causal as well as ontological distinction between object and subject sustained by the ideals of objectivity. Feminist work on these questions has been of two sorts. First, researchers have located and described previously neglected features of scientific knowing: the reflexive properties of psychological observation, the tangible relations between observer and participant, the multiple dimensions of the observer's consciousness, and the limitations imposed on observation created by standardized conventions of research. Second, some researchers have creatively experimented with the scientific knowing process, altering conventional research protocols and assessing how these altered relations of observing affect the empirical findings. These experiments with the experimenter's knowing are varied but not arbitrary. They include acknowledging and integrating the social bases of the relationship between experimenters and participants; describing the identity and situatedness of the observer (exploring how these features impact both the participant and the knowledge produced); and developing innovative, sometimes collaborative, relations with participants. Taken together, these two investigative avenues toward better understanding the knowing of the observer constitute a bold challenge to conventional scientific practice in psychology.

Reexamining the philosophical bases of the discipline's assumptions about human nature prompted feminist scientists to extend yet another issue from the above-mentioned philosophical studies of science: the ethics of knowledge production. That is, investigations of psychology's ready adoption of naive constructs of gender also demonstrate that such presuppositions have served political as well as scientific ends; for instance, claims that gender is fixed, dichotomous, and universal reinforced the *status quo* social order just as they enabled a usable template for experimentation. Science is an inextricable part of culture, and the knowledge it produces has both its origins and influences in culture. Knowledge does not simply correspond with some external reality but, especially in the case of psychology, it also shapes, secures, and sometimes transforms that reality. Accordingly, feminist researchers have proposed more inclusive conceptions of what constitutes valid knowledge, and these conceptions highlight the significance of ethics. The proposals for enhanced validity include the recommendation that scientists be more broadly accountable for their findings; the objective to seek knowledge which is catalytic in that it enhances well-being or transforms common perceptions; and the explicit aim that knowledge contribute to social action and political change.

Feminism has returned to psychology a once revered tradition of philosophical inquiry and debate. This philosophical enrichment, however, has avoided the reintroduction of dense and abstract thought experiments or the reiterative logical games of positivism. To the contrary, the philosophical consciousness introduced through feminist inquiry comprises a remarkable innovation in psychological science. Problems are raised, and unexamined tenets are probed, in direct relation to ongoing empirical projects. Philosophy at last enters the laboratory. These inquiries are forging new and dynamic relations between epistemology, theory, data, and ethics. They require a new intellectual rigor on the part of investigators.

Bibliography

Belenky, M. F., Clinchy, B. M., Goldberger, N. R., & Tarule, J. M. (1986). *Women's ways of knowing: The development of self, voice, and mind.* New York: Basic Books.

Bordo, S. (1986). *The flight to objectivity: Essays on Cartesianism and culture.* Albany: State University of New York Press.

Gilligan, C. (1982). *In a different voice: Psychological theory and women's development.* Cambridge: Harvard University Press.

Harding, S. (1986). *The science question in feminism.* Ithaca, NY: Cornell University Press.

Keller, E. F. (1985). *Reflections on gender and science.* New Haven: Yale University Press.

Morawski, J. G. (1994). *Practicing feminisms, reconstructing psychology: Notes on a liminal science.* Ann Arbor: University of Michigan Press.

Parlee, M. B. (1994). The social construction of premenstrual syndrome: A case study of scientific discourse. In M. G. Winkler & L. B. Cole (Eds.), *The good body: Asceticism in contemporary culture* (pp. 91–107). New Haven, CT: Yale University Press.

Jill Morawski

Feminist Psychology

Feminist psychology incorporates a feminist position, which "acknowledges the inequality of women and men throughout history, and examines the nature of women's oppression, challenges the assumption that male experience and behavior are normal, with females inferior in comparison, and is committed to the eradication of sexism" (From Marie LaFrance, *Contemporary Social Psychology, 13*, p. 63). Feminist psychologists engage in diverse forms of scientific inquiry and applied practices such as therapy, counseling, teaching, and consulting. They are especially concerned with investigating social issues that affect women, such as violence, sexual abuse, and discriminatory social practices. Three forms of scientific inquiry within feminist psychology are distinguished: empirical, feminist standpoint, and postmodern/social constructionist. [*See* Feminism, *article on* Feminist Psychotherapy.]

Background of Current Status of the Field

In the early 1900s, feminist psychology in America evolved as both an intellectual and a social-political endeavor. As suffragettes marched for the vote, the first feminist psychologists, including Christine Ladd-Franklin, Mary Washburn, Helen Thompson Woolley, Mary Whiton Calkins, and Leta Hollingworth asserted their rights to join the profession. Calkins and Washburn succeeded in becoming presidents of the American Psychological Association, in 1905 and 1921, respectively. These early feminist psychologists contested the damaging stereotypes of women and men and the predominant view of the time that women were inferior to men. Hollingworth's 1916 article, "Social Devices for Impelling Women to Bear and Rear Children," challenged the societal wisdom regarding women's capacities and desires for children. (See S. A. Shields, "Ms. Pilgrims' progress: The contributions of Leta Stetler Hollingworth to the psychology of women," *American Psychologist*, 1975, 30, 852–857). This article exposed the social pressures designed to restrict women to domestic roles. Yet, despite this vigorous beginning, feminist psychology languished for most of the century until the rekindling of feminist politics in the 1960s.

The Second Wave of Feminism

Marked by the publication of Betty Friedan's *Feminine Mystique* (New York, 1963), the "second wave of feminism" again focused on the dissatisfaction of women limited to roles as housewives and mothers and the need for concerted political activism to overcome sexist practices in society. In psychology, the founding of the Association for Women in Psychology (AWP) in 1969 signaled the resistance of feminist psychologists to the blatant practices of sex discrimination within psychology. This organization continues as an independent voice in psychology to the present.

Feminist psychologists in the 1970s also concentrated on developing critiques of mainstream, sometimes called "malestream," psychology, arguing that there has been a strong tendency throughout the history of the discipline for researchers to assume a male standard for what is normal human behavior, with women as the deviant or "Other." This critique was popularized by Naomi Weisstein's classic article, "Kinder, Kuche, Kirche as scientific law: Psychology constructs the female" (in R. Morgan, Ed., *Sisterhood Is Powerful*, New York, 1970). She argued that psychology had nothing to say about what women are really like and what they need and want because psychology did not know.

This dissatisfaction encouraged feminists in psychology to lobby for a special division of the American Psychological Association (APA) to be called the Psychology of Women; their efforts were rewarded in 1973. Today Division 35 is an official home for feminist psychology, in the United States and with approximately 5,000 women and men as members, it is now the fourth largest division in APA. The major concern of these feminists has been to create a knowledge base about gender and to correct gender biases in the field. In the United Kingdom, the British Psychological Society has created a similar section of feminist psychology.

In 1974, a compilation of research created by this resurgence, entitled *Psychology of Sex Differences* (Stanford, Calif.), was published by Eleanor Maccoby and Carol Jacklin. The core message was that sex differences had been greatly exaggerated over the centuries and that aside from fairly minor differences in verbal ability favoring women and mathematical, spatial relations and aggressiveness differences favoring men, other measured psychological variables failed to demonstrate significant sex differences. This work contradicted the social stereotype of "opposite sexes" and suggested that women and men were very similar to each other psychologically. This conclusion supported liberal feminist values arguing for equality of the sexes in all fields of endeavor.

Despite advances in feminist psychology, investigations of the mainstream research literature indicated repeatedly that there was little shift in the larger field in terms of research practices, textbook presentations, teaching methods, or other forms of accommodation to feminist ideals. (See F. L. Denmark, *American Psychologist*, 1994, 49, 329–334). However, women's increasing numbers in graduate schools and in junior faculty positions indicated that women were gaining a stronger foothold in psychology. Over time, this influx has resulted in the emergence of three significant approaches to feminist psychology.

The Empiricist Perspective

The majority of feminist psychologists in universities are empirical scientists. They are indistinguishable from their non-feminist colleagues in terms of their scientific standards, research methodologies, and professional accomplishments and goals. Their feminist values encourage them to be vigilant in terms of gender equality, to seek out biases in research practices that discriminate against women, and to develop a knowledge base in gender-related topics of research. Illustrative of feminist empiricism today is the work of feminist psychologists in meta-analysis, a statistical method used to assess the size of gender differences across aggregated empirical studies in various psychological domains such as mathematical ability, persuasibility, or leadership.

Feminist empiricists have also gained recognition for developing personality scales of gender-role identification. Sandra Bem, creator of the Bem Sex Role Inventory in 1974, is widely known for introducing the term *androgyny* to describe the presence of both masculine and feminine traits in a single person. Social psychologists Janet Spence and Robert Helmreich also created a well-known masculinity-femininity scale called the Personality Attributes Questionnaire. Empirical feminists have also been interested in showing how gender differences are substantially moderated by environmental influences, such as sex-differentiated social contexts, social roles, and expectations. (See Kay Deaux, *American Psychologist*, 1984, 39, 105–116.)

Some critics of feminist empirical psychology have questioned whether quantitative methods and laboratory experiments are appropriate for gaining insights into women's experiences. They also question whether the scientific demand for value-neutrality on the part of the researcher is a reasonable standard for feminist psychologists. Some have in fact argued that a strict adherence to scientific methods is not designed to achieve the goals of feminism (see J. G. Morawski, *Practicing Feminism, Reconstructing Psychology: Notes on a Liminal Science*, University of Mich., 1994.)

The Feminist Standpoint Position

In 1982 the publication of Carol Gilligan's highly visible book *In a Different Voice* (Cambridge, Mass.) proposed a feminist standpoint position in psychology. This position calls attention to the special qualities of women, such as nurturance, the importance of women's lived experiences as sources of data, and an appreciation of qualitative research as a means for revealing women's truths. Feminist standpoint theorists regard women's experiences as the grounding for a more comprehensive and less distorted knowledge base than men's do. With *Women's Ways of Knowing* (Mary Belenky, et al., New York, 1986). Jean Baker Miller's *New Psychology of Women* (Boston, 1986), writings from the Stone Center at Wellesley College, and many others, this position has gained a large audience in psychology, women's studies, and within the reading public more generally. In their work, feminist standpoint psychologists often adopt object relations theory, a variant of psychoanalytic theory, which emphasizes the importance of the mother-infant relationship in gender identity development. (See Nancy Chodorow, *The Reproduction of Motherhood*, Berkeley, Calif., 1978.) The theory suggests that this relationship establishes separate developmental paths for girls and boys, with girls valuing connection and closeness with others and boys seeking autonomy and individuality.

Some feminist standpoint theorists, especially in Europe, have adopted a revised Marxist political perspective. For these feminists, the oppression of women is a societal evil that has been overshadowed in Marxist theory by an exclusive focus on men's economic relationships. They urge feminists to declare their gender-specific economic oppression, to reclaim consciousness-raising methods of education in order to emphasize women's status, and to engage in political activism to counteract its effects. This approach is in contrast to American cultural practices, which tend to emphasize the individual and self-actualizing practices and psychotherapy as means of overcoming the effects of sexism in society.

While standpoint positions have attracted a certain degree of acceptance, there have also been criticisms. The divergence of the feminist empiricists' scientific methods and feminist standpoint's value-based qualitative efforts has created tensions within feminist psychology that remain unresolved. Criticisms of feminist standpoint positions have also come from those who argue that the so-called feminist standpoint is the specific standpoint of successful, middle-aged, white academic women and is exclusionary and oppressive to those not included (see J. Yoder & A. Kahn, 1993, *American Psychologist*, 48, pp. 846–850). These critics argue that women can and do oppress other women. For the most part feminist standpoint theorists have taken this criticism to heart; as a result they have attempted to be more cautious about the generality of their claims and more sensitive to their privileged status.

The Feminist Postmodern/Social Constructionist Position

The postmodern movement has strongly influenced many academic disciplines, including academic psychology. For many American feminists, the postmodern movement originated with French writers such as Julia Kristeva, Helene Cixous, and Luce Irigaray. (For a summary see T. Moi, Ed., *French Feminist Thought*, London: 1987.) Of major significance is their critique of language, particularly the discourse of science, which, as a product of male society, they regard as fundamentally oppressive to women. The social constructionist feminist movement in psychology is oriented to considering new ways of constructing reality that are more beneficial to women's interests. One outgrowth of this perspective is the new mission statement of Division 35, which includes the goal "to encourage scholarship on the social construction of gender relations across multicultural contexts." Social constructionist feminists are heavily involved in the critical examination of discourses, in particular how language produces the world of gendered lives. Feminist psychologists within this framework recognize that the "production of knowledge is not set apart from culture but is fully part of it," as Jeanne Marecek has said (*American Psychologist*, 1995, 50, p. 163). Constructionists argue that all social categories—race, class, IQ, ethnicity, sexual orientation, ableness, and even sex and gender are creations of communities of language users, who coordinate their meanings. Outside of these communities, these distinctions are inoperative. Feminist constructionists thus tend to be at odds with feminist empiricists because, for the former, research is not a matter of "fact finding." Rather they regard empirical methods as the process of "fact making." Constructionist views thus differ from both empiricist claims that reality is discovered and feminist standpoint claims that women can tell their own truths on the basis on their personal experiences. A collection of postmodern/social constructionist writings relevant to feminist psychology is *Toward a New Psychology of Gender* (Mary Gergen and Sara N. Davis, Eds., New York, 1997).

Critiques of social constructionism by empiricists focus on the nonfoundational nature of the approach and its lack of methods and standards for evaluating its claims. Feminist standpoint objections to postmodern positions include the fear that "woman" as the subject of inquiry could be challenged or even discarded if the category is "only" a social construction. Socialists object to the loss of material reality, including the reality of oppression and poverty. Feminist standpoint defenders also resist the idea that self-reports and women's experience can be defined as forms of discourse instead of Truth. Social constructionists are also criticized for lacking a strong and clear moral foundation.

All three of these positions—empiricist, feminist standpoint, and social constructionist—have counterarguments to their critics.

Issues of Diversity

Concerns with diversity are of critical interest to feminist psychologists. A special section of Division 35, Psychology of Black Women, was founded in 1978 as a committee and is designed to increase the scientific understanding of those aspects of culture and class pertaining to the psychology of Black women, to increase the quality of education and training in the field of psychology of Black women, and to support African American scholars. Special interest groups for Asian American, Hispanic, and Native American women have also been created within Division 35 to support diversity within the organization and beyond. (See Hope Landrine, Ed., *Bringing Cultural Diversity to Feminist Psychology*, Washington, D.C., 1995).

Training Requirements

There are no specific training requirements in order for psychologists to call themselves feminists. In 1997 Division 35 created a Feminist Academy that offers continuing education credits to psychotherapists and other professionals; these credits will support a new specialization in feminist psychology.

Publications

Feminist psychologists publish in the major journals in psychology as well as in research-oriented journals especially focused on gender issues. These include *Sex Roles: A Journal of Research*, founded in 1975, *The Psychology of Women Quarterly*, begun in 1976 by Division 35, and *Feminism and Psychology*, edited by Sue Wilkinson in England since 1991. Several other journals of interest to feminist psychologists involved in therapy are *Women and Therapy*, *Journal of Feminist Family Therapy*, the *Counseling Psychologist*, *Violence against Women*, *Family Process*, and *Journal of Consulting and Clinical Psy-*

chology. Created in 1993, *masculinities* is a journal of gender studies with a special focus on men.

Future Directions

Feminist psychology is projected to remain a vital forum for many varieties of inquiry well into the twenty-first century. With ever-increasing numbers of feminists in the profession, the "mainstreaming" of feminism within the core of the profession becomes a strong possibility. Feminist psychologists will continue to explore new methods, new publishing opportunities for diverse forms of presentation, and continuing dialogue concerning the nature of scientific research, political goals, and international issues.

As a leading researcher, Alice Eagly has said: "Never before in the history of psychology has such a formidable body of scientific information encountered such a powerful political agenda. The results of this encounter should be instructive to all psychologists who believe that psychology should serve human welfare as it advances scientific understanding" (*American Psychologist*, 1995, 50, 155–156).

Bibliography

Historical Commentary on Feminist Psychology until 1970

Bohan, J. (Ed.). (1994). *Seldom seen, rarely heard: Women's place in psychology*. Boulder, CO: Westview Press. Seventeen chapters covering significant historical events in feminist psychology.

Thompson, H. B. [Woolley]. (1903). *The mental traits of sex: An experimental investigation of the normal mind in men and women*. Chicago: University of Chicago Press. Classic work in feminist psychology (difficult to find).

Commentary on Feminist Psychology after 1970

Crawford, M., & Marecek, J. (1989). Psychology constructs the female: 1968–1988. *Psychology of Women Quarterly*, *13*, 147–165. Evidence for the lack of intersection of feminist psychology and the "malestream."

Russo, N. F., & Dumont, B. A. (1997). A history of Division 35 (Psychology of women): Origins, issues, activities, future. In *A History of the Divisions of the American Psychological Association*. Washington, DC: American Psychological Association.

Sherif, C. (1979). Bias in psychology. In J. A. Sherman & E. T. Beck (Eds.), *The prism of sex: Essays in the sociology of knowledge*. Madison: University of Wisconsin Press. A famous challenge to sexism in the field.

Worell, J., & Johnson, N. (Eds.). (1998). *Feminist visions: New directions for research and practice*. Washington, DC: American Psychological Association. Focused on important issues related to feminist methods of research and practice with an eye to the future of the field. Excellent bibliography.

Empirical Feminist Psychology

Bem, S. (1993). *The lenses of gender: Transforming the debate on sexual inequality.* New Haven: Yale University Press. Follows the prolific author from her early personality trait work on androgyny, through cognitive revisioning, to a flirtation with social constructionism.

Hyde, J. (1994). Can meta-analysis make feminist transformations in psychology? *Psychology of Women Quarterly, 18,* 451–462. A point of view on the values of meta-analysis from one of its leading figures.

Feminist Standpoint Psychology

Jordan, J., Kaplan, A. G., Miller, J. B., Striver, I. P., & Survey, J. L. (Eds.), (1991). *Women's growth in connection: Writings from the Stone Center.* New York: Guilford Press.

Taylor, J., Gilligan, C., & Sullivan, A. M. (1995). *Between voice and silence: Women and girls, race and relationship.* Cambridge, MA: Harvard University Press. A feminist standpoint approach that brings race into the conversation about girl's developmental paths.

Postmodern Feminist Psychology

Gergen, M. M. (2000). *Impious improvisation: Feminist constructions in psychology.* Thousand Oaks, CA: Sage. Demonstrates how one feminist does postmodern psychology.

Bohan, J. S., & Russell, G. M. (1999). *Conversations about psychology and sexual orientation.* New York: New York University Press. Contrasts the essentialist and the constructionist perspectives on what it is to be "gay."

Issues of Diversity

Chrisler, J. C., & Hemstreet, Alyce H. (1995). *Variations on a theme: Diversity and the psychology of women.* Albany: SUNY Press. Covers issues such as violence, achievement, health, friendship, and religion with diverse groups of women including lesbians, the disabled, and the elderly.

Fine, M. (1992). *Disruptive voices: The possibility of feminist research.* Ann Arbor: University of Michigan Press. A creative exploration of ways of doing/writing research that honors voices that are often ignored.

Kimmel, M. (1998). *Manhood: The American quest.* New York: HarperCollins. Exploration of historical and social construction of hegemonic masculinity and alternative masculinities.

General Readers

Unger, R., & Crawford, M. (1996). *Women and gender: A feminist psychology.* (2nd ed.). Philadelphia: Temple University Press. One of many well-known textbooks, this one offers a broad coverage and acknowledges all three approaches to the field.

Tavris, C. (1992). *The mismeasure of women.* A book for the general public that sensitively explores issues of gender differences and similarities.

Mary M. Gergen

Feminist Psychotherapy

Feminist approaches to psychotherapy and counseling have a relatively short history. The reawakening of the women's movement in the late 1960s gave birth to the practice of consciousness raising (CR), in which small groups of women gathered together to consider how their life conditions were connected to their subordinate status in society. In these groups, women discussed how their individual personal problems were rooted in restrictive and stereotyped gender roles or in cultural expectations for how they should live their lives as women in Western society.

The growing awareness in CR groups of widespread discrimination and social injustices for all women led to the theme "the personal is political," which meant that women's personal conflicts and distress are embedded in inequalities in the political, economic, legal, and social structures of society that disempower and disadvantage women. CR groups were leaderless and egalitarian, providing participants with a sense of validation for their problematic feelings and experiences, solidarity with other women, and the impetus to take action toward social change.

The feminist therapies of today bear only partial resemblance to the early CR groups; they are no longer leaderless and they tend to focus more on individual concerns than on radical political activity. Nonetheless, feminist therapies encompass many of the core beliefs of the consciousness-raising era and focus on issues that still confront contemporary women.

A Brief History

In the early 1970s, women in psychology became increasingly aware of the effects of gender stereotyping and bias on clinical judgment, assessment, diagnosis, medication, and approaches to psychotherapeutic intervention. A landmark study by Inge Broverman and her colleagues (1970) revealed that both women and men clinicians evaluated the "healthy woman" differently and less positively than the "healthy man," who was rated as similar to the "healthy adult" (*Journal of Consulting and Clinical Psychology, 34,* 1–7). These findings reflected widespread androcentrism in the mental health community, whereby the lives and experiences of men were taken as the standard for desirable human behavior and psychological well-being. In the same period, books such as Phyllis Chesler's *Women and Madness* (New York, 1972) on women, mental illness, and diagnosis cast additional doubt on the ability of the mental health profession to treat women in an unbiased manner and to take their concerns seriously.

In 1975 a report of the American Psychological Association (APA) Task force on Sex Bias and Sex-Role Stereotyping in Psychotherapeutic Practice (*American*

Psychologist, 30, 1169–1175) brought into sharp focus many of the biases against women that existed in therapeutic practice. Among these practices, sexual misconduct against clients and demeaning interpretations of women's behavior by some therapists were among the more salient reported abuses.

In academia, professional training programs began to introduce feminist practice, and practicing therapists convened at the Seattle Feminist Therapy Institute to share their ideas and concerns. A set of principles of counseling and psychotherapy with women (*Counseling Psychologist, 14,* 180–216) was articulated by Louise Fitzgerald and Roberta Nutt for the APA Division of Counseling Psychology; and the 1993 Boston Conference on Education and Training in Feminist Practice, sponsored by the Division of Psychology of Women, provided visions of the future that are still to be fully realized. From these diverse strands, feminist therapies have emerged as a vital force in the service of women's psychological well-being.

Feminisms and Feminist Therapies

Feminist psychotherapists share with feminists generally the view that women, in all their diversity in contemporary Western societies, are treated unfairly in many ways and that a commitment to improving the status of women is essential. Disagreements among feminists, and among feminist therapists in particular, concern the specific sources of women's disadvantage and distress and which solutions should be endorsed and supported.

Feminist therapies, like feminists in general, are not a homogeneous group. A number of classifications have been proposed to distinguish among them. Carolyn Enns describes six major approaches to feminism: liberal, radical, socialist, cultural, women of color, and postmodern. Although each of these positions contains some distinct characteristics, their applications to feminist therapy can be condensed according to primary themes.

Liberal/reform feminism targets the elimination of inequalities between women and men in legal, political, social, and educational arrangements. This approach to feminism was supported by passage of Title VII of the U.S. Civil Rights Act, which extended civil rights to women and minorities (1964), and by the establishment of the Equal Employment Opportunities Commission (EEOC, 1965) to enforce the provisions of the Civil Rights Act. These two legislations provided opportunities for women and minorities to take legal recourse against many forms of discrimination.

Feminist therapies based on a liberal/reform philosophy assist the client in revisioning herself in the context of gender socialization and its resulting expectations for her roles as a girl, daughter, sweetheart, lover,

wife, mother, and worker. In this perspective, Laura Brown (*Psychotherapy: Theory, Research, and Practice,* 1986) encourages exploration of what each gender role means to the client and how it may influence her satisfaction and distress. A sensitive gender-role analysis helps the client to reduce self-blame and to consider possible alternatives to her present reactions and behaviors. She may be encouraged to move toward androgyny or toward greater flexibility in dealing with self and others whereby she can use behaviors with others in her life that effectively help her attain personal goals. Assertiveness training, or effective confrontation with others, may be used to encourage women to break their silences and to openly voice their pain and needs. Reframing and renaming of experiences assist the woman in turning shame into pride and fear into strength as she is able to acknowledge her ability to cope and survive. Pathology is reconstructed as the woman's best attempt at coping, and formal diagnosis is usually avoided. Women are encouraged to nurture themselves as well as others.

The ethic of equality in liberal/reform therapy also incorporates workplace concerns. Feminist career counseling assists women to explore their work-related conflicts, such as that between family and career, or between "being competent and being feminine" (see Jean Parr Lemkau & Doris Howard (Eds.), *The Dynamics of Feminist Therapy,* New York, 1986). Gender-role analysis can be used in career counseling to help women explore their internalized messages about family and jobs outside the home for women, as well as the meaning of career success and failure. Feminist career counseling assists women to reduce self-blame by identifying the structural barriers to equality in the workplace, including sexual harassment, occupational segregation of women into low paying positions, and the widespread devaluation of women's performance.

Liberal/reform feminism also proposes that traditional gender roles are restrictive for men as well as for women; men must also change if women are to attain equal status. In applying this perspective Michelle Bograd (in *Feminist Approaches to Family Therapy with Men,* New York, 1990), points out that narrowly defined gender roles can lead to both personal and family dysfunction. In particular, societal constructions of masculinity as tied to domination and control provide the foundation for unequal power relationships between women and men. Liberal/reform feminist therapies thus encourage women and men to challenge the status quo and to initiate change within themselves and in their proximal environments.

Radical/socialist feminism, in contrast to liberal/reform feminism, identifies the locus of women's problems in the politics of power and asymmetrical gender relations. Patriarchy, or the dominance of male privilege and possession, is seen as responsible for women's systematic oppression and devaluation, leading women into submissiveness and silence. Patriarchy is also responsible for heterosexism, or viewing as deviant any interpersonal love or sexuality other than between females and males. According to radical feminists women can be free to discover themselves apart from patriarchal structures and institutions only by insisting on the elimination of patriarchy and the establishment of a new order of caring and cooperation. Cultural stereotypes of women as passive, dependent, and nurturant are social constructions designed to maintain women's powerlessness. Such stereotypes are internalized by many women and accepted by others as a natural part of their personality, thereby creating a self-fulfilling prophecy (by believing it, they enact it).

In recognizing patriarchy as a system of control over women and their bodies, Susan Brownmiller, in *Against Our Will: Men, Women, and Rape* (New York, 1975), reinterpreted rape as a manifestation of aggression rather than of sexuality. Violence against women and sexual coercion are also seen as institutionalized control over women to maintain male dominance and women's compliance. Lenore Walker pointed out in *The Battered Woman* (New York, 1979) that women's apparent "submission" to a battering relationship reflects not masochism or enjoyment of pain but signals her best judgment about how to ensure her safety and that of her children in the face of terrifying violence. The outrages of rape and sexual aggression were brought to public attention by radical feminists through rape crisis centers and battered women's shelters. In accord with their recognition of power arrangements, radical feminists also acknowledge and integrate into gender oppression other oppressions, including those associated with ethno-racial status, socioeconomic class, sexual orientation, age, and ableness.

Feminist therapies from a radical perspective expand, rather than replace, the philosophy and strategies of liberal/reform therapies by concentrating on the politics of power. Empowerment of clients becomes critical, and therapists aim to provide an egalitarian relationship with their clients. The challenge of creating an egalitarian relationship leads to a range of procedures, including sharing one's personal values, demystification (informing clients of all aspects of the therapy experience), validating and trusting the lived experiences of the client, and using judicious self-disclosure when appropriate. The client is encouraged to become an expert on herself. Empowerment can also be realized by engaging in social activism.

Several other feminist therapies are currently active. Cultural feminism provides a foundation for self-in-relation therapy, which emphasizes women's "natural" relationship qualities of caring and connection with other women. Lesbian feminism focuses on the multiple oppressions and concerns of women who love women, and multicultural/womanist feminisms focus on ethno-racial issues as the primary basis for their oppression.

Critiques and Controversies

There are a number of critiques of feminist therapies, as follows. Each of these arguments is complex and controversial.

1. Feminist therapy was designed by White, middle-class heterosexual women and has little relevance for the less socioculturally privileged. Gender as central to the analysis of women's lives ignores race and other multicultural variables.
2. Feminist therapy is vaguely defined and is not based on a consistent theory of feminist practice.
3. Liberal feminist therapy assists women in adjusting to an oppressive and patriarchal society; it changes nothing.
4. Feminist therapies have not established a cohesive set of procedures and have failed to demonstrate their effectiveness with outcome studies that document change.

Progress in feminist therapies of all persuasions will be enhanced as satisfactory responses to these concerns are considered and adopted.

Bibliography

Bem, S. L. (1993). *The lenses of gender: Transforming the debate on sexual inequality.* New Haven, CT: Yale University Press. A treatise on the invisibility of polarized and asymmetrical gender arrangements in most societies, whereby the roles and behaviors of women and men appear to be natural characteristics of individuals rather than of cultures. A thoughtful and scholarly discussion of gender.

Brodsky, A. M., & Hare-Mustin, R. T. (1980). *Women and therapy: An assessment of research and practice.* New York: Guilford Press. A synthesis of research and psychotherapy with women that explores issues in women's mental health, gender issues in therapy, and theoretical and research foundations of feminist therapy. One of the groundbreaking publications.

Brown, L. S. (1994). *Subversive dialogues: Theory in feminist therapy.* New York: Basic Books. An advanced and intensely personal exploration of the relationship between feminism and various approaches to feminist psychotherapy. Presents a radical/multicultural view with many case examples. Not for the beginner.

Dutton-Douglass, M. A., & Walker, L. E. A. (Eds.). (1988). *Feminist psychotherapies: Integration of therapeutic and feminist systems.* Norwood, NJ: Ablex.

Enns, C. B. (1997). *Feminist theories and feminist psychotherapies: Origins, themes, and variations.* New York: Harrington Park Press. A survey and examination of the history of feminist thought and how it has shaped the integration of feminist theories and feminist therapies. A very useful reference.

Hare-Mustin, R. T., & Marecek, J. (Eds.). (1991). *Making a difference: Psychology and the construction of gender.* New Haven, CT: Yale University Press. An in-depth exploration of the social construction of gender. Distinguished authors explore social constructions of gender and clarify the concept of gender differences. A valuable introduction to a postmodern feminist perspective.

Jordan, J. V., Kaplan, A. G., Miller, J. B., Stiver, I. P., & Surry, J. L. (Eds.). *Women's growth in connection.* New York: Guilford Press. An overview and exploration of the self-in-relation approach to feminist psychotherapy, emphasizing women's connections to each other as a source of strength, understanding, and change. Reflects Stone Center views.

Mirkin, M. P. (Ed.). (1994). *Women in context: Toward a feminist reconstruction of psychotherapy.* New York: Guilford Press. Covers issues in feminist psychotherapy with a range of women from diverse socioeconomic, racial, ethnic, age, and sexual contexts.

Rave, E. J., & Larsen, C. (Eds.). (1995). *Ethical decision-making in therapy: Feminist perspectives.* New York: Guilford Press. Decision-making issues in psychotherapy when two or more ethical principles conflict are addressed by means of a unique feminist model and case applications.

Rawlings, E. I., & Carter, D. K. (Eds.). (1977). *Psychotherapy for women: Treatment toward equality.* Springfield, IL: Thomas. A landmark book on therapy with women from a radical feminist therapy position. It points out that therapy is never value-free, disentangles feminist from nonsexist therapy, and proposes that feminism and social activism can be therapeutic.

Worell, J., & Johnson, N. (1997). *Shaping the future of feminist psychology: Education, research, and practice.* Washington, DC: American Psychological Association. Provides a cohesive set of principles for feminist practice across the field of psychology, including theory, assessment, therapy, curriculum and pedagogy, research, diversity, supervision, and postdoctoral education.

Worell, J., & Remer, P. (1992). *Feminist perspectives in therapy: An empowerment model for women.* Chichester, UK: Wiley. Presents a model of feminist counseling and psychotherapy that addresses both internal and external sources of women's distress. Case examples and experiential activities for self-exploration of beliefs and values.

Judith Worell

FERENCZI, SANDOR (1873–1933), Hungarian psychoanalyst. Ferenczi's career can be divided into four distinct phases. First, before World War I, he had become acquainted with Sigmund Freud, with whom he quickly gained favor. Ferenczi underwent two short analyses with Freud, in 1914 and 1916. He not only was one of Freud's preferred traveling companions on summer vacations, but he and Freud regularly exchanged ideas. The complete Freud–Ferenczi correspondence will amount to a three-volume edition. Ferenczi was exceptionally charming and imaginative, and many consider Ferenczi to have been the warmest, most human, most sensitive of the early psychoanalytic group. Freud fully appreciated Ferenczi's considerable personal qualities, including his ability to identify with children; Ferenczi was on more than one occasion described as the milk of human kindness.

During the 1920s Ferenczi, always especially interested in the technique of psychoanalytic therapy, began to experiment with ways of improving therapeutic results. Freud was not only uncomfortable about embodying the ideal of becoming a helper but, especially after contracting cancer of the jaw in 1923, Freud withdrew increasingly from his earlier outgoingness as a therapist. In principle Freud was a skeptic, and he could make intellectual fun of humanitarianism. (Supposedly the love of mankind was to be understood as a sublimation of homosexuality.) Ferenczi, however, was increasingly convinced that psychoanalysis was too intellectualist in its approach. So in Ferenczi's second phase he tried to find alternatives to Freud's highly rationalistic approach to treatment. In collaboration with Freud's Viennese disciple Otto Rank, Ferenczi wrote a short book advocating that the analyst aim at the patient's reliving emotional experiences during the course of analysis; this objective was at odds with the earlier psychoanalytic aim of reconstructing the early years of a patient's life. Ferenczi believed that psychoanalysis should not be confined to memory problems but instead should focus on a patient's character as a whole. Ferenczi helped inspire Melanie Klein, a former patient of his, to pioneer in the treatment of children in a way that turned out to be seriously at odds with the path chosen by Freud's daughter Anna.

By around 1930 Ferenczi was boldly striking out in new therapeutic directions. Freud had originally been tolerant of Ferenczi's innovations, despite the warnings from loyalists like Ernest Jones that Ferenczi's work amounted to a heretical revival of the approach of Carl Gustav Jung; although Jung was stigmatized as a so-called deviant before World War I, only in the early 1930s was Freud persuaded that Ferenczi was regressing to a prepsychoanalytic position. In 1896–1997 Freud had entertained the idea that neuroses were due to childhood sexual seduction; he then abandoned this position for the notion that infantile fantasies, not traumas, were at the root of patients' difficulties. Ferenczi, however, picked up on the theme of parents being too cold with their children, which he believed should not be repeated in the course of psychoanalytic therapy. Ferenczi's advocacy of flexibility and "elasticity" in technique alarmed Freud, who feared that beginners might give up on the most distinctive aspects of so-called analytic neutrality. By 1932 Freud opposed Ferenczi's presentation of a paper to a psychoanalytic congress, and at a final meeting he refused to take Ferenczi's hand, even turning his back on Ferenczi. Ferenczi was heartbroken at Freud's intolerance. The pernicious anemia which afflicted Ferenczi led to his death on 22 May 1933.

The third phase in Ferenczi's reputation followed as his stability and sanity were denigrated. Freud wrote a laudatory obituary of Ferenczi, but in private Freud maintained that the physical illness was an expression of psychological conflicts. Jones, once analyzed by Ferenczi, took his revenge in the course of his official biography of Freud. Jones maintained that Ferenczi had had a "latent psychosis," and that this underlying set of problems found expression not only in Ferenczi's final papers, but in his attitude toward Freud. Supposedly Freud's "closest friend" exhibited before his death "violent paranoic and even homicidal outbursts." Although no one intimately acquainted with Ferenczi during his last period of life could confirm any of Jones's attack, the general reading public was unaware of what insiders believed to be Jones's biases.

Starting with Erich Fromm's 1958 challenge to Jones's defense of orthodoxy, outsiders began to wonder what damage he had done to Ferenczi's standing. It took over a generation, though, for people to start to appreciate the merits of Ferenczi's ideas, detached from Jones's polemics. By the 1990s Ferenczi was being hailed as one of the great pathfinders in the history of psychotherapy. It was never possible to tar him with the brush of Jungianism, for Ferenczi remained publicly faithful to the founder of psychoanalysis. Ferenczi's *Clinical Diary* appeared in English (1988) showing the full originality of his therapeutic approach. The publication of the Freud–Ferenczi correspondence documented just how close the two men had been, the extent of the genuine interest Freud took in Ferenczi's private life, and the degree to which the differences between the two men evolved from their contrasting personalities and age discrepancies.

By now Ferenczi has become recognized within classical psychoanalysis as a great proponent of the view that analysts should concentrate on the here-and-now in their work with clients. Ferenczi is acknowledged to have been one of the creators of the interpersonal approach to therapy. Ferenczi taught that analysts should not hide behind their technique, but rather make use of their humanity in trying to heal. Because of the closeness of the personal relationship between Freud and Ferenczi over so many years, it has been impossible to detach Ferenczi from the history of psychoanalysis, and therefore in this fourth part of Ferenczi's career he has successfully inspired a new outlook on the practice of psychoanalytic therapy. Despite what Leo Durocher once said, nice guys do not necessarily finish last.

Bibliography

Ferenczi, S. (1926). *Further contributions to the theory and technique of psychoanalysis.* London: Hogarth Press.

Ferenczi, S. (1955). *Final contributions to the problems and methods of psychoanalysis.* London: Hogarth Press.

Ferenczi, S. (1956). *Sex in psychoanalysis.* New York: Dover.

Ferenczi, S. (1988). *The clinical diary of Sandor Ferenczi* (J. Dupont, Ed., M. Balint & N. Zarday Jackson, Trans.). Cambridge, MA: Harvard University Press.

Fromm, E. (1963). Psychoanalysis: Science or party line. In E. Fromm, *The dogma of Christ, and other essays on religion, psychology and culture.* New York: Holt, Rinehart and Winston.

Jones, E. (1957). *The life and work of Sigmund Freud* (Vol. 3). New York: Basic Books.

Paul Roazen

FERNBERGER, SAMUEL W. (1887–1956), American psychologist. Fernberger, who was born in Philadelphia, contributed to the development of early modern American psychology with his work as an influential teacher, editor of major psychology journals, and officer of several important psychological associations. A general experimental psychologist who published an introductory psychology textbook and numerous articles on an unusually broad range of empirical, theoretical, and applied topics, he was a staunch adherent of the traditions established by Edward Bradford Titchener. He was a member of the faculty of the Psychology Department at the University of Pennsylvania for 35 years, and contributed large collections of books and journals to what was to become the university's Samuel W. Fernberger Library of psychology. [*See the biography of Titchener.*]

Fernberger received all his degrees from the University of Pennsylvania, the institution in which he was to spend almost all of his career: a bachelor's degree in science (1908), a master's degree (1909), and a doctorate in experimental psychology (with F. M. Urban) in 1912. His doctoral dissertation, as were many of his later publications, was on psychophysics; it demonstrated that the method of constant stimuli has some advantages over the method of just noticeable differences; it was published as a monograph in 1913. After teaching at Clark University, Worcester, Massachusetts, for several years, in 1920 he returned to the University of Pennsylvania where he became a full professor in 1927. He was a popular teacher; many students repeated their attendance at his introductory course for no additional credit. Among his teaching innovations was asking students to impersonate important psychologists of the past, which they eagerly did. He was to have become professor emeritus in 1956, but died a month before.

Fernberger edited several major psychological journals for extended periods. A cooperating editor of the *American Journal of Psychology* from 1925 to 1956, he edited the prestigious *Psychological Bulletin* from 1918 to 1930, and then the equally prestigious *Journal of Experimental Psychology* from 1930 to 1946. A prominent member of the American Psychological Association (APA), he served as treasurer from 1922 to 1924 and as secretary from 1926 to 1928, and was president of APA's Division 1 (general psychology), from 1951 to 1952. President of the Eastern Psychological Association from 1936 to 1937, he was also secretary of the Society of Experimental Psychologists from 1928 to 1948, and president of the National Institute of Psychology from 1936 to 1941.

During World War I, as second and then first lieutenant in the U.S. infantry, he earned the Croix de Guerre and the Bronze Star for service in France. During World War II, his work on problems of perception, training, and human engineering for the National Research Council and the National Defense Research Council earned him the President's Certificate of Merit. [*See* Human Factors Psychology; Military Psychology; *and* Perceptual Organization.]

Fernberger's contributions to psychology went beyond his editorial work and his offices in major organizations. His publications were impressive in number and in the breadth of the issues to which they were devoted. Several of his articles on psychophysics, his chief focus, became classics, with papers on such topics as the introspective properties of psychophysical judgments, the status of the middle category of judgments, intraserial effects, the effects of practice and of physical and mental work, the "absolute method," the stimulus error, and the time required for various categories of judgment. He also published on the facial expression of emotion, the memory span, and the range of visual apprehension, and apparent motion, imagery, aphasia, the history of psychology (including the history of APA), experiences resulting from the ingestion of peyote, and the interpretation of the symbolism on Sioux Indian shields. [*See* Memory; Nonverbal Communication; *and* Vision and Sight, Behavioral and Functional Aspects.] He performed statistical studies of a variety of subjects, including the number of articles in psychology published in different languages; the geographical distribution of APA members; the origin of doctoral positions and research interests of men and women in psychology; Wilhelm Maximilian Wundt's students; and the publications of American psychologists. [*See the biography of Wundt.*]

Fernberger was a model general psychologist during the first half of the twentieth century, when "general psychology" represented the highest goal of a typical aspiring psychologist.

Bibliography

Fernberger, S. W. (1936). *Elementary general psychology*. New York: S. F. Crofts. This is Fernberger's introductory psychology textbook; it was favorably reviewed in the *American Journal of Psychology*, 1937, 49, 490–491.

Fernberger, S. W. (1913). On the relation of the methods of just perceptible differences and constant stimuli. *Psychological Monographs*, 14, no. 61, 1–81. This monograph is the published version of Fernberger's doctoral dissertation.

Fernberger, S. W. (1932). The American Psychological Association: A historical summary, 1892–1930. *Psychological Bulletin*, 29, 1–89.

Fernberger, S. W. (1943). The American Psychological Association, 1892–1942. *Psychological Review*, 50, 33–60.

Irwin, F. W. (1956). Samuel Weiller Fernberger: 1887–1956. *American Journal of Psychology*, 69, 676–680. Irwin's obituary was the main source of information for this narrative on Fernberger.

Michael Wertheimer

FERRARI, GIULIO CESARE (1868–1932), Italian psychiatrist and psychologist. Although more known as one of the leading figures of early Italian psychology, Ferrari's institutional career was mainly in the field of psychiatry: director of psychiatric hospitals, and chief editor of the most important Italian psychiatric journal in the age of positivism (*Rivista Sperimentale di Freniatria*). After a period spent in Paris with Alfred Binet, he founded a laboratory of experimental psychology in the Psychiatric Hospital of Reggio Emilia (1896), and began to apply psychological methods (especially mental tests) in research on psychiatric patients with the aim of developing a project of objective experimental diagnosis of mental disorders. Ferrari argued that the variety of psychiatric disorders had one of its fundamental causes in individual differences at the psychological level, and that psychological investigation should represent a preliminary and necessary contribution to psychiatry. In general, his approach was against a reductionistic interpretation of mental disorders in terms of anatomical and physiological abnormalities. He was also actively engaged in improving assistance and care conditions of psychiatric institutions, and in promoting the mental hygiene movement (he was vice president of the first world congress of mental hygiene, held in Washington in 1930).

Moreover, Ferrari founded a settlement for the social rehabilitation of young criminals. His original approach was to put young delinquents and boys and girls with psychiatric disorders together so that delinquents could interact with and help the patients, with a sociopsychological gain for both.

Ferrari's contribution to psychology was especially represented by editorial enterprises. His translation of William James's *Principles of Psychology* in 1901 had a great influence on Italian psychology and culture as well. In fact, this translation (with Ferrari's updatings authorized by James himself) was decisive for the diffusion of pragmatism in Italy (Ferrari also translated James's *Varieties of Religious Experience* and *Talks to Teachers*).

In 1905, Ferrari founded *Rivista di Psicologia*, the first autonomous Italian periodical devoted to psychological research. Ferrari and Italian pragmatists wrote for this new journal, and spread the idea of psychology as a discipline interested in contemporary philosophical, cultural and social problems more than in specialized and experimental fields of psychological investigation. Thus, it is not surprising that in 1916 his *Rivista* published the war diary of the simple soldier Benito Mussolini, the future duce. Many other papers on the psychological and psychiatric problems of soldiers during World War I were written by Ferrari himself. Basically, Ferrari was attracted by James's psychology because its approach was not strictly empirical and was not necessarly linked to laboratory research. Although he made some experimental works, especially in the early period of his activity (probably the most original experiments were on the ergographic responses in females), he spent most of his time in the applied fields of psychiatric rehabilitation and mental hygiene. Although he taught some courses in psychology at the University of Bologna, he did not form a real group of pupils. He represented the Italian scientific community in many international congresses and corresponded with eminent psychologists (e.g., Binet, Edouard Claparède, William James, and Paul Janet).

Bibliography

Babini, V. P. (1996). *La questione dei frenastenici. Alle origini della psicologia scientifica in Italia (1870–1910)*. Milano: Angeli. Ferrari's contributions to the application of psychology in the diagnosis and treatment of mentally retarded children.

Dazzi, N., & Mecacci, L. (1997). Early Italian psychology. In W. G. Bringmann, H. E. Lück, R. Miller, & C. E. Early (Eds.), *A pictorial history of psychology* (pp. 577–581). Chicago: Quintessence.

Ferrari, G. C. (1932). Autobiography. In C. Murchison (Ed.), *A history of psychology in autobiography* (pp. 63–88). Worcester, MA: Clark University Press.

Mucciarelli, G. (Ed.). (1984). *Giulio Cesare Ferrari nella storia della psicologia italiana*. Bologna, Italy: Pitagora Editrice. An exhaustive overview of Ferrari's work in the fields of psychology and psychiatry.

Luciano Mecacci

FESTINGER, LEON (1919–1989), American psychologist. Born the son of Alex and Sara Solomon Festinger, he attended school in New York City and completed his bachelor's degree in psychology at the City College of New York in 1939. He entered graduate school in psychology at the University of Iowa, where Kurt Lewin had recently accepted an appointment at the Iowa Child Welfare Station. Festinger completed his doctoral work in 1942 and remained at the university for an additional year as a research associate. During this time, he authored several articles on the level of aspiration, decision processes, statistics, as well as taste preferences in rats. In 1943 he took an appointment as senior statistician for the Committee on the Selection and Training of Aircraft Pilots, at the University of Rochester, remaining in this position until the end of World War II, when he accepted an appointment as assistant professor in the newly formed Research Center for Group Dynamics at the Massachusetts Institute of Technology.

The head of the new institute was Kurt Lewin, and the other faculty members were Dorwin Cartwright, Ronald Lippitt, and Marian Radke Yarrow. The institute attracted a number of talented graduate students, including Kurt Back, Morton Deutsch, Harold Kelley, Albert Pepitone, Stanley Schachter, and John Thibaut. This distinguished group of faculty and graduate students turned out a number of pioneering research projects on group influence processes. It was from this work that Festinger wrote his influential "Informal Social Communication" (*Psychological Research*, 1950, 57), in which he proposed the concept of pressures toward uniformity. The elegance of this formulation lay in its use of this concept as an intervening variable between various determinants such as group cohesion, the importance and relevance of the issue to the group, and the amount of disagreement within the group, on the one hand, and various dependent effects, on the other, such as attempts to influence deviant group members, tendencies to change one's own position, and tendencies to redefine the group so that deviant members are excluded.

After the death of Lewin in 1947, Festinger moved to the University of Michigan and its Institute for Social Research. Then, in 1951, he accepted an appointment as professor of psychology at the University of Minnesota, where he published his second important theoretical paper in social psychology, "A Theory of Social Comparison Processes" (*Human Relations*, 1954, 57).

Social comparison theory explained a lot of the phenomena of group influence processes, and the theory was more clearly conceptualized as a process within the person rather than within the group. It held that people have a need to evaluate their own opinions and abilities, and in the absence of physical reality checks, they will do so by comparing their own opinions and abilities with those of other people. It further held that comparisons were not particularly helpful unless the position of the comparison person was fairly close to one's own. By this creative stroke, Festinger was able to derive a pressure toward uniformity in the comparison process. Also new in this theory was the idea that people compare their abilities just as they do their opinions and attitudes. While this new theory about social influence processes stimulated a great deal of research, by the time it was published, Festinger was working on yet another theory.

The theory of cognitive dissonance (1957) was Festinger's major contribution to the field of psychology. It had implications for understanding various kinds of persuasion, postchoice reevaluation of choice alternatives, how moral values are strengthened, selective exposure to information, and so on. The basic idea came from an explanation of why people who had experienced an earthquake that produced little visible damage indulged in fear-provoking rumors; the rumors justified their fear. The generalized explanation in terms of the relative strength of cognitions (items of information about the environment and about oneself) that were inconsistent (dissonant) with each other compared to those that were consistent (consonant) made it easily applicable to many of the complex problems with which social psychologists were concerned. Its emphasis on justification of one's own behavior as a method of dissonance reduction put it in a class separate from other theories of cognitive balance and also put it in opposition to traditional behavioristic views about the effect of rewards or threats of punishment on resultant behavioral tendencies. While research on the theory was initiated at the University of Minnesota, it was then continued at Stanford University, where Festinger took a professorship in psychology in 1955. Festinger's work on dissonance theory culminated in his research monograph *Conflict, Decision, and Dissonance* (Stanford, Calif., 1964).

Douglas Lawrence, an animal psychologist at Stanford, and Festinger carried out an extensive program of research with laboratory rats designed to demonstrate that dissonance theory offered an alternative and better way to understand some traditional problems in animal learning. They obtained experimental support for their contention that, in line with dissonance theory, the strength of a learned habit can be increased by relatively low rewards, by infrequent rewards, and by delay of rewards. They published their findings in *Deterrents and Reinforcement* (Stanford, Calif., 1962).

Festinger's attention then turned to the relationship between the person's knowledge and the reality that the knowledge represented. This problem was important in the structure of dissonance theory, and it might

have led to more research on the theory, but Festinger's interest turned to the relationship between the eye and the brain and how they relate to each other. As this new interest in visual perception developed, Festinger left Stanford in 1968 to become the Else and Hans Staudinger Professor at the New School for Social Research in New York City.

For the next 11 years, Festinger followed his interests in visual perception and developed theories about how behavior affects visual location, and how the eye communicates color information to the brain. While this research program was productive, Festinger eventually became impatient with narrow problems in visual perception, and in 1979, he closed his laboratory and launched an investigation that was entirely different from anything he had previously done.

He took up archeology and paleontology in order to address questions about how the development of humans up to the beginning of civilization might influence their adaptation to present day life. To do this, he acquainted himself with the pertinent literature and surrounded himself with world experts about various specific topics that he wished to explore. He spent 4 years in this endeavor, which eventuated in a slim but pithy volume, *The Human Legacy* (New York, 1983). This book explores questions such as why conflict between human groups did not arise until humans began to settle in permanent locations, and the conditions that made slavery widespread and what led to its demise.

Festinger created and chaired the Committee for Transnational Social Psychology during the period after World War 11 when European academic centers had lost much of their talent and influence. Working with the European Association of Experimental Social Psychology, he was instrumental in helping them rebuild and initiate programs and laboratories in social psychology.

Festinger received the Distinguished Scientist Award of the American Psychological Association in 1959. He was a member of the Society of Experimental Psychologists, a Fellow of the American Academy of Arts and Sciences, and a member of the National Academy of Sciences.

[*Many of the people mentioned in this article are the subjects of independent biographical entries.*]

Bibliography

Brehm, J. W. (1998). Leon Festinger: Beyond the obvious. In G. A. Kimble & M. Wertheimer (Eds.), *Portraits of pioneers in psychology* (Vol. 3, pp. 328–344). Mahwah, NJ: Erlbaum.

Festinger, L. (1957). *A theory of cognitive dissonance.* Stanford, CA: Stanford University Press.

Gerard, H. B. (1994). A retrospective review of Festinger's

A theory of cognitive dissonance. Contemporary Psychology, 39, 1013–1017.

Moscovici, S. (1989). Obituary: Leon Festinger. *European Journal of Social Psychology, 19,* 263–269.

Schachter, S. (1994). Leon Festinger, 1919–1989. *Biographical Memoirs, 64,* 98–110.

Schachter, S., & Gazzaniga, M. S. (Eds.). (1989). *Extending psychological frontiers: Selected works of Leon Festinger.* New York: Russell Sage Foundation. An excellent selection of Festinger's work, it includes early papers on level of aspiration and decision theory, the classic theoretical papers on pressures toward uniformity, social comparison processes, and cognitive dissonance, important papers on visual perception, a variety of less systematic contributions, as well as Festinger's commentary on the field of social psychology.

Zajonc, R. B. (1990). Leon Festinger (1919–1989). *American Psychologist, 45,* 661–662.

Zukier, H. (1989). Introduction. In S. Schachter and M. S. Gazzaniga (Eds.), *Extending psychological frontiers: Selected works of Leon Festinger* (pp. xi–xxiv). New York: Russell Sage Foundation.

Jack W. Brehm

FETAL ALCOHOL SYNDROME. Alcohol is a neurobehavioral teratogen, an agent that can cause defects in the structure and function of the developing central nervous system (CNS). Prenatal alcohol exposure can produce a continuum of effects, ranging from subtle functional deficits to the lifelong developmental disability of fetal alcohol syndrome (FAS). Many factors can influence how adverse fetal alcohol effects are expressed from birth to adulthood, including the critical period during pregnancy when exposure occurs, the pattern and amount of maternal alcohol intake, and a host of biological and environmental variables that may impact both the pre- and the postnatal periods. This explains why there is such individual diversity in alcohol effects.

Diagnosis and Nomenclature

FAS is generally associated with heavy maternal alcohol use throughout pregnancy. It is diagnosed by confirming the presence of a characteristic set of craniofacial abnormalities, pre- and/or postnatal growth deficiency, and variable evidence of CNS dysfunction. The partial expression of these teratogenic effects has traditionally been called fetal alcohol effects (FAE). The Institute of Medicine (Stratton, Howe, & Battaglia, 1996) outlined three categories in which there is clear prenatal alcohol exposure and some of the features of FAS occur: partial FAS; alcohol-related birth defects (ARBD, a list of congenital anomalies); and alcohol-related neurodevelopmental disorder (ARND, defined by evidence of CNS neurodevelopmental abnormalities, or evidence of a complex pattern of behavioral or cognitive abnormalities that are inconsistent with developmental level and cannot be explained by familial background or environment alone). Issues of diagnosis and terminology are not yet resolved. One promising system has recently been developed to generate descriptive alcohol-related diagnoses and improve diagnostic reliability, called the 4-Digit Diagnostic Code (Astley & Clarren, 1999).

FAS and related conditions cannot always be recognized in infancy. Indeed, an alcohol-related diagnosis is often made too late to provide early intervention, because a child's problems emerge later in life or diagnostic services were unavailable when the child was young. Efforts are underway to develop better screening methods and surveillance programs.

Scope of the Problem

Literature on the epidemiology of FAS is far from conclusive. The incidence of FAS is estimated to range from 0.5 to 3.0 per 1,000 births in most populations, with much higher rates in some communities. Estimates vary depending on socioeconomic and ethnic factors (Stratton et al., 1996). Based on these figures, 2,000 to 12,000 of children born yearly in the United States will have FAS, with an incidence higher than that of Down syndrome or spina bifida (Streissguth, 1997). The Institute of Medicine states that FAS, ARBD, and ARND designations may occur on average in as many as 6 per 1,000 births (Stratton et al., 1996).

Behavioral Characteristics

Behavioral characteristics of alcohol-affected individuals have been studied across the lifespan, although a final consensus has not been reached. Both "primary" cognitive and behavioral deficits resulting from CNS dysfunction, and "secondary disabilities" in lifestyle and daily functioning, have been examined.

Primary Disabilities. Although FAS and related conditions are associated with a wide variety of neurobehavioral deficits, mental retardation is not always a defining characteristic. Recent data from over 400 alcohol-affected individuals (aged 3 to 51) revealed IQ averaging in the borderline range of intelligence for those diagnosed with FAS (27% with an IQ of 70 or below), and mean IQ in the average range for those labeled with FAE (9% with an IQ of 70 or below). For both groups, there were shortfalls relative to IQ on tests of achievement (especially arithmetic) and adaptive behavior, although individuals with FAE actually had more discrepant scores (Streissguth, Barr, Kogan, and Bookstein, 1996).

Hallmark features of FAS and related conditions include enduring attentional deficits, hyperactivity that may evolve in adolescence into problems of distractibility and cognitive and/or behavioral control, and persistent problems in modulating incoming stimuli. A variety of deficits have been reported in language, motor skills, learning, visuospatial functioning, and memory. There also may be hallmark deficits on measures of executive functions (e.g., planning ability and working memory) and social communicative competence (e.g., understanding another's viewpoint, or clearly communicating complex information).

Secondary Disabilities and Protective Factors. A study of the life history of 415 individuals with FAS or FAE (ages 6 to 51) found a high prevalence of adverse life outcomes (Streissguth et al., 1996). In the full sample, 94% showed mental health problems and/or involvement in mental health treatment. Among alcohol-affected adolescents and adults, 60% had a history of disrupted school experiences, 60% had trouble with the law, 50% underwent a confinement experience, 49% showed inappropriate sexual behavior, and 35% had alcohol/drug problems. These problems were also seen in children, although less frequently.

This correlational study also identified eight protective factors that almost uniformly reduced the odds that several major secondary disabilities would occur. Better outcomes for individuals with FAS/FAE were associated with living in an adequate, stable, nurturant, or good quality home during an important time (or majority) of life, remaining safe from personal violence, applying for and being eligible for social services because of developmental disabilities, and receiving an early diagnosis (before age 6). A diagnosis of FAS was associated with better relative outcomes than a diagnosis of FAE, perhaps because those with the full syndrome more often received services than those with FAE.

Prevention and Treatment Strategies

Many community-based efforts exist to prevent drinking during pregnancy, such as warning signs at points of liquor purchase and educational campaigns. Brief checklists to assess risky drinking have been developed. Once a pregnant woman is identified as being at risk, she may be eligible for high-risk follow-up and referral to women-oriented substance abuse treatment programs. Recent prevention efforts target very high-risk women and involve intensive advocacy programs for chemically dependent mothers, women who are themselves alcohol affected, and women who have already produced a child with FAS.

There are almost no systematic data on the effectiveness of medication or psychosocial treatments for alcohol-affected individuals. Published so far are the experiences and recommendations of families and professionals. Because alcohol-affected individuals have wide-ranging needs, multimodal intervention is recommended, including diagnostic services and appropriate medical, mental health, educational/vocational, legal, and social services. But there are many service gaps, especially for older alcohol-affected individuals, and current eligibility parameters for many services do not capture the deficits of those with alcohol effects, who may then not qualify.

For a young child, early intervention is recommended, including individualized instruction in a consistent, supportive environment, strategies to structure home and school environments and minimize functional problems, and sensory integration treatment. For older individuals, these techniques remain useful, with skill-building, relaxation techniques, instruction in social skills and social communication, positive behavioral management, and help from an advocate also recommended. A major future research focus will be on the effectiveness of recommended intervention techniques.

Bibliography

Astley, S. J., & Clarren, S. K. (1999). *Diagnostic guide for fetal alcohol syndrome and related conditions: The 4-digit diagnostic code.* Seattle: University of Washington Publication Services. This manual presents an efficient method for making descriptive alcohol-related diagnoses, in which diagnosticians determine ratings on clearly defined 4-point scales for the four domains of prenatal alcohol exposure, facial features, growth, and CNS dysfunction. The 4-digit codes that result characterize the individual at an appropriate point on the continuum of alcohol effects. The system also includes ratings of prenatal and postnatal comorbidities. This system is recommended for use within a multidisciplinary team approach for diagnosis and referral.

Coles, C. D., Platzman, K. A., Raskind-Hood, C. L., Brown, R. T., Falek, A., & Smith, I. E. (1997). A comparison of children affected by prenatal alcohol exposure and attention deficit, hyperactivity disorder. *Alcoholism: Clinical & Experimental Research, 21*(1), 150–161. This carefully executed comparison study begins the work of uncovering differences in the neuropsychological profiles of an alcohol-affected sample and a sample of children diagnosed with attention deficit, hyperactivity disorder (ADHD) of nonteratogenic cause.

Institute of Medicine, Division of Biobehavioral Sciences and Mental Disorders, Committee to Study Fetal Alcohol Syndrome. (1996). *Fetal alcohol syndrome: Diagnosis, epidemiology, pevention, and treatment* (K. Stratton, C. Howe, & F. Battaglia, Eds.). Washington, DC: National Academy Press. This is a comprehensive discussion of nomenclature, prevalence, diagnostic issues, approaches to prevention, research recommendations, and the available information on treatment of FAS and other alcohol-related effects.

Jones, K. L., Smith, D. W., Ulleland, C. N., & Streissguth, A. P. (1973). Pattern of malformation in offspring of chronic alcholic mothers. *Lancet*, *1* (7815), 1267–1271. This classic article describes some of the first cases of FAS ever identified and provides a historical context for understanding later research.

Kleinfeld, J., & Wescott, S. (Eds.). (1993). *Fantastic Antone succeeds!: Experiences in educating children with fetal alcohol syndrome*. Anchorage: University of Alaska Press. This easy-to-read book presents the wisdom of practice and includes chapters written by parents, interventionists and researchers. This optimistic resource offers many intervention ideas for young and school-age alcohol-affected children. A companion volume, soon to be published, will focus on the issues of older alcohol-affected individuals: J. Kleinfeld, B. A. Morse, & S. Wescott (Eds.) (in press). *Fantastic Antone grows up Assisting alcohol-affected adolescents and adults*. Anchorage: University of Alaska Press.

Morse, B. A., & Weiner, L. (1996). Rehabilitation approaches for fetal alcohol syndrome. In H. L. Spohr & H. C. Steinhausen (Eds.), *Alcohol, pregnancy, and the developing child* (pp. 249–268). Cambridge: Cambridge University Press. The authors, who are experienced clinicians long familiar with FAS, offer guidelines for treating common problems of alcohol-affected youth. This chapter is part of a book that covers a variety of topics important in the study of alcohol effects.

National Institute on Alcohol Abuse and Alcoholism (NIAAA). (1997). *Ninth special report to the U.S. Congress on alcohol and health*. (NIH Publication No. 97-4017, pp. 193–231). Washington, DC: U.S. Department of Health and Human Services. This handbook is a thorough compendium of research on alcohol and health, and is updated every few years. There is a comprehensive chapter on fetal alcohol effects.

Riley, E. P. (Ed.). (1998). Symposium on the behavioral effects of prenatal alcohol exposure [Special issue]. *Alcoholism: Clinical and Experimental Research*, *22*(2). This collection of scientific papers presents some of the more recent data in the field of FAS. Among other articles, Mattson and Riley provide a review of the neurobehavioral deficits in children with FAS or prenatal exposure to alcohol; Guerri discusses neuroanatomical and neurophysiological mechanisms involved in CNS dysfunction induced by prenatal alcohol exposure; and Steinhausen and Spohr describe the long-term outcome of children with FAS.

Streissguth, A. P. (1997). *Fetal alcohol syndrome: A guide for families and communities*. Baltimore: Brookes. This easily readable book was written by a psychologist and researcher who is a pioneer in the field of FAS. It summarizes extensive clinical knowledge and research data.

Streissguth, A. P., Barr, H. M., Kogan. J., & Bookstein, F. L. (1996). *Understanding the occurrence of secondary disabilities in clients with fetal alcohol syndrome and fetal alcohol effects*. Seattle: University of Washington Publication Services. This report documents findings from psychometric testing and caregiver interviews

of a large clinical sample of fetal alcohol–affected individuals.

Heather Carmichael Olson

FETISHISM involves sexual arousal associated with nonliving objects that occurs primarily among males. Nonliving objects may be less anxiety provoking than actual sexual partners. Fetish objects may be most attractive when they resemble a body part. These objects are commonly women's underpants, bras, stockings, rubber items, shoes, or boots. Masturbation frequently occurs while holding, rubbing, kissing, or smelling the fetish object. In many cases, sexual arousal may not occur in the absence of the object. Thus, a fetishist may ask a sexual partner to wear the object. Most fetishists have more than one fetish object. Fetishism is not diagnosed if the fetish objects are used in cross-dressing, or if the objects have been designed for genital stimulation (e.g., a vibrator). Unlike fetishism, transvestic fetishism involves sexual arousal associated with the act of cross-dressing. Evidence of classical conditioning processes through the experimental pairing of fetishism with sexual arousal to erotic stimuli or with masturbation have been demonstrated (McGuire, Carlisle, & Young, 1965; Rachman & Hodgson, 1968). Presumably, such pairing of sexual arousal and fetish stimuli occurs in real life through masturbation or during interpersonal sexual contact.

Festishists may be most often referred to clinicians after having stolen fetish objects. A second source of clinical referrals may be when a fetish interferes with a sexual relationship with a partner (e.g., sexual dysfunction without the assistance of the fetish object). Thus, fetishists in clinical settings may be those whose interests are most problematic, and such clinical populations are not necessarily representative of all fetishists. Data from a nonclinical sample of 262 gay and bisexual male foot fetishists who belonged to a foot fetish mail correspondence organization may be somewhat more generalizable than findings from clinical samples (Weinberg, Williams, & Calhan, 1995). Results of the survey showed the following: 81% to 94% of the sample indicated that their interest in feet was not associated with negative events during childhood, adolescence, or adulthood; during adolescence, 80% of the sample masturbated while fantasizing about feet or footwear; 44% indicated that feet or footwear fantasies were necessary for their sexual arousal; 69% did not feel that they could stop their fetishistic fantasies if they wanted to; 90% had not attempted to stop their sexual interest in feet and footwear; 36% reported being in a steady relationship at the time of the study; and only

23% experienced high levels of problems (e.g., loneliness, lack of confidence, intimacy problems).

Reliability and Validity of Classification

Clinical diagnoses of fetishism appear to be reliable. The interrater kappa for diagnosing fetishism based on patient records is .85 (Prentky, Knight, & Lee, 1997). Penile tumescence measures are also commonly used to diagnose paraphilias. The reliability of penile tumescence in response to various paraphilic stimuli (e.g., depictions of adult sexual activity with a child) approaches, or is within what would be considered, psychometrically acceptable. However, the reliability of these measures with fetish stimuli is unknown.

Prevalence

The prevalence of fetishism in nonclinical populations is unknown. Fetishism is not illegal and does not necessarily require a partner, and thus it may go undetected. In a sample of psychiatric hospital employees and community men, 3% exhibited clinically significant penile tumescence responses (at least 15% as great as their arousal to their most preferred stimuli) to cross-dressing/fetish slide stimuli (Fedora et al., 1992). The prevalence of sexual arousal to cross-dressing/fetish stimuli was somewhat higher among a large sample of inpatient sexual offenders, with 7% of nonviolent and 17% of violent sexual offenders exhibiting clinically significant penile tumescence (Fedora et al., 1992). However, sexual arousal to a paraphilic stimulus is not equivalent to a sexual preference for the stimulus.

In another sample of adolescent and adult paraphiliacs who underwent outpatient evaluations, 8% of adolescents and 5% of adults were diagnosed as fetishists (Abel, Osborn, & Twigg, 1993). The average age of onset for fetishism in the sample was 16. One fourth of an inpatient sample of convicted rapists and child molesters was diagnosed with fetishism (Barnard, Hankins, & Robbins, 1992). This inpatient sample was generally more pathological than the Abel et al. (1993) outpatient sample. Thus, although most fetishists may not experience other forms of psychopathology, fetishism appears to be a secondary paraphilia among a significant minority of men having other paraphilias, particularly in pathological samples.

Treatment

There are no controlled treatment studies of fetishism. Case reports have described behavioral and pharmacological interventions. It is probable that antiandrogen treatments, which have been demonstrated to be effective in reducing other paraphilic behaviors, would also reduce the sexual motivation for fetishism. Because fetishism may compete or interfere with sexual contact with a partner, enhancing sexual arousal to a partner

would also be important in treatment. Anxiety reduction in the presence of a sexual partner may also be important, to the extent that a fetish is resorted to as a function of social anxiety. It may be possible, at least on a limited basis, to incorporate a fetish into a sexual relationship with a partner in vivo or in fantasy. However, it appears unlikely that large-scale treatment studies of fetishism will be conducted because of the infrequency of the disorder and its lack of harm relative to other paraphilias.

[*See also* Sexual Disorders.]

Bibliography

Abel, G. G., Osborn, C. A., & Twigg, D. A. (1993). Sexual assault throughout the life span: Adult offenders with juvenile histories. In H. E. Barbaree, W. L. Marshall, & S. M. Hudson (Eds.), *The juvenile sex offender* (pp. 104–117). New York: Guilford Press.

Barnard, G. W., Hankins, G. C., & Robbins, L. (1992). Prior life trauma, post-traumatic stress symptoms, and character traits in sex offenders: An exploratory study. *Journal of Traumatic Stress, 5*, 393–420.

Fedora, O., Reddon, J. R., Morrison, J. W., Fedora, S. K., Pascoe, H., & Yeudall, L. T. (1992). Sadism and other paraphilias in normal controls and aggressive and non-aggressive sex offenders. *Archives of Sexual Behavior, 21*, 1–15.

McGuire, R. J., Carlisle, J. M., & Young, B. G. (1965). Sexual deviations as conditioned behavior: A hypothesis. *Behaviour Research and Therapy, 2*, 185–190.

Prentky, R. A., Knight, R. A., & Lee, A. F. S. (1997). Risk factors associated with recidivism among extrafamilial child molesters. *Journal of Consulting and Clinical Psychology, 65*, 141–149.

Rachman, S., & Hodgson, R. J. (1968). Experimentally induced "sexual fetishism": Replication and development. *Psychological Record, 18*, 25–27.

Weinberg, M. S., Williams, C. J., & Calhan, C. (1997). "If the shoe fits . . .": Exploring male homosexual foot fetishism. *Journal of Sex Research, 32*, 17–27.

Gordon C. Nagayama Hall

FIBROMYALGIA SYNDROME (FMS) is a poorly understood chronic musculoskeletal rheumatological condition. Clinical symptoms include diffuse achiness, stiffness, fatigue, disturbed sleep, and the presence of tender points, defined as increased tenderness at muscle and tendon insertion sites.

In 1990, the American College of Rheumatology (ACR) under the direction of Fred Wolfe, published classification criteria for FMS in *Arthritis and Rheumatism*, that include 3-month or longer history of widespread pain that is defined as pain in the left side, right side, above the waist, and below the waist. In addition, axial skeletal pain (chest, spine, or back) must be present, as well as pain in 11 of 18 tender point sites on digital palpation. FMS may be found with other rheumatological conditions such as rheumatoid arthritis or osteoarthritis (Wolfe et al., 1990).

The etiology of FMS is not known. Mechanisms studied include muscle physiology, sleep physiology, neurohormonal function, and psychological status. While research findings are inconclusive, increasingly, central rather than peripheral mechanisms are viewed as important in FMS (Simms, 1996).

Muscle biopsy studies have been nonconclusive. Electromyography EMG studies have been negative. There is no evidence of muscle inflammation; consequently, the *term fibrositis* (referring to inflammation) has been abandoned (Freundlich & Leventhal, 1993).

The role of sleep in the development or maintenance of FMS symptoms has been examined also. Sixty percent of people with FMS report disrupted sleep (Goldenberg, 1987). Harvey Moldofsky (Moldofsky, Scarisbrick, England, & Smythe, 1975) observed that people with FMS have alpha-wave intrusions during deep sleep (Stage 4). This sleep pattern has been referred to as nonrestorative sleep. Transitory symptoms of FMS have been produced in healthy control subjects by reproducing alpha wave intrusions during Stage 4 sleep (Moldofsky & Scarisbrick, 1976). However, the nonrestorative sleep pattern has been found among other patient populations and is not specific to FMS.

Serotonin, a neurochemical known to mediate sleep, pain, and depression has also been examined. Subjective pain ratings of FMS subjects are correlated with tryptophan, a precursor to serotonin. Serum concentration levels of serotonin were significantly lower in people with FMS than matched healthy control subjects. Platelet serotonin receptor density was found to be higher in untreated FMS subjects relative to control subjects. After treatment with ibuprofen and alprazolam, receptor density was normalized (Russell, 1989). Abnormal levels of biogenic amines in cerebrospinal fluid, serum somatomedin C (an analog of growth hormone), prolactin, hypothalamus-pituitary-adrenal markers, and regional cerebral blood flow have also been reported (Simms, 1996). The significance of these findings is not clear but are suggestive of a central processing role for FMS.

Due to the lack of physical findings, the role of psychological factors has been closely examined. Higher levels of psychological disturbance on the MMPI, SCL-90-R, and depression scales relative to control samples have been reported. A study utilizing a community sample of FMS subjects rather than people presenting to tertiary care centers for FMS treatment found no significant difference on psychopathology measures rel-ative to a control sample. This study suggests that selection factors may be important in the study of psychological variables and FMS (Baumstark & Buckelew, 1992; Simms, 1996).

Controlled studies using DSM-III-R criteria found high lifetime rates of major depression (ranging between 34 to 71%) among FMS subjects (Simms, 1996). Although a family history of depression is also more common among FMS subjects than control groups, depression rates at the time of the onset of FMS are not abnormally high. Lifetime rates of migraine, irritable bowel syndrome, and panic disorders are high among subjects with FMS relative to a control sample of subjects with rheumatoid arthritis. James Hudson and Harrison Pope (Hudson & Pope, 1989) have proposed that fibromyalgia, headaches, irritable bowel syndrome, chronic fatigue syndrome, major depression, and panic disorder may represent an "affective spectrum" of disorders with a common physiologic abnormality. Aaron and others (Aaron et al., 1996) studied lifetime incidence of psychiatric disorders among three groups of people: patients with FMS from a tertiary care setting, community residents with FMS who had not received medical care for their FMS symptoms (FMS nonpatients), and healthy controls. This study found that patients with FMS, compared with FMS nonpatients and healthy controls, had a higher incidence of lifetime history of psychiatric disorders. Health care seeking is also related to lower pain thresholds at tender and control points, greater symptom severity and disability. Studies that rely on subjects from tertiary care centers may overestimate the prevalence of depression and may not be representative of the community population of people with FMS (Bradley et al., 1994).

One study found that a history of sexual or physical abuse is higher among FMS subjects (Boisset-Pioro, Esdaile, & Fitzcharles, 1995). This finding has not been replicated (Taylor, Trotter, & Csuka, 1995).

It is estimated that 6 million people in the United States suffer from fibromyalgia. Across clinic settings, 70 to 80% of the people with FMS are female. Average ages range from 34 to 55 (Goldenberg, 1987). It is estimated that the proportion of new patients with FMS range from 10 to 20% in rheumatology clinics and 2.1 to 5.7% in nonspecialized clinics (Wolfe, Ross, Anderson, Russell, & Hebert, 1995). In 1995, in *Arthritis & Rheumatism*, Wolfe and others published a study on the prevalence of FMS in the general population relying on the new ACR criteria for classification of the disorder. A random sample of 3,006 persons in Wichita, Kansas, were contacted. A subsample of 391 persons, including 193 who reported widespread pain, were examined and interviewed in more detail. The prevalence of FMS was 2.0% for both sexes, 3.4% for women, and 0.5% for men. The prevalence of the syndrome increased with age, with the highest percentages falling between 60 and 79 years of age. This is higher than was expected based on previous reports of clinic populations. The prevalence of FMS was six times greater in women than in men for ages 50 and older (Wolfe, Ross, Anderson, Russell, & Hebert, 1995).

The fact that the cause of fibromyalgia has yet to be determined has slowed efforts to identify efficacious treatments. The recommended treatment regimen for FMS is multimodal and consists of patient education, medications (low-dosage tricyclic antidepressants), exercise, and in some cases biofeedback, hypnosis, and cognitive-behavioral interventions for pain management (Baumstark & Buckelew, 1992). Randomized and controlled studies have found that amitriptyline and cyclobenzaprine are each effective in short-term management of FMS symptoms (Goldenberg, 1995). Alprazolam, a benzodiazepine, has been found to be effective in short-term management of FMS symptoms (Russell, Fletcher, Michalek, McBroom, & Hester, 1991). However, concerns about the potential for dependence have tempered its use. In addition, several controlled studies examining exercise interventions for the treatment of FMS revealed that aerobic exercise can result in symptom improvements (Goldenberg, 1995). Aerobic exercise appears more effective than stretching and strengthening exercise interventions (McCain, Bell, Mai, & Halliday, 1988). Two controlled trials of psychologically based interventions have been reported. Carol Burckhardt and others (Burckhardt, Mannerkorpi, Hedenberb, & Bjelle, 1994) examined an education intervention that included a cognitive-behavioral focus; while Susan Buckelew and others (Buckelew et al., 1998) examined a biofeedback/stress management intervention for FMS. Both studies found that the psychologically based interventions resulted in enhanced self-efficacy.

Despite evidence of effective interventions for some symptoms of FMS, natural history studies reveal that many people with FMS have persistent symptoms (Goldenberg, 1987). Research isolating the physiologic and psychologic contributors to the appearance and maintenance of FMS is needed so that effective prevention and treatment interventions can be developed and disability from FMS reduced.

Bibliography

Aaron, L. A., Bradley, L. A., Alarcon, G. S., Alexander, R. W., Triana-Alexander, M., Martin, M. Y., & Alberts, K. R. (1996). Psychiatric diagnosis in patients with fibromyalgia are related to health care-seeking behavior rather than to illness. *Arthritis and Rheumatism, 39* (3), 436–445.

Baumstark, K. E., & Buckelew, S. P. (1992). Fibromyalgia:

Clinical signs, research findings, treatment implications, and future directions. *Annals of Behavioral Medicine, 14* (4), 282–291.

Boisset-Pioro, M. H., Esdaile, J. M., & Fitzcharles, M. A. (1995). Sexual and physical abuse in women with fibromyalgia syndrome. *Arthritis and Rheumatism, 38* (2), 235–241.

Bradley, L. A., Alarcon, G. S., Triana, M., Aaron, L. A., Alexander, R. W., Stewart, K. E., Martin, M., & Alberts, K. (1994). Health care seeking behavior in fibromyalgia: Associations with pain thresholds, symptom severity, and psychiatric morbidity. *Journal of Musculoskeletal Pain, 2* (3), 79–87.

Burckhardt, C. S., Mannerkorpi, K., Hedenberb, L., & Bjelle, A. (1994). A randomized, controlled clinical trial of education and physical training for women with fibromyalgia. *The Journal of Rheumatology 21,* 714–720.

Freundlich, B., & Leventhal, L. (1993). The fibromyalgia syndrome. In *Primer on the rheumatic diseases* (10th ed., pp. 247–249). Atlanta, GA: The Arthritis Foundation.

Goldenberg, D. L. (1987). Fibromyalgia syndrome. An emerging but controversial condition. *Journal of the American Medical Association, 257* (20), 2782–2787.

Goldenberg, D. L. (1995). Fibromyalgia: why such controversy? *Annals of the Rheumatic Diseases, 54,* 3–5.

Hudson, J. I., & Pope, H. G., Jr. (1989). Fibromyalgia and psychopathology: Is fibromyalgia a form of "affective spectrum disorder"? *The Journal of Rheumatology, 16* (19), 15–22.

McCain, G. A., Bell, D. A., Mai, F. M., & Halliday, P. D. (1988). A controlled study of the effects of a supervised cardiovascular fitness training program on the manifestations of primary fibromyalgia. *Arthritis and Rheumatism, 31* (9), 1135–1141.

Moldofsky, H., & Scarisbrick, P. (1976). Induction of neurasthenic musculoskeletal pain syndrome by selective sleep stage deprivation. *Psychosomatic Medicine, 38,* 35–44.

Moldofsky, H., Scarisbrick, P., England, R., & Smythe, H. (1975). Musculoskeletal symptoms and non-REM sleep disturbance in patients with "fibrositis syndrome" and healthy subjects. *Psychosomatic Medicine, 37* (4), 341–351.

Russell, I. J. (1989). Neurohormonal aspects of fibromyalgia syndrome. *Rheumatic Disease Clinics of North America, 15* (1), 149–168.

Russell, I. J., Fletcher, E. M., Michalek, J. E., McBroom, P. C., & Hester, G. G. (1991). Treatment of primary fibrositis/fibromyalgia syndrome with ibuprofen and alprazolam. *Arthritis and Rheumatism, 34* (5), 552–560.

Simms, R. W. (1996). Fibromyalgia syndrome: Current concepts in pathophysiology, clinical features, and management. *Arthritis Care and Research, 9* (4), 315–328.

Taylor, M. L., Trotter, D. R., & Csuka, M. E. (1995). The prevalence of sexual abuse in women with fibromyalgia. *Arthritis and Rheumatism, 38* (2), 229–234.

Wolfe, F., Smythe, H. A., Yunus, M. B., Bennett, R. M., Bombardier, C., Goldenberg, D. L., Tugwell, P., Campbell, S. M., Abeles, M., Clark, P., Fam, A. G., Farber, S. J., Fiechtner, J. J., Franklin, C. M., Gatter, R. A., Hamaty,

D., Lessard, J., Lichtbraun, A. S., Masi, A. T., McCain, G. A., Reynolds, W. J., Romano, T. J., Russell, I. J., & Sheon, R. P. (1990). The American College of Rheumatology 1990 criteria for the classification of fibromyalgia: Report of the Multicenter Criteria Committee. *Arthritis and Rheumatism, 33* (2), 160–172.

Wolfe, F., Ross, K., Anderson, J., Russell, I. J., & Hebert, L. (1995). The prevalence and characteristics of fibromyalgia in the general population. *Arthritis and Rheumatism, 38* (1), 19–28.

Susan P. Buckelew, Margaret S. Nigh, and Kristofer J. Hagglund

FIELD DEPENDENCE AND INDEPENDENCE. In the 1950s, field dependence and independence emerged as a concept out of some classical experiments dedicated to understanding the factors that determine perception of the upright in space. While scientists like J. Gibson and Solomon Asch were debating whether visual external or body internal referents were more important in the judgment of verticality, Herman Witkin, a rather orthodox Gestaltist influenced by Max Wertheimer, raised the question of the individual differences in the process. Instead of asking, Which factor is generally more important? his question was, Which factor is more important for a given individual?

Soon laboratory studies showed that there were individuals who, across a variety of space-orientation tasks and over a long period of time, consistently relied to a greater degree on external referents (the visual field), and other subjects who relied to a greater degree on internal referents (the body state).

The "rod and frame test" provides a good example of the nature of these differences. The subject, seated in a completely darkened room, is required to adjust to vertical a tilted luminous rod, presented within a luminous tilted square frame. In carrying out this task, some subjects (designated as field dependent) align the rod with the tilted frame, thereby indicating that the visual field dominates their perceived location of the rod within it. At the opposite extreme, other subjects, designated as field independent, adjust the rod close to the true upright regardless of the orientation of the surrounding visual frame, utilizing the felt position of the body. Most people fall between these two extremes.

From the observation of self-consistency in performance across different orientation tasks, further studies indicated that the field-dependent and field-independent modes of functioning are not restricted to space perception but embrace other perceptual as well as intellectual domains, that is, field dependence and independence as a cognitive style operates at a general level. Thus, Witkin's question relative to individual differences was very unusual when laboratory experimentalists considered differences among individuals as undesirable "noise." The focus on individual differences and analysis of the processes underlying them created a wealth of theory and research that fostered the emergence of field dependence and independence, probably the most important and widely studied of the so-called cognitive styles that have become identified to date.

In *Personality Through Perception* (1954), a landmark book, Witkin and his associates focused on the role of the status of the perceiver instead of on the perceptual process. Accordingly, Witkin served as one of the small group of psychologists who in the late 1940s introduced the so-called new look in perception. This notion focused on features of the person (values, organismic state, etc.) rather than the sensory input from objects. However, in contrast with other investigators in the "new look group," Witkin focused on stylistic and structural rather than motivational or situational determinants of perceptual activity.

According to the last revision of the theory (Witkin & Goodenough, 1981), the stylistic quality of the field-dependence and field-independence dimension is best characterized as the extent to which there is autonomy from external referents. At the field-independent pole, the availability of internal referents constitutes a central mediating mechanism that fosters the development of cognitive restructuring skills; at the field-dependent pole, the greater reliance on external referents encourages the development of an interpersonal orientation, particularly under conditions of situational ambiguity. A large body of research shows that, whereas field-independent people are more able to segregate and manipulate abstract concepts, field-dependent people are more sensitive to social cues, prefer activities that involve being with people, show emotional openness, and seek physical closeness to people in their social interactions.

In the constant search for unifying constructs to incorporate the large body of new findings, another major theoretical step was the formulation of the theory of "psychological differentiation," fully described in a second important book (Witkin, Dik, Faterson, Goodenough, & Karp 1962), and in a later revision and extension (Witkin, Goodenough, & Oltman, 1979). According to the theory, the individual differences along the field-dependence continuum are considered to be reflecting a higher or lower degree of developmental differentiation in overall psychobiological functioning. In Witkin's view, highly developed differentiation, as a broad organismic process, manifests itself in three significantly interrelated areas: self versus nonself segregation, representing the higher construct from which the extent of autonomy of external referents (or field dependence) is derived; segregation of psychological functions, from which the extent of specialization of personality controls and defences originate; and segre-

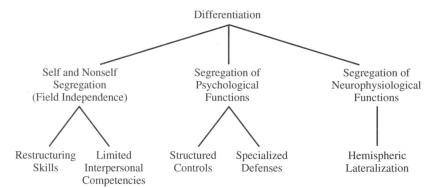

FIELD DEPENDENCE AND INDE-PENDENCE. Figure 1. Differentia-tion model. (From Witkin, Gooden-ough, & Oltman, 1979.)

gation of neurophysiological functions, as revealed, for instance, by the extent of hemispheric lateralization (see Figure 1).

The introduction of this developmental dimension brought to the fore the issue of environmental and biological (genetic, neurophysiological) determinants. Notwithstanding some evidence of hormonal and X-linked genetic factors (see Witkin and Goodenough, 1981, p. 74), a basic socialization hypothesis was initially presented—and later on supported in a variety of settings—that considers autonomy versus excessive control in parenting styles as associated to the development of field independence and field dependence, respectively.

By tracing individual differences in a broad spectrum of situations from the choice of the academic career to the manifestation of psychological symptoms, Witkin and his associates showed that it is not inherently better or worse to be located at one or the other pole of the field dependence–independence dimension; rather, at each pole, there are characteristics that may be adaptive in some circumstances and nonadaptive in others.

Cross-cultural and anthropological studies (Witkin & Berry, 1975; Witkin, 1978) show that the development of a more or less field-dependent mode of functioning is consistent with the requirements of different ecological or socioanthropological environments. These findings have been considered as further proof of the bipolar characteristic of the field dependence and independence dimension as well as of its value-neutral stance, insofar as adaptive qualities are to be found at both poles.

As is to be expected, the work on field dependence and independence has also received criticism and generated controversies, in part at theoretical and in part at methodological levels (Kogan, 1980). To name a particularly recurrent issue, clarification has been requested of the distinction between the ability and stylistic aspects of the dimension, including the instruments to measure it. In the last works published by Witkin and his main collaborator, Don Goodenough (1977, 1979, 1981), important revisions were introduced that take into account a large part of the criticism as well as the new findings that have accumulated. In these publications there is anticipation of research directions aimed not only at implementing the "lacunae and the uncertainties that inevitably characterize an evolving theory" (Witkin & Goodenough, 1981, p. x), but also creating the need for further redefinition and extension of the conceptual framework. Two books published in memory of Witkin (Bertini, Pizzamiglio, & Wapner, 1986; Wapner & Demick, 1991) can give the scientific community an idea of the new directions of this research and of how and in what directions this enterprise will continue to evolve.

Bibliography

Bertini, M., Pizzamiglio, L., & Wapner, S. (Eds.). (1986). *Field dependence in psychological theory, research and application: Two symposia in memory of Herman A. Witkin.* Hillsdale, NJ: Erlbaum.

Kogan, N. (1980). A style of life, a life of style. *Contemporary Psychology, 25,* 595–598.

Wapner, S., & Demick, J. (Eds.). (1991). *Field dependence-independence: Cognitive style across the life span.* Hillsdale, NJ: Erlbaum.

Witkin, H. A. (1978). *Cognitive styles in personal and cultural adaptation.* Worcester, MA: Clark University Press.

Witkin, H. A., Lewis, H. B., Hertzman, M., Machover, K., Meissner, P. B., & Wapner, S. (1954). *Personality through perception.* New York: Harper.

Witkin, H. A., Dik, R. B., Faterson, H. F., Goodenough, D. R., & Karp, S. A. (1962). *Psychological differentiation.* New York: Wiley. (Reprinted by Erlbaum, 1974)

Witkin, H. A., & Berry, J. W. (1975). Psychological differentiation in cross-cultural perspective. *Journal of Cross-Cultural Psychology, 6,* 4–87.

Witkin, H. A., & Goodenough, D. R. (1977). Field dependence and interpersonal behavior. *Psychological Bulletin, 84,* 661–689.

Witkin, H. A., Goodenough, D. R., & Oltman, P. K. (1979).

Psychological differentiation: Current status. *Journal of Personality and Social Psychology, 37,* 1127–1145.

Witkin, H. A., & Goodenough, D. R. (1981). *Cognitive styles: Essence and origins.* New York: International Universities Press.

Mario Bertini

FIELD STUDY. Most social scientists would prefer to study *naturally occurring* behavior with *rigorous* methods. [*See* Data Collection, *article on* Field Research.] Unfortunately, it is typically impossible to maximize both rigor and naturalness in a single study design, because these two criteria impose contradictory restraints. Some social scientists, like anthropologists, have chosen to optimize naturalness at the expense of rigor, while laboratory psychologists have chosen the opposite strategy. Between the anthropological field study and the laboratory experiment is the field experiment, which tries to apply some of the rigor of the laboratory to behavior in the real world.

Muzofer Sherif's "Robbers' Cave" study on intergroup conflict in a summer camp provides a classic example of one type of field experiment: the experiment in a natural setting. Sherif preserved some of the rigor of the laboratory (by randomly assigning campers to groups) while conducting an unobtrusive study of natural behavior in a natural setting (pre-adolescent, white, male, Oklahoma campers around 1950). Though Sherif was able to illuminate intergroup conflict in one real-world setting, the nature of his design limited his ability to generalize to other natural settings. Sherif's design has many virtues, but one cannot be confident that his findings would hold for persons of a different age, race, gender, location, or time period. [*See the biography of Sherif.*]

Limited generalizability, characteristic of many experiments in a natural setting, can typically be avoided by a second type of field study: the found experiment. Here, instead of constructing the experiment, the researcher finds one already constructed by naturally occurring events. For example, a study in *American Sociological Review* (1983, *48,* 560–568) examined the effects of publicized violence by studying U.S. aggression rates before and after prizefights. Similarly, studies by J. D. Kark and others (*Journal of the American Medical Association,* 1995, *273,* 1208–1210) and D. Trichopoulos and others (*The Lancet,* 1993, *1,* 441–444) have examined links between stress and health by studying mortality rates before and after large-scale disasters. These studies, as is typical for the found experiment, examine officially collected data that are available for large, heterogeneous populations in different locations and time periods. Thus, because of its reliance on preexisting, governmental data, the found experiment allows the researcher to generalize to various natural behaviors in real-world settings.

Paradoxically, reliance on these data also limits found experiments, because researchers using found experiments must rely on data collected without their interests in mind. Consequently, investigators often lack information desirable for their analyses. In addition, although the found experiment is well suited for establishing a statistical link between A and B, it is less effective for identifying causal mechanisms that produce this link. In contrast, researchers using the experiment in a natural setting can design studies that address their research interests and explicate causal mechanisms.

The two types of field experiment have complementary limitations and strengths: the one allows superior ability to generalize, while the other allows detailed identification of causal processes. (This strength is even more evident in the laboratory experiment.) Thus, it may be possible to optimize both naturalness and rigor if we employ more than one type of research design. It has been found that a deeper and more useful understanding of psychological phenomena is achieved if those phenomena are studied with experiments in the laboratory, in natural settings, and with found experiments.

Bibliography

Phillips, D. P., & Halebsky, S. C. (1995). The epidemiology of found experiments. *Journal of the American Medical Association, 273,* 1221. A discussion of the strengths and weaknesses of found experiments.

Sherif, M. (1956). Experiments in group conflict. *Scientific American, 195.* A classic discussion of the influence of group structure on intergroup conflict.

David P. Phillips and Laura M. Glynn

FIELD THEORY. In psychology, field theory is identified most cogently with the work of Kurt Lewin. Historically, it is associated with theorizing in other sciences as well. As Harald Mey has noted, "In the physics of the twentieth century there was a shift in scientific emphasis away from the classical mechanics which held sway during the nineteenth century . . . (leading) to a viewpoint which may be characterized as belonging to field theory" (1972, p. ix). In this context, names such as Heisenberg, Planck, and Albert Einstein are prominent. Lewin himself adduces Galileo, in contrast to Newton, as a historic metaphor for field-theoretic conceptualization.

More specifically, in precursors and contemporaries of Lewin, the earlier roots of psychological field theory can be traced to Gestalt psychology, particularly the modes of inquiry exemplified by the works of Wolfgang Köhler, Kurt Koffka, and Max Wertheimer (Koffka, 1935; Köhler, 1929). The influence of Carl Stumpf, who guided—for some time—the doctoral education both of Lewin and Edmund Husserl is felt, albeit from substantively remote areas such as the psychology of sound and musicology (Spiegelberg, 1972). Yet an underpinning of philosophic thought, variously represented as well by Franz Brentano and Cassirer, establishes a basis for field-theoretic thinking (Spiegelberg, 1965). In this framework, we readily observe the nonlinear approach and the conscious consideration of issues relating to direct human perception. The complexity and variability of real-life events, rather than stimulus response or association, move into focus.

With the notion of geographic metaphor (viz. "Continent"), we see how field theory is frequently involved with spatial concepts. This pattern was established early in Lewin's *Kriegslandschaft* ("Battlefieldscape") and later elaborated in the concept of life space. In the paper "Behavior and Development as a Function of the Total Situation" (1951), Lewin makes clear that

> a totality of co-existing (experienced) facts which are conceived of as mutually interdependent is called a *field*. . . . Psychology has to view the life space, including the person and his environment, as one field. . . . In general terms, behavior (B) is a function (F) of the person (P) and of his environment (E), B = F(P,E) . . . to understand or to predict behavior, the person and his environment have to be considered as one constellation of interdependent factors. We call the totality of these factors the life space.

Within the field of the life space a variety of forces coact at a given time. There are valences (the power to attract or repel) and various regions (potential activities), including barriers to "locomotion" . . . viz. slowing over time, impeding or blocking behavior. Graphic representations of life spaces and other constructs abound, both in Lewin's original work and in derivative and applied publication.

The concept of vector—a force of specified magnitude and the direction of its thrust—is of particular significance within the analysis of life spaces and in the study of fields generally. In efforts to understand complex interpersonal and technical situations, as in organization development and systems consultation, force field analysis finds wide application. This approach examines the conditions of equilibrium and nonequilibrium that are associated with conflict, perceptual differences, power, technological innovation, and the like.

Field-theoretic approaches importantly apply to groups: a group is not simply "more than the sum of its parts," but the group-as-a-whole is different than the sum of its parts—the group has unique properties of its own. In field-theoretic terms, Lewin considers a range of group wholes and their dynamic properties. Indeed, his influence on group conceptualization and practice is of defining importance, from the study of group atmospheres to the development of the NTL Institute (originally National Training Laboratories for Group Development).

Field theory has also been (and continues to be) applied to large social entities, in political context and in organizations (e.g., Brown, 1936).

Some aspects of field theory were examined at a conference in 1997 under NTL Institute auspices, observing the fiftieth anniversary of Lewin's death. In addition, the Society for the Advancement of Field Theory and the Society for the Psychological Study of Social Issues have pursued Lewin's themes over the span of many decades. Counterparts throughout the world exist as well, and psychological journals, especially in social psychology, provide current sources in field-theoretic thought and research.

With emphasis on wholes and interdependent parts and the interplay of complex vectors, from individual motivation to processes in large human systems, field theory bears further—and renewed—promise for the deeper understanding of complex human behavior.

[*See also the biography of Lewin.*]

Bibliography

Brown, J. F. (1936). *Psychology and the social order*. New York: McGraw-Hill.
Koffka, K. (1935). *Principles of Gestalt psychology*. New York: Harcourt Brace.
Köhler, W. (1929). *Gestalt psychology*. New York: Horace Liveright.
Lewin, K. (1936). *Principles of topological psychology*. New York: McGraw-Hill.
Lewin, K. (1948). *Solving social conflicts*. New York: Harper & Brothers.
Lewin, K. (1951). *Field theory in social science*. New York: Harper & Brothers.
Marrow, A. (1969). *The practical theorist*. New York: Basic Books.
Mey, H. (1972). *Field theory: A study of its application in the social sciences*. London: Routledge.
Spiegelberg, H. (1965). *The phenomenological movement*. The Hague, The Netherlands: Martinus Nijhoff.
Spiegelberg, H. (1972). *Phenomenology in psychology and psychiatry*. Evanston, IL: Northwestern University Press.

Fred Massarik

FINLAND. Early experimental psychology in Finland was inspired by German research. The institutional date of birth of Finnish psychology is the year 1922, when Eino Kaila (1890–1958) set up the first laboratory of psychology, in Turku. Kaila, a psychologist and philosopher, was for several decades the most prominent figure not only in Finnish psychology but also in Finnish cultural life in general. His experiments on the reactions of the infant on the human face, carried out in Vienna in the early 1930s, were internationally well known. In Finland, his most influential book was *Persoonallisuus* (Personality), published in 1934, three years before G. W. Allport's *Personality*.

Kaila, like Allport, stressed the uniqueness and structural wholeness of the individual and made use of conceptions from psychoanalysis, Gestalt psychology, neurology, and Karl Buehler's philosophy of language. He singled out two leading principles, holism and dynamics, referring to biology and to Freud and Lewin, respectively. Along with his philosophical works, Kaila's *Personality* had a tremendous impact both on the following generations of psychologists and on the educated classes of the country. His influence can be seen even in the movies of the Swedish film director Ingmar Bergman, who reports that reading the Swedish translation of *Personality*, with its notion of needs as determinants of behavior, made a deep impression on him.

Kaila's interest in the positivistic philosophy of science and personality typologies probably contributed to the rise of differential psychology in the 1940s and 1950s, simultaneous with the emergence of a strong school of psychometrics. The foremost representative of this school was Yrjö Ahmavaara (1929–), the developer of transformation analysis of factorial data. Indeed, the excessive use of factor analysis was a peculiarity of Finnish psychological research up to the late 1960s. Factor analysis was put into use in vocational guidance, one of the most active fields of applied psychology in Finland at the time. In 1967, more than one fourth of the members of the Finnish Psychological Association worked in vocational guidance. The centrality of vocational guidance can perhaps be explained by the abrupt transition from an agricultural to an industrial and postindustrial society, which took place faster in Finland than anywhere else in Europe, and by the ideology of social planning then prevalent in all Nordic countries.

After World War II, the United States replaced Germany as the main reference country for Finnish psychologists. This was facilitated by an extensive system of special bilateral Fulbright grants that enabled many young scholars to spend a year in the United States, so that virtually all psychology professors who got their chairs in the 1960s and 1970s had studied there. However, the behaviorist view of the human being was not imported to Finnish psychology. Instead, as part of Kaila's legacy, a more Lewinian picture of human beings as possessing consciousness and being goal-directed was retained.

By the early 1960s, psychology chairs existed in five universities. The generation initially trained by Kaila included Kai von Fieandt (1909–), a specialist in the psychology of perception (in Helsinki), Martti Takala (1924–) in Jyväskylä, and Johan von Wright (1924–) in Turku and later in Helsinki. Both Takala and von Wright have represented a broad functionalist-cognitivistic orientation in the spirit of Kurt Lewin and Frederic Bartlett. Takala, who has also had important national and international administrative duties, was originally oriented toward personality psychology and has enlarged his research interests toward developmental, educational, and social psychology. Von Wright's main interests have been in memory and learning.

The cohorts of psychologists who have been pupils of the Takala and von Wright "generalist" generation were able to specialize more in their research. Consequently, by the mid-1980s psychophysiology and neuropsychology, the psychology of aggressive behavior, and cognitive processes had emerged as fields in which research teams had attained international reputation, according to an internal evaluation (Niemi, 1987). The same evaluation singled out three trends that were common to all subfields of Finnish psychology: First, the systemic approach, which views humans as belonging to different simultaneously operating subsystems; second, seeing human behavior as active and goal-seeking; and third, the shift from a variable-centered approach to an emphasis on more complex real-life activities.

Regarding future prospects for psychology, a recent survey by the Finnish Research Council for the Social Sciences, the central funding agency for psychological research, saw the study of human cognitive processes, their development, and their modifiability as an area of particularly rapid future progress, and stressed the large applicability of this research to schooling and education. The same report also pointed to the important role of psychology in multidisciplinary research networks, for instance, in cognitive science and in the study of childhood.

Approximately two thirds of all psychological research in Finland is carried out in the six universities that train psychologists. The single most important research institute is the Psychological Department of the Institute of Occupational Health. The number of professionally active psychologists is currently about 3,000. A large majority work in medical care, followed by social services and labor force administration. The proportion of private practitioners (5%) and those working in private enterprises (7%) is relatively low. The professional activity of psychologists is regulated by the Act Concerning Health Care Professionals (1994), which restricts the use of the title "psychologist" to those approved by the National Board of Medico-Legal Affairs. This kind of legislation is unique in Europe.

Why does Finland, one of the least densely populated countries in Europe, have one of the highest densities of psychologists (3,000 psychologists for 5 million people) in the world? The rapid social change mentioned above and the ensuing need for psychological services might partly account for this. Another factor the role of which is bound to remain speculative at this point, but which upon further systematic scrutiny might turn out to explain the high proportion of psychologists, or, some of the orientation of Finnish psychological research is the apparent ambivalence of the Finns toward communication. Several studies show that the Finns as a people regard themselves as reserved, taciturn, and uncommunicative, and are not bothered by long silences in interpersonal communication. On the other hand, on some indices of communicativeness, Finland gets or has received top scores, for instance, on the number of amateur play companies or portable phones per capita.

Among the current research traditions, one of the best known is the research program on cognition and its neural basis, which is being carried out by Risto Näätänen (1939–) at the University of Helsinki. It has aimed at clarifying central issues of attention, information processing, and consciousness using event-related brain-potential recordings (ERP) as the main research method. This research relies to a large extent on the mismatch negativity component in the auditory ERP, discovered by Risto Näätänen, Anthony Gaillard, and Sirkka Mäntysalo in 1975. Mismatch negativity has recently received a number of practical applications, for example, in the assessment of auditory abilities and musical talent. Näätänen (with Heikki Summala) has also done some pioneering work on road-user behavior and accidents.

In the areas of developmental, personality, and social psychology, which are not very sharply differentiated in Finland, the Jyväskylä Longitudinal Study of Social Development by Lea Pulkkinen (1939–) has followed the same subjects from age eight up to their midthirties, the initial starting point being a two-dimensional model of self-control and social activity. The more recent focus of the program is on life-styles and emotion regulation. In Turku, Kirsti Lagerspetz (1932–) and her coworkers have studied aggression in mice and humans from a variety of perspectives, including issues of heredity, the impact of TV violence on moral judgments of aggression, as well as bullying in school. In Tampere, Antti Eskola (1934–) has applied the perspective of historical social psychology to personality and personality research and contributed to the development of alternative research methods. Closely related to educational psychology is the approach called developmental work research by Yrjö Engeström (1948–), which draws on the Russian cultural historical school and has applied the concept of an activity system to study "expansive learning" in, for example, courtrooms and health centers.

The Finnish Psychological Society (FPS) was established in 1952. It grew out of the Psychology Society of University Students, established in 1935. Since the creation of the Finnish Psychological Association (FPA), a trade union, in 1957, the FPS has restricted itself to scientific issues. However, from the early 1980s, the two organizations have regularly arranged joint national congresses.

The FPS publishes *Acta Psychologica Fennica* (established in 1950), an English-language journal currently devoted to review articles, a monograph series of applied psychology (in Finnish, since 1987), and a Finnish-language bimonthly journal (*Psykologia*, established in 1966). Since 1960, the FPS has also been involved in the publication of the *Scandinavian Journal of Psychology* together with other Nordic psychological societies. The FPA has a news bulletin, *Psykologiuutiset*. The two organizations own a publishing house that specializes in psychological tests.

Bibliography

Acta Psychologica Fennica. (1980). Vol. 7. Helsinki: The Finnish Psychological Society. Contains chapters dealing with the beginnings of Finnish psychology, with the history of professional psychology and of occupational psychology in Finland, and histories of the university departments.

Acta Psychologica Fennica. (1991). Vol. 12. Helsinki: The Finnish Psychological Society. A survey of the research carried out in Finnish universities from 1980 to 1990, by departments. In addition, a chapter on Eino Kaila by Martti Takala, his student and former assistant.

Ihanus, J. (1993). The sociopsychological thinking of Westermarck. In R. Bourqia & M. Al Harras (Eds.), *Westermarck et la société marocaine* (pp. 27–41). Rabat, Morroco: Faculté des lettres et sciences humaines. An account of the international influences on early Finnish psychological thinking, based on systematic historical research, using the sociologist Westermarck as an example.

Niemi, P. (1987). Evaluation of psychological research: The Finnish experience. *International Journal of Psychology, 22,* 387–392. A summary of the internal evaluation carried out by the Finnish psychological society in the early 1980s.

Takala, M., & Korkiakangas, M. (1981). The development of psychological science in a small country in Europe: A case study of Finland. *Acta Psychologica Fennica, 8,* 5–10. The main focus is on the relative impact of different countries on Finnish psychology and the significance of single scholars on the shaping of research traditions in different time periods.

Klaus Helkama

FISHER, RONALD AYLMER (1890–1962), English statistician and geneticist. Born in London, the youngest of seven children, Fisher graduated from Cambridge in 1912, after studying mathematics and mathematical physics. He won distinction for his papers on optics and pursued an interest in the new sciences of genetics and biometry, reading papers on Mendelism and biometry and on evolution and society before the Cambridge University Eugenics Society.

Fisher's career is remarkable in that he established two much admired reputations, one in statistics and the other in genetics. His most important work in statistics began in 1919 when he joined the staff at Rothamsted, a long-established agricultural research center, north of London. His tasks were to examine the vast amounts of existing data—"raking over the muck-heap" as he was to describe it—and to design and oversee field trials. There he was to develop the technique of *analysis of variance* (ANOVA), which allows for the examination of differences between separate variables, as well as the effect of variables acting in concert, and to sieve the effects of the differences from random error. It is now a routine approach to data appraisal by experimental psychologists. It has profoundly affected psychological research in that the analysis of quantitative data has helped to determine the questions asked in psychology and therefore the development of its subject matter.

Fisher showed that the biometric and the "Mendelian" positions on evolution could be reconciled and thereby firmly established his position in genetics. His paper demonstrating this was rejected by the Royal Society of London after reviews by Karl Pearson, who said that it was not of much interest from the biometric standpoint, and R. C. Punnett (a Cambridge professor of some reputation), who claimed that it held little interest for biologists. It was subsequently published by the Royal Society of Edinburgh.

Nevertheless, Pearson offered Fisher a post at University College, London, at the time that Fisher accepted the Rothamsted job. Unfortunately, however, the initial respect that the two had for each other rapidly deteriorated into the very worst kind of personal animosity. Both men could be infuriatingly obtuse and irascible. Pearson refused, to the end of his days, to recognize the mechanism of Mendelian inheritance, clinging fast to the dogma of his "biometric" school that insisted on continuous variation in biological characteristics and rejecting any "Mendelian" view that could possibly allow for evolution to have a saltatory component.

In the 1920s the statistical rows with Pearson culminated in the X^2 (chi-square) disagreement. Fisher was the leader of a new breed of statisticians interested in the logic and structure of the methods themselves. He pointed out, correctly, that the degrees of freedom in, for example, a fourfold contingency table were determined by the linear constraints imposed by the marginal totals and were therefore one. Pearson, who had developed the X^2 tests, and who was driven mainly by the need to develop tools for his other research interests, wrongly extended the procedure from the X^2 one sample "goodness-of-fit" case, and said that they numbered three. Eventually, Pearson fell silent on the matter. Later, Fisher flatly denied that there was logic or utility in considering the probability of what came to be called the Type II error in statistical analysis—the error of wrongly accepting that an experimental outcome was likely due to chance—pouring scorn on Egon Pearson (Karl Pearson's son) and his coworker, Jerzy Neyman, the proponents of the notion.

But these controversies, that surely reflect the egos of the protagonists, do not detract from Fisher's reputation as a statistician. His books on statistical methods and the design of experiments are the forerunners of the hundreds of such texts that have been published subsequently. He was a mathematician of flair and intuition, sometimes seeing the solution to a problem before developing the steps that were needed for the proof. Nor were all his social relationships tumultuous. He maintained long friendships with W. S. Gosset ("Student" of Student's t-ratio), expanding and rounding out the work of the latter on small-sample statistics. His correspondence with Leonard Darwin, President of the Eugenics Education Society, shows a relationship of warmth and mutual admiration that began in 1915 and lasted for over 25 years.

Fisher was a formidable supporter of the eugenics movement, as was Pearson, whom he succeeded in 1933, as Galton Professor of Eugenics. The latter part of the nineteenth, and the first third of the twentieth century saw the rise of the view that human societies might directly influence human evolution. The fittest should be encouraged to reproduce themselves, while those possessing the least amount of what Galton had described as "civic worth" should be restrained from so doing.

In 1943 Fisher became professor of genetics at Cambridge University where his scholarly reputation and contribution was consolidated. His work was recognized with a knighthood in 1952. After retirement from Cambridge he moved to Australia's University of Adelaide, which, under the meticulous editorship of J. H. Bennett, published his collected papers in five volumes. He died there after a short illness.

Bibliography

Bennett, J. H. (Ed.). (1971). *Collected papers of R. A. Fisher* (Vols. 1–5). Adelaide: University of Adelaide.

Box, J. F. (1978). *R. A. Fisher: The life of a scientist.* New York: Wiley.

Fisher, R. A. (1918). The correlation between relatives on

the supposition of Mendelian inheritance. *Transactions of the Royal Society of Edinburgh, 32*, 399–433.

Fisher, R. A. (1925). *Statistical methods for research workers.* Edinburgh: Oliver & Boyd.

Fisher, R. A. (1935). *The design of experiments.* Edinburgh: Oliver & Boyd.

Michael Cowles

FIVE-FACTOR MODEL OF PERSONALITY. Proponents of the five-factor model (FFM) of personality claim to have resolved one of the longstanding issues in personality psychology: how best to organize and classify the hundreds of personality traits that psychologists have recognized. The FFM has generated a great deal of interest in trait psychology, and has been a focus of research in many diverse fields such as behavior genetics, cross-cultural psychology, industrial/ organizational psychology, and the study of personality disorders. Derived from factor-analytic studies of personality traits, the FFM captures, at a broad level, the commonalities among many of the existing systems of personality description. Although researchers differ somewhat on the details included in the definitions of the five factors, there is reasonably broad agreement on the overarching construct each factor reflects. The first factor, Extraversion or Surgency, is generally characterized as the seeking out and enjoyment of companionship with others. The Agreeableness factor contrasts characteristics such as altruism, nurturance, and emotional support versus hostility, self-centeredness, and jealousy. The Conscientiousness factor refers to conformity or socially prescribed impulse control, an orientation toward work and achievement, and the desire for orderliness in one's activities. The fourth factor, Neuroticism (vs. Emotional Stability), typically includes descriptors such as tense, anxious, nervous, and moody. Finally, the Openness to Experience, or Intellect, factor includes characteristics such as imaginative, curious, artistic, insightful, and sophisticated, but is less well defined.

The FFM has been derived from or replicated in studies intended to capture the way people describe themselves and others in everyday life. The model relies on the assumption that the important aspects of personality will be encoded in language as single terms, an assumption known as the lexical hypothesis. Following this assumption, many researchers turned to natural language dictionaries as a source for such trait attributes. Their studies either laid the foundation for the emergence of the FFM, or were instrumental in clarifying the constructs within the FFM. Other researchers have conducted studies of existing personality questionnaires to show the relations between the questionnaire scales and the FFM. Research from both the lex-

ical and personality questionnaire perspectives has enriched the understanding of the FFM constructs and their relations to various trait theories and assessment instruments (for a brief history of the research from both perspectives, see Goldberg, 1993).

In Wiggins (1996), different theoretical perspectives are offered for interpreting the FFM. Researchers emphasizing the descriptive aspects of the FFM limit the model's role to that of providing a framework for organizing the hundreds of words used to describe an individual's personality. Researchers emphasizing the explanatory, or causal, role of the model suggest that the five factors reflect genetic or biologically based dispositions in the way we perceive, understand, and respond to the events that surround us. Furthermore, some researchers speculate on the emergence of these dispositions as the result of the myriad adaptational tasks that our evolutionary history has provided, particularly those in the social or interpersonal realm. Finally, within the five factors of the model, some researchers focus on the first two factors, Extraversion and Agreeableness, and emphasize interpersonal or dyadic interactional aspects of personality functioning, whereas others believe that the FFM captures traits reflecting competence in acquiring social status and acceptance through roles and agendas played out in various kinds of interactions.

As is true of many areas in the study of personality, the FFM is not without its share of criticism. Several issues have been raised concerning the content and utility of the FFM. Criticisms of the descriptive function served by the FFM typically focus on issues concerning the derivation of the five factors, particularly with respect to the role of factor analysis. Researchers debate the influence of extraction and rotation options on the final factor solution, and more generally, the function that factor analysis serves in theory development (Block, 1995), as well as the effect on factor structure that differing research samples produce (Harkness & McNulty, 1994). In the case of analyses of adjective or trait ratings, terms that are primarily evaluative or describe states (that could also reflect stable emotional temperament traits) and words or concepts that reflect psychological concepts indicative of abnormal personality functioning, have typically been excluded. Expanding the pool of potential trait terms by including, for example, evaluative adjectives or terms specific to personality pathology, has been shown to alter the number, content, and general meaning of the primary factors that emerge from factor analyses (Harkness & McNulty, 1994; Tellegen, 1993). Another criticism concerns the extent to which five broad factors are adequate for describing and predicting personality functioning. Many researchers argue that lower-order facets are really the most informative level of assessment (Briggs, 1989; Clark, 1993). Relatedly, the question has been raised concerning whether or not a model derived from terms essentially reflecting normal personality functioning would be effective in attempting to answer questions about personality disorder. Researchers have argued that the five factors reflect relatively continuous dimensions rather than discrete personality types or disorders (Widiger, Trull, Clarkin, & Costa, 1994). Persons with a personality disorder would have either very high or very low levels on particular dimensions. Critics assert that because instruments assessing the FFM do not generally contain the descriptive terms needed to define personality disorders, a very high or low score may not adequately reflect the characteristics of such disorders (Harkness & McNulty, 1994).

A final issue concerns the role of the FFM in an overall theory of personality. Whereas some FFM proponents and trait theorists have been criticized for suggesting that human personality is adequately captured by such a model, recent researchers have included the five factors as one set of personality dispositions in a framework that also recognizes the influence of situational constraints, motivation, attitudes, values, and cognitive capabilities, as well as the roles of life stories (identity formation) and societal influence (McAdams, 1996).

[*See also* Personality Traits.]

Bibliography

Block, J. (1995). A contrarian view of the five-factor approach to personality description. *Psychological Bulletin, 117*, 187–215.

Briggs, S. R. (1989). The optimal level of measurement for personality constructs. In D. M. Buss & N. Cantor (Eds.), *Personality psychology: Recent trends and emerging directions* (pp. 246–260). New York: Springer.

Clark, L. A. (1993). Personality disorder diagnosis: Limitations of the five-factor model. *Psychological Inquiry, 4*, 100–104.

Costa, P. T., Jr., & McCrae, R. R. (1992). *Revised NEO Personality Inventory (NEO-PI-R) and NEO Five-Factor Inventory (NEO-FFI) professional manual.* Odessa, FL: Psychological Assessment Resources. Widely used in research and practice, the NEO-PI-R has served as one benchmark in mapping the relations between the FFM and several other personality questionnaires and is used in a wide variety of settings for personality assessment.

Costa, P. T., Jr., & Widiger, T. A. (Eds.). (1994). *Personality disorders and the five-factor model of personality.* Washington, DC: American Psychological Association. Contributing authors examine the role of the FFM in understanding the *DSM–III–R* and *DSM–IV* personality disorder diagnoses. Empirical relations between the FFM and personality disorders, characteristics of specific populations and the role of the FFM in treatment planning and practice are explored.

Goldberg, L. R. (1992). The development of markers for the Big Five factor structure. *Psychological Assessment, 4*, 26–42. Following the lexical tradition of the FFM, provides a set of terms for assessing each of the five factors.

Goldberg, L. R. (1993). The structure of phenotypic personality traits. *American Psychologist, 48*, 26–34.

Harkness, A. R., & McNulty, J. L. (1994). The personality Psychopathology Five (PSY-5): Issue from the pages of a diagnostic manual instead of a dictionary. In S. Strack & M. Lorr (Eds.), *Differentiating normal and abnormal personality* (pp. 291–315). New York: Springer.

Hogan, R., & Hogan, J. (1992). *Hogan Personality Inventory manual.* Tulsa, OK: Hogan Assessment Systems. Reflecting the socioanalytic perspective in assessing personality traits, the Hogan Personality Inventory (HPI) incorporates a slightly different, six-factor perspective of personality traits closely related to the FFM. The HPI has been used primarily in organizational settings to facilitate the development of a variety of personnel evaluation, selection, and training programs.

McAdams, D. P. (1996). Personality, modernity, and the storied self: A contemporary framework for studying persons. *Psychological Inquiry, 4*, 295–321.

McCrae, R. R., & Costa, P. T., Jr. (1990). *Personality in adulthood.* New York: Guilford Press. Explores the FFM across the life span, providing evidence for longitudinal and cross-sectional stability of the model.

Tellegen, A. (1993). Folk concepts and psychological concepts of personality and personality disorder. *Psychological Inquiry, 4*, 122–130.

Widiger, T. A., Trull, T. J., Clarkin, J. F., Sanderson, C. S., & Costa, P. T., Jr. (1994). A description of the *DSM–III–R* and *DSM–IV* personality disorders with the five-factor model of personality. In P. T. Costa, Jr., & T. A. Widiger (Eds.), *Personality disorders and the five-factor model of personality* (pp. 41–56). Washington, DC: American Psychological Association.

Wiggins, J. S. (Ed.). (1996). *The five-factor model of personality: Theoretical perspectives.* New York: Guilford Press.

Journals of Interest

Journal of Personality (1992). *60(2)* These articles address many of the issues and applications of the FFM.

Psychological Inquiry (1993). *4(2).* Contributing authors debate the issues concerning the role of dimensional models of personality, particularly the FFM, in assessing the *DSM–III–R* personality disorders.

Psychological Inquiry (1994). *5(2).* Supporters and critics of current trait theory offer their views on a variety of topics concerning the FFM, trait theory, and the structure of personality.

John L. McNulty

FLANAGAN, JOHN C. (1916–1996), American psychologist. A leader in the application of psychology to problems of personnel management, Flanagan made an enormous contribution to the utilization of psychology in many organizational settings. A native of the Pacific Northwest, he received his B.S. degree in physics and mathematics from the University of Washington. He went on to Harvard to earn a Ph.D. degree in psychometrics under Truman L. Kelley in 1934.

In July 1941, Flanagan was commissioned in the Army Air Corps. He began immediately to recruit staff, mostly from academia, for what was to become the Aviation Psychology Program, which included, by the end of the war, about 200 officers, 750 enlisted men, and 30 civilians. The program's primary mission was to provide test results to aid in the selection and classification of inductees for pilot and other aircrew training and for ground duty. From 1944 to 1945, some 600,000 men were tested. Continuous research on the reliability and validity of original and new tests resulted in a steady increase in the composite validities of combinations of tests for each aircrew position. Psychologists were also involved in research on performance measurement, problems in training programs, individual reactions to combat, and approaches to psychometric theory. A detailed, 19-volume report on the operations and research done during the war was printed and distributed by the Government Printing Office. This series has provided a definitive contribution to many areas of applied psychology.

On completion of military service in 1946, Flanagan accepted a professorship at the University of Pittsburgh and, with encouragement from the University, established the American Institutes for Research (AIR). This nonprofit corporation has completed hundreds of sponsored projects of various sizes over the years. Six of the largest projects are described below. Two of these involved the determination of the requirements for two complex jobs and the development of reliable measuring instruments for them. For a period of more than 20 years, one project provided the major airlines with aptitude scores on tests for aircrew positions. The other project furnished the National Board of Medical Examiners with an instrument that could reliably measure the skill of advanced medical students in dealing with patients. Responding to a request from the Agency for International Development, AIR produced a program for selecting, from a pool of non-English candidates, those who would most likely be able to learn to be advanced technicians in nineteen of the new African republics. The educational process in the United States was the area for three large, interlocking projects. In Project TALENT, more than 100,000 high-school students were tested for educational achievement in 1960 and were followed up at intervals thereafter. Patterns of mastery and deficiency provided the basis for curriculum development in Project PLAN (Program for Learning in Accordance with Need). This massive computer-based learning program was developed for grades 1 through 12. Using the "Critical Incident Technique" developed by Flanagan some years before, a quality of life scale was built which served as a criterion measure in subsequent AIR studies.

Flanagan's competence and achievements were recognized in many awards. From the U.S. Air Force he received the Legion of Merit, and from civilian organizations, some half-dozen honors including the Distinguished Professional Award from the American Psychological Association.

Bibliography

Clemans, W. V., Crawford, M. P., & McKeachie, W. J. (1996, July/August). John Clemans Flanagan (1916–1996). *Observer*, pp. 14–15.

Flanagan, J. C. (1947). *The Army Air Force's psychology program research reports* (Report No. 1). Washington, DC: U.S. Government Printing Office.

Flanagan, J. C. (1954). The critical incident technique. *Psychological Bulletin, 51*, 327–358. The critical incident technique is used in job analysis to identify that task which must always be performed to accomplish the job.

Flanagan, J. C. (1971). Project PLAN: Basic assumptions, implementation and significance. *Journal of Secondary Education, 40*, 172–178.

Schwarz, P. A., & Krugg, R. E. (1972). *Aptitude testing in developing countries: A handbook of principles and techniques.* New York: Praeger.

Meredith P. Crawford

FLOODING is a behavior therapy procedure that involves repeated or prolonged exposure to a stimulus for the purpose of extinguishing maladaptive emotional or behavioral responses evoked by the stimulus. Flooding is best known for its use as a treatment for phobias and other anxiety disorders. An example of the use of flooding for therapeutic purposes is an individual with claustrophobia spending extended periods of time in a small room until he or she no longer experiences anxiety. Exposure involved in flooding can be to an actual stimulus, known as in vivo flooding, or to a mental representation of the stimulus, known as imaginal flooding. Although typically thought of as a procedure for eliminating fear and anxiety, flooding has also been used to help people modify other emotional responses, such as anger and guilt.

The flooding procedure was first developed in laboratory settings to study the modification of learned avoidance behavior in animals, a line of research inspired by Pavlov's work on classical conditioning (1927). Pavlov discovered that animals learn to avoid a previously neutral stimulus (e.g., a bell) if it has been paired with an innately aversive stimulus (e.g., an electric shock). In addition, animals actively avoid the previously neutral stimulus long after it ceases to be paired with the aversive stimulus. The persistence of this behavior caught the attention of subsequent researchers who studied different procedures that might eliminate avoidance responses. One such procedure was called flooding, a term first coined by Polin (1959) to refer to an experimental condition in which animals were exposed to a stimulus for extended periods of time despite attempts to escape. Polin reported that flooding was more effective in extinguishing avoidance behavior than procedures that involved shorter periods of exposure.

The term *flooding* first appeared in the clinical literature in the late 1960s as therapists like Isaac Marks, Stanley J. Rachman, and their colleagues at the Maudsley Hospital in London, England, described the use of this procedure to help their patients overcome phobias and obsessive compulsive disorder. Patients were encouraged to remain in feared situations, without escaping, until their anxiety abated. Several other behavioral fear-reduction techniques involving exposure to a feared stimulus were developed around the same time as flooding, but there were some differences between flooding and other exposure therapies. Wolpe's technique, systematic desensitization (1958), emphasizes less intense, more gradual exposure and attempts to maintain patients in a nonanxious state during the procedure. In contrast, proponents of flooding view anxiety as an unavoidable, if not integral, part of exposure therapy.

Another technique similar to flooding is implosive therapy (Stamfl & Levis, 1966). Like flooding, implosive therapy does not attempt to avoid anxiety during exposure. However, implosive therapy usually involves exposure to imagined stimuli, in contrast to the real life (in vivo) exposure often involved in flooding. Another distinction is that implosive therapy attempts to enhance anxiety arousal by adding imaginary exposure cues believed by the therapist to be relevant to the patient's fear, a strategy not characteristic of flooding. Other terms that have been used to describe exposure therapy procedures similar or related to flooding include deconditioning, counterconditioning, ungraded exposure, extinction therapy, detainment, forced reality testing, and behavioral experiments.

The original rationale for the use of flooding in the treatment of anxiety disorders came largely from learning theories. The most influential early model was Mowrer's two-factor theory (1960), which proposed that fear of harmless stimuli is learned through the classical conditioning process described by Pavlov and that avoidance of harmless stimuli is reinforced by relief from anxiety. One important implication of Mowrer's theory was that the elimination of maladaptive fear requires adequate exposure to the feared stimulus and, thus, disruption of avoidance behavior, a principle that remains an important element of contemporary behavior therapy. The two-factor theory stimulated a substantial amount of important research and clinical innovation, but several alternative models were proposed as limitations of Mowrer's model were eventually recognized. Theorists have suggested several other pathways through which maladaptive fear can be learned that do not require the direct experience of an aversive event, including repeated observation of phobic behavior in other people, witnessing aversive events happening to someone else, and receiving inaccurate information. More recent cognitive theories have emphasized the role of an individual's expectations and beliefs in the development and modification of fear. Theorists do not currently agree on the exact mechanism involved in fear development and reduction. However, most believe that extended exposure to a feared, but harmless stimulus is important or even essential for extinction of the fear response.

Like many psychological interventions, flooding has had its share of controversy. Clinicians influenced by psychodynamic theories have questioned the effectiveness of flooding, suggesting that the procedure attends too much to the resolution of symptoms without addressing the core issues that they believe cause symptoms. Accordingly, many critics predicted that flooding would result in little or no benefit or would be followed by "symptom substitution," a hypothetical phenomenon in which the removal of a symptom is followed by the emergence of a new symptom. Other critics have expressed concern that the procedure may actually cause harm, claiming interventions like flooding, which increase unpleasant emotions, could trigger mental instability or result in reinforcement of the fear response. Over the past four decades, a great deal of clinical research has been devoted to studying the effects of flooding and other exposure therapies in human beings. Results of this research suggest that flooding often is an effective treatment for phobias, obsessive compulsive disorder, and a variety of anxiety-related conditions (e.g., Ost, 1996; Stanley & Turner, 1995). Studies have not supported the proposition that flooding induces a state of mental deterioration or insanity, or that it leads to symptom substitution. Flooding usually does involve anxious discomfort and can sometimes temporarily heighten an individual's fear. However, the potential negative side effects of flooding treatments are usually tolerable and can be prevented or managed successfully by properly trained therapists.

[*See also* Behavior Therapy; *and* Specific Phobia.]

Bibliography

Boudewyns, P. A., & Shipley, R. H. (1983). *Flooding and implosive therapy*. New York: Plenum Press.

Mowrer, O. H. (1960). *Learning theory and behavior.* New York: Wiley.

Ost, L. G. (1996). Long-term effects of behavior therapy for specific phobia. In M. R. Mavissakalian & R. F. Prien (Eds.), *Long-term treatments of anxiety disorders.* Washington, DC: American Psychiatric Press.

Pavlov, I. P. (1927). In G. V. Anrep (Ed. & Trans.), *Conditioned reflexes.* New York: Dover.

Polin, A. T. (1959). The effects of flooding and physical suppression as extinction techniques on an anxiety motivated avoidance locomotor response. *Journal of Psychology, 47,* 235–245.

Stampfl, T. G., & Levis, D. J. (1966). Implosive therapy. In R. M. Jurjevich (Ed.), *Handbook of direct and behavior psychotherapies.* Englewood Cliffs, NJ: Prentice Hall.

Stanley, M. A., & Turner, S. M. (1995). Current status of pharmacological and behavioral treatment of obsessive-compulsive disorder. *Behavior Therapy, 26,* 163–186.

Wolpe, J. (1958). *Psychotherapy by reciprocal inhibition.* Stanford, CA: Stanford University Press.

C. Alec Pollard

FLOURENS, PIERRE (1794–1867). French physiologist. At the age of 19, Flourens received his doctorate from the Faculty of Medicine at Montpellier, France. His thesis, "Essai sur quelques points de la doctrine de la revulsion et de la derivation," reflected the philosophy of vitalism, then popular in southeastern France. In 1814 he moved to Paris, where he studied comparative anatomy with George Cuvier and the nervous system with Franz Joseph Gall while both were near the heights of their careers. At first under the patronage of Etienne Geoffroy Saint Hillaire, Flourens was sympathetic to Gall's doctrine of "craniology" (e.g., Flourens, 1819). However, by 1822, after he had switched to the patronage of Georges Cuvier, Flourens became one of Gall's sharpest and most enduring critics (e.g., Flourens, 1824, 1842). Cuvier's patronage guaranteed Flourens a permanent place in France's scientific establishment, and by 1864 he had been elected to the French Academy, become the permanent secretary of the Academy of Sciences and a member of several royal academies of science in Sweden, Russia, Germany, Belgium, Italy, and England, and finally was professor of comparative physiology at the Paris Museum of Natural History and professor at the College of France.

Flourens's main contributions were: an opposition to phrenology; the idea that the cerebellum is responsible for motor coordination; an holistic model of brain function; and the ablation method in experimental physiological psychology. The standard historical account of Flourens begins with his attack on Gall's craniology (Spurzheim's "phrenology") which, in retrospect, was the classic conflict between "lumpers" and "splitters." For Flourens, consciousness was unitary; for Gall, consciousness was multiple. Was his critique a "clear, trenchant annihilation" of phrenology as characterized by Boring (1950)? Hardly. Flourens capitalized on two facts: that Gall had already been linked to the sensualists and thus branded as a materialist and that for years he was a nonestablishment outsider with no links to the patronage system. While this context, along with his interpretation of his ablation studies on birds (and a few mammals) as incompatible with phrenological doctrine, ensured him an audience for his assault on phrenology, it did not win the war. The discrete or punctate model of brain localization remained a topic of intense debate in the academies from the early 1820s until the 1860s, when it was resolved in favor of the phrenologists with the publications of Broca and others.

With respect to the cerebellum, Gall gave it a role in reproduction. Flourens's study of pigeons was a key element in developing the coordination model of cerebellar function—he was the first to distinguish motor coordination from motor control—but this, too, was not readily adopted by others. Cruveilhier (of Salpetriere fame), while unimpressed with Gall's idea that the cerebellum was concerned with sexual function, also saw no evidence to associate it with the coordination of voluntary motion, as suggested by Flourens's experiments of 1823. Cruveilhier and others also rejected the concept of cerebral localization, as suggested by Bouillaud's work on the frontal lobes, for want of clear confirming clinical evidence (Spillane, 1981).

Flourens's holistic view of brain function was, like most such models, a relativistic one: He distinguished the functions of cortex from deep white matter and from cerebellum, and so forth, but denied a discrete or punctate localization of function within broad anatomic divisions. The holistic-focalized pendulum seems to swing back and forth as models, experimental methods, and philosophical assumptions change over time; what one looks for is often what one finds.

Finally, although the ablation method of physiological psychology was invented long before Flourens, it is fair to say that it developed into a major experimental procedure during the nineteenth century in some measure due to Flourens's influence. Fancher discusses how Flourens's work prefigured that of Shepherd Ivory Franz and Karl S. Lashley in the early twentieth century (1996), while Harrington argues that Flourens's influence on orthodox physiology was profound, in part because the crude experimental techniques available at the time limited the amount of counterevidence and in part because a unitary conception of mind and brain was as theologically congenial to most of Flourens's colleagues (1987, p. 10). Note, however, that it is not just with twentieth-century hindsight that one may judge Flourens's experiments as flawed. As early as 1825 Bouillaud criticized the fact that Flourens's animals often failed to survive the crude ablations for long so that they had to be studied while postsurgical trauma and edema-affected areas of the brain other than those that had been lesioned.

As Daniel Robinson clearly points out in his preface (1978), the conflict between Flourens and the nonestablishment science of Gall and Spurzheim was not a question of researching the neuropsychological basis of the mind; everyone agreed on that. There was a conflict over methods: Flourens chose the evidence from the experimental laboratory and ignored the naturalistic observations from the clinic, which the localizationists championed. There was also a conflict over models: Flourens chose a weak, imprecise faculty model that was able to distinguish motor coordination from motor control and sensation from perception, but it analyzed components of intelligence and cognitive functions poorly and never addressed matters of personality. And, of course, there was the issue that remains fundamentally unresolved today: the idealist-dualist versus monist-materialist views of mind and brain; His frequent positive references to Descartes and the occasional dedication of his work to Descartes leaves little doubt that Flourens espoused a dualist philosophy.

Bibliography

Boring, E. G. (1950). *A history of experimental psychology* (2nd ed.). New York: Appleton-Century-Crofts. The discussion of Flourens from pages 61 to 67 of this classic text assured him a place in psychology's history.

Clarke, E., & Jacyna, L. S. (1987). *Nineteenth-century origins of neuroscientific concepts.* Berkeley, CA: University of California Press. See pages 244–307 for a detailed analysis of Flourens and his milieu.

Fancher, R. E. (1996). *Pioneers of psychology* (3rd ed.). New York: Norton. See chapter 3, pages 81–86, for one of the best current treatments of Flourens.

Flourens, P. (1819). Revue de Gall, anatomie et physiologie du systeme nerveux. *Revue Encyclopedique 1,* 417–426.

Flourens, P. (1824). *Recherches expérimentales sur les propriétés et les fonctions du système nerveux, dans les animaux vertebres.* Paris: Crevot.

Flourens, P. (1842). *Examen de la phrenologie.* Paris: Paulin.

Flourens, P. (1851). *De l'instinct eet de l'intelligence des animaux* (3rd ed.). Paris: Hachette.

Flourens, P. (1864). *Ontologie naturelle ou etude philosophique des etres* (3rd ed.). Paris: Garnier Freres.

Flourens, P. (1864). *Psychologie comparee* (2nd ed.). Paris: Garnier Freres. (Originally titled *De la raison, du genie et de la folie.*)

Harrington, A. (1987). *Medicine, mind, and the double brain: A study in nineteenth-century thought.* Princeton, NJ: Princeton University Press.

Robinson, D. N. (Ed.). (1978). *Significant contributions to the history of psychology, 1750–1920. Series E, Physiological psychology: Vol. II. X. Bichat, J. G. Spurzheim, P. Flourens.* Washington, DC: University Publications of America.

Spillane, J. D. (1981). *The doctrine of the nerves.* Oxford, England: Oxford University Press.

Young, R. M. (1970). *Mind, brain and adaptation in the nineteenth century: Cerebral localization and its biological context from Gall to Ferrier.* Oxford, England: Clarendon Press.

Harry Whitaker

FLOURNOY, THÉODORE (1854–1920), Swiss physician and psychologist. Born in Geneva, Switzerland, in 1854, Flournoy received his medical degree from the University of Strasbourg Medical School. He then taught physiological psychology, experimental psychology, philosophy, history, and the philosophy of science at the University of Geneva from 1891 to 1919.

Flournoy is best known for his psychological study of mediums, particularly Élise-Catherine Müller, given the pseudonym "Hélène Smith" in his famous book *From India to the Planet Mars* (Paris, 1900). Although, as was typical of spiritualist mediums, Müller gave people who attended her private séances messages purportedly from the spirits of the dead, she distinguished herself from other mediums by her serial narration of three dramatic "cycles." Two of them dramatized her supposed previous incarnations as Marie Antoinette and a fifteenth-century Hindu princess, Simandini. In the third cycle she spoke as one familiar with the planet Mars and its inhabitants, claiming to know how to speak and write the Martian language. Müller's séances were presided over by "Léopold," a powerful male personality who served as her spirit guide.

Flournoy began participating in the séances of Müller in 1894 and continued his observations of her phenomena up to the publication of his book. He intended from the beginning to provide a purely psychological explanation of her cycles, without reverting to notions of spirits or reincarnation. His analysis of the two reincarnated personalities and Léopold was based on a theory of the subconscious mind that emphasized its creative and dramatic aspect. He believed that the subconscious has the ability to use personal experiences and material drawn from various sources to create personalities and weave stories that then appear in consciousness with the vividness of reality. He also held that these creative productions would sometimes be dramatizations of the individual's unresolved emotionally laden conflicts.

Flournoy did not accept the reality of Léopold and the reincarnated personalities but believed they were characters in romances constructed by Müller's subliminal imagination. Where they exhibited knowledge that Müller believed she could not have gained through any other means, Flournoy held that the explanation was "cryptomnesia," the appearance in awareness of a forgotten memory without the person realizing it is a memory. In *From India to the Planet Mars* and his other writings on mediumship, Flournoy worked out a view of the subconscious mind that had elements that would eventually become common doctrine. Although he accepted the possibility of telepathy, clairvoyance, and psychokinesis, Flournoy believed that paranormal phenomena were not to be easily credited and that natural explanations should be given wherever possible.

The great historian of the unconscious, Henri Ellenberger, called *From India to the Planet Mars* the finest investigation of the unconscious prior to early psychoanalysis, considering Flournoy's book and Freud's *Interpretation of Dreams* as two books published in the same year (1900) that were destined to become classics in the field.

Bibliography

Claparède, E. (1923). Théodore Flournoy: Sa vie et son oeuvre. *Archives de Psychologie, 28*, 1–125.

Flournoy, O. (1986). *Théodore et Léopold: De Théodore Flournoy à la psychoanalyse. Correspondance et documents de Hélène Smith—Ferdinand de Saussure—August Barth—Charles Michel*. Neuchâtel, Switzerland: A La Baconnière.

Flournoy, Théodore. (1994). *From India to the Planet Mars. A case of multiple personality with imaginary languages*. With a foreword by C. G. Jung and commentary by Mireille Cifali. Edited and introduced by Sonu Shamdasani. Princeton, NJ: Princeton University Press.

Ellenberger, H. (1970). *The discovery of the unconscious*. New York: Basic Books.

Ellenberger, H. (1993). *Beyond the unconscious: Essays of Henri F. Ellenberger in the history of psychology*. Princeton, NJ: Princeton University Press.

Adam Crabtree

FLOW refers to a state of optimal experience that people report when they are intensely involved in doing something that is fun to do. It was first identified in a study of artists, athletes, mountain climbers, and chess players, who all gave remarkably similar phenomenological descriptions of how it felt when their favorite activity was going well (M. Csikszentmihalyi, 1975). The same combination of inner states was subsequently reported by studies with a variety of other samples in different cultures (M. Csikszentmihalyi, 1990; M. Csikszentmihalyi & I. Csikszentmihalyi, 1988; Inghilleri, 1999). Flow includes so-called peak experiences first identified by the psychologist Abraham Maslow (1965), although it does not necessarily have the intensity of the latter. Flow also overlaps with the concept of intrinsic motivation developed by Deci and Ryan (1985). [*See the biography of Maslow.*]

Several characteristics are diagnostic of the flow experience. Of these the most universal are: (a) clear sense of what has to be done moment by moment; (b) immediate feedback as to how well one is doing; (c) an intense concentration of attention; (d) a balance between opportunities for action (challenges) and capacity to act (skills); (e) exclusion of irrelevant content from consciousness; (f) a sense of control over the activity; (g) a distortion of sense of time—usually hours pass by in minutes; and (h) a feeling that the activity is intrinsically rewarding, or worth doing for its own sake.

Although these experiences usually occur when one is actively involved in a task or performance, they can also appear when a person reads a book, listens to music, or watches a beautiful landscape. Reading novels is in fact one of the most prevalent sources of flow across cultures. In such cases, the challenges are embedded in the sensory stimuli, and the skills required are the ability to interpret and respond to them. Passive entertainment such as watching television very rarely produces flow because decoding the information requires little personal involvement (Kubey & M. Csikszentmihalyi, 1990).

When these conditions are present in consciousness, a person tends to feel a deep sense of enjoyment that, in retrospect, is interpreted as happiness. During an episode of flow, however, one is too immersed in the activity to be able to feel happy, or for that matter to feel anything else irrelevant to the task. It is important to note that flow is morally neutral. It is possible to experience it in destructive activities such as warfare or various forms of addiction. But because it is such a strong motivating force, it is essential for society to provide opportunities for flow that lead to personal and social well-being. If children do not enjoy learning, they will not get much from schools and will seek out opportunities for enjoyment that often impair their future development.

Every culture contains activities that only exist because they facilitate the experience of flow: Music, dance, art, literature, sports, games, and rituals provide nothing tangible except the opportunity to experience life at its most exciting and meaningful. But the importance of understanding this experiential state consists in the fact that almost any human activity can be made to provide flow if the necessary conditions are present. Thus, work or personal relationships, which take up most of our lives, can be made more rewarding when the principles of flow are applied to them (M. Csikszentmihalyi, 1997).

Not everyone experiences flow, and some people experience it more often than others. About one fifth of the population claims never to have felt it, and a similar proportion claims to experience it several times a day. There is little known about the reasons for such individual differences. Neurological factors may account for them (Hamilton, 1981), but whether these are due primarily to inheritance or learning is not clear. In any case, by early adolescence teenagers develop patterns of activities and experiences that lead either to habitual enjoyment, or to listless passivity. [*See* Boredom.]

The frequency and intensity of flow can be enhanced by two different strategies. The first consists in changing the external conditions to resemble those of a game or a work of art: by clarifying goals, providing more detailed feedback, and creating a better balance between challenges and skills. The second strategy involves changing one's approach to life: choosing appropriate challenges, developing appropriate skills, identifying goals, and recognizing feedback.

The possibility of improving the quality of everyday life by applying the principles of flow has been recognized, for instance, in the practice of clinical therapy (DeVries, 1992), music education (Elliot, 1995), sports (Stein, Kimiecik, Daniels, & Jackson, 1995), and interaction with computers (Hoffman & Novak, 1996). Schools and workplaces are other environments where the introduction of flow promises great benefits.

Bibliography

Csikszentmihalyi, M. (1975). *Beyond boredom and anxiety.* San Francisco: Jossey-Bass.

Csikszentmihalyi, M. (1990). *Flow: The psychology of optimal experience.* New York: HarperCollins.

Csikszentmihalyi, M. (1997). *Finding flow: The psychology of engagement with everyday life.* New York: HarperCollins.

Csikszentmihalyi, M., & Csikszentmihalyi, I. (1988). *Optimal experience: Psychological studies of flow in consciousness.* Cambridge, England: Cambridge University Press.

Deci, E. L., & Ryan, M. (1985). *Intrinsic motivation and self-determination in human behavior.* New York: Plenum Press.

DeVries, M. W. (Ed). (1992). *The experience of psychopathology: Investigating mental disorders in natural settings.* Cambridge, England: Cambridge University Press.

Elliot, D. J. (1995). *Music matters: A new philosophy of music education.* New York: Oxford University Press.

Hamilton, J. A. (1981). Attention, personality, and self-regulation of mood: Absorbing interest and boredom. *Progress in Experimental Personality Research, 10,* 282–315.

Hoffman, D. L., & Novak, T. P. (1996, July). Marketing in hypermedia computer-mediated environments: Conceptual foundations. *Journal of Marketing.*

Inghilleri, P. (1999). *From subjective experience to cultural change.* New York: Cambridge University Press.

Kubey, R., & Csikszentmihalyi, M. (1990). *Television and the quality of life.* Hillsdale, NJ: Erlbaum.

Maslow, A. (1965). Humanistic science and transcendent experience. *Journal of Humanistic Psychology, 5,* 219–227.

Stein, G. L., Kimiecik, J. C., Daniels, J., & Jackson, S. A. (1995). Psychological antecedents of flow in recreational sports. *Personality and Social Psychology Bulletin, 21,* 125–135.

Mihaly Csikszentmihalyi

FMRI. *See* Brain Imaging Techniques.

FMS. *See* Fibromyalgia Syndrome.

FOCUS GROUP. A focus group is a research interviewing procedure specifically designed to uncover insights from a small group of participants. The focus group is distinctive in that it consists of a limited number of homogeneous participants, discussing a predetermined topic, within a permissive and nonthreatening environment. The discussion is guided by a skilled moderator or interviewer who typically exercises limited control over the discussion and moves the conversation from one question to another.

Focus group interviews are used in a variety of ways and have gained popularity because the procedure has helped researchers understand behaviors, customs, and insights of the target audience. This information is used in a variety of ways: creating prevention programs, learning about public policy preferences, preparing social marketing campaigns, or conducting program evaluation and academic research. Focus groups are increasingly used in multimethod studies to complement and augment other methods, such as in the development of a survey instrument, or in the discovery of alternative interpretations of findings obtained from other methodological procedures.

The term *focus group interview* is derived from Robert K. Merton's research just before World War II. Merton and Paul F. Lazarsfeld, sociologists at Columbia University, introduced group interviews that had a focused questioning sequence that elicited comments about behavior, attitudes, and opinions. Merton, along with Patricia L. Kendall and Marjorie Fiske, wrote about their studies on propaganda materials and troop morale in *The Focused Interview* (New York, 1956/1990).

Focus groups gained popularity during the late 1950s as market researchers sought to understand consumer purchasing behavior. From 1950—1980, focus groups were used to study a wide array of topics and helped to uncover consumer psychological motivations.

During this time, focus groups were also referred to as *group depth interviews*. Many prominent focus group practitioners were trained as psychologists and sought to uncover the unconscious connections to consumer behavior. At that time, focus groups consisted of ten to twelve participants, often strangers, and were conducted behind one-way mirrors to allow the sponsor an opportunity to observe.

Since the 1980s academic researchers have used focus groups as a type of qualitative research. Academics used the foundation work of Merton and his colleagues and adapted procedures used by market researchers. These more recent groups place greater emphasis on natural environments (homes, public meeting spaces), smaller groups (often six to eight participants), and additional rigor in the analysis (systematic and verifiable procedures). Focus groups are typically done as a series of interviews. Often at least three or four focus groups are conducted with each particular audience type before conclusions are drawn.

Bibliography

Krueger, R. A. (1994). *Focus groups: A practical guide for applied research* (2nd ed.). Thousand Oaks, CA: Sage. This one-volume (255-page) overview of focus group interviewing provides a description of what focus groups are, how they are used, and strategies that make them successful.

Morgan, D. L. & Krueger R. A. (Eds.). (1998). *Focus group kit*. Thousand Oaks, CA: Sage. A collection of six books (each approximately 100–140 pages) on focus group interviewing: *The focus group guidebook, Planning focus groups, Developing questions for focus groups, Moderating focus groups, Involving community members in focus groups,* and *Analyzing and reporting focus group results.*

Richard A. Krueger

FORENSIC PSYCHOLOGY. The profession of psychology is finding increasing representation in the civil and criminal justice systems. The roles of psychologists are quite broad, and include such activities as the provision of assessment and treatment services, research, and serving as expert witnesses in court. Psychologists are engaged in virtually the full range of settings in the criminal justice system, including police, courts, probation, jails, prisons, and parole, and they work with offenders, victims, and criminal justice personnel. On the civil side, psychologists are involved in areas such as civil commitment, civil competencies (e.g., competency to consent to treatment or research, and guardianship) and other civil issues (e.g., custody and access, and personal injury). Their background in assessment has enabled psychologists to contribute to the development of assessment methods designed to address questions of law, such as the insanity defense, competency to stand trial, civil competency, risk to self or others, and child custody. This work has resulted in improved methods for assessing these and other legal and forensic issues. In a similar manner, psychologists may develop treatment models for forensic populations.

Defining Forensic Psychology

Defining forensic psychology is not a simple task. Some have used the term broadly to encompass any psychologist with an interest in legal issues. The Specialty Guidelines for Forensic Psychologists (Committee on Ethical Guidelines for Forensic Psychologists, 1991) defines forensic psychology to refer to "all forms of professional psychological conduct when acting, with definable foreknowledge, as a psychological expert on explicitly psycholegal issues, in direct assistance to courts, parties to legal proceedings, correctional and forensic mental health facilities, and administrative, judicial, and legislative agencies acting in an adjudicative capacity" (p. 657). This definition would include, for example, social psychologists whose research focuses on jury decision-making or eyewitness behavior. However, most psychologists define the area more narrowly, to refer to clinical psychologists who are engaged in clinical practice within the legal system. This article will focus on the research and practice in the clinical forensic area.

Professional Organizations and Scholarly Journals

As the field of psychology and law has developed, so too have professional organizations and scholarly journals. These include the American Psychology-Law Society (Division 41 of the American Psychological Association), the Law and Society Association, and the American Board of Forensic Psychology. Several journals have also been introduced in North America (e.g., *Law and Human Behavior, Behavioral Sciences and the Law, Law and Society Review,* and *Psychology, Public Policy, and Law*) and in Europe (e.g., *Criminal Behaviour and Mental Health* and *Legal and Criminological Psychology*). Several handbooks have also helped define and shape this growing field of expertise, notably the *Handbook of Forensic Psychology* (I. B. Weiner & A. K. Hess, 1998) and *Psychological Evaluations for the Courts: A Handbook for Mental Health Professionals and Lawyers* (G. B. Melton, J. Petrila, N. J. Poythress, & C. Slobogin, 1997).

Training Requirements

Although most practicing psychologists are trained at the doctoral level, many do not have specific training in the application of psychology to legal issues. In the past decade, however, graduate-level training of psychologists to work in the legal arena has become more common. Programs include forensic specialty programs within clinical psychology programs, and psychology and law degree programs (including joint degree programs in which students obtain both a Ph.D. in psychology and a law degree). This increased emphasis on training in psychology and law is also represented in clinical internship settings. Most graduate clinical programs require students to complete a one-year internship prior to receiving the doctoral degree, and many internships now offer forensic training.

The training of psychologists continues, of course, beyond graduate school. For many psychologists working in the legal system, training may more commonly take place after graduate school, typically in continuing education programs, such as workshops or specialized training programs. While a workshop format is useful for providing the latest information to those already trained in the area, or introducing the area to those with little experience, it is important that the limits of what can be acquired via this format be made explicit. The goal of the continuing education format is not to replace more extensive and formal training, but to supplement it. Ideally, psychologists trained in graduate programs in law and psychology would subsequently take advantage of continuing education programs to update their knowledge or learn new skills.

The research and practice of forensic psychology has focused on assessment and intervention, so each of these areas will be highlighted briefly.

Assessment

Criminal forensic assessment focuses on such legal issues as competency, criminal responsibility, and risk assessment. Developments in two areas, risk assessment and competency to stand trial, illustrate just some of the exciting advances that are taking place in the area of forensic assessment.

Many concerns have been raised about whether psychologists (or other mental health professionals) can predict future violence. Current research shows that predictions of violence are significantly more accurate than chance, although there remain concerns about the still high number of incorrect predictions, especially errors in detaining individuals who would not actually be violent if released. The improved quality of predictions can be partly attributed to the development of actuarial measures, which are are based on specific assessment data, usually static or historical in nature, that have been shown empirically to be predictive of future violence. They provide for consistency in clinical assessments and are more reliable and valid than unstructured clinical judgment approaches. Psychopathy, a psychological construct based on the groundbreaking work of Canadian psychologist Robert Hare, has

emerged as one of the best single predictors of criminal recidivism and is highly useful in assisting forensic psychologists in predictions of future violence (1991). Psychopathy is a form of personality disorder characterized by symptoms that include: superficiality, grandiosity, deceitfulness, lack of remorse, lack of empathy, failure to accept responsibility for one's actions, impulsivity, aggressivity, lack of long-term goals, irresponsibility, early-onset antisocial behavior, and antisocial behavior as an adult. The disorder is usually first evident in childhood and is relatively stable across the life-span. About 25% of incarcerated adult male offenders can be considered psychopaths. The Psychopathy Checklist-Revised, developed by Hare, is a rating scale for the assessment of psychopathy focusing on specific items that reflect the major symptoms of psychopathy. Items are scored on the basis of a review of case history information and an interview, where possible. The PCL-R forms a major component of many risk assessment measures.

Actuarial methods are often useful but have limits. They rely, for the most part, on static, historical variables, so they ignore potentially useful information about an individual's current functioning and risk management strategies that may be employed following release. Some forensic psychologists use what Thomas Grisso, an American clinical psychologist, has referred to as a *forensic assessment instrument* (FAI, 1986). FAIs provide a general framework for conducting assessment; they have also been referred to as *aides memoire* or clinical guidelines. FAIs do not have the characteristics of a true psychological test, but they help to make assessment more uniform and systematic. Unlike actuarial measures, FAIs do not yield a score that is interpreted with reference to norms or cutoffs. Rather, they help the examiner collect relevant information in a consistent manner and follow the decision-making process required under law. The specific content of the assessment (e.g., the questions asked or information collected by the examiner) is tailored to fit the specific evaluation context, and FAIs typically assess both current clinical factors and risk management strategies in addition to historical factors.

Psychologists are often called upon to assess a defendant's competency to stand trial. The determination that an individual is incompetent to stand trial requires the postponement of criminal proceedings on the grounds that such defendants are unable to participate in their defense on account of mental or physical disorder or retardation. Trial competency issues are raised substantially more often than the insanity defense, and between 25,000 and 39,000 competency evaluations are conducted in the United States annually. In the past decade, a considerable amount of research and clinical activity has generated a number of FAIs designed to assist evaluators in making decisions about competency, and these measures have led to more reliable and valid assessments of competency. These new assessments approaches are often based on a functional evaluation of a defendant's ability, matched to the contextualized demands of the case. While an assessment of the mental status of a defendant is important, it is now generally recognized that it is not sufficient as a method of evaluating competency. Rather, the mental status information must be related to the specific demands of the case. Thus, a defendant may be psychotic and still be found competent to stand trial if the symptoms do not impair the defendant's functional ability to consult with his or her attorney and otherwise rationally participate in the legal process.

In the civil arena, psychologists are often asked by divorce courts to provide evaluations of children involved in custody disputes. Obviously, this is a sensitive and demanding responsibility for clinicians. Allegations of child abuse or neglect are becoming more common in divorce cases, making these assessments even more complex. In this, as with other areas of forensic activity, specialized training beyond basic clinical training is essential. Other civil issues include the assessment of the competence of civilly committed patients to consent to treatment or research as well as the assessment of personal injury in civil action cases.

Intervention

Specialized treatment programs have been developed for specific forensic groups, including substance abusers, sex offenders, and defendants found incompetent to stand trial or not guilty by reason of insanity. Psychologists are also involved in providing both individual and group therapy for mentally disordered inmates in jails and prisons. There is considerable controversy about the effectiveness of these interventions, but the conclusion reached in the 1970s that nothing worked is now being replaced with the view that at least some treatment approaches can be effective, especially those based on cognitive behavioral approaches. Perhaps the most promising work is being done in the area of prevention and early intervention, especially with adolescents. This approach has the potential for more long-term impact on adult criminality because it attempts to affect the lives of young people before criminal patterns become more established, through interventions with youths, families, the schools, and the community.

Other Areas

Forensic psychologists are also active in other areas. For example, they provide consultations with police on topics such as police selection, hostage negotiation, police stress, police community relations, and training to deal with domestic violence situations Many forensic psychologists are involved in clinical work with adolescents enmeshed in the legal system or in diversion programs providing alternatives to the juvenile justice system. When the circumstances of a person's death are unclear, as in the case of a possible suicide, psychologists may conduct a psychological autopsy, in which a mental health professional attempts to assess the mental state of a deceased person at some point prior to his or her death. Criminal profiling, although popularized on television shows and in crime novels, is a relatively rare activity in forensic psychology, and the reliability and validity of profiling have not been established.

Future Directions

Forensic psychology has grown dramatically in the past two decades. Advances in the development of specialized forensic instruments has perhaps been the major contribution of the field to date. In the future, as the graduate programs produce forensic psychologists who are better trained for both research and practice, the impact of forensic psychologists on both civil and criminal issues should be substantial. One shortcoming of the field is that most of the contributions have been in applied areas but there have been negligible contributions to theory. The field will be strengthened if the next generation also makes theoretical contributions on such issues as aggression, criminality, and the development of sexual deviance. Another area in need of greater attention is the design of more effective prevention and intervention strategies, especially with young people.

[*See also* Criminality; Law and Psychology; *and* Police Psychology.]

Bibliography

Bersoff, D., Goodman-Delahunty, J., Grisso, J. T., Hans, V. P., Poythress, N. G., & Roesch, R. (1997). Training in law and psychology: Models from the Villanova conference. *American Psychologist, 52,* 1301–1310. This article reports on the National Training Conference on Education and Training in Law and Psychology. Models for training at several levels are described: undergraduate education, graduate programs, including joint J.D./ Ph.D. programs, pre- and postdoctoral internships and fellowships, and continuing education.

Committee on Ethical Guidelines for Forensic Psychologists. (1991). Specialty guidelines for forensic psychologists. *Law and Human Behavior, 15,* 655–665. This article contains the entire set of ethical and professional guidelines of the practice of professional psychology prepared jointly by the American Psychology-Law Society and the American Academy of Forensic Psychology.

Grisso, T., & Appelbaum, P. S. (1998). *Assessing competence to consent to treatment.* New York: Oxford University

Press. This book provides an overview of competence to consent to treatment and discusses issues related to the assessment of treatment competence. In addition, it presents and describes the MacArthur Competence Assessment Tool–Treatment (MacCAT-T), an assessment instrument developed as the result of a comprehensive research project conducted by the authors and their colleagues. The entire assessment process is detailed, from the initial preparation to the final judgment of competence, using case illustrations.

Hare, R. (1991). *The Hare Psychopathology Checklist–Revised.* Toronto: Multi-Health Systems.

Melton, G. B., Petrila, J., Poythress, N. G., & Slobogin, C. (1997). *Psychological evaluations for the courts: A handbook for mental health professionals and lawyers* (2nd ed.). New York: Guilford Press. This edited volume covers virtually all of the areas in which forensic psychologists are engaged. Traditional areas of forensic assessment, like competency to stand trial and criminal responsibility, risk, and dangerousness, as well as more recent topics such as federal antidiscrimination and entitlement laws, are covered. Sample reports are included for most areas of assessment, making this a valuable resource for practitioners.

Weiner, I. B., & Hess, A. K. (Eds.). (1998). *Handbook of forensic psychology.* New York: Wiley. This handbook covers a range of civil and criminal justice topics, including domestic violence, violence and risk prediction, civil and criminal competency, criminal responsibility, and professional issues.

Ronald Roesch

FORGETTING occurs when there is a failure to recover information that has been experienced previously. Obviously, the term "forgetting" applies only to cases in which forgotten information has indeed been experienced directly—in other words, information must be learned, or encoded, before it can be forgotten. This caveat may seem trivial, but it is not; people often claim to have forgotten something, such as someone's name, when in fact the information was never learned in the first place. It is also the case that forgetting, or how much someone has forgotten, can never be measured directly; we can only measure what has been *remembered*, at a particular time, so what appears to have been forgotten may, in fact, turn out to be recoverable at another time or in a different context.

Forgetting has been an important topic of investigation since the earliest days of experimental psychology. The first scientific analysis of forgetting was conducted in the 1880s by the German psychologist Hermann Ebbinghaus. Ebbinghaus's monograph *Memory*, published in 1885, is noteworthy for its experimental rigor, and it helped to establish the analytic "schema" for decades of subsequent memory research: Select a relatively simple experimental situation, such

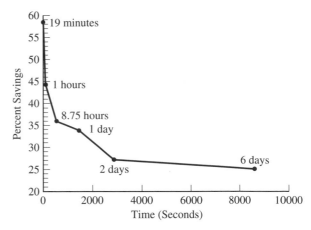

FORGETTING. Figure 1. Ebbinghaus learned lists of nonsense syllables and then measured the time to relearn the same material after various delays. Shown here are the percent "savings" after the delays: 50% savings means it took half as long to relearn the list as it did to learn the list originally; 0% means that it took the same amount of time to relearn the list as it did to learn the list originally.

as learning a set of items in a specified order of occurrence, quantify performance, if possible, and then interpret the performance trends from the perspective of a well-defined set of theoretical ideas (Ebbinghaus, 1885/1964). Not all of Ebbinghaus's methodological contributions remain popular today, such as his invention and use of the nonsense syllable, but the modern study of forgetting still owes much to the pioneering efforts of this remarkable psychologist (Slamecka, 1985).

The Form of Forgetting

One of Ebbinghaus's most enduring contributions was his quantitative analysis of the shape of the forgetting function. What form does forgetting take, and how can it best be described mathematically? Ebbinghaus discovered that when material is learned to some criterion, and retention is tested after various delays, forgetting proceeds in a negatively accelerated fashion; in other words, rather than a linear drop with time, there is a period of rapid loss followed by a long interval of slower decline (see Figure 1). Over the years, researchers have tried to determine the best fitting mathematical description of the so-called forgetting curve. Some of the mathematical candidates have included a logarithmic function (as suggested by Ebbinghaus), as well as versions of exponential, hyperbolic, and power functions. At present, the consensus seems to be that some kind of power function best describes retention data, but the issue remains unresolved and is revisited often by researchers (e.g., Rubin & Wenzel, 1996). One of the advantages of the power function is its generality: many psychophysical functions, such as the relation between the physical intensity of a light and its perceived brightness, also follow power laws (Stevens, 1975).

In addition to studying the general form of forgetting, students of memory have also attempted to determine whether forgetting *rates* are affected by variables such as the degree of original learning, the age of the participant, the meaningfulness of the materials, or by the type of retention test employed. Some methodological problems are associated with measuring the rate of forgetting (see Loftus, 1985; Wixted, 1990), but it is widely believed that forgetting rates are generally unaffected by the kinds of variables listed above. For example, if one measures the slope of the forgetting curve, slope stays relatively constant across a wide range of materials, across different participant age ranges, and across a variety of retention measures. Even well-learned material is apparently forgotten at the same rate as poorly learned material, a conclusion that seems counter to intuition (Slamecka & McElree, 1983). The fact that forgetting rates seem to be largely insensitive to such variables remains a major challenge for theories of forgetting.

The Causes of Forgetting

Why do we forget? Perhaps the most obvious answer is that originally formed impressions fade, or *decay*, spontaneously with the passage of time. Such an idea formed the basis for Edward Lee Thorndike's famous Law of Disuse (Thorndike, 1914), which proposes that dormant, unused, material simply fades away with time. The Law of Disuse seems intuitively plausible, but it has been sharply criticized over the years. One particularly influential critic was the psychologist J. A. McGeoch. McGeoch noted that, at best, forgetting is merely correlated with the passage of time and that time itself is probably not a causative factor. Iron bars left unused in the environment rust with the passage of time, he argued—that is, rust and time are correlated—but it is oxidation, not time, that is responsible for the change. Similarly, it is events that happen *in* time that produce forgetting rather than the passage of time itself.

To help make his case, McGeoch (1932) pointed to two well-known facts: (1) retention can sometimes stay constant or actually improve with the passage of time, and (2) forgetting often depends on the activities that occur during the retention interval. In the first instance, we can all think of examples in which a memory that seemed hopelessly lost to us at Time 1 suddenly reappears at Time 2, or when we try to remember in a different context. In classical conditioning, there is a phenomenon called spontaneous recovery in which a conditioned response that is lost through extinction reappears after a delay. Similarly, when memory for

everyday materials is tested repeatedly, it is not uncommon to find items recalled on a second test that were unavailable on a first test, a condition called reminiscence (Ballard, 1913). Neither spontaneous recovery nor reminiscence can be explained by appealing to decay because decayed information, once lost, should be gone forever.

Simple decay theories also have trouble explaining why forgetting depends on the content of activities that occur during the retention interval. Decades of research on multilist learning showed unequivocally that an initial list is more likely to be forgotten if subsequent lists are learned; moreover, the amount of forgetting depends importantly on the relationships among the lists. Much of this research was conducted using a retroactive interference paradigm: Participants are asked to study a list of arbitrarily paired words, such as CART–TOWN, until they can recall the right-hand member of each pair (TOWN) when given the left-hand word (CART) as a cue. A second list is then learned containing entirely new word pairs, or pairs in which the left-hand words from the first list are paired with new response terms (CART–BACON). The critical finding is that second-list learning impairs retention of the first list, but most significantly in the re-pairing condition; that is, the learning of CART–BACON interferes with the retention of CART–TOWN, a condition known as retroactive interference.

Retroactive interference was considered by most psychologists to be an apt model of how people forget in everyday life. Information is never learned in a vacuum; we are always learning new things, and it seems sensible that new learning potentially interferes with old learning—but how? Interference theorists proposed two factors. First, new learning may sometimes lead to the erasure, or *unlearning*, of old memories; thus learning CART–BACON may eliminate the previously learned association CART–TOWN from memory. Second, if the previous association is not lost, or is not lost completely, any relevant new learning will produce *response competition* at the point of test. After second-list learning, CART is associated with two responses, TOWN and BACON, and the two responses presumably will compete for mnemonic access at retrieval. It is possible, for example, that the association CART–BACON will "block" access to the association CART–TOWN, perhaps because it was the most recently learned association.

The two-factor theory of forgetting just described was widely accepted for many years, but modern psychologists tend to downplay the first factor, unlearning, and appeal more to the second factor, response competition. Unlearning fell out of favor for two reasons: It is virtually impossible to tell whether information has been truly lost, or unlearned, from memory; and it was discovered that proactive interference, like retroactive interference, plays an extremely critical role in forgetting. Proactive interference refers to the effect that prior learning has on the retention of later learning. So, to use our previous example, access to a second-list association CART–BACON will also be impaired by the first-list learning of CART–TOWN. Because prior learning cannot lead to the unlearning of new material, some form of response competition must underlie the retention loss. In a very influential article, Underwood (1957) showed that much of the forgetting that occurs over 24 hours, at least for artificial lists learned in the laboratory, is related to the number of prior lists that a person has learned—not just to the activities that follow during the retention interval.

Most modern theories of forgetting, therefore, essentially boil down to theories of response competition. The cues that are available when we want to remember are often predictive of many things, including things that happen just before or just after the learning of target material, and remembering "correctly" depends on our choosing the right potential response out of many. This means that forgetting is best viewed as a kind of discrimination failure—we always recover some kind of memory when we try to remember, but it may be the "wrong" memory, one that does not help us much in the task at hand. One of the advantages of viewing forgetting in this way is that it helps to explain why memory often seems to fluctuate over time. What we remember will depend on the ensemble of cues that are present, and what those cues best predict. As time passes, so, too, will the nature of the retrieval cues that are present and thereby what will be remembered (Capaldi & Neath, 1995; McGeoch, 1932).

Normal and Abnormal Forgetting

To this point in the discussion, we have treated forgetting as a normal human phenomenon; people forget because the ensemble of cues available at retrieval fails to lead them to the desired memory. Most people view forgetting as a nuisance, or as an undesirable property of the mind, but forgetting actually has many adaptive properties. It is important that we update our memory, that we clear our minds of clutter that is useless or unnecessary. There is no need, for example, for us to remember where we parked our car a week ago, or our phone number from two residences ago. Forgetting therefore plays a very important adaptive role in restricting access to information that is likely to be needed in our current interactions with the environment (Anderson & Schooler, 1991).

However, there are cases in which forgetting is clearly not adaptive, or even debilitating. Physical trauma to the brain, created by injury, stroke, or illness, can lead to chronic memory problems. A severe blow to the head, for example, can produce retrograde amnesia, a condition in which the ability to remember the details of events learned just prior to the injury is lost.

Retrograde amnesia often dissipates with the passage of time, although certain memories immediately surrounding the traumatic event may be lost forever. Anterograde amnesia results from the chronic abuse of alcohol, or from illnesses such as viral encephalitis, and is marked by an inability to remember new information, events that happened after the point of damage. Patients suffering from anterograde amnesia often live in a kind of perpetual present, a world in which each new event is forgotten moments after it occurs.

At present, the psychological underpinnings of amnesia are being hotly debated. One possibility is that damage to the brain creates encoding difficulties such that the affected individual is unable to process incoming material in a way that secures long-term retention. Alternatively, the locus of most forms of amnesia may lie in retrieval, at the point where people attempt to recover stored information through the processing of environmental cues. There is some evidence that people suffering from anterograde amnesia may adequately encode and store new information but lack the ability to recognize that the information has occurred previously at a particular point in time. When these patients are tested indirectly, in tasks that tap prior learning but do not require conscious awareness of occurrence, there are often few or no differences in their performance relative to normal controls.

[See also Amnesia; and Memory.]

Bibliography

Anderson, J. R., & Schooler, L. J. (1991). Reflections of the environment in memory. *Psychological Science, 2,* 396–408.

Ballard, P. B. (1913). Oblivescence and reminiscence. *British Journal of Psychology Monograph Supplements, 1,* 1–82.

Capaldi, E. J., & Neath, I. (1995). Remembering and forgetting as context discrimination. *Learning and Memory, 2,* 107–132.

Ebbinghaus, H. (1964). *Memory: A contribution to experimental psychology.* New York: Dover. (Original work published 1885)

Loftus, G. R. (1985). Evaluating forgetting curves. *Journal of Experimental Psychology: Learning, Memory, and Cognition, 11,* 397–409.

McGeoch, J. A. (1932). Forgetting and the law of disuse. *Psychological Review, 39,* 352–370.

Rubin, D. C., & Wenzel, A. E. (1996). One hundred years of forgetting: A quantitative description of retention. *Psychological Review, 103,* 734–760.

Slamecka, N. J. (1985). Ebbinghaus: Some associations. *Journal of Experimental Psychology: Learning, Memory, and Cognition, 11,* 414–435.

Slamecka, N. J., & McElree, B. (1983). Normal forgetting of verbal lists as a function of their degree of learning. *Journal of Experimental Psychology: Learning, Memory, and Cognition, 9,* 384–397.

Stevens, S. S. (1975). *Psychophysics: Introduction to its perceptual, neural, and social prospects*. New York: Wiley.

Thorndike, E. L. (1914). *The psychology of learning*. New York: Teacher's College Press.

Underwood, B. J. (1957). Interference and forgetting. *Psychological Review, 64*, 49–60.

Wixted, J. T. (1990). Analyzing the empirical course of forgetting. *Journal of Experimental Psychology: Learning, Memory, and Cognition, 16*, 927–935.

James S. Nairne

FOSTER CARE. Every society has faced the challenge of providing for the needs of children who were orphaned or whose parents could not care for them. In America, beginning early in the twentieth century, traditional orphanages became less popular, and foster care placement became the preferred method of caring for such children. Foster care is defined as the placement of a child in a setting outside the family of origin under the supervision of state child welfare agencies. The typical foster placement is with a family that has been approved to care for foster children by a public child welfare agency.

Through the first half of this century, the majority of foster care placements were made voluntarily by parents. Foster care was temporary care, and its goal was often the reunification of the family. By the 1960s, changes in society created greater awareness and concern regarding issues of child abuse and neglect. This led to a growth in the reporting of abuse and neglect, resulting in the involuntary removal of more children from their families by state child welfare agencies. In addition, children were having longer stays in foster care, averaging 5 years, and often were moved from one foster home to another in what became known as "foster care drift."

In 1980, the federal government enacted legislation (Public Law 96-272) to end this "drift" and to move children out of foster care into permanent placements more expeditiously, either through family reunification or through adoption. Efforts to ensure permanency for children initially reduced the numbers of children coming into foster care and shortened the length of time they spent there.

This trend changed again in the mid-1980s as increases in neglect, parental drug addiction, illness, physical and emotional abuse, and the decay of traditional families led to increasing numbers of children being placed in foster care. As a result, children were entering foster care with more severe physical and psychological problems. In addition, children of color were coming into foster care in increasing numbers that were out of proportion to their representation in the general population, which raised significant social concerns. In 1997, Congress enacted the Adoption and Safe Families Act (PL 105-89) with the goal of reducing the length of time children spend in foster care before finding permanent homes and of promoting alternatives to traditional foster care.

In 1982, the federal government mandated that all states maintain a data base that contains comprehensive information about all children in care. As of 1998, not all states have complied with this mandate. The official data that are available can be found in the Adoption and Foster Care Reporting System (AFCARS) and the Multi-State Foster Care Archive. In addition, *Child Abuse and Neglect: A Look at the States* (Petit & Curtis, 1997), includes a wide range of data about children in foster care.

In 1986, 280,000 children were in foster care. By 1994, those numbers had risen to 494,000. The U.S. Department of Health and Human Services estimated that by the late 1990s 700,000 children a year had spent some time in foster care.

Foster Care Goals

A child is placed in foster care to be kept safe from harm. Once in care, the goal for the child is to ensure that he or she is placed in a secure and permanent home with first consideration given to the reunification of the child with his or her family. The public child welfare agency creates a service plan that may include treatment for drug abuse or psychological disorders, vocational services, housing assistance, and other remedial services. Birth parents must comply with the plan requirements in order to be reunited with their children. These plans typically include provisions for contact or visitation between parents and children. Caseworkers supervise the plan and make recommendations regarding family reunification.

Limitations of social service and remedial resources, frequent misunderstandings and adversarial relationships between agencies and birth parents, and administrative pressure to resolve cases, create significant challenges to reunification efforts. When birth parents do not fulfill the requirements of the service plan and the child welfare agency determines that it is not in the child's best interest to return home, the agency will initiate a court proceeding to terminate the birth parents' parental rights. At the same time, the agency will develop an alternative plan for permanent placement, usually a plan for adoption.

Research Issues

Different aspects of foster care have been subjected to empirical study. Some of the areas researchers have examined include social service caseloads and caseload dynamics; permanency goals and factors related to permanency goals; physical and mental health needs of foster children; the functioning of foster families; long-term outcomes of foster care; the frequency and effect of birth parent visitation on the foster child and the foster parents; and the identification of predictors of foster placements and foster care outcomes.

Methodological Challenges in Foster Care Research. There are a number of methodological problems in the existing research on foster care. First, small size, lack of random samples, subject attrition, and lack of control groups limit the conclusiveness and generalizability of many studies. Second, because foster children have unique characteristics, it is questionable whether established norms of standardized instruments apply to this population. Third, research has often relied on the use of reports from parents and social workers; however, the extent to which these reports are accurate is uncertain.

It has also been difficult for research studies to determine the relationship of the complex factors that influence the psychological functioning of foster children. These factors include genetic and biological factors, preplacement history, reasons for placement, and placement experiences. In spite of such limitations, research findings have highlighted critical aspects of the complex world of foster care.

Health, Psychological Functioning, and Resiliency

Children in foster care have a high incidence of serious medical conditions, developmental delays, emotional and behavioral problems, and school failure. Children who experienced abuse are especially vulnerable to attachment and behavioral disorders and major psychopathology. Multiple foster placements, long stays in foster care, separation from parents and siblings, and loss of positive relationships with birth family are critical factors that increase the risk for these problems. Children who have been in foster care are also at greater risk for involvement in delinquent activities. However, research indicates that it is not foster care itself but rather experiences of abuse and neglect that are the most important predictors of delinquent behavior.

Children are removed from their families when they are at great risk. They have typically experienced serious physical and/or psychological injuries. The act of removing children from their families can itself create significant trauma. Frequently children do not know why they are being taken away or what is going to happen to them. They often expect foster parents and other adults to treat them badly. Their experience creates many impediments to developing trusting secure relationships.

In the face of such serious challenges, the question of what potentiates resiliency in foster children is especially important. Good emotional relationships, functioning social support systems, and having at least av-

erage intelligence have been identified as elements that have a positive impact on resiliency. Yet much more knowledge is needed to provide services that support resiliency in foster children.

Kinship Care

The increasing numbers of children entering foster care and a shortage of foster families has led to the development of alternatives to traditional foster care. None has received more attention than formal kinship care, placing children with relatives who are supervised by the public child welfare agency. The premise of kinship care is that keeping a child with relatives maintains continuity of connections for the child and that relatives have a special investment in a member of their own family. This kind of placement is also seen as having greater potential for maintaining ties between the children and their birth parents. At present, there is no indication that children in kinship care fare better than children in traditional foster care, though it is clear that kinship care is one important practical approach to expanding the resources available to children in need.

Challenge for the Future

The number of children entering foster care and the severity of their problems have overwhelmed the traditional public child welfare system. It is unclear whether there is the social and political will to allocate the resources required to protect and serve the best interests of this most vulnerable segment of American society.

For the children in foster care it is essential to develop policies, laws, and practices that, whenever possible, reunite them with their birth parents or relatives. When reunification attempts are unsuccessful, policies, laws, and practice must allow for and provide alternative permanent placements. Either option needs to occur in a timely manner. Doing so requires both resources and an expansion of knowledge that will enable the agencies responsible to provide effective assessments of the children's physical and emotional needs and to implement comprehensive services to ensure that they have every opportunity to develop their individual potential in permanent and nurturing homes.

Bibliography

Fanshel, D., & Shinn, E. B. (1978). *Children in foster care: A longitudinal investigation.* New York: Columbia University Press. Groundbreaking study that examined the effect of out-of-home care on children's personal and social adjustment.

Festinger, T. (1983). *No one ever asked us: A postscript to foster care.* New York: Columbia University Press. Provides a detailed picture of various aspects of the lives of a group of adults who had been discharged from out-of-home care after reaching the age of majority.

McDonald, T. P., Allen, R. I., Westerfelt, A., & Piliavin, I. (1996). *Assessing the long-term effects of foster care.* Washington, DC: CWLA Press. Provides a comprehensive and critical review of research on the impact of out-of-home care on children.

Petit, M. R., & Curtis, P. A. (1997). *Child abuse and neglect: A look at the states. 1997 CWLA Stat Book.* Washington, DC: Child Welfare League of America.

Rosenfeld, A. A., Pilowsky, D. J., Fine, P. (1997). Foster care: An update. *Journal of the American Academy of Child and Adolescent Psychiatry, 36,* 448–457.

Scannapieco, M., Hegar, R. L., & McAlpine, B. C. (1997). Kinship care and foster care: A comparison of characteristics and outcomes. *Families in Society, 78,* 480–488.

Widom, C. S. (1989). The cycle of violence. *Science, 244,* 160–166.

Peter Gibbs

FRAISSE, PAUL (1911–1996), French psychologist. At 17, Paul Fraisse devoted 2 years (1928–1930) to a Jesuit noviciate, but was unable to take holy orders. In 1935 he obtained a degree in scholastic philosophy from the Catholic Faculties in Lyon. He then took up experimental psychology and spent 2 years in Louvain in the laboratory of the Belgian psychologist Albert Michotte (1881–1965). His research focused on the structure of rhythmic movements.

Imprisoned by the Germans during World War II, he escaped on his second attempt in 1943. That same year, he became assistant director of the Laboratory for Experimental Psychology and the Physiology of Sensations at the Ecole Pratique des Hautes Etudes, under Henri Piéron (1881–1964). There he continued his research on rhythm. In 1948, he turned his attention to the perception of time, an area in which he became a world-renowned expert.

In 1952, he succeeded Piéron as director of the laboratory. In 1958, he was appointed professor of experimental psychology at the Sorbonne. In 1961, he became director of the Institute of Psychology, which Piéron had founded in 1921 to provide for the training of psychologists.

Paul Fraisse occupied many other posts in France and abroad. From 1947 to 1994, he edited the journal *L'Année Psychologique*; he was president of the French Psychological Society (1962–1963) and the International Union of Scientific Psychology. He contributed to the foundation of the Association of Francophone Scientific Psychology, and was its secretary general and subsequently president, from 1952 to 1981. He was the recipient of many honors, was made Doctor Honoris Causa by several prestigious universities, and was a member of the New York Academy of Sciences.

In addition to being a world-famous scholar, Paul Fraisse was a politician within the world of psychology. Starting in 1947, he contributed to the gradual emancipation of the psychology curriculum from that of philosophy. He wielded his considerable institutional power to ensure the supremacy of experimental psychology over all other sectors of psychology in the majority of French universities and at the Centre National de la Recherche Scientifique (C.N.R.S.). With Jean Piaget (1896–1980), he coedited *Traité de psychologie expérimentale* in nine volumes, which has been reprinted in several editions and translated into several languages.

Paul Fraisse did not confine himself to psychology. He was also a socialist trade unionist who actively participated in public political life. In addition, he maintained his youthful commitment to the "personnalist" movement of Emmanuel Mournier (1905–1950), a Christian philosopher of subjectivity and founder of the journal *Esprit*.

His scientific work, similarly, was not confined to the themes of rhythm and time. His work on the perception of very short time spans led him to research various forms of information processing, in particular, the processes of verbal and iconic encoding and the perception of language. Fraisse wrote several books and over two hundred articles, and left a lasting mark on French experimental psychology, which remains indebted to him in both scientific and institutional terms.

Bibliography

Fraisse, P. (1957). *The psychology of time.* New York: Harper and Row.

Fraisse, P. (1983). Autobiographie [Autobiography]. In F. Parot & M. Richelle (Eds.), *Psychologues de langue française: Autobiographies* (pp. 79–96). Paris: Presses Universitaires de France.

Fraisse, P., & Piaget, J. (Eds.) (1963–1966). *Traité de psychologie expérimentale* [Treatise on experimental psychology] (Vols. 1–9). Paris: Presses Universitaires de France.

Régine Plas
Translated from French by Chris Miller

FRANCE. The historical foundations of psychology in France can be traced to the names of Alfred Binet, Jean Martin Charcot, and Pierre Janet. Janet was the founder of psychological analysis in France between 1889 and 1893. Charcot, a neuropathologist, belonged to the Salpetrière School. Even though the Salpetrière school's history is closer to medicine than to psychology, we can not ignore that Janet and Binet, who fostered psychology in France, frequented this internationally renowned school, and it was under its influence that they were able to contribute with important concepts in dynamic psychology.

From the Nineteenth to the Twentieth Century

Binet was a promoter of experimental psychology in France. It was he who declared, "One always has to welcome the facts that stand in opposition to our theories." Many accounts of that period state that Alfred Binet was the creator of experimental psychology in France; in 1894, he published his *Introduction to Experimental Psychology*." The following year, Binet was placed in charge of the laboratory of physiological psychology at the Sorbonne. Binet's name will always be associated to the intelligence scale ("echelle d'intelligence"), the success of which strongly contributed to displace the interest in test questionnaires. In *L'Étude experimentale de l'intelligence* (1903), Binet analyzed the intellectual processes, establishing two kinds, the subjective and the objective. In 1904, Theodule Ribot, in his article published in the first issue of the *Journal de psychologie*, also criticized the questionnaire method. There he wrote how one starts to become suspicious toward questionnaires: "The most recent method of the tests, whose value I am not going to examine in this article, seems to me an attempt to replace questionnaires."

In 1903, Janet became a professor in the Collège de France, where he taught his main theories. In 1904, he founded with George Dumas the *Journal de psychologie normale et pathologique*. With Binet's premature death in 1911, Henri Pieron became head of the Sorbonne's laboratory of psychology. On the other hand, Binet's death also left open the direction of the laboratory of psychology attached to Janet's chair at the Collège de France.

Pieron had a physiological approach to experimental psychology, and it may be said that he was the forerunner of French behaviorism. In 1920, he founded the Institute of Psychology at the Sorbonne, and became inaugural president of the International Union of Scientific Psychology.

Janet, in his turn, engaged in the domain of psychopathology. His therapeutic focus was on the patient at the level of consciousness. The patient's words were registered, and previous exposure to treatment carefully considered. Janet was more concerned with the notion of function than that of structure. Janet spoke of transforming the drama into narrative. In 1902, George Du-

mas, a disciple of Théodule-Armand Ribot and Janet's student, succeeded Janet as the person responsible for the course of experimental psychology in the Sorbonne and, in 1912, as professor. Psychopathology prospered under Dumas, and he, along with Charles Blondel, became one of the great names of French psychopathology. He was well known for his outstanding clinical presentations with patients at hospitals such as Sainte-Anne. A cultivated man and a brilliant professor, Dumas had an outstanding influence not only in France but also in Latin America. It was Dumas who created, in 1934, one of the most important universities in São Paulo, Brazil, where Claude Levi-Strauss and Fernand Braudel, invited by Dumas, trained students in human sciences between 1935 and 1937.

Dumas, who was rather against psychoanalysis and Freudian theory, based his outlook on the postulates of Claude Bernard, such as that there was an identity between the normal and pathological mechanism within the organism.

Dumas, in his work *Traité de psychologie* (Treatise of Psychology) published in Paris in 1923, portrayed his fascination with the knowledge and power of the physician. Starting in 1930, the principal psychologists spent ten years reediting his work as a collective work, titled *Nouveau traité de psychologie*.

Paul Guillaume, who occupied the chair in social psychology at the Sorbonne, introduced the theory of form in France. Such theory gives the ground to the obligation, under the Vichy, of the global method of reading training. Guillaume was succeeded by Lagache, who in his turn inherited Janet's legacy. Lagache conceived the separation of psychology from philosophy in 1947. A defender of lay analysis, Lagache promoted the introduction of psychologists to the field of French psychoanalysis and endeavored to give the Freudian approach the place it deserved. On the other hand, he strove to eliminate the multiple cleavages between the clinical/psychoanalytical, the experimental, the social psychological, the ethnological, the humanistic, and the naturalistic. He aspired for a unified discipline of psychology.

The Conflict Between Psychopathology and Psychology

The history of psychology in France testifies to the obstacles to achieving such a unification. The clinician's activities in France are founded in psychopathology. This confronts them with the function of language and the question of the symbolic. At the same time, learning theories, experimentation, behavioral sciences, statistics, psychometrics, all take no account of these crucial functions of language and the symbolic. Moreover, there is a divergence between clinical psychology and analytical practice. Clinical psychology is concerned with the preconscious, analytical practice with the unconscious truth that the transference can mobilize. Even though Lagache's itinerary was followed under the sign of the "unconscious," he finally left to Jacques Lacan the realm of psychoanalysis and occupied a unique place in the psychological domain. Lagache formalized later on a conception of personality that excluded the unconscious dimension.

Lacan himself always held a strong position concerning the deep heterogeneity between psychoanalysis and psychology. He stressed that the object of psychoanalysis was the reality of the unconscious desire, which, he believed, psychology completely ignored. He never ceased to underline how the psychoanalyst thinks differently of his field from how a psychologist thinks of his, and he reaffirmed the radical separation between the domain opened by Freud and that domain inherited by psychology. In a letter to Louis Althusser dated 1 December 1963, Lacan wrote: "It is the freedom to desire that is a new factor not to inspire a revolution—it is always because of a desire that one fights and dies for—but to show that what this revolution wishes for is that its struggle be for the freedom of desire."

Lacan wished to differentiate the transmission of psychoanalysis, which seeks the truth lodged in the unconscious, from the knowledge produced in the university, which according to his conception had the tendency to replace the doctrine of the church. University knowledge would act in the name of a knowledge instead of producing knowledge. The university, according to Lacan's view, would be a kind of tyranic system founded on an ideal pedagogic relation. Lacan always questioned the conditions that would allow the transmission of the Freudian knowledge and was convinced that the university was not a place to favor it.

Nevertheless, there was a "turning point" after this fierce criticism against the university. In 1974, Lacan imposed his teaching in the department of psychoanalysis in Paris VIII-Vincennes and made Jacques Alain Miller his *porte-parole*. It was in 1969 that Serge Leclaire, endowed with a touching humanism, initiated this department of psychoanalysis, the first in the French university system. In Leclaire's eyes, Vincennes was a favorable site for the decentering and avoidance of a dogmatic approach of psychoanalysis. This department of psychoanalysis was part of the philosophy major, and, as such, dispensed credits as a submajor or as electives. No curriculum was imposed on students who could choose their course credits in the order they wished. The Vincennes department offered neither diplomas nor clinical training usable for employment. Under no circumstances could a student through such a program be certified in psychoanalysis. In 1970, Lacan, through a series of political movements that put pressure on the Vincennes team to marginalize Leclaire, forced the latter to resign from Vincennes and

took control of the department with his appointees. Miller, who became, in 1974, Lacan's official delegate at the administrative level, decided to reorganize the department at the University of Vincennes (presently St. Denis) on new grounds, trying also to prevent some positions of the department to be taken over by the psychology section.

Although from 1945 to 1968 psychoanalysis was taught in universities under the rubric of psychology, its orientation was based on Janet rather than Freud. History has proved that, in France, the obstacles to the integration of psychoanalysis into psychology continue because psychoanalysis cannot submit to clinical psychology.

The approach of psychology in France is humanist, in which the psychological facts are assigned to consciousness. In other words, the focus of psychology in France is not so much on behavior as on what has been experienced.

As for the experimental side, Ribot, a disciple of Wilhelm Wundt, pursued experimental psychology. In 1885, he became course director of experimental psychology at the Sorbonne. Despite championing experimental psychology, Ribot himself did not practice it. In his work *The Unconscious Life and Its Movements* (1914), he laid out the primacy of unconscious mechanisms. The well-known Ribot's law is exposed in his work *Diseases of Memory* (1881). This law of memory dissolution, from recent to remote memory, became a cornerstone of psychogerontology.

In 1901, Janet founded La Société Française de Psychologie, a member of the International Union of Scientific Psychology. It is the body that represents France in international psychology forums. It publishes two journals, *Psychologie française* and *Pratiques psychologiques*. The society is an umbrella organization for diverse fields of theoretical and applied psychology. Henri Wallon contributed hundreds of books on psychology. He envisaged the psychogenesis of the child taking into consideration the cultural and hereditary dimensions as well as affective and cognitive aspects. In 1925, he was named professor at the Collège de France. He founded a laboratory of child psychobiology in 1927. His famous work, *The Origins of Child's Character* was published in 1931. From 1937 to 1949, Wallon was professor and chair of psychology and child education at the Collège de France. Wallon's concept of the experience of the body in relation to the mirror image (reported in his text on the psychogenesis of the body proper and the unity of the self) would later serve as the basis for Lacan's celebrated notion of imaginary related to the "stade du miroir." Lacan's elaboration of the register of symbolic was also linked to this process.

Wallon's conceptualization played a fundamental role in the history of psychoanalysis in France. His work also influenced and engendered a myriad of modern theories. For example, his notion of attachment was developed by John Bowlby and Harry Harlow, among others. Psychoanalysts like Donald Woods Winnicott and René Spitz were also influenced by Wallon.

In 1950, René Zazzo became director of the laboratory of child psychobiology. Zazzo developed the notion of "heterochronie," namely, that the mentally deficient, compared to a normal child, develops in a different rhythm according to different aspects of the psychobiological development. He compared endogenous and exogenous debility and applied the concept of debility to the diversity of etiological and psychological dimensions.

Professional Organizations

In France, unlike other industrialized countries, there is no professional statutory board. In keeping with the diversity of psychology, there are several national organizations belonging to the Association Nationale des Organisations de Psychologues (A.N.O.P). These are: Association des Conseillers d'Orientation de France (A.C.O.F.); Association des Enseignants en Psychologie des Universites (A.E.P.U); Association Française des Centres de Consultations Conjugales (A.F.C.C.C.); Association Française des Psychologues Scolaires (A.F.P.S), which publishes the journal *Psychologie scolaire*; Association Nationale des psychologues de l'Enseignement Catholique (A.N.P.E.C.); Ecole des Psychologues Praticiens (E.P.P); Société Française de Psychologie (S.E.P.); Syndicat Nationale des Enseignements de Second degré (S.N.E.S.); Syndicat Nationale de l'Enseignement Superieur (S.N.E.Sup.); Syndicat Nationale des Psychologues (S.N.P.), which publishes the journal *Psychologues et psychologies*; Syndicat National des Praticiens en Psychothérapie (S.N.P.Psy); and Syndicat des Psychologues de l'Éducation Nationale (S.P.E.N.).

Clinical and Academic Preparation

Currently, French universities situate psychology departments within the human and social sciences. Universities actively engaged in the teaching and propagation of psychology are: Aix-Marseille I, Amiens, Angers, Besançon, Bordeaux II, Brest, Caen, Chambery, Clermont-Ferrand II, Dijon, FUPL, Grenoble II, Lille III, Lyon II, Metz, Montpellier III, Nancy II, Nantes, Nice, Paris V, Paris VII, Paris VIII, Paris X, Paris XIII, Poitiers, Reims, Rennes I, Rennes II, Rouen, Strasbourg I, Toulouse II, Tours, and Université Catholique Ouest.

Training in psychology takes five to six years, depending on whether a practicum (known as stage) is included. The *diplôme d'études superieures specialisées* (D.E.S.S.), inaugurated in 1976, marked the establishment of a professional diploma in psychology. The diploma is awarded according to the subspecialty of the graduate.

Experimental Psychology. Rather than being confined to the laboratory and the application of tests, experimental psychology is based on systematic observation. Curiously, its history can be traced also to selection of recruits at the Michelin factory. Clinical psychology in France has been critical of experimental psychology, arguing that laboratory findings cannot be extrapolated to the human situation.

Occupational and Industrial Psychology. Industrial psychology aims to help the integration of groups experiencing difficulties in the workplace. The social situation in France means that this field, which addresses the unemployed, is increasing in importance. Diplomates in this field are better remunerated and more quickly employed than in clinical psychology. It responds to the need of enterprises and recruitment firms. It helps to improve the work environment, reduce professional stress, and industrial accidents.

Social Psychology. The problems of social interaction were formulated in France at the turn of the century by Auguste Comte and Emile Durkheim and gave rise to social psychology, which was formalized in the 1930s. It was Paul Fraisse who, succeeding Lagache at the Institute of Psychology in the Sorbonne, first created his own laboratory of comparative psychology in 1957. He carried a fierce fight against clinicians and against Lagache's students. The current research focus is on the variations in human behavior in society and culture. *Le Journal international de psychologie*, established in 1966, and published in France, is concerned almost entirely with social psychology. Despite an increase in the span of action of social psychology, it has not flourished with the intensity it enjoys in the United States.

Behavioral and Cognitive Psychology. If John Watson, founder of behaviorism, attempted in 1913 in New York to define psychology, Pierre Janet 13 years later in Paris tried to do the same. He prompted one of his disciples, Jean Piaget, to study the intellectual functions, and this work gave rise to the further development of French cognitive psychology. Remy Chauvin, moreover, studied patterns of animal behavior to better grasp the psychological universe and to elaborate the experience of precognition.

Clinical and Pathological Psychology. Clinical psychologists work within the public domain in hospitals and medical-educational associations and in private clinics. Clinical psychology focuses on the individual, and gives no importance to animal behavior. There are three methodological facets in the case study: first, a focus on the conflicts that rule human beings—the psychodynamic; second, the assessment of the development and history of the person—the genesis; third, the notion of Sartre that there is an aspect of incompleteness of being—the totality. Psychoanalysis, as Lagache stated, has contributed enormously to clinical psychology, through key concepts such as transference, resistance, and conflict. It enriches the psychological understanding of pathological (not necessarily abnormal) behavior.

Psychology Today

Given the diversity of psychology in France, one may well speak of the psychologies in the plural. Up to 1947, psychology had no autonomy but was a part of philosophy in the French universities. In that year, the licentiate in psychology in the Facultés des Lettres et Sciences Humaines was established and, through this act, the autonomy of psychology was recognized at the university level.

Nevertheless, it was only in 1965 at the Sorbonne that the psychology section gained autonomy from philosophy. The licentiate in psychology consisted of general psychology, child and adolescent psychology, social psychology, and pathological psychology. The following year, the foundation chair of general psychology was established. Didier Anzieu represented the clinicians and Gilbert Simondon the experimentalists. The two orientations remained divergent, gradually splitting during the 1968 unrest at the Sorbonne. A law implemented by Edgar Fauré, in November 1969, established new bases for universities, which from then on were identified by numbers. As for psychologists, most of the experimentalists gathered in the University of Paris V, while the clinicians in the University of Paris VII. Anzieu was charged with the mission to elaborate a new status for psychologists in the University of Paris VII. Ths university was more open to human sciences and favored a constant reassessment of clinical psychology. Anzieu, along with the Société Française de Psychologie among other organizations, waged a campaign for a ministerial bill to establish the title "psychologist." Even if the academic and professional title (D.E.S.S) were protected, the name of the profession was not. The fact that there was, and still is, no guild of psychologists, dates from the history of France. In 1792, in the course of the French Revolution, corporations were extinguished. No professional groups as such were recognized—that is, until the Vichy regime legalized certain professions and created, among others, the Guild of Medical Doctors, Lawyers, Pharmacists, and Architects.

Thus, all recruitments of psychologists into the public sector are affected through government ministries. The Ministry of Health recruits at the entry-level requirement of D.E.S.S. in clinical psychology. The Ministry of National Education recruits educational psychologists. The Ministry of Justice recruits, by entrance examination, those with the bachelor's degree. The decree of March 1990 established the list of diplomas accredited for the use of the professional title "psychologist." By this criterion, according to the most recently available figures, there were 30,000 psychologists in France in 1996.

It is vital to appreciate the placement of the problem of psychology, in what concerns its object of study and its status in France. Psychology in France, as demonstrated, cannot be dissociated from its peculiar French cultural and historical context.

[*Many of the people mentioned in this article are the subjects of independent biographical entries.*]

Bibliography

Castro D., & Engelhart, D. (1993). De la formation a la professionnalisation. Processus de professionnalisation de la psychologie appliquée en France. *Revue Europeenne de psychologie appliquée, 43* (2) 101–109.

Delay, J., Pichot, P., Fraisse, P., & Zazzo, R. (1958). Commemoration du centenaire de Alfred Binet a la Société Française de Psychologie. *Psychologie Française, 3.*

Lagache, D. (1949). *L'Unité de la psychologie.* Paris: Presses Universitaires de France.

Prevost, C. M. (1994). *La psychologie fondamentale.* Paris: Presses Universitaires de France.

Roudinesco, E. (1990). *A History of Psychoanalysis in France 1925–1985.* (J. Mehlman, Trans.) Chicago: University of Chicago Press.

Roudinesco, E., & Plon, M. (1997). *Dictionnaire de la psychanalyse.* Paris: Fayard.

Renata Volich Eisenbruch and Maurice Eisenbruch

FRANKL, VIKTOR EMIL (1905–1997), Austrian psychiatrist. Frankl, the founder of logotherapy, was born and educated in Vienna, receiving his M.D. at the University of Vienna in 1930. He remained there as professor of neurology and psychiatry until his seizure by the Nazis in 1942. After the war he lectured in Vienna and at numerous universities in the United States, including Harvard and Stanford. He wrote over 32 books, which have been translated into 26 languages, and held 29 honorary doctorates from universities around the world. Called "a monument to the spirit and the heart" by then mayor of Vienna Michael Häupl in an Associated Press obituary, Frankl's theories and his own personal meaning of life were tried and strengthened by his experiences in several Nazi concentration camps during World War II. Logotherapy has been called the third Viennese school of psychotherapy, behind Sigmund Freud's psychoanalysis and Alfred Adler's individual psychology.

According to Frankl's masterwork *Man's Search for*

Meaning (1984), named one of the 10 most influential books by general readers in a 1991 Library of Congress survey, the striving to find meaning in one's life, what Frankl called the will to meaning, is the primary motivational force. In contrast to the atheistic existentialists (e.g., Sartre, Camus, and de Beauvoir) who claimed that life has no meaning, Frankl, as a religious existentialist, believed that one must create meaning in life. Such meaning is unique and specific; it can and must be fulfilled by a person and only by the individual person. Although meaning may vary from person to person and from moment to moment, Frankl described three kinds of values that could be actualized in order to create meaning in one's life: creative values, experiential values, and attitudinal values.

Creative values are actualized by creating something, such as doing a good deed or by taking pride in one's work. One actualizes experiential values by finding meaning in a moment, by appreciating the beauty in nature or in a work of art or a piece of music, or by appreciating the uniqueness of another person through love.

Attitudinal values are actualized by realizing that no matter how dire circumstances are or how little one can do to change a situation—such as when imprisoned in a concentration camp—one can take a stand toward such conditions. That is, one can choose to face the inevitable, such as suffering or death, with dignity: "Human life under any circumstances never ceases to have a meaning . . . this infinite meaning of life includes suffering and dying, privation and death," he wrote in *Man's Search for Meaning* (p. 90), which chronicles his personal experiences. (It was originally subtitled *From Death Camp to Existentialism*.)

Frankl witnessed and wrote about instances of prisoners finding meaning in their lives and dying with dignity, as well as many instances of prisoners succumbing to the degradation of their conditions. Frankl's brother, parents, and wife were killed in the death camps. He himself found meaning in his own concentration camp experience by choosing to help other prisoners find meaning in the final moments of their lives.

If the will to meaning is frustrated, a person may experience a type of spiritual sickness, as opposed to a psychological disorder or a physical illness, called noögenic neurosis, or existential frustration. Noögenic neurosis is frustration in existence itself, in finding the meaning of existence, or in striving to find a concrete meaning in personal experience. This frustration at not being able to see meaning in one's life may be experienced as boredom or depression, and is manifested in escapism, materialism, hedonism, or addictions.

Logotherapy, therefore, is a type of philosophical therapy rather than traditional psychotherapy based on Frankl's philosophy. The therapist helps an individual to create his or her own personal meaning of life and to see meaning in all human life. Happiness comes as a by-product of finding meaning: "[It] must ensue. It cannot be pursued," Frankl says in his book *The Unconscious God* (1975, p. 85).

Although Frankl corresponded with both Freud and Adler, he disagreed with both and went on to found his own philosophy and therapy. His ideas have had great impact on the practice of psychotherapy and especially on pastoral counseling, prison counseling, AIDS counseling, and suicide prevention and recovery.

Bibliography

Fabry, J. B. (1994). *The pursuit of meaning*. Abilene, TX: Institute of Logotherapy Press.

Frankl, V. E. (1967). *Psychotherapy and existentialism*. New York: Washington Square Press.

Frankl, V. E. (1975). *The unconscious God: Psychotherapy and theology*. New York: Simon and Schuster.

Frankl, V. E. (1984). *Man's search for meaning* (3rd ed.). New York: Washington Square Press.

Frankl, V. E. (1997). *Man's search for ultimate meaning*. New York: Plenum Press.

Frankl, V. E. (1997). *Viktor Frankl recollections: An autobiography* (J. Fabry & J. Fabry, Trans.). New York: Plenum Press.

Gould, W. G. (1993). *Viktor E. Frankl: Life with meaning*. Pacific Grove, CA: Brooks/Cole.

Marianne Miserandino

FRANZ, SHEPHERD IVORY (1874–1933), American neuropsychologist. Franz was a pioneer in both basic neurobehavioral research and clinical neuropsychology. He was the first (1902) to combine experimental brain ablations in animals with experimental behavioral testing. He is recognized as being the first (1904) to establish a psychological laboratory in a hospital (McLean Hospital, associated with Harvard Medical School), although Franz attributed that accomplishment to Edward Cowles, his superintendent at McLean; see the dedication in Franz's *Handbook of Mental Examination Methods* (New York, 1912). Franz was the first (1907) to implement routine psychological testing of patients in a psychiatric hospital (St. Elizabeths, then known as the Government Hospital for the Insane, Washington, D.C.), and his *Handbook*, intended for use with psychiatric patients, was among the first of its kind. He was also among the first psychologists to address rehabilitation of neurologically damaged patients.

Franz received his Ph.D. degree at Columbia University under James McKeen Cattell in 1899. Franz's neurological and clinical interests, which remained prevalent throughout his career, developed during his appointments to teach physiology at the Harvard (1899–1901) and Dartmouth medical schools (1901–1904). His animal research investigating the role of the cerebral cortex in learning and memory resulted in his strong theoretical opposition to his contemporaries who argued for localization of brain function. Franz sarcastically referred to their views as the "New Phrenology" (*Science*, 1912). His antilocalization viewpoint influenced his protégé Karl Lashley, who began doing brain research under Franz's supervision in 1915, to develop the principles of mass function and equipotentiality (e.g., *Brain Mechanism and Intelligence*, Chicago, 1929). Franz's and Lashley's theoretical views also influenced Franz's clinical work; for example, equipotentiality (one cortical area can substitute for another) implies the potential for reeducation (see Franz's book cited below) of lost functions following brain damage.

Franz was hired in 1907 as the psychologist at St. Elizabeths Hospital, and he eventually became Director of Scientific Laboratories. In his early years at St. Elizabeths, he and Superintendent William Alanson White, an eminent psychiatrist, got along well, and Franz worked nationally to promote cooperation among psychologists and psychiatrists. Such work, including publications devoted to this cause, resulted in his being made an honorary member of the American Medico-Psychological Association, later renamed the American Psychiatric Association. Over the years, Franz's and White's relationship deteriorated. They began to have theoretical differences when White's early enthusiasm for scientific research yielded to his commitment to psychoanalysis, but it was Franz's being held responsible for minor infractions by subordinates in his administrative charge that resulted in his abrupt demotion, significant salary reduction, and quick resignation in 1924.

Meanwhile, Franz's research and publications including the *Handbook* and textbook, *Nervous and Mental Re-Education* (New York, 1923), helped establish him as the first clinical neuropsychologist in the United States. The latter textbook grew largely out of Franz's assignment, as the government's top psychologist, to address the needs of brain damaged veterans returning from World War I. The book also addressed rehabilitation associated with disorders such as poliomyelitis, tabes dorsalis, cerebral paralysis, speech defects, and psychoses.

Concurrently with his St. Elizabeths appointments, Franz had professorships in physiology and psychology at George Washington University, and, following his resignation from St. Elizabeths, he quickly accepted a faculty position with the newly established University of California, Los Angeles. He chaired the department of psychology and the committee that planned the establishment of UCLA's Graduate School. Franz Hall was opened in 1940 to house UCLA's Psychology Department. Franz was also chief of the Psychological and Educational Clinic at Children's Hospital in Hollywood.

Franz's final books, *Psychology* (New York, 1933) with Kate Gordon and *Persons One and Three: A Study in Multiple Personalities* (New York, 1933), were published in the year of his death, caused by amyotrophic lateral sclerosis. *Persons One and Three*, according to reviewer H. Meltzer (*Journal of Educational Psychology*, 1934), differed from previous works on multiple personality in being "largely on a descriptive, observational level." Franz avoided speculative Freudian and organic explanations, preferring to explain the observed dissociations in terms of specific amnesias which, in this patient, had begun during military service in World War I.

Franz was well recognized during his career as editor of *Psychological Bulletin* (1912–1924) and *Psychological Monographs* (1924–1927) and associate editor of *Journal of General Psychology* (1927–1933). He was president of the American Psychological Association (1920), the Southern Society for Philosophy and Psychology (1911), and the Western Psychological Association (1927–1928), and he was a Fellow in the American Medical Association and in the American Association for Advancement of Science.

Bibliography

Works by Franz

Franz, S. I. (1922). Psychology and psychiatry. *Psychological Review*, 29, 241–249. Exemplary attempt to promote understanding between psychologists and psychiatrists. The tensions of 1922 seem similar to those today.

Franz, S. I. (1926). *The evolution of an idea: How the brain works*. Los Angeles: UCLA Press. Provides good insight into his career in both animal and human brain research.

Franz, S. I. (1932). Shepherd Ivory Franz. In C. Murchison. (Ed.), *A history of psychology in autobiography* (Vol. 2, pp. 89–113). Worcester, MA: Clark University Press. Franz on Franz with few personal details but occasionally pithy jabs at White and others.

Works about Franz

Reisman, J. M. (1991). *A history of clinical psychology* (2nd ed.). New York: Irvington. Consult Reisman's index for citations regarding Franz that show his importance in the history of clinical psychology.

The next three citations include most of the published biographical details of Franz's life and career.

Anonymous. (1926). Franz, Shepherd Ivory. In *The national cyclopedia of American biography being the history of the United States* (pp. 477–478). New York: James T. White.

Thomas, R. K. (1999). Franz, Shepherd Ivory (1874–1933). In John A. Garraty & M. C. Carnes (Gen. Eds.) *American national biography*. (Vol. 8, pp. 405–406). New York: Oxford University Press.

Woodworth, R. S. (1956–1960). Franz, Shepherd Ivory. In J. A. Garraty (Ed.), *Dictionary of American biography* (pp. 316–317). New York: Charles Scribner's.

Roger K. Thomas

FRENKEL-BRUNSWIK, ELSE (1908–1958), American psychologist. At midcentury, Else Frenkel-Brunswik was a major contributor to personality and social psychology, who could draw significantly on perspectives from her Viennese background. After obtaining her doctoral degree at the University of Vienna (1930), she was psychoanalyzed by Ernst Kris, a prominent member of Sigmund Freud's inner circle. She and her husband-to-be, Egon Brunswik, both on the staff of Karl and Charlotte M. Bühler's Institute of Psychology at the University, were also in close communication with the "Vienna Circle" of logical positivist philosophers who promoted a physicalist program for the unity of the sciences. In the United States, the years immediately after World War II were a time when psychoanalysis had its maximum impact on the emerging academic study of personality and on the profession of clinical psychology. It was also a time when the neobehaviorism of Clark Hull, then at its apogee, looked back to the Vienna Circle for philosophical justification. So when Else Frenkel fled Vienna to escape the Nazi occupation of Austria in 1938 and joined and married Egon Brunswik, a theoretically oriented experimental psychologist who had previously been recruited by the University of California at Berkeley, she had unusual resources to offer American psychology.

In her most enduring contribution, she collaborated with Nevitt Sanford, a Berkeley personality psychologist also adept in psychoanalysis, and Daniel Levinson, then their student, in major studies of the psychology of anti-Semitism. They found anti-Semitism to be an aspect of a general pattern of personality that included readiness to reject all out-groups (*ethnocentrism*) and personal orientations similar to those they regarded as underlying German susceptibility to Nazism. Publication of the resulting book, *The Authoritarian Personality* (Adorno, Frenkel-Brunswik, Levinson, & Sanford, New York, 1950) was a major event.

The work was widely acclaimed for bringing the clinical insights of psychoanalysis and the empirical methods of American social psychology to bear on prejudice and proto-fascist attitudes. It was criticized for overplaying the characterological roots of prejudice as compared with class-based or cultural sources, for ignoring left-wing authoritarianism, and for technical defects of the F scale, the quantitative measure of authoritarianism. Subsequent research has supported the authoritarian pattern of conventionality, submission to the strong, and readiness to act hostilely to the weak and socially marginal, though the psychoanalytically based conceptions shared by Frenkel-Brunswik and her colleagues have not fared as well.

In addition to her major part in *The Authoritarian Personality*, Frenkel-Brunswik conducted related research on prejudice in children, wrote on "intolerance of ambiguity" as a cognitive style of personality that emerged prominently in her studies of prejudice (see Heiman & Grant, 1974), and began a major study of ageing, when her life crumbled. The death of her husband by suicide after a long and painful struggle with severe hypertension coincided with profound midlife doubts about both psychoanalysis and logical positivism as pillars of her intellectual life. She died of an overdose of barbitol in her fiftieth year.

Bibliography

Heiman, N., & Grant, J. (Eds.). (1974). Else Frenkel-Brunswik, Selected papers. *Psychological Issues, 31.* Contains Frenkel-Brunswik's most important papers in English; also a biographical essay and an annotated bibliography of her publications in German and English.

Levinson, D. J. (1968). Else Frenkel-Brunswik. *International encyclopedia of the social sciences.*

Smith, M. B. (1980). Frenkel-Brunswik, Else. In B. Sicherman, & C. H. Green (Eds.), *Notable American women: The modern period.* Cambridge, MA: Belknap/Harvard University Press. Contains a rather full account of her life gained from correspondence with her sisters and early colleagues.

Stone, W. F., Lederer, G., & Christie, R. (1993). *Strength and weakness: The authoritarian personality today.* New York: Springer Verlag. A judicious review of the standing of authoritarian personality theory in the light of four decades of research and criticism since the Berkeley studies.

M. Brewster Smith

FREUD, ANNA (1895–1982), Austrian child psychoanalyst. Anna Freud, youngest daughter of Sigmund Freud, was born in Vienna, where she trained first as an elementary school teacher and then as a psychoanalyst, beginning analysis with her father in 1918 and becoming a member of the Vienna Psychoanalytic Society four years later. Henceforth she served as Sigmund Freud's representative in both scientific and administrative capacities, while at the same time making important contributions of her own to the psychoanalytic theory of child development and the technique of child analysis.

One of the first to use psychoanalytic methods in

the treatment of children, Freud began working with the children of her psychoanalytic colleagues and those of the American Dorothy Tiffany Burlingham, who was to become her lifelong friend and companion. In 1926 she gave a series of lectures to teachers and other analysts, which were published as *Introduction to the Technique of Child Analysis* ("Four Lectures on Child Analysis," in *The Writings of Anna Freud: Vol. 1, 1922–1935*, 1974) and which sparked a debate with her contemporary Melanie Klein, the British child analyst, about the proper technique for psychoanalyzing children. Anna Freud's method combined pedagogical experience with psychoanalytical insight, which yielded a cautious approach aimed at strengthening the child's ego, in contrast to Klein's more radical method of probing the child's unconscious phantasy life. For a period in the 1930s, Freud's child seminars were part of the basic training for nursery school teachers in Vienna.

Through the late 1920s and 1930s, as Sigmund Freud's health waned and he began to withdraw from executive positions, Anna Freud took over many important administrative posts. In addition to her duties as editorial assistant and translator for the Internationaler Psychoanalytischer Verlag, a psychoanalytic publishing house, she served as secretary of the International Psychoanalytical Association and, at the age of 26, was made chair of the Vienna Psychoanalytic Society, a position she held until the society was forced to disband in 1938 when Germany invaded Austria.

Her most well-known and important work, *The Ego and the Mechanisms of Defense* (*The Writings of Anna Freud, Vol. 2*, 1966), appeared in 1936 and remains a classic in the psychoanalytic literature. It is widely recognized as a pioneering work in the then new field of ego psychology, the branch of psychoanalysis built on Sigmund Freud's id–ego–superego structural model of the mind, which became the dominant school of psychoanalysis in America. Anna Freud's systematic analysis of the ego's functioning and the mechanisms it uses to defend against unacceptable aspects of the unconscious changed psychoanalysis forever from a technique of id analysis to a therapeutic method that emphasizes analyzing all the structures of the personality equally.

Upon the Nazi invasion of Austria the Freud family fled to London, England, where Anna Freud devotedly nursed her father until his death in 1939. As a new member of the British Psycho-Analytical Society's training committee she immediately became involved in the so-called Controversial Discussions—a scientific debate about the status of Klein's increasingly radical approach to psychoanalysis. Throughout the debate Freud insisted that only classical Freudian psychoanalytic theory and technique should be taught to candidates, and under her guidance the British society instituted two separate training programs for new analysts, one Freudian, the other Kleinian, both of which remain in place today.

Her work during the war years included the development of a new method of study in psychoanalysis, that is, direct observation of children, which she carried out at the Hampstead War Nurseries, set up in 1940 with the help of Dorothy Burlingham. This work is described in detail in *Infants without Families* and *Young Children in Wartime* (in *The Writings of Anna Freud, Vol. 3*, 1967). Soon after the nurseries closed in 1945 the Hampstead Child Therapy Course was instituted and the world-renowned Hampstead Child Therapy Clinic, renamed after her death the Anna Freud Centre for the Psychoanalytic Study and Treatment of Children, opened. Freud's research at the clinic led to the development of the Diagnostic Profile, an instrument for the developmental assessment of childhood disturbances, and the Hampstead Psychoanalytic Index, a method of categorizing psychoanalytic data to allow comparisons among individuals in treatment which enabled her to extrapolate general principles of theory from clinical therapeutic work. In this research, spanning several decades, her focus on normal development was unusual within psychoanalysis. From it she developed a theory of normal development, presented in her 1965 book *Normality and Pathology in Childhood* (*The Writings of Anna Freud, Vol. 6*), which provided a context within which to assess the relative normality or pathology of children at different ages.

In addition to theoretical and methodological contributions, Freud was also concerned with the practical application of psychoanalysis in various areas, including education and child welfare. Thus she often lectured to public audiences on topics as diverse as residential care, child rearing, pedagogy, child development, and family law. Most notably, her commitment to the rights of infants and children led to an invitation in 1961 from the dean of Yale Law School to join the faculty as senior fellow and visiting lecturer. At Yale she met and collaborated with Joseph Goldstein, Sterling Professor of Law, and Albert Solnit, director of the Yale Child Study Center, in producing three influential volumes on *The Best Interests of the Child* between 1973 and 1984; these were instrumental in formulating some of the fundamental social and legal rights of children in America. This socially important work was among Anna Freud's last as she suffered a stroke in the spring of 1982 and died later that year at the age of eighty-seven.

Anna Freud's contribution to psychoanalysis was, in Robert Wallerstein's (1984) characterization, as both a "radical innovator and staunch conservative." Innovative in her pioneering work in understanding both normal and abnormal child development and in the development of ego psychology, yet conservative in her adherence to the principles of Freudian orthodoxy, Anna Freud is a central figure in the history of the psychoanalytic movement.

Bibliography

Dyer, R. (1983). *Her father's daughter: The work of Anna Freud.* New York: Jason Aronson. Brief biography containing a bibliography of her work including shorter works not included in her *Writings.*

Freud, A. (1966–1980). *The writings of Anna Freud* (Vols. 1–8). New York: International Universities Press. Collection of her most important works with prefaces by Anna Freud.

Goldstein, J., Freud, A., & Solnit, A. J. (1973). *Beyond the best interests of the child.* New York: Free Press.

Goldstein, J., Freud, A., & Solnit, A. J. (1979). *Before the best interests of the child.* New York: Free Press.

Goldstein, J., Freud, A., Solnit, A. J., & Goldstein, S. (1984). *In the best interests of the child.* New York: Free Press.

Heller, P. (1990). *A child analysis with Anna Freud* (S. Burckhardt & M. Weigand, Trans.). Madison, CT: International Universities Press. Interesting memoir by a psychoanalyst of his own analysis with Anna Freud, which illuminates both her personality and her approach to child analysis.

King, P., & Steiner, R. (Eds.). (1991). *The Freud–Klein controversies 1941–45.* London: Routledge. Minutes of the British Psycho-Analytical Society meetings at which Anna Freud and Melanie Klein debated the future of psychoanalysis in England, including helpful editorial commentaries.

Sandler, J., & Freud, A. (1980). *The technique of child psychoanalysis: Discussions with Anna Freud.* Cambridge, MA: Harvard University Press.

Sandler, J., & Freud, A. (1985). *The analysis of defense: The ego and the mechanisms of defense revisited.* New York: International Universities Press. Transcripts of conversations with Anna Freud (1980, 1985) which offer a good introduction to her ideas.

Wallerstein, R. (1984). Anna Freud: Radical innovator and staunch conservative. *Psychoanalytic Study of the Child, 39,* 65–80.

Young-Bruehl, E. (1988). *Anna Freud: A biography.* New York: Simon & Schuster. Scholarly and objective biography of Anna Freud and her contribution to psychoanalysis which, unlike other biographies, draws on her unpublished letters and papers.

Gail Donaldson

FREUD, SIGMUND (1856–1937), Austrian physician and psychoanalyst. Born on 6 May 1856 in the Austro-Hungarian town of Freiburg (now Přibor, in the Czech Republic), Freud and his family moved to Vienna in 1860, where he remained until the final year of his life.

An outstanding secondary school student with particular interests in history and literature, he seemed headed for a career in law until a chance hearing of a lecture on nature turned his attention toward science and led him to enroll in the University of Vienna's medical school in 1873. There he studied under the "act psychologist" Franz Brentano (1838–1917) and even more consequentially under the physiologist Ernst Brücke (1819–1892). Brücke taught that all physiological processes, no matter how complex, had to be accounted for "mechanistically" in terms of ordinary physical laws. Freud worked in Brücke's laboratory for 6 years, publishing several papers and aiming at a career as a research physiologist. Only after becoming convinced that an academic research career would not be financially viable did he go to Vienna's General Hospital for clinical training to become a practicing physician.

There, under the tutelage of the psychiatrist and brain anatomist Theodore Meynert (1833–1893), Freud became adept at diagnosing organic brain disorders and earned Meynert's support for a 6-month fellowship to study in Paris with the eminent neurologist Jean Charcot (1825–1893). At that time Charcot was deep into the study of hysteria, a mysterious condition whose symptoms often resembled the effects of localized brain lesions but occurred in their absence. Dismissed as malingering by most physicians, hysteria was explained by Charcot as the result of a generalized weakness of the nervous system that also produced heightened susceptibility to hypnosis. Even though ultimately proved incorrect, Charcot's theories helped elevate the previously disreputable subjects of hysteria and hypnosis to scientific respectability—and first called them to Freud's attention.

Studies on Hysteria

After returning to Vienna, Freud established a practice in neuropathology and wrote well-regarded works on aphasia and cerebral palsy. He could not attract enough "ordinary" neurological patients to make a living, however, and somewhat reluctantly began to treat cases of hysteria. Casting about for an effective therapy for this poorly understood condition, Freud remembered a single case that had been described to him several years earlier by his older doctor friend, Josef Breuer (1842–1925). Together with his patient, a young woman named Bertha Pappenheim (1859–1936), Breuer improvised a "cathartic method." Under hypnosis, Bertha would recall previously forgotten but emotionally charged experiences related to the onset of her symptoms. Upon remembering them and expressing the previously pent-up emotions associated with them—a process Breuer and Freud later called "abreaction"—the symptoms disappeared.

Freud had moderate success when he tried the method on his own patients and persuaded Breuer to collaborate on a "Preliminary Communication" in 1893 and the book *Studies on Hysteria* in 1895. These works hypothesized that hysteria arises when memories for certain emotion-laden experiences become inaccessible to normal consciousness, and the affect associated with these "pathogenic ideas" becomes "strangulated." At moments when the ideas would normally become conscious, the affect discharges into the body's musculature and causes symptoms. Once brought to consciousness via hypnosis and divested of their affect by abreaction, the ideas also lost their pathogenicity.

At this point, Freud sought a nonhypnotic memory recovery technique that could be used with nonhypnotizable patients, as well as an understanding of why pathogenic ideas had become unconscious in the first place. Both problems seemed solved when he developed the technique of "free association" in which patients in the normal waking state were instructed to let their minds wander freely to any and all thoughts aroused by their symptoms, no matter how ridiculous seeming or anxiety arousing. Simple in principle, this procedure was difficult in practice because patients inevitably experienced "resistance"—a blocking, editing, or censoring of their thoughts that could be overcome only with difficulty. Freud became convinced that pathogenic ideas became unconscious because there was something fundamentally anxiety arousing about them, causing them to be actively repressed from consciousness. Unconsciously, patients seemingly preferred the pain of their symptom over the anxiety caused by thinking the thought. Symptoms therefore represented defenses against the conscious acknowledgment of the thought.

Dream Interpretation and Freud's Self-Analysis

While developing these ideas about hysteria, Freud attempted to integrate them with his knowledge of neurology in a draft manuscript that was published only posthumously under the English title, "Project for a Scientific Psychology." Besides presenting Freud's first systematic theory of how unconscious and instinctually driven processes presumably underlie most psychological activity, this work also considered the nature of dreams. It hypothesized that dreams should show certain structural properties in common with hysterical symptoms and further should represent the symbolic gratification of conflict-laden wishes. Freud put these hypotheses to a psychological test by subjecting the remembered, "manifest content" of dreams to free association.

When he did so, a previously unconscious "latent content" seemed to be revealed that stood in many of the same relationships to the manifest content that unconscious pathogenic ideas stood to hysterical symptoms. In both instances, the conscious products were psychologically "safer," that is, less anxiety arousing, than the original unconscious ideas that were recovered through free association. Further, individual symptoms and manifest dream images both seemed to symbolize several different unconscious ideas at once—a phenomenon Freud referred to as "overdetermination" in the case of symptoms and "condensation" in dreams.

When Freud experienced a personal crisis precipitated by the death of his father in 1896, he systematically free-associated to the manifest content of his own dreams in his famous self-analysis. As a result, he discerned within himself a consciously repugnant constellation of attitudes and impulses dating from childhood, which he called the "Oedipus complex." Apparently as a young child, he had wished for the exclusive possession of his mother as a source of sensual, "sexual" gratification, and for the removal or "death" of his father, whom he perceived as the main rival for that gratification.

This self-knowledge suggested a solution to a theoretical problem that had arisen in Freud's understanding and treatment of hysteria. Previously, he had been impressed by the regularity with which his patients' free associations had culminated in recollections of sexual abuse in childhood, usually at the hands of a parent. In 1896, he had publicly proposed a "seduction theory" of hysteria: namely, that childhood sexual abuse was a necessary precondition for the illness. But Freud soon developed doubts. Too often the uncovering of these "memories" failed to produce the expected symptom relief, and too often contrary evidence suggested they could not have been literally true.

Freud now speculated that the traces of childhood sexuality he detected in himself were universal, and that the traditional definition of "sexuality" itself should be revised. Instead of a highly specific, heterosexually oriented instinct to copulate and reproduce, "sexuality" should be thought of as a highly general drive for sensual gratification of many different kinds, present in everyone from infancy onward. Born in a state of "polymorphous perversity," a child typically passes through stages in which the mouth, the anus, and then finally the genital regions become singled out as major sources of gratification. By the age of 5 or 6, many of these pleasures arouse condemnation, and thus anxiety, and become repressed. They do not disappear, however, but remain in the unconscious waiting for opportunities to be expressed indirectly. Thus hysterical pathogenic ideas, like the disturbing latent content of many dreams, were interpretable as representations of repressed childhood impulses and wishes rather than actual experiences.

Freud's Major Works and the Psychoanalytic Movement

With his increasing sense of the pervasiveness of unconscious and sexual motivation and with free association available as a technique for revealing it, Freud turned his attention to other phenomena such as jokes and mistakes. He concluded that these psychic creations are not random, but like symptoms or dreams they express "by allusion" wishful ideas that are too dangerous or embarrassing to be directly stated. By 1905, Freud had published the foundational ideas of a new discipline he called "psychoanalysis," in four major works. *The Interpretation of Dreams* (1900)—which Freud always considered his most important work—not only detailed his dream theory per se but also closed with a theoretical chapter presenting a general model of the psyche, an updated successor to the "Project for a Scientific Psychology." In 1901, he introduced the notion of *parapraxes* or "Freudian slips" in *The Psychopathology of Everyday Life*. In 1905, he published his analysis of humor and wit in *Jokes and Their Relationship to the Unconscious* and his broadened and revolutionary theory of the sexual drive in *Three Essays on the Theory of Sexuality*.

Gradually following publication of these works, Freud began to attract a small following—first from fellow Viennese such as Alfred Adler (1870–1937) and Otto Rank (1884–1939), and later including Karl Abraham (1877–1925) from Berlin, Sandor Ferenczi (1873–1933) from Budapest, and Carl Jung (1875–1961) from Zurich. In April 1908, 40 individuals from five countries gathered to hold the first International Congress of Psychoanalysis in Salzburg, Austria. The following year, at the invitation of the American psychologist G. Stanley Hall (1844–1924), Freud delivered a well-publicized series of lectures about his theories at Clark University in Worcester, Massachusetts. Published in 1910 as *The Origin and Development of Psychoanalysis*, these engaging lectures effectively introduced Freud to the English-speaking world.

Psychoanalysis was now a movement, and Freud the leader of an international organization. Even as some early followers like Jung and Adler soon broke to form rival psychodynamic schools of their own, many more individuals became self-identified "Freudians" and members of the International Psycho-Analytical Association. These followers now became the intended audience for most of Freud's writing, which inevitably became increasingly technical and specialized. In a series of papers on metapsychology in the mid-1910s, Freud explored the fine points of repression and the unconscious. Several other papers from that period presented technical details for conducting psychoanalytic therapy. In *Beyond the Pleasure Principle* (1920), Freud posited an ultimately destructive "death instinct" (Thanatos) in perpetual conflict with a sexually oriented "life instinct" (Eros). In 1923, concern over some technicalities in psychoanalytic terminology stimulated Freud to write *The Ego and the Id*, where he introduced the now famous terms "id," "superego," and "ego" to represent, respectively, the psyche's repository for instinctual demands, the internalized demands of conscience, and the executive agency that attempts to produce compromise responses to conflicting psychic demands.

One of Freud's most controversial technical papers, "Some Psychical Consequences of the Anatomical Distinction between the Sexes" (1925), hypothesized that little boys typically experience "castration anxiety" while little girls feel "penis envy"—a difference that presumably produces stronger and more inflexible superegos in males. Freud presented this view only tentatively and accepted his colleagues' dissent from it with equanimity. He personally welcomed women as professionals in the psychoanalytic movement, including his daughter Anna Freud (1895–1982), who became a distinguished child analyst and theoretician of the "ego defense mechanisms." Yet perhaps understandably, Freud acquired a public reputation of being unfriendly to women following publication of this paper.

In 1923, Freud was diagnosed with mouth cancer and began to undergo a long series of painful and disfiguring operations. The tone of his writing during this period became increasingly philosophical and pessimistic. *The Future of an Illusion* (1927) interpreted all religious beliefs as wishful illusions based on childhood dependency, and *Civilization and Its Discontents* (1930) speculated that the destructive aspects of Thanatos are likely to prevail in the long run over the positive and creative urges of Eros. And in a 1937 paper titled "Analysis Terminable and Interminable," Freud concluded that no therapeutic psychoanalysis can ever be said to be "complete" in any ultimate sense.

In 1938, the Nazi occupation of Vienna led the Jewish Freud to flee to London for sanctuary. A year later at the age of 83, and just before the horrors of World War II seemed to justify his philosophical pessimism, he succumbed to his long illness. Freud's ideas were highly controversial during his lifetime and have remained so up to the present (the following bibliography will highlight some of the major issues involved). Yet despite all the controversy, Freud's basic image of human beings as creatures caught in perpetual conflict between irreconcilable demands from the external world and their inner biology struck a responsive chord. His fundamental concepts of repression and the unconscious nature of much psychological activity have become commonplace. By the end of his life, Freud had become not just an important historical character but in the words of W. H. Auden, "a whole climate of opinion/ Under whom we conduct our differing lives."

Bibliography

Works by Freud

Strachey, J. (Ed.). (1953–1974). *The standard edition of the complete psychological works of Sigmund Freud.* 24 vols. London: Hogarth Press. A uniform English translation of all of Freud's psychological works, each preceded by an invaluable editor's introduction describing the circumstances under which it was written and referring the reader to other works in which Freud dealt with the same topics. Paperback versions of most of Freud's major works, based on this edition, are widely available.

Works about Freud

Crews, F. (Ed.) (1998). *Unauthorized Freud: Doubters confront a legend.* New York: Viking. A collection of articles highly critical of Freud and his theory.

Fancher, R. E. (1973). *Psychoanalytic psychology: The development of Freud's thought.* New York: Norton. Explicates Freud's major works, in the order in which they were written.

Gay, P. (1988). *Freud: A life for our time.* New York: Norton. A sympathetic but comprehensive biography, covering much of the extensive secondary literature on Freud.

Grünbaum, A. (1984). *The foundations of psychoanalysis: A philosophical critique.* Berkeley and Los Angeles, CA: University of California Press. A philosopher criticizes the epistemological bases of Freud's theories.

Holt, R. R. (1989). *Freud reappraised: A fresh look at psychoanalytic theory.* New York: Guilford Press. Sympathetically critical essays about the status and future of Freudian theory.

Masson, J. M. (1983). *The assault on truth: Freud's suppression of the seduction theory.* New York: Farrar, Straus and Giroux. Provocatively argues that Freud abandoned his seduction theory to appease his critics not because of negative evidence.

Ornston, D. G. Jr. (1992). *Translating Freud.* New Haven, CT: Yale University Press. Insightful analysis of the issues involved in translating Freud's works from the German.

Robinson, P. (1993). *Freud and his critics.* Berkeley and Los Angeles, CA: University of California Press. Defends Freud against his critics, particularly Grünbaum, Masson, and Sulloway.

Sulloway, F. (1992). *Freud: Biologist of the mind.* Cambridge, MA: Harvard University Press. Unsympathetically portrays Freud as a mythmaker and extensively documents the biological underpinnings of his theories.

Raymond E. Fancher

FRIENDSHIP. Friendships are a primary source of meaning, happiness, and joy in people's lives. When young adults are asked to generate types of love, friendship is listed most frequently. Moreover, friendship love is seen as capturing the meaning of love—more so than other kinds of love, including romantic love. The importance of friendship is underscored in research by Berscheid, Synder, and Omoto, who asked nearly 250 unmarried undergraduates to identify their "closest, deepest, most involved, and most intimate" relationship (1989). Nearly half (47%) named a romantic partner and 36% named a friend. Only 14% of the respondents named family members.

Although marital and family relationships assume greater prominence in the lives of older adults, friendships retain their significance. For example, in one large-scale study, friends comprised 58% of adults' social networks. Moreover, friends are more likely than kin to be turned to for companionship (Fischer, 1982). Perhaps even more striking are the findings from research on people's daily interactions. Larsen and Bradney found that when teenagers, adults, and retirees were paged at random times, participants of all ages reported higher levels of enjoyment and excitement when they were with friends compared to being alone or with family members (1988). For married adults, time spent with friends was associated with greater happiness than time spent with one's spouse. The greatest amount of happiness was experienced when in the presence of both friends and spouse. Thus, research findings from different traditions using different methodologies converge on a common theme: Friendships occupy a central role in people's lives.

Conceptions of Friendship

There is no single, agreed-upon definition of friendship. As Allan noted:

> "Friend" is not just a categorical label, like "colleague" or "cousin," indicating the social position of each individual relative to the other. Rather it is a relational term which signifies something about the quality and character of the relationship involved. (1989, p. 16)

Different scholars emphasize different qualities or properties of friendships. However, there are at least some commonalities in how both social scientists and laypeople conceptualize friendship.

Experts' Definitions. Friendship is often described as the most voluntary relationship. Friendship is unique in that it is an intimate relationship that operates without social or contractual regulation. Because the voluntariness of friendship sets it apart from other kinds of relationships, it is not surprising that this feature is emphasized in many definitions (e.g., Hays, 1988; Rawlins, 1992). For example, Hartup defined friends as "people who spontaneously seek the company of one another; furthermore, they seek proximity in the absence of strong social pressures to do so" (1975, p. 11).

Friendship also is frequently defined in terms of its relational qualities or attributes. Features such as trust, intimacy, loyalty, affection, and support are central to many social scientists' conceptions of friendship (e.g.,

Hays, 1988; La Gaipa, 1977). Features that are less common, but nevertheless included in some definitions, are equality, conflict, authenticity, and stability. While there is not perfect consensus, social scientists generally conceptualize friendship as as a personal, voluntary relationship characterized by intimacy, trust, loyalty, and enjoyment of one another's company.

Laypeople's Definitions. When young children are asked, What is a friend? their responses reflect a rather concrete conception of friendship. For example, children tend to mention the friend's physical features (e.g., "She has red hair") or possessions ("He has a nice tricycle"), in addition to defining a friend as someone they like or someone who is nice (see Fehr, 1996, for a review). As children develop, their conceptions of friendship become more abstract and relational. By late adolescence, friendship is defined in terms of qualities such as loyalty and intimacy. These continue to be central to lay conceptions of friendship throughout adulthood, along with attributes such as trust, caring, and support (e.g., Weiss & Lowenthal, 1975). For example, Sapadin asked professionals in three major U.S. cities to complete the sentence: "A friend is someone . . ." (1988). The most frequent responses were: with whom you are intimate; you can trust; you can depend on; with whom you share things; who accepts you; with whom you have a caring relationship; with whom you are close; and, you enjoy. Parallel findings have been observed in other cultures (e.g., Great Britain). Thus, there is considerable overlap in the kinds of features of friendship identified by both laypeople and experts— both regard relational features such as intimacy, loyalty, trust, and enjoyment of one another's company, and the provision of help and support as central to the concept.

Development of the Construct

Generally, friendship has received less attention in psychological literature than other relationships such as romantic or familial relationships. However, research cited earlier, demonstrating the importance of friendship in people's lives, has prompted increased attention to this relationship. Much of this work has been conducted in the context of discovery rather than justification. Thus, there is by now a considerable body of research describing the development and deterioration of friendship, age and gender differences in friendships, effects of life events on friendships, and so on. Much less attention has been devoted to theoretical development. When theory-based research on friendships is conducted, scholars generally draw on existing theories of attraction or theories of relationships in general.

Theories of Friendship. Four major theories can be, or have been, applied to the study of friendships: reinforcement, cognitive consistency, social exchange and equity, and developmental.

Reinforcement Theories. The application of reinforcement principles to the study of attraction was spearheaded by Byrne and Clore (1970) and Lott and Lott (1974). These theorists embraced principles of operant conditioning and predicted that we are attracted to people who provide us with rewards. Byrne and Clore assumed that it is reinforcing to learn that others agree with us. They found that if people were led to believe that a stranger held attitudes similar to their own, they reported greater attraction to that person than if they believed that their attitudes were dissimilar (see Byrne, 1971, for a review of these studies). Both pairs of theorists also adopted principles of classical conditioning and predicted that we will be attracted to people who are merely associated with our experience of receiving rewards. To test this idea, Lott and Lott had children play a game in three-person groups (1961). Some received a reward (a candy) while playing the game; others did not. Later, when asked who they would like to accompany them on a family vacation, children who had been previously rewarded were more likely to name their fellow group members than children who had not received a reward.

Social Exchange and Equity Theories. A basic premise of exchange theories is that for people to be satisfied in a relationship, the rewards must outweigh the costs. John Thibaut and Harold Kelley (1959) posited that we evaluate the reward/cost ratio in a relationship by comparing it to reward/cost ratios (outcomes) in other relationships (referred to as the comparison level) as well as to the outcomes we believe we could obtain in alternative relationships (comparison level for alternatives). The theory predicts that we will be satisfied in a relationship to the extent that outcomes exceed our comparison level. Commitment to the relationship is determined by the availability of alternatives; we will remain in a relationship if we do not believe a more attractive alternative is available to us. In an extension of this theory, Rusbult (1980) posited that commitment to a relationship also is determined by the size of our investments in the relationship (e.g., time, money, and emotional energy)—the greater the investments, the greater the commitment.

Equity theory (Walster, Walster, & Berscheid, 1978) also assumes that we seek to maxmize rewards and minimize costs in our relationships. However, rather than compare our outcomes to those obtained in other relationships (or what we might obtain in future relationships), equity theory posits that the critical comparison is with our partner's outcomes. According to this theory, if we believe that our reward/cost ratio is comparable to that of our partner, the relationship is equitable and we will be satisfied. Inequitable relationships are those in which we believe our partner's outcomes are superior to ours (in which case we will feel underbenefited and angry) or that our outcomes are superior to those of our partner (in which case we will feel overbenefited and guilty).

Of all these theories, Rusbult's investment model has been applied most often to friendships. In one study (Rusbult, 1980), participants were asked to assess the rewards (e.g., quality of time together and sense of humor) and costs (e.g., conflicts and friend's annoying habits) in a current friendship. They also were asked to estimate the availability of alternative friendships and their extent of investments in the friendship (e.g., shared memories and amount of time spent together). Consistent with the theory, the more that rewards exceeded costs in the friendship, the greater the satisfaction. Furthermore, commitment to the friendship was predicted by high satisfaction, low availability of alternatives, and high investments.

Cognitive Consistency Theories.
The basic assumption underlying cognitive consistency theories is that people need balance or consistency in their lives (Heider, 1958; Newcomb, 1961). These theories generally focus on the relationship between a perceiver, another person, and an object. A balanced state is said to exist if all possible relations are positive or if two are negative and one is positive. Thus, if two people discover that they hold positive attitudes toward some object (or person), in order to achieve balance they should also like each other. They also should like each other if they discover they both hold negative attitudes toward some object (or person). (Apparently, after meeting a woman, English clergyman Sydney Smith exclaimed, "Madam, I have been looking for a person who disliked gravy all my life; let us swear eternal friendship"!) When relations are unbalanced, people will feel strain and pressure to restore balance by changing either their attitudes toward the other person, or toward the object in question.

In a classic study, Newcomb invited students who were new to the University of Michigan to live in a shared house (1961). Their attitudes and liking for the other students in the house were assessed repeatedly throughout the year. Consistent with his theory, Newcomb found that students were most likely to form friendships with housemates with whose attitudes were similar to theirs and who liked the same people they did.

Developmental Theories.
Developmental theories seek to understand and explain changes in relationships over time. Levinger's ABCDE theory of relationship development is probably most relevant to friendships (Levinger, 1983). According to this theory, relationships begin at the acquaintanceship stage, in which two people become aware of and form positive impressions of each other. In the second stage, buildup, the relationship becomes close through a process of mutual self-disclosure that increases in breadth and depth. Discovering areas of similarity and compatibility

are important at this stage. The next stage, continuation, represents the development of commitment to the relationship. Relationships may remain at this stage. However, external events (e.g., one person moving away) or internal events (e.g., betrayal of trust) can contribute to the deterioration of the relationship. If attempts to repair the relationship are not made, or if repair attempts are unsuccessful, the relationship is likely to enter the final ending stage. To date, the adequacy of this theory as a model of friendship development has not been tested empirically. However, research relevant to each individual stage has been conducted (see Fehr, 1996, for a review).

Formation of Friendships.
The process by which people develop friendships has received considerable research attention. Research suggests that in order for a friendship to develop, four sets of factors must converge: environmental, individual, situational, and dyadic (1996).

Environmental Factors.
A necessary condition for the development of a friendship is that two individuals come into contact with one another. Generally, this contact occurs as people's paths cross in the course of a day (although recently there is evidence of friendship formation through electronic mail or computer networks). For example, people are likely to become friends with those who live close to them. The greater the proximity, the greater the likelihood of friendship formation. In a classic study, Festinger, Schachter and Back asked residents of a student housing complex with whom they socialized (1950). The person most likely to be named lived next door, followed by the person who lived two doors down, and so on. People who lived on different floors were much less likely to become friends than those who lived on the same floor—even when the distance between them was the same. The workplace and school settings also are conducive to the formation of friendships. Finally, when people are asked the sources of their friendships, they frequently mention "other friends and relatives." Thus, social networks play an important role in friendship formation as well.

Individual Factors.
Environmental factors bring us into contact with potential friends. However, we do not cultivate a friendship with every person we meet. Certain qualities in people make it more likely that we will want to pursue a friendship. Research has focused on four individual-level factors that are associated with friendship formation: physical attractiveness, social skills, responsiveness, and similarity. There is evidence that we are more likely to pursue a friendship with someone who is physically attractive rather than unattractive. We also are more likely to form a friendship with someone who is socially skilled—someone who responds to what we are saying, displays appropriate sequencing of gaze or posture, and follows conversational turn-taking norms. Failure to perform such behaviors

can undermine the formation of a friendship. Research also shows that we are attracted to potential friends who are responsive to us by showing interest and concern. For example, individuals who do not answer the other person's questions or give replies that are unrelated are liked less than individuals who are responsive. People who are shy tend to show social skills deficits and failures of responsiveness, which may account for the difficulty they experience in forming friendships.

Finally, probably the most important factor in friendship formation is similarity. There is a large body of research showing that we are likely to form friendships with those who are similar to us in a variety of domains, including demographic characteristics (e.g., age, physical health, education, physical attractiveness, and social status), attitudes, values, communication skills, leisure activity preferences, hobbies, and so on (see Fehr, 1996, for a review).

Situational Factors. Whether or not we form friendships also depends on situational factors. One such factor is the probability of future interaction. People report greater liking for those with whom they anticipate ongoing interactions. In addition, research on the mere exposure effect has shown that the more frequently we see someone, the greater our attraction to that person. Perhaps the most important situational factor that influences the formation of friendships is availability. Even if we are attracted to someone, we may not develop a friendship with them because of other commitments in our lives (e.g., work, romantic partner, family, and existing friendships). These commitments may sap our resources, leaving little time or energy for cultivating new relationships.

Dyadic Factors. The nature of the interaction between potential friends also determines whether or not a relationship will be formed. One important dyadic-level process is reciprocity of liking. In a classic experiment, Backman and Secord led members of a group to believe that they were either liked or disliked by other group members (1959). Participants showed the greatest liking for the group members whom they believed liked them. Self-disclosure is another important dyadic factor that determines whether a friendship will develop. According to social penetration theory (Altman & Taylor, 1973), when we first meet someone we begin by self-disclosing at a superficial level. In order for a relationship to develop, each person must increase the intimacy of their self-disclosures, both in terms of breadth (discussing a wide variety of topics) and depth (discussion of more personal topics). Furthermore, this process must be gradual and reciprocal. Revealing too much too soon can create discomfort and result in disliking. In addition, if only one person is revealing personal information, it is unlikely that a relationship will form.

In conclusion, environmental, individual, situational, and dyadic factors must converge in order for a friendship to develop. Environmental factors bring us into contact with potential friends. We will be more likely to pursue a relationship with a friendship candidate if the person is attractive, socially skilled, responsive, and, most important, similar to us in a variety of ways. The formation of a friendship also depends on situational factors such as whether we are likely to see this person on a frequent basis and whether we have sufficient time and energy to invest in a new friendship. Finally, we are more likely to develop a friendship if we believe the other person likes us and if our self-disclosures are mutual and increasingly more intimate.

Measurement Issues

The major measurement issue in the study of friendship is that most standard relationship scales were devised for romantic or marital relationships, not friendships (e.g., scales to assess love, satisfaction, and conflict). As a result, friendship researchers generally resort to constructing their own measures, tailored to their specific interests. The psychometric properties of these scales are frequently unknown, thereby limiting their usefulness to other researchers. There are some exceptions, however. Rusbult successfully adapted her investment model measures (i.e., questions about rewards, costs, alternatives, and investments) for use with friendships (1980). La Gaipa (1977) developed the Friendship Inventory, in which participants rate their friendships in terms of qualities such as self-disclosure, helping, similarity, strength of character, and so on. Wright constructed a scale, the Acquaintance Description Form (1985), which consists of seven subscales (stimulation value, utility value, maintenance difficulty, ego support value, self-affirmation value, voluntary interdependence, and person-qua-person) as well as a subscale that assesses general favorability toward a friend. Thus, there are currently a few validated friendship scales. However, friendship researchers are asking such a wide range of questions that it is unlikely that three or four scales will be sufficient to answer them.

In conclusion, there is a considerable body of research on friendships, despite insufficiences in theoretical development and measurement instruments. This research has demonstrated the significance of friendships in people's lives and elucidated the processes by which people form these important relationships.

[*See also* Attachment; Intimacy; *and* Love.]

Bibliography

Allan, G. (1989). *Friendship: Developing a sociological perspective.* London: Harvester Wheatsheaf.

Altman, I., & Taylor, D. A. (1973). *Social penetration: The development of interpersonal relationships.* New York: Holt, Rinehart & Winston.

Backman, C. W., & Secord, P. F. (1959). The effect of perceived liking on interpersonal attraction. *Human Relations, 12,* 379–383.

Berscheid, E., Snyder, M., & Omoto, A. M. (1989). Issues in studying close relationships: Conceptualizing and measuring closeness. In C. Hendrick (Ed.), *Review of personality and social psychology: Vol. 10. Close relationships* (pp. 63–91). Newbury Park, CA: Sage.

Byrne, D. (1971). *The attraction paradigm.* New York: Academic Press.

Byrne, D., & Clore, G. L. (1970). A reinforcement model of evaluative responses. *Personality: An International Journal, 1,* 103–128.

Crawford, M. (1977). What is a friend? *New Society, 20,* 116–117.

Fehr, B. (1996). *Friendship processes.* Thousand Oaks, CA: Sage.

Fischer, C. S. (1982). *To dwell among friends: Personal networks in town and city.* Chicago: University of Chicago Press.

Hartup, W. W. (1975). The origins of friendships. In M. Lewis & L. A. Rosenblum (Eds.), *Friendship and peer relations* (pp. 11–26). New York: Wiley.

Hays, R. B. (1988). Friendship. In S. W. Duck (Ed.), *Handbook of personal relationships: Theory, research, and interventions* (pp. 391–408). New York: Wiley.

Heider, F. (1958). *The psychology of interpersonal relations.* New York: Wiley.

La Gaipa, J. J. (1977). Testing a multidimensional approach to friendship. In S. Duck (Ed.), *Theory and practice in interpersonal attraction* (pp. 249–270). London: Academic Press.

Larson, R. W., & Bradney, N. (1988). Precious moments with family members and friends. In R. M. Milardo (Ed.), *Families and social networks* (pp. 107–126). Newbury Park, CA: Sage.

Levinger, G. (1983). Development and change. In H. H. Kelley, E. Berscheid, A. Christensen, J. H. Harvey, T. L. Huston, G. Levinger, E. McClintock, L. A. Peplau, & D. R. Peterson (Eds.), *Close relationships* (pp. 315–359). New York: Freeman.

Lott, A. J., & Lott, B. E. (1961). Group cohesiveness, communication level, and conformity. *Journal of Abnormal and Social Psychology, 62,* 408–412.

Lott, A. J., & Lott, B. E. (1974). The role of reward in the formulation of positive interpersonal attitudes. In T. L. Huston (Ed.), *Foundations of interpersonal attraction* (pp. 171–192). New York: Academic Press.

Newcomb, T. M. (1961). *The acquaintance process.* New York: Holt, Rinehart & Winston.

Rawlins, W. K. (1992). *Friendship matters.* Hawthorne, NY: Aldine de Gruyter Press.

Rusbult, C. E. (1980). Satisfaction and commitment in friendships. *Representative Research in Social Psychology, 11,* 96–105.

Sapadin, L. A. (1988). Friendship and gender: Perspectives of professional men and women. *Journal of Social and Personal Relationships, 5,* 387–403.

Thibaut, J. W., & Kelley, H. H. (1959). *The social psychology of groups.* New York: Wiley.

Walster, E., Walster, G. W., & Berscheid, E. (1978). *Equity: Theory and research.* Boston: Allyn & Bacon.

Weiss, L., & Lowenthal, M. F. (1975). Life course perspectives on friendship. In M. F. Lowenthal, M. Turner, & D. Chiriboga & Associates (Eds.), *Four stages of life* (pp. 48–61). San Francisco: Jossey-Bass.

Wright, P. H. (1985). The acquaintance description form. In S. Duck & D. Perlman (Eds.), *Understanding personal relationships: An interdisciplinary approach* (pp. 39–62). London: Sage.

Beverley Fehr

FROMM, ERICH (1900–1980), German psychologist. Fromm was born in 1900 in Frankfurt am Main, Germany. He received a doctorate from the University of Heidelberg in 1922, after which he received training in psychoanalysis in Munich and Berlin. In 1933, he came to the United States as a lecturer at the Chicago Psychoanalytic Institute and subsequently entered private practice in New York City. Still later in his career, he taught at a number of American universities and institutes before leaving to head the Mexican Psychoanalytic Institute in Mexico City.

In addition to being of interest to psychologists and psychiatrists, Fromm's books have been widely read by philosophers, sociologists, theologians, economists, and political scientists. Many of his books were also widely read by members of the lay public because the almost journalistic style of his writing easily communicated to such readers insights into their personal behavior as well as the threat of authoritarianism to democratic society. Fromm's preoccupation with such authoritarianism was not surprising because many intellectuals who escaped Nazi Germany, especially those who were Jewish, sought to understand how such a destructive dictatorship could emerge within a population of rational and civilized human beings as were the Germans. To the researcher in psychology, Fromm's analyses of the roots of authoritarianism helped generate the classic line of social psychological research of the University of California Group, which postulated the dynamics and behavior of the authoritarian personality as reflected in the 1950 volume *The Authoritarian Personality.*

The roots of Fromm's thinking appear to be many faceted. He has often been described as a psychoanalyst with a neo-Freudian bent, which emphasizes the effects of the cultural context in which the individual lives. However, Fromm accepted many aspects of Freudian theory such as the significance of dream interpretation, which he described as "the forgotten language." He was also influenced by the writings of Karl Marx, particularly Marx's contention that a hierarchy of socioeconomic classes can threaten individual freedom.

Within this context of social determinism tempered by Marxist economic determinism, Fromm's work also reflects a strong spiritual component, which he felt should be integrated within the ultimate self-determinism of the individual. This spiritual component of Fromm's work is reflected in his frequent biblical references and his interest in the work of the theologian Martin Buber. Thus, Fromm believed that the existential question the individual faces should be resolved in a true and free individualism that is essentially humanistic in its focus. In fact, this mixture of direction in his thinking might lead one to define Erich Fromm as a humanistic socio-psychoanalyst.

Among Fromm's concepts that reflect his humanistic socio-psychoanalytical perspectives were his character orientations—productive and nonproductive. Among his nonproductive orientations was being exploitative of the contributions of others rather than creating one's own. Another nonproductive orientation was marketing one's self in the sense of shaping the self to what is necessary for self promotion rather than maintaining a personal authenticity. A key to Fromm's differences with Freud and the orthodox psychoanalysts was the belief that orientations such as the marketing character were not derived from the development of the libido but rather from the character of an individual's parents. He described this as a "social character," specific to every society. Fromm also felt that Freud was too preoccupied with "pregenital" characteristics, essentially narcissistic and nonproductive. Freud had not sufficiently developed the concept of the genital character, which to Fromm was the ultimately mature, productive character capable of maintaining independent creativity yet functioning well within society.

Fromm's distinction between self-love and love of self expressed his humanistic ideology. Self-love to Fromm was a reflection of an immature narcissism. Love of self was a mature, secure self-appreciation of one's independence, self-efficaciousness, and humanistically tempered individuality.

With respect to his concern with the threat of authoritarianism, he articulated various mechanisms of "escape from freedom," such as the individual being willing to function as an automaton in society, being comfortable in an authoritarian submissive role. In fact, Fromm agreed with David Riesman's conception of the "other-directed" individual, which Fromm described as being "alienated." Fromm's therapy also reflected this theme. He treated his patients in terms of encouraging them not to "escape from freedom" but to be self-efficacious and resist the "pseudo-security"

of being overly reactive to the conformist pressures from society.

In spite of his preoccupation with the threats of authoritarianism to human individuality and freedom, most of Fromm's writing reveals an optimistic view that society can overcome the threats of authoritarianism within society and ultimate destruction by nuclear war.

Erich Fromm's books that best reflect his psychological, philosophical, and political perspective include *Escape from Freedom*, *May Man Prevail?*, *The Art of Loving*, and *Man for Himself*.

Bibliography

Evans, R. I. (1981). *Dialogue with Erich Fromm*. New York, NY: Praeger.

Fromm, E. (1941). *Escape from freedom*. New York: Farrar & Rinehart.

Fromm, E. (1947). *Man for himself*. New York: Rinehart.

Fromm, E. (1956). *The art of loving*. New York: Harper & Brothers.

Fromm, E. (1961). *May man prevail?* Garden City, NY: Doubleday.

Richard I. Evans

FROMM-REICHMANN, FRIEDA (1889–1957), psychiatrist. The eldest of three daughters in an Orthodox Jewish family, Reichmann was born in Karlsruhe, Germany on 23 October 1889. Her parents were both from solidly middle-class backgrounds, and she grew up in a warmly supportive household in which she was clearly the favored child. During medical school at the University of Königsberg (where she was one of the first women students), her unusual aptitude for psychiatry was quickly recognized, as she spent hours sitting at the bedsides of psychotic patients, convinced that there was meaning in what they said.

From 1916 to 1918, she served as the unofficial head of a 100-bed military hospital, set up to treat the unprecedented number of brain injuries resulting from trench warfare. A subsequent two years working with Kurt Goldstein's neurological institute in Frankfurt decisively shaped her approach. Emphasizing capacities that remained intact, even after severe injury, she learned to look beyond symptoms to patients' inherent resilience and desire to heal.

After 4 years at a clinic near Dresden where she worked as a psychotherapist with I. H. Schultz, she undertook training at the Berlin Psychoanalytic Institute and then opened her own sanitarium in Heidelberg, seeking to create a utopian community combining psychoanalysis and Orthodox Judaism. During this period, she was briefly married to Erich Fromm, a sociologist 10 years her junior, whom she inspired to become an analyst. Deeply influenced by her friend Georg Groddeck to believe that no patient was ever beyond hope and technique was only a means to an end, she began adapting psychoanalyses to treat disorders (e.g., psychosis, psychosomatic illness) traditionally considered to be outside the scope of the method.

In early 1933, shortly after Hitler's rise to power, she slipped across the border to Strasbourg, pretending to be on a weekend trip, and 2 years later emigrated to the United States. After several months in New York with Fromm (from whom she had previously separated), she moved in June 1935 to Rockville, Maryland, to join the staff of Chestnut Lodge. She lived and worked at the lodge for the rest of her life, training a generation of younger psychiatrists in her methods, and working with her friend and colleague Harry Stack Sullivan to make the institution one of the few places in the world committed to treating psychosis psychoanalytically.

Trusting her intuitions and the patient's own inherent capacities for healing, Fromm-Reichmann evolved a unique clinical style that relied on the therapeutic relationship as the fulcrum for change. Rejecting Freud's claim that psychotics were "unanalyzable," she insisted that errors in the therapist's approach were what made treatment with such patients unsuccessful. In striking contrast to classical analysts, she encouraged colleagues to admit their misunderstandings to validate their patients' often accurate perception of what had happened, and to scrutinize the countertransference reactions that interfered with their own ability to provide the empathy patients deserved.

A popular teacher and supervisor, Fromm-Reichmann was elected president of the Washington-Baltimore Psychoanalytic Society from 1939–1941, was the recipient of the Adolf Meyer Award of the American Psychiatric Association in 1952, was the association's Academic Lecturer in 1954, and was the first woman selected as a Fellow of the Center for Advanced Study in the Behavioral Sciences at Stanford. She died suddenly of an acute coronary thrombosis on 28 April 1957, and was later memorialized to millions as "Dr. Fried" in *I Never Promised You a Rose Garden* (New York, 1964), a slightly fictionalized account of her most successful case, written by patient Joanne Greenberg.

Bibliography

Bullard, D. M. (Ed.). (1959). *Psychoanalysis and psychotherapy: Selected papers of Frieda Fromm-Reichmann*. Chicago: University of Chicago Press.

Fromm-Reichmann, F. (1950). *Principles of intensive psychotherapy*. Chicago: University of Chicago Press.

Silver, A-L. S. (Ed.). (1989). *Psychoanalysis and psychosis*. Madison, CT: International Universities Press.

Gail A. Hornstein

FRONTAL LOBE DISORDERS. The frontal lobes, situated anterior to the Rolandic (central) sulcus and superior to the Sylvian fissure, comprise an enormous expanse of the brain, forming roughly half of the entire cerebral mantle. In humans in particular, this region has expanded disproportionately. Traditionally, the frontal lobes have been subdivided into motor, premotor, prefrontal, and limbic sectors, and the focus here will be on the latter two of these subdivisions. The prefrontal region comprises most of the frontal lobes anterior to the motor/premotor region, and the limbic component comprises the anterior cingulate and posterior orbital sectors. The prefrontal region can be further subdivided into the dorsolateral, mesial, and orbital sectors.

The most common causes of damage to the prefrontal region are stroke, head injury, tumors (and their surgical treatment), and progressive degenerative diseases (e.g., Alzheimer's, Pick's). Many of the victims are relatively young, especially those with head injuries, and this means that many patients may face decades of survival with their condition. Obviously, the rehabilitation and management challenges posed by such patients are enormous. Further complicating the rehabilitation of patients with frontal lobe injuries is their striking tendency to be unaware of, or to vastly underestimate the severity of, their acquired impairments in reasoning, judgment, decision-making, and other cognitive functions. In recent years, though, some effective neuropsychological treatment programs have been developed (Anderson, 1996).

The Frontal Lobes and Personality

Throughout the history of neuropsychology, dating back some 150 years, the psychological capacities associated with the prefrontal region have remained enigmatic and elusive. However, the special significance of this region, particularly the portion formed by the orbital and lower mesial sectors ("ventromedial"), has long been linked to the idea that it provides the neural substrate for a collection of higher-order capacities such as planning, reasoning, decision-making, self-awareness, empathy, and emotional modulation (Benton, 1991). Some authors have gone so far as to consider the ventromedial prefrontal region the neural basis for personality. This notion gained scientific credibility following the description of the now famous "crowbar case" (Bigelow, 1850).

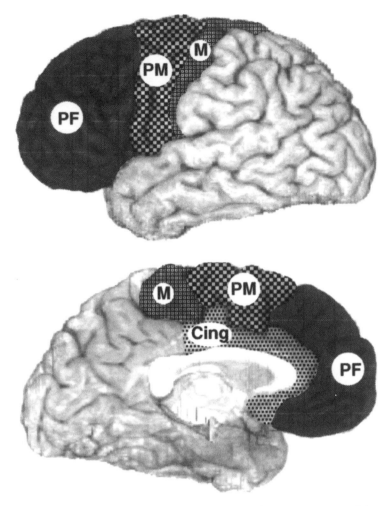

FRONTAL LOBE DISORDERS. Figure 1. The figure shows the major subdivisions of the frontal lobes, including the motor (M), premotor (PM), prefrontal (PF), and limbic/cingulate (Cing) regions. The subdivisions are depicted on lateral (top) and mesial (bottom) views of the left hemisphere; the markings would be the same for the right hemisphere.

On 13 September 1848, Phineas Gage suffered a bizarre accident in which a tamping iron (crowbar) was propelled through the front part of his head. The bar entered his left cheek just under the eye, pierced the frontal lobes of his brain, and exited through the top front part of his head. Gage's medical recovery was nothing short of astonishing, as he survived this onslaught with normal intelligence, memory, speech, sensation, and movement. In fact, the initial interest in the case was focused on the patient's survival from this massive brain injury. As history unfolded, though, the importance of the case came from another quarter: Gage displayed a profound change in personality and social conduct following his prefrontal injury. Before the injury, Gage was responsible, socially well-adjusted, and popular with peers and supervisors. Afterward, he became irresponsible and untrustworthy, irreverent and capricious, unreliable and callous. In a word, he became a psychopath.

Gage's physician, John Harlow, astutely surmised that there was a causative relationship between the prefrontal damage and the profound change in personality and social conduct. Harlow's observations hinted at an idea that has proved remarkably prescient: Structures in the prefrontal region of the brain are dedicated to the planning and execution of personally and socially adaptive behavior, and to the aspect of reasoning known as rationality. Over the past century, a number of case reports supported Harlow's contention, as investigators called attention to the oftentimes bizarre development of abnormal social behavior following prefrontal brain injury (e.g., Eslinger & Damasio, 1985; Stuss & Benson, 1986). The affected patients had a number of features in common (Damasio & Anderson,

1993): inability to organize future activity and hold gainful employment, diminished capacity to respond to punishment, a tendency to present an unrealistically favorable view of themselves, and a tendency to display inappropriate emotional reactions. Making this profile all the more puzzling was the fact that most of these patients, like Gage, retained normal intelligence, language, memory, and perception.

Others have called attention to the striking characteristics of patients with ventromedial prefrontal lobe injury. Blumer and Benson noted that the patients displayed a personality profile that the authors termed "pseudo-psychopathic," featured by puerility, a jocular attitude, sexually uninhibited humor, inappropriate and near-total self-indulgence, and complete lack of concern for others (1975). Stuss and Benson emphasized that the patients demonstrated a remarkable lack of empathy and general lack of concern about others (1986). The patients showed callous unconcern, boastfulness, and unrestrained and tactless behavior. Other descriptors included impulsiveness, facetiousness, and diminished anxiety and concern for the future.

As alluded to above, this personality profile is strikingly similar to that characterized in clinical psychology and psychiatry as psychopathic, or sociopathic (American Psychiatric Association, 1994). In fact, we have designated this condition as "acquired sociopathy" to emphasize the fact that prefrontal injured patients have many personality manifestations that are highly reminiscent of those associated with sociopathy (Tranel, 1994). The qualifier "acquired" signifies that in brain-damaged patients the condition follows the onset of brain injury and occurs in persons whose personalities and social conduct were previously normal. Patients with acquired sociopathy demonstrate a proclivity to engage in decisions and behaviors that have repeated negative consequences for their well-being. The patients are usually not destructive or harmful to others (a feature that distinguishes the "acquired" form of the disorder from the standard "developmental" form); however, they repeatedly select courses of action that in the long run are not in their best interest. They make poor decisions about interpersonal relationships, occupational endeavors, and finances. They act as though they have lost the ability to ponder different courses of action and then select the option that promises the best blend of short- and long-term benefit.

Other Psychiatric Disorders Associated with the Frontal Lobes

Depression and Mania. The development of major depression has been associated with frontal lobe injury. In a series of careful studies of this relationship, Starkstein and Robinson have identified several factors that seem to play a consistent role (1991). First, the side of lesion is important: Major depression is much more strongly associated with *left* frontal lesions, and, in contrast, right frontal lesions tend to produce a sort of apathetic indifference or even cheerfulness. Second, the proximity of the lesion to the frontal pole is important, with lesions closer to the pole being associated with more severe depression. Third, depression has been associated with lesions to the frontal opercular region and the dorsolateral prefrontal sector. By contrast, depression following ventromedial prefrontal lesions of the type described above in connection with acquired sociopathy, is extremely uncommon. In fact, it has been suggested that ventromedial lesions may sometimes produce conditions that are more akin to mania, although this issue has not been carefully studied.

Functional imaging studies have also identified relationships between prefrontal lobe structures and depression and mania. Using positron emission tomography, Drevets and his colleagues found that a region just under the genu of the corpus callosum, known as the subgenual region, was consistently underactivated in patients with either unipolar (depression only) or bipolar (alternating between depression and mania) depression (1997). This same region was activated during periods of mania. Also, Drevets and his colleagues showed that the size of this region (grey matter volume) was consistently reduced in the left hemisphere of depressive patients compared to normal control subjects, a result which is consistent with the ideas proposed by Starkstein and Robinson. The importance of this finding is underscored by the consideration that this region has been implicated in the modulation of neurotransmitters such as serotonin, noradrenaline, and dopamine. The activity of these neurotransmitter systems often appears to be blunted in patients with major depression, and is augmented by antidepressant drugs (Goodwin & Jamison, 1990).

Schizophrenia. Schizophrenia is another psychiatric condition which has been linked to dysfunction of frontal lobe structures (Weinberger, Berman, and Daniel, 1991). It has been noted for a number of years that many of the neuropsychological abnormalities manifest by schizophrenic patients bear a striking resemblance to those evidenced by frontal lobe patients; a good example is the failure of both types of patients on complex decision-making tasks such as the Wisconsin Card Sorting Test and the Tower of Hanoi. More direct support comes from functional imaging studies, which have shown that schizophrenic patients have decreased regional cerebral blood flow (rCBF) in prefrontal regions (Ingvar & Franzen, 1974). This physiological "hypofrontality" has also been found by a number of other studies, particularly those in which patients were engaged in a cognitive task that normally activates frontal lobe structures. It appears that structural brain abnormalities in the frontal lobes are most strongly related to the "negative" symptomatology of schizophrenia, such as apathy, blunted affect, social withdrawal, and impaired attention (Malloy & Duffy, 1994).

Akinetic Mutism. A curious disturbance of motivation and executive behavior, known as akinetic mutism, occurs in relationship to damage to the anterior cingulate gyrus and supplementary motor area (SMA) in the mesial part of the frontal lobes (Damasio & Van Hoesen, 1983). The patient produces no speech, even when spoken to, and makes very few facial expressions. Purposeful, goal-directed movements are also lacking, except for a few "automatic" types of behaviors such as getting up to go to the bathroom. The patients act as though they have lost the will—the drive—to interact with their envirommment. Thus, akinetic mutism can be conceptualized as a disorder of motivation.

Akinetic mutism tends to be more severe and long-lasting when there is bilateral damage to the anterior cingulate/SMA region, while unilateral lesions produce a more transient form of the condition. The side of damage does not seem to be critical, as the same basic syndrome develops in relationship to lesions on either the right or left. Most patients recover fairly well, and, in fact, with unilateral lesions recovery often takes place within the first few weeks after the brain injury.

Cognitive Deficits Associated with Prefrontal Lobe Injuries

Working Memory. Working memory refers to a short window of mental processing, on the order of minutes, during which information is held "on-line" and operations are performed on it—a sort of "mental scratch pad" (Baddeley, 1992). Working memory is used to bridge temporal gaps, to hold representations in a mental work space long enough to make appropriate responses to stimulus configurations or contingencies in which the basic constituents are no longer extant in perceptual space. In essence, working memory is a temporary storage and processing system used for problem-solving and other cognitive operations that take place over a limited time frame.

The prefrontal cortex, especially the dorsolateral sector composed of the cortex and the attendant white matter on the convexity of the hemispheres, has been implicated as an important neural substrate of working memory. After studying nonhuman primates with tasks that have in common the demand for holding stimuli in temporary memory storage over brief periods of time before calling for a response, Goldman-Rakic suggested that working memory may be more or less the exclusive memory function of the entire prefrontal cortex, with different subregions being dedicated to different domains of working memory operation (1995).

Lesion and functional-imaging studies in humans have provided considerable support for the link between the dorsolateral prefrontal cortex and working memory (Bechara et al., 1998). In addition, there is consistent evidence suggesting that the left dorsolateral prefrontal region is specialized for verbal material, whereas the right dorsolateral region is specialized for nonverbal, spatial material (e.g., Smith et al., 1996). Consider the working-memory task used by Smith and his colleagues (Figure 2). Subjects are presented a continous stream of single letters which appear at random locations around an imaginary circle centered on a fixation cross. In the verbal memory condition (lower part of Figure 2), subjects are asked to decide whether or not each letter matches the letter presented three stimuli previously (regardless of location). In the spatial memory condition (top part of Figure 2), subjects are asked to decide whether or not the position of each letter matches the position of the letter presented three stimuli previously (regardless of letter identity). Thus, both tasks require the bridging of a temporal gap. In the study by Smith and his colleagues, and in other similar studies of this type, the verbal condition activated left dorsolateral prefrontal regions, whereas the spatial condition activated right dorsolateral prefrontal regions.

Semantic and Episodic Memory. Another intriguing formulation concerns psychological functions such as retrieval of information from semantic memory, encoding of information into episodic memory, and retrieving information from episodic memory, capacitices which have been associated with different sectors of the frontal lobes. For example, Tulving and his colleagues (1996) have suggested that left frontal structures are specialized for the retrieval of general knowledge (referred to as "semantic memory information"), as well as the encoding of novel aspects of incoming information into episodic memory (unique events). By contrast, right frontal structures are specialized for episodic-memory retrieval and, in particular, for retrieval "attempts" that occur in episodic mode.

Judgments of Recency and Frequency. Judging the recency and frequency of specific events are other capacities that have been associated with the dorsolateral sector of the prefrontal lobes. For example, consider the following question: When was the last time you talked to your mother on the telephone? To arrive at an answer, which may be anywhere from a few minutes ago up to many years ago, you engage in a memory search that requires complex coactivations and associations between the retrieval of various interrelated episodic and semantic memories, and allows you to make a judgment of recency. A similar process occurs when one is asked to judge the frequency of events, for example. How many times was the overnight low temperature below zero last winter? Laboratory studies have suggested some degree of hemispheric specialization for recency and frequency judgments, with the left dorsolateral prefrontal region being relatively more important for verbally coded information, and the right being relatively more important for visuospatial

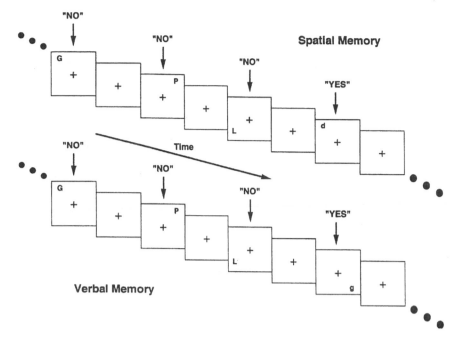

FRONTAL LOBE DISORDERS. Figure 2. The drawing shows a typical working memory task paradigm requiring spatial (top) or verbal (bottom) processing. (Reprinted with permission from *Cerebral Cortex*, Oxford University Press [Smith et al., 1996]).

information. The dorsolateral prefrontal sector has also been linked to other types of "cognitive estimations" that require rough approximations rather than retrieval of rote knowledge, such as ballparking the number of swine that live in Iowa, or the number of mountains higher than 12,000 feet in Montana.

Set Shifting, Planning, and Decision-Making. Formation, maintenance, and shifting of cognitive "sets" are other processes that have been associated with the prefrontal region of the brain, especially the dorsolateral sector. The Wisconsin Card Sorting Test (WCST), widely used in neuropsychology as a measure of set shifting, requires one to sort cards based on contingencies that are never made explicit and that change from time to time throughout the task (not unlike many real-world situations, in which the contingencies for advantageous responding are often vague and changeable over time). One particularly striking impairment that can be identified and quantified by tasks such as the WCST is the tendency to perseverate, that is, to continue responding based on principles that are no longer operative. Perseveration is a frequent manifestation in patients with frontal lobe injuries.

The ability to develop and execute plans, also closely associated with frontal lobe functioning, has been successfully measured with tasks such as the Tower of Hanoi (and other similar "tower" tasks), which require the formulation of subgoals, execution of a series of actions governed by specific rules, and attainment of an overall general objective. In a typical "tower" task, patients are asked to move discs of various diameters from a starting configuration (e.g., stacked on a pole in a certain order) to a final configuration (e.g., stacked on a different pole in a different order), under specific constraints about which discs may and may not be placed on top of one another. Deficits such as perseveration, haphazard subgoal formulation, and rule-breaking are common in patients with frontal lobe injuries.

To investigate decision making, we have developed a paradigm known as the Gambling Task, in which subjects play a card game that contains complex, implicit trade-offs between immediate and long-term rewards and punishments (Tranel, Bechara, & Damasio, 1999). In a nutshell, subjects must learn to accept lower immediate rewards in order to maximize long-term gains, because the task is set up so that higher immediate rewards are accompanied by higher long-term losses. To play the Gambling Task successfully (as is often the case in the real world), one must develop a notion as to the relative merits and hazards of one's decisions in regard to both the immediate and long-term consequences of behavior, a capacity that appears to depend critically on structures in the ventromedial prefrontal cortex. The Gambling Task is nearly always failed, oftentimes quite blatantly, by patients with ventromedial prefrontal lobe injuries. Such patients play the game in a manner that suggests they are insensitive to the future consequences of their behavior, that is, they opt repeatedly for higher short-term reward, even if this eventually leads to long-term punishment.

Binding of Memories and Source Amnesia. Learning new information and retrieving previously learned events normally involves both specific content (e.g., names and faces) and a time-locked association of those contents with one another (knowing that a particular name goes with a particular face, when and where that information was acquired, and even how one felt at the time). The basal forebrain, situated immediately behind the orbital prefrontal cortices, is important for this process of memory binding. Damage to the basal forebrain leads to a characteristic amnesic syndrome, in which patients manifest difficulties associating specific subcomponents of memory episodes with one another. For example, a patient may recall a particular family event but place the event entirely out of context with respect to other events that occurred around the same time period. This errant binding of components of memory episodes affects new learning as well, for example, the patient may learn new proper names but associate these with incorrect faces.

A related phenomenon is what has been termed source amnesia, in which a patient's learning of new facts may be relatively normal, but the patient cannot recall the circumstances under which the learning took place—the patient recalls the content, but not the source, of the learning experience. For instance, the patient learns and can recall a particular name and face but cannot remember where or how that information was acquired. An intriguing characteristic of basal forebrain amnesia, possibly related to the importance of this region for memory binding, is the tendency of patients to produce confabulations, for example, making up stories about bizarre adventures that have no basis in fact.

A Theoretical Formulation

It has been suggested that the primary goal of the prefrontal cortices is to select the responses most advantageous for the organism in a complex social environment (Damasio, 1994, 1995). Relatedly, the prefrontal cortices support the guidance of multistep behaviors, decision making, planning, and creativity. To accomplish these objectives, prefrontal cortices call upon somatic markers, which are understood as patterns of bodily responses composed of the state of viscera, internal milieu, and skeletal musculature that serve as signals to help guide response selection. This idea has led to a theoretical framework known as the somatic marker hypothesis, which has been used to account for the bizarre changes in social conduct, planning, and decision making that characterize patients with damage to the frontal lobes (Damasio, 1994, 1995; Tranel, 1994).

The somatic marker hypothesis is centered on the idea that the frontal lobes subserve the capacity to use emotions and feelings to help guide behavior. Structures in the ventromedial prefrontal cortex provide the substrate for learning associations between complex situations on the one hand, and the types of bioregulatory states (including emotional states) associated with such situations in prior experience. The ventromedial region holds linkages between the facts that comprise a given situation and the emotion previously paired with that situation. The linkages are "dispositional": they do not hold explicitly the representations of the facts or of the emotional state, but, instead, the potential to reactivate an emotion by evoking activity in certain cortical and subcortical structures. In a sense, then, the ventromedial sector performs a memory function: It establishes linkages between dispositions for aspects of various situations and dispositions for the emotions that in the individual's experience have been associated with those situations.

Now, when a situation arises—say, a social scenario calling for certain behaviors and courses of action (e.g., a holiday gathering at one's inlaws')—dispositions are activated in higher-order association cortices, leading to the recall of pertinent facts and related knowledge. The relevant ventromedial prefrontal linkages are activated concurrently, leading to activation of the emotional disposition apparatus (which, neurally, includes various limbic structures, such as the amygdala, cingulate, and insular cortex). The net result is the reconstruction of a previously learned factual-emotional set. Reactivation of the emotional disposition network can occur via a body loop, in which the body (musculoskeletal, visceral, and other internal milieu components) actually changes, with the changes being relayed to somatosensory cortices, or an "as if" body loop, in which reactivation signals bypass the body and get relayed to the somatosensory cortices directly. The establishment of a somatosensory pattern, whether via the body loop or the "as if" loop, can occur either overtly or covertly.

The somatosensory pattern evoked by a particular situation is codisplayed with factual knowledge pertinent to the situation. As far as decision making is concerned, the key idea is as follows: The somatosensory pattern operates to constrain the process of reasoning through multiple options and future outcomes. Specifically, when the somatosensory image which defines a particular emotional response is juxtaposed with the images that describe a particular scenario of a future outcome, the pattern marks the scenario as good or bad. The images of the scenario are judged, and marked, by the juxtaposed images of the somatic state.

When implemented in a complex decision-making space, this process greatly facilitates the operation of logical reasoning. Thus, somatic markers allow certain option-outcome pairs to be rapidly endorsed or rejected, and the decision-making space is made manageable for a logic-based, cost-benefit analysis. Also, in situations in which there is a high degree of uncertainty regarding the future, and the course of action that is optimal (which may be the case at one's inlaws'!), the constraints imposed by somatic markers allow the individual to decide efficiently and within a reasonable time period. In particular, this would apply to many complex social situations and to the on-line navigation required in such situations.

Without somatic markers, which is what happens to patients with ventromedial prefrontal injuries, different response options and outcomes become sort of equalized, and the process of deciding on an option will depend entirely on logic operations over many potential alternatives. This strategy can be extremely slow and laborious, and may fail to take previous experience into account. As a consequence, decision making is not timely or propitious and may even be random or impulsive. The somatic marker hypothesis goes against popular and scientific lore that reasoning and decision-making are optimal when a person is cool, calm, and calculated (unemotional), and explains why too little emotion may be just as bad for decision making as too much.

[*See also* Brain; *and* Hemispheric Functions.]

Bibliography

American Psychiatric Association. (1994). *Diagnostic and statistical manual of mental disorders* (4th ed.). Washington, DC: Author.

Anderson, S. W. (1996). Cognitive rehabilitation in closed head injury. In M. Rizzo & D. Tranel (Eds.), *Head injury and postconcussive syndrome* (pp. 457–468). New York: Churchill Livingstone. A review of current techniques in neuropsychological rehabilitation, with many practical suggestions.

Baddeley, A. D. (1992). Working memory. *Science, 255,* 566–569. A seminal description of the psychological construct of working memory.

Bechara, A., Damasio, H., Tranel, D., & Damasio, A. R. (1998). Dissociation of working memory from decision-making within the human prefrontal cortex. *Journal of Neuroscience, 18,* 428–437. A human-lesion study demonstrating that deficits in working memory are associated with dorsolateral prefrontal lesions, whereas deficits in decision-making are associated with ventromedial prefrontal lesions.

Benton, A. (1991). The prefrontal region: Its early history. In H. S. Levin, H. M. Eisenberg, & A. L. Benton (Eds.), *Frontal lobe function and dysfunction* (pp. 3–32). New

York: Oxford University Press. A superb historical sketch of the neuropsychology of the frontal lobes by an author who has witnessed firsthand nearly a century of the history.

Bigelow, H. J. (1850). Dr. Harlow's case of recovery from the passage of an iron bar through the head. *American Journal of the Medical Sciences, 39,* 13–22. This paper may be difficult to find, but it is one of the most important papers in the history of neuropsychology.

Blumer, D., & Benson, D. F. (1975). Personality changes with frontal and temporal lobe lesions. In D. F. Benson & D. Blumer (Eds.), *Psychiatric aspects of neurologic disease* (pp. 151–169). New York: Grune & Stratton. This paper describes "psychopathiclike" and other psychiatric manifestations of patients with prefrontal lesions.

Damasio, A. R. (1994). *Descartes' error: Emotion, reason, and the human brain.* New York: Grosset/Putnam. This widely known and highly popular book presents an engaging and scientifically rich framework for understanding the relationship between the frontal lobes and rationality.

Damasio, A. R. (1995). On some functions of the human prefrontal cortex. In J. Grafman, K. Holyoak, & F. Boller (Eds.), *Structure and functions of the human prefrontal cortex* (pp. 241–251). New York: New York Academy of Sciences. A concise summary of the somatic marker hypothesis, which explains how emotion and feeling help guide decision-making.

Damasio, A. R., & Anderson, S. W. (1993). The frontal lobes. In K. Heilman & E. Valenstein (Eds.), *Clinical neuropsychology* (3rd ed., pp. 409–460). New York: Oxford University Press. A comprehensive review of the mental capacities associated with the frontal lobes and of various disorders that occur with lesions to different regions of the frontal lobes.

Damasio, A. R., & Van Hoesen, G. W. (1983). Emotional disturbances associated with focal lesions of the limbic frontal lobe. In K. M. Heilman & P. Satz (Eds.), *The neuropsychology of human emotion: Recent advances* (pp. 85–110). New York: Guilford Press. A careful review of emotional disturbances associated with limbic regions of the frontal lobes, with a particularly good description of the condition known as akinetic mutism.

Damasio, H. (1991). Neuroanatomy of the frontal lobe in vivo: A comment on methodology. In H. S. Levin, H. M. Eisenberg, & A. L. Benton (Eds.), *Frontal lobe function and dysfunction* (pp. 92–121). New York: Oxford University Press. A beautiful, highly illustrated presentation of the detailed neuroanatomy of the frontal lobes.

Drevets, W. C., Price, J. L., Simpson, J. R., Todd, R. D., Reich, T., Vannier, M., & Raichle, M. E. (1997). Subgenual prefrontal cortex abnormalities in mood disorders. *Nature, 386,* 824–827. This paper describes a key advance in understanding how specific parts of the frontal lobes participate in the regulation of mood and affect.

Eslinger, P. J., & Damasio, A. R. (1985). Severe disturbance of higher cognition after bilateral frontal lobe ablation: Patient EVR. *Neurology, 35,* 1731–1741. The authors describe in detail a prototypical ventromedial frontal lobe case that exemplifies many of the core features of acquired personality disorder.

Goldman-Rakic, P. S. (1995). Architecture of the prefrontal cortex and the central executive. In J. Grafman, K. Holyoak, & F. Boller (Eds.), *Structure and functions of the human prefrontal cortex* (pp. 71–83). New York: New York Academy of Sciences. A comprehensive review of the neuroanatomy of working memory, based primarily on work on nonhuman primates.

Goodwin, F. K., & Jamison, K. R. (1990). *Manic-depressive illness.* New York: Oxford University Press.

Harlow, J. M. (1868). Recovery from the passage of an iron bar through the head. *Publications of the Massachusetts Medical Society, 2,* 327–347. A key paper in the history of neuropsychology; may be difficult to find.

Ingvar, D. H., & Franzen, G. (1974). Distribution of cerebral activity in chronic schizophrenia. *Lancet, 2,* 1484–1486. This study describes for the first time the notion of "hypofrontality," the idea that reduced frontal lobe activity plays a role in schizophrenia.

Malloy, P., & Duffy, J. (1994). The frontal lobes in neuropsychiatric disorders. In F. Boller & J. Grafman (Eds.), *Handbook of neuropsychology* (Vol. 9, p. 203–232). Amsterdam: Elsevier. A comprehensive and scholarly review of major psychiatric disorders associated with the frontal lobes.

Smith, E. E., Jonides, J., & Koeppe, R. A. (1996). Dissociating verbal and spatial working memory using PET. *Cerebral Cortex, 6,* 11–20. A representative functional-imaging study of working memory, showing the activation of the left dorsolateral prefrontal cortex by a verbal working memory task and the activation of the right dorsolateral prefrontal cortex by a spatial working memory task.

Starkstein, S. E., & Robinson, R. G. (1991). The role of the frontal lobes in affective disorder following stroke. In H. S. Levin, H. M. Eisenberg, & A. Benton (Eds.), *Frontal lobe function and dysfunction* (pp. 288–303). New York: Oxford University Press. The authors summarize their research exploring the relationship between brain damage and depression.

Stuss, D. T., & Benson, D. F. (1986). *The frontal lobes.* New York: Raven Press. This book provides a comprehensive review of neuropsychological deficits associated with frontal lobe injury. A treatment of various theoretical perspectives is included.

Tranel, D. (1994). "Acquired sociopathy": The development of sociopathic behavior following focal brain damage. In D. C. Fowles, P. Sutker, & S. H. Goodman (Eds.), *Progress in experimental personality and psychopathology research* (Vol. 17, pp. 285–311). New York: Springer. A review of empirical evidence supporting the notion of acquired sociopathy associated with ventromedial prefrontal dysfunction, including key findings derived from psychophysiological experiments.

Tranel, D., Bechara, A., & Damasio, A. R. (1999). Decision-making and the somatic marker hypothesis. In M. S. Gazzaniga (Ed.), *The Cognitive Neurosciences* (2nd ed, pp. 1047–1061) Cambridge, MA: MIT Press. A comprehensive review of theoretical and empirical contributions to the understanding of the neural basis of decision-making, including information about how overt and covert aspects of emotion play a critical role in effective decision-making.

Tulving, E., Markowitsch, H. J., Craik, F. I. M., Habib, R., & Houle, S. (1996). Novelty and familiarity activations in PET studies of memory encoding and retrieval. *Cerebral Cortex, 6,* 71–79. A review of empirical findings showing how different prefrontal regions are associated with different types of memory encoding and retrieval.

Weinberger, D. R., Berman, K. F., & Daniel, D. G. (1991). Prefrontal cortex dysfunction in schizophrenia. In H. S. Levin, H. M. Eisenberg, & A. Benton (Eds.), *Frontal lobe function and dysfunction* (pp. 275–287). New York: Oxford University Press. A detailed, scholarly review of evidence pointing to a link between the dysfunction of prefrontal structures and schizophrenic symptomatology.

Daniel Tranel

FRUSTRATION-AGGRESSION HYPOTHESIS. *See* Violence and Aggression.

FUGUE STATES. *See* Dissociative Disorders.

FUNCTIONALISM is a system of psychology founded by a group of early twentieth-century American psychologists at the University of Chicago who defined psychology as the science of mental activities as they function in adapting the individual to the environment. The core concepts of functionalism came to psychology from the writings of William James (1887–1919), philosopher and psychologist, and John Dewey (1855–1952), the renowned American philosopher and educator.

James is known as the father of pragmatism, a point of view in philosophy which asserts that truth and the value of ideas lie in their practical consequences. A prominent role in James's psychology is played by the concepts of adaptation and function. In his *Principles of Psychology*, he held that the function of mental processes is to adapt the individual to the environment. To ensure successful adaptation, learned habits are formed in the course of experience. As James put it in one of his famous phrases, "Habit is the great flywheel of society."

Dewey's philosophy, known as instrumentalism, holds that ideas arising in response to a problem serve the purpose of solving that problem. Consequently, the validity of ideas depends on how well they stand up in the test of experience. Dewey, like James, embraced pragmatism as a fundamental concept in his philosophy.

The impetus for the development of a functional system of psychology originated in an article by John Dewey, then director of the School of Education at the University of Chicago, whose broad interests included the new science of psychology. Dewey's article, published in the *Psychological Review* in 1896, was a criticism of the reflex arc concept in psychology, which reduced behavior to its simplest components, called stimulus-response units. For example, the driver of an automobile approaching a traffic light reacts to a stimulus, red light, by making a response, pressing the brake pedal. The entire reaction is mediated by sensory and motor nerve tracts in the nervous system.

Dewey argues that this elemental analysis is simplistic and artificial, failing to take into account behavior as purposive, adaptive action. To separate it into elemental units is to create abstractions that do not reflect reality any more than reducing water to its elements, hydrogen and oxygen, make for a useful description of water as perceived by a thirsty individual at a water fountain.

In the case of a driver braking at a traffic light, a simple stimulus-response analysis fails to take into account the driver's seeing the light continuously as he brakes, often having to take into account a car ahead that is also coming to a stop. The mental activity of seeing, therefore, is a continuous one inseparable from the response.

The response of braking must also be considered as an ongoing process that begins with seeing but is modified as the driver gets closer and closer to the light or the car ahead. It is also inseparable from ever-changing stimulus conditions that are occurring during the act. The sensation does not precede the response, and the response does not follow the stimulus. Both are continuously interwoven from the beginning to the end of the adaptive act.

It can be further argued, Dewey points out, that reflex acts involve contributions from past experience. The driver had to learn how to press the brake pedal in such a manner as to avoid skidding or, if too late, accidents. Although it is true that long practice makes acts appear automatic, in reality they are complex, involving stimulating and responding processes including individual components that together function continuously, as wholes, not as parts.

Dewey's functional analysis of reflex behavior received a warm reception among psychologists who were dissatisfied with the dominant psychology of the time, known as structuralism, under the leadership of Edward Bradford Titchener (1857–1927) of Cornell University. Titchener defined psychology as the study of consciousness by the method of introspection or objective self-observation. The introspective analysis of consciousness revealed that it could be reduced to three elements: sensations, images, and affective states or feelings.

Critics found structuralism a narrow, static system that ignored the purposeful, adaptive nature of mental and behavioral activities. They characterized it as an atomistic *is* psychology in contrast to a functional *is for* psychology. It was also faulted as excluding areas of interest among functionalists, such as animal behavior, learning, the study of abnormal states, children, the measurement of individual differences, and the application of psychology to business and industry.

Opposition to structuralism coalesced into the functional school of psychology at the University of Chicago under the leadership of Dewey, James Rowland Angell (1869–1949), and Harvey A. Carr (1873–1954). All three wrote introductory textbooks of psychology from the functional point of view that proved highly popular with students. Dewey moved away from psychology to concentrate on his primary interests, philosophy and education; Angell and Carr became leaders of functionalism as it developed toward maturity.

George Herbert Mead (1863–1931), a professor of philosophy at the University of Chicago, along with his departmental colleagues, lent support to functionalism by offering courses in the scientific method, the psychology of language, and social behavior.

Functionalism as a mature system or blueprint for a science of psychology was developed in books and technical articles in professional journals by Angell and Carr. After defining psychology as a study of mental activities as they function in adapting the organism to its environment, they included under mental activities perception, learning, memory, imagination, feeling and emotion, thinking, and will. These processes in Carr's words are involved with the "acquisition, fixation, retention, organization, and evaluation of experience and their subsequent utilization in the guidance of conduct."

Functional psychology views the organism in the environment as subject to stimuli arising both from the environment and from conditions within. Adaptive acts, if successful, must reduce these stimulating conditions to ensure survival.

Adaptive acts, unlike simple reflexes, such as sneezing and the knee jerk, involve motivating conditions. Motives arise from persistent stimuli that dominate behavior until a reaction occurs that eliminates the stimulating conditions. The hungry individual eats to stop the discomfort of stimuli associated with hunger; the thirsty individual drinks to eliminate dryness and stickiness in the mouth. More complex acts, such as winning an Olympic medal, solving a complex mathematical puzzle, or writing a poem, involve complex stimulating conditions that may be difficult to identify but are nevertheless present within the individual.

Carr draws an important distinction between the proximate or immediate stimulating conditions and the distant or delayed consequences of adaptive acts. To eat when hungry ultimately nourishes the body. To drink maintains a safe water level. To paint a portrait may result in earned money. But the act of eating or drinking is not undertaken with nourishment or maintenance of a safe water level as the stimulating condition. Money is not immediately present—indeed, may be delayed for years—to stimulate the artist to begin painting. Present behavior, therefore, cannot be explained by its ultimate consequences.

In higher forms, whose adaptive behavior is characteristically learned rather than instinctive, the functional study of the adaptive process involves an analysis of the roles of motivation, perception, learning, thinking, and, often, the individual's social environment. By introducing these complex processes, functional psychology moved far beyond the narrow boundaries of reflex arc psychology and the analysis of isolated states of consciousness of structuralism.

Functionalism treats all mental activities as psychophysical, involving both mental and physical processes. However, any attempt to separate these two aspects of mental acts can only lead to abstractions without independent existence in reality. The ultimate solution to the mind-body problem—that is, how mind, a nonphysical process, can affect or be affected by the body, a physical entity—is left to philosophy, where it originated in Plato's teachings.

The methods of functional psychology are introspection, when dealing with conscious aspects of mental activities, and experimentation, the method favored by the natural sciences. In practice, functionalists made little use of introspection, favoring instead naturalistic observation and experimentation. They also welcomed mental testing and the methods utilized by sociologists and social anthropologists, including the study of social products, literature, art, inventions, and human social and political institutions as they evolve in society. All these investigatory methods are useful from the functional point of view in understanding human behavior.

When Angell was head of the department and the Chicago functionalists were elaborating a systematic theoretical psychology, they were also teaching and conducting laboratory experiments whose results appeared in technical journals, contributing directly to the growth of American psychology. Many of these publications originated in the research of doctoral candidates and their mentors. Carr, who headed the department after Angell left to become president of Yale University, was one of these. As a graduate student he developed a strong interest in animal psychology, publishing numerous articles describing the results of experiments on maze learning in animals. Later he turned to conducting experiments on visual perception.

Among the Chicago graduates in psychology who became eminent were John Broadus Watson (1878–1955), the founder of behaviorism, who earned the first doctorate awarded at Chicago; Louis Leon Thurstone (1887–1955), whose mathematical analyses of the relationships among aptitudes led to the development of primary abilities tests, the best known of which is the widely used Scholastic Aptitude Test; and Granville Stanley Hall (1846–1924), a pioneer in child and adolescent psychology. There were numerous other candidates working in industrial, educational, personality, and animal psychology, reflecting the catholicity and pragmatic nature of functionalism.

While the Chicago school was the epicenter of functionalism, a closely related orientation developed under the leadership of Robert Sessions Woodworth (1869–1962) at Columbia University. Woodworth called his system dynamic psychology, a functionalism that emphasizes the importance of drives and drive mechanisms in adaptive behavior. The essential principle of Woodworth's dynamic view of behavior is represented by his formula, W–S–O–R–W, where W stands for the world or environment, S for stimuli, O for the organism, and R for the organism's response. Adaptive behavior occurs when drives or motives ready an organism to respond to stimuli with a reaction that reduces the drive by acting on the environment. The organic drives of hunger, thirst, and sex are all characterized by a readiness to respond to stimuli—food, water, sexual objects—by acting on those objects in such a manner as to reduce the drive.

Woodworth emphasizes that mechanisms employed in drive reduction reactions may themselves become drives. The retired worker may express restlessness, even feel impelled to visit the former workplace. The concert pianist plays in the absence of an audience for the enjoyment of playing. The multimillionaire piles up money in the bank far beyond what can be spent for goods or services. By employing the principle that mechanisms tend to become drives, Woodworth greatly expanded the original S–O–R formula to include highly complex behavior.

Like the Chicago functionalists, Woodworth enjoyed a long and distinguished career as a teacher and contributor to the literature of psychology. His texts in introductory and experimental psychology were standards in the field for decades.

Functionalism as a distinct school of psychology associated with specific academic institutions went out of existence by the end of the first half of the twentieth century. This was not the result of its rejection on the part of psychologists but because of its success. Functionalism was quickly absorbed into the mainstream of American psychology, which welcomed its broadly pragmatic and utilitarian point of view. Some of its early opponents were critical of its utilitarian and technological orientation, considering it inferior to a pure science of psychology. Whatever the merits of this criticism, American society has utilized the application of functional psychology in educational testing, business and industry, public opinion polling, advertising, counseling, personnel work, and clinical programs. In the last analysis a pragmatic orientation is characteristic of all sciences, physical and social. A complete absence of interest in the usefulness of scientific discoveries has never been the hallmark of any science in any age.

[See also Psychology, article on Early Twentieth Century.]

Bibliography

Carr, H. A. (1925). *Psychology: A study of mental activity.* New York: McKay. An introductory text that takes the functional point of view.

Chaplin, J. P., & Krawiec, T. S. (1979). *Systems and theories of psychology* (4th ed., rev.). New York: Holt, Rinehart and Winston. A detailed survey of the early and more recent theorists' treatment of psychological processes.

Dewey, J. (1896). The reflex arc concept in psychology. *Psychological Review, 3,* 357–370.

Hilgard, E. R. (1987). *Psychology in America: A historical survey.* San Diego: Harcourt Brace Jovanovich.

Kimble, G. A., Wertheimer, M., & White, C. (Eds.). (1991). *Portraits of pioneers in psychology.* Hillsdale, NJ: Erlbaum.

Koch, S., & Leary, D. E. (Eds.). (1985). *A century of psychology as science.* New York: McGraw-Hill.

James P. Chaplin

FUNCTIONAL MAGNETIC RESONANCE IMAGING. *See* Brain Imaging Techniques.

G

GALEN (c. 130–c. 210 CE), Greek anatomist. Galen, the greatest comparative anatomist of classical antiquity, was born near the ancient city of Pergamum in Asia Minor. His huge volume of works synthesizing the doctrines of ancient medicine became the source material from which scholars of the medieval and early modern West constructed an inclusive psycho-physiological system that influenced European concepts of psychology well into the nineteenth century.

The son of a wealthy architect, Galen began his anatomical studies in his native city and was also educated there in the major philosophical systems of classical Greece—Platonism, Aristotelianism, Stoicism, and Epicureanism—all of which were to influence his thinking about human psychology and physiology. After years of study in the schools of Pergamum, Galen toured the major cosmopolitan centers of the ancient world, including Smyrna, Corinth, and Alexandria, in order to further his medical education. Upon his return to Pergamum, he served for a time as physician and surgeon to the gladiators.

About 161 or 162 Galen first visited Rome, where he practiced medicine for about a year in the capital of the empire. Although he soon returned to Pergamum, he was ordered several years later to serve the empire, first as a military surgeon and then as a physician to the son of Emperor Marcus Aurelius. During his career as court physician (169–192 CE) he used the leisure and resources that the position afforded to devote most of his energy to research and writing. His output on many and diverse topics was prodigious. No medical figure of the ancient world appears to have been more productive, and the bulk and comprehensiveness of his writings led, within three centuries of his death, to his veneration by subsequent medical investigators as the second Hippocrates.

Central to this renown was the theory of cognitive psychology, which Galen's followers constructed out of his diffuse and prolix statements. This theory, based on his own investigative findings as well as those of his predecessors, incorporated many of the philosophical concepts he had studied as a youth. Like the Platonists, Galen asserted that the head was site of all nervous action. This view was denied by prominent Aristotelians, who believed that the *hegemonikon*, or "control center," was localized in the heart, which was said to be the primal organ because it was the first to form.

Denying many of the Epicurean doctrines advocated by his patron, Marcus Aurelius, Galen developed an all-inclusive psycho-physiological system based on the Stoic doctrine of the *pneuma*, or cosmic air. According to this theory, all psychic activity was caused by a rarified spirit or vapor that was elaborated in a network of arteries which Galen, basing his contention on animal dissections, believed existed at the base of the brain. This spirit, which he called *pneuma psychikon* (later translated as "animal spirits" or "spirits of the soul"), was distributed throughout the body in the central nervous system and was responsible for sensation and motion. The animal spirits in the brain effected all mental activity. Galen's successors contended that the mental faculties were localized and operated in the cerebral ventricular system, but Galen refused to localize them in any part of the brain. For Galen, all mental functions resulted from the interaction of the brain and the *pneuma psychikon*.

Nevertheless, some of his comments on brain function seem to imply localization, especially when he associated the anterior of the brain with sensory nerve origins and activity, and the posterior with motor functions. It seemed to him that the anterior part, like most of the sensory nerves, was softer than other cerebral areas, and he identified the olfactory bulbs there. In his study of mental disturbances, he discovered that each of the mental faculties could be disturbed separately, citing a story in which a deranged man, obviously lacking reason, threw pottery and an unfortunate weaver out of a window after asking permission from passersby. (The man clearly did not lack sense perception.) Hence, Galen can be said to have provided some substantiation for later theories that localized the three basic mental faculties of sensation, reason, and memory in the cerebral ventricles.

To the Hippocratic doctrine of the four humors—blood, phlegm, black bile, and yellow bile—Galen added his ideas of personality types, the temperaments—sanguine, phlegmatic, melancholic, and choleric—which he contended were both psychic and somatic. Since these classical temperaments survive as popular psychological types, Galen may thus be claimed as one of the originators of personality typing, which remains today as a very active form of psychological theorizing.

Bibliography

Sources

Galen. (1956). *On anatomical procedures: The later books* (C. Singer, Ed. and Trans.). New York: Oxford University Press.
Galen. (1962). *On anatomical procedures: The later books* (W. L. H. Duckworth, Trans.). Cambridge, England: Cambridge University Press.
Galen. (1968). *On the usefulness of the parts of the body* (M. T. May, Ed. and Trans.). Ithaca, NY: Cornell University Press.
Galen. (1978–1984). *On the doctrines of Hippocrates and Plato* (P. De Lacy, Ed. and Trans.). Berlin: Akademie-Verlag. Corpus Medicorum Graecorum V,4,1,2-V,4,2,1.

Secondary Works

Sarton, G. L. (1954). *Galen of Pergamon.* Lawrence, KS: University of Kansas Press.
Temkin, O. (1973). *Galenism: Rise and decline of a medical philosophy.* Ithaca, NY: Cornell University Press.

Ynez Violé O'Neill

GALL, FRANZ JOSEF. *See* Phrenology.

GALTON, FRANCIS (1822–1911), English scientist. Galton was among the last of the class of wealthy amateurs who dominated science before the increasing professionalization and specialization of the late nineteenth century. Better labeled a "scientist" than with any more specific designation, his personally financed studies contributed importantly to the emerging disciplines of geography, meteorology, criminology, biology, and statistics—as well as psychology. He introduced the idea of intelligence tests, founded the eugenics movement, and popularized the expression "nature and nurture," thus initiating one of the most heated controversies in the history of psychology. Other contributions to psychology included his pioneering studies of mental imagery and word association, twin studies and other foundations of modern behavior genetics, questionnaire methodology, and the techniques of statistical correlation.

Early Life

Galton was born on 16 February 1822 near Birmingham, England. His father was a banker and a descendant of Robert Barclay, one of the founders of the Quaker religion; his mother was a daughter of the eminent physician Erasmus Darwin (1731–1802). Thus, Galton was a younger cousin to Charles Darwin (1809–1882). Under the benevolent tutelage of an older sister, he first seemed to be a child prodigy but then languished in the classics-dominated preparatory schools to which he was sent. After 2 years of medical training, he went to Cambridge with hopes of winning high honors in mathematics but suffered a breakdown and withdrew from honors competition. After Cambridge, he returned briefly to medical study but quit when his father died and left him an ample inheritance. A love of travel kept Galton from becoming a member of the idle rich, as a journey to the Sudan in 1845–1846 whetted his appetite for "serious" travel, and a major exploring expedition to Southwest Africa in 1850–1852 first brought his name to public prominence.

Galton demonstrated a penchant for scientific measurement on that expedition, and his maps and detailed geographical accounts of the present-day country of Namibia won him the Royal Geographical Society's Gold Medal for 1853. His book about the expedition, *Tropical South Africa* (1854), established his reputation as a vivid and entertaining travel writer. Invited to join the governing council of the RGS, he helped plan many of the epic expeditions to the Nile, including those by Richard Burton, John Hanning Speke, and James Grant. In 1855, Galton published the first of several editions of *The Art of Travel*, a practical handbook for travelers in the wild. He combined meteorological with geographical interests in the early 1860s, when he had the inspiration to plot weather data on maps and thus invented the now ubiquitous weather map.

The Darwinian Influence and "Hereditary Genius"

Also during the early 1860s, Galton pondered the implications of his cousin Darwin's recently published *Origin of Species*, of which he had had no foreknowledge. Two related ideas gradually seized Galton's imagination: the likelihood that human intellectual ability was inheritable just like the physical characteristics that Darwin had emphasized in the *Origin*, and consequently that human evolution toward increasing intelligence might be deliberately accelerated through a systematic program of selective breeding. Galton outlined these ideas in his 1865 article in *Macmillan's Magazine*, "Hereditary Talent and Character," and elaborated on them in the 1869 book, *Hereditary Genius*. Both works documented a statistical tendency for intellectual eminence to run in families (such as his own): individuals eminent enough to be listed in biographical dictionaries were far more likely than chance to have one or more close relatives who were also eminent. Galton acknowledged in passing that such patterns might have been produced by environmental similarities as well as heredity and suggested the comparison of adoptive versus biological relatives as one way of sorting out the separate effects. He never seriously acted on that suggestion, however, and in general minimized the importance of environmental factors. Accordingly, he proposed the development of examinations designed to identify young men and women of the highest hereditary "natural ability," who would be encouraged to intermarry and have large numbers of offspring. Here were the original ideas for what became intelligence tests, and the movement he would later call eugenics.

Throughout the early 1870s, Galton corresponded with the Swiss botanist Alphonse de Candolle (1806–1893), who had responded to *Hereditary Genius* with a book of his own arguing for the importance of such environmental factors as family traditions, religion, and national background in producing eminent scientists. While accepting a role for heredity, de Candolle saw these environmental factors as relatively more important. Galton, of course, argued the reverse. Stimulated by his discussion with de Candolle, Galton proposed the catch-phrase "nature and nurture" to represent the heredity-environment interaction and used that term in the titles of two important works. *English Men of Science: Their Nature and Nurture* (1874) summarized the results of questionnaires he sent to the scientific fellows of the Royal Society, inquiring about the origins of their interests in science. The respondents cited many environmental and educational factors but also—of supreme importance to Galton—usually described their love of science as "innate." Galton's 1875 paper, "The History of Twins, as a Criterion of the Relative Powers of Nature and Nurture," reported case studies of several twin pairs, some of whom had developed similarly despite being treated differently, while others differed markedly from each other despite similar upbringing. Galton hypothesized that the former cases must have been monozygotic, the latter dizygotic. Although crude in method and inconclusive in its results, this study inspired the many later and more systematic investigations of twins by behavior geneticists.

Later Works and Influence

In the late 1870s, Galton began grappling with the problem of how to give mathematical expression to the strengths of hereditary relationships. To obtain data, he first planted peas of varying sizes and measured their offspring; later he recorded the heights of several hundred human parents along with those of their grown children. Quite early he learned to cast these data in what are now called scatter plots, leading to his discovery of statistical regression: the offspring of large or small parents differed from the mean in the same direction as their parents, but to a lesser degree that could be mathematically expressed as a fraction between zero and one. Finally, in 1888, he realized that if the measures were converted from inches or feet into statistically defined units such as probable error or standard deviation, the regression fractions would represent genuine "coefficients of correlation." Galton's younger follower Karl Pearson (1857–1936) later refined this idea and provided the computing formulas and systematic rationale for modern correlational analysis.

In 1884, Galton attempted to realize the program of intelligence testing he had first proposed in 1865. In an "anthropometric laboratory" he established in London's South Kensington Science Museum, he collected measures of head size, reaction time, and several kinds of sensory discrimination from several thousand subjects, on the assumption that these variables would reflect the power and efficiency of the subjects' brains and nervous systems—and hence their hereditary "natural ability." Galton, himself, did little to assess the validity of these measures, but his general program of "mental testing" was later taken up by the American psychologist James McKeen Cattell (1860–1944).

In 1901, Cattell's student Clark Wissler (1870–1947) used Pearson's newly introduced formulas to calculate that the correlations between the "mental tests" and academic grades were zero-order. Wissler's study triggered a rapid decline of the neurophysiologically oriented, "Galtonian" approach to intelligence testing—although in recent years more sophisticated measures of "complex reaction time" and "inspection time" have shown somewhat better promise. The first useful approach to intelligence testing, and the model for most intelligence tests today, was introduced in 1905 by Alfred Binet (1857–1911) and Theodore Simon (1873–1961), who used items that tapped complex mental functions much more directly than Galton's tests did.

A man of inveterate curiosity and inventiveness, Galton also investigated diverse topics including fingerprint analysis (another field he helped initiate), composite portaiture (the superimposition of several different portraits, in order to bring out their common features), and a statistical study of "the efficacy of prayer" (showing that monarchs whose health is extensively prayed for do not live longer than average). Of more relevance to psychology, Galton devised questionnaires to study individual differences in the intensity of mental imagery and conducted a word association experiment on himself that may have helped suggest the technique of free association to Freud. Many of these studies were collected together and reprinted in one of Galton's most popular books, *Inquiries into Human Faculty and Its Development* (1883).

Galton was knighted in 1909 and died two years later. His major ideas were controversial during his lifetime and remained so afterward. The idea of eugenics was regarded skeptically by Darwin himself, who saw it as a proposal for artificial as opposed to natural selection, and therefore unlikely to produce permanent changes in the species. Galton himself emphasized "positive" eugenics—the identification of highly able young men and women and the encouragement of them to intermarry and have many offspring. Perhaps naïvely, he believed that the negative side—the discouragement of the less able from having large families—could be effected through education rather than coercion. It is unlikely that he would have endorsed the policies of involuntary sterilization of the retarded adopted by many American states and Canadian provinces following his death, and he could never even have imagined the perversions of his ideas perpetrated by the Hitler regime in Germany, in the name of "race hygiene." Needless to say, the nature-nurture controversy which Galton named and did so much to formulate, remains as alive today as when he debated it with Alphonse de Candolle.

Bibliography

Works by Galton

Galton, F. (1865). Hereditary talent and character. *Macmillan's Magazine, 12,* 157–166, 318–327. Galton's first published account of his theory of hereditary intelligence and the idea (although not yet the names) for intelligence tests and eugenics.

Galton, F. (1869). *Hereditary genius.* London: Macmillan. Galton's most detailed argument for hereditary intelligence, documented with the cases of nearly a thousand eminent figures from three hundred families; here he also argues that intellectual ability is normally distributed in the population.

Galton, F. (1883). *Inquiries into human faculty and its development.* London: Macmillan. Reprints many of Galton's most important shorter works, including papers on mental imagery, word associations, sensory discrimination as an index of intelligence, and the history of twins.

Galton, F. (1888). Co-relations and their measurement. *Proceedings of the Royal Society, 45,* 135–145. Famous paper introducing the method of statistical correlation.

Galton, F. (1908). *Memories of my life.* London: Methuen. Galton's vividly written autobiography.

Works about Galton

Cowan, R. S. (1977). Nature and nurture: The interplay of biology and politics in the work of Francis Galton. In W. Coleman and C. Limoges (Eds.), *Studies in the history of biology* (Vol. 1, pp. 133–208). Baltimore, MD: Johns Hopkins University Press. A critical analysis of Galton's theories, arguing that they were strongly influenced by his conservative political inclinations.

Fancher, R. E. (1983). Alphonse de Candolle, Francis Galton, and the early history of the nature-nurture controversy. *Journal of the History of the Behavioral Sciences, 19,* 341–352. Details Galton's interaction with de Candolle, and his formulation of the nature-nurture controversy.

Fancher, R. E. (1989). Galton on examinations: An unpublished step in the invention of correlation. *Isis, 80,* 446–455. Describes the gradual development of Galton's ideas on correlation and regression.

Fancher, R. E. (1996). *Pioneers of psychology* (3rd ed). New York: Norton. Chapter 7, "The measurement of mind: Francis Galton and the psychology of individual differences" (pp. 216–245). Summarizes Galton's career and importance for psychology.

Forrest, D. W. (1974). *Francis Galton: The life and work of a Victorian genius.* London: Elek.

Kevles, D. (1985). *In the name of eugenics: Genetics and the uses of human heredity.* New York: Knopf. Starts with Galton, then traces the subsequent controversial history of the eugenics movement.

Pearson, K. (1914, 1924, 1930). *The life, letters and labours of Francis Galton,* 3 vols. Cambridge: Cambridge University Press. A detailed, lavishly illustrated, and opinionated account of Galton's life and work by his most important disciple, indispensable for Galton scholars because it reproduces much of his most important correspondence.

Raymond E. Fancher

GAMBLING. *See* Compulsive Gambling.

GAME THEORY is a branch of mathematics concerned with the analysis of the behavior of decision makers (called players) whose choices affect one another. An important distinction exists between the disciplines of individual and interactive decision-making. Individual decision-making, whether under certainty or uncertainty, leads to well-defined optimization problems, like maximizing an objective function (e.g., expected utility) subject to certain constraints. While these problems may be difficult to solve in practice, they involve no conceptual issues. Once the objective function is specified, the meaning of *optimal decision* is clear (even when actual behavior, for one reason or another, is not optimal). In interactive decision-making, the meaning of *optimal decision* is unclear, because no player completely controls the final outcome of the interaction. A formal analysis of interactive decision-making must address the conceptual issue of defining the problem before providing procedures for solving it. Game theory is concerned with both matters. It defines solutions, known as solution concepts, to several classes of interactive decision-making situations that appear in various areas of application and then investigates their properties and provides procedures for their computation.

The theory was first introduced as a scientific discipline by John von Neumann and Oskar Morgenstern in their monumental book *Theory of Games and Economic Behavior*. It has seen rapid expansion in the last 20 years or so. The largest single area of application of game theory has been economics; many modern textbooks in microeconomics and most of the journals in this discipline present or discuss game theoretical models in one form or another. Other important areas of application include political science (e.g., voting systems, power, and international relations), social psychology (e.g., two-person bargaining, social dilemmas, and coalition formation), sociology, evolutionary biology, accounting, marketing, computer science, law, and branches of philosophy such as ethics and epistemology. As is the case with many branches of mathematics, the relationship between theory and application has been two-sided: The theory has helped to structure interactive decision-making situations in these disciplines, understand their logic, prescribe rational solutions, and occasionally account for empirical phenomena and experimental findings, whereas experimental findings and applications have posed new questions and introduced new challenges that have led to new interpretations of existing concepts and additional theoretical developments.

Game theory may be viewed as a sort of umbrella theory for interactive behavior in the social sciences, where "social" is interpreted very broadly to include human beings as well as other kinds of players (collectives such as corporations and nations, animals, plants, computers, etc.). Only the essential aspects of the interactive situation are discussed and formally analyzed, rather than the entire situation with its peculiarities, ambiguities, and subtleties, and as such they can be applied in principle to all interactive situations.

The essential aspects typically include the following: There must be at least two players whose decisions affect each other. The game begins by one or more players making a choice (called a move) among a number of specified alternatives. Following that, a certain situation results determining which player makes the next move and what alternatives are open to her. The choices made by some or all of the players may or may not become known; therefore, when she has to make a choice, the information each player has about the previous choices of all other players must be specified. There is a termination rule determining when the possible plays of the game are completed. Finally, each situation defining an end of a play determines a payoff to each of the bona fide players. The game allows for chance moves by Nature (uncertainty), but if Nature intervenes it is considered a dummy player in the game, deriving no payoff.

Solution concepts are divided in terms of a basic distinction between cooperative games, where agreements, promises, and threats are fully binding and enforceable, to noncooperative games where commitments, even when reached by preplay communication, are not enforceable. The noncooperative approach focuses on the strategic choices of players—how they play the game and what strategies they choose to achieve their objectives. Therefore, it is intimately concerned with and strongly influenced by the details of the interactive process and the rules governing the game. In contrast, the cooperative approach focuses on the options available to the group of players—what coalitions form and how their members disburse their joint payoff.

The basic solution concept for noncooperative games is the Nash equilibrium. A Nash equilibrium is a vector of strategies—one for each player—if no player has an incentive (in terms of improving his payoff) to deviate from his part of the strategy vector given that the other players do not deviate. Thus, if the theory offers the strategy vector $(s_1, \ldots, s_n)$ as the solution but these strategies are not the Nash equilibrium, then at least one player will have an incentive to deviate from the theory's prediction, so the theory will be falsified by the actual play of the game. John Nash proved the existence (but not the uniqueness) of at least one equilibrium for every game with a finite number of strategies for each player. Subsequent research has attempted to eliminate equilibria that rely on noncredible threats (threats that are not to the player's best interests to execute) by "refining" the notion of the Nash equilibrium, has explored alternative interpretations of Nash equilibria for games played repeatedly by players who are not necessarily "rational" and who need not know the structure of the game, and has started to execute the "Nash program," which calls for reformulating cooperative games as noncooperative ones and then solving for their equilibria.

Social psychology has borrowed many of the basic concepts of game theory (e.g., payoff matrix, pure and mixed strategies, and equilibrium) in order to construct theories of social interaction and design experiments to test them. Early experiments were mostly concerned with two-person zero-sum games, where the interests of the two players are diametrically opposed, and with two-person nonzerosum games such as the Prisoner's Dilemma and Chicken, which include some outcomes that are preferred to others by both players. Subsequent research has shifted the focus to assess the descriptive power of various solution concepts in the areas of bargaining, social dilemmas, and coalition formation. However, most of the experimental research on interactive behavior in the last 20 years or so has been conducted outside of psychology within the rapidly growing discipline of experimental economics.

Bibliography

Aumann, R. J. (1987). Game theory. In J. Eatwell, M. Milgate, & P. Newman (Eds.), *The new palgrave*. New York: Norton. Includes a detailed, nontechnical history of game theory that focuses on conceptual issues.

Aumann, R. J., & Hart, S. (1992, 1994). *Handbook of game theory* (Vols. 1–2). Amsterdam: Elsevier. Contains survey articles written by leading professionals in the field on topics varying from chess to auctions that represent the state of the art in the field. A third volume is in production.

Binmore, K. *Fun and games: A text on game theory*. Lexington, MA: Heath. An introductory textbook which is especially strong on issues of rationality and knowledge.

Davis, D. D., & Holt, C. A. (1993). *Experimental economics*. Princeton, NJ: Princeton University Press. Outlines experimental research in economics mostly driven by game-theoretical models.

Fudenberg, D., & Tirole, J. (1991). *Game theory*. Cambridge, MA: MIT Press. A high-level, technical textbook on noncooperative game theory.

Gardner, R. (1995). *Games for business and economics*. New York: Wiley. A low-level textbook whose purpose is to enable students setting up and solving games of strategy that arise in business.

Gibbon, R. *Game theory for applied economics*. Princeton, NJ: Princeton University Press. Introduces noncooperative game theory to those who wish to construct game-theoretical models in applied fields within economics.

Kagel, J. H., & Roth, A. E. (Eds.). (1995). *Handbook of experimental economics*. Princeton, NJ: Princeton University Press. Contains lengthy survey articles on all major aspects of games that have been studied in the behavioral laboratory, including two-person bargaining, public goods provision, industrial organization, coordination, auctions, and individual decision-making.

Kreps, D. M. (1990). *A course in microeconomic theory*. Princeton, NJ: Princeton University Press. The last half of this book is an introductory text on game theory that includes excellent applications to economics.

Myerson, R. B. (1991). *Game theory: Analysis of conflict*. Cambridge, MA: Harvard University Press. A high-level technical textbook on game theory that is especially strong on questions of mechanism design and incomplete information.

Amnon Rapoport and Rami Zwick

GANGS. Understanding street gangs requires recognizing both their general patterns and their variety. The same is true of gang members: understanding them involves discerning both common patterns and their diversity on a number of defining characteristics. There is an unfortunate tendency among the media, both print and broadcast, to stereotype patterns of gang structure and behavior, to overlook the variety of these among gangs, and to focus instead on unique or dramatic extractions such as gang violence or psychopathic leadership. Furthermore, the media tend to overstate simplistic connections, as between street gangs and prison gangs, or between gangs and drug trafficking.

Similarly, agencies and officials engaged in intervening in gang life—police, courts, community-based private agencies, and others—have a tendency to stereotype gang and gang member patterns, and to overlook important differences that might relate to successful interventions. Whether these interventions are psychological, social, economic, enforcement, or judicial, they often ignore much of what is now known about gang patterns and varieties and thus reduce their own effectiveness. This article, therefore, emphasizes both patterns and varieties of gangs and gang members, eschewing dramatic and unique elements that do not lend themselves well to the science of gangs or the practice of gang prevention or intervention.

Definitions

Since gangs are generally informal groups rather than formal organizations, attempts to define "gang" have been both varied and somewhat arbitrary. Scholars and practitioners have not achieved consensus on the definition of gangs; some emphasize gang structure, some stress self-definition by admission of gang status, or use of identifiers such as gang name, tattoos, hand signs, and so on, whereas still others define gangs by their group behavior, especially criminal or even violent behavior. No definition seems to fit all cases, nor fully distinguish gangs from other, more common forms of peer groups. Most, but not all, scholars have come to see the street gang as evolving around its own antisocial behavior as a defining characteristic. That is, in contrast to the myriad other youthful peer groups that form around school, work, or neighborhood, street gangs are now usually defined or characterized by their members' orientations toward, or involvement in, illegal activities, even though these still comprise only a relatively small portion of daily activity.

Descriptive Patterns

In the current era, in contrast to the period roughly prior to 1950 when there were many ethnic White gangs (Irish, Italian, German, Polish, etc.), most street gangs are composed of relatively homogeneous, racial or ethnic minorities; Black gangs and Hispanic gangs predominate, followed by far fewer Asian gangs and Caucasian gangs. Most gangs are principally male. Females may be members of such groups, or may form companion or auxiliary gangs, or, more rarely, may form fully independent female gangs. The proportion of male gang membership has been reported in various studies to range from 100 to virtually zero, but on average may be close to a 3:1 or 4:1 ratio of males to females.

Consonant with minority membership, most street gangs are located within segregated portions of their city. Gangs are found not only in major metropolitan areas, but also in far smaller towns and cities including many with a population below ten thousand. Estimates by Klein (1995) and the National Gang Information Center (1995) have placed the number of cities with established street gangs between 1,100 to over 2,000 jurisdictions.

With the exception of specialty gangs, most street gangs exhibit a versatile pattern of offending, true of females as well as males. They are not crime "specialists." This is true, as well, of individual gang members: they are criminal generalists rather than specialists. The most common forms of crime are of minor seriousness: vandalism, graffiti, petty theft, alcohol and drug use, fighting, and battery. The more serious crimes of property, such as auto theft, burglary, or robbery, are less common but by no means negligible in frequency. Serious violent crimes—homicide, aggravated assault, arson, drive-by shootings, and so on—are even less common but most noted because of their consequences. The most typical victim of such violence is not a stranger or innocent bystander, but someone affiliated with a rival gang. In this sense, gang members are their own worst enemies.

This latter is true in another sense as well. Thornberry, Krohn, Lizotte, and Chard-Wierschem (1993) demonstrated that gangs exacerbate members' criminal behavior, but also tend to close members off from other, more legitimate and positive opportunities. Gang membership often is accompanied by a failure to complete school, failure to learn available work skills and be able to enter a satisfying job market, a lower development of useful adult social and interpersonal skills, and entrapment in low self-esteem and fatalism about life satisfactions. Gang members, that is, often harm themselves most, inadvertently, by cutting themselves off even further from mainstream life than is occasioned by their being raised in urban underclass settings.

Another negative impact, as a function of gang crime and negative public behavior, is the effect of gangs on their own local community. Serious gang activity in a neighborhood leads to fear among residents and local businessmen, a constrained quality of life, and a reduced level of community activity. A seriously impacted gang community can contribute to a rather desultory social situation, often resistant to attempts at gang control or other community involvement. This can be most destructive in gang-infested housing projects.

Since such situations would seem to require early identification of potential gang members in order to prevent their gang involvement, attention has been paid to the personal and psychological characteristics of gang members, including the characteristics that put one at risk of gang membership. But just as there is variety among gangs, so there is variety among gang members; in fact, so much variety that a consensus on what gang members are like has not been attained. Although most scholars find street gang members to be quite similar to nongang members in their same neighborhoods, others have described them as fundamentally different: more hedonistic, or more sociopathic, or more defiant and rationally materialistic.

Factors that put young people at risk of gang membership clearly include minority status and racism, poverty, family conflict, and inadequate local and community resources. But these factors characterize nongang delinquents as well. Finding risk factors specific to gang membership alone has proven difficult, but some consensus across recent research projects suggests that they include individual, family, peer, school, and neighborhood variables. Thus, it should be possible for many disciplines to contribute to gang prevention and intervention.

Public Response

Spergel (1995) outlined five prominent approaches taken by public agencies to reduce gang activity. The first of these is *suppression*, encompassing various procedures employed by law enforcement and the courts to crack down on gang activity. Special antigang legislation, correctional concentration on gang members, creation of gang units in prosecutors' offices and police departments, and cross-agency intelligence operations are examples of gang suppression approaches. A second approach is *social intervention*, including special outreach by street workers, short-term crisis intervention and mediation, counseling, and referral to social service. The street worker approach in particular has been a mainstay of gang intervention for many decades. A third and related approach is referred to as *opportunities provision*, emphasizing the response to gang members' relative exclusion from mainstream opportunities in employment, education, recreation, and community participation. This approach thus opens up jobs and job training, tutoring and alternative schooling, and referrals to special youth activities in the community as alternatives to gang participation. A fourth approach emphasizes youth less and local institutions more. Attempts are made to effect *organizational change* such that unions, schools, social agencies, churches, and the like will become more oriented toward serving gang-prone youth. This is the opposite side of the coin to opportunities provision. The fifth and most comprehensive approach is *community mobilization*, an attempt to reduce gang activity by empowering local community residents and businessmen to exert informal social control in the area on behalf of youth who might engage in gang activity. Such mobilization of community forces is a long-term, complex program based on the notion that gangs thrive in a setting of social disorganization, but will be relatively unnecessary in a community organized for healthy youth development.

Social and Psychological Interventions

The listing here reveals that few modes of gang interventions have been based upon psychological theory. Gang programs have traditionally been the bailiwick of sociology and social work, and these have largely failed to demonstrate their effectiveness. Several reasons can be suggested:

1. *Gang* prevention is different from general delinquency or crime prevention, yet the specifics of this difference seldom guide practitioners.
2. The gang-spawning community is paramount, but modifying it has proven beyond our resources.
3. Gangs are more than their individual parts. There is a group process level that must be engaged. Furthermore, the interaction between group process and the response of families, residents, community, and police is a function of perceived gang *threat*, and evokes punitive responses that produce even stronger gang cohesiveness.
4. Gang *prevention* fails in the absence of gang *control*, because joining gangs is, in part, a response to the appeal of high-status older gang members and perceived need for protection from other (rival) gangs.
5. Concentration has been on gang intervention to reduce their impact on victims and on local residents' quality of life. Far less attention has been paid to the effects of gang membership on the members themselves: injury, reduction of life options, isolation from prosocial adults, damage to self-esteem and social skill development, and the like. These are areas where individual and community psychology might make significant contributions.

A review of gang intervention literature, however, reveals a paucity of involvement by psychologists to date. A fair summary of this situation might be that psychologists have paid little attention to street gangs as an intervenable phenomenon, and in those few instances of attention noted, they have failed to appreciate the important differences between gangs and gang members on the one hand, and disturbed or antisocial or delinquent youth generally on the other. There is much that could be contributed from individual, group, and community psychology; meanwhile, the absence of psychological perspectives leaves the field wide open to interventions by law enforcement and the courts, which largely ignore individual and group concerns.

Bibliography

Cohen, A. K. (1995). *Delinquent boys: The culture of the gang.* New York: Free Press. This early volume established the notion of gang culture and group process as a principal sociological perspective.

Goldstein, H. P., & Huff, R. C. (Eds.). (1993). *The gang intervention handbook.* Champaign, IL: Research Press. An eighteen-chapter collection with sections on psychological, contextual, and criminal justice intervention programs for gangs.

Klein, M. W. (1995). *The American street gang: Its nature, prevalence, and control.* New York: Oxford University Press. A summary of gang research over several decades with the author's perspective on significant gang issues, including the failures of gang intervention programs.

National Gang Information Center. (1995). *1995 National youth gang survey.* Washington, DC: U.S. Department of Justice, Office of Juvenile Justice and Delinquency Prevention. An extensive survey of law enforcement agencies across the country, employing a loosely structural definition of gangs to establish their prevalence.

Sanchez-Jankowski, M. (1993). *Islands in the street: Gangs and American urban society.* Berkeley: University of California Press. A controversial ethnographic study of gangs in three cities that proposes radical changes in street gangs over several decades.

Spergel, I. A. (1995). *The youth gang problem.* New York: Oxford University Press. A text and major overview of gang issues over several decades, this volume details a broad assortment of gang programs revealed in a national survey in the early 1990s.

Thornberry, T. B., Krohn, M. D., Lizotte, H. J., & Chard-Wierschem, D. (1993). The role of juvenile gangs in facilitating delinquent behavior. *Journal of Crime and Delinquency, 30,* 55–87.

Yablonsky, L. (1963). *The violent gang.* New York: Macmillan. An early study of New York gangs that emphasized group process and sociopathic gang leadership.

Malcolm W. Klein

GATE CONTROL THEORY. *See* Pain.

GAY. *See* Homosexuality; *and* Sexual Orientation.

GEMELLI, AGOSTINO (1878–1959), Italian psychologist. He received his medical degree from the University of Padua in 1892, and as Camillo Golgi's assistant devoted himself to research on embryology, histology, and physiology. In 1911, he received a doctorate in philosophy from the University of Louvain.

In 1914, Gemelli wrote a number of theoretical essays and conducted several experimental studies on the relationship between thought and volition (1911) and on the sense of touch (1912). During World War I, he was involved in the selection of air force pilots, and in 1914 he founded and directed the first psychophysiological laboratory of the Italian armed forces.

In 1919, Gemelli founded the Università Cattolica del Sacro Cuore (Catholic University of the Sacred Heart) in Milan, which would subsequently receive the status of *libera università* ("free university") from the Italian government and where Gemelli would serve as rector until his death in 1959.

In 1920, Gemelli and Federico Kiesow founded the journal *L'Archivio di Psicologia, Neurologia e Psichiatria*. He continued teaching experimental psychology (*Introduzione alla psicologia sperimentale*, 1924), being primarily concerned with problems relative to perception (*Introduzione allo studio della percezione*, 1928) and language. In opposition to Gestalt theorists, Gemelli underscored the role of experience in perception and attributed great importance to the study of the origin of the perceptual process. Thus, perception was not only considered a method of obtaining intellectual knowledge, but—by preparing for and anticipating action—an essential tool for adapting to environmental conditions.

In 1938, in Milan, Gemelli founded the journal *L'Archivio di psicologia, neurologia, psichiatria e psicoterapia*, which was published under the auspices of the Consiglio Nazionale delle Ricerche (the National Research Institute). This journal substituted for Levi Bianchini's *Archivio di psicologia, neurologia, psichiatria e psicoanalisi*, which could no longer be published due to the introduction of racial laws at the time.

Despite the war raging in Italy, Gemelli's journal continued to make many contributions to medical psychology, psychiatry, and psychopharmacology. From its pages, Gemelli continued to arouse interest in psychological research, although, in conforming to the anti-Anglo-Saxon propaganda of the fascist regime, he assumed a number of ambiguous positions that would increase the provincialism and isolation of Italian psychology. As president of the Psychology Section of the Consiglio Nazionale delle Ricerche (National Research Institute), Gemelli organized a conference for Italian and German psychologists that was held in Rome and Milan on 16–21 June 1941. It proved to be emblematic in this respect: The conference was entirely dedicated to establishing a close coordination between the two countries in meeting the demands of warfare within the field of psychology.

Gemelli's investigations in applied psychology were extremely important, from his initial research on the personality of aircraft pilots and on the criteria used for their selection, to his work on industrial psychology (*La psicologia applicata all'industria*, 1944), and his studies on the problems of professional guidance (*L'orientamento professionale dei giovani nella scuola*, 1947). His contributions devoted to the discussion of the epistemological status of psychology are also of great interest. He defined psychology as "the science that has as its object, the study . . . of the characteristics of man's life, namely, psychic activity and its functions, also considered in their biological foundations." According to Gemelli, it is only through perceiving man "in his admirable unity," that it becomes possible for psychology to obtain the status of an autonomous science, thus achieving independence from both philosophy and biological science. Gemelli claimed that psychology could find its own method of investigation in observation and experimental studies and its privileged object, the study of conduct. He asserted that "the methodological approach to the study of personality is based on the correspondence existing between inner life and behavior" ("Introduzione alla psicologia," written with G. Zunini, 1947).

Gemelli's attitude toward psychoanalysis was also not always clear or coherent. While opposing the complete dismissal of psychoanalysis, he nevertheless attacked the deterministic, instinctual and atheistic "psychoanalytic philosophy." Furthermore, he attempted to retrieve various methodological aspects of psychoanalysis in accordance with the distinctive eclectic approach that he had previously adopted toward behaviorism and Gestalt psychology. Emblematic in this regard are his efforts to underline the existing connections between psychology and medicine, as well as his acceptance of the Freudian hypothesis, although he limits its application to a strictly clinical context.

Gemelli's activity was not, however, limited to psychological research: in 1914 he founded the publishing house *Vita e Pensiero*, and in 1936 he became president of the Pontifical Academy of Science. He was the director of the journal *Rivista di filosofia neoscolastica* (founded by him in 1909), rector of the Sacred Heart University, and president of the Committee for the Application of Psychology of the Consiglio Nazionale delle Ricerche (National Research Council). Gemelli exerted a lasting influence on Italian Catholic culture as a whole.

Nino Dazzi

GENDER, SEX, AND CULTURE. [*This entry comprises three articles*:

> Gender and Culture
> Sex and Culture
> Sex Differences and Gender Differences

The first article describes how appropriate gender roles and behaviors vary across cultures. The second article provides a wide-ranging cross-cultural overview of standards of sexual behavior. The third article profiles sex differences and (or versus) gender differences.]

Gender and Culture

Sex refers to the physiological, hormonal, and genetic makeup (XX or XY chromosome) of an individual. Gender is a cultural category that contains the roles, behaviors, rights, responsibilities, privileges and personality traits assigned by that specific culture to men and women (Cyrus, 1997; Wade & Tavris, 1994). Gender roles may be seen as the constellation of behaviors a culture deems appropriate for males and females and may include the attitudes and emotions that are seen as fundamental to being a man or a woman (Carroll & Wolpe, 1996). Gender identity is a psychological construct that reflects an individual's psychological sense of who and what they are. In most individuals gender identity is consistent with their biological sex but this is not automatically true for everyone. Masculinity and femininity represent the ideal constellation of traits that a specific culture assigns to each gender. Traditional definitions of masculine behavior include the presence of physical strength, mechanical ability, ambition, the capacity for assertiveness, control of emotions, knowledge about the world, and the capacity to be a good provider (Cyrus, 1997). Feminine behavior is characterized by passivity, domesticity, dependency, emotional expressiveness, a preoccupation with one's physical appearance, the presence of nurturing and maternal instincts (Cyrus, 1997). Socialization is the process that teaches a culture's members the roles it has assigned as the correct role.

Traditional definitions of masculinity and femininity, and gender roles, differ across cultures and change over time within the same culture. As gender is a category that is explicitly shaped by culture, it represents a socially constructed identity rather than one that is biologically determined. Roles and behaviors assigned to men and women reflect the attitudes and practices of the culture that assigns them at a particular point in time. Understanding the construction of a specific culture's gender roles requires an analysis of its history, political system, economy, how the economy is affected by geography, available natural resources and weather (Wade & Tavris, 1994). Such an analysis also requires information about who controls and distributes resources, the relative safety of community members from hostile outsiders, the kinds of work people do, how they structure that work and whether there is pressure to produce or restrict the production of children (Wade & Tavris, 1994).

Gilmore (1991) observes that rigid concepts of manhood are found in cultures where there is great competition for few resources. It is under these conditions that the men of the culture are taught to hunt, compete for work, and go off to war to fight their enemies. Gilmore explains that this frequently entails great risk and raises the question of what kinds of rewards would be needed or are present in cultures that would persuade men to adopt roles that involve threats to their physical safety. Giving males social prestige, power, and women is viewed as the payoff for doing the culture's "dirty and dangerous work." Of course, in such arrangements Gilmore (1991) points out that the culture must socialize its women to be obedient and accept a position in the hierarchy that is subservient to its males.

Changes in the kind of work a culture requires inevitably produces changes in gender roles and relationships. Wade and Tavris (1994) suggest that the Industrial Revolution in the United States required men to work away from the home to a much greater degree than they had before. As a result, a greater distinction was made between work within and outside of the home with men working outside and women working inside. However, as the nature of the kinds of work a culture does changes from that which once required brute strength to work requiring service or technical skill, gender roles will reflect these changes. This highlights the degree to which practical conditions may have a greater influence on gender roles than genetic or biological determinants (Gilmore, 1991; Wade & Tavris, 1994).

Wade and Tavris (1994) observe that women's roles are affected by the social control of specific opportunities, such as: the measure of economic security, access to education, access to birth control, and medical care, the degree of self-determination, participation in public and political life, the power to make family decisions, and the degree of physical safety. Among countries surveyed, Scandinavian countries offer the greatest range of these opportunities while Bangladesh offers the least (Williams & Best, 1994).

Most presumptions about gender are based on the assumption that gender is a dichotomous category in which people are either male or female. It is also assumed that biological sex, gender identity and gender roles are consistent and that satisfaction with one's biological sex is normative. Such assumptions are challenged by the presence of transsexuals and transgendered persons. Assumptions that presume a dichotomy of gender are further challenged by cross-cultural studies that reveal the presence of cultures that have a legitimate identity for persons who are regarded as neither male or female.

Wade and Tavris (1994) observe that well into the late 1800s, the Plains Indians and many western tribes responded with understanding when a young member of the tribe wanted to live the role that was not assigned to that individual's biological sex. Crossing traditional gender roles was not merely allowed but was made legitimate by the existence of socially acceptable and specific status in the tribe. Tafoya (1996) contends these practices were at variance with established European and Euro-American orthodoxy and that many of the groups who conquered native tribes killed their members on learning their beliefs and practices about sexuality. Consequently, Native American people learned to avoid any open discussion of gender and sexuality as they could be killed because of it (Tafoya, 1996). Genocide in these cases decreased the number of people left to tell the pre-colonial tribal stories and left the survivors in fear of being killed if they were to continue to pass the stories along. As a consequence, many of the tribes' stories were lost, even to many contemporary Native American people themselves.

Categories for people who were neither male nor female were reserved in many tribes for what were deemed two-spirit people (Blackwood, 1994; Williams, 1986). The term "two spirit" has its origins in the belief that an individual has a male and female spirit within, but that most must work at achieving the balance that a two-spirit person exemplifies (Tafoya, 1996). Tafoya (1997) cautions that concepts and roles for what constitutes a two-spirit person may differ between tribes such that descriptions within one tribe may not be generalized to another. Tafoya (1996) observes that in over half of surviving native languages there are terms for members of tribes that are neither male nor female, but are something else. This is consistent with Native American traditions that presume that all individuals have male and female constituents. Two-spirit people however are believed to view the world through the eyes of male and female, to "see" further than either male or female and to have the potential to exist on a more integrated level (Tafoya, 1996; Williams, 1986). A two-spirit person was often a biological male who took on the role of a female, but was not considered a female or male. Such a person might sometimes marry a male (Blackwood, 1984; Williams, 1986). Other persons with nontraditional gender roles found in Native American tribes (also referred to as Berdache) were bi-

ological females who had demonstrated as a child an interest in activities associated with males. Such a person would be initiated into puberty as a male and considered a male (with respect to roles and activities) thereafter. A female Berdache could marry a woman, remain childless and had the potential of becoming a prominent member of the tribe (Carroll & Wolpe, 1996; Tafoya, 1996). Among Alaskan natives, Ingalik (Carroll & Wolpe, 1996; Tafoya, 1996) were biological females who were allowed in nude sweat baths and treated as males.

Scholars (Blackwood, 1984; Williams, 1986) have historically reported that two-spirit people were believed to have special powers and accorded a special level of respect on the basis of those powers. Tafoya (1996) warns that non-Native American scholars may have observed that two-spirit people were respected and incorrectly attributed that respect to their status as two-spirited. He suggests that in native tribes, people were not accorded or denied the respect of the tribe because of their gender or their sexual orientation. Being two-spirited did not automatically accord respect any more than it would elicit the kind of revulsion observed in Western cultures when members do not neatly fit the confines of one gender or the other. According to Tafoya (1996), respect was not accorded on the basis of gender or sexual orientation (as it is understood by modern westerners); rather it was more specifically person based.

Native Americans are not the only cultural group who have a category for those who do not fit traditional gender dichotomies. In the Persian Gulf territory of Oman there is a group of individuals who are biologically male but are exempt from traditional Islamic rules that restrict men's interactions with women (Wikan, 1977). Xanith (Wikan, 1977) have men's names but are not considered men nor neuter within the culture. In Thailand a class of biological males who dress and behave as women but display pride in their male genitalia, Kathoey, serve a function similar to that of Xanith. In India, a class of males known as Hijra undergo ritual castration. While they dress as women, some have facial hair and are considered a third gender. Most spend their lives worshiping Mother Goddess Bahuchara Mata (Nanda, 1990). Many Indians believe that Hijra can curse or bless male children and as such, many Hijra make a living selling blessings to new parents. Others serve as male prostitutes. Herdt (1997) observes that in old Hawaii, at the time of Captain Cook, the Aikane represented a class of males who commonly transformed to a third gender in which some men took on the roles and sexuality of women (Morris, 1990). In Tahiti, the Mahu represented a third gender that did not consistently dress or behave as the other sex (Herdt, 1997). Some Mahu are males who take on women's dress and roles, and whose sexual partners are men, while others assumed appearances that were more like men. While most Mahu were males, the existence of women in this group has been reported. Herdt (1997) notes that some of the Mahu, as they existed in old Polynesia, may have been what would now be considered bisexual, individuals who were primarily attracted to members of the other sex but sometimes desired sexual relations with members of their own sex. In contemporary Tahitian society, the Mahu may be viewed by Westerners as a transvestite, or someone taking on the physical appearance (clothing, makeup) of women (Herdt, 1997). These examples serve to highlight social contexts and cultures in which dichotomous categories of gender were not the tradition.

Cross-Cultural Studies of Gender

Behaviors that are considered suitable for members of one gender in one culture may be considered inappropriate for members of that gender in another culture. For example, women are permitted to engage in premarital sex in many parts of Polynesia, however it is forbidden and severely punished in Iran and parts of the Sudan (Williams & Best, 1994). Similarly, extramarital affairs are acceptable for women who are part of the Toda of India but are expressly forbidden in Islamic countries. Permission to express emotions and the degree to which they may be expressed varies along gender lines as well. While in many cultures women are given greater license to be emotionally expressive than men, in many Asian countries, both sexes are expected to contain the outward expression of emotions. In the middle east, men are permitted and expected to be as emotionally expressive as women (Williams & Best, 1994).

Williams and Best (1994) conducted perhaps the most extensive, large scale studies on gender stereotypes in over 30 countries over a period of 15 years. University students in different cultures were asked to consider a list of 300 adjectives and indicate which words, in their culture, would be associated with men, women or both. The identified characteristics associated with gender revealed a high degree of pancultural agreement across the countries studied (Williams & Best, 1994). Male stereotypes were more favorable than female stereotypes, with respect to attributed characteristics in Japan, South America, and Nigeria. Female stereotypes were more favorable than male stereotypes in Italy, Peru, and Australia. Stereotypes of men tended to suggest that maleness is seen as generally physically stronger and more active than femaleness. Both genders identified the person they wanted to be, or their ideal self, in terms that were more in keeping with masculine rather than feminine stereotypes, as stronger and more active. In studies measuring sex role ideology, students in 14 countries were asked what they thought

they should believe about gender roles (Williams & Best, 1994). The most egalitarian gender ideologies were found in the Netherlands, Germany, and Finland. The most male-dominated ideologies were found in Nigeria, Pakistan, and India. The United States fell somewhere in the middle of this distribution. Generally, women held more modern views than men. Findings also suggest that culture contributes more to variations in sex role ideology than gender. For example, there was more agreement about sex role ideology between men and women of the same culture than between women of different cultures or between men of different cultures. Gender roles appeared to be more sharply differentiated in Protestant rather than Catholic countries in ways that often reflected the differing place of women in the religion's theology and in the religious practices of the group (Williams & Best, 1990, 1994). Williams and Best (1990, 1994) cross-cultural studies included samples of 5- and 8-year-old middle class children from 25 countries. In all countries studied, by the time children are 5 years old they show beginning knowledge of gender stereotypes. Their sex stereotype knowledge increases significantly between ages 5 and 8. Brazilian children revealed the least and Pakistani children revealed the greatest knowledge of gender stereotypes within their cultures when 5-year-olds were sampled. These findings suggest that repeated exposure to gender stereotypes in an individual's culture socializes individuals in that culture into viewing the appropriateness of certain roles more similarly than not.

Asexuality and Hermaphroditism

There are individuals who are born with XX and XY chromosomes, giving them a genetic gender identity, however they have no sex organs. Such individuals are considered asexual. Individuals who are born asexual are often assigned a gender at birth, and subsequently given surgery and hormone treatments to facilitate the development of secondary sex characteristics consistent with the identity they have been assigned. In most cases they live out the role of the gender to which they were assigned, however, there are some cases of individuals who live as asexual beings (Carroll & Wolpe, 1996).

While some individuals are born with no sex organs, hermaphrodites are born with male and female gonadal tissue (one ovary and one testicle). Hermaphrodites have a genetic sex represented by the presence of XX chromosomes for females and XY chromosomes for males. True hermaphroditism is rare, however, pseudohermaphroditism is less uncommon. Pseudohermaphrodites are born with testicles or ovaries, usually not both; however, their sex organs are not consistent with their genetic sex. Others may have ambiguous genitalia. To correct these problems a gender identity is assigned at birth or early in the child's life and a combination of surgical and hormonal treatments may be used to assist in the development of genitals and other physical characteristics that approximate or conform to those of the assigned gender. Pseudohermaphrodites acquire the gender identity and gender roles of the gender they are assigned to despite the fact that their genetic gender is not consistent with their assigned gender. While there are exceptions, the adjustment of these individuals suggests that gender identity and gender roles are strongly influenced by cultural factors. The environmental context of a culture plays a significant role in influencing what specific roles or behaviors the culture assigns to its men and women. While the vast majority of gender-specific behaviors differ widely in different parts of the world, most appear to be determined primarily by cultural context (Rathus, Nevid, & Fichner-Rathus, 1993; Williams & Best, 1994).

Bibliography

Blackwood, E. (1984). Sexuality and gender in certain Native American tribes: The case of the cross-gender females. *Signs: Journal of Women in Culture and Society, 10,* 27–42.

Carroll, J. L., & Wolpe, P. R. (1996). *Sexuality and gender in society.* New York: HarperCollins.

Cyrus, V. (Ed.). (1997). Gender identity. In V. Cyrus (Ed.), *Experiencing race, class and gender in the United States* (pp. 64–65). Mountain View, CA: Mayfield.

Gilmore, D. (1991). *Manhood in the making.* New Haven, CT: Yale University Press.

Harris, M. (1974). *Cows, pigs, wars and witches: The riddles of culture.* New York: Random House.

Herdt, G. (1990). Developmental continuity as a dimension of sexual orientation across cultures. In D. McWhirter, J. Reinisch, & S. Sanders (Eds.), *Homosexuality and heterosexuality: The Kinsey scale and current research* (pp. 208–238). New York: Oxford University Press.

Herdt, G. (1994). *Ritualized homosexuality in Melanesia.* Berkeley, CA: University of California Press.

Herdt, G. (1997). *Same sex, different cultures: Exploring gay and lesbian lives.* Boulder, CO: Westview Press.

Morris, R. J. (1990). Aikane: Accounts of Hawaiian same sex relationships in the journals of Captain Cook's third voyage (1776–1780). *Journal of Homosexuality, 19,* 21–54.

Nanda, S. (1990). *Neither man, nor woman.* Belmont, CA: Wadsworth.

Rathus, S., Nevid, J., & Fichner-Rathus, L. (1993). *Human sexuality in a world of diversity.* Boston: Allyn & Bacon.

Tafoya, T. N. (1996). Native two-spirit people. In R. P. Cabaj & T. S. Stein (Eds.), *Textbook of homosexuality and mental health* (pp. 603–617). Washington, DC: American Psychiatric Press.

Wade, C. & Tavris, C. (1994). The longest war: Gender and culture. In W. J. Lonner & R. S. Malpass (Eds.), *Psychology and culture* (pp. 121–126). Boston: Allyn & Bacon.

Wikan, U. (1977). Man becomes woman: Transsexualism in Oman as a key to gender roles. *Man, 12,* 304–391.

Williams, W. (1986). *The spirit and the flesh: Sexual diversity in American Indian culture.* Boston: Beacon Press.

Williams, J. E., & Best, D. L. (1990). *Measuring sex stereotypes: A multi-nation study.* Newbury Park, CA: Sage.

Williams, J. E., & Best, D. L. (1994). Cross-cultural views of women and men. In W. J. Lonner & R. S. Malpass (Eds.), *Psychology and culture* (pp. 191–197). Boston: Allyn & Bacon.

Beverly Greene

Sex and Culture

Sexual behavior includes the constellation of behaviors and physical activities that are involved in the expression of erotic feelings or desires. While the capacity for sexual feelings and desires has biological origins, the way that capacity is understood and the way it may be expressed is culturally embedded, varies significantly across cultures and varies within a culture over time. Sexual activities may be characterized by factors such as specific physical activities, frequency, the presence or absence of a sexual partner, number of partners over a lifetime, number of concurrent partners, the gender of the partner, and age of initiation and termination. The role of procreation in sexual relationships across cultures ranges in importance from being the only purpose for sex that is culturally sanctioned in some cultures and relationships to having no role at all in others.

Sex and sexuality can only be meaningfully understood in the context of culture. It is in the culture that we find the rationale or meaning for the sexual practices and beliefs that are specific to members of the group. Its meaning is embedded in the interaction of all that comprises a culture or society. Cultural beliefs and values about sex are influenced by the culture's political history, geographical location, weather, economic needs, natural and other resources, religion, the degree to which religion and state laws are separate or merged, and other factors. Cultural institutions such as family, religion, economy, law, and media shape and in some cases completely dictate the role and scope of sexuality in an individual's life.

The culture's institutions also communicate values about sexuality and regulate the practice of sexual relationships among the culture's members. For example, the specifics of a culture determine the kinds of relationships in which sanctioned sexual activity may take place and is likely to determine how those relationships are to be structured. Carroll and Wolpe (1996) observe that social value judgments and not science ultimately determine which behaviors are considered appropriate and which are not, as well as what structures in relationships are appropriate and what structures are considered inappropriate. For example, some cultures sanction sexual relations only when they occur within the context of a marital relationship; for others, marital status is irrelevant. Even in the context of cultures that require marriage as a prerequisite for sexual activity, different cultures define marriage differently. While some cultures consider monogamous fidelity an inherent characteristic of marriage, others do not require monogamy. In some cultures men may have more than one wife or have license to engage in extramarital relations, and in some cultures women may engage in extramarital relations as well. The rules a culture establishes about sexual contact, patterns or rules that regulate sexual behavior between or among the sexes, what is considered normal or abnormal, natural or unnatural, sinful or morally correct is the result of the interaction of many of the variables that define the culture itself. Taken as a whole, these factors affect all aspects of sexuality and sexual practices in any specific culture. For example, in a culture where resources are scarce, the production of children may increase the competition for few resources, particularly food. In this context, there may be pressure to restrict the production of children, reflected in sexual beliefs, taboos and values that restrict sexual activities that could result in pregnancy and perhaps encourage activities that do not result in pregnancy. The rules that regulate sexual behavior in this context may be more directly related to limiting the production of children than with concerns about sex per se. On the other hand, in cultures where there are large areas of uncultivated land or farms, more members may be needed to develop the land and maintain it. In this context, one may see attitudes about sex that encourage early marriage or sanction the initiation of sexual activity at younger ages. Wade and Tavris (1994) observe that one New Guinea tribe, located in an inhospitable climate of the highlands where food is scarce, believes that sex is powerful and mysterious, that it weakens men and that women are unclean. This group also believes that if sexual activity is conducted in a garden it will lead to a blight of the crop. Because of these attitudes, antagonism between men and women is common and men tend to remain single longer, marrying later in life. This behavior leads to lower birth rates, conserving the group's resources. However, in another New Guinea tribe beliefs about sex are completely different (Wade & Tavris, 1994). In this tribe, sex was encouraged as an activity that revitalized men and fostered plant growth. The latter tribe was located in a geographical region with large areas of uncultivated terrain. More individuals were needed to supply the labor required to cultivate the land and defend the group. The way that this group structured its

beliefs about sexual activity facilitated the creation of needed group members (Wade & Tavris, 1994).

While many rules regulating sexual behavior are based on the culture's characteristics, within a culture, gender and socioeconomic class may further determine that certain forbidden behaviors are allowed for some individuals, often those with greater social privilege, but not for others. For example, while the incest taboo appears to be in place across cultures, the degree to which it is strictly enforced and which family members are included varies. Thornhill & Thornhill (1987) observe that divine rulers of ancient Egypt and royal families of the Incas and Himalayas permitted marriage between brothers and sisters, however marriage between siblings in these cultures was forbidden among commoners. Marriage between close and distant cousins was not uncommon among twentieth-century European royalty, as well as some members of American aristocratic families; however, it has not been routine among commoners. In fact, a stereotype of poor southern and Appalachian Whites, intended as a slur or indication of their lack of worth, is the belief that cousins and other family members have sex with one another or marry routinely. That this behavior would be regarded as a defect among poor and disenfranchised members of the population, yet permitted among the privileged classes and royalty speaks directly to the issues of class and culture. Rathus, Nevid, and Fichner-Rathus (1993) and Carroll and Wolpe (1996) observe that marriage among family was a means of keeping the family wealth within that group and preserving the divisions between the social classes. We might also surmise that among the aristocracy, only other aristocracy would be deemed worthy enough for a union. Since their numbers were and continue to be finite and since many royal families share some common ancestors, the choices among them would be far fewer than those available in the general population. Marriage to someone with whom there may be family ties would be difficult to avoid.

Studies of sexual behavior suggest that universal trends across cultures are uncommon, however general findings have been observed. According to Marshall and Suggs (1971) masturbation is rare in preliterate groups; foreplay is used prior to intercourse in most cultures; when used, foreplay is generally initiated by males; sexual intercourse occurs most commonly at night before participants fall asleep; women's orgasms vary greatly from culture to culture. These represent general trends observed at that time. They do not apply with uniformity to all members of any cultural group. Laumann, Gagnon, and Michael (1994) find that more educated individuals tend to have a greater number of partners over the lifespan when compared to their less well-educated counterparts; men are likely to have a larger number of sexual partners over the lifespan compared to women and that for both men and women the majority of sexual partners are accumulated during their twenties. Observations and generalizations about sexual behavior tend to be based on research with heterosexual participants. These findings must be viewed with caution in our attempts to understand lesbian and gay male sexual relationships.

Blumstein and Schwartz (1983) research suggests that just as gender differences play a role in the sexual behavior of heterosexual couples, it plays a role in the behavior of lesbian and gay couples as well. However, those gender differences will be a reflection of the gender roles in a specific culture. We may not assume that the differences observed in lesbians and gay men socialized in the United States will be the same as for their counterparts in other cultures and societies. For example, Blumstein and Schwartz (1983) observe that gay male couples have a higher frequency of sexual activity than lesbian couples. We may argue that since heterosexual coitus cannot be used to define sex among lesbian and gay couples that the definition of the behavior being observed requires refining. Nonetheless, Blumstein and Schwarz (1983) attribute the disparity in frequency to differences in gender role socialization that result in males being more apt to initiate sexual activity than women. While they also consider the possibility of lower sex drive in women, and the possibility that women are less apt to express emotional feelings sexually, these findings must be limited to lesbians and gay men in the United States. In a culture where women are encouraged from a young age, rather than discouraged, to be assertive about their sexual and other needs, lesbians in that culture may not have sex with less frequency than gay males or heterosexual couples. More cross-cultural research on lesbian and gay men is needed to more adequately address this issue.

When we examine non-Western cultures we see a variety of different sexual practices within varied cultural groups. In the South Pacific islands of Mangaia, attitudes about sexuality are more open than in Western cultures. For example, women are encouraged to be sexually aggressive, to initiate sexual activity and from an early age are taught directly by elders how to have multiple orgasms (Carroll & Wolpe, 1996). Both male and female children are encouraged to masturbate (Rathus, Nevid, & Fichner-Rathus, 1993). The sexual beliefs on Inis Beag, an island off the coast of Ireland, stand in stark contrast to those of Mangaia. On Inis Beag, sexual intercourse is viewed negatively and is considered appropriate only for procreation. Members of this community believe that if a woman experiences sexual pleasure or achieves orgasm during sex, she is abnormal (Messinger, 1971). Accordingly, sanctioned sexual relations may take place only within marriage. The presence of premarital sexual relations is not observed (Messinger, 1971) and marriage is delayed until

the middle thirties for men and middle twenties for women (Rathus, Nevid, & Fichner-Rathus 1993). Prior to marriage, men and women tend to be socialized separately. The way sexual relationships are conducted and structured in this culture is consistent with the view of sex as an activity that is a part of one's marital obligation but not an activity that should result in any pleasure. Couples have sex clothed with minimal foreplay (Carroll & Wolpe, 1994; Messinger, 1971; Rathus, Nevid, & Fichner-Rathus 1993).

Other practices in varied cultures are a reflection of significant differences in beliefs about sex from conventional Western notions. Among the Toda of South India (Carroll & Wolpe, 1994; Howard, 1989) women are allowed to have sexual relations outside of their marriage, with their husband's knowledge. Among the Chukchee men in the Siberian arctic, sex with one's wife may be exchanged or offered to friends (Rathus, Nevid, & Fichner-Rathus, 1993). In sub-Saharan Africa, marriage is structured such that men are allowed to have multiple sex partners (concurrently), more than one wife, and concubines while wives are expected to be faithful to their husbands. These practices stand in stark contrast to the requirement of sexual fidelity contained in Christian marriage. Carroll and Wolpe (1996) and Leslie and Korman (1989) observe that Western cultural practices reflected in customs in the United States are among less than 5% of all cultures that forbid extramarital sexual relationships. They attribute this to the Judeo-Christian values that serve as underpinnings for moral customs.

Just as sexual practices vary across cultures, they also change over time within a culture. In Western cultures, anal and oral sex were once considered perversions, as were same-sex relationships and masturbation. Indeed, homosexuality was once considered a mental illness. While prejudice and discrimination against those who identify themselves as lesbians and gay men persists, the American Psychiatric Association removed it from the diagnostic nomenclature in 1973. The American Psychological Association and other mental health organizations urged its members to abandon the pathology models of homosexuality as there is no scientific basis for the assumptions contained within the pathology models. While anal and oral sex are still against the law in some states in the United States, they are no longer considered sexual perversions nor are they considered signs of poor mental health. Indeed, if one examines attitudes toward homosexuality over time there are periods of more and periods of less tolerance depending on the sociopolitical context, the nature of the theology of the religious group that influences or controls social policy and law, as well as changes in that theology over time.

Sexual taboos represent a set of rules about sexuality in the culture. The most prominent sexual taboo and one that seems to appear across over 200 preliterate and literate cultures is the incest taboo (Ford & Beach, 1951; Carroll & Wolpe, 1996; Rathus, Nevid, & Fichner-Rathus, 1993). This does not mean that sexual behavior never takes place between consenting adults who are related, however it appears to be sanctioned only in very specific circumstances. In some cultures, an adult family member may initiate a young member of the group sexually; however, this usually occurs in the context of culturally sanctioned rituals that are for that specific purpose. It does not appear that this occurs in the context of an erotic or romantic relationship between the two. This raises relevant questions about how child sexual abuse is defined cross culturally. It appears that coercive sexual relations between an adult and a child are not endorsed; however, elders in the group may initiate a younger group member in the context of a cultural ritual with a specific purpose.

Rape represents a form of coercive sexual behavior. The degree to which it is disapproved of is culturally embedded however. Western cultures disapprove of rape, generally have sympathy for the victim, and punish the rapist. In violent cultures and in cultures where women are treated as the property of men, rape is observed to be more common (Sanday, 1981). Forty-five societies that Sanday (1981) observed to be freer of rape were those in which women and men have more egalitarian roles, where power and resources are shared, and where women are less economically dependent on men.

Prostitution is another form of sexual behavior that has been a part of the landscape of most cultures. However, the extent to which it is sanctioned, regarded as a necessary evil, or penalized by law varies from culture to culture. By definition, prostitution represents commercial sex. It involves sexual activity that not only does not occur within the sanctioned relationship of marriage, but does not occur within the context of a personal or romantic relationship at all. It is sex without a relationship and there is no intent to procreate. In fact, procreation must be scrupulously avoided as it will interfere with the prostitute's ability to make a living. There can be no illusion that sexual behavior in this context occurs for any reason other than simply for the sake of sexual behavior itself, sexual variety, money, and for some participants, the absence of the responsibilities that a relationship entails. In cultures where sex is viewed as a sinful or immoral activity that is only redeemed in the context of marriage and used to procreate, prostitution is considered not only immoral but, in Western cultures, violates the law.

In summary, sexuality represents an aspect of human behavior that is complex but is always relative. It is relative to specific cultural values and practices but it is also relative to that culture's practices at a specific point in time. Sexual values and beliefs change over time. Some practices may change with changes in beliefs and others may not. All however are embedded in a cultural matrix that is essential to understand if the behavior is to be properly contextualized.

Bibliography

Blumstein, P., & Schwartz, P. (1983). *American couples.* New York: Morrow.

Carroll, J. L., & Wolpe, P. R. (1996). *Sexuality and gender in society.* New York: HarperCollins.

Ford, C. S., & Beach, F. A. (1951). *Patterns of sexual behavior.* New York: Harper & Row.

Howard, M. C. (1989). *Contemporary cultural anthropology* (3rd ed). Glenview, IL: Scott, Foresman & Co.

Laumann, E. C., Gagnon, J. H., & Michael, R. T. (1994). *Social organization of sexuality.* Chicago: University of Chicago Press.

Leslie, G. R., & Korman, S. K. (1989). *The family in social context.* New York: Oxford University Press.

Marshall, D., & Suggs, R. (Eds.). (1971). *Human sexual behavior: Variations in the ethnographic spectrum.* New York: Basic Books.

Masters, W., Johnson, V., & Kolodny, R. C. (1995). *Human sexuality* (5th ed.). New York: HarperCollins.

Messinger, J. C. (1971). Sex and repression in an Irish folk community. In D. S. Marshall & R. C. Suggs (Eds.), *Human sexual behavior: Variations in the ethnographic spectrum* (pp. 3–37). New York: Basic Books.

Rathus, S., Nevid, J., & Fichner-Rathus, L. (1993). *Human sexuality in a world of diversity.* Boston: Allyn & Bacon.

Sanday, P. R. (1981). The sociocultural context of rape: A cross cultural study. *Journal of Social Issues, 40,* 117–136.

Thornhill, N. W., & Thornhill, R. (1987). Evolutionary theory and rules of mating and marriage pertaining to relatives. In C. Crawford, M. Smith, & D. Krebs (Eds.), *Sociobiology and psychology: Ideas, issues and applications* (pp. 373–400). London: Erlbaum.

Wade, C., & Tavris, C. (1994). The longest war: Gender and culture. In W. J. Lonner & R. S. Malpass (Eds.), *Psychology and culture* (pp. 121–126). Boston: Allyn & Bacon.

Beverly Greene

Sex Differences and Gender Differences

Some psychologists refer to differences in the behavior of females and males as *sex differences,* and others refer to them as *gender differences.* Although each term can be considered correct, psychologists who prefer one over the other generally have reasons for their preference. A common rationale for preferring the term *sex difference* begins with a statement that *the sexes* refers to the grouping of people into female and male categories on the basis of their socially identified biological sex. Therefore, the terms *sex differences* and *similarities* are applied to describe the results of comparing these two groups. Ordinarily, psychologists who use the term *sex difference* to refer to a demonstrated difference do not intend to give priority to any particular class of causes as explaining differences and similarities. Also, psychologists who use the term *sex* to refer to male and female categories typically reserve the term *gender* to refer to the meanings that societies and individuals ascribe to these categories. Consequently, psychologists generally use the terms *gender stereotypes* and *gender roles* because these constructs are based on the meanings ascribed to sex categories. In this article, the terms *sex* and *gender* follow this usage, and therefore all differences between males and females are referred to as sex differences. This school of thought about sex and gender terms appears to be the majority position among contemporary researchers in psychology.

Other investigators prefer to refer to at least some of the differences in female and male behavior as *gender differences*. These psychologists generally take the view that the term *sex* connotes biology or sexuality, whereas the term *gender* connotes culture and learning. In labeling certain female-male differences as gender differences, these researchers express their preference for interpreting or investigating such differences as a product of learning and culture rather than of intrinsic, biological factors that differ between the sexes. However, any attempt to provide a priori classification of female-male differences as sex or gender differences on the basis of biological versus cultural causation is problematic for scientists because understanding the causes of differences is the end product of scientific research, not a claim that should be made in the absence of evidence. Scientists continually debate the causes of differences and produce new research, with the result that the weight given to biological and social factors in the scientific consensus may change over time. Moreover, often certain differences between females and males are ascribed to a mix of biological and social causes, making especially difficult the choice of the sex or gender label. To avoid the obvious complications inherent in giving differences varying labels that signify their presumed causes, some psychological researchers use a single term to refer to all male-female differences—either gender difference or sex difference. Those who label all behavioral differences as gender differences usually are expressing their assumption that the majority of differences are learned and thus reflect the society and culture, whereas, as already noted, most psychologists who label all differences as sex differences intend to avoid this or any other causal implication of their descriptive label.

Psychological sex differences are typically investigated in controlled settings in which contemporaneous factors other than sex are held constant. Very often the relevant observations are made in laboratory settings, and, when they are made in natural settings, such as in organizations, the men and women who are compared typically occupy the same social role. For example, an investigator would compare male and female managers rather than male managers and female clerical workers. Psychologists are thus interested in general tendencies to behave in particular ways, aside from the constraints of specific situational demands that may commonly differ by sex because women and men tend to occupy different social roles.

When psychologists or other scientists refer to a difference between the sexes, they rarely mean that all men differ from all women in a particular respect. Instead, what is demonstrated in research data is a difference in the central tendency of the two sexes. Ordinarily, an investigator compares the mean performance of women and men on a particular measuring instrument and declares that the comparison yields a difference if the two means differ according to the criterion of statistical significance. As in other comparisons that researchers make (e.g., between groups of people who have received different treatments or who differ in personality), the underlying distributions of the groups that are compared may be highly overlapping even though the means are statistically different. Therefore, the appropriate way to think about psychological sex differences is in terms of overlapping distributions of women and men. It is in this spirit that sex differences in height might be thought to provide an appropriate and easily understood analogy for describing psychological sex differences because some women are taller than many men and some men are shorter than many women. However, the height sex difference is actually relatively larger than almost all psychological sex differences. Therefore, distributions of men and women on the majority of psychological attributes should be considered highly overlapping. Nonetheless, these psychological sex differences are often large enough to be noticeable in daily life, and their magnitudes show a range of values that is probably fairly typical of the range of values produced for findings in areas of psychological research unrelated to sex and gender (Eagly, 1995).

Because conclusions about sex differences and similarities are laden with political meaning, the research area is frequently controversial, and some psychologists maintain that the territory is too politically charged and scientifically difficult to warrant expending scientific effort. Other researchers believe that understanding sex differences is no more difficult than understanding many other problems studied by psychologists, such as mental illness. Moreover, proponents of studying sex differences argue that it is precisely such socially significant, politically charged questions that should receive priority in research, because the answers that research produces are important to society (see Kitzinger,

1994, for this debate). Nonetheless, the political ramifications of the research area should encourage researchers who do study differences not only to exercise utmost care that their conclusions are scientifically appropriate but also to reflect on the political meaning of their findings. They should in particular consider the implications of the language by which they describe particular differences, because their terminology can imply a deficit or an advantage in the female sex or the male sex. For example, the tendency for women to be more readily influenced by other people, especially in group contexts (Eagly & Carli, 1981), could be described negatively in terms of female gullibility and suggestibility or male stubbornness and hostility. Alternatively, this tendency could be described positively in terms of female open-mindedness and cooperativeness or male independence and autonomy. Because descriptions of the results of sex comparisons can reflect favorably or unfavorably on men or women, they are thus fraught with political meanings.

A Brief History of the Study of Psychological Sex Differences

Although research psychologists have compared the sexes throughout the twentieth century (Morawski & Agronick, 1991; Shields, 1975), systematic attempts to draw conclusions about differences and similarities did not become a prominent part of psychological research until the publication of Maccoby and Jacklin's (1974) wide-ranging book on sex differences. On the basis of their cataloging and evaluation of the extant psychological research that had compared the sexes, Maccoby and Jacklin maintained that there are sex differences in several aspects of intellectual abilities (namely, verbal, quantitative, and spatial abilities) and in aggression. With respect to other aspects of behavior, they either reasoned that evidence was insufficient to draw a definitive conclusion or concluded that there is no sex difference.

The generalizations stated in Maccoby and Jacklin's (1974) book have been much contested, in part because of the methods that they used to review research findings. Maccoby and Jacklin's methods of research integration followed traditional practices that became known as *narrative reviewing*. Like other narrative reviewers, they stated a general conclusion about a sex difference based on what appeared to be the overall trend of findings in the research literature, after they had classified studies according to whether they yielded a significant difference in the male or female direction or no difference. This "voting method" of aggregating research findings is not statistically appropriate and is likely to lead to erroneous conclusions (Hedges & Olkin, 1985).

In the late 1970s, reviewers began to apply an improved set of methods to the task of drawing conclusions from psychological studies that had reported comparisons of the sexes. In contrast to Maccoby and Jacklin's (1974) informal methods of producing generalizations, the methods referred to as *quantitative synthesis* or *meta-analysis* provide statistically justified methods for synthesizing research (Johnson & Eagly, in press). Meta-analysts typically represent the comparison between male and female behavior for each relevant study in terms of its *effect size* (or d), which expresses the sex difference in units of the study's standard deviation. With each finding represented in this common metric, studies that compared women and men can be collectively represented by taking an average of their effect sizes. This central tendency is located somewhere along a quantitative continuum that runs from no difference to large differences and thus does not provide a simple yes or no answer to the question of whether the sexes differed in general in the available studies.

In interpreting research findings, meta-analysts are particularly attentive to the consistency of the findings across the studies. When an appropriate statistical test shows that the findings are inconsistent or highly variable, the meta-analyst attempts to explain *why* they differ. This task, which can be described as a search for moderator variables, requires that meta-analysts classify the studies on various dimensions and determine the extent to which studies with different characteristics are associated with differing findings. For example, a meta-analysis of sex differences in aggressive behavior showed that men's general tendency to be more aggressive than women was considerably more pronounced for aggression that had physical impact compared with aggression that had psychological impact (Eagly, 1987). To identify such moderator variables, meta-analysts generally make use of their theories of difference and similarity but remain alert to discovering unexpected relationships as well. Careful application of these methods induces reviewers to scrutinize the particular ways in which the studies in a research literature differ from one another in their results and their methods. This scrutiny of studies' characteristics ordinarily includes an evaluation of their quality, especially focusing on attributes of studies that could produce artifactual findings.

Meta-analysis is hardly a panacea for all of the difficulties that reviewers may encounter when attempting to produce sound conclusions concerning sex differences and similarities. Meta-analysts must make many subjective decisions about what studies to include and how to represent their characteristics. Yet, the method brings the process of reviewing into the scientific tradition because the reviewers make their exact procedures and decision rules public in a written document and thus open to criticism, just as researchers who conduct individual studies make their methods and findings available for scrutiny to an audience of other scientists. Moreover, the reviewer's rules for aggregating and comparing findings are statistically appropriate. Because claims concerning sex differences and similarities should take into account all of the available evidence, rather than just a few selected studies, conclusions can be based on scores or even hundreds of studies—far too many to be appropriately aggregated using intuitive or informal methods. The meta-analytic method allows more reliable and valid conclusions to be drawn from this evidence.

Even though most contemporary scientific discussions of sex differences draw heavily from meta-analytic integrations of research findings, individual studies comparing the sexes continue to attract attention, particularly when these studies report differences that have received little prior investigation. Finally, psychologists and scholars trained in other disciplines have very often used predominantly qualitative methods to examine sex differences (e.g., Gilligan, 1982), and work in this tradition has also been influential (see review by Kimball, 1995).

Sex Differences in Cognitive Abilities

Sex differences in cognitive abilities have been intensely scrutinized by psychologists (see summaries by Halpern, 1997; Hyde, 1996). Reviewers have examined, not merely whether the sexes differ, but whether any sex differences changed in magnitude over the life cycle or over the decades for which research data are available. The generalizability of sex-related differences has also been examined to some extent cross-nationally and across ethnic and racial groups within the United States. The result of all of this effort is a large and complex research literature, most of whose conclusions rest on meta-analytic integrations.

Considerable controversy surrounds the proper interpretation of the sex differences and similarities displayed in research literatures on cognitive abilities. Some psychologists have argued that their meta-analyses challenge Maccoby and Jacklin's (1974) conclusions by showing that sex differences in cognitive abilities are negligible in magnitude, whereas other psychologists have maintained that the available findings show some important sex differences. Despite these disagreements, there is consensus that two of the tendencies that Maccoby and Jacklin (1974) noted, male superiority in quantitative ability and female superiority in verbal ability, are very weak when the available findings are aggregated across all age groups and all types of tests. Decreases over time in the magnitude of these sex differences in adolescent populations have been

noted by some reviewers but appear to be quite small in data sets that are representative of the entire school population of the United States (Hedges & Nowell, 1995).

Meta-analyses and individual research projects have begun to pinpoint certain aspects of cognitive abilities for which sex differences are larger. For example, the sex difference in quantitative ability is largest for mathematical problem solving and remains substantial among adults and older adolescents. Men's advantage on mathematical problem solving may reflect a more general advantage on a variety of tasks requiring fluid reasoning (e.g., mechanical reasoning, scientific reasoning, and even verbal analogies). In the verbal area, differences favor females on measures of writing ability and reading comprehension. Also, differences favoring females are substantial on measures of verbal fluency, particularly on tests requiring that respondents produce words or sentences meeting certain requirements of meaning or form. This sex difference may reflect a more general superiority of women on tasks that require rapid access to and use of information from long-term memory, because women perform better than men on a variety of memory tasks that require such access (Halpern, 1997). Women also have an advantage on tests of speech production requiring rapid and accurate speech. In addition, males have some superiority on the majority of tests of spatial ability, and these differences are especially large on tests involving the mental rotation of three-dimensional figures. This better performance may reflect a general male superiority in tasks that require transformations in visual working memory. However, females exceed males on tests of spatial location memory, the ability to remember where objects are located.

As these descriptions of sex differences imply, the traditional categorization of cognitive tasks into quantitative, verbal, and spatial domains may not be very helpful for revealing the most common sex differences. Instead, psychologists are beginning to favor classifications based on underlying cognitive processes, because sex differences in task performance may reflect some differences in basic cognitive and memorial processes (Halpern, 1997).

Some researchers have emphasized that the proportions of males and females who exceed or fall below a certain level of test performance can differ especially strongly in the tails of the distribution. This augmentation of sex differences in extreme samples is consistent with the overrepresentation of boys in groups of gifted children and adolescents who have been selected for high quantitative skills as well as with boys' overrepresentation at the low-ability end of many distributions (e.g., encompassing mental retardation, attention deficit disorder, dyslexia, and learning disabilities).

This disproportionate representation of one sex in highly selected samples appears to be a product of sex differences in the variability of test scores as well as their central tendency (Feingold, 1994).

Sex Differences in Social Behavior and Personality

Social psychologists were very quick to take up quantitative reviewing after Maccoby and Jacklin's (1974) work raised many questions about the extent to which some aspects of social behavior are sex related (see overviews by Eagly, 1995; Hyde, 1996). Most of the early meta-analyses examined research literatures from experimental social psychology. Hall (1984) carried out numerous meta-analyses on sex differences in nonverbal behaviors, including the ability to decode and encode nonverbal cues. Meta-analyses on conformity and influenceability followed rapidly. Female and male behavior was carefully examined in studies of empathy as well as helping behavior and aggressive behavior. Meta-analyses of social interaction in task-oriented small groups investigated whether women are friendlier and more social than men and whether men are more narrowly task oriented than women, whether men are more likely than women to emerge as leaders, and whether group performance differs between all-male and all-female groups. In syntheses that included predominantly organizational studies, meta-analysts examined whether the style and the effectiveness of leaders and managers differ according to their sex.

Quantitative reviewers have examined sex differences in other tendencies important to social behavior, for example, in the qualities they prefer in mates and their disclosure of personal concerns to others. Other meta-analyses have concerned sex differences in sexual behavior and attitudes, the life satisfaction or happiness that women and men report in surveys, and the incidence of mental illness, especially depression. Syntheses have examined sex differences in personality traits, as assessed by personality tests and inventories, and personality growth in adolescence and adulthood. Finally, other meta-analyses have concerned sex-related differences in activity level and in motor behaviors such as reaction time, flexibility, throw distance, and grip strength.

Each meta-analysis of research findings produced a complex set of results: Conclusions about an overall difference between the sexes were accompanied by a series of conclusions about moderator variables that showed how under specific conditions, the overall difference became larger or smaller or even sometimes reversed its usual direction. Despite these complexities, the reviewers who have conducted most of these syntheses of sex differences in social behavior and personality are in general agreement that their findings yielded evidence of at least some consequential differences. Although the complexity of typical meta-analytic findings makes it potentially misleading to provide a simple list of these sex differences, the best overall description is that the results of quantitative syntheses generally conform to people's ideas about the sexes. For example, thematic analysis of demonstrated sex differences in social behavior and personality suggests that they conform to stereotypic expectations that women are communal and men are agentic (Bakan, 1966; see review by Eagly & Wood, 1991). In general, women, more than men, tend to manifest behaviors that can be described as socially sensitive, friendly, and concerned with others' welfare, whereas men, more than women, tend to manifest behaviors that can be described as dominant, controlling, and independent. More formal evidence of the stereotypic quality of sex differences was provided by demonstrations that research participants' estimates of differences between the sexes (i.e., their gender stereotypes) predicted with considerable success the mean effect sizes representing the sex differences obtained in the available meta-analyses on social behavior and personality and various cognitive abilities (Hall & Carter, 1999; Swim, 1994).

Finally, there are large research literatures on sex differences and similarities in communication styles and language behavior (Canary & Dindia, 1998). Particularly based on Tannen's (1990) writings for a popular audience, claims of differences in conversational style have received considerable publicity. Although only portions of these findings have been meta-analyzed, there are some differences in the explicit and implicit meanings of the communicative behavior of women and men, despite an absence of sex differences in most aspects of language and communication. These sex differences also appear to warrant description as gender stereotypic. Specifically, as manifested in communicative behavior, women, more than men, are emotionally expressive and engage in behavior that appears to be oriented to maintaining relationships, whereas men, more than women, control their emotional displays and engage in behavior that appears to be oriented to achieving or maintaining control and dominance.

Theories of Sex Differences and Similarities

Empirical findings on sex differences and similarities take on meaning and importance to the extent that they become interpretable within theories that explain the findings. A wealth of theories from psychology and related disciplines contend for the territory of explaining differences between the sexes (see Beall & Sternberg, 1993; Canary & Dindia, 1998; Deaux & LaFrance, 1998). Favored by social psychologists are several theories that explain sex differences by calling on differing status, social roles, and gender-based expectancies about one's own and others' behavior. Sex-differentiated behavior is viewed as an accommodation to the differing roles occupied by men and women. One principle of these social structural theories, deriving from the greater power and status associated with male-dominated roles, is that women's adaptations to roles with lesser power and status produce a pattern of behavior that can be described as subordinate, and men's adaptations to greater power and status produce more dominant behavior (Ridgeway & Diekema, 1992). Subordinate behavior is more compliant to social influence, less overtly aggressive, and more cooperative and conciliatory. Dominant behavior is controlling, assertive, directive, autocratic, authoritative, and competent.

Social structural theories also emphasize that women and men seek to accommodate to sex-typical roles by acquiring skills and resources that facilitate successful role performance and by adapting their social behavior to role requirements. A variety of sex-specific skills and beliefs arise from men's and women's typical family and economic roles, which in many Western societies can be described as resource provider and homemaker. To the extent that this division of labor remains, women and men seek to accommodate to these roles by acquiring role-related skills, such as women learning domestic skills and men learning skills that are marketable in the paid economy. The social behaviors associated with these roles have been characterized in terms of Bakan's (1966) distinction between communal and agentic characteristics (Eagly, 1987). Thus, women's accommodation to the domestic role and to female-dominated occupations produces a pattern of interpersonally facilitative and friendly behaviors that can be termed *communal*. In contrast, men's accommodation to the employment role, especially to male-dominated occupations, fosters a pattern of assertive and independent behaviors that can be termed *agentic*.

These social structural theories provide an overall interpretation of sex differences. Yet, the influence of gender roles on behavior is mediated by individual and social factors, because sex differences arise as a by-product of social interaction. Social psychologists, especially Deaux and Major (1987), have been particularly effective in analyzing the detailed features of social situations and of people's gender schemas that determine the extent to which expectancies about women and men get transformed into gendered behavior.

Favored by developmental psychologists (and some other social scientists) is the idea that women and men are socialized into somewhat different cultures—women into a culture that emphasizes cooperation and the maintenance of relationships, and men into a culture that emphasizes independence, competition, and achievement. Of course, these separate cultures may reflect the underlying differences in men's and women's

role obligations. Emphasized in this tradition is the idea that children learn rules for social interaction from their experience in largely sex-segregated peer groups in childhood and then carry this learning into adult social interaction, with the result that their behavior is marked by different communicative patterns and styles of social interaction (e.g., Maccoby, 1990; Maltz & Borker, 1982). Other developmental psychologists continue to pursue a range of perspectives that reveal aspects of sex-typed socialization; these perspectives include social learning theory, cognitive developmental theory, and gender schema theory. Research related to these theories displays the mechanisms by which people acquire sex-typed behaviors.

Other theories of sex differences derive from evolutionary psychology (Buss & Kenrick, 1998). Evolutionary psychologists see human sex differences as deriving from adaptations built into the human species in the primeval period during which the human species evolved to its modern anatomical form. Evolutionary psychologists especially emphasize the differing situation of the sexes in relation to reproduction, and their predictions pertain in particular to sex differences in sexuality and mating. The sex-differentiated psychological mechanisms featured by evolutionary psychologists are considered to be genetic and hereditary. Some evolutionary accounts posit that genetic factors trigger biochemical processes that mediate psychological sex differences, by means of sex differences in hormone production. Also, biopsychologists investigate in considerable detail the genetic and hormonal mechanisms that may mediate some psychological sex differences.

The discourse surrounding these and other theories of sex differences is sometimes contentious. Comparative evaluations of the strength of scientific evidence supporting competing theoretical positions has only just begun, and scientists are beginning to learn to take sophisticated versions of competing theories into account. Once more researchers become knowledgeable concerning the range of theoretical positions that can be deployed to interpret sex differences and similarities, they will be prepared to develop more integrative theories of sex differences.

Bibliography

Bakan, D. (1966). *The duality of human existence: An essay on psychology and religion.* Chicago: Rand-McNally.

Beall, A. E., & Sternberg, R. J. (Eds.). (1993). *The psychology of gender.* New York: Guilford Press. Provides chapters reviewing major theories of sex differences.

Buss, D. M., & Kenrick, D. T. (1998). Evolutionary social psychology. In D. T. Gilbert, S. T. Fiske, & G. Lindzey (Eds.), *The handbook of social psychology* (4th ed., Vol. 2, pp. 982–1026). Boston: McGraw-Hill.

Canary, D. J., & Dindia, K. (Eds.) (1998). *Sex differences and similarities in communication: Critical essays and empirical investigations of sex and gender in interaction.* Mahwah, NJ: Erlbaum. Chapters review a range of research programs and theories pertaining to the communicative behavior of women and men.

Deaux, K., & LaFrance, M. (1998). Gender. In D. T. Gilbert, S. T. Fiske, & G. Lindzey (Eds.), *The handbook of social psychology* (4th ed., Vol. 1, pp. 788–827). Boston: McGraw-Hill. Provides a comprehensive review of research on gender, including theories that predict sex differences and similarities.

Deaux, K., & Major, B. (1987). Putting gender into context: An interactive model of gender-related behavior. *Psychological Review, 94,* 369–389.

Eagly, A. H. (1987). *Sex differences in social behavior: A social-role interpretation.* Hillsdale, NJ: Erlbaum.

Eagly, A. H. (1995). The science and politics of comparing women and men. *American Psychologist, 50,* 145–158.

Eagly, A. H., & Carli, L. L. (1981). Sex of researchers and sex-typed communications as determinants of sex differences in influenceability: A meta-analysis of social influence studies. *Psychological Bulletin, 90,* 1–20.

Eagly, A. H., & Wood, W. (1991). Explaining sex differences in social behavior: A meta-analytic perspective. *Personality and Social Psychology Bulletin, 17,* 306–315.

Feingold, A. (1994). The additive effects of group differences in central tendency and variability are important in distributional comparisons between groups. *American Psychologist, 50,* 5–13.

Gilligan, C. (1982). *In a different voice: Psychological theory and women's development.* Cambridge, MA: Harvard University Press.

Hall, J. A. (1984). *Nonverbal sex differences: Communication accuracy and expressive style.* Baltimore: Johns Hopkins University Press.

Hall, J. A., & Carter, J. D. (1999). Gender-stereotype accuracy as an individual difference. *Journal of Personality and Social Psychology, 77,* 350–359.

Halpern, D. F. (1997). Sex differences in intelligence: Implications for education. *American Psychologist, 52,* 1091–1102.

Hedges, L. V., & Nowell, A. (1995, 7 July). Sex differences in mental test scores, variability, and numbers of high-scoring individuals. *Science, 269,* 41–45.

Hedges, L. V., & Olkin, I. (1985). *Statistical methods for meta-analysis.* Orlando, FL: Academic Press.

Hyde, J. S. (1996). Where are the gender differences? Where are the gender similarities? In D. M. Buss & N. M. Malamuth (Eds.), *Sex, power, conflict: Evolutionary and feminist perspectives.* New York: Oxford University Press.

Johnson, B. T., & Eagly, A. H. (in press). Quantitative synthesis of social psychological research. In H. T. Reis & C. M. Judd (Eds.), *Handbook of research methods in social psychology.* London: Cambridge University Press. Provides a compact, yet comprehensive review of meta-analytic methods.

Kimball, M. M. (1995). *Feminist visions of gender similarities and differences.* Binghamton, NY: Haworth Press. Reviews work by a range of feminist scholars, many of whom investigate sex differences with qualitative methods.

Kitzinger, C. (Ed.). (1994). Special feature: Should psychologists study sex differences? *Feminism & Psychology, 4,* 501–546.

Maccoby, E. E. (1990). Gender and relationships: A developmental account. *American Psychologist, 45,* 513–520.

Maccoby, E. E., & Jacklin, C. N. (1974). *The psychology of sex differences.* Stanford, CA: Stanford University Press. The classic narrative review of psychological sex differences.

Maltz, D. N., & Borker, R. A. (1982). A cultural approach to male-female miscommunication. In J. J. Gumperz (Ed.), *Language and social identity* (pp. 196–216). New York: Cambridge University Press.

Morawski, J. G., & Agronick, G. (1991). A restive legacy: The history of feminist work in experimental and cognitive psychology. *Psychology of Women Quarterly, 15,* 567–579.

Ridgeway, C. L., & Diekema, D. (1992). Are gender differences status differences? In C. L. Ridgeway (Ed.), *Gender, interaction, and inequality* (pp. 157–180). New York: Springer-Verlag.

Shields, S. A. (1975). Functionalism, Darwinism, and the psychology of women. *American Psychologist, 30,* 739–754.

Swim, J. K. (1994). Perceived versus meta-analytic effect sizes: An assessment of the accuracy of gender stereotypes. *Journal of Personality and Social Psychology, 66,* 21–66.

Tannen, D. (1990). *You just don't understand: Women and men in conversation.* New York: William Morrow.

Alice H. Eagly

GENDER CONSTANCY. In 1966 Lawrence Kohlberg introduced a novel theoretical perspective on gender development called cognitive-developmental theory, based on Piagetian principles of general cognitive development. In contrast to learning theory perspectives that dominated the empirical literature in the field, he proposed that the motivation to act in accordance with gender norms is internally generated, originating from children's constructions of and identification with their gender, rather than externally generated through receiving reinforcement from parents for playing with dolls or trucks. The central construct of the theory was gender constancy, children's emerging sense of the permanence of being either a boy or a girl. Numerous studies have confirmed that an understanding of gender constancy occurs in a series of stages: first, gender identity or labeling (correctly identifying one's own and others' sex); then gender stability (understanding that a person's sex does not change over time); and finally, gender consistency (understanding that a person's sex is fixed across situations, not altered by superficial transformations in appearance or activities) (Slaby & Frey, 1975). Research in other cultures has found the identical stages (Munroe, Shimmin, & Munroe, 1984).

The cognitive developmental perspective implies that understanding constancy is linked to the Piagetian stage of concrete operational thought and would thus emerge at 5 to 7 years of age, with identity and stability emerging a year or two earlier. Although gender constancy is correlated with measures of operational thought, as expected, the exact age of attainment varies considerably across studies, which may be partly due to how constancy is measured. The use of dolls, schematic drawings, and hypothetical questions may lead to an underestimation of gender constancy because children may think they are supposed to pretend that sex is changing. In contrast, measures that do not assess children's reasoning about the judgment they make may lead to an overestimation of performance, because children may give correct answers without fully understanding that one's sex is immutable. Indeed, several studies have reported a U-shaped trend in constancy development, with a drop in performance occurring in the range of ages 4 to 6 (Ruble & Martin, 1998). Emmerich (1982) has used the term *pseudo-constancy* to refer to young children who answer the questions correctly but whose justifications for their answers do not reflect a true grasp of constancy. Such problems raise important questions about what constancy is and how it should be related theoretically to other aspects of gender development.

The exact role that gender constancy plays in other aspects of gender development is controversial. Kohlberg's basic hypothesis was that children's understanding of gender constancy provided a stable organizer of children's gender attitudes and initiated their motivation to learn gender norms and behave in accordance with them. But there have been alternative hypotheses concerning the relation between gender constancy and gender typing (see Ruble & Martin, 1998, for a review). According to some investigators, children adhere most strongly to gender norms prior to understanding gender constancy because they fear that cross-gender behaviors may turn them into the other sex; once they have attained constancy, however, they become more flexible (e.g., Urberg, 1982). According to other investigators, children are predicted to be most rigid in their application of gender norms at the point they understand gender constancy, and they do not become more flexible until at least a few years later (e.g., Frey & Ruble, 1992).

Although numerous studies have tested these hypotheses, conclusions remain unclear. Many studies fail to find any relation (Huston, 1988; Ruble & Martin, 1998). Nevertheless, a pattern of results does appear to be emerging (Ruble & Martin, 1998). Children who have attained gender *identity* are more likely than children who have not to play with gender-typed toys (e.g., Weinraub, Clemens, Sockloff, Ethridge, Gracely, & Myers, 1984). Children who have attained gender *stability* show several indications of greater attention and affect associated with gender relative to children who have not, such as increased imitation of same-sex models (e.g., Ruble, Balaban, & Cooper, 1981), and more positive feelings about one's own sex and same-sex peers (e.g., Yee & Brown, 1994). Finally, children who have attained gender *consistency* are more likely than children who have not to prefer gender-typed activities under conditions of conflict, such as when the same-sex choice is less attractive than the other-sex choice (Frey & Ruble, 1992; Newman, Cooper, & Ruble, 1995).

Simply knowing that one is a boy or a girl may be sufficient to orient a child to gender-related features of the world and to make corresponding choices, as long as they do not conflict with other desires. When such choices do involve a conflict, however, a more advanced level of gender understanding appears to be required, perhaps because of its association with greater cognitive sophistication or perhaps because, consistent with Kohlberg's emphasis on motivational processes, knowing that one will always be a boy or a girl regardless of time or circumstances provides an additional impetus to regulate one's choices and behaviors in accordance with gender norms. Interestingly, gender constancy often affects boys more than girls, perhaps because girls are granted greater freedom to engage in other-sex activities or because boys' activities are more prestigious, resulting in less motivation for girls to embrace female-typed and reject male-typed behaviors (Frey & Ruble, 1992).

In summary, a number of questions remain concerning the time at which gender constancy is fully understood and what implications it has for other aspects of gender development. The findings indicate that lower levels, especially stability, show many of the associations Kohlberg predicted to occur with full constancy. Definite conclusions about the effects of understanding gender consistency are hard to draw, however, because of the difficulties in accurately assessing children's true level of understanding and the resulting inconsistencies across studies in the age of attainment. Clearly, gender typing is evident prior to an understanding of consistency, and thus full gender constancy does not serve the initial organizing function that Kohlberg proposed. It may have other functions, however, such as serving as a period of consolidation for conclusions about gender-appropriate behaviors and increasing motivation to adhere to gender norms (Ruble, 1994). Further research is needed to elucidate the different effects of attaining each stage of constancy and to ascertain whether such effects are best understood in terms of the motivational processes Kohlberg described or in terms of other mechanisms.

Bibliography

Emmerich, W. (1982). Nonmonotonic developmental trends in social cognition: The case of gender identity. In S. Strauss (Ed.), *U-shaped behavioral growth* (pp. 249–269). New York: Academic Press.

Frey, K. S., & Ruble, D. N. (1992). Gender constancy and the "cost" of sex-typed behavior: A test of the conflict hypothesis. *Developmental Psychology, 28,* 714–721.

Huston, A. C. (1983). Sex typing. In E. M. Hetherington (Ed.), *Handbook of child psychology: Socialization, personality, and social development* (Vol. 4, pp. 388–467). New York: Wiley.

Kohlberg, L. A. (1966). A cognitive-developmental analysis of children's sex role concepts and attitudes. In E. E. Maccoby (Ed.), *The development of sex differences* (pp. 82–173). Stanford, CA: Stanford University Press.

Munroe, R. H., Shimmin, H. S., & Munroe, R. L. (1984). Gender understanding and sex role preference in four cultures. *Developmental Psychology, 20,* 673–682.

Newman, L. S., Cooper, J., & Ruble, D. N. (1995). Gender and computers: II. The interactive effects of gender knowledge and constancy on gender-stereotyped attitudes, *Sex Roles, 33,* 325–351.

Ruble, D. N. (1994). A phase model of transitions: Cognitive and motivational consequences. In M. Zanna (Ed.), *Advances in experimental social psychology, 26,* 163–214.

Ruble, D. N., Balaban, T., & Cooper, J. (1981). Gender constancy and the effects of sex-typed televised toy commercials. *Child Development, 52,* 667–673.

Ruble, D. N., & Martin, C. L. (1998). Gender development. In W. Damon (Series Ed.) & N. Eisenberg (Vol. Ed.), *Handbook of child psychology: Vol. 3. Social, emotional, and personality development* (5th ed., pp. 933–1016). New York: Wiley.

Slaby, R. G., & Frey, K. S. (1975). Development of gender constancy and selective attention to same-sex models. *Child Development, 52,* 849–856.

Urberg, K. A. (1982). The development of the concepts of masculinity and femininity in young children. *Sex Roles, 8,* 659–668.

Weinraub, M., Clemens, L. P., Sockloff, A., Ethridge, R., Gracely, E., & Myers, B. (1984). The development of sex role stereotypes in the third year: Relationships to gender labeling, gender identity, sex-typed toy preferences, and family characteristics. *Child Development, 55,* 1493–1503.

Yee, M., & Brown, R. (1994). The development of gender differentiation in young children. *British Journal of Social Psychology, 33,* 183–196.

Diane N. Ruble

GENDER DIFFERENCES. *See* Gender, Sex, and Culture, *article on* Sex Differences and Gender Differences.

GENDER IDENTITY. The meanings of gender identity and gender role have changed over time, and debate continues about the appropriate use of these terms. Nonetheless, most researchers have adopted a tripartite concept that distinguishes between gender identity, gender role, and sexual orientation. Gender identity is the fundamental sense of belonging to one sex. Gender role refers to the behaviors, attitudes, and traits that are associated with being male or female. In contrast to these two terms is sexual orientation, which refers to one's responsiveness to sexual stimuli (Zucker & Bradley, 1995).

At a basic level, the designation of gender identity is anatomical. It is unclear, however, in terms of measurement and conceptual definition, to what extent gender identity is an inner knowledge and/or an outer expression of one's sex (Fagot, 1985). Debates also have arisen over the extent to which gender identity and roles reside in individuals, which has been the dominant approach in psychology for many years, or in broader contexts such as interactions, societal structures, and cultural expectations, which has been a newly emerging view, especially within social psychology (Deaux & LaFrance, 1998).

The Development of Gender Identity

Two distinct groups of children have been studied to understand how gender identity forms. Developmental psychologists have studied typical children to investigate the timing of different aspects of gender understanding. Clinical and developmental psychologists have studied atypical children to investigate the extent to which gender identity depends on biological factors, such as chromosomes or hormones, or on one's sex of rearing. Studies of gender identity have also focused on identifying the consequences associated with the development of gender identity that is consistent with or different from one's chromosomal sex.

The prominent view has been that gender identity develops in three stages in typical children. First, children learn to identify themselves and others by sex, usually around the age of 2½ years, which is called gender labeling or gender group membership. Gender labeling is measured by asking children to label the sex of men, women, boys, and girls and to label their own sex. Second, children learn to recognize that sex is stable over time, often called gender stability, and this understanding occurs at 3½ years. Measuring gender stability involves asking children whether they were baby girls or baby boys when they were little and whether they will grow up to be mommies or daddies. Third, between age 4 and 5 children learn to recognize the constancy of gender over situational changes and changes in one's motivation, often called gender constancy or consistency. Before reaching this stage, a child might believe that a boy who wears a dress or plays with dolls or wants to be a girl really is a girl. Once achieving consistency, children understand that one's sex stays constant and can explain why sex does not change (Ruble & Martin, 1998).

The research on gender identity in atypical children has moved in a very different direction, with the emphasis being on identifying the major contributors to gender identity. At one extreme is the idea that children develop a gender identity in line with their chromosomal sex, and at the other extreme is the idea that gender identity is more influenced by the way one is raised.

The issue about the contributions of biology and environment has yet to be resolved. For many years, the predominant view was based on John Money's research on children with various sorts of medical conditions, in which either their sex was not clear because of having ambiguous genitalia or they had mismatched indicators of sex. For instance, the classic case was a set of monozygotic male twins one of whom was raised as a female after a very early surgical accident destroyed his penis. Based on a number of case studies of atypical children, Money concluded that the major factor influencing gender identity was how the child was raised. In several cases, genetic boys raised as girls appeared to develop the gender identity of a girl. Furthermore, based on case studies of children with ambiguous genitalia who were given gender labels early versus later in life, Money argued that there is a critical period for learning one's sex. Children who were given gender labels by age 2 or 3 were more likely to develop a clear sense of gender identity than children who were not labeled until they were older. In the cases in which gender labeling was postponed, children were uncomfortable even discussing the issue and showed many problems in psychological adjustment (e.g., Money & Ehrhardt, 1972).

Evidence has accumulated that suggests that gender identity is influenced by both environmental and biological factors. A group was identified in the Dominican Republic of XY-chromosome children who had a genetic disorder (5-alpha-reductase deficiency) that interfered with the final stages of prenatal sexual development. Although they were exposed to normal male levels of testosterone prenatally, their external genitalia were more female-like when they were born and they were raised as females. However, because they were genetic males, they began to develop sexual characteristics of males as they entered puberty; for instance, they developed penises and male secondary sexual charac-

teristics. In the original reports, many of these girls successfully changed their gender identities to male identities and began to live as males (Imperato-McGinley, Peterson, Gautier, & Sturla, 1979). Based on the successful conversion of gender identity in adolescence in most of these cases, Imperato-McGinley and colleagues argued that gender identity must be more influenced by biological factors than was previously believed.

These conclusions have been challenged, however. First, a male gender identity was not clearly established for all the cases. Second, parents of these "girls" may have realized that their children were not like other girls and they may have treated them differently, which may have lead to easier transitions to a male identity. Finally, more recent reports suggest that the cultural attitudes may determine the ease of changing gender identity. In countries such as the Dominican Republic where males are more valued than females, the conversion is much easier than in countries, such as the United States, where less imbalance occurs (see Ruble & Martin, 1997).

Additional evidence of the role of biological factors has come to light in the last few years through research on the importance of hormones on gender development and in recent reports about the later development of the male twin who was raised as a girl. Although initially the child seemed to be adjusting to the female role, by age 14, the twin decided to live as a male and received hormone treatment and surgery to facilitate the change. At age 25, he married and adopted two children. Although some researchers are now recommending that the best medical practice may be to follow the chromosomal sex of the child, the ideal course of treatment has not yet been resolved because of the complexity of the social and biological factors involved in gender identity (Zucker & Bradley, 1995).

Clinical psychologists also study children and adults with gender identity problems whose biological sex is not in doubt. These individuals may be labeled as having gender identity disorders if they wish to be the other sex and show behavior typical of the other sex (see Zucker & Bradley, 1997). About 2 to 5% of the population has gender identity disorder (GID), and boys are referred for treatment much more frequently than girls. The onset of GID typically occurs in the preschool years but may occur earlier. Some children with GID will be rejected by their peers. Evidence suggests that in extreme cases of GID for boys, there is a greater likelihood of bisexual and homosexual behavior in adulthood (see Zucker & Bradley, 1995).

The Development of Gender Roles

Psychologists have been conducting research to understand the consequences of identification of oneself as masculine and/or feminine, that is, how such self-identification relates to one's behavior, appearance, and traits. The major emphasis in this research has been on how masculinity and femininity are measured and the coherence of these constructs.

The traditional view in Western culture was that boys should be socialized to be masculine and girls to be feminine. The underlying belief was that masculinity and femininity were unidimensional, with each representing opposite ends of a single continuum. Individuals were labeled according to their degree of fit with the traditional expectations.

Critiques of this view during the early 1970s caused significant changes in the conception and measurement of masculinity and femininity. Most psychologists now consider that masculinity and femininity are multidimensional and independent constructs. Masculinity generally is conceived of as instrumental and agentic behaviors, such as assertiveness and dominance; femininity is conceived of as expressive behaviors, such as nurturance and sensitivity to others. A new construct arose from the idea that masculinity and femininity are best measured separately, called psychological androgyny, which is the idea that a person may have both masculine and feminine characteristics. Many psychologists assume that androgyny represents the new ideal, since androgynous individuals have a wider set of behaviors they can enact, which should then allow them to be more adaptable than sex-typed individuals.

Based on these new ideas about the nature of masculinity and femininity, two new questionnaires were developed, the Bem Sex Role Inventory (BSRI; Bem, 1974) and the Personal Attributes Questionnaire (PAQ; Spence, Helmreich, & Stapp, 1974). For both, individuals rate the extent to which they personally endorse various personality traits that tap into the two broad dimensions of masculinity and femininity. Individuals are classified using a two-by-two table (high versus low on masculinity; high versus low on femininity) into people who are sex-typed, androgynous, and undifferentiated. Using these instruments, femininity and masculinity have been shown to be heterogeneous dimensions.

Developmental researchers have used a variety of methods to assess masculinity and femininity in children. In some studies, children's preferences for toys, activities, or future occupations; parents' ratings of children's preferences; or observations of children's toy and playmate preferences have been used as indicators of levels of femininity and masculinity. In the 1980s, personality questionnaires were developed for children that were similar to the PAQ and BSRI, except that behaviors were used to represent personality traits, thereby making it possible for younger children to answer the questions.

Although personality questionnaires continue to be the most typical methods of assessing masculinity, femininity, and androgyny in adults, there are some measurement issues that need to be recognized when they are employed. First, the meaning of the subscales has been debated. Spence and colleagues suggest that these subscales measure only narrow subsets of personality traits that relate to masculinity and femininity: specifically, instrumentality/agency and expressiveness/communality. Second, the separability of the two subscales of masculinity and femininity is not clear. Third, trait measures may be inappropriate for assessing the kinds of behavioral capabilities that are thought to be associated with androgyny. Fourth, concern has been raised about describing characteristics as being masculine or feminine, as these labels may serve to reify these distinctions, making them a constructed reality (see Ruble & Martin, 1998).

Theories of Gender Development

The first psychological theory about gender development was Freud's psychoanalytic approach. Freud argued that children develop traditional gender roles as they gradually begin to identify with parents of the same sex. Although this theory provided the intellectual driving force for many other theorists, this perspective has not received much empirical support.

With their introduction in the 1960s, the two central theories of gender development were social learning theory, as proposed by Mischel (1966) and later Bandura (1977) and cognitive developmental theory, as proposed by Kohlberg (1966). Social learning theory was based on the idea that children learn gender roles by the rewards and punishments they receive for different kinds of play and through observation and modeling, especially of their same-sex parent. Social learning theory has changed somewhat to focus more on cognitive factors, such as remembered expectancies about contingencies. The theory has provided important insights into the processes involved in observational learning and has been central in much of the research on parents' socialization practices as they influence gender development.

Cognitive developmental theory was based on a revolutionary view, namely, that the child plays a central role in learning about gender. According to Kohlberg, once children understood which sex they were and the irreversibility of being female or male, they become motivated to seek out and learn about how members of their own sex act and what is appropriate (and not) for their own behavior. Much of the research on typical children's gender identity has been driven by this theory, and it has been very influential in the field in emphasizing the idea that children actively construct their own gender typing.

As a result of the cognitive revolution in psychology, in the 1980s, gender schema theories were proposed as a new way to explain gender development (Bem, 1981; Martin & Halverson, 1981). Gender schemas are dynamically changing, culturally determined networks of gender-related information that children learn because gender is a functional category, one loaded with meaning in our culture. Gender schemas influence children's and adults' thinking and behavior. For instance, children attend to and remember information better if they believe it is relevant to their own sex versus information that they believe is not. Information that does not fit schemas may be distorted to confirm expectations (see Martin & Halverson, 1981). These theories have provided useful insights into the cognitive processes related to the development and maintenance of gender-related beliefs.

Social psychological views of gender development have emphasized the importance of context and situations in understanding gendered behavior. Rather than situating gender within the individual, these theories shift the focus to the broader context of situations and society. One example of this shift is social role theory, in which the major idea is that sex differences have emerged because of the different roles that males and females occupy because roles are seen to encourage or discourage particular behaviors (Eagly, 1987). Another example is Deaux and Major's (1987) model of how contextual/situational variations change gender-related responding. Perceivers and targets negotiate gender. Targets will exhibit varying degrees of gender-related behavior depending on expectations of the perceiver, the goals and self-conceptions of the target, and the situational factors that influence the salience of gender. These approaches share the assumption that gender is a dynamically changing feature that is constructed within situations.

Several approaches to gender development have been proposed that provide a greater emphasis on biological factors, including evolutionary, ethological views and brain structure and hormone approaches. Evolutionary views of gender emphasize the importance of adaptation and natural selection in the evolution of social behavior, especially in differences between men and women. Hormonal theories, which emphasize prenatal and postnatal exposure to hormones as determining gender, have been described as viable vehicles for understanding how and why males and females develop different sorts of neural pathways and structures and how these differences may relate to behavior.

The Coherence or Multidimensional Nature of Gender

A major issue in understanding gender identity concerns the coherence or multidimensional nature of the various aspects of gender. For years, many researchers have assumed that tapping into one aspect of gender gives information about all others; for instance, a child who likes to play with dolls is assumed to be feminine and thus will be nurturant and expressive. The coherence of gender was brought under fire in the 1980s as Huston (1983) and others argued that there are many aspects of gender and that not all of them are necessarily related or predictive of one another. For instance, Huston described a matrix of gender typing that included various content domains such as biological sex, interests, personality attributes, social relationships, and styles/symbols. Within each domain there are various constructs such as concepts, self-perception, preferences, and behavioral enactment. Rather than assuming unity in all these aspects, Huston recommended that researchers investigate where relations hold and where they do not.

The multidimensionality versus coherence debate has gained attention, especially in its possible impact on theories of gender development. In particular, two issues have been paramount. The first has been more prevalent in the social psychological literature, namely, the question concerning the extent to which masculine and/or feminine personality characteristics are predictive of other aspects of gender. Generally, research suggests that personality characteristics do not predict other aspects of gender very well. The second has been a concern in the developmental literature, namely, the issue about the extent to which gender cognitions relate to other aspects of behavior and thinking. Although early evidence suggested that gender cognitions may develop later than behaviors, more recent research on infants and toddlers suggest that there may be rudimentary gender cognitions in place during the early years that may be guiding behavior (Ruble & Martin, 1998). Further research is necessary before either issue will be completely resolved.

Bibliography

Bandura, A. (1977). *Social learning theory.* Englewood Cliffs, NJ: Prentice Hall.

Bem, S. L. (1981). Gender schema theory: A cognitive account of sex typing. *Psychological Review, 88,* 354–364.

Deaux, K., & LaFrance, M. (1998). Gender. In D. Gilbert, S. Fiske, & G. Lindzey (Eds.), *The handbook of social psychology* (4th ed.). Current review of social psychological views on gender.

Deaux, K., & Major, B. (1987). Putting gender into context: An interactive model of gender-related behavior. *Psychological Review, 94,* 369–389.

Eagly, A. H. (1987). *Sex differences in social behavior: a social-role interpretation.* Hillsdale, NJ: Erlbaum.

Fagot, B. I. (1985). Gender identity: Some thoughts on an old concept. *Journal of the American Academy of Child Psychiatry, 24,* 684–688.

Huston, A. C. (1983). Sex typing. In E. M. Hetherington (Ed.), *Handbook of child psychology: Socialization, person-*

ality, and social development (Vol. 4, pp. 388–467). New York: Wiley. Classic comprehensive review of gender development and issue of multidimensionality.

Imperato-McGinley, J., Peterson, R. E., Gautier, T., & Sturla, E. (1979). Androgens and the evolution of male gender identity among male pseudohermaphrodites with 5-alpha-reductase deficiency. *New England Journal of Medicine, 300,* 1233–1237.

Kohlberg, L. A. (1966). A cognitive-developmental analysis of children's sex role concepts and attitudes. In E. E. Maccoby (Ed.), *The development of sex differences.* Stanford, CA: Stanford University Press. This book provides reviews of the major early theories of gender development.

Martin, C. L., & Halverson, C. F. (1981). A schematic processing model of sex typing and stereotyping in children. *Child Development, 54,* 563–574.

Mischel, W. (1966). A social-learning view of sex differences in behavior. In E. E. Maccoby (Ed.), *The development of sex differences* (pp. 57–81). Stanford, CA: Stanford University Press.

Money, J., & Ehrhardt, A. A. (1972). *Man & woman, boy & girl.* Baltimore: Johns Hopkins University Press. Reviews classic cases of intersex gender identity.

Ruble, D. N., & Martin, C. L. (1998). Gender development. In N. Eisenberg (Ed.), *Handbook of child psychology: Social, emotional, and personality development.* New York: Wiley. Current comprehensive review of gender identity and gender roles in children.

Spence, J. T., Helmreich, R., & Stapp, J. (1974). The Personal Attributes Questionnaire: A measure of sex role stereotypes and masculinity-femininity. *Journal of Supplemental Abstract Service Catalog of Selected Documents in Psychology, 4,* 43.

Zucker, K. J., & Bradley, S. J. (1995). *Gender identity disorder and psychosexual problems in children and adolescents.* New York: Guilford Press. Comprehensive review of gender identity issues.

Carol Lynn Martin

GENDER ROLES are those shared expectations that apply to individuals on the basis of their socially identified sex. According to this definition, people hold expectations about the behaviors that are appropriate to an individual because they identify the person as a member of the social category that consists of either females or males. The idea that gender roles are shared implies that many of the expectations associated with men and women tend to be consensual in society. This definition suggests that, at an implicit or explicit level, most people endorse the expected behaviors as appropriate for men or for women.

This definition of gender roles derives from the general concept of social role, which is central to the social sciences and refers to the shared expectations that apply to persons who occupy a certain social position or are members of a particular social category. At an individual level, roles exist as schemas, understood as abstract knowledge about a particular entity—in this case, about a group of people. Because role schemas tend to be consensual (i.e., shared among members of a society), they are important structures at the societal as well as the individual level. Roles are thus aspects of social structure, which can be understood as "persisting and bounded patterns of behavior and interaction among people or positions" (House, 1995, p. 390). According to the role construct, people who have the same social position within a social structure such as an organization or family, or who are classified in the same general societal category (e.g., as women, as African Americans), experience common situational constraints that tend to maintain their characteristic patterns of behavior. These constraints arise from the shared role schemas that people in their society hold. For example, people who have a particular paid occupation (e.g., as dental hygienists or auto mechanics) are subjected to a set of expectations concerning the work they should do and the style in which they should do it. If they deviate from these expectations by behaving in ways that are perceived as atypical and regarded as inappropriate for people in their occupation, negative sanctions follow.

In contrast to specific roles based on occupations, family relationships, and memberships in other groups such as volunteer organizations, gender roles are rather diffuse because they apply to people who have membership in the extremely general social categories of male and female. Gender roles thus pertain to virtually all people. These roles, like other diffuse roles based on qualities such as age, race, and social class, have great scope or generality because they are applicable to all portions of one's daily life. In contrast, more specific roles based on factors such as family relationships (e.g., mother, son) and occupation (e.g., kindergarten teacher, firefighter) are mainly relevant to one's behavior in a particular group or organizational context—at work, for example, in the case of occupational roles. Gender roles coexist with specific roles and are relevant to most social interactions, including encounters that are also structured by these specific roles. This general applicability of gender roles means that they continue to have impact on behavior, even though specific roles also constrain behavior. For example, because gender roles are relevant in the workplace, people have somewhat different expectations for female and male occupants of the same workplace role. More generally, research suggests that people combine or average the expectations associated with specific roles and more diffuse roles such as gender roles.

Evidence that gender roles are important features of social structure follows in part from research on gender stereotypes, which has consistently documented the existence of differing beliefs about men's and women's typical behavior. For example, factor analytic studies of gender stereotypes have shown that the content of many of these beliefs can be summarized in terms of differences on two dimensions, which are frequently given Bakan's (1966) labels of *communal* and *agentic*. Women, more than men, are thought to behave in a manner that can be described as communal (i.e., friendly, unselfish, concerned with others, and emotionally expressive). Men, more than women, are thought to behave in a manner that can be described as agentic (i.e., independent, masterful, assertive, and instrumentally competent). Gender stereotypes also encompass beliefs about many other aspects of individuals, including their physical characteristics, typical roles, specific skills, and emotional dispositions. Nonetheless, such beliefs about the typical characteristics of women and men are not sufficient to demonstrate the existence of gender roles, because roles are built, not merely from expectations about how people typically behave, but also from expectations about how they should behave. Thus, most research on gender stereotypes describes what Cialdini and Trost (1998) labeled as *descriptive norms*, which are expectations derived from observations of what people do. In contrast, social roles encompass what Cialdini and Trost labeled as *injunctive norms*, which are expectations about what people should do.

Demonstrations that many aspects of gender stereotypes describe injunctive norms as well as descriptive norms can be found in research showing that stereotypic ways of behaving are perceived as generally desirable for people of each sex, at least insofar as researchers examine the evaluatively positive aspects of gender stereotypes. To understand what behaviors are thought to be desirable for women and men, some stereotype researchers have investigated people's beliefs about the ideal woman and man (Broverman, Vogel, Broverman, Clarkson, & Rosenkrantz, 1972; Spence & Helmreich, 1978). These beliefs about ideal behavior tend to parallel beliefs about what is typical of women or men. Such findings show that people tend to think that women and men ought to differ in many of the ways that they are perceived to differ. This "oughtness" transforms gender stereotypes into gender roles.

The distinction between descriptive and injunctive norms informs analyses of the power of gender roles to influence behavior. In general, observations of deviations from descriptive norms produce surprise, whereas observations of deviations from injunctive norms produce social disapproval and efforts to induce compliance. Because descriptive norms describe what is normal or typical, they can provide guidance concerning what behaviors are likely to be effective in a situation. People thus refer to others of their own sex to find out what sorts of behaviors are usual for people of their own sex in a situation. They may tend to imitate these sex-typical behaviors, especially if a situation is ambiguous or confusing and they therefore turn to others for guidance. Because injunctive norms describe what is desirable and admirable, these norms provide guidance concerning what behaviors are likely to elicit approval from others. People thus refer to what is desirable for persons of their sex when they endeavor to satisfy their motives to build and maintain social relationships. In summary, the power of gender roles to induce role-consistent behavior derives from these roles' descriptions of what is typical of men and women and what is desirable for them.

The idea that expectations about appropriate male and female behavior are shared implies that a social consensus exists about typical and appropriate behaviors and that people are aware of this consensus. This relative consensus about perceived sex differences and the desirability of these differences has been shown repeatedly in stereotype research. Despite some individual differences in gender stereotype data, researchers have found that largely similar beliefs are held by men and women, students and older adults, and people who differ in social class and income (e.g., Broverman et al., 1972). Moreover, social cognitive researchers such as Devine (1989) have argued that virtually everyone has acquired the stereotypic beliefs that are associated with important social categories such as sex, race, and age. In addition, people are aware that gender-stereotypic beliefs are consensual in society. Awareness of the society's apparent consensus about the characteristics of men and women has been shown very directly in research that asks people to report the characteristics that they believe are associated with each sex in their culture (e.g., Williams & Best, 1982). Respondents readily reported their beliefs about the stereotypes held in their own cultures.

In summary, the power of gender roles to influence behavior derives, not only from their description of typical and desirable behavior, but also from their tendency to be relatively consensual and for people to be aware of this consensus. The ability of gender roles, like other social roles, to produce role-consistent behavior follows from the overall validity of the assumption that most other people hold these expectations. People thus believe that the typical other person holds these beliefs and thus would react approvingly to role-consistent behavior and disapprovingly to inconsistent behavior. Therefore, an individual does not have to inquire of another person what he or she thinks would be typical or appropriate male and female behavior. Instead, a person is generally correct in assuming that others endorse some version of the consensual gender roles. Therefore, the most likely route to social approval in most situations and a smoothly functioning social interaction is to behave consistently with one's gender role or at least to avoid strongly deviating from this role.

Consequently, it is not surprising that, compatible with well-known social psychological concepts such as normative influence and self-fulfilling prophecy, research on the behavioral confirmation of gender stereotypes has shown that, under many circumstances, men and women act to confirm the stereotypic expectations that others hold about their behavior (e.g., Skrypnek & Snyder, 1982).

Social Consequences of Deviating from Gender Roles

A key assumption of a gender role analysis is that both women and men are penalized by other people for deviating from their gender roles. Behavior inconsistent with gender roles is often negatively sanctioned and tends to disrupt social interaction. The sanctions for role-inconsistent behavior may be overt (e.g., losing a job) or subtle (e.g., being ignored, disapproving looks).

Evidence abounds for negative reactions to deviations from gender roles. For example, one early study demonstrated that men who behave passively and women who behave assertively were rated less favorably than men who behaved assertively and women who behaved passively (Costrich, Feinstein, Kidder, Marecek, & Pascale, 1975). In a meta-analysis of 61 studies of evaluations of male and female leaders, Eagly, Makhijani, and Klonsky (1992) showed that women who adopted a male-stereotypic assertive and directive leadership style were evaluated more negatively than men who adopted this style, whereas women and men who adopted more democratic and participative styles were evaluated equivalently. In small-group interaction, women's competent, task-oriented contributions are more likely to be ignored and to elicit negative reactions than comparable contributions from men. Moreover, women tend to lose likability and influence over others when they behave in a dominant style by expressing clear-cut disagreement with another person, using direct rather than tentative speech, and behaving in an extremely competent manner (e.g., Carli, 1995). Such research details some of the processes involved in the norm-sending mechanism that helps regulate behavior in groups. Group members thus elicit conformity to gender-role norms by dispensing rewards such as liking and cooperation in return for conformity to these norms and dispensing social punishments such as rejection and neglect in return for nonconformity.

In general, social psychological research has established that one mechanism by which gender roles regulate social interaction derives from people's tendency to judge the value and appropriateness of others' behavior according to its conformity with gender roles. Because people often sanction behavior that is inconsistent with gender roles, these roles have a conservative impact on men and women by exacting costs from those who deviate from norms concerning male and female behavior. Weighing these negative outcomes in a cost-benefit analysis, people would not engage in nonconformity with their gender role unless it produced substantial benefits that would outweigh these costs. Part of these perceived benefits for women, as members of a subordinate group in society, may be having some chance to gain access to rewards and opportunities formerly reserved for men.

Impact of Gender Roles on the Self-Concept

Gender roles can produce sex differences in behavior not only by affecting the rewards and punishments received from others but also by affecting the self-concepts of women and men. Research showing that people's self-concepts tend to be gender stereotypic suggests that gender roles influence people's ideas about themselves (e.g., Spence & Helmreich, 1978). Consistent with stereotypic communal and agentic qualities, women's construals of themselves are oriented toward interdependence in the sense that representations of others are treated as part of the self. In contrast, men's construals of themselves are oriented toward independence, separation, and dominance in the sense that representations of others are separate from the self (Cross & Madsen, 1997). Because self-definitions are important in regulating behavior, sex-typed selves can underlie sex-differentiated behavior.

The internalization of gender-stereotypic qualities results in people adopting sex-typed norms as personal standards for judging their own behavior. They tend to evaluate themselves favorably to the extent that they conform to these personal standards and to evaluate themselves unfavorably to the extent that they deviate from these standards. In a demonstration of such processes, Wood, Christensen, Hebl, and Rothgerber (1997) investigated normative beliefs that men are powerful, dominant, and self-assertive and that women are caring, intimate with others, and emotionally expressive. They found that to the extent that these gender role norms were personally relevant to participants, experiences that were congruent with gender norms (i.e., involving dominance for men and communion for women) yielded positive feelings about the self and brought participants' actual self-concepts closer to the standards represented by their ought and ideal selves. This evidence suggests that one of the processes by which gender roles affect behavior is that they are incorporated into people's self-concepts and then operate as personal standards.

The link between gender roles and people's self-construals helps explain why there are substantial individual differences in the extent to which women and men engage in behavior consistent with the gender roles of their culture. People raised in culturally atypical environments may not internalize conventional gender-role norms and thus may have self-construals atypical of their gender. Consistent with research showing substantial relationships between sex-typed behaviors and self-reported masculinity and femininity (see Taylor & Hall, 1982), people who have self-concepts that differ from those that are typical of people of their sex are less likely to show traditionally sex-typed behavior.

Gender Roles as Cultural Constructions

Because gender roles are composed of norms about male and female behavior, they are products of the culture. They form an important part of the culture and social structure of every society. Just as cultures differ in features such as family structure and religious practices, they differ in their definition of gender roles. Demonstrating cross-cultural variation in gender roles is Best and Williams's (1993) research on ideologies about gender in fourteen countries. Classifying countries' gender ideologies on a dimension that ranged from conservative, or male-dominant, to modern, or egalitarian, substantial cross-cultural differences emerged. The most conservative definitions of gender roles were found in Nigeria and Pakistan, and the most modern in the Netherlands and Germany. In general, gender roles were more modern in more economically developed nations, as well as in countries that were more heavily Christian, more urbanized, and located at higher latitudes.

In another cross-cultural project, Best and Williams (1993) examined gender stereotypes among university students in 25 nations. This research produced considerable cross-cultural commonality in beliefs about the characteristics of men and women, such that men were generally viewed as more active, strong, dominant, autonomous, aggressive, achievement-oriented, and exhibitionistic and women were viewed as more passive, weak, deferent, succorant, nurturing, and affiliative. Despite the generality of these themes across the nations, the research also established some evidence for cross-cultural variability. In particular, the tendency for men to be perceived as more agentic (e.g., stronger and more active) than women was less pronounced in nations that were more economically developed and in which literacy rates and the percentage of women attending universities were high. These findings suggest that in countries in which the division of labor between the sexes is less sex-typed and the sexes have greater social and political equality, gender stereotypes and roles become less traditional. Another interesting trend was that the tendency for women to be viewed as more affiliative than men was less evident in Muslim than Christian countries, a trend that may reflect the relative confinement of Muslim women in the home (Williams & Best, 1982). To the extent that the beliefs documented by Williams and Best reflect the injunctive and descriptive norms embodied in gender roles, they establish some variability across cultures in the definition of gender roles.

Even though gender roles are products of the culture, they are not arbitrary cultural constructions. Instead, consistent with Best and Williams's (1993) findings, they are firmly rooted in a society's division of labor between the sexes. The differing distributions of men and women into social roles form the basis for gender roles (Eagly, 1987). Thus, the typical division of labor in industrial nations (and, to a lesser extent, in postindustrial nations) assigns a disproportionate share of domestic activities to women and of other activities to men. Mainly women occupy the domestic role, somewhat more men than women occupy the employee role, and women are more likely than men to be employed part-time or part-year (e.g., Shelton, 1992). Although most women are employed in the paid labor force in the United States and many other industrial and postindustrial nations, women and men tend to be employed in different occupations in a largely sex-segregated labor force.

The link between gender roles and the specific family and employment roles of the sexes follows from the principle that men and women are expected to have attributes that equip them for their sex-typical roles (Eagly, 1987). Women and men are expected to accommodate to their family and employment roles by acquiring role-related skills, such as women learning domestic skills and men learning skills that are useful in paid occupations, particularly male-dominated occupations. Also, women's association with the domestic role and female-dominated occupations lends the female role its pattern of interpersonally facilitative and friendly behaviors that can be termed *communal*. In particular, the assignment to women of the majority of child-rearing duties leads people to expect communal behaviors from women, including nurturant behaviors that facilitate care for children and other dependent individuals. The importance of close relationships to women's nurturing role favors superior interpersonal skills and ability to communicate nonverbally. In contrast, men's association with the employment role, especially male-dominated occupations, produces expectations of assertive and independent behaviors that can be termed *agentic* (Eagly & Steffen, 1984). This argument is not to deny that paid occupations show wide variation in the extent to which they favor more masculine or feminine qualities. Suggesting that expectations about the personal qualities of each sex may be shaped by their paid occupations are demonstrations that to the extent that occupations are male dominated, success in them is perceived to follow from agentic personal qualities, whereas to the extent that occupations are female dominated, success in them is perceived to follow from communal personal qualities (Cejka & Eagly, 1999).

Roles that offer the greatest amount of power and status are male dominated. Because people in less powerful roles are expected to behave in a less dominant and more submissive style than people in powerful roles, gender roles take on these prescriptions as well. Men are expected to be more dominant and women to be more subordinate. In particular, subordinate behavior is more compliant to social influence, less overtly aggressive, and more cooperative and conciliatory, and dominant behavior is controlling, assertive, and relatively directive and autocratic. Gender roles therefore encompass expectations about these more subordinate and more dominant styles of behavior that follow from the societal subordination of women relative to men.

Change in Gender Roles

The view that gender roles are rooted in the division of labor between the sexes implies that these roles should change if the division of labor changes. Remarkable in the second half of the twentieth century was the rapid increase in the extent to which women were employed in the paid labor force in the United States and those of many other nations (Reskin & Padavic, 1994). Women's greatly increased education, by which their rates of high-school graduation and university degrees exceed those of men in the United States and some other nations, has qualified them for jobs with more status and income than the jobs that women typically held in the past. More modest changes have occurred in men's domestic life, with some tendency for men to increase their responsibility for child care and other domestic work. These changes, especially women's entry into paid employment, should result in some erosion of acceptance of the traditional gender roles and a redefinition of the patterns of behavior that are most appropriate to women and men.

Such changes have been documented in research on attitudes toward the appropriate roles and responsibilities for women and men. Twenge (1997) meta-analytically demonstrated a general shift toward more egalitarian definitions of women's rights and responsibilities between 1970 and 1995 and found that the change in women's attitudes was somewhat larger than the change in men's attitudes. However, some portion of people in Western nations still endorse traditional gender roles, as displayed in researchers' ability to successfully capture individual differences with attitude scales assessing acceptance versus rejection of traditional norms about male and female behavior (e.g., Swim, Aikin, Hall, & Hunter, 1995). Such research suggests that gender roles are in considerable flux, at least in Western societies. Although these shifts suggest that a loss of consensus may lessen the power of gender roles to influence behavior, the traditional consensus may be intact in some of the more conservative segments of society, and a new consensus may have emerged in less traditional segments of society. Nonetheless, the new consensus may share some features with the old consensus, such as the expectation that men provide financially for their families (Riggs, 1997).

Conclusion

Gender roles can have powerful effects on individuals, who strive to take these roles into account as they try to reach important goals, enhance their self-esteem, and gain approval from others. Other social roles, especially those pertaining to occupations and family relationships, are also very important, and the influence of these other roles combines with gender roles to influence behavior. In all social settings, people must negotiate social interactions as a man or a woman and therefore must contend with their own and others' expectations concerning the behavior that is typical and appropriate for individuals of their sex. Violating others' expectations about male or female behavior can bring a variety of negative reactions, whereas meeting their expectations can bring rewards of social approval and cooperation. In addition, living up to one's own personal expectations about gender-appropriate behavior can yield rewards of self-esteem and satisfaction. Yet, this prescription that conformity with gender roles yields social and personal rewards is overly simple in societies in which women's position in the social structure is undergoing rapid change and gender roles are in flux. Although shifting gender roles can loosen the constraints of traditional rules about how men and women should behave and thus allow more behavioral flexibility, these changes can also produce ambiguity, confusion, and debates concerning what is the proper place of women and men in society.

Bibliography

Bakan, D. (1966). *The duality of human existence: An essay on psychology and religion.* Chicago: Rand-McNally.

Best, D. L., & Williams, J. E. (1993). A cross-cultural viewpoint. In A. E. Beall & R. J. Sternberg (Eds.), *The psychology of gender* (pp. 215–248). New York: Guilford Press. Reviews research on the cross-cultural aspects of gender stereotypes and roles.

Broverman, I. K., Vogel, S. R., Broverman, D. M., Clarkson, F. E., & Rosenkrantz, P. S. (1972). Sex-role stereotypes: A current appraisal. *Journal of Social Issues, 28*(2), 59–78.

Carli, L. L. (1995). Nonverbal behavior, gender, and influence. *Journal of Personality and Social Psychology, 68,* 1030–1041.

Cejka, M. A., & Eagly, A. H. (1999). Gender-stereotypic images of occupations correspond to the sex segregation of employment. *Personality and Social Psychology Bulletin, 25,* 413–423.

Cialdini, R. B., & Trost, M. R. (1998). Social influence: Social norms, conformity, and compliance. In D. T. Gilbert, S. T. Fiske, & G. Lindzey (Eds.), *The handbook of social psychology* (4th ed., Vol. 2, pp. 151–192). Boston: McGraw-Hill.

Costrich, N., Feinstein, J., Kidder, L., Marecek, J., & Pascale, L. (1975). When stereotypes hurt: Three studies of penalties for sex-role reversals. *Journal of Experimental Social Psychology, 11,* 520–530.

Cross, S. E., & Madson, L. (1997). Models of the self: Self-construals and gender. *Psychological Bulletin, 122,* 5–37. Provides a comprehensive analysis of the impact of gender roles on the self.

Devine, P. G. (1989). Stereotypes and prejudice: Their automatic and controlled components. *Journal of Personality and Social Psychology, 56,* 5–18.

Eagly, A. H. (1987). *Sex differences in social behavior: A social-role interpretation.* Hillsdale, NJ: Erlbaum. Presents a social role of theory of sex differences in social behavior.

Eagly, A. H., Makhijani, M. G., & Klonsky, B. G. (1992). Gender and the evaluation of leaders: A meta-analysis. *Psychological Bulletin, 111,* 3–22.

Eagly, A. H., & Steffen, V. J. (1984). Gender stereotypes stem from the distribution of women and men into social roles. *Journal of Personality and Social Psychology, 46,* 735–754.

House, J. S. (1995). Social structure, relationships, and the individual. In K. S. Cook, G. A. Fine, & J. S. House (Eds.), *Sociological perspectives on social psychology* (pp. 387–395). Boston: Allyn & Bacon.

Reskin, B. F., & Padavic, I. (1994). *Women and men at work.* Thousand Oaks, CA: Pine Forge Press.

Riggs, J. M. (1997). Mandates for mothers and fathers: Perceptions of breadwinners and care givers. *Sex Roles, 37,* 565–580.

Shelton, B. A. (1992). *Women, men and time: Gender differences in paid work, housework, and leisure.* New York: Greenwood Press. Presents a cogent analysis and empirical description of changes in women's and men's occupational and domestic roles.

Skrypnek, B. J., & Snyder, M. (1982). On the self-perpetuating nature of stereotypes about women and men. *Journal of Experimental Social Psychology, 18,* 277–291.

Spence, J. T., & Helmreich, R. (1978). *Masculinity & femininity: Their psychological dimensions, correlates, & antecedents.* Austin: University of Texas Press.

Swim, J. K. (1994). Perceived versus meta-analytic effect sizes: An assessment of the accuracy of gender stereotypes. *Journal of Personality and Social Psychology, 66,* 21–36.

Swim, J. K., Aikin, K. J., Hall, W. S., & Hunter, B. A. (1995). Sexism and racism: Old-fashioned and modern prejudices. *Journal of Personality and Social Psychology, 68,* 199–214.

Taylor, M. C., & Hall, J. A. (1982). Psychological androgyny: Theories, methods, and conclusions. *Psychological Bulletin, 92,* 347–366.

Twenge, J. M. (1997). Attitudes toward women, 1970–1995. *Psychology of Women Quarterly, 21,* 35–51. A meta-analysis of changes in attitudes toward women's rights and roles.

Williams, J. E., & Best, D. L. (1982). *Measuring sex stereotypes: A thirty-nation study.* Newbury Park, CA: Sage.

Wood, W., Christensen, P. N., Hebl, M. R., & Rothgerber, H. (1997). Conformity to sex-typed norms, affect, and the self-concept. *Journal of Personality and Social Psychology, 73,* 523–535.

Alice H. Eagly

GENDER SCHEMA. There is probably no area in psychology about which so much has been written with so little agreement as the area of gender role development. Many theories have been proposed, but no single theory has adequately explained the process (Constantinople, 1979). Social learning theory emphasizes environmental influences, while psychodynamic theorists focus on the role of affect, and cognitive-developmental theorists point to the child's own influence in gender role development. Children, however, live in a world where these influences interact with one another in complex ways and cannot be neatly divided into separate realms of experience (Mischel, 1966).

Research in this field has been shaped primarily by social learning and cognitive-developmental theories, though the two approaches have come closer together in recent years (Kohlberg, 1966). Social learning theorists focus on how the environment shapes boys' and girls' development differently. Children are exposed to sex-differentiated information from birth and are continually bombarded with it throughout childhood. Studies have confirmed that boys and girls receive different information in both home and school environments (Fagot, 1974; Serbin, O'Leary, Kent, & Tonick, 1973).

Kohlberg (1966) presented stages which included identifying one's own sex (gender identity), understanding that sex remains stable over time (gender stability), and understanding that sex remains constant despite perceptual changes (gender constancy). Cognitive developmentalists have emphasized regularities in children's understanding of gender and have developed a stage theory of gender role development. Research has shown that this sequence appears to be consistent (Emmerich, Goldman, Kirsh, & Sharabany, 1977; Fagot, 1985).

Beginning with Martin and Halverson's recent article, children have been seen to actively contribute to their own gender role development. Martin and Halverson (1981) adopted the term *schema* to describe an organized knowledge structure. The term *gender schema*, developed in this context, is a knowledge structure organized around gender or sex.

Children form categories to help organize and understand the flood of information that constantly inundates them, and sex is a readily available organizing principle, relevant to the child's own self. Gender role adoption is expected to occur as the self-concept is assimilated to the gender schema and as children adopt standards of sex appropriateness. Schema formation undoubtedly depends upon the child's own mental effort and developmental status, but the information processed also reflects the degree and importance of gender typing the child's surroundings. Schema theory offers a framework for describing and integrating the development of gender understanding with environmental information and values.

Specific ways that information about gender is processed have been further developed as additional research has been conducted on gender schema theory. Martin (1993) proposed that gender information is not organized in a hierarchical fashion, but into components. Information is placed into context domains (e.g., family-role behaviors) and the components are placed into two overriding groups, male and female. Because information can come from different sources and at different times, the components are not necessarily highly related, but are held together loosely by the categories of male and female.

Living in a sex-typed world leads children to develop gender schemas that guide the choice of "sex-appropriate" behaviors. They also develop the knowledge of the action patterns necessary to carry them out. These action patterns are called *scripts*, which are generalized or temporally ordered representations. Research shows that boys appear to be more knowledgeable about scripts relating to events and action patterns about masculine-typed activities, while girls are equally knowledgeable about scripts relating to masculine- or feminine-typed activities (Boston & Levy, 1991). Research indicates that this is due to an avoidance of feminine scripts by boys, rather than simply more knowledge of the male stereotype (Bauer, 1992; Boston & Levy, 1991).

Separating cognitive understanding from motivation to perform is difficult. Girls and boys may have different understandings of gender schemas, or it may be that boys are given more negative feedback when they engage in opposite-sex play than girls (Fagot, 1989). There is also evidence that gender schemas not only contain information about using objects and participating in activities, but also information about dimensions of meaning that underlie the concepts of masculinity and femininity.

Leinbach, Fagot, and Hort (1997) found that 4-year-olds assigned bears, fire, and something rough to males; butterflies, hearts, and flowers were assigned to females. These notions are probably not taught directly to children, but it seems plausible that children associate gentler qualities with females and qualities such as strength or aggressiveness with males.

As with many areas of study, research on gender schema and gender role development is impacted by the way variables are defined and measured, as well as by characteristics of the samples studied. In looking at the differential roles of mothers and fathers on the socialization of sex differences and the creation of gender schema, studies using natural settings and studies of younger children have found larger effect sizes (Fagot, 1995). Longitudinal samples may also give us more information than cross-sectional data about the relationship of the acquisition of gender labels and the onset of sex-typed behaviors.

The way children use information from their environments is a function of their underlying human abilities to process that information. Boys and girls receive different information from their environments and the schemas they develop around this information appear to influence their behavior and patterns of thinking. When we talk about sex differences, we are talking about differences in the content of gender schemas, not the process by which children put these schemas together.

Bibliography

Bem, S. L. (1983). Gender schema theory and its implications for child development: Raising gender-aschematic children in a gender-schematic world. *Signs: Journal of Women in Culture and Society, 8,* 598–616.

Carter, D. B. (1987). Sex role research and the future: New directions for research. In D. B. Carter (Ed.), *Current conceptions of sex roles and sex typing* (pp. 243–355). New York: Praeger.

Carter, D. B. (Ed.). (1987). *Current conceptions of sex roles and sex typing.* New York: Prager.

Fagot, B. I., & Leinbach, M. D. (1993). Gender-role development in young children: From discrimination to labeling. *Developmental Review, 13,* 203–224.

Levy, G. D., & Fivush, R. (1993). Scripts and gender: A new approach for examining gender-role development. Special Issue: Early gender-role development. *Developmental Review, 13,* 126–146.

Maccoby, E. E. (Ed.). (1966). *The development of sex differences.* Stanford, CA: Stanford University Press.

Martin, C. A. (1993). New directions for investigating children's gender knowledge. *Developmental Review, 13,* 184–204.

Martin, C. A., & Halverson, C. F. (1981). A schematic processing model of sex typing and stereotyping in children. *Child Development, 52,* 1119–1134.

Beverly Fagot and Carie Rodgers

GENDER SOCIALIZATION. Identification theories, social learning theories, and social-cognitive developmental theories will be discussed as they relate to gender socialization.

Grand Theories of Gender-Role Socialization: Identification Theories

In the Freudian view, identification is the psychological mechanism by which children acquire complex sets of both behaviors and beliefs through the incorporation of the personality of another person into their own. To the extent that children identify with their same-sex parent, identification is the process by which children incorporate their parents' gender-role behaviors into their own identity system (Freud, 1933/1964). As a consequence, and as long as women and men engage in different patterns of behaviors and roles, girls and boys will be motivated to acquire different complexes of behaviors, attitudes, mannerism, and goals.

Over the past seventy years, Freud's ideas have been reworked into a number of modified theories differing from one another primarily in terms of the psychodynamic processes assumed to underlie and motivate the identification process. For example, Freud argued that fear of castration and the Oedipus conflict motivated little boys to identify with their fathers. More recently, feminist psychodynamic theorists such as Chodorow (1978) argue that gender awareness and gender identity motivate children to identify with their same-sex parent.

It is very difficult to either prove or disprove either the existence of identification or its power in the socialization process. Social learning theorists, in particular, have questioned the need for a global construct such as identification to explain behavior. Clinical theorists disagree and cite case studies and other clinical evidence to support their point of view (e.g., Fast, 1984). The continuing heat of this debate is a testament to how difficult it is to use scientific methods to study such covert and broad psychological constructs as identification.

Grand Theories of Gender-Role Socialization: Social Learning Theories

Cognitive social learning theorists (e.g., Bandura, 1977) argue that gender-role behaviors are learned by reinforcements (rewards and punishments) and observational learning.

Reinforcement. Learning theorists suggest that children are rewarded differentially by their parents and their society for exhibiting behaviors appropriate to their gender role. As a result, gender-appropriate behaviors take on greater value for the child and are exhibited with greater frequency. Reinforcements also inform girls' and boys' expectations regarding which behaviors are likely to yield either rewards or disapproval and rejection. Anticipated rewards and punishments, in turn, influence whether or not they engage in particular behaviors (Ruble & Martin, 1998). To the extent that gender becomes an important cue regarding which behaviors will be rewarded and which will be punished, females and males learn to expect different consequences for the same behaviors.

Finally, rewards and punishments shape the patterns of interpersonal behaviors and attitudes found among adults (Deaux & Major, 1987). Females learn not to be assertive in their interactions with males. Males learn that they should be the initiators of intimate relations and that they should engage in risky behavior to impress their peers. Girls learn that success in life is a successful husband who can take care of her and her children. Boys learn that success is a good job and an attractive female partner. These attitudes then shape the goals and aspirations of boys and girls as well as the types of interaction patterns they are comfortable with as adults.

Modeling and Observational Learning. Social learning theorists also suggest that individuals learn by watching the behavior of those around them (models) especially if the models are reinforced for their behavior. But individuals do not imitate all of the behaviors they observe. Instead, individuals are more likely to imitate the behavior of someone of their own sex than of someone of the opposite sex (Bandura, 1977).

Extensive empirical evidence exists to support the importance of reinforcement and observational learning in gender-role socialization (Ruble & Martin, 1998). Peers in particular provide strong reinforcement for gender stereotypic behaviors (Maccoby, 1998).

Grand Theories: Social-Cognitive Developmental Theories

Social-cognitive developmentalists argue that children play an active role in their own socialization (e.g., Kohlberg, 1966; Ruble & Martin, 1998). That is, children are motivated to learn gender roles because they want to master the demands of their culture in order to become "good" members of their society. Advocates of the social-cognitive perspective believe that early in life children learn that people can be classified as either females or males. They also learn that they, themselves, are either a female or a male. At this point most children incorporate their gender into their identity (their subjective view of whom they are). Once the knowledge of gender and gender identity emerge, social cognitive theorists believe that children begin to use gender as a social category. That is, they organize much of the social information available to them according to gender. In keeping with their active view of the child, these theorists assume that children create these categories and seek out the information needed to fill out the content of each category (that is, male and female). In building up the content of these categories, children are assumed to use all available information.

Having formed these gender-role categories, children then strive to become like the categories they have created. They imitate behaviors they assume to be important characteristics of their gender and adopt attitudes congruent with their image of a "good" boy or girl. For social-cognitive theorists, this process of monitoring one's own behavior is the crux of gender-role acquisition. Ample empirical evidence supports these assumptions and predictions (Ruble & Martin, 1998).

Developmental Changes

Social-cognitive theorists believe that children's understanding of gender roles and scripts is tempered in part by their level of cognitive development (e.g., Kohlberg, 1996). The quality and rigidity of these concepts change with the child's age. For example, because 3-year-olds are very concrete in their thinking and because they tend to overgeneralize newly discovered facts, they hold very rigid beliefs regarding gender roles (e.g., doctors simply cannot be women, and nurses simply cannot be men). In addition, because beliefs and behaviors are not well integrated during the preschool years, children's behaviors are likely to be more under the influence of direct reinforcement contingencies than gender-role schema.

Similarly, social-cognitive theorists suggest that gender-role transcendence (overcoming one's gender stereotyped notions of appropriate behavior for males and females and overcoming one's identity with the traditional gender role) depends on cognitive abilities not common in individuals prior to the adolescent and adult years. Most individuals do not develop the cognitive capacity to imagine new social orders until they reach adolescence. At this point, adolescents are capable of questioning the validity of traditional gender roles and can begin to modify their own gender-role identity. Whether they will engage in this questioning and reevaluation depends on the social environment in which they live. Social-cognitive developmentalists assume that change in social-cognitive structures depend on both cognitive development and the necessary social stimuli. Social-cognitive structures will change only to the extent that the information in the social environment is incompatible with the existing social schema. Consequently, individuals will continue to hold stereo-

typed gender-role schemas until they have both the cognitive capacity to imagine a different schema and the opportunity to observe examples of gender-role transcendence. In addition, it is unlikely that individuals will seriously consider the alternative unless encouraged to do so by their social groups. If the individual lives in a culture that has well-defined gender roles and rigid rules governing behavior, then she or he will develop rigid gender-role concepts as a young child and these concepts are likely to remain rigid throughout the individual's life. In contrast, if the individual lives in a society with more egalitarian gender-role prescriptions, then gender-role concepts should become less rigid and more tolerant of variation as the person grows older.

But even in the optimal social environment, this process of change and reevaluation may not proceed smoothly. Eccles and Bryan (1994) suggested that there may be times in people's development when individuals cling to more rigid views of their world. Early adolescence is likely to be such a time because individuals are forced by social and physical changes to move from a largely sex-segregated social system into a heterosocial world. They must learn new ways of interacting and must establish new social hierarchies based on popularity with members of the opposite sex. To cope with these changes, early adolescents may cling to the rigid ideas they acquired early in life about male-female interactions. Furthermore, society may increase its pressure to conform to gender-role stereotypes. But, as individuals gain confidence in their new social roles, as they gain the cognitive skills necessary to imagine a new social order, and if they are encouraged to question traditional role and values by their peers and other key socializers, the process of derigidification should begin again in later adolescence.

[*See also* Gender Roles.]

Bibliography

Bandura, A. (1977). *Social learning theory*. Englewood Cliffs, NJ: Prentice Hall.

Chodorow, N. (1978). *The reproduction of mothering: Psychoanalysis and the sociology of gender*. Berkeley, CA: University of California Press.

Deaux, K., & Major, B. (1987). Putting gender into context: An interactive model of gender-related behavior. *Psychological Review, 94*, 369–389.

Eccles, J. S., & Bryan, J. (1994). Adolescence and gender-role transcendence. In M. Stevenson (Ed.), *Gender-roles across the life span* (pp. 111–148). Muncie, IN: Ball State University Press.

Fast, I. (1984). *Gender identity: A differentiation model*. Hillsdale, NJ: Analytic Press.

Freud, S. (1964). *New introductory lectures in psychoanalysis*. In (J. Strachey, Ed., Trans.), *The standard edition of the complete psychological works of Sigmund Freud* (Vol.

22, pp. 1–182). London: Hogarth Press. (Original work published 1933)

Kohlberg, L. A. (1966). A cognitive developmental analysis of children's sex-role concepts and attitudes. In E. E. Maccoby (Ed.), *The development of sex differences* (pp. 82–173). Stanford, CA.: Stanford University Press.

Maccoby, E. E. (1998). *The two sexes: Growing up apart, coming together*. Cambridge, MA: Belknap Press/Harvard University Press.

Maccoby, E. E., & Jacklin, C. N. (1974). *Psychology of sex differences*. Stanford, CA: Stanford University Press.

Ruble, D. N., & Martin, C. L. (1998). Gender development. In W. Damon & N. Eisenberg (Eds.), *Handbook of child psychology: Vol. 3, Social, emotional, and personality development* (5th ed.). New York: Wiley.

Jacquelynne S. Eccles

GENDER STEREOTYPES. *See* Stereotypes.

GENERAL SYSTEMS THEORY AND PHILOSOPHY. The philosophical foundation for the family therapy movement that rose to prominence in the 1970s under the influence of the anthropologist Gregory Bateson was provided by General Systems Theory (GST). The philosophical legacy of GST remains alive within family therapy, which is often called *systemic* or *systems therapy*, terms that makes the influence of GST explicit. Family systems theorists extended and applied certain principles derived from GST, namely, holism, circular or cybernetic causality, and an epistemology that eliminated the distinction between the observer and the observed.

Definition and Scope of GST

The biologist Ludwig von Bertalanffy is credited with formulating GST. In *General Systems Theory* (New York, 1968), as in his earlier articles, he defined a system as "sets of elements standing in interaction" (p. 38), and he set the goal of GST as the search for "those principles which are valid for 'systems' in general" (p. 32). In their edited volume *General Systems Theory and Psychiatry* (Boston, 1969), psychiatrists William Gray, Frederick Duhl, and Nicholas Rizzo emphasized how GST seeks general structural "isomorphisms" (or corresponding parts) among systems of all sorts. They defined GST as "a new approach to the unity-of-science problem" (p. 7), although their focus on mental health led them to seek isomorphisms among "biological, behavioral, and social phenomena and sciences" (p. 37). James G. Miller, who coined the term "behavioral science" in 1949, attempted to develop an interdisciplinary or "general theory of behavior" and then a "general living systems theory."

Doctrine of Holism

GST advances a holistic rather than a reductionistic approach to the scientific study of all systems. Von Bertalanffy specified that the whole is not reducible to the sum of its parts, and he led other systems theorists toward an "organismic approach" that emphasized such concepts as wholeness, growth, differentiation, integration, and hierarchical order. According to Gray, Duhl, and Rizzo, the goal of GST was to find the "organizing relationships themselves that result from dynamic interaction and make the behavior of parts different, when studied in isolation, than when studied within the whole" (p. 11). James Miller similarly claimed that the state of each element in the system is determined by the state of the other elements in that system. Gregory Bateson also expressed this concern when he emphasized the search for "the pattern which connects," a phrase echoed by many family systems theorists and therapists in the 1980s.

The general systems theorists' holistic focus on pattern, relationship, order, information, and organization had close ties to developments in the discipline of cybernetics, which informed their thinking. According to systems theorist and family therapist Bradford Keeney, Norbert Wiener, Warren McCulloch, Heinz von Foerster, Gregory Bateson, and John von Neumann were among the scientists involved in a series of meetings in the 1940s that came to be titled "Feedback Mechanisms and Circular Causal Systems in Biological and Social Systems." Feedback is a key concept of cybernetics, which the mathematician Norbert Wiener, in *Cybernetics* (New York, 1948), defined as "the entire field of control and communication theory, whether in the machine or in the animal" (p. 19). (W. Ross Ashby was also influential in defining this new discipline.) Cybernetics examined how the output of a system is fed back into the same system in the form of information or input that regulates the (functional) pattern or organization of the system as a whole.

Circular Causality, Stability, and Change

Systems as wholes were said to maintain themselves through homeostatic or self-regulatory mechanisms involving circular or cybernetic feedback loops. Thus, traditional linear, cause-effect (A → B) sequences came under attack as an erroneously reductionistic way to understand the nature of systems as wholes. Von Bertalanffy emphasized this in saying that the problem of (living) systems consists in the interaction of many variables; simple linear, one-way, cause-effect sequences do not apply because of the goal-directed or teleological nature of those systems. William Gray and Nicholas Rizzo, in *General Systems Theory and Psychiatry* (Boston, 1969), linked cybernetics, information theory, and GST when they said that the "most fundamental property of the living organism [is] its ability to maintain and further its organized state against a constant tendency toward disorganization" (p. 21). Bradford Keeney called "lineal" causality "atomistic, reductionistic, and anticontextual," while calling "nonlinear" causality "systemic, ecological, ecosystemic, circular, recursive, or cybernetic." The notion of holism, then, is clearly linked to circular or cybernetic causality and is seen as antithetical to linear causality. These notions became the cornerstones of family systems theory and therapy, which defined the patient's family—rather than the patient in isolation—as the relevant systemic whole, wherein an interpersonal set of patterns of organization (i.e., circular feedback loops) held the family's behavior in a stable equilibrium.

Family systems theorists imported a host of other concepts from the general systems/cybernetic scientists. The concept of *homeostasis* focused attention on interactions within the system that resulted in feedback that maintained the system (i.e., circular causality). Family therapists used that cybernetic notion to account for the "resistance" of family systems to the change-inducing interventions of the therapist. (This alleged resistance to change motivated what became known as *strategic therapy*, which generated much debate.) Members of the Mental Research Institute (MRI) in Palo Alto, California, adopted these and other ideas (e.g., the theory of logical types) in their research on the family dynamics of schizophrenia. Through such MRI members as Gregory Bateson, Don Jackson, Paul Watzlawick, John Weakland, and Jay Haley, the "cybernetic revolution" took flight within family therapy.

But these therapists also needed to account for the possibility of change. Therefore, family therapists turned to such scientists as the Nobel Prize–winning chemist Ilya Prigogine and Magoroh Maruyama to explain not only system consistency and stability, but also the possibility of change or "morphogenesis" within a cybernetic system. David Speer's oft-cited 1970 article "Family Systems: Morphostasis and Morphogenesis, or 'Is Homeostasis Enough?'" which appeared in the journal *Family Process*, marked the onset of this trend. Several sets of distinctions emerged: positive (deviation-amplifying) versus negative (deviation-counteracting) feedback, first-order versus second-order learning and change, and first-order versus second-order cybernetics. First-order cybernetics (or simple cybernetics) was the science of feedback control already discussed. Second-order cybernetics had two meanings, although the second one ultimately prevailed within family therapy: (a) emphasizing morphogenesis over homeostasis and (b) putting the observer into the feedback system or loop so that the "observing system" and the "observed system" are no longer distinct. Systems theorist and family therapist Paul Dell adopted this latter view in his 1982 call (in a famous issue of *Family Process*) to eliminate the concept of *causality* altogether in favor of noncausal "fit" or "coherence." He based his ideas on the "structure determinism" of biologist Humberto Maturana, who claimed that only the structure of the system itself could determine what "perturbed" or changed it.

"Cybernetic Epistemology"

Second-order cybernetics and structure determinism marked the start of the epistemological phase of the family therapy movement and of the problematic term *cybernetic epistemology*. In cybernetic epistemology, circular causality is not there, ontologically, in the system itself, but is a way for an observer to "punctuate" or ascribe causality to the system. The causality, then, is in the observer, not in the observed. Gregory Bateson was foundational in making this shift from objectivity to subjectivity, followed by systems theorists Paul Watzlawick, Paul Dell, and Bradford Keeney, among others in the early 1980s.

When Bateson said in *Steps to an Ecology of Mind* (New York, 1972, p. 163) that there are "various habits of punctuating the stream of experience so that it takes on one or another sort of coherence and sense," he was advocating subjectivity, or an antirealist epistemology, that eliminated the distinction between the knower and the known. He thus set the tone for the antirealist epistemology still seen in certain family therapy circles. Systems theorists Paul Dell, Bradford Keeney, Lynn Hoffman, Paul Watzlawick, Heinz von Foerster, and Ernst von Glasersfeld, among many others, propounded antirealism by claiming that we construct or create reality in language rather than discovering an objective or mind-independent reality. This epistemology ultimately became known as *constructivism*.

For Bateson and Keeney, cybernetic epistemology—that is, punctuating the stream of experience to perceive circular causality—was the "epistemologically correct" way of knowing; punctuating to perceive linear causality was deemed "epistemologically incorrect." This view has been criticized by Held and Pols (1985) because these theorists sometimes claimed that systems operate by way of circular causality; this is a conventional ontological or metaphysical claim about reality that contradicts the subjective or antirealist epistemology of these theorists. Thus, the term *epistemology* developed two meanings: (a) the conventional one about the nature of knowing (in this case, that all knowing is subjective) and (b) the unconventional one about the nature of what is known (in this case, that the world operates by way of circular causality). Hence the conflation of ontology/metaphysics and epistemology embodied in the term *cybernetic epistemology*, a conflation that has persisted in the family therapy literature.

The epistemological claim that we make reality in language led many family theorists and therapists to adopt the constructivism that became popular in the humanities and social sciences in the 1980s and 1990s. Many family therapists left traditional models of family functioning and turned to what was originally called *strategic/systemic* therapy and is now known as *narrative* therapy, a movement led by such theorist/therapists as Harold Goolishian, Harlene Anderson, Michael White, and Steve de Shazer. Narrative therapy seeks to help clients develop new narratives of their life situations so that new options and solutions become apparent. Held (1995) has argued that narrative therapy produces practical as well as theoretical problems, since narrative therapists must avoid the "imposition" of any predetermined theoretical constructs, such as the notion of a rigid family structure, because such hypothetical constructs are supposedly nothing more than antirealist fictions that obstruct the co-construction of therapeutic narratives. Thus, current forms of family systems theory and therapy, guided by an antirealist epistemology and an allegiance to circular causality and holism, continue to advance certain philosophical presuppositions of GST.

[*See also* Family Therapy; Metaphysics; and Philsophy, *article on* Philosophy of Science.]

Bibliography

Works on General Systems Theory

Ashby, W. R. (1956). *An introduction to cybernetics.* New York: Wiley.

Buckley, W. (1968). *Modern systems research for the behavioral scientist: A sourcebook.* Chicago: Aldine. Contains classic essays by von Bertalanffy, von Neumann, Ashby, von Foerster, Wiener, McCulloch, Rosenblueth, Maruyama, and other systems/cybernetic theorists.

Maruyama, M. (1963). The second cybernetics: Deviation-amplifying mutual causal processes. *American Scientist, 51,* 164–179.

Maturana, H. R. (1978). Biology of language: The epistemology of reality. In G. A. Miller, & E. Lenneberg (Eds.), *Psychology and biology of language and thought* (pp. 27–63). New York: Academic Press. Employs systems concepts to advance notions of structure determinism and antirealism, notions used by family systems theorists.

Miller, J. G. (1978). *Living systems.* New York: McGraw-Hill. Examines the structure and processes of "seven hierarchical levels of living systems": cell, organ, organism, group, organization, society, and supranational system.

Prigogine, I. (1976). Order through fluctuation: Self-organization and social system. In E. Jantsch & C. H. Waddington (Eds.), *Evolution and consciousness: Human systems in transition* (pp. 93–133). Reading, MA: Addison-Wesley.

Works on the Extension of General Systems Theory by Family Systems Theorists

Anderson, H., & Goolishian, H. A. (1988). Human systems as linguistic systems: Preliminary and evolving ideas about the implications for clinical theory. *Family Pro-*

cess, 27, 371–393. A seminal paper in the narrative therapy movement in which an antirealist epistemology is put forth.

Bateson, G. (1979). *Mind and nature: A necessary unity.* New York: Bantam Books.

Held, B. S. (1995). *Back to reality: A critique of postmodern theory in psychotherapy.* New York: Norton.

Held, B. S., & Pols, E. (1985). The confusion about epistemology and "epistemology"—and what to do about it. *Family Process, 24,* 509–517. Explains and illustrates the double use of the term *epistemology* by family systems theorists in the 1970s and 1980s and how that confusion perpetuated certain logical contradictions.

Keeney, B. (1983). *Aesthetics of change.* New York: Guilford Press. Provides an overview of the development of cybernetic epistemology within family therapy, especially as it relates to GST and the ideas of Gregory Bateson.

Simon, F. B., Stierlin, H., & Wynne, L. C. (1985). *The language of family therapy: A systemic vocabulary and sourcebook.* New York: Family Process Press.

Watzlawick, P., Weakland, J. H., & Fisch, R. (1974). *Change: Principles of problem formation and problem resolution.* New York: Norton. A seminal work of the strategic therapy movement that provides practical applications of the work of Bateson and other systems thinkers.

Barbara S. Held

GENERATIVITY. Introduced to psychology through the writings of Erik H. Erikson, generativity refers to an adult's concern for and commitment to promoting the next generation. Adults can express generativity through parenting, teaching, mentoring, and generating products and outcomes that aim to benefit youth and foster the development and well-being of individuals and social systems that will outlive the self. Generativity is an inherently psychosocial concept. From a psychological standpoint, generativity is experienced both as an inner desire or need and an age-appropriate demand whose successful engagement is viewed to be a sign of psychological maturity in the adult years. From the standpoint of society and culture, generativity is a critical resource that may undergird social institutions, encourage citizens' contributions and commitments to the public good, motivate efforts to sustain continuity from one generation to the next, and initiate social change.

Erikson's Theory of Generativity

In his landmark book *Childhood and Society* (1950), Erikson conceived of the human life course as a sequence of eight stages, with each stage defined by a central psychosocial issue. After moving through the fifth (late-adolescent) stage of *identity versus role confusion,* and the sixth (young adult) stage of *intimacy versus isolation,* the adult confronts *generativity versus stagnation*—the key issue of Erikson's seventh stage, associated with the long period of the middle adult years. In the ideal Eriksonian scenario, the adult first consolidates a sense of who he or she is and how he or she fits into society (identity) and then commits himself or herself to others through marriage and friendship (intimacy) before he or she is psychosocially ready to devote considerable time and effort to the well-being of generations to come. Parenting is perhaps the prototypical expression of generativity, but adults can be generative in many other ways as well, especially through creative and productive activities and through leadership and teaching. Failures and frustrations in generativity may be experienced as stagnation, wherein the adult feels that he or she is unable to create or produce a satisfying legacy of the self, or as self-preoccupation, wherein the adult focuses attention mainly on the care and maintenance of the self rather than others.

Erikson identified care as the signal virtue associated with the generativity stage. A primary arena for the expression of care is the family, and the primary objects of generativity for many adults are their own children and the young people in their immediate community. But generativity can also be expressed on a larger public stage, even to the point of caring for society as a whole. In *Gandhi's Truth* (1969), Erikson showed how one man's generativity mission came to encompass the well-being of an entire nation. As a spiritual leader and a fatherly care giver for his own people, Gandhi played out his generativity in a dramatic public fashion even as he failed to be a good father to his very own children at home.

Erikson described generativity as stemming both from inner needs or drives and external forces in society. He speculated that generativity may ultimately stem from some kind of biological urgings, related perhaps to sexuality and procreation, but he also underscored how society's expectations for generative behavior shape the expression of generativity and care in adulthood. Furthermore, while Erikson's stage model suggests that generativity versus stagnation is a normative psychosocial issue, adults still differ significantly from one another with respect to the strength and scope of their generative feelings, attitudes, and expressions.

Individual differences in generativity may stem from many causes, Erikson argued. Among the more intriguing may be what Erikson (1950, p. 267) called a "belief in the species"—a faith in the ultimate goodness and worthwhileness of the human enterprise. Generativity always involves hard work, and people who lack a belief in the species may find it difficult to summon forth the energy and commitment that are needed to support that work and sustain the hope that it will all pay off in the long run. It is difficult to be generative, Erikson maintained, if one is not at least moderately optimistic about the future and about the fate of one's family, community, or people.

Generativity motivates behavior aimed at promoting a greater good. But Erikson also emphasized how generativity can be good for the generative person. Not only is generativity a sign of psychosocial maturity in Erikson's developmental scheme, it should also be associated with psychological health and well-being. Psychoanalytically informed theorists and clinicians have argued that generativity represents the kind of full expression of love and work that Freud viewed to be the key to healthy adult living. In *Adaptation to Life* (1977), George Vaillant placed generativity at the center of healthy adaptation in the adult years. Vaillant suggested that in early-to-middle adulthood, generativity is often expressed through parenting and one's activities in the workplace, but that as adults move through midlife their generative expressions expand to encompass the maintenance of important social institutions. In mid-life, Vaillant wrote, especially generative adults may come to function as society's "keepers of the meaning."

Theoretical Extensions

Although Erikson introduced his stage model shortly after World War II, it was not until the 1980s that theorists began to elaborate further on the concept of generativity itself. One of the first to do so was John Kotre, whose book *Outliving the Self: Generativity and the Interpretation of Lives* (1984) expanded the concept of generativity in three ways. First, Kotre distinguished among four different forms of generativity: biological (bearing offspring), parental (raising children), technical (teaching skills), and cultural generativity (creating or conserving symbol systems and cultural meanings). Second, Kotre pointed to two different thematic lines in generative expressions. While some forms of generativity are especially communal in that they involve nurturance and care for others, other forms of generativity are more agentic in that they encompass creative and/or powerful extensions of the self, as in some forms of leadership, entrepreneurial activity, scientific and artistic achievement, and so forth. Third, Kotre underscored the extent to which generativity involves an adult's personal project of symbolic immortality. For Kotre, generativity is "the desire to invest one's substance in forms of life and work that will outlive the self" (1984, p. 10). As such, generativity may be used for good or ill. One person's efforts to produce legacies that will outlive the self may be seen by others as misguided, destructive, or even evil. Kotre emphasizes the dark side of generativity, for example, how generativity can sometimes lead to fanaticism, and how the outcomes of one's own generative efforts can sometimes turn out to be bad. At the same time, one's generativity can also take the form of transforming a bad legacy into a good one, or of assuring that something bad from the past (e.g., a family history of abuse, a destructive cultural practice) is actively blocked so that it will not be repeated in future generations. In the latter example, the generative person functions as an intergenerational buffer, filtering out the negative legacies and seeking to pass on only those meanings and practices from the past that are deemed to be positive.

Beginning in *Power, Intimacy, and the Life Story: Personological Inquiries into Identity* (1985), Dan McAdams has drawn on the writings of Erikson and Kotre, as well as other theorists and researchers, to articulate an integrative model of generativity. McAdams argues that generativity is a configuration of seven psychosocial features that center on the individual and social goal of providing for the next generation. Generativity begins with: (1) agentic and communal *desires* that motivate a person to seek out opportunities for both symbolic immortality and caring nurturance for others, and (2) age-graded cultural *demands* that provide standards and expectations concerning how people may and should begin to take responsibility for the next generation as they move into and through middle adulthood. Then, motivated by inner desire and shaped by cultural demand, adults develop (3) a conscious *concern* for the next generation that, when supported by (4) a *belief* in the species, may lead them to formulate plans and goals which constitute (5) generative *commitments*. Ideally, such commitments are translated into (6) generative *actions*, which typically take the form of behaviors aimed at creating new things, maintaining good things, and caring for those things created and maintained so that they may ultimately be let go or offered up to society as a whole. Finally, the adult constructs (7) a personal *narration* of generativity which becomes part of his or her overall life story and specifies how he or she has worked and will continue to work to fashion something positive for the future. One's narration of generativity functions to provide an adult with a satisfying "ending" for his or her self-defining life story in that it anticipates how one's life may ultimately result in the generation of offspring, products, and outcomes that will outlive the self.

A number of other psychologists have begun to articulate further the concept of generativity. For example, Abigail Stewart and Bill Peterson have argued that generative motivation should be distinguished from generative realization. Young adults may have strong motivations to be generative, but they are not able to actualize or fulfill these desires until they have achieved the necessary resources that may attend mid-life. By then, their generative motivations may have flagged somewhat, but their behavioral realizations of generativity are likely to reach their peak. Other theorists have underscored the variability of ge-

nerativity across different life domains. Like Gandhi, many people may be specialists in generativity, expressing high levels of care and commitment in some social roles but not in others. Beyond the strength and scope of generativity, therefore, individual differences in generative expression can be understood with respect to a person's idiosyncratic patterning of their social roles.

Research and Applications

Until the 1980s, psychologists did very little empirical research on generativity. Early research relied on clinical ratings and case examples to buttress Erikson's claim that generativity is an important feature of the psychosocial landscape of midlife. But rigorous, hypothesis-testing studies awaited the development of quantifiable measures of individual differences in generativity. A number of measures have been developed in recent years. These include self-report scales such as McAdams's Loyola Generativity Scale, the generativity Q-sort profiles developed by Peterson, behavioral checklists, semiprojective measures of generative goals and strivings, and content-analysis procedures for assessing generativity themes in imaginative stories and autobiographical recollections.

A small body of research has examined Erikson's developmental assumptions concerning generativity. Unfortunately, most of this work has been cross-sectional rather than longitudinal, so it is difficult to sort out developmental trends from cohort effects. Different measures show different results, but the general tendency in the studies suggests that some forms and aspects of generativity (such as Stewart's notion of generative realization and McAdams's measures of generative acts and commitments) appear to manifest themselves at higher levels among mid-life adults (in their 40s and 50s) compared to younger adults (generally in their 20s). It is not clear, however, when and whether such generative inclinations decrease thereafter, as Erikson's stage model seems to suggest they should. In any case, contemporary thinking about generativity tends to deemphasize the extent to which it can be neatly located within a clearly demarcated stage of life, while retaining the more general idea that generativity may become an increasingly salient psychosocial issue, and in some cases a problem, as people move through early adulthood and into mid-life, and perhaps beyond.

Is generativity related to psychological well-being? The answer appears to be yes. A number of studies have documented statistically significant, though generally modest, positive associations between measures of generativity on the one hand and self-report measures of psychological well-being on the other. Generativity appears to be positively correlated with assessments of life satisfaction, happiness, self-esteem, and sense of coherence in life, and negatively associated with self-report measures of depression and anxiety. Adults high in generativity also report more social support from friends and families and high levels of satisfaction with the quality of that support.

Various measures of generativity also appear to predict patterns of parenting, at least among working-class and middle-class Americans. For example, high levels of generativity have been associated with authoritative parenting styles that blend parental warmth with high demands for achievement among children. In addition, parents high in generativity appear to be more invested in their children's education, showing more involvement in school activities and helping their children with their homework to a greater extent than parents scoring low in generativity. Among African American and Anglo American adults, both working class and middle class, generativity is positively associated with higher levels of political participation, church attendance, volunteer work, and involvement in community activities.

A small body of research has examined the ways in which highly generative adults construct meaning in their lives. Stimulated by Kotre's delineation of agentic and communal themes in the discourse of generativity, researchers have shown that highly generative adults describe their own lives in ways that emphasize both agentic and communal qualities, though the relative emphasis is typically on the communal. McAdams and his colleagues have explored the kinds of themes that highly generative adults emphasize in their self-defining life stories. They have identified a cluster of themes that comprise a prototypical commitment story, the features of which tend to be significantly more salient in the self-narratives of highly generative adults compared to their less generative counterparts. In the commitment story, the protagonist (a) enjoys an early family blessing or advantage, (b) is sensitized to the suffering of others at an early age, (c) is guided by a clear and compelling personal ideology that remains relatively stable over time, (d) transforms or redeems bad scenes into good outcomes, and (e) sets goals for the future to benefit society.

As an internalized narrative of the self, the commitment story may help to sustain and reinforce the modern adult's efforts to contribute to the next generation in positive ways.

Other researchers have examined themes of generativity in the life stories of political activists, creative artists and scientists, and even reformed criminals. These studies in autobiography tend to underscore how some adults find personal meaning and even psychological and spiritual redemption through generativity. In keeping with this emphasis, the cultivation of generativity has become an increasingly explicit theme in some brands of counseling and psychotherapy, as in the approach to generative parenting developed by David Dollahite and colleagues in family therapy. In addition, generativity has begun to appear in the discourse of business consultants and practitioners in industrial-organizational psychology, as they have argued that highly productive and effective managers and leaders are likely to adopt an especially generative approach to their work and life pursuits.

[*See also* Parenting; *and the biography of Erikson.*]

Bibliography

Browning, D. (1975). *Generative man.* New York: Dell. Browning reviews and analyzes how a number of psychoanalytically informed theorists, including Erich Fromm and Erik Erikson, construe psychosocial health and maturity, emphasizing the role of generativity.

Erikson, E. H. (1950). *Childhood and society.* New York: Norton. In Erikson's most influential book, he outlines his stage model of psychosocial development and introduces the concept of generativity.

Erikson, E. H. (1969). *Gandhi's truth: On the origins of militant nonviolence.* New York: Norton. In this classic psychobiography, Erikson highlights the problems and triumphs of Gandhi's struggles to be a generative father for his own children and for the entire nation of India.

Kotre, J. (1984). *Outliving the self: Generativity and the interpretation of lives.* Baltimore, MD: Johns Hopkins University Press. Kotre extends generativity theory and illustrates the dynamics of generativity in eight powerful case studies.

Kotre, J. (1999). *Make it count: How to generate a legacy for a meaningful life.* New York: Free Press. Kotre synthesizes research and clinical insights within a broad life-span framework for understanding generativity, underscoring both the positive potentials and the potentially destructive aspects of generative expressions.

McAdams, D. P. (1985). *Power, intimacy, and the life story: Personological inquiries into identity.* New York: Guilford Press. McAdams situates generativity within his life-narrative theory of identity in the adult years and reinterprets the construct of generativity in light of ancient myths, life stories of contemporary adults, and the writings of Ernest Becker and David Bakan.

McAdams, D. P., & de St. Aubin, E. (Eds.). (1998). *Generativity and adult development: How and why we care for the next generation.* Washington, DC: APA Books. This interdisciplinary collection brings together the most influential contemporary theory, research, and applications in the realm of generativity, incorporating large-scale national surveys, laboratory-based research, case studies and psychobiographies, and historical and philosophical analyses, and features the contributions of psychologists such as John Kotre, John Snarey, Abigail Stewart, Bill Peterson, Carol Ryff, Bertram Cohler, Shelley MacDermid, and David Dollahite.

McAdams, D. P., Diamond, A., de St. Aubin, E., & Mansfield, E. D. (1997). Stories of commitment: The psychosocial construction of generative lives. *Journal of Personality and Social Psychology, 72,* 678–694. The authors describe a quantitative exploration of the life stories of highly generative adults.

Peterson, B., & Stewart, A. J. (1990). Using personal and fictional documents to assess psychosocial development: A case study of Vera Brittain's generativity. *Psychology and Aging, 5,* 400–411. In this case study, the authors illustrate how generativity themes wax and wane over the life course.

Smelser, N. J., & Erikson, E. H. (Eds.). (1980). *Themes of love and work in adulthood.* Cambridge, MA: Harvard University Press. In this interdisciplinary collection, generativity proves to be a central theme in clinically informed studies of the sociocultural patterning of adult life and individual adaptation and development in adulthood.

Snarey, J. (1993). *How fathers care for the next generation: A four-decade study.* Cambridge, MA: Harvard University Press. In this rich and extensive longitudinal study, Snarey documents the role of generativity in the lives of fathers and their children, illustrating many central tenets of Erikson's theory, documenting impressive relationships between indices of generativity on the one hand and social and psychological outcomes on the other, and introduces some new concepts in generativity theory, such as the notion of "generativity chill."

Vaillant, G. E. (1977). *Adaptation to life.* Boston: Little, Brown. Vaillant situates generativity within his own psychoanalytically informed theory of adaptation in the adult years.

Vaillant, G. E., & Milofsky, E. (1980). The natural history of male psychological health: IX. Empirical evidence for Erikson's model of the life cycle. *American Journal of Psychiatry, 137,* 1348–1359. In one of the best examples of early research on generativity, Vaillant and his colleagues provide empirical evidence for the psychosocial salience of generativity in the middle adult years.

Dan P. McAdams

GENETIC COUNSELING. Sheldon Reed is credited with first using the term *genetic counseling* less than 50 years ago. The term is used to refer both to a profession and to a clinical service. As a profession, genetic counseling is a relatively new specialty, and there are about 1,500 genetic counselors in the United States. Genetic counseling training programs confer a master's degree, with certification contingent on completion of a clinical internship and passage of an examination. Genetic counselors typically work as team members affiliated with clinical genetic services within a department of pediatrics, obstetrics, or oncology of an academic medical center or a large hospital. Local genetic counselors can be identified by contacting the National Society of Genetic Counselors, a professional membership organization.

As a clinical service, genetic counseling is also provided by nurses, physicians, psychologists, and other health-care professionals who may or may not have specialized training. Although medical genetics is a board-certified specialization in the field of medicine, many of the physicians who refer to or provide genetic testing as a service have no formal training in genetics or genetic counseling. The rapid growth in genetic technologies and the availability of clinical genetic testing will increase the need for continuing education in genetics for all health-care professionals, psychologists included.

Development of the Profession

As the profession of genetic counseling has developed, a variety of models of practice have been considered, and some, such as the eugenic model, have been discarded. In the mid-1940s, several "hereditary clinics" were established to provide families with information about genetic diseases. Concerns about the eugenics movement led most of those clinics to provide health care and reproductive information in a neutral manner, a "nondirective" philosophy that remains central to much genetic counseling today. However, some of the early clinics subscribed to the belief that, with appropriate information, clients would make the rational decisions that would ultimately promote the societal goal of reducing the incidence of genetic disease.

With the general shift in medicine in the 1970s toward increasing the value of patient autonomy, genetic counseling moved to incorporate the concept of helping clients to make their own decisions, regardless of the benefit to society. The provision of genetic and medical information to individuals or families in a comprehensive and understandable manner is viewed as an essential prerequisite for informed decision making. In addition, the contemporary psychotherapeutic genetic counseling model recognizes the larger ramifications of coping with current issues as well as understanding the impact of the decisions on the client's future. Meshing the education that is necessary to make decisions with the counseling required to assimilate those decisions can be a challenge, especially with the increasing limitation of one or two visits.

The Process of Genetic Counseling

A distinctive feature of genetic counseling is the fact that genetic information can have implications for biological relatives. An individual's diagnosis or test result has direct implications for the risk status of parents, siblings, and children. As a result, family interactions and dynamics are inseparable aspects of the genetic counseling process. As a member of a team of professionals providing genetic counseling and testing services, a psychologist can evaluate and address the impact of familial disease and risk information.

Genetic counseling begins with intake, which often

includes not only the individual's medical and social history, but also the formulation of a family history. The family history contains both the biological relationships within the family and the health status of extended family members. This process allows the clinician to collect information to assist in making the diagnosis of inherited disease. In addition, this "pedigree assessment" increases the clinician's understanding of the family dynamics and the family's response to the condition. Many opportunities for educating occur during the family history intake, such as correcting misconceptions concerning the pattern of inheritance or the nature of the genetic condition.

Absolutely essential to the genetic counseling process is making a correct diagnosis, since natural history, inheritance pattern, treatment, and reproductive alternatives are dependent on it. The increasing availability of biochemical, cytogenetic, and molecular laboratory testing plays a central role in this part of the process. It is important to note, however, that even the most sophisticated technology may provide a test result that is not clinically meaningful. Good genetic counseling clarifies not only what is known about the significance of a particular gene mutation but also what is unknown.

Genetic counseling can occur at various stages during the life cycle, most commonly in prenatal, pediatric, and adult settings. Often a prenatal session occurs because there is reason to be concerned about the health of the developing fetus. Although historically one of the most common reasons for referral was the recognized increase in fetal chromosome abnormalities with increasing maternal age, screening of pregnant women for serum markers has grown significantly, with patients who have abnormal results often being referred to a tertiary center for genetic evaluation. Abnormal ultrasound findings, teratogenic exposures, and family histories of genetic conditions are also reasons for referral for prenatal genetic counseling.

Genetics clinics for adult-onset disorders emerged in the 1980s. Potential clients for this type of genetic counseling can be divided into two groups, those who are clinically symptomatic and those who are presymptomatic. Often, testing is first offered to a member of the family who has already been diagnosed with the disease. If a disease-related mutation is identified, counseling and testing are then offered to unaffected (presymptomatic) relatives. Although controversial, presymptomatic testing is now offered for a variety of diseases. Survey data have shown a high degree of interest in presymptomatic genetic testing among the public. Studies indicate, however, that hypothetical interest greatly overestimates actual utilization.

Genetic counseling, because of its unique involvement of and implications for the extended family, requires that close attention be paid to privacy and con-

fidentiality. Clients should understand the risk of discrimination and other ethical issues related to the exchange of genetic information. The decisions that clients make impact not only their own lives, but also those of future generations.

Bibliography

Baty, B., Venne, V., McDonald, J., Croyle, R. T., Halls, C., Nash, J., & Botkin, J. R. (1997). BRCA1 testing: Genetic counseling protocol development and counseling issues. *Journal of Genetic Counseling, 6*, 223–244. Focuses on genetic counseling within the context of genetic testing for inherited susceptibility to breast and ovarian cancer.

Croyle, R. T., & Lerman, C. (1995). Psychological impact of genetic testing. In R. T. Croyle (Ed.), *Psychosocial effects of screening for disease prevention and detection* (pp. 11–38). New York: Oxford University Press. Reviews empirical research concerning psychological reactions to genetic screening and testing.

Kessler, S. (Ed.). (1979). *Genetic counseling: Psychological dimensions*. New York: Academic Press. A classic work in the field that continues to be cited.

Marteau, T. M., & Richards, M. (Eds.). (1996). *The troubled helix: Social and psychological implications of the new human genetics*. New York: Cambridge University Press. Reviews a wide range of social issues concerning genetics and includes first-person accounts from members of high-risk families.

McKinnon, W. C., Baty, B. J., Bennett, R. L., Magee, M., Neufeld-Kaiser, W. A., Peters, K. F., Sawyer, J. C., & Schneider, K. A. (1997). Predisposition genetic testing for late-onset disorders in adults: A position paper of the National Society of Genetic Counselors. *Journal of the American Medical Association, 278*, 1217–1220. Recommends components that should be incorporated into genetic counseling protocols.

Shiloh, S. (1996). Genetic counseling: A new area of interest for psychologists. *Professional Psychology: Research and Practice, 27*, 475–486. Discusses the current and potential roles of psychologists within medical genetics.

Vickie L. Venne and Robert T. Croyle

GENETIC DISORDERS. As science unlocks the mysteries of the human genome, we have learned a great deal about genes and the roles that genetic factors play in mood, behavior, and psychological well-being. In spite of this genetic revolution, the influence of genetics in the development of mental health disorders remains unclear. Twin (monozygotic and dyzygotic), adoption, and developmental studies have observed a strong heritable component for these disorders. Epidemiological studies have confirmed that familial risks for some disorders are significant and have estimated the magnitude of genetic contributions to the presentation of these disorders. However, these studies generally assume that the genetic transmission of psychological disorders involves a complicated interplay between genetic factors and shared and nonshared environmental factors. One of the more common problems in this research is disentangling genetic and environmental contributions to these disorders. Improved understanding in identifying these individuals whose genetic vulnerability interact with environmental risk factors will lead to improved treatment and prevention strategies (Kendler, 1995).

Research has clearly established that there is a genetic basis for schizophrenia. Risk for schizophrenia in siblings or offspring of schizophrenic patients is approximately 9 to 13 times greater than the risk for the general population (Gottesman & Moldin, 1997). Much of this research has been driven by a hypothesis that excessive dopaminc activity may be a cause of schizophrenia. Research on dopaminergic genes and tobacco use and the frequently observed link between schizophrenia and tobacco use suggests circumstantially a dopaminergic gene syndrome. Higher rates of schizophrenia among certain populations have drawn attention to reasons for population patterns. Recently, Hutchinson et al. (1996) examined the potential genetic influence associated with the high rate of schizophrenia among second-generation African Caribbean residents in England, concluding that genetic predisposition alone could not account for the very high rates of this disorder. The phenotypic expression of schizophrenia was more influenced by environmental factors that placed African Caribbean residents at greater risk.

Existing data suggest a wide range of variance in terms of genetic vulnerability toward other psychiatric disorders (Kendler et al., 1995; Lloyd & Weich, 1997; Sullivan & Kendler, 1998; Thapar & McGuffin, 1996). Kendler et al. conducted a multivariate twin analysis and examined the risk factor domains for mood disorders, anxiety disorders, bulimia, and alcoholism in twins. They observed heritability estimates for depression ranging from 43 to 73% and for anxiety disorders (including phobias, generalized anxiety disorder, and panic disorder) ranging from 32 to 44%. For bulimia nervosa, heritability estimates were about 30%. Alcoholism exhibited the most heritability (59%). Family environment accounted for only 4% of the variance for risk for mood disorders, anxiety disorders, and alcoholism but had a stronger impact in the manifestation of bulimia. These data are consistent with the notion that depression, mood disorders, and alcoholism have substantial genetic components but that bulimia was more affected by environmental factors.

Researchers have also examined the genetic transmission of personality disorders. While they have had little success in identifying links for specific personality disorders, several distinct personality dimensions have demonstrated clear genetic influence (Jang, Livesly, Vernon, & Jackson, 1998; Livesly, Jang, & Vernon, 1998).

Smoking and Genetics

Increasingly, interest in the interaction of genetic and environmental determinants of mood and behavior has turned to social problems like tobacco use or cigarette smoking. Evidence suggests that genetic influences are important in both the initiation of smoking and its maintenance over time (Heath et al., 1993; Heath & Madden, 1995; True et al., 1997). Much of this research is based on the premise that a specific gene or specific genes reduce one's sensitivity to nicotine effects and allow for more rapid tolerance (Pomerleau & Kardia, 1999). One study found that for initiation of smoking genetic factors accounted for 50% of the variance in risk and that shared environmental factors accounted for 30% of this variance (True et al., 1997). In contrast, genetic factors appeared to be primarily responsible for persistence of smoking among regular smokers, accounting for 70% of the variance of this risk. A major new study of tobacco use among twins found that genetic factors have substantial influence on smoking and the ability to quit smoking (Lerman et al., 1999). Examining the genetic polymorphisms in the dopamine transporter (SLC6A3) and the D-sub-2 dopamine receptor (DRD2) genes, they found that individuals with SLC6A3-9 and DRD2-A2 genotypes were less likely to become smokers.

Hostility/Aggression and Genetics

Another issue that has received attention from behavioral geneticists is hostility. As antisocial behavior and aggression increase, interest in causes of hostility has also increased, and there is a growing literature examining the influence of genetic factors on hostility and hostility-related traits. Pedersen et al. (1989) examined the genetic and environmental contributions among 700 pairs of monzygotic and dizygotic twins reared apart or together. Between 27 and 43% of Type A characteristics were accounted for by genetic influences, but shared family environment appeared to exert a greater influence on hostility and aggression. The findings of Manuck et al. (1998) support the role of a neurobehavioral dimension in the expression of aggression and hostility involving the central serotonergic system function. Specifically, evidence suggests a negative relationship between serotonin and aggression in nonhuman primates. Reductions in plasma cholesterol appear to increase the tendency to engage in impulsive or aggressive behavior through a mechanism involving central serotonergic activity (Kaplan, Muldoon, Manuck, & Mann, 1997). The cholesterol–serotonin–behavior association is speculated to have evolved in response to nutritional threat, which causes increased hunting. These data imply that alterations in brain chemistry may cause behavior under certain environmental conditions.

Psychosocial Factors in Genetic Testing

Not all research on genetics and behavior focuses on whether genetic factors determine traits or disorders. Some of this work addresses the impact of genetic technology that allows risk identification at a better level of precision. As advances in genetic testing continue and identification of individuals at risk becomes increasingly possible, a number of psychological issues and challenges emerge. The results generated from such tests may have troubling implications. Different consequences may emerge pending the notification of the genetic testing results. Risk status (negative or positive) may result in increased levels of distress but may reduce uncertainty that may lead to the underuse or overuse of preventive behaviors directed toward reducing the likelihood of disease onset (Baum, Friedman, & Zakowski, 1997). It is expected that some distress will result from testing, particularly when results indicate elevated risk, and genetic testing may enhance psychological vulnerability and long-term difficulties; on the other hand, it can decrease stress by reducing uncertainty. People considering undergoing such testing may benefit from interventions designed to decrease distress and the perceived absence of control over developing disease (Audrain et al. 1997).

Bibliography

Audrain, J., Schwartz, M. D., Lerman, C., Hughes, C., Peshkin, B. N., & Biesecker, B. (1997). Psychological distress in women seeking genetic counseling for breast-ovarian cancer risk: The contributions of personality and appraisal. *Annals of Behavioral Medicine, 19*(4), 370–377.

Baum, A., Friedman, A. L., & Zakowski, S. G. (1997). Stress and genetic testing for disease risk. *Health Psychology, 16*(1), 8–19.

Gottesman, I. I., & Moldin, S. O. (1997). Schizophrenia genetics at the millenium: Cautious optimism. *Clinical Genetics, 52*(5), 404–407.

Heath, A. C., Cates, R., Martin, N. G., Meyer, J., Hewitt, J. K., Neele, M. C., & Eames, L. J. (1993). Genetic contribution to risk of smoking initiation: Comparisons across birth cohorts and across cultures. *Journal of Substance Abuse, 5*(3), 221–246.

Heath, A. C., & Madden, P. A. F. (1995). Genetic influences on smoking behavior. In J. R. Turner, L. R. Cardon et al. (Eds.), *Behavior genetic approaches in behavioral medicine. Perspectives on individual differences* (pp. 45–66). New York: Plenum.

Hutchinson, G., Takei, N., Gilvarry, C., Sham, P., Bhugra, D., Mallett, R., Leff, J., Murray, R. M., Fahy, T. A., & Moran, P. (1996). Morbid risk of schizophrenia in first-degree relatives of white and African-Caribbean patients with psychosis. *British Journal of Psychiatry, 169*(6), 776–780.

Jang, K. L., Livesly, W. J., Vernon, P. A., & Jackson, D. N. (1996). Heritability of personality disorder traits: A twin study. *Acta Psychiatrica Scandinavica, 94*(6), 438–444.

Kaplan, J. R., Muldoon, M. F., Manuck, S. B., & Mann, J. J. (1997). Assessing the observed relationship between low cholesterol and violence-related mortality: Implications for suicide risk. In D. Stoff & J. Mann (Eds.), *The neurobiology of suicide: From the bench to the clinic. Annals of the New York Academy of Sciences* (Vol. 836, pp. 57–80). New York: New York Academy of Sciences.

Kendler, K. S. (1995). Genetic epidemiology in psychiatry: Taking both genes and environment seriously. *Archives of General Psychiatry, 52*(11), 895–899.

Kendler, K. S., Walters, E. E., Neale, M. C., Kessler, R. C., Heath, A. C., & Eaves, L. J. (1995). The structure of the genetic and environmental risk factors for six major psychiatric disorders in women: Phobia, generalized anxiety disorder, panic disorder, bulimia, major depression, and alcoholism. *Archives of General Psychiatry, 52*(5), 374–383.

Lerman, C., Caporaso, N., Audrain, J., Main, D., Bowman, E. D., Lockshin, B., Boyd, N. R., & Shields, P. G. (1999). Evidence suggesting the role of specific genetic factors in cigarette smoking. *Health Psychology, 18*(1), 14–20.

Livesly, W. J., Jang, K. L., & Vernon, P. A. (1998). Phenotypic and genetic structure of traits delineating personality disorder. *Archives of General Psychiatry, 55*(10), 941–948.

Lloyd, K. R., & Weich, S. (1997). The epidemiological toolbox in psychiatry: Population-based methods in the study of mental disorders. *Current Opinion in Psychiatry, 10*(2), 149–152.

Manuck, S. B., Flory, J. D., McCaffery, J. M., Matthews, K. A., Mann, J. J., & Muldoon, M. F. (1998). Aggression, impulsivity, and central nervous system serotonergic responsivity in a nonpatient sample. *Neuropsychopharmacology, 19*(4), 287–299.

Pedersen, N. L., Lichtenstein, P., Plomin, R., DeFaire, U., McLean, G. E., & Matthews, K. A. (1989). Genetic and environmental influences for Type A–like measures and related traits: A study of twins reared apart and twins reared together. *Psychosomatic Medicine, 51*(4), 428–440.

Pomerleau, O. F., & Kardia, S. L. R. (1999). Introduction to the featured section: Genetic research on smoking. *Health Psychology, 18*(1), 3–6.

Sullivan, P. F., & Kendler, K. S. (1998). Genetic epidemiology of "neurotic" disorders. *Current Opinion in Psychiatry, 11*(2), 143–147.

Thapar, A., & McGuffin, P. (1996). A twin study of antisocial and neurotic symptoms in childhood. *Psychological Medicine, 26*(6), 1111–1118.

True, W. R., Heath, A. C., Scherrer, J. F., Waterman, B., Goldberg, J., Lin, N., Eisen, S. A., Lyons, M. J., & Tsuang, M. T. (1997). Genetic and environmental contributions to smoking. *Addiction, 92*(10), 1277–1287.

Andrew S. Baum and John P. Garofalo

GENIUS. Geniuses are admired and valued for a number of reasons, not least because their achievements touch the lives of millions of ordinary people: Copernicus, Galileo, and Newton transformed our understanding of the physical world, as did Darwin and Einstein; Bach and Mozart have enriched and uplifted vast audiences; Shakespeare not only opened people's minds, but also extended the powers of the English language. Broadly speaking, a genius is a person who has created literary, artistic, or scientific masterpieces of exceptional power or inventiveness, or who has produced insights or ideas of great originality. This is a rather vague definition, but it is virtually impossible to provide a more precise one, or even a definitive list of attributes. The reason for this is because when people decide to call someone a genius, they do so as an acknowledgment of what the person has actually done, rather than a description of what the person is like. By saying that someone is a genius, we draw attention to the individual's extraordinary creative powers and achievements. If it is widely considered that someone has made dazzlingly innovative or creative contributions, the chances are that others will refer to that person as a genius. Consequently, despite appearances, calling someone a genius is more a matter of bestowing an accolade, rather than providing a description of that person.

The modern use of the word *genius* is fairly recent. The term comes from Latin, in which *gens* means family. For the Romans, a genius was a kind of household spirit, which accompanied a person throughout life. Yet it was always partly outside the person, in the way that poets' muses have been seen as essences that attend on individuals and are, to some extent, distinct from them, rather than being attributes fully under the person's control. The Middle Ages retained this notion of a genius as a kind of personal spirit that offered an individual help and protection.

Using the word *genius* to designate an exceptional kind of individual was largely unknown until the eighteenth century. Our modern meaning derives as much from the Latin word *ingenium* as from the Latin *genius*. The former term refers to a person's natural disposition or innate ability. However, shades of the idea of genius as an attendant spirit have persisted, contributing to the common, but largely unsubstantiated, belief that genius and madness are closely connected. The same partly external power of genius that inspired creative ideas was also believed to impart thoughts that could drive people out of their minds.

To a considerable extent, whether or not a creative person acquires the reputation of being a genius depends on factors outside the individual's control. Had Einstein been born 30 years earlier, or 30 years later, the impact of his particular skills and qualities might have been less than it was. Fashion and chance also help determine the manner in which a person's creative achievements will be received, and as reputations wax and wane, so too can people's views about whether somebody merits being called a genius. Few music lovers today would deny that Bach was a genius, and yet, until fairly recently, his reputation was not what it is now; nor was that of some other major composers, such as Vivaldi. Similarly, Botticelli was not regarded as having been a great artist until perceptive nineteenth-century critics such as John Ruskin drew attention to his qualities; when Rembrandt was alive, he was reputed to be a lesser artist than his contemporary Jan Lievens. With scientists, too, scholars have differed in their appraisals. In the case of the geneticist Gregor Mendel, for example, some authorities have regarded him as an undoubted genius and the great founding figure of genetic science, whereas others have seen him as a lesser scientist who had the good fortune to produce some immensely important findings.

The fact that genius is not the kind of concept that enables the word to be straightforwardly defined has another important consequence: It is impossible to have total agreement about who does and does not belong in the genius category. A relatively small number of famous individuals are almost universally recognized to have been geniuses. In the English-speaking world, the majority of educated people would include in a list of undoubted geniuses various well-known figures, including Archimedes, Plato, Copernicus, Galileo, Michelangelo, Newton, Darwin, Bach, Beethoven, Mozart, Shakespeare, and Einstein. Other frequently nominated individuals include Milton, Dickens, Picasso, Manet, George Eliot, Faraday, Balzac, Tolstoy, Dostoevsky, Schubert, Verdi, and Puccini. But there are numerous other creative and innovative men and women who would be regarded as geniuses by some people but not by others. Was Emily Brontë a genius, for instance? Was Jane Austen? Should Marie Curie be considered a genius, or Edgar Allan Poe, Benjamin Franklin, or van Gogh? It would be possible to nominate hundreds, if not thousands, of creative individuals on whose behalf a serious claim could be made. As long as the chances of inclusion in the genius category continue to be determined by the degree to which others value a person's contributions, there will never be agreed right answers to these questions. To some extent at least, genius is a social construct.

There have been efforts to introduce more objectivity into the task of trying to define genius, but these have been largely unsuccessful. For instance, Francis Galton, who happened to be a cousin of a genius, Charles Darwin, was in favor of referring to one individual in 4,000 as being "eminent," and one person in a million as being "illustrious." However, that proposal merely raises further problems. For example, it is not at all clear how those individuals would be chosen.

Another conceivable solution is to allocate individuals to the genius category on the basis of their exceptionally high scores on some broadly measurable dimension, such as intelligence. Yet that would not be a satisfactory procedure, as is immediately evident if we consider how certain universally acknowledged geniuses would fare if it were adopted. Mozart, for example, would probably not have done particularly well on an IQ test. So we would have to stop regarding him as a genius, creating an absurd state of affairs. Conversely, many individuals who do gain extremely high scores on intelligence tests never make any outstanding achievements at all. But if test scores formed the chosen basis for making decisions, we would nevertheless have to include these people in the genius category. Moreover, although IQ scores are moderately predictive of certain kinds of success at near-average levels of capability, at the very highest degrees of accomplishment, people who gain exceptionally high IQ scores do little if at all better, on average, than people with only moderately high scores. And alternative kinds of test scores which might be considered to be candidates as possible indicators of genius, have similar limitations.

In certain respects, geniuses are often similar to one another. The vast majority are people who have displayed an extraordinary single-mindedness and commitment to the work they have undertaken. Most geniuses possess a very strong sense of direction: They know what they want to do and refuse to be distracted. They work extremely hard at acquiring the capabilities they need. They may appear to make progress fluently and without effort, but that is only possible because of the enormous efforts that have gone into mastering the skills on which their achievements depend. Other activities tend to be neglected.

Mozart, for example, was described as having the ability to focus all his attention on whatever he was doing. Even as a young child he gave himself so completely to the activity he was engaged in that all other thoughts were put aside. When working on music he appeared totally unaware of anything else. Similarly, when Newton was asked how he discovered the law of universal gravitation, he replied that he did so by thinking about it continuously, and when he set his mind to a problem he would neglect everything else. Mealtimes and guests were liable to be forgotten. As a young man, teaching himself mathematics from Descartes's treatise on geometry, he would return again and again to the passages he found difficult, with a determination that refused to be defeated. Charles Darwin described himself as someone who could reflect for years on an unexplained problem, and he attributed his success to sheer industry and determination, coupled with a sustained capacity for careful observation. Einstein, who like Darwin attributed his achievements to curiosity, determination, and hard work, had a similar capacity for maintaining ferocious concentration for lengthy periods of time on questions that engaged his curiosity. Like Newton, he could be totally oblivious of social niceties. Interestingly, although geniuses often cheerfully admit to being unusually curious and especially diligent and single-minded, they tend to deny that they are intrinsically more intelligent than other people. Darwin, for example, was convinced that he was in no respect particularly clever or quick.

In other respects, geniuses have varied enormously. Charles Darwin came from a wealthy background, but Michael Faraday's family was very poor, and he had to leave school when he was thirteen. Fortunately, Faraday had a helpful employer and his job as an apprentice bookbinder gave him plenty of opportunities to read. Mozart was given intensive training from a very early age by his father. So was John Stuart Mill, whose acquaintances perceived with some accuracy that he had the qualities and limitations of a "manufactured" scholar. However, a few geniuses have educated themselves by their own largely unaided efforts. For instance, George Stephenson, the great engineer who was responsible for making the possibility of steam trains into a reality, thereby revolutionizing passenger travel and the transportation of goods, grew up in considerable poverty and never went to school at all. Not until he was 18 and employed as a colliery worker could he afford to pay a local teacher to help him learn to read.

Among scientists, those who have made major achievements have usually come from stable home backgrounds. Investigations of the backgrounds of Nobel prizewinners in the sciences have shown that they have often come from professional homes. In many cases their fathers were involved in science or teaching. However, a different picture emerges among Nobel prizewinners in literature, with home backgrounds that were disturbed or unstable being much more common, often as the result of the death of a parent.

Geniuses also vary considerably in the extent to which they display early indications of their superior capabilities. Many have been precocious in childhood to the extent that they have been regarded as child prodigies. Mozart is a particularly well-known example, but a substantial number of other famous composers were also considered prodigies as children. Even among those geniuses who were never said to be child prodigies, biographical records of their early lives often point to unusually advanced abilities acquired at an early age. That was true of Einstein. Examples of geniuses who never gave signs of being at all exceptional in childhood are relatively sparse, although not unknown. Charles Darwin, for instance, seems to have been a remarkably ordinary child.

Although it is the intellectual and creative qualities of geniuses that strike us most forcibly, in many cases other personal attributes are just as crucial. Take the case of Darwin, for example. In the popular imagination he is perceived as a reclusive scientist who was preoccupied with his poor health and rarely left the house he inhabited for almost 40 years. The real picture is very different. His great achievements were only possible because, along with his impressive intellectual capacities, he was socially accomplished and very good at getting along with other people. He cooperated with others in many scientific activities. He relied in various ways on a large number of friends and collaborators. His career also depended upon the cooperation of a number of distinctly prickly individuals, ranging from his own father to the captain of the HMS *Beagle*, on which he passed the 5 crucial years of its voyage round the world.

It is not uncommon for people to believe that genius is a complete mystery, and that geniuses are a race apart, with the causes of their extraordinary abilities being unknown. Similarly, it is sometimes assumed that asserting that the creative achievements of a certain person were possible because that individual was a genius is tantamount to saying that the causes are mysterious. However, there are no genuine grounds for concluding that the origins of genius are a mystery. There is no denying that the creative achievements of geniuses are often dazzling and quite extraordinary, and that the skills of such individuals may be far removed from anything that ordinary people can achieve, but that is no reason for assuming that the origins are entirely mysterious. In fact, on those occasions in which it has been possible to trace the early life of a genius in detail, it has usually been found that the influences shaping the person's progress were not totally different from those affecting the less remarkable lives of other people.

We may extend our understanding of geniuses more effectively by looking at the ways in which they are like other people, rather than concentrating only on their unique contributions. When we are able to examine closely the early lives of individual geniuses, it becomes very clear that there are no shortcuts to genius. Reaching the highest standards of achievement demands thousands of hours of concentrated effort, and that is just as true for geniuses as it is for others. Even Mozart did not begin to produce his major contributions as a composer until he had devoted about 15 years to intensive musical training. His childhood compositions, remarkable as they were in one so young, were neither substantial nor innovative.

It is undeniable that the challenge of explaining how particular individuals became capable of the remarkable accomplishments that lead to a person being recognized as a genius is a difficult one. However, provided that detailed records of the individual's progress can be made available, there is no reason to conclude that the task is totally impossible. Darwin's theory of evolution has enabled us to understand that even the develop-

ment of the physical universe, marvelous and awesome as it is, is not intrinsically mysterious. It is explicable in principle, even if we are yet unable to provide a full description of precisely how it took place. Similarly, when we confront works of genius, although we may admire them and be moved and dazzled by them, and may find ourselves quite unable to understand how they were constructed, we are not compelled to believe that the origins of genius are inexplicable.

There is no single cause of genius. Genetic sources of human variability may play a part, although nobody is ever born possessing a special ability. It is conceivable that genetic influences take the form of innate talents that, in one way or another, provide certain individuals with qualities that selectively facilitate the acquisition of particular mental skills. However, despite the fact that the talent account of the causes of exceptional capabilities is widely believed in, it has been strongly challenged. It is entirely possible that unusual experiences are especially crucial, rather than exceptional inborn endowments. So it would be quite wrong to deduce that simply because someone's achievements are remarkable, that person must have begun life possessing some special gift. Yet the probability that experiences rather than talents account for exceptional accomplishments does not rule out the involvement of genetic influences. Genetic sources of individual variability may act indirectly, by affecting the manner in which men and women experience and react to events in their lives, rather than by directly imparting special innate powers.

Bibliography

Eysenck, H. J. (1995). *Genius: The natural history of creativity*. Cambridge, England: Cambridge University Press.

Howe, M. J. A. (1997). Beyond psychobiography: Towards more effective syntheses of psychology and biography. *British Journal of Psychology 88*, 235–248.

Howe, M. J. A. (1999). *Genius explained*. Cambridge, England: Cambridge University Press.

Weisberg, R. (1993). *Creativity: Beyond the myth of genius*. New York: Freeman.

Zuckerman, H. (1977). *Scientific elite: Nobel laureates in the United States*. New York: Free Press.

Michael J. A. Howe

GENOCIDE. The U.N. Genocide Convention, passed on 9 December 1948, defined genocide as "acts committed with intent to destroy in whole or in part, a national, ethnical, racial or religious group." Although political groups were not included, most students of genocide consider such acts against political groups as genocide.

Some call it politicide. United Nations conventions and statements of principles have created a body of "international law" to inhibit human rights violations, including genocide. However, enforcement mechanisms have been nonexistent, highly limited, or ad hoc, like the tribunals created to try perpetrators in Bosnia and Rwanda.

The Origins of Genocide

To understand the origins of genocide it is necessary to consider societal conditions, the political system, cultural characteristics, the psychology of perpetrators, and the behavior and psychology of internal bystanders (members of the society in which genocide takes places who are not themselves perpetrators) as well as external bystanders (especially other nations) (Staub, 1989).

Social Conditions. Difficult life conditions are a frequent starting point for genocide. They include intense economic problems, intense political conflict, and great and rapid social changes. A combination of such conditions brought the Nazis to power in Germany and was therefore the starting point for the Holocaust, the genocide against the Jews. Such conditions activate fundamental psychological needs in people: for security, for a feeling of effectiveness and control, for a positive identity, for positive connections and support, for a comprehension of reality in the midst of chaos.

A number of group processes arise under difficult life conditions that do not necessarily improve conditions but partially satisfy basic psychological needs. One of them is increased identification with some group, usually an ethnic or religious group. Another is scapegoating a subgroup of society for life problems. A third one is creating or adopting an ideology which promises a better life, either for the group (nationalistic ideology) or for all humanity (a "better world" ideology, like communism). Often the ideology has both nationalistic and universalistic components, as did the Nazi ideology. Almost inevitably, the ideology identifies some group as standing in the way of its fulfillment.

Evolution. Intense group identification, scapegoating, and a destructive ideology turn the group against an "enemy." Harmful actions against this enemy change the perpetrators. Individuals and groups "learn by doing," changing as the result of their own actions. The norms of conduct in the group change. Perpetrators further devalue their victims, exclude them from the moral universe or from the realm of moral obligation, and create institutions to harm and kill them. Individuals and the group move toward genocide with "steps along a continuum of destruction" (Staub, 1989).

Predisposing Cultural Characteristics. All this is more likely to happen in cultures with certain characteristics. One of these is a history of devaluation of a group, which becomes the victim. The division into "us" and "them" can be along varied lines. In Germany there was a long history of anti-Semitism. In Cambodia there was hostility between peasants living in the countryside and inhabitants of the city, who traditionally ruled over the peasants. This became a major dividing line for the "autogenocide" in Cambodia.

At times instead of devaluation by one group of another there is a history of conflict and violence between groups. One form of this is conflict between a dominant group and a subordinate group that is poor and has limited rights. State response to rebellion by "ethnoclasses" excluded from power has been a frequent cause of genocide since World War II. Another form is a history of intense conflict and violence, which leads to a perception of the other as an enemy that represents a danger to the existence of oneself, and a perception of one's group as an enemy of the other. This characterized group relations in Rwanda. A long history of minority Tutsi dominance was followed by Hutus coming to power when the country gained independence from colonial rule. There was repeated large-scale violence, primarily by Hutus against Tutsis. However, in neighboring Burundi, where the minority Tutsis retained power, in several cycles of violence the Hutus were the primary victims (Kressel, 1996). With the psychological groundwork already laid, there was a relatively sudden flare-up of violence.

Strong respect for authority is another relevant cultural characteristic. It makes difficult life conditions, and the inability of those with authority to offer protection, especially threatening. It also makes it especially difficult for members of a group to oppose discrimination and violence practiced by their group. A history of violence in dealing with conflict is another predisposing characteristic.

The presence of unhealed wounds in a group due to past victimization also appears to be a predisposing characteristic. Not only direct survivors, but even members of the victimized group who were geographically removed are deeply affected. Their identity and perception of the world is affected. They are likely to respond to threat to the group with violence, which they see as necessary to defend themselves (Staub, 1999).

Pluralism and Democracy. A monolithic society with limited values and views and/or limited freedom to express them, in contrast to a pluralistic society, is another predisposing cultural characteristic. Democracies are pluralistic and rarely engage in genocide. However, less established democracies can turn into autocratic or totalitarian states, as Germany did after the Nazis came to power. Or they may have deep internal divisions, as in Colombia, with extreme violence, which might be pregenocidal. It is "mature" democracies, with pluralistic cultures and well-established traditions and institutions of civil society, that are unlikely to engage in genocide.

Leaders, Follower, Perpetrators. Cultural characteristics and difficult life conditions combine to create a readiness to turn to leaders who promote group identification through scapegoating and destructive ideologies. Thus followership is essential to genocide. Such leaders, in turn, advance destructive ideologies. They intensify antagonism through propaganda. They create parmilitary groups, which become tools of genocide, as they did in Germany, Rwanda, Turkey, and elsewhere. The behavior of such leaders is usually seen as oppportunistic, aimed at strengthening their power (Fein, 1990). In the present view, however, leaders, like followers, are motivated to a substantial extent by intense human needs that arise from a combination of social conditions and culture.

The role of leaders was also shown in European countries occupied by or allied with Germany. The greater the preexisting institutionalized anti-Semitism, and the more national leaders (at home or in exile) and Church leaders accepted and supported rather than opposed Nazi policies against the Jews, the larger was the percentage of Jews killed in that country (Fein, 1979).

The preceding analysis of the psychology of perpetrator groups in part derives from and is consistent with research on direct perpetrators. Many of them voluntarily *joined* the genocidal movement. Many came from authoritarian homes and either selected themselves or joined and were selected for their roles based on their ideological orientation, respect for authorities, and career goals. While obedience had a role (Kelman & Hamilton, 1984), it was probably obedience based on personality and rooted in culture, rather than obedience resulting from specific circumstances.

Lifton (1986) suggested that certain perpetrators, particularly Nazi doctors at Auschwitz, dealt with their participation by "doubling," a form of splitting of self into an Auschwitz self and a non-Auschwitz self. It is possible, however, that rather than splitting of the self, they embraced the "higher ideals" of their ideology, developed extreme devaluative orientations to their victims, and focused on their tasks.

Passive Bystanders. The evolution toward genocide is usually made possible by the passivity of both internal and external bystanders (Staub, 1989). Bystanders are witnesses who know or are in a position to know what is happening. Their passivity affirms the perpetrators. The Nazis were emboldened by the passivity and cooperation of the German people. Passivity and going along in turn change bystanders, who distance themselves from victims to reduce their empathy and guilt. Scholarship by sociologists and political scientists has viewed genocide as a state crime. As the preceding analysis suggests, however, citizens are involved in significant ways.

The passivity of the rest of the world also emboldened Germans. After political enemies were killed and while the Jews were increasingly persecuted, the whole world went to Berlin in 1936 to participate in the Olympics. During the 1930s U.S. corporations were busy doing business in Germany. Only about one tenth of the legal quota of Jewish immigrants was actually allowed to enter the United States (Wyman, 1984). During the war, the allies refused to bomb Auschwitz or the railroad leading to it. Germany, Turkey's supporter and ally in World War I, did very little to stop the genocide of the Armenians. Many Western nations continued to support Iraq, before it invaded Kuwait, while it was using chemical weapons against its Kurdish citizens.

The influences that give rise to genocide also create other forms of group violence, including mass killings, like the disappearances in Argentina, and war. As violence evolves, it extends to new victims, sometimes to other countries. In Argentina the disappearances of the late 1970s were followed by the Falklands War. At times war provides a cover for genocide, or the violence of war contributes to an evolution toward genocide, as in Nazi Germany and Turkey.

Rescuers of Jews. In most genocides there are some people who attempt to help victims. Some Turks helped Armenians, and some Serbs helped Muslims. But extensive research only exists on "rescuers" of Jews in Nazi Europe. The danger to them was great not only because of German brutality, but also because in most European coutries the population abandoned the Jews.

About half the rescuers were asked to help by Jewish friends or former work associates or by intermediaries, whereas the other half initiated help. Extensive interviews with them found characteristics and socializing experiences (Oliner & Oliner, 1988) similar to those that have been found in basic research on the determinants and origins of helping and altruism. Some were guided by moral principles, others by empathy, and still others by a prosocial orientation that combines caring about other people with a feeling of personal responsibility to help others. Many hated Nazism.

Their childhood experiences included parental warmth and reasoning, in cultures where physical punishment was common. Their parents did not draw the sharp division between ingroup and outgroups, including their own ethnic group and Jews, that was characteristic of their society. Some rescuers, for example, those in Belgium, acted on the basis of their identification with their group, which resisted Nazis or helped Jews. Some came from families that were marginal to the rest of the community—a foreign parent, a different religion, or some other difference (Tec, 1986). Many evolved, in that they agreed to help in a limited way but changed as a result of their own actions and became intensely committed to helping (Staub, 1989).

Prevention of Genocide

The prevention of genocide requires, first and foremost, response by external bystanders: individuals, groups, and especially nations and the international community (Staub, 1989, 1999). Both research in psychology and real-life events show the power of bystanders. Their words and actions can affect other bystanders and even perpetrators. Early strong reactions by bystander nations, like protests, boycotts, and sanctions, occurring before the perpetrators have developed strong commitment to their ideology and murderous course, could inhibit the evolution toward genocide. The international boycott against South Africa was an unusual example of this, with positive results. When intense violence has already started, only the use of force is likely to stop it. Such intervention has been rare. The U.N. and the community of nations did not respond to information about plans for an impending genocide in Rwanda or intervene to stop the genocide (des Forges, 1999). Perhaps the response to mass killing in Bosnia, after long delay, and then the speedy but problematic response in Kosovo, will begin to set a precedent as well as bring attention to effective modes of response.

Individuals must help develop an international climate in which nations and the international community assume responsibility for the life of human beings wherever they live. Early and effective action also depends on the development of standards about when to act, who is to act, and what actions should occur, as well as the development of institutions to initiate action. Early reactions can inhibit perpetrators' evolution toward genocide.

Prevention through third-party efforts aimed at healing, reconciliation, and conflict resolution (Rothman, 1992; Staub 1999) can be especially effective. Both early response and prevention require good theories and assessment tools to identify the beginning of a genocidal process or conditions that make it probable. Since similar influences may result either in genocide or in lesser violence, preventive action must aim at stopping collective violence of any kind.

Prevention also requires punishment of perpetrators. International tribunals created for this purpose also have the important function of truth commissions. By convincingly establishing what has taken place, as the Nuremberg tribunal did, they make it less likely that members of the perpetrator society feel like victims. By showing to the world the victims' suffering, they also help with healing. Both make reconciliation more likely and a renewed cycle of violence less likely.

The Effects on Survivors

Most of the research on the effects of genocide has focused on survivors of the Holocaust. The literature based on observation and study of those who have sought therapeutic help tends to report traumatic effects. The research literature based on a representative sample has reported somewhat varied findings.

Some researchers report that survivors they interviewed are well adjusted and effective in the world, but the predominant finding has been of negative physical and psychological consequences in survivors of the Holocaust (Eitinger & Krell, 1985). Survivors are a high-risk group for emotional problems later in life. The experience of the Holocaust appears to have also enhanced the stress of aging and reduced well-being in old age. Perhaps the most reasonable conclusion is that many survivors function effectively in the world, but with disturbances in memory and affect and a painful internal life. Their functioning probably also depends on pregenocidal history, their age at the time of the genocide, and what happened to them both during and after the genocide. After a period of silence the world has paid attention to the Holocaust and to the great suffering of its victims and survivors. In contrast, there has been limited acknowledgment of the suffering of the Armenians, partly as a result of Turkey denying, and exerting influence on others to deny, that a genocide took place.

Research beginning around 1980 has shown that the trauma of the Holocaust has been transmitted through the generations. Children of survivors have been impacted both by parents who are silent about their experiences and by parents who frequently talk about their painful past. They tend to feel the need to take care of wounded parents, which makes separation from them more difficult.

Scholarship on genocide has been the work of historians, sociologists, political scientists and psychologists. Increasingly, however, the study of the causes and prevention of genocide is informed by the interdisciplinary approach of political psychology. This approach concerns itself with the psychological bases of social and political phenomena. It recognizes that in understanding group behavior like genocide, and applying this understanding to prevention, it is necessary to consider the joint and interconnected influence of political phenomena, social processes, culture, and the psychology of individuals and groups.

[See also Bystander Phenomenon; Enemy Image; and Intergroup Relations.]

Bibliography

Chalk, K., & Jonassohn, K. (1990). *The history and sociology of genocide: Analyses and case studies.* New Haven, CT: Yale University Press. Presents and analyzes a wide range of cases, from antiquity to the present.

Charny, I. (Ed.). (1988–1993). *Genocide: A critical bibliographic review* (Vols. 1–3). New York: Facts on File. Brief review articles about modern genocides.

des Forges, A. (1999). *Leave none to tell the story: Genocide in Rwanda*. New York: Human Rights Watch. A detailed description and examination of how the genocide in Rwanda developed and was perpetrated, written by an eminent scholar on Rwanda.

Eitinger, L., & Krell, R. (1985). *The psychological and medical effects of concentration camps and related persecutions of survivors of the Holocaust*. Vancouver, BC: University of British Columbia Press. Reviews research showing the effects of the Holocaust on survivors.

Fein, H. (1979). *Accounting for genocide: Victims and survivors of the Holocaust*. New York: Free Press. Through both quantitative and qualitative methods, explores the reasons for differences in the extent Jewish populations were destroyed in different European countries during the Holocaust.

Fein, H. (1990). Genocide: A sociological perspective [Special issue]. *Current Sociology, 38*, 1–126. Reviews a substantial body of research and theory on genocide.

Kelman, H., & Hamilton, L. (1984). *Crimes of obedience*. New Haven, CT: Yale University Press.

Kressel, N. J. (1996). *Mass hate: The global rise of genocide and terror*. New York: Plenum Press. A psychological perspective, including chapters on Rwanda and Bosnia.

Lifton, R. J. (1986). *The Nazi doctors: Medical killing and psychology of genocide*. New York: Basic Books. An in-depth interview study and exploration of the psychology of doctors who directly participated in perpetrating the Holocaust, especially doctors at Auschwitz.

Oliner, S. B., & Oliner, P. (1988). *The altruistic personality: Rescuers of Jews in Nazi Europe*. New York: Free Press. An extensive and important study of rescuers, using both qualitative and quantitative approaches.

Rothman, J. (1992). *From confrontation to cooperation: Resolving ethnic and regional conflict*. Beverly Hills, CA: Sage. Examines approaches to conflict resolution, focusing on the involvement of "third parties."

Staub, E. (1989). *The roots of evil: The origins of genocide and other group violence*. New York: Cambridge University Press. Examines the psychological, cultural, societal roots of genocide and mass killing, including the role of bystanders; develops and applies a conception to the Holocaust and three other contemporary cases.

Staub, E. (1999). The origins and prevention of genocide, mass killing, and other collective violence. *Peace and Conflict: Journal of Peace Psychology, 5*, 303–336. Briefly reviews a conception of the origins of collective violence, applies it to the genocide in Rwanda, and explores in detail avenues to halt collective violence after it begins and to prevent such violence.

Tec, N. (1986). *When light pierced the darkness: Christian rescue of Jews in Nazi-occupied Poland*. New York: Oxford University Press. One of the important studies of rescuers of Jews.

Wyman, D. S. (1984). *The abandonment of Jews: America and the Holocaust, 1941–1945*. New York: Pantheon Books. A history of U.S. resistance to taking in and helping

Jews in the course of increasing persecution in Germany and the subsequent genocide.

Ervin Staub

GERMAIN, JOSÉ (1897–1986), Spanish neuropsychiatrist and psychologist, mainly responsible for the institutionalization of Spanish psychology after the Civil War. After receiving his doctorate in medicine from the University of Madrid in 1923, Germain furthered his training abroad under some of the most eminent European neurologists (Sicard, Alajouanine, Guillain), psychiatrists (Dumas, Janet), and psychologists (Claparède, Rupp) of the time. Although his earliest writings have a neuropsychiatric character, he soon concentrated in psychology, specifically, in the elaboration of mental tests within the Institute for the Reeducation of Handicapped Workers. His adaptation of Terman's revision of Binet's tests in 1930 had a wide impact, and represented a significant step toward the establishment of psychology as a profession in Spain.

In 1928, the Spanish government officially acknowledged the relevance of professional guidance and selection. As a result, two main centers were organized in Madrid and Barcelona, Germain being appointed head of the former and Mira y López of the latter. The assessment and guidance of young and/or handicapped workers, as well as the testing of future drivers as part of a traffic safety plan were some of the tasks undertaken. Together with the neuropsychiatrist Lafora, Germain also played an essential role in the organization of Spanish neuropsychiatry in a number of official positions.

At the outbreak of the Civil War in 1936, Germain was forced to leave the country. On his return, thanks to the influence that the Italian psychologist Gemelli had with the new authorities, he was appointed head of the small Department of Experimental Psychology within the recently founded Higher Council for Scientific Research. There, with a group of young psychologists (Yela, Pinillos, Siguan, and some others), Germain undertook the task of restoring the interrupted psychological tradition. One of the most ambitious projects carried out by Germain and his collaborators was the adaptation of U.S. Air Force pilot selection tests, which enabled them to introduce psychological techniques into the Spanish Air Force and other private companies, thereby increasing the group's professional prestige.

Germain's main achievement, however, was of an institutional nature. In 1946 he founded the *Revista de Psicología General y Aplicada* [Journal of General and Applied Psychology], a journal making possible both the expression of Spanish psychology and the reception of foreign psychological research. Germain also founded the Spanish Psychological Society in 1952. As its first president, he promoted research and communication among professionals through the organization of meetings and conferences. In 1953 Germain promoted the creation of a Psychological and Psychotechnical School at the University of Madrid, thereby paving the way toward rigorous psychological training.

In 1956 Germain was installed as head of the National Institute of Psychology and Psychotechnology, a position he held until his retirement in 1972. In his later years he devoted much effort to the development of the International Association of Professional Guidance and Selection, of which he became president. Thus, Germain's significance for Spanish psychology lies mainly in the establishment of an institutional framework to provide continuity in psychological training, application, and research.

Bibliography

Works by Germain

Germain, J. (1933). La práctica de la orientación profesional [The practice of professional guidance]. *Revista de Medicina del Trabajo e Higiene Industrial, 4,* 19–20.

Germain, J. (1953). Sociedad Española de Psicología. Acta de la Sesión Inaugural: Palabras del Presidente Germain [Spanish Society of Psychology. Proceedings of the inaugural session: President Germain's address]. *Revista de Psicología General y Aplicada, 8,* 713–724.

Germain, J. (1980). Autobiografía [Autobiography]. *Revista de Historia de la Psicología, 1*(1), 7–32; *1*(2), 139–169.

Germain, J., & Pinillos, J. L. (1958). Validación de la U.S.A.F. Aircrew Classification Battery en una muestra de pilotos españoles [Validation of the U.S.A.F. Aircrew Classification Battery in a sample of Spanish pilots]. *Revista de Psicología General y Aplicada, 13,* 551–560.

Germain, J., & Rodrigo, M. (1930). *Pruebas de inteligencia* [Tests of intelligence]. Madrid: Espasa-Calpe.

Works about Germain

Carpintero, H. (Ed.). (1981). *José Germain y la psicología española* [José Germain and Spanish psychology]. Madrid: Anejos de la Revista de Psicología General y Aplicada. A monographic volume on Germain's work and personality by various specialists.

Carpintero, H. (1994). *Historia de la psicología en España* [History of psychology in Spain]. Madrid: Eudema. The most complete overall view of the history of Spanish psychology.

Mora, J. A. (1992). *El Dr. José Germain: Hitos principales de su biografía* [Dr. José Germain: Milestones of his biography]. Málaga: Edinford.

Tortosa, F., & Martí, C. (1996). José Germain. In M. Saiz & D. Saiz (Eds.), *Personajes para una historia de la psicología en España* [Figures in the history of Spanish psychology] (pp. 398–422). Madrid: Pirámide. A biographical

account including a discussion of Germain's neuropsychiatric, psychotechnological, and institutional contributions.

Enrique Lafuente

GERMANY. Psychology has its roots in philosophical and natural science theorizing. The influence of both approaches and of the relationship between the two on psychology in Germany has varied at different times.

Historical Developments

The development of modern psychology in Germany can be seen as a process spanning about 200 years and described by six characteristics and stages:

- The thematic and methodical development of modern psychology as an empirical science around the beginning of the nineteenth century.
- Institutionalization, that is, the establishment of experimental psychological institutes, beginning in Leipzig in 1879
- Division into dominant schools and their gradual integration from about 1890 to 1940
- The development of applied psychology, starting around 1890
- Professionalization (i.e., university-trained psychologists working outside universities), starting during World War I
- The development of a service-oriented psychology, which has intensified since World War II.

Development Trends in the Nineteenth and Their Continuation in the Twentieth Century.
The history of psychology in Germany can be characterized by seven trends that entail specific concepts, ideas, and methodological approaches that have influenced modern psychology.

1. "The physics of inner experience" was mainly successful as mathematical psychology, including modeling. Nineteenth-century representatives include Herbart and Beneke.
2. Objective psychology is based on the study of behavior. It was later imported into the United States as behaviorism and the theory of the higher nervous system. Nineteenth-century representatives include F. A. Lange.
3. Physiology of the soul influenced physiological psychology. Nineteenth- and early twentieth-century representatives include J. P. Müller, Lotze, von Helmholtz, and G. E. Müller.
4. Psychophysics influenced the psychology of perception, measurement and scaling methods, and methodology. Nineteenth- and early twentieth-century representatives include E. H. Weber, Fechner, and G. E. Müller.
5. The concept of psychology as "experimental," as well as "nonexperimental" psychology, was espe-

cially successful with respect to institutionalization. Many institutes of psychology were founded on this basis (e.g., the world's first, founded in Leipzig by Wundt in 1879). Dual psychology also led to endless controversies concerning an experimental-natural science versus a *geisteswissenschaftliche* (humanistic), cultural science, or social science psychology. Nineteenth- and early twentieth-century representatives included Lotze and Wilhelm Wundt.

6. Psychophysics of the higher mental processes influenced cognitive psychology (including memory), psychology of volition (*Willenspsychologie*), and of emotions. Nineteenth- and early twentieth-century representatives included: Fechner, Ebbinghaus, Stumpf, G. E. Müller, Schumann, Pilzecker, and Jost.

7. Developmental psychology started as "general developmental psychology," focusing on the "empirical study of the mind of the child." Nineteenth- and early twentieth-century representatives included Preyer, W. Stern, and C. Stern.

At this time, the first psychological journals were founded. Primary examples include, *Zeitschrift für Völkerpsychologie und Sprachwissenschaft*, founded by Lazarus and Steinthal in 1860; *Philosophische Studien*, founded by Wundt in 1881; *Zeitschrift für Psychologie und Physiologie der Sinnesorgane*, founded by Ebbinghaus and König in 1890. In 1904, the Gesellschaft für experimentelle Psychologie (Society for Experimental Psychology), later called the Deutsche Gesellschaft für Psychologie (DGPs, German Society for Psychology) was founded by G. E. Müller. The first international psychological congress ever held in Germany took place in Munich in 1896 (the third meeting of the International Association of Psychology, later called the International Union of Psychological Science, or IUPsyS).

Dominant Schools of Psychology. The history of psychology in the first half of the twentieth century is characterized by the impact of "schools." These were scientific communities of psychologists collaborating, for example, with respect to certain theoretical approaches or empirical methods. Schools were founded and influenced by a dominant personality as the main figure; they typically started from specific phenomena (e.g., Gestalt psychology started as experimental psychology of thinking and perception; psychoanalysis started as research on hysteria, analyzing Freudian "slips" [para plaxes], dreams, and free association), gradually included additional subjects and areas for application, and finally claimed a monopoly. Such schools included Wundt and the first Leipzig School; Felix Krueger and the second Leipzig School (holistic psychology); Oswald Külpe, Ach, Karl Bühler, Marbe, and the Würzburg School (thinking); G. E. Müller, Schumann, Pilzecker, Jost, Ach, and the Göttingen School (psychophysics, memory, color perception, and volition). Gestalt psychology, primarily associated with Max Wertheimer, Wolfgang Köhler, and Kurt Koffka, focused on:

- Holistic thinking: The whole is more than the sum of its parts (suprasummativity, transposability).
- Analysis of phenomena: Directly experienced phenomena [*das unmittelbar Erscheinende*]—not the condition of their genesis—must constitute the starting point of any empirical study.
- Methods: experiments must be constructed in a way that they correspond to the type of event [*Geschehenstyp*].
- psychological isomorphism: "Psychological facts and the brain events that underlie them are similar in all their structural characteristics." (Köhler, cited by Ash, 1995, p. 177)

Field theory, developed by Lewin and his Berlin students (e.g., Zeigarnik, Dembo, and Karsten), focused on:

- Principle of dynamics: analysis and explanation of mental events must occur from the perspective of their dynamic foundations (i.e., needs, motives, emotions, affects, etc.)
- Principle of the type of event [*Geschehenstyp*]: the research paradigm must reflect in its structure and function as large a class of real situations as possible.

Psychodynamic psychology [*Tiefenpsychologie*] was based on the work of Sigmund Freud, Carl Jung, and Alfred Adler. In his studies on hysteria conducted in collaboration with Josef Breuer, Freud recognized the importance of the unconscious for mental phenomena (primarily for mental disorders); he viewed experimental methods developed for the analysis of conscious phenomena as invalid and therefore used methods of free association, Freudian-slip analysis, and dream interpretation. Freud influenced developmental psychology, personality theory, and psychotherapy. Later on, he extended his studies to the development of cultures and societies.

Applied Psychology. The development of psychology is also characterized by the expansion of applied psychology, through which the institutionalization and professionalization of psychology has profited a great deal. Some key concepts and important figures are pharmacopsychology (Emil Kraepelin), experimental pedagogics (Ernst Meumann), industrial psychology (Hugo Münsterberg in Freiburg, and later in Boston), and forensic psychology (W. Stern and Karl Marbe). Examples of institutionalization are the founding of the Institute for Industrial Psychotechnics by Moede and Schlesinger in 1918 and the founding of a commercial psychological service organization by Lipmann and Stern, the Institute for Applied Psychology and Depot for Psychological Research, in 1906. Rupp set up the Department of Applied Psychology at Berlin University in 1922. In 1920, Piorkowski and Lipmann founded the Institute for Occupational and Industrial Psychology in Berlin. The growing interest of physicians like Moll and Kronfeld in psychology led to the development of clinical psychology. In 1908, Abraham, a physician trained in psychoanalysis, set up as a physician in Berlin, where he founded the Berlin Psychoanalytic Association in 1910. In 1920, the first Psychoanalytic Outpatient Clinic followed. In 1918, Hirschfeld founded the Institut für Sexualforschung in Berlin and developed the psychology of sexual behavior. In the 1920s, Goldstein developed clinical neuropsychology.

Personality Theories, Characterologies, and Typologies.

In addition, the development of German psychology was influenced by a heterogeneous flow of ideas, dominated by personality theories, characterologies, and biotypologies that affected the image of psychology from the late 1920s until the 1960s. Here, partly phenomenologically oriented, partly biological macromodels of personality in the normal and the psychopathological area were developed. Some of the approaches were associated with results from neuroscientific research concerning the neuronal localization of mental functions, and others with psychiatric issues or racial psychological hypotheses. The theories were linked to qualitative behavioral diagnostics and diagnostics of action. The typologies of Ernst Kretschmer and the brothers E. R. Jaensch and W. Jaensch serve as examples.

Kretschmer's biotypology aimed to prove the relationship between three types of physical constitution (leptosomic, pyknic, and athletic) and three types of character (schizothymic, cyclothymic, and viscous). The first two types were associated with the clinical forms of schizophrenia and manic-depressive psychosis, respectively, and the third type with epilepsy. Sheldon refined Kretschmer's approach and developed an area known as somatotyping.

Jaensch and Jaensch's typology was formulated according to the characteristic of the "eidetic disposition," which has to do with a certain ability to form and maintain subjective (optic, acoustic, haptic, and olfactory) imageries [Anschauungsbilder]. According to E. R. Jaensch, the "eidetic disposition" is manifest in different expressional and behavior characteristics as well as in the style and vigor of actions. For political reasons, especially due to E. R. Jaensch's sympathies with Nazi ideology, this typology acquired broader recognition in the era of National Socialism.

The personality theories and characterologies of that time are also connected to names like Eduard Spranger and his phenotypology of the "life forms." Spranger differentiated six ideal fundamental types of individuality: the theoretical, economical, aesthetic, social, religious, and powerful. Other representatives of these kinds of conceptions are: Gottschaldt (the human-ontogenetic approach: methodology of "personality research in genetic psychology"), Lersch (the theory of "the construction of the character"), Rothacker ("layers of personality"), and Wellek ("polarity in the construction of the character").

Psychology During National Socialism.

The end of the Weimar Republic and the beginning of the Nazi era affected psychology in Germany both quantitatively and qualitatively. On the one hand, psychology profited with respect to its institutionalization; applied psychology, especially, expanded. Between 1933 and 1942, the number of positions for psychologists in and outside universities increased; new research programs and new areas for applied psychology (e.g., in industry and service sectors) were established. After 1935, military psychology developed; the reintroduction of compulsory military service created new positions for psychologists. The increasing demand affected the professionalization of psychology. This can be seen in the first officially recognized curriculum of 1941 and the simultaneous accreditation of Diplom-Psychologe (approximately equivalent to a North American master's degree in psychology). The title Diplom-Psychologe and characteristics for qualifications are still valid, and professional activities were thereby officially established.

On the other hand, psychology lost its qualitative variety and originality. After the emigration of outstanding scholars, important theoretical and methodological approaches were excluded from the further development of psychology, especially Gestalt psychology (e.g., Wolfgang Köhler) and field theory (Kurt Lewin). In the beginning of the Nazi regime, one third of the main figures of psychology lost or gave up their positions as professors and left Germany (or Austria). Among these were Karl and Charlotte Bühler, Freud, Gelb, Katz, Köhler, Lewin, Peters, Selz, Stern, and Wertheimer. After 1933, 14% of the members of the German Society for Psychologie emigrated. Some became influential outside of Germany (e.g., Lewin), while others are only recently being rediscovered (e.g., Selz).

Psychology After the War.

After World War II, research and teaching at universities in Germany's four occupation zones resumed immediately. The three zones in the West fell under the influence of the American "reeducation" program, while the Eastern zone was under Russian influence. In the first two decades after the war, the prewar regulations for graduation (Diplom) consolidated the training program in East and West Germany until the early 1960s in structure and partly in content; the research programs of the remaining leading representatives of psychology in Germany of the 1930s and 1940s were continued until the early 1960s. In 1949, two German states were created: the Federal Republic of Germany (FRG) and the German Democratic Republic (GDR). The building of the Berlin Wall in 1961 led to the separation of German psychologists on the organizational level. A separate Society for Psychology in the GDR was founded in 1963, had held seven meetings by 1990, and was dissolved shortly thereafter. Most of its members were then admitted to the DGP.

Generation Shift and Changes in Science Policies from the 1960s to the 1990s. In the 1960s and 1970s, in both East and West Germany, a new generation of psychologists adopted mainstream psychology from the United States. Many psychologists from the FRG went to the United States for additional training. In the GDR, psychologists oriented themselves to the Soviet Union as well and some had studied on a graduate or postgraduate level there. The new generation intensified the experimental traditions of the psychology of the nineteenth century. In the FRG, this resulted in the formation of a group of *experimental psychologists* in 1959 in Marburg. These developments increased the experimental focus in the 1960s in the FRG and somewhat later in the GDR.

The thematic and methodical changes can be seen in book titles, congress programs, and journals. New topics were: information psychology, cognitive psychology, cybernetic psychology, the psychology of action regulation. New curricula included test theory, multivariate statistics, methodology, mathematical psychology, and later evaluation and research methods. In the 1970s, new key words within the area of applied psychology indicated the practical fields into which psychology had advanced (e.g., clinical, ecological, organizational, media, and engineering psychology).

In the 1970s, in both parts of Germany, major changes in science policies positively affected institutionalization and professionalization. In the FRG, these were related to an expansion of the university system, including the founding of universities and new institutes, new academic positions, increased numbers of students, new positions in applied fields, research projects, and opportunities to publish in newly founded journals. In the GDR in the late 1960s and 1970s, there was also some increase in scientific personnel and students. New positions in applied fields and research projects opened up and opportunities to publish increased. From 1968 to 1973, new training programs including more practical experience were introduced. New job descriptions for main areas of psychologists (i.e., clinical, industrial and engineering, educational, and social psychology) were developed. Starting in 1968, a postgraduate training system for certified psychologists was arranged, and a group for experimental psychology was established within the Academy of Sciences of the GDR.

After the unification of East and West Germany, psychology in East Germany was reorganized according to the West German model. This involved a considerable transfer of psychologists from West to East Germany, the reestablishment of previously existing, the founding of new as well as an expansion of already existing institutes (personnel and technical equipment) in East Germany.

Relationships Between Culture and Psychology in Germany

From a cultural and social psychological point of view, psychology is a sociocultural endeavor embedded in ways of thinking that are prominent in specific historical periods and sociocultural contexts. In line with Jahoda (1992), we refer to "culture" as a certain commonality of meaning implying a complex pattern of behavior and values shared by a certain group of people (e.g., shared history, language, *Zeitgeist*).

Development of Psychology in Cultural Context. There are characteristics of psychology prominent for Germany, at least in the beginning of its development (cf. Metzger, 1965):

- A focus on personality theories and studies of character by developing various typologies (Klages et al.).
- A trend toward phenomenological perspectives in order to describe mental phenomena adequately.
- Skepticism against trends in American and Russian psychology aiming to establish psychology as a science dealing merely with behavior; belief that a proper psychological methodology must be based on the examination of conscious phenomena [*Bewußtseinsphänomene*].
- A skeptical attitude toward elementarist approaches while favoring positions of psychological holism (e.g., Dilthey's *geisteswissenschaftliche* psychology, Brentano's conception of a holistic psychology, Krueger's developmental psychology, and Gestalt psychology). Felix Krueger, the founder of holistic psychology, viewed a specific German contribution in a German *Weltanschauung* and in the qualification of German psychologists to focus on the inner world to explain its function.

That scientific psychology emerged in Germany was mainly fostered by three contextual factors:

- The significant progress in natural sciences in Germany
- The achievements of the German *Geisteswissenschaften* (humanities)
- The specific development of German universities

The progress of the natural sciences in Germany is documented by the seminal work of physicists, such as Röntgen, von Laue, Planck, Albert Einstein, Heisenberg, and others, and can also be exemplified by the fact that from 1901 to 1931, of the 30 Nobel laureates in chemistry, 14 were Germans. On the other hand, German history and philosophy had produced outstanding achievements as documented by the works of Immanuel Kant, Fichte, Hegel, Ranke, Karl Marx, Friedrich Nietzsche, Dilthey, Brentano, Husserl, and Windelband.

The developments in both disciplines, their disagreement with respect to fundamental issues on theorizing and methodology, and the challenge to foster their respective academic status influenced the intellectual climate during the nineteenth century, and hence the development of psychology. For example, Herbart, successor to Kant's chair in Königsberg, introduced Karl Leibniz's concept of "apperception" into psychology and pedagogy. His *Lehrbuch der Psychologie* (Textbook of Psychology, 1816) called for an application of mathematical methods and is thought to be the first textbook on psychology as an independent discipline. Gustave Fechner, Hermann von Helmholtz, and G. E. Müller were the first to systematically observe and test relationships between physical and psychological phenomena. Wundt founded psychology as an academic discipline by institutionalizing experimental psychology based on the methods of the natural sciences (e.g., isolating elements according to the physics model).

The status of psychology as an independent discipline was certainly supported by the rapid progress in the natural sciences, and the development of psychology took place in the context of the specific relations between the natural sciences and German *Geisteswissenschaften*. For example, Kant's criticism of David Hume's empiricism laid the groundwork for the skeptical attitude in Germany toward positivistic approaches and experimental studies, while at the same time encouraging "holistic" theories. On this basis, Dilthey promoted the ideographic and hermeneutic methods as opposing the nomothetic approach of experimental psychology. Methodological problems concerning the nature of psychological phenomena stimulated debates beyond the boundaries of philosophy, biology, and physics. Wundt's concept of a dual psychology can be seen as an attempt to reconcile the dominant intellectual traditions of German thinking by following the humanistic ideal of interdisciplinary, one of the main features of early scientific psychology in Germany.

Another specific aspect of the development of psychology in Germany is related to Humboldt's university reform, emphasizing research and the "unity of research and teaching." German universities provided an institutional setting in which an unusually intellectual, innovative climate was espoused, including unusual interdisciplinary approaches. Psychology in Germany profited considerably from this *Zeitgeist*. This is documented in the rapid increase in institutes of psychology at German universities until the turn of the century. Several psychologists (e.g., Wundt) held a chair in philosophy and at the same time founded an independent institute of experimental psychology. The expansion of German-language psychological institutes went beyond the present borders of Germany (e.g., to Austria, Switzerland, Poland, and Russia). In other European countries, the institutionalization of psychology occurred much later (e.g., teaching was often carried out as part of departments of philosophy, social sciences, or medicine). On the other hand, in the United States, institutionalization was rapid.

One may ask whether additional cultural specifics (e.g., the cosmopolitan climate of early twentieth-century Vienna and Berlin, the intellectual and social situation of Jewish communities in Germany, the atmosphere of the German *Bildungsbürgertum*, or the sociopolitical situation of intellectuals under Nazism) also contributed to the *Zeitgeist* in which the development of specific schools, topics, and methods in psychology took place. Ash's 1995 study on Gestalt psychology in Germany elaborates on questions on the role of culture and society in the development of psychology.

While the above-mentioned contextual conditions for the development of psychology in Germany are historical facts, the impact of these conditions as aspects of German culture and *Zeitgeist* remains problematic from the point of view of empirical psychology. This results from the fact that the concepts "culture" and "*Zeitgeist*," and "typical" traits of psychology in Germany are difficult to define and empirically measure. Whether a "German psychology" ever existed or exists now is a question reminiscent of nineteenth-century holistic psychological theories on a "group mind" or "national character." Such questions are no longer respectable, even though the notion persists under other labels (Jahoda, 1992). Neither the definition nor the measurement of a complex variable like culture or German psychology is culture free. Therefore, simple relationships between German culture and German psychology cannot be empirically verified. However, modern historiography may illuminate possible relationships between culture and the development of psychology.

Culture as Topic in and of Psychology

Historical Perspective. The focus on culture has a long tradition in psychology, dating back to the interest in culture and history in the nineteenth century (e.g., comparisons of "civilized" and "primitive" cultures; belief in cultural evolution). Main figures are Lazarus and Steinthal, founders of the first journal of psychology (often ignored by widely cited histories of psychology, e.g., Boring, 1950), who believed in the sociocultural nature of man and are regarded as founders of a *Völkerpsychologie*—an independent social and cultural psychology (Cole, 1996; Jahoda, 1992). Both were influenced by Herbart's metaphysical and quasi-mechanical understanding of mental processes ("mechanisms of the soul"), by Hegel's idealism, and by W. von Humboldt (the first to use the term *Völkerpsychologie*). Assuming that culture and mind are intimately linked and mediated by developmental processes over time, Wundt conceived of *Völkerpsychologie* (encompassing methods of ethnology and descriptive sciences) as complementary to experimental psychology. The impact of this idea was mainly restricted to Germany, and even there it was forgotten until recently.

Another historical root is related to Kurt Lewin, who laid theoretical ground for the study of human mind in context. Lewin's interactional understanding of behavior as resulting from and also influencing environment, and his concept of "life space" [*Lebensraum*], rooted in physics and philosophy, carry important theoretical implications, though the focus of his work was not on culture. Lewin, who had considerable influence in America (e.g., his leadership typology) had only little direct impact on cross-cultural and cultural psychology in Germany. The influence of Freud, another important figure in the study of culture and mind (e.g., *Totem and Taboo*, 1913), shifted from Europe to America. Malinowski, a student of Wundt, observed matrilineal Trobriand Island people to test the universality of Freud's Oedipus complex. Psychoanalytic theorizing has influenced American anthropologists engaged in culture-and-personality research. In Germany, Freud's theorizing affected typologies and studies of the national character (e.g., Fromm, Adorno).

To summarize, there is no direct link between the writings of Wundt, Lewin, or Freud—main figures in psychology who studied questions on culture and mind—and present-day cultural psychology, or cross-cultural psychology in Germany.

Recent Influences. Culture did not play an important role until the 1960s. Then a critical attitude toward ethnocentric theorizing and experimental methods arose, and a renewed search for relationships between society and mind reentered psychology, partially reflecting Hegelian and Marxist ideas (e.g., Holzkamp's "critical psychology"). At about the same time, European social psychologists claimed a "crisis psychology" and promoted a shift toward social constructivism ("social representations"). However, these approaches differ from cultural psychology and cross-cultural psychology.

The work of the very few German psychologists focusing on culture is reviewed by Trommsdorff (1986), presented in a selection of contributions by Thomas (1993), and discussed under specific theoretical considerations by Kornadt, Eckensberger, and Emminghaus (1980).

The first scholar in German culture-psychological research was Boesch. In his studies on human behavior in a cultural environment (starting in the 1960s), polyvalence of action and related symbolism became an integral part of his symbolic action theory (1991), which integrates parts of psychoanalysis, Gestalt theory, constructivism, and cognitivism and opens a rich view on complex psychological processes (cf., a special issue of *Culture and Psychology*, Vol. 3, p. 3, 1997). In the 1960s,

Boesch founded the Institute of Psychology for Developing Countries. Its work, continued by Eckensberger and Kornadt for a while in the 1980s, is a rare example of basic and applied research on culture and mind. Eckensberger, Boesch's student, follows a constructivist and action-theoretical approach, viewing action as a dynamic interface to study the unity of interactions between individual and culture.

Research topics of scholars combining cross-cultural and cultural perspectives include cultural conditions of the development of social motivation (aggression and altruism, by Kornadt and Trommsdorff), the development of moral thinking (by Edelstein and M. Keller), and adolescents' concepts of human mind (by Oerter). Research topics from a human ethology approach are attachment as the sociobiological foundation of socioemotional development (K. E. Grossmann and K. Grossmann) and universal patterns of primary care-givers' behavior toward their infants (sensitivity and contingency of reactions, by H. Keller). A new research topic is culture contact, bridging basic and applied psychology. Specific areas are the identification of cultural standards as a basis for a culture assimilator training device (by Thomas) and processes of acculturation in adolescents from different cultural environments, including developmental risks (by Silbereisen).

Presently, a "cultural turn" can be observed in Germany that goes beyond cross-cultural and cultural psychology. This is reflected by theories on the evolution of mind and culture (by Klix), on biological and environmental factors in human development (by Weinert), and on the biogenetic and sociocultural architecture of human development across the life-span (by Baltes). This research demonstrates the necessity of understanding interactions between genetic-biological and cultural-environmental influences with respect to their specific function for human behavior and indicates that complex psychological processes may be better understood by bridging different approaches, including a focus on culture.

Current Status of Psychology in Germany

Associations. Since German unification, there are two main associations of psychologists. The Deutsche Gesellschaft für Psychologie (DGPs), with 1,484 full and 270 associate members, represents academic psychology. It holds biannual meetings and includes various sections indicating the diversification of psychology. The Berufsverband Deutscher Psychologen [Professional Association of German Psychologists], founded in 1946 (20,940 members) represents psychologists working outside universities. Besides the DGPs' bimonthly journal Psychologische Rundschau [Psychological Review], several journals have been founded by various subdisciplines (e.g., experimental psychology, differential psychology, cognition, language, emotion, development, social psychology, clinical psychology, industrial and organizational psychology, neuropsychology, and artificial intelligence).

Training. The admission of students majoring in psychology is restricted by law. Presently, the admission rate is about 4,000 annually. Altogether, about 25,000 students major in psychology (64% women in 1997). The *Diplom-Psychologe* certificate (obtained by about 2,000 students annually) underlies nationwide regulations and involves a specific curriculum. Textbooks on nearly all subdisciplines of psychology are published regularly. Thirty-five volumes of the 90-volume German-language *Encyclopedia of Psychology* have been published. The topics include the history of psychology, methodology, and theory and research in basic and applied psychology.

Postgraduate Studies. In order to increase the participation of young scientists in research, the Volkswagen Foundation initiated and financed university-based *Graduiertenkollegs* (special postgraduate programs) in the 1980s. In 1990, the Deutsche Forschungsgemeinschaft (DFG, the German Research Foundation) continued this initiative, which focuses, for example, on cognitive sciences, artificial intelligence, neuroscience, linguistic foundations of language processing, intercultural communication in science, and social psychology.

Research. Various institutions offer research grants for psychologists. The DFG establishes special research programs [*Sonderforschungsbereich,* or SFB], whose duration may amount to 15 years. So far, only a few psychologists participate in this interdisciplinary program. The first SFB for psychological research, founded in the late 1960s, focused on social-psychological and economic aspects of decision making (directed by Irle). This has promoted social psychology and its integration into an international scientific network. A recent SFB specializes in language and communication in context (directors included Graumann and Herrmann).

Furthermore, psychological research is carried out at five prestigious Max Planck Institutes (MPIs). The MPI for Human Development and Education in Berlin, founded in 1963, studies human development and education from a life-span and life-course perspective, including psychology, education, and sociology (present directors are Baltes, Baumert, Gigerenzer, Mayer). The MPI for Psychological Research in Munich, founded in 1981, includes a section on the biogenetic basis of cognitive development (directed by Weinert) and on cognition and action (directed by Prinz). The former section on motivation and volition was directed by Heckhausen. The Institute for Psychiatry in Munich, integrated into the Max Planck Society in 1954, specializes partly in clinical psychology and neuropsychology. The MPI of Neuropsychology in Leipzig (directed by Friederici and von Crammon) was founded in 1994.

The MPI for Psycholinguistics in Nijmegen (The Netherlands), integrated into the Max Planck Society in 1980, researches mental processes in language (directed by Levelt). Another indicator of prominent research areas are the topics of scholars awarded a special grant (the renowned Leibniz Award); these include problem solving, experimental research in cognition, psychophysiology, and neuropsychology.

Role of Psychology in Society. In the last few decades, professionalization has expanded. This can be seen in the recent passing of the federal law concerning psychotherapy, which now permits psychologists trained in specific therapies to offer their services directly to clients without the supervision of a physician. Furthermore, psychologists developed the Test for Medical School Admission (TMS), which has been used to test over 300,000 students after its predictive validity had been tested for a decade.

Furthermore, several psychologists have held influential positions in science policy or education, for example, as members or chairpersons of the Wissenschaftsrat (National Science Advisory Council), as advisers in numerous government committees, as vice president of the DFG, or as president of a university.

Internationalization. Besides a European orientation, an increasing internationalization of German-speaking psychologists is documented by the rapid growth of citations from U.S. journals; increasing importance to publish in major international journals; and an increasing number of German scholars being trained in the United States, holding chairs in the United States, acting as consulting editors of international journals, or holding influential positions in international associations (e.g., as president of the IUPsyS: Klix from 1980 to 1984, Pawlik from 1992 to 1996).

Summary and Outlook

The development of psychology began in Germany in the nineteenth century and was influenced by the natural sciences and philosophical approaches. At the end of the twentieth century, the formal criteria for the development of a scientific discipline are fully applicable. Psychology in Germany today covers a broad range of subdisciplines, is institutionalized, is interrelated with several other disciplines (e.g., biology, neuroscience, sociology, and education), and offers a wide area of services. Psychology in Germany generally follows mainstream psychology in the United States. At the beginning of a new millennium, one can assume that besides internationalization, professionalization and institutionalization will continue in the following areas: basic research in a multidisciplinary context, applied research, and practical work.

More specifically, we expect intensified development in the following areas:

- Biological psychology and neuroscience
- Cognitive psychology, including artificial intelligence
- Psychology of action, motivation, volition, and emotion, focusing on their biological and social conditions
- Developmental psychology, including a life-span-oriented research approach with a focus on biogenetic and cultural-environmental influences
- Social psychology, with an emphasis on intra- and interpersonal processes
- Clinical psychology, including psychotherapy, psychodiagnostics, and counseling
- Applied psychology, including industrial and organizational psychology, psychology of law, and educational psychology
- Methods and methodology comprising basic research, diagnostics, intervention, and evaluation methods
- Theoretical psychology, including the history of psychology, the theory of science, methodology, and mathematical psychology

These developments will profit from theoretical and technological developments outside the boundaries of psychology and will be based on increased specialization and, at the same time interdisciplinary cooperation. It can be expected that these scientific advancements will further the capacity of psychology in Germany to solve present and future problems in human life.

Bibliography

Ash, M. G. (1995). *Gestalt psychology in German culture, 1890–1967: Holism and the quest for objectivity.* New York: Cambridge University Press.

Boesch, E. E. (1991). *Symbolic action theory and cultural psychology.* Berlin/New York: Springer.

Boring, E. G. (1950). *A history of experimental psychology* (2nd ed.). New York: Appleton-Century-Crofts.

Bringman, W. G., Lück, H. E., Miller, R., & Early, C. E. (Eds.). (1997). *A pictorial history of psychology.* Chicago: Quintessence.

Cole, M. (1996). *Cultural psychology: A once and future discipline.* Cambridge, MA/London: Belknap Press.

Eckardt, G., Bringmann, W. G., & Sprung, L. (Eds.). (1985). *Contributions to a history of developmental psychology.* Berlin: Mouton.

Graumann, C. F. (Ed.). (1985). *Psychologie im Nationalsozialismus* [Psychology in national socialism]. Berlin/Heidelberg/New York/Toronto: Springer.

Jahoda, G. J. (1992). *Crossroads between culture and mind: Continuities and change in theories of human nature.* New York/London/Toronto: Harvester Wheatsheaf.

Klix, F., Kossakowski, A., & Mäder, W. (Eds.). (1980). *Psychologie in der DDR—Entwicklung, Aufgaben, Perspektiven* [Psychology in the GDR—Development, tasks, perspectives] (2nd ed., rev.). Berlin: VEB Deutscher Verlag der Wissenschaften.

Kornadt, H.-J., Eckensberger, L. H., & Emminghaus, W. B. (1980). Cross-cultural research on motivation and its contribution to a general theory of motivation. In H. C.

Triandis & W. J. Lonner (Eds.), *Handbook of cross-cultural psychology* (Vol. 3, pp. 223–322). Boston: Allyn & Bacon.

Metzger, W. (1965). The historical background for national trends in psychology: German psychology. *Journal of the History of the Behavioral Sciences, 1,* 109–115.

Sprung, H., & Sprung, L. (1996). Carl Stumpf (1848–1936), a general psychologist and methodologist, and a case study of a cross-cultural scientific transition process. In W. Battmann & S. Duttke (Eds.), *Processes of the moral regulation of behavior* (pp. 327–342). Lengerich, Germany: Pabst.

Thomas, A. (Ed.). (1993). *Kulturvergleichende Psychologie: Eine Einführung* [Cross-cultural psychology: An introduction]. Göttingen/Bern/Toronto: Hogrefe.

Trommsdorff, G. (1986). German cross-cultural psychology. *German Journal of Psychology, 10*(3), 240–266.

Gisela Trommsdorff and Lothar Sprung

GERONTOLOGY. "How can we try to transform to a normal and physiological condition old age, at present utterly pathological, unless we first understand the most intimate details of its mechanism?" asked Nobel laureate Elie Metchnikoff (1903/1908, p. 289). "I think it is extremely probable that the scientific study of old age and of death, two branches of science that may be called *gerontology* and *thanatology*, will bring about great modifications in the course of the last period of life" (1903/1908, pp. 297–298). In these two sentences, the renowned director of the Pasteur Institute in Paris not only coined a name for a new domain of knowledge, but he also invited his scientific colleagues to engage in basic research into processes and mechanisms of senescence.

Metchnikoff realized that philosophers, theologians, physicians, poets, novelists, and other social commentators since ancient times had pondered the significance and experience of what it means to grow older. Like many of his predecessors, Metchnikoff had a personal stake in the subject; he wished to increase his chances for living longer than did his parents and grandparents. Convinced that an imaginative blend of theory building could dispel scientific nihilism, Metchnikoff incorporated ideas from cytology, pathology, and zoology to hypothesize that parasites in the intestines caused aging. Scientists quickly rejected both Metchnikoff's theory of senile phagocytosis and his recommendation that people eat yogurt every day. Nonetheless, his commitment to scientific method, his multidisciplinary approach to problem solving, no less than his failure to find a "cure" for old age, remain emblematic of the promise and shortcoming of this relatively young field of inquiry.

Since World War II there has been an explosion of biomedical studies, behavioral experiments, and social surveys that have tried to establish patterns of "normal" aging, "successful" aging, and "productive" aging. Like Metchnikoff, most contemporary investigators have focused on participants who were over fifty years old. Scientists still try to differentiate between pathological and physiological aspects of senescence. Without question, twentieth-century researchers on aging have advanced our knowledge of continuities and changes over the human life course across a wide range of physical, psychological, mental, and social capacities, decrements, and potentials. Whether they have created a new science or discipline or profession is debatable.

Scientific Precedents

The oldest information about aging in Western civilization comes from Hebrew Scripture. The oral traditions of the great patriarchs (ca. 2000–1500 BCE), the Pentateuch, the psalms and proverbs, the visions of the prophets, provide a rich vein of ideas and imagery concerning changes throughout the life span (Isenberg, 1992). So did the earliest documents of the Jesus movement and fledgling Christian communities (*Eph.* 4.7, 4.13–16; Bouwsma, 1978). Along with its portrayals of hoary heads, the Bible presents grim descriptions of physical decay, of older people's foibles, of their rejection by family and friends, and of death. Graeco-Roman culture provides the other major source of wide-ranging perceptions about aging. For instance, Seneca's dictum, "*senectus morbidus est*" (aging is a disease), anticipated prevailing nineteenth-century presumptions about the pathological nature of senescence. Galen emphasized hygiene as a way of warding off senility long before public health interventions came into vogue.

Later writers embellished archetypal ideas. Chaucer, Boccaccio, and Shakespeare stressed differences among the aged; their gendered images of late-life wisdom and lunacy received full elaboration in John Bunyan's two-part *Pilgrim's Progress* (1678, 1684). Between the fourteenth and eighteenth centuries, portrayals of the "steps of ages" by folk artists and great masters connected chronological age, biological condition, and social function (Philibert, 1968). Luigi Cornaro's *Sure and Certain Method of Attaining a Long and Healthful Life* (1558), published when the Venetian noble was 85, was translated into Latin, English, Dutch, German, and French. Encyclopedists describing old age accepted its scientific validity for the next three centuries (Cole, 1992). *The Angel of Bethesda* (1724) by the Puritan divine Cotton Mather was probably the first North American catalog of the elderly's ailments and attitudes (Haber 1983). On both sides of the Atlantic during the Revolutionary era, tables of longevity were constructed: the presence of vigorous centenarians was said to demonstrate the salubrity of the natural and political environments.

Foundations for the modern science of gerontology were laid in Europe in the mid-nineteenth century. Social scientists took cues from Adolphe Quetelet, who claimed that the growth of *l'homme moyen* ("the average man") could be measured according to a social physics that determined averages over the course of human development (Birren, 1986). Toward the end of the century, private foundations and government agencies commissioned large surveys to measure the extent of poverty among the aged. G. Stanley Hall's *Senescence* (1922, cited in Achenbaum, 1978) synthesized a variety of historical, literary, anthropological and behavioral insights into aging and death in an effort to demonstrate the existence of an "intelligent and well-conserved senectitude" (p. 127).

New instruments, clinical advances, and the rise of novel theories of disease created fresh interest in the processes of aging among biomedical researchers after the 1840s. Unlike eighteenth-century physicians who viewed senescence as inevitable "natural" decay, subsequent experts increasingly accentuated its pathological features. They sought cures besides yogurt. Pierre Delbet proposed magnesium chloride. Still others thought that ionizing elderly endocrines, or replacing them with goats' testicles, would rejuvenate elders. Another line of investigation challenged pathological models at the beginning of the twentieth century. Biologist Edmund Wilson, citing Darwinian arguments, thought that *Cell Development and Inheritance* (1896) naturally ceased after a certain point. The physician and sociologist I. L. Nascher, who established geriatrics as a specialty in 1915, emphasized the physiology of aging: "Senility is a distinct period of life . . . a physiological entity as much so as the period of childhood" (Nascher, 1909, p. 358). Bench scientists began to examine the aging of various organs in a systematic manner.

Setting the Parameters for Gerontologic Inquiry

Although they had hitherto lagged behind European scientists, U.S. researchers, through a series of publications and networks, increasingly set the parameters for gerontologic inquiry in the 1930s. The Josiah Macy, Jr. Foundation asked Edmund Vincent Cowdry, an anatomist by training who also achieved fame as a cytologist, to invite two dozen biomedical investigators and social scientists to discuss pathological and physiological aspects of aging from various perspectives. Out of their multidisciplinary conversations emerged *Problems of Ageing* (Cowdry, 1939), the first of many handbooks on aging produced in America.

In his Introduction to Cowdry's volume, John Dewey affirmed that "ageing" was a dynamic, interactive, multifaceted "problem":

> There is a problem and one of scope having no precedent in human history. Biological processes are at the

roots of the problem and of the methods of solving them, but the biological processes take place in economic, political, and cultural contexts. They are inextricably interwoven with those contexts so that one reacts upon the other in all sorts of intricate ways. We need to know the ways in which social contexts react back into biological processes as well as to know the ways in which the biological processes condition social life. This is the problem to which attention is invited. (Dewey in Cowdry, 1939, p. xxvi)

Dewey articulated a research agenda for aging that remains as valid today as it did 60 years ago. Gerontology builds on disciplinary-specific perspectives; its own orientation perforce is multidisciplinary. Scholars still attempt to make broad connections between intrinsic and extrinsic factors of aging. They focus on continuities and changes in biomedical and behavioral patterns that in turn interact with broader cultural and social forces.

Although World War II diverted attention from gerontologic issues, several outposts were established that became very influential. With support from the Macy Foundation, the U.S. Public Health Service authorized a unit on gerontology within the National Institutes of Health. When Nathan W. Shock arrived on Pearl Harbor Day to take over the unit, he had one lab assistant. By the time he retired in 1975, Shock was overseeing the work of 175 scientists in a building with 200,000 square feet of lab space. During his tenure, Shock published more than 350 scientific articles; he created a valuable bibliographic guide for researchers. Shock is probably best known for starting the Baltimore Longitudinal Studies of Aging (BLSA) in 1968, which remains the biggest and best survey of its kind. *Normal Human Aging* (1984), the first comprehensive analysis based on the BLSA survey, sharpened researchers' awareness of the differences between longitudinal and cross-sectional studies.

Meanwhile, several universities began to focus social science research in gerontology. Under the direction of Ralph Tyler, community studies involving the elderly and "social adjustment to old age" became a major thrust of work after 1938 at the Committee on Human Development at the University of Chicago. Ernest Burgess, Robert Havighurst, and Bernice Neugarten made Chicago the premier place in the world to study the social psychology of aging from the 1950s through the 1970s. After World War II the Universities of Minnesota and Michigan launched adult education courses in aging. With the support of a large endowment, the backing of the central administration, and eventually grants from federal agencies, Michigan's Wilma Donahue and her successor Harold Johnson made summer institutes in Ann Arbor a mecca for teachers and policy analysts wanting to learn the essentials about gerontology. Finally, U.S. researchers institutionalized their common professional interests. To sustain the exchanges begun

at the Cowdry conference, participants started a Club for Research on Ageing, which became incorporated as the Gerontological Society of America (GSA) in 1945

to promote the scientific study of aging, in order to advance public health and mental hygiene, the science and art of medicine, and the cure of disease; to foster the gowth and diffusion of knowledge relating to problems of aging and of the sciences contributing to an understanding thereof; to afford a common meeting ground for . . . scientific fields interested in such problems. (Certification of incorporation, 1946, pp. 134–135)

The American Geriatrics Society, founded in 1942, still collaborates with GSA.

Britain probably has been the United States' closest rival in networking. A British Society for Research on Aging was established in 1939. Six years later the Oxford Gerontological Research Unit began to function under the direction of a Russian-born pathologist, V. Korwenchevsky. In both instances Lord Nuffield's generosity made good things possible. By 1950, a dozen or so investigators in virtually every European country and Canada had established similar research clubs (Shock & Baker, 1988). At the first International Congress of Gerontology in Belgium in 1950, most of the scientific papers focused on pathological and physiological aspects of senescence.

Current Status and Future Prospects

The United States remains central in efforts to advance gerontologic knowledge. Its citizens have dominated the International Association of Gerontology. Its scientific meetings, wherein organizers compartmentalize sessions according to disciplines, are the protoype for symposia elsewhere. Specialized journals of gerontology proliferate; major disciplines regularly allocate space for aging-related articles. Roughly 500 U.S. colleges and universities offer more than 1,000 different programs in gerontology; two major universities offer Ph.D.s in the field. The University of Southern California has emerged as the foremost training site for students at all levels who wish to pursue careers in aging (Lobenstine, Wendt, & Peterson, 1994).

The North American grip on the "aging enterprise" (Estes, 1979) is not hegemonic, however. United States gerontologic research thus far has been data rich and theory poor. On the social science side, centers such as the Institute for Social Research in Ann Arbor have generated an impressive array of longitudinal data concerning poverty trends and retirement patterns in later years, as well as assessments of the elderly's capacity for mobility. Empirical analyses have proven more enduring than U.S. conceptual models. Hence, disengagement theory—the assumption that people gradually and inevitably withdraw from all spheres of activity with age (Cumming & Henry, 1961)—has been the most important multidisciplinary idea set forth by U.S. gerontologists, but it was discredited fairly quickly. In its place have arisen, in turn, continuity and activity theories of aging.

On the biomedical side, there has been an extraordinary range of hypotheses about the causes of senescence, but none has gained a large following. Arguably the most important idea has been the notion that the longevity of rats can be extended if their food intake is limited. This finding has been reaffirmed in countless other species (though not humans). Hayflick (1994) made the most controversial assault on conventional biological thinking with his demonstration that cells reproduce only a finite number of times. Evolutionary models of aging, which began to circulate in the 1950s, have become popular again (Rose, 1991).

European scholars have had more success in theory building than U.S. gerontologists. Perhaps two examples will suffice. On the one hand, British gerontologists have developed a set of working hypotheses about "the political economy of aging," which builds on Marxist concepts, as well as notions about the human body. On the other hand, scholars associated with the Max Planck Institute in Berlin, particularly the work of Paul and Margret Baltes on the selective optimization of functioning in later years (1993), have developed fascinating ideas about the practical nature of wisdom that incorporates insights about computers and basic behavioral processes.

Furthermore, several industrial nations have been more responsive than the U.S. in coming to terms with population aging. The Japanese government, for instance, acknowledges that its population is rapidly aging amidst many changes in intergenerational relations. Japan has allocated considerable resources for planning to meet future conditions. Similarly, western European leaders are downsizing their social welfare programs because they lack resources to deal with pensioners' needs. In the United States, such discussions are quite formative.

Gerontology remains a relatively young and immature field of inquiry (Achenbaum, 1995). Investigators effectively borrow from a variety of disciplines and professions. Still, gerontologists have not yet created scientific paradigms that are generally accepted by colleagues in the field or by scholars who hew to disciplinary-specific approaches. Too often their insights do not make their way into mainstream disciplinary thinking, which reinforces a sense of marginalization. Researchers on aging have not perfected techniques for doing longitudinal analyses or developed original methods for measuring phenomena that are widely shared. Most middle-range theories of aging are partial and tentative.

The future of gerontology nonetheless is bright. Increases in life expectancy at birth and at maturity, as well as the growing awareness of the policy implications of societal aging on retirement funds and medical care, heighten interest in the elderly. The intellectual excitement generated by current studies, not to mention the increasing availability of public and private dollars earmarked for gerontological research, bode well. There are dangers in the years ahead: Just as alchemists in the Middle Ages used to offer nostrums that proved illusory, so too the opinions of present-day charlatans and popularizers could undercut appreciation for basic scientific research.

As a new millennium unfolds, it seems more likely that gerontology will emerge as a major focus of scholarly inquiry and public interest. The foundations for a new age-based paradigm that transcends disciplinary boundaries will doubtless result from the proliferation of scientifically executed, incremental studies. No magic bullet or revolutionary insight is likely to transform the field overnight. Advances in the behavioral sciences merit close scrutiny since the psychologists (especially those who interact with social scientists) have positioned themselves as the *media via*, thanks to good contacts with biomedical researchers on the one hand, and applied researchers on the other.

[*See also* Clinical Geropsychology.]

Bibliography

Achenbaum, W. A. (1978). *Old age in the new land: The American experience since 1790*. Baltimore: Johns Hopkins University Press.

Achenbaum, W. A. (1995). *Crossing frontiers: Gerontology emerges as a science*. New York: Cambridge University Press.

Baltes, P. B., & Baltes, M. M. (1993). *Successful aging*. New York: Cambridge University Press.

Birren, J. E. (1986). The process of aging. In A. Pifer & L. Bronte (Eds.), *Our aging society* (pp. 263–282). New York: Norton.

Bouwsma, W. J. (1978). Christian adulthood. In E. Erikson (Ed.), *Adulthood* (pp. 81–97). New York: Norton.

Certification of incorporation of the Gerontological Society, Inc. (1946, January). *Journal of Gerontology, 1*, 134–135.

Cole, T. R. (1992). *Journey of life: A cultural history of aging in America*. New York: Cambridge University Press.

Cowdry, E. V. (Ed.). (1939). *Problems of ageing*. Baltimore: Williams & Wilkins.

Cumming, E., & Henry, W. (1961). *Growing old: The process of disengagement*. New York: Basic Books.

Estes, C. (1979). *The aging enterprise*. San Francisco: Jossey-Bass.

Haber, C. (1983). *Beyond sixty-five*. New York: Cambridge University Press.

Hayflick, L. (1994). *How and why we age*. New York: Ballantine Books.

Isenberg, S. (1992). Aging in Judaism. In T. R. Cole, D. D. Van Tassel, & R. Kastenbaum (Eds.), *Handbook of the humanities and aging* (pp. 16–40). New York: Springer.

Lobenstine, J. C., Wendt, P. F., & Peterson, D. A. (1994). *National directory of educational programs in gerontology and geriatrics* (6th ed.). Washington, DC: Association for Gerontology in Higher Education.

Metchnikoff, E. (1908). *The nature of man: Studies in optimistic philosophy*. New York: Putnam. (Original French edition published 1903.)

Nascher, I. L. (1914). *Geriatrics*. Philadelphia: Blakiston.

Philibert, M. (1968). *L'échelle des ages* [The steps of ages]. Paris: Seuil.

Rose, M. R. (1991). *Evolutionary biology of aging*. New York: Oxford University Press.

Shock, N. W., & Baker, G. T., III (1988). *The international association of gerontology*. New York: Springer.

W. Andrew Achenbaum

GESELL, ARNOLD LUCIUS (1880–1961), American psychologist and physician. Gesell was born 21 June 1880 in Alma, Wisconsin, and died 29 May 1961 in New Haven, Connecticut. After graduating from Alma High School in 1896, he attended Stevens Point Normal School, where he was taught psychology by Edgar Swift, and graduated in 1899. He was employed at Stevens Point High School for one year "as a teacher of U.S. history, ancient history, German, accounting, and commercial geography, and coach and referee of football" (Miles, 1964, p. 58). He then attended the University of Wisconsin–Madison where he was instructed in psychology by Joseph Jastrow, and received his Ph.B. in 1903. He then worked for one year as a high school principal in Chippewa Falls, Wisconsin. With the assistance of Swift, Gesell received a tuition scholarship to Clark University, and received his Ph.D. in psychology in 1906. His dissertation was on the topic of jealousy (Gesell, 1906). Gesell's career was significantly influenced by Clark faculty, especially G. Stanley Hall.

Gesell had several minor pursuits before being lured by the California climate and the friendship of Lewis M. Terman to a position with the Los Angeles Normal School. There he met, and in 1909, married Beatrice Chandler, a University of Chicago graduate and member of the Normal School faculty. They had two children, Catherine and Gerhardt. His wife was a lifelong supporter, and together they published a book (Gesell & Gesell, 1912). To understand child development better, Gesell studied medicine, first at the University of Wisconsin and then at Yale University where he taught in the Department of Education while pursuing his M.D. degree, which he completed in 1915. He founded the Yale Psycho-Clinic in 1911, which in various forms continued throughout his career, eventually becoming the Gesell Institute of Human Development. From 1915–1919, Gesell served jointly as a full professor of child hygiene in the Yale Graduate School and state director of child hygiene for the Connecticut State Board of Education. In this latter capacity, Gesell "formalized what would become the first position titled 'school psychologist' in the United States" (Fagan, 1987b, p. 399). Collaborating with Norma Cutts in New Haven, his efforts led to the creation of special educational classrooms and a Division for Educationally Exceptional Children under the State Board of Education. However, his most notable contributions were in developmental pediatric medicine and child psychology.

For the remainder of his career, Gesell worked at Yale University conducting research on child hygiene and development while blending his knowledge of medicine, psychology, special education, and child study. Gesell was well connected to several important psychologists of the period including Terman, Goddard, Witmer, Sanford, Burnham, and Hall. His Yale research associates had distinguished careers of their own including Catherine Amatruda, Louise Bates Ames, Frances Ilg, and Helen Thompson. Over the course of his career, his interests shifted from child study and clinical psychology to the study of normal development, though with a persistent interest in, using the terminology of the time, the "defective and deficient child."

Gesell never practiced psychology or medicine privately, although he was an attending pediatrician at the New Haven Hospital for many years. Supported by Yale and externally (e.g., Laura Spelman Rockefeller Memorial, Carnegie Corporation, American Optical Company), he pioneered research methodologies such as the co-twin technique to study the impact of learning and heredity, and cinematography for the recording of developmental sequences frame-by-frame. Following upon Hall's earlier popularization of child study, Gesell and his colleagues established norms for infant and child development that established standards for evaluating both normal and abnormal children. The results were documented in an impressive number of popular and scientific publications (see Miles, 1964).

Gesell emphasized a maturational explanation of child development that had difficulty competing with Freudian and Watsonian psychology, and later with cognitive theorists, and was often misunderstood (Ames, 1989; Thelen & Adolph, 1992). Ames analyzed the themes of Gesell's work, including the still popular interest in school readiness, and defended Gesell's viewpoint as interactionist, not merely maturational. Ames identified Gesell's most well known books: *Infant and Child in the Culture of Today* (1943), *The Child From Five to Ten* (1946), and *Youth: The Years from Ten to Sixteen* (1956). An earlier work, *The Preschool Child from the Standpoint of Public Hygiene and Education* (1923), was recognized by the American Library Association as one of the 37 "most notable books published in 1925" (Miles, 1964, p. 65).

Following his retirement from Yale in 1948, Gesell became an associate with the Harvard Pediatric Study, at Yale he studied child vision with Gerald N. Getman, and he consulted at the Gesell Institute. Gesell made significant contributions to applied and developmental psychology, pediatric psychology, and developmental pediatric medicine. Although his contributions have been overshadowed, his legacy is observed in contemporary developmental psychology (Thelen & Adolph, 1992). Elected to Phi Beta Kappa and Sigma Xi as a student, Gesell was president (1952–1953) of the American Academy of Cerebral Palsy, and was elected to the National Academy of Sciences in 1947. Gesell was a fellow in the American Academy of Pediatrics and the American Psychological Association. He held an honorary doctorate from Clark University, conferred in 1930, served as vice president of the Association Internationale pour la Protection de l'Enfance, and served on several national and state commissions.

Bibliography

Works by Gesell

Gesell, A. L. (1906). Jealousy. *American Journal of Psychology, 17,* 437–496.

Gesell, A. L. (1923). *The preschool child from the standpoint of public hygiene and education.* Boston: Houghton Mifflin.

Gesell, A. L. (1952). Autobiography. In E. G. Boring, H. Werner, H. S. Langfeld, & R. M. Yerkes (Eds.), *A history of psychology in autobiography* (Vol. 4, pp. 123–142). Worcester, MA: Clark University Press.

Gesell, A. L., & Gesell, B. C. (1912). *The normal child and primary education.* Boston: Ginn.

Gesell, A. L., Ilg, F. L., Ames, L. B., & Learned, J. (1943). *Infant and child in the culture of today.* New York: Harper.

Gesell, A. L., Ilg, F. L., Ames, L. B., & Bullis, G. E. (1946). *The child from five to ten.* New York: Harper.

Gesell, A. L., Ilg., F. L., & Ames, L. B. (1956). *Youth: The years from ten to sixteen.* New York: Harper.

Works about Gesell

Ames, L. B. (1989). *Arnold Gesell—Themes of his work.* New York: Human Sciences Press.

Fagan, T. K. (1987a). Gesell: The first school psychologist. Part I. The road to Connecticut. *School Psychology Review, 16,* 103–107.

Fagan, T. K. (1987b). Gesell: The first school psychologist. Part II. Practice and significance. *School Psychology Review, 16,* 399–409.

Miles, W. R. (1964). Arnold Lucius Gesell 1880–1961. A biographical memoir. In National Academy of Sciences, *Biographical memoirs* (Vol. 37, pp. 55–96). New York: Columbia University Press.

Thelen, E., & Adolph, K. E. (1992). Arnold L. Gesell: The paradox of nature and nurture. *Developmental Psychology, 28,* 368–380.

Thomas K. Fagan

GESTALT PSYCHOLOGY. Gestalt theory was one of the major schools of psychology of the first half of the twentieth century. While its main early focus was a protest against the atomism or elementism that characterized its rival schools (such as structuralism and functionalism and, later, behaviorism), its emphasis on the organized, integrated nature of psychological entities and processes has continued to influence the field throughout the remainder of the century. The German word *Gestalt,* roughly meaning "structure," "whole," "form," or "configuration," has no exact equivalent in English, so the term has become part of the technical vocabulary of psychology.

Gestalt psychologists rejected the "constancy hypothesis" that was generally taken for granted early in the twentieth century, namely that there is a constant point-for-point correspondence between physical characteristics of a stimulus and the psychological attributes of the resulting sensation. In numerous experiments they demonstrated that local perceptual qualities vary not just with the local stimulus but with the contexts that surround the stimulus. Percepts are not immutable correlates of the local physical stimuli that give rise to them, but reflect specific interactive relational aspects of a stimulus complex. The well-known perceptual constancies (size, shape, color, brightness, etc.) are all inconsistent with the "constancy hypothesis"; for example, the perceived brightness of a small spot in a large visual field depends upon not only the light intensity of the spot itself but also the intensity of the spot's surround. Comparably, color contrast phenomena disprove the "constancy hypothesis"; the same gray circle will appear greenish if surrounded by violet, or yellow if surrounded by blue. Perceptual attributes such as size, shape, color, brightness, movement, etc., are *relationally determined.*

Relational determination also plays a crucial role in many cognitive (and physiological) functions other than sensation and perception. While it is central in perceptual organization (as in controlling what aspects of a complex sensory input will be perceived as figure and which as ground), it is also at the core of productive thinking. To solve a problem productively, it is necessary to understand what aspects of it are essential and which superficial or irrelevant, as well as the critical interrelations among the core aspects. In most psychological wholes or Gestalten the parts are not indifferent to each other, but are mutually interdependent;

indeed the attributes of the separate component parts of the Gestalt are determined by their place, role, and function within the whole of which they are parts. Productive thinking involves transforming a confused, fuzzy, meaningless view of a problem into a clear conception of it that takes all the relevant features into account; such reorganization or restructuring of the problem results in insight, understanding, and its solution, if the reorganization is adequate to the central features of the problem.

This view of problem solving, and of learning, contrasted sharply, in its emphasis on meaningfulness, with the views of learning that prevailed in other schools, which instead emphasized blind contiguity in space and time (as in traditional associationism and as in the process of classical conditioning that was considered prototypic of learning by behaviorists). The top-down approach of the Gestalt theorists, making the whole primary, was the opposite of the bottom-up approach typical of psychologists in other schools, which began with "elements" (such as sensations, or stimuli and responses) and studied how they combine to add up to a whole.

The Gestalt psychologists contrasted their "dynamic" view with what they called the static "machine theory" of their opponents. Natural systems—in physics and physiology as well as in psychology—undergo "dynamic self-distribution," as in electrical or magnetic fields, such that the organization of any Gestalt or whole will be as "good" as the prevailing conditions allow. This "principle of Prägnanz," as the Gestalt psychologists called it, makes unnecessary the arbitrary connections or mechanical constraints that "andsum" theorists use in explaining natural processes in physics, physiology, and psychology: consider the form of a soap bubble or of a drop of oil in water; they are the result not of an artificial constraining mold but of dynamic self-distribution.

Antecedents of Gestalt Psychology

That a whole may be more than a mere sum of its parts had been recognized since antiquity, even by Plato. During the nineteenth century several philosophers emphasized that a thoroughgoing simple elementism is inadequate. For example, John Stuart Mill objected to his father James Mill's theory of mind as the sum total of sensations and images associated via contiguity in space and time. He argued that the properties of chemical compounds may not be deducible from the properties of their constituent elements in isolation, and proposed a "mental chemistry" in contrast with his father's "mental mechanics." Even Wilhelm Maximilian Wundt, one of whose objectives was to analyze the contents of consciousness into their constituent "mental elements," had been compelled to acknowledge that mental compounds may display emergent qualities that are not to be found in their constituent elements in isolation—a result that he proposed is due to a principle of "creative synthesis" that characterizes human mental processes.

In 1890, Christian von Ehrenfels argued that "form qualities" such as squareness, circularity—or a melody—are separate elements over and above the component elements of a whole. Thus a square is, in effect, the sum of four equal straight lines plus four right angles—plus the "Gestalt quality" of "squareness." The lengths of the lines or their color can be changed, but this will not alter the squareness of the square; you can transpose a melody into a different key, changing every note, yet the melody remains unchanged. He proposed that it is the transposability of Gestalt qualities, their independence of the specific qualities of the other elements, that is the criterion for their existence.

The Emergence of Gestalt Theory

In 1910 Max Wertheimer pointed out that the "primitive" music of a tribe in Ceylon had a complex structure, in which early parts of a melody set up requirements for the melody's continuation. Two years later (1912a) he analyzed examples of numerical thinking in aboriginal peoples that is not purely summative but that takes into account the dynamic and structural features of the problem to which the numerical thinking is applied. For example, if one divides a chain of eight links in half one has two chains of four links each; another division yields four sets of two links each; but with yet another division there no longer is a chain. In certain situations "one, a couple, a few, many" is an appropriate quantitative scale; and no reasonable person would specify an amount of rice in terms of the number of kernels it contains.

Structural and dynamic features take precedence over "elements" and their "andsums." It is not appropriate to think of wholes as the sum total of their parts, or, as in von Ehrenfels's case, as "more" than the sum total of their parts (the "elemental parts" plus the element of "Gestalt quality"). Rather, wholes are entirely different from any summation; they have their own inherent properties that in turn determine the nature of the parts. There is no need to refer to "elements," whether they be in the form of James Mill's elementism, Wundt's product of creative synthesis, or Ehrenfels's constituent elements plus form quality.

Another 1912 article by Max Wertheimer (1912b) on the perception of apparent movement is generally viewed as the founding publication of the Gestalt school (see Ash, 1995, for a thorough account of the emergence of the Gestalt school of psychology in Germany). When two adjacent stationary visual stimuli are presented successively under appropriate spatial and temporal conditions, the result is a compelling perception not of two successively presented stationary stimuli nor of two simultaneously presented ones, but of a single object moving from one location to another. The Gestalt of the entire exposure is such that the perceived motion is entirely different from the characteristics of the two sensations in isolation, and no combination of "elements" can explain the percept; it is totally different from any "sum" of its "parts." This demonstration also convincingly disproved the "constancy hypothesis" of an immutable relation between stimulus and sensation; the motion is in the percept but nowhere in the stimuli. The whole, the Gestalt, had become primary perceptually and ontogenetically.

Wolfgang Köhler and Kurt Koffka were among the participants in Wertheimer's experiments on apparent motion. They joined Wertheimer in promoting Gestalt psychology during the ensuing decades.

Major Proponents and Landmarks of Gestalt Psychology

Wertheimer, Köhler, and Koffka are generally viewed as the three original Gestalt theorists. All of them had been students of Carl Stumpf at Berlin, and had been influenced by Stumpf's holism and his advocacy of the phenomenological method in experimental psychology. Erich Moritz von Hornbostel was an early advocate of the school, but went on to devote himself primarily to ethnomusicology. Kurt Lewin, younger than the three founders, broadened the Gestalt approach into a somewhat looser "field theory" and applied it to motivation, personality, and social psychology. Gestalt psychologists of the second generation include the following: Rudolf Arnheim applied the theory to the psychology of art. Karl Duncker performed experiments on problem solving using verbal protocols. His experimental work on induced motion established that if an object and its surrounding environment move relative to each other the movement is perceived as occurring in the object rather than in the frame. Hans Wallach did extensive experimental work primarily in perception. Solomon E. Asch, in addition to experiments in perception, association, and personality, developed a Gestalt perspective on social psychology. Abraham S. Luchins performed experiments on the debilitating effects of set on problem solving. George Katona's work on organizing and memorizing summarized experiments demonstrating the superiority of Gestalt-based meaningful learning over rote memorization. He later became a pioneer in the new discipline of psychological economics. Mary Henle, an experimental psychologist, published significant papers on the nature and history of the Gestalt approach and prepared several anthologies of Gestalt work. Wolfgang Metzger promulgated the Gestalt per-

spective in Germany after the three founders had emigrated to the United States.

Soon the Gestalt school expanded its perspective into almost all subfields of psychology. During the 1920s Wertheimer published articles with many examples of productive thinking, and also wrote on how the principle of Prägnanz results in the organized perception of integrated objects in the world through the operation of the principles of perceptual organization. Koffka applied the Gestalt perspective to the psychology of mental development. Köhler reported pioneering studies of problem solving in chimpanzees, demonstrating their capacity for meaningful insight; experiments on transposition that generated international interest; and detailed explorations of the implications of the Gestalt approach in physics, biology, chemistry, and physiology. During the 1930s and later, Köhler published a number of books on Gestalt psychology that were to become world renowned; Koffka wrote a mid-1930s major text on Gestalt theory summarizing its experimental foundations and developing systematic theoretical positions about most of the significant psychological issues of the time. Wertheimer's posthumous book on productive thinking was published in the 1940s. Condensed English translations of significant Gestalt publications were made available by Willis D. Ellis in 1938 (and reissued thereafter). Wertheimer's book on productive thinking was reissued in 1959, 1978, and 1982, and translated into several foreign languages. German translations of Wertheimer's late essays on truth, ethics, freedom, and democracy were prepared during the 1990s. An international multidisciplinary quarterly journal, *Gestalt Theory*, the official journal of the Society for Gestalt Theory and Its Applications, has been published by Westdeutscher Verlag in Wiesbaden, Germany, since 1979. Although all the first, and most of the second, generation of Gestalt psychologists had died, Gestalt theory continued to be highly visible.

By the end of the twentieth century, Gestalt thought was evident in a wide array of contemporary research. The Gestalt work on productive thinking was frequently viewed as posing challenging problems for cognitive psychology (e.g., Murray, 1995; Sternberg & Davidson, 1995), and the early experimental work on the perceptual constancies, on the perception of movement, and on the organization of perception continued to interest visual physiologists and cognitive neuroscientists (e.g., Rock & Palmer, 1990; Spillmann & Ehrenstein, 1996). Writers on social psychology, personality, and psychopathology continued to use a Gestalt perspective, some explicitly and many implicitly. A Gestalt orientation continued to permeate a significant number of theoretical and empirical approaches in almost all areas of psychology.

[*See also* Bender-Gestalt Visual Motor Test; Humanistic Psychology; Psychology, *articles on* Early Twentieth Century *and* Nineteenth Century through Freud.]

Bibliography

Ash, M. G. (1995). *Gestalt psychology in German culture, 1890–1967: Holism and the quest for objectivity.* New York: Cambridge University Press.

Ellis, W. D. (1967). *A source book of Gestalt psychology.* New York: Harcourt, Brace. (Original work published 1938)

Koffka, K. (1935). *Principles of Gestalt psychology.* New York: Harcourt, Brace.

Murray, D. J. (1995). *Gestalt psychology and the cognitive revolution.* London: Harvester Wheatsheaf.

Rock, I., & Palmer, S. (1990). The legacy of Gestalt psychology. *Scientific American, 263* (6), 84–90.

Spillmann, L., & Ehrenstein, W. H. (1996). From neuron to Gestalt. In R. Greger, & V. Windhorst (Eds.), *Comprehensive human physiology: Mechanisms of visual perception* (Vol. 1, pp. 861–893). Heidelberg: Springer.

Sternberg, R. J., & Davidson, J. E. (Eds.). (1995). *The nature of insight.* Cambridge, MA: Bradford/MIT Press.

von Ehrenfels, C. (1890). Über Gestaltqualitäten [On Gestalt qualities]. *Vierteljahresschrift für wissenschaftliche Philosophie, 14,* 249–292.

Wertheimer, M. (1910). Musik der Wedda [The music of the Veddas]. *Sammelbände der internationalen Musikgesellschaft, 11,* 300–309.

Wertheimer, M. (1912a). Über das Denken der Naturvölker: I. Zahlen und Zahlgebilde [On the thinking of aboriginal people: I. Numbers and numerical concepts]. *Zeitschrift für Psychologie, 60,* 321–378.

Wertheimer, M. (1912b). Experimentelle Studien über das Sehen von Bewegung [Experimental studies of the perception of movement]. *Zeitschrift für Psychologie, 61,* 161–265.

Wertheimer, M. (1982). *Productive thinking.* Chicago: University of Chicago Press. (Original work published 1945)

Michael Wertheimer

GESTALT THERAPY. Fritz Perls, the German-born American founder, along with his wife, Laura Perls, and American-born Paul Goodman, all contributed to the development of Gestalt therapy. The major theoretical work *Gestalt Therapy: Excitement and Growth in the Human Personality* (F. Perls, Hefferline, & P. Goodman, New York) was published in 1951. Gestalt therapy is currently based on three fundamental principles: phenomenology, field theory, and dialogue (Resnick, 1995).

Theory

Gestalt therapists use the phenomenological method of working with people's awareness in the here and now to promote current experience. Experience is seen as occurring at the boundary between the organism and the environment, and contact is seen as the primary datum of experience. *Contact* is defined as the forming, in awareness, of a figure against a background. This concept attempts to capture the moment of lived experience as the organism contacts the environment. Experience is not viewed as the result of compromise formation between unconscious and conscious forces, as in psychoanalysis, or as epiphenomenal, as in behaviorism, but rather as a vital aspect of creative adjustment to the environment.

One of the themes of Gestalt therapy is that growth occurs by assimilation of what is needed from the environment, and that psychopathology arises as a disturbance of contact with the environment. Disturbances of contact, which prevent the necessary assimilation, are caused either by interruptive processes (introjection, projection, and retroflection) or by past unfinished situations intruding into the present (unfinished business). People are seen as self-organizing, growth-oriented individuals adjusting to changes at the contact boundary. Introjection of social control, or "shoulds," is seen as a major cause of interruption of growth.

Method

The Gestalt approach proposed a unique form of therapy. This involved increasing awareness of experience by focusing attention on feelings, sensations, and motoric processes. Therapy was aimed at helping people become aware of their agency in constructing their realities, as well as at identifying and reworking unfinished business that impeded present contact. In therapy, client awareness is followed in a disciplined manner as contact with or withdrawal from the environment is made; as a need is recognized, acted on, and satisfied; or as a goal is met or an interest is followed. In doing this, Gestalt therapists often focus on people's nonverbal behavior and their use of language.

The graded experiment was introduced as a major method of intervention as opposed to the predominant interventions of the time: interpretation, reflection, or goal setting. This experimental method set up in-session tasks for clients, not to be completed, but to be tried out to discover something. Experiments in the session with tasks like two-chair work and dream work were emphasized, but many other experiments were created in the moment to help clients intensify and embody their experiences. Creative experiments were designed to meet the client's situation: experiments such as asking the client to express resentment to an imagined other, to assert or disclose something intimate to the therapist, to curl up into a ball, or to express a desire in order to make it more vivid. The client's experience and expression were then analyzed for what prevented or interrupted completion of these experiments. The experimental method focused on bringing people's difficulties with task completion to the surface. Therapists asked clients to become aware of and experience the interruptive processes that prevented their feelings or needs from being expressed or acted on. In this manner, clients were seen as gaining insight into their own experience by discovery rather than interpretation.

The experiment involved "try this" followed by "what do you experience now?" In addition to the experiment, Gestalt therapists used a set of key questions designed to get at particular aspects of clients' functioning and promote creative adjustment to the environment. Key questions oriented at experience were "What are you aware of?", "What do you experience?", "What do you need?", and "What do you want or want to do?" Identity-related questions of the form "Who are you?" or "What do you want to be?" were also used.

With more fragile clients who have not developed a strong sense of self or a boundary between self and other, the development of awareness is a more long-term objective. Promoting experience and asking these clients feeling-oriented questions are viewed as premature, as they have yet to develop an awareness of their internal world. With these clients, a more relational form of work is used in which the process of contact with the therapist becomes the focus.

Gestalt therapy evolved from an individualistic form of practice, one that emphasized the development of self-support, to a field theoretic, interpersonal one in which support from the field was seen as important. The recent shift to this more dialogical form of Gestalt therapy has brought the "I-thou" dialogue (M. Buber, I & Thou, New York, 1937) into the foreground as the foundation of practice. Greater emphasis has been placed on respecting clients, providing support, validating clients as authentic sources of experience, and relating to clients less confrontationally or authoritatively.

This perspective is guided by a view of relationship emphasizing that encounters between individuals should be characterized by qualities of presence, inclusion, nonexploitativeness, authenticity, and commitment to dialogue. This more recent form of Gestalt therapy, rather than viewing relational problems as client projections, sees them as arising from an interpersonal field. Problems in the relationship between client and therapist are seen as a source of new learning for both client and therapist. Therapists are highly aware of their own impact on clients' momentary experience, focusing on disruptions in relational contact as both a source of discovery and an opportunity for new experience.

L. S. Greenberg, Elliott, and Lietaer (*Handbook of Psychotherapy and Behavior Change*, New York, 1995) have summarized research on this approach and found evidence for its effectiveness in dealing with specific types of in-session problems (conflicts), specific problems (unfinished business), and specific disorders (depression).

[*See also* Bender-Gestalt Visual Motor Test.]

Bibliography

Polster, I., & Polster, I. (1973). *Gestalt therapy integrated*. New York: Bruner Mazel.

Resnick, R. (1995). Gestalt Therapy: Principles, prisms and perspectives. *British Gestalt Journal, 4*, 3–13.

Wheeler, G. (1991). *Gestalt reconsidered*. New York: Gardner Press.

Yontef, G. M. (1993). *Awareness, dialogue and process: Essays on Gestalt therapy*. Highland, NY: Gestalt Journal Press.

Leslie S. Greenberg

GHISELLI, EDWIN E. (1907–1980), American psychologist. If there is some sense to the notion of "generations" of applied psychologists, Ghiselli belonged to the third generation. The first generation was defined by Hugo Münsterberg, James McKeen Cattell, Walter V. Bingham, and Walter D. Scott. The second generation included Harold Burtt, Bruce Moore, Morris Viteles, Edward K. Strong, Jr., Charles S. Myers, and John G. Jenkins.

Ghiselli was born in San Francisco in 1907 and matriculated at the University of California at Berkeley, majoring in Italian. After completing his undergraduate education, he waded into the world of commerce, working in the banking industry. While working, he decided to take a graduate course in psychology being offered by Robert C. Tryon. The course was a galvanizing experience, and Ghiselli abandoned banking for the life of a graduate student in psychology. Tryon introduced Ghiselli to the concepts of mental measurement and individual differences, the same siren that had called to Cattell 45 years earlier. In 1933, he received his M.A. from Berkeley, and in 1936, his doctorate. His dissertation was a study of learning discrimination tasks in animals, carried out under task direction of Edward C. Tolman.

Subsequently, Ghiselli spent a postdoctoral year with another well-known discrimination theorist and researcher at Harvard University—Karl Lashley. This was followed by a short stay as a teaching fellow at Cornell University. The topic of his lectures at Cornell was individual differences; John G. Jenkins became his new mentor. Jenkins influenced Ghiselli greatly and awakened in him a heretofore inchoate fascination with application. When Jenkins moved to the University of Maryland in 1938, Ghiselli went with him.

In 1939, Ghiselli was offered the opportunity to begin a program in applied psychology at Berkeley, and he accepted the opportunity with great enthusiasm. A similar program had been launched at the Carnegie Institute of Technology 23 years earlier by Bingham. Ghiselli patterned the Berkeley program after the Carnegie model with two major exceptions. The Carnegie program did not offer formal courses nor did it grant degrees, it simply served applied clients. The Berkeley program was to be a traditional degree-granting program in all respects.

In 1942, Ghiselli was commissioned as a captain in the Aviation Research Program of the U.S. Air Force. He left the service in 1945, having been promoted to lieutenant colonel. After his return to Berkeley, he served two terms as the department chair. In 1955, he was elected the tenth president of Division 14 of the American Psychological Association.

Ghiselli published widely and was the author of over 100 research articles and 8 books. In 1948, with C. W. Brown, he published *Personnel and Industrial Psychology* (New York). In 1964, he published *Theory of Psychological Measurement* (New York). The work he is best known for, however, is a partly descriptive, partly inferential *Validity of Occupational Aptitude Tests* (New York, 1966). This monumental effort summarized the available evidence on the validity of various categories of tests for differing occupational groupings. It was a precursor to meta-analysis. This text is still widely cited in treatment of test validity.

In the years preceding his retirement in 1973, Ghiselli became interested in patterns of international management and collaborated with Mason Haire and Lyman Porter in the publication of *Managerial Thinking: An International Study* (New York, 1966).

In 1972, the American Psychological Association presented Ghiselli with the Distinguished Scientific Contribution Award. Ghiselli retired in 1973. In 1983, the Society of Industrial and Organizational Psychology (also known as Division 14) changed the name of the James McKeen Cattell Award for Research Design Excellence to the Ghiselli Award in recognition of his many contributions to the application of design and measurement principles to the study of work behavior.

[*Many of the people mentioned in this article are the subjects of independent biographical entries.*]

Bibliography

Works by Ghiselli

Ghiselli, E. E., & Brown, C. W. (1955). *Personnel and industrial psychology* (Rev. ed.). New York: McGraw-Hill.

Ghiselli, E. E. (1978). From Jack London to Luigi Pirandello: Influences in the career of an industrial psychologist. In T. S. Krawicc (Ed.), *The psychologists: Autobiographies of distinguished living psychologists* (Vol. 3, pp. 60–81). Brandon, VT: Clinical Psychology.

Ghiselli, E. E., Campbell, J. P., & Zedeck, S. (1981). *Measurement theory for the behavioral sciences*. San Francisco: Freeman.

Works about Ghiselli

Beach, F. A. (1981). Obituary: Edwin E. Ghiselli (1907–1980). *American Psychologist. 36* (7), 794–795.

Benjamin, L. T., Jr. (1997). The early presidents of Division 14: 1945–1954. *The Industrial Organizational Psychologist, 35*(2), 33–34.

Postman, L. (Ed.). (1962). *Psychology in the making: Histories of selected research problems*. New York: Knopf.

Frank J. Landy

GIBSON, ELEANOR J. (1910–), American psychologist. Eleanor Jack was born in Peoria, Illinois, where she grew up in a middle-class home. In 1931 she received a bachelor's degree in psychology from Smith College, a women's college in Northampton, Massachusetts, where she studied with and married American experimental psychologist James J. Gibson.

Eleanor J. Gibson pursued a doctorate at Yale University. For her dissertation research, she had initially wished to follow a comparative approach utilizing the chimpanzee population housed in Robert Yerkes's laboratory. When Yerkes refused to allow her to work in his laboratory because she was a woman, she persuaded Clark Hull to allow her to work with him. Although Hull's behaviorist perspective emphasized the association of stimuli and responses in learning by rats, Gibson extended this theoretical perspective to the study of verbal learning and forgetting in human participants. Gibson received her doctorate in 1938, and the concept of differentiation explored in her doctoral research was to become a central component of her later work.

The development of Gibson's career following her doctorate was influenced by a number of factors, including the financial realities of the 1930s, as well as having to put her husband's career concerns above her own. One consequence was that an academic position was virtually impossible for her to obtain, either during World War II or afterward. Without a faculty position, Gibson did not obtain research funding. Despite her growing recognition by the academic world, Gibson did not obtain a faculty position until 1965, when her husband's departure for another position prompted Cornell University, her husband's employer since 1949, to appoint her as professor of psychology, although on a half-time basis only. After 1965, however, Gibson was the recipient of numerous awards and honors. She was the Susan Linn Sage Professor of Psychology at Cornell from 1972 to 1979, and she was professor emeritus after 1979. Far from retiring, she continued her professional contributions through a number of visiting professorships. She also received recognition through honorary degrees, as well as numerous awards, ranging from the Distinguished Scientific Contribution Award (1968) and the Gold Medal Award (1968) of the American Psychological Association to the National Medal of Science (1992) and election to the National Academy of Sciences.

Gibson's contributions to psychology were both numerous and of major importance. She was perhaps best known for her work with the visual cliff, with which she demonstrated the primacy of depth perception. Several themes characterized her career, including a comparative approach firmly rooted in exploring relationships between organisms and their environments, her ongoing interests in perception and development, and her ability both to transform a serendipitous observation into a research question and to design an innovative methodology with which to explore it.

The process of differentiation, which was a focus of Gibson's doctoral dissertation, became a concept central to perceptual learning, a research focus that occupied her over a 15-year period. In one sense, perceptual learning involves extracting previously unused information from what is perceived as a result of experience, so that there is a change in what is perceived. Perceptual learning involves differentiating among distinctive features and higher-order invariants as an organism is actively involved in relating to its environment. Gibson's ongoing work demonstrated that perceptual learning could not be accounted for by existing theories, and thus she defined a new field, which she gradually expanded to include perceptual development as well. One result of these efforts was the book *Principles of Perceptual Learning and Development* (1969). At the time this book appeared, the study of perception in preverbal children had received very little attention. However, this book greatly stimulated the development of new methodologies to study infant perception. A common theme in many of these studies was to utilize a baby's exploratory activities, such as looking, listening, and mouthing, as indicators of what was perceived.

Gibson's work on perceptual learning and development provided an excellent foundation for the exploration of the process of reading, which was the next major topic that she addressed. Just as Gibson viewed the perceiver as an active searcher for information rather than a passive recipient of environmental stimulation, she also came to view the process of reading as an active search for information. Gibson and her colleagues brought to the study of reading an innovative interdisciplinary perspective that meshed theory and research concerning such reading-related issues as memory, cognition, development, and language, in addition to perception. This work was described in the book *The Psychology of Reading* coauthored with Harry

Levin (1975). Whereas the study of reading had essentially been abandoned by experimental psychology decades earlier, the work of Gibson and her colleagues made the psychology of reading once again a flourishing area of research.

Although Eleanor J. Gibson and James Gibson worked independently, they did draw on each other's research and theory. In his ecological theory of perception, James J. Gibson emphasized perceivers' direct perception of information from the environment rather than their processing of such information in stages, as was suggested by a cognitive approach. An ecological approach views the perceiver as actively seeking information from the environment in order to act appropriately in ways that the environment affords or allows. Eleanor J. Gibson has applied this theory to infant perceptual development, thus establishing an additional major field of psychology.

Besides influencing theory and research on verbal learning, on perceptual learning, and on the psychology of reading and establishing infant perceptual development as a major field, another of Gibson's most important contributions to psychology has been through her students, with whom she has collaborated throughout her professional life. During her career Eleanor J. Gibson has excelled at identifying significant theoretical issues, devising methodologies to explore them, and motivating others both to build upon her work and to develop their own views.

Bibliography

Works by Gibson

Gibson, E. J. (1963). Perceptual learning. *Annual Review of Psychology, 14,* 29–56.

Gibson, E. J. (1969). *Principles of perceptual learning and development.* New York: Appleton-Century-Crofts.

Gibson, E. J. (1980). Autobiography. In G. Lindzey (Ed.), *A history of psychology in autobiography* (pp. 239–271). San Francisco: Freeman.

Gibson, E. J. (1984). Perceptual development from the ecological approach. In M. E. Lamb, A. L. Brown, & B. Rogoff (Eds.), *Advances in developmental psychology* (Vol. 3, pp. 243–286). Hillsdale, NJ: Erlbaum.

Gibson, E. J. (1988). Exploratory behavior in the development of perceiving, acting, and the acquiring of knowledge. *Annual Review of Psychology, 39,* 1–41.

Gibson, E. J. (1991). *An odyssey in learning and perception.* Cambridge, MA: MIT Press. Includes reprints of Eleanor Gibson's most important papers, together with her own reappraisals of their significance and indications of how her own views have changed and developed. Also includes some previously unpublished material.

Gibson, E. J., & Levin, H. (1975). *The psychology of reading.* Cambridge, MA: MIT Press.

Gibson, E. J., & Walk, R. D. (1960). The "visual cliff." *Scientific American, 202*(4), 64–71.

Works about Gibson

Caudle, F. M. (1989). Eleanor J. Gibson. In A. N. O'Connell & N. F. Russo (Eds.), *Women in psychology* (pp. 104–116). New York: Greenwood Press. Summarizes major aspects of Eleanor J. Gibson's life, with discussion of issues that she faced as a woman pursuing her academic and research interests in a professional world in which women were not welcomed for many years.

Epstein, W. (Ed.). (1987). The ontogenesis of perception [special issue]. *Journal of Experimental Psychology: Human Perception and Performance, 13*(4). An issue devoted to research on perception in infants, an area influenced by Eleanor J. Gibson; includes an introductory essay by Gibson.

Pick, A. D. (Ed.). (1979). *Perception and its development: A tribute to Eleanor J. Gibson*. Hillsdale, NJ: Erlbaum. A collection honoring Eleanor J. Gibson's continuing contribution to psychology's understanding of perception. Contributions are organized into topics influenced by Gibson, including learning and generalization, development of spatial perception, perception of pattern and structure, perception of meaning, and exploration and selectivity in perceptual development. Includes a foreword by James J. Gibson.

Pick, H. L. (1992). Eleanor J. Gibson: Learning to perceive and perceiving to learn. *Developmental Psychology, 28* (5), 787–794. One of a series of articles prepared for the centennial of the American Psychological Association; describes major contributions of Eleanor J. Gibson.

Fairfid M. Caudle

GIBSON, JAMES JEROME (1904–1979), American psychologist. During a long career at Smith College and Cornell University, Gibson developed his distinctive ecological approach to perception, establishing an influential theory that wedded functional psychology with strains of philosophical realism.

Born in McConnelsville, Ohio, Gibson attended Princeton University in the 1920s during the heyday of American pragmatism and progressivism. He completed his doctorate at Princeton in 1928 under the psychologist Herbert S. Langfeld, who had studied German experimental psychology and phenomenology under Carl Stumpf. Also among Gibson's teachers at Princeton was the psychologist-philosopher Edwin B. Holt, a top student and an intimate of William James. Holt's "new realist" philosophy and response theory of cognition had a lasting influence on Gibson's approach to perception, most notably with respect to Holt's view of awareness as an integrated adjustment of an observer to the environment. Gibson's tough-minded approach to perception was, however, moderated by a respect for phenomenology that was probably drawn from Langfeld and motivated by the work of the Gestalt psychologist Kurt Koffka, Gibson's senior colleague at

Smith College from 1928 to 1941. Also among Gibson's influences at Smith, and throughout his career, was Eleanor J. Gibson, whom he married in 1932. Eleanor Gibson was to become a notable psychologist in her own right, making fundamental contributions in the area of perceptual development.

Gibson's insights into perception paralleled technological advances, such as the automobile and the airplane, that raised problems related to visually guided activity. In his autobiography, Gibson recalled childhood memories of riding on a train with his father, Thomas, an employee of the Wisconsin Central Railroad. From the locomotive, the young Gibson noticed that the visual world seemed to expand in the direction in which the train was headed, but that when he looked back from the rear platform, the visual world seemed to contract. Later, as a young adult, Gibson was impressed by the flow of optical information that accompanies driving an automobile and by the control that drivers have over the pattern and velocity of the optical flow. Many of Gibson's ground-breaking ideas would become explicit during World War II, after he entered the U.S. Army in 1941 to become the director of the U.S. Army Air Force's Psychological Test Film Unit.

As a captain in the Air Force, Gibson studied visual perception as it pertained to flying and landing airplanes. Of primary importance was his finding that the visual world remains stable during flight despite the illusory vestibular and kinesthetic feedback caused by the rotation, tilt, and yaw of a moving aircraft. Earlier theories had attempted to explain the perception of the environment's horizontal and vertical spatial axes in terms of nonvisual sensations from the vestibular organs. Although Gibson found such theories to be persuasive at first, he soon found them unworkable for explaining visual constancy during flight. Indeed, how could the constancy of a pilot's visual world be explained in terms of illusory vestibular and kinesthetic feedback? Gibson was also led to reformulate the classical problem of the ambiguity of the retinal image: the problem of how a stable, three-dimensional visual world can be reconstructed by a visual system that begins with a flat, projectively ambiguous, two-dimensional retinal image. Rather than appeal to "mentalistic" constructive or organizational processes to account for perceptual constancy, however, Gibson developed what he called a *ground theory of perception*.

Gibson's ground theory begins with direct awareness of a stable ground terrain with a limiting edge (the horizon) that separates the ground below from the untextured sky above. In his first book, *The Perception of the Visual World* (1950), published after his first year at Cornell, Gibson advanced the concept of a *retinal texture gradient*. He showed that the textured ground plane projects an increasing gradient of density to the retina as it extends toward the horizon. The ground plane thus provides a background scale against which the relative sizes, shapes, and distances of objects arrayed against the extended ground surface can be assessed directly, without recourse to inner constructive or organizational processes. Gibson further postulated that the retinal texture gradient of the ground surface, together with the horizon, was sufficient to determine orientation with respect to the environmental upright. Gibson's answer to the problem of visual constancy was thus to redefine the stimulus for vision to include "higher-order invariant information," such as the relationship of ground to sky, the stable horizon, and retinal texture gradients.

Gibson also introduced the concept of a *retinal motion gradient*, a gradient of changes in velocities, superimposed on the texture gradient of the ground surface. He showed that retinal motion gradients directly specify the direction of movement by virtue of motion-based retinal velocities that radiate outward from a point, called the *center of expansion*, toward which a perceiver is moving. Gibson further demonstrated that optical information is available to specify a perceiver's approach to a surface. For example, the stimulation reaching a perceiver from the horizon remains constant, whereas the stimulation from nearby sources undergoes rapid changes, and the velocity of global changes within the motion gradient can specify the speed of a perceiver's approach to a surface, as well as the speed of self-movement generally.

In brief, Gibson argued that the "ambient optic array," the light surrounding an active, exploring observer, is sufficiently structured to enable the direct perception of self-movement and the layout of perceivable space. In *The Senses Considered as Perceptual Systems* (1966), Gibson offered a functional, ecological taxonomy of the senses based on modes of activity, such as orienting, looking, listening, smelling, tasting, and touching, and the external information obtained by these means. In *The Ecological Approach to Visual Perception* (1979), Gibson put forth his *theory of affordances*: that perceivers guide their behavior by detecting what the environment offers or affords for action. By the end of his life, Gibson therefore argued that the adaptive value of objects and events can be directly perceived. The concept of affordances marked a radical departure from mainstream ways of conceptualizing perceptually meaningful stimuli. Gibson continued to explore his highly controversial approach to perception until he succumbed to cancer in December 1979.

Bibliography

Works by Gibson

Gibson, J. J. (1950). *The perception of the visual world.* Boston: Houghton Mifflin. Gibson's psychophysical theory of the correlation between textured stimuli and spatial vision.

Gibson, J. J. (1966). *The senses considered as perceptual systems.* Boston: Houghton Mifflin. Gibson's theory of functional perceptual systems as modes of activity that obtain information about the environment and the self.

Gibson, J. J. (1979). *The ecological approach to visual perception.* Boston: Houghton Mifflin. Gibson's description of a visual environment replete with ecological information that can directly specify meaningful affordances for action.

Works about Gibson

Gibson, J. J. (1967). James J. Gibson. In E. G. Boring, & G. Lindzey (Eds.), *A history of psychology in autobiography* (Vol. 5, pp. 127–143). New York: Appleton-Century-Crofts.

Lombardo, T. J. (1987). *The reciprocity of perceiver and environment: The evolution of James J. Gibson's ecological psychology.* Hillsdale, NJ: Erlbaum. A theoretical history of Gibson's approach to perception, with special emphasis on his account of the functional complementarity of organism and environment.

Mace, W. M. (1977). James J. Gibson's strategy for perceiving: Ask not what's inside your head, but what your head's inside of. In R. Shaw, & J. Bransford (Eds.), *Perceiving, acting, and knowing* (pp. 43–66). Hillsdale, NJ: Erlbaum. Arguably the most readable and concise introduction to Gibson's ecological approach to perception.

Neisser, U. (1976). *Cognition and reality.* San Francisco: Freeman. A synthesis of Gibsonian thinking and mainstream cognitive psychology that was instrumental in stimulating cognitive psychologists' interest in Gibson's work.

Reed, E. S. (1988). *James J. Gibson and the psychology of perception.* New Haven, CT: Yale University Press. A biography of Gibson that draws on a rich archive of his working notes, drafts, and correspondence. The book also attempts to reconstruct, for the first time, the social psychology of Gibson's pre–World War II career.

David M. Boynton

GIFTEDNESS. Most people agree that some individuals are more intellectually gifted than others. Unfortunately, people do not always agree on what it means to be intellectually gifted. This lack of agreement arises for at least three reasons. First, giftedness is societally constructed and, at different times and in different places, societies change the meaning of giftedness. Second, the criteria frequently change across the life span. In the United States, childhood giftedness is often determined on the somewhat arbitrary basis of intelligence quotients (IQs) of 130 or higher on standardized intelligence tests (Horowitz & O'Brien, 1986). This means a child must have an IQ that is at least two standard deviations above the average IQ of 100. In contrast, adulthood giftedness is generally determined on the basis of creativity and distinction in a specific domain (Siegler & Kotovsky, 1986). In other words, childhood giftedness is usually based on exceptional acquisition of domain-general information, whereas adult giftedness is based on exceptional discovery of a new way to conceptualize information in a specific domain. A final reason why giftedness has been difficult to define is that there are several fields of giftedness and each one has its own set of research problems and agendas. Until recently, none of these fields has been especially aware of the others.

In order fully to understand and foster the talents of gifted individuals, it is necessary to have a reasonably clear idea of what intellectual giftedness consists of, and how it can be assessed across the life span. Indeed, any instructional program for capitalizing on abilities assumes as a prerequisite some understanding of what giftedness is and how it can be identified. Fortunately, researchers are conducting theory-based research and merging approaches to form a more complete picture of giftedness from early childhood through adulthood. A review of these theories and the mental processes involved in giftedness, followed by a discussion of how giftedness is identified and fostered, will help illuminate this important construct.

Theories of Giftedness

IQ plays a major role in conceptions of giftedness that focus on academically talented children. Perhaps the best known view of giftedness as a unitary construct was held by Lewis M. Terman, a pioneer of intelligence testing in the United States, who defined gifted individuals as those who scored in the top 1% on conventional intelligence tests. He viewed intellectual giftedness as genetically inherited, stable, and psychometrically measurable. In the 1920s, Terman initiated a longitudinal study of the physical, emotional, cognitive, and personality traits of approximately 1,500 California children who had IQs of at least 135 on the Stanford–Binet Intelligence Scales (Terman, 1925; Terman & Oden, 1959). Terman's results showed these children to be superior to other children in social adjustment, coordination, physical health, and school achievement.

One of Terman's primary interests was whether gifted children would become successful adults. In general, this turned out to be the case. As adults, the male participants in Terman's study received more college degrees, awards, and higher salaries than average. They were also highly represented in honorary societies and *Who's Who in America*. The female participants showed a similar pattern of distinction except, like most women of that time period, they were less likely than the males to have advanced degrees and professional careers at midlife.

IQs are fairly good predictors of school-related achievements. However, it should be noted that none of Terman's sample participants excelled in creative pursuits, such as extraordinary musical, scientific, or artistic accomplishments. It should also be noted that the Stanford–Binet Intelligence Scales and other conventional intelligence tests are frequently criticized for cultural bias and for failing to correlate with creativity and special talents. Today, many psychologists go beyond Terman's IQ-based definition to identify a wider range of gifted individuals. For example, Joseph Renzulli, director of the National Research Center on the Gifted and Talented at the University of Connecticut, developed a "three-ring" conception of giftedness. According to this conception, giftedness consists of high levels of creativity, strong commitment to a specific area of interest, and above-average general and specific abilities (Renzulli, 1986).

Like Renzulli, Yale psychologist Robert Sternberg also believes that intellectual giftedness encompasses more than a high IQ. According to Sternberg (1986), there are at least three ways an individual can demonstrate intellectual giftedness. The first, componential intelligence, is internal to the individual and involves superior analytic skills, such as those needed in school and on conventional intelligence tests. This type of intelligence includes information-processing skills, such as defining a problem, selecting and employing an effective strategy for solving the problem, and evaluating the results. The second way, experiential intelligence, involves capitalizing on one's experiences in order to solve novel problems creatively and quickly automatize procedures. Finally, a gifted individual may be particularly adept at adapting to, shaping, or selecting real-world environments. This type, called contextual intelligence, allows one to acquire tacit knowledge in environments where strategies for success are not explicitly taught. Individuals who are gifted in one of these three types of intelligence are not necessarily gifted in the other two. Sternberg believes that the gifted are particularly good at capitalizing on their strengths and improving on, or compensating for, their weaknesses. Moreover, students who are taught in a way that matches their componential, experiential, or contextual abilities achieve at higher levels than when instruction does not match these abilities (Sternberg, Ferrari, Clinkenbeard, & Grigorenko, 1996).

Howard Gardner, Professor of Education at Harvard University Graduate School of Education, also rejected the conception of intellectual giftedness as a general ability, even though his view of intelligence differs from Sternberg's. According to Gardner (1983/1993a), individuals can be gifted in one or more of at least seven autonomous types of intelligence. Each type has its own developmental course and utilizes different areas of the brain. Three of the types—linguistic, logical-mathematical, and spatial—are related to abilities measured by conventional intelligence tests. The remaining four—musical, bodily-kinesthetic, intrapersonal, and interpersonal—are valued in most cultures, even though they are not measured by conventional intelligence tests. Individuals become gifted in one or more of these seven intelligences through genetic inheritance, training, and socialization of cultural values. In addition, gifted individuals often have a crystallizing experience that exposes them to a domain related to their particular latent abilities and ignites their interest in this domain (Walters & Gardner, 1986).

Mihaly Csikszentmihalyi (1996) adopted a systems approach that takes into account both internal and external factors related to giftedness. According to this approach, giftedness involves a positive interaction between an individual, a domain, and a field. Giftedness results when (a) an individual's knowledge, talents, and interests are a good match for the particular domain to which the individual contributes, and (b) the individual's contributions are evaluated favorably by knowledgeable judges in the larger field, or context, of the domain. Csikszentmihalyi, Rathunde, and Whalen (1993) found that gifted adolescents achieved flow states, or periods of intense concentration, while working in domains that matched their interests and talents. These flow states increased the likelihood that material within a domain would be mastered. Individuals who achieved flow tended to be curious, open to new experience, and sensitive to sensory information.

Only a representative sample of theories of giftedness has been presented here. In general, new views of giftedness differ from Terman's in two important ways. First, whereas Terman's approach identifies the gifted in terms of quantitative differences in IQs, newer approaches view gifted individuals as qualitatively different in terms of their skills and styles of thinking. Even though the newer approaches differ in the emphasis they place on information-processing skills, environmental influences, and personality traits, they all maintain that giftedness involves more than a quantitative difference in IQ. Second, Terman's definition of giftedness is based on general ability. More recent approaches define giftedness as multidimensional and largely domain specific. These domains are not limited to academic ones; they can include art, music, and athletic skills.

In general, the new views are less narrow than an IQ-based definition of giftedness. They also begin to bridge the gap between childhood and adult giftedness. More specifically, these theories help explain both the extraordinary acquisition of knowledge by gifted children, and the extraordinary creation of new forms of domain-specific knowledge by gifted adults. For example, intrinsic motivation, absorption in a particular area, and creative approaches to problem solving are components of many current theories. Unlike IQs, these components have been found to predict gifted behavior across the life span.

Mental Processes

What are the cognitive antecedents of giftedness? Although efficient information-processing skills do not account for all gifted behavior, they do seem to play an important role. In general, gifted individuals appear to have above-average metacognitive skills (Jackson & Butterfield, 1986). These skills involve knowledge about one's own mental processes and the ability to regulate and evaluate these processes. However, metacognition may, to some extent, be specific to the domain of one's gifts; this can contribute to uneven problem-solving performance across different content areas.

Gifted individuals spontaneously and effectively use three metacognitive processes when they do not know routine procedures for solving novel problems (Davidson, 1986; Davidson & Sternberg, 1984). These processes are selective encoding, selective combination, and selective comparison. Selective encoding involves distinguishing information that is relevant for one's purposes from information that is irrelevant. Many problem situations often contain large amounts of information, only some of which is needed to solve the problem. Selective encoding helps restructure one's mental representation so that information originally viewed as being irrelevant is now coded as relevant to the solution. Similarly, information thought to be quite important may now be ignored. Selective combination allows a problem solver to piece together elements of a problem situation in an appropriate, yet nonobvious, way. This new method of combining the elements also results in a change in the solver's mental representation of the problem. Selective comparison occurs when one finds a nonobvious relationship between new information and information one has already learned. Seeing nonobvious relationships allows one to use analogies, metaphors, and models to solve problems successfully. Effective use of these three processes leads to insightful thinking and creative solutions.

Research on selective encoding, selective combination, and selective comparison revealed that gifted children spontaneously applied these processes when solving novel problems, and they were far less likely than other students to need hints or guidance. When average students were explicitly told what information to encode, how to combine information, and what information to compare, their problem-solving performance was similar to the performance of gifted students. However, unlike the gifted students, the average students did not spontaneously search for and select the relevant elements, combinations, and prior knowledge that would help them solve the problems. Gifted children's use of these three processes helps explain why they learn more independently than other children.

Identifying and Fostering Giftedness

Gifted children have at least three characteristics that distinguish them from other children (Winner, 1996). First, gifted children are precocious and tend to learn material in a domain at an earlier and more rapid rate than other children. Second, their learning is qualitatively different. For example, gifted children are more likely than other children to create novel ways of understanding information. Finally, gifted children are intrinsically motivated and have a "rage to master" their domains of interest. These three characteristics imply that standard educational programs do not promote the talents of children who learn more independently and more rapidly than their age-related peers.

However, identifying children for gifted programs is a controversial issue. These programs are often viewed as elitist, and it is not obvious how gifted children should be selected. Identification and education of gifted children depends, in large part, on cultural values and the operational definition of giftedness used by school systems. Many schools use a definition based on general intelligence and, therefore, require children to have IQs of 130 or above for admission to gifted programs. The Stanford–Binet Intelligence Scales, the Weschler Intelligence Scale for Children (WISC–III), and the Goodenough-Harris Draw-A-Person Test are the most widely used measures for this type of selection. When creativity is included in the definition of giftedness, the Torrance Tests of Creative Thinking or the Wallach and Kogan Creative Battery are often administered. A talent search started at Johns Hopkins University identifies mathematically and verbally precocious youth on the basis of their math and verbal scores on the Scholastic Assessment Test (SAT) or the American College Test (ACT). Seventh- and eighth-grade students whose performance on these tests is at the level of college-bound high school seniors are eligible for special programs offered by the Study of Mathematically Precocious Youth and the Center for Talented Youth.

Because of the narrowness of an IQ-based definition of giftedness, and because of concerns about the validity of standard intelligence and creativity tests, new methods are being considered for gifted identification. These methods are derived from some of the theories of giftedness described earlier. For example, some schools select children on the basis of Renzulli's three-ring conception of giftedness. In these cases, teachers often identify children by using the Renzulli–Smith Early Childhood Checklist (Renzulli & Smith, 1981). Other schools use Gardner's (1993b) theory of multiple intelligences to identify students' talents.

Once gifted children are identified, two standard options exist for their education: enrichment and acceleration (Horowitz & O'Brien, 1986). Enrichment involves keeping gifted children at a grade level consistent with their chronological ages and supplementing their curriculum with advanced material and experiences. This supplementation can occur for all school subjects or only for particular ones. In some school systems, this enrichment occurs in the regular classroom. In others, gifted children leave their regular classrooms two to three hours a week to interact with other gifted children on special projects and trips. In general, schools are not the sole source, or even the primary source, of enrichment. Parents typically provide their gifted children with responsive and stimulating environments (Feldman, 1986).

Acceleration allows intellectually gifted children to skip grades and enter one that is consistent with their mental age or to enroll in advanced courses. For example, the Study of Mathematically Precocious Youth and the Center for Talented Youth provide intensive summer programs where a one-year curriculum is covered in three weeks; through these programs, precocious youth complete college courses and often attain early enrollment to college. A common fear that skipping grades places children at a social disadvantage because they are not with same-age peers appears to be unfounded. Gifted children who are accelerated show equal social competence and greater academic achievement when compared to gifted children who have not been accelerated (Brody & Benbow, 1987).

As children progress in school, the number of girls receiving enriched or accelerated education decreases. Gifted programs for kindergarten through third-grade students contain approximately equal numbers of girls and boys. However, girls make up less than 30% of the population in programs for gifted junior high and high school students. In addition, fewer girls than boys are identified as mathematically gifted in the Johns Hopkins' talent searches. By junior high age, high-ability girls have lower career goals and self-confidence than high-ability boys, respond less favorably to invitations to enter gifted programs, and are more likely to disguise their abilities in order to be socially accepted (Winner, 1996). The reasons for these gender differences are not yet clear.

To summarize, giftedness is invented by members of a society rather than discovered by them, and its conceptualization can change over time and place. Understanding a society's view of giftedness and making this view explicit means that valuable talents can be fostered rather than wasted.

Conceptions of giftedness are moving away from an unidimensional, IQ-based definition, toward a broader, multidimensional view. In theory and in practice, it is starting to be acknowledged that there are numerous ways to be gifted; performing well on intelligence tests is only one of these ways. Giftedness is now viewed as largely domain specific, rather than as a purely general characteristic. Current theories focus on internal traits, mental processes, and environmental influences that characterize giftedness across the life span. Even though the criteria for giftedness change from childhood to adulthood, many of the underlying skills and mental processes remain the same. Adult giftedness requires more domain-specific knowledge and creative contributions than does childhood giftedness. However, intrinsic motivation, absorption in a particular area, and creative approaches to problem solving in childhood are good predictors of giftedness in adulthood.

Identification and education of gifted children are starting to reflect the current theories. Although IQs are still the most common method of selecting children for special programs, theory-based forms of identification are now being used by some school systems. Gifted individuals are a valuable resource for a society. New theories, assessment devices, and interventions are being developed and implemented in an attempt to nurture the varied gifts of these individuals.

[See also Prodigies; and Talent.]

Bibliography

Brody, L. E., & Benbow, C. P. (1987). Accelerative strategies: How effective are they? *Gifted Child Quarterly, 3*, 105–110.

Csikszentmihalyi, M. (1996). *Creativity*. New York: HarperCollins.

Csikszentmihalyi, M., Rathunde, K., & Whalen, S. (1993). *Talented teenagers: The roots of success and failure*. New York: Cambridge University Press.

Davidson, J. E. (1986). The role of insight in giftedness. In R. J. Sternberg & J. E. Davidson (Eds.), *Conceptions of giftedness* (pp. 201–222). New York: Cambridge University Press.

Davidson, J. E., & Sternberg, R. J. (1984). The role of insight in intellectual giftedness. *Gifted Child Quarterly, 28*, 58–64.

Feldman, D. (1986). *Nature's gambit: Child prodigies and the development of human potential*. New York: Basic Books.

Gardner, H. (1993a). *Frames of mind: The theory of multiple intelligences*. (10th anniversary ed.). New York: Basic Books. (Original work published 1983)

Gardner, H. (1993b). *Multiple intelligences: The theory in practice*. New York: Basic Books.

Horowitz, F. D., & O'Brien, M. (1986). Gifted and talented children: State of knowledge and directions for research. *American Psychologist, 41*, 1147–1152.

Jackson, E. N., & Butterfield, E. C. (1986). A conception of giftedness designed to promote research. In R. J. Sternberg & J. E. Davidson (Eds.), *Conceptions of giftedness* (pp. 151–181). New York: Cambridge University Press.

Renzulli, J. S. (1986). The three-ring conception of giftedness: A developmental model for creative productivity. In R. J. Sternberg & J. E. Davidson (Eds.), *Conceptions of giftedness* (pp. 53–92). New York: Cambridge University Press.

Renzulli, J. S., & Smith, L. H. (1981). The Early Childhood Checklist. In J. S. Renzulli, S. M. Reis, & L. H. Smith (Eds.), *The revolving door identification model* (p. 181). Mansfield Center, CT: Creative Learning Press.

Siegler, R. S., & Kotovsky, K. (1986). Two levels of giftedness: Shall ever the twain meet? In R. J. Sternberg & J. E. Davidson (Eds.), *Conceptions of giftedness* (pp. 417–435). New York: Cambridge University Press.

Sternberg, R. J. (1986). A triarchic theory of intellectual giftedness. In R. J. Sternberg & J. E. Davidson (Eds.), *Conceptions of giftedness* (pp. 223–247). New York: Cambridge University Press.

Sternberg, R. J., Ferrari, M., Clinkenbeard, P. R., & Grigorenko, E. L. (1996). Identification, instruction, and assessment of gifted children: A construct validation of a triarchic model. *Gifted Child Quarterly, 40*(3), 129–137.

Terman, L. M. (1925). *Genetic studies of genius: Vol. 1. Mental and physical traits of a thousand gifted children*. Stanford, CA: Stanford University Press.

Terman, L. M. & Oden, M. H. (1959). *Genetic studies of genius: Vol. 5. The gifted group at mid-life: Thirty-five years' follow-up of the superior child*. Stanford, CA: Stanford University Press.

Walters, J., & Gardner, H. (1986). The crystallizing experience: Discovering an intellectual gift. In R. J. Sternberg & J. E. Davidson (Eds.), *Conceptions of giftedness* (pp. 306–331). New York: Cambridge University Press.

Winner, E. (1996). *Gifted children*. New York: Basic Books.

Janet E. Davidson

GILBRETH, LILLIAN (1878–1972), American psychologist. Lillian Evelyn Moller Gilbreth was born in Oakland, California, one of ten children of William Moller, a successful businessman, and Annie Delger Moller, a typical nineteenth-century housewife and mother. The Moller family and home were the center of life for every family member. The parents taught their children that girls should accept responsibilities for home and family, and would not attend college. Consequently, Gilbreth studied music, read literature, and wrote poetry, rather than preparing for college.

Despite initial opposition from her father, Gilbreth enrolled in college classes and completed her bachelor's degree in 1900 at the University of California in Berkeley where she was the first female commencement speaker. In her speech, "Life—A Means or an End," Gilbreth presented her view of life and stated that individuals should live every day for the day and not as a preparation for the future. After completing a master's degree in literature in 1902 at the University of California, Berkeley, Gilbreth enrolled in the doctoral program in English there, with a minor in psychology.

In 1904, she married Frank Bunker Gilbreth, a contracting engineer and pioneer of motion and time studies. Shortly thereafter, Gilbreth changed her major to psychology because she and her husband recognized the value of psychological theory for their work. She submitted a doctoral dissertation to the University of California, Berkeley, which was accepted; however, the doctorate was not conferred because the requirement of a final year in residence was not fulfilled by Gilbreth (she refused to leave her family responsibilities). Her dissertation was published as a book (*Psychology of Management*, New York, 1914), which has been considered one of the most influential textbooks on industrial relations. She asserted that managers need to know psychology so they can understand their workers, and she explained how psychological theories are essential for effective management.

While working as an apprentice and partner in her husband's construction and engineering business, Gilbreth noted that engineers were addressing their technical problems scientifically, but appeared to be unaware of what psychology had to offer as a science. She became intrigued with applying psychology, and enrolled in a new doctoral program at Brown University to study applied psychology. She was awarded a doctorate in psychology in 1915. Gilbreth's dissertation was entitled "The Elimination of Waste" and it was the application of scientific management principles and psychology to the work of classroom teachers. She may have been the first recipient of a Ph.D. in industrial psychology.

The Gilbreths established themselves worldwide as management experts. They used time and motion studies to identify the best way for completing a job so worker efficiency could be enhanced and productivity improved. Their methods were similar to Frederick Taylor's scientific management system; however, they believed Taylor neglected attention to individual rights and needs in the work setting. Gilbreth wanted to know if the best and most efficient motions provided the happiest results for the workers, and would ask them how they felt about their tasks. Jobs would then be designed to fit the needs of the worker, a new philosophy for the emerging discipline of industrial psychology [now known as industrial and organizational (I/O) psychology].

After her husband died in 1924, Gilbreth consulted and researched applications of psychology for the next 45 years. Her work was responsive to many issues, and was grounded by an underlying theme: Whenever possible, a human component must be included. Workers' physical and mental capacities should be considered, as well as their perceptions when identifying ways to improve performance. Gilbreth researched in both applied settings and laboratories, and examined several areas of industrial psychology including selection criteria and methods, acquisition of skills, work methods, job design, job satisfaction, hiring individuals with disabilities, and nonfinancial incentives. In her article entitled "The Present State of Industrial Psychology" (*Mechanical Engineering*, 1925), Gilbreth offered many current applications of I/O psychology such as biodata, tests, promotions, job evaluations, training, and group cooperation.

Gilbreth also expanded applications of psychology to problems outside traditional industrial settings. She focused on challenges faced by women, including managing homes, raising families, and working in jobs outside the home. She was hired by the General Electric Company and other appliance manufacturing companies to assist in redesigning kitchen and household appliances to match the needs of homemakers and to maximize efficiency and effectiveness. Two of her most notable inventions were the shelves inside refrigerator doors and the foot-pedal trash can.

In addition to consulting and researching, Gilbreth taught college and university courses at Bryn Mawr, Newark College of Engineering (Chair, Department of Personnel Relations), and Rutgers. In 1935, she was appointed professor of management at Purdue University, the first woman to receive such an appointment. She was appointed resident lecturer at MIT in 1964 at 86 years of age.

Gilbreth's contributions to engineering, management, and psychology brought her many honors. She was included in *American Men of Science*, *Who's Who in American Women*, and *Notable American Women: The Modern Period*. She became a Fellow of the American Psychological Association in 1921. She has been called the "mother of scientific management," the "first lady of management," and the "mother of industrial psychology." She served on a number of committees appointed by Presidents Hoover, Roosevelt, Truman, Eisenhower, Kennedy, and Johnson. She received over 20 honorary degrees and numerous awards, primarily in areas of engineering and management. In 1984, a commemorative postage stamp was issued in her honor, the only psychologist to receive this honor.

Gilbreth was a pioneer in many respects. Because of her strong sympathy and empathy for individuals, she realized the need to compensate for Taylor's omission of human aspects. She generated innovative applications of psychology to work, and generalized her ideas and methods to societal problems. Gilbreth managed a consulting business from her home, an atypical work style for women, and in later years attributed her achievements to having a supportive spouse and family (of 12 children). Gilbreth exemplified the modern I/O psychologist by blending successfully research, practice, service, and a personal life.

[*See also* Industrial and Organizational Psychology.]

Bibliography

Gilbreth, F., Jr. (1970). *Time out for happiness*. New York: Crowell.

Gilbreth, F., Jr., & Carey, E. G. (1949). *Cheaper by the dozen*. New York: Bantam.

Gilbreth, F., Jr., & Carey, E. G. (1950). *Belles on their toes*. New York: Bantam.

Gotcher, J. M. (1992). Assisting the handicapped: The pioneering efforts of Frank and Lillian Gilbreth. *Journal of Management, 18*, 5–13.

Kelly, R. M., & Kelly, V. P. (1990). Lillian Moller Gilbreth. In A. N. O'Connell & N. F. Russo (Eds.), *Women in psychology: A bio-bibliographic sourcebook* (pp. 117–124). New York: Greenwood Press.

Perloff, R., & Naman, J. L. (1996). Lillian Gilbreth: Tireless advocate for a general psychology. In G. A. Kimble, C. A. Boneau, & M. Wertheimer (Eds.), *Portraits of pioneers in psychology* (Vol. 2, pp. 106–116). Washington, DC: American Psychological Association.

Spriegel, W. R., & Myers, C. E. (1953). *The writings of the Gilbreths*. Homewood, IL: Irwin.

Stevens, G., & Gardner, S. (1982). *The women of psychology. Vol. 1: Pioneers and innovators*. Cambridge, MA: Schenkman.

Yost, E. (1943). *American women of science*. New York: Stokes.

Yost, E. (1949). *Frank and Lillian Gilbreth: Partners for life*. New Brunswick, NJ: Rutgers University Press.

Laura L. Koppes

GINER DE LOS RÍOS, FRANCISCO (1839–1915), Spanish jurist and pedagogue. Giner was professor of philosophy of law at the University of Madrid. He belonged to a group of progressive intellectuals deeply influenced by the ideas of the German idealist philosopher K.C.F. Krause (1781–1832). The leading purpose of the group was to achieve a moral and intellectual renewal of Spanish society. In 1875, Krausist professors protested against a governmental measure restricting the freedom of science and conscience, which was one of their most fundamental tenets. As a result, most of them were dismissed from office, including Giner, who was imprisoned.

Giner then founded a private educational center where, free from governmental constraints, new men and women could be trained with a Europeanizing aim. Thus, the Free Institution of Education came into existence in 1876 and soon succeeded in transforming the Spanish cultural scene. Inspired by educational principles similar to those guiding the New School move-ment, the Free Institution had an open attitude toward modern science that favored the reception of the new scientific psychology in Spain.

After writing his 1869/1922 paper on comparative psychology, in which he discussed the issue of continuity between animals and humans, Giner remained attentive to contemporary psychological and psychiatric research, mainly in regard to child and educational problems. In 1874 he published a short systematic treatise of Krausist psychology, his *Brief Lessons on Psychology*, which was soon used as a textbook in secondary education.

In a second edition of this book (1877), the original Krausist outlook was completed with references to recent psychophysical and psychophysiological findings. Relevant authors, such as Wundt, Fechner, Lotze, Helmholtz, and Spencer, were cited and issues such as the speed of nervous transmission, brain localization, and the Weber–Fechner law were introduced. Thus, in spite of Giner's generally idealistic, spiritualistic approach, *Brief Lessons* was of great significance, because it represented a first step toward a more positivistic, scientific outlook that clearly indicated a path to follow.

Giner's wide intellectual influence determined the new course taken by Spanish psychology. The Free Institution of Education soon became the main center for the reception and dissemination of modern psychological ideas in Spain. A journal was published, and such eminent psychologists as Binet, Baldwin, Claparède, Dewey, William James, and Stanley Hall became familiar to readers. Also, many of the most significant contributors to subsequent Spanish psychology (Barnés, Besteiro, Lafora, Navarro, Simarro, and Viqueira, to name a few) were students of Giner or linked to the Free Institution in other ways. Through the contributions and translations made by these and other "institutionists," the works of Binet, Baldwin, Claparède, James, Münsterberg, Piaget, Preyer, Ribot, and many other modern psychologists, mostly of a functionalistic bent, succeeded in reaching a wide Spanish audience.

Thus, Giner's original approach to the findings of the "new psychology" initiated a period of continuous psychological development in Spain that only the outbreak of the Civil War in 1936 was able to interrupt.

Bibliography

Works by Giner de los Ríos

Giner de los Ríos, F. (1874). *Lecciones sumarias de psicología* [Brief lessons on psychology]. Madrid: Noguera.

Giner de los Ríos, F. (1877). *Lecciones sumarias de psicología* [Brief lessons on psychology] (2nd ed., rev.). Madrid: Alaria.

Giner de los Ríos, F. (1916–1936). *Obras completas* [Complete works] (Vols. 1–20). Madrid: La Lectura/Espasa-Calpe.

Giner de los Ríos, F. (1922). Psicología comparada. El alma de los animales [Comparative psychology. Animals' souls]. In F. Giner de los Ríos (Ed.), *Obras completas* (Vol. 3, pp. 31–60). Madrid: La Lectura. (Original work published 1869.) Giner's works are long out of print and not readily available, but may be accessible in libraries specializing in nineteenth- and early twentieth-century Spanish history and culture.

Works about Giner de los Ríos

Carpintero, H. (1982). The introduction of scientific psychology in Spain. In W. Woodward & M. G. Ash (Eds.), *The problematic science: Psychology in nineteenth-century thought* (pp. 255–275). New York: Praeger. A short overview, in English, of the origins of modern psychology in Spain.

Carpintero, H. (1994). *Historia de la psicología en España* [History of psychology in Spain]. Madrid: Eudema. The most complete overall view of Spanish psychology history.

Jiménez-Landi, A. (1996). *La Institución Libre de Enseñanza* [The Free Institution of Education] (Vols. 1–4). Madrid: Editorial Complutense. The most comprehensive treatment of both Giner's life and the history of the Free Institution of Education.

Lafuente, E. (1996). El pensamiento psicológico de Francisco Giner de los Ríos [The psychological ideas of Francisco Giner de los Ríos]. In M. Saiz & D. Saiz (Eds.), *Personajes para una historia de la psicología en España* (pp. 167–183). Madrid: Pirámide. Focuses on Giner's contribution to psychology and includes an annotated bibliography.

Lafuente, E., & Carpintero, H. (1996). *Francisco Giner de los Ríos y la Institución Libre de Enseñanza en la psicología española* [Francisco Giner de los Ríos and the Free Institution of Education in Spanish psychology]. Madrid: UNED. A videotaped account of Giner's life and times, with particular emphasis on his psychological significance; includes a booklet with an annotated bibliography.

Enrique Lafuente

GOALS. The goal concept is commonly defined by the two related concepts of need and incentive. An animal's need (e.g., hunger) points to a respective incentive (i.e., food), and it is the animal's efforts to approach the incentive that qualify as goal pursuit. Animal psychologists focus on the attributes of goal pursuit as observed from the outside (e.g., persistence) and thus on the objective goal as defined by the researcher (i.e., the incentive the researcher chooses as a reference point for describing observed behavior). Psychologists interested in human goal pursuit analyze the subjective goal or intention of the individual. A person's need for approval, for instance, includes various classes of incentives (e.g., being popular with one's friends), and it is the person's

intention to attain these incentives that is analyzed as the goal. The intention to attain the incentives is understood as the higher-order goal that may be served by a multitude of lower-order goals focusing on specific behaviors (e.g., giving a party).

The analysis of human goal pursuit has, first and foremost, addressed the question of what determines goal attainment. There are two answers to this question. The first answer is provided by "content theories of goal pursuit." These theories explain differences in goal attainment in terms of what the specified goal entails. Various relevant structural features of goal content have been identified. Challenging, specific goals lead to better performances than challenging, vague goals (so-called do-your-best goals), and this is true whether goals are self-set or assigned. What matters is that people feel committed to the goal in question. The goal specificity effect is based on feedback and self-monitoring advantages, as is the goal proximity effect (i.e., proximal goals lead to better performances than distal goals). As proximal goals relate to what is to be done in the present and the near future, people find it easier to monitor their progress compared to progress toward distal goals. The latter specify intended behaviors and desired outcomes too far removed in time to monitor one's progress effectively and to provide small successes that promote self-efficacy and interest.

But thematic features of goal content are also relevant. Goals that serve the needs of autonomy, competence, and social integration foster goal attainment via intrinsic motivation, whereas goals that serve the feeling of obligation hamper goal attainment. Similar performance benefits have been observed for mastery goals (i.e., learning how to perform a given task) and for performance goals (i.e., finding out through task performance how capable one is). Mastery goals allow the individual to cope more effectively with failure. Performance goals are more effective when they are framed as approach goals (i.e., I intend to achieve good grades) rather than as avoidance goals (i.e., I intend to avoid bad grades).

"Self-regulation theories of goal pursuit" provide a different answer to the question of what determines goal attainment. They explain differences in goal attainment in terms of how effectively people solve the problems associated with goal implementation. These problems pertain to initiating goal-directed actions and bringing them to a successful conclusion. For example, it is observed that planning the implementation of a goal creates a cognitive orientation (implemental mind set) that facilitates the initiation of goal-directed actions. Moreover, forming implementation intentions that link a good opportunity to act to a special goal-directed behavior furthers the initiation of this behavior in the critical situation (i.e., action initiation becomes immediate and efficient and does not need a conscious intent). To prevent the derailing of an ongoing goal pursuit, people may use further action control strategies (e.g., emotion control, environmental control) geared toward removing distractions. If actual failure occurs, the experienced goal discrepancy is reduced by goal-directed behaviors when the perceived feasibility of goal attainment is high and goal commitment is strong. The resumption of a disrupted goal pursuit also depends on the person's goal commitment. However, people may take precautionary measures to avoid the disruption of goal pursuits through competing pursuits by using various goal negotiation strategies (e.g., creative integration of two different goal pursuits).

Whereas in social, organizational, industrial, and educational psychology goal pursuit is analyzed primarily in terms of effective goal attainment, personality psychologists focus on the side effects of goal pursuit in terms of subjective well-being and personality development. Commitment to personal goals (either communal or agentic) and the perceived attainability of these goals jointly predict a person's experience of well-being; this effect is mediated by the perceived progress in goal achievement. However, when the selected personal goal is poorly matched with the person's chronic needs (e.g., a communal goal with a strong power need), subjective well-being is impaired. Research on social cognition has also addressed the side effects of goal pursuit. For example, it is observed that interpersonal goals (e.g., to collaborate on solving a given problem) affect the processing of information about others (i.e., produce more accuracy-driven, less stereotypic impression formation).

Recently, the issues of goal setting and goal disengagement have received a more systematic analysis. The distal factors of age and personality attributes influence the content of the goals people set for themselves or disengage from. For instance, older people set health and leisure activity goals and disengage from occupational and material goals held in middle adulthood. In addition, fear of failure motivates individuals to set performance goals and give up mastery goals, whereas the reverse is true for success-motivated individuals. The proximal psychological processes that account for goal setting and goal disengagement, however, are based on mentally contrasting the desired outcomes with those aspects of the present status quo that impede the realization of the desired future. This creates a readiness to act, which in turn triggers feasibility-related reflections. If the perceived feasibility is high, the desired future becomes a goal that is associated with a strong commitment; if the perceived feasibility is low, the person's commitment becomes weakened.

[See also Achievement Motivation; and Motivation.]

Bibliography

Gollwitzer, P. M., & Bargh, J. A. (1996). *The psychology of action: Linking cognition and motivation to behavior.* New York: Guilford Press. Documents the importance of the goal concept in present theories of the control of action.

Gollwitzer, P. M., & Moskowitz, G. B. (1996). Goal effects on action and cognition. In E. T. Higgins & A. W. Kruglanksi (Eds.), *Social psychology: Handbook of basic principles* (pp. 361–399). New York: Guilford Press. Presents a comparative analysis of modern goal theories.

Karoly, P. (1993). Mechanisms of self-regulation: A systems view. *Annual Review of Psychology, 44,* 23–52. Suggests a cybernetic, control-theoretical approach.

Locke, E. A., & Latham, G. P. (1990). *A theory of goal setting and task performance.* Englewood Cliffs, NJ: Prentice Hall. Discusses moderators and mediators of goal effects and applies goal theory to issues of work motivation.

Maehr, M., & Pintrich, P. (Eds.). (1991). *Advances in motivation and achievement* (Vol. 7). Greenwich, CT: JAI Press. Documents the importance of the goal concept in educational environments.

Martin, L. L., & Tesser, A. (1996). *Striving and feeling. Interactions among goals, affect, and self-regulation.* Mahwah, NJ: Erlbaum.

Pervin, L. A. (1989). *Goal concepts in personality and social psychology.* Hillsdale, NJ: Erlbaum.

Peter M. Gollwitzer

GOD CONCEPTS. For believers, the concept of God probably constitutes the most central aspect of their religious system. Unless there is a need for such awareness, these images are usually covert and function implicitly. Conscious attributions to the qualities of a deity constitute the essence of this approach. Following the psychoanalytic object relations tradition, Ana-Maria Rizzuto, in her seminal work, *The Birth of the Living God: A Psychoanalytic Study* (Chicago, 1979), employs the notion of God representation, with unconscious cognitive preconceptual and nonlinguistic contents. Though there is overlap between attributional and representational perspectives, the correspondence between the two has yet to be exactingly researched.

Given the complexity of God images, factor analysis has usually been employed to dimensionalize these expressions. One thus reads of traditional Christian, transcendent-imminent, imminent-companionable, deistic, kind, wrathful, omni (-potent, -present, -scient), kingly, personal-benevolent, unconventional, punitive, creator, healer, friend, redeemer, father, and lover, among other possibilities. Most such systems are atheoretic and suffer from considerable undirected variation among the items utilized in factor studies. Further, curbs are rarely placed on the nature of the samples examined. A strong need exists for theory to inform this approach.

The dominant perspective regarding views of God was advanced by Freud in his classic *The Future of an Illusion The Standard Edition of the Collected Works of Sigmund Freud* (Vol. 21, London, 1927). He treated the idea of deity as a projection of the father image. B. Biet-Hallahmi and M. Argyle provided some support for this view (God as a father-projection: The theory and the evidence, *British Journal of Medical Psychology*, 1975, 48, 71–75); however, research has also found ties to perceptions of one's mother, preferred parent, an amalgam of fantasized and reality-based images of both parents, and self-perceptions. Further, as noted, Rizzuto and others stress unconscious determinants of God representation in their object relations approach as opposed to empirical attributional methods. Both orientations find expression in this work, but to date, little or no effort has been directed toward the resolution of variant views and findings.

Though most of this work has been conducted with adults, the situation is no less complex when dealing with children and adolescents. Empirical research designed to assess God representational views is primarily developmental and relies largely on phenomenological methods.

Current theories from mainstream psychology have also entered this realm. Dominating this work are attachment theory and attribution theory for which rather sophisticated frameworks have been proposed. Both have shown promise.

Probably the richest work on God concepts has been conducted in the developmental sphere. European ideas and studies have dominated this literature. The theoretical and methodological approach of Piaget has usually guided these efforts in both Europe and America. Most impressive is the massive research of Tamminen which he reported in his rather definitive *Religious Development in Childhood and Youth* (Helsinki, 1991). He studied some thousands of Finnish children, adolescents, and their parents with replications over a twelve-year period. Employing a broad spectrum of methods to obtain data, Tamminen observed that "different measures bring out different aspects of" the God concept (p. 192). This finding has not gained the appreciation it merits. He also found the main characterization of deity to be "trustworthy, forgiving, loving and helping" (p. 193).

Americans such as Fowler, in his highly regarded *Stages of Faith: The Psychology of Human Development and the Quest for Meaning* (New York, 1981), have made significant theoretical and research contributions to our understanding of God cognitions. As a rule, these variants on Piagetian themes picture the development of God concepts along dimensions such as concrete to abstract, undifferentiated to differentiated, preoperational to operational, anthropomorphic to nonhuman abstractions. Others have viewed development as mul-

tifaceted, and examined God images verbally, intellectually, emotionally, morally, and aesthetically. Fowler's theory involves six stages and seven aspects. The former are essentially Piagetian, ranging from an initial preoperational stage to one of formal operations. His aspects include form of logic, perspective taking, moral judgment, social awareness, locus of authority, world coherence, and symbolic function. Critiques and extensions of his system have, however, been made relative to God concepts. This is an instance of fine thinking buttressed by often subjective methods. The need for developing more rigorous and demanding objective methodology is evident. With these perspectives in mind, Helmut Reich (1993) has offered a life-span unified theory of religious development that can serve as a research guide.

God concepts have further been studied in relation to personality, adjustment, coping behavior, social factors, and influences and other religious expressions. Much of this work has primarily concerned self-concept and locus of control. Apparently, images of self and deity relate positively. With regard to God images and locus of control, though findings have not been consistent, a sense of God control is suggestive of effective coping behavior.

In terms of where God concepts fit in one's religious system, patterns of God images have been associated with religious commitment and forms of prayer. Favorable God images relate broadly to ideas of prayer's efficacy and virtually all forms of prayer. Threatening and punitive God attributions tie similarly, but less strongly to most kinds of prayer, though ties with confession and petition and ritualistic prayer forms dominate. Interestingly, prayers of thanksgiving and meditation are unrelated to threatening God concepts but do associate with positive images.

As the above indicates, God concepts appear to be a fruitful theoretical and research avenue for studying the integration of religion with other aspects of life.

Bibliography

Goldman, R. (1964). *Religious thinking from childhood to adolescence*. London: Routledge & Kegan Paul. This classic investigation not only covers God concepts but a broad range of religious content, and seems to have served as a model for many succeeding studies of children and youth.

Hood, R. W. Jr., Spilka, B., Hunsberger, B., & Gorsuch, R. L. (1996). *The psychology of religion: An empirical approach*. New York: Guilford Press. Clearly the definitive work on empirical research in the psychology of religion, this scientifically demanding volume also stresses theoretical frameworks that eventuate in research.

Hyde, K. E. (1990). *Religion in childhood and adolescence*. Birmingham, AL: Religious Education Press. An exhaustive and exacting overview of the developmental literature on the role of religion in early life.

Kirkpatrick, L. A. (1992). An attachment-theory approach to the psychology of religion. *International Journal for the Psychology of Religion, 2,* 3–28. The initial groundbreaking theoretical entré to the concept of attachment and how it can be researched in the psychology of religion.

Koenig, H. G. (1994). *Aging and God: Spiritual pathways to mental health in mid-life and later years.* New York: Haworth. Both developmental and clinical in orientation, this constructive and critical work extends our understanding of the place of religion in adult life.

Pargament, K. I. (1997). *The psychology of religion and coping.* New York: Guilford Press. A rigorous theoretically and empirically oriented overview of the role religion plays in coping with life and its adversities. A truly definitive work.

Reich, K. H. (1993). Integrating different theories: The case of religious development. *Journal of Empirical Theology, 6,* 39–49. A necessary integrative effort to unite the best in a variety of theoretical perspectives that deals with religion within a life-span perspective. It appears to have much research potential.

Spilka, B., Shaver, P., & Kirkpatrick, L. A. (1985). A general attribution theory for the psychology of religion. *Journal for the Scientific Study of Religion, 24,* 1–20. Broadening the concept of attribution from simply defining emotional states, this paper offers a wide-ranging theoretical framework that has proved fruitful in both psychological research and applied religious and pastoral work.

Vergote, A., & Tamayo, A. (1980). *The parental figures and the representation of God.* The Hague: Mouton. This is a compilation of a large number of psychological and cross-cultural studies undertaken by the authors on the correspondence of God and parental images.

Wulff, D. (1997). *Psychology of religion: Classic and contemporary views* (2nd ed.). New York: Wiley. An impressively written, scholarly overview of the historical and contemporary psychology of religion. It is extremely broad in its coverage of research, theory, and cross-cultural work.

Bernard Spilka

GODDARD, HENRY HERBERT (1866–1957), American psychologist, was the first American intelligence tester. His writings focused largely on what was then called "feeblemindedness" and later called mental retardation. Although most of Goddard's ideas would be rejected by later generations of psychologists, physicians, geneticists, and educators, they proved extremely influential in the early decades of the twentieth century.

Goddard was born in East Vassalboro, Maine, the fifth (and third surviving) child of Henry Clay and Sarah Goddard. His father, a farmer, died when he was 7. His mother became a traveling Quaker missionary, and Goddard spent much of his boyhood in Quaker boarding schools. After graduating from Haverford College in 1887, he taught briefly at the University of Southern California and also coached this school's first football team. In 1889, he earned a master's degree in mathematics from Haverford. That same year he married Emma Robbins, and they spent the next 7 years teaching together in small Quaker academies.

Goddard's career in psychology began in 1896, when he entered Clark University to study with G. Stanley Hall. His 1899 dissertation, "The Effects of Mind on Body as Evidenced in Faith Cures," reflected both his religious upbringing and his new faith in science, for it offered psychological explanations for popular religious beliefs. After graduating, Goddard taught psychology and pedagogy at the State Normal School in West Chester, Pennsylvania, where he became very active in the child study movement. Through these activities he met Edward Johnstone, superintendent of a school for "feebleminded" children in Vineland, New Jersey. In 1902, Johnstone, Goddard, and educator Earl Barnes founded Vineland's "Feebleminded Club," a semiannual gathering of educators, physicians, scientists, and others interested in questions relating to institutional medicine and special education. In 1906 Johnstone hired Goddard to open a psychological laboratory on the grounds of his school to see what the "new psychology" could contribute to the study of "feeble minds."

Seeking new ideas on how psychologists might help such children, in 1908 Goddard toured Europe, where he learned of the "intelligence" tests developed in 1905 by French psychologist Alfred Binet. Goddard tried out Binet's tests in his own institution and found them useful. By 1910, he had convinced American institutional physicians to use Binet's tests to diagnose and classify different degrees of mental deficiency. Following his recommendations, these doctors transformed their medical vocabulary to reflect Binet's ideas. Thus an "idiot" was redefined as an individual who tested to a mental age below 3 on Binet's intelligence scale and an "imbecile" as one testing between 3 and 7. Since there was no commonly accepted medical term for the highest group, persons testing to a mental age of between 8 and 12, Goddard coined a new word from a Greek root that as yet had no English connotation: "moron."

Goddard also used intelligence testing in other ways. In 1910, he became the first psychologist to try out Binet's tests in a public school system and advocated their use for determining placement in special classes. In 1914, he introduced these tests into American courts to argue against the death penalty for defendants he considered feebleminded. He also tried the tests at Ellis Island to see if they could be used to diagnose feebleminded immigrants. In 1917, Goddard was one of seven American psychologists who prepared the controversial World War I army intelligence tests.

During the same years, Goddard also became interested in determining the causes of mental deficiency. In 1909, he met Charles Davenport, leader of the American eugenics movement. Working with this biologist, Goddard began to conceptualize low intelligence as a single recessive trait inherited according to Mendel's laws and impervious to all environmental improvements. Such a finding had moral as well as medical significance, Goddard insisted, for he saw feebleminded persons as particularly prone to social delinquency or economic dependency. The only way to stop such individuals from passing on their feeble inheritance to future generations, Goddard argued, was through institutionalization or sterilization.

Goddard explained these ideas in his first and most famous book, *The Kallikak Family* (New York, 1912), which traced the relatives of an institutionalized woman pseudonymously called "Deborah Kallikak." According to Goddard, this family had two distinct branches: one descended from a Revolutionary War soldier and his wife, which contained only good citizens, and one started by this same soldier and "a feebleminded tavern girl," and which included paupers, prostitutes, criminals, and feebleminded persons (such as Deborah). Goddard invented this family's pseudonym to contrast good and bad inheritance, for "Kallikak" combined the Greek roots for beautiful (*kallos*) and bad (*kakos*). By the decade's end, Goddard had also written *Feeble-Mindedness: Its Causes and Consequences, School Training of Defective Children, The Criminal Imbecile, Psychology of the Normal and Subnormal*, and *Human Efficiency and Levels of Intelligence*. In these works, he linked low intelligence to nearly every social problem of the day, including crime, poverty, prostitution, truancy, alcoholism, and unemployment.

In 1918, Goddard left Vineland to direct the Ohio Bureau of Juvenile Research. In 1922, he became professor of abnormal and clinical psychology at Ohio State University. During the 1920s, Goddard wrote monographs on juvenile delinquency, multiple personality disorders, and education for the gifted; like many scientists during this decade, he gradually moved away from theories stressing heredity and increasingly emphasized education. In 1927, Goddard conceded that many of his conclusions concerning feeblemindedness had been in error. Still, his earlier writings continued to be used by far more ardent eugenicists promoting their own theories about the meaning of good and bad inheritance.

As the century progressed, Goddard's ideas were increasingly challenged by numerous critics; these included geneticists rejecting eugenic doctrines, psychol-

ogists questioning hereditarian interpretations of intelligence testing, physicians advocating deinstitutionalization, and educators promoting mainstreaming. In recent decades, his writings have most often been cited to illustrate how social biases can distort supposedly objective science. Even so, this psychologist left a complex and multifaceted legacy, particularly in promoting the study of child development, mental retardation, and special education, and in institutionalizing psychological testing within American hospitals, courtrooms, and classrooms.

Bibliography

Fancher, R. R. (1985) *The intelligence men: Makers of the IQ controversy*. New York: Norton. Summarizes the lives and ideas of major contributors to the heredity-environment controversy, including Goddard.

Gelb, S. A. (1986). Henry H. Goddard and the immigrants, 1910–1917: The studies and their social context. *Journal of the History of the Behavioral Sciences, 22,* 324–332. A balanced assessment of Goddard's efforts to test the minds of Ellis Island immigrants.

Gould, S. J. (1981). *The mismeasure of man*. New York: Norton. A detailed and sharp critique of biased techniques frequently used by scientists attempting to measure human differences; includes analyses of Goddard's Kallikak study and the World War I army tests.

Haller, M. H. (1963). *Eugenics: Hereditarian attitudes in American thought*. New Brunswick, NJ: Rutgers University Press. A detailed history of the rise and demise of the American eugenics movement.

Kevles, D. J. (1985). *In the name of eugenics: Genetics and the uses of human heredity*. New York: Knopf. A comparative study of the eugenics movements in England and the United States.

Paul, D. B. (1995). *Controlling human heredity: 1865 to the present*. Atlantic Highlands, NJ: Humanities Press. An overview of the broad diversity of eugenic ideas found around the world, including in the United States, England, Germany, and Scandinavia.

Sarason, S. B., & Doris, J. (1979). *Educational handicap, public policy, and social history: A broadened perspective on mental retardation*. New York: Free Press. Analyzes the history of ideas concerning mental retardation and special education, including those found in Goddard's Kallikak study.

Sokal, M. M. (1987). *Psychological testing and American society, 1890–1930*. New Brunswick, NJ: Rutgers University Press. Case studies focusing on the work of early American intelligence testers; two essays explore Goddard's research on mental retardation and juvenile delinquency.

Trent, J. W. (1994). *Inventing the feeble mind: A history of mental retardation in the United States*. Berkeley: University of California Press. Focuses on the shaping of social attitudes and policies toward mental retardation, including institutionalization and deinstitutionalization.

Zenderland, L. C. (1998). *Measuring minds: Henry Herbert Goddard and the origins of American intelligence testing.* New York: Cambridge University Press. A biography of Goddard and a history of the early American intelligence testing movement.

Leila Zenderland

GOLDSTEIN, KURT (1875–1965), German neurologist and philosopher. Goldstein was born in Katowice, Upper Silesia, the seventh of nine children in a prosperous Jewish family. Through his mother, he was related to Ernst Cassirer, a German philosopher, with whom he had close intellectual as well as family ties.

Goldstein's first loves were literature and philosophy. The rich vision of human potential that he found in them informed his life work in neurology and biology. Goldstein earned a medical degree under the supervision of Carl Wernicke at the University of Breslau (1903) with a dissertation on the posterior columns of the spinal cord. He became disillusioned with the therapeutic nihilism he found in his first full-time position at the Psychiatric Clinic of the University of Koningsberg and in 1914 accepted a position as chief assistant to Ludwig Edinger at the Neurological Institute of the University of Frankfurt.

In 1916, Goldstein organized the Institute for Research into the Consequences of Brain Injuries. Here Goldstein focused on diagnosis, treatment, and rehabilitation, with remarkable success in returning patients to a high level of functioning. Goldstein's research program at the Institute included cortical injuries, sensorimotor defects, perceptual disturbances, visual agnosia, cerebellar function, and aphasia. The last topic, aphasia, became a principal focus for many years. From this clinical variety, Goldstein developed his central insight: the behavior of organisms should be understood as a series of adaptations toward maximal self-actualization.

Goldstein argued that brain injury often led to the inability to form a gestalt; that is, the brain could no longer organize the world into coherent relationships. The lack of ability to see the whole was most evident in the patient's regression to concrete thinking and an inability to abstract and categorize. Goldstein viewed this regression as adaptive; it allowed the patient to avoid the anxiety caused by the loss of normal functioning. Goldstein interpreted his data as reflecting the organism's inherent drive to live as completely as possible.

In the 1920s, Goldstein's influence grew. He served as one of the founding editors of the Gestalt psychology journal *Psychologische Forschung*; he helped found the International Society for Psychotherapy; and he was instrumental in the attempts to establish a truly psychosomatic medicine in Germany. In the context of postwar doubt about the efficacy of positivistic science, Goldstein's work offered a holistic alternative that served to revitalize Weimar Germany.

Goldstein accepted a professorship of neurology at the University of Berlin in 1930. He was stripped of his position and forced into exile by the Nazis in 1933. Going first to Switzerland and then to Amsterdam, Goldstein finally settled in the United States in 1935. He further developed his organismic concepts and continued to ground his work in clinical practice, explaining aphasia, for example, as impairment in the ability to abstract.

Goldstein's influence was not confined to neurology. The "Third Wave" movement of humanistic psychology was indebted to Goldstein, exemplified by Abraham Maslow's concept of the self-actualizing person. A variety of figures in the arts and sciences, including W. H. Auden, René Dubos, Werner Heisenberg, Paul Tillich, and Loren Eiseley, acknowledged an intellectual debt to Goldstein. The development of psychosomatic medicine in the United States was also influenced by Goldstein's holism. Finally, his clinical work and his philosophy remain an inspiration to many who refuse to accept a strict reduction of human functioning to physicochemical processes.

Bibliography

Works by Goldstein

Bolles, M., & Goldstein, K. (1938). A study of the impairment of "abstract behavior" in schizophrenic patients. *Psychiatric Quarterly, 12,* 42–65.

Goldstein, K. (1934/1995). *The organism: A holistic approach to biology derived from pathological data in man.* New York: Zone Books. The first major publication of Goldstein's views in English. A dense, rich exploration of adaptation drawn from his clinical work and placed in the context of holistic biology.

Goldstein, K. (1940). *Human nature in the light of psychopathology.* Cambridge, MA: Harvard University Press.

Goldstein, K. (1948). *Language and language disturbance.* New York: Grune & Stratton. A synthesis of his work on aphasia and other language problems.

Goldstein, K. (1954). The concept of health, disease, and therapy: Basic ideas for an organismic psychotherapy. *American Journal of Psychotherapy, 8,* 745–764.

Goldstein, K., & Scheerer, M. (1941). Abstract and concrete behavior: An experimental study with special tests. *Psychological Monographs, 53* (2), 1–29.

Works about Goldstein

Goldstein, K. (1967). Autobiography. In E. G. Boring & G. Lindzey (Eds.), *A history of psychology in autobiography* (Vol. 5, pp. 145–166). New York: Appleton-Century-Crofts.

Harrington, A. (1996). *Reenchanted science: Holism in German culture from Wilhelm II to Hitler.* Princeton, NJ:

Princeton University Press. Currently, the best source for biographical information about Goldstein. Harrington intelligently analyzes his work and shows how it reflected and shaped its cultural context.

Simmel, M. L. (1966). Obituary. Kurt Goldstein, 1878–1965. *Journal of the History of the Behavioral Sciences, 2,* 185–191. A fine, sympathetic piece by someone who knew Goldstein well in the latter years of his life.

Wade E. Pickren

GOODENOUGH, FLORENCE LAURA (1886–1959), American psychologist. Goodenough received her doctorate from Stanford University under Lewis Terman in 1924 and spent her career as a developmental psychologist at the University of Minnesota. Shortly after arriving at Minnesota, she published her Draw-a-Man test, a scale for measuring the intelligence of children by analyzing their drawings. From its inception, the Draw-a-Man test enjoyed widespread popularity, which continued for many years. Dale Harris later developed an extensive revision of the test (1950). Known as the Goodenough-Harris Drawing Test, the revision featured new standardization as well as a companion Draw-a-Woman test and introduced a drawing quality score.

Following her work on the Draw-a-Man test, Goodenough turned her attention to developing more traditional verbal tests of intelligence for children. With the publication of the Minnesota Preschool Scale, she sought to extend the Stanford–Binet scale downward in age. It offered both language and nonlanguage scores and was designed to be compact and inexpensive. Although not as well known as her Draw-a-Man test, it remained in wide use into the 1940s.

In her early work on testing, Goodenough presented frequent references to methodological issues and limitations of research. In 1928, she developed what has become known as time sampling. In time sampling, a particular behavior such as thumb sucking is targeted for observation. Researchers agree on a uniform series of brief time intervals for observing subjects. By taking a series of observations, a record is produced showing the frequency of occurrence of the behavior under observation. The technique has been used widely since its initial publication.

Following her work on testing and methodological issues, Goodenough turned her attention to the social and emotional development of young children. In the 1920s, researchers had concentrated much effort on investigating John Watson's claim that the newborn is capable of three basic emotions—fear, rage, and love—and that more complex emotions are learned from these. Goodenough's *Anger in Young Children* (Minne-apolis, 1931) was an early attempt to extend work on the development of emotions beyond infancy. It remains one of the most systematic and detailed works concerning emotional development in childhood.

Goodenough's most noted controversy was over the effect of environmental input on IQ. When a group of University of Iowa researchers reported significant improvement in IQ scores of children who had been removed from an orphanage and placed in what was argued to be a more suitable environment, Goodenough defended the concept of fixed IQ in a series of rather heated criticisms (1939). By 1942, however, she revised her views, admitting that intellectual development was far more flexible than she had previously believed.

During her later years at Minnesota, Goodenough contracted an illness that led to an early retirement in 1947. In spite of nearly total blindness and partial loss of hearing, she, nevertheless, produced three of her best-known works, *Mental Testing* (New York, 1949), *Exceptional Children* (New York, 1956), and, with Leona Tyler, the final edition of her textbook *Developmental Psychology* (New York, 1959).

[*Many of the people mentioned in this article are the subjects of independent biographical entries.*]

Bibliography

Goodenough, F. L. (1928). Measuring behavior traits by means of repeated short samples. *Journal of Juvenile Research, 12,* 230–235.

Goodenough, F. L. (1939). Look to the evidence! A critique of recent experiments on raising the I.Q. *Educational Methods, 19,* 73–79.

Goodenough, F. L., & Harris, D. B., (1950). Studies in the psychology of children's drawings: II. 1928–1949. *Psychological Bulletin, 47,* 369–433.

Harris, D. B. (1963). *Children's drawings as measures of intellectual maturity: A revision and extension of the Goodenough Draw-a-Man test.* San Diego: Harcourt Brace Jovanovich. Prepared in collaboration with Goodenough, the revision of her Draw-a-Man test.

Stevens, G., & Gardner, S. (1982). Florence Laura Goodenough. In G. Stevens & S. Gardner (Eds.), *The women of psychology: Vol. 1. Pioneers and innovators* (pp. 193–197). Cambridge, MA: Schenkman.

Thompson, D. (1990). Florence Laura Goodenough, 1886–1959. In A. N. O'Connell & N. F. Russo (Eds.), *Women in psychology: A bio-bibliographic sourcebook* (pp. 125–133). Westport, CT: Greenwood.

Wolf, T. H. (1980). Florence Laura Goodenough, August, 6, 1886–April 4, 1959. In B. Sicherman & C. Green (Eds.), *Notable American women: The modern period* (pp. 284–286). Cambridge, MA: Harvard University Press.

Dennis N. Thompson